Rabbi Yitzḥak Frank

THE PRACTICAL TALMUD DICTIONARY

The Practical Talmud Dictionary
Published 1991, Second Edition, 1994
Third Edition, 2016

Maggid Books: An imprint of Koren Publishers Jerusalem Ltd.

POB 8531, New Milford, CT 06776-8531, USA
& POB 4044, Jerusalem 9104001, Israel
www.korenpub.com

Ariel United Institutes
HaPisga 5
POB 16002
Jerusalem, Israel

This book is published with the assistance of the
Ministry of Religious Affairs, State of Israel

הספר יוצא לאור בסיוע המשרד לעניני דת
אגף ארגונים ומוסדות תורה, המחלקה לישיבות

Editorial supervisor: Rav Dr. Ezra Zion Melamed ז"ל
Production and Design: Rabbi David Landesman ז"ל

Comments and suggestions concerning the contents of
this book are welcome. They should be addressed to
Rabbi Yitzḥak Frank at yitzfrank@gmail.com

ISBN 978-1-59264-451-3, *hardcover*

A CIP catalogue record for this title is
available from the British Library

Printed and bound in Israel

לרעיתי המסורה מרשה:
שלי ושלהם שלך הוא.

לילדינו – שושנה, חביבה, שלומית ציונה, אוריאל, וחיים – שתרמו כל אחד בדרכו להכנת הספר:

יהי רצון שנזכה כולנו לעסוק כל ימינו
בתורה, בעבודה, ובגמילות חסדים.

זכרון לאבי מורי
אברהם שניאור בן צבי דב ז״ל
הלך לעולמו כ״ז אדר שני, תשמ״ד.

תהא נפשו צרורה בצרור החיים.

זכרון לחמי היקר
דב אריה בן חיים מנחם ז״ל
הלך לעולמו כ״ה אייר, תשנ״ג.

תהא נפשו צרורה בצרור החיים.

Table of Contents:

שאר-ישוב כהן

RABBI SHE'AR YASHUV COHEN

Chief Rabbi of Haifa

It is recounted in Masekheth S^{e}maḥoth, that when the tanna Sh^{e}muel HaKatan passed away, his colleagues placed his key and his notebook in his burial casket. Rabban Gamliel and R. El'azar ben Azaryah then eulogized him and said: "Sh^{e}muel HaKatan has taken all of the beautiful things in this world and has departed."

The "key and the notebook" which enable man to enter the vaults that protect the Torah's treasures are, in truth, the words and concepts that our sages utilised to explain the meaning of the written Torah. Thus, the publication of a Talmudic dictionary in English — the mother tongue of so many people today — is a significant event, for it provides vast numbers of committed and serious students with "the key and the notebook" needed by them to study the Talmudic and Rabbinic literature and their commentaries. The words and concepts that form the entries in *The Practical Talmud Dictionary* are the very soul of our people for they form our link to all of "the beautiful things in this world."

The present work is another in a continuing effort on the part of Ariel — United Israel Institutes, to provide superior and critical works of benefit to both the advanced scholar and the layman. The underlying principle shared by all of Ariel's many divisions — including the postgraduate training centers, both those for Judges in the Religious Courts and those for Rabbis, as well as the training center for Russian immigrants, and also the *Complete Rashi* project, the *Complete Tosafoth* project, the *Ḥoshen Mishpat* project and many additional projects in the fields of *Halakhah* and *Aggadah* — is that "there is no life without Torah and there is no Torah without life." It is the dedication to this tenet that has led Ariel to assume a leadership role in making the masterworks of our heritage accessible to all.

Upon publication of this volume, we offer a sincere prayer that we be granted the ability to continue our work "for the glory of the Torah and those who study its words." May it be G-d's will that this work be privileged to serve as a means of drawing more and more of our people to the study of Torah and thus hasten the coming of the Messiah, speedily and in our days.

Rabbi She'ar Yashuv Cohen
Chief Rabbi of Haifa
President of Ariel Institutes

RABBI NATHAN KAMENETSKY
9/B Sorotzkin St., Jerusalem 94423

15th of Av, 5750

בס"ד

During the years I was privileged to serve as Rosh Yeshiva of Shapell College of Jewish Studies, I worked together with Rabbi Yitzhak Frank in teaching young men who, after having mastered a secular discipline, were taking their first steps in the study of Gemara. Our students, especially those with a background in the exact sciences, pressed for an exact translation, a rudimentary knowledge of the rules of grammar, and a correct pronunciation of the text as preliminary to tackling its content. At that time, I suggested to my colleague, an erudite and diligent lover-of-Torah, that he undertake the arduous task of compiling a work that will satisfy this need. To this end, I introduced Rabbi Frank to the great scholar and prominent Rav in the Persian community in Israel, Rav Professor E.Z. Melamed, who collaborated with him in the laborious 13 year pursuit. It is therefore personally gratifying to witness the completion of this important work.

It is obvious that the elucidation that this volume provides for the unique language of Talmudic reasoning is crucial for novices in Gemara study. But *The Practical Talmud Dictionary* is important for experienced students as well – even for those who began learning Gemara as youngsters.

As recorded in the preface to the first volume of my revered father's זצ"ל writings, he deliberated on whether to include in his עיונים במקרא the insights on the language of the Torah, its grammar and its notes (*trop*). Initially, he was apprehensive that these comments would be of no benefit to the readers, "since the world of לומדים is not concerned with such matters." Finally this very lack of concern persuaded him to proceed with their publication. He stated: "Let this neglected part of Torah, in which our masters, the Rishonim, invested so much toil, be redeemed; let the לומדים of our age devote some time to it."

At the beginning of פרשת וישב the Rashbam attributes the lack of his contemporaries' interest in פשט to their piety ("מתוך חסידותם") – people studied Torah only for the purpose of applying its instructions to their actions. His analysis suggests a rationalization for the neglect of a "part of Torah" by the present-day "world of "לומדים" that my father ז"ל laments. However commendable this rationale is, my father זצ"ל pointed out that it was ultimately rejected by the Rishonim. Be that as it may, piety is a feeble excuse for the sorry state of ignorance of gemara-language on the part of some experienced Gemara students, which this dictionary is capable of overcoming.

Yet another factor makes *The Practical Talmud Dictionary* a welcome addition to the *shtender* of every student of Gemara, tyro and *talmid hakham*. חז"ל teach us that when one quotes a sage, he should visualize that the sage is standing before him (ירושלמי שבת פ"א ה"ב ועוד). What disrespect we show that sage when we repeat his words in corrupt form! Does not the reverence due to the Tannaim and Amoraim enjoin us to appreciate the fullness of meaning of every one of their phrases? I am confident that בע"ה this dictionary will enhance the love of Talmud, and increase the respect towards its teachings and its teachers זי"ע.

At this time in Jewish history, when we are witnessing a revival of Torah study (see משך חכמה ופ' בחקותי), *The Practical Talmud Dictionary* will be of great significance for all who utilize it בע"ה.

נתן בהגר"י קמנצקי

דוד קאהן

ביהמ״ד גבול יעבץ
ברוקלין, נוא יורק

בס״ד

I have seen fragments of *The Practical Talmud Dictionary* by Rabbi Yitzchok Frank נ״י and was impressed by both its clarity and the scholarship of the author. It is no doubt that this work shall enhance the study of the Talmud, since it serves both the scholar and the student.

I have seen and heard of approbations by noted Talmidei Chachamim and I humbly add mine to this noble undertaking.

Rabbi David Cohen
אלול תש״נ

צבי שכטר
ר״מ בישיבת רבנו יצחק אלחנן
נוא יארק

יום ה׳ לס׳ שופטים, ב׳ לחודש הרחמים, שנת תש״נ

לכב׳ יקירי ידידי-מנוער הר״ר יצחק הי״ו,

עיינתי פה ושם בחיבורו אשר הוא עומד להוציא לאור בקרוב ואמינא לפעלא יישר. בעו״ה, יש בזמננו הרבה תלמידים בישיבות השואפים לגדולות, ושבאמת יש להם הכשרונות לכך, אלא שחסרים להם הכלים הכי-יסודיים ללימוד הגמרא בגלל שלא חונכו בקטנותם בגרסא דינקותא בבאור המלות, ועל כן לפי דעתי דבר גדול עשה כב׳ בעריכת מלונו התלמודי, אשר ברצות ד׳ הוא יהי׳ לתועלת גדולה בהרבצת התורה. ויה״ר שנזכה כולנו לראות בקרוב בהרמת קרן התורה.

הכותב והחותם ביקרא דאורייתא,
צבי שכטר

PREFACE

The initiative for this book was born out of the frustration of my English-speaking Talmud students who were suffering from the lack of a convenient reference work. I had long admired the Hebrew booklet אשנב התלמוד by HaRav Ezra Zion Melamed, whose last edition was published by Kiryat Sepher Ltd., Jerusalem in 5736 (1976). Since this brief but useful work had clarified many important Talmudic terms and expressions for me, I reasoned that an English edition would help make my students' learning more efficient. HaRav Nathan Kamenetsky, head of the yeshiva where I was teaching, encouraged this idea and helped me forge a link with Rav Melamed in 1977 that has lasted until this day. Even if this project had never come to fruition, I would owe many thanks to Rav Kamenetsky for the special relationship I have enjoyed with Rav Melamed, which has benefited me personally in many ways. With Rav Melamed's blessing, I began a translation of אשנב התלמוד. Moreover, when I subsequently decided that my students really needed a far more extensive work, I received Rav Melamed's assistance in expanding the project. Eventually, a new reference work evolved that contains many more Aramaic entries, some Hebrew entries (which are especially important for non-Israelis), and numerous Talmudic illustrations — all translated into English.

Rav Melamed and I spent so much time working together on this project in its early stages that, in retrospect, it is difficult to differentiate between his contribution and mine. Furthermore, even my own direct contribution was enhanced significantly by what I learned from him during the many hours we spent together at his home. Without Rav Melamed's cooperation and encouragement, this project could not have been undertaken; without his participation, it would never have been completed. Our work proceeded in the following manner: I undertook most of the technical research, combing the forty-one volumes of the concordance of the Talmud for new entries and illustrations. Rav Melamed examined my material and criticized it, sometimes proposing alternatives or additions. On the rare occasions when we did not agree — usually with regard to the needs of English-speaking students — I took upon myself the responsibility for the final decisions. In the later stages, I made some additions and alterations on my own, but I continued to consult with Rav Melamed, who critically proofread the Hebrew and Aramaic text of the dictionary proper. As a rule of thumb, the reader should assume that the positive features of this work are to Rav Melamed's credit and that the errors are mine. In spite of his crucial role in this project, Rav Melamed, the recipient of the *Israel Prize for Torah Literature* in 5747 (1987) for the many scholarly works he produced, graciously recommended that I be regarded the author of this work.

The contributions of two other individuals, Dr. Aryeh Siegel and my wife Marcia, were indispensable in the creation of *The Practical Talmud Dictionary*. Both of them spent innumerable hours scrutinizing the material, armed with extraordinary linguistic skills and great perseverance. Each one pressed me almost relentlessly for greater comprehensibility and clarity.

Other individuals who voluntarily contributed their critical skills to this project include my cousin, Howard Harrison, Professor Emeritus of English at the State University of New York, who served as my authoritative guide on English diction and punctuation, whom I consulted very frequently; my late hometown rabbi, Joseph J. Gold ז"ל, of Worcester, Massachusetts; Rav M. S. Feldblum of Yeshiva University; my former students: Dr. Deena (Cohen) Zimmerman and the late Sara Levinson ז"ל, who served as proofreaders during the early stages of this project; my brothers-in-law: Leonard Davis who proofread during the Gulf War and Rav Menachem Davis who has given me important advice throughout. I also wish to express gratitude to Naḥum Wengrov of The Ariel Institute for his careful proofreading and to Rav David Strauss, Menachem Goldberger and my son Uriel for their assistance with the acronyms (ראשי תיבות).

For whatever competence I have developed over the years in handling a Talmudic text, I owe thanks to my *gemara* teachers, namely (in chronological order): Rav Joseph J. Gold ז"ל, Hyman Steinberg ז"ל, and Arnold J. Miller ז"ל, in Worcester; HaRav Dr. Moshe Tendler, HaRav Joseph Weiss, and HaRav Yerucham Gorelick ז"ל at Yeshivath Rabbenu Yitzhak Elchanan, Yeshiva University in New York; HaRav Chaim Stein and HaRav Mordechai Gifter at the Telshe Yeshiva in Wickliffe, Ohio; HaRav HaGaon Dr. Joseph B. Soloveitchik at the S^emikha program of Yeshiva University and HaRav Dr. Aharon Lichtenstein at the Kollel of Yeshiva University both in New York and Jerusalem. I am grateful to my late teacher, HaRav Dr. Michael Bernstein ז"ל of Yeshiva University, who provided me with the foundation in Hebrew, Aramaic, and Syriac that gave me the confidence (or perhaps: the ḥutzpa) to undertake this project.

I wish to express my gratitude to my late father Abraham S. Frank ז"ל and my mother Mrs. Sylvia Frank, may the Lord grant her many more pleasant years; to my in-laws, Dr. and Mrs. Benjamin L. Davis, and to our aunt Mrs. Bertha Sokol — for their encouragement and support. I thank Mrs. Els Bendheim for her support and her extraordinary efforts to get this volume published.

During my sabbatical years from teaching, 5743 and 5750, the Memorial Foundation for Jewish Culture provided me with grants that enabled me to concentrate on this project. The assistance was deeply appreciated.

My special thanks are due to Rav Yeḥeskel Fogel, Director General of the Ariel Institute for his energetic devotion to *The Practical Talmud Dictionary*. From the moment he became aware of this project, he took a personal interest in it and spared no effort in its behalf. Through a rare combination of persistence and patience, he skillfully guided the publication to its successful completion.

Rav David Landesman and his staff at the Girls' Town Computer Project at Kfar Chasidim succeeded in transforming my index cards into a real dictionary. Their work was difficult, exacting, and — at times — very frustrating. I sincerely appreciate their labor in producing this handsome volume and the remarkable patience Rav Landesman exhibited towards me throughout the process.

The final acknowledgement is to the Holy One Blessed Be He for granting us the strength to see this project through in spite of the obstacles along the way.

Yitzḥak Frank
Jerusalem, Elul 5751

PREFACE TO THE SECOND EDITION

I am deeply gratified that the *Practical Talmud Dictionary* has been well received by both students and teachers and has won the Prize of the Israeli Minister of Education in 5752 for the academic year 5753 (1992–3). Over the years I had received some dire warnings from people involved in Jewish education that my work would be either unnecessary because of existing dictionaries or irrelevant because yeshiva students are concerned exclusively with matters of greater import, e.g., conceptual analysis. Nevertheless, the popularity of the *PTD* indicates that many students of the Talmud seriously care about understanding the text properly. They realize that most of us should first learn to walk before learning to run or fly.

A work of this size contains so many computer bytes that in spite of many hours of careful proofreading, some typographical errors occurred. Those which were discovered by my wife and me upon proofreading the first edition have now been corrected. Some readers, moreover, graciously accepted the invitation on the credit page of this book to forward comments and suggestions. Specifically, I would like to express my gratitude to my teacher, Prof. Neḥama Leibowitz, to my brother-in-law, Rabbi Menachem Davis, and to my friends and colleagues, Rabbi Yoseph Kramer and Rabbi Chaim Pollack, for their suggestions that have been incorporated into the text of this second edition.

I thank the Almighty for granting me the opportunity to learn and teach Torah through the medium of the printed word, and I pray that He will enable me to continue to learn and to teach through other media as well for many years to come.

* * * * *

Between the publication of the first edition of this work and the publication of the second edition, on the third day of the Passover festival, 5753, we were bereaved of our great master, whom we loved and revered,

HARAV HAGAON YOSEPH DOV SOLOVEITCHIK,
May the memory of the righteous be forever blessed.

The Rav — with his wonderful mastery of Torah and general culture, his profound insight into Talmudic concepts, his deeply religious personality, his unique ability to communicate with our generation, and his extraordinary humility — will remain alive in our hearts forever. May it be Thy Will, O God, that even this modest work, written by one of his minor disciples, serve to honor his sacred memory.

Yitzḥak Frank
Jerusalem, Shevat 5754

I. SPECIAL FEATURES OF *THE PRACTICAL TALMUD DICTIONARY*

In recent years, the study of Talmud has become increasingly widespread among English-speaking Jewry. Many teachers and students, however, are well aware of the need for educational materials that would ease the student's entry into the world of the Babylonian Talmud.

In the field of language study, *the learner's dictionary* has become an important tool for many students the world over. This type of reference work takes little for granted. It aims to help students master the essential vocabulary and terminology of an extensive literature. Even the scholar who has become familiar with much of the literature and is now concerned with concepts and principles can benefit from the precision and clarity of such a work. In Jewish tradition, moreover, the term *learning*, as in the expression *learning Torah*, refers to Torah study that is undertaken in fulfillment of a Divine commandment — not merely as an intellectual exercise. It is our hope and prayer that *The Practical Talmud Dictionary*, a learner's dictionary in both senses, will enhance the intellectual-religious experience of learning Torah for many students.

The Talmudic reference work that is most widely used today — Marcus Jastrow's *Dictionary of the Targumim, the Talmud Bavli and Yerushalmi, and the Midrashic Literature* — was first published in 1903. Jastrow's dictionary is a serious work that has assisted many students over the years. With all due respect to the author's achievement, however, many students and teachers have been frustrated by certain shortcomings that limit its usefulness — especially for the student who is not yet a scholar. The present work is designed to overcome those shortcomings in order to render more practical assistance to students who are struggling to understand the Talmudic text. Here are some of the features of *The Practical Talmud Dictionary*:

A. User Friendliness

In Semitic languages, the verb is the most crucial part of speech. The verbal systems of both Hebrew and Aramaic feature three-letter roots from which many different verbal forms evolve. Most Semitic dictionaries list verbs only by their roots. As a result, a student who does not possess grammatical sophistication experiences great difficulty in locating verbal forms. For example, if one searches Jastrow's dictionary for such important Talmudic verbs as אִיבְּעִי *(it was necessary* or *it was asked)*, מוֹתִיב *(refuting)*, or תִּיפּוֹק *(let it be derived)* according to their spelling, he will find nothing — not even a cross-reference. Jastrow listed these words only under their roots: תוב, בעי, and נפק, respectively. In *The Practical Talmud Dictionary*, each of these key verbal forms is presented as a separate entry item, spelled as in the Talmud.

B. Words and Expressions

The entry items in most dictionaries are single words. When a student is trying to figure out a Talmudic passage, however, he is sometimes stymied by a phrase or an expression — even if he does know the translation of each individual word. In such cases, the meaning of the whole is greater and more significant than the sum of its parts. For example, the Aramaic expression אִיכָּא בֵּינַיְיהוּ means much more than its literal translation, *there is between them*. In this respect, the present dictionary is more comprehensive than other Talmudic dictionaries: It contains many entries of more than one word that are crucial for understanding Talmudic methodology. In addition to translating such expressions, *The Practical Talmud Dictionary* explains how they function in a Talmudic context. Many of the contextual explanations are based on the work of HaRav Ezra Zion Melamed in his אשנב התלמוד. Others were developed by Rav Melamed and the author especially for this dictionary.

C. Accuracy

Many of the definitions and usages presented in *The Practical Talmud Dictionary* were formulated after consulting the *Arukh* of R. Nathan b. Y^eḥiel of Rome, the commentary of Rashi on the Talmud, and other classical commentaries. In addition, the present work makes use of some of the more recent advances in Semitic-language scholarship. In both areas, we have drawn upon the expertise of Rav Melamed, since he is both a traditional *talmid hakham* and a noted scholar of Semitics.

D. Trilingualism: Aramaic, Hebrew, and English

The Practical Talmud Dictionary is primarily an Aramaic-English dictionary designed for English speakers. Nevertheless, experience indicates that a knowledge of Hebrew is helpful to the student who is trying to master the Talmud. Accordingly, this work takes advantage of opportunities to teach Hebrew:

1. A large majority of the entries are Aramaic, and the Aramaic words are translated into *both* Hebrew and English. These Hebrew translations are useful because of the close relationship between Hebrew and Aramaic. They serve to reinforce the student's knowledge of the Aramaic entry.
2. Besides the Aramaic entries, this dictionary contains more than five hundred entries of words and expressions in Mishnaic Hebrew (e.g., אַזְהָרָה and אַב בֵּית דִּין). The student can discern that these entry items are Hebrew and not Aramaic by virtue of the fact that they are translated *only* into English.
3. There are also some *co-entries* that feature both a Mishnaic Hebrew word and an Aramaic word, when both forms are used in the Talmud in the same way. For an example, see SAMPLE III below.
4. Lastly, the notes in this dictionary sometimes point out that some form of the word or expression presented in the entry has entered Modern Hebrew. Such an association is often meaningful for students, especially for those who have spent some time in Israel and have been exposed to Hebrew as a spoken language. For an example, see the second note on the entry אֲזַל.

E. Scope

Many students have found Jastrow's work to be intimidating. Its 1,736 pages contain a great deal of material from the Targumim, the Midrashim, and the Talmud Yerushalmi that is irrelevant to the Talmud Bavli. A student often has to wade through many extraneous entries and usages before he finds what he seeks. The *Practical Talmud Dictionary,* on the other hand, focuses upon the Babylonian Talmud exclusively. Furthermore, it does not attempt to include every Aramaic word found in the Babylonian Talmud. The decisions as to which words and phrases qualify to be *entry items* were made according to the following criteria:

1. In general, Aramaic words that occur at least ten times in the Talmud are presented. The omission of rare words is not a terrible loss, especially since so many of them have been explained in Rashi's commentary on the Talmud.
2. In practice, however, this policy is applied with flexibility. There is a deliberate tendency to be generous and include words that occur less frequently — if they are used in Talmudic tractates commonly studied nowadays or if they are Aramaic verbal forms or terms that are important for understanding Talmudic

methodology. This policy is more restrictive, however, with regard to nouns (especially names of plants, animals, diseases, etc.) and words from tractates rarely studied.

3. As noted above, even though *The Practical Talmud Dictionary* is primarily an Aramaic dictionary, it contains a substantial number of Hebrew entries. In reality, they were chosen on a subjective basis, i.e., the author's assessment of what material students will find most helpful. Hebrew terms and phrases relating to Talmudic methodology, e.g., יָצָא and (וְ)הִיא הַנּוֹתֶנֶת, are presented as entry items. Common words that are used in the Mishna or in the Talmud in a special sense, e.g., מַה, or words that are likely to confuse the student, e.g., מְטַמֵּא and מִיטַמֵּא, are also included — even if they do appear in standard Hebrew-English dictionaries.

4. The analysis of specific *halakhic concepts* is beyond the scope of this dictionary. In our opinion, such matters are best left to the classroom teacher. Except for very general categories, e.g., הֲלָכָה and בְּנֵי חוֹרִין, relatively few Hebrew halakhic concepts are presented as entry items. Thus, we have omitted such specific halakhic concepts as יֵאוּשׁ שֶׁלֹּא מִדַּעַת, at the beginning of the chapter אֵלּוּ מְצִיאוֹת, and דָּבָר שֶׁלֹּא בָּא לָעוֹלָם, at the beginning of הַמַּפְקִיד — two chapters that are often taught in the classroom. It is the primary task of *The Practical Talmud Dictionary* to explain the terminology and the vocabulary that make up the skeleton of Talmudic discussions in general, rather than to encompass the specific concepts that are debated on a particular page.

F. Examples

For most entries — whether single words or expressions consisting of more than one word — illustrations are quoted from the Talmud.[1] A conscious effort was made to choose passages that would be readily understandable and to quote enough of the Talmudic text to illustrate the use of the entry, but not more of it than necessary. The illustrations are fully vocalized and fully translated into English. For students interested in studying the illustration in its broader context, the location of the Talmudic source is given as well (within parentheses).[2] In entries where a search through the Talmudic concordance[3] did not produce an example suitable for quotation in the dictionary, the student is at least referred to a Talmudic source. For a small percentage of entries — e.g., measures, weights, coins and numbers — illustrations are not provided since their usage is quite clear.

G. Acronyms (רָאשֵׁי תֵּיבוֹת) and Abbreviations

One of the stumbling blocks that confront the student of the Talmud is the many acronyms (ראשי תיבות) that appear in the text. Appendix I of the present work contains a comprehensive list of the Hebrew and Aramaic acronyms found in the Babylonian Talmud and a selection of Talmudic abbreviations. Each acronym has been resolved into its component parts and translated into English.

1 – In some of the illustrations, the text of our printed editions of the Talmud is a bit problematic. When a manuscript version is smoother and/or more consistent grammatically, it has been quoted as the illustration. In such cases, the designation עפ״י כת״י has been printed immediately after the Talmudic source — meaning עַל פִּי כְּתַב יָד, *according to a manuscript version*. These illustrations have been taken from the famous Munich manuscript or from one of the other manuscripts used by R.N. Rabbinovics in his דקדוקי סופרים.

2 – Since a page of the Babylonian Talmud is quite large, it may be difficult for a student to locate a specific passage. In order to expedite this process, this dictionary indicates where on the page the passage is located. The following abbreviations are used: רע״א (= רֵישׁ עַמּוּד א) and רע״ב (= רֵישׁ עַמּוּד ב) indicating that the passage is located near *the top of the Talmudic page*, and סע״א (= סוֹף עַמּוּד א) and סע״ב (= סוֹף עַמּוּד ב) indicating that the passage is located near *the bottom of the Talmudic page*. Of course, the absence of these designations is also meaningful, for it indicates that the passage is located neither at the top nor at the bottom of the page but rather towards the middle.

3 – C. J. Kasowski, אוצר לשון התלמוד, Jerusalem 1954–1982.

H. Measures and Numbers

Appendix II of the present work contains tables listing linear measures, measures of area and volume, weights, coins, as well as Aramaic numbers and fractions. These tables serve to clarify the relationships among these data. In addition, the translation of these data into their modern equivalents makes them more realistic for the student.

I. Vocalization

What is the correct way to vocalize (i.e., to mark with vowels) the Aramaic of the Babylonian Talmud? In contrast to the Biblical text, whose vocalization has been handed down to us with very few controversies, the standard editions of both the Mishna and the Talmud have no vowels. For the Mishna, a serious vocalized edition has been published, based on some vocalized Mishna manuscripts and oral reading traditions.[4] The situation regarding the Babylonian Talmud, however, is more complicated: Little vocalized material is available in manuscripts, and the reading traditions among the various Jewish communities are widely divergent. There is no easy solution.

The most scientific way to handle the problem would be to play it safe and not vocalize at all. Such an approach would avert scholarly criticism, but at the same time it would probably frustrate the *student* for whom this volume has been produced. In our view it is better to furnish the student with a reasonable vocalization — which may be dubious or even erroneous in some of its details — than to leave the student in the lurch, without any vocalization.

At first glance, one might assume that Biblical Aramaic should be a guide for the vocalization of the Aramaic of the Talmud, since the books of Ezra and Daniel both have an authoritative vocalized text. Babylonian Aramaic, however, is a different dialect. Just as it would be a mistake to equate Mishnaic Hebrew with Biblical Hebrew,[5] it would also be a mistake to equate Talmudic Aramaic with Biblical Aramaic.

The Aramaic of Targum Onkelos, which was known among Babylonian Jewry as תַּרְגּוּם דִּידַן,[6] *our Targum,* is certainly closer to Babylonian Aramaic and would seem to be a more reliable guide.[7] Indeed, Yemenite Jews have painstakingly preserved a careful vocalization of Targum Onkelos both in their manuscripts and their books.[8] Recent studies of the Yemenite reading tradition, however, have shown that their pronunciation of the Babylonian Aramaic of the Talmud differs from their own pronunciation of Targum Onkelos.[9] Nevertheless, to vocalize this dictionary in accordance with the Yemenite tradition would be impractical. Most of the students who will use this volume are non-Yemenites who study in non-Yemenite institutions of learning where the reading tradition of the Talmud differs markedly from the Yemenite pronunciation.

---

4 – Ḥ. Albeck (commentary) and Ḥ. Yalon (vocalization), *The Six Orders of the Mishna.* Jerusalem and Tel Aviv: Bialik Institute and Dvir, 1958. See also: Ḥ. Yalon, *Introduction to the Vocalization of the Mishna.* Jerusalem: Bialik Institute, 1964.

5 – See Y. Frank, *Grammar for Gemara.* Jerusalem: Ariel — United Israel Institutes, 1992, Chapter 1.

6 – For an example — see קידושין מט,א.

7 – Onkelos lived in Erets Yisrael, but according to some scholars (e.g., J.N. Epstein, E.Y. Kutscher) at least the final editing and the vocalization of his Targum are of Babylonian origin. When quotations from Targum Onkelos are quoted in the Babylonian Talmud, they are almost always introduced by the word וּמְתַרְגְּמִינַן, *and we (= Babylonian Jews) translate.* Later, the Gaonim of Babylonia regularly called it תַּרְגּוּם דִּידַן, *our Targum.*

8 – Alexander Sperber, *The Bible in Aramaic.* Leiden: E.J. Brill, 1959, vol. 1.

9 – Shelomo Morag, ארמית במסורת תימן: לשון התלמוד בבלי (with an English abstract and table of contents entitled *Babylonian Aramaic: The Yemenite Tradition*). Jerusalem: Ben Zvi Institute, 1988, pp. 41–45.

The Practical Talmud Dictionary adopts a somewhat eclectic approach towards this problem. On the one hand, an attempt is made to vocalize the Aramaic in a manner that makes sense grammatically and historically — sometimes in the face of a popular pronunciation.[10] For example, the common form מִיפַּלְגִי is vocalized in that manner, since no way was found to justify the popular pronunciation מִיפְּלְגִי. In such cases, the vocalization based upon the popular pronunciation is mentioned in a note, so that the student will recognize what he hears. On the other hand, *wherever possible*, the popular pronunciation is used. For example, the traditional pronunciation of תָּנוּ — rather than תְּנוּ — is preserved in vocalizing the expression תָּנוּ רַבָּנַן. Although this vocalization may be subject to criticism, nevertheless it can be defended according to grammatical principles.

We fully realize that the fine points of vocalization and pronunciation are often insignificant for the understanding of the Talmudic text. In Judaism, there is a fundamental difference between the study of תּוֹרָה שֶׁבִּכְתָב, *the written law*, and the study of תּוֹרָה שֶׁבְּעַל פֶּה, *the oral law*: While a Jew can fulfill the mitzva of learning Torah by reading mechanically from the text of Scripture, reading תּוֹרָה שֶׁבְּעַל פֶּה mechanically — without at least trying to *understand* the content — does not fulfill the mitzva. Reading the words properly is important only as a means to enhance understanding, but not as an end in itself. Indeed, my revered teacher, HaRav Dr. Michael Bernstein of blessed memory, used to say: *Know* the correct pronunciation, but *read* the *Gemara* in the traditional way!

J. Punctuation

1. IN HEBREW AND ARAMAIC ENTRY ITEMS

a. In general, an entry item is presented without any punctuation as in the standard text of the Babylonian Talmud. Exception: *Ellipsis points* (...) are used to indicate that a word or more has been omitted from the Talmudic text.

b. A *slash* (/) is placed between two different spellings of the same Hebrew or Aramaic word.

c. A *semicolon* (;) is used to separate between a Hebrew word and its Aramaic counterpart.

2. IN ENGLISH TRANSLATIONS

While entry items are presented without punctuation, English and Hebrew translations are fully punctuated:

a. A *semicolon* (;) is used to separate between different translations — leaving commas free for their ordinary use within an individual translation.

b. A *slash* (/) is used to separate between different alternatives of various kinds (not between alternate spellings as in the Hebrew and Aramaic entry items).

c. Both *parentheses* ( ) and *square brackets* [ ] are used to enclose words that are not actually part of a literal translation. The following distinction in their use has been adopted in this dictionary:

(1) *Square brackets* are used to enclose additional words that are needed merely to make the English read more smoothly.

(2) *Parentheses* are used to enclose explanatory material, which is usually preceded by an equal sign (=) immediately after the first parenthesis.

10 – Particularly useful have been: Yaakov Naḥum HaLevi Epstein, דקדוק ארמית בבלית (A Grammar of Babylonian Aramaic) ed. by E.Z. Melamed. Jerusalem: Magnes and Tel Aviv: Dvir, 1960, and the critical review of the work by Yeḥeskel Kutscher, reprinted in his מחקרים בעברית ובארמית, Jerusalem, 1977, pp. 226–55.

d. Traditionally, foreign words that have not been absorbed into the English language are printed in *italics*, whereas those words that have been absorbed into the language are printed in normal type. This dictionary uses some Hebrew and Aramaic terms in explanations and translations that have become so familiar to students of the Talmud that they have become absorbed into *Talmudic English*. Here is a list of such transliterated words that have not been italicized in this dictionary — together with the Hebrew or Aramaic spelling of those that appear as entries: amora (אָמוֹרָא), baraitha (בָּרַיְיתָא), b'rakha, Beth HaMikdash, Haggada, ḥakham, halakha (הֲלָכָה), ḥametz, matza, mishna (מִשְׁנָה), mitzva, Nasi (נָשִׂיא), pasuk, Pesaḥ, Rosh HaShana, Sanhedrin (סַנְהֶדְרִין), Sukkoth, Shavu'oth, tanna (תַּנָּא), Torah, and Yom Kippur.

e. The combination of a *question mark and an exclamation point* (?!), which is not a conventional punctuation mark in English, has been consistently used in this volume after *rhetorical questions* to distinguish them from ordinary questions and exclamations. For an example, see SAMPLE IV.

3. IN ILLUSTRATIONS FROM THE TALMUD (and their translations)

a. The Talmudic quotations are punctuated *according to their original contexts*. Only if a quotation constitutes a complete sentence in its original context is it punctuated as a complete sentence in this dictionary. Otherwise — even in cases where the quotation could be regarded as a complete sentence when taken out of context — it is punctuated as a fragment, not as a sentence. Strictly speaking, three *ellipsis points* (...) should be placed both before and after such quotations, but they are omitted for the sake of brevity. In a few illustrations, the Talmudic quotation begins with a capital letter and ends with ellipsis points in order to emphasize that it comprises the beginning of a complete sentence in the original text.

b. These Talmudic illustrations are easily recognizable as such since they are printed in a smaller typeface, followed by the Talmudic source in parentheses and by an English translation in *italics*. *Quotation marks* are *not* used to enclose these quotations — even when they are presented as the words of a specific tanna or amora. However, when a Biblical passage is quoted within a Talmudic illustration, it is set off by quotation marks. Its Biblical source in Hebrew — preceded by the abbreviation ע״פ (= עַל פִּי, *according to*) — is stated after the Talmudic source and both are included within the same parentheses, e.g., (ברכות ב,א ע״פ בראשית א:א).

4. NOTES AND THEIR DESIGNATIONS

Notes are printed in a smaller typeface towards the end of an entry, before any cross-references. A note is indicated in the text by an asterisk (*) in superscript, and the same symbol introduces the note itself. For multiple notes in the same entry, this dictionary uses two asterisks (**), then three asterisks (***), one diamond (°), and two diamonds (°°).

K. Transliteration Rules for Hebrew and Aramaic in this Dictionary

1. CONSONANTS

Hebrew Letter	Transcription	Hebrew Letter	Transcription
א[1]	’	מ	m
בּ	b	נ	n
ב	v	ס	s
ג	hard g	ע[1]	’
ד	d	פּ	p
ה[2]	h	פ	f
ו	v	צ	tz
ז	z	ק	k
ח	h	ר	r
ט	t	שׁ	sh
י	y	שׂ	s
כּ	k	תּ	t
כ	kh	ת	th
ל	l		

2. VOWELS

Hebrew Vowel Sign (the letter א indicates placement)	Name	Transcription	Sound
אָ	קָמֶץ גָּדוֹל	*a*	*a* in *father*
אָ	קָמֶץ קָטָן	*o*	*o* in *soft*
אַ	פַּתַח	*a*	*a* in *father*
אֶ	סֶגוֹל	*e*	*e* in *set*
אֵ	צֵרֵי	*e, é*	*é* in *passé*[3]
אִ	חִירִיק	*i*	*i* in *siesta*
אוֹ, אֹ	חוֹלָם	*o*	*o* in *bold*
אוּ	שׁוּרוּק	*u*	*u* in *rule*
אֻ	קֻבּוּץ	*u*	*u* in *rule*
אְ	שְׁוָא נָע	*ᵉ*	*e* in *guarded*
אְ	שְׁוָא נָח	–	silent

3. DEGESHIM

In both Hebrew and Aramaic, a dot (called a דָּגֵשׁ, *dagesh*) is sometimes inserted into a consonant to indicate a certain type of pronunciation. In some cases, it is used as a "light *dagesh*" to show that certain consonants (such as בּ, כּ, פּ) are to be pronounced as *plosives (b, k, p),* rather than as *fricatives (v, kh, f).* In other cases, it is used as a "strong *dagesh*" to indicate the "doubling" (= lengthening) of a consonant. In this work, we have transcribed Hebrew/Aramaic consonants that have a "strong *dagesh*" as doubled English consonants. Thus, the letter נ in the word תַּנָּא has been transliterated as *nn* in *tanna*. There is, however, one exception to this policy: When a Hebrew consonant with a "strong *dagesh*" immediately follows the definite article ה, its English counterpart has been capitalized, but not doubled. For example, הַמָּזוֹן has been transliterated *haMazon.*

---

1 – In the middle of a word, the slanted apostrophe is occasionally used to represent either א or ע. Otherwise, these two letters are not represented in English in this dictionary.

2 – When ה serves as a vowel letter, e.g., in מִשְׁנָה, it is not pronounced, and hence it need not be transliterated in English. For example, מִשְׁנָה is transcribed *mishna*. On the other hand, תּוֹרָה is transliterated as *Torah*, because the English reader is so familiar with that spelling.

3 – This transliteration is used only at the end of a word. Otherwise, a plain *e* is used.

L. Acronyms and Abbreviations Used in this Dictionary

1. HEBREW

Bava Bathra (name of a tractate[1])	בָּבָא בָּתְרָא	ב"ב
Bayith Ḥadash (a commentary on the *Tur*)	בַּיִת חָדָשׁ	ב"ח
*Bava M*ᵉ*tsia* (name of a tractate[1])	בָּבָא מְצִיעָא	ב"מ
Bava Kama (name of a tractate[1])	בָּבָא קַמָּא	ב"ק
Divré HaYamim (= the Book of Chronicles)	דִּבְרֵי הַיָּמִים	דבה"י
the discussion that begins [with]	דִּבּוּר הַמַּתְחִיל	ד"ה
*Dikduké Sof*ᵉ*rim* (by R. N. Rabbinovics)	דִּקְדּוּקֵי סוֹפְרִים	דק"ס
halakha; law	הֲלָכָה (ה"א = הלכה א; ה"ב = הלכה ב, וכו')	ה"...
the (author of) *Bayith Hadash*	הַ(מְּחַבֵּר שֶׁל) בַּיִת חָדָשׁ	הב"ח
the *halakhoth* of; the laws of	הִלְכוֹת	הל'
R. Moshe Isserles	הָרַב מֹשֶׁה אִיסֶרְלִישׂ	הרמ"א
the six orders (of the Mishna); the Talmud	הַ"שִּׁשָּׁה סְדָרִים"	הש"ס
and so on	וְכוּלֵּיהּ	וכו'
and study ...! and look carefully at ...!	וְעַיֵּין!	וע'
and according to; and based on	וְעַל פִּי	וע"פ
and [a list of sources] has been presented there	וְשָׁם נִסְמַן	וש"נ
[May] his memory be a blessing.	זִכְרוֹנוֹ לִבְרָכָה	ז"ל
manuscript; mansucripts	כְּתָב יָד; כִּתְבֵי יָד	כת"י
the Munich manuscript (of the Babylonian Talmud)	כְּתָב יַד מִינְכֶן	כתי"מ
mishna	מִשְׁנָה (מ"א = משנה א; מ"ב = משנה ב, וכו')	מ" ...
our teacher R. Shᵉlomo Luria	מוֹרֵנוּ הָרַב שְׁלֹמֹה לוּרְיָא	מהרש"ל
A Guide for the Perplexed	מוֹרֵה נְבוּכִים	מו"נ
Mo'ed Katan (name of a tractate[1])	מוֹעֵד קָטָן	מו"ק
Ma'aser Sheni (name of a tractate of Mishna)	מַעֲשֵׂר שֵׁנִי	מע"ש

---

1 – i.e., a tractate of the Mishna or of the Talmud

the end of the first page[2]	סוֹף עָמוּד א'	סע"א
the end of the second page[2]	סוֹף עָמוּד ב'	סע"ב
Study ...! Look carefully at ...!	עַיֵּין!	ע'
Avoda Zara (name of a tractate[1])	עֲבוֹדָה זָרָה	ע"ז
according to; based upon	עַל פִּי	ע"פ
chapter	פֶּרֶק (פ"א = פרק א)	פ"
Rabbi	רַבִּי	ר'
R. Avraham (b. Méir) Ibn Esra	ר' אַבְרָהָם (בֶּן מֵאִיר מִמִּשְׁפַּחַת) אִבְּן עֶזְרָא	ראב"ע
Rabbenu Asher	רַבֵּינוּ אָשֵׁר	רא"ש
Rosh HaShana (name of a tractate[1])	רֹאשׁ הַשָּׁנָה	ר"ה
Rabbenu Ḥananel	רַבֵּנוּ חֲנַנְאֵל	ר"ח
R. Yom Tov b. Avraham (of Seville)	ר' יוֹם טוֹב בֶּן אַבְרָהָם (אַלְאִשְׁבִּילִי)	ריטב"א
R. Yitsḥak of Fes	ר' יִצְחָק אַל־פָּסִי	רי"ף
R. Moshe b. Maimon; Maimonides	ר' מֹשֶׁה בֶּן מַיְמוֹן	רמב"ם
R. Méir HaLevi (Abulafia)	ר' מֵאִיר הַלֵּוִי (אַבּוּלָעְפְיָה)	רמ"ה
R. Nissim (b. Rᵉuven)	רַבֵּנוּ נִסִּים (בֶּן רְאוּבֵן)	ר"ן
the top of the first page[2]	רֹאשׁ עָמוּד א'	רע"א
the top of the second page[2]	רֹאשׁ עָמוּד ב'	רע"ב
R. Shᵉmuel b. Méir (grandson of Rashi)	ר' שְׁמוּאֵל בֶּן מֵאִיר	רשב"ם
R. Shᵉlomo Yitsḥaki	ר' שְׁלֹמֹה יִצְחָקִי	רש"י
R. Shᵉmuel Shtrashun	ר' שְׁמוּאֵל שְׁטְרַאשׁוּן	רש"ש
Shita Mᵉkubbetzeth (an anthology of Talmudic commentaries)	שִׁיטָה מְקֻבֶּצֶת	שטמ"ק
Targum Onkelos	תַּרְגּוּם אוֹנְקְלוֹס	ת"א
Tosafoth	תּוֹסָפוֹת	תוס'
the *Tosafoth* of Rabbenu Asher	תּוֹסָפוֹת רַבֵּנוּ אָשֵׁר	תוס' הרא"ש

1 – i.e., a tractate of the Mishna or of the Talmud

2 – The pagination in the Babylonian Talmud, runs from right to left. Each leaf (in Hebrew, דַּף), which would be considered two pages in an ordinary book, is given *one* Hebrew page number. The front side of the leaf (= a page in an ordinary book) is referred to in Hebrew as עָמוּד א' (= ע"א), and the back side as עָמוּד ב' (= ע"ב). In a Talmudic tractate, the first page of text is numberd ב at its upper left-hand corner and called דַּף ב עָמוּד א' (= ב, ע"א), and the second page (i.e., the reverse side) is דַּף ב עָמוּד ב' (ב' ע"ב).

2. ENGLISH

a.	active
abs.	absolute (state of a noun)
act.	active
adj.	adjective
adv.	adverb
b.	*ben; bar;* the son of
c.	*circa*; approximately
cf.	*confer*; compare
cm.	centimeters
cnstr.; constr.	construct (state of a noun)
demons.	demonstrative
e.g.	*exempli gratia;* for example
etc.	*et cetera;* and others
f.	feminine
f. pl.	feminine plural
f.s	feminine singular
fut.	future
gm.	grams
Heb.	Hebrew
ibid.	*ibidem*; in the same place
i.e.	*id est*; that is; namely
imp.	imperative
in.	inches
inf.	infinitive
km.	kilometers
lit.[1]	literally
lit.[2]	liter

m.[1]	masculine
m.[2]	meters
m. pl.	masculine plural
m.s.	masculine singular
mi.	miles
ms.	manuscript
n.	noun
oz.	ounces
p.[1]	page
p.[2]	passive
pass.	passive
pers.	person
pl.	plural
pp.	pages
prep.	preposition
pron.	pronoun
prt.	present tense; participle
R.	*Rabbi*
s.	singular
s.v.	*sub verbo*; the discussion that begins with
yd.	yard

II. SAMPLE ENTRIES FROM *THE PRACTICAL TALMUD DICTIONARY*

In order to help the learner use this dictionary efficiently, we will present samples of four different types of entries and explain their component parts.

SAMPLE I: A TECHNICAL TERM

2 1

וְ**אִיתֵּימָא** (וְאִי+תֵּימָא)*

4 3

"and if you would say"; and some say "וְאִם תֹּאמַר"; וְיֵשׁ אוֹמְרִים

5

This term is placed between the names of two hakhamim to indicate that there are two different traditions as to which ḥakham is really the author of what is about to be quoted.

8 7 6

Sh^emuel and some say R. Yoḥanan stated שְׁמוּאֵל וְאִיתֵּימָא ר׳ יוֹחָנָן אָמַר (ביצה ו, סע״א)

9

* This etymology is one of several possibilities. It is also possible to regard the term as a contraction of אִית+אָמַר, *there is [someone who] says* or as a variant form of the passive verb אִתְאֲמַר, *it was said.*

10

SEE: (וְ)אָמְרִי לָהּ

This entry consists of the following elements:

1 – The Aramaic term in **boldface** type.

NOTE: The prefix -וְ, *and*, is printed in smaller regular type, because the word is alphabetized in this dictionary according to the letter א.

2 – An etymology of the term (within parentheses).

NOTE: The asterisk (*) in superscript refers the learner to a note (See #9).

3 – Hebrew translations of the term.

NOTE: If the literal translation fails to convey the meaning in Talmudic contexts, it is enclosed within quotation marks. It is immediately followed by a more practical, contextual translation.

4 – English translations in **boldface** type. See note on previous element.

5 – An explanation of the function of this term in a Talmudic context.

6 – A Talmudic quotation, printed in a smaller font, illustrating the use of this term.

7 – The source of the Talmudic quotation (in parentheses).

NOTE: The acronym סע״א (= סוף עמוד א׳) means at the end of the first side of the leaf. See the second note on page XXI above.

8 – An *italicized* English translation of that quotation.

9 – A note introduced by an asterisk (*). This particular note proposes two additional etymologies.

NOTE: The words in square brackets are *not* part of the literal English translation. They have been added so that the translation will read more smoothly.

10 – A cross-reference to another entry, introduced by the word SEE.

NOTE: The prefix letter וְ of (וְ)אָמְרִי is enclosed within parentheses in order to indicate that the entry is listed in this dictionary under אָמְרִי.

SAMPLE II: A BASIC VERBAL ENTRY

5 4 3 2 1

אִיתְחֲזִי (חזי* אִתְפְּעֵל: מִתְחֲזֵי/מִיחְזֵי .prt)

8 7 6

it was seen; it appeared (1) נִרְאָה

11 10 9

it appeared to them in a dream אִיתְחֲזִי לְהוּ בְּחִילְמָא (תענית כא,ב)

8 7 6

it was fit; it was suitable (2) הָיָה רָאוּי

10 9

בְּעִידָּנָא דְאִיתְחֲזַאי קַמַּיְיתָא, לָא אִיתְחֲזַאי בָּתְרַיְיתָא (יומא סב,א)

11

at the time when the first was fit, the last was not fit

12

* For the full conjugation of this verb, see *Grammar for Gemara*: Chapter 4, Verb 12.

This entry consists of the following elements:

1 – The basic form of the Aramaic verb — the 3rd person masculine singular of the past tense — printed in **boldface** type.

The next four elements (2–5) appear within the parentheses:

2 – The *root* of the verb.

NOTE: The asterisk (*) in superscript refers the learner to a note below (see #12).

3 – The *binyan* (conjugation) — unless it is the קַל *binyan*, in which case this element is omitted.

4 – Another *principal* part of the verb, in this instance: the *present tense* or *participle* (masculine singular). Other forms that are sometimes listed in verbal entries as principal parts are the *future tense* (third person masculine singular), the *imperative* (masculine singular), and the *infinitive* — whichever forms occur in the Talmud with some frequency.

NOTE: This particular participle has two alternate spellings, which are separated by a slash (/).

5 – An abbreviation of the English name for the principal part, i.e., "prt." for *present tense* or *participle.*

6 – The numbers (1) and (2), respectively introducing two distinct meanings of this particular verb.

Each of the next five elements (7–11) appears twice in this entry — once for meaning (1) and once again for meaning (2).

7 – Hebrew translations of this basic form of the Aramaic verb.

8 – English translations in **boldface** type of the same basic form.

9 – Examples of the use of this verb from the Talmud — either the same form, i.e., אִיתְחֲזִי, or a slightly different form, i.e., אִיתְחֲזַאי, the 3rd person *feminine* — are presented in a smaller font.

10 – Sources of the Talmudic quotations (in parentheses).

11 – *Italicized* English translations of the Talmudic quotations.

12 – A note introduced by an asterisk (*). This particular note refers the student to *Grammar for Gemara*, a companion volume to this dictionary.

SAMPLE III: A SECONDARY VERBAL ENTRY

9 8 7 6 5 4 3 2 1

מְסַיֵּיעַ prt. (סיע פִּעֵל); מְסַיַּיעַ* prt. (סיע פַּעֵל)

10

assisting; supporting (a ḥakham in his statement)

13 12 11

וּמִקְרָא מְסַיְּעוֹ (סנהדרין צא,ב) *and a pasuk supports him*

14

* The first form is Hebrew, and the second is Aramaic.

This *co-entry* features a Hebrew form — מְסַיֵּיעַ — and its Aramaic counterpart — מְסַיַּיעַ — indicating that both the Mishnaic Hebrew form and the Aramaic form are used in the Talmud in the same way. It consists of the following elements:

1 – A Hebrew verb in the *present tense* or *participle*, masculine singular.

2 – An abbreviation of the name of this verbal form, prt.

The next two elements are within parentheses:

3 – The *root* of the Hebrew verbal form.

4 – The name of the Hebrew *binyan* (conjugation).

5 – A semicolon (;) separating this Hebrew form from its Aramaic counterpart.

6 – An Aramaic verb in the *present tense* (= *participle*), masculine singular.

NOTE: The asterisk (*) refers to a note at the end of the entry (element 14).

7 – Same as element 2.

The next two elements are within parentheses:

8 – The *root* of the Aramaic verbal form.

9 – The name of the Aramaic *binyan* (conjugation).

10 – English translations in boldface type, which apply equally to both the Hebrew and Aramaic forms.

NOTE: This grammatical form is technically a *participle*, i.e., a verbal adjective. It can be used with any person (1st, 2nd or 3rd) like any other adjective, and it is not limited to the present tense. Thus an English verb with an *–ing* suffix, e.g., *assisting*, is a proper translation. But when this form functions in the Talmud as a *present tense* would in English, it is convenient to translate as a present tense, as in the translation of the Talmudic example in this entry.

11 – An example of the use of one of the two verbal forms (in this case, the Hebrew one) from the Talmud.

12 – The source of the Talmudic quotation within parentheses.

13 – An *italicized* English translation of the Talmudic quotation.

14 – A note introduced by an asterisk (*). This particular note regularly appears at or near the end of Hebrew-Aramaic co-entries in this dictionary.

SAMPLE IV: A MULTIWORD ENTRY

1

הֵיכִי מַשְׁכַּחַתְּ לַהּ

3 2

How can you find it (= such a case)?! כֵּיצַד אַתָּה מוֹצֵא אוֹתָהּ?!

4

This rhetorical question points to a *difficulty* in setting up the case that has been formulated in the mishna or baraitha under discussion.

6 5

בּוֹר שֶׁל שְׁנֵי שׁוּתָּפִין — הֵיכִי מַשְׁכַּחַתְּ לַהּ?! (בבא קמא נא,א)

7

[As for] a pit belonging to two partners — how can you find it (= such a case)?!

This sample entry consists of the following elements:

1 – The Aramaic expression that is to be explained in this entry in boldface type.

2 – A Hebrew translation.

3 – An English translation in boldface type.

NOTE: (Within parentheses) there is an explanation of what "it" refers to.

4 – An explanation of the function of this expression in context.

NOTE: The term *difficulty*, printed in *italics*, characterizes the nature of the expression. Some of the other terms that this dictionary uses in this manner are *controversy, contradiction, halakhic problem, inference, interpretation, proof, refutation, resolution*, and *rule of Biblical interpretation*.

5 – A Talmudic quotation, in a smaller font, that illustrates the use of the expression.

6 – The source of the Talmudic quotation (in parentheses).

7 – An *italicized* English translation of that quotation.

NOTE: The translation contains a set of square brackets at the beginning, which encloses a phrase that is added to make the English read more smoothly, and a set of parentheses at the end, which encloses a clarification.

III. GUIDELINES FOR USING *THE PRACTICAL TALMUD DICTIONARY*

A. Spelling

The entry items in this dictionary are spelled as they appear in the Talmud. When the same word has been spelled in different ways in the Talmud, the more frequent spelling is used. When the second spelling is also fairly common, it is presented to the left of the more frequent spelling, with a slash (/) separating the two forms (e.g., זוּטָא/זוּטַר).

In cases of multiple spellings, a word is sometimes spelled with a vowel letter (e.g., דִּילְמָא or יוֹשֵׁב) and sometimes without a vowel letter (e.g., דִּלְמָא or יֹשֵׁב). The former spelling is called כְּתִיב מָלֵא, *full spelling,* while the latter is called כְּתִיב חָסֵר, *defective spelling.* Full spelling is more common in the Talmud and hence in this dictionary as well.

B. Prefixes

In *The Practical Talmud Dictionary*, entry items appear in alphabetical order with one important exception: Words with common prefixes that have distinct, translatable meanings (e.g., the מ in מֵהָכָא, ***from** here* or the ב in בְּמַאי פְּלִיגִי, ***about** what do they differ?*) are listed according to their spellings *without* the prefixes. Therefore, it is important for anyone who is about to look up an entry in this dictionary to *disregard* the following prefixes.[1]

1. PREFIXES THAT ARE USED IN BOTH HEBREW AND ARAMAIC

-בְּ = *on; in; in a case of; with*
-וְ = *and; but; or*
-כְּ = *like; as*
-לְ = *to; for; according to*
-מִ = *from; than*
Example: קַשְׁיָא לְרָבָא, *it is difficult **according to** Rava[’s opinion]*

2. HEBREW PREFIXES

-כְּשֶׁ = *when*
-שֶׁ = *that; which; who; because; for*
-מִשֶּׁ and -כְּשֶׁ = *when; since; once*
Example: מִשֶּׁנִּכְנָס אֲדָר, ***once** Adar enters*

3. ARAMAIC PREFIXES

-דְּ = *of*
-דְּ = *that; which; who; because; for*
-כִּדְ = *like [the statement] of/that; as*
-מִדְּ = *from [the fact] that; since*
-אַ = *on; upon; by; at; against; with reference to*
Example: דַּאֲמַר רַב, *for Rav said* (Note the vocalization דַּ before אֲ.)
The prefix -קָ[2], which is also in this category, is usually not translated.

---

1 – For a discussion of *verbal* prefixes, see *Grammar for Gemara*: Chapter 3. Assigning distinct translations to verbal prefixes is much more difficult than assigning translations to the prefixes discussed here. It is therefore much more convenient to regard a verbal prefix, e.g., the מ in מְסַיֵּיעַ, as an integral part of the word.

2 – Instead of the prefix -קָ, the Talmud sometimes uses קָא as a separate word. Multiword entries in this dictionary that begin with the word קָא, such as קָא מַשְׁמַע לַן, are listed alphabetically at קָא.

This policy of ignoring prefixes in alphabetizing the entries applies only to prefixes with a distinct meaning. When one of these prefixes (other than -קָ) cannot be translated separately, it is treated as an integral part of the word. For example, לְגַמְרֵי, *completely*, is alphabetized without dropping the initial ל.

C. One-word Entries

The great majority of the entries in *The Practical Talmud Dictionary* are individual words. To locate a one-word entry in this work, it is helpful for the learner to recognize what part of speech is confronting him in the Talmud — or, at least, to determine whether he is dealing with a verb or not. In both Hebrew and Aramaic, some parts of speech always appear in the same form and are easy to locate in a dictionary. Others, especially verbs, appear in a variety of grammatical forms that may confuse the learner.

CONJUNCTIONS (such as אֶלָּא, *but*) and ADVERBS (such as אַכַּתִּי, *still*) do not change.

PREPOSITIONS are also stable, except for the personal-pronoun suffixes that are sometimes added. For example, suffixes are added to the preposition -כְּוָות, *like*, yielding the forms: כְּוָותִי, *like me;* כְּוָותָךְ, *like you;* and so on. See the table of the most common prepositions with pronoun suffixes in *Grammar for Gemara*: Chapter 7. Some of the prefixes listed above, such as -בְּ and -לְ, are prepositions that are sometimes combined with personal-pronoun suffixes to form בֵּיהּ and לֵהּ and so on.

CARDINAL NUMBERS may be either masculine or feminine. For example, the number *one* is חַד (masculine) or חֲדָא (feminine). The common Aramaic cardinal numbers — whether masculine or feminine — appear as separate entries. See Appendix II for the table containing all the cardinal numbers that appear in the Talmud.

ORDINAL NUMBERS occur infrequently in the Talmud, except for קַמָּא, *first*, the only one presented as an entry item in this dictionary. See Appendix II for the table containing all the ordinal numbers in the Talmud.

PRONOUNS also vary according to gender and number, producing several different forms. Since they do occur frequently, all the common Aramaic forms appear as entry items — irrespective of gender and number. See the entries הַאי (m.s.), הָא (f.s.), meaning *this*, and אִילֵּין (pl.), meaning *these*. For tables of Aramaic pronouns, see *Grammar for Gemara*: Chapter 7.

NOUNS are either masculine or feminine. They appear in one of three different states: the absolute state (for example, גְּבַר, *a man*); the construct state (גְּבַר, *a man of*) and the emphatic state (גַּבְרָא, *the man* or *a man*). There are also plural forms for each state. Since the singular of the *emphatic* state is the most common form, we have presented noun entries in that form and added any other common forms of the particular noun within parentheses. See the table of Aramaic nouns in *Grammar for Gemara*: Chapter 6.
Example: גַּבְרָא (abs. גְּבַר, pl. גַּבְרֵי/גּוּבְרִין)

ADJECTIVES also vary according to gender, number, and state. Adjective entry items are presented in the masculine singular of the *emphatic* state, with other forms added in parentheses if they are common. See the table of Aramaic adjectival forms in *Grammar for Gemara*: Chapter 6.
Example: רַבָּא/רַבָּה (abs. רַב, f.s. רַבְּתָא/רַבָּתִי, m. pl. רַבְרְבֵי)

VERBS are by far the most difficult part of speech to locate in a dictionary of a

Semitic language, because many different verbal forms develop from the same root. They vary according to *binyan* (conjugation), tense, person, gender and number, as explained in detail in Chapters 3 and 4 of *Grammar for Gemara.* Unlike most dictionaries that list verbs only according to their roots, *The Practical Talmud Dictionary* presents verbal entries according to those forms that actually occur in the Talmud. As we explained above, the forms אִיבָּעֵי, מוֹתֵיב, and תֵּיפּוֹק appear as entry items, so that the learner does not have to recognize the grammatical roots — בעי, תוב, and נפק, respectively. While it is beyond the scope of this work to list every Aramaic verbal form that occurs in the Talmud, nevertheless the following verbal forms are presented as entry items in this dictionary, since they are the forms most likely to be of assistance to the student:

A *basic verbal entry* has been presented for almost every Aramaic verb. The entry item is the third person, masculine singular form of the *past tense* of any *binyan.*

Examples: אֲזַל (*binyan* קַל), *he went;* צַלִּי (פַּעֵל), *he prayed;* אַפִּיק (אַפְעֵל), *he took out;* אִיכְּסִיף (אִתְפְּעֵל), *he was embarrassed.*

In many cases, the verbal form in the Talmud that confronts the student will resemble the form presented in a basic verbal entry closely enough for him to see the connection between them. In some cases, however, it may be be difficult for the student to make the association. In order to alleviate this problem, *The Practical Talmud Dictionary* also presents common verbal forms as entry items in secondary verbal entries when the initial letter of these forms is different from the initial letter of the form in the basic verbal entry:

1. For all *binyanim* except the simple *binyan* (the קַל), the masculine singular form of the *present tense* or *participle.* This form, which is labeled prt., is always spelled with a -מ prefix that may confuse the student.

Examples: מְזַבֵּין (*binyan* קַל), *selling;* מַפִּישׁ (אַפְעֵל), *increasing;* מִימְּלִיךְ (אִתְפְּעֵל), *reconsidering.*

NOTE: In this dictionary, these verbal prefixes are regarded as an integral part of the word, since they cannot be translated separately. Therefore, these entry items are alphabetized with their prefixes intact.

2. For any *binyan* — the third person, masculine singular of the *future tense.* This form, which is labeled fut., may be confusing because the -ל or -נ prefix for the 3rd person masculine singular differs from the Hebrew usage.

NOTE: In the course of Talmudic argumentation, it is often best translated as *let him/it ...* It is termed the "jussive" by many grammarians.

Examples: לֶיהֱוֵי (*binyan* קַל), *let it be;* נַיְיתֵי (אַפְעֵל), *let him bring.*

3. The *infinitive* of *binyan* קַל. Unlike its Hebrew counterpart, this form (labeled inf.) always has a -מ prefix. Since many students do not recognize the -מ prefix as such and fail to associate this form with its *basic verbal entry,* this dictionary presents the קַל infinitive under the letter מ separately as a secondary verbal entry. When this form precedes a different form of the same verb to strengthen the latter, it is best rendered in English as an *adverb,* such as *very, surely,* or *certainly.* This infinitive is called *the infinitive absolute* by grammarians.

Example: מִיזְהַר זְהִירֵי, *they are very careful.*

When an infinitive is preceded by a -ל prefix with the distinct meaning *to,* it is used like an English infinitive. Grammarians call it *the infinitive construct.* The -ל prefix is ignored in the alphabetization of the entries in this dictionary, since it is not so difficult to recognize.

Example: לְמֵידַע, *to know.*

If the student has still not succeeded in finding the word he seeks, after having followed the above guidelines, he should search for the verbal entry closest to that word by disregarding the following *personal-pronoun suffixes*:
The following suffixes indicate the subject of the verb:[3]

PRESENT TENSE	
I	־נָא
you (s.)	־ַתְּ
she/it (f.)	־ָה, ־ָא
we	־נַן
you (pl.)	־תּוּ, ־תּוּן
they (m.)	־ִי, ־ִין
they (f.)	־ָן

Example: בָּעֵינַן, *we need*

PAST TENSE	
I	־ִ, ־ִי, ־ִית
you (s.)	־תְּ
she/it (f.)	־ָא, ־ָה, ־ַת
we	־ַן, ־נָא, ־נַן
you (pl.)	־תּוּ, ־תּוּן
they (m.)	־וּ
they (f.)	־ָא, ־ָה, ־ָן

Example: בְּעֵינַן, *we needed*

Other suffixes indicate the object of the verb:

me	־ן, ־ַן
you (m.s.)	־ךְ, ־ָךְ
you (f.s.)	־ִיךְ
him, it (m.)	־הּ, ־הוּ, ־ֵיהּ
her, it (f.)	־ָהּ, ־ָהָא, ־ֵהּ
us	־ן, ־נָן, ־ִינַן
you (m. pl.)	־כוּ
you (f. pl.)	־כִי
them (m.)	־נוּן, ־ִינוּן, ־נְהוּ, ־ִינְהוּ
them (f.)	־נְהִי, ־ִינְהִי

Example: שְׁחְטֵיהּ, *he slaughtered it*

The student must also take into account the fact that some of the entry items presented in this dictionary contain a *vowel letter* that does not appear in the form that confronts him in the Talmud. Examples: אַפֵּיק, *he took out*; מְפֵּישׁ, *increasing*.

---

3 – For a fuller presentation of these suffixes and other suffixes for the future tense and the imperative, see *Grammar for Gemara*: Chapter 3 and Chapter 7.35.

D. Multiword Entries

Many terms and expressions in the Talmud are crucial for the proper understanding of the text. Some of them consist of more than one word. The meaning of the whole expression and an understanding of its function in context are more important than the literal translation of its components. The whole is greater than the sum of its parts. Such entries have been listed alphabetically according to their first word, even if the *first* word is of minor importance. When the learner senses that several words form a significant expression, he should look for such an entry according to its *first* word. Otherwise, he can locate a multiword entry through a cross-reference under one of the *important* words in the expression. Thus, the entries אִם תִּמְצָא לוֹמַר and הֵיכִי מַשְׁכַּחַתְּ לַהּ are alphabetized according to אִם and הֵיכִי respectively. They are also cross-referenced under תִּמְצָא and מַשְׁכַּחַתְּ respectively. See SAMPLE IV above.

E. The Publication of an Introduction to Aramaic Grammar

When searching for a Talmudic word or expression in this dictionary, it is very helpful to have a basic knowledge of Aramaic grammar. For this very reason, a companion volume to this dictionary has been prepared, entitled *Grammar for Gemara*. It is a practical introduction to Babylonian Aramaic that features extensive paradigms of the forms found in the Talmud — especially conjugations of verbs.

THE PRACTICAL TALMUD DICTIONARY

א

אַ-

This Aramaic prefix is usually equivalent to the Hebrew preposition עַל with all its various meanings and nuances. It is a contraction of עַל: the ע is replaced by א whose pronunciation was similar to it in Babylonia, and the ל is replaced by a strong *dagesh* in the first letter of the next word whenever possible.

on; upon (1) עַל
יְתִיב אַאַרְעָא (חולין סג,א) *it is sitting on the ground*

at; by; in front of (2) עַל; עַל יַד; לִפְנֵי
אֲתָא עַנְיָא וְקָאֵי אַבָּבָא. (בבא מציעא נט,ב)
A poor man came and stood at the door.

against (3) עַל; נֶגֶד
רְמָא ... מַתְנִיתִין אַבָּרַיְיתָא (ברכות מג, רע"א)
he hurled ... our mishna against a baraitha (= he pointed out a contradiction between them)

with reference to (4) עַל; בְּנוֹגֵעַ ל-
אַסֵּיפָא קָאֵי! (שבת לז,א)
He "stands with reference to" the latter clause! (= The amora is referring to the latter clause of the mishna!)

according to (5) עַל; עַל פִּי
אַלִּיבָּא ד- (בבא קמא כט, רע"ב ועוד)
according to the opinion of

because of; on account of (6) עַל; בִּגְלַל
אַקַּמְצָא וּבַר קַמְצָא חֲרוּב יְרוּשָׁלַיִם. (גיטין נה, סע"ב)
On account of [the incident involving] Kamtza and Bar Kamtza, Jerusalem was destroyed.

for; towards (7) עַל; לְמַעַן
ר' חִיָּיא בַּר יוֹסֵף — יְהַבוּ לֵיהּ זוּזֵי אַמִּלְחָא. (ב"מ מח, רע"ב)
[As for] R. Ḥiyya b. Yosef — [some people] gave him money towards [the purchase of] salt.

(8) אֶת
Sometimes this Aramaic prefix serves as an indicator of a direct object — like the word אֶת in Hebrew. It is not translated into English.
גַּלֵּית אַדַּעְתָּךְ (ב"מ קט,א) *you revealed your intention*
SEE: אַגַּב, אַדַּעְתָּא ד-, אַדְּרַבָּה, אַהָא, אַהֲדָדֵי, אַהֲיָיא, אַיְּדֵי, אַלִּיבָּא ד-, אַפּוּמָּא ד-

אָב (אַב/אֲבִי .constr, אָבוֹת .abs. pl, אֲבוֹת .constr. pl)

father; head; principal category; prototype
SEE: בִּנְיַן אָב

אַב בֵּית דִּין

head of the court; vice president
In the Sanhedrin, this title was held by the ḥakham who was second in rank to the *Nasi*.
יוֹסֵי בֶּן יוֹעֶזֶר ..., יוֹסֵי בֶּן יוֹחָנָן ...; שְׁמַעְיָה ... אַבְטַלְיוֹן .... הָרִאשׁוֹנִים הָיוּ נְשִׂיאִים, וְהַשְּׁנִיִּים אֲבוֹת בָּתֵּי דִּינִין. (חגיגה טז, רע"ב: משנה פ"ב מ"ב)
Yosé b. Yo'ezer ..., Yosé b. Yoḥanan ...; Sh^ema'ya, ... Avtalyon .... The first ones (of each pair) were N^esi'im, and the second ones heads of the court.

אַב מְלָאכָה

principal category of labor (forbidden on the Sabbath)
אֲבוֹת מְלָאכוֹת אַרְבָּעִים חָסֵר אַחַת (שבת עג, סע"א: משנה פ"ז מ"ב)
thirty-nine principal categories of labor

אַבָּא (pl. אֲבָהָן, אֲבָהָתָא)

father (1) אָב
כָּל מִצְוָתָא דִמְחַיַּיב אַבָּא לְמֶיעֱבַד לִבְרֵיהּ ... (קידושין ל,ב)
All duties that a father must perform for his son ...

my father; Father (2) אָבִי
אַבָּא גָּדוֹל מֵאָבִיךָ! (סנהדרין לז, סע"ב: משנה פ"ד מ"ה)
My father is superior to yours!

Abba ... (3) ... אַבָּא
This word is sometimes used as a title of respect before a proper name.
אַבָּא שָׁאוּל (ברכות לא,א ועוד) *Abba Sha'ul*

Abba (4) אַבָּא
This word itself is sometimes used as a proper name.*
ר' אַבָּא (סנהדרין יז,ב ועוד) *R. Abba*

* In addition to several ḥakhamim who were called by this name in the Talmud, *Abba* was most likely the proper name of the famous amora who was known as *Rav*. See Rashi on חולין קלז, סע"ב and Rashbam on בבא בתרא נב,א — as opposed to Rashi's comment on ברכות מז,א.
SEE: אִמָּא

אַבָּרַאי

outside בַּחוּץ
וְלֵיתֵּיב אִיהוּ מִגַּוַּאי וְאֶינָשׁ אַחֲרִינָא מֵאַבָּרַאי (גיטין סט,א)
and he should sit inside and another man outside
SEE: בָּר; גַּוַּאי

אַבָּתְרֵיהּ/בָּתְרֵיהּ

after him אַחֲרָיו
SEE: בָּתַר

אַגַּב (אַ+גַּב) "עַל גַּב"; עַל יְדֵי

on the basis of; by means of; by virtue of

אַגַּב אוֹרְחֵיהּ לְפִי דַּרְכּוֹ; דֶּרֶךְ אַגַּב

by the way; in passing; incidentally
For an example, see מִילְּתָא אַגַּב אוֹרְחֵיהּ קָא מַשְׁמַע לַן.

אַגַּב גְּרָרָא "עַל יְדֵי גְּרִירָה"; דֶּרֶךְ אַגַּב

"through dragging"; incidentally

הָכָא עִיקָר; הָתָם אַגַּב גְּרָרָא נְסָבָהּ. (בבא מציעא ד, סע"ב)
Here (= this mishna) is the principal (source); there (in another mishna) he mentioned it incidentally.

אַגַּב ד- "עַל יְדֵי שֶׁ-"; כֵּיוָן שֶׁ- **since**

אַגַּב דַּחֲשִׁיבִי, מַשְׁמוּשֵׁי מְמַשְׁמֵשׁ בְּהוּ. (בבא מציעא כא,ב)
Since [these items] are valuable, he frequently gropes for them.

אַגַּב מְקַרְקְעֵי/קַרְקַע עַל יְדֵי קַרְקָעוֹת/קַרְקַע
by virtue of [the transfer of] land

According to Torah law, certain modes of transferring ownership (קִנְיָנִים) are effective only for land, while others are effective only for movable objects. Through קִנְיַן אַגַּב (קרקע), it is possible to make a "package deal" wherein one of the modes for transferring land (for example, the payment of money) effects not only the transfer of land, but the transfer of some movables as well.

מִטַּלְטְלֵי אַגַּב מְקַרְקְעֵי הִקְנָה לָהֶם (בבא מציעא יא,ב)
he transferred movables to them by virtue of [his transfer of] land

אַגְבִּי (גבי אַפְעֵל: מַגְבֵּי .prt, לְאַגְבּוּיֵי .inf) הִגְבָּה
he caused/ordered to be collected; he confiscated

רַב פָּפָּא אַגְבִּי אַרְבַּע מְאָה זוּזֵי לְבוֹשֶׁת. (בבא קמא פד,ב)
Rav Pappa ordered four hundred zuz to be collected [as payment] for [causing] embarrassment.

SEE: גְּבִי

אַגָּדָה/ הַגָּדָה, אַגַּדְתָּא* **aggada; narration**

The aggada comprises all the teachings presented in the Talmud and Midrash that are not directly concerned with halakha. These include Biblical interpretations, the amplification of the Biblical narrative, maxims, doctrines, reasons for the commandments, anecdotes, and historical data about the Talmudic period. Occasionally, הַגָּדָה and אַגַּדְתָּא refer to the Pesaḥ Haggada.

מָר אָמַר לֵיהּ: לֵימָא מָר שְׁמַעְתָּא; וּמָר אֲמַר לֵיהּ: לֵימָא מָר אַגַּדְתָּא. (בבא קמא ס,ב)
One said to him: Will the master (= you) state a halakha; while the other said to him: Will the master state an aggada.

דְּבָרִים שֶׁמּוֹשְׁכִין לִבּוֹ שֶׁל אָדָם כְּאַגָּדָה* (שבת פז, סע"א)
matters that attract the heart of a person like aggada

* The root of both the Hebrew noun אַגָּדָה/הַגָּדָה and the Aramaic noun אַגַּדְתָּא is נגד, as in the Hebrew verb הִגִּיד, *he told*. The characterisation of aggada as *attractive*, in the second Talmudic example, may have been inspired by the Aramaic verb נְגַד from the same root, which means *he pulled* or *he attracted*.

אַגְמַר (גמר אַפְעֵל) לִמֵּד **he taught**

אַגְמְרֵיהּ (אַגְמַר+ֵיהּ) לִמֵּד אוֹתוֹ **he taught him**

אַגְמְרֵיהּ רַחֲמָנָא לְמֹשֶׁה (עירובין טו,ב)
*the Merciful [God] taught Moshe**

* Literally: *(he) taught him, Moshe.* The pronoun *him*, which is redundant in English, anticipates the direct object *Moshe*.

SEE: גְּמַר

אֲגַר (אגר: אָגַר .act. prt, אֲגִיר .pass. prt, לְמֵיגַר .inf)
שְׂכַר **he hired; he rented**

הַאי מָאן דַּאֲגַר אֲגִירֵי (בבא מציעא עו, סע"ב)
someone who hired laborers

אֲגַר נְטַר לֵיהּ/לִי שְׂכַר הַמְתֵּן לוֹ/לִי
compensation for waiting for him/me

This is an interest charge that a seller adds to the purchase price (or a lessor to the rental fee) in exchange for postponing the collection of the payment that is due. It comes under the prohibition of usury.

כְּלָלָא דְרִבִּיתָא: כָּל אֲגַר נְטַר לֵיהּ אָסוּר. (בבא מציעא סג,ב)
The general principle of usury is: Any compensation for waiting for him is forbidden.

אַגְרָא (אֲגַר .abs. and constr)
שָׂכָר **a reward; compensation; rent; wages**

לְפוּם צַעֲרָא אַגְרָא. (משנה אבות סוף פרק ה)
According to the suffering is the reward.

אַד- (אַד+ד- = עַד+ד-)

(1) עַד שֶׁ-; בִּזְמַן שֶׁ- **until; while; by the time that**

דִּלְמָא אַדְּאָתֵית, שָׁכֵיב ר' אַבָּא. (בבא קמא קד,ב ורש"י שם)
Perhaps by the time you come [back], R. Abba will die.

(2) עַד שֶׁ-; בִּמְקוֹם שֶׁ- **instead of; rather than**

For examples, see אַדְּמִיפַּלְגֵי בּ- ... לִיפְלְגוּ בּ- as well as אַדְּתָנֵי ... לִיפְלוֹג וְלִיתְנֵי בְּדִידָהּ.

אַדְבַּר (דבר אַפְעֵל)
הִנְהִיג; הוֹלִיךְ **he led; he directed**

SEE: דְּבַר

אַדְבְּרֵיהּ* (אַדְבַּר+ֵיהּ)
הוֹלִיךְ אוֹתוֹ **he led him; he brought him**

אַדְבְּרֵיהּ רַב חִסְדָּא לְרַבָּנָא עוּקְבָא וּדְרַשׁ. (ביצה כט, סע"א ורש"י שם; אבל עי' ר"ח שם)
Rav Hisda brought Rabbana Ukba forward [into the beth midrash] and [the latter] expounded.

* See note under אַגְמְרֵיהּ.

אַדְהָכִי (אַד+ד+הָכִי)
עַד כָּךְ; בֵּינְתַיִם **meanwhile**

אַדְהָכִי וְהָכִי עַד כָּךְ וְכָךְ; בֵּינְתַיִם **meanwhile**

אַדְהָכִי וְהָכִי אֵיזִיל וְאֶשְׁמַע מִלְּתָא מִבֵּי מִדְרְשָׁא. (ברכות טז, רע"א ע"פ כת"י)

Meanwhile I will go and listen to a pronouncement from the beth midrash.

אַדְכַּר (דכר אַפעל: מַדְכַּר .prt, לְאַדְכּוּרֵי .inf)

(1) הִזְכִּיר; אָמַר **he mentioned; he recited**

אַדְכַּר לֵיהּ בִּקְרִיאַת שְׁמַע (ברכות כא,א)

he mentioned it (= the exodus from Egypt) during the reading of Sh'ma

(2) הִזְכִּיר; גָּרַם שֶׁמִּישֶׁהוּ יִזָּכֵר **he reminded**

אַדְכְּרֵיהּ חוּרְבַּן בֵּית הַמִּקְדָּשׁ. (כתובות סב,א)

He reminded him [about] the destruction of the Beth HaMikdash.

אִדְּכַר

SEE: אִידְּכַר

אַדְמִיפַלְגִי ב-... לִיפַלְגוּ ב-...

עַד שֶׁחֲלוּקִים הֵם בְּ-..., יֵחָלְקוּ בְּ-...

Instead of their disagreeing about ... [that case], let them disagree about ... [this case]!

This formula points out that there is a *difficulty* with the proposed interpretation of a tannaitic controversy. It is argued that if that interpretation were indeed correct, a different case would have been presented in the tannaitic text as the subject of the controversy.

אַדְמִיפַלְגִי בִּסְפֵיקוֹ, לִיפַלְגוּ בְּוַדַּאי! (מכות יז, רע"א)

Instead of [R. Eliezer and the Ḥakhamim] disagreeing about [a case where there is] a doubt [whether the produce has been tithed], let them disagree about [a case of] certainty [that it has not been tithed]!*

* Literally: "about its doubt"

SEE: אַד-

אַדַּעְתָּא ד- עַל דַּעַת; לְדַעַת

with intention for

SEE: דַּעַת, לָאו אַדַּעְתַּאי

אַדַּעְתָּא דְהָכִי עַל דַּעַת כָּךְ

with this intention; with such an understanding

אַדַּעְתָּא דְהָכִי לָא יְהַב. (בבא קמא קי, סע"ב ורש"י שם)

He did not give [the money] with this intention.

אַדַּעְתָּא דְנַפְשֵׁיהּ עַל דַּעַת עַצְמוֹ; בְּיָזְמָתוֹ

of his own accord; on his own initiative

נָכְרִי אַדַּעְתָּא דְנַפְשֵׁיהּ קָא עָבֵיד. (יבמות קיד,א ע"פ כת"י)

The non-Jew is acting on his own.

אַדְּרַבָּה/אַדְּרַבָּא* (אַ+דְּ+רַבָּה)

"עַל הַגְּדוֹלָה"; גְּדוֹלָה מִזּוֹ; לְהֶפֶךְ **on the contrary**

שְׁחוּנָה מַעַלְיוּתָא הִיא? אַדְּרַבָּה, גְּרִיעוּתָא הִיא! (תענית כד,ב)

Is [a] hot [year] an advantage? On the contrary, it is a disadvantage!

* This word should not be confused with אַדְּרַבָּה (as in בבא מציעא יח, סע"א), *against that [opinion] of Rabba*, or אַדְּרָבָא (as in בבא בתרא ל,א), *against that [opinion] of Rava*. The student can determine the appropriate meaning from the context.

אַדְּרַבָּה אִיפְכָא מִסְתַּבְּרָא

גְּדוֹלָה מִזּוֹ: הַהֵפֶךְ מִסְתַּבֵּר! **On the contrary! The reverse makes [more] sense!**

This expression presents a *logical objection* to the argument that was just quoted in the Talmud.

אֲמַר רַבָּה: מִסְתַּבְּרָא: עֲבוֹדָה זָרָה, דִּלְיָם הַמֶּלַח קָא אָזְלָא, לָא בָּעְיָא שְׁחִיקָה; חָמֵץ, דִּלְשְׁאָר נְהָרוֹת קָאָזֵיל, בָּעֵי פֵּירוּר. אֲמַר לֵיהּ רַב יוֹסֵף: אַדְּרַבָּה! אִיפְכָא מִסְתַּבְּרָא! עֲבוֹדָה זָרָה, דְּלָא מְמִיסָה, בָּעֵי שְׁחִיקָה; חָמֵץ, דְּמָמֵיס, לָא בָּעֵי פֵּירוּר. (פסחים כח,א)

Rabba said: It stands to reason: An idol, which is going [to be cast] into the Dead Sea, does not require crushing (since it is unlikely that it will be retrieved); ḥametz, which is going [to be cast] into any river, requires crumbling. Rav Yosef said to him: On the contrary! The reverse makes [more] sense! An idol, which does not dissolve, requires crushing; ḥametz, which dissolves, does not require crumbling!

אַדְּתָנֵי ... לִיפְלוֹג וְלִיתְנֵי בְּדִידַהּ

עַד שֶׁהוּא שׁוֹנֶה ..., יַחֲלֹק בָּהּ בְּעַצְמָהּ וְיִשְׁנֶה ...!

Instead of stating ... [an additional clause], [he] should have formulated a distinction in [this clause] itself and stated ...!

An interpretation of a tanna's halakha is sometimes challenged in the following manner: If that interpretation were indeed correct, the tanna would have drawn a distinction within the same clause of the mishna or baraitha — instead of formulating a separate clause to express that distinction.

משנה: הָיָה בַּעַל קוֹרָה רִאשׁוֹן וּבַעַל חָבִית אַחֲרוֹן: (1) נִשְׁבְּרָה הֶחָבִית בַּקּוֹרָה — פָּטוּר; (2) וְאִם עָמַד בַּעַל הַקּוֹרָה — חַיָּיב; (3) וְאִם אָמַר לְבַעַל הֶחָבִית "עֲמוֹד" — פָּטוּר. (בבא קמא לא,א: משנה פ"ג מ"ה)

תלמוד: [חַיָּיב] כְּשֶׁעָמַד לָפוּשׁ [אֲבָל פָּטוּר כְּשֶׁעָמַד לְכַתֵּף]. אַדְּתָנֵי סֵיפָא: וְאִם אָמַר לוֹ לְבַעַל חָבִית "עֲמוֹד", פָּטוּר — לִיפְלוֹג וְלִיתְנֵי בְּדִידַהּ: בַּמֶּה דְּבָרִים אֲמוּרִים? כְּשֶׁעָמַד לָפוּשׁ — אֲבָל עָמַד לְכַתֵּף, פָּטוּר! (שם לא,א)

MISHNA: The carrier of a beam was [walking] first, and the carrier of a barrel behind: (1) If the barrel broke by [colliding with] the beam, he (= the carrier of the beam) is exempt. (2) But if the carrier of the beam stopped [suddenly], he is liable. (3) But if he had cried out to the carrier of the barrel "Halt!" — he is exempt.

TALMUD: [The ruling in the second clause, "he is liable," applies only] where he stopped to rest [but not where he had stopped merely to adjust the beam on his shoulder. Against this qualification the Talmud argues that, if it were true] instead of stating [in] the last clause: "But if he had cried out to the carrier of the barrel 'Halt!', he is exempt," [the tanna] should have formulated a distinction [in the second clause] itself and stated: "Under what circumstances [is he liable]? Where he stopped to rest — but if he stopped to adjust

the beam on his shoulder, he is exempt" (and most certainly if he had cried out "Halt!")!
SEE: אַד־

אַהָא (אַ+הָא)

on this; with reference to this — עַל זֹאת

אִיכָּא דְמַתְנֵי לַהּ אַהָא. (מכות ח, רע"ב ועוד)
There is [an authority] who teaches it (= the same statement) with reference to this [text].

אַהֲדָדֵי (אַ+הֲדָדֵי)

upon each other — (1) זֶה עַל זֶה

מַנְחֵי אַהֲדָדֵי (בבא מציעא כה, סע"א)
they are resting upon each other

one against the other — (2) זֶה נֶגֶד זֶה

קָשׁוּ קְרָאֵי אַהֲדָדֵי! (קידושין ב,ב)
The p^{e}sukim are difficult one against the other (= they contradict each other)!

each other — (3) זֶה אֶת זֶה

In this sense, the אַ־ prefix indicates a direct object, but it is not translated in English.
they remind each other — מַדְכְּרֵי אַהֲדָדֵי (עירובין ג,א)
SEE: אַ־

אַהְדַּר (הדר אַפְעֵל: מְהַדַּר .prt, לְאַהְדּוּרֵי .inf)

he returned; he restored — (1) הֶחֱזִיר

אַהְדַּרְנִיךְ לִמְדִינְתִּיךְ. (כתובות נא,א: משנה פ"ד מ"ח)
I will return you to your city.

he replied; he answered — (2) הֵשִׁיב; עָנָה

לָא אַהְדַּר לֵיהּ רָבָא. (בבא בתרא ט,א)
Rava did not answer him.

he turned (his face) — (3) הֶחֱזִיר (פָּנָיו); הָפַךְ (פָּנָיו)

אַהְדְּרִינְהוּ אִיהוּ לְאַפֵּיהּ לְגַבֵּי שְׁרָגָא. (שבת קכב, רע"ב)
He turned his face towards the lamp.
SEE: הֲדַר

אַהֵיָּא (אַ+הֵיָּא)

on which? about which? — עַל אֵיזוֹ?

The Talmud has quoted a halakhic text — either a mishna, a baraitha, or an amora's statement — that comprises several clauses. The last clause presents either a dissenting opinion or a modification or a comment. Now the Talmud uses the term אַהֵיָּא to raise the *question:* Which of the earlier clauses or elements in the text that was quoted is being disputed, modified, or commented upon by the last clause? In most cases, this question is followed by a tentative reply introduced by the term אֵילֵימָא.

ברייתא: (1) אֵין חוֹתְכִין שְׁפוֹפֶרֶת בְּיוֹם טוֹב, וְאֵין צָרִיךְ לוֹמַר בְּשַׁבָּת. (2) נָפְלָה — מַחֲזִירִין אוֹתָהּ בְּשַׁבָּת, וְאֵין צָרִיךְ לוֹמַר בְּיוֹם טוֹב. (3) וְר' יֹאשִׁיָּה מֵקֵל.
תלמוד: ר' יֹאשִׁיָּה אַהֵיָּא? אִילֵימָא אַרֵישָׁא — הָא קָמְתַקֵּן מָנָא! אֶלָּא אַסֵּיפָא — תַּנָּא קַמָּא נָמֵי מִישְׁרָא קָשָׁרֵי! (שבת קמו,ב)

BARAITHA: (1) One must not cut a tube (for a pipe or a faucet) on a festival — and certainly not on the Sabbath. (2) [If] it has fallen (from the bottle where it served as a pipe), one may replace it on the Sabbath — and certainly on a festival. (3) R. Yoshiyya rules leniently.
TALMUD: About which (of the two halakhoth does R. Yoshiyya rule leniently)? If we say [he is talking] about the first clause —[the person] is surely preparing a utensil (an act that is clearly forbidden)! But [if he is talking] about the latter clause — even the first (anonymous) tanna, permits [such an act], (and there is no point to R. Yoshiyya's lenient ruling)!
SEE: אֵילֵימָא

אַהֲנִי* (הני אַפְעֵל: מְהַנֵּי .prt) — הֶהֱנָה; הוֹעִיל

he benefited; it was effective; it took effect

אַהֲנִי גְּזֵירָה שָׁוָה, וְאַהֲנִי קְרָא. (בבא קמא ו,ב)
The גְּזֵירָה־שָׁוָה *analogy was effective (in establishing one halakhic point), and the pasuk (itself) was effective (in establishing another point).*

* Do not confuse אַהֲנִי with אַהָנֵי (= אַ+הָנֵי), *on these!*

אוֹגַר (אגר אַפְעֵל: מוֹגַר .prt, לְאוֹגוּרֵי .inf)

he rented out; he hired out — הִשְׂכִּיר

הַהוּא גַּבְרָא דְּאוֹגַר לֵיהּ חֲמָרָא לְחַבְרֵיהּ ... (בבא מציעא פא,ב)
There was a man who hired out a donkey to his friend...
SEE: אֲגַר

אוֹדֵי (ידי אַפְעֵל: מוֹדֵי .prt, אוֹדִי .imp, אוֹדוּיֵי .inf)

he admitted (responsibility) — (1) הוֹדָה

כְּפַר בְּמִקְצָת, וְאוֹדִי בְּמִקְצָת. (שבועות לט,ב)
He denied part (of the claim against him), and he admitted part.

he accepted (his opponent's view); he agreed (with) — (2) הוֹדָה; הִסְכִּים

וְאוֹדִי לֵיהּ הִלֵּל לְשַׁמַּאי (עבודה זרה לט, סע"ב)
but Hillel accepted [the view of] Shammai

he thanked; he acknowledged — (3) הוֹדָה; הִבִּיעַ תּוֹדָה

עַבְדָּא דְּמַפֵּיק לֵיהּ מָרֵיהּ לְחֵירוּת וְיָהֵיב לֵיהּ כַּסְפָּא וְדַהֲבָא ... בָּעֵי לְאוֹדוּיֵי וּלְשַׁבּוּחֵי. (פסחים קטז, סע"א)
A slave whose master releases him to freedom and gives him silver and gold ... needs to thank [his master] and praise [him].
SEE: לְדִידֵי... אֶלָּא לְדִידְכוּ אוֹדוּ לִי מִיהָא ד־

אוֹדַע (ידע אַפְעֵל: מוֹדַע .prt, לְאוֹדוּעֵי .inf)

he informed — הוֹדִיעַ

אוֹדְעֵיהּ לְבַעַל שָׂדֶה, וְאוֹדְעִינְהוּ לְסָהֲדֵי (בבא קמא קב, סע"ב)
he informed the owner of the field, and he informed the witnesses

אוֹזִיף (יזף אַפְעֵל: מוֹזִיף .prt)

he loaned — הִלְוָה

(usually money with the understanding that it may be spent and the same amount paid back)

... אוֹזְפֵיה וּפַרְעֵיהּ. (שבועות מא, סע"ב)

... [the plaintiff] had loaned him [the money] and [the defendant] had paid him back.

SEE: יְזַף, אוֹשִׁיל

אוּכָּמָא שָׁחוֹר **black**

עוֹרֵב אוּכָּמָא (חולין סג,א) *a black raven*

אוּלְמָא כֹּחַ; חֹזֶק **strength; superiority**

SEE: (וּ)מָאי אוּלְמֵיהּ ד־... מִ־

אוֹמֶד **assessment; estimate**

תְּרוּמָה גְדוֹלָה נִיטֶּלֶת בְּאוֹמֶד (גיטין לא, רע"א)

the great t^e^ruma may be set aside by estimate

אוּמְדָּנָא אוֹמֶד דַּעְתּוֹ שֶׁל אָדָם **"estimation"; an assumption (with respect to the motive or intention of a person in a specific legal situation)**

מָאן תַּנָּא דְאָזְלִינַן בָּתַר אוּמְדָּנָא? אֲמַר רַב נַחְמָן: ר' שִׁמְעוֹן בֶּן מְנַסְיָא הִיא, דְּתַנְיָא: הֲרֵי שֶׁהָלַךְ בְּנוֹ לִמְדִינַת הַיָּם, וְשָׁמַע שֶׁמֵּת בְּנוֹ, וְעָמַד וְכָתַב כָּל נְכָסָיו לְאַחֵר, וְאַחַר כָּךְ בָּא בְנוֹ .... ר' שִׁמְעוֹן בֶּן מְנַסְיָא אוֹמֵר: אֵין מַתְּנָתוֹ מַתָּנָה, שֶׁאִלְמָלֵא הָיָה יוֹדֵעַ שֶׁבְּנוֹ קַיָּים, לֹא הָיָה כּוֹתְבָן. (בבא בתרא קמו,ב)

Who is the tanna [who holds] that we follow an assumption? Rav Naḥman said: It is [the view of] R. Shim'on b. M^e^nasya, for it is taught (in a baraitha): [If] a person's son went overseas, and he (= the father) heard that his son died, and he went and assigned in writing all his property to someone else, but subsequently his son reappeared .... R. Shim'on b. M^e^nasya says: His gift is not a [legally valid] gift, for had he known that his son was alive, he would not have assigned it [to another].

אוּמָּן; אוּמָּנָא* **artisan; craftsman**

הָאוּמָּנִין קוֹרִין בְּרֹאשׁ הָאִילָן. (ברכות טז,א: משנה פ"ב מ"ד)

Craftsmen may read [the Sh^e^ma while they are] at the top of a tree.

* The first form of the word is Hebrew. The second, which is Aramaic, sometimes refers to a person who treats the ill through bloodletting (as in ב"מ צז,א ורש"י שם).

אוּמָּנוּת; אוּמָּנוּתָא* **handicraft; trade**

ר' יְהוּדָה אוֹמֵר: כָּל שֶׁאֵינוֹ מְלַמֵּד אֶת בְּנוֹ אוּמָּנוּת מְלַמְּדוֹ לִיסְטוּת. (קידושין כט,א)

R. Y^e^huda says: Anyone who does not teach his son a trade teaches him robbery.

* The first form is Hebrew, the second is Aramaic.

וְאוֹמֵר SEE: וְאוֹמֵר

אוֹנֶס*; אוֹנְסָא** **force; duress; accident; inevitable circumstances**

תְּחִילָּתוֹ בִּפְשִׁיעָה, וְסוֹפוֹ בְּאוֹנֶס. (בבא קמא כא,ב)

Its inception (= the beginning of the damaging act) was due to negligence, but its culmination was due to inevitable circumstances.

אוֹנְסָא דִשְׁכִיחַ (כתובות ג,א) *an accident that is frequent*

* Do not confuse this Hebrew noun with the next entry!

** This form is Aramaic.

SEE: אָנַס, אֲנַס

אוֹנֵס (אנס .prt) **rapist**

הָאוֹנֵס נוֹתֵן אֶת הַצַּעַר, וְהַמְפַתֶּה אֵינוֹ נוֹתֵן אֶת הַצַּעַר. (כתובות לט,א: משנה פ"ג מ"ד)

A rapist must pay for the pain (he caused), while a seducer does not have to pay for pain.

SEE: אָנַס, אֲנַס

אוֹסֵיף (יסף אַפְעֵל: מוֹסֵיף .prt, לוֹסֵיף .fut, לְאוֹסוֹפֵי .inf) הוֹסִיף **he added; he increased**

מִשְׁנֵה תוֹרָה לְאוֹסוֹפֵי הוּא דַּאֲתָא. (חולין סג, רע"ב)

The book of D^e^varim has come to add (mitzvoth not mentioned in the earlier books of the Torah).

אוֹקִי/אוֹקִים (קום אַפְעֵל: מוֹקֵים .prt, לוֹקֵים .fut, אוֹקִי .imp, לְאוֹקוֹמֵי .inf)

(1) הֶעֱמִיד; הֵקִים **he had (someone) stand**

אוֹקִי רָבָא אָמוֹרָא עֲלֵיהּ וּדְרַשׁ. (בבא בתרא קכז, סע"א)

Rava had an interpreter stand by his side and lectured.

(2) הֶעֱמִיד **he set up; he maintained (the status quo)**

אוֹקִי מָמוֹנָא בְּחֶזְקַת מָרֵיהּ! (קידושין מה,ב ושי"נ)

Maintain the money (or property) in the possession of its owner (in accordance with the status quo)!

(3) הֶעֱמִיד; פֵּרֵשׁ **he set up (a text as referring to a specific case or as presenting the opinion of a particular tanna); he interpreted (a mishna or a baraitha)***

וְהָא אוֹקִימְנָא: רֵישָׁא בִּמְצִיאָה וְסֵיפָא בְּמִקָּח וּמִמְכָּר?! (ב"מ ח,א)

But have we not interpreted: The first clause [of our mishna refers] to [finding] a lost article and the latter clause to buying and selling?!

* Such an interpretation is called an אוֹקִימְתָּא by Rashi.

SEE: (בְּ)מָאי אוֹקִימְתָּא

אוֹרַח אַרְעָא

(1) דֶּרֶךְ אֶרֶץ **"the way of the land"; proper conduct; good manners**

כַּרְעֵיהּ — לָאו אוֹרַח אַרְעָא לְגַלּוֹיֵי קַמֵּיהּ רַבֵּיהּ. (חגיגה יג,ב)

It is not [considered] good manners to uncover one's leg in the presence of his teacher.

(2) דַּרְכּוֹ שֶׁל עוֹלָם **"the way of the world"; the usual practice**

אוֹרַח אַרְעָא לְמִשְׁדָּא אוּמְצָא לְכַלְבָּא. (שבת קנה,ב)

It is the usual practice to throw raw meat to a dog.

אוֹרְחָא דְמִילְּתָא קָתָנֵי*

דַּרְכּוֹ שֶׁל הָעִנְיָן הוּא שׁוֹנֶה

"the normal way of the matter" he is teaching; he is presenting the usual case

This *explanation* of a mishna or baraitha rejects an attempt to draw halakhic conclusions from the wording of the text. It is argued that the tanna speaks of a particular situation — not because he restricts the halakha to that particular case — but because that situation is most common.

משנה: מִיַּד הַתִּינוֹקוֹת שׁוֹמְטִין אֶת לוּלְבֵיהֶן וְאוֹכְלִין אֶתְרוֹגֵיהֶן. (סוכה מה,א: משנה פ"ד מ"ז)

תלמוד: תִּינוֹקוֹת — אִין, גְּדוֹלִים — לָא?! הוּא הַדִּין דַּאֲפִילּוּ גְּדוֹלִים, וְהָא דְקָתָנֵי "תִּינוֹקוֹת" — אוֹרְחָא דְמִלְּתָא קָתָנֵי. (שם מו,ב ועי' רש"י)

MISHNA: From the hands of the children they take their lulavim (= the children's) and eat their ethrogim [on the seventh day of the Sukkoth festival].

TALMUD: [From] children — but not [from] adults?! — The same law applies even to [those of] adults, and [the reason] that [the tanna] states "children" [is that] he is presenting the usual case.

* A similar idea is sometimes expressed in the Mishna:

דִּבֵּר הַכָּתוּב בַּהוֹוֶה (בבא קמא נד,ב: משנה פ"ה מ"ז)

Scripture has spoken about the usual situation.

דִּבְּרוּ חֲכָמִים בַּהוֹוֶה (שבת סה,א; סו,ב: משנה פ"ו מ"ו ומ"ט)

The hakhamim have spoken about the usual situation.

אוֹרְחֵיהּ דַּרְכּוֹ

his normal way; its usual manner; its custom

קֶרֶן, כֵּיוָן דַּעֲבַד תְּרֵי וּתְלָתָא זִימְנֵי, אוֹרְחֵיהּ הוּא. (ב"ק כו,א)

[As for an animal that causes damage with its] horn, after it has done [so] two or three times, this is [considered] its usual manner.

SEE: אַגַּב אוֹרְחֵיהּ, מִילְּתָא אַגַּב אוֹרְחֵיהּ קָא מַשְׁמַע לַן

אוֹרְחֵיהּ דִּקְרָא דֶּרֶךְ הַכָּתוּב

normal Biblical style (as opposed to an extraordinary expression whose uniqueness would teach a certain point)

"אִישׁ" אֲמַר רַחֲמָנָא — וְלָא "אִשָּׁה", אוֹ דִלְמָא אוֹרְחֵיהּ דִּקְרָא הוּא? (בבא קמא קט, רע"ב ע"פ במדבר ה:ח)

Has the Torah (specifically) stated a "man" — but not a "woman" (thereby excluding women from this halakha), or perhaps this is normal Biblical style (and so women are not necessarily excluded)?

אוֹרֵי (ירי אַפְעֵל: מוֹרֵי .prt, אוֹרוּיֵי .inf)

he taught; he issued a ruling הוֹרָה; פָּסַק

כֵּיוָן דְּאוֹרֵי בַּהּ חָכָם, הֵיכִי אֲכַל מִינַּהּ?! (חולין מד,ב)

Since a hakham had issued a ruling [forbidding] it, how did he eat from it?

SEE: אוֹרָיָין, אוֹרַיְיתָא

אוֹרָיָין/אוֹרָיָאן תּוֹרָה

Torah

בְּרִיךְ רַחֲמָנָא דִּיהַב אוֹרָיָאן תְּלִיתָאֵי לְעַם תְּלִיתָאֵי ... (שבת פח,א ורש"י שם;בכת"ים: אוריין)

Blessed is the Merciful (God) who has given the tripartite Torah (תנ"ך) to the tripartite nation ...

SEE: בַּר אוֹרָיָין

אוֹרַיְיתָא תּוֹרָה

Torah

This term — usually with a ־ד prefix — designates a mitsva to be of Torah origin and Torah status, as opposed to a law enacted by the hakhamim.

מַצָּה בִּזְמַן הַזֶּה דְּאוֹרַיְיתָא, וּמָרוֹר דְּרַבָּנָן. (פסחים קכ,א)

[The eating of] matza nowadays is [a mitzva] of Torah [status], whereas [the eating of] bitter herbs is [a law] of the hakhamim.

בְּדִיקַת חָמֵץ דְּרַבָּנָן הוּא, דְּמִדְּאוֹרַיְיתָא בְּבִיטּוּל בְּעָלְמָא סַגִּי (פסחים ד,ב)

searching for hametz is [a mitzva] of Rabbinic status, because according to Torah law, mere (verbal) nullification is sufficient

אוּרְתָּא עֶרֶב; תְּחִלַּת הַלַּיְלָה

evening; beginning of the night

וְדָוִד בְּפַלְגָא דְּלֵילְיָא הֲוָה קָאֵי? מֵאוּרְתָּא הֲוָה קָאֵי! (ברכות ג,ב ורש"י שם)

Did [King] David get up at midnight? He used to get up at the beginning of the night!

אוֹשִׁיל (שאל אַפְעֵל: מוֹשִׁיל .prt, אוֹשׁוֹלֵי .inf)

he lent (something to be returned intact) הִשְׁאִיל

אוֹשְׁלַהּ מָקוֹם (גיטין עז, סע"ב ורש"י שם)

he lent her a place [in his courtyard]

SEE: אוֹזִיף, שְׁאֵיל

אוּשְׁפִּיזָא

lodging place; inn* (1) מָקוֹם לִינָה; אַכְסַנְיָא

אִית לֵיהּ אוּשְׁפִּיזָא בְּאֶרֶץ יִשְׂרָאֵל (גיטין מד,ב)

he has a lodging place in Eretz Yisrael

host; innkeeper** (2) מְאָרֵחַ; בַּעַל מָלוֹן

מִשְׁתַּתַּפְנָא בִּפְרִיטֵי בַּהֲדֵי אוּשְׁפִּיזַאי (שבת כג,א ע"פ כת"י)

I used to participate (in the cost of the Hannukka lights) with my host by [paying] money

* Compare the Latin ***hospitium*** and the English ***hospice***.

** Compare the Latin ***hospes*** and the English ***host***. In the ***Zohar*** the word means ***guest*** in the notion of the אוּשְׁפִּיזִין who visit the ***sukka***.

אוּשְׁפִּיזְכָן

innkeeper; host אוּשְׁפִּיזָא; מְאָרֵחַ

זָכָה בִנְיָמִין הַצַּדִּיק וְנַעֲשָׂה אוּשְׁפִּיזְכָן לַגְּבוּרָה. (יומא יב,א)

Binyamin the righteous had the merit, and he became the host of the Omnipotent (since the Holy of Holies is located within the territory of his tribe).

* The suffix ־כָן, ***khan***, may be of Persian origin.

אוֹתֵיב[1] (תוב אַפְעֵל: מוֹתִיב/מְתִיב prt., לוֹתִיב fut., לְאוֹתוּבֵי inf.)

he refuted — הֵשִׁיב; הִקְשָׁה

אוֹתְבֵיהּ ר' אַבָּא בַּר מֶמֶל לְר' אַמִי (בבא מציעא לו,ב)

R. Abba b. Memel refuted R. Ammi

SEE: (וְ)לָאו אוֹתְבִינֵיהּ חֲדָא זִימְנָא, אִיתִיבֵיהּ, מֵיתִיב, מֵיתִיבֵי, מוֹתֵיב[1], תְּיוּבְתָּא

אוֹתֵיב[2] (יתב אַפְעֵל: מוֹתִיב prt., לוֹתִיב fut., לְאוֹתוּבֵי inf.)

he seated; he placed — הוֹשִׁיב; הִנִּיחַ

לָא יָדַעְנָא הֵיכָא אוֹתְבִיתִינְהוּ. (ב"מ לה,א; מב,א ע"פ כת"י)

I know not where I placed them.

SEE: מוֹתֵיב[2]

אֲזַד* (אזד: אָזְדָא prt. f.s., אָזְדוּ prt. m. pl.)

it went — הָלַךְ

* The same verb appears in דניאל ב:ה — according to Rashi's commentary there. See the next two entries.

וְאָזְדָא ר' ... לְטַעְמֵיהּ

וְ[הַהֲלָכָה שֶׁל] ר' ... הוֹלֶכֶת לְשִׁיטָתוֹ.

And [the halakha of] R. ... goes according to his principle.

The halakha that was just quoted in the name of a certain amora or tanna follows the same principle that underlies another halakha of his, which is about to be quoted in the Talmud.

For an example — see (ר' יוחנן) פסחים קא, סע"א.

SEE: טַעַם

וְאָזְדוּ לְטַעֲמַיְיהוּ — וְהוֹלְכִים לְשִׁיטוֹתֵיהֶם

and they go according to their principles

In this controversy, these tannaim or amoraim are consistent with their respective principles that are manifested in another controversy of theirs, which is quoted immediately in the Talmud.

For example, see (ר' יוחנן וריש לקיש) יבמות סב,א.

SEE: טַעַם

אַזְהָרָה

a warning (from the Torah); a Biblical prohibition

עוֹנֶשׁ שָׁמַעְנוּ, אַזְהָרָה מְנַיִן? תַּלְמוּד לוֹמַר: "אֱלֹהִים לֹא תְקַלֵּל". (סנהדרין סו,א ע"פ שמות כב:כז ועוד)

We have [now] derived the punishment [for cursing a judge], [but] from where [do we derive] a warning [from the Torah]? Scripture teaches: "You shall not curse judges."

SEE: הַתְרָאָה

אַזֵּיק (נזק אַפְעֵל: מַזִּיק prt., לְאַזּוֹקֵי inf.)

he damaged; he caused damage — הִזִּיק

הוּא דְּאַזֵּיק אַנַּפְשֵׁיהּ. (בבא קמא כז, רע"ב)

It is he who caused damage to himself.

אֲזַל* (אזל: אָזֵיל prt., לֵיזִיל fut., זִיל imp., לְמֵיזַל inf.)

(1) הָלַךְ — **he went**

אָזְלִינַן בָּתַר רוּבָּא. (בבא קמא מו,ב)

We go after (= we follow) the majority.

(2) אָפֵס; תַּם — **it went away; it was finished; it was used up****

אָזַל כְּתָב, אָזְלָא קְדוּשְׁתֵיהּ. (שבת קטז,א)

[When] the writing has gone away, its sanctity has gone away.

* For the full conjugation of this verb, see *Grammar for Gemara:* Chapter 4, Verb 9.

** The second meaning is also found in Biblical Hebrew: הַלֶּחֶם אָזַל מִכֵּלֵינוּ (שמואל א ט:ז), *the bread was used up from our vessels*, and in Modern Hebrew: אָזַל מִן הַשּׁוּק, *it is out of stock.*

SEE: וְאָזֵיל, (כְּ)מַאן אָזְלָא הָא

כְּאֶחָד SEE: כְּאֶחָד

אֶחָד ... וְאֶחָד... (אַחַת ... וְאַחַת ... f.)

(1) both ... and ...

כָּל מִצְוַת עֲשֵׂה שֶׁלֹּא הַזְּמַן גְּרָמָהּ — אֶחָד אֲנָשִׁים וְאֶחָד נָשִׁים חַיָּיבִים. (קידושין כט,א: משנה פ"א מ"ז)

[In] all positive commandments that are not time-bound — both men and women are obligated.

(2) one (way) ... and another (way) ...

הַמְדַבֵּר אֶחָד בַּפֶּה וְאֶחָד בַּלֵּב (פסחים קיג,ב)

one who talks one [way] with his mouth and another [way] in his heart (= insincerely)

אֶחָד אֶחָד (אַחַת אַחַת f.) — **one by one**

טוֹבֵל אֶחָד אֶחָד בַּמֶּלַח וְאוֹכֵל (משנה מעשרות פ"ד מ"ג)

he may dip [the olives] in salt one by one and eat

אַחְוֵי (חוי אַפְעֵל: מַחְוֵי prt., לַחְוֵי fut., אַחְוֵי imp.)

he showed; he told; he indicated (by gesture) — הֶרְאָה; הִגִּיד; רָמַז

רֵישׁ לָקִישׁ אַחְוֵי לֵיהּ דִּינָרָא לְר' אֶלְעָזָר. (בבא קמא ק,א)

Resh Lakish showed a dinar (coin) to R. Elazar.

SEE: מַחְוֵי

אַחְזֵיק (חזק אַפְעֵל: מַחְזִיק prt., אַחְזוֹקֵי inf.)

(1) הֶחֱזִיק — **he took possession (of); he maintained possession (of); he occupied**

הַאי מַאן דְּאַחְזֵיק מִגּוּדָא דְּעָרוֹדֵי וּלְבַר — לָא הָוֵי חֲזָקָה. (בבא בתרא לו,א)

[As for] one who has occupied [a strip of field] outside of the wild animals' fence — [it] does not constitute an act of acquisition.

(2) הֶחֱזִיק; תָּפַס — **he took hold; he grasped**

כֵּיוָן דְּאַחְזֵיק בֵּיהּ, זָכָה בֵּיהּ. (סוטה מה, סע"א)

Since he took hold of it, he acquired ownership of it.

(3) הֶחֱזִיק; חָשַׁב — **he presumed; he considered**

לְאַחְזוֹקֵי אִינִישׁ בְּגַנָּבֵי לָא מַחְזְקִינַן. (שבועות מו,ב)

We certainly do not presume a person [to be in the category of] thieves.

SEE: הֶחֱזִיק, חֲזָקָה

אַחֵיךְ (חוך אַפְעֵל: מְחַכוּ .prt. pl, אַחוֹכֵי .inf)

he laughed צָחַק

אַחִיכוּ עֲלֵיהּ .... אֲמַר רַב כָּהֲנָא: גַּבְרָא רַבָּה אֲמַר מִילְּתָא; לָא תַחִיכוּ עֲלֵיהּ! (ברכות יט,ב)

They laughed at him .... Rav Kahana said: A great man has made a statement; don't laugh at him!

SEE: מְחַכוּ עֲלָהּ בְּמַעֲרְבָא, מְחַיֵּיךְ, חוּכָא

אַחֵיל (חלל אַפְעֵל: מַחֵיל .prt, אַחֵיל .imp, אַחוֹלֵי .inf)

(1) חִלֵּל **he desecrated; he profaned**

אַחִילוּ עֲלוֹהִי יוֹמָא רַבָּא דְשַׁבְּתָא (שבת קנו,א)

they desecrated the great day of the Sabbath on his account

(2) חִלֵּל; פָּדָה **he transferred sanctity from (produce designated for the second tithe, מַעֲשֵׂר שֵׁנִי, or from fruit during their fourth year of growth, רְבָעִי, onto money); he redeemed**

אַחְלֵיהּ, וַהֲדַר אַכְלֵיהּ! (ברכות לה,א ע"פ ויקרא יט:כד)

Redeem it (= the produce), and [only] then eat it!

(3) מָחַל; וִתֵּר **he forgave; he yielded**

וְחַד מִינַּיְיהוּ אַחוֹלֵי אַחְלֵיהּ לְמָנְתֵיהּ גַּבֵּי חַבְרֵיהּ (ב"מ כו,ב)

and one of them yielded his portion to his partner

אַחֵית (נחת אַפְעֵל: מַחֵית .act. prt, מַחַת .pass. prt, אַחֵית .imp, אַחוֹתֵי .inf) הוֹרִיד

he took down; he lowered; he deposed

כֵּיוָן דְּאַחְתִּינֵיהּ, לָא מַסְּקִינַן לֵיהּ. (בבא בתרא לב,א)

Once we have deposed him (from serving as a kohen), we do not reinstate him.

SEE: נְחַת

אַחֲרָיוּת **responsibility; guarantee**

אֵין בֵּין נְדָרִים לִנְדָבוֹת אֶלָּא שֶׁהַנְּדָרִים חַיָּיב בְּאַחֲרָיוּתָן, וּנְדָבוֹת אֵינוֹ חַיָּיב בְּאַחֲרָיוּתָן. (מגילה ח, רע"א: משנה פ"א מ"ו)

There is no difference between vow-offerings and free-will offerings except that [in] vow-offerings [where one says: I take upon myself to bring an offering] he has the responsibility for [replacing] them, but [in] free-will offerings [where one says: Behold this is an offering], he has no responsibility for [replacing] them.

SEE: נְכָסִים שֶׁיֵּשׁ לָהֶן אַחֲרָיוּת, נְכָסִים שֶׁאֵין לָהֶן אַחֲרָיוּת

אַחֲרִינָא (אַחֲרִיתִי* .f.s, אַחֲרִינֵי .m. pl)

another; else אַחֵר

מַפֵּיק לֵיהּ לְהַאי קְרָא לִדְרָשָׁא אַחֲרִינָא (קידושין מא, סע"ב)

he uses this pasuk for another interpretation

* Our printed editions sometimes have אחריתא instead.

SEE: לִישָּׁנָא אַחֲרִינָא, מִידֵי אַחֲרִינָא

אַטּוּ

(1) מִשּׁוּם; בִּשְׁבִיל **on account of; because of**

קְנַסוּ שׁוֹגֵג אַטּוּ מֵזִיד. (שבת ג, סע"ב)

They established a penalty for the unwitting offender on account of the [case of a] deliberate one.

(2) כְּלוּם ...?! וְכִי ...?! **is it ...?!**

This word sometimes introduces a *rhetorical question*. In English its force is best expressed by a change in word order and by the speaker's interrogative intonation — rather than by a specific translation. *It is*, for instance, becomes *Is it?*

אַטּוּ בְּשׁוֹפְטָנֵי עָסְקִינַן?! (בבא בתרא קכב, סע"א)

Are we dealing with fools?!

אַטּוּ יִרְאַת שָׁמַיִם מִילְּתָא זוּטַרְתִּי הִיא?! (ברכות לג, סע"ב)

Is the fear of Heaven a small matter?!

SEE: מִידֵי, כְּלוּם, (וְ)כִי

אַטּוּ כּוּלְּהוּ בַּחֲדָא מַחִיתָא מְחִיתִינְהוּ הֵיכָא דְּאִיתְּמַר אִיתְּמַר הֵיכָא דְּלָא אִיתְּמַר לָא אִיתְּמַר*

וְכִי אֶת כֻּלָּם בַּאֲרִיגָה אַחַת אֲרַגְתֶּם?! בְּמָקוֹם שֶׁנֶּאֱמַר, נֶאֱמַר; וּבְמָקוֹם שֶׁלֹּא נֶאֱמַר, לֹא נֶאֱמַר.

Would you weave all of them into one web?! [In the case] where it was stated, it was stated; [in the case] where it was not stated, it was not stated.

This argument means the following: Do *not* equate the two cases! The statement made by the amora regarding one case does not necessarily apply to the other case.

אֲמַר לֵיהּ רַב כָּהֲנָא לְרַב אַשִׁי: הָתָם אֲמַר רָבָא: אַף עַל גַּב דְּתַנְיָא תְּיוּבְתָּא דִשְׁמוּאֵל, הִלְכְתָא כְּוָתֵיהּ; הָכָא מַאי? אֲמַר לֵיהּ: אַטּוּ כּוּלְּהוּ בַּחֲדָא מַחִיתָא מְחִיתִינְהוּ?! הֵיכָא דְּאִיתְּמַר, אִיתְּמַר; הֵיכָא דְּלָא אִיתְּמַר, לָא אִיתְּמַר. (ברכות כד,א ע"פ כת"י, וש"נ)

Rav Kahana said to Rav Ashi: In that case Rava stated: Even though [a baraitha] has been taught [that contains] a refutation of Shmuel, the halakhic ruling is in accordance with his opinion; what is [the halakhic ruling] in this case? [Rav Ashi] said to him: Would you weave all of them into one web?! [In the case] where it was stated, it was stated; where it was not stated, it was not stated.

* In a few cases, ... הֵיכָא דְּאִיתְּמַר has a somewhat different meaning, as in עירובין מו, סע"ב – מז, רע"א.

אִי[1]*/הִי **alas! woe!**

אִי עָנָיו! אִי חָסִיד! מִתַּלְמִידָיו שֶׁל אַבְרָהָם אָבִינוּ! (ברכות ו,ב)

Alas the humble man! Alas the pious man! One of the disciples of Avraham our father [has departed]!

* Compare: אִי לָךְ אֶרֶץ שֶׁמַּלְכֵּךְ נָעַר (קהלת י:טז).

אִי[2]* **not**

עֲקִיבָא! אִי אַתָּה מִתְיָירֵא מִפְּנֵי מַלְכוּת? (ברכות סא,ב)

Akiva! Are you not afraid of the [Roman] Empire?

* Sephardic Jews pronounce this word אֵי — apparently as a contraction of אֵין. Nevertheless, the vocalisation אִי is supported by the Biblical Hebrew אִי כָבוֹד in שמואל א ד:כא.

אִי[3] אִם **if; whether**

See the examples in the following entries.

אִי ... אִי ...

whether ... or ... (1) אִם ... אִם ...*

מְסַפְּקָא לֵיהּ אִי מוּקֶּפֶת חוֹמָה מִימוֹת יְהוֹשֻׁעַ בִּן נוּן הִיא, אִי לָא. (מגילה ה, סע"ב)

He is in doubt whether [the city] was surrounded by a wall from the days of Y'hoshua bin Nun or not.

either ... or ... (2) אוֹ ... אוֹ ...

מַתְנִיתִין מַנִּי? אִי רַבִּי אִי ר' יוֹסֵי. (מגילה ד,ב)

Whose [opinion] is [presented in] our mishna? Either [that of] Rebbi or [that of] R. Yosé.

* Compare. אם בהמה אם איש (שמות יט:יג).

אִי אִיתָא

SEE: אִם אִיתָא

אִי אִיתְּמַר הָכִי אִיתְּמַר

SEE: אֶלָּא אִי אִיתְּמַר הָכִי אִיתְּמַר

אִי אָמְרַתְּ בִּשְׁלָמָא;* אֶלָּא אִי אָמְרַתְּ ...

בְּשָׁלוֹם אִם אַתָּה אוֹמֵר ..., אֶלָּא אִם אַתָּה אוֹמֵר ... (יֵשׁ קֻשְׁי).

It is well if you say ..., but if you say ... (and thereby adopt the opposing view, there will be a difficulty).

This formula *supports* a proposition by showing that the authoritative text that has just been quoted in the Talmud is in harmony with that proposition alone — not with the opposing view.

ברייתא: בֶּהֱמַת נָכְרִי מְטַפֵּל בָּהּ כְּבֶהֱמַת יִשְׂרָאֵל.
תלמוד: אִי אָמְרַתְּ בִּשְׁלָמָא צַעַר בַּעֲלֵי חַיִּים דְּאוֹרָיְיתָא, מִשּׁוּם הָכִי "מְטַפֵּל בָּהּ כְּבֶהֱמַת יִשְׂרָאֵל"; אֶלָּא אִי אָמְרַתְּ צַעַר בַּעֲלֵי חַיִּים לָאו דְּאוֹרָיְיתָא, אַמַּאי מְטַפֵּל בָּהּ כְּבֶהֱמַת יִשְׂרָאֵל? (בבא מציעא לב,ב)

BARAITHA: One must tend to an [incapacitated laden] animal of a non-Jew, just as [one must tend] to the animal of a Jew.

TALMUD: It is well if you say [that relieving] the suffering of animals is [a duty] from the Torah — then it follows that one must tend to it (= the animal of a non-Jew), just as [one must tend] to the animal of a Jew; but if you say [that relieving] the suffering of animals is not [a duty] from the Torah — why must he tend to it, just as [one must tend] to the animal of a Jew?

* This introductory expression equals בִּשְׁלָמָא אִי אָמְרַתְּ.
SEE: אָמְרַתְּ, (בִּ)שְׁלָמָא

אִי אֶפְשִׁי

"It is not desirable to me"; I do not want

אִי אֶפְשִׁי לָזוּז מִבֵּית אַבָּא. (כתובות קג,א: משנה פי"ב מ"ג)

I do not want to move from my father's house.

SEE: [1]אִי and its note.

אִי אֶפְשָׁר

impossible; it is impossible

אִלְמָלֵא מִקְרָא כָּתוּב, אִי אֶפְשָׁר לְאוֹמְרוֹ! (ראש השנה יז,ב)

Were it not for the fact that the pasuk is written [in the Torah], it would be impossible to say this!

SEE: [1]אִי and its note.

אִי בָּעֵי

אִם רוֹצֶה; אִלּוּ רָצָה

if he wants; if he would want

אִי בָּעֵי, אָכֵיל; אִי בָּעֵי, לָא אָכֵיל. (סוכה כז,א)

If he wants, he eats; if he wants, he does not eat.

SEE: בְּעָא

אִי בָּעֵית אֵימָא

SEE: אִיבָּעֵית אֵימָא

אִי הָכִי

if so אִם כֵּן

This expression usually introduces an *argument* that refutes the solution or explanation which was proposed in the Talmud. In several passages, however, this expression introduces a proof.*

For an example — see מִיבָּעֵי לֵיהּ.

* See שבת כח,א (and Rashi's commentary there) and קידושין מו,א (and Rashi and Tosafoth there).

SEE: אֶלָּא מֵעַתָּה

אִי מִשּׁוּם הָא לָא אִירְיָא

אִם מִפְּנֵי זֹאת, אֵין רְאָיָה.

If [your argument is] because of this [text], there is no proof.

This expression introduces a *refutation* of a proof. It is argued that the textual evidence just now presented can be refuted, because the text is subject to a different interpretation.

תלמוד: בְּעָא מִינֵּיה רַב אַדָּא בַּר מַתְנָה מֵאַבָּיֵי: מוֹכִין שֶׁטָּמַן בָּהֶן — מַהוּ לְטַלְטְלָן בְּשַׁבָּת? [אַבָּיֵי אָסַר.] לֵימָא מְסַיֵּיעַ לֵיהּ?
ברייתא: טוֹמְנִין ... בְּמוֹכִין, וְאֵין מְטַלְטְלִין אוֹתָן.
תלמוד: אִי מִשּׁוּם הָא, לָא אִירְיָא. הָכִי קָאָמַר: אִם לֹא טָמַן בָּהֶן, אֵין מְטַלְטְלִין אוֹתָן. (שבת מח,א)

TALMUD: Rav Adda b. Mathna asked Abbayé: Is it permissible [on the Sabbath] to handle cloth material in which one had kept food warm? [Abbayé forbade it.] Shall we say [that the following baraitha] supports him?

BARAITHA: One may keep food warm in ... cloth material, but one may not handle it [on the Sabbath].

TALMUD: If [your argument is] because of this [baraitha], there is no proof, [because] this is [what the baraitha] may mean: [One may keep food warm in ... cloth material, but as for cloth material in general] if one did not keep food warm in it, he may not handle it [because it is considered "muktze," since it was not intended for Sabbath use].

SEE: אִירְיָא

אִי נַמִּי

or else; or alternatively (1) "אִם גַּם"; אוֹ*

This expression introduces an *alternative* — usually an alternative solution to a difficulty or to a problem.

תלמוד: וְכָבְתָה, אֵין זָקוּק לָהּ?! וּרְמִינְהִי:
ברייתא: מִצְוָתָהּ מִשֶּׁתִּשְׁקַע הַחַמָּה עַד שֶׁתִּכְלֶה רֶגֶל מִן הַשּׁוּק.
תלמוד: מַאי? לָאו דְּאִי כָּבְתָה, הֲדַר מַדְלִיק לַהּ?! לָא! דְּאִי לָא אַדְלִיק, מַדְלִיק; וְאִי נַמִּי לְשִׁיעוּרַהּ. (שבת כא,ב)

TALMUD: And if it became extinguished, one does not need [to relight] it (= the Ḥanukka light)?!

BARAITHA: Its mitzva is from [the time] that the sun sets until the feet [of the firewood merchants] leave the market.

TALMUD: What [are the circumstances]? Does not [the text mean that] if it became extinguished, he must light it again?! No! [The text means] that if he has not [yet] lit, he may [still] light (until the last of the merchants leave the market); or alternatively [the text refers to] its quantity (that is, the minimum amount of oil that must be placed in the vessel in the first place).

even if **(2) אֲפִילוּ**

אִי נַמִּי אֱינַשׁ אַחֲרִינָא שְׁמַע וַאֲזַל וּשְׁחַט, רוֹב מְצוּיִין אֵצֶל שְׁחִיטָה מוּמְחִין הֵן (חולין יב,א ע"פ כתי"ם וע' רש"י שם)

even if another man heard and went [ahead] and slaughtered [the animal, it is considered kosher, since] most people involved in slaughtering are experts

For additional examples, see סנהדרין לג,א; פד,ב.

* The Hebrew words אוֹ, which usually means *or*, and אִם, which usually means *if*, are sometimes interchangeable (רש"י ויקרא ד:כג).

SEE: נַמִּי, אִיבָּעֵית אֵימָא

אִי קַשְׁיָא הָא קַשְׁיָא   אִם קָשֶׁה, זוֹ קָשָׁה.

If there is [anything] difficult, [it is] the following [point that] is difficult.

The *difficulty* that has already been pointed out regarding the halakha under discussion can easily be resolved. However, if indeed there is a serious difficulty, it is the difficulty here it is.

See סוכה לח,א for an example.

SEE: קַשְׁיָא

אִי תַּנְיָא תַּנְיָא   אִם שְׁנוּיָה, שְׁנוּיָה.

If it has been taught (in a baraitha), **it has [indeed] been taught.**

With this statement an amora responds to a difficulty that was raised against his halakha from a baraitha. The actual meaning of this response may be explained in two different ways:

(1) If there is in fact such a baraitha, I retract my opinion in deference to it.

For an example — see חגיגה יט,ב ורש"י שם.

(2) I personally stand by my halakha, since I have received it on good authority; however, if my opponent has a baraitha expressing a different opinion, he is certainly entitled to follow it.

For examples — see נדה כג,ב ורש"י שם, שבת קטו,ב וש"נ and נדרים יט,ב and ר"ן there.

SEE: תַּנְיָא

אִיבָּעֵי* (= אִתְבָּעֵי: בעי אִתְפְּעֵל: מִיבָּעֵי .prt)

it was necessary; it was needed **(1) הָיָה צָרִיךְ**

מַאי אִיבָּעֵי לֵיהּ קְרָאֵי? (בבא קמא סא, רע"א)

Why did he need [two] pᵉsukim [to make one point]?

אִיבָּעֵי לֵיהּ לְמַחוֹיֵי. (בבא בתרא לה,ב)

It was necessary for him to protest (= he should have protested).

it was asked; **(2) נִשְׁאַל**
[a halakhic problem] was raised

See the next entry for an example.

* We have vocalized this verb אִיבָּעֵי, as the *binyan* אִתְפְּעֵל (the passive of the פְּעַל) in accordance with the popular pronunciation. Since בְּעָא, in the קַל *binyan*, serves as the active form, we would have expected the passive form to be אִיבְּעֵי, the passive of the קַל, in the אִתְפְּעֵל *binyan*. See the note on the entry אִישְׁתְּכַח, which indicates that Aramaic is not always consistent in this regard. For the full conjugation of the verb בעי, see *Grammar for Gemara*: Chapter 4, Verb 11.

SEE: בְּעָא, מִיבָּעֵי

אִיבַּעְיָא לְהוּ

They had a halakhic problem. **נִשְׁאֲלָה לָהֶם.**

This expression introduces a *halakhic problem* (a בַּעְיָא) that confronted the ḥakhamim in the beth midrash.

אִיבַּעְיָא לְהוּ: סִימָנִין — דְּאוֹרָיְיתָא אוֹ דְּרַבָּנָן? (ב"מ כז, סע"א)

They had a halakhic problem: [Is the law of using] identification marks (as the basis for determining ownership of a lost article) of Torah status or of Rabbinic status?

SEE: בַּעְיָא

אִיבָּעֵית* אֵימָא

If you want, say ... **אִם אַתָּה רוֹצֶה, אֱמֹר ...**

This expression introduces an *alternative* solution to the same difficulty or problem, or an *alternative* explanation of the same point.

ברייתא: חֲכָמִים עָשׂוּ סְיָג לְדִבְרֵיהֶם ... אָדָם בָּא מִן הַשָּׂדֶה בָּעֶרֶב, נִכְנָס לְבֵית הַכְּנֶסֶת ... וְקוֹרֵא קְרִיאַת שְׁמַע וּמִתְפַּלֵּל ... וְכָל הָעוֹבֵר עַל דִּבְרֵי חֲכָמִים חַיָּיב מִיתָה.
תלמוד: מַאי שְׁנָא הָכָא דְּקָתָנֵי "חַיָּיב מִיתָה"? אִיבָּעֵית אֵימָא: מִשּׁוּם דְּאִיכָּא אוֹנֶס שֵׁינָה; וְאִיבָּעֵית אֵימָא: לְאַפּוּקֵי מִמַּאן דְּאָמַר תְּפִלַּת עַרְבִית רְשׁוּת; קָא מַשְׁמַע לַן דְּחוֹבָה. (ברכות ד,ב)

BARAITHA: The ḥakhamim made a fence around their words ... [so that] a man coming from the field in the evening ... should enter the synagogue ... and recite the Shᵉma and recite the Amida ... and whoever transgresses the words of the ḥakhamim deserves death.

TALMUD: Why is it unique here that [the tanna] states: "He deserves death"? If you want, say: Because [here] there is a danger of sleep overpowering him; and if you want, say: To exclude the opinion of the one who says: The evening Amida is optional; [this] teaches us that it is obligatory.

* אִיבָּעֵית may be written as two separate words אִי בָּעֵית.
SEE: אִי נָמֵי, בְּעָא

אִיבָּעֵית אֵימָא קְרָא אִיבָּעֵית אֵימָא סְבָרָא
אִם אַתָּה רוֹצֶה, אֱמֹר: פָּסוּק; אִם אַתָּה רוֹצֶה, אֱמֹר: סְבָרָה.

If you want, say it is [based on] a pasuk; if you want, say it is [based on] reasoning.
This formula introduces two alternative answers, solutions, or interpretations of the same point — one derived from a Biblical source and another derived through reasoning.

רָעָב קָשֶׁה מחרב. אִיבָּעֵית, אֵימָא קְרָא; וְאִיבָּעֵית, אֵימָא סְבָרָא. אִיבָּעֵית, אֵימָא סְבָרָא: הַאי קָא מִצְטַעֵר, וְהַאי לָא קָא מִצְטַעֵר. אִיבָּעֵית, אֵימָא קְרָא: "טובים הָיוּ חַלְלֵי חרב מֵחַלְלֵי רָעָב". (ב"ב ח,ב ע"פ כת"י וע"פ איכה ד:ט. ע' ברכות ד,ב וש"נ)
[Death by] famine is worse than [death by] the sword. If you want, say it is [based on] a pasuk; and if you want, say it is [based on] reasoning. If you want, say it is [based on] reasoning: One suffers [prolonged agony], while the other does not suffer. If you want, say it is [based on] a pasuk: "[Those] slain by the sword were better off than [those who] died in the famine."

אִיבְּרָא/אִבְּרָא בֶּאֱמֶת **indeed**
אִיבְּרָא מַלְכָּא אַתְּ (גיטין נו, רע"ב) *indeed you are a king*

אִיגַּלַּאי מִילְּתָא
נִגְלָה הַדָּבָר; נוֹדַע הַדָּבָר; נִתְבָּרֵר
the matter was revealed; it was discovered; it was clarified
This expression is frequently used with the adverbs לְסוֹף, *at the end, ultimately,* and לְמַפְרֵעַ, *retroactively.*

לְסוֹף אִיגַּלַּאי מִילְּתָא דִּבְלָא דַּעְתֵּיהּ שְׁקַלֵיהּ. (בבא מציעא פא,ב)
Ultimately it was discovered that he had taken it without his (= the owner's) consent.
SEE: אִיגְּלֵי

אִיגְּלֵי* (= אִתְגְּלֵי: גלי אִתְפְּעֵל: מִיגְּלֵי .prt, לְאִיגַּלּוּיֵי .inf)
נִגְלָה **it was revealed; it came to light**
מִילְּתָא דַּעֲבִידָא לְאִיגַּלּוּיֵי (ראש השנה כב,ב וש"נ)
a matter that is likely to come to light
* The third person f.s. form is אִיגַּלַּאי, as in אִיגַּלַּאי מִילְּתָא, the previous entry.

אִיגָּרָא (.pl אִיגָּרֵי) גַּג* **roof**
הָנֵי שְׁמַעְתָּתָא דִּידִי מְרַפְסָן אִיגָּרֵי! (קידושין סג,ב ורש"י שם)
These halakhic teachings of mine "will shatter roofs" (= they are difficult to understand)!
* Since a flat roof was sometimes used for living quarters, it has occasionally been translated עֲלִיָּה, *an upper story.*
ע' פסחים קא,א ורש"י לתענית כג, רע"ב.

אִיגַּרְתָּא אִגֶּרֶת; מִכְתָּב **letter; document**
קָרְיָינָא דְאִיגַּרְתָּא — אִיהוּ לֶיהֱוֵי פָּרְווֹנְקָא! (סנהדרין צו,א*)
[As for] the reader of the letter — let him be the messenger! (= Let the one who offers the advice carry it out himself!)
* See Rashi on במדבר כה:ו.

אִידְּחִי (= אִתְדְּחִי: דחי אִתְפְּעֵל: מִידְּחִי .prt)
נִדְחָה **it was postponed; he was disqualified**
משום דַהֲוָה ליה חולה, אידחי ליה מִנְּשִׂיאוּתֵיהּ?! (הוריות י,א)
Because [the Nasi] was ill, has he been disqualified from his position (of Nasi)?!
SEE: דְּחָא

אִידִי וְאִידִי זֶה וָזֶה; אֵלּוּ וָאֵלּוּ; כָּאן וְכָאן
this and that; these and those; here and there; both (usually: both sources or cases)
אידי ואידי בִּזְמַן שבית הַמִּקְדָּשׁ קַיָּים. (סוכה מד, רע"א)
Both [mishnayoth] are [talking] about a time when the Beth HaMikdash [was] standing.

אִידָךְ (.pl אִינָךְ)
(1) אַחֵר; שֵׁנִי; חֲלַף **another; a second;**
the other one (usually: the other opinion or the other hakham)
הָנֵי תְּלָת מִילֵּי שַׁוְּינְהוּ רַבָּנַן כְּהִלְכְתָא בְּלָא טַעְמָא: חֲדָא — הָא, אִידָךְ ..., אִידָךְ .... (בבא בתרא קמד,א)
The following three things the hakhamim have enacted as halakhoth without [giving] a reason: one is this (= the halakha previously quoted in the Talmud), another is ..., [and] another is ....
בְּאִידָךְ גִּיסָא (פסחים קיא,א ועוד) *on the other side*

(2) הַשְּׁאָר **the rest**
דַּעֲלָךְ סְנֵי לְחַבְרָךְ לָא תַּעֲבִיד — זו היא כל הַתּוֹרָה כולה, וְאִידָךְ פֵּירוּשָׁא הוּא; זִיל גְּמוֹר! (שבת לא,א)
That which is hateful to you do not do toward your fellow man — this is the whole Torah, and the rest is [merely] commentary; go (and) study!
SEE: אִינָךְ, וְאִידָךְ

אִידְּכַר/אִדְּכַר (= אִתְדְּכַר: דכר אִתְפְּעֵל: מִידְּכַר .prt)
נִזְכַּר **he was reminded; he remembered**
אִדְּכַר קודם "שׁוֹמֵעַ תְּפִלָּה" (ברכות כט, סע"א)
he remembered [his omission] before [he recited the b^erakha] "shoméa t^efilla"
SEE: דְּכַר

אִידַּמֵּי (= אִתְדַּמֵּי: דמי אִתְפְּעֵל)
נִדְמָה **he appeared** (like or in the guise of)
חֲלַף אֵלִיָּהוּ, חֲזְיֵיהּ; אִידַּמֵּי לֵיהּ כְּטַיָּיעָא. (ברכות ו,ב)
Eliyyahu passed by, [and] he saw him; [Eliyyahu] appeared to him in the guise of a Bedouin.
SEE: דְּמֵי

אִיהוּ* הוּא **he**

אִיהִי* הִיא **she**

קָם אִיהוּ בְּחֲדָא זָוִיתָא וְאִיהִי בְּחֲדָא זָוִיתָא. (תענית כג,ב)
He stood in one corner and she in another corner.

* For a full listing of the independent personal pronouns in Babylonian Aramaic, see *Grammar for Gemara*: Chapter 7.2.

אִיזְדְּהַר/אִזְדְּהַר (= אִתְזְהַר: זהר אִתְפְּעֵל: מִיזְדְּהַר .prt, נִיזְדְּהַר .fut, אִיזְדְּהַר .imp)

he was careful; he took care נִזְהַר
טְוֵי לִי בַּר אַוְוזָא, וְאִזְדְּהַר מֵחֲרוֹכָא! (ביצה לב,ב)
Roast a duck for me, and be careful not to burn [it]!
SEE: מִיזְּהַר

אִיזִי* אֵיפוֹא;** נָא **then; now**
אֵימָא לִי, אִיזִי, גּוּפָא דְעוּבְדָא הֵיכִי הֲוָה? (גיטין לט, סע"ב)
Tell me, then, how was the incident itself (= what really happened)?

* In some instances where our editions read אִיזוּ, the form אִיזִי may be more correct (בבא מציעא ע, רע"א ועוד).
** In his Biblical commentary on בראשית כז:לג, Rashbam writes that the Biblical Hebrew word אֵיפוֹא has the same meaning as the Aramaic אִיזִי.

אִיחַיַּיב (= אִתְחַיַּיב: חוב אִתְפְּעֵל: מִיחַיַּיב .prt, לִיחַיַּיב .fut, אִיחַיּוּבֵי .inf)

he was/became obligated נִתְחַיֵּיב
אִיחַיַּיב לֵיהּ בָּעִיר (בבא מציעא ל, רע"ב)
he became obligated to [return] it to him in the city
SEE: לִיחַיַּיב, מִיחַיַּיב

לְאִיחַלּוּפֵי (= לְאִתְחַלּוּפֵי) .inf (חלף אִתְפְּעֵל)

to be interchanged לְהַחְלִף
אָתֵי לְאִיחַלּוּפֵי בְּגִיטָּא (יבמות נב, סע"א)
[this document] may come to be interchanged with an (ordinary) bill of divorce
SEE: מִיחַלַּף

אִיטַּמִּי (= אִתְטַמִּי: טמי אִתְפְּעֵל: מִיטַּמָּא .prt, לִיטַּמָּא .fut, אִיטַּמּוּיֵי .inf)

he/it became [ritually] unclean נִטְמָא
אִי בְּשֶׁרֶץ אִטַּמִּי, אִי בִּנְבֵלָה אִיטַּמִּי (שבועות יח,ב)
whether it became unclean by contact with a creeping thing or with an animal carcass
SEE: לִיטַּמָּא, מִיטַּמָּא

אַיְּדֵי (אַ+יְדֵי)

by means of; through עַל יְדֵי
אִיסּוּרָא אַיְּדֵי בְּהֵמָה הוּא דְּאָתֵי (נזיר ב, סע"א)
it is through the animal that a prohibition comes about
SEE: -אַ

אַיְּדֵי ד-

since; because "עַל יְדֵי שֶׁ-"; הוֹאִיל וְ-; כֵּיוָן שֶׁ-

אַיְּדֵי דְּאַתְיָא לֵיהּ מִדְּרָשָׁא, חֲבִיבָא לֵיהּ (ב"ב קח, רע"ב)
since [the tanna] derived it from an interpretation, it is dear to him (and he taught it first)

אַיְּדֵי דְּבָעֵי לְמִיתְנֵי/לְמִיתְנָא סֵיפָא ... תְּנָא נַמֵּי רֵישָׁא ....

כֵּיוָן שֶׁרוֹצֶה לִשְׁנוֹת בְּסוֹפָהּ ..., שָׁנָה אַף בְּרֹאשָׁהּ ...
Since [the tanna] wants to state ... [in] the latter clause, he has also stated ... [in] the first clause
For examples — see שבת ל, רע"א and the example under the entry מִשּׁוּם דְּקָא בָּעֵי לְמִיתְנֵי סֵיפָא.

אַיְילוֹנִית* **a barren woman; a woman who cannot bear children**
אַיְילוֹנִית דּוּכְרָנִית, דְּלָא יָלְדָה. (כתובות יא, רע"א ורש"י שם)
"Ailonith" [means] "like a male," for she does not give birth.

* The word is thus derived from the Hebrew אַיִל, a *male (sheep)*, which is equivalent to the Aramaic דְּכַר.

אַיַּיקַר* (= אִתְיַקַּר: יקר אִתְפְּעֵל)

it became dearer; it rose in value נִתְיַקֵּר
אַיַּיקַר חַלָּא וְאִזְדַּבַּן בִּדְמֵי חַמְרָא. (ברכות ה,ב)
Vinegar became dearer and sold at the price of wine.

* The expression אַיַּיקַר לֵיהּ תַּלְמוּדָהּ (עבודה זרה מו,ב) or אִתְיַקַּר תַּלְמוּדֵיהּ (שבת קמז,ב) or אִיעַקַּר תַּלְמוּדֵיהּ (בבא בתרא ט,ב) means *his learning was forgotten* — either from the root יקר, *to become heavy*, or from עקר, *to be uprooted*.
SEE: אִיעַקַּר

אַיְירֵי (ארי* אַפְעֵל: מַיְירֵי .prt)
הָיָה מְעֹרָה (ב-); עָסַק (ב-)

he was connected (with); he was dealing (with); he was speaking (of)
אַיְּדֵי דְּאַיְירֵי בְּאִיסּוּר אַחְוָתָא, תְּנָא "אֲחוֹת אִשְׁתּוֹ" (יבמות ג,א)
since [the tanna] was dealing with a prohibition due to sisterhood, he [also] stated "his wife's sister"

* According to Rav Hai Gaon, the Aramaic root ארי is equivalent to the Hebrew ערי. For example, מְעוֹרָה, *connected*, occurs in the Mishna (טבול יום פ"ג מ"א). See the explanation of the *gaon* quoted in the *Arukh* (end of entry ער). The Yemenite pronunciation, however, is אִיָּירֵי, the equivalent of אִתְיְרֵי, the אִתְפְּעֵל form from the root ירי meaning *it was pointed out* or *it was discussed*. (See S. Morag, *Babylonian Aramaic, The Yemenite Tradition*, Jerusalem 1988, p. 85 and p. 282)
SEE: (וּד)קָאָרֵי לָהּ מַאי קָאָרֵי לָהּ, מַיְירֵי, אִירְיָא

אַיְיתִי (אתי* אַפְעֵל: מַיְיתֵי .prt, לַיְיתֵי .fut, אַיְיתִי .imp, לְאַתוּיֵי/לְאֵיתוּיֵי .inf)

he brought (1) הֵבִיא
אֲתָא וְאַיְיתִי מַתְנִיתָא בִּידֵיהּ (בבא קמא מב, סע"א)
he came and brought a baraitha with him

he included; he extended (2) הֵבִיא; רִבָּה

This verb is often used to mean *include* in the following context: A general expression in a mishna, a baraitha, or in a pasuk is usually interpreted as *including* borderline cases into a halakhic category. Sometimes, the Talmud explicitly asks the question לְאֵתוּיֵי מַאי? *([the expression comes] to include what?)* and responds with an explanation beginning with the infinitive לְאֵתוּיֵי *(to include ...)*. In other instances, that question is implicit.

משנה: כָּל מָקוֹם שֶׁאֵין מַכְנִיסִין בּוֹ חָמֵץ אֵין צָרִיךְ בְּדִיקָה. (פסחים ב, רע"א: משנה פ"א: מ"א)
תלמוד: "כָּל מָקוֹם" — לְאֵתוּיֵי מַאי? לְאֵתוּיֵי הָא דְתָנוּ רַבָּנַן: חוֹרֵי בַיִת הָעֶלְיוֹנִים וְהַתַּחְתּוֹנִים, וְגַג הַיָּצִיעַ ... אֵין צְרִיכִין בְּדִיקָה. (שם ח,א)

MISHNA: Every place into which hametz is not brought need not be searched.

TALMUD: What [does] "every place" [come] to include? [It comes] to include this [baraitha] that the hakhamim taught: The very high and low holes in the house, the roof of the balcony ... need not be searched.

* For the full conjugation of this verb, see *Grammar for Gemara*: Chapter 4, Verb 14.

SEE: אֲתָא, (לְ)אַפּוֹקֵי, רִיבָּה, רַבִּי

אִיְיתַּר (= אִתְיְתַר: יתר אִתְפְּעֵל)

it remained superfluous נוֹתַר; נַעֲשָׂה מְיֻתָּר **(and was therefore available for an interpretation)**

אִיְיתַּר לֵיהּ חַד "הִילּוּל" לִבְרָכָה. (ברכות לה,א ע"פ ויקרא יט:כד)

One [mention of] "praising" (as implied by the plural form הִלּוּלִים*) remained superfluous (and hence available) for [teaching about] a bᵉrakha.*

SEE: מְיַיתַּר

אִיכָּא (אִית+כָּא) יֵשׁ כָּאן; יֵשׁ

here there is; there is; there are; it is possible (to); there are grounds (to)

For examples, see the entries that follow.

SEE: אִית

אִיכָּא בֵּינַיְיהוּ יֵשׁ בֵּינֵיהֶם

there is [the following halakhic difference] between them

This expression introduces the Talmud's *response* to the question מַאי בֵּינַיְיהוּ? *(what is [the halakhic difference] between them?)*.

See an example of both the question and the response under מַאי בֵּינַיְיהוּ.

אִיכָּא דְאָמְרִי יֵשׁ אוֹמְרִים

there are [some authorities] who say; some say; others say

This term introduces *another version* of a statement in the Talmud or *another version* of an entire

Talmudic discussion.

(1) In some instances, the two versions are substantially different.

אֲמַר רַב פָּפָּא ... : שׁוֹאֵל שֶׁאוֹמֵר "הֲרֵינִי מְשַׁלֵּם" לָא מַקְנֵי לֵיהּ כְּפֵילָא. אִיכָּא דְאָמְרִי אֲמַר רַב פָּפָּא: שׁוֹאֵל נַמִּי, כֵּיוָן שֶׁאָמַר "הֲרֵינִי מְשַׁלֵּם" מַקְנֵי לֵיהּ כְּפֵילָא ... (בבא מציעא לד,א)

Rav Pappa said: ... [If] a borrower (of the animal) says: "I am ready to pay [for the missing animal]," [the owner] does not transfer (the rights to receive) a double payment (from the thief) to him. Some say: Rav Pappa said: Even [with respect to] a borrower, once he says "I am ready to pay," the owner does transfer (the rights to) a double payment to him.

(2) In some instances, the two versions differ — not about the content of the statement — but about its authorship or about the structure of a Talmudic discussion.

וְכַמָּה? אֲמַר רַב יְהוּדָה בַּר חֲבִיבָא אֲמַר שְׁמוּאֵל: שְׁלֹשָׁה יָמִים. אִיכָּא דְאָמְרִי: תָּנֵי רַב יְהוּדָה בַּר חֲבִיבָא קַמֵּיהּ דִּשְׁמוּאֵל: שְׁלֹשָׁה יָמִים.* (כתובות ס, סע"ב ורש"י שם)

And how long [did the infant stop nursing]? Rav Yᵉhuda b. Habiva said in the name of Shᵉmuel: Three days. Some say: Rav Yᵉhuda b. Habiva [was] teaching [a baraitha] before Shᵉmuel (which says): Three days.

* Although the content of the statement is the same, one version ascribes it to the amora Shᵉmuel himself, while the other says it was stated in a baraitha that was recited before Shᵉmuel.

אִיכָּא דְמַתְנֵי לַהּ/לְהָא אַ- יֵשׁ שֶׁמְּשַׁנֶּה אוֹתָהּ/אֶת־זֹאת עַל ...

there is someone who teaches it/this as referring to ...

After the Talmud has presented a statement of an amora as referring to a mishna or a baraitha, this formula is used to introduce a *different tradition* that contends that the same amoraic statement refers to a different mishna or baraitha.

משנה: לְחָיַיִן שֶׁאָמְרוּ ... רָחְבָּן ... כָּל שֶׁהוּא. ר' יוֹסֵי אוֹמֵר: רָחְבָּן שְׁלֹשָׁה טְפָחִים. (עירובין יד,ב: משנה פ"א מ"ו)
תלמוד: אֲמַר לֵיהּ רָבָא בַּר רַב חָנָן לְאַבַּיֵי: הִילְכְתָא מַאי? אֲמַר לֵיהּ: פּוּק, חֲזִי מַאי עַמָּא דָבַר! אִיכָּא דְמַתְנֵי לַהּ אַהָא:
משנה: הַשּׁוֹתֶה מַיִם לִצְמָאוֹ אוֹמֵר שֶׁהַכֹּל ... ר' טַרְפוֹן אוֹמֵר: בּוֹרֵא נְפָשׁוֹת ... (ברכות מה,א: משנה פ"ו מ"ח)
תלמוד: אֲמַר לֵיהּ רַב חָנָן לְאַבַּיֵי: הִילְכְתָא מַאי? אֲמַר לֵיהּ: פּוּק, חֲזִי מַאי עַמָּא דָבַר! (עירובין יד, סע"ב)

MISHNA: The side-posts of which they spoke may be of any width. R. Yosé says: Their width must be [at least] three handbreadths.

TALMUD: Rava b. Rav Hanan said to Abbayé: What is the halakha? He (= Abbayé) said to him: Go out [and] see what people do! There is someone who teaches it (= the dialogue between Rava b. Hanan and Abbayé) as referring to the following:

MISHNA: [If] one drinks water to [quench] his thirst, he recites: שֶׁהַכֹּל. *R. Tarfon says:* בּוֹרֵא נְפָשׁוֹת.

TALMUD: Rav Ḥanan said to Abbayé: What is the halakha? He (= Abbayé) said to him: Go out [and] see what people do!

SEE: מַתְנֵי

וְאִיכָּא דְּמַתְנֵי לַהּ* לְהָא שְׁמַעְתָּא בְּאַפֵּי/ בְּאַנְפֵּי נַפְשַׁהּ

וְיֵשׁ שֶׁמְּשַׁנֶּה אֶת הַשְּׁמוּעָה הַזֹּאת בִּפְנֵי עַצְמָהּ.

And there is someone who teaches this halakha independently (usually as a *controversy* not connected with our mishna).**

משנה: קְרִיכוֹת בִּרְשׁוּת הָרַבִּים ... הֲרֵי אֵלּוּ שֶׁלּוֹ. (בבא מציעא כא,א: משנה פ"ב מ"א)
תלמוד: אָמַר רַבָּה: וַאֲפִילּוּ בְּדָבָר שֶׁיֵּשׁ בּוֹ סִימָן — אַלְמָא קָסָבַר רַבָּה: סִימָן הֶעָשׂוּי לִידָּרֵס לָא הָוֵי סִימָן. רָבָא אָמַר: לֹא שָׁנוּ אֶלָּא שֶׁאֵין בּוֹ סִימָן, אֲבָל יֵשׁ בּוֹ סִימָן חַיָּיב לְהַכְרִיז — אַלְמָא קָסָבַר: סִימָן הֶעָשׂוּי לִידָּרֵס הָוֵי סִימָן. וְאִיכָּא דְּמַתְנֵי לַהּ לְהָא שְׁמַעְתָּא בְּאַנְפֵּי נַפְשַׁהּ: סִימָן הֶעָשׂוּי לִידָּרֵס — רַבָּה אָמַר: לָא הָוֵי סִימָן, רָבָא אָמַר: הָוֵי סִימָן. (ב"מ כב,ב ע"פ כת"י)

MISHNA: Small sheaves [found] in a public thoroughfare belong to the finder.

TALMUD: Rabba said: Even something that has an (identifying) mark — it follows that Rabba must hold that a mark that is liable to be trampled is not [considered] an [identifying] mark. Rava said: [The mishna] refers only to something without an [identifying] mark, but he must announce [an object] that has a mark — consequently, he (= Rava) must hold that a mark that is liable to be trampled is [considered] an [identifying] mark. And there is someone who teaches this halakha independently: A mark that is liable to be trampled — Rabba says it is not [considered] an [identifying] mark, [while] Rava says it is [considered] an [identifying] mark.

* The word לַהּ is sometimes omitted.

** A different usage occurs in כתובות יא,ב. See Rashi there.

SEE: מַתְנֵי

וְאִיכָּא דְּרָמֵי לְהוּ* מִירְמָא

יֵשׁ שֶׁמֵּטִיל אוֹתָם הָטֵל.

There is someone who "hurls" them (= pits the two tannaitic texts against each other).

After one tradition has presented an amora's interpretation of our mishna without reference to any other tannaitic text, a second tradition now reports that the amora used the same interpretation of our mishna to resolve a *contradiction* between our mishna and (usually) a baraitha.

משנה: לֹא יִטַּע אָדָם אִילָן סָמוּךְ לִשְׂדֵה חֲבֵירוֹ, אֶלָּא אִם כֵּן הִרְחִיק מִמֶּנּוּ אַרְבַּע אַמּוֹת. (בבא בתרא כו,א: משנה פ"ב מי"ב)
תלמוד: אָמַר שְׁמוּאֵל: לֹא שָׁנוּ אֶלָּא בְּאֶרֶץ יִשְׂרָאֵל, אֲבָל בְּבָבֶל שְׁתֵּי אַמּוֹת .... וְאִיכָּא דְּרָמֵי לְהִי מִירְמָא: תְּנַן לֹא יִטַּע ... אַרְבַּע אַמּוֹת, וְהַתַּנְיָא: שְׁתֵּי אַמּוֹת! אָמַר שְׁמוּאֵל: לָא קַשְׁיָא — כָּאן בְּבָבֶל, כָּאן בְּאֶרֶץ יִשְׂרָאֵל. (שם ע"פ כת"י**)

MISHNA: One should not plant a tree close to his neighbor's field except at a distance of four cubits from it.

TALMUD: Sh°muel said: They taught [this] only with respect to Eretz Yisrael, but for Babylonia [a distance of] two cubits [is sufficient]. There is someone who "hurls" them (= who points out a contradiction between our mishna and a baraitha): We have stated [in our mishna]: One should not plant ... [unless at a distance of] four cubits, but [a baraitha] states: two cubits! Sh°muel said: There is no difficulty — here (in the baraitha) [it refers] to Babylonia, there (in our mishna) [it refers] to Eretz Yisrael.

* Instead of לְהוּ, sometimes the f.s. לַהּ, *it*, or, as in our example, the f. pl. לְהִי appears in a manuscript.

** See ראש השנה כז,ב and Rashi's comment there.

SEE: (לְ)מִירְמָא, רְמָא and its note

אִיכָּא לְמֵימַר

it is [possible] to say יֵשׁ לוֹמַר

הָתָם וַדַּאי אִיכָּא שְׁבוּעַת שָׁוְא; הָכָא אִיכָּא לְמֵימַר דְּלֵיכָּא שְׁבוּעַת שָׁוְא. (בבא מציעא ב,ב)

In that case there is certainly a false oath; in this case it is [possible] to say that there is no false oath.

SEE: מַאי אִיכָּא לְמֵימַר

אִיכָּא לְמִיפְרַךְ יֵשׁ לְהַקְשׁוֹת

there are grounds to refute (the קַל־וָחֹמֶר analogy)

For an example, see מָה לְ- ... שֶׁ-... תֹּאמַר בְּ- ... שֶׁ-.

SEE: (לְ)מִיפְרַךְ, קַל וָחֹמֶר

אִיכּוּ (אִי+כּוּ) אִם אֵיפוֹא; אִילּוּ

if then; if

אִיכּוּ הַשְׁתָּא לָא אֲתַאי, סַכַּנְתּוּן לִבְרִי. (ברכות כה, סע"ב)

If I had not come now, you would have endangered my son.

SEE: כּוּ

אִיכַּוַּון/אִיכַּוֵּין (אִתְכַּוַּן: כוון אִתְפְּעַל: מִיכַּוֵּין .prt)

he intended; he had intention (for) נִתְכַּוֵּן

לָא אִיכַּוַּון לְמָרוֹר (פסחים קיד, רע"ב)

he did not intend to [fulfill the mitzva of eating] a bitter herb

אִיכְּסִיף/אִכְּסִיף (אִתְכְּסִיף: כסף אִתְפְּעִל: מִיכְּסִיף .prt, לִיכְּסִיף .fut) הִלְבִּין; נִתְבַּיֵּשׁ

he grew pale like silver; he was embarrassed

אֵיתִיבֵיהּ רָבִינָא לְרָבָא .... אִיכְּסִיף. (עבודה זרה כב,א)

Rabina refuted [the halakha of] Rava (from a baraitha) .... [Rava] was embarrassed (by the refutation and unable to respond).

SEE: אִישְׁתּוֹמַם כְּשָׁעָה חֲדָא, כִּיסוּפָא

אִיכַּפַּל (אִתְכַּפַּל: כפל אִתְפְּעַל) טָרַח; נִתְיַגֵּעַ

he took pains; he troubled himself

אִיכַּפַּל

וְאִיכַּפַּל תַּנָּא לְאַשְׁמוֹעִינַן
וְכִי טָרַח הַתַּנָּא לְהַשְׁמִיעֵנוּ ...?!

Did the tanna take pains to teach us [such an exceptional case]?!

This formula raises a *difficulty* against an explanation of a mishna or a baraitha on the grounds that the explanation is far-fetched.

וְאִיכַּפַּל תַּנָּא לְאַשְׁמוֹעִינַן גַּבְרָא עַרְטִילָאֵי דְּלֵית לֵיהּ וְלָא כְלוּם?! (בבא מציעא מו, רע"א)

Did the tanna take pains to teach us [a case of] a naked man who possesses nothing at all?!

אִיכְּפַּת* (= אִתְכְּפַת: כפת אִתְפְּעֵל)
it concerned (him); he cared נוֹגֵעַ (לוֹ)

This verb is always followed by -ל with a personal-pronoun suffix.

הַיְינוּ הַאי דְּלָא אִיכְּפַת לֵיהּ אַמָּמוֹנָא דְּחַבְרֵיהּ! (ב"מ כד,א)

This is the one who was not concerned about the property of his fellow man!

* The etymology of this word is obscure. We have presented it as an Aramaic verb, the אִתְפְּעֵל *binyan* from the root כפת. Nevertheless, we do not really understand why the *dagesh*, which one would expect to appear in the כ (אִיכְּפַת), has shifted to the פ (אִיכַפַּת). In fact, the Yemenite tradition reads this form אִיכְּפַת! This word is occasionally used in Mishnaic Hebrew (משנה ב"מ פ"ג מ"ז; פ"ט מ"ד) and often in Modern Hebrew, where a new noun אִכְפַּתִיּוּת, *concern*, has developed from it.

אִילּוּ/אִלּוּ* (אִם+לוּ)
if; were

This Hebrew conjunction introduces an unfulfilled condition.

אִלּוּ פִינוּ מָלֵא שִׁירָה כַּיָּם ..., אֵין אָנוּ מַסְפִּיקִין לְהוֹדוֹת לְךָ ה'. (ברכות נט,ב)

Were our mouths filled with song like the sea ..., we could not give sufficient thanks to You, O God.

* See: וְאִלּוּ לַעֲבָדִים וְלִשְׁפָחוֹת נִמְכַּרְנוּ, הֶחֱרַשְׁתִּי (אסתר ז:ד)

וְאִילּוּ/וְאִלּוּ*
but as for; whereas; while

מֵעִיקָּרָא כְּתִיב: "שִׂמְחָה וּמִשְׁתֶּה וְיוֹם טוֹב", וּלְבַסּוֹף כְּתִיב: "לַעֲשׂוֹת אוֹתָם יְמֵי מִשְׁתֶּה וְשִׂמְחָה" — וְאִילּוּ "יוֹם טוֹב" לָא כְּתִיב. (מגילה ה,ב ע"פ אסתר ט:יט, כב)

First it is written (about the celebration of the miraculous Jewish victory on Purim): "Rejoicing and drinking and a holyday (implying abstaining from work)," and later (in Mord^ekhai's letter regarding the establishment of Purim) it is written: "To make them days of drinking and rejoicing" — whereas "a holyday" is not written (and so it is permitted to do work).

* This conjunction may have a precedent in Biblical Hebrew, although the vocalisation is different:

כִּי אִם יִפֹּלוּ, הָאֶחָד יָקִים אֶת חֲבֵרוֹ; וְאִילוֹ הָאֶחָד שֶׁיִּפּוֹל, וְאֵין שֵׁנִי לַהֲקִימוֹ. (קהלת ד:י ותרגום שם)

אִילֵּימָא (אִי+לֵימָא)
if we say ... אִם נֹאמַר ...

This term introduces a *tentative interpretation* of a text that is immediately refuted and then replaced by a different interpretation.

אִילֵימָא אַרֵישָׁא, פְּשִׁיטָא! אֶלָּא אַסֵּיפָא. (ברכות יח,א)

If we say [this statement refers] to the first clause, it is obvious (and hence superfluous)! Rather [it refers] to the latter clause.

See אֶהֱיֵיא for a more extensive example.

אִילֵּין/אִלֵּין
these אֵלּוּ

אִלֵּין יוֹמַיָּא דְּלָא לְהִתְעַנָּאָה בְּהוֹן ... (תענית יז,ב ע"פ מגילת תענית)

These are the days on which it is forbidden to fast ...

וְאֵילָךְ
and onwards; and henceforth

שֶׁבַע מֵעֶזְרָא וְאֵילָךְ. (משנה פרה פ"ג מ"ה)

There were seven [red heifers prepared] from [the time of] Ezra and henceforth.

אֵילָךְ וְאֵילָךְ
hither and thither; to one side and the other; in both directions

וּפִנָּה גֶחָלִים אֵילָךְ וְאֵילָךְ (יומא מג,ב: משנה פ"ד מ"ג)

and he cleared away the coals to one side and the other

SEE: (מ)כָּאן וְאֵילָךְ

אֵימָא[1] (אמר) imp.
say! אֱמֹר!

This word often introduces a *resolution* of a difficulty or a *rejection* of a proposal — achieved either by reinterpreting a text or by changing it.

וְאָמַר ר' יְהוֹשֻׁעַ בֶּן לֵוִי: לְעוֹלָם יַשְׁכִּים אָדָם לְבֵית הַכְּנֶסֶת כְּדֵי שֶׁיִּזְכֶּה וְיִמָּנֶה עִם עֲשָׂרָה הָרִאשׁוֹנִים; שֶׁאֲפִילּוּ מֵאָה בָּאִים אַחֲרָיו, נוֹטֵל שְׂכַר כּוּלָּן. "נוֹטֵל שְׂכַר כּוּלָּן" סָלְקָא דַעְתָּךְ?! אֶלָּא אֵימָא: נוֹתְנִין לוֹ שָׂכָר כְּנֶגֶד כּוּלָּן. (ברכות מז, סע"ב ע"פ כת"י)

And R. Y^ehoshua b. Levi said: A person should always come early to the synagogue so that he merit to be counted among the first ten; for even if one hundred [more] come after him, he receives the reward of them all. Do you [really] think: "He receives the reward of them all"!? Rather say (= change the text): "He receives a reward equal to [the reward of] all of them."

SEE: אֲמַר, אֵימוּר, אֵימַר

אֵימָא[2] (אמר) fut. 1st person singular
I will say; I would say אֹמַר

לְעוֹלָם, אֵימָא לָךְ ... (ברכות כו,ב ועוד)

In reality, I will say to you ...

SEE: אֲמַר, לְעוֹלָם

אִימָּא
SEE: אִמָּא

וְאֵימָא הָכִי נַמִי
But say [it is] really so! וֶאֱמֹר אַף כֵּן!

After a proposal that a halakhic statement rejects is presented, the Talmud sometimes "turns the tables" and argues that the proposal may be correct after all.

בריתא: בֵּית הָאִשָּׁה ... חַיֶּיבֶת בִּמְזוּזָה.
תלמוד: פְּשִׁיטָא! מַהוּ דְּתֵימָא "בֵּיתְךָ" — וְלֹא "בֵּיתָהּ" ... קָמַשְׁמַע לַן. וְאֵימָא הָכִי נַמֵּי! (יומא יא,ב ע"פ דברים יא:כ)

BARAITHA: A woman's house ... must have a m^e^zuza.

TALMUD: It is obvious! (Why, then, does the baraitha need to state it?) What might you say: [The Biblical precept that] "your house" [requires a m^e^zuza may imply] — but not "her house"? [Hence the baraitha is needed to] teach us [that a woman's house needs a m^e^zuza]. But say [it is] really so (that a woman's house is indeed excluded from m^e^zuza)?

וְאֵימָא כּוּלֵּיהּ לְהָכִי הוּא דְּאָתָא

וֶאֱמֹר כֻּלּוֹ לְכָךְ הוּא בָּא!

But say that all of it has come for that!

After a Scriptural passage has been explained as a source for one halakhic point, the Talmud sometimes raises a *difficulty*: Perhaps the whole passage is needed for that point alone — leaving another point, for which the passage was supposed to provide a Scriptural source, without any basis whatsoever?

For an example — see בבא קמא נח, רע"ב.

אֵימָא לָא

I would have said: No! אֱמֹר: לֹא!

This expression is frequently used in the course of a צְרִיכוּתָא argument that seeks to show that both of the elements stated in the text under discussion are necessary, because without one of them I would have reached a wrong conclusion.

See example under צְרִיכָא.

אֵימָא סֵיפָא

Say the end! אֱמֹר אֶת הַסּוֹף!

Take note of the latter clause (of the mishna, baraitha, or of the amora's statement)!*

After the Talmud has just presented an interpretation or a comment about an earlier clause in the text under discussion, this expression is often used to introduce a latter clause in the same text that seems to be a *contradiction* to that interpretation or comment.

משנה: בְּאֶחָד בְּנִיסָן רֹאשׁ הַשָּׁנָה ... לָרְגָלִים. בְּאֶחָד בֶּאֱלוּל, רֹאשׁ הַשָּׁנָה לְמַעְשַׂר בְּהֵמָה. ר' אֶלְעָזָר וְר' שִׁמְעוֹן אוֹמְרִים: בְּאֶחָד בְּתִשְׁרִי. (ראש השנה ב, רע"א: משנה פ"א מ"א)
תלמוד: לָרְגָלִים. מַנִּי? ר' שִׁמְעוֹן הִיא. אֵימָא סֵיפָא: ר' אֶלְעָזָר וְר' שִׁמְעוֹן אוֹמְרִים: בְּאֶחָד בְּתִשְׁרִי. (שם ז,ב ורש"י שם)

MISHNA: On the first of Nisan it is the New Year ... for festivals. On the first of Elul it is the New Year for the tithe from cattle. R. El'azar and R. Shim'on say: On the first of Tishri.

TALMUD: [The first of Nisan is the New Year] for festivals. Who is [the authority for] it? It is R. Shim'on. [But] take note of the latter clause: R. El'azar and R. Shim'on say: On the first of Tishri [is the New Year for the tithe from cattle, indicating that the anonymous author of the earlier clause in the mishna is not R. Shim'on]!

* Occasionally, "the latter clause" is a baraitha that was taught as an addendum to a mishna as in ברכות כז, רע"א.

אֵימָא רֵישָׁא

אֱמֹר אֶת הָרֹאשׁ!

Say the beginning! Take note of the earlier clause!

This expression introduces a *contradiction* from a previous clause.

For an example — see בבא מציעא לו, סע"ב.
SEE: אֵימָא סֵיפָא

אֵימוּר/אֵימַר imp. (אמר)

say! one could say אֱמֹר!

This term often introduces an interpretation that serves as a *tentative* resolution* of a difficulty or a *tentative* refutation* of an argument.

משנה: וְלֹא יִתֵּן לְתוֹכוֹ מַיִם, מִפְּנֵי שֶׁהוּא מְכַבֶּה. (שבת מז,ב: משנה פ"ג מ"ו)
תלמוד: לֵימָא תְּנַן סְתָמָא כְּר' יוֹסֵי דַּאֲמַר: גּוֹרֵם לְכִיבּוּי אָסוּר? וְתִסְבְּרָא?! אֵימוּר דַּאֲמַר ר' יוֹסֵי בְּשַׁבָּת — בְּעֶרֶב שַׁבָּת מִי אֲמַר?! (שם מז,ב)

MISHNA: But (even on Friday) one must not pour water into it (= a vessel placed under a lamp to catch sparks), since he would be extinguishing (and thus desecrating the Sabbath).

TALMUD: Shall we say we have learned an anonymous mishna in accordance with [the halakha of] R. Yosé, who said: Indirect extinguishing is forbidden? But does it make sense?! One could say that R. Yosé stated [his halakha] about [an act done on] the Sabbath [itself, but] did he state [it] about [an act done on] the eve of the Sabbath (= Friday)?!

* This *tentativeness* is sometimes evident in the Talmud, e.g.:
לָא לֵימָא מָר "אֵימוֹר" אֶלָּא "וַדַּאי" ...! (ערובין צג,ב)
Let the master not say "one could state" but "definitely" ...!
SEE: אֲמַר, אֵימָא

אִימְלִיךְ/אִמְלִיךְ (= אִתְמְלִיךְ: מלך אִתְפְּעֵל: מִימְלִיךְ prt., אִימְלוֹכֵי inf.)

he consulted (with); he sought advice (from) (1) נִמְלַךְ; נוֹעַץ

אֲזַל וְאִמְלִיךְ בִּדְבֵיתְהוּ. (ברכות כז, סע"ב)
He went and consulted with his wife.

he reconsidered; he changed his mind (2) נִמְלַךְ; חָזַר בּוֹ

כָּתְבָהּ מֵעִיקָּרָא לְהַאי וְאִמְלִיךְ וְלָא יַהֲבָהּ לֵיהּ. (ב"מ יט,ב)
He originally wrote it (= the document) for this [person] but reconsidered and did not give it to him.

אֵימַר imp. (אמר)

say! one could say אֱמֹר!

For further explanation with an example, see אֵימוּר.

אִימְשִׁיךְ (= אִתְמְשִׁיךְ: משך אִתְפְּעֵל: מִימְשִׁיךְ .prt, אִימְשׁוֹכֵי .inf)

he was drawn; it was protracted נִמְשַׁךְ

וְלֹא לֶאֱכוֹל בִּסְעוּדָה קְטַנָּה ... דִּילְמָא אָתֵי לְאִמְשׁוֹכֵי (שבת ט,ב)
[One should] not [begin to] eat [even] a small meal (before the afternoon prayer) ... lest [the meal] come to be protracted.

אֵימַת אֵימָתַי; מָתַי **when**

זְמַן קְרִיאַת שְׁמַע דִּ"שְׁכִיבָה" — אֵימַת? (ברכות ב,א)
*When is the time for reciting the Sh*ᵉ*ma of "lying down" (= of the night)?*

SEE: כָּל אֵימַת

אֵימְתָא אֵימָה; מוֹרָא **fear; awe**

אֵימְתָא דִשְׁמַיָּא (שבת קנו,ב) *the fear of Heaven*

אִין הֵן; כֵּן **yes; indeed**

This affirmative word is often used in contrast to the negative לָא.

הָנֵי — אִין; אוֹרֶז וְדוֹחַן — לָא! (פסחים לה,א)
these (= species of grain) — yes; rice and millet — no!

SEE: אִין הָכִי נַמֵי, אִין וְלָאו וְרַפְיָא בִידֵיהּ

אֵין ... אֶלָּא ...

not ... but ...; not ... except ...; only

This formula may be rendered into English affirmatively as *only* (like the French *ne ... que ...*).

רֵאשִׁית הַגֵּז אֵינוֹ נוֹהֵג אֶלָּא בָאָרֶץ. (ברכות כב,א; חולין קלו,א)
[The law of] the first shearing does not apply except in Eretz Yisrael. (= It applies only in Eretz Yisrael.)

אֵין יְשִׁיבָה אֶלָּא לְשׁוֹן עַכָּבָה, שֶׁנֶּאֱמַר: "וַתֵּשְׁבוּ בְקָדֵשׁ יָמִים רַבִּים". (מגילה כא, סע"א ע"פ דברים א:מו)
[The verb] ישב (in this context) is only an expression of "staying," as it is written: "And you stayed in Kadesh many days."*

* This formula does *not* necessarily denote exclusiveness. Here, for example, it is *not* claimed that the verb ישב always means *staying*, for sometimes it does mean *sitting* as in ויקרא טו:ו.

SEE: אֶלָּא

אֵין בֵּין ... לְ- ... אֶלָּא ... **There is no [difference] between ... and ... except ...**

אֵין בֵּין יוֹם טוֹב לְשַׁבָּת אֶלָּא אוֹכֶל נֶפֶשׁ בִּלְבָד. (מגילה ז,ב: משנה פ"א מ"ח*)
There is no [difference] between a festival and the Sabbath [with regard to forbidden labors] except for [the preparation of] food for people.

* See the subsequent mishnayoth in that chapter.

אִין הָכִי נַמֵי הֵן, אַף כָּךְ!

Yes, it is indeed so! Your point is well taken!

With this conciliatory *response*, the Talmud or a specific ḥakham concedes the point that was just now stated.

ברייתא: "כָּל זְכוּרְךָ" — לְרַבּוֹת אֶת הַקְּטַנִּים.
תלמוד: קָטָן שֶׁהִגִּיעַ לְחִינּוּךְ דְּרַבָּנָן הִיא! אִין, הָכִי נַמֵי, וּקְרָא אַסְמַכְתָּא בְּעָלְמָא! (חגיגה ד,א ע"פ שמות כג:יז)
BARAITHA: "All your males [must appear before God on the three pilgrim festivals]" — including children.
TALMUD: A child who has reached [the age of] education is [obligated only because of] an enactment of the ḥakhamim (so how can this obligation be derived from a Biblical passage)! Yes, it is indeed so (that the obligation has been enacted by the ḥakhamim), and [thus] the Biblical passage is merely a support (for that rabbinic obligation).

אִין וְלָאו וְרַפְיָא בִידֵיהּ

"Yes" and "no," for it was unsteady in his hand "הֵן" וְ"לֹא", וְרָפָה בְּיָדוֹ

In response to a problem that was posed to him on several occasions, the amora sometimes answered "yes" and sometimes "no." He did not reach a clear-cut decision.

For an example — see קידושין ס"ה,א ורש"י שם וש"נ.

אֵין לִי אֶלָּא ... מִנַּיִן? **I have [established] only ..., from where [can I derive] ...?**

This formula, which is common in baraithoth of Midrash halakha, presents the following *difficulty*: Whereas the Biblical passage quoted previously is a source for one halakhic point, it does not appear to be a source for a related point or another case. What, then, is the source for the latter?

"עַל מַצּוֹת וּמְרוֹרִים יֹאכְלוּהוּ" — אֵין לִי אֶלָּא בִּזְמַן שֶׁבֵּית הַמִּקְדָּשׁ קַיָּים. בִּזְמַן שֶׁאֵין בֵּית הַמִּקְדָּשׁ קַיָּים, מִנַּיִן? (פסחים קכ, סע"א ע"פ במדבר ט:יא)
"They shall eat it (= the Pesaḥ offering) with unleavened bread and bitter herbs" — I have [established the obligation to eat unleavened bread] only at a time when the Beth HaMikdash is in existence. From where [can I derive that obligation] for a time when the Beth HaMikdash is not in existence (when there is no Pesaḥ offering)?

אֵין מִיעוּט אַחַר מִיעוּט אֶלָּא לְרַבּוֹת

[One] limitation [that occurs in the Torah] after [another] limitation really [comes] to extend [the scope of the law].

This *rule of Biblical interpretation*, which seems to defy logic, is probably a received tradition. It interprets the occurrence of two limiting words regarding the same point as extending the halakhic category to include an additional case.*

"וְכִי יִהְיֶה בְאִישׁ חֵטְא [מִשְׁפַּט מָוֶת וְהוּמָת, וְתָלִיתָ אֹתוֹ עַל עֵץ]." ... אָמַר רַב נַחְמָן בַּר יִצְחָק: לְרַבּוֹת "בֵּן סוֹרֵר וּמוֹרֶה". מַאי טַעְמָא? דְּאָמַר קְרָא: "וְכִי יִהְיֶה בְאִישׁ חֵטְא" — אִישׁ וְלֹא בֵן.

"חֵטְא" — מִי שֶׁעַל חֶטְאוֹ נֶהֱרָג, יָצָא בֵּן סוֹרֵר וּמוֹרֶה, שֶׁעַל שֵׁם סוֹפוֹ נֶהֱרָג. הָוֵי מִיעוּט אַחַר מִיעוּט, וְאֵין מִיעוּט אַחַר מִיעוּט אֶלָּא לְרַבּוֹת. (סנהדרין מו,א ע' רש"י ויד רמ"ה שם ע"פ דברים כא:כב)

*"And if a man has [committed] a sin [subject to the death penalty and is executed, you shall hang him on the gallows]." ... Rav Nahman b. Yitzhak said: [This is] to include "the stubborn and rebellious son" [in the law of hanging]. What is the source? Since the pasuk stated: "And if a man has [committed] a sin" — "a man," not a son [excluding the case of "the stubborn and rebellious son," who is too young to be called a "man"]; "a sin [subject to the death penalty]," [implying] one who is executed on account of a sin — excluded is "the stubborn and rebellious son," who is executed on account of his [criminal] destiny.** [Thus] there is [one] limitation after [another] limitation, and [one] limitation after [another] limitation really [comes] to extend [the scope of the law, so as to include "the stubborn and rebellious son" in the law of hanging].*

* The converse is אֵין רִיבּוּי אַחַר רִיבּוּי אֶלָּא לְמַעֵט, *[one] extension after [another] extension really [comes] to limit [the scope of the law].* It appears in פסחים כג,א and בבא קמא מה,ב.

** According to the baraitha in סנהדרין עא,א, the case of *"the stubborn and rebellious son" never occurred and never will occur,* but the Torah has taught us the law for study only — not for its actual implementation.

אֵין צָרִיךְ/צוֹרֶךְ לוֹמַר

it is not necessary to state; it goes without saying

This expression introduces the most obvious case where a particular halakha certainly applies — in contrast to a case where we need to be taught that the halakha applies.

"בֶּחָרִישׁ וּבַקָּצִיר תִּשְׁבּוֹת" — אֵין צָרִיךְ לוֹמַר חָרִישׁ ... שֶׁלַּשְּׁבִיעִית, אֶלָּא חָרִישׁ שֶׁלְּעֶרֶב שְׁבִיעִית שֶׁהוּא נִכְנָס בַּשְּׁבִיעִית ... (משנה שביעית פ"א מ"ד ע"פ שמות לד:כא)

"You must refrain from plowing and harvesting" — it is not necessary to state [that you must refrain from] plowing during the Sabbatical year, but [you must refrain from] plowing on the eve of the Sabbatical year entering the Sabbatical year ...

שֶׁאֵין תַּלְמוּד לוֹמַר ...

"There is no teaching that [the Biblical passage comes] to say ..."; It was not necessary for the Torah to state ...

This formula indicates that there seems to be a *superfluous word* or *expression* in the pasuk that was just quoted. It is always followed by the question (וּ)מַה תַּלְמוּד לוֹמַר?, *what does ... [come] to teach?*

דָּרַשׁ ר' עֲקִיבָא: "אָז יָשִׁיר מֹשֶׁה וּבְנֵי יִשְׂרָאֵל אֶת הַשִּׁירָה הַזֹּאת לַה', וַיֹּאמְרוּ לֵאמֹר." שֶׁאֵין תַּלְמוּד לוֹמַר "לֵאמֹר". וּמַה תַּלְמוּד לוֹמַר "לֵאמֹר"? (סוטה כז,ב: משנה פ"ה מ"ד)

R. Akiva expounded: "Then Moshe and the children of Yisrael sang this song unto God, and they spoke saying." It was not necessary [for the Torah] to state לֵאמֹר *("saying"). But what does* לֵאמֹר *[come] to teach?*

SEE: תַּלְמוּד לוֹמַר

אִינְגִּיד/אִיתְנְגִיד (נגד אִתְפְּעֵל) נֶחֱלַשׁ; הִתְעַלֵּף

he became weak; he became faint

אִינְגִּיד וְאִיתְּנַח (מגילה טז,א) *he became faint and sighed*

אֵינָהּ מִשְׁנָה

[it] is not an [authoritative] teaching

בֵּית שַׁמַּאי בִּמְקוֹם בֵּית הִלֵּל אֵינָהּ מִשְׁנָה. (ברכות לו, רע"ב וש"נ ורש"י שם)

[The opinion of] Beth Shammai when in conflict with [that of] Beth Hillel is not an [authoritative] teaching.

SEE: מִשְׁנָה

אִינְהוּ* הֵם — they (m.)

אִינְהִי* הֵן — they (f.)

אִינְהוּ עֲדִיפֵי מִינֵּיהּ (מגילה ג,א) *they are superior to him*

* For a full listing of the independent personal pronouns in Babylonian Aramaic, see *Grammar for Gemara:* Chapter 7.2.

אֵינוֹ דִין שֶׁ- ...

is it not logical that ...?!

This formula is often used to mark the conclusion of a קַל-וָחוֹמֶר argument.

For an example — see (וּ)מָה ... אֵינוֹ דִין שֶׁ-.

וְאֵינוֹ חוֹשֵׁשׁ

and he need not be concerned (that such activity is forbidden)

מִי שֶׁנָּשְׁרוּ כֵלָיו בַּדֶּרֶךְ בְּמַיִם מְהַלֵּךְ בָּהֶן וְאֵינוֹ חוֹשֵׁשׁ (שבת קמו, סע"ב: משנה פכ"ב מ"ד)

One whose clothes fell into water [on the Sabbath] on the way may continue walking in them and he need not be concerned (that people may suspect that he washed the clothes on the Sabbath).

SEE: לְכַתְּחִילָּה

אִינּוּן הֵם

they

וּמָאן אִינּוּן? מֹשֶׁה וְאַהֲרֹן. (ברכות לא,ב)

And who are they? Moshe and Aharon.

SEE: אִינְהוּ, the more common form, and its note.

אִינִי (אִין+הִיא) כָּךְ הִיא?!

Is it so?!

This term introduces a *contradiction* to the statement just quoted in the Talmud.

אֲמַר רַבִינָא: שְׁמַע מִינַּהּ הַמְבַשֵּׁל בְּחַמֵּי טְבֶרְיָה בְּשַׁבָּת חַיָּיב ... אִינִי?! וְהָאֲמַר רַב חִסְדָּא: הַמְבַשֵּׁל בְּחַמֵּי טְבֶרְיָה בְּשַׁבָּת פָּטוּר! (שבת מ, סע"ב)

Rabina said: This proves that [if] one cooks in the hot springs of Tiberias on the Sabbath, he is guilty [of desecrating the Sabbath]. Is it so?! But did not Rav Ḥisda say: [If] one cooks in the hot springs of Tiberias on the Sabbath, he is exempt!

אֱינִישׁ*/אֱינָשׁ (pl. אֱינָשֵׁי)

man; person אָדָם; אִישׁ

another person אֱימַשׁ אַחֲרִינָא (בבא מציעא כו, רע״ב)

* This form is popularly pronounced אִינִישׁ.

SEE: אֱינָשֵׁי בֵּיתֵיהּ

אִינָךְ (s. אִידָךְ)

those; the others הָהֵם; הָאֲחֵרִים

תְּלָתָא — הָנֵי דַּאֲמַרַן; אִינָךְ ... (כתובות קיא,א)

Three (of the six oaths) are these that we have (just) stated; the others are ...

אִינְסִיבָא/אִינְסִיב* f. (= אִתְנְסִיבָא; נסב אִתְפְּעֵל; מִינַסְבָא .prt. f., אִינְסוּבֵי .inf)

she got married נִשְּׂאָה

שָׁמוּ לָהּ לְאִשָּׁה, וְאִינְסִיבָא (בבא מציעא לה, סע״א)

[if] they appraised [the estate] for a woman [creditor], and she got married

* This verb always has a feminine subject, yet אִינְסִיב — without the feminine suffix — is also found in our printed editions, as in יבמות קכ,א.

SEE: אַנְסִיב, נְסַב

לְאִינְצוּיֵי (= לְאִתְנְצוּיֵי: נצי אִתְפְּעֵל)

to quarrel לָרִיב

תַּקִּינוּ רַבָּנַן דְּלָא לֵיתוֹ לְאִינְצוּיֵי. (בבא מציעא י,א ע״פ כת״י)

The ḥakhamim enacted [the halakha] so that [people] would not come to quarrel

אֱינָשׁ

SEE: אֱינִישׁ

אִינְשִׁי (= אִתְנְשִׁי: נשי* אִתְפְּעֵל: מִינְשֵׁי .prt)

he forgot שָׁכַח

שְׁבוּעָתֵיהּ אִינְשִׁי; חֶפְצָא דְּכִיר (שבועות כו,א ורש״י שם)

he has forgotten [the language of] his oath; (but) he has recalled the object [mentioned in his oath]

* See מְנַשֶּׁה, כִּי נַשַּׁנִי אֱלֹקִים אֶת כָּל עֲמָלִי (בראשית מא:נא)

אֱינָשֵׁי* (s. אֱינִישׁ) אֲנָשִׁים

men; people

* This form is popularly pronounced אִינְשֵׁי.

אֱינָשֵׁי בֵּיתֵיהּ אַנְשֵׁי בֵּיתוֹ; אִשְׁתּוֹ

members of his household; his wife

לָא מִיקַבְּלִי עֲלַי אֱינָשֵׁי בֵּיתִי. אֲמַר לֵיהּ: מָה שְׁמַהּ? חַנָּה. (תענית כג, סע״ב ורש״י שם)

My wife is not acceptable to me. He said to him: What is her name? Ḥanna.

SEE: אַנְשֵׁי בֵּיתוֹ, בַּיִת

לְאִינְתּוּ

in matrimony; for a wife לְאִישׁוּת

הֲרֵי אַתְּ לִי לְאִינְתּוּ! (קידושין ה,ב)

Here you are to me in matrimony! (= Be my wife!)

אִינְתְּתָא/אִנְתְּתָא

woman; wife

SEE: אִיתְּתָא

אִיסּוּר; אִיסּוּרָא*

(1) a prohibition

אֵין אִיסּוּר חָל עַל אִיסּוּר. (יבמות יג,ב; חולין קיג,ב)

*A prohibition does not take hold where there is already a prohibition.***

(2) ritual law — as opposed to civil law

כִּי אָזְלִינַן בָּתַר רוּבָּא — בְּאִיסּוּרָא; בְּמָמוֹנָא — לָא. (בבא בתרא צב, רע״ב ורשב״ם שם)

In ritual law we follow the majority [practice] — not in civil law (where the status quo is the determining factor).

* The first form is Hebrew, and the second is Aramaic.

** For example, eating the meat of a pig does not entail an additional punishment if the pig had not been halakhically slaughtered.

אִיסּוּר לָאו

a prohibition [forbidden] by an [ordinary] negative commandment (punishable only by flogging)

שַׁבָּת, דְּאִיסּוּר סְקִילָה, גְּזַרוּ רַבָּנַן; יוֹם טוֹב, דְּאִיסּוּר לָאו, לָא גְּזַרוּ בֵּיהּ רַבָּנַן. (יבמות קיד, סע״א)

[With regard to the] Sabbath, where the prohibition [of labor] is subject to [death by] stoning, the ḥakhamim issued a decree; [with regard to] a festival, where the prohibition [is forbidden] by an [ordinary] negative commandment (punishable only by flogging), the ḥakhamim did not issue a decree.

SEE: לֹא תַעֲשֶׂה, לָאו

אִיסּוּר עֲשֵׂה*

a prohibition [forbidden by implication] from a positive commandment

נְשִׂיאַת כַּפַּיִם, דְּאִיסּוּר עֲשֵׂה (כתובות כד,ב ורש״י שם)

*"lifting up the hands" (= birkath kohanim), which [if performed by a non-kohen] constitutes a prohibition [forbidden by implication] from a positive commandment***

* Aside from the example quoted above, this halakhic term occurs once more in עירובין פו,ב — according to our printed editions of the Talmud, but not according to the famous Munich Manuscript. The more common Talmudic term is לָאו הַבָּא מִכְּלַל עֲשֵׂה (see that entry). אִיסּוּר עֲשֵׂה is sometimes used in Talmudic commentaries and in halakhic codes. See also the Rambam's use of this terminology in משנה תורה, הלכות אישות א:ח, ד:יד.

** In his commentary on this passage, Rashi states that the primary source for the halakha that this mitsva must be performed by kohanim *exclusively* is:

״כֹּה תְבָרְכוּ״ (במדבר ו:כג) — אַתֶּם וְלֹא זָרִים!

"Thus you shall bless" — you, but not non-kohanim!

אֶיסַמְיַיהּ/ אֶיסַמְיַהּ fut. (סמי פַּעֵל)

Shall I erase it? אֶמְחֹק אוֹתָהּ?

(1) An amora presented a mishna or a baraitha. (2) Subsequently, a difficulty was pointed out with regard to the halakha he had presented. (3) The amora sometimes acknowledges the difficulty and asks: Should I eliminate that problematic halakha

from the material I teach?*

(1) תָּנֵי רַבָּה בַּר בַּר חַנָּה קַמֵּיהּ דְּרַב: שׁוֹרִי הָרַגְתָּ! ... אַתָּה אָמַרְתָּ לִי לְהוֹרְגוֹ! ... פָּטוּר. (2) אֲמַר לֵיהּ: לָא שָׁבְקַתְּ חַיֵּי לִבְרִיָּיתָא! כָּל קְמֵינֵיהּ?! (3) אֲמַר לֵיהּ: אֵיסְמְיֵהּ? (ב"ק צא,ב ע"פ כת"י)

(1) Rabba, the grandson of Ḥanna, recites [the following baraitha] before Rav: "You killed my ox!" -[claimed the plaintiff, and the defendant replied:] "You told me to kill it!" He is exempt [from responsibility]. (2) He (= Rav) said to him (= Rabba): You are not allowing people to live! How can his claim ("you told me to kill it") be believed? (3) He (= Rabba) said to him: Shall I erase it?

* See Rashi on בבא מציעא כז, רע"א; נח, רע"ב

SEE: סָמֵי, סוּמָא

אִיסָּר*

issar

This coin is worth eight *p*e*rutoth.*

* See the table of coins in the appendix.

אִיעֲנַשׁ (= אִתְעֲנַשׁ: ענשׁ אִתְפְּעֵל: מִיעֲנַשׁ .prt)

he was punished נֶעֱנַשׁ

וְדָנִיֵּאל מְנָלַן דְּאִיעֲנַשׁ? (בבא בתרא ד,א)

And [as for] Daniel, from where do we derive that he was punished?

אִיעֲסַק (= אִתְעֲסַק: עסק אִתְפְּעֵל)

he occupied himself (with) נִתְעַסֵּק

רַבִינָא אִיעֲסַק לֵיהּ לִבְרֵיהּ בֵּי רַב חֲבִיבָא (כתובות ח, סע"א ורש"י שם)

Rabina occupied himself with [preparations for] his son['s wedding] at Rav Ḥabiva's house.

SEE: עֲסַק

אִיעֲקַר/אִיתְעֲקַר (עקר אִתְפְּעֵל)

(1) it was uprooted; it was torn away; it moved from its place (1) נֶעֱקַר; זָז מִמְּקוֹמוֹ

אִיעֲקוּר אִיעֲקוֹרֵי (חולין מד, סע"א)

they were completely torn away

(2) it was forgotten (2) נִשְׁכַּח

אִיעֲקַר תַּלְמוּדֵיהּ (שבת קמז,ב) *his learning was forgotten*

(3) he became sterile (3) נַעֲשָׂה עָקָר

אִיעַקְרָא דְבֵיתְהוּ (כתובות סב,ב ורש"י שם)

his wife became sterile

SEE: אִיַּיקַר

לְאִיעֲרוֹמֵי* (= לְאִתְעֲרוֹמֵי) .inf (ערם אִיתְפְּעֵל)

to be subtle; to act deceptively; to employ a stratagem לְהַעֲרִים

מְבַשֵּׁל הוּא דְּלָא אָתֵי לְאִיעֲרוֹמֵי (שבת לח, רע"א)

cooking [on the Sabbath] is [something regarding] which one would not come to act deceptively (by feigning ignorance of the prohibition)

* Occasionally, אַעֲרוֹמֵי (*binyan* אַפְעֵל) is used with the same meaning as in בבא מציעא ד,ב.

SEE: מִיעֲרַם, מַעֲרִים

אִיעֲתַר (= אִתְעֲתַר: עתר אִתְפְּעֵל)

he became wealthy הִתְעַשֵּׁר; הֶעֱשִׁיר

מִן שִׁית מִילֵּי אִיעֲתַר ר' עֲקִיבָא. (נדרים נ, סע"א)

From six things (= sources) R. Akiva became wealthy.

אֵיפָה*

éfa

This measure of volume equals three *s*e*as.*

* See the table of measurements in the appendix.

אֵיפוּךְ .imp (אפך)

reverse! interchange! הֲפֹךְ! הַחֲלֵף!

In order to resolve a difficulty, the Talmud sometimes uses this term to introduce a *textual change* in a baraitha or a mishna.

(1) In some instances, the authorship of two opinions in a controversy is reversed, so that the opinion formerly attributed to one ḥakham is now attributed to his colleague and vice versa.

ברייתא: נָפַל לְיַד דַּיָּין, לֹא יוֹצִיאוֹ עוֹלָמִית. ר' יוֹסֵי אוֹמֵר: הֲרֵי הוּא בְחֶזְקָתוֹ. (בבא מציעא ז,א)

תלמוד: אֵיפוּךְ! נָפַל לְיַד דַּיָּין, לֹא יוֹצִיאוֹ עוֹלָמִית — דִּבְרֵי ר' יוֹסֵי; וַחֲכָמִים אוֹמְרִים: הֲרֵי הוּא בְחֶזְקָתוֹ. (שם ז,ב)

BARAITHA: [According to the Ḥakhamim, if a note of indebtedness] fell into the hands of a judge, it must never be produced [for collection]. R. Yosé says: It retains its validity (and the debt may be collected).

TALMUD: (Because of a contradiction between R. Yosé's statement here and his statement in another baraitha:) Reverse [this baraitha so that it will read: If] it fell into the hands of a judge, it must never be produced [for collection; this is] the opinion of R. Yosé, but the Ḥakhamim say: It retains its validity.

(2) In other instances, two elements within a statement are reversed. Thus the predicates of two clauses may be interchanged, so that what was predicated at first about one subject is now predicated about the other subject, and vice versa.

ברייתא: סַנְטֵר אֵינוֹ מָכוּר; אַנְקוֹלְמוֹס מָכוּר.

תלמוד: אֵיפוּךְ! ... סַנְטֵר מָכוּר; אַנְקוֹלְמוֹס אֵינוֹ מָכוּר. (בבא בתרא סח,ב)

BARAITHA: [If one sells a town] the watchman is not sold; the town clerk is sold (even though both individuals are slaves).

TALMUD: Reverse [the clauses]! ... The watchman is sold; the town clerk is not sold.

Sometimes, the Talmud later rejects the proposed textual change and exclaims: לְעוֹלָם לָא תֵּיפוּךְ!, *In reality, do not reverse [them]!* Then it presents another opinion that resolves the difficulty differently. See the Talmudic passage from which our first example was taken.

SEE: מוּחְלֶפֶת הַשִּׁיטָה

אֵיפוּךְ אֲנָא (אפך) fut. 1st pers. s.

I should reverse [the order]! אֶהֱפֹךְ אֲנִי!

With this expression the Talmud challenges the order of the data that has been presented and proposes a different order.

רִאשׁוֹנָה בְּשׁוֹמֵר חִנָּם; שְׁנִיָּיה בְּשׁוֹמֵר שָׂכָר. אֵיפוּךְ אֲנָא! (בבא מציעא צד,ב ע"פ שמות כב:ו־יב)

The first [paragraph refers] to an unpaid guardian; the second [paragraph refers] to a paid guardian. I should reverse [the order] (and explain that the first paragraph refers to a paid guardian, and the second to the unpaid guardian)!

אִיפְּטַר/אִפְּטַר (= אִתְפְּטַר: פטר אִתְפְּעִל: מִיפְּטַר .prt, לִיפְּטַר .fut)

(1) נִפְטַר (= נִהְיָה פָּטוּר) **he was exempt**

וְשׁוֹמֵר קַמָּא אִפְּטַר לֵיהּ לְגַמְרֵי (בבא קמא נו,ב)

and the first guardian would be exempt altogether

(2) נִפְרַד **he departed; he took leave**

ר׳ שִׁמְעוֹן בֶּן חֲלַפְתָּא אִפְּטַר מִינֵּיהּ דְּרַב (מועד קטן ט,ב)

R. Shim'on b. Ḥalafta took leave of Rav.

SEE: מִיפְּטַר, לִיפְּטַר

אִיפְּכָא

מַהֲפָךְ; לְהֶפֶךְ **the opposite; the reverse**

For examples — see: אַדְּרַבָּה אִיפְּכָא מִסְתַּבְּרָא, (וְ)תָא אִיפְּכָא שָׁמְעִינַן לְהוּ, (וְ)הָתַנְיָא אִיפְּכָא

אִיפְּלִיג (אִתְפְּלִיג: פלג* אִתְפְּעִל: מִיפְּלִיג .prt, לְאִיפְּלוֹגֵי .inf)

(1) נֶחֱלַק **he disagreed; he disputed**

For examples — see: תָּא אִיפְּלִיגוּ בָּהּ חֲדָא זִימְנָא, מִיפַּלְגִי.

(2) נִתְחַלֵּק **it was divided**

אֶרֶץ יִשְׂרָאֵל — לִשְׁבָטִים אִיפְּלְגָא? (ב"ב קכא, סע"ב ע"פ כת"י)

Was Eretz Yisrael divided according to the tribes (into twelve equal portions)?

* For the full conjugation of this verb, see *Grammar for Gemara:* Chapter 4, Verb 1.

SEE: פְּלַג

אִיפְּסִיל (= אִתְפְּסִיל: פסל אִתְפְּעִל: מִיפְּסִיל .prt, לִיפְּסִיל .fut, לְאִיפְּסוֹלֵי .inf)

נִפְסַל **it was disqualified; it became unfit**

אָתֵי לְאִיפְּסוֹלֵי (גיטין סז,ב)

[the bill of divorce] may come to be disqualified

אִיצְטְרוֹפֵי/אִצְטְרוֹפֵי* .inf (צרף אִתְפְּעַל: מִצְטָרֵף .prt) הִצְטָרֵף

"join"; "be counted" (as part of a quorum)

ברייתא: אֲפִילּוּ לֹא ... אָכַל עִמָּהֶם אֶלָּא גְרוֹגֶרֶת אַחַת מִצְטָרֵף.
תלמוד: אִצְטְרוֹפֵי מִצְטָרֵף, אֲבָל ... (ברכות מח, סע"א)

BARAITHA: Even if he ate only one fig he may be counted [as part of a quorum for Birkath haZimmun].

TALMUD: He may indeed be counted, but ...

* This form (without -ל), the absolute infinitive, is used to strengthen the verbal form that follows. It is best translated into English by an adverb, e.g., *surely* or *indeed*.

אִיצְטְרִיךְ/אִצְטְרִיךְ (צרך* אִתְפְּעִל)

נִצְרַךְ; הָיָה צָרִיךְ **it was needed; it was necessary [to be stated]**

This term is often used to indicate that a Biblical passage or a halakhic statement (or any part of either) is *not superfluous* — in spite of any explicit or implicit arguments to the contrary.

הֲלָכָה כְּרִ׳ יְהוֹשֻׁעַ בֶּן קָרְחָה — אִיצְטְרִיךְ. סָלְקָא דַעְתָּךְ אֲמִינָא: יָחִיד וְרַבִּים הֲלָכָה כְּרַבִּים. קָא מַשְׁמַע לַן: הֲלָכָה כְּיָחִיד. (עבודה זרה ז,א)

[That] the halakhic ruling is in accordance with [the opinion of] R. Yᵉhoshua b. Korḥa, needed [to be stated]. You would [otherwise] think [that] I should say: [When the opinion of] an individual opposes the majority [opinion], the halakhic ruling follows the majority. [This statement] teaches us that [in this case I do not invoke that rule, but] the halakhic ruling [here] is in keeping with the minority [view].

* For the full conjugation of this verb, see *Grammar for Gemara:* Chapter 4, Verb 3.

SEE: סֵיפָא אִיצְטְרִיכָא לֵיהּ

אִיקְּטִיל (= אִתְקְטִיל: קטל אִתְפְּעִל: מִיקְּטִיל .prt)

נֶהֱרַג **he was killed; he was executed**

כֵּיוָן דְּאִיקְּטוּל, קָרֵי לְהוּ "עֲבָדֶיךָ". (סנהדרין מז, סע"א ע"פ תהלים עט:ב)

Once they have been executed (by the Gentile government), [Scripture] calls them "Your servants."

אִיקַּיַּים (אִתְקַיַּים: קום* אִתְפַּעַל; מִיקַּיַּים .prt)

נִתְקַיֵּים **it was established; it was fulfilled**

לָא אִיקַּיַּים תְּנָאֵיהּ (גיטין לד, סע"א)

his stipulation was not fulfilled

* For the full conjugation of this verb, see *Grammar for Gemara:* Chapter 4, Verb 17.

אִיקְּלַע (אִתְקְלַע: קלע אִתְפְּעִל: מִיקְּלַע .prt)

נִקְלַע*; נִזְדַּמֵּן **he happened to come; he chanced upon**

מָר זוּטְרָא אִיקְּלַע לְבֵי רַב אַשִׁי. (ברכות מו,ב)

Mar Zutra happened to come to the home of Rav Ashi.

* In Modern Hebrew usage, נִקְלַע usually has a negative connotation, which is not present in the Aramaic verb.

אִיקַּפַּד* (אִתְקַפַּד: קפד אִתְפַּעַל) הִקְפִּיד; כָּעַס

he was annoyed; he became angry

שְׁמַע ר׳ יוֹחָנָן וְאִיקַּפַּד. (ראש השנה כא,א)

R. Yoḥanan heard [about the incident] and became angry.

* This verb is often pronounced אִיקְפִּיד, a variation of the אַפְעֵל *binyan*, which is parallel to the Hebrew הִקְפִּיד in the

הפעיל *binyan*. In fact, it is spelled איקפיד in some printed editions of the Talmud.
SEE: קְפִיד

אִיקְרִי/אִקְרִי[1] (= אתקרי: קרא אתפעל: מקרי .prt)

it was called; it was termed נִקְרָא

ראש חודש איקרי מועד (פסחים עז, רע"א)
the first of the month has been termed a festival

אִיקְרִי/אִקְרִי[2] (= אתקרי: קרי אתפעל)

he happened (to) קָרָה; נִזְדַּמֵּן

ודלמא איקרו ויהבו ליה? (כתובות כו,א)
But perhaps they happened to give [it] to him?

אִירְיָא*

proof; a determination (1) רְאָיָה; קְבִיעָה

For examples — see מידי איריא, אי משום הָא לָא איריָא.

"seizing"; a determination (2) תְּפִיסָה; נְקִיטָה

See example under the entry מַאי איריָא.

* This noun is based on the Aramaic verb ארי, the equivalent of the Hebrew verb ערי.

SEE: אַיירי, (וד)קָארי לַהּ מַאי קָארי לַהּ

אִירְכַס (= אתרְכַס: רכס אתפעל: מירְכַס .prt)

it was lost אָבַד

שְׁטָרָא מעַלְיָא הֲוָה לי ואירכַס! (בבא בתרא לב, רע"ב)
I had a valid document, but it got lost!

אִירְתַת (אתרְתַת: רתת אתפעל: מירתַת .prt, אירתותי .inf)

he was trembling/afraid רָתַת; רָעַד

הֵיכָא דאיכָא עדים, אירְתוּתֵי מירתַת (ב"ב קכח,ב ע"פ כת"י)
where there are witnesses, he is certainly afraid

אֶישְׁתּוֹמַם

SEE: אֶשְׁתּוֹמַם

אִישְׁתִּי*/אִשְׁתִּי* (שתי: שָׁתֵי .prt, לְמִישְׁתֵּי .inf)

he drank שָׁתָה

יוֹמָא חַד אִשְׁתִּי טוּבָא, וְלָא הֲוָה יָדַע כַּמָּה שָׁתֵי. (פסחים קי,ב)
One day he drank a lot, and he did not know how much he was drinking.

* The initial ("prosthetic") א is prefixed for phonetic reasons, but the *binyan* is still considered קַל.

אִישְׁתַּיַּיר/אִשְׁתַּיַּיר (שאר אתְפְעַל: מִשְׁתַּיַּר .prt)

he remained; he was left נִשְׁתַּיֵּר; נִשְׁאַר

לָא אִישְׁתַּיְירָא מִינַּיְיהוּ אֶלָּא הַהִיא יְנוּקְתָּא (ב"ב ג, סע"ב)
only one young girl was left from them

אִישְׁתִּיק*/אִשְׁתִּיק*/שְׁתֵיק (שתק: שָׁתֵיק .prt, מִישְׁתַּק .fut, לִישְׁתּוֹק .inf)

he was silent שָׁתַק

In some cases, an amora remains silent in the face of a halakhic question or an objection. There are several possible explanations for his silence:

(1) The amora did not know the answer.

(2) He agreed with the objection that was raised

against his opinion.**

(3) He ignored what was said to him, because he was not impressed by it.***

אֲמַר ליה רַב חסדָא לְרַב יצחָק: ... הָכָא מַאי? אִישְׁתִּיק וְלָא אֲמַר ליה וְלָא מידי. (ברכות כז,א)
Rav Ḥisda said to Rav Yitzḥak: ... What is [the halakha] here? [Rav Yitzḥak] was silent and said nothing to him.

* The initial ("prosthetic") א is prefixed for phonetic reasons, but the *binyan* is still considered קַל.

** שתיקה כהודָאָה, as in בבא מציעא לז, רע"ב

*** בבא בתרא סב,א ותוס' ד"ה "ומודה רב"

אִישְׁתְּכַח/אִשְׁתְּכַח (שכח אתפעל: משתכַח .prt, לשתכַח .fut)

it was discovered; (1) נִמְצָא*; נִתְבָּרֵר

it became clear; it resulted; consequently

ינוקָא מקני קָני, אַקְנויי לָא מָקני, ואישתכַח דקָא נָפיק בלולָב שאינו שלו. (סוכה מו,ב)
A child can acquire possession [of a lulav, but] he cannot transfer possession, and consequently [an adult who has recovered the lulav he had given to a child] is performing the mitzva with a lulav that is not his own.

it was forgotten (2) נִשְׁכַּח**

דאישתכַח — אישתכַח (תמורה טו,ב ורש"י שם)
that (halakhic material) which was forgotten — was forgotten

* In spite of the fact that the active form of this sense of the verb is אַשְׁכַּח, the אַפְעֵל *binyan*, nevertheless the passive form אִישְׁתְּכַח is in the אִתְפְּעֵל *binyan*, the passive of the קַל. Our vocalisation is confirmed by manuscripts of the Talmud and Targum Onkelos and by the popular pronunciation.

** This meaning of the root שכח is common in Hebrew but rare in Aramaic.

SEE: אַשְׁכַּח

אִישְׁתְּלִי (שלי אִתְפְּעַל: מִשְׁתְּלֵי .prt)

he forgot; he erred שָׁכַח; שָׁגַג

אֲכַל, וְאִשְׁתְּלִי וְלָא בָּרֵיךְ. (ברכות נג,ב)
He ate, and he forgot to recite Birkath HaMazon.

אִישְׁתְּמִיט/אִשְׁתְּמִיט (שמט אִתְפְּעַל: מִשְׁתְּמִיט .prt, לִישְׁתְּמִיט .fut, לְאִישְׁתְּמוּטֵי .inf)

נִשְׁמַט; נִשְׁכַּח

it slipped (his mind); it was overlooked

אִישְׁתְּמִיטְתֵּיהּ הָא דַּאֲמַר שְׁמוּאֵל. (ראש השנה יג, סע"ב)
This (halakha) which Sh[e]*muel said was overlooked by him (= R. Zera).*

אִישְׁתַּמֵּיט (שמט אִתְפַּעַל: מִשְׁתַּמֵּט .prt, לִישְׁתַּמֵּיט .fut, לְאִשְׁתַּמּוּטֵי .inf)

he slipped away; (1) הִשְׁתַּמֵּט; הִתְחַמֵּק

he escaped

אִשְׁתַּמּוּטֵי הוּא דְּקָא מִשְׁתַּמֵּט מִינֵּיהּ. (בבא מציעא ג, רע"ב)
He is actually slipping away from him. (= The defendant is trying to put off the claimant.)

he omitted (2) הִשְׁתַּמֵּט; דִּלֵּג

לָא לִישְׁתְּמֵיט תַּנָּא וְלִיתְנֵי "הֶעָרֵל וְהַטָּמֵא"! (יבמות עב,ב)
Let the tanna not omit stating [the case of] "the uncircumcised and the ritually unclean"!

אִישְׁתְּמַע (שמע אִתְפְּעֵל: מִשְׁתְּמַע prt., לִישְׁתְּמַע fut.)
it was heard נִשְׁמַע
אִישְׁתְּמַע מִילְּתָא בֵּי מַלְכָּא. (בבא מציעא פג,ב)
A report was heard at the king's residence.

אִישְׁתַּמַּשׁ/אִשְׁתַּמַּשׁ/אִישְׁתַּמֵּישׁ (שמש אִתְפְּעֵל: מִשְׁתַּמֵּשׁ prt., לִישְׁתַּמֵּשׁ fut., לְאִישְׁתַּמּוֹשֵׁי inf.)
he used הִשְׁתַּמֵּשׁ
שְׁרוּ לֵיהּ רַבָּנַן לְאִשְׁתַּמּוֹשֵׁי בְּגַוַּייהוּ (בבא מציעא כט,ב)
The ḥakhamim permitted him (= the finder) to use them (= the lost articles).

אִישְׁתְּעֵי (שעי אִתְפְּעֵל: מִשְׁתְּעֵי prt., לִישְׁתְּעֵי fut., לְאִשְׁתְּעוֹיֵי inf.)
he spoke; he discussed (1) דִּבֵּר
אִשְׁתְּעֵי אִיהוּ בִּלְשׁוֹן הַקּוֹדֶשׁ (סוטה לו, סע"ב)
he spoke in the holy tongue
he told; he related (an incident) (2) סִפֵּר
אִשְׁתְּעֵי לִי רַב חָמָא (בבא מציעא פו, רע"א)
Rav Ḥamma told me

אִישְׁתְּרֵי (שרי אִתְפְּעֵל: מִישְׁתְּרֵי prt., לִישְׁתְּרֵי fut., אִישְׁתְּרוּיֵי inf.)
it was permitted הֻתַּר
נְהִי דְּאִישְׁתְּרֵי בְּעִידָּן עֲבוֹדָה, בְּלָא עִידָּן עֲבוֹדָה לָא אִישְׁתְּרֵי. (מנחות מג, סע"א)
Even though [a kohen] has been permitted [to wear sha'atnez] at a time [when he is performing] the Temple service, he has not been permitted [to do so] at a time [when] not [performing] the Temple service.
SEE: שְׁרָא

אִית יֵשׁ **is; are; exists; has validity**
The word אִית, like the Hebrew יֵשׁ, is often used with pronoun suffixes that represent the grammatical subject. The following forms are the most common:*

it (m.) is; it has substance/validity יֶשְׁנוֹ אִיתֵיהּ
it (f.) is; it has substance/validity יֶשְׁנָהּ אִיתָא/אִיתַהּ
they are; they have substance/validity יֶשְׁנָם אִיתַנְהוּ

מַתָּנָה מִדַּעְתַּהּ אִיתָא, בְּעַל כּוּרְחַהּ לֵיתָא (גיטין כא, א)
[if] a gift [is granted] with her consent, it has validity; [if granted] against her will, it has no validity
הוֹאִיל וְאִיתַנְהוּ בִּשְׁמִירָה, אִיתַנְהוּ בִּזְכִירָה (ברכות כ, ב)
since they (= women) are [included] in observing [the Sabbath], they are [included] in reciting [Kiddush]

* For the complete paradigm, see *Grammar for Gemara*: Chapter 7.313.
SEE: לֵית

אִית בֵּיהּ (בַּהּ f.s.; בְּהוּ m. pl.)
there is in it; it has; it contains יֵשׁ בּוֹ
אִית בֵּיהּ שָׁוֶה פְּרוּטָה (קידושין יב, סע"א)
it has the value of a p'ruta (coin)
SEE: לֵית בֵּיהּ

אִית לֵיהּ (לַהּ f.s.; לְהוּ m. pl.) יֵשׁ לוֹ
(1) he has; he possesses
אִית לֵיהּ חַמְרָא לְלֹוֶה (בבא מציעא סב,ב)
the debtor possesses wine
(2) he is entitled to; he has a right of
קָטָן אִית לֵיהּ זְכִיָּיה לְנַפְשֵׁיהּ (בבא מציעא יב, א)
a minor has [the right of] acquisition for himself
(3) he holds (an opinion); **he agrees with**
רַבָּנַן אִית לְהוּ דְּרַב חִסְדָּא (בבא מציעא מז, סע"ב)
the Ḥakhamim agree with [the opinion] of Rav Ḥisda
SEE: לֵית לֵיהּ

אִיתָא/אִיתַהּ יֶשְׁנָהּ
it (f.) is; it has substance/validity
For examples, see אִית and אִם אִיתָא.

לְאִיתוֹיֵי/לְאָתוֹיֵי inf. (אתי אַפְעֵל)
to bring; to include לְהָבִיא
See example under אַיְיתִי.

אִיתּוֹסַף (יסף אִתְפְּעַל) נוֹסַף
it was added
אִיתּוֹסַף אִיסּוּר לְגַבֵּי בַּעְלָהּ. (כריתות יד, רע"ב)
A prohibition was added with regard to her husband.

אִיתּוֹתַב (תוב אִתְפְּעַל) הוּשַׁב
he was refuted
וְלָאו אִיתּוֹתַב רֵישׁ לָקִישׁ? (בבא מציעא יב,ב)
Has Resh Lakish not been refuted?
SEE: אֵיתִיב, אֵיתִיבֵיהּ, תְּיוּבְתָּא

אִיתַּזַם (זמם אִתְפְּעַל) הוּזַם
it was refuted
SEE: הוּזַם and its note.

אִיתַּזַק (נזק אִתְפְּעַל: מִיתַּזַק prt., לִיתַּזַק fut.)
it was damaged הֻזַּק; נִזַּק
אִילּוּ אִיתַּזַק מֵעָלְמָא (בבא קמא יג,ב)
if [my ox] had been damaged by someone else's [ox]

אִיתְחֲזִי (חזי* אִתְפְּעֵל: מִתְחֲזֵי/מִיחֲזֵי prt.)
it was seen; it appeared (1) נִרְאָה
אִיתְחֲזִי לְהוּ בְּחֶילְמָא (תענית כא,ב)
it appeared to them in a dream
it was fit; it was suitable (2) הָיָה רָאוּי
בְּעִידָּנָא דְּאִיתְחֲזַאי קַמַּיְיתָא, לָא אִיתְחֲזַאי בָּתְרַיְיתָא (יומא סב,א)
at the time when the first was fit, the last was not fit

* For the full conjugation of this verb, see *Grammar for Gemara:* Chapter 4, Verb 12.
SEE: מיחזי, חזא

אִיתְחֲזַק* (חזק אתפעל) הָחְזַק
it was established; it has taken hold
איתחזק איסורא דאשת איש (גיטין ב,ב)
the status of [being] a married woman [who is thus forbidden to other men] has (already) taken hold

* We have vocalised this verb אִיתְחֲזַק, as the *binyan* אִתְפְּעֵל, in accordance with the popular pronunciation. Since אַחְזֵק in the אַפְעֵל *binyan* serves as the active form, it would be more consistent for the passive form to be vocalised אִיתַּחְזַק from the אִתַּפְעַל *binyan*, the passive of אַפְעֵל. Compare the entry אִישְׁתְּכַח, which indicates that Aramaic is not always consistent in this regard.

אֵיתִיב (תוב אַפְעֵל: מְתִיב/מוֹתִיב .prt, לוֹתִיב .fut, אוֹתִיב .imp, לְאוֹתוּבֵי .inf)
he replied; he refuted הֵשִׁיב; הִקְשָׁה

אֵיתִיבֵיהּ* (איתיב+ליה) הֱשִׁיבוֹ; הִקְשָׁה לוֹ
he replied to him; he raised a difficulty against him; he refuted him
This term introduces a *difficulty*** raised by an amora against the halakha of another amora because of a contradiction from a more authoritative source — a pasuk, a mishna, a baraitha, or from the standard text of the siddur.
שׁוֹמֵר שֶׁמָּסַר לְשׁוֹמֵר ... ר׳ יוֹחָנָן אָמַר חַיָּיב ... דְּאָמַר לֵיהּ: "אֵין רְצוֹנִי שֶׁיְּהֵא פִּקְדּוֹנִי בְּיַד אַחֵר." אֵיתִיבֵיהּ ר׳ אַבָּא בַּר מֶמֶל לְרִ׳ אַמִי: הַשּׂוֹכֵר פָּרָה מֵחֲבֵירוֹ וְהִשְׁאִילָהּ לְאַחֵר וּמֵתָה כְּדַרְכָּהּ, יִשָּׁבַע הַשּׂוֹכֵר שֶׁמֵּתָה כְּדַרְכָּהּ ... וְאִם אִיתָא, לֵימָא לֵיהּ: אֵין רְצוֹנִי שֶׁיְּהֵא פִּקְדּוֹנִי בְּיַד אַחֵר! (בבא מציעא לו,א)
[If] one guardian handed over [a deposit] to [another] guardian ... R. Yoḥanan said [the first] is liable ... because [the owner] can say: "I did not want my property to be in someone else's hand." R. Abba b. Memel raised a difficulty against R. Ammi (from a mishna): [If] one rented a cow from his fellow man and lent it to another person and it died of natural causes, the renter must take an oath that it died of natural causes [and he does not have to pay compensation] ... But if [R. Yoḥanan's opinion] is true, let [the owner] say to him: "I did not want my property to be in someone else's hand," (and the renter should pay compensation because of his irresponsibility)!

* The Yemenite pronunciation is אִתִּיבֵיהּ, ignoring the first י. Among Ashkenazim, it is popularly pronounced אֵיתִבֵיהּ, ignoring the second י.
** On rare occasions, this term introduces a *proof* — as in עירובין כו, רע"א. See Rashi's comment there.
SEE: אוֹתִיב, תְּיוּבְתָּא, מְתִיב, מֵיתִיבִי

אִיתֵיהּ יֶשְׁנוֹ **it is; it has substance/validity**
SEE: אית

אִיתְיְלִיד/אִתְיְלִיד (ילד אִתְפְּעֵל)
he was born נוֹלַד
אִיתְיְלִיד לֵיהּ הַהוּא יְנוּקָא כְּשֶׁהוּא מָהוּל. (שבת קלה,א)
A child was born to him [already] circumcised.

וְאִיתֵּימָא (ואי+תימא)* וְאִם תֹּאמַר; וְיֵשׁ אוֹמְרִים
"and if you say"; and some say
This term is placed between the names of two ḥakhamim to indicate that there are two different traditions as to which one of them is the author of what is about to be quoted in the Talmud.
שְׁמוּאֵל וְאִיתֵּימָא ר׳ יוֹחָנָן אָמַר (ביצה ו,א)
Sh^e^muel — and some say R. Yoḥanan — stated

* This etymology is one of several possibilities. Others regard the term as a contraction of אִית+אָמַר, *there is [someone who] says*, or as a variant form of the passive verb אִתְאֲמַר, *it was said*.
SEE: (וְ)אָמְרֵי לָהּ

אִיתְכְּשַׁר* (כשר אִתְפְּעֵל: מִיתְכְּשַׁר .prt, לִיתְכְּשַׁר .fut)
it became fit; הֻכְשַׁר (לָרֹב: לְקַבֵּל טוּמְאָה)
it became susceptible to ritual defilement
משנה: הֶחָלָב טָמֵא (שבת קמד, סע"ב: משנה טהרות פ"ג מ"ג)
תלמוד: ... בְּמַאי אִיתְכְּשַׁר? (שבת שם)
MISHNA: the milk is ritually unclean
TALMUD: ... through what did it become susceptible to defilement?

* We have vocalised this verb אִיתְכְּשַׁר as the *binyan* אִתְפְּעֵל in accordance with the popular pronunciation. Since אַכְשַׁר in the אַפְעֵל *binyan* serves as the active form, it would be more consistent for the passive form to be vocalised אִיתַּכְשַׁר from the אִתַּפְעַל *binyan*, the passive of אַפְעֵל. See the entry אִישְׁתְּכַח, and its note.

אִיתְּמַר/אִתְּמַר (= אִתְאֲמַר: אמר* אִתְפְּעֵל)
it was stated נֶאֱמַר
This word is used to introduce the words of an amora or a controversy between two amoraim.**
אִתְּמַר: שׁוֹמֵר שֶׁמָּסַר לְשׁוֹמֵר — רַב אָמַר: פָּטוּר, וְר׳ יוֹחָנָן אָמַר: חַיָּיב. (בבא מציעא לו,א)
It was stated: [If one] guardian handed over [the object in his custody] to [another] guardian — Rav said: He (= the first guardian) is exempt, and R. Yoḥanan said: He is liable.

* For the full conjugation of this verb, see *Grammar for Gemara:* Chapter 4, Verb 10.
** Rarely, it introduces a controversy between tannaim. See יומא נז, סע"ב וריטב"א ותוס׳ ישנים (מודפסות נח,ב שם).
SEE: (וְ)אִיתְּמַר עֲלָהּ, אֶלָּא אִי אִיתְּמַר הָכִי אִיתְּמַר, אֶלָּא הֵיכָא דְּאִיתְּמַר אִיתְּמַר הֵיכָא דְּלָא אִיתְּמַר לָא אִיתְּמַר, כִּי אִיתְּמַר

וְאִיתְּמַר/וְאִתְּמַר עֲלָהּ ... וְנֶאֱמַר עָלֶיהָ ...
and it was stated in connection with it ...
This term introduces a comment by an amora that qualifies or interprets a text — either a mishna, a baraitha, or a statement of an early amora — that has just been quoted in the Talmud.

בריית: רַבָּן שִׁמְעוֹן בֶּן גַּמְלִיאֵל אוֹמֵר: שְׁנֵי אַכְסְנָיִים אוֹכְלִין עַל שֻׁלְחָן אֶחָד — זֶה בָּשָׂר וְזֶה גְּבִינָה.
תלמוד: וְאִיתְּמַר עֲלַהּ: אָמַר ... שְׁמוּאֵל: לֹא שָׁנוּ אֶלָּא שֶׁאֵין מַכִּירִין זֶה אֶת זֶה, אֲבָל מַכִּירִין זֶה אֶת זֶה, אָסוּר. (שבת יג,א)
BARAITHA: Rabban Shim'on b. Gamliel says: Two travellers may eat at the same table — one [eating] meat and the other cheese.
TALMUD: And it was stated in connection with it: ... Sh'muel said: They taught [this] only where they are not acquainted with each other, but [in a case where] they are acquainted with each other, it is forbidden.
SEE: הָא אִיתְּמַר עֲלַהּ

אִיתַנְהוּ יֶשְׁנָם
they are; they have substance/validity
See example under the entry אִית.

אִיתְנִיס (= אִתְאֲנִיס: אנס אִתְפְּעֵל: אִיתְנוּסֵי .inf)
he was forced; נֶאֱנַס
he was unavoidably prevented
אִיתְנִיס, וְלָא אֲתָא. (נדרים כז,א)
He was unavoidably prevented [from travelling], and he did not arrive.
SEE: אוֹנֶס, אָנוּס

אִיתַסִּי/אִתַּסִּי (= אִתְאַסִּי: אסי אִתְפְּעֵל: מִיתַּסֵּי .prt)
he was cured; he recovered נִרְפָּא
בְּעוֹ רַבָּנַן רַחֲמֵי עֲלֵיהּ, וְאִתַּסִּי. (ברכות ו,א)
The hakhamim begged for mercy (= prayed) in his behalf, and he recovered.

אִיתְּסַר (= אִתְאֲסַר: אסר אִתְפְּעֵל: מִיתְּסַר .prt, לִיתְּסַר (.fut
it was forbidden נֶאֱסַר
כֵּיוָן דַּאֲמַר: "הַב לַן וְנִבְרִיךְ", אִיתְּסַר לֵיהּ לְמִשְׁתֵּי חַמְרָא. (חולין פו, סע"ב)
As soon as one says: "Let us say Birkath HaMazon," it is forbidden for him to drink wine (without reciting a new b'rakha).

אִיתְעֲבִיד/אִתְעֲבִיד (עבד* אִתְפְּעֵל: מִיתְעֲבִיד)
it was done; it was made נַעֲשָׂה
הוֹאִיל וְאִתְעֲבִיד בֵּיהּ מִצְוָה, נַעֲבִיד בֵּיהּ מִצְוָה אַחֲרִיתִי. (ברכות לט, סע"ב)
Since one mitsva has [already] been done with it, let us do another mitsva with it.
* For the full conjugation of this verb, see *Grammar for Gemara*: Chapter 4, Verb 4.
SEE: עֲבַד

אִיתְעֲקַר SEE: אִיעֲקַר

אִיתְּעַר* (עור אִתְפְּעֵל: מִתְּעַר .prt) הִתְעוֹרֵר; נֵעוֹר
he was awakened; he roused himself
אִיתְּעַר בְּהוּ ר׳ יוֹחָנָן, אֲמַר לְהוּ ... (שבת קמח,א)
R. Yohanan was awakened by their [conversation, and] he told them ...
* תִּיר, which may be an abbreviated form of this verb, occurs in the expression תִּיר וְלָא תִּיר (פסחים קכ, רע"ב ורש"י), *he was awake and not awake.*

אִיתְּקַשׁ (נקש אִתְפְּעֵל) הֻקַּשׁ
it was compared
הָא אִיתְּקַשׁ הַשְׁבָּתַת שְׂאוֹר לַאֲכִילַת חָמֵץ! (פסחים ה, סע"א ע"פ שמות יב:טו)
Has not the destruction of leaven been compared to the eating of hametz!
* We have vocalised this verb אִיתְּקַשׁ as the *binyan* אִתְפְּעֵל, in accordance with the popular pronunciation. Since אַקֵּישׁ in the אַפְעֵל *binyan* serves as the active form, it would be more consistent for the passive form to be vocalised אִיתַּקַּשׁ from the אִתַּפְעַל *binyan*, the passive of אַפְעֵל. See the entry אִישְׁתְּכַח and its note.
SEE: הוּקַשׁ, הֶיקֵּשׁ

אִיתְרַבִּי (רבי אִתְפְּעֵל: מִיתְרַבֵּי .prt) נִתְרַבָּה; נִכְלַל
it was included (into a halakhic category)
חָצֵר מִשּׁוּם "יָדָהּ" אִתְרַבְּאִי. (ב"מ י, סע"ב ע"פ דברים כד,א)
[Her] courtyard was included under the category of "her hand." (= Placing a bill of divorce in her courtyard is halakhicly equivalent to placing it in her hand.)
SEE: רִיבָּה, לְרַבּוֹת

אִיתְרְחִישׁ (רחש אִתְפְּעִיל: מִתְרְחִישׁ .prt)
it was done נַעֲשָׂה

אִיתְרְחִישׁ* לֵיהּ נִיסָּא
a miracle was done for him נַעֲשָׂה לוֹ נֵס
For an example — see ברכות כח, רע"א.
* In the Talmud and in the Targumim — e.g., in the Targum to קהלת ד:יג — this verb always occurs with נִיסָּא, *miracle.* In Modern Hebrew, however, the verb הִתְרַחֵשׁ, is used in a general sense to mean *it happened.*

אִיתְרְמִי/אִתְרְמִי (רמי אִתְפְּעֵל: מִיתְרְמֵי .prt, אִיתְרְמוּיֵי (.inf
it happened נִזְדַּמֵּן
כִּי הֵיכִי דְּאִתְרְמִי לְדִידָךְ, אִתְרְמִי נַמִּי לְחַבְרָךְ. (ב"ם כג,ב)
Just as it happened to you, it may have also happened to your fellow man.

אִיתְּרַע[1]* (רעע אִתְפְּעֵל: מִיתְּרַע .prt) הוּרַע; נִתְרוֹעֵעַ
it was impaired; it was weakened
אִיתְּרַע שְׁטָרָא (שבועות מב,א)
The document has been impaired.
* The vocalisation אִיתְּרַע from the אִיתְּפְעַל *binyan* may be more correct. Compare the note on אִישְׁתְּכַח.

אִיתְּרַע[2] (ארע אִתְפְּעֵל: מִיתְּרַע .prt)
it happened; it befell אֵרַע
In the Babylonian Talmud, this verb appears only in the euphemism that comprises the next entry.

אִיתְּרַע בֵּיהּ מִילְּתָא
"Something befell him." אֵרְעוֹ דָּבָר.*
(= A death occurred in his family.)

See example in מועד קטן יא, סע"ב.

* The parallel Hebrew euphemism, אִרְעוֹ דָּבָר, appears in the Mishna (מדות פ"ב מ"ב). Compare אִרְעוֹ אֵבֶל, *mourning befell him*, in מועד קטן יא, רע"ב: משנה פ"ב מ"א.

אִיתְּשִׁיל (שאל אתפעל: מִיתְּשִׁיל .prt, לְאִיתְּשׁוּלֵי .inf)

"he was asked"; נִשְׁאַל (עַל נִדְרוֹ אוֹ עַל שְׁבוּעָתוֹ)

he submitted to questioning before a ḥakham (in order to be absolved from his vow or oath)**; he applied for absolution from his vow**

שְׁמַע כַּלְבָּא שָׂבוּעַ ... וְאִיתְּשִׁיל עַל נִידְרֵיהּ, וְאִישְׁתְּרִי. (נדרים נ,א)

Kalba Savua heard [about his son-in-law, R. Akiva] ... and applied for absolution from his vow, and it was annulled.

אִיתְּתָא/אִתְּתָא/אִינְתְּתָא

woman; wife אִשָּׁה

כִּי נָסֵיב אֱינָשׁ אִיתְּתָא (ברכות ח,א)

when a man marries a woman

SEE: הַהִיא אִיתְּתָא, (לְ)אִינְתּוּ

אַכְשַׁר (כשר אפעל: מַכְשַׁר .prt, לַכְשַׁר .fut, אַכְשׁוּרֵי .inf)

he rendered fit; he declared qualified הִכְשִׁיר

בַּדְקָהּ רַב אַשִׁי לְסַכִּינֵיהּ, וְנִמְצֵאת יָפָה, וְאַכְשְׁרֵיהּ. (חולין יח,א)

Rav Ashi examined his (= the ritual slaughterer's) knife, and it was found to be good, and he declared him [a] qualified [slaughterer].

אַכַּתִּי עֲדַיִן

still; yet

וְאַכַּתִּי מִיבְּעֵי לֵיהּ! (מגילה ב,א ועוד)

But still it is needed by him!

אַל תִּקְרֵי ... אֶלָּא ...

read not ..., but rather ... אַל תִּקְרָא ... אֶלָּא ...

This formula is used to present *Scriptural support* for a halakha or an aggada. Two different usages may be distinguished:

(1) Read this Biblical word not only in accordance with its Masoretic vocalisation, but in accordance with its spelling that allows for a different vocalisation as well!

"וְכָל בָּנַיִךְ לִמּוּדֵי ה', וְרַב שְׁלוֹם בָּנָיִךְ". אַל תִּקְרֵי "בָּנָיִךְ", אֶלָּא "בּוֹנָיִךְ"! (ברכות סד,א ע"פ ישעיה נד:יג)

"And all your children (בָּנַיִךְ) [shall be] the disciples of the Lord, and great [shall be] the peace of your children (בָּנָיִךְ)." Read not בָּנָיִךְ *(= your children), but* בּוֹנָיִךְ *(= your teachers*)!*

(2) Read this word not only in accordance with the way it is actually spelled, but read it also *as if* two of its letters were transposed!**

"קִרְבָּם בָּתֵּימוֹ לְעוֹלָם". אַל תִּקְרֵי "קִרְבָּם", אֶלָּא "קִבְרָם"! (מועד קטן ט,ב ע"פ תהלים מט:יב)

"Their inner [thoughts are that] their houses [will exist] forever." Read not קִרְבָּם *(= their inner), but* קִבְרָם *(= their grave, indicating that their houses will be their grave).*

* According to this reading, בּוֹנָיִךְ is derived from the Hebrew root בין, *understand*, and it means *those who instill in you understanding*, in other words, *your teachers*. This is the explanation of S. Baer in his siddur, *Avodath Yisrael (Roedelheim, Germany, 1868), p. 195*. Others take בנה as the root of בּוֹנָיִךְ and translate *your builders*, which also refers to *your teachers*.

** In one instance in the Talmud, a word is read and explained *as if* two of its letters (נן) were *replaced* by two different letters (לש):

אַל תִּקְרֵי "וְשִׁנַּנְתָּם" אֶלָּא "וְשִׁלַּשְׁתָּם"! (קידושין ל,א)

וְאַל תִּתְמַהּ שֶׁ-

And do not be amazed (by the statement I have just made), **for ...**

A ḥakham uses this formula in defending his halakha or aggada against anticipated criticism.

עֶצֶם שֶׁיֵּשׁ בּוֹ מוֹחַ — שׁוֹבֵר וְאוֹכֵל. וְאַל תִּתְמַהּ, שֶׁהֲרֵי יָבֹא עֲשֵׂה וְיִדְחֶה לֹא תַעֲשֶׂה. (פסחים פה,א ע"פ שמות יב:ח, מו)

One may break a bone [from the Pesaḥ offering] that has marrow, and he may eat [it]. And do not be amazed [at this halakha], for the positive command [of eating from this offering] comes and overrides the negative command [of not breaking a bone].

SEE: תְּמַהּ

אֶלָּא*

(1) but; rather

In this sense, אֶלָּא lends emphasis to whatever follows. It expresses *contrast* between the following statement and a previous statement, or it stresses the following point to the *exclusion* of all other possibilities.

"וְהָיָה, כַּאֲשֶׁר יָרִים מֹשֶׁה יָדוֹ, וְגָבַר יִשְׂרָאֵל ...." וְכִי יָדָיו שֶׁל מֹשֶׁה עוֹשׂוֹת מִלְחָמָה אוֹ שׁוֹבְרוֹת מִלְחָמָה?! אֶלָּא לוֹמַר לָךְ: כָּל זְמַן שֶׁהָיוּ יִשְׂרָאֵל מִסְתַּכְּלִים כְּלַפֵּי מַעְלָה וּמְשַׁעְבְּדִין אֶת לִבָּם לַאֲבִיהֶם שֶׁבַּשָּׁמַיִם, הָיוּ מִתְגַּבְּרִים; וְאִם לָאו, הָיוּ נוֹפְלִים. (ראש השנה כט,א: משנה פ"ג מ"ח ע"פ שמות יז:יא)

"And it came to pass — when Moshe would raise his hand, [the army of] Israel prevailed ...." Did the hands of Moshe make or break war? Rather [the Torah comes] to tell you: As long as [the people of] Israel looked on high and subjugated their hearts to their Father Who is in Heaven, they prevailed — and otherwise, they failed.

(2) except for; but; only (when used after a negative, like לא)

In this sense, אֶלָּא introduces an *exception*.

לֹא הִתְקִין רַבָּן יוֹחָנָן בֶּן זַכַּאי אֶלָּא בְּיַבְנֶה בִּלְבָד. (ראש השנה כט,ב: משנה פ"ד מ"א)

Rabban Yoḥanan b. Zakkai did not legislate [this enactment] except for Yavne exclusively. (= He legislated only for Yavne.)

* Targum Onkelos translated אִם לֹא in בראשית כד:לח as אֱלָהֵן, the equivalent of אֶלָּא. Accordingly, Ḥ. Yalon

suggested that אֶלָּא may be a contraction of אִין+לָא, *if not*. (See his מבוא לניקוד המשנה, Jerusalem 5724, pp. 104–07.)

אֶלָּא אִי אִיתְּמַר הָכִי אִיתְּמַר

אֶלָּא אִם נֶאֱמַר כָּךְ נֶאֱמַר ...

Rather if [something] was stated, thus it was stated ...

After a statement of an amora has been refuted, the Talmud sometimes uses this formula to introduce a different version of the same statement that is not subject to the refutation.

משנה: אוֹ שֶׁהָיוּ עֲנָבָיו מְרוּבִּין מֵעָלָיו — פָּסוּל. (סוכה לב,ב: משנה פ"ג מ"ב)

תלמוד: אָמַר רַב חִסְדָּא: ... לֹא שָׁנוּ אֶלָּא בְּמָקוֹם אֶחָד, אֲבָל בִּשְׁנַיִם אוֹ שְׁלֹשָׁה מְקוֹמוֹת — כָּשֵׁר. אֲמַר לֵיהּ רָבָא: שְׁנַיִם וּשְׁלֹשָׁה מְקוֹמוֹת הָוֵי מְנוּמָּר וּפָסוּל! אֶלָּא אִי אִיתְּמַר, הָכִי אִיתְּמַר:

משנה: אוֹ שֶׁהָיוּ עֲנָבָיו מְרוּבִּין מֵעָלָיו — פָּסוּל.

תלמוד: אָמַר רַב חִסְדָּא: ... לֹא שָׁנוּ אֶלָּא עֲנָבָיו שְׁחוֹרוֹת, אֲבָל עֲנָבָיו יְרֻקּוֹת — מִינוֹ דַהֲדַס הוּא וְכָשֵׁר. (סוכה לג, סע"א-רע"ב)

MISHNA: Or if its (= the myrtle branch's) berries are more numerous than its leaves, it is disqualified (for use as one of the "four species" for Sukkoth).

TALMUD: Rav Ḥisda said: ... they taught [that the myrtle branch is disqualified] only [if the berries are] in one place, but [if they are] in two or three places, it is fit. Rava said to him: [If the berries are] in two or three places, it is [considered] speckled and (thereby) disqualified! Rather if [something] was stated [by Rav Ḥisda on this mishna], thus it was stated:

MISHNA: Or if its berries are more numerous than its leaves, it is disqualified.

TALMUD: Rav Ḥisda said: ... they taught [that the myrtle branch is disqualified] only [if] its berries are black, but [if] its berries are green — it is a species of myrtle, and it is fit.

אֶלָּא אִם כֵּן

"but if indeed"; unless

לֹא יְגַדֵּל אָדָם אֶת הַכֶּלֶב, אֶלָּא אִם כֵּן הָיָה קָשׁוּר בְּשַׁלְשֶׁלֶת. (בבא קמא עט,ב: משנה פ"ז מ"ז)

One should not breed a dog, unless it is [kept] tied with a chain.

אֶלָּא לָאו

but is it not ...?!

This expression — which is often followed by the term שְׁמַע מִינַּהּ, *"there is a proof from here"* — introduces a *tentative inference.*

אֶלָּא לָאו שְׁמַע מִינַּהּ: מִצְוָה לְהַנִּיחָהּ בְּתוֹךְ עֲשָׂרָה?! (ב"ק סב,ב)

But is there not a proof from here [that] it is required to place it (= the Ḥanukka lamp) within the [first] ten handbreadths [from the ground]?!

In many instances, שְׁמַע מִינַּהּ (also) appears immediately after the inference, indicating that the inference is regarded by the Talmud as conclusive.

אֶלָּא לָאו שְׁמַע מִינַּהּ: כָּאן בְּסַפָּר נָכְרִי, כָּאן בְּסַפָּר יִשְׂרָאֵל?! שְׁמַע מִינַּהּ. (בבא מציעא מח, סע"א)

But is there not a proof from here [that] one [case] refers to a non-Jewish barber and the other to a Jewish barber?! There is [indeed] a proof from here.

SEE: לָאו, שְׁמַע מִינַּהּ

וְאֶלָּא מַאי

but what? אֶלָּא מָה?

(1) But what (do you propose as an alternative)? But (if not this) what (then)?

לֵימָא מַתְנִיתִין דְּלָא כְּסוּמְכוֹס ...? וְאֶלָּא מַאי? רַבָּנַן?! (בבא מציעא ב,ב)

Shall we say [that] our mishna is not in accordance with [the opinion of] Sumkhus ... (because of a contradiction between them)? But [if it is not according to Sumkhus], what [then]?! (Can the mishna really follow the opinion of the Ḥakhamim?!)

(2) But what [does ... mean or refer to]?

This question seeks a *definition* or an *identification.*

אֶלָּא מַאי "תַּרְגּוּם"? תַּרְגּוּם דִּידַן. (קידושין מט, סע"א)

But what [does] "targum" [refer to]? Our Aramaic translation (= Targum Onkelos).

אֶלָּא מַאי אִית לָךְ לְמֵימַר

אֶלָּא מָה יֵּשׁ לְךָ לוֹמַר?!

But what do you have to say?!

This *rhetorical question* is used in the course of a Talmudic debate with the following thrust: "Since you, my opponent, must anyhow accept the validity of this point in one context, why don't you accept its validity in the present case as well?!"

For an example — see ברכות כד,א; לח,א.

אֶלָּא מֵהָא לֵיכָּא לְמִשְׁמַע מִינַּהּ

אֶלָּא מִזּוֹ אֵין לִלְמֹד מִמֶּנָּה.

But from this [text] one cannot derive [a definitive conclusion].

This declaration marks the end of a discussion that consisted of the following stages:

(1) The first clause (רֵישָׁא) of a mishna or baraitha was quoted as a *proof* for a particular proposition.

(2) In rebuttal, the latter clause* (סֵיפָא) was quoted as a refutation of the same proposition.

(3) Now, אֶלָּא מֵהָא לֵיכָּא לְמִשְׁמַע מִינַּהּ is used to indicate that the mishna or baraitha that was quoted does not constitute solid evidence — neither in favor of, nor against, the proposition under discussion. Thus, the issue remains unsettled.

אִיבַּעְיָא לְהוּ: תַּעֲנִית צִבּוּר בְּכַמָּה? ... תָּא שְׁמַע: (1) בְּרָאשֵׁי חֳדָשִׁים וּבְחוּלּוֹ שֶׁלַּמּוֹעֵד קוֹרִין אַרְבָּעָה — הָא בְּתַעֲנִית צִבּוּר שְׁלֹשָׁה! אֵימָא רֵישָׁא: (2) בַּשֵּׁנִי וּבַחֲמִישִׁי וּבְשַׁבָּת בְּמִנְחָה קוֹרִין שְׁלֹשָׁה — הָא בְּתַעֲנִית צִבּוּר אַרְבָּעָה! (3) אֶלָּא מֵהָא לֵיכָּא לְמִשְׁמַע מִינַּהּ. (מגילה כב,א)

*They had a halakhic problem: [On] a public fast day (excluding Yom Kippur) how many [must read from the Torah scroll]? ... Come [and] hear (what is stated in the mishna): (1) On Rosh Ḥodesh and on Ḥol HaMoed four must read [from the Torah scroll] — here it implies [that] on a public fast day (only) three [must read]!** Take note of the earlier clause (in the mishna): (2) On Monday and Thursday and at the Minḥa [service] on the Sabbath three must read — here it implies [that] on a public fast day four [must read]! (3) But from this (mishna) one cannot derive [a definite conclusion].*

For another example — see ברכות כה, סע"א וש"נ.

* Occasionally, rather than the latter clause of the same text, a halakha of an earlier amora is quoted in rebuttal as in בבא מציעא פא,ב.

** Since the *Musaf Amida* is not recited on a public fast day, its status may be inferior.

אֶלָּא מְחַוְּורְתָּא כִּדְשַׁנִּינַן מֵעִיקָּרָא

אֶלָּא [הַתְּשׁוּבָה] הַבְּרוּרָה הִיא זוֹ שֶׁתֵּרַצְנוּ מִתְּחִלָּה.

Rather the clear [reply] is [the one] that we had answered originally.

After the second of two solutions to a difficulty has been refuted, the Talmud sometimes emphasizes that the *first solution* remains intact.

For an example — see מכות ב, רע"ב.

SEE: מְחַוְּורְתָּא

אֶלָּא מֵעַתָּה

"but from now ...!"

but according to that proposal ...!

This expression introduces a *difficulty* that is raised against a proposal that had been presented in the Talmud. It is usually argued that adopting that proposal would lead to an unacceptable conclusion.

"אַךְ בַּיּוֹם הָרִאשׁוֹן תַּשְׁבִּיתוּ שְּׂאֹר מִבָּתֵּיכֶם" ... רַב נַחְמָן בַּר יִצְחָק אָמַר: "רִאשׁוֹן" דְּמֵעִיקָּרָא מַשְׁמַע ... אֶלָּא מֵעַתָּה "וּלְקַחְתֶּם לָכֶם בַּיּוֹם הָרִאשׁוֹן", הָכִי נַמֵי "רִאשׁוֹן" דְּמֵעִיקָּרָא מַשְׁמַע?! (פסחים ד, סע"ב־ה,א ע"פ שמות יב:טו, ויקרא כג:מ)

"But on the רִאשׁוֹן *day you shall eliminate ḥametz from your houses" ... Rav Naḥman b. Yitzḥak said:* רִאשׁוֹן *means "the preceding day" [thus the ḥametz must be eliminated on erev Pesaḥ, the fourteenth of Nisan]. But according to that proposal, would* רִאשׁוֹן *mean "the preceding day" even [in the pasuk]: "And you shall take for yourselves on the* רִאשׁוֹן *day [the four species of the Sukkoth festival]"?! (That is certainly not true, for there it means "on the first day" of Sukkoth — not on the day before.)*

SEE: אִי הָכִי

אֵלּוּ*

(1) these; these are

אֵלּוּ דְּבָרִים שֶׁאֵין לָהֶם שִׁיעוּר (משנה פאה פ"א מ"א)

These are the mitzvoth for which there is no fixed measure.

(2) which? (pl.)**

אֵלּוּ מְצִיאוֹת שֶׁלּוֹ וְאֵלּוּ חַיָּיב לְהַכְרִיז? אֵלּוּ מְצִיאוֹת שֶׁלּוֹ: מָצָא פֵּירוֹת מְפוּזָּרִין .... וְאֵלּוּ חַיָּיב לְהַכְרִיז: מָצָא פֵּירוֹת בִּכְלִי .... (בבא מציעא כא,א; כד,סע"ב: משנה פ"ב מ"א - מ"ב)

*Which objects [that are] found belong to him (= the finder) and which is he obligated to announce?*** These are the found objects that belong to him: [If] he found scattered fruit .... And these are the found objects [that] he is obligated to announce: [If] he found fruit in a container ....*

* This Mishnaic Hebrew form is the equivalent of אֵלֶּה in Biblical Hebrew.

** The singular forms are אֵיזֶה (m.) and אֵיזוֹ (f.).

*** The fact that the mishna then explains אֵלּוּ מְצִיאוֹת שֶׁלּוֹ indicates that we probably have a question *(Which...?)* followed by an answer *(These are ....)*.

אֵלּוּ ... וְאֵלּוּ ...

these ... and those ...

אֵלּוּ הוֹלְכִים בָּאַכְסַדְרָא דֶּרֶךְ הַמִּזְרָח, וְאֵלּוּ הוֹלְכִים בָּאַכְסַדְרָא דֶּרֶךְ הַמַּעֲרָב. (משנה תמיד פ"א מ"ג)

These walk in the portico eastwards, and those walk in the portico westwards.

אֵלּוּ וְאֵלּוּ

these and those; both; all

אֵלּוּ וְאֵלּוּ דִּבְרֵי אֱלֹקִים חַיִּים הֵן. (עירובין יג,ב; גיטין ו,ב)

Both [opinions] are the words of the living God.

אַלִּיבָּא דְ-   "עַל חֲלָב שֶׁל"; לְדַעַת; לְשִׁיטַת

according to the opinion of; with regard to the opinion of; according to the system of

See the next three entries for examples.

SEE: אָמוֹרָאֵי נִינְהוּ וְאַלִּיבָּא דְּרִ' יוֹחָנָן

אַלִּיבָּא ד- פּוּלֵּי עָלְמָא לָא פְּלִיגִי כִּי פְּלִיגִי אַלִּיבָּא ד-

לְשִׁיטַת...כָּל הָעוֹלָם אֵינָם חֲלוּקִים; כְּשֶׁנֶּחְלְקוּ לְשִׁיטַת...

According to the system of [Tanna A], all the disputants do not disagree; they disagree according to the system of [Tanna B].

This formula states that the *controversy* between amoraim that is under consideration must be understood within the framework of an earlier controversy, usually between tannaim. The two amoraim agree what the halakha would be in their case according to the position of one tanna (R. Méir in our example), but they dispute what the halakha would be according to the position of his opponent (the Ḥakhamim in our example).

אַלִּיבָּא דְּרִ' מֵאִיר, כּוּלֵּי עָלְמָא (= ר' יוחנן ור' אלעזר) לָא פְּלִיגִי, כִּי פְּלִיגִי אַלִּיבָּא דְּרַבָּנַן ... (בבא קמא כט, רע"ב)

According to the system of R. Méir, all the disputants (the amoraim, R. Yoḥanan and R. El'azar) do not disagree; they disagree according to the system of the Ḥakhamim ...

אַלִיבָּא ד- לָא תִיבָּעֵי לָךְ כִּי תִיבָּעֵי לָךְ אַלִיבָּא ד- לְשִׁיטַת ... לֹא תִהְיֶה לְךָ שְׁאֵלָה; אִם תִּהְיֶה לְךָ שְׁאֵלָה, לְשִׁיטַת ...

According to the system of [Tanna A], you have no problem; you do have a problem according to the system of [Tanna B].

This formula contends that the *halakhic problem* posed by an amora (Rav Pappa in our example) is a problem only if we adopt one side of an earlier, usually tannaitic, controversy (that of the Ḥakhamim in our example). According to the other side (the opinion of R. Yosé b. R. Yᵉhuda in our example), the halakha is clear.

בָּעֵי רַב פָּפָּא .... אַלִיבָּא דְר׳ יוֹסֵי בְּרִ׳ יְהוּדָה, לָא תִיבָּעֵי לָךְ ...; כִּי תִיבָּעֵי לָךְ, אַלִיבָּא דְרַבָּנָן .... (כתובות נד, רע״א)

Rav Pappa poses a (halakhic) problem .... According to the system of R. Yosé b. R. Yᵉhuda, you have no problem ...; you do have a problem according to the system of the Ḥakhamim ....

אַלִיבָּא דְמַאן אִי אַלִיבָּא ד-... וְאִי אַלִיבָּא ד- לְדַעַת מִי? אִם לְדַעַת ... וְאִם לְדַעַת ...!

According to the opinion of whom? If [it is understood] according to the opinion of [Tanna A, there is a difficulty]; and if according to the opinion of [Tanna B, there is a difficulty]!

This formula points out a *difficulty*. It is usually argued that an amora's statement or a halakhic problem that has been raised is not consistent with either side of a controversy between two tannaim.

For an example — see בבא קמא מה, סע״ב.

אַלִּים (f. אַלִּימָא) חָזָק; תַּקִּיף **strong; powerful**

כָּל דְּאַלִּים גָּבַר. (גיטין ס,ב; בבא בתרא לד, סע״ב)

Whoever is stronger prevails (and wins the dispute).

SEE: (וּ)מִי אַלִּימָא מִמַּתְנִיתִין

אִלֵּין

SEE: אִילֵּין

אִלֵּם (f. אִלֶּמֶת) **a mute**

שׁוֹמֵעַ וְאֵינוֹ מְדַבֵּר זֶהוּ "אִלֵּם". (גיטין עא,א ע״פ תהילים לח,יד)

One who can hear but not speak is "a mute."

SEE: חֵרֵשׁ

אַלְמָא הֲרֵי שֶׁ-; נִמְצָא שֶׁ-; מִכָּאן אָנוּ לְמֵדִים ...

consequently ...; it follows that ...; from here we may derive ...

משנה: כְּרִיכוֹת בִּרְשׁוּת הָרַבִּים הֲרֵי אֵלּוּ שֶׁלּוֹ.
תלמוד: אָמַר רַבָּה: וַאֲפִילּוּ בְּדָבָר שֶׁיֵּשׁ בּוֹ סִימָן. אַלְמָא קָסָבַר רַבָּה: סִימָן הֶעָשׂוּי לִידָּרֵס לָא הָוֵי סִימָן. (בבא מציעא כב,ב)

MISHNA: Small sheaves [found] in a public thoroughfare belong to the finder.

TALMUD: Rabba said: Even something that has an [identifying] mark. It follows that Rabba must hold that a mark that is liable to be stepped on is not [considered] an [identifying] mark.

אַלָּמָה (אַ+לָמָּה) עַל לָמָּה ...?! לָמָּה ...?! **why ...?!**

This word introduces a *difficulty* that can often be paraphrased as follows: (In light of your opinion,) why does the following text state ...?!

מַתְקִיף לָהּ ר׳ זֵירָא: אִי הָכִי, אֲפִילּוּ גִיזּוֹתֶיהָ וּוַלְדוֹתֶיהָ נָמֵי! אַלָּמָּה תַנְיָא: חוּץ מִגִּיזּוֹתֶיהָ וּוַלְדוֹתֶיהָ?! (ב״מ לד, רע״א)

R. Zera attacked it (= Rava's opinion): If so, even its shearings and offspring [should belong to the man who looked after the animals]! Why has it been stated (in a baraitha): [He receives the value of the animal] with the exception of its shearings and its offspring?!

לְאַלְתַּר **immediately**

SEE: לְאַלְתַּר

אִלְמָלֵא/אִלְמָלֵי*

(1) (אִלּוּ+אִם+לֹא) **if not; were it not for**

In this sense, this word is a preposition, and it precedes *a noun*.

הֱוֵי מִתְפַּלֵּל בִּשְׁלוֹמָהּ שֶׁל מַלְכוּת; שֶׁאִלְמָלֵא מוֹרָאָהּ, אִישׁ אֶת רֵעֵהוּ חַיִּים בְּלָעוֹ. (משנה אבות פ״ג מ״ב)

Pray for the welfare of the government; for were it not for the fear of it, man would swallow his fellow alive.

(2) (אִלּוּ+אִם+לוּ) **if indeed**

In this sense, this word is a conjunction. It usually precedes *a verb* and introduces an unfulfilled condition.

אִלְמָלֵי מְשַׁמְּרִין יִשְׂרָאֵל שְׁתֵּי שַׁבָּתוֹת כְּהִלְכָתָן, מִיָּד נִגְאָלִים. (שבת קיח,ב)

If the Jewish people would indeed observe two Sabbaths properly, they would be redeemed immediately.

* According to the manuscripts available to us, it is difficult to prove a consistent differentiation in spelling between the two different meanings. Such a distinction, however, was proposed by Rabbenu Tam (תוספות למגילה כא, סע״א).

אֵם (pl. אִמָּהוֹת)

(1) a mother; my mother; Mother

אֲמַר אַבָּיֵי: אָמְרָה לִי אֵם ... (קידושין לא,ב)

Abbayé said: My mother told me ...

(2) womb

פָּרָה שֶׁנִּיטְלָה הָאֵם שֶׁלָּהּ (בכורות כח,ב ורש״י שם: משנה ד:ד)

a cow whose womb was removed

(3) authority

For an example — see יֵשׁ אֵם לַמִּקְרָא.

SEE: אִמָּא

אִם אֵינוֹ עִנְיָן ל- ... תְּנֵהוּ עִנְיָן ל- ...

If it has no bearing upon [this subject], let it have bearing upon [that subject].

This *rule of Biblical interpretation* operates as follows: When a pasuk cannot be explained as referring to its own subject matter (because it would then be either redundant or difficult), it may be explained as referring to a related matter.*

(1) חִילּוּק מְלָאכוֹת מְנָלַן? אֲמַר שְׁמוּאֵל: אָמַר קְרָא "מְחַלְלֶיהָ מוֹת יוּמָת", הַתּוֹרָה רִבְּתָה מִיתוֹת הַרְבֵּה עַל חִילּוּל אֶחָד. (2) הַאי בְּמֵזִיד כְּתִיב! (3) אִם אֵינוֹ עִנְיָן לְמֵזִיד, דִּכְתִיב "כָּל הָעוֹשֶׂה בוֹ מְלָאכָה יוּמָת", תְּנֵהוּ עִנְיָן לְשׁוֹגֵג! (שבת ע,א ע"פ שמות לא:יד ולה:ב)

(1)From where do we derive the separate treatment of the labors (forbidden on the Sabbath, so that when a Jew performs several forbidden labors on the Sabbath, he incurs a punishment for each one of them)? Sh^emuel said: The Torah has stated: "Those who defile it shall surely be put to death (מוֹת יוּמָת), *the Torah has included multiple deaths for one desecration (by using those two verbal forms). (2) [But] this is written with reference to willful desecration! (3) If it has no bearing upon willful desecration, since it is (already) written: "Whoever does any work on it shall be put to death," let it have bearing upon unwitting desecration.*

* This method corresponds to the twentieth rule in the list of *Rules of Biblical Interpretation* ascribed to R. Eliezer b. R. Yosé the Galilean.

אִם אִיתָא; אִי אִיתָא

If it were true; if it were valid אִם יֶשְׁנָהּ

This expression introduces an argument in the Talmud.

אִם אִיתָא דְאִיגָּרְשָׁא, קָלָא אִית לַהּ לְמִילְּתָא! (כתובות כג,א)

If it were true that she had been divorced, [then] there would have been public knowledge of the matter!

וְאִם נַפְשְׁךָ לוֹמַר

And if it is your desire to say (otherwise) ...

After a baraitha has presented one proof for a certain point from a pasuk, it uses this expression to introduce an *alternative proof* — as if to say: "If you find fault with my first proof, here is another."*

יָכוֹל סִימֵּא אֶת עֵינוֹ, נְסַמֵּא אֶת עֵינוֹ ...? תַּלְמוּד לוֹמַר: "מַכֵּה אָדָם" וּ"מַכֵּה בְהֵמָה" — מָה "מַכֵּה בְהֵמָה" לְתַשְׁלוּמִין, אַף "מַכֵּה אָדָם" לְתַשְׁלוּמִין. וְאִם נַפְשְׁךָ לוֹמַר: הֲרֵי הוּא אוֹמֵר: "לֹא תִקְחוּ כוֹפֶר לְנֶפֶשׁ רוֹצֵחַ" — לְנֶפֶשׁ רוֹצֵחַ אִי אַתָּה לוֹקֵחַ כּוֹפֶר, אֲבָל אַתָּה לוֹקֵחַ כּוֹפֶר לְרָאשֵׁי אֵבָרִים שֶׁאֵינָן חוֹזְרִין. (בבא קמא פג,ב ורש"י שם ע"פ ויקרא כד:כא ובמדבר לה:לג)

Could [you say] if he blinded the eye of another, we should blind his eye ...? Scripture teaches: "One who kills a person ..." and "one who kills an animal" — just as "one who kills an animal" [must pay] compensation, so too "one who kills a person" [must pay] compensation. And if it is your desire to say (otherwise): Behold He states: "Do not accept ransom for the life of a murderer" — (only) for the life of a murderer may you not accept ransom, but you may accept ransom for the [loss of] principal limbs that do not grow back.

* After quoting the whole baraitha, the Talmud proceeds to ask: מַאי "וְאִם נַפְשְׁךָ לוֹמַר"? See that entry.

אִם תִּמְצָא/תִּמְצֵי לוֹמַר

If (upon examining the problem) you conclude and say ...

After one halakhic problem has been presented, this formula is often used to link a second problem to the first.* According to one of the two alternatives presented by the first problem, the second problem may be raised; but, according to the other alternative, the second problem has no logical basis.**

(1) עַכְבָּר נִכְנָס וְכִכָּר בְּפִיו, וְעַכְבָּר יוֹצֵא וְכִכָּר בְּפִיו — מַהוּ? מִי אָמְרִינַן: הַיְינוּ הַאי דְעָל וְהַיְינוּ הַאי דִנְפַק, אוֹ דִלְמָא אַחֲרִינָא הוּא? (2) אִם תִּמְצָא לוֹמַר: הַיְינוּ הַאי דְעָל וְהַיְינוּ הַאי דִנְפַק — עַכְבָּר לָבָן נִכְנָס וְכִכָּר בְּפִיו, וְעַכְבָּר שָׁחוֹר יוֹצֵא וְכִכָּר בְּפִיו — מַהוּ? הַאי וַדַּאי אַחֲרִינָא הוּא, אוֹ דִלְמָא אַרְמוֹיֵי אַרְמְיֵהּ מִינֵּיהּ? (פסחים י,ב ורש"י שם)

(1) [If] a mouse enters with bread in his mouth, and a mouse leaves with bread in his mouth — what is the halakhic ruling (about the need for a search for ḥametz)? Do we assume the same one that has entered has left (and so the room need not be searched for ḥametz), or perhaps it is a different [mouse]? (2) If you conclude and say the same one that has entered has left — [if] a white mouse enters with bread in his mouth and a black mouse leaves with bread in his mouth — what is the halakhic ruling? Is this one certainly a different [mouse] (and some bread remains inside requiring a search), or perhaps [the black mouse] seized it (= the bread) from him?

* Other uses of this expression also occur in the Talmud. ע' ברכות כו,א ומב,ב ורש"י שם; בבא מציעא ח,א ורש"י שם.

** According to Gaonic authorities, the fact that the second problem is based on the first alternative of the first problem indicates that the first alternative has been accepted as a halakhic norm.

אִמָּא/אִימָּא

a mother; my mother; Mother (1) אֵם; אִמִּי

כָּל שֶׁנֵּיעוֹר מִשְּׁנָתוֹ וְאֵינוֹ קוֹרֵא: "אִמָּא! אִמָּא!" (סוכה כח,ב)

Any [child] who awakens from his sleep and does not call out: "Mother! Mother!" [must dwell in a sukka].

***Imma*; Madam** (2) אִמָּא

This word is sometimes used as a title of respect for a woman.

Madam so-and-so אִמָּא פְּלוֹנִית (ברכות טז,ב ורש"י שם)

SEE: אַבָּא

אַמַּאי (אַ+מַאי)

for what? why? עַל מָה? לָמָּה?

מָעוֹת מְפוּזָּרוֹת הֲרֵי אֵלּוּ שֶׁלּוֹ. אַמַּאי?! (בבא מציעא כא,ב)

Scattered coins belong to him (= the finder). Why (should this be so)?!

אָמַד (אמד: אוֹמֵד .prt);
אֲמַד* (אמד: אָמֵיד .act. prt, אֲמִיד** .pass. prt)

he estimated; he approximated

אוֹמְדִין כַּמָּה יָמִים מִכָּאן עַד מָקוֹם פְּלוֹנִי. (נזיר ח,א: משנה א:ו)
They estimate how many days' [journey] it is from here until that particular place.

* The first verb is Hebrew, and the second is Aramaic.
** Sometimes, the passive participle אֲמִיד, *evaluated (as having wealth)*, may be regarded as an adjective, *wealthy*, like אָמִיד in Modern Hebrew. See Rashi on ב"ב ח,ב; גיטין נב,ב.
SEE: אוֹמֶד

אַמָּה (אַמּוֹת .pl)

(1) forearm; cubit

A cubit is a measure of length corresponding to the distance between a man's elbow and the tip of his middle finger. It equals six טְפָחִים, *handbreadths*.*

סוּכָּה שֶׁהִיא גְבוֹהָה לְמַעְלָה מֵעֶשְׂרִים אַמָּה פְּסוּלָה. (סוכה ב, רע"א; משנה פ"א מ"א)
A sukka which is higher than twenty cubits is disqualified.

(2) waterway; canal; sewer

הָיָה מְהַלֵּךְ בְּשַׁבָּת וּפָגַע בְּאַמַּת הַמַּיִם** (שבת קיג, רע"ב)
[if a Jew] were walking on the Sabbath and came upon a waterway

(3) the male sexual organ

For an example — see יבמות קה, סע"א.

* See the table of distances in the appendix at the end of this work. According to the Talmud (מנחות יא, רע"א), the middle finger is itself called אַמָּה because of its function in measuring a cubit.
** In this sense, אַמָּה is sometimes used with the word מַיִם and sometimes without.
SEE: אַמְתָא

אָמָה (אֲמָהוֹת .pl) **maidservant**

This Hebrew noun refers to *a Hebrew maidservant*, אָמָה עִבְרִיָּה (as in קידושין ד,ב), in contradistinction to the שִׁפְחָה כְּנַעֲנִית, *a Canaanite (heathen) maidservant.*
SEE: אַמְתָא

אֱמוֹר מֵעַתָּה

"say from now"; say as a consequence (of that Biblical quotation) ...

This expression introduces an aggadic teaching that is derived from a pasuk.

"עַד יַעֲבוֹר עַמְּךָ ה'" — זוֹ בִיאָה רִאשׁוֹנָה; "עַד יַעֲבוֹר עַם זוּ קָנִיתָ" — זוֹ בִיאָה שְׁנִיָּה. אֱמוֹר מֵעַתָּה: רְאוּיִים הָיוּ יִשְׂרָאֵל לַעֲשׂוֹת לָהֶם נֵס בְּבִיאָה שְׁנִיָּה כְבִיאָה רִאשׁוֹנָה. (סנהדרין צח,ב ע"פ שמות טו:טז)
"Until Your people pass over, O God" — this refers to the first entry [into Eretz Yisrael]; "until this people that You have acquired pass over" — this refers to the second entry. Say as a consequence: The Jewish people were as worthy of a miracle being performed for them at the second entry as at the first entry.

אֱמוֹר מֵעַתָּה: בְּמִצְרַיִם לָקוּ עֶשֶׂר מַכּוֹת, וְעַל הַיָּם לָקוּ חֲמִשִּׁים מַכּוֹת. (הגדה של פסח; מכילתא לשמות ח:טו)
Say as a consequence [of that pasuk]: In Egypt they were inflicted with ten plagues, and at the sea they were inflicted with fifty plagues.

אָמוֹרָא מְתוּרְגְּמָן; מְפָרֵשׁ

***amora;* speaker; transmitter; interpreter**

This term has two distinct uses:

(1) It denotes a scholar who lived in either Erets Yisrael or Babylonia during the period between the compilation of the Mishna and the compilation of the Talmud. The amoraim were engaged in the transmission and interpretation of the teachings of the tannaim.

כּוּלְּהוּ אָמוֹרָאֵי וְתַנָּאֵי בְּדעֶזְרָא קָמִיפַּלְגִי. (ברכות כב, רע"ב)
All the amoraim and tannaim disagree about [the interpretation of the enactment] of Ezra.

(2) This term was also applied in Talmudic times to the man who stood near the ḥakham while the latter was delivering his lecture and repeated what the ḥakham said to the audience in a loud voice. Occasionally, the amora also explained some of the points mentioned in the ḥakham's lecture and translated some Hebrew words into Aramaic, the language which was more widely understood at the time.

אַטּוּ כּוּלֵּי עָלְמָא לְתַנָּא צָיְיתִי? לְאָמוֹרָא צָיְיתִי! (חולין טו,א ופירושי רש"י ו"רבינו גרשום" שם)
Is everybody [in the audience] listening to the tanna? They are listening to the amora!
SEE: תַּנָּא, תּוּרְגְּמָן

אָמוֹרָאֵי נִינְהוּ וְאַלִּיבָּא דְּר' יוֹחָנָן

אָמוֹרָאִים הֵם וְעַל דַּעַת ר' יוֹחָנָן.

They (= these two statements) are [rulings transmitted by two different] amoraim, and [they disagree] with regard to the opinion of R. Yoḥanan.

A *resolution* of a difficulty: After two contradictory statements have been quoted in the name of R. Yoḥanan, the Talmud sometimes replies that there is no real difficulty, because one amora has reported one version of R. Yoḥanan's statement, while the other amora has reported a different version of his statement.*

(1) אֲמַר ר' אַבָּא בַּר יַעֲקֹב אֲמַר ר' יוֹחָנָן: הֲלָכָה כְּר' שִׁמְעוֹן בֶּן גַּמְלִיאֵל ... (2) וּמִי אֲמַר ר' יוֹחָנָן הָכִי?! וְהָא אֲמַר רַבָּה בַּר בַּר חַנָּה אֲמַר ר' יוֹחָנָן: בְּכָל מָקוֹם שֶׁשָּׁנָה ר' שִׁמְעוֹן בֶּן גַּמְלִיאֵל בְּמִשְׁנָתֵנוּ הֲלָכָה כְּמוֹתוֹ ...?! (3) אָמוֹרָאֵי נִינְהוּ וְאַלִּיבָּא דְר' יוֹחָנָן (כתובות עז,א ע"פ כת"י ורש"י שם)
(1) R. Abba b. Ya'akov said quoting R. Yoḥanan: The halakhic ruling is in accordance with Rabban Shim'on b. Gamliel [in this particular instance] ... (2) But did R. Yoḥanan [really] say so?! Didn't Rabba, the

grandson of Hanna, say quoting R. Yohanan: Wherever Rabban Shim'on b. Gamliel taught [a halakha] in our Mishna, the halakhic ruling is according to him?! (In other words, since R. Yohanan himself said that the halakha is always like Rabban Shim'on b. Gamliel, why did R. Yohanan have to rule explicitly in favor of this specific halakha of R. Shim'on b. Gamliel?) (3) They (= these two statements) are [rulings transmitted by two different] amoraim (namely, R. Abba b. Ya'akov and Rabba, the grandson of Hanna), and [they disagree] with regard to the opinion of R. Yohanan.

* This formula, which deals with amoraic statements, occurs in the Talmud only with regard to the amora R. Yohanan — except for one instance (יבמות ת,ב) where it was proposed with regard to the amora Rav but subsequently rejected. As for statements of tannaim, see the formula תְּרֵי תַּנָּאֵי אַלִּיבָּא דְ-.

אַמְטוּ

See the next two entries.

אַמְטוּל בִּשְׁבִיל; מִשּׁוּם

because of

אַמְטוּל הָכִי*

because of this; therefore מִשּׁוּם כָּךְ; הִלְכָּךְ

אַמְטוּל הָכִי פָּטְרִי רַבָּנַן (ב"ק עא, סע"א-ע"ב, רע"ב ע"פ כת"י)

because of this the Hakhamim declare [him] exempt

* In many editions of the Talmud, this phrase is written אַמְטוּ לְהָכִי, but Talmudic manuscripts read אַמְטוּל הָכִי.

אַמְטִי (מטי אַפְעֵל: מַמְטֵי .prt, אַמְטוּיֵי .inf)

he presented; he brought הִמְצִיא; הֵבִיא

מַאי דִּשְׁקַלִי מֵהָכָא אַמְטַאי לְהָתָם. (תענית כא, סע"א ע"פ כת"י)

What I took from here I brought there.

אֲמִיד

SEE: אָמַד

אֲמִינָא (אֲמִיר+אֲנָא*) "אוֹמֵר אֲנִי"

I say; I state; I would say; I speak (of); I mean

See examples under the next three entries and also under סָלְקָא דַעְתָּךְ אֲמִינָא and מַנָּא אֲמִינָא לָהּ, הֲוָה אֲמִינָא.

* According to this explanation, אמינא is a contraction of the passive participle אֲמִיר (with the ר deleted) and אֲנָא, *I*. This etymology accounts for the popular pronunciation, אֲמִינָא. On the other hand, it may be a contraction of the active participle אָמַר (without the ר) and אֲנָא. It would then be pronounced אָמֵינָא or, according to the Yemenite tradition, אַמֵינָא (in the manner of verbs with final root letter י like חָזֵינָא or חַזֵינָא).

SEE: אֲמַר

קָאֲמִינָא* (קָא+אֲמִינָא) "אוֹמֵר אֲנִי"

I say; I state; I would say; I speak (of); I mean

אִין! הָכִי קָאֲמִינָא! (בבא מציעא נד, סע"ב)

Yes! This [is what] I mean!

אַלִּיבָּא דר' שִׁמְעוֹן לָא קָאֲמִינָא; כִּי קָאֲמִינָא אַלִּיבָּא דְרַבָּנַן. (בבא מציעא מז, סע"ב)

I am not stating [my halakha] according to [the system of] R. Shim'on; I am stating [it] according to the Hakhamim.

* Do not confuse with the entry קָאֵימְנָא.

SEE: (קָ)אָמַר and its note.

אֲמִינָא: כִּי נָיֵים וְשָׁכֵיב רַב אֲמַר לְהָא שְׁמַעְתָּא אוֹמֵר אֲנִי: כְּשֶׁהָיָה רַב מְנַמְנֵם וְשׁוֹכֵב, אָמַר אֶת הַשְּׁמוּעָה הַזֹּאת.

I would say: Rav must have made this halakhic statement while he was dozing or sleeping.

Occasionally, Rav Shesheth thus expresses his reservations about a halakha of Rav, because it is contradicted by a mishna or a baraitha. Rav Shesheth proceeds to quote that source.

For an example — see יבמות כד,ב ושי"נ.

אֲמִינָא לָךְ אֲנָא ... וְאַתְּ אָמְרַתְּ לִי ... אֲנִי אוֹמֵר לְךָ ..., וְאַתָּה אוֹמֵר לִי ...!

I speak to you ..., while you tell me ...!

This formula is used by a hakham in a *refutation* of his colleague's statement on the grounds that the latter has failed to take an important distinction into consideration.

אֲמִינָא לָךְ אֲנָא מְלָאכָה דְרַבָּנַן, וְאַתְּ אָמְרַתְּ לִי חָמֵץ דְּאוֹרָיְיתָא! (פסחים ב, סע"ב)

I speak to you [of] a labor [whose prohibition was established] by the hakhamim, while you tell me [about] hametz [which is forbidden] by the Torah!

אֲמָנָה

trust; faithfulness

מְחוּסְּרֵי אֲמָנָה (בבא מציעא מט, רע"א)

[people] lacking faithfulness (because they do not keep their word)

אַמְצִי (מצי אַפְעֵל: מַמְצֵי .prt)

he made available; he furnished הִמְצִיא

וּמַמְצֵי נַפְשֵׁיהּ לְבֵי עַנְיֵי (כתובות סז, סע"ב)

and he makes himself available to the poor people

אֲמַר (אמר*: אָמַר .prt, לֵימָא/ נֵימָא .fut, אֵימָא/ אֵימַר/ אֵימוּר .imp, לְמֵימַר .inf)

he said; he stated אָמַר

This verb is often used by the Talmud in presenting an amora's statement. Occasionally, two different traditions are reported concerning the authority of a statement made by an amora. According to one tradition, the statement is really a baraitha that the amora is quoting, and as such it is introduced by some form of the Aramaic verb תְּנָא, *he taught*. According to the other tradition, the statement is the amora's own (or that of his amoraic teacher), and thus it is introduced by the verb אמר.

אָמַר רַב יְהוּדָה בַּר חֲבִיבָא ... אִיכָּא דְּאָמְרִי: תָּנֵי רַב יְהוּדָה בַּר חֲבִיבָא ... (כתובות ס, סע"א ורש"י שם)

Rav Y"huda b. Habiva states ... There are some who report: Rav Y"huda b. Habiva teaches (the same halakha in a baraitha) ...

For further examples, see the entries that follow.

* For the full conjugation of this verb, see *Grammar for Gemara:* Chapter 4, Verb 10.

SEE: אֵימָא, אֵימוּר, לֵימָא, (לְ)מֵימַר, מֵימְרָא, אָמְרִי, אָמְרִינַן, אָמְרִיתוּ, אָמְרַתְּ, אַמִינָא

אָמַר לָךְ ר' ... אוֹמֵר לְךָ ר' ...; יָכוֹל לוֹמַר לְךָ ר' ...

R. ... says to you; R. ... would say to you; R. ... might say to you

With this formula, the Talmud introduces an *argument* that the tanna or amora could have presented, had he participated in the Talmudic debate.

See an example under the entry אֲנָא דְּאָמְרִי אֲפִילּוּ לְר' ....

אָמַר מָר הָאָדוֹן אָמַר; אָמַרְתָּ*

The master has stated; you have stated*

This formula usually introduces the quotation of one or more excerpts from a baraitha, an amoraic statement, or occasionally from a mishna, that was quoted in full during the previous Talmudic discussion. Now the Talmud proceeds to comment on that excerpt or to discuss it in detail.

For an example — see בבא קמא ב, סע"ב.

* The second translation takes אָמַר מָר as a polite expression that is used in place of the direct mode of address, *you said*.

SEE: גּוּפָא and note the difference!

אָמַר קְרָא הַכָּתוּב אָמַר ...

Scripture said; the pasuk has stated ...

SEE: עָלֶיךָ אָמַר קְרָא, אָמַר רַחֲמָנָא

אָמַר ר' ... אָמַר ר' ... אָמַר ר' ...: אָמַר ר' ...

R. (Amora A) said (quoting) R. (B)

In this introduction to a teaching of an amora (or sometimes to that of a tanna), the amora whose name appears first is saying that he received a direct, face-to-face communication from the earlier amora or tanna whose name appears second. In many instances, the first hakham was a direct disciple of the second.

אָמַר רַב יְהוּדָה: אָמַר רַב ... (בבא קמא ו,ב ועוד)

Rav Y"huda said quoting Rav ...

אָמַר ר' ... מִשּׁוּם ר' ...;
אָמַר ר' ... מִשְּׁמֵיהּ דְּר' ...*

R. ... said in the name of R. ...

This formula introduces a teaching of an amora or a tanna that was not necessarily transmitted through direct, face-to-face communication.** In some instances, the two hakhamim were not even contemporaries.

אָמַר ר' יוֹחָנָן מִשּׁוּם ר' שִׁמְעוֹן בֶּן יוֹחַי. (ברכות ז, סע"ב)

R. Yohanan said in the name of R. Shim'on b. Yohai.

וְהָאָמַר שְׁמוּאֵל מִשּׁוּם ר' אֱלִיעֶזֶר ...?! (חולין קיג,ב ורש"י שם)

But didn't Sh"muel say in the name of R. Eliezer?!

* The first formula is Hebrew, and the second is Aramaic.

** Occasionally, copyists or printers have omitted some intermediate links in the chain of tradition, so that only the first name and the last name in the chain have been preserved in our printed editions. For example, our editions read: אָמַר רַב שְׁמוּאֵל מִשְּׁמֵיהּ דְּר' יוֹחָנָן (נדה טו,ב), but in the Munich manuscript, the text reads: אָמַר רַב שְׁמוּאֵל בַּר אַבָּא אָמַר רַב אַבָּא אָמַר רַב אַסִּי אָמַר ר' יוֹחָנָן.

אָמַר רַחֲמָנָא "הָרַחֲמָן אָמַר"; הַתּוֹרָה אָמְרָה

"the Merciful [God] has said"; the Torah has stated

"שׁוֹר רֵעֵהוּ" אָמַר רַחֲמָנָא — וְלֹא שׁוֹר שֶׁל הֶקְדֵּשׁ. (בבא קמא ז, רע"א ע"פ שמות כא:לה)

"The ox of his fellow man" the Torah has stated — but not an ox [that is the property] of the Beth HaMikdash. (If the latter ox is gored by another ox, the owner of the attacking ox need not pay compensation.)

SEE: אָמַר קְרָא

קָאָמַר (קָא*+אָמַר)

he says; he states; he means הוּא אוֹמֵר

וְהָא קְרָא קָאָמַר! (בבא מציעא ה,א)

But behold he is stating (= quoting) a pasuk (hence the halakha under discussion is from the Torah)!

אַף עַל גַּב דְּלָא אָמַר "תְּחִילָּה", "תְּחִילָּה" קָאָמַר! (ב"מ י, רע"א)

Although he did not say: "(I acquired it) first," he means "first"!

* The קָא element, which is not translated in English, is discussed in its own separate entry.

SEE: הָכִי קָאָמַר, חֲדָא וְעוֹד קָאָמַר, מַאי קָאָמַר, שַׁפִּיר קָאָמַר

אָמְרוּ דָּבָר אֶחָד

[These tannaim] have said the same thing.

With this formula an amora asserts that the halakha of one tanna, which has just been quoted, is in harmony with the halakha of another tanna or with those of several tannaim, which he is about to quote.

ברייתא: אֶתְרוֹג הַבּוֹסֶר — ר' עֲקִיבָא פּוֹסֵל, וַחֲכָמִים מַכְשִׁירִין.
תלמוד: אָמַר רַבָּה: ר' עֲקִיבָא וְר' שִׁמְעוֹן אָמְרוּ דָּבָר אֶחָד: ר' עֲקִיבָא - הָא דַּאֲמַרַן, ר' שִׁמְעוֹן — מַאי הִיא? דִּתְנַן:
משנה: ר' שִׁמְעוֹן פּוֹטֵר אֶת הָאֶתְרוֹגִים בְּקוֹטְנָן. (סוכה לו,א ע"פ כת"י)

BARAITHA: [With regard to] an immature ethrog, R. Akiva declares [it] invalid [to be taken as one of the four species on Sukkoth], but the Hakhamim declare [it] valid.

TALMUD: Rabba said: R. Akiva and R. Shim'on have said the same thing: R. Akiva [in] the statement we

have [just] quoted; [but as for] R. Shim'on, what is it [that he said]? [The halakha] that we learned [in the following mishna]:

MISHNA: R. Shim'on declares ethrogim exempt [from tithing] when they are small.

The halakhic statements of the tannaim that are quoted are not identical. In fact, in some instances where an amora uses this formula, his colleague challenges his assessment and argues that the halakhoth are not compatible, as in the continuation of our example from סוכה לו,א:

אֲמַר לֵיהּ אַבַּיֵי: וְדִלְמָא לָא הִיא! עַד כָּאן לָא קָאָמַר ר' עֲקִיבָא הָכָא, דְּבָעִינַן "הָדָר" וְלֵיכָּא; אֲבָל הָתָם כְּרַבָּנַן סְבִירָא לֵיהּ.

Abbayé said to him: Perhaps it is not [so]! So far [we have only heard that] R. Akiva maintains his view here [regarding the mitzva of taking the four species], for we require a "goodly" [ethrog], but [an immature one] is not "goodly," but there [regarding tithing] he may agree with the Ḥakhamim (who disagree with R. Shim'on and hold that immature ethrogim are subject to the law of tithing).

אֲמַרִי* (אמר) 1st pers. s.

I said; I stated　　　　אָמַרְתִּי

See example under ... אֲנָא דַּאֲמַרִי אֲפִילוּ לְר'.

* Do not confuse with the next entry אָמְרִי.

SEE: אֲמַר

אָמְרִי* prt. m. pl. (אמר); **קָאָמְרִי** (קָא+אָמְרִי)

they say; they state　　　　אוֹמְרִים

This word often introduces an anonymous *difficulty* or an anonymous *resolution* of a difficulty. In the example below, it is used twice — once each way.

משנה: גָּנַב וְטָבַח בְּיוֹם הַכִּפּוּרִים ... מְשַׁלֵּם תַּשְׁלוּמֵי אַרְבָּעָה וַחֲמִשָּׁה.

תלמוד: אָמְרִי: אַמַּאי? נְהִי דִקְטָלָא לֵיכָּא, מַלְקוֹת מִיהָא אִיכָּא, וְקַיְימָא לַן דְּאֵינוֹ לוֹקֶה וּמְשַׁלֵּם! אָמְרִי: הָא מַנִּי? ר' מֵאִיר הִיא דַּאֲמַר: לוֹקֶה וּמְשַׁלֵּם. (בבא קמא עא, רע"א)

MISHNA: [If] one stole [an animal] and slaughtered it on Yom Kippur ..., he must make a four-fold or five-fold payment (as punishment for stealing).

TALMUD: They say (raising a difficulty): Why [does he have to pay]? Granted that there is no capital punishment (for desecrating Yom Kippur), there is at least the punishment of lashes (for desecrating Yom Kippur), and we have established that [one who] receives lashes, does not [have to] pay [compensation for the same act]! They say (resolving the difficulty): Who is [the authority for this [halakha]? It is R. Méir who has stated: [One who] receives lashes must pay. (But our established halakha follows the opinion of the Ḥakhamim who disagree with him.)

* Do not confuse with the previous entry, אֲמַרִי.

SEE: אֲמַר, קָא

people say　　אוֹמְרִים בְּנֵי אָדָם　　**אָמְרִי אֱינָשֵׁי***

This expression is used to introduce a popular saying.

For examples, see the entries הַיְינוּ דְּאָמְרִי אֱינָשֵׁי and מְנָא הָא מִילְּתָא דְּאָמְרִי אֱינָשֵׁי.

* See note on אֱינָשֵׁי. Some midrashim use a parallel Hebrew expression: מָשָׁל הֶדְיוֹט אוֹמֵר, *a popular proverb says*, as in the midrash quoted by Rashi on דברים א:ז.

וְאָמְרִי לַהּ　　וְאוֹמְרִים אוֹתָהּ; וְיֵשׁ אוֹמְרִים

and they say it; and some say it; but some quote it

This formula is used in two different senses:

(1) Like (וְ)אִיתֵימָא, it is used between the names of two authorities — indicating that one tradition ascribes the statement that it is now quoted to one authority, while a different tradition ascribes it to the other.

אָמַר ר' אַבָּהוּ וְאָמְרִי לַהּ בְּמַתְנִיתָא תְּנָא (ברכות נא,ב)

R. Abbahu said but some quote it [as a statement that a tanna] taught in a baraitha

(2) In some instances, it introduces a different tradition as to the *content* of a statement.

אֲמַר רָבָא: ... שְׁרָגָא בִּמְטַלַּלְתָּא, וְאָמְרִי לַהּ: בָּר מִמְּטַלַּלְתָּא. (סוכה כט, רע"א)

Rava said: ... a lamp [may be kept] within the sukka, but some quote it (= Rava's statement): [that a lamp must be kept] outside the sukka.

SEE: (בְּ)מַתְנִיתָא תְּנָא

וְאָמְרִי לַהּ כְּדִי*　　וְיֵשׁ אוֹמְרִים אוֹתָהּ סְתָם

and some state it anonymously

This expression introduces the suggestion that the statement about to be quoted was transmitted anonymously — not necessarily by the specific amora to whom others have attributed it.

אֲמַר רַב פָּפָּא ... וְאָמְרִי לַהּ כְּדִי ... (בבא מציעא ב, סע"א, וע' מהרש"ל שם)

R. Pappa stated ... and some state it anonymously ...

* Rashi explains כְּדִי, *anonymously*, in his commentary on גיטין פח, סע"ב (ד"ה "ולורכיה"). According to all the filmed manuscripts at the Institute of Microfilmed Hebrew Manuscripts, Hebrew University, Jerusalem, the text of Rashi's comment reads בלא חכם. R. Avraham Zacuto, in his *Sefer HaYuḥasin*, quotes Rashi: בלא שם חכם. The erroneous reading in printed editions, שם חכם, has misled various scholars over the centuries to regard כדי as the proper name of an otherwise unknown amora.

SEE: כְּדִי

דְּאָמְרִי תַּרְוַיְיהוּ

... both of whom say　　... שֶׁאוֹמְרִים שְׁנֵיהֶם

This expression appears immediately after the names of two amoraim to indicate that both of them have stated the halakha that is now being quoted. The pairs of amoraim whose halakhoth

are presented in this manner are: Rav and Sh^emuel, Abbayé and Rava, Rabba and Rav Yosef, R. Yoḥanan and R. El'azar, R. Yoḥanan and Resh Lakish (pairs who were often halakhic opponents) and Abbayé b. Abin and Rav Ḥanina b. Abin (a pair of brothers).

ר׳ יוֹחָנָן וְרֵישׁ לָקִישׁ דְּאָמְרִי תַּרְוַיְיהוּ* (שבועות ג,ב)
R. Yoḥanan and Resh Lakish both of whom say

* In this example, the two amoraim agree about the halakha but disagree about the reason behind it.

אָמְרִינַן (אָמְרֵי+אֲנַן)**;** קָאָמְרִינַן (קָא+אָמְרִינַן)

we say; we mean "אוֹמְרִים אֲנַחְנוּ"

See example under אֲנַן הָכִי קָאָמְרִינַן.
SEE: אֲמַר, קָא

אָמְרִיתוּ (אָמְרֵי+אַתּוּ)**;** קָאָמְרִיתוּ (קָא+אָמְרִיתוּ)

you (pl.) say/mean "אוֹמְרִים אַתֶּם"

SEE: אֲמַר, קָא

אָמְרַתְּ* (אָמַר .prt + אַתְּ)**;** קָאָמְרַתְּ (קָא+אָמְרַתְּ)

you say; you speak "אוֹמֵר אַתָּה"

קָאָמְרַתְּ is often used to emphasise the difference between two cases in order to refute an argument that was based on an analogy between them.

(1) מָהוּ לִמְכּוֹר סֵפֶר תּוֹרָה יָשָׁן לִיקַּח בּוֹ חָדָשׁ? ... (2) תָּא שְׁמַע: מַנִּיחִין סֵפֶר תּוֹרָה עַל גַּבֵּי תוֹרָה ... (3) הַנָּחָה קָאָמְרַתְּ?! שָׁאנֵי הַנָּחָה דְּלָא אֶפְשָׁר. (מגילה כג,א)

(1) What is the halakhic ruling [about] selling an old Torah scroll in order to buy a new [one] with it (= the proceeds)? (2) Come (and) hear: We may place [one] Torah scroll on top of [another] Torah (implying that one Torah scroll may be utilized in behalf of another one). (3) Are you speaking of placing? [The question of] placing [the Torah scrolls] is different (from the question of selling one to buy another), because [we are dealing with a case where] it is impossible [to place them other than one scroll on top of another].

* The past tense אֲמַרְתְּ, *you said*, is also used in the Talmud.
SEE: אֲמַר, שַׁפִּיר קָאָמְרַתְּ

וּדְקָאָמְרַתְּ ...**;** וּדְקָא אָמְרַתְּ ...
וּמָה שֶׁאַתָּה אוֹמֵר ...

and [as for] what you have been saying ...

This expression ***reintroduces*** **an argument that had been presented earlier in the Talmudic discussion. Now, however, a new response is presented.**

משנה: כְּרִיכוֹת בִּרְשׁוּת הָרַבִּים הֲרֵי אֵלּוּ שֶׁלּוֹ, בִּרְשׁוּת הַיָּחִיד נוֹטֵל וּמַכְרִיז (בבא מציעא כא,א: משנה פ״ב מ״א).

תלמוד: (1) הֵיכִי דָּמֵי? אִי דְּלֵית בְּהוּ סִימָן, בִּרְשׁוּת הַיָּחִיד מַאי מַכְרִיז? אֶלָּא לָאו דְּאִית בְּהוּ סִימָן ...! (2) אָמַר לָךְ רָבָא: לְעוֹלָם דְּלֵית בְּהוּ סִימָן; וּדְקָא אָמְרַתְּ: בִּרְשׁוּת הַיָּחִיד מַאי מַכְרִיז? מַכְרִיז מָקוֹם. (בבא מציעא כב,ב)

MISHNA: Sheaves found on public property belong to him (= the finder), [whereas those found] on private property he must take and announce.

TALMUD: (1) What is the case [of which the text is speaking]? If they have no marks of identification, [with regard to those found] on private property what is he to announce? Rather isn't it [a case] where they have marks of identification ...! (2) Rava would say to you: In reality they have no marks of identification and [as for] what you have been saying: [as for those found] on private property what is he to announce (if they have no marks of identification)? He should announce the location [where they were found].

אַמְתָּא (pl. אַמִּין/אַמְהָתָא)

forearm; cubit אַמָּה

כָּל אַמְתָּא בְּרִיבּוּעַ — אַמְתָּא וּתְרֵי חוּמְשֵׁי בַּאֲלַכְסוֹנָא. (עירובין נז,א ושי״נ)

*Whenever a cubit is [the length of a side] of a square, one and two fifths cubits is the (approximate) length of the diagonal.**

* According to the Pythagorean Theorem, the diagonal is the square root of 2 (= 1.4142135).
SEE: אַמָּה

אַמְתָּא (pl. אַמְהָתָא)

maidservant אָמָה

הַהִיא אַמְתָּא דַּהֲוַיָא בְּבֵי רַבִּי (שבת קנב,א)
[there was] a maidservant [working] in Rebbi's home
SEE: אָמָה

אֲנָא* אֲנִי **I**

* See note under אֲנַן.

אֲנָא דַּאֲמַרִי אֲפִילּוּ לְר׳ ....
מַה שֶּׁאֲנִי אָמַרְתִּי [מַתְאִים] אֲפִילּוּ לְ[דַעַת] ר׳ ....

[The halakha] that I have stated is [in keeping] even with [the opinion of] R. ....

In the course of a Talmudic discussion, it had been stated that the opinion of one amora could be maintained, according to only one side of a controversy between tannaim. Now, however, it is argued that the amora can explain his opinion in such a manner that it would fit ***either side*** **of the tannaitic controversy.**

משנה: וְעַל כּוּלָּם אִם אָמַר "שֶׁהַכֹּל נִהְיֶה בִּדְבָרוֹ", יָצָא. (ברכות מ, רע״ב: משנה פ״ו מ״ב)

תלמוד: (1) אִתְּמַר: רַב הוּנָא אֲמַר: חוּץ מִן הַפַּת וּמִן הַיַּיִן; וְר׳ יוֹחָנָן אֲמַר: אֲפִילּוּ פַּת וְיַיִן. (2) נֵימָא כְּתַנָּאֵי? רָאָה פַּת וְאָמַר: "כַּמָּה נָאָה פַּת זוֹ! בָּרוּךְ הַמָּקוֹם שֶׁבְּרָאָהּ" — יָצָא ... דִּבְרֵי ר׳ מֵאִיר. ר׳ יוֹסֵי אוֹמֵר: כָּל הַמְשַׁנֶּה מִמַּטְבֵּעַ שֶׁטָּבְעוּ חֲכָמִים בִּבְרָכוֹת — לֹא יָצָא יְדֵי חוֹבָתוֹ. נֵימָא רַב הוּנָא דְּאָמַר כְּר׳ יוֹסֵי, וְר׳ יוֹחָנָן דְּאָמַר כְּר׳ מֵאִיר? (3) אָמַר לָךְ רַב הוּנָא: אֲנָא דַּאֲמַרִי אֲפִילּוּ לְר׳ מֵאִיר. עַד כָּאן לָא קָאָמַר ר׳ מֵאִיר הָתָם, אֶלָּא הֵיכָא דְּקָא מַדְכַּר שְׁמֵיהּ דְּפַת, אֲבָל הֵיכָא דְּלָא מַדְכַּר שְׁמֵיהּ דְּפַת, אֲפִילּוּ ר׳ מֵאִיר מוֹדֶה. (ברכות מ, רע״ב)

MISHNA: Over all [foods] if one said [the blessing] ... שֶׁהַכֹּל, he has fulfilled his duty.

TALMUD: (1) It was stated: Rav Huna said: [The law of the mishna applies to all foods] with the exception of bread and wine, but R. Yoḥanan said: [it applies] even [to] bread and wine. (2) Shall we say [their controversy] is the same as [the controversy between] tannaim [in the following baraitha]?

BARAITHA: One who saw bread and [before eating it] said: "How nice is this bread! Blessed be the Omnipresent who has created it!" has fulfilled his duty — [according to] the opinion of R. Méir. R. Yosé says: Whoever alters the formula that the ḥakhamim have coined for b^{e}rakhoth has not fulfilled his duty.

TALMUD: Shall we say it is Rav Huna who has followed R. Yosé (since both insist upon a specific formula), whereas it is R. Yoḥanan who has followed R. Méir (since both expressed a more flexible point of view)? (3) [Not necessarily, because] Rav Huna might say to you: [The halakha] I have stated is [in keeping] even with [the opinion of] R. Méir. R. Méir only goes so far as to state [his halakha] in that case where one does mention the word "bread" [in his b^{e}rakha]; however, where one does not mention the word "bread" [in the b^{e}rakha, as in שֶׁהַכֹּל נִהְיָה בִּדְבָרוֹ], even R. Méir might concede [that he has not fulfilled his duty].

SEE: אָמַר לָךְ ר׳ ..., עַד כָּאן לָא קָאָמַר, אֲפִילּוּ תֵּימָא

אַנְדְרוֹגִינוֹס

hermaphrodite; a person who has reproductive organs of both sexes

See example in יבמות פא,א: משנה פ״ח מ״ו.

forced (אנס) pass. prt. **אָנוּס**

See example under אָנַס.

אַנַּח (נוח אַפְעֵל: מַנַּח .prt, לֵינַּח* .fut, לְאַנּוֹחֵי .inf)

he placed; he left (1) הִנִּיחַ

אַנַּח כּוּזָא דְמַיָּא אַפּוּמָא דְקוּמְקוּמָא (שבת מח, רע״א)

he placed a cup of [cold] water on the spout of a kettle

"he gave rest"; he put at ease; he calmed (2) הֵנִיחַ

בְּעָא אַבַּיֵי לְאַנּוֹחֵי דַעְתֵּיהּ דְּרַב יוֹסֵף. (ברכות כח, רע״ב)

Abbayé sought to calm the mind of Rav Yosef.

*** Sometimes the letter י appears after the prefix letter in the future — indicating the vocalisation לֵינַּח instead of the usual לַנַּח. Similar forms occur in the future אַפְעֵל of other verbs as well. The reason for this vowel shift is unclear.**

SEE: מַנַּח

for I say; for I assume **שֶׁאֲנִי אוֹמֵר**

This expression sometimes introduces a *halakhic assumption.*

שְׁתֵּי קוּפּוֹת (אַחַת שֶׁל חוּלִּין וְאַחַת שֶׁל תְּרוּמָה) וְלִפְנֵיהֶם שְׁתֵּי סְאִין (אַחַת שֶׁל חוּלִּין וְאַחַת שֶׁל תְּרוּמָה) וְנָפְלוּ אֵלּוּ בְּתוֹךְ אֵלּוּ — הֲרֵי אֵלּוּ מוּתָּרִים, שֶׁאֲנִי אוֹמֵר: תְּרוּמָה לְתוֹךְ תְּרוּמָה נָפְלָה, וְחוּלִּין לְתוֹךְ חוּלִּין נָפְלָה. (יבמות פב, סע״א)

[There are] two baskets (one containing ordinary fruit and the other t^{e}ruma) and in front of them there are

two s^{e}as (one of ordinary fruit and one of t^{e}ruma). [If] the latter (= the two s^{e}as) fell into the former (that is, one s^{e}a fell into each basket) — behold they are permitted; for I assume the t^{e}ruma fell into t^{e}ruma and the ordinary fruit fell into ordinary fruit.*

*** A s^{e}a is a measure of volume.**

SEE: תִּלָא, סְאָה

forced אָנוּס (אנס) pass. prt. **אֲנִיס**

SEE: אָנַס

we אָנוּ; אֲנַחְנוּ **אֲנַן***

*** For a full listing of independent personal pronouns in Babylonian Aramaic, see *Grammar for Gemara:* Chapter 7.2.**

אֲנַן הָכִי קָאָמְרִינַן אָנוּ, כָּךְ אָנוּ אוֹמְרִים ...

So we are saying; This [is what] we mean ...

With this formula, the Talmud introduces a *reinterpretation* of a question or a proof that was presented earlier in the discussion.

בריתא: ר׳ יוֹסֵי אוֹמֵר: אָדָם נִידּוֹן בְּכָל יוֹם, שֶׁנֶּאֱמַר "וַתִּפְקְדֶנּוּ לִבְקָרִים". ר׳ נָתָן אוֹמֵר: אָדָם נִידּוֹן בְּכָל שָׁעָה, שֶׁנֶּאֱמַר "לִרְגָעִים תִּבְחָנֶנּוּ".

תלמוד: ... אֲמַר רַב חִסְדָּא: מַאי טַעְמָא דְּר׳ יוֹסֵי? כִּדְקָאָמַר טַעְמֵיהּ: "וַתִּפְקְדֶנּוּ לִבְקָרִים"! אֲנַן הָכִי קָאָמְרִינַן: מַאי טַעְמָא לָא אָמַר כְּר׳ נָתָן? (ראש השנה טז,א ע״פ איוב ז:יח)

BARAITHA: R. Yosé says: A person is judged every day, as it says, "And you visit him every morning." R. Nathan says: A person is judged every moment, as it says, "You test him every moment."

TALMUD: Rav Ḥisda said: What is R. Yosé's reason? (How can you ask this?) His reason is as he has stated: "And you visit him every morning!" [Rather] this [is what] we mean: [For] what reason did he (= R. Yosé) not say like R. Nathan?

SEE: וְהָא אֲנַן תְּנַן, אַף אֲנַן נַמֵי תְּנֵינָא, נֵיחְזֵי אֲנַן

אֲנַס (אנס: אוֹנֵס .act. prt, אָנוּס .pass. prt);

אֲנַס* (אנס: אָנֵס .act. prt, אֲנִיס .pass. prt)

he forced; he compelled; he raped

לִבְּךָ אֲנָסְךָ. (שבועות כו,א)

Your heart compelled you [to take a false oath].

אָנוּס רַחֲמָנָא פַּטְרֵיהּ. (נדרים כז,א וש״נ)

The Torah has exempted [one who was] forced (that is, one who was prevented from carrying out his responsibility because of unavoidable circumstances).

*** The first verb is Hebrew, and the second is Aramaic.**

man of violence; outlaw; bandit **אַנָּס***

מִשֶּׁרַבּוּ הָאַנָּסִין (סנהדרין כד,ב: משנה פ״ג מ״ג)

when outlaws became numerous

*** In Modern Hebrew, an אַנָּס is usually a *rapist* (= אוֹנֵס in Mishnaic Hebrew).**

אַנְסֵיב* (נסב אַפְעֵל) הִשִּׂיא

he caused to marry; he married off; he

granted permission to remarry

אַנְסְבָה רָבָא לִדְבִיתְהוּ. (יבמות קכא,א)
Rava granted his (= the drowned man's) wife permission to remarry.

* A similar verbal form (usually without the נ) occurs in the sense of *giving advice,* as in (ב"ב ג,ב) אַסְבֵּיה לֵיהּ עֵצָה, *he gave him advice.*

SEE: אִינְסִיבָא, נְסַב

אַנְפֵּי /בְּאַנְפֵּי

SEE: אַפֵּי /(בְּ)אַפֵּי

אַנְשֵׁי בֵיתוֹ*

members of his household; his wife

מְשַׁגְּרוֹ בְּמַתָּנָה לְאַנְשֵׁי בֵיתוֹ (ברכות נא, סע"א ורש"י שם)
he sends it as a gift to his wife

* Compare אֹיְבֵי אִישׁ אַנְשֵׁי בֵיתוֹ in מיכה ז:ו.

SEE: אֱינָשֵׁי בֵּיתֵיהּ, בֵּיתוֹ

אַנְתְּ/אַתְּ

you אַתָּה

זִיל אַנְתְּ אַיְיתִי סָהֲדֵי ...! (בבא מציעא לט, סע"ב)
You go [and] bring witnesses ...!

SEE: אַתְּ

אַסָּא

a myrtle branch הֲדַס

מֵעִיקָּרָא הֲוָה לֵיהּ "אַסָּא", וְהַשְׁתָּא "הוֹשַׁעְנָא". (סוכה ל, סע"ב)
Originally, it was [called] "a myrtle branch" by him, but now it is [called] a "hoshana."

אַסְבַּר (סבר: מַסְבַּר .prt)

he explained הִסְבִּיר

מַאי לְשׁוֹן "מוֹסֵירָה"? אֲמַר רָבָא: אִידִי אַסְבְּרָא לִי "כְּאָדָם הַמּוֹסֵר דָּבָר לַחֲבֵירוֹ". (בבא מציעא ח,ב)
What is [the etymology of] the word מוֹסֵרָה *(= the reins on an animal)? Rava said: Idi explained it to me "like a person who hands over something to his friend."*

SEE: סְבַר

אַסְהִיד (סהד אַפְעֵל: מַסְהִיד .prt, לְאַסְהוֹדֵי .inf)

he testified הֵעִיד

אַסְהִידוּ בֵיהּ תְּרֵי סָהֲדֵי (סנהדרין כה,א)
two witnesses testified against him

SEE: סָהֲדָא

אָסוּתָא

remedy; cure רְפוּאָה

כָּל מִילֵּי יָדַעְנָא אַסְוָתַיְיהוּ — לְבַר מֵהָנֵי תְּלָת ... (ב"מ קיג,ב)
I know the remedies for everything — except for these three ...

SEE: מַסֵּי, אָסְיָא

אַסַּח (נסח אַפְעֵל: מַסַּח .prt, אַסּוֹחֵי .inf) הִסִּיחַ

he removed; he abandoned; he discovered

אַסַּח דַּעְתֵּיהּ הִסִּיחַ דַּעְתּוֹ

he withdrew his mind (from); he diverted his attention (from)

כֵּיוָן דְּלָא חֲזֵי לְאוּרְתָּא, אַסּוֹחֵי מַסַּח דַּעְתֵּיהּ מִינֵּיהּ, וְלָא אָתֵי לְחַתּוֹיֵי גֶחָלִים. (שבת יח,ב)
Since [the raw meat] will not be ready for the [Sabbath] evening [meal], he is certainly withdrawing his mind from it, and [so] he will not come to stir coals.

אָסְיָא

doctor; physician רוֹפֵא

דְּכָאֵיב לֵיהּ כְּאֵיבָא אָזֵיל לְבֵי אָסְיָא. (בבא קמא מו,ב)
One who is suffering pain goes to the doctor's.

SEE: מַסֵּי, אָסוּתָא

אַסִּיק (סלק* אַפְעֵל: מַסִּיק .prt, לַסִּיק .fut, אַסּוֹקֵי .inf)

he brought up; he raised (1) הֶעֱלָה

אַסִּיק חֲמָרֵיהּ לְמַבָּרָא (בבא קמא קיז,ב)
he brought his donkey up onto the ferry-boat

he had in mind; he thought (2) הֶעֱלָה (עַל דַּעַת)

In this sense, the verb is followed by some form of the noun דַּעְתָּא, *mind.*

לָא אַסִּיק אַדַּעְתֵּיהּ (בבא קמא מה,ב)
he did not have [it] in [his] mind

he named; he termed; he designated (3) קָרָא

אַסִּיקוּ לְרַ' מֵאִיר "אֲחֵרִים" וּלְרַ' נָתָן "יֵשׁ אוֹמְרִים". (הוריות יג, סע"ב ועי' תוס' לסוטה יב,א)
They designated R. Méir as "others," and R. Nathan as "some say."

he brought to a conclusion (4) הִסִּיק (מַסְקָנָה)

אַסּוֹקֵי שְׁמַעְתָּא אַלִּיבָּא דְהִלְכְתָא (יומא כו,א)
to bring the matter to a [proper] halakhic conclusion

* For the full conjugation of this verb, see *Grammar for Gemara:* Chapter 4, Verb 7.

SEE: מַסִּיק, סָלְקָא דַעְתָּךְ

אַסְמַךְ (סמך אַפְעֵל)

he supported; he found support הִסְמִיךְ

אֲתָא יְחֶזְקֵאל וְאַסְמְכָהּ אַקְּרָא (יומא עא,ב וש"נ)
Y°ḥezkel came [along] and found support for it (= this halakha) in a pasuk

SEE: אַסְמַכְתָּא

אַסְמַכְתָּא

a support; an intimation (1) סְמָךְ; סַעַד; זֵכֶר

Sometimes there is an *allusion* in a Biblical text to a halakha whose real source is either a Rabbinical enactment or an oral tradition from Sinai, but not the pasuk itself.*

"כָּל חֵלֶב" מִדְּרַבָּנַן, וּקְרָא אַסְמַכְתָּא בְּעָלְמָא. (יומא עד, סע"א ע"פ ויקרא ז:כג)
"Any fat" (teaches that even the slightest amount of forbidden food must not be eaten) according to Rabbinic law, and the (other) pasuk (which was previously quoted in the Talmud) is merely a support.

הִלְכְתָא נִינְהוּ, וּקְרָא אַסְמַכְתָּא בְּעָלְמָא הוּא. (סוכה ו,א)
They are halakhic traditions, and the pasuk is merely a support.

(2) הִסְתַּמְּכוּת (בְּלִי הִתְחַיְּבוּת גְּמוּרָה)
"reliance" (upon a particular eventuality); a conditional (monetary) obligation undertaken without full commitment, (because it is contingent upon the fulfillment of a condition that each party anticipates will not be fulfilled — as in gambling where the players do not expect to lose)

מְשַׂחֵק בְּקוּבְיָא ... הֲוָה אַסְמַכְתָּא, וְאַסְמַכְתָּא לָא קָנְיָא. (סנהדרין כד,ב)

[The case of] a dice player is a conditional obligation undertaken without full commitment, and [such an] obligation is not binding (according to Rami b. Ḥama).

*** As to the nature of these allusions, there is some disagreement among the classical commentators. In his *Introduction to the Commentary on the Mishna*, the Rambam speaks of a mitsva being linked to a pasuk by an interpretation of the Ḥakhamim in order for it to be known and remembered, even though the interpretation is artificial and not an integral part of the pasuk. On the other hand, the Ritva (ראש השנה טז,א) insists that the pasuk really alludes to the mitsva and recommends the mitsva act, but it is for the Ḥakhamim to decide whether or not to make such conduct obligatory.**

SEE: אַסְמַךְ, זֵכֶר

אֲסַר (אסר: אָסַר **a. prt.**, אֲסִיר **p. prt.**, לְמֵיסַר **inf.**)

(1) אָסַר; קָשַׁר **he bound; he tied**

קָא אָסַר וְשָׁרֵי (בבא מציעא פו, סע"ב ורש"י שם)

he was binding [the wound] and untying [it]

(2) אָסַר; הֵטִיל אִסּוּר
he forbade; he prohibited

מַאי דְּקָא אָסַר תַּנָּא קַמָּא, קָא שָׁרֵי ר' דּוֹסָא. (ביצה ט,ב)

What the first tanna forbids, R. Dosa permits.

SEE: איתסר

אַף אֲנַן נַמֵּי תְּנֵינָא

We have also learnt ... אַף אָנוּ שָׁנִינוּ ...

This formula introduces a mishna (or occasionally a baraitha) that contains implicit* corroboration of an amora's statement that was previously presented in the Talmud.

(1) אֲמַר ר' אַבָּהוּ אֲמַר ר' יוֹחָנָן: כָּל אִיסּוּרִין שֶׁבַּתּוֹרָה — אֵין לוֹקִין עֲלֵיהֶן אֶלָּא דֶּרֶךְ הֲנָאָתָן .... (2) אֲמַר ר' זֵירָא: אַף אֲנַן נַמֵּי תְּנֵינָא: אֵין סוֹפְגִין אֶת הָאַרְבָּעִים מִשּׁוּם עָרְלָה אֶלָּא עַל הַיּוֹצֵא מִן הַזֵּיתִים וּמִן הָעֲנָבִים בִּלְבָד; וְאִילּוּ מִתּוּתִים, תְּאֵנִים, וְרִימּוֹנִים — לֹא. מַאי טַעְמָא? לָאו מִשּׁוּם דְּלָא קָאָכֵיל לְהוּ דֶּרֶךְ הֲנָאָתָן?! (פסחים כד,ב ע"פ משנה תרומות פי"א מ"ג)

(1) R. Abbahu said in the name of R. Yoḥanan: [As for] all the foods forbidden by the Torah — one is not punished with lashes on account of them, unless [he eats them] in the normal manner of their consumption. (2) R. Zera said: We have also learnt: One does not receive forty lashes on account of "orla" — except for that which issues forth from olives or grapes alone; but not on account of that which issues forth from mulberries, figs or pomegranates. What is the reason? Is it not because he is not eating them in the usual manner of their consumption?!

*** When an amora's statement is found to be stated *explicitly* in a mishna, an objection is usually raised in the Talmud in the form of** מַאי קָא מַשְׁמַע לָן?, ***what [new point] is he teaching us?*** **See that entry.**

SEE: תְּנֵינָא

אַף עַל גַּב ד- אַף עַל פִּי שֶׁ-

even though; in spite of [the fact] that

אַף עַל גַּב דְּקָא מִשְׁתְּבַע לִי, לָא מְהֵימַן לִי. (בבא מציעא ג,א)

Even though he swears to me, he is not trustworthy in my eyes.

אַף עַל פִּי שֶׁאֵין רְאָיָה לַדָּבָר זֵכֶר לַדָּבָר

Although there is no (Biblical) proof for the matter, there is an allusion to the matter (in the pasuk that is about to be quoted).

מִנַּיִן לְסִיכָה שֶׁהִיא כִּשְׁתִיָּיה בְּיוֹם הַכִּיפּוּרִים? אַף עַל פִּי שֶׁאֵין רְאָיָה לַדָּבָר, זֵכֶר לַדָּבָר, שֶׁנֶּאֱמַר: "וַתָּבֹא כַמַּיִם בְּקִרְבּוֹ וְכַשֶּׁמֶן בְּעַצְמוֹתָיו". (שבת פו,א: משנה פ"ט מ"ד ע"פ תהלים קט:יח)

From where [do we learn that] annointing is like drinking [and is thus forbidden] on Yom Kippur? Although there is no proof for the matter, there is an allusion to the matter, for it is stated: "And it entered like water within him and like oil within his bones."

SEE: רְאָיָה, זֵכֶר, אַסְמַכְתָּא

אַפּוּמָא ד- "עַל הַפֶּה שֶׁל"

(1) עַל פִּי עֵדוּתוֹ שֶׁל **through the testimony of**

אִינְהוּ מַפְקֵי מָמוֹנָא אַפּוּמָא דְּחַד. (ב"ק קיג,ב - קיד,א)

They collect money through the testimony of one [witness].

(2) עַל פִּי; עַל שְׂפַת; עַל פֶּתַח **on the mouth of; on the edge of; at the opening of**

מַנַּח מִידֵּי אַפּוּמָא דַּחֲבִיתָא (בבא קמא קטו,ב)

he may place something on the edge of the barrel

SEE: פום

לְאַפּוּקֵי* inf. (נפק אַפְעֵל)

to take out; to rule out; to exclude לְהוֹצִיא

This verb is often used in explaining why a particular element in a text is *not superfluous*. Two different kinds of explanations are expressed by this term:

(1) The mishna, baraitha, or occasionally a pasuk has used a certain word or expression in order to exclude a potentially debatable case from the halakhic rule that is stated. In some instances, the question לְאַפּוּקֵי מַאי? ***(to rule out what?)*** **is explicitly asked in the Talmud. Then this explanation is presented, introduced by** לְאַפּוּקֵי. **(See example below.) In other instances, the question is implicit.**

משנה: הַשּׁוֹתֶה מַיִם לִצְמָאוֹ אוֹמֵר: "שֶׁהַכֹּל נִהְיֶה בִּדְבָרוֹ". (ברכות מד,א: משנה פ"ו מ"ח)
תלמוד: לְאַפּוֹקֵי מַאי? ... לְאַפּוֹקֵי לְמַאן דְּחַנְקְתֵיהּ אוּמְצָא. (שם מד,סע"ב - מה, רע"א)
MISHNA: If one drinks water to [quench] his thirst, he recites שֶׁהַכֹּל נִהְיֶה בִּדְבָרוֹ.
TALMUD: What [case does the term "to quench his thirst" come] to exclude [from requiring a b^e^rakha]? [It comes] to exclude [a case of] one whom a piece of meat was choking (who needs a drink of water — but not to quench his thirst).

(2) Sometimes, the Talmud explains that the mishna or baraitha was formulated in its present form in order *to express opposition to* the opinion of another tanna. In this sense, the verb לְאַפּוֹקֵי is followed by the prefix -מְ.

משנה: ... אֵלּוּ אֲבוֹת מְלָאכוֹת אַרְבָּעִים חָסֵר אַחַת. (שבת ע"ג, סע"א: משנה פ"ז מ"ב)
תלמוד: "חָסֵר אַחַת" — לְאַפּוֹקֵי מִדְּר' יְהוּדָה, דְּתַנְיָא: ר' יְהוּדָה מוֹסִיף אֶת הַשּׁוֹבֵט וְהַמְדַקְדֵּק. (שם עה,ב)
MISHNA: These are the principal labors [forbidden on the Sabbath] — forty less one.
TALMUD: "Less one" — to exclude [the opinion] of R Y^e^huda, for it is taught (in a baraitha): R Y^e^huda adds the closing up of the web and the beating of the woof. (Thus R Y^e^huda reaches a total of forty-one labors — rather than the thirty-nine of the mishna.)

* This word is popularly pronounced לְאַפּוּקֵי.

SEE: אַפֵּיק, הוֹצִיא, מִיעֵט, מַעֵט, אַיְיתֵי

אַפֵּי/אַנְפֵּי/אַפִּין* pl. פָּנִים **face; presence**

This Aramaic noun appears almost exclusively in the construct state or with personal-pronoun suffixes. In most cases, it also has a -ב or a -ל prefix, as presented in the next three entries. Some of the forms with suffixes are from the singular noun אַף, which also means *nose, face,* or *anger.* The following forms with pronoun suffixes are the most common:

his face; his/its (m.) presence אַפֵּיהּ/אַנְפֵּיהּ
her face; her/its (f.) presence אַפַּהּ/אַנְפַּהּ
their faces; their presence אַפַּיְיהוּ/אַנְפַּיְיהוּ
he turns his face מְהַדַּר אַפֵּיהּ (ברכות ו,ב)

* The Aramaic noun is plural, but its English translation is singular. In Biblical Hebrew, אַפַּיִם (the dual form) means *face,* as in וַיִּשְׁתַּחוּ אַפַּיִם אַרְצָה (בראשית יט:א).

בְּאַפֵּי/בְּאַנְפֵּי
in the face of; in the presence of בִּפְנֵי
בְּאַפֵּי סָהֲדֵי פַּרְעֵיהּ (שבועות מב,א)
he paid him in the presence of witnesses

בְּאַפֵּי נַפְשֵׁיהּ (בְּאַפֵּי נַפְשַׁהּ .f.s, בְּאַפֵּי נַפְשַׁיְיהוּ .m. pl)
by itself; independently בִּפְנֵי עַצְמוֹ
For example, see אִיכָּא דְּמַתְנֵי לַהּ לְהָא שְׁמַעְתָּא בְּאַפֵּי נַפְשַׁהּ.

לְאַפֵּי "לִפְנֵי"; לִקְרָאת; מוּל
"to the face of"; facing; towards; opposite
תַּרְתֵּי עֲנָנֵי דְּסָלְקֵי — חֲדָא לְאַפֵּי חֲבֶרְתָּהּ (ברכות נט,א)
two clouds that rise — one facing the other

אַפֵּיךְ (אפך: אָפֵיךְ .prt, לֵיפוּךְ .fut, אֵיפוּךְ .imp, לְמֵיפַךְ
he reversed; he interchanged הָפַךְ (inf.
מַאי חָזֵית דְּאַפְּכַתְ בְּתַרְיֵיתָא? אֵיפוּךְ קַמַּיְיתָא! (ברכות כה,ב)
Why did you reverse the [order of the statements in the] last [baraitha]? Reverse the first [baraitha]!

SEE: מַאי חָזֵית

אֲפִילוּ תֵּימָא ר' ... אֲפִילוּ תֹּאמַר ר' ...
You may say [that the text is compatible] even [with the opinion of] R. ...

After it was asserted that an anonymous halakha in a mishna or a baraitha is consistent with only one side of a controversy between tannaim, it is now argued that the halakha may also be *consistent with the opposing opinion,* after all.

זְרִיעָה וַחֲרִישָׁה בִּשְׁבִיעִית מִי שְׁרִי?! אָמַר אַבָּיֵי: בִּשְׁבִיעִית בַּזְּמַן הַזֶּה, וְרַבִּי הִיא ... רָבָא אָמַר: אֲפִילוּ תֵּימָא רַבָּנַן — אָבוֹת אֲמַר רַחֲמָנָא; תּוֹלָדוֹת לָא אֲמַר רַחֲמָנָא. (מועד קטן ב, סע"ב)
Can [irrigation, which comes under the heading of] either sowing or plowing, be permissible during the Sabbatical year?! Abbayé said: [The mishna speaks] of the Sabbatical year nowadays, and it [follows the opinion of] Rebbi (who holds that the Sabbatical year is of only Rabbinic status; hence essential irrigation is permissible). Rava said: You may say [that the mishna is compatible] even [with the opinion of] the Ḥakhamim (who disagree with Rebbi and hold that the Sabbatical year has Torah status even nowadays) — [irrigation is permissible, because] the Torah has stated [only] main categories of labor; secondary categories (like irrigation) the Torah has not stated [as being forbidden].

אַפֵּיק (נפק* אַפְעֵל: מַפֵּיק .act. prt, מַפַּק .pass. prt, אַפֵּיק .imp, לְאַפּוֹקֵי .inf)

Besides the basic meaning *he took out* or *he brought forth* (like its Hebrew parallel הוֹצִיא), this Aramaic verb is used in the following senses:

he expressed (1) הִבִּיעַ
אַפְקֵיהּ רַחֲמָנָא בִּלְשׁוֹן "מַחְמֶצֶת" (פסחים כח,ב ע"פ שמות יב:כ)
the Torah expressed it with the term "leavening" (= something that causes fermentation)

he derived (from a pasuk) (2) לָמַד
אִית תַּנָּא דְּמַפֵּיק לֵיהּ לְיָדוֹת מִן "לִנְדּוֹר נֶדֶר" (נדרים ג,ב ע"פ במדבר ו,ב)
there is a tanna who derives abbreviated formulas [for vows] from [the passage] "to vow a vow"

he used (a Biblical passage to teach) (3) הִשְׁתַּמֵּשׁ

הַאי "אִם הִמָּצֵא תִמָּצֵא" מַפֵּיק לֵיהּ לְגַנָּב עַצְמוֹ. (בבא קמא סד,ב ע"פ שמות כב:ג)
This [passage] "if it indeed be found" he uses for [the law of] the thief himself.

(4) הוֹצִיא (בִּפְקֻדַּת בֵּית דִּין); עִקֵּל
he dispossessed (through the judicial process)
וְאִי תָּפַס, לָא מַפְּקִינַן מִינֵּיהּ. (בבא קמא טו,ב)
But if he has [already] seized [the property], we (= the court) do not dispossess him [of it].

(5) הוֹצִיא יְדֵי חוֹבָתוֹ
he caused another to fulfill his obligation; he performed [a duty] in behalf of another
אָתֵי דְאוֹרַיְיתָא וּמַפֵּיק דְאוֹרַיְיתָא (ברכות כ,ב)
[one who is obligated by] Torah law can come and perform [a duty] in behalf of [another who is obligated by] Torah law

(6) הוֹצִיא; מִעֵט
he excluded; he ruled out
אַפְּקַהּ רַחֲמָנָא לִשְׁבוּעַת עֵדוּת מִכְּלַל שְׁבוּעַת בִּיטּוּי (שבועות כח,ב)
the Torah has excluded the oath pertaining to testimony from the category of the oath confirming a statement

* For a full conjugation of this verb, see *Grammar for Gemara:* Chapter 4, Verb 6.

SEE: נְפַק, הוֹצִיא, לְאַפּוֹקֵי, מַפֵּיק, מַפַּק

אַפֵּישׁ (נפש אַפְעֵל: מַפֵּישׁ prt., אַפּוֹשֵׁי inf.)
he increased; he extended הִרְבָּה
דִּילְמָא אָתֵי לְאַפּוֹשֵׁי בִּשְׁבִיל יִשְׂרָאֵל (שבת קכב,א)
perhaps he will come to increase [the amount of water he draws] for the sake of a Jew

אַפְסֵיד (פסד אַפְעֵל: מַפְסֵיד prt., לַפְסֵיד fut., לְאַפְסוֹדֵי inf.) הִפְסִיד; הִזִּיק
he caused a loss; he damaged; he spoiled
אִיהוּ הוּא דְּאַפְסֵיד אַנַּפְשֵׁיהּ. (כתובות ב, סע"ב ועוד)
It is he who has caused a loss to himself.
SEE: פְּסֵיד

אַפְסֵיק (פסק אַפְעֵל: מַפְסֵיק prt., לְאַפְסוֹקֵי inf.)
he separated; he stopped הִפְסִיק
רַב אִיקְלַע לְבָבֶל. חַזְיִנְהוּ דְּקָא קָרוּ הַלֵּילָא בְּרֵישׁ יַרְחָא, סְבַר לְאַפְסוֹקִינְהוּ. (תענית כח,ב)
Rav happened to come to Babylonia. He saw them (= people) who were reciting Hallel on Rosh Ḥodesh (and) he considered stopping them.
SEE: פְּסַק

אַפְקַהּ (אַפֵּיק+לַהּ) SEE: אַפֵּיק

אַפְקֵיהּ (אַפֵּיק+לֵיהּ) SEE: אַפֵּיק

אַפְקַע (פקע אַפְעֵל: מַפְקַע prt., לְאַפְקוֹעֵי inf.)
he cancelled; he invalidated; he removed הִפְקִיעַ; בִּטֵּל; הוֹצִיא
אַפְקְעִינְהוּ רַבָּנָן לְקִידּוּשִׁין (כתובות ג, רע"א וש"נ)
the ḥakhamim invalidated the marriage
SEE: פְּקַע

אַפְקַר (פקר אַפְעֵל: מַפְקַר prt., אַפְקוֹרֵי inf.) הִפְקִיר
he renounced ownership; he abandoned
נְפִישׁ טִרְחַיְיהוּ ... אַפְקוֹרֵי* מַפְקַר לְהוּ. (בבא מציעא כא,א)
[In a situation where] it is too much bother [to collect] them ... he would certainly abandon them.

* The infinitive אַפְקוֹרֵי is used to strengthen מַפְקַר, *he would abandon*, and is best translated in English by an adverb such as *certainly* or *really*.

אַפְרֵישׁ (פרש אַפְעֵל: מַפְרֵישׁ prt., לְאַפְרוֹשֵׁי inf.)
he separated; he kept away הִפְרִישׁ; הִרְחִיק
לְאַפְרוֹשֵׁי מֵאִיסּוּרָא (שבת מ,ב)
to keep [people] away from sin
SEE: פְּרַשׁ

לְאַצּוֹלֵי inf. (נצל אַפְעֵל: מַצִּיל prt.)
to save; to rescue לְהַצִּיל
קָאֵי בְּתְרֵי עִיבְרֵי דְנַהֲרָא, דְּלָא מָצֵי אַצּוֹלֵיהּ. (סנהדרין עב,ב)
They are standing on two opposite sides of the river, so that he cannot save him.

אַצְנַע (צנע אַפְעֵל: מַצְנַע prt., לְאַצְנוֹעֵי inf.)
he hid; he concealed; he put aside הִצְנִיעַ; הִטְמִין; שָׁמַר
הָנֵי — אֱינָשׁ אַצְנְעִינְהוּ. (בבא מציעא כה,ב)
These a person put aside.

אַקְדֵּים (קדם אַפְעֵל: מַקְדֵּים prt., לַקְדֵּים/לִיקְדֵּים* fut., לְאַקְדוֹמֵי inf.) הִקְדִּים
he made first or earlier; he put first; he acted earlier; he preceded; he anticipated
אַיְּידֵי דַּחֲבִיבָה לֵיהּ, אַקְדְּמַהּ. (יבמות ל,א; לב,א)
Since it is dear to him, he put it first [in the mishna].

* Regarding this form of the future, see אֲנָח and its note.

SEE: קְדַם

אַקֵּיל (קלל אַפְעֵל: מַקֵּיל prt., לְאַקּוֹלֵי inf.)
he ruled leniently הֵקֵל
מִשּׁוּם עִיגּוּנָא אַקִּילוּ בַהּ רַבָּנָן. (גיטין ג, רע"א; יבמות פח,א)
Because of the "aguna" (= anchored-wife) problem, the ḥakhamim ruled leniently about her.

אַקֵּישׁ (נקש אַפְעֵל: מַקֵּישׁ prt., לַקֵּישׁ fut., אַקֵּישׁ imp., לְאַקּוֹשֵׁי inf.) הִקִּישׁ
he compared; he drew an analogy (between two matters, usually because of their juxtaposition in Scripture)
לְאַקּוֹשֵׁיהּ לְחַג הַמַּצּוֹת (ראש השנה ד, סע"ב ע"פ דברים טז:טז)
to compare it (= the Sukkoth festival) to the festival of unleavened bread (= Pesaḥ)
SEE: הֶיקֵּשׁ, הִקִּישׁ, מַקֵּישׁ

אַקְנֵי (קני אַפְעֵל: מַקְנֵי .prt, לַקְנֵי/לִיקְנֵי* .fut, לְאַקְנוּיֵי .inf)

he transferred possession; he sold הִקְנָה

יְנוּקָא מַקְנֵי קָנֵי, אַקְנוּיֵי לָא מַקְנֵי. (סוכה מו,ב ורש"י שם)

Children can acquire possession; [but] they cannot transfer possession.

* See note under אֵנַח regarding this form of the future.

SEE: קָנֵי

אַקְרַאי* **chance; casual occurrence** מִקְרֶה

מֵעִיקָּרָא, סָבוּר אַקְרַאי בְּעָלְמָא הוּא (סנהדרין כה,ב)

initially, they thought it was mere chance

* Do not confuse with אַקְרָאֵי (= אַ+קְרָאֵי), *on p^esukim or with reference to p^esukim.*

אַקְרֵי (קרא אַפְעֵל: מַקְרֵי .prt, לְאַקְרוּיֵי .inf)

he taught to read; he taught Scripture הִקְרִיא; לִמֵּד מִקְרָא

אֲנָא "זָכָר" אַקְרְיוּן! (בבא בתרא כא, רע"ב ע"פ דברים כה:יט)

[As for] me — they taught me to read זָכָר *(= the male Amalekites — instead of* זֵכֶר*, the memory of Amalek)!*

אַקְרְיֵיה, וְאַתְנְיֵיה, וְשַׁוְּיֵיה גַּבְרָא רַבָּא. (בבא מציעא פד,א)

He (= R. Yoḥanan) taught him (= Resh Lakish) Scripture, and he taught him mishna, and he made him a great man.

SEE: קְרָא

אִקְרֵי SEE: אִיקְרֵי

אַקְרֵיב (קרב אַפְעֵל: מַקְרֵב .prt, לַקְרֵיב/לִיקְרֵיב* .fut, לְאַקְרוּבֵי .inf) הִקְרִיב

he brought near; he offered (as a ***korban*****)**

אַפְרֵישׁ, וְלָא אַקְרֵיב (ראש השנה ו,א)

he set aside [the animal], but he has not offered [it as a korban]

* See note under אֵנַח regarding this future form.

אַקְשֵׁי (קשי אַפְעֵל: מַקְשֵׁי .prt, אַקְשׁוּיֵי .inf)

he raised a difficulty; he objected; he pointed out a contradiction הִקְשָׁה

אֲמַר שְׁמַעְתָּא, וְאַקְשֵׁי. (בבא קמא קיז, סע"א לפי כת"י)

He presented a halakha, and [the other scholar] raised a difficulty.

* Do not confuse with אַקִּישׁ from the root נקש.

SEE: מַקְשֵׁי

אַרְבָּא **boat** סְפִינָה

הֲווּ קָאָזְלֵי בְּאַרְבָּא (חולין קח,ב)

[they] were travelling in a boat

אַרְבֵּיסַר/אַרְבְּסַר **fourteen** אַרְבָּעָה עָשָׂר

אַרְבְּסְרֵי **fourteen (f.)** אַרְבַּע עֶשְׂרֵה

אַרְבַּע/אַרְבְּעִי **four (f.)** אַרְבַּע

אַרְבְּעָא **four** אַרְבָּעָה

אַרְבְּעִין **forty** אַרְבָּעִים

אַרְוַוח (רוח אַפְעֵל: מַרְוַוח .prt, לְאַרְווֹחֵי .inf)

(1) רֵוַח; הִרְחִיב; הֶאֱרִיךְ **he extended**

אַרְוַוח לַהּ זִימְנָא (קידושין ו,ב)

he extended the time [for repayment] for her

(2) הִרְוִיחַ **he profited; it was profitable**

מַרְוַוח עִסְקָךְ (ברכות נו,א) *your business will be profitable*

SEE: רְוַח, רְוָחָא

אֲרֵי (ארי); **קָאָרֵי** (קָ+אָרֵי) .prt

attached; involved מְעֹרֶה; עוֹסֵק

SEE: אֵיירִי, אִירְיָא

וּדְקָאָרֵי לַהּ מַאי קָאָרֵי לַהּ

וּמִי שֶׁעוֹסֵק בָּהּ, מָה הוּא עוֹסֵק בָּהּ?!

And [as for the one] who is involved with it (and has pointed out a difficulty with the mishna or baraitha), how [does it happen that] he has become involved with it!

With this ***question*** **the Talmud expresses amasement at the ḥakham who raised a difficulty, because its resolution is too obvious.**

(1) ר' יוֹחָנָן אָמַר: קָדְשׁוּ בְּכוֹרוֹת בְּמִדְבָּר, וְרֵישׁ לָקִישׁ אָמַר: לֹא קָדְשׁוּ בְּכוֹרוֹת בְּמִדְבָּר ... (2) אֵיתִיבֵיהּ ר' יוֹחָנָן לְרֵישׁ לָקִישׁ: "עַד שֶׁלֹּא הוּקַם הַמִּשְׁכָּן, הָיוּ הַבָּמוֹת מוּתָּרוֹת וַעֲבוֹדָה בִּבְכוֹרוֹת". (3) אֲמַר לֵיהּ: בְּאוֹתָן שֶׁיָּצְאוּ מִמִּצְרַיִם ... (4) וּדְקָאָרֵי לַהּ, מַאי קָאָרֵי לַהּ?! (בכורות ד,ב)

(1) R. Yoḥanan said: The first-born [sons] in the wilderness were sanctified (for Divine service), but Resh Lakish said: The first-born in the wilderness were not sanctified. (2) R. Yoḥanan raised an objection against Resh Lakish (from a mishna): Before the tabernacle was erected, the high places were permitted [for offerings], and the [Divine] service [was performed] by the first-born. (3) He (= Resh Lakish) said to him: By those [first-born] who had departed from Egypt (not by those born in the wilderness) ... (4) And (as for the one) who is involved with it (= R. Yoḥanan, who raised the objection from the mishna), how [does it happen that] he has become involved with it (since it is an obvious answer that the first-born were those who had left Egypt, since they were old enough to perform the Divine service)!

וע' כתובות טז, רע"א וש"נ בגליון הש"ס ושם לו,א ורש"י שם.

אַרְיָא **lion** אֲרִי

(1) Sometimes, אַרְיָא is a metaphor in Aramaic for an outstanding Torah scholar, as in our example:*

אֲמַר לֵיהּ שְׁמוּאֵל לְחִיָּיא בַּר רַב: בַּר אַרְיָא!** תָּא, אֵימָא לָךְ מִילְּתָא מֵהָנֵי מִילֵּי מַעַלְיָיתָא דַּהֲוָה אָמַר אֲבוּךְ. (חגיגה יד, רע"א)

Sh^emuel said to Ḥiyya, the son of Rav: Son of the *lion! Come, I will tell you a statement from among these excellent statements that your father used to utter.* (2) Occasionally, אַרְיָא is used metaphorically to indicate a prohibition, as in אַרְיָא הוּא דִּרְבִיעַ עִילָּוֵיהּ (שבועות כב,ב ורש"י שם), *"a lion" is resting on it****.

* Compare the Hebrew metaphor אֲרִי שֶׁבַּחֲבוּרָה, *the lion of the group,* which appears in סנהדרין ח, רע"ב and elsewhere.

** The *lion* is Rav. Shᵉmuel addressed Ḥiyya as *son of the lion,* since he was about to quote him a statement from Rav, Ḥiyya's father. Such is the significance of this term in ברכות יב, סע"א and עבודה זרה לא, סע"ב (according to the Munich Manuscript).

*** See בַּר אֲכִילָה for a fuller quotation of this passage.

אֲרִיךְ

tall; long   (1) אָרֹךְ

הַנְהוּ בֵּי תְרֵי דַּהֲווֹ מַסְגוּ בְּאוֹרְחָא, חַד אֲרִיךְ וְחַד גּוּצָא (בבא מציעא פא, רע"ב)

two men were travelling on the road, one tall and the other short

befitting; proper*   (2) כָּשֵׁר; רָאוּי

וְאָתוּ בְּנֵי קְרִיָּתָא וּמְקַשְׁקְשִׁין בְּכַרְמַיָּא וְאוֹכְלִין בְּזֵיתַיָּא — אֲרִיךְ אוֹ לָא אֲרִיךְ? (סוכה מד,ב ורש"י שם)

and the inhabitants of the cities come [during the Sabbatical year] and hoe in the vineyards and eat olives [as payment] — is [this] proper or improper?

* This usage is also found in Biblical Aramaic in the pasuk לָא אֲרִיךְ לַנָא לְמֶחֱזֵא (עזרא ד:יד).

אָרִיס; אֲרִיסָא*

a tenant-farmer (who cultivates a field or an orchard and receives a certain percentage of the produce as payment)

בְּאַתְרָא דְּשָׁקֵיל אֲרִיסָא פַּלְגָא (בבא מציעא קי, א)

in a place where the tenant-farmer receives half (of the produce)

* The first form is Hebrew, and the second is Aramaic.

SEE: חוֹכֵר

אֲרַמָּאָה

an Aramean;   אֲרַמִּי; לֹא יְהוּדִי
a non-Jew (of any nationality)

לִיטַעְמֵיהּ קַפִּילָא אֲרַמָּאָה! (חולין צז,א ורש"י שם)

Let a non-Jewish cook taste it!

אָרַע (רעע אַפְעֵל: מָרַע .prt, לְאוֹרוֹעֵי .inf)

he impaired; he weakened   הֵרַע; הֶחֱלִישׁ

וְנֵימָא: "שְׁבוּעָה שֶׁחֶצְיָהּ שֶׁלִּי"! מָרַע לֵיהּ לְדִיבּוּרֵיהּ. (ב"מ ה,ב)

But let him state: "I swear that half of it (= the garment) is mine!" He would be weakening his own statement (because he previously claimed that all of it was his).

אַרְעָא (.pl אַרְעָתָא)   אֶרֶץ; קַרְקַע

land; country; ground; field; the earth

מַלְכוּתָא דְּאַרְעָא כְּעֵין מַלְכוּתָא דִּרְקִיעָא. (ברכות נח,א)

The earthly realm is like the Heavenly realm.

SEE: אוֹרַח אַרְעָא

אַשְׁבַּח (שבח אַפְעֵל: מַשְׁבַּח .prt, אַשְׁבּוֹחֵי .inf)

he improved (something);   הִשְׁבִּיחַ; שִׁפֵּר
it appreciated (in value)

אַיְיתוֹ יַתְמֵי רְאָיָה דְּאִינְהוּ אַשְׁבְּחוּ. (בבא מציעא קי,ב)

The orphans produced evidence that they had improved [the property].

אַשְׁגַּח (שגח אַפְעֵל: מַשְׁגַּח .prt)   הִשְׁגִּיחַ; שָׂם לֵב

he cared (about); he paid attention (to)

אֲמַר לֵיהּ: ... מְחוֹל לִי! לָא אַשְׁגַּח בֵּיהּ. (ברכות כח,א)

[Rabban Gamliel] said to him (= R. Yᵉhoshua): ... Forgive me! [R. Yᵉhoshua] paid no attention to him.

לְאַשְׁווֹיֵי .inf (שוי אַפְעֵל)

to make even; to level   לְהַשְׁווֹת ; לְיַשֵּׁר

דִּילְמָא אָתֵי לְאַשְׁווֹיֵי גּוּמוֹת (שבת צה,א ועוד)

so that he won't come to level depressions [in the ground on the Sabbath]

אַשְׁכַּח (שכח אַפְעֵל: מַשְׁכַּח .prt)   מָצָא

he found

אַשְׁכְּחַן ... מְנָלַן   מָצָאנוּ ... , ... מִנַּיִן לָנוּ?

We found ..., from where do we [derive] ...?

This formula poses the following *question:* Now that we have discovered the basis (usually in Scripture) for one of the cases or items under discussion, what is the basis for the other one?

אַשְׁכְּחַן סִיכָה, רְחִיצָה מְנָלַן? (יומא עו,ב)

We have found [a source for the prohibition of] annointing [on Yom Kippur], from where do we [derive the prohibition of] washing?

לְאַשְׁמוֹעִינַן (לְאַשְׁמוֹעֵי+לָן)

to inform us; to teach us   לְהַשְׁמִיעַ לָנוּ

רַב חִסְדָּא מַתְנִיתִין אֲתָא לְאַשְׁמוֹעִינַן?! (ראש השנה ח, סע"א)

Did Rav Ḥisda [merely] come to teach us [the halakha stated in] our mishna?!

SEE: אַשְׁמַע

אַשְׁמַע (שמע אַפְעֵל: מַשְׁמַע .prt, לַשְׁמַע .fut, לְאַשְׁמוֹעֵי .inf)   הִשְׁמִיעַ; לִמֵּד

"he caused to hear"; he informed; he taught

SEE: אַשְׁמְעִינַן, מַשְׁמַע, לַשְׁמְעִינַן, (ל)אַשְׁמוֹעִינַן

אַשְׁמְעִינַן (אַשְׁמַע+לָן)

he informed us; he taught us   הִשְׁמִיעַ לָנוּ

מִמִּשְׁנָה יְתֵירָה אַשְׁמְעִינַן דִּרְאִיָּה לָא קָנֵי. (בבא מציעא ב, סע"א)

Through the additional [clause in the] mishna, [the tanna] has taught us that sighting [an article without taking hold of it] does not acquire possession [of it].

SEE: אַשְׁמַע, לַשְׁמְעִינַן

אַשְׁקִי (שקי אַפְעֵל: מַשְׁקֵי .prt, לַשְׁקֵי .fut, אַשְׁקִי .imp, לְאַשְׁקוֹיֵי .inf)   הִשְׁקָה

he gave to drink

קָרִיבוּ תַּכָּא קַמֵּיהּ וְאַשְׁקְיוּהּ תְּרֵי כָּסֵי (ב"מ פו,א ע"פ כת"י)
they brought a tray before him and they gave him two goblets [of liquor to] drink

אִשְׁתּוֹמֵם/אִישְׁתּוֹמֵם (שמם אתפעל)
he was perplexed — הִשְׁתּוֹמֵם; תָּמַהּ

אִשְׁתּוֹמֵם כְּשָׁעָה חֲדָא* — תָּמַהּ כְּרֶגַע אֶחָד.
He was perplexed for a moment (by the difficulty, and then he proposed a solution).
See example in מועד קטן ג,ב ורש"י.
* This sentence is a quotation from דניאל ד:טז, even though the last word is spelled חֲדָה in the Biblical text.

אֶשְׁתָּקַד* — בְּשָׁנָה שֶׁעָבְרָה — **last year**
אֶשְׁתָּקַד הָיְתָה מְלֵאָה פֵּירוֹת תְּרוּמָה (משנה מע"ש פ"ד מ"א)
last year [the barrel] was filled with fruits of t'ruma
* The prosthetic א is prefixed for phonetic reasons. The other four letters may derive from the first two letters of the Aramaic words: שַׁתָּא, *year*, and קַדְמָאָה, *previous*. This word is used in Modern Hebrew.

אֶת
(1) According to the plain sense of Scripture, the Biblical Hebrew אֶת is usually an indicator of a direct object, which is not translated into English, e.g., אֶת ה' אֱלֹקֶיךָ תִּירָא (דברים י:כ), *you shall revere the Lord your God.** Nevertheless, אֶת is often the focus of a Talmudic דְּרָשָׁא *(= interpretation)* that amplifies the scope of the next word in the pasuk. Thus one tanna had interpreted every אֶת in the Torah as an amplification, until he reached a passage where he was unable to do so. R. Akiva, however, intervened and presented an appropriate interpretation even for that instance, as reported in the following Talmudic source:
בָּא ר' עֲקִיבָא וְדָרַשׁ: "אֶת ה' אֱלֹקֶיךָ תִּירָא" — לְרַבּוֹת תַּלְמִידֵי חֲכָמִים (פסחים כב, סע"ב ע"פ דברים י:כ)
R. Akiva came and interpreted: "You shall revere the Lord your God" — [the word] אֶת [has been written] to include [reverence towards] Torah scholars.

(2) In Mishnaic Hebrew, אֶת is sometimes used as a demonstrative pronoun meaning *that.***
לֹא נֶאֱמַר אֶלָּא "אֱלֹהֵיהֶם" — אֶת שֶׁנּוֹהֵג בּוֹ מִשּׁוּם אֱלוֹהַּ אָסוּר, וְאֶת שֶׁאֵינוֹ נוֹהֵג בּוֹ מִשּׁוּם אֱלוֹהַּ מוּתָּר. (עבודה זרה מד,ב: משנה פ"ג מ"ד ע"פ דברים יב: ב-ג)
It is specifically stated [in the Torah]: "[You must destroy] their gods" — that which [the heathen] treats as a deity is forbidden [for the Jew to use for any purpose], but that which he does not treat as a deity is permitted.
Sometimes, this אֶת is used, with a third-person suffix attached, as a demonstrative adjective meaning *that* or *the same*. The forms thus created are אוֹתוֹ, אוֹתָהּ, אוֹתָם and אוֹתָן. The suffix agrees in gender and number with the noun it precedes.
the same day — אוֹתוֹ הַיּוֹם (מכות ה,א: משנה פ"א מ"ד)
at that time — בְּאוֹתָהּ שָׁעָה (ברכות לד, רע"א: משנה ה:ג)
* Sometimes, however, אֶת is the equivalent of the preposition עִם, *with*, and is so translated by Onkelos. See בראשית לז:ב, where it occurs twice in this sense.
** This usage is found in Biblical Hebrew in the pasuk:
וְטוֹב מִשְּׁנֵיהֶם אֵת אֲשֶׁר עֲדֶן לֹא הָיָה (קהלת ד:ג).

אַתְּ*/אַנְתְּ — **you (m. or f.)**
אֲמַר לֵיהּ: מֵהֵיכָן אַתְּ? (פסחים סב,ב)
He said to him: Where are you from?
* (1) The use of אַתְּ as a *masculine* pronoun in the singular is common both in Mishnaic Hebrew and in Aramaic. In a few instances, this usage occurs in Biblical Hebrew, for example: וְאִם כָּכָה אַתְּ עֹשֶׂה לִּי in במדבר יא:טו.
(2) Both אַתְּ and אַנְתְּ are used in Aramaic, but אַתְּ is much more common in the Talmud, and it is always used in Targum Onkelos. Biblical Aramaic, however, consistently uses אַנְתְּ, which is spelled אנתה throughout the book of Daniel. For a full listing of independent personal pronouns in Babylonian Aramaic, see *Grammar for Gemara:* Chapter 7.2.

וְאַתְּ אָמְרַתְּ — וְאַתָּה אוֹמֵר...! — **but you say ...!**
SEE: אָמֵינָא לָךְ אֲנָא ... וְאַתְּ אָמְרַתְּ לִי

וְאַתְּ לָא תִּסְבְּרָא — וְאַתָּה אֵינְךָ סָבוּר כָּךְ?!
But do you [really] not hold it (= this opinion)?!
With this formula an amora introduces an *argument* against the halakhic position of his opponent.
אֲמַר לֵיהּ אַבָּיֵי לְרַב יוֹסֵף: וְאַתְּ לָא תִּסְבְּרָא דְּשׁוֹמֵר אֲבֵידָה כְּשׁוֹמֵר חִנָּם דָּמֵי?! (בבא קמא נו, סע"א)
Abbayé said to Rav Yosef: But do you [really] not hold that a person who minds a lost article is [treated] like an unpaid guardian?!
SEE: (וְ)תִסְבְּרָא

אֲתָא (אתי*: אָתֵי .prt, לֵיתֵי .fut, תָּא .imp, לְמֵיתֵי .inf)
(1) בָּא — **he came; it came (to teach)**
אֲתָא לְקַמֵּיהּ דְּרַב (בבא מציעא כב,ב ועוד)
he came before Rav (for a halakhic ruling)
קְרָא לְמַאי אֲתָא? (פסחים צו,ב ועוד)
What did the pasuk come [to teach]?
(2) נִלְמַד — **it was derived**
For an example, see אַתְיָא.
* For the full conjugation of this verb, see *Grammar for Gemara:* Chapter 4, Verb 14.
SEE: אֲתָאן, אֲתוּ, אָתֵי, אַתְיָא, אַתְיָא, אַתְיָא מִבֵּינַיְיא, אָתֵית, תָּא, הוֹאִיל וְאַתָא לִידָן נֵימָא בֵּיהּ מִילְּתָא, כִּי אֲתָא ר' ..., תֵּיתֵי

אֲתָאן (אתי) 1st pers. pl. — בָּאנוּ — **we came**
SEE: אֲתָא

אֲתָאן לְ-
בָּאנוּ לְ- — **we have come to; we have reached**
This term indicates that one of the clauses in the

mishna or baraitha that the Talmud is discussing is compatible with only one side of a controversy between tannaim or that the scope of the clause is limited to certain circumstances. Usually, this comment refers to a later clause (סיפא) that is found to be of different authorship from that of the first clause (רישא). The Talmud considers such a split authorship unsatisfactory.

ברייתא: שבח — מזיק נותן כשעת הנזק.
תלמוד: מני? ר׳ ישמעאל היא .... אימא סיפא: כחש — כשעת העמדה בדין. אתאן לר׳ עקיבא! ... רישא ר׳ ישמעאל, וסיפא ר׳ עקיבא?! (בבא קמא לד,א)

BARAITHA: [Where there is subsequent] improvement [of the damaged property] — the offender pays compensation according to [its value at] the time of the damage.

TALMUD: [In accordance with] whose [opinion is this halakha]? It is R. Yishmael's .... Take note of the latter clause: [Where there is subsequent] depreciation — [he pays] according to [its value at] the time of [the case's] being brought to court. [With this halakha] we have come to [the opinion of] R. Akiva! Is the first clause [according to] R. Yishmael, and the latter clause [according to] R. Akiva?!

SEE: אתאן, סיפא אתאן ל־, רישא ר׳ ... וסיפא ר׳ ...

אתאן לתנא קמא באנו לתנא הראשון.

We have come [back] to the first tanna.

The Talmud makes this comment with regard to a statement in a baraitha. (1) The baraitha stated a halakha in the name of one tanna (the תנא קמא). (2) It stated a dissenting halakhic opinion of a second tanna. (3) A halakha is stated in the baraitha anonymously. The Talmud's comment, *"we have come back to the first tanna,"* now declares that this anonymous statement is *a resumption of the first tanna's utterance* — not a continuation of the second tanna's words.

ברייתא: (1) חמץ — בין לפני זמנו בין לאחר זמנו — עובר עליו בלאו ... דברי ר׳ יהודה. (2) ר׳ שמעון אומר: חמץ לפני זמנו ולאחר זמנו אינו עובר עליו בלא כלום ... (3) ומשעה שאסור באכילה אסור בהנאה.
תלמוד: אתאן לתנא קמא. (פסחים כח, סע״א־רע״ב ורש״י שם)

BARAITHA: (1) Hametz — both before its time (= from noon until darkness on the 14th of Nisan) and after its time (= after Pesah if it had been possessed by a Jew during Pesah) — is subject to the Biblical prohibition [of eating]. [This is] the opinion of R. Y"huda. (2) R. Shim'on says: Hametz — both before and after its time — is not subject to the prohibition at all ... (3) And from the time eating is forbidden, benefiting [from it] is forbidden.

TALMUD: We have come back to the first tanna (= R. Y"huda, so that the last clause that equates the time of the eating prohibition with the benefiting prohibition means that R. Y"huda forbids benefiting from hametz even without eating it from noon before Pesah).

אתה אומר ... או אינו אלא ...

Do you say ..., or [perhaps] it is really ...?

This formula is used frequently in Midrash halakha. After quoting one Biblical interpretation, the Midrash asks whether that interpretation or an alternative interpretation is in fact the correct one. Ultimately, the first interpretation is chosen.

"עין תחת עין" — ממון. אתה אומר ממון — או אינו אלא עין ממש? (בבא קמא פג, סע״ב ע״פ שמות כא:כד)

"An eye for an eye" [means] monetary compensation. Do you say [it means] monetary compensation, or [perhaps] it is really an eye?

אתו prt. pl. (אתי) קאתו (= קא+אתו)

they are coming הם באים

בהדי הדדי קאתו (שבת צט,ב) *they come simultaneously*

SEE: אתא

לאתויי

SEE: אייתי

אתון* אתם

you (m. pl.)

אתון מהתם מתניתו לה; אנן מהכא מתנינן לה. (תענית ז,ב)

You derive it from there (= that pasuk); we derive it from here.

* For a full listing of independent personal pronouns in Babylonian Aramaic, see *Grammar for Gemara:* Chapter 7.2.

אתחיל (תחל אפעל: מתחיל .prt, אתחולי .inf)

he began התחיל

אתחולי בפורענותא לא מתחלינן. (בבא בתרא יד, סע״ב)

We do not begin with punishment.

אתי prt. (אתי: אתיא .f.s); קאתי (קא+אתי)

he/it is coming הוא בא

גירושין דלרחוקה קאתי ... קידושין דלקרובה קאתי (גיטין עד,א)

divorce, which comes to send her away (from her husband) ... marriage, which comes to bring her close

SEE: אתא

אתיא prt. f.s. (אתי)

she comes; it is derived באה; נלמדת

This word is used to introduce a גזרה־שוה analogy.

אתיא "לחם" — "לחם". כתיב הכא: "לחם עוני", וכתיב התם: "והיה באכלכם מלחם הארץ." מה להלן משלכם, אף כאן משלכם. (פסחים לח,א ע״פ דברים טז:ג; במדבר טו:יט)

[The halakhic definition of] "bread" [here] is derived [from] "bread" [elsewhere]. Here (= regarding matsa on Pesah) it is written: "the bread of affliction," while there (= regarding setting aside halla) it is written: "and it will be when you will eat of the bread of the land." Just as there [halla must be] from your own

[property], here too [matza must be] your own.
SEE: אַתָא

אַתְיָא מִבֵּינַיְיא נִלְמֶדֶת מִבֵּין שְׁנֵיהֶם.
It is derived from [a combination of] the two of them.
For an example — see ביצה כ,א.
SEE: בִּנְיַן אָב ,(הַ)צַּד הַשָּׁוֶה שֶׁבָּהֶן

אַתֵית (אתי) בָּאתָ 2nd pers. m.s. **you came**
For an example — see הַשְׁתָּא דַּאֲתֵית לְהָכִי.
SEE: אַתָא

אַתְלִי (תלי אַפְעֵל)
הֶאֱחִיז (אֵשׁ); הִדְלִיק; הִבְעִיר **he lit; he kindled**
אַדְּשִׁימְשָׁא בְּרֵישׁ דִּיקְלֵי, אַתְלוּ שְׁרָגָא! (שבת לה,ב ורש"י שם)
When the sun is at the top of the palm trees, light the lamp!

אַתְמוֹהֵי inf. (תמה אַפְעֵל: מַתְמַהּ prt.)
הַתְמֵהַּ **"wonder"; "express astonishment"**

אַתְמוֹהֵי קָא מַתְמַהּ* הַתְמֵהַּ מַתְמִיהַּ
he is really expressing astonishment; he really is asking a rhetorical question
אַתְמוֹהֵי קָא מַתְמַהּ: "אֶכְתּוֹב לוֹ רוּבֵּי תּוֹרָתִי?!" (גיטין ס, רע"ב ע"פ הושע ח:יב)
[God] is really asking a rhetorical question: "Shall I write most of my Torah for him (= the Jewish people)?!" (No! Most of the Torah is to remain oral.)
* The participle מַתְמַהּ is strengthened by קָא and by the absolute infinitive אַתְמוֹהֵי. See note under אַפְּקַר.
SEE: (בְּ)אַתְמִיהָה, קָא

אִתְּמַר SEE: אִיתְּמַר

אַתְנִי (תני אַפְעֵל: מַתְנֵי prt. ,אַתְנוּיֵי inf.)
(1) הִשְׁנָה; לִמֵּד **he taught (mishna); he transmitted (the text of a halakha)**
מַתְנִיתִין נַמִּי אִיפְּכָא אַתְנְיוּהָ! (בבא קמא צו, סע"ב)
[As for] our mishna — they also taught it in reverse (= with the names of the tannaim transposed)!

(2) הִתְנָה **he stipulated**
וְהָכִי אַתְנוּ בַּהֲדָדֵיהוּ: אִי מִינָּן מַלְכֵי, מִנַּיְיכוּ הַפַּרְכֵי; אִי מִנַּיְיכוּ מַלְכֵי, מִינָּן הַפַּרְכֵי. (עבודה זרה ח,ב)
And so they stipulated with one another: If the kings will be from us, the governors will be from you; if the kings will be from you, the governors will be from us.
* For the full conjugation of this verb, see *Grammar for Gemara*: Chapter 4, Verb 13.
SEE: אַקְרֵי, מַתְנֵי, תְּנָא (and its second example)

אִתְעֲבִיד SEE: אִיתְעֲבִיד

אַתְקֵין (תקן אַפְעֵל) הִתְקִין **he established; he instituted (a Rabbinic enactment)**
אַתְקֵין ר' אַבָּהוּ בְּקֵיסָרִי. (ראש השנה לד, סע"א)
R. Abbahu instituted in Caesarea [the order of blowing the shofar on Rosh HaShana].
SEE: תַּקֵּין

אַתְקָפְתָּא
אַתְקָפָה; קֻשְׁיָא **objection; refutation**
סָלְקָא דַּעְתָּךְ אָמִינָא כְּאַתְקָפְתָּא דְּרַב שִׁישָׁא בְּרֵיהּ דְּרַב אִידִי. (חגיגה ט,ב)
You would have thought [the halakha is] in accordance with the objection of Rav Shisha, the son of Rav Idi.
SEE: מַתְקִיף

אַתְרָא (אַתַר* abs.) מָקוֹם **place; locality**
מָר כִּי אַתְרֵיהּ, וּמָר כִּי אַתְרֵיהּ. (פסחים ג,א ושי"נ)
One authority [is speaking] according to [the practice in] his locality, while the other [is speaking] according to [the practice in] his locality.
* The phrase בְּכָל אֲתַר וַאֲתַר appears in the special *Kaddish* that is recited after Torah study. In Modern Hebrew אֲתַר means *site*, and the verb אִתֵּר means *localized* or *located*.
SEE: לְאַלְתַּר

אַתְרֵי (תרי אַפְעֵל) הִתְרָה
he warned (the accused just before the crime)
אַתְרוּ בֵּיהּ מַלְקוּת, וְלָא אַתְרוּ בֵּיהּ קַטְלָא. (סנהדרין ט, רע"א)
They warned him about [the punishment of] lashes, but they did not warn him about capital punishment.
SEE: הַתְרָאָה

אִתְּתָא SEE: אִיתְּתָא

ב

בֶּאֱמֶת אָמְרוּ*

in reality [the hakhamim] said

This expression is used in a mishna or a baraitha to introduce a specific statement that comprises an exception to the rule previously formulated.

וְלֹא יִקְרָא לְאוֹר הַנֵּר. בֶּאֱמֶת אָמְרוּ: הַחַזָּן רוֹאֶה הֵיכָן הַתִּינוֹקוֹת קוֹרְאִים ... (שבת יא, סע״א: משנה פ״א מ״ג)

And one may not read by the light of a candle (on the night of the Sabbath). In reality [the hakhamim said: The supervisor may see [by candlelight] where [in the Torah] the pupils are reading ...

Statements introduced by this expression have considerable authority, as the amora R. El'asar has emphasised:

כָּל "בֶּאֱמֶת אָמְרוּ" הֲלָכָה הִיא.** (ב״מ ס,א ורש״י ושטמ״ק שם)

Every [statement that is introduced by] "in reality they said" is a halakhic norm.

* In some instances, e.g., משנה בבא מציעא פ״ד מ״א, the word אָמְרוּ is missing, but the meaning of the expression is the same. See also the text quoted in the next note.

** According to Rav Hai Gaon and the *Arukh*, the text reads כָּל "בֶּאֱמֶת" הֲלָכָה לְמֹשֶׁה מִסִּינַי הִיא, *Every [statement that is introduced by] "in reality" is a halakha transmitted to Moshe from Sinai.*

בָּאנוּ לְמַחְלוֹקֶת

we have come to the [issue in] dispute [between the tannaim] ...

The halakha regarding the case now under consideration in the Talmud depends upon the outcome of an earlier *controversy* between two tannaim, since the same issue is at stake in both cases.

See, for example, the controversy between R. Méir and the Hakhamim in שבת ז, סע״ב.

בָּאנֵי

SEE: בֵּי בָאנֵי

בְּאַפֵּי; בְּאַפֵּי נַפְשֵׁיהּ

SEE: אַפֵּי

בָּבָא (pl. בָּבֵי)

(1) פֶּתַח **gate**

וְקָאֵי אַבָּבָא (בבא מציעא מט, סע״א)

and he was standing at the gate

(2) מִשְׁפָּט **clause (in a mishna or baraitha)**

בָּבָא דְרֵישָׁא ... בָּבָא דְסֵיפָא (שבת ג, רע״א)

the first clause (in the mishna) ... the last clause

(3) שַׁעַר; חֵלֶק **section; volume (of a book)**

The first three tractates of *Seder N*e*zikin*, which originally comprised a single tractate, are named בָּבָא קַמָּא, בָּבָא מְצִיעָא, and בָּבָא בָּתְרָא, *the first section, the second section*, and *the last section*, respectively. Similarly, in the Tosefta only, the tractate *Kelim* in *Seder T*e*haroth* is divided into three parts that are named בָּבָא קַמָּא, בָּבָא מְצִיעָא, and בָּבָא בָּתְרָא.

בְּבַת* אַחַת **at once; together**

לֹא כָל גּוּפוֹ בְּבַת אַחַת אֶלָּא אֵבֶר אֵבֶר. (שבת מ, רע״א)

[He may] not [wash] his whole body at once but limb by limb.

* The literal meaning of בַּת in this expression is obscure.

בְּגַוֵּהּ/בְּגַוֵּוהּ/בְּגַוַּייהוּ

SEE: (בְּ)גוֹ

בְּדוּתָא בְּדוּי **an invention; a mistake**

SEE: בְּרוּתָא

בָּדַח (בדח: בָּדֵח .prt)

שָׂמַח **he was cheerful; he rejoiced**

מִקַּמֵּי דְפָתַח ..., אָמַר מִילְּתָא דִבְדִיחוּתָא וּבָדְחִי רַבָּנַן. (שבת ל,ב)

Before [Rabba] would begin [his lecture] ..., he would say something cheerful, and the scholars would rejoice.

* In Modern Hebrew, a בְּדִיחָה is a *joke*.

בְּדִידִי

בְּשֶׁלִּי; בִּי עַצְמִי **in my [case]; with me myself**

בְּדִידִי הֲוָה עוּבְדָא בִּי עַצְמִי הָיָה הַמַּעֲשֶׂה.

The incident happened with me myself. (= I myself participated in the incident.)

For an example — see בבא מציעא מט, סע״א ורש״י שם.

בְּדִיל[1] (בדל) pass. prt.

בָּדֵל; פּוֹרֵשׁ **keeping aloof; abstaining**

חָמֵץ — לָא בְּדִיל מִינֵּיהּ (פסחים יא,א)

[as for] hametz — one does not abstain from it (easily, because it is permitted most of the year)

בְּדִיל[2] (בְּ+דִי+ל) בְּשֶׁל; בִּשְׁבִיל; בַּעֲבוּר

on account of; because of; for the sake of

בְּדִיל רַבָּה אָכִיל תַּלְמִידָא (יומא עה,ב* ורש״י שם; ע׳ ר״ח שם)

because of the teacher the student eats

* This is the only passage in the Talmud where this word occurs, but it is common in the Targumim and elsewhere.

בְּדִין **logical; proper**

SEE: (בְּ)דִין

בְּדִיעֲבַד

SEE: דִּיעֲבַד

בְּדַק (בדק: בָּדֵיק .prt)

(1) בָּדַק; נִסָּה — **he searched; he examined; he tested**

אֲמַר רַב פָּפָּא: בָּדֵיק לַן רָבָא. (עירובין נא, סע"א ורש"י שם וש"נ)

Rav Pappa said: Rava was testing us (and asked a question, which I answered).

(2) הִגִּיהַּ — **he repaired; he added as a correction**

בַּדְקַהּ לֵוִי בְּמַתְנִיתֵיהּ (יבמות י, סע"א; ב"מ מח, סע"א)*

Levi added it as a correction to his baraitha

* This explanation is given by Rashi in his commentaries on both of these Talmudic passages. Compare it with the next entry. The Ramban, however, in his commentary on the passage in בבא מציעא, understood the verb בַּדְקַהּ to mean *he searched for it*. See also the רש"ש and דקדוקי סופרים on that passage.

בֶּדֶק הַבַּיִת* — **repair of the Beth HaMikdash**

קָדְשֵׁי בֶּדֶק הַבַּיִת (סנהדרין מז,א)

donations dedicated for the repair of the Beth HaMikdash (as opposed to those that are dedicated to the altar as sacrifices, which are termed קָדְשֵׁי מִזְבֵּחַ)

* See וְהֵם יְחַזְּקוּ אֶת בֶּדֶק הַבַּיִת (מלכים ב יב:ז ורד"ק שם).

בְּדַר (בדר: בָּדַר .prt) פִּזֵּר — **he scattered**

בַּדַּר (בדר פָּעֵל: מְבַדַּר .prt) פִּזֵּר — **he scattered**

אִי בָּדְרִי לַהּ סַמָּא (חולין נד,א ורש"י שם)

if they scatter medicine over it

בַּהֲדֵי עִם — **with; in the presence of**

לְעוֹלָם לִישַׁתֵּף אֱינִישׁ נַפְשֵׁיהּ בַּהֲדֵי צִיבּוּרָא. (ברכות ל, רע"א)

A person should always associate himself with the community.

This preposition is frequently used with personal–pronoun suffixes, especially in these forms:*

בַּהֲדֵיהּ	עִמּוֹ	with him/it (m.s.)
בַּהֲדַהּ	עִמָּהּ	with her/it (f.s.)
בַּהֲדַיְיהוּ	עִמָּהֶם	with them

* For a table of all the forms, see *Grammar for Gemara:* Chapter 7.326.

SEE: לַהֲדֵי

בַּהֲדֵי ד- עִם שֶׁ- — **while**

בַּהֲדֵי דְאָזְלוּ (בבא קמא ג,ב) — *while they were moving*

בַּהֲדֵי הֲדָדֵי זֶה עִם זֶה — **with each other; together; simultaneously**

אִלּוּ עָבֵיד שְׁתֵּי אָבוֹת בַּהֲדֵי הֲדָדֵי (בבא קמא ב,א)

if he performs two principal [labors] simultaneously

SEE: הֲדָדֵי, בְּבַת אַחַת

בְּהֶדְיָא בְּפֵירוּשׁ; מְפֹרָשׁ; בְּגָלוּי

clearly; explicitly; openly; directly

תַּנָּא מִילְּתָא דִכְתִיבָא בְּהֶדְיָא קָתָנֵי; דְּאָתְיָא מִדְּרָשָׁא לָא קָתָנֵי. (בבא מציעא צח, סע"א־רע"ב)

The tanna states the matter that is written explicitly [in the Torah]; he does not state that which is derived through an interpretation.

בּוֹ בַּיּוֹם* — **on that very day**

כָּל הֵיכָא דְאָמְרִינַן "בּוֹ בַּיּוֹם", הַהוּא יוֹמָא הֲוָה. (ברכות כח,א וראה משנה סוטה פ"ה מ"ב־מ"ה)

Wherever we say (= use the expression) "on that very day," it was that day (on which R. El'azar b. Azaria was installed as Nasi).

* Literally: *on it, on the day.* The pronoun suffix וֹ–, *it*, anticipates the noun יוֹם, *day*, like the Biblical Aramaic suffix ה ֵ in בֵּהּ זִמְנָא, *at that time*, in דניאל ג:ז.

בּוֹגֶרֶת* f. — **an adult young woman**

This term refers to a girl who has reached the age of twelve and one-half years and has attained maturity and adulthood according to Jewish law.

For an example — see כתובות מח, סע"ב ע"פ דברים כב:כג.

* In Modern Hebrew, this term often means *a graduate.* The masculine form is בּוֹגֵר.

SEE: נַעֲרָה

בּוּקֵי סְרִיקֵי

כַּדִּים רֵקִים — **"empty vessels"; absurd opinions**

לָא תִתְלוּ בֵּיהּ בּוּקֵי סְרִיקֵי! (חולין נ, סע"א־רע"ב ורש"י שם)

Don't attribute absurd opinions to him!

SEE: סְרַק, סְרִיק

בּוּרְכָא/בּוּרְכְתָא בּוּרוּת; דְּבַר בּוּרוּת

ignorance; statement without foundation

This term is used by Rava to express his rejection of halakhoth proposed by Rav Naḥman b. Ḥisda in כתובות סג,ב שבועות יב, רע"ב and חולין פח,ב.

See Rashi on all three passages and the *Arukh* s.v. ברך.

בְּטֵיל (בטל: בְּטִילָן .pass. prt)

בָּטַל — **it was invalidated; it was abolished; it was neutralised**

מִית קֵיסָר וּבְטֵיל גְּזֵירְתֵיהּ (שבת לג,ב)

the emperor has died, and his decree has been abolished

בְּטִיל בְּרוּבָּא (בבא מציעא נג,א)

[the forbidden object] is neutralized by the majority

בַּטֵּיל (בטל פָּעֵל: מְבַטֵּל .prt)

בִּטֵּל — **he abolished; he nullified**

אִי אִיַּישַׁר חֵיל, אֲבַטְלִינֵיהּ! (גיטין לו, ב)

If I would have authority, I would abolish it!

בָּטְלָה דַעְתּוֹ אֵצֶל כָּל אָדָם

His intention has been voided in view of [the practice of] all people.

לָא קָבְעִי אֱינָשֵׁי סְעוּדְתַיְיהוּ עִלָּוֵיהּ ... אִי קָבַע עִלָּוֵיהּ סְעוּדְתֵיהּ, מַאי? ... בָּטְלָה דַעְתּוֹ אֵצֶל כָּל אָדָם. (ברכות לה, סע"ב וש"נ)

People do not base their meal on it (= wine, and therefore Birkath HaMazon is not recited after it) ... If one does base his meal on it, what is the halakha [regarding Birkath HaMazon]? ... His intention has been voided in view of [the practice of] all people.

בֵּי

(1) בֵּית **house of; home of; school of**

אַפִּיתְחָא דְבֵי נְשִׂיאָה (קידושין לא,א)

at the gate of the house of the Nasi

In this sense, this word is often used before nouns to produce compounds, which comprise some of the entries that follow.

(2) בֵּין **between; among**

בֵּי חָלְתָא (ב"מ כו,ב ורש"י שם) *among the sand dunes*

For another example, see בֵּי שִׁמְשֵׁי.

(3) קְבוּצָה שֶׁל **a group of**

בֵּי is used in this sense with cardinal numbers.

For examples, see בֵּי תְרֵי and בֵּי עַשְׂרָה.

SEE: דְּבֵי

בֵּי בָאנֵי/בָנֵי

בֵּית מֶרְחָץ **bathhouse**

ר' אַבָּהוּ עָל לְבֵי בָנֵי. (ברכות ס, סע"א ורש"י שם)

R. Abbahu entered a bathhouse.

בֵּי דִינָא

בֵּית דִּין **court**

לְבֵי דִינָא קָמַזְהַר רַחֲמָנָא (בבא קמא לג, סע"א)

the Torah is warning the court

בֵּי דָרֵי

גֹּרֶן **granary; threshing floor**

בְּמַכְנַשְׁתָּא דְבֵי דָרֵי עָסְקִינַן. (בבא מציעא כא,א ורש"י שם)

We are dealing with the gathering (of grain) at the threshing floor.

בֵּי כְנִישְׁתָּא

בֵּית כְּנֶסֶת **synagogue**

הֲוָה ... מְצַלֵּינָא בְּבֵי כְנִישְׁתָּא (ברכות ח,א)

I used to pray in the synagogue

בֵּי מִדְרְשָׁא

בֵּית מִדְרָשׁ **beth midrash; schoolhouse**

מָאן אָמַר הֲלָכָה בֵּי מִדְרְשָׁא? (ברכות כח, סע"א ורש"י שם)

Who stated the halakhic ruling [in] the beth midrash?

בֵּי מְסוּתָא/מַסְחוּתָא*

בֵּית מֶרְחָץ **bathhouse**

ר' חִיָּיא הֲוָה יָתֵיב בֵּי מַסְחוּתָא (קידושין לג,א וע' רש"י שם)

R. Ḥiyya was sitting [in] the bathhouse

* This noun is derived from the verb אַסְחֵי, *he washed,* which is the standard translation of רחץ in Targum Onkelos, e.g., תרגום אונקלוס לבראשית מג:לא.

בֵּי נָשָׁא

בֵּית אֲבִי הָאִשָּׁה (אַחֲרֵי מוֹת הָאָב) **the property of a (deceased) father-in-law**

אַפִּיתְחָא דְּבֵי נָשָׁא דְּרַב שִׁיזְבִי (שבת כג,ב וע' רש"י ותוס' שם)

at the gate of the property of Rav Shizbi's (deceased) father-in-law

בֵּי סַדְיָא

מְרַאֲשׁוֹת*; כַּר (תַּחַת הָרֹאשׁ) **(that which is) underneath the head; pillow**

לָא מְזַגֵּינָא רֵישִׁי אַבֵּי סַדְיָא (שבת קיט, רע"א ע"פ כת"י)

I do not place my head on the pillow

* Targum Onkelos renders the Hebrew word מְרַאֲשֹׁתָיו as איסדוחי in בראשית כח:יא.

בֵּי עַשְׂרָה

עֲשָׂרָה; קְבוּצָה שֶׁל עֲשָׂרָה; מִנְיָן שֶׁל עֲשָׂרָה **ten; group of ten (people); minyan**

הֲווֹ מְכַנְּפִי בֵּי עַשְׂרָה בְּשַׁבְּתָא דְרִגְלָא וּמְצַלּוּ (ברכות ל,א)

they would gather together a minyan on the Sabbath of the festival and pray

בֵּי־רַב*/בֵּי־רַבָּנַן

בֵּית מִדְרָשׁ **beth midrash**

יָתֵיב תַּרְתֵּי סְרֵי שְׁנִין בְּבֵי רַב (כתובות סב, סע"ב)

[R. Akiva] sat (and studied) twelve years in the beth midrash

* In some instances, however, בֵּי רַב means the *school of (the amora) Rav,* as in כתובות ו, רע"א. The standard meaning is *beth midrash,* as Rashi emphasizes in his commentary on קידושין מז,ב.

SEE: בַּר בֵּי רַב

בֵּי שִׁמְשֵׁי

"בֵּין הַשְּׁמָשׁוֹת"; כְּנִיסַת הַשַּׁבָּת **the onset of the Sabbath**

כָּל בֵּי שִׁמְשֵׁי הֲוָה אָתֵי לְבֵיתֵיהּ (כתובות קג,א וע' ברש"י שם)

every [week at] the onset of the Sabbath he would come to his house

בֵּי תְרֵי

שְׁנַיִם; קְבוּצָה שֶׁל שְׁנַיִם **two; pair**

קַבְּלֵיהּ עֲלֵיהּ כְּבֵי תְרֵי (סנהדרין כג,א)

he has accepted [the testimony of] him upon himself like [the testimony of] two [witnesses]

בֵּינֵי

בֵּין **between; among**

ר' אַמֵּי וְר' אַסִּי ... לָא הֲווֹ מְצַלּוּ אֶלָּא בֵּינֵי עַמּוּדֵי הֵיכָא דַּהֲווֹ גָּרְסִי. (ברכות ח,א וע' רש"י שם; ושם ל,ב)

R. Ammi and R. Assi ... would only pray between the pillars (of the beth midrash) where they studied.

בֵּינֵי־בֵּינֵי/בֵּינֵי־וּבֵינֵי

בֵּינְתַיִם; בֵּינֵיהֶם **in the meantime; in between**

דִּלְמָא אַפְסְקָה לַהּ שְׂכִירוּת בֵּינֵי בֵּינֵי (בבא מציעא צח,ב)

perhaps the rental in between (the two borrowings) has interrupted it

בֵּינַיְיא

בֵּין שְׁנֵיהֶם **between the two of them**

SEE: אָתְיָא מִבֵּינַיְיא

בֵּינַיְיהוּ

בֵּינֵיהֶם **between them**

For examples — see אִיכָּא בֵּינַיְיהוּ and מַאי בֵּינַיְיהוּ.

בֵּיעֲתָא (pl. בֵּיעֵי) בֵּיצָה **egg**

אֲפִילוּ בֵּיעֲתָא בְכוּתְחָא, לָא לִישְׁרֵי אִינִישׁ בִּמְקוֹם רַבֵּיהּ. (כתובות ס,ב)

Even [a case as obvious as eating] an egg together with a milk product, [a person] should not rule as permissible in his teacher's jurisdiction.

בִּיעֲתוּתָא בְּעָתָה; פַּחַד **fright; fear**

מִשּׁוּם בִּיעֲתוּתָא דִגְמַלִּים אוֹרְחָא הִיא (פסחים ג, סע"א)

on account of the fear of [falling off] camels, it is normal [for women to ride in a more secure fashion]

SEE: בְּעִית

בִּישָׁא (abs. בִּישׁ; f. בִּישְׁתָא, f. abs. בִּישָׁא)

רַע **bad; evil**

עֵסֶק בִּישׁ* (בבא קמא צט, סע"ב ורש"י שם) *a bad business*

* This expression is used in Modern Hebrew to mean a *disastrous affair or a fiasco.*

SEE: לִישָּׁנָא בִּישָׁא, עֵינָא בִּישָׁא

בִּישׁוּ/בִּישׁוּת רוֹעַ; בְּרוֹעַ

evil; wickedness; [with] displeasure

חֲדַר חַזְיֵיהּ לְרִ׳ אֱלִיעֶזֶר בִּישׁוּת. (מכות ה,ב ועוד ורש"י שם)

Thereupon he (= Resh Lakish) looked upon R. Eliezer with displeasure.

בַּיִת (constr. בֵּית), **בֵּיתָא*** (constr. בֵּי)

house; school; *Beth HaMikdash*

For examples, see the entries that follow.

* The first form is Hebrew, and the second is Aramaic.

SEE: בְּדֶק הַבַּיִת, בַּעַל הַבַּיִת, בֵּי, דְּבֵי

בֵּית הַפְּרַס SEE: פְּרַס

בֵּית עוֹלָמִים*

"the eternal house"; the *Beth HaMikdash*

בִּשְׁלֹשָׁה מְקוֹמוֹת שָׁרְתָה שְׁכִינָה עַל יִשְׂרָאֵל: בְּשִׁילֹה, וְנוֹב וְגִבְעוֹן, וּבֵית עוֹלָמִים. (זבחים קיח,ב)

The Divine Presence rested on Israel in three places: in Shilo, Nov-Giv'on, and [in] the Beth HaMikdash (in Jerusalem).

* In one instance in the Tosefta (ברכות פ"ג הכ"ד), the same expression means *a cemetery* — like the Aramaic בֵּית עָלְמִין, the next entry. Both the Aramaic בֵּית עָלְמִין and the Hebrew בֵּית עוֹלָם are used in Modern Hebrew in that sense.

בֵּית עָלְמִין בֵּית קְבָרוֹת **cemetery**

שְׁאֵילִית ... בְּבֵית עָלְמִין דְּהוּצָל (סנהדרין יט,א)*

I asked ... in the cemetery of Hutzal

* See, however, the comment of מהרש"ל there.

בֵּיתָהּ

her house; marital relations with her husband; her private parts

אֲסוּרָה לְבֵיתָהּ (סוטה ב,א: משנה פ"א מ"ב)

she is forbidden to [have] marital relations with her husband

בֵּיתוֹ **his house; his wife**

"בֵּיתוֹ" זוֹ "אִשְׁתּוֹ". (יומא ב,א: משנה פ"א מ"א)

"His house" means "his wife."

SEE: דְּבֵיתְהוּ, אַנְשֵׁי בֵּיתוֹ

מִבֵּיתוֹ

out of his own pocket; from his money

מְשַׁלֵּם מִבֵּיתוֹ. (משנה שקלים פ"ה מ"ד)

He must pay out of his own pocket.

בִּכְדֵי **within [the amount or time] needed ...**

בִּכְדֵי אֲכִילַת פְּרַס (ברכות לז,ב ועוד)

within [the time] needed to eat half [a loaf]

SEE: כְּדֵי

בִּכְדִי*

לְחִנָּם; לְלֹא צֹרֶךְ **for nothing; needlessly**

אַטְרוֹחֵי בֵּי דִינָא בִּכְדִי, לָא מַטְרְחִינַן. (בבא קמא כט, רע"ב)

We do not trouble the court needlessly.

* The expression לֹא בִּכְדִי, *not for nothing (but for a very good reason)*, is used in Modern Hebrew.

SEE: כְּדִי

בַּל **not**

This Hebrew word appears in the Talmud, chiefly as a substitute for לא in quotations of Biblical prohibitions.*

עוֹבֵר מִשּׁוּם "בַּל יֵרָאֶה" וּ"בַל יִמָּצֵא" (פסחים ה,ב ע"פ "לא יֵרָאֶה" בשמות יג:ז ו"לא יִמָּצֵא", שם יב:יט)

He is in violation of the prohibition "[ḥametz] shall not be seen" and "it shall not be found."

* It sometimes occurs in the Biblical text itself, for example in בַּל תַּנִיחֵנִי לְעֹשְׁקָי (תהלים קיט:קכא).

בְּלָא גַבְרֵי "בְּלֹא אֲנָשִׁים"; בְּלִי מוֹסְרִים בִּשְׁמָם

"without people"; without [intermediary] scholars (who transmitted the halakha in the name of the original authors)

וְהָאָמַר רַב חִיָּיא בַּר אַשִׁי אָמַר רַב: הֲלָכָה כְּרִ׳ יְהוּדָה, וְרַב חָנָן בַּר אַמִּי אָמַר שְׁמוּאֵל: הֲלָכָה כְּרִ׳ שִׁמְעוֹן?! וְרַב חִיָּיא בַּר אַבִין מַתְנֵי בְּלָא גַבְרֵי: רַב אָמַר הֲלָכָה כְּרִ׳ יְהוּדָה, וּשְׁמוּאֵל אָמַר הֲלָכָה כְּרִ׳ שִׁמְעוֹן?! (שבת קיא, רע"ב ורש"י שם)

But did Rav Ḥiyya b. Ashi not say [that] Rav said: The halakha is in accordance with R. Yehuda, and Rav Ḥanan b. Ammi said quoting Shemuel: The halakha is in accordance with R. Shim'on?! And R. Ḥiyya b. Abin teaches it without [intermediary] scholars: Rav said: The halakha is in accordance with R. Yehuda, and Shemuel said: The halakha is in accordance with R. Shim'on?!

בִּלְבַד **only; exclusively**

רִ׳ טַרְפוֹן אוֹמֵר: אֵין מַדְלִיקִין אֶלָּא בְשֶׁמֶן זַיִת בִּלְבַד. (שבת כד,ב: משנה פ"ב מ"ב)

R. Tarfon says: We may not kindle [the Sabbath lights] except with olive oil exclusively.

וּבִלְבַד שֶׁ- **but only if; provided that**

נָתַן עָלֶיהָ נֶסֶר שֶׁהוּא רָחָב אַרְבָּעָה טְפָחִים — כְּשֵׁרָה, וּבִלְבַד שֶׁלֹּא יִישַׁן תַּחְתָּיו. (סוכה יד,א: משנה פ"א מ"ו)

[If] one placed a board that is four handbreadths wide on it (= the sukka), [the sukka] is valid provided that he does not sleep under it (= the board).

בְּמַאי

SEE: (בְּ)מַאי

בַּמֶּה

SEE: (בְּ)מָה

בֶּן דַּעַת **an intelligent being**

נָפַל לְתוֹכוֹ בֶּן דַּעַת — פָּטוּר. (בבא קמא נד, רע"ב ע"פ כת"י)

[If] an intelligent being fell into it (= a pit), [the person who dug it] is exempt [from paying damages].

בֶּן זוּג; בַּר זוּגָא* **partner; mate**

הָיוּ כוֹתְבִין עַל קַרְשֵׁי הַמִּשְׁכָּן לֵידַע אֵיזֶה בֶּן זוּגוֹ. (שבת קג, א: משנה פי"ב מ"ג)

They used to write on the boards of the Mishkan (= Tabernacle), so that they would know which [board] is its mate.

* The first expression is Hebrew, and the second is Aramaic.

SEE: זוּג

בֶּן חוֹרִין (pl. בְּנֵי חוֹרִין)**; בַּר חוֹרִין*** (pl. בְּנֵי חֲרֵי)

"son of noblemen"; a free man

See example under the plural, בְּנֵי חוֹרִין.

* The first form is Hebrew, and the second is Aramaic.

SEE: חוֹרִין

בֶּן יוֹמוֹ (pl. בְּנֵי יוֹמָן)

within its [twenty-four-hour] day; less than one-day old

שׁוֹר בֶּן יוֹמוֹ קָרוּי "שׁוֹר". (בבא קמא סה,ב)

An ox within its [first] day is [already] called "an ox."

SEE: בַּת יוֹמָא

בֶּן קַיָּימָא

capable of living; viable יָכוֹל לְהִתְקַיֵּים

נִתְכַּוֵּין ... לִנְפָלִים וְהָרַג בֶּן קַיָּימָא — פָּטוּר. (בבא קמא מד,א: משנה פ"ד מ"ו)

[If] he aimed for ... non-viable infants and killed a viable [one] — he is exempt [from responsibility].

בְּנֵי חוֹרִין; בְּנֵי חֲרֵי*

(1) "sons of noblemen"; free men

"בְּנֵי חוֹרִין" — לְמַעוֹטֵי עֲבָדִים. (בבא קמא טו, רע"א ע"פ משנה שם יד, רע"ב)

[The mishna specifies] "free men" — excluding slaves.

(2) free properties

A creditor may collect his debt from property that has remained in the possession of a debtor (usually a borrower) who still owes him money.

נְהִי דְּלָא גָּבֵי מִמְּשַׁעְבְּדֵי, מִבְּנֵי חֲרֵי מִגְבָּא גָּבֵי. (ב"מ יב,ב)

Granted that [the creditor] may not collect from subjugated properties [that have been transferred to a third party], he may certainly collect from free properties.

* The first form is Hebrew, and the second Aramaic. Compare: אֶל הַזְּקֵנִים וְאֶל הַחֹרִים (מלכים א כא:ח).

SEE: נְכָסִים בְּנֵי חוֹרִין, נְכָסִים מְשׁוּעְבָּדִים, חוֹרִין, חֲרֵי

בְּנֵי

SEE: בֵּי בָאנֵי

בִּנְיַן אָב **"the building of a father"; the establishment of a prototype**

According to this rule of Biblical interpretation, one topic — or an abstraction based on the common properties shared by two or more topics — is set up as a *prototype*, in order to teach us the meaning of a term in the Torah or to apply a halakha to other comparable topics.

(1) When the prototype is one topic, the formula מָה (מָצִינוּ) ... אַף ... or the expression חֲדָא מֵחֲדָא may be used in the Talmud. In the list of thirteen rules of interpretation of R. Yishmael, this method is termed בִּנְיַן אָב מִכָּתוּב אֶחָד, *the establishment of a prototype from one pasuk.**

תָּנֵי דְּבֵי יִשְׁמָעֵאל: הוֹאִיל וְנֶאֶמְרוּ "בְּגָדִים" בַּתּוֹרָה סְתָם, וּפָרַט לְךָ הַכָּתוּב בְּאֶחָד מֵהֶן "צֶמֶר וּפִשְׁתִּים" — מָה לְהַלָּן "צֶמֶר וּפִשְׁתִּים", אַף כָּל "צֶמֶר וּפִשְׁתִּים". (שבת כו, רע"ב ועי' רש"י שם ע"פ ויקרא יג:מז)

The school of R. Yishmael teaches: Since "garments" have been mentioned in the Torah without specification, and Scripture has specified one of them for you (elsewhere) as "wool and flax" — just as there [the "garment" mentioned is one made of] "wool and flax," so all ["garments" mentioned are those made of] "wool and flax."

(2) When the prototype is a theoretical construct based upon הַצַּד הַשָּׁוֶה, *the common denominator (of two topics)* — we deal with בִּנְיַן אָב מִשְּׁנֵי כְתוּבִים, *the establishment of a prototype from two p^e^sukim.**

אַזְהָרָה מִנַּיִין? תַּלְמוּד לוֹמַר: "אֱלֹהִים לֹא תְקַלֵּל ...." אִם הָיָה אָבִיו דַּיָּין, הֲרֵי הוּא בִּכְלַל "אֱלֹהִים לֹא תְקַלֵּל"; וְאִם הָיָה אָבִיו נָשִׂיא, הֲרֵי הוּא בִּכְלַל "וְנָשִׂיא בְעַמְּךָ לֹא תָאוֹר". אֵינוֹ לֹא דַּיָּין וְלֹא נָשִׂיא — מִנַּיִין? אָמַרְתָּ: הֲרֵי אַתָּה דָּן בִּנְיַן אָב מִשְּׁנֵיהֶן: לֹא רְאִי נָשִׂיא כִּרְאִי דַּיָּין, וְלֹא רְאִי דַּיָּין כִּרְאִי נָשִׂיא ... — הַצַּד הַשָּׁוֶה שֶׁבָּהֶם שֶׁהֵן "בְּעַמְּךָ" וְאַתָּה מוּזְהָר עַל קִלְלָתָן, אַף אֲנִי אָבִיא אָבִיךָ שֶׁ"בְּעַמְּךָ" וְאַתָּה מוּזְהָר עַל קִלְלָתוֹ. (סנהדרין סו,א ע"פ שמות כב:כז)

From where [do we derive] a warning [against cursing one's father]? Scripture teaches: "You shall not curse judges ...." If his father be a judge, he is included in "You shall not curse judges"; and if his father be a ruler, he is included in "and a ruler of your people you shall not curse." [If] he be neither a judge nor a ruler, from where [do we derive a warning]? You may say [that] here you derive [the warning from] the establishment of a prototype from the two of them: A ruler is not like a judge, nor is a judge like a ruler ... — the common denominator between them is that they are "of your nation" and you are forbidden to curse them, I too include your father who is "of your nation" [so that] you are forbidden to curse him.

* Our explanation follows the opinion of Rashi in his commentary on the first example in this entry. A different explanation is presented by R. Shimshon of Chinon in his *Sefer K*e*rithoth* III:3.

בְּסִים

pleasant; tasty; sweet — **נָעִים; טָעִים**

טַעֲמֵיהּ, הֲוָה בְּסִים טוּבָא. (פסחים קז,א)

He drank [some of] it, and it was very tasty.

בְּעָא (בעי: בָּעֵי .prt, לִיבְעֵי .fut, לְמִיבְעֵי .inf)

(1) שָׁאַל — he asked

For examples, see the next three entries.

(2) בִּקֵּשׁ — he asked for; he requested

בְּעוֹ רַבָּנַן רַחֲמֵי עֲלֵיהּ וְאִתְּסֵי. (ברכות ו,א)

The hakhamim asked for mercy (= prayed) for him, and he was cured.

(3) רָצָה — he wanted; he desired

בְּעָא לְמִיסַק לְאֶרֶץ יִשְׂרָאֵל. (כתובות קי, סע"א)

He wanted to go up (= to immigrate) to Eretz Yisrael.

(4) הָיָה צָרִיךְ — he required; he needed

לָא בָּעְיָא גִיטָּא. (גיטין צא,א)

She does not need a bill of divorce [in order to remarry].

* For the full conjugation of this verb, see *Grammar for Gemara*: Chapter 4, Verb 11.

SEE: בְּעָיָא, אִי בָּעֵי, אִיבָּעִית אֵימָא, אִיבָּעֵי

בְּעָא מִינֵּיהּ

he asked him — **שָׁאַל אוֹתוֹ**

This expression introduces a *problem* that an amora posed to his teacher or his colleague.

בְּעָא מִינֵּיהּ אַבָּיֵי מֵרַבָּה: מַהוּ לְכַבּוֹת אֶת הַדְּלֵיקָה בְּיוֹם טוֹב? (ביצה כב,א)

Abbayé asked Rabba: What is [the halakhic ruling about] extinguishing a fire on a festival?

בְּעוֹ מִינֵּיהּ

they asked him — **שָׁאֲלוּ אוֹתוֹ**

This formula introduces a *problem* that was addressed to a specific amora, usually by unidentified questioners.

בְּעוֹ מִינֵּיהּ מֵרַבִּי יְהוֹשֻׁעַ בֶּן לֵוִי: מַהוּ לְהִסְתַּפֵּק מִנּוֹיֵי סוּכָּה כָּל שִׁבְעָה? (שבת כב,א)

*They asked R. Y*e*hoshua b. Levi: What is [the halakhic ruling with regard to] taking from decorations of the sukka during all seven days [of Sukkoth]?*

בָּעֵי .prt

he asks; he poses a problem — **שׁוֹאֵל**

This term introduces a *problem* that a specific amora raises before an authority who is not identified in the Talmud.

בָּעֵי רָבָא: כִּכָּר בִּשְׁמֵי קוֹרָה — צָרִיךְ סוּלָּם לְהוֹרִידָהּ אוֹ אֵין צָרִיךְ? (פסחים י,ב)

Rava poses a problem: [As for] a loaf [of hametz] on the top rafters — is one obligated [to ascend] a ladder to take it down [before Pesah] or not?

בְּעָיָא[1]* (= בְּעָיָהּ: בְּעָא + ־הּ)

he asked it — **שְׁאֵלָהּ; שָׁאַל אוֹתָהּ**

For an example — see בָּתַר דִּבְעָיָא הֲדַר פְּשָׁטָהּ.

* In this *verbal* form (which should not be confused with the noun בְּעָיָא), the final א is equivalent to a final consonantal ה in the third-person-feminine-singular suffix.

SEE: אִיבְּעֵי, מִיבְּעֵי

בְּעָיָא[2] (בְּעָיָין .pl)

a (halakhic) problem — **שְׁאֵלָה**

In a בְּעָיָא, the questioner seeks an answer to a problem about which he has a genuine doubt. Both sides of the issue are often explained in the Talmud — separated by the expression אוֹ דִלְמָא, *or perhaps*, or מִי אָמְרִינַן, *shall we say*. (In a קוּשְׁיָא, however, the questioner points out a *difficulty* with regard to a statement or an argument previously quoted in the Talmud, with a view towards refuting it.)

The issues that a בְּעָיָא seeks to clarify include:

(1) A halakhic ruling about a new case.

(2) The source or reason for a halakha.

(3) The proper interpretation or the correct wording of a tannaitic text.

וְתִפְשׁוֹט בְּעָיָא דְּרַב פָּפָּא (מכות כ,א)

and you may solve the (halakhic) problem raised by Rav Pappa

Since a בְּעָיָא is introduced by some form of the verb בעי, examples of *halakhic problems* appear in the entries בָּעֵי, אִיבַּעְיָא לְהוּ, and בְּעָא מִינֵּיהּ.

בְּעֵינָא* / בְּעֵינֵיהּ* / בְּעֵינַיְיהוּ*

בְּעֵינָא* בְּעֵינָהּ; כְּמוֹת שֶׁהִיא — **as it (f.) is; intact**

בְּעֵינֵיהּ* בְּעֵינוֹ; כְּמוֹת שֶׁהוּא — **as it (m.) is; intact**

בְּעֵינַיְיהוּ* בְּעֵינֵיהֶם; כְּמוֹת שֶׁהֵם — **as they are**

מְפָרֵר וְזוֹרֶה לָרוּחַ, אֲבָל מָטִיל לַיָּם בְּעֵינֵיהּ. (פסחים כח,א)

He must crumble [his hametz] and [only then] throw [it] to the wind, but he may cast [it] into the sea intact.

* Besides these Aramaic forms, this word also occurs in Biblical Hebrew, e.g., הַנֶּגַע עָמַד בְּעֵינָיו (ויקרא יג:ה ות"א), *the plague remained intact*, and in Talmudic Hebrew in גְּזֵלָה חוֹזֶרֶת בְּעֵינֶיהָ (ב"ק צד, רע"ב; צה,א ורש"י שם), *the stolen article must return intact*. In post-Talmudic Hebrew, this word is used without a suffix with the same meaning: בְּעַיִן (or בְּעֵין, as pronounced by many Ashkenazic Jews), e.g., in Rashi's commentary on כתובות צג,ב.

SEE: עַיִן

כִּדְבָעֵינַן לְמֵימַר לְקַמָּן
כְּמוֹ שֶׁאָנוּ רוֹצִים לוֹמַר לְפָנֵינוּ

as we are going to (lit. "want to") say later on

This expression indicates *a cross-reference* to the original halakhic text, which is quoted in the Talmud a bit further on — usually within a page or two.

בְּזוּטוֹ שֶׁל יָם וּבְשִׁלּוּלִיתוֹ שֶׁל נָהָר — אַף עַל גַּב דְּאִית בֵּיהּ סִימָן, רַחֲמָנָא שַׁרְיֵיהּ, כִּדְבָעֵינַן לְמֵימַר לְקַמָּן. (בבא מציעא כא,ב) מִנַּיִן לַאֲבֵידָה שֶׁשְּׁטָפָהּ נָהָר שֶׁהִיא מוּתֶּרֶת? דִּכְתִיב ... (שם כב,ב)

[If a lost article is found swept up] by the tide of the sea or by the flooding of a river — even if it has a mark of identification, the Torah permits [the finder to keep] it, as we are going to say later on. (One page later the Talmud quotes the halakha in the name of R. Yoḥanan.) From where [do we learn] that a lost article that a river swept up is permissible [to be kept by the finder]? As it is written [in the Torah] ...

בָּעִית pass. prt. (בעת)
frightened; afraid נִבְעַת; מְפַחֵד

גָּנַב מִשֶּׁל אָבִיו וְאָכַל בִּרְשׁוּת אָבִיו ... בָּעִית. (סנהדרין עא,א)

[If] he stole [money] from his father and ate [food he had bought with it] on his father's property ... he is afraid (to persist with such conduct on a regular basis).

SEE: בִּיעֲתוּתָא

בַּעַל[1] (pl. בְּעָלִים)
husband

SEE: בְּעָלִים

בַּעַל[2] constr. (בַּעֲלַת .f.s ; בַּעֲלֵי .m. pl)
owner/master of; possessed of; subject to

This Hebrew noun often forms a compound with the noun that immediately follows it. The more common compounds comprise some of the following entries.

בַּעַל דְּבָרִים*
plaintiff

לָאו בַּעַל/בַּעֲלַת דְּבָרִים דִּידִי אַתְּ! (בבא קמא ח, סע"ב; כתובות פא, סע"ב)

You are not my plaintiff! (= You have no standing in this dispute!)

* See (שמות כד:יד) מִי בַעַל דְּבָרִים יִגַּשׁ אֲלֵהֶם, Targum Onkelos and Rashi's commentary on that pasuk, and its interpretation in בבא קמא מו,ב.

בַּעַל דִּין
litigant; opponent (in court)

מִנַּיִן לַדַּיָּין שֶׁלֹּא יִשְׁמַע דִּבְרֵי בַּעַל דִּין קוֹדֶם שֶׁיָּבֹא בַּעַל דִּין חֲבֵירוֹ? (שבועות לא,א)

From where [do we learn that] a judge should not listen to the words of [one] litigant before his fellow litigant enters?

בַּעַל הַבַּיִת
owner of the house; landlord; owner; host; private individual; ordinary person (in contrast to a person engaged in a particular profession)

הַחֶנְוָנִי כְּבַעַל הַבַּיִת — דִּבְרֵי ר' מֵאִיר. ר' יְהוּדָה אוֹמֵר: הַחֶנְוָנִי כְּשׁוּלְחָנִי. (בבא מציעא מג,א; משנה פ"ג מ"א)

*A shopkeeper is [considered] like a private individual (hence he may not use money, which was deposited with him for safe keeping) — [this is] the opinion of R. Méir. R. Y*e*huda says: A shopkeeper is [considered] like a money-changer (hence he is allowed to use the money).*

בַּעַל חוֹב*
"an owner of a debt"; creditor; lender

אֲתָא בַּעַל חוֹב, טַרְפָהּ מִינֵּיהּ. (בבא מציעא יד,א)

A creditor came, [and he] seized it from him (as payment of his debt).

* In post-Talmudic Hebrew, this expression is often used in the opposite sense: *subject to a debt, debtor, borrower.* See, e.g.: רש"י לכתובות פו, סע"א ד"ה "פריעת בעל חוב"; רמב"ם הל' מלוה ולוה פ"א ה"ג.

בַּעֲלֵי חַיִּים* pl.
animals

צַעַר בַּעֲלֵי חַיִּים דְּאוֹרַיְיתָא. (בבא מציעא לב, רע"ב)

[The prohibition of causing] suffering to animals is of Torah authority.

* The singular, בַּעַל חַיִּים, does not occur in the Mishna or in the Talmud, but it is used in Modern Hebrew.

בְּעַל/עַל כָּרְח- נֶגֶד רְצוֹנ-
against the will of

This expression is used with personal-pronoun suffixes exclusively. The following forms are the most common ones:

against your will	בְּעַל/עַל כָּרְחָךְ
against his will	בְּעַל/עַל כָּרְחֵיהּ
against her will	בְּעַל/עַל כָּרְחָהּ
against their will	בְּעַל כָּרְחַיְיהוּ

נְקַט מִתַּרְוַיְיהוּ — מֵחַד מִדַּעְתֵּיהּ וּמֵחַד בְּעַל כָּרְחֵיהּ. (ב"מ ב,ב)

He received [money] from both of them — from one [he received it] willingly and from the other one [it was forced upon him] against his will.

בַּעַל מוּם
having a blemish; defective

שְׁחָטוֹ, וְנִמְצָא בַּעַל מוּם (פסחים עא, סע"ב: משנה פ"ו מ"ו)

[if] he slaughtered it (= the animal), and it was found to have a blemish

בַּעַל תְּשׁוּבָה
a repentant sinner

אִם הָיָה בַּעַל תְּשׁוּבָה, אַל יֹאמַר לוֹ: "זְכוֹר מַעֲשֶׂיךָ הָרִאשׁוֹנִים!" (בבא מציעא נח,ב: משנה פ"ד מ"י)

If [someone] is a repentant sinner, one should not say to him: "Remember your former deeds!"

בְּעָלִים
(1) the owner; the owners

When used in this sense, this Hebrew noun always

appears in the plural form — even though the owner may be a single individual.

מַעֲשֵׂר שֵׁנִי שֶׁאֵין דָּמָיו יְדוּעִין — פּוֹדִין אוֹתוֹ בִּשְׁלֹשָׁה לָקוֹחוֹת ..., אֲפִילּוּ אֶחָד מֵהֶם בְּעָלִים. (סנהדרין יד,ב)

A second tithe whose value is not known may be redeemed according to [the evaluation of] three dealers ..., even if one of them is the owner [himself].

The noun בְּעָלִים usually takes a plural verb, even when it is singular in meaning.*

the owner has given up hope נִתְיָאֲשׁוּ הַבְּעָלִים (ב"מ כב,א)

(2) husbands

יֵשׁ מוּתָּרוֹת לְבַעֲלֵיהֶן. (יבמות פד,א: משנה פ"ט מ"א)

Some are permitted to their husbands.

* Biblical Hebrew, however, uses a singular verb if the meaning is singular as in: וְלָקַח בְּעָלָיו וְלֹא יְשַׁלֵּם (שמות כב:י).

SEE: בַּעַל

בְּעָלְמָא בְּעוֹלָם **in the world**

Besides this literal meaning, the following two usages are often found in the Talmud:

(1) בְּדֶרֶךְ כְּלָל; בִּמְקוֹמוֹת אֲחֵרִים

in general; in other cases; elsewhere

בְּעָלְמָא דְּקָתָנֵי: מְצָאתִיהָ (בבא מציעא ב, סע"א ורש"י שם)

in other cases where [a tanna] states: I found it

(2) בִּלְבַד **merely; alone**

וּקְרָא אַסְמַכְתָּא בְּעָלְמָא (יומא עד, סע"א)

and the pasuk is merely a support

SEE: עָלְמָא

בַּעֲלַת constr. f.s. SEE: בַּעַל

בְּצִיר pass. prt. (בצר) **less**

See example under בְּצַר.

בְּצַר* (בצר: בּוֹצֵר .prt, לִבְצוֹר .inf)

he cut (grapes for harvesting)

שְׁנַיִם שֶׁבָּצְרוּ אֶת כַּרְמֵיהֶם ... (משנה דמאי פ"ו מ"ז)

two [people] who cut [grapes from] their vineyards

* This verb is Hebrew, and the next two are Aramaic.

בְּצַר (בצר: בְּצַר .act. prt, בְּצִיר .pass. prt, לְמִיבְצַר .inf)

פָּחַת **it was less; it was missing**

בְּצִיר מֵעַשְׂרָה לָאו אוֹרַח אַרְעָא. (מגילה כג,ב)

It is not proper [to have] less than ten.

בַּצַּר (בצר פַּעֵל: מְבַצַּר .prt, לְבַצּוֹרֵי .inf)

פִּחֵת **he reduced; he deducted**

אַהֲנֵי מָסוֹרֶת* לְבַצּוֹרֵי חֲדָא. (זבחים לז, סע"ב)

The accepted (Masoretic) spelling (of the word קרנת *without a* ו*, so that it could theoretically be read as a singular noun) has the effect of deducting (from the halakhic requirement) one (sprinkling of the blood of the offering on a corner of the altar).*

* See יֵשׁ אֵם לַמָּסוֹרֶת.

בַּר **outdoors; outside; the wild**

ox of the wild; wild ox שׁוֹר בָּר* (משנה כלאים פ"ח מ"ו)

אֵין תּוֹכוֹ כְּבָרוֹ (ברכות כח,א)

his inside is not like his outside (= he is insincere)

* In Modern Hebrew, חַיּוֹת בָּר means *wild animals.* It is similar to חֵיוַת בָּרָא in Biblical Aramaic (as in דניאל ד:ט) and in the Targumim (as in ת"א לויקרא כו:כב).

SEE: בָּרָא

בַּר*/לְבַר* מִ- חוּץ מִ- **outside of; except for**

כָּל פְּטוּרֵי דְשַׁבָּת פָּטוּר אֲבָל אָסוּר לְבַר מֵהָנֵי תְּלָת דְּפָטוּר וּמוּתָּר. (שבת ג, רע"א ורש"י שם)

All [occurrences of the term] פָּטוּר *with reference to the Sabbath [mean] "exempt [from punishment] yet forbidden" except for these three [cases] where [it means] "exempt [from punishment] and permissible."*

* Although this word is popularly pronounced בָּר by Ashkenazim, the vocalization בַּר is probably more correct, and it serves to distinguish בַּר from the noun בַּר, *son.*

SEE: בַּר מִינָּהּ דְּהַהִיא, בַּר מִינֵּיהּ ד-, אַבְּרַאי, בָּרַיְיתָא

לְבַר/ לְבָרָא/ לְבָרַאי חוּצָה **outside**

See example under (לְ)גָיו.

SEE: פּוּק תְּנֵי לְבָרָא

מִלְּבַר מִבַּחוּץ **from the outside**

For an example — see בבא מציעא נג, סע"א.

בַּר cnstr. (pl. בְּנֵי) בֶּן **son of**

Besides its literal sense, this construct form — like its Hebrew counterpart בֶּן — is combined with other words and expresses a variety of meanings, including: *capable of, fit for, subject to, obligated in, possessing, belonging to,* and *worthy of.* The more common compounds thus created are presented in fourteen of the next sixteen entries.

SEE: בְּרָא, בַּת

בַּר אוֹרְיָין* בֶּן תּוֹרָה **a Torah scholar**

בַּר אֲבָהָן וּבַר אוֹרְיָין (מנחות נג,א)

[he is] a son of noble ancestors, and [he is] a Torah scholar

* This expression should not be confused with בַּר אַרְיָא, which is discussed in the note on the entry אַרְיָא.

בַּר אֱינָשׁ; בַּר נָשׁ* בֶּן אָדָם **"son of man"; a human being**

לֵית דִּין בַּר אֱינָשׁ! (שבת קיב,ב ורש"י שם, וש"נ)

This is no [ordinary] human being!

* The form בַּר נָשׁ, which has entered Modern Hebrew, is common in the Palestinian Talmud but rare in the Babylonian Talmud.

בַּר אֲכִילָה (בַּת אֲכִילָה .f, בְּנֵי אֲכִילָה .m. pl)

רָאוּי לַאֲכִילָה **fit for eating; edible**

עָפָר לָאו בַּר אֲכִילָה הוּא כְּלָל; נְבֵילָה בַּת אֲכִילָה הוּא וְאַרְיָא הוּא דִּרְבִיעַ עִילָּוָהּ. (שבועות כב,ב ורש"י שם)

Dust is not edible at all; carrion is edible, but "a lion" (= a prohibition) is resting on it.

בַּר בֵּי רַב

בֶּן יְשִׁיבָה; תַּלְמִיד **[yeshiva] student; disciple**

בַּר בֵּי רַב דְּחַד יוֹמָא (חגיגה ה; סע"ב)

a student for one day (who attends lectures only occasionally and is therefore not a serious scholar)

בַּר הָכִי (בַּת הָכִי .f)

"בֶּן כָּךְ"; רָאוּי לְכָךְ; יָכוֹל **capable of this**

דְּדָחֵיל מֵרַבָּנַן הוּא גוּפֵיהּ הָוֵי רַבָּנַן; וְאִי לָאו בַּר הָכִי הוּא, מִשְׁתַּמְעָן מִילֵּיהּ כְּצוּרְבָא מֵרַבָּנַן. (שבת כג,ב ע"פ כת"י)

One who stands in awe of the ḥakhamim will himself be a ḥakham; but if he is not capable of this (= of scholarship), his words will be listened to like [those of] a Torah scholar.

בַּר זוּגָא

בֶּן זוּג **partner; mate**

SEE: בֶּן זוּג

בַּר חִיּוּבָא (בַּת חִיּוּבָא .f.s, בְּנֵי חִיּוּבָא .m. pl)

בֶּן חִיּוּב; חַיָּב בְּדָבָר

subject to obligation; obligated

גּוֹי לָאו בַּר חִיּוּבָא הוּא; יִשְׂרָאֵל בַּר חִיּוּבָא הוּא. (חולין קלה,ב)

A non-Jew is not obligated (in this mitzva); a Jew is obligated.

בַּר מִינַּהּ* דְּהַהִיא

"חוּץ מִמֶּנָּה שֶׁל הַהִיא"; חוּץ מֵהַהִיא

"except for that"; exclude that [baraitha from our discussion]

This formula is used by an amora or by the Talmud to introduce a *rejection* of a proof from a baraitha — either because the baraitha can be interpreted differently (for example, it may refer to special circumstances) or because it is not authoritative (for example, its text is faulty).

מֵת וּמְשַׁלֵּם לֵית לֵיהּ? וְלָא?! וְהָתַנְיָא: גָּנַב וְטָבַח בְּשַׁבָּת ... מְשַׁלֵּם אַרְבָּעָה וַחֲמִשָּׁה — דִּבְרֵי ר' מֵאִיר ... אָמְרִי: בַּר מִינַּהּ דְּהַהִיא, דְּהָא אִיתְּמַר עֲלַהּ ... מִשְּׁמֵיהּ דְּר' יוֹחָנָן .... בְּטוֹבֵחַ עַל יְדֵי אַחֵר! (בבא קמא עא,א)

And he (= R. Méir) does not hold that one condemned to death may also be required to pay? Does he not?! But it is stated (in a baraitha): [If a person] stole [an animal] and slaughtered [it] on the Sabbath ..., he must make the four-fold or five-fold restitution (even though he would also face the death penalty for Sabbath desecration) — [according to] the opinion of R. Méir ...! They say [in the beth midrash]: Exclude that [baraitha from our discussion], for [the following interpretation] has been stated about it ... in the name of R. Yoḥanan .... [It refers to a case] where he [had the] slaughtering [done] by another person (and so he did not really desecrate the Sabbath and he is punished only with the monetary penalty; hence there is no proof that one incurs both punishments where the death penalty is applicable as well)!

* The feminine singular suffix הַ- anticipates the pronoun הַהִיא, literally: *except for it, for that.*

SEE: בַּר מִינֵּיהּ דְּ-

בַּר מִינֵּיהּ

בֶּן מִינוֹ **one of his own kind; a person of his own status**

לָא שְׁנָא דְּקָטַל בַּר מִינֵּיהּ, וְלָא שְׁנָא דְּקָטַל דְּלָאו בַּר מִינֵּיהּ. (מכות ט,א)

It makes no difference whether he killed a person of his own status or a person not of his own status.

בַּר מִינֵּיהּ דְּ-

"חוּץ מִמֶּנּוּ שֶׁל"; חוּץ מִ-

"except for him ..."; exclude [him from our discussion]

בַּר מִינֵּיהּ דְּרַב יְהוּדָה, דְּכֵיוָן דִּמְסוּכָּן הוּא, אֲפִילּוּ בְּשַׁבָּת נַמִּי שְׁרֵי לְמֶעְבַּד לֵיהּ! (שבת לז,ב)

Exclude Rav Y^ehuda [from our discussion], for since he is dangerously ill, even on the Sabbath it is also permitted to do [this] for him!

SEE: בַּר מִינַּהּ דְּהַהִיא

בַּר מִצְוָה* (בַּת מִצְוָה .f, בְּנֵי מִצְוָה .m. pl)

בֶּן מִצְוָה **subject to the commandments; obligated by the commandments**

שְׁלִיחַ דְּבַר מִצְוָה הוּא (בבא מציעא צו, סע"א)

an agent who is obligated by the commandments (as opposed to an agent who is not Jewish)

* In post-Talmudic Hebrew, this term denotes a Jewish youth who has reached the age of thirteen and is now obligated by the commandments of Judaism.

בַּר מֶצְרָא (בְּנֵי מֶצְרָנֵי .pl)

"בֶּן הַגְּבוּל"; אָדָם שֶׁיֵּשׁ לוֹ זְכוּת קְדִימָה לִקְנוֹת נִכְסֵי שְׁכֵנוֹ

the owner of adjacent property

The person who owns the property adjacent to the property that is about to be sold has the prerogative of acquiring that property.

מִשּׁוּם דִּינָא דְּבַר מֶצְרָא מְסַלְּקִינַן לֵיהּ. (בבא מציעא קח,א)

Because of the law of the owner of adjacent property, we remove him (= the would-be purchaser).

בַּר מָתָא (בְּנֵי מָתָא .pl)

בֶּן הָעִיר **a citizen of a town**

בַּר מָתָא אַבַּר מָתָא אַחֲרִיתִי מָצֵי מְעַכֵּב. (ב"ב כא, סע"ב)

A citizen of [one] town can prevent a citizen of another town [from setting up a competing enterprise in his town].

בַּר סַמְכָא (בְּנֵי סַמְכֵי .pl)

"בֶּן סָמָךְ"; מֻסְמָךְ **a reliable person; an authority**

ר' אָבִין בַּר סַמְכָא הוּא? (קידושין מד, סע"א)

Is R. Abin an authority (in halakhic matters)?

בַּר פְּלוּגְתָּא* בֶּן מַחֲלֹקֶת

disputant; opponent (in a Talmudic dispute)

לְמַאן מוֹדֶה? לְר' עֲקִיבָא, בַּר פְּלוּגְתֵּיהּ. (בבא מציעא לז,ב)
To whom does he concede [this point]? To R. Akiva, his opponent.

* Although this compound occurs only once in the Talmud, it occurs more frequently in the commentaries and in Modern Hebrew.

SEE: פְּלוּגְתָּא

בַּר קְטָלָא (pl. בְּנֵי קְטָלָא) בֶּן מָוֶת

(1) liable to [the] death [penalty]

לָאו בַּר קְטָלָא הוּא, וְלָאו בַּר מָמוֹנָא הוּא. (סנהדרין עט,ב)
He is not liable to the death penalty, nor is he obligated to pay monetary compensation.

(2) sentenced to be executed; condemned to death

בְּעִידָּנָא דְקָא מַסְהֲדִי, גַּבְרָא בַּר קְטָלָא הוּא. (מכות ה, סע"א)
At the time they were testifying, he was [already] a man condemned to death.

בָּרָא חִיצוֹן **outside**

See example under תְּנָא בָּרָא.

SEE: בַּר

בְּרָא (abs./cnstr. בַּר, pl. בְּנֵי/ בְּנִין) בֵּן **son**

This noun is often used with personal-pronoun suffixes, creating the following forms:

my son	בְּנִי	בְּרִי/בְּרַאי
his son	בְּנוֹ	בְּרֵיהּ
her son	בְּנָהּ	בְּרַהּ

In addition, the third-person suffix הּ- sometimes anticipates the noun that follows in such expressions as רַב אַחָא בְּרֵיהּ דְּרָבָא (שבת ד,א) *Rav Aha, his son [that] of Rava (= Rav Aha, son of Rava).* Thus -בְּרֵיהּ ד is equivalent to בַּר, *son of.*

SEE: בַּר

בְּרַבִּי

SEE: בְּרִיבִּי

בָּרוּתָא* [הֲלָכָה] חִיצוֹנָה

"an outside [halakha]"; a mistake

This term is used by the Talmud to indicate that an amora's statement is outside the halakhic canon. It serves as a polite rejection of a halakha in the face of a difficulty.

וְהָא דְר' אַבָּהוּ בָּרוּתָא הִיא. (בבא מציעא ט,א)
But this [statement] of R. Abbahu is a mistake.

* In other editions of the Talmud (e.g., in the Munich Manuscript version of our Talmudic example) and sometimes in printed editions, the text reads בְּדוּתָא, *an invention.* The connotation of the latter term may be a bit harsher than בָּרוּתָא *an outside [halakha].* See the quotation from the *Arukh* in the margin of the same Talmudic passage we have quoted above. A list of all the occurrences of both terms appears in the margin of פסחים יא,א.

SEE: בַּר, בּוּרְכָא

בָּרִי בָּרִיא **certain; sure; definite**

"בָּרִי" וְ"שֶׁמָּא" — בָּרִי עָדִיף. (בבא קמא קיח,א)
[If one litigant issues a plea of] "definite" and [his opponent counters with a plea of] "perhaps" — [the] "definite" [plea] wins.

בְּרִיבִּי/ בְּרַבִּי* ***B^eRebbi***

(1) This title is an expression of deep respect that is used *after* the names of certain tannaim.

יוּדָן בריבי הָיָה דוֹרֵשׁ. (קידושין כא,ב ורש"י שם)
Yudan B^eRebbi was expounding.

(2) It is sometimes used by itself by some tannaim with regard to other tannaim.

אָמַר לֵיהּ רַבָּן שִׁמְעוֹן בֶּן גַּמְלִיאֵל לְר' יוֹסֵי: בְּרַבִּי! (פסחים ק,א ורשב"ם שם)
Rabban Shim'on b. Gamliel said to R. Yosé: B^eRebbi!

(3) This word is sometimes the name of a tanna.

בריבי אומר ... (חולין יא,ב ורש"י שם) *B^eRebbi says ...*

* The meaning of the prefix ב here is obscure. However, when בְּרַבִּי appears *before* a proper name, the prefix ב, stands for בֶּן, *son of,* so that ר' יִשְׁמָעֵאל בְּרַבִּי יוֹסֵי (שבת נא,א) means *R. Yishmael, son of R. Yosé.*

בָּרַיְיתָא

baraitha; an outside teaching מִשְׁנָה חִיצוֹנָה

Both this term and the term מַתְנִיתָא are used instead of the full expression מַתְנִיתָא בָּרַיְיתָא, *a teaching [of tannaim that has remained] outside [the Mishna of R. Y^ehuda HaNasi].** The terms בָּרַיְיתָא and מַתְנִיתָא are practically synonymous, but בָּרַיְיתָא provides a clearer contrast to מַתְנִיתִין, *our mishna.* It is therefore preferred in those contexts where both a baraitha and a mishna are quoted or referred to during the Talmudic discussion.**

* Rabbenu Hananel (סנהדרין יב,א) designates a *baraitha* by the Hebrew word חִיצוֹנָה.

** See the note on the next entry.

SEE: תְּנָא בָּרָא

בָּרַיְיתָא/מַתְנִיתָא* לָא שְׁמִיעַ לֵיהּ

הוּא לֹא שָׁמַע אֶת הַבָּרַיְיתָא.

He has not heard the baraitha.

The amora who presented his own halakhic opinion was apparently unaware of the baraitha, which has just been quoted in the Talmud, that had already decided the same halakhic point. It is not shocking that an amora was sometimes unacquainted with a particular baraitha, because there were so many baraithoth taught by many different tannaim from various yeshivoth. On the other hand, the Mishna is such a vital and influential work that every amora was presumed to be familiar with its contents. It is never proposed in the Talmud that an amora was unaware of a particular mishna.

* The statement בָּרַיְיתָא לָא שְׁמִיעַ לֵיהּ occurs four times in the Talmud: in שבת יט,ב; עירובין יט,ב; גיטין מה, רע"א; and

ערכין ל, רע"א. In every case, the term *baraitha* expresses contrast to a specific *mishna* that is being referred to in the course of the Talmudic discussion. On the other hand, מַתְנִיתָא לָא שְׁמִיעַ לֵיהּ appears just twice in the Talmud: in שבת סא,א and פסחים קא,ב. In both cases, there is no mishna involved in the Talmudic discussion. This data confirms the distinction in usage between the terms בָּרַיְיתָא and מַתְנִיתָא that was stated at the end of the previous entry.

בְּרַם

but; however (1) אֲבָל

דְּבָרִים שֶׁאָמַרְתִּי לִפְנֵיכֶם טָעוּת הֵן בְּיָדִי, בְּרַם כָּךְ אָמְרוּ ... (שבת סג, סע"ב ורש"י)

The things that I told you were erroneous, but this [is what] they said ...

indeed (2) אָמְנָם

בְּרַם, זָכוּר אוֹתוֹ הָאִישׁ לְטוֹב ... (סנהדרין יג, סע"ב ועוד)

Indeed, may this man be remembered for a blessing ...

בְּרַתָּא (cnstr. בַּת, pl. בְּנָתָא/בְּנָן)

daughter בַּת

This noun is often used with personal-pronoun suffixes, creating the following forms:

his daughter	בִּתּוֹ	בְּרַתֵּיהּ
daughter of	בִּתּוֹ שֶׁל; בַּת	בְּרַתֵּיהּ ד-*

בְּרוּרְיָה דְּבֵיתְהוּ דְּרִ' מֵאִיר בְּרַתֵּיהּ דְּרִ' חֲנִינָא בֶּן תְּרַדְיוֹן. (פסחים סב,ב; עבודה זרה יח,א)

B^{e}ruria, the wife of R. Méir, the daughter of R. Hannina b. T^{e}radyon.

* This form is parallel to בְּרֵיהּ ד- *son of*, in the entry בְּרָא.

בִּשְׁלָמָא

SEE: (בְּ)שְׁלָמָא

בְּשֵׁם

SEE: (בְּ)שֵׁם

בָּת (בית: prt. בָּיֵית)

he stayed overnight לָן

מַיָּא דְּבִיתוּ* (פסחים מב,א ורש"י שם)

water that stayed overnight

* In Hebrew: מַיִם שֶׁלָּנוּ.

בַּת constr.

daughter of בַּת

Some of the compounds formed by using בַּר with other words have feminine counterparts as well. See בַּר and the compound entries that follow it.

בַּת חִיּוּבָא (סוכה מב,א) *obligated*

בַּת אַחַת

SEE: בְּבַת אַחַת

בַּת יוֹמָא*/יוֹמָהּ

within its day בַּת יוֹמָהּ

This term refers to a utensil that has been used for cooking within the previous twenty-four hours.

קְדֵירָה בַּת יוֹמָא (פסחים מד, סע"ב וש"נ ורש"י שם; בכת"י: בַּת יוֹמָהּ)

a pot within its day.

* The final אָ- is often substituted for הָ-, the suffix for the third-person feminine singular.

SEE: בֶּן יוֹמוֹ

בָּתַר

after; according to אַחֲרֵי

אָזְלִינַן בָּתַר רוּבָּא (בבא קמא מו,ב ע"פ שמות כג,ב)

we go after (= according to) the majority

The preposition בָּתַר is used with personal-pronoun suffixes, creating the following forms:

after me	אַחֲרַי	בָּתְרַאי
after him/it (m.)	אַחֲרָיו	בָּתְרֵיהּ
after her/it (f.)	אַחֲרֶיהָ	בָּתְרַהּ
after them	אַחֲרֵיהֶם	בָּתְרַיְיהוּ

See example under (ו)כְתִיב בָּתְרֵיהּ.

בָּתַר/לְבָתַר ד-

after אַחֲרֵי שֶׁ-

הָא מִקַּמֵּי דְּשַׁמְעָהּ מֵר' יוֹחָנָן; הָא לְבָתַר דְּשַׁמְעָהּ מֵר' יוֹחָנָן. (חולין לט,א)

This [opinion was expressed by Resh Lakish] before he heard it (= the new interpretation) from R. Yohanan; the other [opinion was expressed] after he heard it from R. Yohanan.

בָּתַר דִּבְעָיָא הֲדַר פַּשְׁטַהּ

אַחַר שֶׁשְּׁאָלָהּ, חָזַר וּפְשָׁטָהּ.

After he had asked it, he subsequently answered it.

The amora who posed the problem is the same one who found a solution to it.

בָּעֵי רָבָא: מִקְרָא מְגִילָּה וּמֵת מִצְוָה — הֵי מִינַּיְיהוּ עֲדִיף? ... בָּתַר דִּבְעָיָא, הֲדַר פַּשְׁטַהּ: מֵת מִצְוָה עֲדִיף. (מגילה ג,ב)

Rava raised a problem: [As for] reading the scroll [of Esther on Purim] and the commandment of [attending to] a dead body [where no one else is available] — which one of them takes precedence? ... After he had asked it, he (himself) subsequently answered it: The commandment of [attending to] a dead body takes precedence.

בָּתְרָא (בָּתְרַיְיתָא f.s., בָּתְרָאֵי m. pl., בָּתְרַיְיתָא f. pl.)

last; latest אַחֲרוֹן

For examples, see the entries בָּבָא and לִישָּׁנָא בָּתְרָא.

ג

גַּב **back; outside; the outside part**

תוֹכוֹ טָהוֹר, וְגַבּוֹ טָמֵא. (ברכות נב, סע"א)

Its inside is ritually clean, and its outside is ritually unclean.

SEE: אַגַּב, עַל גַּב/גַּבֵּי, אַף עַל גַּב ד־

גַּבָּאי* **collector** (of taxes or alms for the poor)

הַגַּבָּאִין שֶׁנִּכְנְסוּ לְתוֹךְ הַבַּיִת (חגיגה כו,א: משנה פ"ג מ"ו)

the (tax) collectors who came into the house

* Nowadays, this word usually denotes a person who manages a synagogue.

SEE: גַּבֵּי

הַגָּבוֹהַּ* **the Most High** (= God)

אֲמִירָתוֹ לַגָּבוֹהַּ כִּמְסִירָתוֹ לַהֶדְיוֹט. (קידושין כח, סע"ב: משנה פ"א מ"ו)

One's verbal [dedication of an object] to the Most High is [equivalent to] his delivery [of the object] into [the hands of] a common person (in a private transaction).

* The correct pronunciation is gaVOah — with the final vowel pronounced before the consonantal ה.

בִּגְבוּלִין **beyond the boundaries**

(1) beyond the boundaries of (the courtyard of) the Beth HaMikdash

אֵין אוֹמְרִים שֵׁם הַמְּפוֹרָשׁ בַּגְּבוּלִין. (יומא סט, רע"ב ורש"י שם)

We may not pronounce the specific name (of God) beyond the boundaries of the Beth HaMikdash.

(2) beyond the boundaries of Y^e^rushalayim

עֶשְׂרִים וְאַרְבַּע מַתְּנוֹת כְּהוּנָּה נִיתְּנוּ לְאַהֲרֹן וּלְבָנָיו ... עֶשֶׂר בַּמִּקְדָּשׁ ... וְאַרְבַּע בִּירוּשָׁלַיִם ... וְעֶשֶׂר בַּגְּבוּלִין. ... (ב"ק קי,ב)

Twenty-four gifts for the kohanim were given to Aharon and to his sons ... ten in the Beth HaMikdash ... four in Y^e^rushalayim ... and ten beyond the boundaries of Y^e^rushalayim ....

הַגְּבוּרָה **the Omnipotent** (= God)

"אָנֹכִי" וְ"לֹא יִהְיֶה לְךָ" מִפִּי הַגְּבוּרָה שְׁמַעֲנוּם. (מכות כד, רע"א ע"פ שמות כ:ב,ג)

[The commandments] "I [am the Lord your God]" and "Thou shalt not have [other gods before Me]" we heard directly from the Omnipotent (= God).

גָּבֵי prt. (גבי: לְמִיגְבָּא .inf) **גּוֹבָה** **collecting** (usually a debt, taxes, or a contribution)

יַתְמֵי מִיגְבָּא גָּבוּ; אַגְבּוֹיֵי לָא מַגְבִּינַן מִינַּיְיהוּ. (כתובות קי,א)

Orphans are certainly entitled to collect [a debt owed them, but] we may not recover a debt from them.

SEE: גַּבָּאי, גּוּבַיְינָא, אַגְבֵּי

גַּבֵּי/לְגַבֵּי

אֵצֶל **next to; with; with regard to**

גַּבֵּי הֲדָדֵי תַּנְיָין. (בבא מציעא לד, סע"א)

[The two baraithoth] are taught next to each other [in the Tosefta].

גַּבֵּי מַתָּנָה דִּזְכוּת הוּא לוֹ זָכִין לְאָדָם שֶׁלֹּא בְּפָנָיו. (ב"מ יב,א)

With regard to a gift that is [considered] an advantage for him, we may confer an advantage upon a person in his absence.

גַּבֵּי is also used with personal-pronoun suffixes. The following forms are the most common:

גַּבָּךְ **next to you; with regard to you**

גַּבֵּיה **next to him/it (m.); with regard to him/it**

גַּבָּהּ **next to her/it (f.); with regard to her/it**

גַּבַּיְיהוּ **next to them; with regard to them**

מַאי עֲבִידְתֵּיהּ גַּבֵּיהּ? (בבא מציעא כד, סע"א)

What is his business with it? (= What right does he have to handle it?)

גַּבְרָא (pl. גַּבְרֵי/גּוּבְרִין ,abs. גְּבַר)

גֶּבֶר; אִישׁ **man; person**

אֲמַר רָמֵי בַּר חָמָא: הָא גַּבְרָא, וְהָא תְּיוּבְתָּא! אֲמַר רָבָא: גַּבְרָא קָא חָזֵינָא וּתְיוּבְתָּא לָא קָא חָזֵינָא! (בבא מציעא טז,א)

Rami b. Ḥama said [with regard to an objection raised by Rav Shesheth]: Here is a [great] man (= Rav Shesheth), and here is a refutation [by him]! Rava said: I do see a [great] man, but I do not see a refutation!

מִי סָבְרַתְּ חוֹבַת גַּבְרָא הוּא?! חוֹבַת טַלִּית הוּא! (מנחות מא,א)

Do you think [that tzitzith] is an obligation upon the person?! It is an obligation for [each] garment!

SEE: הַהוּא גַּבְרָא, חֶפְצָא

גַּבְרָא אַגַּבְרָא קָא רָמֵית

אָדָם עַל אָדָם אַתָּה מֵטִיל?!

"Are you hurling a man against a man?!" Are you pitting one amora's opinion against another's?!

When an amora's halakha is contradicted by a halakha from a more authoritative source — such as a mishna or a baraitha — the amora's halakha faces a difficulty, a קוּשְׁיָא. However, when the halakhoth of two different amoraim contradict each other, such a contradiction does not usually cause difficulty for either amora.* Each amora is entitled to his own opinion — even if it is disputed by a fellow amora. Sometimes, this latter principle is expressed by the *rhetorical question* that comprises this entry.

אָמַר ר׳ יוֹחָנָן: הֲלָכָה כְּר׳ יְהוּדָה ... וְאָמַר ר׳ אֶלְעָזָר: הֲלָכָה כְּרַבָּן גַּמְלִיאֵל! גַּבְרָא אַגַּבְרָא קָא רָמֵית?! (תענית ד,ב)

*R. Yoḥanan said: The halakhic ruling is in accordance with [the opinion of] R. Y'huda ..., but R. El'azar said: The halakhic ruling is in accordance with [the opinion of] Rabban Gamliel!** Are you pitting one amora's opinion against another's?!*

* In some instances where the opinions of two amoraim conflict, the Talmud does regard one opinion as more authoritative than the other. This phenomenon has been explained in several different ways by the classical commentators on the Talmud. See the article by Prof. Eliav Shochetman in *Sidra*, vol. VI, pp. 93–107, that supplies the following sources that deal with this issue:

תוספות למועד קטן ב,ב: סוף ד״ה ״חייב שתים״; רמב״ן לבבא בתרא ב,ב: סוף ד״ה ״אלמא״; רשב״א שם ד״ה ״שאני התם״.

** The halakhic issue in dispute is from what date must one insert the prayer for rain into the Amida.

SEE: מֵימְרָא

גַּבְרָא רַבָּה   אָדָם גָּדוֹל*; תַּלְמִיד חָכָם

a great man (in Torah learning); an outstanding halakhic authority

גַּבְרָא רַבָּה אָמַר מִילְּתָא; לָא תַחִיכוּ עֲלֵיהּ! (ברכות יט,ב)

An outstanding halakhic authority has made a statement; do not laugh at him!

* In Hebrew, the phrase אָדָם גָּדוֹל is used in the sense of a Torah scholar (קידושין כט, סע״ב ועוד).

בְּגוֹ   בְּתוֹךְ   **within; inside; about**

עֲבִיד אֱינִישׁ דְּפָרַע בְּגוֹ זִמְנֵיהּ. (בבא בתרא ה, סע״א)

A person usually repays within his [allotted] time.

בְּגוֹ is also used with personal-pronoun suffixes, especially in the following forms:

within it (m.); in it; about it   בְּגַוֵּיהּ/בְּגַוִּיהּ

within it (f.); in it; about it   בְּגַוַּהּ/בְּגַוָּהּ

within them; in them; about them   בְּגַוַּיְיהוּ

he is certain about it   קִים לֵיהּ בְּגַוֵּיהּ (בבא מציעא לה,א)

וְגוֹ׳   וְגוֹמֵר   SEE: וגו׳

לְגוֹ   לְתוֹךְ; בִּפְנִים   **into; inside**

נָפֵיל אִיסּוּרָא לְגוֹ הֶיתֵּרָא (עבודה זרה עג,א)

the forbidden [substance] falls into the permitted

מִגּוֹ   מִתּוֹךְ   **from; out of**

two out of three   תְּרֵי מִגּוֹ תְּלָתָא (בבא מציעא לב, רע״א)

SEE: (מְ)אִלְגָיו

מִגּוֹ/מִיגּוֹ דְּ-   מִתּוֹךְ שֶׁ-; מִפְּנֵי שֶׁ-   **since**

For an example, see מִגּוֹ דְּ-.

גַּוָּאֵי adj. m. pl.   פְּנִימִיִּים   **inside; interior**

הָא בְּבָתֵּי גַּוָּאֵי; הָא בְּבָתֵּי בָּרָאֵי. (קידושין לג,א)

One [refers] to the inner chambers; the other to the outer chambers.

לְגַוָּאֵי adv.   פְּנִימָה   **inside**

לְגַוָּואֵי עֲבִידִי, וּלְבָרַאי לָא עֲבִידִי (סוכה יט,א)

[the walls] are made for inside, but they are not made for outside

גּוּבַיְינָא*   גְּבִיָּה   **collection**

שְׁטָרָא לְגוּבַיְינָא קָאֵי (בבא מציעא קג,א)

the document is "standing" (ready) for collection

* This Aramaic word is used in Modern Hebrew. For example, a *collect telephone call* is שִׂיחַת גּוּבַיְינָא.

SEE: גְּבֵי

גוּד imp. (נגד)   מְשֹׁךְ!   **pull! extend!**

גּוּד אוֹ אֱגוֹד! (בבא בתרא יג,א ורש״י שם)

"Pull or I will pull!" (= Either buy out my portion and take possession of the property, or let me buy out your portion and take it!)

גּוּד, אַחִית מְחִיצָתָא! (שבת קא,א ורש״י שם)

Extend [and] bring the partitions down! (= Treat the case halakhically as if the walls reach the ground!)

גּוּדָא

(1) גָּדָה; חוֹף   **bank (of a river); shore**

אַגּוּדָא דְנַהֲרָא (בבא מציעא קג, סע״א ועוד)

on the bank of the river

(2) כֹּתֶל   **wall**

מַאי "מְחִיצָה"? גּוּדָא. (בבא בתרא ב, סע״א ורש״י שם)

What is [meant by] "a separation"? A wall.

בְּגַוּוֹה/בְּגַוַּהּ
בְּגַוֵּיה/בְּגַוֵּיהּ
בְּגַוַּיְיהוּ

SEE under (בְּ)גוֹ

גַּוְונָא (גוֹן constr. גַּוְונֵי; pl.)

(1) גָּוֶן; צֶבַע   **color; nuance**

כּוּלָּהּ בְּחַד גַּוְונָא הֲוָה קָאֵי (נדה כד,ב ע״פ דפוס ונציה)

all of it would have remained in one color

(2) מִין; אֹפֶן   **type; manner**

For examples — see תְּרֵי גַּוְונֵי, כִּי־הַאי/כְּהַאי גַּוְונָא, and כְּגוֹן.

גּוּזְמָא   גֻּזְמָה; הַפְרָזָה

exaggeration (used as a figure of speech)

This term indicates that the expression that the hakham employed must not be taken literally; he was exaggerating for rhetorical effect.

הִשְׁקוּ אֶת הַתָּמִיד בְּכוֹס שֶׁל זָהָב. אָמַר רָבָא: גּוּזְמָא! (חולין צ,ב ע״פ משנה תמיד פ״ג מ״ד)

They gave [the lamb designated for] the daily offering to drink from a cup of gold. Rava said: It is an exaggeration! (In reality, a golden cup is not required.)

גּוֹסֵס prt. (גסס) **dying; a dying man**

עָיֵיל כְּשֶׁהוּא גּוֹסֵס (נזיר מג,א)

[the kohen] enters when he (= the other man) is dying

גּוּף; גּוּפָא*

(1) body

בָּתַר רֵישָׁא גּוּפָא אָזֵיל (עירובין מא,א)

the body must follow the head

(2) person

חוֹבַת הַגּוּף נוֹהֶגֶת בֵּין בָּאָרֶץ בֵּין בְּחוּצָה לָאָרֶץ (יבמות ו,ב)

an obligation upon a person (as opposed to an obligation linked to the soil) is in effect both within the land [of Israel] and outside the land

(3) substance

שְׁטָרוֹת ... אֵין גּוּפָן מָמוֹן (בבא מציעא נז,ב)

[as for] documents ... their substance (= the paper itself) is not the [true] value

(4) the essence

גּוּפוֹ שֶׁל גֵּט: הֲרֵי אַתְּ מוּתֶּרֶת לְכָל אָדָם. (גיטין פה, סע״א: משנה פ״ט מ״ג)

The essence of a letter of divorce [is the statement]: "You are hereby permitted to [marry] any man."

(5) This noun is also used with third-person singular suffixes as a *reflexive* pronoun, *-self*, in both Hebrew and Aramaic — like עַצְמוֹ and עַצְמָהּ, the more common Hebrew forms.

himself; itself (m.) — **גּוּפוֹ, גּוּפֵיהּ***

herself; itself (f.) — **גּוּפָהּ, גּוּפָהּ/גּוּפָא***

פֵּירָא גּוּפֵיהּ "זַיִת" אִקְרֵי. (ברכות לה,ב)

The fruit itself is called "an olive."

* The first form is Hebrew, and the second is Aramaic.

SEE: הָא גוּפָא קַשְׁיָא, (וְ)הַאי מִיבְּעֵי לֵיהּ לְגוּפֵיהּ, הִיא גוּפָא גְּזֵירָה וַאֲנַן נֵיקוּם וְנִגְזוֹר גְּזֵירָה לִגְזֵירָה

גּוּפָא "הַגּוּף"; [הָבָה נַחֲזוֹר לַמַּאֲמָר] עַצְמוֹ.

"the body"; [Let us now return to] the statement itself.

This term regularly introduces the text of an amoraic statement, or a baraitha, or occasionally a mishna* that has been quoted *in part* during the course of a previous Talmudic discussion.** Now the Talmud quotes that text *in full* and discusses it further, usually presenting one of the following:

(1) *an explanation* of it, as in בבא מציעא כא,א;

(2) *an objection* to it, as in מגילה כב,ב;

(3) *a corroboration* of it from another source, as in סנהדרין כג,א;

(4) *a dissenting view*, as in בבא בתרא מט, רע״א;

(5) *another statement* (or several others) from the same author, as in בבא קמא קי, סע״א.

* See Rashi's comment on סוכה יד,א (ד״ה "משום").

** This point is emphasised by Rashi, Tosafoth, and the Rosh on נזיר יח,ב. In some cases, a text is quoted that was mentioned several pages earlier, as in סנהדרין ח, סע״ב, where Sh^e^muel's halakha from סנהדרין ג,א is discussed.

SEE: אָמַר מָר, and note the difference!

גּוּפָא דְעוּבְדָא הֵיכִי הֲוָה

אֵיךְ הָיָה הַמַּעֲשֶׂה עַצְמוֹ?

How was the incident itself? (= What actually happened?)

This *question* is asked in an attempt to clarify the facts of the case that has just been presented.

For an example — see בבא קמא כז,ב.

גּוּפַהּ; גּוּפֵיהּ See under גּוּף

גּוּפְנָא גֶּפֶן **vine**

בֵּינֵי גּוּפְנֵי קָיְימָא. (בבא קמא צב, רע״א)

It was standing among the vines.

SEE: עֲמַר גּוּפְנָא

גּוֹרְעִין וּמוֹסִיפִין וְדוֹרְשִׁין

[We] may subtract [a letter from a word] and add [that letter to an adjacent word] and [then] expound [the Biblical passage].

This method of Biblical interpretation is used in the Talmud on several occasions to establish a Scriptural basis for a halakha of a tanna.

ברייתא: "וְלָקַח מִדַּם הַפָּר" ... דָּם מֵהַפָּר יְקַבְּלֶנּוּ.

תלמוד: ... וְקָסָבַר: גּוֹרְעִין וּמוֹסִיפִין וְדוֹרְשִׁין. (יומא מח,א ע״פ ויקרא ד:ה)

BARAITHA: "And [the kohen] shall take from the blood of the ox" ... — the blood [straight] from the ox shall he receive.

TALMUD: And [the tanna] holds: [We] may subtract [the מ from the word מִדַּם in the phrase מִדַּם הַפָּר] and add [that מ to the word הַפָּר, so that the clause is explained as if it read "וְלָקַח דָּם מֵהַפָּר"] and [then] expound ["And he shall take the blood directly from the ox"].

גּוּשְׁפַּנְקָא* חוֹתָם **seal; signet-ring**

וְלֶחְתְּמֵיהּ בְּגוּשְׁפַּנְקָא דְפַרְזְלָא! (ברכות ו,א)

Let him seal it with a "seal of iron"!

* This word is used in Modern Hebrew in the sense of *official approval* or *authorisation*.

גִּזְבָּר **treasurer**

This term specifically denotes an official in charge of the treasury of the Beth HaMikdash who may act in its behalf.

הִקְדִּישׁ מָנֶה לְבֶדֶק הַבַּיִת וְנִגְנַב אוֹ שֶׁאָבַד - ר׳ יוֹחָנָן אָמַר: חַיָּיב בְּאַחֲרָיוּתוֹ עַד שֶׁיָּבוֹא לִידֵי הַגִּזְבָּר. (חולין קלט,א ע״פ כת״י)

[If] one dedicated a "maneh" (= one hundred zuz) for the repair of the Beth HaMikdash, and it was stolen or lost, R. Yohanan said: He is responsible for it until it reaches the hands of the (Temple) treasurer.

גְּזֵירָה/גְּזֵרָה

decree; prohibition; Rabbinic safeguard

גְּזֵירָה שֶׁמָּא יִטְּלֶנּוּ בְּיָדוֹ ... וְיַעֲבִירֶנּוּ אַרְבַּע אַמּוֹת בִּרְשׁוּת הָרַבִּים. (ראש השנה כט,ב)

[The prohibition against blowing the shofar on the Sabbath is] a Rabbinic safeguard, so that one will not take it in his hand ... and carry it four cubits in the public domain.

גְּזֵירָה לִגְזֵירָה

[one] Rabbinic safeguard for [the protection of] a[nother] Rabbinic safeguard

For an example — see הִיא הִיא.

SEE: הִיא גוּפָהּ גְּזֵירָה וַאֲנַן נֵיקוּם וְנִיגְזוֹר גְּזֵירָה לִגְזֵירָה

גְּזֵירָה שָׁוָה

g*[e]*zera shava*

This *rule of Biblical interpretation* compares two passages that contain either an identical word or expression, verbal forms from the same grammatical root, or (occasionally) words that are synonymous though different. The comparison either (1) clarifies the meaning of an ambiguous passage by comparing it with another passage, or (2) applies a halakha derived from one passage to another. The rule is listed among the seven rules of interpretation of Hillel, the thirteen rules of R. Yishmael, and the thirty-two rules of R. Eliezer b. R. Yosé, the Galilean. Hillel presented the following גְּזֵירָה שָׁוָה in order to prove that the Pesaḥ offering must be brought even on the Sabbath:

נֶאֱמַר "מוֹעֲדוֹ" בְּפֶסַח, וְנֶאֱמַר "מוֹעֲדוֹ" בְּתָמִיד. מָה "מוֹעֲדוֹ" הָאָמוּר בְּתָמִיד דּוֹחֶה אֶת הַשַּׁבָּת, אַף "מוֹעֲדוֹ" הָאָמוּר בְּפֶסַח דּוֹחֶה אֶת הַשַּׁבָּת. (פסחים סו,א ע"פ במדבר ט:ג ושם כח:ב)

It has been stated [in the Torah]: "at its prescribed time" with regard to the Pesaḥ offering, and it has been stated: "at its prescribed time" with regard to the daily offering. Just as "at its prescribed time" that is stated with regard to the daily offering [means that the offering] supersedes the Sabbath, so too does "at its prescribed time" stated with regard to the Pesaḥ offering [mean that the offering] supersedes the Sabbath.

* We have merely *transliterated* this term, since its literal meaning is so uncertain. Possible translations include: *the same law, a comparison with the equal*, and *an equivalent form* (vocalising גְּזֵרָה שָׁוָה).

SEE: אָתְיָא, מוּפְנֶה

גְּזֵירַת הַכָּתוּב

SEE: גְּזֵירַת מֶלֶךְ

גְּזֵירַת־הַמַּלְכוּת/גְּזֵרַת־הַמַּלְכוּת

"decree of the kingdom"; religious persecution on the part of the government

In current editions of the Talmud, this expression has been substituted for the original term הַשְּׁמָד, *the destruction [of Judaism]*, which appears in uncensored manuscripts. It denotes campaigns against the Jewish religion by the (Roman) government.

בִּשְׁעַת גְּזֵרַת הַמַּלְכוּת, אֲפִילּוּ עַל מִצְוָה קַלָּה, יֵהָרֵג וְאַל יַעֲבוֹר (סנהדרין עד, סע"א. בכת"י: "בִּשְׁעַת הַשְּׁמָד")

in a period of religious persecution on the part of the government, even for [the infringement of] a minor commandment, one must let himself be killed rather than transgress

גְּזֵירַת מֶלֶךְ*; גְּזֵירַת הַכָּתוּב

a Divine (lit. Royal) decree; a decree of Scripture

Both expressions are used with reference to various Torah laws and principles that seem arbitrary, either because they appear to contradict common sense or because they are exceptions to other Torah regulations.

בְּדִין הוּא שֶׁתְּהֵא בַּת רְאוּיָה לִהְיוֹת כְּ"בֵן סוֹרֵר וּמוֹרֶה" ... אֶלָּא גְּזֵירַת הַכָּתוּב הִיא: "בֵּן" — וְלֹא בַּת. (סנהדרין סט, סע"ב - ע, רע"א ע"פ דברים כא:יח)

It would have been logical that a daughter be eligible to be [judged] "a stubborn and rebellious child" ... but it is a decree of Scripture: "a son" — but not a daughter.

מֹשֶׁה וְאַהֲרֹן לְחוֹתְנָם — מִשּׁוּם דְּלָא מְהֵימְנֵי הוּא?! אֶלָּא גְּזֵירַת מֶלֶךְ הוּא שֶׁלֹּא יָעִידוּ לָהֶם. (ב"ב קנט,א ע"פ דברים כד:טז)

Is it because they are not trustworthy [that] Moshe and Aharon are [disqualified to testify] with regard to their [respective] fathers-in-law?! Rather it is a Divine decree that [even] they may not testify about them.

* This expression must not be confused with גְּזֵירַת הַמַּלְכוּת, the previous entry.

גַּזְלָנָא גַּזְלָן

robber

The robber who openly takes something from his victim by force is not obligated to pay double its value.

גַּזְלָנָא הוּא דִּנְקִיט לַהּ לְאַרְעִי בְּגַזְלָנוּתָא (ב"ב לח, סע"ב)

he is a robber who has taken [possession of] my land through robbery

SEE: גַּנָּבָא

גְּזַר (גזר: גָּזַר .prt)

(1) גָּזַר **he decreed**

גְּזַר תַּעֲנִיתָא (תענית כד,א) *he decreed a fast day*

(2) גָּזַר; אָסַר; עָשָׂה סְיָג לַתּוֹרָה **he prohibited; he enacted a Rabbinic safeguard**

גָּזְרִינַן שֶׁמָּא יַעֲלֶה וְיִתְלוֹשׁ. (פסחים נו,ב)

We prohibit [gathering fallen dates on the Sabbath], so that one not go up and pick [from the branches].

SEE: מִילְּתָא דְּלָא שְׁכִיחָא לָא גְּזַרוּ בַהּ רַבָּנַן

גְּזַר דִּין

"the decree of judgment"; the Divine verdict

הַכֹּל נִידּוֹנִים בְּרֹאשׁ הַשָּׁנָה, וּגְזַר דִּין שֶׁלָּהֶם נֶחְתָּם בְּיוֹם הַכִּפּוּרִים. (ראש השנה טז,א)
Everybody is judged on Rosh HaShana, and their verdict is sealed (by the Almighty) on Yom Kippur.
SEE: גְּמַר דִּין

גְּחֵין (גחן: גָּחֵין .prt) שָׁחָה **he bent over**
גְּחֵין, לְחֵישׁ לֵיהּ לְרַבָּה. (בבא בתרא לב, רע"ב)
He bent over [and] whispered to Rabba.

גֵּט; גִּיטָּא*

a (legal) document; (usually) letter of divorce
כָּל הַגִּיטִּין שֶׁנִּכְתְּבוּ בַּיּוֹם וְנֶחְתְּמוּ בַּלַּיְלָה פְּסוּלִין — חוּץ מִגִּיטֵּי נָשִׁים. (גיטין יז, סע"א: משנה פ"ב מ"ב)
All documents that were written during the day and signed at night are invalid — except for letters of divorce.
הֲרֵי זֶה גִּיטֵּיךְ! (גיטין יט,ב) *Here is your letter of divorce!*
גֵּט חוֹב (בבא קמא צה, סע"א)
a document of indebtedness (= an IOU)
* The first form is Hebrew, and the second is Aramaic.

לְגָיו/לְגָאו

לִפְנִים; כְּלַפֵּי פְּנִים **inside; to the inside**
וְלִיחֱזֵי אִי קַתָא לְגָאו אִי קַתָא לְבָר. (בבא מציעא כו, רע"א)
Let us see whether the handle [points] to the inside or to the outside.
SEE: (לְ)גוֹ

מִלְּגָיו מִבִּפְנִים **from the inside; from within**
For an example — see בבא מציעא נג, סע"ב.
SEE: (לְ)גוֹ

גָּיֵיז .prt (גזז: לְמֵיגַז .inf)
גּוֹזֵז; חוֹתֵךְ **shearing; cutting off**
דִּלְמָא גָּיֵיז לְעֵילָּאֵי וְכָתֵיב מַאי דְּבָעֵי (בבא בתרא קסג,ב)
perhaps he will cut off the upper [part of the document] and write whatever he wishes

גִּילּוּי מִילְּתָא SEE: גַּלּוּיֵי מִילְּתָא בְּעָלְמָא הוּא

גִּימַטְרִיָּא*

numerical value
This term denotes a *method of Biblical interpretation*, based on the numerical value of the letters in the Hebrew alphabet. It is listed as one of the thirty-two rules of R. Eliezer b. R. Yosé, the Galilean.**
"תּוֹרָה צִוָּה לָנוּ מֹשֶׁה מוֹרָשָׁה ...." "תּוֹרָה" בְּגִימַטְרִיָּא שִׁית מְאָה וְחַד סְרֵי הָווּ, "אָנֹכִי" וְ"לֹא יִהְיֶה לְךָ" מִפִּי הַגְּבוּרָה שְׁמַעְנוּם. (מכות כג, סע"ב - כד, רע"א ע"פ דברים לג:ד)
"Moshe commanded [the] Torah to us as an inheritance ...." [The word] "Torah" according to the numerical value corresponds to 611 (ת = 400; ו = 6; ר = 200; ה = 5): *"I [The Lord am your God]" and "Thou shalt not have [other gods besides Me]" (the first two commandents at Sinai) we heard directly from God (so that those two, together with the 611 heard from Moshe constitute a total of 613 commandments).*
* The vocalization is uncertain. גִּימַטְרִיָּא is an alternative.
** The numerical value of the letters is as follows:

א = 1	ו = 6	ל = 30	צ = 90
ב = 2	ז = 7	מ = 40	ק = 100
ג = 3	ח = 8	נ = 50	ר = 200
ד = 4	ט = 9	ס = 60	ש = 300
ה = 5	י = 10	ע = 70	ת = 400
	כ = 20	פ = 80	

גִּיסָא* צַד **side; direction**
חֲדָא בְּהַאי גִּיסָא דִּשְׁבִילָא, וַחֲדָא בְּאִידָּךְ גִּיסָא (פסחים קיא,א)
one [was sitting] on one side of the path, and one on the other side
יַיִן — אִיתְּמַר מִשְּׁמֵיהּ דְּרַב נַחְמָן: צָרִיךְ הֲסִיבָּה, וְאִיתְּמַר מִשְּׁמֵיהּ דְּרַב נַחְמָן: אֵין צָרִיךְ הֲסִיבָּה. וְלָא פְּלִיגֵי: הָא בְּתַרְתֵּי כָּסֵי קַמָּאֵי, הָא בְּתַרְתֵּי כָּסֵי בָּתְרָאֵי. אָמְרִי לַהּ לְהַאי גִּיסָא, וְאָמְרִי לַהּ לְהַאי גִּיסָא. אָמְרִי לַהּ לְהַאי גִּיסָא: תְּרֵי כָּסֵי קַמָּאֵי בָּעוּ הֲסִיבָּה ... וְאָמְרִי לַהּ לְהַאי גִּיסָא: אַדְּרַבָּה, תְּרֵי כָּסֵי בָּתְרָאֵי בָּעוּ הֲסִיבָּה .... (פסחים קח,א)
[As for drinking] wine (at the Pesaḥ Seder) — it was stated in the name of Rav Naḥman [that] it requires reclining, and it was stated in the name of Rav Naḥman [that] it does not require reclining. And [the two reports] do not disagree: one [refers] to the first two cups; the other [refers] to the last two cups. Some explain it in one direction some explain it in the other direction. Some explain it in one direction: The first two cups require reclining ... and some explain it in the other direction: On the contrary, the last two cups require reclining ....
* גִּיסָא (Hebrew: גִּיס) meaning *brother-in-law* is also derived from the some basic meaning, *side*, in family terms.

גִּירָא חֵץ **arrow**
גִּירֵי דִּידֵיהּ הוּא דְּאַהֲנוּ לַהּ. (בבא מציעא מד,א ורש"י שם)
It was "his arrows" (= his action) that caused it.

גִּירְסָא* לִמּוּד **learning; reciting by heart**
גִּירְסָא דְּיַנְקוּתָא (שבת כא,ב) *the learning of youth*
* In later Hebrew, גִּירְסָה means *a text* or *a version [of a text]*, and חִלּוּפֵי גִּרְסָאוֹת are *variant readings [of a text]*.
ע' רש"י לע"ז יט,א ד"ה "ילמד" ותוס' לברכות כא,א ד"ה "הכי".
SEE: גְּרַס

גִּלְגּוּל שְׁבוּעָה* **the extension of an oath**
If a defendant has to take an oath in court in response to one claim of a plaintiff, he can be required by that plaintiff to include within his oath a response to another outstanding claim from the same plaintiff. This *extension* applies even to affirmations that the defendant would not have been required to make otherwise.**
עַד הֵיכָן גִּלְגּוּל שְׁבוּעָה? ... דְּאָמַר לֵיהּ: הִישָּׁבַע לִי שֶׁאֵין עַבְדִּי

אַתְּ! (קידושין כח,א ורש"י שם)

How far does the extension of an oath [go]? ... [The plaintiff] can say to him (= the defendant): Swear to me that you are not my slave!

* The word גִּלְגּוּל literally means *rolling*.

** This halakhic principle is sometimes expressed without the word שְׁבוּעָה — either by the phrase עַל יְדֵי גִלְגּוּל, *by extension* (as in בבא מציעא צח,ב) or by the verb מְגַלְגְּלִין, *they extend* (as in שבועות מח, סע"ב).

גַּלּוּיֵי* מִילְּתָא בְּעָלְמָא הוּא

הוּא [בָּא] רַק לְגַלּוֹת הַדָּבָר.

It [comes] merely to reveal the fact.

This expression is used in several different ways, of which the following two are the most common:

(1) In certain cases, a statement is accepted in court even though it does not meet the strict standards required for formal testimony, since it merely reveals a fact but does not testify directly about the issue at hand.

"וְאִשְׁתְּמוֹדְעֻנוּהִי דַּאֲחוּהִי דְּמִיתְנָא מֵאַבָּא נִיהוּ" ... וְהִילְכְתָא: גַּלּוּיֵי מִילְּתָא בְּעָלְמָא הוּא, וַאֲפִילּוּ קָרוֹב וַאֲפִילּוּ אִשָּׁה. (יבמות לט,ב ע"פ כת"י, וע' הלכות הרי"ף שם ורמב"ם הל' יבום וחליצה פ"ד הל"א)

"and we ascertained that he is the paternal brother of the deceased ..." And the halakhic ruling is: It [comes] merely to reveal the fact, and [hence] even a relative or even a woman [may identify him].

(2) A Biblical interpretation sometimes merely clarifies the meaning of a word but does not provide a source for a new halakha.

ברייתא: "כִּי יִגַּח ..." — אֵין נְגִיחָה אֶלָּא בְּקֶרֶן, שֶׁנֶּאֱמַר: "וַיַּעַשׂ לוֹ קַרְנֵי בַרְזֶל וַיֹּאמֶר: ... 'בְּאֵלֶּה תְּנַגַּח אֶת אֲרָם'"
תלמוד: וְכִי תֵימָא: דִּבְרֵי תוֹרָה מִדִּבְרֵי קַבָּלָה לָא יָלְפִינַן! ... וְהַאי מֵילַף הוּא?! גַּלּוּיֵי מִילְּתָא בְּעָלְמָא הוּא דִּנְגִיחָה בְּקֶרֶן הוּא. (בבא קמא ב,ב ע"פ כת"י. בדפוסים: גילוי. ע' שמות כא:כח ומלכים א כב:יא ורש"י שם)

BARAITHA: "If it gores ..." — goring is only with a horn, as it is written: "And he made him horns of iron and he said: ... 'With these you shall gore the Arameans.'"

TALMUD: And if you say: We cannot derive Torah law from the words of tradition (as formulated in the N^evi'im)! ... Is this [a matter of] derivation?! It [comes] merely to reveal fact that goring is [done] with a horn.

* The correct spelling according to manuscripts is indeed גַּלּוּיֵי, the Aramaic פַּעֵל infinitive — rather than גלוי or גילוי (apparently the Hebrew noun גִּלּוּי), which frequently appears in our printed editions.

גַּלִּי (גלי פַּעֵל: מְגַלֵּי .prt, לְגַלּוּיֵי .inf) גִּלָּה

he revealed; he uncovered; he published

SEE: אִיגַּלִּי, תְּנָא סֵיפָא לְגַלּוּיֵי רֵישָׁא

גַּלִּי דַעְתֵּיהּ/אַדַּעְתֵּיהּ גִּלָּה דַעְתּוֹ

"he revealed his mind"; he made his intention clear

כֵּיוָן דִּנְפַל, גַּלִּי דַעְתֵּיהּ דִּבְנְפִילָה נִיחָא לֵיהּ דְּנִקְנֵי. (ב"מ י,ב)

Since he fell [upon the object], he has made his intention clear that he acquire [it] by falling [on it].

גַּלִּי רַחֲמָנָא הָרַחֲמָן גִּלָּה; גִּלְּתָה הַתּוֹרָה

The Merciful (God) has revealed; the Torah has revealed

This expression usually indicates that the Torah has explicitly stated a point about one case that also applies to a second case.

אִי סָלְקָא דַעְתָּךְ עֲבוֹדָה הִיא, יֵשׁ לָךְ עֲבוֹדָה שֶׁכְּשֵׁרָה בִּשְׁנֵי כֵלִים?! וְר' יוֹחָנָן: גַּלִּי רַחֲמָנָא בְּכֻתּוֹנֶת וּמִכְנָסַיִם — וְהוּא הַדִּין לְמִצְנֶפֶת וְאַבְנֵט. (יומא כג,ב ע"פ ויקרא ו:ג)

If you think [that the removal of the ashes] is a [Temple] service, do you have a service that is performed by [a kohen who is wearing only] two [priestly] garments?! And R. Yoḥanan [would reply]: The Torah has revealed [the duty] to [wear] the undercoat and the breeches — [but] the same duty applies to [wearing] the mitre and the belt (thus all four garments are required, as in all services in the Beth HaMikdash).

גְּלִימָא טַלִּית; בֶּגֶד עֶלְיוֹן **garment; cloak**

מִינֵּיהּ — אֲפִילּוּ מִגְּלִימָא דְעַל כַּתְפֵּיהּ! (בבא קמא יא, סע"ב)

From him — even from the cloak on his shoulder [may the debt be collected]!

גָּמוּר pass. prt. (גמר)

(1) finished; complete; absolute

צַדִּיק גָּמוּר (ברכות ז,א) *a complete(ly) righteous person*

(2) real; actual

גָּזֵל גָּמוּר (גיטין נט,ב: משנה פ"ה מ"ח) *actual robbery*

SEE: מַמָּשׁ

גְּמִיר pass. prt. (גמר: גְּמִירֵי .pl)

(1) לָמֵד learning; deriving

In this active sense, this passive form consistently refers to a *tradition* that was received from earlier authorities — as opposed to a derivation from Scripture.*

גְּמָרָא גְּמִירֵי לַהּ. (סנהדרין כב, סע"ב ושי"נ)

They learn it as an oral tradition.

(2) מְלֻמָּד learned; well-versed

גְּמִיר וּסְבִיר (הוריות ב, רע"ב)

learned and capable of logical reasoning

(3) נִגְמַר; נִפְסַק decided; concluded

כֵּיוָן דִּגְמִיר לֵיהּ דִּינָא לִקְטָלָא, מִיקְטַל קָטְלֵי לֵיהּ. (גיטין כח,ב)

Once a death verdict has been decided regarding him, they (= a heathen court) will certainly execute him.

* The **active participle** גָּמַר is used in the case of **derivation from Scripture**.

SEE: גְּמַר, נְקִטִינַן/נְקִיטִינַן

גַּמְלָא

camel — (1) גָּמָל

לֵיחוּשׁ לְגַמְלָא פָּרַח? (מכות ה,א)

Shall we take into consideration [that he may have travelled on] a flying (= swift) camel?

bridge — (2) גֶּשֶׁר

הֲוָה קָא מְעַבַּר חֵיוָתָא אַגַּמְלָא דְנַרֶשׁ (בבא מציעא צג,ב)

he was crossing the animals over the bridge of Narash

גָּמַר* (גמר: גּוֹמֵר .act. prt, גָּמוּר .pass. prt)

he finished; he decided; he resolved

נִמְנוּ וְגָמְרוּ (משנה ידים פ"ד מ"א)

[the judges] were counted (in a vote), and they decided

* This verb is Hebrew, and the next entry is Aramaic.

גְּמַר (גמר גָּמַר .act. prt, גְּמִיר .pass. prt, לִיגְמַר/לִגְמוֹר .fut, גְּמוֹר .imp, לְמִיגְמַר .inf)

he learned; he derived — (1) לָמַד

מִבָּשָׂר בְּחָלָב לָא גָמְרִינַן, דְּחִידּוּשׁ הוּא. (פסחים מד,ב)

We do not derive [a general rule] from meat [cooked] with milk, for it is a unique [prohibition].

he finished; he made up his mind; he decided — (2) גָּמַר; גָּמַר בְּדַעְתּוֹ; הֶחְלִיט

גָּמַר וּמַקְנֵי לֵיהּ (בבא מציעא סז,א)

he makes up his mind and transfers [it] to him (in other words, he does it wholeheartedly)

SEE: גְּמִיר and its note

גְּמַר דִּין

the conclusion of the judgment; verdict

הֵיכִי דָּמֵי גְמַר דִּין? ... "אִישׁ פְּלוֹנִי אַתָּה חַיָּיב, אִישׁ פְּלוֹנִי אַתָּה זַכַּאי!" (סנהדרין ו, סע"ב)

What is considered the conclusion of the judgment (after which point arbitration is forbidden)? ... [When the judges say:] "So and so, you are guilty! So and so, you are innocent!"

SEE: גְּזַר דִּין

גְּמָרָא

an oral tradition; a halakha received from tradition — (1) שְׁמוּעָה; מָסֹרֶת

גְּמָרָא אוֹ סְבָרָא? (יבמות כה, סע"ב; בבא בתרא עז, רע"א)

[Is this] a halakha received from tradition or [is it based on] reason?

גְּמָרָא גְּמִירִי לַהּ, וַאֲתָא יְחֶזְקֵאל וְאַסְמְכַהּ אַקְּרָא. (יומא עא,ב)

They were learning it [as] an oral tradition, and Y'hezkel came [along] and found support for it in a pasuk.

learning; discussion;* analysis — (2) לִמּוּד; תַּלְמוּד

גְּמָרָא גְּמוֹר זְמוֹרְתָא תְּהֵא!? (למשל שבת קו,ב ורש"י שם)

Recite [your] learning, [and] let it be [like] a song?!

חַד שָׁקִיל וְטָרֵי בַּהֲדֵי רַבֵּיהּ, וְאִידָךְ מַצְלֵי אוּדְנֵיהּ לִגְמָרָא. (חגיגה יא,ב ורש"י שם)

One [disciple] discusses [the halakha] with his teacher, and the other inclines his ear to the discussion.

"לְהוֹרוֹתָם" — זֶה גְּמָרָא** (ברכות ה,א ורש"י שם ע"פ שמות כד:יב. בכתי"ם: "תלמוד" וע' דקדוק סופרים שם)

"to teach them" — this [refers to] analysis

* The abbreviation גמ' is regularly used in the Talmud to mark the beginning of the discussion that follows each mishna of a tractate.

** In this passage, the Aramaic noun גְּמָרָא in our printed editions is a substitution for the Hebrew noun תַּלְמוּד, which is found in manuscripts and in early printed editions. This substitution came about because of the censorship of the word תַּלְמוּד.

SEE: גְּמִירֵי, מִשְׁמֵיהּ דִּגְמָרָא, תַּלְמוּד

לַגְמְרֵי

SEE: לְגַמְרֵי

גְּנָא (גני: גָּנֵי .prt, לִיגְנֵי .fut, לְמִיגְנָא .inf)

he lay down; he slept — שָׁכַב; יָשַׁן

דַּאֲכַלוּ וּשְׁתוּ וּגְנוּ בְּבֵי כְנִישְׁתָּא (פסחים קא, רע"א)

who ate and drank and slept in the synagogue

גַּנָּבָא

thief — גַּנָּב

The thief who steals something without his victim's knowledge, e.g., a pickpocket, has to pay double its value.

הַהוּא אַרְנְקָא ... אֲתוּ גַּנָּבֵי וּגְנַבוּהּ. (בבא קמא צג, סע"א)

There was a purse ... thieves came and stole it.

SEE: לִיסְטִים, גַּזְלָנָא

גַּס* (גסס) act. prt.

(1) intimate; familiar

אֵין לִבּוֹ גַּס בָּהּ (גיטין פא, סע"א: משנה פ"ח מ"ט ועוד)

His heart is not intimate with her.

(2) large; excessive

בְּהֵמָה גַּסָּה (קידושין כה,ב)

large cattle (= cows and oxen, in contradistinction to sheep and goats, which are called בְּהֵמָה דַקָּה*)*

excessive eating — אֲכִילָה גַסָּה (פסחים קז, רע"ב)

גַּס רוּחַ (משנה אבות פ"ד מ"ז)

"excessive of spirit" (= arrogant)

* גִּיס, pass. prt. in Aramaic, is also used in the first sense, as in כתובות פה,ב.

גְּרִידָא* (גרד) pass. prt.

mere; unqualified

לָא תַעֲשֶׂה גְּרִידָא (יבמות ג, סע"ב)

a mere prohibition (that does not incur a punishment more severe than flogging)

* This Aramaic word is sometimes used in Modern Hebrew in the same sense.

גְּרִיס (pl. גְּרִיסִין)

a split granule (of grain or pulse)

כַּגְּרִיס (שֶׁל פּוֹל)* the area of a split bean

This measure denotes the area of the surface that was formed by splitting a bean widthwise into two equal parts.

רַב חִסְדָּא אָמַר: כַּגְּרִיס תּוֹלָה ... (נדה נח,ב)

Rav Ḥisda said: [If the bloodstain is] the area of a split bean, she may attribute [it to a louse that was killed] ...

* See the measures of area in Appendix II.

גְּרִיעוּתָא חִסָּרוֹן; נֶזֶק disadvantage; harm

שְׁחוּנָה מַעַלְיוּתָא הִיא? אַדְּרַבָּה! גְּרִיעוּתָא הִיא! (תענית כד,ב)

Is a hot [year] a benefit? On the contrary! It is a disadvantage!

SEE: מַעַלְיוּתָא

גָּרֵיר act. prt. (גרר) גּוֹרֵר; מוֹשֵׁךְ

"dragging"; stimulating; attracting

חַמְרָא מִיגְרַר גָּרֵיר (פסחים קז, סע"ב)

wine certainly stimulates [the appetite]

גְּרִיר pass. prt. (גרר) נִגְרָר; נִמְשָׁךְ

dragged along; attracted to; influenced by

כֵּיוָן דְּאִיכָּא מִינֵּיהּ, בָּתַר מִינֵּיהּ גְּרִיר. (בבא מציעא צא,ב)

Since [an animal] of his own species is present, it is attracted to its own species.

SEE: אַגַּב גְּרָרָא

גָּרַם (גרם: גּוֹרֵם .prt)**;** **גְּרַם*** (גרם: גָּרֵים .prt)

he/it caused; it determined

מִצְוַת עֲשֵׂה שֶׁהַזְּמַן גְּרָמָהּ** (קידושין כט,א: משנה פ"א מ"ז)

a positive commandment that time has determined [when] it [is to be performed]

* The first verb is Hebrew, and the second is Aramaic.

** This is the spelling found in our editions of the Mishna. In our editions of the Talmud, however, the word is spelled גְּרָמָא — with the final א replacing the final ה as the personal-pronoun suffix. While this substitution is rare in Hebrew, it is fairly common in Aramaic.

SEE: גְּרָמָא

גַּרְמָא עֶצֶם bone

גַּרְמָא וּבִישׁוּלָא (פסחים קיד, סע"ב)

a [meat] bone and the soup (it was cooked in)

גְּרָמָא* גְּרִימָה עֲקִיפָה indirect causation

גְּרָמָא בִּנְזָקִין אָסוּר.** (ב"ב כב, סע"ב ע"פ כת"י ורש"י שם)

The indirect causation of damages is forbidden (however, a court cannot impose payment for it).

"לֹא תַעֲשֶׂה כָל מְלָאכָה" — עֲשִׂיָּיה הוּא דְּאָסוּר, גְּרָמָא שָׁרֵי. (שבת קכ,ב ע"פ שמות כ:י)

"Thou shalt not do any labor [on the Sabbath]" — [direct] action is what is forbidden, the indirect causation [of a labor] is permitted.

Most commentators on the Talmud and the codifiers of Jewish law distinguish between cases of גְּרָמָא and cases of דִּינָא דְּגַרְמֵי. The former are definitely not subject to payment in court, whereas in the latter case there is a controversy among tannaim as to whether a court imposes payment for damages.

* גְּרָמָא is also an alternate spelling for גְּרָמָהּ. See גְּרַם and the note thereon.

** See also the statement of Rav Ashi in בבא קמא ס,א.

גַּרְמֵי SEE: דִּינָא דְּגַרְמֵי

לְגַרְמֵיהּ לְעַצְמוֹ; עַל דַּעַת עַצְמוֹ

for himself; in keeping with his own opinion

שִׁמְעוֹן בֶּן שָׁטַח דַּעֲבַד — לְגַרְמֵיהּ הוּא דַּעֲבַד. (ברכות מח,א ורש"י שם וש"נ)

Shim'on b. Shetaḥ acted in keeping with his own opinion (which was not generally accepted).

גְּרַס* (גרס: גָּרֵיס .prt, לְמִיגְרַס .inf)

גָּרַס; לָמַד; שִׁנֵּן he studied by heart; he learned by rote; he recited and reviewed (in order to commit to memory)

כִּי בָּעֵיתוּ לְמֵיעַל לְמִיגְמַר קַמֵּי רַבְּכוֹן, גְּרוֹסוּ מֵעִיקָּרָא מַתְנִיתָא, וַהֲדַר עוּלוּ קַמֵּי רַבְּכוֹן! (כריתות ו, רע"א; ועי' הוריות יב,א)

When you want to go before your teacher to study, first learn the mishna by heart, and then go before your teacher!

* (1) The Talmud connects this verb with גָּרְסָה נַפְשִׁי לְתַאֲבָה in תהלים קיט:כ (עבודה זרה יט,א).

(2) Rashi and other commentators on the Talmud regularly use this verb in establishing or rejecting a particular version of the text — often in such expressions as: הָכִי גָּרְסִינַן ... (as in רש"י לפסחים ב, רע"א), *Thus we should read [the text] ...*, and לָא גָּרְסִינַן ... (as in רש"י שם), *We do not read [these words in the text of the Talmud] ....*

SEE: גִּירְסָא

גְּרַע (גרע: גָּרַע .act. prt, גְּרִיעַ .pass. prt, מִיגְרַע .inf)

נִגְרַע it was less; it was inferior

מִי גָּרַע מְקַלֵּל אֶת חֲבֵירוֹ בַּשֵּׁם מִמּוֹצִיא שֵׁם שָׁמַיִם לְבַטָּלָה?! (תמורה ג, סע"ב)

Is one who curses his fellow man with the [Divine] Name inferior to (= less criminal than) one who pronounces the Name in vain?!

גָּרַע (גרע פָּעֵל: מְגָרַע .act. pass, גְּרוּעֵי .inf)

גֵּרַע; מִעֵט he subtracted; he reduced

שׁוֹמֵר שָׂכָר שֶׁמָּסַר לְשׁוֹמֵר חִנָּם דְּהַשְׁתָּא גָּרוּעֵי גָּרְעָהּ לִשְׁמִירָתוֹ (בבא קמא יא,ב ע"פ כת"י)

a paid guardian who handed over [that which was deposited with him] to an unpaid guardian, for now [the first guardian] has certainly reduced the care of it

SEE: גּוֹרְעִין וּמוֹסִיפִין וְדוֹרְשִׁין

גְּרָרָא SEE: אַגַּב גְּרָרָא

ד

ד-

Although in Biblical Aramaic דִּי appears as a separate word, in the Talmud it has been shortened and has become the prefix -ד.

(1) אֲשֶׁר; שֶׁ-

which; that; that which; who; for; as

תִּסְתַּיֵּים דְּר׳ זֵירָא הוּא דַּאֲמַר פָּטוּר. (סנהדרין עז,א)

Let it be proved that it is R. Zera who said [he is] exempt.

(2) שֶׁל — **of**

מִילֵּי דְבֵיתָא (בבא מציעא נט,א) — *matters of the home*

SEE: (וּדְקָ)אָמְרַתְּ, (וּדְקָ)אָרֵי לַהּ מַאי קָאָרֵי לַהּ, דִּי

דָּא f. זֹאת — **this**

דָּא עָקָא! (סנהדרין כו,א). — *This is the problem!*

SEE: דֵּין, הָדָא, הָא

דְאוֹרָיְיתָא — SEE: אוֹרָיְיתָא

דָּאֵין/דָּיֵין prt. (דון: דָּיְינֵי .pl) דָּן — **judging**

הֲוָה יָתֵיב וְקָא דָאֵין דִּינָא (כתובות קח,ב)

he was sitting and judging a case

דְּאָמְרִי תַּרְוַיְיהוּ — SEE: (דְּ)אָמְרִי תַּרְוַיְיהוּ

דְּבֵי שֶׁל בַּיִת; בֵּית מִדְרָשׁוֹ שֶׁל

of the house of; the school of

אָמְרִי דְבֵי ר׳ יַנַּאי (ברכות ט,א ועוד)

the school of R. Yannai states (an amoraic statement)

תְּנָא דְבֵי ר׳ יִשְׁמָעֵאל (סוטה ג,א ועוד)

the school of R. Yishmael taught (a baraitha)

דְּבִיתְהוּ*

"שֶׁל בֵּיתוֹ"; אִשְׁתּוֹ — **"of his house"; his wife**

אֲזַל וְאִימְּלִיךְ בִּדְבִיתְהוּ. (ברכות כז, סע״ב)

He went and consulted with his wife.

* This expression is used only with the personal-pronoun suffix -הוּ.

SEE: אַנְשֵׁי בֵּיתוֹ, אֱינָשֵׁי בֵיתֵיהּ, בֵּיתוֹ

דְּבַר (דבר: דָּבַר .prt)

(1) לָקַח; הִנְהִיג; הוֹלִיךְ — **he took; he led**

דְּבָרֵיהּ וְעַיְילֵיהּ לְגַן עֵדֶן. (בבא מציעא קיד,ב)

He took him and brought him into Paradise.

(2) נָהַג — **he acted; he did**

For an example, see .פּוּק חֲזִי מַאי עַמָּא דָּבַר

SEE: נְסִיב, אַדְבְּרֵיהּ

דַּבָּר — **leader**

דַּבָּר אֶחָד לְדוֹר, וְאֵין שְׁנֵי דַבָּרִין לְדוֹר. (סנהדרין ח,א)

[There can be] one leader for a generation, but [there can] not [be] two leaders for a generation.

דָּבָר אַחֵר — **another matter; another reason; something else**

(1) This expression often introduces an *additional reason* for a halakha or an *additional interpretation* of a Biblical passage.*

בֵּית הִלֵּל אוֹמְרִים: מְבָרֵךְ עַל הַיַּיִן וְאַחַר כָּךְ מְבָרֵךְ עַל הַיּוֹם, שֶׁהַיַּיִן גּוֹרֵם לְקִידּוּשׁ שֶׁתֵּאָמֵר. דָּבָר אַחֵר: בִּרְכַּת הַיַּיִן תְּדִירָה, וּבִרְכַּת הַיּוֹם אֵינָהּ תְּדִירָה; תָּדִיר וְשֶׁאֵינוֹ תָּדִיר — תָּדִיר קוֹדֵם. (ברכות נא, סע״א; פסחים קיד,א).

Beth Hillel says: One must recite the b°rakha on the wine and subsequently recite the b°rakha on the day (= kiddush), for the wine causes kiddush to be said. Another reason: The b°rakha on the wine is a frequent [obligation] and the b°rakha on the day is infrequent; [when it is a question of] frequent and infrequent — the frequent precedes.

"וּבְכָל מְאֹדֶךָ" — בְּכָל מָמוֹנְךָ. דָּבָר אַחֵר: "בְּכָל מְאֹדֶךָ" — בְּכָל מִדָּה וּמִדָּה שֶׁהוּא מוֹדֵד לְךָ, הֱוֵי מוֹדֶה לוֹ בִּמְאֹד מְאֹד. (ברכות נד,א: משנה פ״ט מ״ה, ע״פ דברים ו:ה)

[The expression] "וּבְכָל מְאֹדֶךָ" [means] with all your money. Another interpretation: "בְּכָל מְאֹדֶךָ" [means] with whatever measure (= treatment) He metes out to you, give a great deal of thanks to Him.

(2) This expression is also used as a *euphemism* in place of one of the following:**

(a) **idolatry; an idol** — עֲבוֹדָה זָרָה

הַכֹּהֲנִים שֶׁשִּׁמְּשׁוּ בְּבֵית חוֹנְיוֹ לֹא יְשַׁמְּשׁוּ בְּמִקְדָּשׁ בִּירוּשָׁלַיִם, וְאֵין צָרִיךְ לוֹמַר לְדָבָר אַחֵר. (מנחות קט,א ורש״י שם: משנה פי״ג מ״י)

The kohanim who have ministered in the Temple of Onias may not minister in the Beth HaMikdash in Jerusalem, and it goes without saying [that they are disqualified if they ministered] for idolatry.

(b) **pig; swine; pork** — חֲזִיר

עֲבַד לֵוִי עוּבְדָא... בִּגְדִי וְדָבָר אַחֵר. (פסחים עו,רע״ב ורש״י שם)

Levi issued a ruling ... in the case of a goat and a pig [which had been roasted together].

(c) ***tzara'ath;* skin disease** — צָרַעַת

קַשְׁיָא לְרֵיחָא וּלְדָבָר אַחֵר. (פסחים עו,ב ורש״י שם)

It is detrimental to the smell [of one's breath] and to [one's susceptiblity to] tzara'ath.

(d) **sexual matters; sexual relations** — חַיֵּי אִישׁוּת

וּצְנוּעִין בְּדָבָר אַחֵר (ברכות ח,ב ורש״י שם)

and they are chaste in sexual matters

(e) **a charitable donation from a non-Jew** — צְדָקָה מִגּוֹי

אוֹכְלֵי דָבָר אַחֵר (סנהדרין כו,ב ורש"י ותוס' שם)
those who accept a charitable donation from a non-Jew

* Occasionally the Talmud asks ?"מָאי "דָּבָר אַחֵר, *why [is there a need for] an additional reason?* This question is similar to ?"מָאי "וְאוֹמֵר.

** E.Z. Melamed, "לישנא מעליא וכינויי סופרים", reprinted in his *Essays in Talmudic Literature*, Jerusalem 1986, p. 286.

a matter **דָּבָר הַלָּמֵד מֵעִנְיָנוֹ**
that may be explained from its context

This expression comprises a *rule of Biblical interpretation* that is employed to elucidate an ambiguous word or passage. This rule is listed among the *Seven Rules of Hillel* and the *Thirteen Rules of R. Yishmael.*

"לֹא תִגְנֹב" — בְּגוֹנֵב נְפָשׁוֹת הַכָּתוּב מְדַבֵּר ... צֵא וּלְמַד מִשְּׁלֹשׁ עֶשְׂרֵה מִדּוֹת שֶׁהַתּוֹרָה נִדְרֶשֶׁת בָּהֶן: דָּבָר הַלָּמֵד מֵעִנְיָנוֹ. בַּמֶּה הַכָּתוּב מְדַבֵּר? בִּנְפָשׁוֹת, אַף כָּאן בִּנְפָשׁוֹת. (סנהדרין פו,א ע"פ שמות כ)

"Thou shalt not steal" — Scripture refers to kidnapping ... Go out and learn from [one of] the thirteen rules through which the Torah is interpreted: A matter that may be explained from its context. Of what is Scripture speaking? Of crimes involving capital punishment (e.g., "Thou shalt not murder!"), here too [Scripture refers to] a crime involving capital punishment (i.e., kidnapping — as opposed to ordinary stealing).

Torah law **דְּבַר תּוֹרָה**

This term designates a mitsva obligation to be of Torah origin and Torah status, as opposed to a law enacted by the ḥakhamim.

נָשִׁים חַיָּיבוֹת בְּקִידּוּשׁ הַיּוֹם דְּבַר תּוֹרָה. (ברכות כ,ב)
Women are obligated in the sanctification of the day (= kiddush) [by] Torah law.

SEE: אוֹרָיְיתָא

field שָׂדֶה **דַּבְרָא**

אִשָּׁה בְּדַבְרָא לָא שְׁכִיחָא (ברכות ג, רע"ב)
a woman is not usually in the field

דִּבְּרָה תּוֹרָה כִּלְשׁוֹן בְּנֵי אָדָם

The Torah has spoken in the [ordinary] language of people.

This *rule of Biblical interpretation* is employed by certain tannaim to indicate that an emphatic verbal usage (see example below)* does not broaden the scope of a mitsva. Instead, it may be regarded as normal Hebrew style.**

"הַעֲבֵט תַּעֲבִיטֶנּוּ".* ... יֵשׁ לוֹ וְאֵינוֹ רוֹצֶה לְהִתְפַּרְנֵס — מִנַּיִן? תַּלְמוּד לוֹמַר: "תַּעֲבִיטֶנּוּ" — מִכָּל מָקוֹם. וּלְרִ' שִׁמְעוֹן דְּאָמַר: יֵשׁ לוֹ וְאֵינוֹ רוֹצֶה לְהִתְפַּרְנֵס, אֵין נִזְקָקִין לוֹ — "תַּעֲבִיטֶנּוּ" לָמָּה לִי? דִּבְּרָה תּוֹרָה כִּלְשׁוֹן בְּנֵי אָדָם. (בבא מציעא לא, סע"ב ע"פ דברים טו:ח)

"You shall surely lend him." ... [If] he has [his own possessions] but does not want to support himself — from where [do we know that you still have to lend to him]? A [Biblical] teaching states [the emphatic form]: "You shall lend him" — in any case. But according to R. Shim'on who said: [if] he has [his own possessions] but does not want to support himself, we do not attend to him — why do we need [the emphatic form] "You shall lend him"? The Torah has spoken in the [ordinary] language of people.

* In the example, the infinitive of a verb (הַעֲבֵט) precedes the future tense of the same verb (תַּעֲבִיטֶנּוּ).

**This rule of interpretation has been explained in this entry as it is used in the Talmud Bavli and the Midr^e^shé Halakha. In the works of the Rambam, however, the same rule is applied in a different sense to Biblical expressions (anthropomorphisms) that portray God in human terms, which are more readily understandable by ordinary people. According to the Rambam, *the Torah speaks in the language of people,* e.g., in וַיֵּרֶד ה' לִרְאוֹת (בראשית יא:ה), *"and the Lord descended to see."* Such an expression is a *metaphor* and is not meant to be taken literally. In fact, the Aramaic translation of Onkelos is וְאִתְגְּלִי ה' לְאִתְפְּרָעָא, *the Lord manifested Himself to punish.*

SEE: רמב"ם הל' יסודי התורה פ"א הי"ב; מו"נ ח"א:כו־כז

the (ten) statements; **הַדִּבְּרוֹת***
the Decalogue; "the ten commandments"

בַּדִּבְּרוֹת הָרִאשׁוֹנִים ... וּבַדִּבְּרוֹת הָאַחֲרוֹנִים ... (בבא קמא נד,ב ע"פ שמות ה:ב־יג ודברים ה:ו־יז)
in the first [version of] the Decalogue (in Sh^e^moth) ... and in the last [version of] the Decalogue

* The singular form is probably דִּבֵּר, a noun that appears in ירמיהו ה:יג. Some manuscripts of the Pesaḥ Haggada have the reading אָנוּס עַל פִּי הַדִּבֵּר, *forced by the Word* — instead of הַדִּיבּוּר in our printed editions. The Biblical Hebrew expression is עֲשֶׂרֶת הַדְּבָרִים, and it is found in שמות לד:כח, in דברים ד:יג, and in דברים י:ד.

SEE: (הַ)דִּיבּוּר

דִּבְרֵי חֲכָמִים

SEE: דִּבְרֵיהֶם

words of prophecy **דִּבְרֵי נְבִיאוּת**

This expression has been interpreted by different commentators in two opposite senses. Some take it positively, in praise of a halakhic opinion that is so extraordinary that it must have been Divinely inspired. Others regard the expression as having a derogatory connotation suggesting that a halakhic opinion lacks proper rationale and substantiation.

אֵין אֵלּוּ אֶלָּא דִּבְרֵי נְבִיאוּת! (עירובין ס, סע"ב וש"נ. ע' רש"י ותוס' שם)
These are nothing but words of prophecy!

words of the Sof^e^rim **דִּבְרֵי סוֹפְרִים***

This term denotes laws, not explicitly stated in the Torah text, that have been transmitted orally by the Sof^e^rim, the ḥakhamim of the early tannaitic period.

(1) In some instances, they had received halakhic traditions of Biblical status and transmitted them to their disciples.

הָאוֹמֵר ... חָמֵשׁ טוֹטָפוֹת, לְהוֹסִיף עַל דִּבְרֵי סוֹפְרִים, חַיָּב. (סנהדרין פח, סע"ב: משנה פי"א מ"ג)

[A rebellious elder] who states [that the t^e^fillin placed on the head must contain] five compartments (instead of four) [thus] adding to the words of the Sof^e^rim, is liable [to the death penalty].

(2) In other instances, the Sof^e^rim themselves enacted new halakhoth whose status is thus Rabbinic.

רַבָּן שִׁמְעוֹן בֶּן גַּמְלִיאֵל אוֹמֵר: כְּתוּבַּת אִשָּׁה אֵינָהּ מִדִּבְרֵי תוֹרָה אֶלָּא מִדִּבְרֵי סוֹפְרִים. (כתובות י, רע"ב)

Rabban Shim'on b. Gamliel says: The k^e^thuba of a wife is not from Torah law but from the words of the Sof^e^rim.

* The Rambam's use of this term has been a source of much analysis and speculation. ע' פירושו למשנה כלים פי"ז מי"ב; משנה תורה הל' אישות פ"א ה"ב; וספר המצוות: שורש שני.

דִּבְרֵי קַבָּלָה

words of received tradition (as recorded either in the books of נְבִיאִים or כְּתוּבִים)*

יוֹם שֶׁנֶּהֱרַג בּוֹ גְּדַלְיָה בֶּן אֲחִיקָם ... דִּבְרֵי קַבָּלָה הוּא. (ראש השנה יט,א ע"פ זכריה ח:יט)

[The fast commemorating] the day when G^e^dalya b. Aḥikam was assassinated is [based upon] the words of received tradition.

* See Rashi's commentary on חולין קלז, סע"א and the תוספות מאן דהו quoted in the commentary attributed to Rashi on the mishna in תענית טו,א.

SEE: קַבָּלָה

דִּבְרֵיהֶם/דִּבְרֵי־חֲכָמִים

their words; the words of the ḥakhamim

(1) Both Talmudic expressions often serve as technical terms indicating the Rabbinic status of halakhoth enacted by tannaim or amoraim.

עַד כָּאן — שֶׁל תּוֹרָה; מִכָּאן וְאֵילָךְ — שֶׁל דִּבְרֵיהֶם. (ב"מ סא,ב)

[The examples listed in the mishna] until here [constitute usury] according to Torah law; [those listed] from here on [constitute usury] according to the enactments of the ḥakhamim.

מִצְוָה לִשְׁמוֹעַ דִּבְרֵי חֲכָמִים. (יבמות כ,א ושי"נ)

It is a duty to obey the words of the ḥakhamim.

(2) In some instances, these expressions merely refer to a statement of anonymous tannaim, the Ḥakhamim,* without indicating whether the halakha involved is of Torah or Rabbinic status.

מַה בֵּין דִּבְרֵי ר' אֶלְעָזָר לְדִבְרֵי חֲכָמִים? (תמורה כ,ב: משנה פ"ג מ"ד)

What is [the difference] between R. El'azar and the words of the Ḥakhamim?

* In this dictionary, we have adopted the practice of capitalizing the word *Ḥakhamim* when it refers to *anonymous tannaim* who differed with a specific tanna who was mentioned by name. We have not capitalized *ḥakhamim* when it refers to *Torah scholars* in a more general sense.
SEE: רַבָּנָן, חֲכָמִים

דְּבָרִים בְּגוֹ

There is something in it.

There must be some profound inner meaning to this statement that requires further analysis.

For an example — see כתובות קיא,א ורש"י שם.

דַּהֲבָא (abs. דְּהַב) זָהָב

gold

כַּסְפָּא טִבְעָא, וְדַהֲבָא פֵּירָא. (בבא מציעא מד,ב)

Silver is [regarded as] coin, and gold is a commodity.

דְּהָא (= דְּ+הָא)

(1) שֶׁהֲרֵי; מִפְּנֵי שֶׁ־ **"for behold"; because**

"אם לא תִמְצָא חֵן בְּעֵינָיו ..." — דְּהָא מָצָא בָהּ עֶרְוַת דָּבָר (גיטין צ,א ע"פ דברים כד:א)

"if she does not find favor in his eyes ..." — because he discovered a matter of unchastity about her

(2) שֶׁזֹּאת **for this (f.)**

דְּהָא בְּהָא תַּלְיָא (מגילה ו,ב) *for this is dependent on that*

(3) שֶׁל זֹאת **of this (f.)**

גִּיטָּא דְּהָא גִּיטָּא (יומא יג, רע"ב)

the letter of divorce of this [woman] is a [valid] letter of divorce

דּוּ*/דְּיוּ

two; double

דּוּ פַּרְצוּפִין (ברכות סא,א) *two faces*

* The prefix ־דּוּ, which is of Greek origin, is often used in Modern Hebrew in such compounds as דּוּ-שִׂיחַ, *dialogue*.
SEE: טַנְדּוּ

דּוּבְשָׁא דְּבַשׁ

honey

דּוּבְשָׁא דְּתַמְרֵי (ברכות לח, רע"א) *date honey*

דּוּחַק; דּוּחְקָא

SEE: דְּחַק

דּוּכְתָּא מָקוֹם

place

מַאי שְׁנָא בְּכָל דּוּכְתָּא דְּלָא קָתָנֵי חַיָּיב מִיתָה, וּמַאי שְׁנָא הָכָא דְּקָתָנֵי חַיָּיב מִיתָה? (ברכות ד,ב)

What is the difference between every [other] place where it does not state [that one who violates Rabbinic law is] deserving of death and here (= in this case) where it does state he is deserving of death?

דּוּמְיָא ד־ "דִּמּוּי שֶׁל", בְּדוֹמֶה לְ־

"a resemblance of"; analogous to; like

משנה: הַדַּיָּינִים חוֹתְמִים לְמַטָּה אוֹ הָעֵדִים. (שביעית פ"י מ"ד)
תלמוד: מַאי לָאו דַּיָּינִים דּוּמְיָא דְעֵדִים? מָה עֵדִים שְׁנַיִם, אַף דַּיָּינִים נַמֵי שְׁנַיִם! (גיטין לג, רע"א)

MISHNA: The judges or the witnesses sign at the bottom (of the document).

TALMUD: Are not the judges analogous to the witnesses? Just as [there must be] two witnesses, so too [there must be] two judges (but three are not required)!

דון מִינָהּ וְאוֹקֵי בְּאַתְרָהּ

דּוּן מִמֶּנָּה וְהַעֲמֵד בִּמְקוֹמָהּ!

Deduce [a halakhic point about B] from it (= A), but apply [that point] within its (= B's) own context!

See explanation under the next entry.

דון מִינָהּ וּמִינָהּ   דּוּן מִמֶּנָּה [וַחֲזוֹר] וְדוּן מִמֶּנָּה!

Deduce [a halakhic point about B] from it (= A), and [deduce further] from it (= A)!

This expression and the expression in the previous entry represent two sides of a controversy between tannaim regarding the derivation of a halakhic point by analogy (usually a * גְּזֵירָה שָׁוָה) from one case (= A) to another (= B). According to one opinion, not only is a primary halakhic point that is stated in the Torah regarding A transferred to B, but other related points are also transferred. This approach is expressed by דּוּן מִינָהּ וּמִינָהּ. According to the other opinion, the primary halakhic point alone is transferred from A to B. In all other respects, however, B retains its own halakhic character. This approach is expressed by the rule דּוּן מִינָהּ וְאוֹקֵי בְּאַתְרָהּ.

משנה: דְּבַשׁ תְּמָרִים וְיֵין תַּפּוּחִים ... וּשְׁאָר מֵי פֵּירוֹת שֶׁל תְּרוּמָה — ר' אֱלִיעֶזֶר מְחַיֵּיב קֶרֶן וָחוֹמֶשׁ, וְר' יְהוֹשֻׁעַ פּוֹטֵר.

תלמוד: בְּמַאי פְּלִיגִי? בְּדוּן מִינָהּ וּמִינָהּ וּבְדוּן מִינָהּ וְאוֹקֵי בְּאַתְרָהּ קָמִיפַּלְגִי, דְּר' אֱלִיעֶזֶר סָבַר דּוּן מִינָהּ וּמִינָהּ: מָה בִּיכּוּרִים — מַשְׁקִין הַיּוֹצְאִין מֵהֶן כְּמוֹתָן, אַף תְּרוּמָה נַמִּי — מַשְׁקִין הַיּוֹצְאִין מֵהֶן כְּמוֹתָן. וּמִינָהּ: מָה בִּכּוּרִים — אֲפִילּוּ שְׁאָר מַשְׁקִין, אַף תְּרוּמָה נַמִּי — אֲפִילּוּ שְׁאָר מַשְׁקִין. וְר' יְהוֹשֻׁעַ סָבַר: דּוּן מִינָהּ וְאוֹקֵי בְּאַתְרָהּ: מָה בִּכּוּרִים — מַשְׁקִין הַיּוֹצְאִין מֵהֶן כְּמוֹתָן, אַף תְּרוּמָה — מַשְׁקִין הַיּוֹצְאִין מֵהֶם כְּמוֹתָן. וְאוֹקֵי בְּאַתְרָהּ: מָה מַשְׁקִין דְּקָדְשֵׁי בִּתְרוּמָה — תִּירוֹשׁ וְיִצְהָר, אִין; מִידֵי אַחֲרִינָא, לָא; אַף מַשְׁקִין הַיּוֹצְאִין מֵהֶן — תִּירוֹשׁ וְיִצְהָר, אִין; מִידֵי אַחֲרִינָא, לָא. (חולין קכ,ב ע"פ כת"י וע' רש"י שם)

MISHNA: [If a non-kohen drank in error] date-honey, apple-cider, ... or any other juices (except for wine or oil) of t^eruma — R. Eliezer declares [him] liable [to pay its] value and an [added] fifth, but R. Y^ehoshua exempts him.

TALMUD: About what [principle] do they differ? [They differ whether to say:] "Deduce [a halakhic point] from it and [deduce further] from it!" or "Deduce from it, but apply [that point] within its own context!" R. Eliezer holds: Deduce from it and [deduce further] from it. Just as in the case of first-fruits — liquids that exude from them are like [the fruits] themselves, so too [in the case of] t^eruma — liquids that exude from them are like [the fruits] themselves. And [deduce further] from it: Just as [the law of] first-fruits [applies] even [to] other juices [besides wine and oil], so too [with regard to] t^eruma [the law applies] even [to] other juices. But R. Y^ehoshua holds: Deduce from it, but apply [that point] within its own context. Just as [in the case of] first-fruits — liquids that exude from them are like [the fruits] themselves, so too [in the case of] t^eruma — liquids that exude from them are like [the fruits] themselves. But apply [that point] within its own context: Just as the [only] liquids that [can be] consecrated for t^eruma are wine and [olive] oil [but] not other liquids, so too [the rule that] liquids that exude from it are like [the fruits] themselves [applies only to] wine and oil — but not to other liquids.

SEE: דַּיּוֹ לַבָּא מִן הַדִּין לִהְיוֹת כַּנִּדּוֹן

דַּוְקָא

exactly; literally (1) בְּדִיּוּק

ברייתא: הַמּוֹכֵר עַבְדּוֹ לְעוֹבֵד כּוֹכָבִים קוֹנְסִין אוֹתוֹ עַד עֲשָׂרָה בְּדָמָיו.

תלמוד: דַּוְקָא אוֹ לָאו דַּוְקָא? (גיטין מד,א ע' רש"י ותוס' שם)

BARAITHA: [If] one sells his slave to a heathen, we penalize him [to ransom the slave, even if it costs him] up to ten times his (= the slave's) value.

TALMUD: [Is the number ten to be taken] literally or loosely?

exclusively; necessarily; only (2) רַק כָּךְ; בִּלְבַד

משנה: מִיָּד תִּינוֹקוֹת שׁוֹמְטִין אֶת לוּלְבֵיהֶן וְאוֹכְלִין אֶתְרוֹגֵיהֶן. (סוכה מה,א: משנה פ"ד מ"ז)

תלמוד: מַאי לָאו הוּא הַדִּין לִגְדוֹלִים? לָא, תִּינוֹקוֹת דַּוְקָא. (סוכה מו,ב ורש"י שם)

MISHNA: From the hands of the children they take their lulavim and eat their (= the children's) ethrogim [on the seventh day of Sukkoth].

TALMUD: Does this not apply to [the ethrogim of] adults, too? No, only [those of] children [may be eaten].

SEE: לָאו דַּוְקָא

דּוּקְיָא/דִּיּוּקָא   דִּיּוּק

"precision"; an inference (derived by an amora from the choice of wording in a mishna or baraitha text)

דּוּקְיָא דְּרָבָא מְהֵיכָא? (בבא קמא עד,א)

From where is Rava's inference [derived]?

See an example of such an inference under דַּיְקָא נַמִּי.

SEE: דָּיֵיק

דְּחָא (דחי: דָּחֵי .prt, לִידְחֵי .fut, לְמִידְחֵי .inf)

he pushed aside; he superseded דָּחָה

אָתֵי עֲשֵׂה וְדָחֵי לֹא תַעֲשֶׂה. (שבת קלב,ב)

A positive commandment comes and supersedes a negative commandment.

דְּחוּיֵי .inf (דחי פַּעֵל)

"push aside"; "put off" דַּחֵה

דְּחוּיֵי* קָא מְדַחֵי לֵיהּ דְּחִיָּה הוּא דוֹחֶה אוֹתוֹ.

He is really putting him off (hence his statement does not accurately reflect his own position).

For an example — see בבא קמא צט,א ורש"י שם.

* The infinitive דְּחוּיֵי serves to add emphasis to the main verb מְדַחֵי, which has been expressed in the English translation by the adverb *really*.

SEE: מְדַחֵי

דָּחֵיל* prt. (דחל)

afraid; fearing פּוֹחֵד; יָרֵא

גְּבַר דָּחֵיל חֲטָאִין הוּא. (שבת לא, רע"ב)

He is a man [who] fears sin.

* The Modern Hebrew word דַּחְלִיל means *a scarecrow*.

דְּחַק (דחק: דָּחֵיק, act. prt. דְּחִיק, pass. prt.)

he pressed; he forced; he strained דָּחַק

דָּחֲקִינַן וּמוֹקְמִינַן מַתְנִיתִין בִּתְרֵי טַעֲמֵי, וְאַלִּיבָּא דְחַד תַּנָּא (קידושין סג, רע"ב)

we strain to interpret [the phrase that occurs twice in] our mishna with two [different] meanings, and [thus all of its clauses will be] consistent with [the opinion of] one tanna

שִׁנּוּיָא דְּחִיקָא לָא מְשַׁנֵּינָא לָךְ. (בבא בתרא מג, סע"א)

I will not answer you [with] a forced reply.

דְּחָק/דּוֹחַק; דּוּחְקָא*

pressure; an emergency; distress

דּוּחְקָא דְסַכִּינָא (חולין ח,ב) *the pressure of the knife*

עַל יְדֵי הַדְּחָק (בבא מציעא כב,א ועוד) *under pressure; with difficulty*

בִּשְׁעַת הַדְּחָק (ברכות ט,א ועוד) *in time of emergency*

בִּשְׁעַת דָּחְקוֹ (משנה אבות פ"ב מ"ג) *in the time of his distress*

* The first two forms are Hebrew, and the last is Aramaic.

SEE: מַאי דּוּחְקֵיהּ דְּר' ... לְאוֹקְמֵי מַתְנִיתִין

דַּי (constr. דֵּי)

enough; sufficient

This word is often used with personal-pronoun suffixes.

SEE: דַּיָּהּ, דַּיּוֹ, כְּדַי, כְּדֵי

דִּי אֲשֶׁר **that**

In Biblical Aramaic, דִּי is used frequently. In the Talmud, however, the use of this word is almost entirely* restricted to quotations from the books of Daniel and Ezra. Otherwise, the abbreviated form, the prefix ־ד, occurs. The fuller form דִּי is often used with suffixes — either with ל followed by a personal-pronoun suffix (e.g., לֵיהּ as in דִּילֵיהּ) or, more frequently, with a second ד followed by a personal-pronoun suffix (as in דִּידֵיהּ).**

אֲנַן בְּדִידַן, וְאִינְהוּ בְּדִידְהוּ! (ברכות ת, סע"א)

We [do] our [thing], while they [do] theirs!

* For the exceptions, see מגילה טז,א and סנהדרין צו,ב.

**For a complete list of the forms thus created, see *Grammar for Gemara*: Chapter 7.33.

SEE: דִּידִי, דִּידֵיהּ, ־ד

"the speech"; the [Divine] Revelation הַדִּיבּוּר

חֲגִיגָה עֲדִיפָא, דְּיָשְׁנָה לִפְנֵי הַדִּיבּוּר. (חגיגה ו,א ורש"י שם)

The festival-offering is superior, because it was [commanded] prior to the Revelation (at Sinai).

speech; expression דִּבּוּר **דִּיבּוּרָא**

מִדְּשַׁנֵּי קְרָא בְּדִיבּוּרֵיהּ (קידושין לה,ב)

since the Torah has changed its [style of] expression

of mine; my שֶׁלִּי **דִּידִי/דִּילִי**

וְאֵימָא טַעֲמָא דִּידִי, וְאֵימָא טַעֲמָא דִּידְהוּ. (עירובין ח,ב)

And I will state my reason, and I will state their reason.

in my [case]; with me myself **בְּדִידִי**

SEE: בְּדִידִי

according to my [opinion] **לְדִידִי**

SEE: לְדִידִי

of his; his; its (m.) שֶׁלּוֹ **דִּידֵיהּ/דִּילֵיהּ**

... דִּידֵיהּ אֲמַר ... [דַּעְתּוֹ] שֶׁלּוֹ אָמַר

... he stated his own [opinion]

After the Talmud has quoted a halakhic statement of an amora that he taught in the name of his teacher, the Talmud sometimes quotes the amora's own independent teaching about the same halakha. In his own teaching, the amora either cites a different halakhic source, or offers a different interpretation, or disagrees with his teacher's statement.

אָמַר רַב נַחְמָן אָמַר שְׁמוּאֵל: הֲלָכָה כְּר' אֶלְעָזָר בֶּן עֲזַרְיָה, וְרַב נַחְמָן דִּידֵיהּ אָמַר: אֵין הֲלָכָה כְּר' אֶלְעָזָר בֶּן עֲזַרְיָה. (כתובות נו, רע"א)

Rav Naḥman said quoting Shᵉmuel: The halakhic ruling is in accordance with [the opinion of] R. El'azar b. Azarya, but R. Naḥman stated his own [opinion]: The halakhic ruling is not in accordance with R. El'azar b. Azarya.

SEE: הָא דִּידֵיהּ הָא דְּרַבֵּיהּ, (וּ)פְלִיגָא דִּידֵיהּ אַדִּידֵיהּ

[it is] enough for her/it (f.) **דַּיָּהּ**

דַּיָּהּ לְצָרָה בְּשַׁעְתָּהּ. (ברכות ט,ב ורש"י שם)

[It is] enough for a calamity [to trouble us] at its time. (= We will worry about it when it happens.)

SEE: דַּו **דֵּיו**

[it is] enough for him/it (m.) **דַּיּוֹ**

וּבִשְׁעַת הַסַּכָּנָה מַנִּיחָהּ עַל שׁוּלְחָנוֹ וְדַיּוֹ (שבת כא,ב)

and in time of danger (from the gentiles) he may place it (= the Ḥanukka candle) on his table (rather than at the window) and it is enough for him

דַּיוֹ לַבָּא מִן הַדִּין לִהְיוֹת כַּנִּדּוֹן

It is sufficient for [the law] derived from a logical inference to be like [the law from which the inference] has been drawn (but not superior to it!).

This rule limits the application of a קַל־וָחוֹמֶר argument. It means that when a law is transferred from case A to case B, its application to B cannot exceed its application to A.*

(1) גַּנָּב עַצְמוֹ מְנָא לֵיהּ? (2) וְכִי תֵּימָא: לֵיתֵי בְּקַל וָחוֹמֶר מִטּוֹעֵן טַעֲנַת גַּנָּב! (3) דַּיּוֹ לַבָּא מִן הַדִּין לִהְיוֹת כַּנִּדּוֹן: מָה לְהַלָּן בִּשְׁבוּעָה, אַף כָּאן בִּשְׁבוּעָה. (בבא קמא סג, סע"ב ע"פ שמות כב:ז,ח וע' רש"י שם)

(1) From where does he derive [that] the thief himself [must pay a double payment], (since, in his opinion, the Torah does not explicitly state such a halakha)? (2) And if you should say: Let it be derived through a קַל־וָחוֹמֶר *argument from the law of [a guardian of an object falsely] alleging the claim [that there was] a thief (where the guardian certainly has to pay a double payment)! (3) (That derivation is not valid, because) it is sufficient for [the law] derived from a logical inference] to be like [the law from which the inference] has been drawn (but not superior to it!): Just as there [a double penalty is imposed only] after [the guardian had taken a false] oath, here too [only] after [the thief had taken a false] oath.*

* See a Biblical example of this principle in במדבר יב:יד as explained in Rashi's commentary there.

SEE: קַל וָחוֹמֶר

דִּיוּקָא

an inference

(derived from the precise wording of the text)

SEE: דוּקְיָא

דָּיֵין

SEE: דָּאִין

דָּיֵיק (דוק) act. prt. מְדַיֵּיק; מְדַקְדֵּק

he is particular; he draws an inference (from the exact wording of a tannaitic text); **he deduces**

רָבִינָא דָּיֵיק מֵרֵישָׁא; רַב חִסְדָּא דָּיֵיק מִסֵּיפָא. (כתובות לא,ב)

Rabina deduces [his halakhic position] from [the wording of] the first clause [in the mishna]; Rav Ḥisda deduces [his halakhic position] from the latter clause.

SEE: דָּק

דִּיכְרָא

(1) זָכָר **male**

בְּנִין דִּכְרִין (כתובות נב,ב: משנה פ"ד מ"י) *male children*

(2) *אַיִל **a male sheep; a ram**

דִּיכְרָא גְּנַבִי מִמָּךְ?! (בבא קמא סה,ב)

Did I steal a ram from you?!

* In Mishnaic Hebrew too, זָכָר may sometimes mean *a ram*, as in ראש השנה כו,ב: משנה פ"ג מ"ד. As for Biblical Hebrew, see וְיֵשׁ בְּעֶדְרוֹ זָכָר (מלאכי א: יד).

דִּילִי; דִּילֵיהּ

SEE: דִּידִי, דִּידֵיהּ

דִּילְמָא/דִּלְמָא שֶׁמָּא

(1) perhaps

In this sense, this word is often used in the following three contexts — in the formulation of:

(a) a halakhic problem (בְּעָיָא)

אוֹ דִילְמָא ...? (שבת לז,א ועוד)

or perhaps (the halakhic ruling should be different than proposed according to the first side of the problem) ...?

(b) a difficulty (קוּשְׁיָא)

וְדִילְמָא לָא הִיא! (ביצה ט, סע"ב)

But perhaps it is not so (and there is a difficulty)!

(c) a refutation of a difficulty (שִׁינּוּיָא)

דִּילְמָא שָׁאנֵי הָתָם ...! (שבת לז,א)

Perhaps it is different in that case (and the difficulty is resolved) ...!

(2) lest; that ... not ...; that*

אֲנָא יָכֵילְנָא לְחַדּוּשֵׁי בַּהּ מִילְּתָא וּמִסְתְּפֵינָא דִּלְמָא מִטְרֵידְנָא. (ברכות כט,ב)

I can insert a novel addition (into my recitation of the Amida), but I fear that I may become confused.

* With verbs of fearing or expressions of danger, the negative is not stated explicitly. It is implied.

SEE: בְּעָיָא, קוּשְׁיָא, שִׁינּוּיָא

דֵּין/דָּן (f. דָּא) זֶה

this

This demonstrative pronoun occurs almost exclusively in official documents or in certain Talmudic tractates that are written in an Aramaic dialect that is different from the Aramaic of most of the Babylonian Talmud. The tractates are נְדָרִים, נָזִיר, כְּרֵיתוֹת, תְּמוּרָה, and מְעִילָה.*

דֵּין הוּא אֲדָר. (סנהדרין יח,ב)

This is [the month of] Adar.

* In his commentary on תמורה כג,ב, Rashi designates the dialect as לְשׁוֹן יְרוּשַׁלְמִי, *the Jerusalem dialect*.

SEE: הָדֵין

דִּין; דִּינָא*

(1) law; a judgment

דִּינָא דְמַלְכוּתָא דִּינָא. (נדרים כח,א וש"נ)

The law of the government is law.

(2) a lawsuit; a legal claim

דִּין וּדְבָרִים אֵין לִי עַל שָׂדֶה זוֹ. (בבא בתרא מג, רע"א)

I have no legal claim or arguments with respect to this field.

(3) a rule of Biblical interpretation; a logical inference (usually, a קַל־וָחוֹמֶר argument)

אֵין עוֹנְשִׁין מִן הַדִּין. (סנהדרין נד,א ועוד)

We do not impose punishment on the strength of a logical inference.

* The first form is Hebrew, and the second is Aramaic.

SEE: דָּן, בֵּי דִינָא, בַּעַל דִּין, דַּיּוֹ לַבָּא מִן הַדִּין לִהְיוֹת כַּנִּדּוֹן, (וּ)מָה ... אֵינוֹ דִין שֶׁ- ...

בְּדִין

in accordance with logic; logical; proper

For an example — see ברכות יד,ב.

...וּבְדִין הוּא דְּ-

and it would have been logical that ...

This formula is used by the Talmud to express what the halakhic formulation in the text *should have been* according to logic or propriety — were it not for another consideration that is then presented in the Talmud.

חָלוּק ר' שִׁמְעוֹן אַף בָּרִאשׁוֹנָה ... וּבְדִין הוּא דְּנִפְלוֹג ר' שִׁמְעוֹן בְּרֵישָׁא, אֶלָּא נָטַר לְהוּ לְרַבָּנָן עַד דִּמְסַיְּימִי לְמִילְּתַיְיהוּ וַהֲדַר פְּלֵיג עֲלַיְיהוּ. (יבמות יח,ב ורש"י שם)

R. Shim´on is in disagreement with the first [clause in the mishna] as well (even though he states his opposition to the Ḥakhamim only after their second clause has been completed). It would have been logical for R. Shim´on to [explicitly] dispute the first clause, but he waits until the Ḥakhamim have completed their [full] statement (in two clauses), and then he disagrees with them (regarding both clauses).

and it is a logical inference ... ...וְדִין הוּא

This expression introduces a logical inference — usually a קַל־וָחֹמֶר argument that begins with the word וּמָה.

For examples, see (וַ)הֲלֹא דִין הוּא, (וּ)מָה ... אֵינוֹ דִין שֶׁ-.

And logic indicates ... ...וְהַדִּין נוֹתֵן

This expression, which occurs regularly in baraithoth of Midrash halakha, introduces a logical inference — usually a קַל־וָחֹמֶר argument.

For an example — see סוכה לו, סע"ב.

SEE: (וְ)הוּא הַדִּין, (וְ)הִיא הַנּוֹתֶנֶת

דִּינָא דְגַרְמִי* דִּין הַגּוֹרְמִים הָעֲקִיפִים

the case of indirect causes [of damage]

ר' מֵאִיר הוּא דְּדָאֵין דִּינָא דְגַרְמִי. (בבא קמא ק,א)

It is [the opinion of] R. Méir who [advocates] prosecuting the case of indirect causes [of damage].

* The second word is popularly pronounced גַּרְמִי.

SEE: גְּרָמָא

dinar (pl. דִּינָרִין) דִּינָר; (pl. דִּינָרֵי) *דִּינָרָא

(1) A *silver dinar* is a coin or a weight equal to half a *shekel*.** It is also called a *zuz*.**

(2) A *golden dinar* equals twenty-five *silver dinars*.**

* Both the Hebrew דִּינָר and the Aramaic דִּינָרָא are derived from the Latin *denarius*.

** See the table of coins and weights in Appendix II.

דִּיעֲבַד (= דְּאִיעֲבַד*)

מִשֶּׁנַּעֲשָׂה; לְאַחַר שֶׁכְּבָר נַעֲשָׂה; לְאַחַר מַעֲשֶׂה

once/after it has been done; after the fact

This term indicates an after-the-fact perspective towards an act whose performance may have been forbidden (or at least not recommended) by Jewish law. Once the act has been performed, we may consider whether it is subject to punishment or exempt therefrom or whether or not it constitutes a valid procedure. According to the Babylonian Talmud, the following terminology in a mishna or a baraitha indicates that an act is regarded as an acceptable procedure after the fact, דִּיעֲבַד (even though it was not proper for it to have been performed in the first place, לְכַתְּחִילָּה):

(1) the adjective כָּשֵׁר, *valid* or *fit*;

(2) the verb יָצָא or the fuller expression — יָצָא יְדֵי חוֹבָתוֹ, *he has fulfilled his obligation*;

(3) the use of the past tense of a verb (e.g., חָלַץ) — rather than the participle (e.g., חוֹלֵץ);

(4) the use of a participle preceded by the definite article (e.g., הָרוֹחֵץ).**

Each of the four usages is illustrated by one of the following four examples:

(1) משנה: ... שְׁחִיטָתָן כְּשֵׁרָה. (משנה חולין ב, רע"א)
תלמוד: דִּיעֲבַד! (בבלי שם)

MISHNA: ... their slaughtering is valid.

TALMUD: [Only] after the fact! (In other words, meat of animals slaughtered under certain circumstances under which slaughtering should not have been undertaken may nevertheless be eaten.)

(2) משנה: אִם הִשְׁלִים בַּתּוֹרָה, יָצָא. (ראש השנה לב,ב: משנה פ"ד מ"ו)

תלמוד: וְהָא "אִם הִשְׁלִים, יָצָא" קָתָנֵי — דִּיעֲבַד, אִין; לְכַתְּחִילָּה, לָא! (בבלי שם ע"פ כת"י)

*MISHNA: If he completed [his recitation of, for example, the "malkhiyoth" series of p*ᵉ*sukim] with [a pasuk from] the Torah, he has fulfilled his obligation.*

TALMUD: But [the tanna] states: "If he completed [his recitation] with [a pasuk from] the Torah, he has fulfilled his obligation" — after the fact, yes; [but] in the first place, [the procedure is] not [recommended]!

(3) משנה: ... וְחָלַץ לְזוֹ, אֵין אַחַר חֲלִיצָה כְּלוּם. (יבמות נ, סע"א: משנה פ"ה מ"ד)

תלמוד: מִי קָתָנֵי "חוֹלֵץ"?! "חָלַץ" קָתָנֵי — בְּדִיעֲבַד! (שם נג,א)

MISHNA: ... and he performed the ḥalitsa [ceremony] with respect to this [sister-in-law], there is nothing at all required after ḥalitsa.

TALMUD: Does [the tanna] state "he may perform the ḥalitsa"?! He states: "... he performed the ḥalitsa" — after the fact (implying that even though the ḥalitsa was effective, it was not really proper for it to be performed)!

(4) משנה: הָרוֹחֵץ בְּמֵי מְעָרָה ... (שבת קמ"ז, סע"א: משנה פכ"ב מ"ה)

תלמוד: "הָרוֹחֵץ" — דִּיעֲבַד, אִין; לְכַתְּחִילָּה, לָא! (שם)

MISHNA: One who is [already] bathing [on the Sabbath] in the [hot] water of a pit ...

TALMUD: "One who is [already] bathing" — after the fact yes; [but] in the first place, [the activity is] not [permissible on the Sabbath]!

* According to this etymology, דִּיעֲבַד is derived from the combination of ד־, *that*, and the אִתְפְּעֵל *binyan* of עבד, אִתְעֲבֵד = אִיעֲבַד, *it was done*. A different etymology regards דִּיעֲבַד as a combination of three elements: ד+אִי+עֲבַד, *that if he did [it]*.

** See the comments of Rashi and Tosafoth on סוטה ב,א.

דִּיקָא* (דוק) pass. prt. f.

precise; exact מְדֻיֶּקֶת

* Many pronounce this word דִּיקָא, while the Yemenites read it as an active participle, דָּיְקָא.

SEE: דוקְיָא

דִּיקָא נַמֵּי דְּקָתָנֵי אַף מְדֻיֶּקֶת, שֶׁהוּא שׁוֹנֶה ...

[The wording of the following text] is also precise (and hence supportive of what was just proposed), for [the tanna] states ...

This formula introduces a *proof* that is derived from the particular wording of a baraitha or mishna.

ברייתא: "מְעֻוָּת לֹא יוּכַל לִתְקוֹן" — זֶה שֶׁבִּטֵּל ... תְּפִלָּה שֶׁל עַרְבִית אוֹ תְּפִלָּה שֶׁל שַׁחֲרִית.

תלמוד: אֲמַר ר' יִצְחָק אֲמַר ר' יוֹחָנָן: הָכָא בְּמַאי עָסְקִינַן? שֶׁבִּטֵּל בְּמֵזִיד. אֲמַר רַב אַשִׁי: דִּיקָא נַמֵּי, דְּקָתָנֵי "בִּטֵּל" וְלָא קָתָנֵי "טָעָה". (ברכות כו, סע"א ע"פ קהלת א:טו)

BARAITHA: "That which is crooked cannot be made straight" — this [refers to a person] who omitted the Amida of the evening or the Amida of the morning.

TALMUD: R. Yitzhak said quoting R. Yohanan: With what [case] are we dealing here? With [a person] who deliberately omitted [the Amida]. Rav Ashi said: The wording [of the baraitha] is precise [and hence supportive of this interpretation], for [the tanna] states "omitted" and he does not state "erred."

SEE: מַתְנִיתִין נַמֵּי דִּיקָא דְּקָתָנֵי

דִּכְוָותֵיהּ SEE: דְּ(כְוָותֵיהּ)

דְּכִירִ* (דכר) pass. prt. **remembering** זָכוּר

כָּל מִילֵּי דְּכְדִי לָא דְּכִירִי אֱנָשֵׁי. (סנהדרין כט, רע"ב)

[As for] all matters of no consequence people do not remember [them].

* This passive participle form is active in meaning.

דְּכַר **he mentioned** הִזְכִּיר

This form, in the קַל *binyan*, is used only in the rhetorical question מַאן דְּכַר שְׁמֵיהּ?!, *who mentioned its name?!* This meaning is similar to the Midrash Halakha's interpretation of the parallel Hebrew

verb זכר, which is applied to such p^esukim as:

זָכוֹר אֵת אֲשֶׁר עָשָׂה לְךָ עֲמָלֵק (דברים כה:יז)

*Recite what Amalek did to you.**

Hebrew usually expresses this meaning with the הִפְעִיל *binyan* of זכר, הִזְכִּיר, which is parallel to the Aramaic אַפְעֵל, אַדְכַּר. **

* See תורת כהנים, ריש פרשת בחוקותי.

** מָאן אַדְכַּר שְׁמֵיהּ appears as an entry in the dictionary compiled by R. Sh^emuel b. Ḥofni Gaon, which was published by S. Abramson, in ספר אברהם אבן שושן, Jerusalem 5745. See p. 56.

SEE: אדְכַר, אַדְכַר, מָאן דְּכַר שְׁמֵיהּ

דַּל (דלל) imp.

Deduct! Take away! Eliminate! הַחְסֵר!

דַּל אֲנָא מֵהָכָא, מַתְנְיָיתָא מִי לָא קַשְׁיָן אַהֲדָדֵי?! (עירובין ג, רע"ב ורש"י שם).

[Even if you] eliminate me (= my halakhic statement) from here, will the two baraithoth not contradict each other?!

דְּלָא (דלי: דָּלֵי prt.)

he lifted; he raised; he drew (water from a well) הִגְבִּיהַּ; הֵרִים; דָּלָה

אִי לָאו דִּדְלַאי לָךְ חַסְפָּא, מִי מַשְׁכַּחַת מַרְגָּנִיתָא תוּתֵיהּ?! (מכות כא,ב; יבמות צב,ב; בבא מציעא יז,ב)

If I had not lifted up the shell for you, would you have found the pearl under it?!

דִּלְמָא SEE: דִּילְמָא

דָּמֵי (דמי: דָּמְיָא .f.s, דָּמוּ .m. pl, דָּמְיָין .f. pl.) prt.

resembling; is like דּוֹמֶה

This word usually appears at the end of a clause.

גֵּר שֶׁנִּתְגַּיֵּיר כְּקָטָן שֶׁנּוֹלַד דָּמֵי. (יבמות כב,א וש"נ)

A proselyte who has converted is like a newborn infant.

SEE: הֵיכִי דָּמֵי, מִי דָּמֵי

דָּמִים (דָּם .s); **דְּמֵי*** (דְּמָא .s)

(1) blood; bloodguiltiness

"דָּמִים" תַּרְתֵּי מַשְׁמַע. (מגילה יד, רע"ב ורש"י שם)

*[The word] דָּמִים means two [different things] (menstrual blood and the shedding of blood, i.e., murder).***

(2) value

לְפִי מִדָּה מְשַׁלֵּם אוֹ לְפִי דָּמִים מְשַׁלֵּם? (פסחים לב, רע"א)

Must he repay according to the quantity [of the stolen produce] or according to [its] value?

(3) money

דְּמֵי קָא יָהֵיב. (בבא מציעא ב,ב) *He is paying money.*

* The first form is Hebrew, and the second is Aramaic.

** This is the correct explanation of the Talmudic statement in context. In Modern Hebrew, however, the same statement is quoted out of context to indicate that דָּמִים means both *blood* and *money*.

דָּן (דון: דָּן **prt.**, לָדוּן **inf.**, דּוּן **imp.**);
דָּן* (דָּאֵין **prt.**, לְמֵידָן **inf.**, דּוּן **imp.**)

(1) he judged

דָּן אֶת הַדִּין (בכורות כח,ב: משנה פ"ד מ"ד)
[if] he judged the case

(2) he derived (through analogy, according to one of the rules of Biblical interpretation)

דָּנִין תַּשְׁלוּמִין מִתַּשְׁלוּמִין, וְאֵין דָּנִים תַּשְׁלוּמִין מִמִּיתָה. (בבא קמא מד,ב)
We may derive [a ruling regarding] payment from [a ruling regarding] payment, but we may not derive [a ruling regarding] payment from [a ruling regarding] killing.

(3) he discussed; he argued

הַדָּנִין לִפְנֵי חֲכָמִים (משנה עדיות פ"א מ"י)
*[the scholars] who discuss [halakhic matters] before the hakhamim***

* The first verb is Hebrew, and the second Aramaic.
** See סנהדרין יז,ב where the identity of these scholars is discussed.
SEE: דָּאֵין, דִּין

vessel; jug; barrel חָבִית **דַּנָּא**
רָמֵי אַרְבְּעִין וְתַמְנֵי כּוּזֵי בְּדַנָּא. (ב"מ מ, סע"א ורש"י שם)
They pour forty-eight cups [of wine] into a jug.

this זֶה demon. pron. **דְּנָא**
מִן קַדְמַת דְּנָא* (בבא מציעא קד,א ועוד)
"from before this" (= formerly; from days of old)
* This expression, in a slightly different form, מִקַּדְמַת דְּנָה, occurs in עזרא ה:יא.

this זֶה demon. adj. **דְּנָן**
this bill of divorce גִּיטָא דְּנָן (בבא מציעא יח,א)

one-sixth שְׁתוּת*; שִׁשִּׁית **דַּנְקָא**
* See the table of fractions in Appendix II.

דְּעָלְמָא SEE: (דְּ)עָלְמָא

דַּעַת; דַּעְתָּא*

(1) mind

וְכִי תַּעֲלֶה עַל דַּעְתְּךָ ...? (סנהדרין כח, סע"ב)
Would it enter your mind ...?

(2) understanding; reason; opinion

דַּעַת נוֹטָה. (חולין צ, סע"ב)
Reason inclines (towards a particular decision).

(3) awareness; knowledge

לְדַעַת — צָרִיךְ דַּעַת. (בבא קמא קיח, סע"א)
[If the theft was carried out] with [the] knowledge [of the owner], [the thief's return of the stolen goods] requires [the] knowledge [of the owner].

(4) consent

"יָדָהּ" אִיתָא, בֵּין מִדַּעְתָּהּ בֵּין בְּעַל כּוּרְחָהּ. (גיטין כא,א ע"פ דברים כד,א)
[If he places a bill of divorce in] "her hand," it constitutes [a valid divorce] — whether [it was placed there] with her consent or against her will.

(5) intent; intention; purpose

וְדַעְתּוֹ לְגָרְשָׁהּ (יבמות לז,ב)
and it is his intent to divorce her

* The Hebrew noun is דַּעַת and occasionally דֵּעָה; the Aramaic form is דַּעְתָּא.
SEE: סָלְקָא דַעְתָּךְ, בֶּן דַּעַת, אַדַּעְתָּא ד־

דָּק (דוק: דָּיֵיק **act. prt.**, דִּיק **pass. prt.**, לְמֵידַק **inf.**)

(1) דַּיֵּק; דִּקְדֵּק **he was exact/particular**
אָמַר שְׁמוּאֵל: שִׁיעוּר הֲדַס וַעֲרָבָה שְׁלֹשָׁה .... לָא דָּק. (סוכה לב,ב)
*Sh*muel stated: The [minimum] length of the myrtle and willow branches must be three [handbreadths] .... He was not exact (since a length of two and a half is really sufficient).*

(2) בָּדַק **he examined; he investigated**
For an example, see נְפַק דָּק וְאַשְׁכַּח.
SEE: דָּיֵיק, דִּיקָא

small; thin; fine **דַּק**
בְּהֵמָה דַקָּה (בבא קמא עט,ב: משנה פ"ז מ"ז)
"small cattle" (= sheep and goats)

דְּרַבָּנָן SEE: (דְּ)רַבָּנָן

step; level מַדְרֵגָה; מַעֲלָה **דַּרְגָּא***
חוּת דַּרְגָּא, נְסִיב אִיתְּתָא! (יבמות סג,א ע"פ כת"י ורש"י שם)
Go down a step [socially when you] take a wife!
* This word is used frequently in Modern Hebrew with a Hebraised spelling דַּרְגָּה.

child; schoolboy תִּינוֹק **דַּרְדְּקָא**
דַּרְדְּקֵי! לָא כָּךְ אָמַרְתִּי לָכֶם ...?! (שבת קמח,ב וע' רש"י שם)
Children! Did I not say to you thus ...?!
SEE: סָקְרֵי דַרְדְּקֵי

הַדָּרוֹם; דָּרוֹמָא*

the Darom; the South; Judea (especially Lod and its vicinity — as opposed to the Galilee)

וְהָיָה הָעוֹלָם שָׁמֵם עַד שֶׁבָּא ר' עֲקִיבָא אֵצֶל רַבּוֹתֵינוּ שֶׁבַּדָּרוֹם וּשְׁנָאָהּ לָהֶם (יבמות סב,ב)
and the world remained desolate until R. Akiva came to our teachers who [live] in the Darom and taught it (= Torah) to them
* The first form is Hebrew, and the second Aramaic.

דָּרֵי SEE: בֵּי דָרֵי

the ways of peace **דַּרְכֵי שָׁלוֹם**
The hakhamim instituted certain regulations in order to encourage peaceful relationships between

people and to discourage quarreling and controversy.

וְאֵילּוּ דְּבָרִים אָמְרוּ מִפְּנֵי דַּרְכֵי שָׁלוֹם: כֹּהֵן קוֹרֵא רִאשׁוֹן וְאַחֲרָיו לֵוִי ... (גיטין נט, סע"א: משנה פ"ה מ"ח)

And these are matters [the ḥakhamim] stated to promote the ways of peace: a kohen [is called up to] read the Torah first, and a levi after him ...

דְּרָרָא זִיקָה; הֶפְסֵד **stake; risk; a loss**

דְּרָרָא דְּמָמוֹנָא (בבא מציעא ב, סע"ב וע' רש"י ושטמ"ק שם)

a monetary stake; a loss of money

דְּרַשׁ (prt. דָּרֵשׁ) דָּרַשׁ

(1) he interpreted (a Biblical passage)

לְרִ' שִׁמְעוֹן דְּדָרֵישׁ טַעְמָא דִקְרָא (קידושין סח,ב וש"נ ע"פ דבו'ים ז:א־ד)

according to R. Shim'on who interprets the reason [expressed or implied] in the pasuk (as a basis for halakhic conclusions)

(2) he lectured; he delivered a public lecture (in the beth midrash)

ר' אַבָּהוּ דְּרַשׁ בְּאַגַּדְתָּא; ר' חִיָּיא בַּר אַבָּא דְּרַשׁ בִּשְׁמַעְתָּא. (סוטה מ,א)

R. Abbahu lectured on aggada; R. Ḥiyya b. Abba lectured on halakha.

SEE: מַאי דְּרַשׁ

דְּרָשָׁא מִדְרָשׁ

a (Biblical) interpretation (that serves as a basis for either a halakhic or an aggadic teaching)

For an example, see חַבִּיב.

SEE: מִדְרָשׁ

דָּשׁ (דוש: prt. דָּיֵישׁ)

דָּרַךְ; דָּרַס; דָּשׁ; הָרְגַּל **he tread; he trampled; he threshed; he became familiar**

כֵּיוָן דְּדָשׁ בֵּיהּ, כְּהֶתֵּירָא דָּמֵי לֵיהּ. (חולין ד,ב)

Since he has trampled upon it, it appears like a permissible act to him.

דַּשָּׁא דֶּלֶת **door; entrance**

תְּלָא נַפְשֵׁיהּ בְּעִיבּוּרָא דְּדַשָּׁא (סוכה נב, סע"א ורש"י שם)

he leaned against the bolt of the door

ה

הָ-

This prefix is a contraction of הָא, the next entry.

SEE: הָנִיחָא, (וְ)הָתַנְיָא, (וְ)הָתְנַן

הָא

this **(1) זוֹ***

this statement הָא מילְתָא (ברכות מה,ב ועוד)

behold; this implies; from here **(2) הֲרֵי**

(a) הָא often introduces an *inference* that is derived from a statement that has just been quoted in the Talmud. The fuller expression הָא לָמַדתָּ, *thus you have derived*, is sometimes used.

"מָשַׁח ה' אותי לְבַשֵּׂר עֲנָוִים" — "חֲסידים" לא נֶאֱמַר אֶלָּא "עֲנָוִים"! הָא לָמַדתָּ שֶׁעֲנָוָה גְדוֹלָה מכּוּלָן. (עבודה זרה כ,ב ע"פ ישעיה סא:א)

"God has annointed me to bring good tidings to the humble" — "the pious" is not stated but rather "the humble"! Thus you have derived that humility is greater than all of these (character traits).

(b) Sometimes, הָא introduces an *inference* based upon *contrast* between the case that has been stated in a text and a different case.

משנה: כִּכָּרוֹת שֶׁלַּנַּחְתּוֹם ... הֲרֵי אלו שלו. (בבא מציעא כא,א: משנה פ"ב מ"א)

תלמוד: הָא שֶׁלְּבַעַל הַבַּיִת חַיָּיב לְהַכְרִיז. (שם כג,א)

MISHNA: A baker's loaves belong to him (= the finder).

TALMUD: This implies [that for] homemade [loaves, the finder] is obligated to make an announcement.

Behold ...! Is it not ...?! **(3) הֲרֵי ...!**

הָא sometimes has *rhetorical* force that can be expressed in English either by an exclamation introduced by *behold* or by the use of interrogative word order with a negative.

הָא אַדְכַּר לֵיהּ בִּקְרִיאַת שְׁמַע! (ברכות כא,א)

Behold he has mentioned it during the recitation of the Sh^ema! or *Has he not mentioned it during the recitation of the Sh^ema?!*

ago **(4) זֶה**

זְבַנִי לֵיהּ מִינֵּיהּ הָא אַרְבְּעִי שְׁנֵי (בבא בתרא ל, סע"ב)

I bought it from him four years ago

here is; here are **(5) הִנֵּה****

here is the document הָא שְׁטָרָא (בבא בתרא לב, סע"א)

* As a demonstrative adjective, הָא almost always modifies a *feminine* noun – but there are some exceptions, especially in our printed editions. The proper masculine form is הַאי.

** Similarly, in the phrase הָא לַחְמָא עַנְיָא in the Pesaḥ Haggada, הָא is probably best translated *here is*.

SEE: (וְ)הָא גוּפָא קַשְׁיָא, הָא דִידֵיהּ הָא דְרַבֵּיהּ, הָא ... הָא ... (וְ)הָא ...,
הָא כִּדְאִיתָא וְהָא כִּדְאִיתָא, הָא כֵּיצַד, הָא מַנִּי, הָא קָא מַשְׁמַע לַן, הָא תוּ לָמָּה לִי, טַעְמָא ד- ... הָא, (וְ)תוּ לֵיכָּא וְהָא אִיכָּא, (וְ)הָא אִיפְּכָא שָׁמְעִינַן לְהוּ, הָא איפְלִיגוּ/פְּלִיגִי בַּהּ חֲדָא זִימְנָא, (וְ)הָא אֲמַרְהָ ... חֲדָא זִימְנָא, (וְ)הָא אֲנַן תְּנַן, (וְ)הָא כְּתִיב, (וְ)הָא/לָאו אִיתְמַר עֲלַהּ, (וְ)הָא עֲלַהּ קָתָנֵי, הָא תְּנָא לֵיהּ רֵישָׁא

הֵא*

here is

הא גיטיך. (גיטין עח,א: משנה פ"ח מ"ב)

Here is your bill of divorce.

* This word is found in Biblical Hebrew: הא לָכֶם זֶרַע in בראשית מז:כג.

SEE: הֵילָךְ

וְהָא אִיפְּכָא שָׁמְעִינַן לְהוּ

וַהֲרֵי חִילּוּף אָנוּ שׁוֹמְעִים אוֹתָם?!

But have we not heard them (= the two disputing tannaitic opinions) in reverse?!

This expression introduces a *contradiction* between two versions of the same tannaitic controversy — one version that the Talmud has just quoted and a different version that the Talmud is about to quote where the names of the same disputing tannaim are transposed.

משנה: עַד כַּמָּה מְזַמְּנִין? עַד כַּזַּיִת. ר' יְהוּדָה אוֹמֵר: עַד כַּבֵּיצָה.
תלמוד: לְמֵימְרָא דר' מאיר חָשִׁיב לֵיהּ כַּזַּיִת וְר' יְהוּדָה כַּבֵּיצָה? וְהָא אִיפְּכָא שָׁמְעִינַן לְהוּ! דתְנַן: ... ר' מאיר אוֹמֵר: ... בְּכַבֵּיצָה, ור' יְהוּדָה אוֹמֵר: ... בְּכַזַּיִת! (ברכות מט,ב ע"פ משנה שם פ"ז מ"א ומשנה פסחים פ"ג מ"ח)

MISHNA: How much [do people have to eat in order to] recite Birkath HaZimmun? As much as an olive. R Y^ehuda says: As much as an egg.

TALMUD: Is that to say that for R Méir the size of an olive is significant (since an anonymous opinion in the mishna is regularly ascribed to R Méir) and for R Y^ehuda the size of an egg? But have we not heard them in reverse?! For we have learnt [in another mishna]: ... R Méir says: ... as much as an egg, and R Y^ehuda says: ... as much as an olive!

In the continuation of the passage and in some other cases as well, the Talmud proceeds to quote an amora who resolves the contradiction through the argument מוּחְלֶפֶת הַשִּׁיטָה, *the line [of opinions] must be reversed*.

SEE: מוּחְלֶפֶת הַשִּׁיטָה

הָא אִיפְּלִיגוּ/פְּלִיגִי בַּהּ חֲדָא זִימְנָא

הֲרֵי נֶחְלְקוּ/חֲלוּקִים בָּהּ פַּעַם אַחַת?!

Haven't they [already] disputed this [point] once [before]?!

A *difficulty*: Why is the same controversy, between the same ḥakhamim, presented a second time?! The Talmud usually responds that the two

formulations of the controversy differ in some significant way, so that they are really two independent controversies.

For an example — see the controversies between Rav and Sh^e^muel in בבא מציעא טו,ב.

וְהָא /וְלָאו אִיתְּמַר עֲלַהּ
וַהֲרֵי /וַהֲלֹא נֶאֱמַר עָלֶיהָ ...?!

But has it not been stated in connection with it (= the text) ...?!

A *difficulty:* A mishna, a baraitha, or a statement of an early amora has been quoted in the Talmud as proof for a proposition. This formula is now used to introduce a comment on that text by an amora that interprets it in such a manner that the proof is undermined.

הֵיכָא דְאִיכָּא דֵיעוֹת שָׁאנֵי, דְּקָתָנֵי סֵיפָא: רַבָּן שִׁמְעוֹן בֶּן גַּמְלִיאֵל אוֹמֵר: שְׁנֵי אַכְסְנָיִים אוֹכְלִין עַל שֻׁלְחָן אֶחָד — זֶה בָּשָׂר וְזֶה גְּבִינָה — וְאֵין חוֹשְׁשִׁין. וְלָאו אִתְּמַר עֲלַהּ: אָמַר ... שְׁמוּאֵל: לֹא שָׁנוּ אֶלָּא שֶׁאֵין מַכִּירִין זֶה אֶת זֶה אֲבָל מַכִּירִין זֶה אֶת זֶה, אֲסוּרִים?! (שבת יג,א)

[A case] where there are [two or more] people is unique (and so it is permitted for one to eat meat and the other to eat cheese at the same table), as [the tanna] states [in] the latter clause: Rabban Shim'on b. Gamliel says: Two travellers may eat at the same table — one [eating] meat and the other cheese — and they need not be concerned [about any transgression]. But has it not been stated in connection with it: ... Sh^e^muel said: They taught [this] only where [the two people] are not acquainted with each other, but [in a case where] they are acquainted with each other, they are forbidden (hence the case where there are two people is not always permissible)?!

SEE: (וְ)הָא עֲלַהּ קָתָנֵי, (וְ)אִיתְּמַר עֲלַהּ

וְהָא אָמְרַהּ ... חֲדָא זִימְנָא
הֲרֵי ... אָמַר אוֹתָהּ פַּעַם אַחַת?!

But didn't ... [already] state it once?!

A *difficulty:* Why did the ḥakham make a halakhic statement that is essentially the same as the statement he made on a previous occasion?!

אָמַר רַבָּה בַּר בַּר חָנָה אָמַר ר׳ יוֹחָנָן: "הַטּוֹב וְהַמֵּטִיב" צְרִיכָה מַלְכוּת. מַאי קָא מַשְׁמַע לַן? כָּל בְּרָכָה שֶׁאֵין בָּהּ מַלְכוּת לֹא שְׁמָהּ בְּרָכָה? וְהָא אָמְרַהּ ר׳ יוֹחָנָן חֲדָא זִימְנָא?! (ברכות מט,א)

Rabba, grandson of Ḥanna, said quoting R. Yoḥanan: [The recitation of] הַטּוֹב וְהַמֵּטִיב [in Birkath HaMazon] requires [the mention of God's] Kingship. What [new halakha] is he teaching us? [That] any b^e^rakha that does not contain a mention of Kingship is not called a [proper] b^e^rakha? But didn't R. Yoḥanan [himself already] state it once?!

וְהָא אֲנַן תְּנַן, וְהָאֲנַן תְּנַן
וַהֲרֵי אָנוּ שָׁנִינוּ [בְּמִשְׁנָתֵנוּ] ...?!

But have we not learnt [in our mishna] ... ?!

This formula introduces a *contradiction* between our mishna, which the Talmud is about to quote, and the halakha that has just been quoted. Sometimes, instead of quoting an entire clause from our mishna, the Talmud quotes only the crucial word or phrase, inserting it between the words אֲנַן and תְּנַן.

For an example, see חוּא דְּאָמַר כִּי/כִּ־.

SEE: (וְ)הָתְנַן

הָא גוּפָא קַשְׁיָא   זוֹ עַצְמָהּ קָשָׁה!

This [text] itself is difficult!

This expression introduces a *contradiction* between two clauses of the same mishna or baraitha. In most instances, the contradiction is not obvious, but it is inferred from the implications of the clauses.

בריית‎א: הָעוֹסְקִין בַּמִּקְרָא — מִדָּה וְאֵינָהּ מִדָּה. בַּמִּשְׁנָה — מִדָּה וְנוֹטְלִין עָלֶיהָ שָׂכָר. בַּתַּלְמוּד — אֵין לְךָ מִדָּה גְּדוֹלָה מִזּוֹ, וּלְעוֹלָם הֱוֵי רָץ לַמִּשְׁנָה יוֹתֵר מִן הַתַּלְמוּד.

תלמוד: הָא גוּפָא קַשְׁיָא! אָמְרַתְּ "בַּתַּלְמוּד — אֵין לְךָ מִדָּה גְּדוֹלָה מִזּוֹ", וַהֲדַר אָמְרַתְּ "וּלְעוֹלָם הֱוֵי רָץ לַמִּשְׁנָה יוֹתֵר מִן הַתַּלְמוּד"! (בבא מציעא לג, סע״א)

BARAITHA: [As for] those who study the [written] Torah — it is meritorious but not [so] meritorious. [The study of] the Mishna is meritorious, and one receives reward for it. [As for the study of] the Talmud — you have nothing more meritorious than this, yet you should always run to the Mishna more than [to] the Talmud.

TALMUD: This [baraitha] itself is difficult! You said: "[As for the study of] the Talmud — you have nothing more meritorious than this," and then you said: "Yet you should always run to the Mishna more than [to] the Talmud"!

הָא דִּידֵיהּ הָא דְּרַבֵּיהּ   זוֹ שֶׁלּוֹ; [וְ]זוֹ שֶׁל רַבּוֹ.

This [halakhic statement] is his own; [while] the other is [the opinion] of his teacher.

In order to arrive at a *resolution* of a contradiction between two statements of the same ḥakham, it is sometimes argued that one statement truly represents his own personal opinion, while the other is the opinion of his teacher, which he has presented even though he disagrees with it.

For an example — see בבא קמא ל, רע״א.

הָא ...(וְ)הָא ...   זוֹ ... (וְ)זוֹ ...

This ..., (while) that ...; One ..., (while) the other ...

This formula is often used to point out a *distinction* between two halakhic statements.

(1) In some instances, it is proposed that the statements were formulated by two different authors who are in disagreement.*

הָא ר' מֵאִיר; הָא ר' יְהוּדָה. (ברכות טו, סע"א ועוד)
This [halakha is the opinion of] R. Méir; [while] that [halakha is the opinion of] R. Y°huda.

(2) In other instances, it is proposed that the two statements deal with different circumstances.*

הָא דְאִיכָּא אָדָם חָשׁוּב; הָא דְלֵיכָּא אָדָם חָשׁוּב. (ברכות נג,א)
One [baraitha speaks of a situation] where a distinguished person is present; [while] the other [speaks of a situation] where there is no distinguished person present.

* For further examples, see לָא קַשְׁיָא and לָא פְּלִיגִי.

הָא כִּדְאִיתָא וְהָא כִּדְאִיתָא

זוֹ כְּמוֹת שֶׁהִיא, וְזוֹ כְּמוֹת שֶׁהִיא.

This one is as it is, and the other is as it is.

A *rejection* of a comparison: In spite of the juxtaposition of the two cases in the text before us, it is now contended that each case is unique and follows its own particular rules. Therefore the previous proposal comparing them is rejected.

See example under מִידֵי אִרְיָא, which often introduces this formula.

SEE: אִיתָא

הָא כֵּיצַד   זוֹ אֵיךְ?!   **How [can] this [be]?!**

This rhetorical question is used to point out a *contradiction* — often between two p°sukim.

תְּרֵי קְרָאֵי כְּתִיבִי. כְּתִיב: "שִׁבְעַת יָמִים שְׂאוֹר לֹא יִמָּצֵא בְּבָתֵּיכֶם", וּכְתִיב: "אַךְ בַּיּוֹם הָרִאשׁוֹן תַּשְׁבִּיתוּ שְּׂאוֹר מִבָּתֵּיכֶם". הָא כֵּיצַד?! (פסחים ד, סע"ב ע"פ שמות יב:יט,טו)
Two p°sukim are written. It is written: "Seven days it is forbidden for leavening to be found in your houses," and it is written: "Even on the first day you must destroy leaven from your houses!" How [can] this [be]?

הָא כְּתִיב   הֲרֵי כָּתוּב ...?!   **is it not written ...?!**

This formula introduces a *difficulty* that arises from a Biblical passage.

בריתא: קְרִיאַת שְׁמַע כִּכְתָבָהּ — דִּבְרֵי רַבִּי. וַחֲכָמִים אוֹמְרִים: בְּכָל לָשׁוֹן.
תלמוד: ... וְרַבָּנָן, מַאי טַעְמַיְיהוּ? אָמַר קְרָא: "שְׁמַע" — בְּכָל לָשׁוֹן שֶׁאַתָּה שׁוֹמֵעַ. וּלְרַבִּי נַמִי הָא כְּתִיב: "שְׁמַע"?! ... (ברכות יג, סע"א)
BARAITHA: The Sh°ma is to be recited, as it is written (= i.e., in the Hebrew language) — the words of Rebbi. But the Ḥakhamim say: In any language.
TALMUD: ... And what is the reason of the Ḥakhamim? The Torah states: שְׁמַע (= understand!) [implying] in any language that you understand. But according to Rebbi also, is it not written שְׁמַע?! (= How could he explain the choice of this verb?!)

הָא לָא קַשְׁיָא   זוֹ אֵינָהּ קָשָׁה ...

This is not difficult (but another point is difficult) ...

With this expression, the Talmud presents a *resolution* of one difficulty facing the halakha under discussion — but then it proceeds to raise another, more serious difficulty.

For an example — see שבועות כג, סע"ב (ורש"י שם).

הָא מַנִּי

whose [halakha] is this?   זוֹ [שֶׁל] מִי הִיא?

This *question* seeks to determine which tanna's opinion is presented in an anonymous mishna or baraitha. In many instances, the purpose of this investigation is the resolution of a difficulty (e.g., in שבת ד, סע"א); sometimes the purpose is to raise a difficulty (e.g., בבא קמא קיד, סע"א).

SEE: מַנִּי, מַתְנִיתִין מַנִּי

וְהָא עֲלַהּ קָתָנֵי   וַהֲרֵי עָלֶיהָ הוּא שׁוֹנֶה ...?!

But in connection with it (= this text) doesn't [a tanna] teach ... ?!

This formula is used in presenting a *refutation*. After a mishna or a baraitha has been quoted in the Talmud as proof for a proposition, this formula introduces an explanatory tannaitic text that interprets that mishna or baraitha in a way that undermines the proof. This tannaitic text may be a separate baraitha (e.g., יומא סט, סע"ב) or a later clause in the same mishna (e.g., ב"מ פ,ב) or in the same baraitha (e.g, ב"מ עו,ב).

SEE: (וְ)הָא אִיתְּמַר עֲלַהּ, (וְ)תָנֵי עֲלַהּ

הָא קָא מַשְׁמַע לַן   זוֹ הוּא מַשְׁמִיעַ לָנוּ ...

This [is what the tanna of the mishna or baraitha] teaches us ...

בריתא: מֶלֶךְ שֶׁעָמַד בְּעֶשְׂרִים וְתִשְׁעָה בַּאֲדָר — כֵּיוָן שֶׁהִגִּיעַ אֶחָד בְּנִיסָן, עָלְתָה לוֹ שָׁנָה.
תלמוד: הָא קָא מַשְׁמַע לַן דְּנִיסָן רֹאשׁ הַשָּׁנָה לִמְלָכִים. (ראש השנה ב, סע"א־רע"ב)
BARAITHA: [As for] a king who ascends [the throne] on the twenty-ninth of Adar — as soon as the first of Nisan arrives, it is reckoned as [the completion of] one year of his reign.
TALMUD: This [is what the tanna of the baraitha] teaches us that [the first of] Nisan is the new year for kings.

הָא תוּ לָמָּה לִי   זוֹ עוֹד לָמָּה לִי?!

Why do I need this, too?!

This question points out a *difficulty*: The halakha formulated in the text before us is redundant, because it is essentially the same as a halakha that has already been stated — either earlier in the same text or in another text. In some instances, the question הָא תוּ לָמָּה לִי? is followed by the exclamation הַיְינוּ הָךְ! *(this is [the same as] that!)* in order to dramatise the point. Usually, the

Talmud proceeds to explain away the difficulty by showing that the halakha does contain at least one novel element, and so it is not redundant after all.

ברייתא: נוֹתְנִין מְזוֹנוֹת לִפְנֵי הַכֶּלֶב בֶּחָצֵר. נְטָלוֹ וְיָצָא, אֵין נִזְקָקִין לוֹ. כַּיּוֹצֵא בוֹ נוֹתְנִין מְזוֹנוֹת לִפְנֵי הַנָּכְרִי בֶּחָצֵר. נְטָלוֹ וְיָצָא, אֵין נִזְקָקִין לוֹ.
תלמוד: הָא תּוּ לָמָּה לִי?! הַיְינוּ הָךְ! (שבת יט, רע"א)

BARAITHA: We may place food before a dog in a courtyard [on the Sabbath]. If it (= the dog) takes it and goes out [carrying the food], we are not obliged [to restrain the dog from carrying in the street]. Similarly, we may place food before a non-Jew in a courtyard [on the Sabbath]. If he takes it and goes out [carrying the food], we are not obliged [to restrain him from carrying].

TALMUD: Why do I need this (= the latter clause), too?! The latter [clause] is [the same as] the former!

SEE: הַיְינוּ הָךְ, תַּרְתֵּי לָמָּה לִי

הָא תָּנָא לֵיהּ רֵישָׁא

הֲרֵי [הַתַּנָּא] שָׁנָה אוֹתוֹ [בָּ]רֹאשׁ?!

Hasn't [the tanna already] stated it in an earlier clause?!

This *rhetorical question* points out a redundancy in the text of a mishna or baraitha, in that the halakha of a later clause has already been stated in an earlier clause.

משנה: לֹא יֵשֵׁב אָדָם לִפְנֵי הַסַּפָּר סָמוּךְ לְמִנְחָה עַד שֶׁיִּתְפַּלֵּל ... וְאִם הִתְחִילוּ אֵין מַפְסִיקִין. מַפְסִיקִין לִקְרִיאַת שְׁמַע, וְאֵין מַפְסִיקִין לִתְפִלָּה. (שבת ט, רע"ב: משנה פ"א מ"ב)
תלמוד: הָא תָּנָא לֵיהּ רֵישָׁא: אֵין מַפְסִיקִין?! (שם יא,א)

*MISHNA: A man should not sit down before a barber close to minḥa until he has said the Amida. But if they have begun [the haircut], they need not interrupt [for the Amida]. They must interrupt for the reading of the Sh*e*ma, but need not interrupt for the Amida.*

TALMUD: Hasn't [the tanna already] stated it in an earlier clause: They need not interrupt [for the Amida]?!

SEE: תְּנָא/תָּנָא

הַאי (f. הָא) זֶה
this; the latter

Besides its regular use as a demonstrative adjective or pronoun, הַאי is often used before a Biblical or tannaitic quotation in the sense of *this word, this expression,* or *this clause.*

הַאי "וְכָתַב" — מַאי עָבְדִי לֵיהּ?! (גיטין כא,ב ע"פ דברים כד:א)

[as for] this expression "and he shall write" — what would they (= the Ḥakhamim) do with it?

SEE: כּוּלֵּי הַאי

כְּהַאי גַּוְונָא
SEE: כִּי הַאי גַּוְונָא

הַאי דְּ- זֶה שֶׁ- ...
this [one] that ...; the fact that ...; the reason why ...

אָמַר רַב חִסְדָּא: הַאי דַּעֲדִיפְנָא מֵחַבְרַאי דִּנְסֵיבְנָא בְּשִׁיתְסַר.

(קידושין כט, סע"ב)

Rav Ḥisda said: The reason why I am superior to my colleagues is that I married at [the age of] sixteen.

הַאי ... וְהַאי ... זֶה ... וְזֶה ...
this ... and that ...; one ... and the other ...

הַאי לְחוּדֵיהּ קָאֵי, וְהַאי לְחוּדֵיהּ קָאֵי. (סנהדרין פח, סע"ב ועוד)

This [species] stands by itself, and that [species] stands by itself. (In other words, there is no real halakhic connection between them.)

SEE: הָא ... הָא

הַאי מַאי זֶה מַהוּ?!
what is this?! how now?!

This *rhetorical question* expresses opposition to a comparison that was stated explicitly or assumed implicitly in the Talmud, as if to say: How can two such cases be equated?! This expression is immediately followed by a more detailed objection, usually beginning with the term בִּשְׁלָמָא or the term אִי אָמְרַתְּ בִּשְׁלָמָא.

For an example — see קידושין יח, סע"ב.

SEE: אִי אָמְרַתְּ בִּשְׁלָמָא, (בִּ)שְׁלָמָא, מַאי הַאי, הָכִי הַשְׁתָּא, מִי דָּמֵי

הַאי מַאן דְּ-* מִי שֶׁ-
one who

This formula often introduces a halakhic statement or a general truth.

הַאי מַאן דְּאַרְתַּח כּוּפְרָא חַיָּיב מִשּׁוּם מְבַשֵּׁל. (שבת עד,ב)

One who boils pitch [on the Sabbath] is subject to punishment on account of "cooking."

הַאי מַאן דְּיָהִיר בַּעַל מוּם הוּא. (מגילה כט,א)

One who is haughty is blemished.

* הַאי means *this* so that the literal translation is *this who that*, which is not idiomatic English.

וְהַאי מִיבָּעֵי לֵיהּ לְגוּפֵיהּ וְזֶה נִצְרָךְ לוֹ לְעַצְמוֹ!
But this is needed for it itself!

After a midrashic interpretation of a Biblical passage was cited in support of a halakha, it is now argued that the interpretation is not well founded, because the passage can be understood in a sense that is closer to the Biblical context.

משנה: מְגִילָּה נִקְרֵאת בְּי"א, בְּי"ב, בְּי"ג, בְּי"ד, בְּט"ו. (מגילה ב, רע"א: משנה פ"א מ"א)
תלמוד: ... הֵיכָא רְמִיזָא? ... אָמַר ר' יוֹחָנָן: אָמַר קְרָא: "לְקַיֵּם אֶת יְמֵי הַפּוּרִים הָאֵלֶּה בִּזְמַנֵּיהֶם" — זְמַנִּים הַרְבֵּה תִּקְנוּ לָהֶם. הַאי מִיבָּעֵי לֵיהּ לְגוּפֵיהּ! (שם ע"פ אסתר ט:לא)

MISHNA: The scroll [of Esther] may be read on the eleventh, the twelfth, the thirteenth, the fourteenth, or the fifteenth [of Adar].

TALMUD: Where is [the reading on the eleventh, twelfth, thirteenth] alluded to [in Scripture]? ... R. Yoḥanan said: Scripture has stated: "To confirm these days of Purim in their times" — [indicating that] they enacted many times for them. [But] this [text] is needed for it itself (= its literal meaning, that the reading takes place on the fourteenth or fifteenth)!

הַאי מֵרַבָּנַן

"זֶה מֵהַחֲכָמִים"; אֶחָד מִן הַחֲכָמִים

"this one of the ḥakhamim"; this scholar

This term is sometimes used contemptuously.

דָּמֵי הַאי מֵרַבָּנַן כִּדְלָא גְמִירִי אֱינָשֵׁי שְׁמַעְתָּא. (ב"מ יא, רע"ב)

This scholar is like people who have not learnt halakha.

וְהַאי תַּנָּא מַיְיתֵי לַהּ מֵהָכָא

וְתַנָּא זֶה מֵבִיא אוֹתָהּ מִכָּאן.

And this tanna deduces it from here.

The Talmud has quoted one tanna as having derived the halakha or aggada under consideration from one Biblical passage. After some discussion, the Talmud now presents another tanna's derivation of the same halakha from a different Biblical passage.

משנה: וְהָאִישׁ אֶת אִשְׁתּוֹ. (בבא בתרא קח,א: משנה פ"ח מ"א)
תלמוד: מְנָהָנֵי מִילֵּי? דְּתָנוּ רַבָּנַן: "שְׁאֵרוֹ" — זוֹ אִשְׁתּוֹ, מְלַמֵּד שֶׁהַבַּעַל יוֹרֵשׁ אֶת אִשְׁתּוֹ ... וְהַאי תַּנָּא מַיְיתֵי לַהּ מֵהָכָא, דְּתַנְיָא: "וְיָרַשׁ אוֹתָהּ" — מְלַמֵּד שֶׁהַבַּעַל יוֹרֵשׁ אֶת אִשְׁתּוֹ, דִּבְרֵי ר' עֲקִיבָא. (שם קיא,ב ע"פ במדבר כז:יא)

MISHNA: And the husband [inherits] his wife.

TALMUD: From where [do we derive] these matters? As the ḥakhamim have taught: "His relative" — this [refers to] his wife, teaching that the husband inherits the wife ... And this tanna deduces it from here, as it is taught: "And he shall inherit her," teaching that the husband inherits his wife. [This is] the opinion of R. Akiva.

SEE: (וְ)תַנָּא מַיְיתֵי לַהּ מֵהָכָא

הָאִידָּנָא (הַאי+עִידָּנָא)

now; today (1) עַכְשָׁיו;

זִיל הָאִידָּנָא וְתָא לְמָחָר! (ביצה ד, סע"א ועוד)

Go today and come [back] tomorrow!

nowadays (2) בַּזְּמַן הַזֶּה

כְּמַאן מְצַלִּינַן הָאִידָּנָא: "זֶה הַיּוֹם תְּחִלַּת מַעֲשֶׂיךָ ..."? כְּמַאן? כְּרִ' אֱלִיעֶזֶר, דַּאֲמַר: בְּתִשְׁרִי נִבְרָא הָעוֹלָם. (ראש השנה כז,א)

*According to whom (= whose opinion) do we pray (on Rosh HaShana) nowadays: "This is the day of the beginning of your work ..."? According to whom? According to R. Eliezer, who said: The world was created in Tishri (as opposed to R. Y*hoshua who held that the world was created in Nisan).*

SEE: עִידָּנָא

הַאיְךְ* (f. הָךְ)

that (one); the former הַהוּא; הַלָּה

הַאי לַחֲגִיגַת חֲמִשָּׁה עָשָׂר, וְהַאיְךְ כּוּלֵּיהּ קְרָא לַחֲגִיגַת אַרְבָּעָה עָשָׂר (פסחים עא,ב ע"פ ויקרא ז:טז ודברים טז:ד)

this [pasuk refers] to the festive offering of the fifteenth (of Nisan), and that entire pasuk [refers] to the festive offering of the fourteenth

* The suffix ךְ- is added to הַאי, *this* (m.), and to הָא, *this* (f.) — forming הַאיְךְ and הָךְ respectively, *that*. In some instances, our editions have erroneously printed הֵיאַךְ, a word that really means *how* — instead of הַאיְךְ, the correct reading, which is found in manuscripts. See the example under שְׁלָמָא(ב).

וְהָאֲנַן תְּנַן SEE: (וְ)הָא אֲנַן תְּנַן

הַב imp. (יהב: הַבוּ .pl) תֵּן!

give!

Besides this common, literal meaning — this imperative form is occasionally used before another verb in the future, first person, to express urging or encouragement. In this sense, it is rendered in English by the expression *let us!**

הַב וְנִיבְרֵיךְ! (פסחים קג, רע"ב ע"פ רש"י ותוס' ור"ח שם)

Let us say Birkath HaMazon!

* A similar usage is found in Biblical Hebrew e.g., the pasuk הָבָה נִבְנֶה לָנוּ עִיר! (בראשית יא:ד) and in the Modern Hebrew song הָבָה נָגִילָה.

SEE: יְהַב

הֲבַאי/הֲוַואי

nonsense; exaggeration

נִדְרֵי הֲבַאי (נדרים כד,ב: פ"ג מ"ב) *vows of exaggeration*

SEE: לְשׁוֹן הֲבַאי/הֲוַואי

הַבוּ דְלָא לוֹסִיף עֲלַהּ

הָבָה שֶׁלֹּא נוֹסִיף עָלֶיהָ!

Let us not add to it!

The thrust of this expression is the following: Even if we do accept this controversial halakhic principle, we must at least refrain from extending it to any case that is significantly different from the original one.

For an example — see שבועות מח,ב (ורש"י שם).

הֵבִיא (בוא הִפְעִיל: מֵבִיא .prt, יָבִיא .fut, הָבֵא .imp, לְהָבִיא .inf)

he brought; he included

Besides its common Biblical meaning, this verb is sometimes used in the Mishna and in the Talmud to *amplify the scope of a halakha* based upon an extra word or expression in Scripture.

"לְמַעַן תִּזְכּוֹר אֶת יוֹם צֵאתְךָ מֵאֶרֶץ מִצְרַיִם כֹּל יְמֵי חַיֶּיךָ" ... וַחֲכָמִים אוֹמְרִים: "יְמֵי חַיֶּיךָ" — הָעוֹלָם הַזֶּה, "כֹּל יְמֵי חַיֶּיךָ" — לְהָבִיא לִימוֹת הַמָּשִׁיחַ.* (ברכות יב, סע"ב: משנה פ"א מ"ח ע"פ דברים טז:ג)

"So that you recall the day of your departure from the land of Egypt all the days of your life" ... And the Ḥakhamim say: "The days of your life" [means] this world, "all the days of your life" [is written] to include the days of the Mashiaḥ (in the mitzva of mentioning the departure from Egypt).

* Some manuscripts read לְהָבִיא אֶת יְמוֹת הַמָּשִׁיחַ.

SEE: רִיבָּה, רַבִּי, אַיְיתִי, הוֹצִיא

הָדָא .f זֹאת

this

SEE: הָדֵין, דָא

הֲדָדֵי (הֲדָדֵי: חַד חַד) **זֶה זֶה** **each other**

This word is often used with prefixes:

אַהֲדָדֵי upon each other; each other

בַּהֲדָדֵי with each other; together

כַּהֲדָדֵי like each other; equal

מֵהֲדָדֵי from each other; one from another

כֵּיוָן דְּכוּלְּהוּ כִּי הֲדָדֵי נִינְהוּ, מֵהֲדָדֵי יָלְפִינַן. (סנהדרין מ, רע״ב ע״פ כת״י ע׳ רש״י שם)

Since all of them (= the p^e^sukim) are like each other, we may derive one from another.

SEE: אַהֲדָדֵי, (בְּ)אַהֲדֵי הֲדָדֵי, כִּי הֲדָדֵי נִינְהוּ

בַּהֲדֵי **with; in the presence of**

SEE: בַּהֲדֵי

לַהֲדֵי/לְבַהֲדֵי **against; at**

SEE: לַהֲדֵי

בְּהֶדְיָא **clearly; explicitly**

SEE: בְּהֶדְיָא

לְהֶדְיָא **openly; directly; immediately**

SEE: לְהֶדְיָא

הֶדְיוֹט (pl. הֶדְיוֹטוֹת) **common; ordinary**

The connotation of this word depends upon which term is contrasted to it.

(1) a layman — as opposed to an אוּמָן, a professional

עוֹשִׂין מַעֲקֶה לַגַּג וְלַמִּרְפֶּסֶת מַעֲשֵׂה הֶדְיוֹט אֲבָל לֹא מַעֲשֵׂה אוּמָן. (מועד קטן יא,א: פ״א מ״י)

We may construct a parapet for a roof or a balcony [during the intermediate days of a festival if it is] the work of a layman, but not the work of a professional.

(2) secular — as opposed to הֶקְדֵּשׁ or גָּבוֹהַּ, sacred

ר׳ מֵאִיר סָבַר: מַעֲשֵׂר שֵׁנִי מָמוֹן גָּבוֹהַּ הוּא, וְרַבָּנַן סָבְרִי: מָמוֹן הֶדְיוֹט. (סנהדרין קיב, סע״ב)

R. Méir holds: The second tithe is sacred property, and the Ḥakhamim hold: [It is] secular property.

(3) a layman — as opposed to a מוּמְחֶה, an ordained judge

דִּינֵי מָמוֹנוֹת בִּשְׁלֹשָׁה הֶדְיוֹטוֹת; גְּזֵילוֹת וַחֲבָלוֹת בִּשְׁלֹשָׁה מוּמְחִין. (סנהדרין ג,א)

Monetary cases may be tried by three laymen; [but] larceny and bodily damages must be tried by three ordained judges.

(4) a common priest, כֹּהֵן הֶדְיוֹט — as opposed to the כֹּהֵן גָּדוֹל, the high priest

אִיסּוּר קְדוּשָּׁה: אַלְמָנָה לְכֹהֵן גָּדוֹל, גְּרוּשָׁה וַחֲלוּצָה לְכֹהֵן הֶדְיוֹט. (יבמות כ,א: משנה פ״ב מ״ד)

A prohibition by virtue of sanctity [refers to] a widow forbidden to a high priest; a divorcee or a woman who had performed ḥalitsa [even] to a common priest.

הָדֵין (f. הָדָא) **זֶה** **this**

מִן הָדֵין קְרָא (נדרים לח,א)

[the point is derived] from this pasuk

SEE: דֵּין

הֲדַר (הדר:* הָדַר .prt, לֶיהְדַּר .fut, לְמֶיהְדַּר .inf)

(1) חָזַר **he went back; he repeated; he returned**

אִי טָעֵי, הָדַר. (ברכות מט,ב)

If he makes [such] a mistake, he must go back [and recite Birkath HaMazon again].

(2) חָזַר בּוֹ **he reversed himself; he retracted; he changed his mind**

In this sense, the verb is usually followed by -ב with a personal-pronoun suffix, like -חזר ב in Hebrew.

הֲדַר בֵּיהּ רָבָא מֵהַהִיא. (שבת כז,א ועוד)

Rava reversed himself with respect to that (= the halakha he had previously stated).

(3) חָזַר; אַחַר כָּךְ

upon reconsideration; then; subsequently

This verb often precedes another verb in an adverbial sense. Sometimes the form הֲדַר is used irrespective of the form of the other verb, while in other instances the הדר form matches the subsequent verbal forms.

הֲדַר אֲמַר רָבָא: לָאו מִילְּתָא הִיא דַּאֲמַרִי. (מכות ח, סע״א)

Upon reconsideration, Rava said: What I stated [previously] is not a [valid] statement (but an error).

וְנָטְרִי לֵיהּ לְר׳ מֵאִיר עַד דִּמְסַיֵּים לַהּ לְמִילְּתָא וַהֲדַר פְּלִיגֵי עִילָּוֵיהּ (חולין פו,א)

and [the Ḥakhamim] wait for R. Méir to complete his statement and then disagree with him

הדור** קַבְּלוּהָ** בִּימֵי אֲחַשְׁוֵרוֹשׁ (שבת פח,א ע״פ אסתר ט:כז)

subsequently, they accepted it (= the Torah) in the days of Aḥashverosh

* For the full conjugation of this verb, see *Grammar for Gemara*: Chapter 4, Verb 5. Upon completing the study of a Talmudic tractate, it is customary to recite the formula, ... הדרן עֲלָךְ מַסֶּכֶת, which is usually printed at the conclusion of each tractate. The meaning of הדרן is somewhat obscure. It may be the first-person plural form of the past tense of our Aramaic verb הֲדַרַן or הֲדַרְן, the equivalent of the Hebrew חָזַרְנוּ, *we have returned (to you)* or *we have reviewed (you)*. Alternatively, it may be understood as a noun with a pronoun suffix, *may our glory be upon you*. The latter interpretation is supported by the continuation of this formula הֲדָרָךְ עֲלָן, which most probably means *may your glory be upon us*. See the discussion of this problem in D. Sperber's מִנְהֲגֵי יִשְׂרָאֵל (מוסד הרב קוק, ירושלים תשמ״ט), pp. 129–134.

** Both verbal forms are third-person masculine plural of the present tense.

SEE: הֲדַר קוּשְׁיָין לְדוּכְתַּיְיהוּ, תָּנֵי וַהֲדַר מְפָרֵשׁ

הַדַּר* (הדר פַּעֵל: מְהַדֵּר .prt, יְהַדֵּר .fut)

he honored; he glorified; he adorned

יָכוֹל יְהַדְּרֶנּוּ בְּמָמוֹן? (קידושין לב,ב ע"פ ויקרא יט:לב)
Could it be [that] one must honor him (= a scholar) with money?

* This entry is Hebrew, but the next one is Aramaic.

הֲדַר (הדר פָּעַל: מְהַדַּר prt., לְהַדַּר fut., הֲדוּרֵי inf.)

he pursued (zealously); he sought — חִזֵּר

הֲדוּרֵי אַפֵּירְכֵי לָמָּה לָךְ? אוֹתִיב מִמַּתְנִיתִין! (חולין עו,ב ורש"י)
Why do you seek refutations [from a baraitha]? Refute [the amora's statement] from our mishna (which is widely known and more authoritative)!

SEE: מְהַדַּר

הֲדַר קוּשְׁיָין לְדוּכְתֵּיהּ

חָזַר הַקֹּשִׁי שֶׁלָּנוּ לִמְקוֹמוֹ.

Our difficulty has returned to its place.

After a difficulty has been presented and then resolved, the resolution is sometimes refuted. Thus the original difficulty is reinstated.

For an example — see קידושין טו,ב.

הוּא (הִיא f., הֵן pl.)

he/it (m.); it is

Besides its common meanings, this personal pronoun is also used where English would use the linking verb *is*, especially in identifications.

Avram is Avraham. — אַבְרָם הוּא אַבְרָהָם. (ברכות יג,א)

Sometimes הוא appears twice for emphasis — once before the subject and once before the predicate.

אָמַר אַבָּיֵי: הוּא יַנַּאי הוּא יוֹחָנָן. (ברכות כט,א)
Abbayé said: Yannai is [identical with] Yoḥanan.

SEE: היא

הַהוּא (הַהִיא f.)

(1) that (one)

This masculine pronoun often refers to a Biblical passage and introduces an argument that limits the scope of the passage to particular circumstances, in order to resolve a difficulty or to raise an objection.

קְרִיאַת שְׁמַע דְּרַבָּנַן ... מְתִיב רַב יוֹסֵף: "[וְדִבַּרְתָּ בָּם ...] בְּשָׁכְבְּךָ וּבְקוּמֶךָ"! אָמַר לֵיהּ אַבָּיֵי: הַהוּא בְּדִבְרֵי תוֹרָה כְּתִיב. (ברכות כא,א ע"פ דברים ו:ז)
The recitation of Sh^e^ma is [a commandment] of Rabbinic status ... Rav Yosef raises an objection: [The Torah states that "you must recite them...] at the time of retiring" (at night) "and at the time of getting up" (in the morning — hence reciting the Sh^e^ma seems to be a Torah commandment). Abbayé said to him: That [pasuk] is written about [the commandment of studying] the words of the Torah.**

(2) someone; one; a man

This pronoun is sometimes used in the first sense of the expression הַהוּא גַּבְרָא, the next entry.

הַהוּא דַּאֲתָא לְקַמֵּיהּ דְּרַ' חֲנִינָא ... (בבא בתרא קכו,ב)
There was someone who came before R. Ḥanina ...

* Rav Yosef holds that בָּם, *them*, refers to the words of Sh^e^ma, whereas Abbayé holds that it refers to words of Torah in general.

SEE: (הַ)הִיא, הַהוּא מִיבָּעֵי לֵיהּ

הַהוּא גַּבְרָא

there was a man ... — (1) מַעֲשֶׂה בְּאָדָם אֶחָד ...

This expression is often used to introduce a narrative passage.

הַהוּא גַּבְרָא דְאַפְקִיד זוּזֵי גַּבֵּי חַבְרֵיהּ ... (בבא מציעא מב,א)
There was a man who deposited some money with his neighbor ...

"that man"; a certain man — (2) אוֹתוֹ אִישׁ

Sometimes it is used as a euphemism in place of the first-person or second-person singular pronoun.

לָא תִסְפְּדוּהּ לְהַהוּא גַּבְרָא! (סנהדרין מו, סע"ב)
Don't eulogize "that man" (= me)!

הַהוּא גַּבְרָא בְּעֵיל דְּבָבֵיהּ דְּהַהוּא גַּבְרָא הוּא. (גיטין נה, סע"ב)
"That man" is the enemy of "that man" (= You are my enemy.)

SEE: (הַ)הוּא, (הַ)הִיא אִיתְּתָא

הוּא ד-

it is ... that/who ...; that is where ... — הוּא שֶׁ-

This expression usually implies *exclusiveness*.

אִיהוּ הוּא דְאַפְסֵיד אַנַּפְשֵׁיהּ. (בבא מציעא טז,ב ועוד)
It is he (rather than another party) who caused the loss to himself.

Sometimes, an exclusion is stated explicitly.

תּוֹךְ אַרְבַּע הוּא דְאָסוּר; חוּץ לְאַרְבַּע אַמּוֹת חַיָּיב (ברכות יח,א)
within four cubits [of the dead] that is where it is forbidden [to read the Sh^e^ma]; beyond four cubits he is obligated (to read the Sh^e^ma)

וְהוּא ד-

provided that — וְהוּא שֶׁ-

This expression introduces a *stipulation*.

הִשְׁקָה מֵהֶן לְבָנָיו וְלִבְנֵי בֵיתוֹ — יָצָא. אָמַר רַב נַחְמָן בַּר יִצְחָק: וְהוּא דְאִשְׁתִּי רוּבָּא דְכָסָא. (פסחים קח,ב)
[If] he gave his sons and his household to drink [from one of "the four cups"], he has [nevertheless] fulfilled his own duty. Rav Naḥman b. Yitzḥak said: Provided that he [himself] drank the major portion of the cup.

הוּא דַאֲמַר* כִּי/כְּ- — הוּא שֶׁאָמַר כְּ-

He who has stated [this amoraic halakha has thereby ruled] in accordance with [another tanna].

After a mishna or a baraitha has been quoted contradicting the halakha of an amora, this formula is sometimes used to defend his halakha on the grounds that it is consistent with the opinion of a different tanna that the Talmud is about to quote from a mishna or a baraitha.

אָמַר ר' אֶלְעָזָר: בְּהֵמָה גַסָּה נִקְנֵית בִּמְשִׁיכָה. וְהָא אֲנַן בִּמְסִירָה תְּנַן?! הוּא דְּאָמַר כִּי הַאי תַּנָּא, דְּתַנְיָא: וַחֲכָמִים אוֹמְרִים: זוֹ וָזוֹ בִּמְשִׁיכָה. (בבא קמא יא,ב ע"פ כת"י)

R. El'azar said: Large cattle may be acquired by [the new owner's] pulling [the animal into his possession]. But did we not learn (in the mishna): By delivery (= the current owner's handing it over, e.g., by its reins)?! He (= R. El'azar) who has stated [this amoraic halakha has thereby ruled] in accordance with the following tanna, as it is stated (in a baraitha): And the Hakhamim say: Both [types of cattle may be acquired] by pulling.

* Occasionally, this formula is used in the plural, as in אינהו דאמור כי האי תנא (שבת מז, סע"א).

SEE: תַּנָּאֵי הִיא

וְהוּא הַדִּין

and that is (also) the rule

וּתְנָא שׁוֹמֵר חִנָּם, וְהוּא הַדִּין לְשׁוֹמֵר שָׂכָר (בבא מציעא צה,ב)

and he states [the law of] the unpaid guardian, and that is (also) the rule with regard to the paid guardian

הוּא מוֹתִיב לַהּ וְהוּא מְפָרֵק לַהּ

הוּא מַקְשֶׁה אוֹתָהּ, וְהוּא מְתָרֵץ אוֹתָהּ.

He raises it (= the objection), and he [himself] answers it.

The same amora who has pointed out a *difficulty* based on a mishna or a baraitha now resolves it through his own reinterpretation of that text.

For an example — see גיטין ו,א (ר' ירמיה).

SEE: מוֹתִיב, מְפָרֵק

הוּא תָּנֵי לַהּ וְהוּא אָמַר* לַהּ

הוּא שׁוֹנֶה אוֹתָהּ, וְהוּא מְפָרֵשׁ אוֹתָהּ.

He states it (= the text), and he [himself] explains it.

The same amora who has presented a baraitha — just as he received it from his teacher — now offers his own explanation of that baraitha or issues a halakhic ruling about it.

כִּי אֲתָא ר' אַחָא בַּר חֲנִינָא מִדָּרוֹמָא, אַיְיתִי מַתְנִיתָא בִּידֵיהּ: "וּבְנֵי אַהֲרֹן הַכֹּהֲנִים יִתְקְעוּ בַּחֲצוֹצְרוֹת" .... מַה תַּלְמוּד לוֹמַר "יִתְקְעוּ"? הַכֹּל לְפִי הַמּוּסָפִים תּוֹקְעִין. הוּא תָּנֵי לַהּ וְהוּא אָמַר לַהּ: לוֹמַר שֶׁתּוֹקְעִין עַל כָּל מוּסָף וּמוּסָף. (סוכה נד,א ע"פ במדבר י:ח; וע' רש"י לחולין כב,ב)

When R. Aha b. Hanina came from the Darom, he brought a baraitha with him: "And the sons of Aharon, the kohanim, shall blow trumpets" .... What teaching does "they shall blow" [mean] to convey? [That] they blow entirely according to the Additional offerings. He (= R. Aha) states it (= the baraitha), and he (himself) explains it. [That is] to say that they blow for every single Additional offering (even when two Additional offerings are brought on the same day, for example when a festival coincides with the Sabbath).

* אָמַר here means *explains* or *interprets* (as in אָמוֹרָא).

הַהוּא מִיבָּעֵי לֵיהּ

הַהוּא נִצְרָךְ לוֹ

that is needed by him; he requires that

During the course of a Talmudic debate between two parties to a halakhic controversy, it is argued that according to one party there is either a superfluous Biblical expression or an unusual choice of words in a Biblical passage. In response, the Talmud uses this formula to introduce a *resolution* of that difficulty.

וּלְרַבִּי נַמִי, הָא כְּתִיב "שְׁמַע"?! הַהוּא מִיבָּעֵי לֵיהּ: הַשְׁמַע לְאָזְנֶיךָ מַה שֶּׁאַתָּה מוֹצִיא מִפִּיךָ! (ברכות יג, סע"א)

*But according to Rebbi too, is it not written "Sh*e*ma"?! He requires that (for the teaching): Make your ears hear what you utter from your mouth! (In other words, pronounce the words of the Sh*e*ma audibly!)*

SEE: (וְ)הַאי מִיבָּעֵי לֵיהּ לְגוּפֵיהּ

הַהוּא מֵרַבָּנַן

one of the hakhamim אֶחָד מִן הַחֲכָמִים

This term refers to a mature Torah scholar* whose statement is quoted anonymously. In some instances, the Talmud proceeds to identify the scholar (an amora) by name.

אֲמַר לְהוּ הַהוּא מֵרַבָּנַן, וְר' יַעֲקֹב שְׁמֵיהּ (שבת קלד,ב)

one of the hakhamim said to them, and R. Ya'akov is his name

* See "Rashi" on תענית ד, רע"א ד"ה "צורבא".

SEE: צוּרְבָא מֵרַבָּנַן

הֲוַאי (הוי)

she was; it (f.) was (1) הָיְתָה

בַּת אָחִיו הֲוַאי! (סנהדרין נח, רע"ב)

She (= Sara) was his (= Avraham's) niece!

I was (2) הָיִיתִי

if I had been there אִי הֲוַאי הָתָם (מגילה ז,א ועוד)

SEE: הֲוָה

הוֹאִיל וּ-*

since; now that; because

הוֹאִיל וְעָלֶיךָ מִצְוָה, אִם רְצוֹנְךָ לִפְרוֹק — פְּרוֹק! (בבא מציעא לב,א: משנה פ"ב מ"י)

Since you have a Torah obligation [to help], if you wish to unload [my donkey that is having difficulty with its burden], unload [it]!

* The ו, prefixed to the next word (like -שֶׁ in -כֵּיוָן שֶׁ), is an integral part of this expression and must not be translated separately (as *and*) in English. The etymology of the expression is obscure.

הוֹאִיל וַאֲתָא לִידַן, נֵימָא בֵּיהּ מִילְּתָא

הוֹאִיל וּבָא לְיָדֵינוּ, נֹאמַר בּוֹ דָּבָר.

Now that [this topic] has come up in the course of our discussion,* let us now present another halakhic point relating to it.

For an example — see בבא מציעא טז, סע"ב.

* Literally: "it came to our hand"

לְהוֹדִיעֲךָ כֹּחוֹ דְ-

to inform you of the force of ...

This mishna or baraitha was formulated in its present form, referring to this particular case, only to indicate how broad is the scope of one tanna's opinion — but with no intention of limiting the scope of the second tanna's opinion to that same case.

משנה: מי שֶׁאָכַל וְשָׁכַח וְלֹא בֵרַךְ — בֵּית שַׁמַּאי אוֹמְרִים: יַחֲזוֹר לִמְקוֹמוֹ וִיבָרֵךְ, וּבֵית הִלֵּל אוֹמְרִים: יְבָרֵךְ בִּמְקוֹם שֶׁנִּזְכַּר. (ברכות נא,ב: משנה פ"ח מ"ז)

תלמוד: הוּא הַדִּין אֲפִילּוּ בְּמֵזִיד, וְהַאי דְּקָתָנֵי "וְשָׁכַח" — לְהוֹדִיעֲךָ כֹּחָן דְּבֵית שַׁמַּאי (שם נג,ב)

MISHNA: [If] one had eaten and had forgotten to say Birkath HaMazon — Beth Shammai says: He must return to his place and say Birkath HaMazon, and Beth Hillel says: He may say [Birkath HaMazon] wherever he remembers.

TALMUD: That is the rule (= that Birkath HaMazon may be recited wherever he remembers) even [if he failed to say it] on purpose, and the reason why [the tanna of the mishna] states "and [he] had forgotten" is to inform you of the force of (the opinion of) Beth Shammai (that their opinion that one must return to his place for Birkath HaMazon applies not only if he had deliberately omitted it, but even if he had forgotten to say it).

הֲוָה (הוי*: הָוֵי .prt, לֶיהֱוֵי/יְהֵא .fut, הֲוֵי .imp, לְמֶיהֱוֵי (inf.

he was; it (m.) was הָיָה

See next entry for an example.

* For the full conjugation of this verb, see *Grammar for Gemara*: Chapter 4, Verb 15.

SEE: הֲוָה אָמֵינָא, הֲוָה לֵיהּ לְ-, לָא הֲוָה בִּידֵיהּ, מַאי דַּהֲוָה הֲוָה, מִידֵּי דַּהֲוָה אַ-, הֲוַאי, הָוֵי, הֵוִי, הֲוֵינָא, הָוְיָא, הֲוֵינַן

participle + הֲוָה   participle + הָיָה

he was ...; he used to ...; he would ...

This verb is often used as a *"helping verb"** before the participle of another verb to form a compound tense. Sometimes, person is indicated by a pronoun suffix that is appended to that participle, while the helping verb הֲוָה remains unchanged.**

זִמְנִין סַגִּיאִין הֲוָה קָאֵימְנָא קַמֵּיהּ דְּרַב (פסחים קו, רע"ב)

many times I used to stand before Rav

* The modern grammatical term is *modal auxiliary.*

** This Aramaic usage is different from its Hebrew parallel where the personal-pronoun suffix is appended to the helping verb — not to the participle. Consider, for example:

פַּעַם אַחַת הָיִיתִי מְהַלֵּךְ בַּדֶּרֶךְ (משנה אבות פ"ו מ"ט)

one time I was walking along the road

SEE: הֲוֵי

הֲוָה אָמֵינָא   הָיִיתִי אוֹמֵר

(1) I would have said; I might have thought

משנה: הָאִשָּׁה נִקְנֵית בְּשָׁלֹשׁ דְּרָכִים .... (קידושין ב, רע"א)

תלמוד: וְנִיתְנֵי הָכָא "הָאִישׁ קוֹנֶה" ...! אִי תְּנָא "קוֹנֶה", הֲוָה אָמֵינָא אֲפִילּוּ בְּעַל כּוֹרְחָהּ. (שם ב,ב)

MISHNA: A wife is acquired in one of three ways ....

TALMUD: But let [the tanna] state: "A husband acquires ..."! If he had stated "acquires," I might have thought [that it may be done] against her will.

(2) I used to think

מֵרֵישׁ הֲוָה אָמֵינָא: לֵיכָּא קוּשְׁטָא בְּעָלְמָא (סנהדרין צז,א)

at first I used to think: there is no truth in the world

SEE: אָמֵינָא

הֲוָה לֵיהּ לְ-

he had to; he should have הָיָה לוֹ לְ-

The ל in this expression is a prefix to an infinitive.

מַאי הֲוָה לֵיהּ לְמֶיעֱבַד?! (בבא מציעא מב, רע"א ועוד)

What was there for him to do?! (= What should he have done?!)

הֲווֹת

SEE: חֲוַת

הוּזַם* (זמם הָפְעַל)

he was refuted

(and incriminated by other witnesses)

וְהוּזְמוּ עַל הַגְּנֵיבָה (בבא קמא עג,א*)

and [the witnesses] were refuted regarding the theft

* The Aramaic אִיתְזַם (אִתְפְּעַל), from the same root, also occurs there on the same page with the same meaning.

SEE: הֲזָמָה

הוּחְזַק (חזק הָפְעַל: מוּחְזָק .prt)

he/it was established; he/it was ascertained

הוּחְזַק כַּפְרָן (ב"מ ד,א) *he was ascertained [to be] a liar*

הָוֵי (הוי: הָוְיָא .f; הָווּ .m. pl; הָוְיָין .f. pl)

it is [a case of]; it constitutes הוֹוֶה; הוּא

הָוֵי מָמוֹן הַמּוּטָל בְּסָפֵק, וּמָמוֹן הַמּוּטָל בְּסָפֵק חוֹלְקִין. (יבמות לז,ב)

It is [a case of] money [whose ownership] is cast into doubt, and money [whose ownership] is cast into doubt must be divided.

SEE: מַאי הָוֵי, מַאי הָוֵי עֲלָהּ, הָוְיָא

הֵוִי* (הוי פַּעֵל) דָּן; הִקְשָׁה

he discussed; he raised a difficulty

הֵוִי בָּהּ ר' זֵירָא (כתובות עב, רע"ב ורש"י שם)

R. Zera raised a difficulty about it

* This form may have developed from the Biblical Aramaic verb חַוִּי, *he told.*

SEE: הֵוֵינַן, הֲוָיוֹת

הֱוֵי*; הֲוִי** (הוי) .imp

be!

הֱוֵי מִתַּלְמִידָיו שֶׁל אַהֲרֹן! (משנה אבות א:יב)

Be of the disciples of Aharon!

* This Hebrew imperative is often used as a "helping verb" before a participle — most commonly in the expression הֱוֵי אוֹמֵר, the next entry. Occasionally in the Talmud (and more commonly in the Midrashim), הֱוֵי is used as a contraction of the expression הֱוֵי אוֹמֵר, *you have to say*, or

חֲוֵי לוֹמֵד, *you must deduce*, as in יבמות מב, רע"א ורש"י שם.
See the entry "participle + הֲוָה" and its first note.
** This form is the Aramaic imperative.

הֱוֵי אוֹמֵר*

you have to say ...; you must conclude

אֵיזֶהוּ חָג שֶׁהַחוֹדֶשׁ מִתְכַּסֶּה בּוֹ? הֱוֵי אוֹמֵר: זֶה רֹאשׁ הַשָּׁנָה. (ראש השנה ח, סע"א-רע"ב)

Which is the festival [that occurs] when the moon (literally: "the month") is hidden? You have to say: It is Rosh HaShana.

* See the previous entry and its first note.

הֲוָיָה (pl. הֲוָיוֹת)

being; becoming; status; condition

"וְהָיוּ [הַדְּבָרִים הָאֵלֶּה ...]" — בַּהֲוָיָתָן יְהוּ. (ברכות יג,א ע"פ דברים ו:ז)

"[These words] shall be" — [implying that] they must remain in their (original) status (= in Hebrew).

הֲוָיוֹת לִיצִיאוֹת מַקְשִׁינַן? (קידושין ט, סע"א ע"פ דברים כד:ב)

Do we compare "becomings" (= the modes of marriage) to "departures" (= modes of divorce)?

For more examples, see קידושין ה, רע"א וש"נ.

הֲוָיוֹת

problems; investigations; objections

הֲוָיוֹת דְּאַבַּיֵי וְרָבָא* (סוכה כח,א ורש"י שם; בבא בתרא קלד, סע"א ורשב"ם ודק"ס שם)

the [halakhic] investigations of Abbayé and Rava

* In the *Mishné Torah*, the Rambam uses this expression as a general term for the Talmudic dialectical process. See הלכות יסודי התורה פ"ד הי"ג.

SEE: הֲוֵי, הֲוֵינַן

הֲוֵינָא/הֲוֵינַן (הוי) 1st pers. pl.

we were הָיִינוּ

בְּמוֹתַב תְּלָתָא הֲוֵינָא (בבא בתרא קסה,ב)

we were in a session of three [judges]

הֲוֵינָא (הָוֵי + prt. אֲנָא)

I am; I would be; I will be הֹוֶה אֲנִי; אֶהְיֶה

אִי כָּתְבַתְּ לִי כּוּלְּהוּ נִכְסִיךְ, הֲוֵינָא לָךְ. (בבא בתרא מ, סע"ב)

If you write [a document granting] me all your property, I will be your [wife].

הֲוֵינַן/הֲוֵינָא (הוי) 1st pers. pl.

we were הָיִינוּ

כִּי הֲוֵינַן בֵּי רַב הוּנָא, אֲמַר לַן (ברכות לט,א)

when we were at Rav Huna's house, he said to us

הֲוֵינַן (הוי פָּעֵל) 1st pers. pl.

we raised a difficulty הִקְשִׁינוּ

SEE: הֲוֵי, הֲוָיוֹת

וַהֲוֵינַן בָּהּ וְהִקְשִׁינוּ עָלֶיהָ

and we raised a difficulty about it

This term introduces a *difficulty* concerning the halakhic text we have just quoted. This difficulty — which was first raised elsewhere, in the original Talmudic treatment of the text — is now quoted by the Talmud immediately after quoting that text.

וְהָתְנַן: אֲבוֹת מְלָאכוֹת אַרְבָּעִים חָסֵר אַחַת, וַהֲוֵינַן בָּהּ: מִנְיָנָא לָמָּה לִי? (שבת ו,ב ע"פ משנה שם ע"ג,א)

But did we not learn (in the mishna): Thirty-nine are the categories of forbidden labor on the Sabbath, and we raised a difficulty about it: Why do I need the number (thirty-nine) [to be mentioned in the mishna]?

הוֹלֵךְ[1] prt. (הלך)

walking; going

Besides the common meaning of this Hebrew participle, it is sometimes used in a special sense with a -ו prefix, which is presented under וְהוֹלֵךְ.

הוֹלֵךְ[2] imp. (הלך הִפְעִיל)

take! deliver!

הוֹלֵךְ מָנֶה לִפְלוֹנִי שֶׁאֲנִי חַיָּיב לוֹ! (גיטין יד,א)

Deliver to Mr. So-and-So the "maneh" (= a sum of money) that I owe him!

הוֹצִיא (יצא הִפְעִיל: מוֹצִיא .prt, יוֹצִיא .fut, הוֹצֵא .imp, לְהוֹצִיא .inf)

he took out; he brought forth; he released

Besides these basic meanings in Biblical Hebrew, this verb is also used in two special senses in Mishnaic Hebrew.

(1) he excluded (from a halakha or a category)

וּמָה רָאִיתָ לְרַבּוֹת אֶת אֵלּוּ וּלְהוֹצִיא אֶת אֵלּוּ? (יומא מב,ב)

But on what grounds did you determine to include these [instances] and to exclude those?

(2) he caused another to fulfill his obligation; he performed a duty on behalf of another

לְהוֹצִיא אֶת שֶׁאֵינוֹ בָּקִי (ראש השנה לד, סע"ב)

to perform the duty [of prayer] on behalf of one who is not well-versed

SEE: יָצָא, נְפַק, אַפֵּיק, מִיעֵט, מָעֵט, הֵבִיא, רִיבָּה

הוּקַּשׁ (= הֻקַּשׁ: נקש הָפְעַל)

it was compared

An analogy was drawn between two matters — usually because of their juxtaposition in Scripture.

הוּקַּשׁ כְּבוֹדָן לִכְבוֹד הַמָּקוֹם. (סנהדרין נ,א)

Honor for them (= parents) has been compared to honor for the Omnipresent.

SEE: אִיתְקַשׁ, הִקִּישׁ, הֶיקֵּשׁ

הוֹרָאָה/הוֹרָיָה

a teaching; instruction; a halakhic decision

הוֹרָאַת שָׁעָה

a decision for the moment; an ad hoc decision

This term denotes a halakhic ruling that was made because of unique circumstances and is therefore not regarded as a precedent.

"מְקוֹשֵׁשׁ" הוֹרָאַת שָׁעָה הָיְתָה. (סנהדרין פ,ב ורש"י שם ע"פ במדבר טו:ב)

[The case of] "the stick-gatherer [on the Sabbath]" was an ad hoc decision (in that the offender was punished without having been properly warned before his crime).

הֲוַת/הֲווֹת הָיְתָה **she was**

SEE: הֲוַאי, הֲוָה

הוּתַּר (= הֻתַּר: נתר הִפְעַל)

it was permitted; it was exempted

הוּתַּר מִכְּלָלוֹ (הוּתְּרָה מִכְּלָלָהּ .f)

it was exempted from its category; there was an exemption from its general [prohibition]

הַיּוֹצֵא מִן הַגֶּפֶן לֹא הוּתַּר מִכְּלָלוֹ, וְטוּמְאָה וְתִגְלַחַת הוּתְּרוּ מִכְּלָלָן. (נזיר מד,א: משנה פ"ו מ"ה)

[With regard to] a product of the vine (which is prohibited to a nazirite) — there was no exemption from its general [prohibition]; whereas [with regard to] defilement and hair-cutting — there were exemptions from their general [prohibitions].

SEE: כְּלָל

הִזְהִיר (זהר הִפְעִיל: מַזְהִיר .act. prt, מוּזְהָר .pass. prt)

he warned; he prohibited

This verb refers to a warning from the Almighty that is expressed in the Torah.

לֹא עָנַשׁ אֶלָּא אִם כֵּן הִזְהִיר. (יומא פא,א ועוד)

[The Torah] did not state a punishment [for an offence] unless it prohibited [that offence].

SEE: אַזְהָרָה, הַתְרָאָה

הֵזִיד (זוד הִפְעִיל: מֵזִיד .prt, יָזִיד .fut)

he sinned with full awareness

הֵזִיד בְּשַׁבָּת (שבת סט,א)

He sinned (by performing a forbidden labor on the Sabbath) with full awareness of [its being] the Sabbath day.

הֵזִים (זמם הִפְעִיל: לְהָזִים .inf)

he refuted (and incriminated witnesses)

עֵדוּת שֶׁאִי אַתָּה יָכוֹל לַהֲזִימָהּ לָא הָוְיָא עֵדוּת. (ב"ק עה, סע"ב)

Testimony that you cannot refute (and incriminate the witnesses) is not valid testimony.

SEE: הוּזַם, הֲזָמָה

הֲזָמָה **refutation**

This term refers to the refutation and consequent incrimination of witnesses through the testimony of other witnesses who testify that the first witnesses were with them at the same time that the crime or transaction was alleged to have occurred, at a place from which they could not possibly have witnessed it.

For an example — see בבא מציעא ד,א.

SEE: הַכְחָשָׁה

הֶחֱזִיק (חזק הִפְעִיל: מַחֲזִיק .prt, יַחֲזִיק .fut)

(1) he took possession of; he maintained possession of; he occupied

כָּל שֶׁהֶחֱזִיקוּ עוֹלֵי בָבֶל (משנה שביעית פ"ו מ"א)

all [the territory] that the immigrants from Babylonia occupied

(2) he took hold (of); he grasped

זֶה שֶׁהֶחֱזִיק בָּהּ, זָכָה בָּהּ. (בבא מציעא י,א: משנה פ"א מ"ד)

The one who took hold of it has acquired it.

(3) he accounted it as merit; he gave credit; he was grateful

In this usage the direct object is טוֹבָה.*

רַבָּן יוֹחָנָן בֶּן זַכַּאי ... הָיָה אוֹמֵר: אִם לָמַדְתָּ תּוֹרָה הַרְבֵּה, אַל תַּחֲזִיק טוֹבָה לְעַצְמְךָ, כִּי לְכָךְ נוֹצַרְתָּ.** (משנה אבות פ"ב מ"ח)

Rabban Yohanan b. Zakai used to say: If you have learned a lot of Torah, don't give yourself credit, because you have been created for that.

* אַחְזֵיק טֵיבוּתָא is the parallel expression in the Aramaic of the Talmud. (ברכות יט, רע"א ועוד)

** Some manuscripts read: אִם עָשִׂיתָ תּוֹרָה הַרְבֵּה

SEE: אַחְזֵיק, מַחֲזִיק, חֲזָקָה

הֵי*/אִי **alas!**

This word is an expression of grief.

הֵי חָסִיד! הֵי עָנָיו! תַּלְמִידוֹ שֶׁל עֶזְרָא! (סנהדרין יא,א)

Alas the pious man! Alas the humble man! The disciple of Ezra [has departed]!

* Compare the Biblical Hebrew הִי in יחזקאל ב:י.

SEE: אִי

הֵי אֵיזֶה? אֵיזוֹ? אֵלּוּ? **which?**

This pronoun is usually interrogative.

הֵי מִינַּיְיהוּ אֵיזֶה מֵהֶם? **Which one of them?**

For an example — see מגילה ג,ב.

הֵי נִיהוּ אֵיזֶהוּ? **Which is it?**

הֵי נִיהוּ קְנֵה הַלֵּב? (חולין מה,ב) *Which is the aorta?*

הֵי נִינְהוּ

אֵלּוּ הֵם? אֵלּוּ הֵן? **Which are they?**

ברייתא: הָאָב שֶׁנִּשְׁבָּה, וּמֵת בְּנוֹ בִּמְדִינָה ... יוֹרְשֵׁי הָאָב וְיוֹרְשֵׁי הַבֵּן יַחְלוֹקוּ.

תלמוד: הֵי נִינְהוּ יוֹרְשֵׁי הָאָב, וְהֵי נִינְהוּ יוֹרְשֵׁי הַבֵּן? (בבא בתרא קנט,ב)

BARAITHA: [If] a father was taken captive [and died], and his son died in the city ..., the heirs of the father and the heirs of the son split [the inheritance].

TALMUD: Which (= who) are the heirs of the father, and which are the heirs of the son?
SEE: הַיְינוּ

הֵי ר' ...

Which [halakha of] R. ...? אֵיזֶה ר' ...?
After an amora or the Talmud itself has proposed that a halakha in the mishna or baraitha under discussion follows the opinion of a specific tanna, the Talmud sometimes inquires: Which specific halakha of that tanna is meant?*

אֲמַר רַב יוֹסֵף: הָא מַנִּי? רֶבִּי הִיא. הֵי רֶבִּי? (שבת ד,ב)
*Rav Yosef said: This [halakha in our mishna] is according to whom? It [follows the opinion of] Rebbi. Which halakha of Rebbi [does it follow]?**

In response, another mishna or baraitha is quoted that presents the appropriate halakha of the tanna.

* In תענית ג,א (ע' דק"ס שם), there is also uncertainty whether the ר' יְהוֹשֻׁעַ referred to is ר' יְהוֹשֻׁעַ בֶּן חֲנַנְיָה or ר' יְהוֹשֻׁעַ בֶּן בְּתֵירָה and whether the בֶּן בְּתֵירָה referred to is ר' יְהוּדָה בֶּן בְּתֵירָה or ר' יְהוֹשֻׁעַ בֶּן בְּתֵירָה. In most cases, however, the identity of the tanna is known, but it is uncertain as to which of his statements is intended.

הֵי תֵּיתֵי

Which one will be deduced? אֵיזוֹ תָּבוֹא?

תֵּיתֵי חֲדָא מִתַּרְתֵּי! הֵי תֵּיתֵי? (בבא מציעא סא,א)
Let one [of the prohibitions under discussion] be derived from [the other] two! Which one will be deduced?*

* robbery, usury, and overcharging

מֵהֵי תֵּיתֵי

מֵאֵלּוּ תָּבוֹא?
From which [cases] will it be deduced?
For an example — see יבמות ה,ב.

הִיא

she/it (f.); it is
SEE: הוא, (וְ)לָא הִיא

הַהִיא

that (one)
This feminine pronoun often refers to a mishna or a baraitha and introduces an argument that limits the scope of that text or attributes its halakha to a specific tanna in order to resolve a difficulty or to raise an objection.

רָבָא כָּרַע בְּהוֹדָאָה — תְּחִלָּה וְסוֹף .... וְהָתַנְיָא: הַכּוֹרֵעַ בְּהוֹדָאָה הֲרֵי זֶה מְגוּנֶּה?! הַהִיא בְּהוֹדָאָה שֶׁבְּהַלֵּל. (ברכות לד,ב)
*Rava kneeled in the thanksgiving [b^erakha] — at the beginning and at end .... But has it not been taught (in a baraitha): One who kneels in the end "thanksgiving" is reprehensible?! That [baraitha] is speaking of [the] thanksgiving [portion] of Hallel**

* At first, the Talmud understood that the baraitha opposed kneeling at מוֹדִים, the thanksgiving b^erakha of the Amida. Subsequently, it was proposed that the baraitha refers only to kneeling at הוֹדוּ לַה' כִּי טוֹב, the thanksgiving portion of Hallel.
SEE: כִּי תַנְיָא הַהִיא, (הַ)הוּא

הַהִיא אִיתְּתָא

אוֹתָהּ אִשָּׁה; אִשָּׁה אַחַת; מַעֲשֶׂה בְּאִשָּׁה אַחַת
that woman; a certain woman; there was a woman
This expression sometimes introduces a narrative passage in the Talmud.

הַהִיא אִיתְּתָא דְעָלַת לְמֵיפָא בְּהַהוּא בֵּיתָא ... (בבא קמא מח,א)
There was a woman who went into a house to bake ...
SEE: (הַ)הוּא גַּבְרָא

הִיא גוּפָא גְּזֵירָה וַאֲנַן נֵעֲמֹד וְנִגְזוֹר גְּזֵירָה לִגְזֵירָה

הִיא עַצְמָהּ גְּזֵרָה, וְאָנוּ נַעֲמֹד וְנִגְזוֹר גְּזֵרָה מִשּׁוּם גְּזֵרָה?!
It is itself a Rabbinic safeguard, and shall we [then] arise and enact [another] safeguard for [the protection of that] safeguard?!
This *rhetorical question* argues that the prohibition under discussion is difficult to justify — since Rabbinic safeguards are enacted to discourage the violation of Torah commandments, not to support other Rabbinic safeguards.
For examples, see the end of the example in the next entry and ביצה ג, רע"א (ושי"נ).

הִיא הִיא

It is it. It is the same. הִיא הִיא
This assertion usually constitutes a *solution* to a halakhic problem that has been raised in the Talmud, as if to say: This case is halakhically the same as the other one.

משנה: לֹא יַעֲמוֹד אָדָם בִּרְשׁוּת הַיָּחִיד וְיִשְׁתֶּה בִּרְשׁוּת הָרַבִּים ... (עירובין צט, סע"א: משנה פ"י מ"ו)
תלמוד: אִיבַּעְיָא לְהוּ: כַּרְמְלִית מַאי? אֲמַר אַבָּיֵי: הִיא הִיא. אֲמַר רָבָא: הִיא גוּפָא גְּזֵירָה, וַאֲנַן נֵיקוּם וְנִגְזוֹר גְּזֵירָה לִגְזֵירָה?! (עירובין שם ושבת יא, רע"ב ורש"י שם)

MISHNA: A person must not stand in a private domain [on the Sabbath] and drink in a public domain.
TALMUD: They had a halakhic problem: What is [the halakha regarding] karm^elith (= a domain that is considered a public domain only by virtue of a Rabbinic enactment)? Abbayé said: It is the same. Rava said: It (= the prohibition against carrying from karm^elith into a private domain) is itself a Rabbinic safeguard, and shall we [then] arise and enact [another] safeguard (= a prohibition against drinking from karm^elith while standing in a private domain) for [the protection of that] safeguard?!

וְהִיא הַנּוֹתֶנֶת

but it points [to the opposite conclusion]!

A *refutation:* The very distinction that has just been presented as an argument in behalf of one conclusion is in fact an even stronger argument in behalf of the opposite conclusion!

For an example — see מכות ב, רע"ב (ורש"י שם).

SEE: (וְהַ)דין נותן

הֵיאַךְ (=אֵיךְ?) **how?**

(1) how can (it be that) ...?!

Sometimes, this interrogative introduces a *rhetorical question.*

הֵיאַךְ מַנִּיחִין דִּבְרֵי חֲכָמִים וְעוֹשִׂין כְּר׳ אֱלִיעֶזֶר?! (שבת קל, ב)

How can we abandon the opinion of the Ḥakhamim and conduct ourselves according to [the view of] R. Eliezer?!

(2) how is it? what is the law?

In other cases, it introduces an *ordinary question.*

בָּעֵי ר׳ ירמְיָה: בְּמַתָּנָה היאַךְ? (בבא מציעא יא,ב)

R. Yirmᵉya asked: What is the law with regard to [acquiring] a gift [in that manner]?

SEE: היכי and the note on הֵאיךְ

הֵיָיא אֵיזוֹ? **which**

This word occurs only with the prefix -אַ.

SEE: אַהֵיְיא

הַיָּיא מַהֵר **quickly; rapidly**

קָטָן, סָלֵיק ביה בישְׂרָא הַיָּיא. (שבת קלד,ב)

[As for] an infant, [his] flesh heals quickly.

הַיְינוּ[1] (הַאי+נִיהוּ) זֶהוּ

This is it. This is the same as the following.

For examples, see the four entries that follow the next entry.

הַיְינוּ[2]* (הֵי+נִיהוּ) אֵיזֶהוּ? **Which one is ...?**

For an example, see ... הַיְינוּ ... הַיְינוּ.

* In this interrogative sense, the vocalization הֵינוּ may be better, since the word is derived from הֵי, *(which?)*.

... הַיְינוּ ... [דַּעְתּוֹ שֶׁל] ... שָׁוָה לְ[דַעְתּוֹ שֶׁל ...] !

[The opinion of] ... is the same as [that of] ...!

This formula expresses the following *difficulty:* How can the opinions of two tannaim that are formulated separately in the same mishna or baraitha be identical?! Unless there is a real distinction between them, one of them is redundant.

משנה: אֵין מַדְלִיקִין ... בְּחֵלֶב (דברי תנא קמא); נָחוּם הַמָּדִי אוֹמֵר: מַדְלִיקִין בְּחֵלֶב מְבוּשָּׁל, וַחֲכָמִים אוֹמְרִים: אֶחָד מְבוּשָּׁל וְאֶחָד שֶׁאֵינוֹ מְבוּשָּׁל אֵין מַדְלִיקִין בּוֹ. (שבת כ,ב: משנה ב:א)
תלמוד: חֲכָמִים הַיְינוּ תַּנָּא קַמָּא! (שם כד,ב)

MISHNA: We may not kindle with tallow [for the Sabbath lights, in the opinion of the first tanna]. Naḥum, the Mede, says: We may kindle with boiled tallow. But the Ḥakhamim say: We may not kindle with it — whether boiled or not.

TALMUD: The opinion of the Ḥakhamim is the same as that of the first tanna!

SEE: מַאי בינַייהו

הַיְינוּ דְאָמְרִי אֱנָשֵׁי זֶהוּ שֶׁבְּנֵי אָדָם אוֹמְרִים ...

this is what people say ...

This formula links an incident or a situation with a popular saying.

אֲמַר לְהוּ: "אֲנָא חוני הַמְעַגֵּל"! לָא הֵימנוּהּ ... וְלָא נְהַגוּ בֵיהּ יְקָרָא כדמיבְּעֵי ליה. בְּעָא רַחֲמֵי, ונָח נַפְשֵׁיהּ. אֲמַר רָבָא: הַיְינוּ דְאָמְרי אינָשֵׁי: "או חַברוּתָא או מיתוּתָא"! (תענית כג, רע"א ע"פ הגדות התלמוד)

He said to them (after he had been absent for seventy years): "I am Ḥoni, the circle-drawer!" They did not believe him ..., and they did not treat him with the respect that was due him. He prayed for Divine mercy, and died. Rava said: This is what people say: "[Give me] friendship or [give me] death!"

הַיְינוּ דְקָתָנֵי

This is why [the tanna] states ... זֶהוּ שֶׁשּׁוֹנֶה ...

This formula indicates that the text of the mishna or baraitha that is about to be quoted matches one (and only one) of the two amoraic opinions under consideration.* Usually this formula appears within an *objection* introduced by (ב)שלָמָא.

משנה: חָמֵץ של ... ישְׂרָאל אָסור בַּהֲנָאָה, שנאֱמַר "לא יֵרָאֶה לְךָ שאור". (פסחים כח, סע"א: משנה פ"ב מ"ב ע"פ שמות יג:ז)
תלמוד: רָבָא אֲמַר: ... קְנָסָא קָנֵיס, הואיל וַעֲבַר עֲלֵיה בְּבַל יֵרָאֶה ... בשלָמָא לְרָבָא, הַיְינוּ דקָתָנֵי של ישְׂרָאל אָסור, משום שנֶאֱמַר "לא יֵרָאֶה", אֶלָּא לְרַב אַחָא בַּר יַעֲקב ... (שם כט,א)

MISHNA: Ḥametz belonging to a Jew is forbidden for [even after Pesaḥ], because it is stated (in the Torah): "Your leavening shall not be seen."

TALMUD: It is well according to Rava, this is why [our tanna] states: [Ḥametz] belonging to a Jew is forbidden for use, because it is stated: "Your leavening shall not be seen," but according to Rav Aḥa b. Ya'akov ...

* This expression is also used in a somewhat different sense in the course of other objections. See אִי הָכִי הַיְינוּ דְקָתָנֵי in יבמות כח,א and Rashi's commentary there.

SEE: (וְ)הָא עֲלַהּ קָתָנֵי

הַיְינוּ ... הַיְינוּ ...[1] זֶהוּ ... זֶהוּ ...

"This ... is that ..."; ... is the same as ...

הַיְינוּ כַּד הַיְינוּ חָבִית. (בבא קמא כז, סע"א)

כַּד *is [the same as]* חָבִית. *(They both mean a jug.)*

הַיְינוּ ... הַיְינוּ ...[2] אֵיזֶהוּ ...? אֵיזֶהוּ ...?

Which is ...? Which is ...?

This formula is used to present a *difficulty*, i.e., a redundancy in the tannaitic or amoraic text. The Talmud asks: What is the uniqueness of each of these terms? Are they not identical and consequently redundant?!

משנה: אֲבוֹת מְלָאכוֹת ... הַזּוֹרֶה, הַבּוֹרֵר ... וְהַמְרַקֵּד ... (שבת עג, סע"א: משנה פ"ז מ"ב)

תלמוד: הַיְינוּ זוֹרֶה? הַיְינוּ בּוֹרֵר? הַיְינוּ מְרַקֵּד? (שבת עג, סע"ב ורש"י שם)

MISHNA: The main categories of [forbidden] labors [are] ... winnowing, selecting, ... and sifting ...

TALMUD: Which [labor] is "winnowing"? Which is "selecting"? Which is "sifting"? (Since all three are acts of separating, why should they all be listed in the Mishna as distinct categories of labor?)

See also: כתובות י,ב (ורש"י ושיטה מקובצת שם)

SEE: הַיְינוּ[2]

הַיְינוּ הָךְ

This is the same as that! זָהוּ זֶה!

The two are identical!

This expression is used to point out a redundancy.

See the example quoted under הָא תוּ לָמָּה לִי, which sometimes precedes this expression.

SEE: הִיא הִיא

הֵיכָא

where? in what case? הֵיכָן? אֵיפֹה?

משֶׁה הֵיכָא הֲוָה יָתֵיב? (סנהדרין מג,א)

Where was Moshe sitting?

הֵיכָא אָמְרִינַן דְּאָתֵי עֲשֵׂה וְדָחֵי לֹא תַעֲשֶׂה...? (שבת קלב, סע"ב)

In what case do we say that a positive commandment comes and supersedes a negative commandment ...?

הֵיכָא ד-

where; in a case where בְּמָקוֹם שֶׁ-

הֵיכָא דְּאִיתְּמַר אִיתְּמַר; הֵיכָא דְּלָא אִיתְּמַר לָא אִיתְּמַר. (ברכות כד,א ושי"ן)

In the case where [the halakhic ruling] was stated — it was stated; in the case where it was not stated — it was not stated (and it does not apply there).

SEE: כָּל הֵיכָא ד-, אַטּוּ כּוּלְּהוּ בְּחֲדָא מְחִיתָא מְחִיתִינְהוּ

הֵיכִי

how? אֵיךְ? כֵּיצַד?

(1) In what manner?

Sometimes, this interrogative introduces an *ordinary question*.

הֵיכִי עֲבִיד? (ביצה כז, סע"ב; כח, סע"ב ורש"י שם)

How shall he do (this)? (= What procedure should he follow?)

(2) how can (it be that) ...?!

In other cases, it introduces a *rhetorical question*.

הֵיכִי עָבִיד הָכָא הָכִי וְהֵיכִי עָבִיד הָתָם הָכִי?! (יבמות יד,א)

How can he act here in this manner, and how can he act there in a different manner?!

SEE: הֵיאַךְ, כִּי הֵיכִי ד-

הֵיכִי דָמֵי

how? "אֵיךְ דּוֹמֶה?" כֵּיצַד?

(1) What is a case of ...? What is the case of

which the text is speaking?

הֵיכִי דָמֵי חִילּוּל הַשֵּׁם? אֲמַר רַב: כְּגוֹן אֲנָא אִי שָׁקִילְנָא בִּישְׂרָא מִטַּבָּחָא וְלָא יָהֵיבְנָא דְמֵי לְאַלְתַּר. (יומא פו,א)

What is a case of desecration of the Divine Name? Rav said: If someone like me would take meat from a butcher and not pay [for it] on the spot.

(2) What is the case?

This interrogative often introduces a *difficulty* that takes the form of a dilemma:

קַב בְּאַרְבַּע אַמּוֹת — הֵיכִי דָמֵי? אִי דֶּרֶךְ נְפִילָה, אֲפִילּוּ טוּבָא נַמִי! וְאִי דֶּרֶךְ הִינּוּחַ, אֲפִילּוּ בְּצִיר מֵהָכִי נַמִי לָא! (ב"מ כא,א)

[If one finds] a "kav" (= a certain quantity of fruit) within an area of four cubits [he may keep it]. What is the case? If [the fruit appears to have been] dropped accidentally, even if there is a greater quantity [of fruit, it should] also [belong to the finder]! And if [it appears to have been] deliberately set down, even a smaller quantity than this should not [be his]!

הֵיכִי מַשְׁכַּחַתְּ לַהּ

כֵּיצַד אַתָּה מוֹצֵא אוֹתָהּ?!

How can you find it (= such a case)?!

This rhetorical question points to a *difficulty* in setting up the case that has been formulated in the mishna or baraitha under discussion.

בּוֹר שֶׁל שְׁנֵי שׁוּתָּפִין — הֵיכִי מַשְׁכַּחַתְּ לַהּ?! (בבא קמא נא,א)

[As for] a pit belonging to two partners — how can you find it (= such a case)?!

הֵיכִי קָאָמַר

אֵיךְ הוּא אוֹמֵר?

"How is he talking?" What does he mean? How should these words be interpreted?

This *question* seeks to clarify the statement that has just been quoted in the Talmud.

משנה: מְפָרֵר וְזוֹרֶה לָרוּחַ אוֹ מַטִּיל לַיָּם. (פסחים כא,א: משנה פ"ב מ"א)

תלמוד: אִיבַּעְיָא לְהוּ: הֵיכִי קָאָמַר? מְפָרֵר וְזוֹרֶה לָרוּחַ וּמְפָרֵר וּמַטִּיל לַיָּם — אוֹ דִילְמָא מְפָרֵר וְזוֹרֶה לָרוּחַ, אֲבָל מַטִּיל לַיָּם בְּעֵינֵיהּ? (שם כח,א)

MISHNA: He may crumble [the ḥametz] and throw [it] to the wind or cast [it] into the sea.

TALMUD: They had a halakhic problem: What does he mean? He may crumble [it] and throw [it] to the wind or he may crumble [it] and cast [it] into the sea — or perhaps [it means] he may crumble [it] and throw [it] to the wind, but he may cast [it] into the sea intact (= without first crumbling)?

הֵיכָן

(= הֵי+כָּאן)

where?

הֵיכָן פִּקְדוֹנִי? (בבא קמא קח, סע"ב: משנה פ"ט מ"ז)

Where is my deposit?

SEE: עַד הֵיכָן

הֶיכֵּר; הֶיכֵּירָא/הֶיכֵּרָא*

a distinction; something distinctive

בָּעֵינַן תְּרֵי טִיבּוּלֵי, כִּי הֵיכִי דְּתֶיהֱוֵי הֶיכֵּרָא לַתִּינוֹקוֹת. (פסחים קיד,ב)

We require two dippings (at the Seder) so that there be something distinctive to [attract the attention of] the children.

* These nouns — the first Hebrew and the second Aramaic — are derived from נכר, like הִכִּיר, *he recognised.*

הֵילָךְ (= הֵא+לָךְ)

"here it is for you"; it is yours הִנֵּה לְךָ

אֵין לָךְ בְּיָדִי אֶלָּא חֲמִשִּׁים זוּז וְהֵילָךְ! (ב"מ ד,א ורש"י שם)

I have only fifty zuz of your [money] and here it is! (= Take it!)

הִילְכְתָא SEE: הֲלָכָה

הֵימֶנּוּ (הֵימֶנָּה .f)

from him/it (m.); than he/it (m.) מִמֶּנּוּ

הַשֵּׁנִי נוֹחַ לִי, וְהָרִאשׁוֹן קָשֶׁה הֵימֶנּוּ. (כתובות קט, סע"א: משנה פי"ג מ"ו)

The second [person] is easy for me [to deal with], while the first is more difficult than he.

SEE: לֹא כָל הֵימֶנּוּ

הֵימְנוּתָא אֱמוּנָה **trust; faith**

כִּי לֵית בְּהוּ הֵימְנוּתָא ... מִיקְרוּ בָּנִים (קידושין לו,א)

when they (= the Jewish people) do not have faith ... they are [still] called "children [of God]"

הֵימְנֵיהּ (= הֵימַן+ֵיהּ הימר*: מְהֵימַן ,act. prt. מְהֵימַן

he believed him; הֶאֱמִינוֹ (inf. מְהֵימוֹנֵי ,pass. prt.

he trusted him; he gave credence to him

כְּבֵי תְּרֵי הֵימְנֵיהּ** (שבועות מב,א)

he gave credence to him like two [witnesses]

* This Aramaic root consists of three consonants (ה, מ, and נ) and the semivowel י, so that it is in effect a four-letter root like גלגל or תרגם. It may have developed from the causative הַפְעֵל *binyan* of the root אמן which appears in Biblical Aramaic (e.g., הֵימִין in דניאל ו:כד) — a parallel of הֶאֱמִין from the Hebrew הִפְעִיל *binyan.*

** In a few other instances, this verb is used with a plural subject and singular suffix, הֵימְנוּהּ, *they believed him.*

See: כתובות כב,ב ע"פ כת"י (בדפוס: הימנוהו)

SEE: מְהֵימַן, מְהֵימָן

הֶיקֵּשׁ; הֶיקֵּישָׁא/הֶקֵּישָׁא*

a comparison; an analogy

This term usually denotes a halakhic analogy, based upon the connection between two items in the Torah.

(1) In some instances, the analogy is explicitly formulated in the Torah.

דָּם ... אִיתְקַשׁ לְמַיִם, דִּכְתִיב: "לֹא תֹאכְלֶנּוּ, עַל הָאָרֶץ תִּשְׁפְּכֶנּוּ כַּמָּיִם". (פסחים כב, סע"א ע"פ דברים יב:כד)

Blood ... has been compared to water, for it is written: "You shall not eat it (= blood); you shall spill it on the ground like water."

From this analogy the Talmud finds support for a halakha: מַה מַיִם מוּתָּרִין, אַף דָּם מוּתָּר. (פסחים שם)

Just as water is permitted [for use], so is blood permitted (for all uses – except for eating or drinking).

(2) More frequently, however, the analogy is not explicit, but it is based upon the juxtaposition of two items — usually in the same pasuk but occasionally in adjacent p[e]sukim.**

הֶקֵּישָׁא הוּא, דִּכְתִיב: "לֹא תוּכַל לֶאֱכוֹל בִּשְׁעָרֶיךָ מַעְשַׂר דְּגָנְךָ וְתִירוֹשְׁךָ וְיִצְהָרֶךָ, וּבְכוֹרוֹת בְּקָרְךָ וְצֹאנֶךָ, וְכָל נְדָרֶיךָ אֲשֶׁר תִּדֹּר, וְנִדְבוֹתֶיךָ ..." (פסחים כד, סע"א ורש"י שם ע"פ דברים יב:יז)

It is an analogy, for it is written: "You may not eat within your gates the tithe of your grain, your wine, or your oil, or the first-born of your herd or of your flock, nor any of your vows that you may vow nor your voluntary offerings ..." (The analogy is between "vows" and "voluntary offerings," on the one hand, and "tithe," on the other, with respect to punishment.)

* The first noun is Hebrew, and the second is Aramaic. Both are derived from the root נקשׁ, like the verb הִקִּישׁ, *he compared.*

**See: אנציקלופדיה תלמודית כרך י' "הֶקֵּשׁ"

SEE: סְמוּכִים, (וּ)סְמִיךְ לֵיהּ

הָךְ* (הָא+דְ)** .f

that; the former הַהִיא; אוֹתָהּ

בְּהָא קָאָמַר ר' יוֹסֵי, אֲבָל בְּהָךְ אֵימָא מוֹדֵי לְהוּ לְרַבָּנַן (בבא מציעא לז, סע"ב)

in this [case] R. Yosé maintains [his own position], but in that [case] I might say that he agrees with the Hakhamim

הָךְ קַמַּיְיתָא (בבא מציעא שם ועוד) *that first (case)*

* This word is pronounced הַךְ by Ashkenasim. The הָךְ vocalization, however, is probably more correct, since it is related to הָא.

** See the note under הָאִיךְ.

SEE: הַיְינוּ הָךְ

לְהָךְ לִישָּׁנָא לְפִי אוֹתוֹ לָשׁוֹן ...

according to that version (of the amora's statement) ...

For an example — see בבא קמא יב, סע"א.

הָכָא (= הָא+כָא) כָּאן **here; in this case**

See the examples under the entries that follow.

מֵהָכָא מִכָּאן **from here; from this pasuk**

After one Biblical source has been cited for a halakha or an aggada, this term is used to introduce a different source.

אָמַר רָבָא בַּר רַב הוּנָא: כֵּיוָן שֶׁנִּפְתַּח סֵפֶר תּוֹרָה, אָסוּר לְסַפֵּר אֲפִילּוּ בִּדְבַר הֲלָכָה, שֶׁנֶּאֱמַר: "וּכְפִתְחוֹ עָמְדוּ כָל הָעָם" — וְאֵין עֲמִידָה אֶלָּא שְׁתִיקָה ... ר' זֵירָא אָמַר רַב חִסְדָּא: מֵהָכָא, "וְאָזְנֵי כָל הָעָם אֶל סֵפֶר הַתּוֹרָה". (סוטה לט, רע"א ע"פ נחמיה ח,ג-ה)

Rava b. Rav Huna said: Once the Torah scroll has been unrolled [to be read before the congregation], it is forbidden to converse even about a halakhic matter, as it is written: "And when he opened it, all the people were still" — [the verb] עמד *indicates "being quiet" ... R. Zera quoted Rav Ḥisda saying: From here: "And the ears of all the people were [attentive] to the Torah scroll."*

הָכָא בְּמַאי עֲסִיקִינַן/עָסְקִינַן

כָּאן בַּמֶּה אָנוּ עֲסוּקִים?

With what (situation) are we involved here?

הָכָא בְּ... עֲסִיקִינַן/עָסְקִינַן

כָּאן בְּ... אָנוּ עֲסוּקִים

Here we are dealing with...

This expression — whether in the form of a question or a statement — introduces a *resolution* of a difficulty, achieved by restricting the scope of the case under discussion.

וְאוֹצְרוֹת יַיִן אֵין צָרִיךְ בְּדִיקָה?! וְהָתַנְיָא: אוֹצְרוֹת יַיִן צָרִיךְ בְּדִיקָה ...! הָכָא בְּמַאי עֲסִיקִינַן? בְּמִסְתַּפֵּק. (פסחים ח,א)

But do storehouses of wine not require searching [for ḥametz]?! But has it not been taught (in a baraitha): Storehouses of wine require searching! With what circumstances are we involved here (= in the baraitha)? In [a case where the owner regularly] takes his supplies [from the storehouse] (and so there is some likelihood that ḥametz has fallen inside).

SEE: עֵסֶק, (וְ)הִלְכְתָא

הָכָא נַמֵּי

here too; in our case as well אַף כָּאן

This expression indicates that the same statement originally made in another context should be applied to the present case too.

הַלּוֹקֵחַ בַּיִת בְּאֶרֶץ יִשְׂרָאֵל כּוֹתְבִין עָלָיו אוֹנוּ אֲפִילּוּ בְּשַׁבָּת. בְּשַׁבָּת סָלְקָא דַעְתָּךְ?! אֶלָּא כִּדְאָמַר רָבָא הָתָם: אוֹמֵר לְנָכְרִי וְעוֹשֶׂה, הָכָא נַמֵּי: אוֹמֵר לְנָכְרִי וְעוֹשֶׂה. (בבא קמא פ, סע"ב)

[If] one purchases a house in Eretz Yisrael, they may write its bill of sale even on the Sabbath. Do you [really] think [that the writing may be done] on the Sabbath?! Rather, just as Rava had stated in another context: He may tell a non-Jew, and [the non-Jew] does [it], here too: He may tell a non-Jew, and [the non-Jew] does [it].

הָכָא תַּרְגִּימוּ

כָּאן תִּרְגְּמוּ; כָּאן פֵּרְשׁוּ

here (in Babylonia) they translated; here they explained

The Talmud uses this expression to introduce a translation or an explanation of a difficult expression or a reason for a halakha that was stated by unnamed Babylonian amoraim. Then the Talmud quotes a different explanation (almost always) from Erets Yisrael — either introduced anonymously by the term בְּמַעֲרָבָא, *in the West (= Erets Yisrael)*, or presented by a specific amora from Erets Yisrael.

מַאי שְׁטָרֵי בֵירוּרִין? הָכָא תַּרְגִּימוּ: שְׁטָרֵי טַעֲנָתָא. ר' יִרְמְיָה אָמַר: זֶה בּוֹרֵר לוֹ אֶחָד, וְזֶה בּוֹרֵר לוֹ אֶחָד. (ב"מ כ, סע"א)

What are documents of clarification? Here they explained [it as] documents containing records of claims. R. Yirm'ya stated: [Documents stating] this party has chosen one [judge], and the other party has chosen one [judge].

הַכְחָשָׁה

contradiction; refutation

This invalidation of the testimony of witnesses is accomplished either by means of a contradiction between their testimonies or through the testimony of other witnesses that contradicts the content of their testimony.

For an example — see כתובות יט, סע"ב.

SEE: הֲזָמָה

הָכִי כָּךְ

so; thus; in this manner; this

See the examples under the entries that follow.

SEE: בַּר הָכִי

הָכִי הַשְׁתָּא כָּךְ עַכְשָׁיו?!

Now, [is it] so?!

Now, [is the analogy] correct?!

This exclamation introduces a *refutation* of an analogy that has been drawn between two cases, as if to say: Are the two cases really analogous?!

כִּשְׁכְּשָׁה בִּזְנָבָה — מַהוּ? אֲמַר לֵיהּ אִידָךְ: וְכִי יֹאחֲזֶנָּה וְיֵלֵךְ?! אִי הָכִי, קֶרֶן נַמֵּי — וְכִי יֹאחֲזֶנָּה בְּקֶרֶן וְיֵלֵךְ?! הָכִי הַשְׁתָּא?! קֶרֶן לָאו אוֹרְחֵיהּ; הַאי אוֹרְחֵיהּ! (בבא קמא יט,ב)

[If] an animal wagged its tail [and thereby caused damage], what is the halakha? Another [ḥakham] said to him: Must one walk holding it (= the animal, by its tail)?! If so, with regard to [damage by] the horn also, must one walk holding it by the horn? Now, [is the analogy] correct?! [Damage by the] horn [is caused by] its unusual behavior; this (= damage caused by wagging its tail) [is caused by] its usual behavior!

הָכִי נַמֵּי

so also (1) כָּךְ גַּם

For an example, see הָכִי נַמֵּי מִסְתַּבְּרָא.

It is indeed so! (2) כָּךְ הוּא!

For examples, see אִין הָכִי נַמֵּי and (וְ)אֵימָא הָכִי נַמֵּי.

הָכִי נַמֵּי מִסְתַּבְּרָא

so it also stands to reason כָּךְ אַף מִסְתַּבֵּר

This expression introduces a *proof* — either from a text or from a logical argument — corroborating a point that has just been presented in the Talmud.

קָא מַשְׁמַע לַן דְּשׁוּמָא מִילְּתָא הִיא. הָכִי נַמֵּי מִסְתַּבְּרָא, דִּתְנַן: אֵלּוּ עוֹבְרִים בְּלֹא תַעֲשֶׂה — הַמַּלְוֶה וְהַלֹּוֶה, הֶעָרֵב וְהָעֵדִים. בִּשְׁלָמָא כּוּלְּהוּ עֲבוּד מַעֲשֶׂה, אֶלָּא עֵדִים מַאי עֲבוּד? אֶלָּא לָאו שְׁמַע מִינַּהּ: שׁוּמָא מִילְּתָא הִיא?! שְׁמַע מִינַּהּ. (ב"מ סב,א)

It teaches us that arranging [an interest-bearing loan]

is a matter [that is blameworthy]. So it also stands to reason, for we learned (in the mishna): The following [people] transgress a prohibition [with regard to interest]: The lender, the borrower, the guarantor, and the witnesses. It is understandable [that] all the others have [transgressed, since they] performed an act, but what did the witnesses do? Rather is there not a proof from here [that] arranging [an interest-bearing loan] is a matter [that is blameworthy]?! There is a proof from here.

הָכִי קָאָמַר כָּךְ הוּא אוֹמֵר **so he says**
הָכִי קָתָנֵי כָּךְ הוּא שׁוֹנֶה **so he teaches**

These expressions introduce a *resolution* of a difficulty that is achieved either by reinterpreting a mishna or a baraitha, as if to say: "The following is what the tanna really means," or by presenting a different version of the text: "The following is what the tanna really says." In the latter sense, the term חַסּוּרֵי מִחַסְּרָא sometimes precedes הָכִי קָתָנֵי.

For an example — see מַאן דְּכַר שְׁמֵיהּ.

SEE: אַדְּהָכִי, (וְ)אִימָא כּוּלֵּיהּ לְהָכִי הוּא דַּאֲתָא, חַסּוּרֵי מִחַסְּרָא, תַּנְיָא נָמֵי הָכִי

הֲלֹא **Is it not ...!**

This negative interrogative term often introduces *rhetorical* questions.

SEE: הָא

וַהֲלֹא דִּין הוּא

But is it not [derivable from] a logical inference (chiefly a קַל־וָחֹמֶר argument)?!

This rhetorical question points out a *difficulty*: Why must a special Biblical interpretation be invoked to teach this halakhic point? It can be deduced from the data already available through a קַל־וָחֹמֶר argument! Then the Talmud proceeds to reject this contention, by proving that the Biblical source is needed after all.

"כִּי יִקַּח אִישׁ אִשָּׁה ..." אֵין "קִיחָה" אֶלָּא בְּכֶסֶף, וְכֵן הוּא אוֹמֵר: "נָתַתִּי כֶּסֶף הַשָּׂדֶה, קַח מִמֶּנִּי". וַהֲלֹא דִּין הוּא! וּמָה אָמָה הָעִבְרִיָּה, שֶׁאֵינָהּ נִקְנֵית בְּבִיאָה, נִקְנֵית בְּכֶסֶף — זוֹ, שֶׁנִּקְנֵית בְּבִיאָה, אֵינוֹ דִּין שֶׁתִּקָּנֶה בְּכֶסֶף?! (קידושין ד, רע״ב ע״פ דברים כד:א ובראשית כג:ג)

"When a man takes a wife ..." "Taking" means through money, and thus [the Torah] says: "I am giving the money for the field, take it from me." But is it not [derivable from] a logical inference?! Since the Hebrew maidservant, who cannot be acquired through intercourse, can be acquired through [the transfer of] money — then is it not a logical inference that [a wife], who can (theoretically) be acquired through intercourse, can be acquired through [the transfer of] money?!

הַלָּה (pl. הַלָּלוּ) **that (one)**

כֵּיצַד הַלָּה עוֹשֶׂה סְחוֹרָה בְּפָרָתוֹ שֶׁל חֲבֵירוֹ?! (בבא מציעא לה,ב: משנה פ״ג מ״ב)

How can that [fellow] make a profit from the cow of his fellow man?!

הִלּוּלָא* חֻפָּה **wedding**

רַב אַשִׁי עֲבַד הִלּוּלָא לִבְרֵיהּ (ברכות לא, רע״א)

Rav Ashi made a wedding for his son

* Compare תהלים עח:סג and Rashi's comment there. Under the influence of the *Zohar*, this word came to denote the celebration of the anniversary of the death of a righteous man whose soul rejoices before God — for example, the celebration at the grave of R. Shim'on b. Yoḥai on the thirty-third day of the counting of Omer, the 18th of Iyyar.

SEE: בֵּי הִלּוּלָא

הָלֵין* אֵלּוּ **these**

לָמָּה לִי לְמִיתְנָא כָּל הָלֵין?! (נזיר ד,א) *Why do I have to state all these [expressions in the mishna]?*

* This word appears mostly in the tractates נדרים, נזיר and כריתות.

הֲלָכָה; הִלְכְתָא/הִילְכְתָא* (pl. הִלְכָתָא)

(1) a halakha; a law (in contrast to אַגָּדָה, the non-legal material in the Talmud)

מְלַמְּדוֹ ... הֲלָכוֹת וְהַגָּדוֹת (נדרים לו, רע״א: משנה פ״ד מ״ג)

he may teach him ... halakhoth and aggadoth

לְמַאי הִלְכְתָא כְּתָבֵיהּ רַחֲמָנָא? (ב״מ לב, סע״א ע״פ שמות כג:ה)

For what halakha did the Merciful One write it (= the pasuk)?

(2) a halakhic tradition; a law based upon a received oral tradition (rather than upon a derivation from Scripture or a Rabbinic enactment)

אִם הֲלָכָה, נְקַבֵּל; וְאִם לְדִין, יֵשׁ תְּשׁוּבָה! (יבמות עו,ב ורש״י שם: משנה פ״ח מ״ג)

If [the basis of your position] is a halakhic tradition, we shall accept [it]; but if it is a logical argument, there is an objection!

הֲלָכָה לְמֹשֶׁה מִסִּינַי** (משנה פאה פ״ב מ״ו ועוד)

a halakhic tradition [transmitted] to Moshe from [the Divine Revelation at] Sinai

הִלְכְתָא נִינְהוּ וְאַסְמְכִינְהוּ רַבָּנַן אַקְּרָאֵי. (סוכה כח,א)

They are halakhic traditions, but the Rabbis attached them to p^esukim.

(3) a halakhic ruling

הֲלָכָה לְמַעֲשֶׂה (בבא בתרא קל, ב)

a halakhic ruling [intended as a guide] for practice

הִלְכְתָא לִמְשִׁיחָא (סנהדרין נא,ב)

a halakhic ruling for [the days of] the Mashiaḥ (without any practical application nowadays)

* The first noun is Hebrew, and the second one is Aramaic.

**In certain cases, one of the classical Talmudic commentaries understands הֲלָכָה לְמֹשֶׁה מִסִּינַי as referring to an old established law — even if it is really of Rabbinic origin. See the commentary of Rabbenu Asher on the Mishna: ידים פ"ד מ"ג and his הלכות מקואות.

הֲלָכָה וְאֵין מוֹרִין כֵּן*

[This is the] halakha (that the practice is permitted), but [we] do not issue a ruling to that effect.

In certain cases, the Rabbis withhold a lenient halakhic decision fearing that the public might treat it too lightly and exaggerate its scope.

שַׁמָּשׁ שֶׁאֵינוֹ קָבוּעַ בִּדְמִשְׁחָא — מַהוּ? אָמַר רַב: הֲלָכָה, וְאֵין מוֹרִין כֵּן. (שבת יב, סע"ב ורש"י שם)

[As for] a temporary attendant [examining dishes on the Sabbath] by [the light of an] oil [lamp] — what is the halakhic ruling? Rav said: The halakha [really permits this practice], but we do not issue a ruling to that effect.

* In Modern Hebrew, this expression is used in the opposite sense, as if to say: Legally, this particular activity is forbidden, however the prohibition is not enforced in practice, and most people engage in the activity anyhow.

הֲלָכָה מִכְּלָל דִּפְלִיגִי

"הֲלָכָה" — מִתּוֹךְ [כָּךְ יוֹצֵא] שֶׁחוֹלְקִים.

[The fact that] a halakhic ruling [had to be explicitly issued in favor of one tanna's opinion] indicates that [the two tannaim] disagree.

משנה: הַצָּד ... צְבִי לְגִינָּה וְלֶחָצֵר וּלְבֵיבָרִין חַיָּיב. רַבָּן שִׁמְעוֹן בֶּן גַּמְלִיאֵל אוֹמֵר: לֹא כָּל הַבֵּיבָרִין שָׁוִין. (שבת קו, רע"ב: משנה פי"ג מ"ח)

תלמוד: אָמַר רַב יוֹסֵף אָמַר רַב יְהוּדָה אָמַר שְׁמוּאֵל: הֲלָכָה כְּרַבָּן שִׁמְעוֹן בֶּן גַּמְלִיאֵל. אָמַר לֵיהּ אַבָּיֵי: "הֲלָכָה" מִכְּלָל דִּפְלִיגִי. (שם)

MISHNA: [If] one hunts a deer driving him into a garden, a courtyard, or a vivarium (= a pen), he is liable [for desecrating the Sabbath]. Rabban Shim'on b. Gamliel says: Not all vivaria are alike.

TALMUD: Rav Yosef said quoting Rav Y'huda who quoted Sh'muel: The halakhic ruling is in accordance with Rabban Shim'on b. Gamliel. Abbayé said to him (= Rav Yosef): [The fact that] a halakhic ruling [had to be explicitly issued in favor of one tanna's opinion] indicates that [the two tannaim] disagree.

הִלְכָּךְ (= הוֹאִיל+וְכָךְ)*

therefore; accordingly

הִלְכָּךְ נֵימְרִינְהוּ לְתַרְוַיְיהוּ. (מגילה כא,ב ורש"י)

Therefore (in light of the two different versions that have been proposed) let us recite both of them.

* The spelling הולכך in some Talmudic manuscripts and in Gaonic literature corroborates this etymology. See also the commentary of Rashi on חולין סח,א that paraphrases הִלְכָּךְ as הוֹאִיל וְאָמְרִינַן הָכִי, *since we say so.*

וְהִלְכְתָא   וַהֲלָכָה ...

(1) and the halakhic ruling is ...

This term introduces a halakhic ruling at the conclusion of a discussion in the Talmud.

וְהִלְכְתָא: אוֹמֵר "זְמַן" בְּרֹאשׁ הַשָּׁנָה וּבְיוֹם הַכִּיפּוּרִים. (עירובין מ, סע"א)

And the halakhic ruling is: One does recite [the b'rakha] "SheHeḥeyanu" on Rosh HaShana and Yom Kippur.

(2) and the halakha applies ...

Sometimes, this term introduces a *resolution* of a difficulty, achieved by limiting the scope of a text.

וְהִלְכְתָא בִּכְפוּתָ. (גיטין כא,א)

And the halakha [that the text speaks of] applies where [the slave is] bound.

SEE: הָכָא בְּמַאי עָסְקִינַן

הִלְכְתָא

SEE: הֲלָכָה

הַלָּלוּ (s. הַלָּה)

those

As an adjective, this word follows the noun it modifies.

בֵּין הַכּוֹסוֹת הַלָּלוּ אִם רוֹצֶה לִשְׁתּוֹת, יִשְׁתֶּה; בֵּין שְׁלִישִׁי לִרְבִיעִי לֹא יִשְׁתֶּה. (פסחים קיז, סע"ב: משנה פ"י מ"ז)

Between those cups (= the second and third cups of wine at the Seder) if he wishes to drink [more], he may drink; between the third and fourth cup he must not drink.

לְהַלָּן

SEE: לְהַלָּן

הֵן¹

they (m./f.)

הֵן הֵן הַדְּבָרִים שֶׁנֶּאֶמְרוּ לוֹ לְמֹשֶׁה בְּסִינַי! (פסחים לח, סע"ב)

They are the very words that were said to Moshe at Sinai!

הֵן² / הֵין

yes

אַתָּה הוּא הִלֵּל שֶׁקּוֹרִין אוֹתְךָ נְשִׂיא יִשְׂרָאֵל? אָמַר לוֹ: הֵן. (שבת לא,א)

Are you the Hillel who is called the Patriarch of Yisrael? He said to him: Yes.

הַנְהוּ

they; those; the aforementioned אוֹתָם; הָהֵם

This word introduces a narrative passage. It is sometimes best left untranslated in English.

הַנְהוּ תְּרֵי תַּלְמִידֵי דַּהֲווֹ יָתְבֵי קַמֵּיהּ דְּרַב ... (פסחים ג,ב)

Those two disciples who were sitting before Rav ... (= Two disciples were sitting before Rav)

הָנֵי*

these** אֵלּוּ

תְּנָא הָנֵי — וְהוּא הַדִּין לְהָנָךְ. (פסחים פד,א)

He listed these [items] — and that is (also) the rule with regard to the others.

וְהָנֵי נָשֵׁי הוֹאִיל וְאִיתְנְהוּ בִּשְׁמִירָה, אִיתְנְהוּ בִּזְכִירָה (ברכות כ,ב)

and women, since they are commanded "to observe" they are commanded "to remember"

* This word is pronounced הָנֵי by Ashkenazim. Cf. הָךְ.
** In some instances, this demonstrative is so weak that it need not be translated in English, as in the second example.
SEE: הָנָךְ

הָנֵי ... וְהָנֵי ...

these ..., but those/others ... אֵלּוּ ... וְאֵלּוּ ...

הָנֵי חֲשִׁיבֵי לֵיהּ, וְהָנֵי לָא חֲשִׁיבֵי לֵיהּ. (בבא מציעא נח,ב)

These are important for him, but others are not important for him.

הָנֵי מִילֵּי "דְּבָרִים אֵלּוּ"; בַּמֶּה דְבָרִים אֲמוּרִים

"these words"; it applies only [in a case]

This expression is used in the Talmud to limit the scope of the text or case now under discussion.

אוֹנֵס רַחֲמָנָא פַּטְרֵיהּ .... וְכִי תֵימָא: הָנֵי מִילֵּי לְעִנְיַן קְטָלָא, אֲבָל לְעִנְיַן נְזָקִין — חַיָּיב ... (בבא קמא כח, סע"ב)

The Torah has exempted [from punishment] an act carried out because of unavoidable circumstances .... And if you say [this halakha] applies only in a case involving the death penalty, but in a case involving the payment of damages he is liable ...

SEE: בַּמֶּה דְבָרִים אֲמוּרִים, מְנָא הָנֵי מִילֵּי

וְהָנֵי תַנָּאֵי כִּי* הָנֵי תַנָּאֵי

וְתַנָּאִים אֵלּוּ כְּתַנָּאִים אֵלּוּ

and these tannaim are like those tannaim

The *controversy* between tannaim that was previously quoted in the Talmud is parallel to another controversy between two different tannaim.

For example, see the comparison of the controversy between R. Akiva and R. El'azar with the controversy between R. Eliezer and R. Y^{e}hoshua in ברכות ט,א.

* Sometimes כְּהָנֵי, *like those*, is written as one word.
SEE: תַּנָּאֵי הִיא

הָנִיחָא (= הָא נִיחָא)

this is appropriate; this is good; this is reasonable זוֹ נוֹחָה

SEE: בִּשְׁלָמָא, תֵּינַח

הָנִיחָא לְ... אֶלָּא לְ... מַאי אִיכָּא לְמֵימַר

זוֹ נוֹחָה לְ... אֶלָּא לְ... מַה יֵּשׁ לוֹמַר?

This [approach] is good according to ... (one of the two opinions), but according to ... (the other opinion), what is there to say?

This formula points out a *difficulty* with regard to an explanation (or some other point) that has just been proposed — on the grounds that it is inconsistent with one of the two opinions under discussion.*

משנה: יוֹם הַכִּפּוּרִים אָסוּר בַּאֲכִילָה וּבִשְׁתִיָּה ...
תלמוד: אָמַר ר' אִילָא ...: לָא נִצְרְכָה אֶלָּא לַחֲצִי שִׁיעוּר. הָנִיחָא לְמַאן דְּאָמַר: חֲצִי שִׁיעוּר אָסוּר מִן הַתּוֹרָה, אֶלָּא לְמַאן דְּאָמַר חֲצִי שִׁיעוּר מוּתָּר מִן הַתּוֹרָה, מַאי אִיכָּא לְמֵימַר? (יומא עג,ב)

MISHNA: On Yom Kippur it is forbidden to eat and to drink ...
TALMUD: R. Ila said ...: [The mishna] must be referring to [eating] half (= less than) the minimum quantity [necessary for punishment]. This [answer] is good according to the one who says: Half the minimum quantity is forbidden by the Torah, but according to the one who says: Half the minimum quantity is permitted by the Torah, what is there to say?

* Compare תֵּינַח — a term that introduces a difficulty on the grounds that the proposal is inconsistent with one of the *cases* under discussion.

הָנָךְ (= הָנֵי+ךְ)

those; the others אוֹתָם; הָהֵם

For an example — see הָנֵי.
SEE: הָאֵיךְ, הָנְהוּ

הִסִּיק (סלק הִפְעִיל: מַסִּיק .prt, יַסִּיק .fut, לְהַסִּיק .inf)

he heated; he kindled; he fired (an oven)

תַּנּוּר שֶׁהִסִּיקוּהוּ בְּקַשׁ (שבת לח,ב: משנה פ"ג מ"ב)

an oven that they fired with straw

SEE: אַסִּיק, the parallel Aramaic verb.

הֶסֵּק/הֶיסֵּק/הַסָּקָה

heating; kindling

לֹא נִיתְּנוּ עֵצִים אֶלָּא לְהַסָּקָה. (ביצה לג,א)

Wood is made only for kindling.

הֶעְלֵם/הַעֲלָמָה

forgetfulness (with respect to a prohibition)

הַכּוֹתֵב שְׁתֵּי אוֹתִיּוֹת בְּהֶעְלֵם אֶחָד — חַיָּיב. (שבת קד, רע"ב: משנה פי"ב מ"ד)

One who writes two letters [of the alphabet] within one [period of] forgetfulness is liable [to punishment for Sabbath desecration].

הִקִּישׁ (נקש הִפְעִיל: מַקִּישׁ .prt, לְהַקִּישׁ .inf)

(1) he struck; he knocked

הִקִּישׁ עַל הַדֶּלֶת (משנה זבים פ"ד מ"ג)

he knocked on the door

(2) he compared; he drew an analogy (between two matters, usually because of their juxtaposition in the Torah)

"עַל פִּי שְׁנַיִם עֵדִים אוֹ שְׁלֹשָׁה עֵדִים יוּמַת הַמֵּת ..." לְהַקִּישׁ שְׁלֹשָׁה לִשְׁנַיִם: מָה שְׁלֹשָׁה מְזִמִּין אֶת הַשְּׁנַיִם, אַף הַשְּׁנַיִם יְזוֹמּוּ אֶת הַשְּׁלֹשָׁה. (מכות ה, סע"ב: משנה פ"א מ"ז ע"פ דברים יז:ו)

"From the testimony of two witnesses or three witnesses, the criminal is to be executed" ... [This juxtaposition of "two" and "three" teaches us] to draw an analogy between [the law of] three and [the law of] two: Just as three [witnesses] can refute [and incriminate] two, so can two refute three.

SEE: הֶיקֵּשׁ and אַקִּישׁ, the parallel Aramaic verb.

הֲרֵי*

(1) here is

הֲרֵי שֶׁלְּךָ לְפָנֶיךָ! (בבא מציעא עח,א: משנה פ״ו מ״ג)

Here is your property before you! (= Take it in its present condition!)

(2) behold; now; consider [the case of] ...

וַהֲרֵי תְּפִלָּה דְּדָבָר שֶׁהַצִּבּוּר עֲסוּקִין בּוֹ ...

But consider [the case of] prayer, which is a matter that the congregation is engaged in ...

(3) behold ...! is it not ...?!

הֲרֵי sometimes has a rhetorical force that can be expressed in English either by an exclamation introduced by *behold* or by the use of interrogative word order with a negative.

אַל תְּהִי רָגִיל לַעֲשׂוֹת כֵּן, שֶׁהֲרֵי שָׁנִינוּ ... (יומא נג,ב)

Don't become accustomed to doing that, for behold we have learned ...! (or *have we not learned ...?!)*

* The word הֲרֵי in the idiom ... לֹא הֲרֵי ... כַּהֲרֵי is of uncertain etymology; hence, it is difficult to determine its literal translation.

SEE: הָא

הֲרֵינִי (= הֲרֵי+אֲנִי)

here I am; behold I am; I hereby am

הֲרֵינִי נָזִיר. (נזיר ח, רע״ב: משנה פ״ב מ״א ועוד)

I hereby [undertake to be] a nazirite.

הַשְׁתָּא* (= הָא+שַׁתָּא) הַשָּׁנָה הַזֹּאת **this year**

שַׁתָּא קַמַּיְיתָא דִּיהַבְתְּ, אֲכַלְתְּ; הַשְׁתָּא אֲנַן יָהֲבִינַן, אֲנַן אָכְלִינַן. (גיטין נח,ב)

The first year you paid [the tax] — you ate [the produce]; this year we will pay [the tax] — we will eat [the produce].

* See הַשַּׁתָּא הָכָא in the Pesaḥ Haggada.

הַשְׁתָּא (= הָא+שַׁעְתָּא) שָׁעָה זוֹ; עַכְשָׁיו; מֵעַתָּה

"this hour"; now; now that; since

In addition to the meaning *now* in a temporal sense, this word is often used in a logical sense — as in the example below.

הַשְׁתָּא כָּתַב אוֹת אַחַת פָּטוּר, הִגִּיהַּ אוֹת אַחַת חַיָּיב?! (שבת קד, סע״ב)

Now that [we have learned that if] one wrote one letter [of the alphabet on the Sabbath], he is exempt [from punishment], [if] he corrected one letter, is he subject to punishment?!

SEE: הָכִי הַשְׁתָּא

הַשְׁתָּא דְּאָתֵית לְהָכִי עַכְשָׁיו שֶׁבָּאתָ לְכָךְ ...

now that you have come to this ...

In view of the fact that you have adopted this explanation to solve one difficulty, you may apply the same explanation to solve another difficulty that was mentioned earlier in the Talmudic discussion (instead of accepting the solution that had been proposed there).

ברייתא: הַמּוֹצֵא מָעוֹת בְּבָתֵּי כְנֵסִיּוֹת וּבְבָתֵּי מִדְרָשׁוֹת ... הֲרֵי אֵלּוּ שֶׁלּוֹ, מִפְּנֵי שֶׁהַבְּעָלִים מִתְיָאֲשִׁין מֵהֶן ...

תלמוד: הָכָא בְּמַאי עָסְקִינַן? בְּבָתֵּי כְנֵסִיּוֹת שֶׁל גּוֹיִים. בָּתֵּי מִדְרָשׁוֹת — מַאי אִיכָּא לְמֵימַר? בָּתֵּי מִדְרָשׁוֹת דִּידַן דְּיָתְבֵי בְּהוּ גּוֹיִים. הַשְׁתָּא דַּאֲתֵית לְהָכִי, בָּתֵּי כְנֵסִיּוֹת נַמֵי דִּידַן דְּיָתְבֵי בְּהוּ גּוֹיִים. (בבא מציעא כד, סע״א ע״פ כת״י)

MISHNA: [If] one finds money in a synagogue or a beth midrash ... it belongs to him (= the finder), because the owner gives up hope.

TALMUD: With what circumstances are we involved here? With a "synagogue" (= meeting place) of non-Jews. [But] what is there to say [about] "a beth midrash"?! [It refers to] a beth midrash of ours in which non-Jews are sitting. Now that you have come to this, a synagogue may also be explained [as one of] ours in which non-Jews are sitting.

הַשְׁתָּא ... מִיבַּעְיָא מֵעַתָּה ..., ... צָרִיךְ לוֹמַר?!

now [that] ..., is it necessary to state ...!

This formula presents a קַל־וָחוֹמֶר argument.

הַשְׁתָּא עַל לֹא תַעֲשֶׂה מְכַפֵּר, עַל עֲשֵׂה מִיבַּעְיָא?! (יומא פה, סע״ב)

Now [that] it atones for [the transgression of] a negative commandment, is it necessary to state [that it atones for the violation of] a positive commandment (which is less severe)?!

SEE: קַל וָחוֹמֶר

הָתִינַח/הָא־תִּינַח זוֹ תְּהֵא נוֹחָה

this would be appropriate; this would be good; this would be reasonable

See the explanation under תֵּינַח.

הָתָם (= הָא+תָּם)

there; in that case; in another context שָׁם

מֵהָכָא לְהָתָם (סנהדרין ה,א)

from here (= Babylonia) to there (= Eretz Yisrael)

For another example — see הָכָא נַמֵי.

SEE: תְּנַן הָתָם

וְהָתַנְיָא/וְהָא־תַּנְיָא*

(1) וַהֲרֵי שְׁנוּיָה ...?!

but has it not been taught (in a baraitha) ...?!

This *rhetorical question* usually introduces a baraitha (or an excerpt from a baraitha) that contradicts an amora's halakha.

אָמַר רַב חִסְדָּא: בֵּי דָגִים אֵין צָרִיךְ בְּדִיקָה. וְהָתַנְיָא: צְרִיכִין בְּדִיקָה?! (פסחים ח,א)

Rav Ḥisda said: A fish pantry does not require a search (for ḥametz). But has it not been taught: [Fish pantries] require a search?!

(2) וְזֹאת שְׁנוּיָה ...

and this has been taught (in a baraitha) ...

This term sometimes introduces a baraitha that is cited as a *proof*. To distinguish this less common usage from the first, Rashi often comments: בְּנִיחוּתָא, *gently*, or occasionally: סַיַּיעְתָּא, *a proof.*

אִם לֹא גִילַּח עֶרֶב הָרֶגֶל, אָסוּר לְגַלֵּחַ אַחַר הָרֶגֶל. וְהָתַנְיָא: ... אִם לֹא גִילַּח עֶרֶב הָרֶגֶל, אָסוּר לְגַלֵּחַ אַחַר הָרֶגֶל. (מועד קטן יט, סע"א-רע"ב ורש"י שם: סייעתא)

If [the mourner] did not shave the day before the festival, he is forbidden to shave after the festival. And this has been taught (in a baraitha): If he did not shave the day before the festival, he is forbidden to shave after the festival.

* The two different usages do not depend upon the two different spellings.

SEE: תַּנְיָא

וְהָתְנַן/וְהָא־תְנַן*

(1) וַהֲרֵי שָׁנִינוּ ...?!

but have we not learned (in a mishna) ...?!

This *rhetorical question* usually introduces a mishna (or an excerpt from a mishna) that contradicts a baraitha or a halakha of an amora.

ברייתא: חָבִיּוֹת שֶׁל יַיִן וְשֶׁל שֶׁמֶן ... הֲרֵי אֵלּוּ שֶׁלּוֹ.

תלמוד: וְהָא תְנַן: כַּדֵּי יַיִן וְכַדֵּי שֶׁמֶן חַיָּיב לְהַכְרִיז?! (בבא מציעא כג,ב ע"פ משנה שם פ"ב מ"ב)

BARAITHA: [If one finds] barrels of wine or oil ..., they belong to him (= the finder).

TALMUD: But have we not learned (in a mishna): Jars of wine and jars of oil must be announced [publicly to locate the owner]?!

(2) וְזֹאת שָׁנִינוּ ...

and we have learned this (in a mishna) ...

This term occasionally introduces a mishna that is cited as a *proof*. In order to distinguish this rare usage from the first, Rashi often comments: בְּנִיחוּתָא, *gently*.

אֲמַר לֵיהּ רַב פָּפָּא לְאַבָּיֵי: וְסָבַר ר' שִׁמְעוֹן: חוּלִּין שֶׁנִּשְׁחֲטוּ בָּעֲזָרָה דְאוֹרַיְיתָא הִיא?! אֲמַר לֵיהּ: אִין, וְהָתְנַן: ר' שִׁמְעוֹן אוֹמֵר: חוּלִּין שֶׁנִּשְׁחֲטוּ בָּעֲזָרָה יִשָּׂרְפוּ בָּאֵשׁ ... (חולין פה,ב ורש"י שם)

Rav Pappa said to Abbayé: But does R. Shim'on (really) hold: Unconsecrated [animals slaughtered] in the Temple court [must not be eaten] according to Torah law?! He (=Abbayé) said to him: Yes, and we have learned this (in a mishna): R. Shim'on says: Unconsecrated [animals] that were slaughtered in the Temple court must be burned by fire ...

* The two different usages do not depend upon the two different spellings.

SEE: תְּנַן

הַתְרָאָה*

a warning

the oral warning issued to an offender just prior to his commiting an offense

חָבֵר אֵינוֹ צָרִיךְ הַתְרָאָה, לְפִי שֶׁלֹּא נִיתְּנָה הַתְרָאָה אֶלָּא לְהַבְחִין בֵּין שׁוֹגֵג לְמֵזִיד. (סנהדרין ח, סע"ב)

A scholar does not require a (formal) warning [in order to be punished for his offense], because a warning has been required only [as a means] to distinguish between an ignorant offender and a willful one.

* See Rashi's commentary on בראשית מג:ג.

SEE: אַזְהָרָה

הִתְרָה (תרי הִפְעִיל: מַתְרֶה .prt)

he warned (the accused prior to the alleged offense)

מַכִּירִין אַתֶּם אוֹתוֹ? הִתְרֵיתֶם בּוֹ? (סנהדרין מ, רע"א: משנה פ"ה מ"א)

Do you (witnesses) recognize him? Did you warn him?

SEE: הִזְהִיר

ו - ז

ו-* **and**

Besides its common meaning, this prefix has two other important usages in the Mishna and the Talmud:

(1) or

הַקּוֹרֵא אֶת הַמְּגִילָּה — עוֹמֵד וְיוֹשֵׁב (מגילה כא,א: משנה ד:א)

one who reads the scroll (of Esther) [may do so either] standing or sitting

(2) but

In this sense, this prefix often introduces a *rhetorical question.*

וּמִי מָצֵית אָמְרַתְּ הָכִי?! (שבת קג,ב ועוד)

But can you really say so?!

* In this dictionary, most entries beginning with the prefix ו- are alphabetized without that prefix. Some of the more common ones are listed below, and the reader is referred to the main entry.

וְאוֹמֵר **and [Scripture also] states**

One text has been quoted from Scripture in a mishna or baraitha as a proof — usually introduced by the term שֶׁנֶּאֱמַר, *as it has been stated.* Then, the term וְאוֹמֵר is used to introduce an additional Biblical proof text. Sometimes, the Talmud proceeds to challenge the need for the additional proof and asks: מַאי "וְאוֹמֵר"?, *What is [the need for] "and [Scripture also] states"?*

"בָּנִים אַתֶּם לַה' אֱלֹקֵיכֶם" — בִּזְמַן שֶׁאַתֶּם נוֹהֲגִים מִנְהַג בָּנִים, אַתֶּם קְרוּיִים בָּנִים; אֵין אַתֶּם נוֹהֲגִים מִנְהַג בָּנִים, אֵין אַתֶּם קְרוּיִים בָּנִים; דִּבְרֵי ר' יְהוּדָה. ר' מֵאִיר אוֹמֵר: בֵּין כָּךְ וּבֵין כָּךְ אַתֶּם קְרוּיִים בָּנִים, שֶׁנֶּאֱמַר: "בָּנִים סְכָלִים הֵמָּה", וְאוֹמֵר: "בָּנִים לֹא אֵמֻן בָּם", וְאוֹמֵר: "זֶרַע מְרֵעִים, בָּנִים מַשְׁחִיתִים" ... (קידושין לו,א ע"פ דברים יד:א, ירמיהו ד:כב, דברים לב:כ, וישעיהו א:ד)

"You are sons of the Lord your God" — when you behave like sons, you are called sons; [when] you do not behave like sons, you are not called sons; [this is] the opinion of R. Y'huda. R. Méir says: In both cases you are called "sons," as it has been stated: "They are foolish sons," and [Scripture also] states: "They are sons [who] have no faithfulness," and [Scripture also] states: "Wicked children, sons that deal corruptly" ...

SEE: מַאי וְאוֹמֵר

וְאָזְדָא ר' ... לְטַעְמֵיהּ SEE: אָזְדָא

וְאָזְדוּ לְטַעְמַייהוּ SEE: אָזְדוּ

... וְאָזֵיל ... וְהוֹלֵךְ

going on and ...; going ahead and ...

This Aramaic participle with the prefix ו is used to modify another participle that immediately precedes it.

קָאָכֵיל וְאָזֵיל (שבת מה, סע"א)

he is going on and eating (= he is engaged in the process of eating)

כּוּלֵי יוֹמָא מְצַלֵּי וְאָזֵיל. (ברכות כו,א)

During any time of the day he may go ahead and pray.

SEE: וְהוֹלֵךְ

וְאִידָךְ וּ[לְדַעַת הֶחָכָם] הַשֵּׁנִי?

And [as for the opinion of] the other [ḥakham]?

After explaining the position of one disputant, the Talmud now addresses the other disputant. It asks how he would maintain his position in light of the data that has just been presented explaining his opponent's position.

וּלְהָנֵךְ תַּנָּאֵי ... הֲנָאַת עוֹרוֹ מְנָא לְהוּ? נָפְקָא לְהוּ מֵ"אֶת בְּשָׂרוֹ" — אֶת הַטָּפֵל לִבְשָׂרוֹ. וְאִידָךְ? "אֶת" לָא דָרֵישׁ. (פסחים כב,ב ע"פ שמות כא:כח)

But according to those tannaim ... from where do they derive [the prohibition against] the use of its hide (= the hide of an ox killed by order of the court)? They derive it from אֶת בְּשָׂרוֹ *— that which is joined to its flesh [may not be used]. And [as for the opinion of] the other [tanna: How would the word* אֶת *be explained]? He would not interpret* אֶת *(as indicative of an extension of meaning).*

וְאִי אִיתָא SEE: אִם אִיתָא

וְאִיכָּא דְּמַתְנֵי לַהּ לְהָא שְׁמַעְתָּא בְּאַפֵּי נַפְשַׁהּ SEE: ... אִיכָּא דְּמַתְנֵי

וְאִיכָּא דְּרָמֵי לְהוּ מִירְמָא SEE: ... אִיכָּא דְּרָמֵי

וְאִילוּ SEE: אִילוּ

וְאִילֵּךְ SEE: (וְ)אֵילָךְ

וְאֵינוֹ חוֹשֵׁשׁ SEE: (וְ)אֵינוֹ חוֹשֵׁשׁ

וְגוֹ' (= וְגוֹמֵר)

and it concludes; and so on; et cetera (= etc.)

This term is placed immediately after the quotation of part of a pasuk in order to indicate the continuation of that pasuk. In some instances, it is the *continuation of the pasuk,* which was not explicitly quoted in the Talmud, that contains the point for which the pasuk was cited.

וְר' יְהוּדָה, כְּתִיב קְרָא אַחֲרִינָא: "הִשְׁבַּעְתִּי אֶתְכֶם, בְּנוֹת יְרוּשָׁלַיִם, בִּצְבָאוֹת אוֹ בְּאַיְלוֹת הַשָּׂדֶה" וְגוֹ' (כתובות קיא, רע"א ע"פ שיר השירים ב:ז)
*And [as for] R. Y^ehuda, there is another pasuk written (in support of his view against immigrating to Eretz Yisrael): "I impose an oath upon you, O daughters of Jerusalem, by the gazelles or by the deer of the field," et cetera.**

For another example — see: פסחים כד,א ע"פ דברים יב:יז.

* It is the continuation of the pasuk — *"that you not awaken nor stir up the love" (between the Lord and the Jewish people)* — that provides support for R. Y^ehuda's view.

SEE: וכו'

וְדִלְמָא לָא הִיא — וְאוּלַי לֹא [כָּךְ]?!

But perhaps it is not [so]?!

This formula is used to introduce a *difficulty* with regard to a statement that the Talmud has previously quoted.

For an example — see the quotation from סוכה לו,א at the end of the entry אָמְרוּ דָּבָר אֶחָד.

... וְהוֹלֵךְ

going on and ...; going ahead and ...

This Hebrew participle with the prefix ו is used to modify another participle that immediately precedes it.

בֵּית שַׁמַּאי אוֹמְרִים: יוֹם רִאשׁוֹן מַדְלִיק שְׁמוֹנֶה, מִכָּאן וְאֵילָךְ פּוֹחֵת וְהוֹלֵךְ; וּבֵית הִלֵּל אוֹמְרִים: יוֹם רִאשׁוֹן מַדְלִיק אַחַת, מִכָּאן וְאֵילָךְ מוֹסִיף וְהוֹלֵךְ. (שבת כא,ב)
The school of Shammai says: The first night [of Ḥanukka] he kindles eight [candles]; henceforth he goes on and decreases; but the school of Hillel says: The first night he kindles one; henceforth he goes on and increases.

SEE: וְאָזִיל

וָי"ו מוֹסִיף עַל עִנְיָן רִאשׁוֹן

[The letter] ו adds to the preceding subject.

The coordinating conjunction *and* links the two passages together, so that a halakha mentioned in one is applied to the other as well.

וְשׁוֹמֵר שָׂכָר גּוּפֵיהּ מְנָלַן? גָּמְרִי חִיּוּבָא דְשׁוֹמֵר שָׂכָר מֵחִיּוּבָא דְשׁוֹאֵל — מָה לְהַלָּן בִּבְעָלִים פָּטוּר, אַף כָּאן בִּבְעָלִים פָּטוּר. בְּמַאי גָּמַר? ... אָמַר קְרָא: "וְכִי יִשְׁאַל" — וָי"ו מוֹסִיף עַל עִנְיָן רִאשׁוֹן, וְיִלְמַד עֶלְיוֹן מִתַּחְתּוֹן. (ב"מ צה,א ע"פ שמות כב:יג)
And from where do we derive that a paid guardian himself [is exempt from responsibility for his charge if he was in the service of the owner]? [Since we] derive the responsibility of the paid guardian from the responsibility of the borrower (stated in the next Torah section) — just as there [the borrower] is exempt [if he was] in the service of the owner, here too [the paid guardian] is exempt [if he was] in the service of the owner. How does one derive [this]? ... The pasuk stated: "And if a man borrows" — [The letter] ו adds to the preceding case, and so the former case (i.e., of the paid guardian) will derive from the latter case (i.e., of the borrower).

SEE: הֶיקֵּשׁ

וְכוּ' (= וְכוּלֵיהּ*)

and all [the rest] of it; et cetera וְכֻלּוֹ

This term is usually placed after the quotation of part of a mishna or baraitha in order to indicate the continuation of that text. In many instances, the purpose of the quotation is a point that appears in the continuation of the tannaitic text — rather than in the part actually quoted in the Talmud.

וּבַמֶּה אָמְרוּ: "שְׁתֵּי שׁוּרוֹת" וְכוּ'? "מַרְתֵּף"! מַאן דְּכַר שְׁמֵיהּ? (פסחים ח,ב ע"פ משנה שם פ"א מ"א)
*And under what conditions did they say: "Two rows," et cetera? "A wine cellar!" Has it been stated (earlier in the mishna)?***

* This Aramaic form is also used in Modern Hebrew.

** The Talmud objects to the sudden mention of the word מַרְתֵּף, *wine cellar*, in the mishna, which is out of context since it does not appear earlier in the mishna. The word מַרְתֵּף, however, is not quoted by the Talmud as part of the mishna, but it is the first word in the continuation of the mishna that is indicated by וְכוּ', *et cetera*.

SEE: מַאן דְּכַר שְׁמֵיהּ, וְגוֹ'

וְכִי

SEE: כִּי

וְלָא הִיא

But it is not [so]! וְלֹא הִיא!

This expression rejects the proposal that has just been presented in the Talmud.

הַנַּח לְיִשְׂרָאֵל! מוּטָב שֶׁיְּהוּ שׁוֹגְגִין וְאַל יְהוּ מְזִידִין. סְבוּר מִינָּהּ: הָנֵי מִילֵּי — בִּדְרַבָּנַן, אֲבָל בִּדְאוֹרַיְיתָא — לָא. וְלָא הִיא! לָא שְׁנָא בִּדְרַבָּנַן, וְלָא שְׁנָא בִּדְאוֹרַיְיתָא ...* (שבת קמח,ב)
Let the Jewish people alone! It is better that they sin out of ignorance than deliberately (since they are likely to sin even if we rebuke them). They (= some students in the beth midrash) understood from it [that this principle] applies only to a law enacted by the ḥakhamim, but not to a law with a Scriptural basis. But it is not [so]! There is no difference between a law enacted by the ḥakhamim and a law with a Scriptural basis ...

* For the halakhic ruling that has been accepted on this issue, see שולחן ערוך, אורח חיים תרח:ב והגהת הרמ"א שם.

וּמַאי אוּלְמֵיהּ דְּ- מִ-

SEE: (וּ)מַאי אוּלְמֵיהּ דְּ- מִ-

וְעוֹד

SEE: עוֹד

וְתוּ

SEE: תוּ

זֹאת אוֹמֶרֶת

this says ...; this indicates ...

This expression introduces an inference drawn by an amora, as if to say: From the aforementioned halakha, the following halakha may be derived.

כְּפָאוֹ וְאָכַל מַצָּה — יָצָא ... אָמַר רָבָא: זֹאת אוֹמֶרֶת: הַתּוֹקֵעַ לְשִׁיר — יָצָא. (ראש השנה כח, סע"א)

[If someone] forced him to eat matza (on the first night of Pesaḥ) — he has fulfilled his duty (even though he did not intend to perform the mitzva). Rava said: This indicates [that] one who blows the shofar (just) for music (on Rosh HaShana) has fulfilled his duty.

זְבוּנָא

SEE: זְבִינָא

זַבֵּין (זבן פַּעֵל: מְזַבֵּין .prt, לְזַבּוֹנֵי .inf)

he sold מָכַר

תַּגָּרָא דְזָבֵין וּמְזַבֵּין (בבא מציעא עד,ב)

a merchant who buys and sells

SEE: זְבַן and its note

זְבִינָא/זְבוּנָא

buyer; customer קוֹנֶה; לָקוֹחַ

מִידִי דְקָפֵיץ עֲלֵיהּ זְבִינָא (פסחים לב,א)

something that a customer would "jump at" (= would be eager to buy)

זְבִינֵי

sale מֶכֶר; מְכִירָה

זְבִינֵיהּ זְבִינֵי (ב"ב מז, סע"ב)

his sale is a [valid] sale

זְבַן* (זבן: זָבֵין .prt, לְמִיזְבַּן .inf)

he bought קָנָה

See example under זַבֵּין.

* In the popular Pesaḥ song, חַד גַּדְיָא, the correct vocalization should be: דִּזְבַן אַבָּא בִּתְרֵי זוּזֵי, *which Father bought for two susim.* For the complete conjugation of this verb, see *Grammar for Gemara*: Chapter 4, Verb 2.

SEE: מִזְדַּבַּן

זָדוֹן

deliberate wrongdoing

דָּבָר שֶׁחַיָּיבִין עַל זְדוֹנוֹ כָּרֵת וְעַל שִׁגְגָתוֹ חַטָּאת (סנהדרין סו, רע"א: משנה פ"ז מ"ח)

an offense [whose perpetrators] are liable to (Divine) cutting off [when it is] a deliberate wrongdoing and [to] a sin offering [when it is] an unintended wrongdoing.

SEE: הֵזִיד, מֵזִיד

זֶהוּ ;זֶה

this is; this refers to; this is equivalent to

The demonstrative pronoun זֶה is sometimes combined with the personal pronoun הוּא to form the word זֶהוּ, which is frequently used in equations and definitions:

הֶפְשֵׁרוֹ זֶהוּ בִּישׁוּלוֹ. (שבת מ,ב)

Warming it (= oil) — this is equivalent to cooking it (since it is thus prepared for use).

"הַיָּרֵא וְרַךְ הַלֵּבָב" זֶהוּ הַמִּתְיָירֵא מִן הָעֲבֵירוֹת שֶׁבְּיָדוֹ. (סוטה מד, סע"א: משנה פ"ח מ"ה ע"פ דברים כ:ח)

"One who is fearful and faint-hearted" — this refers to one who is frightened because of the sins "in his hand" (= that he has committed).

Sometimes, זֶה by itself is used in the same manner as זֶהוּ in the above examples — especially in the interpretation of words from Scripture.

"מְפוֹרָשׁ" זֶה תַּרְגוּם. (מגילה ג,א ע"פ נחמיה ח:ח)

"Explained" — this refers to translation (i.e., Targum Onkelos).

SEE: זוֹ; זוֹהִי

זֶה בָּנָה אָב

this [passage] has established a prototype

This formula is used to introduce a בִּנְיַן אָב derivation.

מִמַּשְׁמַע שֶׁנֶּאֱמַר: "לֹא יָקוּם עֵד" — אֵינִי יוֹדֵעַ שֶׁהוּא אֶחָד?! מָה תַּלְמוּד לוֹמַר: "אֶחָד"? זֶה בָּנָה אָב: כָּל מָקוֹם שֶׁנֶּאֱמַר "עֵד" — הֲרֵי כָּאן שְׁנַיִם, עַד שֶׁיִּפְרֹט לְךָ הַכָּתוּב: "אֶחָד". (סנהדרין ל, סע"א ע"פ דברים יט:טו)

From the meaning of what is stated (in the Torah): "[A] witness shall not rise up ..." do I not know that one [is meant]?! What teaching does [the expression] "one [witness]" come to convey? This [passage] has established a prototype: Wherever [the word] עד is written (in the Torah) it means two [witnesses] unless Scripture clearly specifies to you: "one."

SEE: בִּנְיַן אָב

זוֹ* f.

this

הִתְקַדְּשִׁי לִי בִּתְמָרָה זוֹ. (קידושין מו,א: משנה פ"ב מ"א)

Be married to me by [accepting] this date (fruit).

* This form is the feminine singular demonstrative in Mishnaic Hebrew. In Biblical Hebrew, זאת is the standard form, but זֹה is found occasionally, e.g., תהילים קלב:ב and הושע ז:טז. In the former verse, however, it is a relative pronoun meaning *that which* (like זו in שמות טו:יג,טז). In the latter verse, its meaning is uncertain (see Rashi and Radak there).

זוֹ; זוֹהִי

this is; this refers to; this is equivalent to*

קְרִיָּיתָהּ זוֹ הִיא הַלֵּילָא. (ערכין י,ב)

Its reading (= that of Mgillath Esther) — this is equivalent to [reciting] Hallel.

* See the entry זֶה; זֶהוּ where this usage is explained.

זוֹ וְאֵין צָרִיךְ לוֹמַר זוֹ

this and needless to say that

Sometimes cases are listed in a mishna or baraitha in an anticlimactic sequence, starting with the most novel case and proceeding in sequence to the most obvious case.

משנה: וְאֵין חוֹתְכִין אוֹתוֹ — בֵּין בְּדָבָר שֶׁהוּא מִשּׁוּם שְׁבוּת וּבֵין בְּדָבָר שֶׁהוּא מִשּׁוּם לֹא תַעֲשֶׂה (ר"ה לג, רע"א: משנה פ"ד מ"ח)
תלמוד: זוֹ וְאֵין צָרִיךְ לוֹמַר זוֹ קָתָנֵי. (בבלי שם)

MISHNA: and we may not cut it (= a shofar on Rosh HaShana) — neither with an implement whose use is forbidden by a Rabbinic safeguard nor with an implement forbidden by a Torah prohibition

TALMUD: *[The tanna] is listing (in the mishna) this (= the Rabbinic safeguard) and needless to say that (= the Torah prohibition).*

SEE: לא זו אף זו

זוג; זוגא/זוזא/זָוְוא* (זוגי/זוזי pl.)

(1) pair; couple

אין הֲלָכָה כאותו הַזּוּג. (ביצה יז,א)

The halakhic ruling is not in accordance with [the joint opinion of] that pair [of tannaim].

שְׁדַר אַבַּיֵי זוגא דְרַבָּנָן לְמִיבְדְקֵיה (תענית כא, סע"ב*)

Abbayé sent a pair of ḥakhamim to test him

(2) a pair of scissors

זוג שֶׁל סְפָרִים (משנה כלים פי"ג מ"א)

a pair of barbers' scissors

וְאַיְיתִי זוזא מִבֵיתֵיה (מגילה טז,א ורש"י שם)

and he brought a pair of scissors from his house

(3) bell; the body of a bell

הַחִיצוֹן זוג, וְהַפְּנִימִי ענבָל. (נזיר לד,ב)

The outer part is the bell, and the inner part is the tongue.

* The first form is Hebrew, and the others are Aramaic. *Dikduké Soferim* on the two Aramaic examples quotes the different spellings of this word.

SEE: בן זוג, בר זוגא

הַזּוּגוֹת **the *Zugoth***

This term is applied to the five pairs of leaders of the Great Sanhedrin, one a *Nasi* and the other an *Av beth din*, who functioned during the period of the second Beth HaMikdash. Their names appear in the first chapter of *Pirké Avoth.**

מְקוּבָּל אֲנִי מֵרִ׳ מְיָאשָׁא, שֶׁקִּיבֵּל מֵאַבָּא, שֶׁקִּיבֵּל מִן הַזּוּגוֹת, שֶׁקִּיבְּלוּ מִן הַנְּבִיאִים הֲלָכָה לְמֹשֶׁה מִסִּינַי. (פאה פ"ב מ"ו).

I received [a tradition] from R. Myasha, who received [it] from my father, who received [it] from the Zugoth, who received [it] from the Nvi'im as a halakhic tradition [transmitted] to Moshe from [the Divine Revelation at] Sinai.

* See משנה אבות פ"א מ"ד-י"ב.

SEE: סַנְהֶדְרִין, אַב בֵּית דִּין, נָשִׂיא

זוז; זוזא* (זוזי/זוזין pl.) **a *zuz***

This silver coin, which is equal to 192 *p*ʳ*rutoth*, is sometimes called a *dinar.*

* The first form is Hebrew, and the second is Aramaic. See the table of coins at the end of this volume.

SEE: דִּינָר

זוזא (זוזי pl.) SEE: זוג; זוגא

זוזי ***zuzim*; money (in general)** זוּזִים; מָעוֹת

וְלֶחֱזֵי זוזי מֵמָאן נְקַט! (בבא מציעא ב,ב)

But let us see from whom he took money!

זוטא/זוטר (זוטרא m.s. emphatic*, זוטַרְתִּי f.,

small; insignificant קָטָן (זוטֵי/זוטְרֵי m. pl.)

אַטוּ יִרְאַת שָׁמַיִם מִילְּתָא זוטַרְתִּי הִיא?! (ברכות לג, סע"ב ע"פ כת"י)

Is the fear of Heaven an insignificant matter?!

* The emphatic form expresses the definite article (*the* in English). See *Grammar for Gemara*, Chapter 6.

זוֹמֵם prt. (זמם) **plotting evil**

הָעֵדִים הַזּוֹמְמִים (מכות ה,ב: משנה פ"א מ"ו ע"פ כת"י)

the evil-plotting witnesses (who have been refuted through הֲזָמָה *and are thereby subject to the same penalty that their testimony would have caused their intended victim)*

* See the Biblical source: וַעֲשִׂיתֶם לוֹ כַּאֲשֶׁר זָמַם לַעֲשׂוֹת לְאָחִיו (דברים יט:יט).

SEE: הזים, הוּזַם, הֲזָמָה

זיבורא דְּבוֹרָה **bee**

רַב הוּנָא חֲזְיֵיה לְהַהוּא גַּבְרָא דְּקָא קָטֵיל זיבורא. (שבת קכא,ב)

Rav Huna saw a certain man who was killing a bee.

זיבורית/זבורית **the worst land (of an estate)**

הַנִּזָּקִין שָׁמִין לָהֶן בָּעִידִית וּבַעַל חוֹב בְּבֵינוֹנִית וּכְתוּבַּת אִשָּׁה בְּזִיבּוּרִית. (גיטין מח,ב: משנה פ"ה מ"א)

Claimants for damage are compensated out of the best land, a creditor out of average land and a woman's (= a divorcee's or a widow's) marriage-settlement out of the worst land.

זַיֵּיף (זיף פָּעֵל: מְזַיֵּיף act. prt., מְזַיַּיף/זַיֵּיף pass. prt.,

he falsified; he forged זִיֵּף (זִיוּפֵי inf.)

שְׁטָרָא זַיְיפָא הוּא. (ב"ב לב,ב)

It is a forged document.

זִיכָּה SEE: זכה

זיל¹ imp. (אזל) **go!** לֵךְ!

זיל בָּתַר רובָּא! (חולין יא, רע"א)

Go after (= follow) the majority!

SEE: אֲזַל

זיל² pass. prt. (זִילָא f.) (זלל)

cheap; worthless; contemptible זוֹל; מְזֻלְזָל

זִילָא בֵיהּ מִילְּתָא. (מנחות סז,ב)

The matter is contemptible to him. (= It is beneath his dignity.)

SEE: זַל

זיל קְרִי בֵּי רַב הוּא

"לֵךְ, קְרָא בְּבֵית מִדְרָשׁ" הוּא.

[It is a case of] "go, read [it] in the schoolhouse."

This expression indicates that the halakhic point is so obvious that any schoolboy can tell it to you.

For an example — see סנהדרין לג,ב.

זִילוּתָא זִלְזוּל; פְּחִיתוּת כָּבוֹד

cheapening; disgrace; disrepute

ברייתא: בְּמָקוֹם שֶׁחוֹלְקִין מַעֲשַׂר עָנִי, נוֹתְנִין לְאִשָּׁה תְּחִלָּה.
תלמוד: מַאי טַעְמָא? מִשּׁוּם זִילוּתָא. (יבמות ק,א ורש"י שם)

BARAITHA: In the place where they distribute the tithe of the poor, they give to women first.
TALMUD: What is the reason? Because of the disgrace (for women to stand around waiting).

SEE: זָל, זִילֹ²

זִימְנָא/זִמְנָא זְמַן; פַּעַם **time;**

an appointed time; date; occasion

זִימְנָא חֲדָא פַּעַם אַחַת **one time; once**

This expression is used to introduce a narrative passage.

זִימְנָא חֲדָא הֲוָה אָזְלִינַן בִּסְפִינְתָּא ... (בבא בתרא עג,ב)

Once we were travelling in a boat ...

SEE: חֲדָא זִימְנָא

זִימְנִין/זִמְנִין pl. זְמַנִּים **times**

This plural form of the noun זִמְנָא has two special usages.

(1) פְּעָמִים sometimes (usually followed by -ד)

זִימְנִין דְּנָפֵיל וְאָתֵי לְמֵיכְלֵיהּ (פסחים י,ב ע"פ כת"י)

sometimes it will fall, and he might come to eat it (= ḥametz on Pesaḥ)

(2) פַּעַם אַחֶרֶת on another occasion

זִימְנִין הֲווֹ יָתְבִי קַמֵּיהּ דְּר' יוֹחָנָן, אֲתָא כִּי הַאי מַעֲשֶׂה לְקַמַּיְיהוּ. (מכות ה,ב ורש"י שם)

On another occasion, they were sitting before R. Yoḥanan, [and] a similar case came before them.

זִימְנִין ... זִימְנִין ... פְּעָמִים ... פְּעָמִים ...

on some occasions ... on other occasions ...

זִמְנִין סַגִּיאִין הֲוָה קָאֵימְנָא קַמֵּיהּ דְּרַב: זִימְנִין דַּחֲבִיבָא עֲלֵיהּ רִיפְתָּא, מְקַדֵּשׁ אַרִיפְתָּא; זִימְנִין דַּחֲבִיבָא לֵיהּ חַמְרָא, מְקַדֵּשׁ אַחַמְרָא. (פסחים קו,ב)

Many times I stood before Rav: on some occasions when bread was preferable to him, he would recite Kiddush over bread, on other occasions when wine was preferable to him, he would recite Kiddush over wine.

זִימְנִין סַגִּיאִין

פְּעָמִים רַבּוֹת **many times; often**

See example under previous entry.

זָכָה (זכי: זוֹכֶה .prt); **זְכָא*** (זכי: זָכֵי .prt)

(1) he merited; he was worthy (of)

זָכֵי לְעָלְמָא דְאָתֵי (גיטין סח,ב)

he will be worthy of the world-to-come

(2) he was entitled; he acquired; he gained

זָכִין לְאָדָם שֶׁלֹּא בְּפָנָיו. (גיטין יא,ב: משנה פ"א מ"ו; קידושין כג,א וש"נ)

We may acquire [something beneficial] on behalf of a person in his absence.

(3) he won; he was victorious** נָצַח

בְּהָא זְכַנְהוּ ר' נָתָן לְרַבָּנָן. (חולין לא,ב ורש"י שם)

In this [matter] R. Nathan was victorious over the Ḥakhamim.

* The first form is Hebrew and the second Aramaic.

** See: משנה ברכות פ"א מ"ו ור' עובדיה מברטנורא שם

זִכָּה/זִיכָּה (זכי פִּעֵל: מְזַכֶּה .prt); **זַכִּי*** (מְזַכֵּי .prt)

(1) he transferred possession

זִיכָּה לוֹ עַל יְדֵי אַחֵר (גיטין מ,ב; בבא בתרא קלח, רע"א)

he transferred possession [of the document] to him through a third party

For an example of זַכִּי, see example under יָד.

(2) he acquitted; he voted for acquittal; he voted in favor of

אֲנִי מְזַכֶּה, וַחֲבֵירַי מְחַיְּיבִין. (סנהדרין כט,א: משנה פ"ג מ"ז)

I have voted for acquittal, and my colleagues have voted for conviction.

שְׁטָרָא מְזַכֵּי לְבֵי תְרֵי הוּא! (פסחים עח,א ורש"י שם)

It is a document ruling in favor of the two [conflicting parties]! (= His statement is paradoxical.)

* The first forms are Hebrew, and the last is Aramaic.

זֵכֶר

(1) remembrance; memorial

לוּלָב נִיטָל... שִׁבְעָה זֵכֶר לַמִּקְדָּשׁ. (סוכה מא,א: משנה פ"ג מי"ב)

The palm branch must be taken ... [on all] seven [days of Sukkoth] as a remembrance of the Beth HaMikdash.

(2) allusion

an intimation in the Biblical text of a halakhic or aggadic statement whose actual source is not the text itself but either a Rabbinic enactment or an oral tradition from Sinai

For an example — see אַף עַל פִּי שֶׁאֵין רְאָיָה לַדָּבָר, זֵכֶר לַדָּבָר.

SEE: אַסְמַכְתָּא

זָל (זלל: זִיל .pass. prt)

הוּזַל **it became cheaper**

וּלְסוֹף זָל עִיבִידְתָּא (בבא מציעא עז,א)

and subsequently labor became cheaper

SEE: זִילֹ²

זְעִירָא קָטָן **small; minor**

פִּסְחָא זְעִירָא (חולין קכט, סע"ב)

[the day of] the minor Pesaḥ offering (= Pesaḥ Sheni on the fourteenth of Iyyar)

זָקוּק (זקק) pass. prt.

having an obligation; obliged; bound

אִם הָיָה עָלָיו יָתֵר עַל מַשָּׂאוֹ, אֵין זָקוּק לוֹ. (בבא מציעא לב,א: משנה פ"ב מ"י)

If there was more than its [normal] burden on it (= the animal), he has no obligation to [help] him (= the owner).

זְקוּקָה לְיָבָם (קידושין ס,ב ע"פ דברים כה:ה־יא)
[she is] bound to the brother-in-law (by the יִבּוּם *relationship)*

SEE: נִזְקַק

זָר

(1) strange; foreign

"strange service"; idolatry עֲבוֹדָה זָרָה (בבא בתרא קי,א)

(2) "a stranger"; a (Jewish) non-kohen

הַשְּׁחִיטָה כְּשֵׁרָה בְּזָרִים. (זבחים לא, סע"ב: משנה פ"ג מ"א)
The slaughtering (of an offering) by non-kohanim is proper.

ח

חֲבוּרָה; חֲבוּרְתָּא*

group; a company (of people)

אֲנִי וַאֲרִי שֶׁבַּחֲבוּרָה (שבת קיא, רע"ב וש"נ)

*I together with the "lion" (= the most outstanding member) of the group***

בְּנֵי חֲבוּרָה (פסחים פט, רע"ב: משנה פ"ח מ"ד)

members of a company (that was organized for the Pesaḥ offering)

* The first form is Hebrew, and the second is Aramaic.

** Compare אַרְיָא

חַבּוּרָה

wound; bruise

"חָבַלְתָּ בִּי" וְ"עָשִׂיתָ בִּי חַבּוּרָה" (שבועות לו,ב: משנה פ"ה מ"ה)

"you have injured me" or "you have caused me a wound"

חָבִיב (חֲבִיבָא .f) — חָבִיב

beloved; favored

כֵּיוָן דְּאָתְיָא מִדְּרָשָׁא, חֲבִיבָא לֵיהּ. (יבמות ב, סע"ב)

Since it is derived from a Biblical interpretation, it is beloved to him (= the tanna, and he lists it first in the mishna).

חֲבִיבִי — דּוֹדִי

my uncle

This word is used by the amora Rav when referring to his uncle, R. Ḥiyya.

אָמַר רַב: הֲוָה יָתִיבְנָא קַמֵּיהּ דַּחֲבִיבִי (ב"ב מא,ב ורשב"ם שם)

Rav said: I was sitting before my uncle

חָבֵר (חֲבֵרָה .f); חַבְרָא* (חַבִירְתָּא .f)

(1) friend; colleague; fellow man

חַבְרָךְ — חַבְרָא אית ליה, וְחַבְרָא דְּחַבְרָךְ — חַבְרָא אית ליה! (בבא בתרא כח,ב וש"נ)

Your friend has a friend, and your friend's friend has a friend (and thus the story will spread)!

הוּנָא חַבְרִין (כתובות סט, סע"א ועוד)

(Rav) Huna our colleague

(2) a fellow; a parallel; an equal; another

שלא מָצִינוּ לוֹ חָבֵר בְּכָל הַתּוֹרָה כּוּלָּהּ (שבת פג, רע"ב וש"נ)

for which we have not found a parallel in the whole Torah

בְּרָכָה הַסְּמוּכָה לַחֲבֶרְתָּהּ (ברכות מו, סע"א)

a bᵉrakha immediately following another (bᵉrakha)

(3) ḥaver; a fellow; a scholar

This title is applied to a Torah scholar who has undertaken to observe special restrictive measures with regard to ritual purity and some other matters.

אַתּוּן חַכִּימֵי וַאֲנָא חָבֵר. (קידושין לג,ב)

You are ḥakhamim, while I am (merely) a ḥaver.

* The first form is Hebrew, and the second is Aramaic.

SEE: תַּלְמִיד חָבֵר, חֲדָא מִכְּלַל חֲבֶירְתָּהּ אִיתְּמַר

חַבָּר; חַבָּרָא*

a member of a fanatical sect of fire-worshippers from Persia who forbade the lighting of fire outside their own temples on their festivals

For an example — see גיטין יז, רע"א ורש"י שם.

* The first form is Hebrew, and the second is Aramaic.

חַבְרוּתָא — חֲבֵרוּת

friendship

אוֹ חַבְרוּתָא אוֹ מִיתוּתָא! (תענית כג, סע"א)*

[Give me] friendship or [give me] death!

* See a more complete excerpt from this source under the entry הַיְינוּ דְּאָמְרֵי אֱינָשֵׁי.

חַבְרַיָּיא — חֲבֵרִים; בְּנֵי הַיְשִׁיבָה

the ḥaverim; the scholars (in the beth midrash who were not ordained)

וְנִסְבִּין חַבְרַיָּיא לְמֵימַר (חולין יד, רע"א ורש"י שם)

and the ḥaverim ventured to say

חַג

festival

Besides the common meaning, there are two additional usages that should be noted.

(1) an offering*

חַגֵּי נְדָבָה (ברכות לג,ב)

free-will offerings

(2) the festival, i.e., *Sukkoth***

מִן הָעֲצֶרֶת עַד הֶחָג מֵבִיא וְקוֹרֵא (משנה ביכורים פ"א מ"ו)

From Shavu'oth until Sukkoth one may bring [the first fruits to the Beth HaMikdash] and recite [the designated Biblical passage דברים כו:ג, ה-י].

* This usage occurs in the Torah: ולא יָלִין חלב חַגִּי עד בקר (שמות כג:יח).

** In this sense, הֶחָג is used with the definite article. Even the common phrase שֶׁל חַג (e.g., in סוכה כז,א: משנה ב:ו) appears as שֶׁלֶּחָג (= שֶׁל הֶחָג), *of the festival*, in manuscripts.

חַד — אֶחָד

one

חַד אָמַר ... וְחַד אָמַר ...

אֶחָד אוֹמֵר ..., וְאֶחָד אוֹמֵר ...

one says ..., and the other says ...

When presenting a *controversy* between two amoraim, the Talmud sometimes uses this formula to indicate that there is no clear tradition matching the two amoraim with their respective opinions.

(1) This phenomenon occurs in halakhic controversies, chiefly between Rav Aḥa and Rabina.

פליגי בה רב אחא ורבינא — חד אמר מעשה שבת דאורייתא, וחד אמר: דרבנן. (בבא קמא עא, סע"א)

Rav Aha and Rabina are in disagreement about it — one says: Whatever was prepared [unlawfully] on the Sabbath is [forbidden to use] according to Torah law, and the other says: [It is forbidden] because of Rabbinic legislation.

(2) This phenomenon also occurs in aggadic controversies, chiefly between Rav and Sh^e^muel.

"ויקם מלך חדש על מצרים" — רב ושמואל: חד אמר: "חדש" ממש, וחד אמר: שנתחדשו גזירותיו. (עירובין נג,א)

"And a new king arose over Egypt" — Rav and Sh^e^muel [differ]: One says: [He was] actually [a] new [king], and the other says: [He] issued new decrees.

When dealing with halakhic controversies, the Talmud often tries to clarify which amora should be associated with which opinion, by quoting another statement of one of the two amoraim that coincides with one of the two opinions under consideration. See the term תסתיים, which always introduces such clarifications.

חד מתרי (ותלתא) טעמי נקט

אחד משנים (ושלשה) טעמים תפס.

He (= the tanna) has mentioned one of two (or three) explanations.

SEE: חדא מינייהו נקט

חד סר/חדסר אחד עשר — **eleven**

חד סרי f. אחת עשרה — **eleven**

חדא f. אחת — **one**

חדא ועוד קאמר: חדא ... ועוד ...

"אחת" "ועוד" הוא אומר: אחת ... ועוד ...

"First of all" "and furthermore" he is stating: First of all ..., and furthermore ...

This formula introduces a *resolution* of the difficulty that a tanna (or rarely an amora) has stated one reason for a halakha but has ignored the primary reason. In response, it is argued that there is no difficulty, for the tanna would have certainly endorsed the primary reason, if asked. He stated his reason, however, as an additional argument for his halakha.

משנה: אמר ר' יהושע בן קרחה: למה קדמה פרשת "שמע" ל"והיה אם שמוע"? כדי שיקבל עליו עול מלכות שמים תחלה, ואחר־כך יקבל עליו עול מצוות. (ברכות יג,א: משנה פ"ב מ"ב)
תלמוד: תניא: ר' שמעון בן יוחאי אומר: ... שזה ללמוד (וללמד ולעשות). ותיפוק ליה מדר' יהושע בן קרחה? "חדא" "ועוד" קאמר: חדא, כדי שיקבל עליו עול מלכות שמים תחלה ..., ועוד משום דאית בה הני מילי אחרנייתא. (שם יד,ב)

MISHNA: R. Y^e^hoshua b. Korha says: Why does the section of "Sh^e^ma" precede [that of] "V^e^Haya im Shamo'a"? So that one first accept upon himself the yoke of the kingdom of Heaven and then accept upon himself the yoke of commandments.
TALMUD: It is taught (in a baraitha): R. Shim'on b. Yohai says: ... because the former [prescribes] learning, (teaching, and doing) ... But should he not derive it from the reason of R. Y^e^hoshua b. Korha? "First of all" "and furthermore" he is stating: First of all, so that one accept upon himself the yoke of the kingdom of Heaven at the outset ..., and furthermore, because the former (= Sh^e^ma) has these other features.

חדא זימנא פעם אחת — **one time; once**

For examples — see the entries: הא איפליגו בה חדא זימנא, הא אמרה ... חדא זימנא, זימנא חדא, תנינא חדא זימנא, (ו)לאו אותביניה חדא זימנא

חדא מינייהו נקט אחת מהם תפס.

He has mentioned one of them.

A *resolution* of a difficulty: Granted that there are one or more additional explanations or items that are as appropriate as the ones mentioned in the text, nevertheless this state of affairs presents no difficulty: The tanna selected only one of them — merely by way of example; he did not intend to exclude others.

For examples — see בבא קמא קו,ב; יבמות מח,ב וש"נ.
SEE: תנא ושייר

חדא מכלל חבירתה איתמר; חדא מכללא דחברתה איתמר

אחת מכלל חברתה נאמר.

One [halakha] was stated by inference from "its colleague" (= another halakha).

A difficulty has been pointed out: Why was the same halakha of an amora (or the same controversy between two amoraim) stated with regard to two similar cases? In response, the following *resolution* is sometimes presented: The amora himself stated the halakha in just one of the two cases. A disciple subsequently applied that halakha by inference to the second case, even though that case is somewhat different from the first. Ultimately, this applied halakha was attributed to the amora, as if he had actually said it himself.

אמר ר' יצחק נפחא: ראש חדש אדר שחל להיות בשבת — מוציאין שלש תורות ... ואמר ר' יצחק נפחא: ראש חדש טבת שחל להיות בשבת מביאין שלש תורות ... וליפא הא ולא בעי הך?! חדא מכלל חבירתה איתמר. (מגילה כט, סע"ב וש"נ)

R. Yitzhak the smith said: [When] the first of the month of Adar falls on the Sabbath, we take out three Torah scrolls ... And R. Yitzhak the smith said: [When] the first of the month of Teveth falls on the Sabbath, we bring three Torah scrolls ... But let him

(= R Yitzḥak) state the former [halakha only], and he would not need [to state] the latter?! One [halakha] was stated by inference from the other [halakha].
SEE: מִכְּלָלָא

חָדֵי* prt. (חדי) שָׂמֵחַ **rejoicing**
וּמִי חָדֵי הַקָּדוֹשׁ בָּרוּךְ הוּא בְּמַפַּלְתָּן שֶׁל רְשָׁעִים? (מגילה י,ב)
But does the Holy One Blessed Be He rejoice over the downfall of evildoers?!
* The Hebrew noun חֶדְוָה, *joy*, is derived from the same root. The verb occurs in Biblical Hebrew: וַיִּחַדְּ יִתְרוֹ (שמות יח:ט).

חֲדַת (חַדְתָּא .f, חַדְתֵי .m. pl) חָדָשׁ **new**
חֲדָא הִיא לָךְ אוֹ חֲדַת הִיא לָךְ? (ברכות כח, סע"א ורש"י שם)
Is this [point] the [only] one you [learned from R Yoḥanan] or is it (= the fact that R Yoḥanan is its author) new to you?

חוֹב m. (חוֹבוֹת pl.)
debt; detriment; disadvantage
חוֹב הוּא לָהּ, וְאֵין חָבִין לְאָדָם שֶׁלֹּא בְּפָנָיו. (יבמות קיח, סע"ב)
It is to her detriment, and we do not cause a disadvantage to a person in his/her absence.
שְׁטַר חוֹב (כתובות קי, רע"א: משנה פי"ג מ"ח ועוד)
a note of indebtedness; an IOU
SEE: בַּעַל חוֹב

חוֹבָה f. (חוֹבוֹת pl.)
obligation; duty; guilty verdict
תְּפִלַּת עַרְבִית רְשׁוּת אוֹ חוֹבָה? (ברכות כז,ב)
Is the evening prayer optional or a duty?
יָצָא יְדֵי חוֹבָתוֹ (משנה חלה פ"א מ"ב ועוד)
he has fulfilled his obligation
דִּינֵי נְפָשׁוֹת — מַחֲזִירִין לִזְכוּת וְאֵין מַחֲזִירִין לְחוֹבָה. (סנהדרין לב,א: משנה פ"ד מ"א)
[In] capital cases, we (= the court) may reverse [the decision] towards an acquittal, but we may not reverse [it] towards a guilty verdict.
SEE: יָצָא

חוּכָּא צְחוֹק **laughter**
כִּי הֵיכִי דְּלָא לֶיהֱווּ מִילֵּי דְּרַבָּנַן כְּחוּכָּא וּטְלוּלָא* (עירובין סח,ב ורש"י שם)
so that the words of the ḥakhamim not be [subject to] laughter and jest
* Some texts read חוּכָּא וְאִיטְלוּלָא. This expression has entered Modern Hebrew in the sense of *a laughing stock*.
SEE: אַחֵיךְ, מְחַכוּ

חוֹכֵר **a tenant-farmer**
(who receives a fixed salary paid in cash or in goods for cultivating a field or an orchard)
For an example — see בבא מציעא קד,א.
SEE: אָרִיס

חוּמְרָא* חֹמֶר **strictness**
מִשּׁוּם חוּמְרָא דְּשַׁבָּת מִבְדָּל בְּדִילִי** (פסחים יא,א)
on account of the strictness of the Sabbath, they will surely keep away [from transgression]
* In Modern Hebrew, a חֻמְרָה often means a *restriction* that an individual or a group of people have voluntarily imposed upon themselves beyond the normative Halakhic requirement.
** The Aramaic infinitive מִבְדָּל, which adds emphasis to the participle בְּדִילֵי, is expressed in English by the adverb *surely*.
SEE: קַל וָחוֹמֶר

לְחוּמְרָא **strictly**
וְכָל סְפֵיקָא דְאוֹרָיְיתָא לְחוּמְרָא (ביצה ג,ב)
and every [case of] doubt regarding Torah law [must be treated] strictly
SEE: (לְ)קוּלָּא

חוּמְשָׁא חֹמֶשׁ **one-fifth**

חוֹרִין pl. **noblemen**
In the Talmud, חורין always appears as part of a compound. See the entries בֶּן חוֹרִין and בְּנֵי חוֹרִין.*
* In Biblical Hebrew, however, חֹרִים occurs in the phrase הַזְּקֵנִים וְהַחֹרִים (מלכים א כא:ח), *the elders and the noblemen*.
SEE: בֶּן חוֹרִין, בְּנֵי חוֹרִין

חוּרְפָּא חֲרִיפוּת **sharpness; brilliance**
לְפוּם חוּרְפָּא, שִׁבְשְׁתָּא! (בבא מציעא צו, רע"ב וש"נ)
As great as the brilliance [so is] the error!

חוֹשֵׁשׁ prt. (חשש) **worrying; concerned**
For an example — see (וְ)אֵינוֹ חוֹשֵׁשׁ.

חֲזָא (חזי*: חָזֵי .act. prt, חֲזֵי .pass. prt, לֶיחֱזֵי .fut, חֲזִי .imp, לְמֶחֱזֵי .inf) רָאָה **he saw; he noticed**
חֲזָא סָמְיָא דַּהֲוָה קָא טָעֵי בְּאוֹרְחָא. (גיטין סח, רע"ב)
He saw a blind man who had lost his way.
* For the complete conjugation of this verb, see *Grammar for Gemara*: Chapter 4, Verb 12.
SEE: (וּ)מַאי חֲזֵית, פּוּק חֲזִי מַאי עַמָּא דָּבַר

חֲזֵי pass. prt. (חזי: חֲזְיָא .f.s, חֲזוּ .m. pl, חֲזְיָין .f. pl)
(1) רָאוּי **fit; proper; worthy**
לְמַאי חֲזֵי? (שבת לה, סע"ב)
For what is [a ram's horn] fit (on the Sabbath)?
(2) נִרְאֶה **seen**
For an example — see (לְ)דִידִי חֲזֵי לִי.
SEE: מִיחֲזֵי

חַזְיֵיה רָאָה אוֹתוֹ **he saw him/it (m.)**

חַזְיַיהּ/חַזְיָא רָאָה אוֹתָהּ **he saw her/it (f.)**

חַזָּן; חַזָּנָא* (חזי)
supervisor; attendant; overseer
הַחַזָּן רוֹאֶה הֵיכָן הַתִּינוֹקוֹת קוֹרְאִים. (שבת יא, סע"א ורש"י שם: משנה פ"א מ"ג)

[On the night of the Sabbath] the supervisor may see [by candlelight] where [in the Torah] the pupils are reading.

* The first form is Hebrew, and the second is Aramaic.

חַזַּן הַכְּנֶסֶת* שַׁמָּשׁ בֵּית הַכְּנֶסֶת

the sexton; the superintendent of the synagogue

For an example — see מגילה כה,ב.

* The *sexton* would also lead the prayers in the synagogue when no other qualified person was available, hence from Gaonic times onwards חַזָּן came to refer to the one who leads the public prayer, *the cantor* or *the reader*, whom the Talmud calls שְׁלִיחַ צִיבּוּר, the *representative of the congregation*.

חֲזָקָה; חֶזְקָא*

(1) legal status (regarding ownership or kashruth)

אוֹקֵי מִילְּתָא אַחֶזְקֵיהּ! (חולין י,ב)

Determine the matter according to its [current] legal status!

(2) possession (of movables); **occupation** (of real estate for three years)

כָּל חֲזָקָה שֶׁאֵין עִמָּהּ טַעֲנָה אֵינָהּ חֲזָקָה. (בבא בתרא מא, רע"א: משנה פ"ג מ"ג)

Any occupation that is not accompanied by a claim of [legal acquisition] is not an occupation (and it does not constitute proof of ownership).

(3) "a taking hold"; a legal mode of acquisition (of real estate accomplished by the acquiring party)

נָעַל וְגָדַר וּפָרַץ כָּל שֶׁהוּא — הֲרֵי זוֹ חֲזָקָה. (בבא בתרא מב, סע"א: משנה פ"ג מ"ג)

[If] he locked up [the field] or fenced [it] or made any [useful] opening [in it] whatsoever — this is a legal mode of acquisition.

(4) legal presumption

חֲזָקָה: לָא עָבֵיד אִינִישׁ דְּפָרַע בְּגוֹ זִימְנֵיהּ. (ב"ב ה, סע"ב)

[There is] a legal presumption: A person does not usually pay [his debt] within his [allotted] time.

* The first noun is Hebrew, and the second is Aramaic.

SEE: הֶחֱזִיק, אַחְזֵיק, אוֹקֵי מָמוֹנָא בְּחֶזְקַת מָרֵיהּ, אוּמְדָּנָא

חָזַר (חזר: חוֹזֵר .prt, יַחֲזוֹר .fut, לַחֲזוֹר .inf)

Besides the common meanings of this Hebrew verb, *he returned* and *he repeated*, there are several other important usages in Mishnaic Hebrew.

(1) he reversed himself; he retracted; he changed his mind

In this sense, the verb is usually followed by the preposition -ב with a personal-pronoun suffix — such as בִּי, בָּךְ, בּוֹ, בָּהּ.

וְכָל הַחוֹזֵר בּוֹ — יָדוֹ עַל הַתַּחְתּוֹנָה (בבא מציעא עו, רע"א: משנה פ"ו מ"ב)

and whoever retracts [from the commitment] is at a halakhic disadvantage

(2) "he went back (and)"; thereupon; subsequently; again; in turn

In this adverbial sense, the verb is followed by another verb with a -ו prefix.

... והמתין שָׁעָה אַחַת, חָזַר וְאָמַר: מִי כָּאן הִלֵּל? (שבת לא,א)

... and he waited a while, [and] he said again: Is Hillel here?

(3) he went around; it revolved

For an example — see the next entry.

SEE: הֲדַר, the Aramaic equivalent

וְחָזַר הַדִּין: לֹא רְאִי זֶה כִּרְאִי זֶה וְלֹא רְאִי זֶה כִּרְאִי זֶה הַצַּד הַשָּׁוֶה שֶׁבָּהֶן שֶׁ- ... אַף אֲנִי אָבִיא ... שֶׁ-

Now the inference resolves: [Although] this [case] is not like that, and that is not like this, the common factor shared by [both of] them is that ...; I shall also propose [a new case] that [shares that factor and is therefore analogous].

With this formula the Talmud presents a conclusion that is derived from הַצַּד הַשָּׁוֶה, *the common denominator* of two cases.

For an example — see קידושין כא,א ושי"נ.

SEE: (ה)צַּד הַשָּׁוֶה

חִיּוּבָא

obligation; conviction; responsibility חִיּוּב

לָא מְטָא זְמַן חִיּוּבָא דְּפֶסַח (סוכה כה,ב)

the time of the Pesaḥ obligation had not arrived

SEE: בַּר חִיּוּבָא

לְחַיּוּבֵי (חוב פַּעֵל) .inf

to obligate; to make liable לְחַיֵּיב

וּמְמַאי דִּלְחַיּוּבֵי בָּתְרָא? דִּלְמָא לְחַיּוּבֵי קַמָּא! (ב"ק נא, סע"א)

But from where [do you know] to make the last (= the person who completed the pit) liable? Perhaps [you should] make the first (= the one who began the digging) liable!

לְחַיֵּי

SEE: לְחַיֵּי

חַיָּיב

(1) guilty; subject to punishment

הַזּוֹרֵק מֵרְשׁוּת הַיָּחִיד לִרְשׁוּת הָרַבִּים ... חַיָּיב. (שבת צו,א: משנה פי"א ה"א)

One who throws [an object] from a private domain into a public domain is subject to punishment (on account of desecrating the Sabbath).

(2) obligated (to carry out a mitsva)

חַיָּיב אָדָם לְבָרֵךְ עַל הָרָעָה, כְּשֵׁם שֶׁהוּא מְבָרֵךְ עַל הַטּוֹבָה. (ברכות נד,א: משנה פ"ט מ"ה)

A person is obligated to recite a b^erakha on misfortune, *just as he must recite a bᵉrakha on good fortune.*

(8) obligated (to pay)

הַחוֹפֵר בּוֹר בִּרְשׁוּת הָרַבִּים, וְנָפַל לְתוֹכוֹ שׁוֹר אוֹ חֲמוֹר וָמֵת, חַיָּיב. (בבא קמא נ,ב: משנה פ"ה מ"ה)

One who digs a pit in a public domain into which an ox or a donkey falls and dies is obligated (to pay damages).

חַיָּיבֵי עֲשֵׂה

[those] guilty of [violating] a positive commandment

Since some of the commandments that are formulated positively in the Torah as מִצְוֹות עֲשֵׂה actually prohibit certain acts by implication,* one who violates such a prohibition is guilty of *violating a positive commandment.*

חַיָּיבֵי עֲשֵׂה — מִצְרִי וַאֲדוֹמִי (שבועות ל, רע"א ורש"י שם ע"פ דברים כג:ח־ט)

*[those] guilty of [violating] a positive commandment — [by having marital relations with] an Egyptian or an Edomite***

* See the entries אִיסּוּר עֲשֵׂה and לָאו הַבָּא מִכְּלַל עֲשֵׂה and the examples presented there.

** The Torah states that a third-generation converted Egyptian or Edomite is permitted to marry into the Jewish fold, implying that neither the first generation (i.e., the convert himself) nor the second generation (i.e., the son of a convert) is eligible for marriage to a Jew or Jewess.

חָיֵיל prt. (חול)

occurring; resting; taking effect חָל

מֵראשׁ הַשָּׁנָה חָיֵיל יוֹבֵל (ראש השנה ז, סע"ב)

the Jubilee year takes effect from Rosh HaShana

SEE: חָל

חַיִּים

SEE: בַּעֲלֵי חַיִּים

חָיֵישׁ prt. (חשש: חָיְישָׁא ,f. חָיְישֵׁי .m. pl)

suspecting; concerned; afraid; taking into consideration חוֹשֵׁשׁ

SEE: חָשׁ

חָיְישִׁינַן (חָיְישֵׁי+אֲנַן) חוֹשְׁשִׁים אָנוּ

we suspect; we are concerned; we are afraid

חָיְישִׁינַן לְפֵירָעוֹן (בבא מציעא ז, רע"ב)

We suspect payment (i.e., that the loan has already been repaid, and thus the lender is demanding money fraudulently).

SEE: חָשׁ

חִילּוּף הַדְּבָרִים

The reverse of the statements [is correct].

After one tanna has presented his (halakhic) opinion regarding two different cases — deciding one case more strictly and the other more leniently, a second tanna is sometimes quoted who distinguishes between the two cases in the opposite direction. This second opinion is introduced by the expression חִילּוּף הַדְּבָרִים.

עֲבוֹדָה זָרָה שֶׁל נָכְרִי אֵינָהּ אֲסוּרָה עַד שֶׁתֵּיעָבֵד, וְשֶׁל יִשְׂרָאֵל אֲסוּרָה מִיָּד — דִּבְרֵי ר׳ יִשְׁמָעֵאל. ר׳ עֲקִיבָא אוֹמֵר: חִילּוּף הַדְּבָרִים. עֲבוֹדָה זָרָה שֶׁל נָכְרִי אֲסוּרָה מִיָּד, וְשֶׁל יִשְׂרָאֵל מִשֶּׁתֵּיעָבֵד. (עבודה זרה נא, סע"ב)

[Deriving benefit from] the idol of a non-Jew is not prohibited until it has been worshipped, but that of a Jew is prohibited immediately — [this is] the opinion of R. Yishmael. R. Akiva says: The reverse of the statements [is correct]. The idol of a non-Jew is prohibited immediately, but that of a Jew [only] from when it was worshipped.

SEE: מוּחְלֶפֶת הַשִּׁיטָה

חֲכָמִים

(1) *hakhamim*; the Torah sages

This Hebrew noun is sometimes used in a general sense with reference to tannaim or Torah sages from the earlier generations — without referring to a particular Torah sage and without even pointing to a specific generation of Torah sages. When used in this general sense, the word *hakhamim* is spelled without a capital *ḥ* in this work.

מַטְבֵּעַ שֶׁטָּבְעוּ חֲכָמִים (ברכות מ, רע"ב)

a text that the ḥakhamim have formulated

See also לֹא מָסְרָהּ הַכָּתוּב אֶלָּא לַחֲכָמִים.

(2) the *Ḥakhamim*; the Torah Sages

Sometimes this noun is used in a mishna or a baraitha to refer to a group of specific tannaim or even to a single tanna. These tannaim often advocate an opinion which is in conflict with the opinion of another tanna who is mentioned by name. The fact that an opinion is attributed to *Ḥakhamim* (in the plural) does not necessarily indicate that it was the majority view among the tannaim. The compiler of the Mishna, R. Yᵉhuda HaNasi (= Rebbi), sometimes expressed his own halakhic preference in favor of a minority view by designating a halakhic statement of a single tanna as the opinion of the *Ḥakhamim*, as in the example below. Whenever the word *Ḥakhamim* refers to tannaim who advocate one particular opinion versus the opinion of other tannaim, it is regarded as a proper noun in this work and is capitalized. In some cases, the Talmud attempts to identify them and inquires: מָאן חֲכָמִים?, *Who are the Ḥakhamim?* See that entry as well.

משנה (פרק "אותו ואת בנו"): הַשּׁוֹחֵט וְנִמְצָא טְרֵפָה ... ר׳ שִׁמְעוֹן פּוֹטֵר, וַחֲכָמִים מְחַיְּיבִין. (חולין פא,ב: משנה פ"ה מ"ג ע"פ ויקרא כב:כח)

משנה (פרק "כסוי הדם"): הַשּׁוֹחֵט וְנִמְצָא טְרֵפָה ... ר׳ מֵאִיר מְחַיֵּיב, וַחֲכָמִים פּוֹטְרִין. (חולין פח,א: משנה פ"ו מ"ב ע"פ

ויקרא יז:יג)

תלמוד: אָמַר ר׳ חִיָּיא בַּר אַבָּא אָמַר ר׳ יוֹחָנָן: רָאָה רַבִּי אֶת דְּבָרָיו שֶׁל ר׳ מֵאִיר בְּ״אוֹתוֹ וְאֶת בְּנוֹ״ וּשְׁנָאוֹ בִּלְשׁוֹן ״חֲכָמִים״, וּדְרִ׳ שִׁמְעוֹן בְּ״כִסּוּי הַדָּם״ וּשְׁנָאוֹ בִּלְשׁוֹן ״חֲכָמִים״. (שם)

MISHNA 1: [If] one slaughters [an animal and its young] and it is found to be terefa ..., R. Shim'on exempts [him from the prohibition: "It and its young you shall not slaughter in one day"], but the Ḥakhamim declare [him] guilty.

MISHNA 2: [If] one slaughters [a wild animal or a fowl] and it is found to be terefa ..., R. Mé'ir declares [him] obligated [to cover its blood], and the Ḥakhamim exempt [him].

TALMUD: R. Ḥiyya b. Abba quoting R. Yoḥanan said: Rebbi preferred the opinion of R. Mé'ir with reference to [the law of] "it and its young" (in the former mishna) and presented it under the label "[the] Ḥakhamim," and [he preferred the opinion] of R. Shim'on with reference to [the law of] "covering the blood" (in the latter mishna) and presented it under the label "[the] Ḥakhamim."

* See טְרֵיפָה

חָל (חול: חָיֵיל .prt, לֵיחוּל .fut, לְמֵיחַל .inf)

it came; it occurred; חָל
it took effect; it was in force

לָא חָל שַׁמְתָּא עֲלֵיהּ תְּלָתִין יוֹמִין. (מועד קטן טז,א)
The ban has not been in force upon him thirty days.

חֲלִיפִין

exchange; barter

This term refers to a method of transfer of ownership accomplished by exchanging one article for another.

(1) Sometimes, חֲלִיפִין operates as a real barter, so that one commodity constitutes the price of the other.

הֶחְלִיף שׁוֹר בְּפָרָה אוֹ חֲמוֹר בְּשׁוֹר — כֵּיוָן שֶׁזָּכָה זֶה, נִתְחַיֵּיב זֶה בַּחֲלִיפָיו. (קידושין כח, סע״א: משנה פ״א מ״ו)
[If] one exchanged an ox for a cow or a donkey for an ox — as soon as one party has taken possession [of one animal], the other party has assumed liability for [the animal] exchanged for it (wherever it is).

(2) Sometimes, חֲלִיפִין operates as a fictional barter: An article, such as a handkerchief, is handed over by one party to the other party. By accepting it, the recipient expresses his commitment to transfer the ownership of something else, in the manner of a barter. This type of חֲלִיפִין may also be used to confirm other agreements between two parties. The commentators on the Talmud (e.g., Rashi on בבא מציעא יא,ב) term this procedure קִנְיַן סוּדָר, *affirmation by means of a scarf*. The Rambam writes (in הל׳ מכירה פ״ה ה״ה) that it is simply called קִנְיָן as indicated by the Talmud (in ב״ב מ, רע״א).

וְכִי לָא הֲוָה לְהֶם סוּדָר לִקְנוֹת מִמֶּנּוּ בַּחֲלִיפִין?! (ב״מ יא,ב)
But didn't they possess a cloth (literally, "a scarf") to acquire [the produce] from him by means of exchange?!

SEE: קִנְיָן, סוּדָר

חֲלַף (חלף: חָלֵיף .prt)

he passed by חֲלַף; עָבַר

ר׳ סִימוֹן וְר׳ אֶלְעָזָר הֲווּ יָתְבִין; חָלֵיף וְאָזֵיל ר׳ יַעֲקֹב בַּר אַחָא ... (שבת לא, רע״א)
R. Simon and R. El'azar were sitting; R. Ya'akov b. Aḥa was passing by ...

חַלֵּף (חלף פַּעֵל: מְחַלֵּף .prt, חַלּוֹפֵי .inf)

he exchanged הֶחֱלִיף

מַהוּ דְּתֵימָא חַלּוֹפֵי חַלְּפֵיהּ?* (גיטין יט, סע״ב)
What would you say: He has surely exchanged it [for a different document]?

* The Aramaic infinitive חַלּוֹפֵי, which adds emphasis to the past tense חַלְּפֵיהּ, has been expressed in English by the adverb *surely*.

חֲלַף prep.

instead of; in exchange for; for תַּחַת

נַפְשָׁא חֲלַף נַפְשָׁא (שבת קכט,א)
life for life

חֲלַשׁ (חלש: חָלֵישׁ .prt)

he became weak; he became ill חָלַשׁ; נֶחֱלַשׁ

רַב אַוְיָא חֲלַשׁ וְלָא אֲתָא לְפִרְקָא דְּרַב יוֹסֵף. (ברכות כח, רע״ב)
Rav Avia became ill and did not attend the lecture of R. Yosef.

חֲלַשׁ/חֲלַשָׁה דַּעְתֵּיהּ　חָלְשָׁה דַּעְתּוֹ; הִצְטַעֵר

he was upset; he became depressed;
he became discouraged

חָלְשָׁא דַּעְתֵּיהּ, סָבַר: קָא חָדֵי בִּי. (סנהדרין יט,א)
He might be depressed, thinking: [My rival] rejoices at my loss.

חֵמָה

heat; anger; fury

SEE: מֵחֲמַת

חֲמֵיסַר

fifteen חֲמִשָּׁה עָשָׂר

חֲמִיר (חֲמִירָא .f, חֲמִירֵי .m. pl)

strict; stringent; grave חָמוּר

שַׁבָּת דַּחֲמִירָא וְלָא אָתֵי לְזַלְזוּלֵי בַּהּ (ביצה ב, רע״ב ורש״י שם)
[regarding] the Sabbath that is stringent so that [people] will not come to treat it lightly

חֲמִירָא

leaven; yeast (1) שְׂאוֹר

חֲמִירָא דְחִיטֵי וַחֲמִירָא דִשְׂעָרֵי (עבודה זרה סו,א)
yeast from wheat and yeast from barley

leavened bread; ḥamets (2) חָמֵץ

עַל הַמַּשְׂכִּיר לִבְדּוֹק דַּחֲמִירָא דִידֵיהּ הוּא ...? (פסחים ד,א)
Is it incumbent upon the renter (of the house) to search (for ḥametz), since the ḥametz is his ...?

חַמָּר; חַמָּרָא* donkey-driver

חַמָּר־גַּמָּל (עירובין לה,א ורש"י ור"ח שם: משנה פ"ג מ"ד)
*[one individual who is simultaneously serving as both] a donkey-driver [and] a camel-driver***

* The first form is Hebrew, and the second is Aramaic.

** Since a donkey is driven from behind, while a camel is led by pulling on its reins from the front, it is difficult to drive both animals simultaneously; hence, this expression is used to describe a person who is confronted by a paradoxical halakhic situation.

חַמְרָא* (abs. חֲמַר) יַיִן wine

See example under the next entry.

* A Biblical Hebrew parallel appears in וְדַם עֵנָב תִּשְׁתֶּה חָמֶר (דברים לב:יד).

חֲמָרָא (abs. חֲמָר) חֲמוֹר donkey

חֲמָר לְמִירְכַּב אוֹ חֲמַר לְמִישְׁתֵּי? (עירובין נג,ב)
[Does he mean] חֲמָר, a donkey to ride, or חֲמַר, wine to drink?

חַמְשָׁא/חַמְשָׁה חֲמִשָּׁה five

חַמְשִׁין חֲמִשִּׁים fifty

חֶנְוָנִי storekeeper

הַחֶנְוָנִי עַל פִּנְקָסוֹ (שבועות מה,א: משנה פ"ז מ"ה)
the storekeeper with regard to his account book

חָנוּת (pl. חֲנוּיוֹת); **חֲנוּתָא***

a store (or shop) where (prepared) foods and drinks are sold and also served

For an example — see בבא מציעא ס,א.

* The first form is Hebrew, and the second is Aramaic. In Modern Hebrew, this word means any type of a store.

חַסּוּרֵי מְחַסְּרָא וְהָכִי קָתָנֵי

חָסֵר מְחֻסֶּרֶת, וְכָךְ הוּא שׁוֹנֶה ...

[The text] is surely lacking, and thus he is teaching ...

In response to a difficulty about the text of a mishna or a baraitha, this formula is used to propose the following *resolution:* One or more words have been omitted from the original version of the text under discussion. If the missing words are restored, however, the corrected reading of the text contains no difficulty.* Sometimes, this formula may be understood as presenting an interpretation of a text, rather than an actual alteration of its wording. In such cases, the tanna of the mishna or baraitha formulated his halakha in an abbreviated form, which should be interpreted *as if* there were something missing.**

משנה: קָטָן שֶׁאֵינוֹ צָרִיךְ לְאִמּוֹ חַיָּב בְּסֻכָּה. מַעֲשֶׂה וְיָלְדָה כַּלָּתוֹ שֶׁל שַׁמַּאי הַזָּקֵן, וּפִיחֵת אֶת הַמַּעֲזִיבָה, וְסִיכֵּךְ עַל גַּבֵּי הַמִּטָּה בִּשְׁבִיל הַקָּטָן. (סוכה כח,א: משנה פ"ב מ"ח)
תלמוד: מַעֲשֶׂה לִסְתּוֹר?! חַסּוּרֵי מְחַסְּרָא, וְהָכִי קָתָנֵי: וְשַׁמַּאי מַחְמִיר, וּמַעֲשֶׂה נַמִי בְּכַלָּתוֹ שֶׁל שַׁמַּאי ... (שם כח,ב ע"פ כת"י)

MISHNA: A child who is not dependent upon his mother is obligated [to fulfill the duty of] sukka. Once it happened that the daughter-in-law of Shammai the Elder gave birth [to a baby boy], and [Shammai] broke away the plaster of the roof and put sukka-roofing over the bed for the child.

TALMUD: Is [this] incident [quoted] in order to contradict [the halakha previously stated]?! [Rather the text] is surely lacking, and thus he teaches: But Shammai rules strictly, and once it happened to Shammai's daughter-in-law ...

* רש"י לזבחים קיד,ב ד"ה דרב ששת; לסנהדרין י,ב ד"ה והא

** תוס' שבת קב,א ד"ה רב אשי

חַסְפָּא (abs. חֲסַף)

clay; shard; a fragment of pottery חֶרֶס

This word is often used metaphorically to indicate worthlessness,* most commonly with reference to documents.

וְהַאי שְׁטָרָא חַסְפָּא בְּעָלְמָא הוּא! (גיטין י,ב)
This document is a mere fragment of pottery (since it was signed by invalid witnesses)!

* Compare the Hebrew expression כְּחֶרֶס הַנִּשְׁבָּר in the *Maḥzor* for Rosh HaShana and Yom Kippur.

חֶפְצָא חֵפֶץ; דָּבָר **(1) thing; object; matter**

תְּנָא נְדָרִים דְּמִיתְּסַר חֶפְצָא עֲלֵיהּ ... לְאַפּוֹקֵי שְׁבוּעוֹת דְּקָאָסַר נַפְשֵׁיהּ מִן חֶפְצָא.* (נדרים ב,ב)
[The tanna of our mishna] listed vows where the object is forbidden to the person ... to the exclusion of oaths where he forbids himself from the object.

(2) a sacred object; an object used for the performance of a mitsva

צְרִיךְ לְאַתְפּוֹשֵׁי חֶפְצָא בִּידֵיהּ. (שבועות לח, סע"ב ורש"י שם)
[The judge] must have him hold a sacred object in his hand (at the time he takes an oath).

For another example, see the verb נְקַט.

* For further elaboration of this distinction, see the commentary of R. Nissim Gerondi — הר"ן לנדרים יח,א.

חֲרֵי חוֹרִים; שָׂרִים **noblemen**

See example in יומא כ,ב.

SEE: חוֹרִין, בְּנֵי חֲרֵי

חֲרִיף

(1) חַד; שָׁנוּן **sharp; keen**

סַכִּינָא חֲרִיפָא מְפַסְקָא קְרָאֵי! (ב"ב קיא,ב ושי' ע' רשב"ם)
A sharp knife is dissecting the p°sukim! (= Your interpretation does violence to the Biblical syntax!)

חֲרִיפֵי דְפוּמְבְּדִיתָא* (סנהדרין יז,ב)
the keen [scholars] of Pumb°ditha

(2) עוֹבֵר לַסּוֹחֵר; סָחִיר

current (as a medium of exchange); circulating

כַּסְפָּא דְחָרִיף הָוֵי טִבְעָא; דַּהֲבָא דְלָא חָרִיף הָוֵי פֵּירָא. (בבא מציעא מד, רע״ב ורש״י שם)

Silver [coin], since it is [more] current, is regarded as money; gold [coin], since it is not [so] current, is regarded as a commodity.

* The Talmud identifies them as Efa and Avimé, the sons of R^eḥava.

חֵרֵשׁ (חֵרֶשֶׁת .f); חֵרְשָׁא*

(1) deaf-mute

״חֵרֵשׁ״ שֶׁדִּבְּרוּ בוֹ חֲכָמִים בְּכָל מָקוֹם — שֶׁאֵינוֹ לֹא שׁוֹמֵעַ וְלֹא מְדַבֵּר (משנה תרומות פ״א מ״ב ופירוש הרמב״ם שם)

The "ḥeresh" to which the ḥakhamim generally refer is one who can neither hear nor speak (i.e., a deaf-mute).

(2) a deaf person

הַמְדַבֵּר וְאֵינוֹ שׁוֹמֵעַ — זֶהוּ חֵרֵשׁ; שׁוֹמֵעַ וְאֵינוֹ מְדַבֵּר — זֶהוּ אִלֵּם. (חגיגה ב,ב ורש״י שם)

One who can speak but cannot hear is [called] a deaf person; one who can hear but cannot speak is [called] a mute.

* The first form is Hebrew, and the second is Aramaic.

חָרָשָׁא

sorcerer מְכַשֵּׁף

לָא חַרְשֵׁי דְחָרָשָׁא (ברכות סב, סע״א ורש״י שם)

not the magic of a sorcerer

חָשׁ (חשש: חָיֵישׁ .prt, לֵיחוּשׁ .fut, לְמֵיחַשׁ .inf)

he was concerned; חָשׁ
he was afraid; he took into consideration

הֲוָא עוּבְדָא וְחָשׁ לֵיהּ רַב לְהָא דְרַב אַסִי. (מגילה ה, רע״א)

There was a case, and Rav took into consideration this [opinion] of Rav Assi.

לָא חָשׁ לְקִימְחֵיהּ (פסחים פד,א ושי״נ)

"he was not concerned with his flour" (A ḥakham who is not precise in his halakhic formulations is compared to a miller who does not do his work carefully, and so the flour he produces is intermingled with bran.)

SEE: חָיֵישׁ, חֲשָׁשָׁא

חֲשָׁדָא

suspicion (about a person's conduct) חֲשַׁד

חָצֵר שֶׁיֵּשׁ לָהּ שְׁנֵי פְתָחִים צְרִיכָה שְׁתֵּי נֵרוֹת ... מִשּׁוּם חֲשָׁדָא. (שבת כג, סע״א)

A courtyard that has two entrances requires two [Ḥanukka] lamps (one at each entrance) ... because of suspicion (on the part of passers-by that the owner has neglected to perform the mitzva).

SEE: חֲשִׁיד, חֲשָׁשָׁא

חָשֵׁיב (חשב) act. prt.

considering; חוֹשֵׁב
reckoning; counting; enumerating

תַּנָּא דִידַן קָא חָשֵׁיב תְּקִיעָה דְכוּלְּהוּ בָבֵי וּתְרוּעוֹת דְכוּלְּהוּ בָבֵי. (ראש השנה לג,ב)

Our tanna counts the t^eki'a notes of all the sets and the t^eru'a notes of all the sets.

SEE: לִיחְשׁוּב

חֲשִׁיב (חשב) pass. prt. חָשׁוּב

considered (important); significant; valuable

כֵּיוָן דַּחֲשִׁיבִי, לָא מַפְקַר לְהוּ (בבא מציעא כא,א)

since they are valuable, he would not [readily] abandon them

חֲשִׁיד (חשד) pass. prt. חָשׁוּד

suspected

מִגּוֹ דַּחֲשִׁיד אַמָּמוֹנָא, חֲשִׁיד אַשְׁבוּעֲתָא. (בבא מציעא ה,ב)

Since he is suspected of [fraudulent] money [dealings], he is also suspected of a [false] oath.

SEE: חֲשָׁדָא

חֲשָׁשָׁא

concern; fear; apprehension חֲשָׁשׁ

הָכָא וַדַּאי שְׁדֵי בֵּיהּ מוּמָא?! חֲשָׁשָׁא הוּא. (בכורות לו,א)

In this case, is it certain [that] he has inflicted a blemish [on the animal so that it may be permitted to be slaughtered and eaten]?! (No!) There is merely apprehension [that he might have done so].

SEE: חָשׁ, חֲשָׁדָא

ט – י

טָב (טָבָא .emph, טָבֵי/טָבִין .m. pl, טָבָא .f, טָבְתָא (.f. emph
good — טוֹב

זִיל, שַׁלֵּים לַהּ טָבִין וּתְקִילִין! (בבא מציעא מד,ב)
Go [and] pay her good and full-weight [coins]!

טָבַח (טבח: טוֹבֵחַ .prt); **טְבַח*** (טָבַח .prt)
he slaughtered

טָבַח וּמָכַר — מְשַׁלֵּם תַּשְׁלוּמֵי אַרְבָּעָה וַחֲמִשָּׁה. (בבא מציעא לג,ב: משנה פ"ג מ"א ע"פ שמות כא:לז)
[If] he slaughtered or sold (a sheep or an ox that he stole), he must pay a payment of four or five times.

* The first form is Hebrew, and the second is Aramaic.

טַבָּח; טַבָּחָא*

slaughterer-butcher — (1) שׁוֹחֵט־קַצָּב

הַטַּבָּח צָרִיךְ שָׁלֹשׁ סַכִּינִים: אַחַת שֶׁשּׁוֹחֵט בָּהּ, וְאַחַת שֶׁמְּחַתֵּךְ בָּהּ בָּשָׂר, וְאַחַת שֶׁמְּחַתֵּךְ בָּהּ חֲלָבִים. (חולין ח,ב)
A slaughterer-butcher needs three knives: one with which he slaughters, one with which he cuts meat, and one with which he cuts [away forbidden] fats.

cook; chef — (2) מְבַשֵּׁל

cooks' dough — עֵמִילָן שֶׁלַּטַּבָּחִין (פסחים מב,א: משנה פ"ג מ"א)

* The first form is Hebrew, and the second is Aramaic. In Biblical Hebrew, both meanings of this noun are found. See שמואל א ח:יג, מלכים ב כה:ח, and the controversy among the commentators on בראשית לז:לו. In Modern Hebrew, a טַבָּח is a *cook*, who does his work in a מִטְבָּח, a *kitchen;* a שׁוֹחֵט is a *ritual slaughterer*, who works in a בֵּית הַמִּטְבָּחַיִים (e.g., in משנה אבות פ"ה מ"ה), a *slaughterhouse;* a קַצָּב (e.g., in ביצה כה, סע"א) is a *butcher* who works in an אִטְלִיז (e.g., in בכורות לא, סע"א: משנה פ"ה מ"א), and a מְנַקֵּר, a *porger*, cuts away the forbidden fats and sinews.

טָבַל (טבל: טוֹבֵל .act. prt, טָבוּל .pass. prt);
טְבַל* (טבל: טָבֵיל .prt)

(1) he dipped (an object)

טוֹבֵל בָּהֶן פִּתּוֹ (שבת קח, רע"ב: משנה פי"ד מ"ב)
one may dip his bread in it (= salt water)

(2) he immersed himself

כֵּיוָן דְּלָא טָבֵיל, נָכְרִי הוּא. (יבמות מו,א)
Since he has not immersed himself, he is (still) a non-Jew.

טְבוּל יוֹם (שבת יד, רע"ב ועוד)
[a ritually unclean person who has immersed himself during the day (but does not become ritually clean until nightfall)

(3) it created the status of *tevel*; he made subject to tithing

מָה תְּרוּמָה טוֹבֶלֶת, אַף מַעֲשֵׂר רִאשׁוֹן נַמֵּי טוֹבֵל. (יבמות פו,א)
Just as t^eruma creates the status of tevel, so does the first tithe create the status of tevel as well.

* The first form is Hebrew, and the second is Aramaic.
SEE: מַטְבִּיל, טֶבֶל

טֶבֶל; טִבְלָא*

produce from which *t^eruma* and/or tithes have not been separated

For an example — see מכות יג, סע"א: משנה פ"ג מ"ב.

* The first form is Hebrew, and the second is Aramaic.

טַבְלָא/טַבְלָה — **tablet; board; plank**

נוֹטֵל אֶת הַטַּבְלָה כּוּלָּהּ וּמְנַעֲרָהּ. (שבת קמג,א: משנה כא:ג)
He takes the whole board and shakes it out.

טוּבָא

much; a great deal; many — (1) הַרְבֵּה

טוּבָא קָא מַשְׁמַע לַן! (שבת נא,א; קח, רע"א; קמה,ב)
[The amora] is teaching us a great deal [that is not stated in our mishna]!

וְהָאִיכָּא טוּבָא?! (מגילה י,ב)
But are there not many [cases]?!

very — (2) מְאֹד

he is very intelligent — חַכִּים טוּבָא (סנהדרין ה, רע"ב)

טוֹבַת הֲנָאָה — **a goodwill benefit**

This term denotes the right of a person to select a particular individual to be the recipient of a gift that he is obligated to bestow — for example, the right of an ordinary Jew to give the first tithe to the levite of his own choosing.

For an example — see קידושין נח, סע"א וש"נ.

טוֹל imp. (נטל: טְלִי .f, טְלוּ .m. pl) — **take**

טוֹל אֶת שֶׁלְּךָ! (בבא מציעא פ,ב: משנה פ"ו מ"ו)
Take your own [property]!

טוּלָּא — צֵל — **shade; shadow**

אֲנָא אַפֵּיקְתֵּיהּ לְמָר שְׁמוּאֵל מִשִּׁמְשָׁא לְטוּלָּא (ביצה כה,ב)
I took out the master Sh^emuel from the sunlight into the shade

טוּנָא (= טְעוּנָא) — מַשָּׂא — **burden; load**

מִטּוּנָךְ (= מִן טְעוּנָךְ)
"from your load" — מִן מַשָּׂאֲךָ*

This term, which is used in the course of Talmudic debates, may be paraphrased as follows: From your refutation of the halakhic position of others, there is an argument that undermines your own position.

For an example — see ראש השנה ד, רע"א וש"נ ורש"י שם.
* This translation follows Rashi's explanation in his commentary on ראש השנה ד, רע"א. Nevertheless, on another passage (חולין קלב, רע"א) he explains the term differently.
SEE: טָעוּן, הִיא הַנּוֹתֶנֶת

טוֹפֶס; טוֹפְסָא*

the standard formula of a legal document; a blank (document)

הַכּוֹתֵב טוֹפְסֵי גִיטִּין צָרִיךְ שֶׁיַּנִּיחַ מְקוֹם הָאִישׁ, וּמְקוֹם הָאִשָּׁה, וּמְקוֹם הַזְּמַן. (גיטין כו,א: משנה פ"ג מ"ב)
One who writes blank bills of divorce (for sale) must leave open place for [the name of] the husband, and [the name of] the wife, and the date.

* The first form is Hebrew, and the second is Aramaic.
SEE: תּוֹרֶף

טִיב **nature; character**

מָצָא שְׁטָר בֵּין שְׁטָרוֹתָיו וְאֵינוֹ יוֹדֵעַ מַה טִּיבוֹ (בבא מציעא כ,א: משנה פ"א מ"ח)
[if] one has found a document among his documents, but he does not know what its nature is (for example, who deposited it with him and under what circumstances)

טִיבוּתָא/טִיבוּ

goodness; good deed; favor טוֹבָה; חֶסֶד
For an example — see שְׁקַל.

טִיהֲרָא צָהֳרַיִים **daylight; midday; noon**

שְׁרָגָא בְּטִיהֲרָא מַאי אַהֲנֵי?! (חולין ס,ב ורש"י שם)
What good does a lamp do in (broad) daylight?!

טַיָּיעָא עַרְבִי; בֶּדְוִי **an Arab; a Beduin**

הֲוָה קָא אָזְלִינַן בְּמַדְבְּרָא וְאִתְלְוִי בַּהֲדַן הַהוּא טַיָּיעָא (בבא בתרא עג, סע"ב ורשב"ם שם)
we were walking in the desert and a certain Beduin accompanied us

טִינָא

(1) טִיט; טִין **clay; mud**
אִי חַבְרֵיהּ בְּטִינָא (ב"ב ו,ב) *if he attached it with clay*

(2) מַחְשָׁבָה פְסוּלָה **impurity (of thought)**
טִינָא הָיְתָה בְלִבָּם. (חגיגה טו, סע"ב)
There was impurity in their hearts.

טַלְטֵל (טול פִּלְפֵּל: מְטַלְטֵל, act. prt. מִיטַּלְטַל, pass. prt. לְטַלְטוּלֵי .inf)

טַלְטֵל **he moved; he handled; he carried**
שְׁרָגָא דְמִשְׁחָא שְׁרֵי לְטַלְטוּלֵהּ. (שבת מו,א)
*[As for] an (olive-) oil lamp, it is permitted to handle it (on the Sabbath).**
וְלָא גָּזְרִינַן דִּילְמָא אָתֵי לְטַלְטוּלֵי (עירובין כב,א)
and we do not enact Rabbinic safeguard legislation (in this case) so that he not come to carry (on the Sabbath)

* i.e., under certain conditions.
ע' רש"י ותוס' שם קכב,ב ד"ה "רחת"

טַלִּית (טַלִּיוֹת/טַלִּיתוֹת .pl)

(1) a cloak
טַלִּית שֶׁל תַּלְמִיד חָכָם — כֵּיצַד? כָּל שֶׁאֵין חֲלוּקוֹ נִרְאֶה מִתַּחְתָּיו טֶפַח. (בבא בתרא נז,ב)
How [long] should the cloak of a Torah scholar be? Long enough that a handbreadth of his undergarment is not visible beneath it.

(2) a *tallith*
טַלִּית מְצוּיֶּיצֶת (מנחות מג,א)
a tallith with tzitzith attached

טַן דּוּ כִּשְׁנֵי גוּפוֹת; בְּיַחַד

as two people; as a couple; together
טַב לְמֵיתַב טַן דּוּ מִלְּמֵיתַב אַרְמְלוּ. (קידושין ז,א ורש"י שם)
It is better to live as [part of] a [married] couple than to live in widowhood.

טְעָא (טעי: טָעֵי .prt, לְמִיטְעֵי/מִיטְעָא .inf)

(1) טָעָה **he erred; he was mistaken**
בֵּין יְמָמָא לְלֵילְיָא לָא טָעוּ אִינָשֵׁי. (פסחים יב, סע"א)
People do not make a mistake between day and night.

(2) תָּעָה **he wandered; he was lost**
כִּי חֲזִיתֵיהּ לְהַהוּא רָוְיָא דַּהֲוָה קָטָעֵי בְּאוֹרְחָא (גיטין סח,ב)
when you saw a drunkard who was lost on the way

טָעוּן (טען) .pass. prt

(1) loaded; laden; carrying
גָּמָל שֶׁהָיָה טָעוּן פִּשְׁתָּן (בבא קמא סב, רע"א: משנה פ"ו מ"ו)
a camel that was laden with flax

(2) requiring; needing
כָּל הַטָּעוּן בְּרָכָה לְאַחֲרָיו טָעוּן בְּרָכָה לְפָנָיו. (ברכות מד,ב: משנה נדה פ"ו מ"י)
Whatever [food] that requires a b^erakha after [eating] it requires a b^erakha before [eating] it.
SEE: טְעַן

טְעוּנָא/טוּנָא מַשָּׂא **load; burden**

רְמוּ אִינְהוּ וּטְעוּנַיְיהוּ בְּאוֹרְחָא. (בבא מציעא לב, סע"א)
Both they (= the animals) and their burdens are cast on the road.
SEE: (מ)טוּנָךְ

טְעֵים (טעם: טָעֵים .prt, לִטְעוּם .fut, לְמִיטְעַם .inf)

טָעַם **he tasted; he ate (or drank) a little bit**
אִישְׁתְּלֵי וּטְעֵים מִידֵּי (פסחים קו,ב)
he made a mistake and tasted something (before Havdala)

טַעַם; טַעְמָא*

(1) taste; flavor

טַעַם כְּעִיקָּר. (פסחים מד, רע"ב)

The flavor [of a forbidden substance] is [forbidden] like the substance itself.

(2) reason; reasoning; argument; sense; (Scriptural or logical) basis

sensible words — דְּבָרִים שֶׁל טַעַם (עבודה זרה יח,א)

הִלְכְתָא כְּרַבָּן שִׁמְעוֹן בֶּן גַּמְלִיאֵל — וְלָא מִטַּעְמֵיהּ. (כתובות פג, סע"ב)

The halakha is in accordance with Rabban Shim'on b. Gamliel — but not because of his reason.

(3) opinion; (halakhic) position

For an example — see three of the next five entries.

(4) teaching; meaning

מִקְרָא אֶחָד יוֹצֵא לְכַמָּה טְעָמִים, וְאֵין טַעַם אֶחָד יוֹצֵא מִכַּמָּה מִקְרָאוֹת. (סנהדרין לד,א)

*One pasuk may convey several meanings, but one meaning may not be deduced from several p*e*sukim.*

*** The first form is Hebrew, and the second is Aramaic.**

SEE: טַעְמָא ד- ... הָא ..., מַאי טַעְמָא, טַעְמָא מַאי, מַה טַעַם קָאָמַר, (וְ)אָזְדָא ... לְטַעְמֵיהּ, (וְ)אָזְדוּ לְטַעְמַיְיהוּ, מְתָרֵץ לְטַעְמֵיהּ, טַעְמָא דְנַפְשֵׁיהּ קָאָמַר, (וְל)טַעְמָיךְ

טַעְמָא ד- ... הָא ...

הַטַּעַם [שֶׁל הַהֲלָכָה הַזֹּאת] הוּא מִשּׁוּם שֶׁ- ..., הֲרֵי ...

The reason [for this halakhic ruling] is that ..., this implies (that in other situations the ruling would be different).

This formula presents a *deduction* based on a careful reading of the text of a mishna or baraitha.

משנה: וְאֵלּוּ חַיָּיב לְהַכְרִיז: מָצָא פֵּירוֹת בִּכְלִי ... מָעוֹת בְּכִיס ... (בבא מציעא כד, סע"ב: משנה פ"ב מ"ב)

תלמוד: טַעְמָא, דְּמָצָא פֵּירוֹת בִּכְלִי וּמָעוֹת בְּכִיס — הָא כְּלִי וּלְפָנָיו פֵּירוֹת, כִּיס וּלְפָנָיו מָעוֹת — הֲרֵי אֵלּוּ שֶׁלּוֹ! (שם כה, רע"א)

MISHNA: The following [objects the finder] must announce publicly: [If] he found fruit in a vessel ... money in a purse ...

TALMUD: The reason [why he has to announce] is that he found fruit in a vessel or money in a purse, this implies [that if he would find] a vessel with fruit in front of it or a purse with money in front of it — they would be his (= the finder's)!

טַעְמָא דְנַפְשֵׁיהּ קָאָמַר

דַּעְתּוֹ שֶׁלּוֹ הוּא אוֹמֵר.

He is stating his own position.

רַבָּן גַּמְלִיאֵל לָאו מַכְרִיעַ הוּא; טַעְמָא דְנַפְשֵׁיהּ קָאָמַר. (פסחים יג,א ע"פ כת"י)

Rabban Gamliel is not making a compromise (ruling in favor of one tanna's opinion on one point and in favor of the other tanna on a second point); [rather] he is stating his own position.

טַעְמָא מַאי (מִשּׁוּם ...)*

What is the reason [for this halakha]? (The reason is that ...) — מַהוּ הַטַּעַם? (מִשּׁוּם ...)

This formula is usually employed to call attention to the reason for a specific halakha in order to lay a foundation for the next point. Seldom does it present a real question that seeks to uncover a reason that was not recognised previously.**

תִּשְׁעָה אָכְלוּ דָּגָן וְאֶחָד אָכַל יָרָק — מִצְטָרְפִין. אֲמַר ר' זֵירָא, בְּעַאי מִינֵיהּ מֵרַב יְהוּדָה: שְׁמוֹנָה מַהוּ? שִׁבְעָה מַהוּ? אֲמַר לִי: לָא שְׁנָא. שִׁשָּׁה ... לָא מִבַּעְיָא לִי. אֲמַר לֵיהּ ר' יִרְמְיָה: שַׁפִּיר עֲבַדְתְּ דְּלָא אִיבַּעְיָא לָךְ. הָתָם טַעְמָא מַאי? מִשּׁוּם דְּאִיכָּא רוּבָּא; הָכָא נַמִּי אִיכָּא רוּבָּא. (ברכות מח,א)

*[If] nine [people] ate bread, and one ate vegetables, they may combine [for Birkath HaZimmun]. R. Zera said, I asked Rav Y*e*huda: What about eight? What about seven? He said to me: It makes no difference (and they do combine). About six I had no question. R. Yirm*e*ya said: You acted properly [in] that you had no question (because) there (= with seven or eight men eating bread) the reason is that there was a majority [who ate bread]; here, too, there is a majority.*

* In most cases טַעְמָא מַאי is followed by ... מִשּׁוּם.

** Questions of that type are introduced by וְטַעְמָא מַאי and מַאי טַעְמָא.

... לְטַעְמֵיהּ

[ר' ...] לְשִׁטָּתוֹ.

[R. ... is going] according to his own opinion (which he expressed in another halakhic statement).

רָבָא שְׁרָא לֵיהּ לְרַ' אַחָא בַּר אַדָּא לְמִגְנָא בָּר מִמְּטַלַּלְתָּא מִשּׁוּם סִירְחָא דְגַרְגִּישְׁתָּא. רָבָא לְטַעְמֵיהּ, דַּאֲמַר רָבָא: מִצְטַעֵר פָּטוּר מִן הַסּוּכָּה. (סוכה כו,א)

Rava permitted Rav Aḥa b. Adda to sleep outside the sukka on account of the odor of clay. Rava [is going] according to his own opinion, for Rava said: One who is suffering (because of conditions in the sukka) is exempt from [the obligation of] sukka.

SEE: (וְ)אָזְדָא ר' ... לְטַעְמֵיהּ, (וְ)אָזְדוּ לְטַעְמַיְיהוּ

וְלְטַעֲמָיךְ/וְלִיטַעֲמָיךְ

וּלְטַעַמְךָ ...! וּלְשִׁיטָתְךָ ...!

but according to your position ...!

With this introductory term, an amora (or the Talmud itself) launches a *counterattack* against his opponent who has just now attacked his position — as if to say: How can you attack my position?! I can show you that your own position is at least equally vulnerable!

אֲמַר ר' זֵירָא אֲמַר רָבָא בַּר יִרְמְיָה: מֵאֵימָתַי מְבָרְכִין עַל הָרֵיחַ? מִשֶּׁתַּעֲלֶה תִּמְרָתוֹ. אֲמַר לֵיהּ ר' זֵירָא לְרָבָא בַּר יִרְמְיָה: וְהָא לָא קָא אָרַח! אֲמַר לֵיהּ: וְלִיטַעֲמָיךְ, הַמּוֹצִיא לֶחֶם מִן הָאָרֶץ דִּמְבָרֵךְ, וְהָא לָא אֲכַל! אֶלָּא דַּעְתֵּיהּ לְמֵיכַל, הָכָא נַמִּי דַּעְתֵּיהּ לְאָרוֹחֵי. (ברכות מג,א)

*R. Zera said quoting Rava b. Yirm*e*ya: When do we recite a b*e*rakha over [the smell of] incense? As soon as the column of smoke ascends. R. Zera said to Rava* *b. Yirm^e ya: But he has not yet smelt it! He (= Rava) said to him: But according to your position, [how can you explain that] one recites "HaMotzi ..." although he has not [yet] eaten! Rather his intention is to eat [and that is enough to enable him to recite a b^e rakha]; here too his intention is to smell*

טְעַן (טען: טָעֵין act. prt., טְעִין pass. prt.) טָעַן

(1) טָעַן טַעֲנָה; תָּבַע; הִגִּיב לְטַעֲנָה
he claimed; he sued; he pleaded (in court)

טָעֲנִינַן לְהוּ לְיָתְמֵי (בבא בתרא נב, סע"א)
we (= the judges) claim on behalf of orphans

(2) נָשָׂא; עָמַס **he carried; he bore; he loaded**

לָא טָעֵין פֵּירֵי עַד תְּלָת שְׁנִין (ראש השנה טו,א)
it does not bear fruit until three years [have passed]

טַעֲנְתָּא טַעֲנָה **a claim; a lawsuit; a plea**

טַעֲנְתָּא מְעַלַּיְיתָא הִיא, וּמָמוֹנָא אִית לֵיהּ גַּבֵּיהּ! (ב"מ עט,ב ע"פ כת"י)
It is a valid claim, and he owes him money!

טְפָא (טפי: טָפֵי prt.)

הוֹסִיף **he added; he increased**

טְפָא לְהוּ אַאַגְרַיְיהוּ (בבא מציעא פג, סע"א ורש"י שם)
he increased their wages for them

טֶפַח **handbreadth**

This length is equal to the width of four fingers.*

* See the table of distances in the appendix at the end of this volume.

טְפֵי יוֹתֵר **more**

הַאי — צְלִיל נְהוֹרֵיהּ טְפֵי. (שבת כג,א)
[As for] this (= olive oil) — its light is clearer.

אֲכַל טְפֵי, מַפְּקִינַן מִינֵּיהּ. (בבא מציעא סז, סע"א)
[If] he used up more (than the amount of the loan), we take [the field] away from him.

טָפֵל

(1) **secondary; of lesser importance**

כָּל שֶׁהוּא עִיקָּר וְעִמּוֹ טְפֵלָה — מְבָרֵךְ עַל הָעִיקָּר וּפוֹטֵר אֶת הַטְּפֵלָה. (ברכות מד, רע"א: משנה פ"ו מ"ז)
Whenever [one eats] a primary [food] together with a secondary [one] — he may recite a b^e rakha over the primary and (thereby) exempt the secondary.

(2) **attached; subordinate**

כָּל הַטָּפֵל לַשֵּׁם ... מִלְּפָנָיו ... נִמְחָק. (שבועות לה,ב)
Whatever is attached to the name (of God) ... before it (as a prefix) may be erased.

SEE: תָּפֵל

טְרָא (טרי: טָרֵי prt.)

נָתַן; הֵטִיחַ **he gave; he cast**

שְׁקַל מֵהַנְהוּ מַיָּא, טְרָא בְּאַפֵּיהּ. (תמיד לב,ב)
He took some of that water, [and] he cast [it] on his [own] face.

SEE: שָׁקֵיל וְטָרֵי

טְרַח (טרח: טָרַח act. prt., טְרִיחַ pass. prt., לְמִיטְרַח inf.) טָרַח **he took pains;**
he went to the trouble; he troubled himself

לְמִטְרַח בְּאוֹכְלָא טָרְחִינַן, לְשַׁוּוֹיֵי אוֹכְלָא לָא מְשַׁוִּינַן. (שבת קנה,א)
We may trouble ourselves with (prepared) foodstuffs, [but] we may not make [something into] a foodstuff (on the Sabbath).

SEE: מִילְּתָא דְאָתְיָא בְּקַל וָחוֹמֶר טְרַח וּכְתַב לַהּ קְרָא

טְרִיד pass. prt. (טרד) טָרוּד

preoccupied (by); engrossed (in); troubled

טְרִיד טִרְדָא דְמִצְוָה (ברכות יא,א; סוכה כה, סע"א)
he is engrossed in preoccupation with a mitzva

טְרֵיפָה/טְרֵפָה; טְרֵיפְתָּא* *t^e refa*

This term refers to an animal that has been fatally attacked by a beast of prey or afflicted with a fatal organic disease. Eating of the flesh of a *t^e refa* animal is prohibited, even after the animal has been slaughtered in accordance with Jewish law;** but proper slaughtering does prevent the carcass from conveying ritual uncleanliness.***

כָּל שֶׁשְּׁחִיטָתָהּ כְּרָאוּי וְדָבָר אַחֵר גָּרַם לָהּ לִיפָּסֵל — טְרֵפָה. (חולין לב, סע"א: משנה פ"ב מ"ד)
Any [animal] whose slaughtering was proper, but another factor (= a physical defect) rendered it unfit [for eating] is [classified as] t^e refa.

* The first two forms are Hebrew, and the third is Aramaic.

** The Biblical prohibition is וּבָשָׂר בַּשָּׂדֶה טְרֵפָה לֹא תֹאכֵלוּ (שמות כב:ל).

*** Occasionally this term is applied to a human being who is so ill that his survival is deemed impossible from a medical point of view. For an example — see סנהדרין עח,א.

SEE: נְבֵילָה

טָרַף (טרף: טָרֵף prt.); **טְרַף*** (טרף: טָרֵיף prt.)

(1) **he attacked; he struck; he knocked**

טָרְפָה בְּהֵמָה וְאָכְלָה בָּשָׂר (בבא קמא טז,ב)
[a beast] attacked an animal and ate [its] flesh

(2) **he inflicted an organic defect** (on an animal); **he declared [an animal to be]** ***t^e refa***

הֲוָה עוּבְדָא, וּטְרַף רַב יוֹסֵף עַד תְּלֵיסַר חֵיוָתָא. (חולין י, רע"ב)
It once happened that Rav Yosef declared as many as thirteen animals (to be) t^e refa.

(3) **he seized** (property as payment for an outstanding debt) **from****

וְקָא טָרֵיף לָקוֹחוֹת שֶׁלֹּא כַּדִּין (בבא מציעא יט,א)
and he might seize [property] from the purchasers illegally

* The first form is Hebrew, and the second is Aramaic.

** The court authorizes a creditor to seize property for the debt owed by the borrower, even if that property has been purchased from the borrower by a third party after the loan was made. The document issued by the court to authorise the seizure is called a טִירְפָּא. See (ב"ק ט, רע"א (ורש"י שם.

"יַגִּיד עָלָיו רֵיעוֹ"

"Let its fellow tell about it."

This Biblical quotation (from איוב לו:לג) is used by Abbayé to introduce his explanation of certain mishnayoth. In its Talmudic context, this expression means: Let the same halakha that was explicitly stated in the mishna with regard to one case be applied to a similar case as well.

For examples — see בבא מציעא לא,א; בבא בתרא יט,א.

יָד; יְדָא*

hand

Besides this basic meaning, the following usages also occur in the Mishna and in the Talmud:

(1) handle**

כָּל יְדוֹת הַכֵּלִים (יומא לז,א: משנה פ"ג מ"י)

all the handles of the utensils

(2) an abbreviated expression (whose meaning must be understood from its context)

יָדַיִים שֶׁאֵינָן מוֹכִיחוֹת (קידושין ה, סע"ב ורש"י שם וש"נ)

abbreviated expressions that are not clear

(3) power; authority

יְדָא יְתֵירְתָא זַכֵּי לַהּ רַחֲמָנָא. (גיטין סד,ב)

The Merciful [God] has granted her extra power.

(4) possession

שְׁבוּעָה שֶׁאֵין לְךָ בְּיָדִי! (שבועות לו,ב: משנה פ"ה מ"ב)

[I hereby take] an oath that your property is not in my possession.

* The first form is Hebrew, and the second is Aramaic.

** Modern Hebrew uses the noun יָדִית in this sense.

יָדוֹ עַל הָעֶלְיוֹנָה

"His hand is on the top." He has the upper hand (and so he wins the legal dispute).

For an example — see ב"מ מד,א: משנה פ"ד מ"ב.

יָדוֹ עַל הַתַּחְתּוֹנָה

"His hand is on the bottom." He is at a disadvantage (and so he loses the legal dispute).

For an example — see ב"מ עו, רע"א: משנה פ"ו מ"א.

בְּיָדוּעַ* pass. prt. (ידע)

it is well known; it is certain

כָּל הַמְרַחֵם עַל הַבְּרִיּוֹת — בְּיָדוּעַ שֶׁהוּא מִזַּרְעוֹ שֶׁלְּאַבְרָהָם אָבִינוּ. (ביצה לב,ב)

Whoever acts compassionately towards [God's] creatures — it is certain that he is [descended] from the seed of Avraham our father.

* This -בְּ prefix, which is not translated into English, merely adds emphasis. In a few instances, however, a -בְּ prefix before יָדוּעַ means *in* — for example בְּיָדוּעַ נַמִּי מַחְלוֹקֶת (בבא קמא קיד,א), *in [a case where] it is known (that the owner has given up hope of recovering the article) there is also a controversy.*

יָדַע (ידע*: יָדַע .a. prt ,יָדִיעַ .p. prt ,לֵידַע .fut ,לְמִידַע (inf. יָדַע

he knew; he recognized יָדַע

From where does he know? מְנָא יָדַע? (כתובות ס,א ועוד)

* For the complete conjugation of this verb, see *Grammar for Gemara*: Chapter 4, Verb 8.

יְהֵא fut. (היי: תְּהֵא .f ,יְהוּ .pl)

he/it will be; let him be

SEE: יֵימַר, הֲוָה, לא יְהֵא אֶלָּא and its note

יְהֵא רַעֲוָא

May it be the will [of God] יְהִי רָצוֹן

יְהֵא רַעֲוָא דְּתֶהֱוֵי כְּוָותֵיהּ! (נדה לג,ב)

May it be the will [of God] that you be like him!

יְהַב (יהב:* יָהֵיב .prt ,הַב .imp)

he gave נָתַן

כֵּיוָן דַּחֲבִיב, יָהֵיב דַּעְתֵּיהּ וְשָׁמַע (ראש השנה כז,א)

since it (= the blowing of the shofar) is beloved, one will pay (lit. "give") attention and listen [to it closely]

* In the infinitive and the future (= imperfect), the Talmud uses forms of the verb נתב — e.g., לְמִיתַּב, *to give*, and לִיתֵּיב, *let him give*.

SEE: הַב, לִיתֵּיב, (לְ)מִיתַּב

יְהִיר*

arrogant; haughty יָהִיר

הַאי מַאן דְּיהִיר בַּעַל מוּם הוּא. (מגילה כט,א)

One who is haughty is blemished.

* See חבקוק ב:ה ותרגום יונתן שם ע"פ כת"י.

יוֹהֲרָא

arrogance; haughtiness יְהִירוּת

כֵּיוָן דְּכוּלֵּי עָלְמָא עָבְדֵי מְלָאכָה וְאִיהוּ לָא קָא עָבֵיד, מִיחֲזֵי כְּיוֹהֲרָא (ברכות יז,ב)

since everyone is doing work (on the fast day of the ninth of Av) and he is not doing [work], it seems like arrogance

יוֹכִיחַ fut. (יכח הִפְעִיל: תּוֹכִיחַ .f)

Let it (= this case) prove! Let it serve as evidence!

This term is used in a *refutation* of an analogy, e.g., a קַל וָחוֹמֶר.

אָמַר ר' אֱלִיעֶזֶר: וַהֲלֹא דִּין הוּא, מָה אִם שְׁחִיטָה שֶׁהִיא מִשּׁוּם מְלָאכָה דּוֹחָה אֶת הַשַּׁבָּת — אֵלּוּ שֶׁהֵן מִשּׁוּם שְׁבוּת לֹא יִדְחוּ אֶת הַשַּׁבָּת?! אָמַר לוֹ ר' יְהוֹשֻׁעַ: יוֹם טוֹב יוֹכִיחַ, שֶׁהִתִּירוּ בוֹ מִשּׁוּם מְלָאכָה וְאָסוּר מִשּׁוּם שְׁבוּת! (פסחים סה, סע"ב: משנה ו:ב)

R. Eliezer said: But is it not a kal-vahomer argument, since [an act of] slaughtering that is within the category of a [forbidden] labor [nevertheless] supersedes the Sabbath (in the case of the Pesah offering) — should not these [activities] that are within the category of a Rabbinic safeguard [also] supersede the

Sabbath?! R. Y'hoshua said to him: Let [the case of] a festival serve as evidence (against your argument), for [certain activities that are] within the category of a labor (such as cooking) have been permitted on it, but [those] within the category of a Rabbinic safeguard are prohibited on it!

יוֹמָא

day; period of twenty-four hours (1) יוֹם

יְמָמָא וְלֵילְיָא חַד יוֹמָא הוּא. (נזיר ז, סע"א)

Daytime and [the previous] night constitute one day.

the day; Yom Kippur (2) הַיּוֹם; יוֹם הַכִּפּוּרִים

Yoma, one of the tractates of the Mishna and the Talmud, deals with Yom Kippur.

the sun* (3) הַשֶּׁמֶשׁ

וְלוֹקְמֵיה לְהָדֵי יוֹמָא (שבת קלד,א ורש"י שם)

and one should place him in the sun

* The Biblical Hebrew יוֹם may also be explained in this way in some cases: e.g., כחם היוֹם (בראשית יח:א ורש"י שם) or הִנֵּה הַיּוֹם בָּא בֹּעֵר כַּתַּנּוּר, וְהָיוּ כָל זֵדִים ... קַשׁ, וְלִהַט אֹתָם הַיּוֹם הַבָּא (מלאכי ג:יט ורש"י שם).

SEE: יְמָמָא, בֶּן יוֹמוֹ, בַּת יוֹמָא

כְּיוֹצֵא בְּדָבָר

SEE: כַּיּוֹצֵא בְּדָבָר

כְּיוֹצֵא בוֹ

SEE: כַּיּוֹצֵא בוֹ

יְזַף (יזף: יָזֵיף .prt, לְמֵיזַף .inf)

he borrowed לָוָה

(chiefly money — with the understanding that he may spend it and pay back the same amount)

עֲבִיד אֱינִישׁ דְּיָזֵיף לְיוֹמֵיהּ. (כתובות קי,א)

A person is likely to borrow for a day.

SEE: אוזיף, שאיל

יְחִידָאָה יָחִיד; יְחִידָה; הַיָּחִיד

alone; individual; the lone (authority)

בֶּן בַּג בַּג יְחִידָאָה הוּא, וּפְלִיגִי רַבָּנַן עֲלֵיהּ. (ב"ק כח, רע"א)

The son of Bag Bag is alone [in his opinion], and the Ḥakhamim disagree with him.

יֵימַר fut. (אמר) יֹאמַר

he will say

This form, with a -י prefix,* is used almost exclusively in the formula -מִי יֵימַר ד (*who can say that ...?*). See that entry for an example.

* This -י prefix for the third-person masculine singular of the future tense is rare in Babylonian Aramaic, where the prefix is usually -ל (as in לֵימָא) or -נ (as in נֵימָא). See the conjugation of the future of the verb אמר in *Grammar for Gemara*, Chapter 4, Verb 10.

SEE: לֵימָא, אֲמַר

יִישַׁר fut. (ישר)

May he/it be strong!
Well done!

רַבָּה בַּר מָרִי אִיקְלַע לְבֵי רָבָא בְּחוֹל. חַזְיֵיהּ דְּבָרֵיךְ לִפְנֵי הַמָּזוֹן, וַהֲדַר בָּרֵיךְ לְאַחַר הַמָּזוֹן. אֲמַר לֵיהּ: יִישַׁר! (ברכות מב, רע"ב ורש"י שם וש"נ)

Rabba b. Mori chanced upon the house of Rava on a weekday. He saw him reciting a b'rakha (over wine) before the meal and again after the meal. He said to him: Well done!

יִישַׁר כֹּחֲךָ* שֶׁשִּׁיבַּרְתָּ! (שבת פז,א וש"נ)

May your power be strong (= more power to you) in that you (Moshe Rabbenu) have broken [the tablets]!

* Some pronounce this expression יְיַשֵּׁר כֹּחֲךָ, *May He strengthen your power!*

יָכוֹל (= יָכוֹל אַתָּה לוֹמַר ...?)

Could you say [that] ...? Could it be [that] ...?
This term, which occurs frequently in Midrash Halakha, tentatively introduces a proposal that is promptly rejected because of Scriptural evidence (which is introduced by the term תַּלְמוּד לוֹמַר, *Scripture teaches*).

יָכוֹל יִתְפַּלֵּל אָדָם לְכָל רוּחַ שֶׁיִּרְצֶה? תַּלְמוּד לוֹמַר: "נֶגֶד יְרוּשָׁלֶם". (ברכות לא,א ע"פ דניאל ו:יא)

Could it be [that] a person can pray (the Amida) facing any direction he wishes? Scripture teaches: "Toward Jerusalem."

כִּבְיָכוֹל

SEE: כִּבְיָכוֹל

יְכֵיל (יכל: יָכֵל .prt) יָכֹל; הָיָה יָכוֹל

(1) he was able; he could

יְכֵילְנָא לְשַׁנּוּיֵי לָךְ ... (ב"ק מג,א) — *I can answer you ...*

(2) he overcame

לָא יְכֵיל לֵיהּ (סנהדרין מט,א) — *he did not overcome him*

יְלַמְּדֵנוּ רַבֵּנוּ

Will our teacher instruct us ...
This expression introduces a *halakhic problem* that was presented to a Torah scholar for resolution.

For an example — see תְּנָא וְשַׁיֵּיר.

יְלַף (ילף: יָלֵיף .prt, נֵילַף/לֵילַף .fut, לְמֵילַף .inf)

he learned; he derived לָמַד

דִּבְרֵי תוֹרָה מִדִּבְרֵי קַבָּלָה לָא יָלְפִינַן. (חגיגה י,ב; ב"ק ב,ב)

We do not derive [a conclusion concerning] Torah law from the words of received tradition.

יְמָמָא* יוֹם; יוֹמָם

daytime; daylight

עַד צֵאת הַכּוֹכָבִים יְמָמָא הוּא. (פסחים ב,א)

Until the appearance of the stars it is [considered] daytime.

* In Modern Hebrew, יְמָמָה is used to mean a calendar day — a twenty-four hour period including day and night.

SEE: יוֹמָא

יְנוּקָא* תִּינוֹק; יֶלֶד

"suckling"; child; schoolboy

זִיל אַיְיתֵי יְנוּקָא דְּלָא חַכִּים וְלָא טִפֵּשׁ ... (מנחות כט, רע"ב)

(2) he fulfilled his obligation**

אִם כִּוֵּן לִבּוֹ, יָצָא. (ברכות יג,א: משנה פ״ב מ״א)

If he directed his heart (with proper intention), he has fulfilled his obligation.

* For parallel usages of the causative (הִפְעִיל) of this verb, see הוֹצִיא and מוֹצִיא. See also the Aramaic נְפַק and אַפֵּיק.

** Sometimes, the fuller expression יָצָא יְדֵי חוֹבָתוֹ is used, as in סוכה כ,ב: משנה פ״ב ה״א.

יְקָרָא
honor; respect יְקָר; כָּבוֹד

הֶסְפֵּידָא — יְקָרָא דְחַיֵּי הָוֵי אוֹ יְקָרָא דְשָׁכְבֵי? (סנהדרין מו,ב)

Is a eulogy [made at a funeral because of] respect for the living [relatives] or [because of] respect for the deceased?

SEE: אַיְיקַר

יַרְחָא
month יֶרַח; חֹדֶשׁ

תְּרֵיסַר יַרְחֵי שַׁתָּא (ב״מ לה,א) *twelve months of the year*

יְרַת (ירת: יָרֵית .prt, לֵירוֹת .fut)
he inherited יָרַשׁ

בְּרָא יָרֵית אַבָּא (ב״ק פח, סע״ב) *a son inherits a father*

יֵשׁ אֵם לַמָּסוֹרֶת
The accepted (Masoretic) spelling [of the Biblical text] has authority.

This method of Biblical interpretation discovers intimations of halakhoth in the accepted *spelling* (the כְּתִיב) of words in the text, even where different spellings do not affect how they are read. Thus it takes into account whether a word has a full spelling (with vowel letters like the ו in the word סֻכּוֹת in the example below) or a defective spelling (without vowel letters, as in סֻכֹּת).

רַבָּנַן סָבְרִי: יֵשׁ אֵם לַמָּסוֹרֶת. "בַּסֻּכֹּת", "בַּסֻּכֹּת", "בַּסֻּכּוֹת" — הֲרֵי כָּאן אַרְבַּע; דַּל חַד קְרָא לְגוּפֵיהּ, פָּשׁוּ לְהוּ תְּלָת. (סנהדרין ד,א ע״פ ויקרא כג:מב-מג)

The Hakhamim hold: The accepted spelling has authority. [The word] בַּסֻּכֹּת [is spelled twice without the letter ו *before the final* ת*, so that its spelling does not indicate plurality, and once with a* ו*, indicating plurality, i.e., two] — hence there is [intimation of] four [walls]; subtract one term needed for [the commandment] itself, [and] three [walls] are left.*

יֵשׁ אֵם לַמִּקְרָא
The accepted (Masoretic) reading [of the Biblical text] has authority.

This method of Biblical interpretation discovers intimations of halakhoth in the accepted *reading* (the קְרִי) of the words of the text. According to this method, the words are understood as they are read, whether their spelling is full (i.e., with vowel letters, like the ו in סֻכּוֹת in the example below) or defective (without vowel letters, as in סֻכֹּת).

Go [and] get a child who is neither [especially] intelligent nor [especially] dull (to read the word in question from the Torah scroll).

* This noun — derived from the verb יָנַק, *he suckled* — has entered Modern Hebrew, in the sense of a *boy-rebbi* in a Hassidic dynasty.

יַנְקוּתָא
youth; boyhood יַלְדוּת

גִּירְסָא דְיַנְקוּתָא (שבת כא,ב) *the learning of youth*

יִסְתָּאֵב .fut (סאב התפעל)
Let it become disqualified (by means of a blemish)!

יִרְעֶה עַד שֶׁיִּסְתָּאֵב! (בבא קמא קי,א: משנה פ״ט מי״א ועוד)

Let it (= the animal designated for sacrifice) go to pasture until it [develops a blemish and thus] becomes disqualified [for sacrifice and hence permitted to be redeemed, slaughtered, and eaten by its owner]!

SEE: מְסָאַב

יָפֶה
beautiful; appropriate; good;

Besides its Biblical meanings, this adjective has the following meanings in the Mishna and the Talmud:

(1) worth

שְׁנֵי כֵלִים — אֶחָד יָפֶה מָנֶה וְאֶחָד יָפֶה אֶלֶף זוּז (ב״מ לז,א: משנה פ״ג מ״ה)

two utensils — one worth a "maneh" (= one hundred zuz) and one worth one thousand zuz

(2) effective; great (used with כֹּחַ, *strength*)

יָפֶה כֹּחַ הַכֶּסֶף מִכֹּחַ הַשְּׁטָר. (קידושין כז, סע״א)

The power of money is greater than the power of a document.

מַה כֹּחַ בֵּית דִּין יָפֶה? (גיטין לג,א; לג סע״ב; לד, רע״א)

How [will] the authority of the court [be] effective (if we do not fulfill their decision strictly)?

יִפָּה (יפי פִּעֵל: מְיַיפֶּה .prt, לְיַיפּוֹת .inf)
he beautified; he improved

לְיַיפּוֹת כֹּחוֹ* שֶׁלַּמּוֹכֵר (ב״ב קג, סע״ב: משנה פ״ז מ״ב)

to improve the power of the seller

* In Modern Hebrew יִפּוּי כֹּחַ means *authorisation* or *power of attorney.*

יָצָא (יצא: יוֹצֵא .prt, יֵצֵא .fut, לָצֵאת .inf)
he went out; he departed

Besides this basic meaning in Biblical Hebrew, this verb is found in special senses in Mishnaic Hebrew and beyond.*

(1) it was excluded (from a halakha or a category)

יָצְאוּ קַרְקָעוֹת, שֶׁאֵינָן מִטַּלְטְלִין (ב״מ נז,ב ע״פ שמות כב:ח)

land has been excluded (from the law of double payment by a thief), because it is not movable

ר׳ שִׁמְעוֹן סָבַר: יֵשׁ אֵם לַמִּקְרָא. ״בַּסֻּכּוֹת״, ״בַּסֻּכּוֹת״, ״בַּסֻּכּוֹת״ — הֲרֵי כָּאן שֵׁשׁ; דַּל חַד קְרָא לְגוּפֵיהּ, פָּשׁוּ לְהוּ אַרְבַּע. (סנהדרין ד,א ע״פ ויקרא כג:מב־מג)

R. Shim´on holds: The accepted reading has authority. [The word] בַּסֻּכּוֹת [that occurs] three times [is read as a plural indicating a minimum of two in each case, even though two of the occurrences are spelled without the letter ו, בַּסֻּכֹּת] — hence, here is [an intimation of] six [walls]; [however] subtract one term needed for [the commandment] itself, [and just two occurrences of בַּסֻּכּוֹת*, indicating] four [walls] are left.*

יָת   אֶת

This Aramaic word is an indicator of a direct object, and it is not translated into English. Its use is rare in the Babylonian Talmud, except for the tractate נדרים. For the most part, it appears only in proverbs, official documents, and in the translation of Biblical passages.*

אַתְקֵין רָבָא בְגִיטֵי: אֵיךְ פְּלָנְיָא בַּר פְּלָנְיָא פְּטַר וְתָרֵיךְ יָת פְּלוֹנִית אִנְתְּתֵיהּ. (גיטין פה, סע״ב)

Rava instituted [the following formula] in letters of divorce: [We testify] how So-and-so, son of So-and-so, has dismissed and divorced So-and-so, his wife.

יָת is also used with personal-pronoun suffixes:

me	אוֹתִי	יָתִי
you	אוֹתְךָ	יָתָךְ
him/it (m.)	אוֹתוֹ	יָתֵיהּ
them	אוֹתָם	יָתְהוֹן

וְלַשְׁבַּע יָתְהוֹן! (נדרים כה,א)

But let him make them swear!

* In the Targumim, יָת is the standard translation of the Biblical Hebrew אֶת when it is a direct-object indicator, as in בְּרָא ... יָת שְׁמַיָּא וְיָת אַרְעָא (בראשית א:א). When אֶת means *with*, it is translated עִם (שם לז:ב).

יְתֵיב (יתב: יָתֵיב .prt, לֵיתֵיב .fut, לְמֵיתַב .inf)

(1) יָשַׁב   he sat; he was seated (at his studies)

יָתֵיב רַב יוֹסֵף קַמֵּיהּ דְּרַב הוּנָא, וְיָתֵיב וְקָאָמַר ... (עירובין ז,א)

*Rav Yosef was seated (at his studies) before Rav Huna, and [while] he was seated, he (= Rav Yosef) stated ...**

(2) יָשַׁב; גָּר   he lived; he dwelled

וְרַחֲמָנָא הֵיכָא יָתֵיב? (ברכות מח, רע״א)

And where does the Merciful God dwell?

* Rav Yosef, the student, was seated before his teacher Rav Huna — in keeping with the usual practice. See the inference drawn at the beginning of תוס׳ לב״ב לד,א ד״ה ״הוה יתיב״.

SEE: לֵיתֵיב, לְמֵיתַב

יַתֵּיב (יתב פַּעֵל: pass. prt. מְיַתַּב, inf. לְיַתּוּבֵי)

יִשֵּׁב   he set at ease; he quieted

אִיבָּעֵי לֵיהּ לְיַתּוּבֵי דַּעְתֵּיהּ (סוכה כה,ב)

it is incumbent upon him to set his [own] mind at ease

SEE: מְיַתְּבָא דַעְתֵּיהּ

יַתִּירָא (יַתִּירְתָּא .f.s, יַתִּירֵי .m. pl, יַתִּירָתָא .f. pl)

יָתֵר   more; extra; superfluous; redundant

לִישָּׁנָא יַתִּירָא (בבא בתרא קלח,ב) *a redundant expression*

קְרָא יַתִּירָא (בבא קמא ג,א ועוד)

a superfluous Biblical passage (or word)

יַתְמָא   יָתוֹם   orphan

This term usually denotes an heir to an estate who has not yet reached the legal age of adulthood according to Jewish law.

נָפְלֵי נִכְסֵי קַמֵּי יַתְמֵי. (כתובות מח, סע״א)

The estate falls before the orphans (as an inheritance).

יַתֵּר* (יַתִּירָה .f.s, יַתִּירִין .m. pl, יַתִּירוֹת .f. pl)

more; extra; superfluous; redundant

* This is the proper vocalization of the adjective, which has the same form as its opposite חָסֵר. When this word is pronounced יֶתֶר, however, it is really a noun meaning *remainder, abundance,* or *excess.*

SEE: יַתִּירָא, the Aramaic equivalent

יָתֵר עַל כֵּן אָמַר ר׳ ...   Moreover, said R. ...

This expression introduces a second more radical statement of a tanna in a baraitha concerning the same halakhic topic.

For an example — see R. Yᵉhuda's statement quoted in שבת ו, סע״א.

כ

כְּאֶחָד (f. כְּאַחַת) **at the same time; together**

SEE: שְׁנֵי כְתוּבִים הַבָּאִים כְּאֶחָד אֵין מְלַמְּדִין

כָּאן **here; now; in this case**

SEE the entries that follow and ... עַד כָּאן לֹא ... אֶלָּא

מִכָּאן*

(1) from here

אֵינִי זָז מִכָּאן עַד שֶׁתְּרַחֵם עַל בָּנֶיךָ (תענית כג,א)

I (= Honi, the circle-maker) will not move from here until You show mercy towards Your children

(2) from now

אִם לֹא בָאתִי מִכָּאן וְעַד שְׁנֵים עָשָׂר חֹדֶשׁ (כתובות ב,ב)

if I don't come from now until [the end of] twelve months

(3) from this case; from this pasuk [it may be derived]

דְּבֵי ר׳ יִשְׁמָעֵאל אוֹמֵר: "וְרַפֹּא יְרַפֵּא" — מִכָּאן שֶׁנִּיתְּנָה רְשׁוּת לָרוֹפֵא לְרַפְּאוֹת. (בבא קמא פה,א ע"פ כת"י ע"פ שמות כא:יט)

The school of R. Yishmael says: "And he must certainly heal" — from this pasuk [it may be derived] that permission has been given to a doctor to heal.

* In a few instances, this word is spelled מִיכָּן, for example, in כתובות ב, סע"ב.

מִכָּאן וְאֵילָךְ **from now on; henceforth**

הַקּוֹרֵא מִכָּאן וְאֵילָךְ לֹא הִפְסִיד. (ברכות ט,ב: משנה פ"א מ"ב)

*[If] one recites [the Sh*ᵉ*ma] henceforth (after the first quarter of the day), he has not lost out (completely).*

כָּאן וְכָאן **here and there; in both cases**

ר׳ שִׁמְעוֹן מַתִּיר כָּאן וְכָאן. (משנה תרומות פי"א מ"י)

R. Shim'on permits [the practice] in both cases.

כָּאן ... כָּאן ...

here ..., there ...; the latter ..., the former ...

This formula is often used in presenting a ***resolution*** **of a difficulty, usually after the introductory term** לָא קַשְׁיָא, ***it is not difficult.*** **The difficulty is resolved by proposing that the conflicting passages refer to different situations.**

לָא קַשְׁיָא: כָּאן בְּמִקְדָּשׁ רִאשׁוֹן, כָּאן בְּמִקְדָּשׁ שֵׁנִי. (ב"מ כח,א)

There is no difficulty: The latter (= the baraitha) [refers] to the [period of the] first Beth HaMikdash [and] the former (= our mishna) to the [period of the] second Beth HaMikdash.

SEE: הָא ... (וְ)הָא ... לָא קַשְׁיָא

לְכָאן וּלְכָאן **to here and there; both ways**

ר׳ יְהוּדָה דְּאָמַר: שְׁנַת חֲמִשִּׁים עוֹלָה לְכָאן וּלְכָאן (ר"ה ט, רע"א)

*R. Y*ᵉ*huda who said: The fiftieth year counts both ways (that is, as the Jubilee year and as the first year of the new Sabbatical cycle)*

כָּאן שָׁנָה רַבִּי

Here Rebbi (the compiler of the Mishna) **has taught** (by implication).

This expression is usually employed by an amora to introduce a halakhic principle, implied by the halakha formulated in a mishna.

משנה: אִם אָמַר לוֹ: טוֹל לִי הֵימֶנָּה חֵפֶץ פְּלוֹנִי — לֹא יְשַׁלְּחֶנּוּ בְּיַד אַחֵר, שֶׁאֵין רְצוֹנוֹ שֶׁיְּהֵא פִּקְדּוֹנוֹ בְּיַד אַחֵר. (גיטין כט,א: משנה פ"ג מ"ה)

תלמוד: אָמַר רֵישׁ לָקִישׁ: כָּאן שָׁנָה רַבִּי — אֵין הַשּׁוֹאֵל רַשַּׁאי לְהַשְׁאִיל, וְאֵין הַשּׂוֹכֵר רַשַּׁאי לְהַשְׂכִּיר. (שם כט, סע"א)

MISHNA: If [the husband] said to him (= his agent): Bring me a specific object (of mine) from her (when you hand her a bill of divorce from me) — [the agent] may not send it through the agency of another [agent], because it is not his (= the husband's) desire that his property be in the possession of another.

TALMUD: Resh Lakish said: Here Rebbi has taught (by implication) that a borrower [of an object] is not permitted to lend [that object to a third party], nor is one who has received something for rent permitted to rent it out [to a third party].

כִּבְיָכוֹל **as if it were possible (to speak in this manner);* as it were**

This term introduces an ***anthropomorphic*** **statement.****

מִפְּנֵי מָה הֶחֱמִירָה תוֹרָה בְּגַנָּב יוֹתֵר מִגַּזְלָן? ... כִּבְיָכוֹל, עָשָׂה עַיִן שֶׁלְּמַעְלָה כְּאִילּוּ אֵינָה רוֹאָה וְאֹזֶן שֶׁלְּמַעְלָה כְּאִילּוּ אֵינָה שׁוֹמַעַת. (בבא קמא עט,ב ורש"י ליומא ג, רע"ב)

Why was the Torah more severe towards a thief than towards a robber? ... [Because], as it were, he (= the thief, who steals in secret) has treated the heavenly Eye as if It does not see and the heavenly Ear as if It does not hear.

* See Rashi's definition in his commentary on יומא ג,ב.

** In post-Talmudic Hebrew, this expression is sometimes used as a designation for God.

כְּגוֹן כְּמוֹ; כְּעֵין; לְדוּגְמָא **"like the color of"; like [the following case]; for example**

רַבָּן שִׁמְעוֹן בֶּן גַּמְלִיאֵל אוֹמֵר: כָּל מִצְוָה שֶׁקִּבְּלוּ עֲלֵיהֶם בְּשִׂמְחָה כְּגוֹן מִילָה ... עֲדַיִין עוֹשִׂין אוֹתָהּ בְּשִׂמְחָה. (שבת קל,א)

Rabban Shim'on b. Gamliel says: Every commandment that they accepted upon themselves with joy, for example, circumcision ... they still observe with joy.

כְּגוֹן שֶׁ-; כְּגוֹן דְּ-* **in a case where/when**

כִּי אָמְרִינַן הַכּוֹפֵר בְּפִקָּדוֹן פָּסוּל לְעֵדוּת — כְּגוֹן דַּאֲתוֹ סָהֲדֵי וְאַסְהִידוּ בֵּיהּ ... (בבא מציעא ה,ב)

When do we say that one who denies [having received] a deposit is disqualified for being a witness — in a case where witnesses came and testified against him ...

* The first form is Hebrew, and the second is Aramaic.

כְּדְ- כְּמוֹ שֶׁ- **"like that which"; as**

כִּדְאָמְרֵי בְּמַעַרְבָא (בבא קמא סד,ב)

as they say in the west (= Eretz Yisrael)

כַּד כַּאֲשֶׁר **when**

כַּד הֲווֹ מְטַיְּילִין טַלְיָא וְטַלְיְיתָא בְּשׁוּקָא (בבא בתרא צא,ב)

when a boy and girl would go for a walk in the market

כַּד; כַּדָּא* **vessel; jug; pitcher**

הַמַּנִּיחַ אֶת הַכַּד בִּרְשׁוּת הָרַבִּים (ב"ק כז,א: משנה פ"ג מ"א)

one who places a pitcher in the public domain

* The first form is Hebrew, and the second is Aramaic.

כְּדַי/כְּדַאי (כְּ+דַי)

(1) worthy; deserving

כְּדַאי הוּא ר' שִׁמְעוֹן לִסְמוֹךְ עָלָיו בִּשְׁעַת הַדְּחָק. (ברכות ט,א וש"נ ופסחים נא, רע"ב ורש"י שם)

R. Shim'on is worthy [enough] to be relied upon (as an authority) in an emergency.

(2) proper

אֲנִי אֵינִי כְּדַי לַעֲמוֹד מִפְּנֵי בְנִי. (קידושין לג,ב)

It is not proper for me to stand up (as a sign of respect) before my son.

כְּדִי*

(1) לְלֹא צֹרֶךְ **needlessly; for no purpose**

For an example — see כְּדִי נְסַבָהּ.

(2) סְתָם; בְּלֹא שֵׁם אוֹמְרוֹ **anonymously**

For an example — see (וְ)אָמְרֵי לַהּ כְּדִי.

(3) לְבַד **without anything else; by itself**

יֵאוּשׁ כְּדִי לָא קָנֵי. (ב"ק קיד,א ורש"י שם; גיטין נה,א ורש"י)

[The owner's] despairing [of recovering the goods stolen from him] by itself does not grant possession [of them to the robber].

* The etymology of this word is uncertain. It may be a contracted form of כְּדִיב (= כָּזָב), *falseness, nothingness* or of כִּדְהִיא (= כְּמוֹת שֶׁהִיא), *as it is*.

SEE: בִּכְדִי; מִכְּדִי

כְּדֵי **enough for ...; as much as needed for; as long as it takes to**

כְּדֵי הִילּוּךְ מֵאָה אַמָּה (סוכה כו, רע"ב)

as long as it takes to walk one hundred cubits

SEE: תּוֹךְ כְּדֵי דִיבּוּר; בִּכְדֵי

כְּדֵי לְ- **so that; in order that**

נוֹתֵן הוּא ... לְתוֹךְ הַכּוֹס כְּדֵי לְהַפְשִׁירָן (שבת מא, סע"א: משנה פ"ג מ"ה)

he may put [a large quantity of cold water] into a cup [of hot water] in order to cool it off

SEE: כְּדֵי שֶׁ-

כְּדִי נְסַבַהּ/נַסְבָא לְלֹא צֹרֶךְ תְּפָסָהּ.

He mentioned it for no purpose.

This argument is used in *refutation* of a proof based upon the mention of one element in a text.

ברייתא: מַה "שִׂמְלָה" מְיוּחֶדֶת שֶׁיֵּשׁ לָהּ סִימָנִין, וְיֵשׁ לָהּ תּוֹבְעִין, חַיָּיב לְהַכְרִיז — אַף כָּל דָּבָר שֶׁיֵּשׁ לוֹ סִימָנִין וְיֵשׁ לוֹ תּוֹבְעִין חַיָּיב לְהַכְרִיז.

תלמוד: תַּנָא תּוֹבְעִין אִיצְטְרִיכָא לֵיהּ; סִימָנִין כְּדִי נַסְבָא. (בבא מציעא כז, רע"ב [ע"פ דברים כב:ג] וע' רש"י ור"ח שם; ע' ראש השנה ה, סע"א וש"נ)

BARAITHA: Just as a "garment" is distinctive in that it has identification marks and there are claimants for it [and so] it must be announced — every item that has identification marks and for which there are claimants must also be announced.

*TALMUD: It was only necessary for the tanna [to mention] "claimants"; he mentioned "identification marks" for no purpose.**

* The law that the finder must publicly announce an object which has claimants — i.e., the owner has apparently not given up hope — is of Torah status and is the primary topic of the baraitha. The law that he must announce an object that has a mark of identification may be of Rabbinic origin. Accordingly, its mention in the baraitha in connection with a Biblical passage may be, strictly speaking, unnecessary or incidental.

SEE: אַגַּב אוֹרְחָא, אַגַּב גְּרָרָא

כְּדֵי שֶׁ- **so that; in order to**

כְּדֵי שֶׁיַּכִּירוּ תִינוֹקוֹת וְיִשְׁאֲלוּ (פסחים קטו,ב)

so that children will take notice and inquire

SEE: כְּדֵי לְ-

כְּהַאי גַּוְונָא SEE: כִּי הַאי גַּוְונָא

כַּהֲדָדֵי SEE: כִּי הֲדָדֵי

כּוּ אֵיפוֹא **then**

This word is not found in our printed editions of the Talmud, but it does appear in manuscripts.* It has a logical — not a temporal — sense.

מַאן, כּוּ, מִיחַיַּיב? (ראש השנה כט,א ע"פ כת"י)**

Who, then, is obligated?

אֶלָּא בְּמַאי, כּוּ, מִקַּדְשָׁא? (קידושין מח, סע"א ע"פ כת"י)**

But through what, then, is she to become married?

* See J. N. Epstein, *A Grammar of Babylonian Aramaic* (Hebrew), Jerusalem 1960, p. 141.

** In the first example, the word is omitted in our printed editions; in the second, the word בו appears in its stead.

SEE: אִיכּוּ

כו' (= כּוּלֵּיהּ) SEE: וְכוּ'

כַּוְורָא דָּג **a fish**

זִימְנָא חֲדָא הֲוָה קָא אָזְלִינַן בִּסְפִינְתָּא וְחָזֵינַן הָהוּא כַּוְורָא דְּאַפְּקֵיה לְרֵישֵׁיה מִיַּמָּא ... (בבא בתרא עד, סע"א)

Once we were travelling in a boat and we saw a fish that raised its head out of the sea ...

כְּוָות-* כְּמוֹ **like**

like me	כָּמוֹנִי	כְּוָותִי
like you	כָּמוֹךָ	כְּוָותָךְ
like him/it (m.)	כָּמוֹהוּ	כְּוָותֵיהּ
like her/it (f.)	כָּמוֹהָ	כְּוָותַהּ

וְלֵית הִלְכְתָא כְּוָותֵיהּ. (ברכות כב,ב ועוד)

But the halakhic ruling is not like him (= in accordance with his opinion).

* The Aramaic -כְּוָות (used only with suffixes attached) is equivalent to the Hebrew כְּמוֹת, since the letters "ו" and "מ" are phonetically close. For a complete list of the forms with suffixes, see *Grammar for Gemara*, Chapter 7.324.

SEE: כְּמוֹת

כְּוָותֵיהּ* דְּ- "כָּמוֹהוּ שֶׁל"; כְּמוֹ **like; according to [the opinion of]**

כְּוָותֵיהּ דְּרַב מִסְתַּבְּרָא. (ברכות מ,ב)

It makes sense according to [the opinion of] Rav.

* The pronoun suffix ־ֵיהּ is added in anticipation of the following noun, so that the literal translation of our example would be *according to him, [that] of Rav* — which is equivalent to *according to Rav*. Similarly, בְּאַתְרֵיהּ דְּרַב הוּנָא (פסחים ג,א) means *in his locality, [that] of Rav Huna (= in Rav Huna's locality)*. For further discussion, see *Grammar for Gemara*: Chapter 9.2.

SEE: תַּנְיָא כְּוָותֵיהּ דְּ-

דִּכְוָותֵיהּ (דִּכְוָותַהּ f.)
that which is like it; similar to it שֶׁכְּמוֹתוֹ

שֶׁכֵּן עָנִי חוֹפֵר גּוּמָא לְהַצְנִיעַ בָּהּ פְּרוּטוֹתָיו, דִּכְוָותֵיהּ גַּבֵּי מִשְׁכָּן: שֶׁכֵּן תּוֹפְרֵי יְרִיעוֹת חוֹפְרִין גּוּמָא לְהַצְנִיעַ בָּהּ מַחֲטֵיהֶן (שבת קב,ב)

because a poor man digs a hole to hide his coins in it; similar to it in the [construction of the] Tabernacle: because those who sewed [the] curtains would dig a hole to hide their needles in it

כּוּז; כּוּזָא* **pitcher; an earthenware vessel**

אַתְקֵין רַב אַשִׁי בְּהוּצַל כּוּזָא בַּת רְבִיעְתָּא. (חולין קז,א ורש"י)

*Rav Ashi instituted in Hutzal an earthenware vessel holding a quarter of a "log" (for washing the hands).***

* The first form is Hebrew, and the second is Aramaic.

** See the table of weights and measurements in the appendix to this volume.

כַּוֵּין (כון פִּעֵל: מְכַוֵּין .prt) כִּוֵּן

he directed; he concentrated; he intended

לָא כַּוֵּין דַּעְתֵּיהּ (ברכות ל,ב)

he did not direct his mind (to his prayer)

SEE: כִּיוֵּן, the Hebrew parallel

כּוּלָּא (= כֹּלָא: כּוּלֵּי .constr)

all; the whole; the entire

As in Hebrew, pronoun suffixes are often attached to this noun.

all of it (m.)	כֻּלּוֹ	כּוּלֵּיהּ
all of it (f.)	כֻּלָּהּ	כּוּלַּהּ
all of them	כֻּלָּם	כּוּלְּהוּ

כּוּלַּהּ ר' מֵאִיר הִיא. (בבא מציעא צד,א)

All of it (= the whole mishna) is [in accordance with the opinion of] R. Méir.

כּוּלֵּי הַאי כָּל זֶה; כָּל כָּךְ

all of this; so much; to that extent

וּמִי בָּעֵינַן כּוּלֵּי הַאי? (סנהדרין מה,א ועוד)

But do we require so much?

כּוּלֵּי עָלְמָא

(1) כָּל הָעוֹלָם; כָּל בְּנֵי אָדָם

the whole world; all humanity; everybody

קָרוֹב — כּוּלֵּי עָלְמָא יָדְעִי דְּקָרוֹב הוּא. (גיטין פא,ב)

[As for] a relative — everybody knows that he is a relative.

(2) כָּל בְּנֵי הַמַּחֲלֹקֶת; דִּבְרֵי הַכֹּל

all the disputants

In this sense, the term refers to all the participants in the controversy previously quoted in the Talmud, but not necessarily all the ḥakhamim who have expressed an opinion on the matter.

לְכוּלֵּי עָלְמָא, מַקְשִׁינַן פְּשָׁרָה לְדִין. (סנהדרין ו,א ועי' תוס' שם)

According to all the disputants, we equate [the law of] arbitration with [the law of] judgment.

כּוּלֵּי עָלְמָא לָא פְּלִיגִי

all the disputants do not disagree (= they all agree) כָּל הָעוֹלָם אֵינָם חוֹלְקִים

For an example — see אַלִּיבָּא דְּ- ... כּוּלֵּי עָלְמָא לָא פְּלִיגִי

כּוֹר; כּוֹרָא* שְׁלֹשִׁים סְאָה ***kor***

This measure of volume equals thirty *seah*.**

בֵּית כּוֹר (בבא בתרא קב,ב: משנה פ"ז מ"א)

an area requiring a kor of seed (= seventy-five thousand square cubits)

* The first form is Hebrew, and the second is Aramaic.

** See the table of measurements at the end of this volume.

כּוּתִי (כּוּתִים/כּוּתִיִּים; כּוּתָאֵי** .pl)

a Cuthean; a Samaritan

This term properly denotes a descendant of the colonists who were brought to Samaria from Cuth (near Babylon) by the Assyrians after Assyrian forces had destroyed the northern Kingdom of Israel (c. 586 B.C.E.). According to the Biblical narrative (מלכים ב יז: כד־מא), the Cutheans converted to Judaism because of their fear of marauding lions; the status of their conversion is debated by tannaim in יבמות כד,ב.

וְהַכּוּתִי מְזַמְּנִין עָלָיו. (ברכות מה,א: משנה פ״ז מ״א)

And we may invite a Cuthean to participate in Birkath HaMazon.

* In some later editions of the Talmud, the word כותי is sometimes used instead of the terms גוי and נָכְרִי, *a non-Jew*, which appear in manuscripts and early printed editions. The change came about because of censorship or because of the fear thereof. For example, consider the following:

תֵיתֵי לִי, דְלָא עֲבַדִי שוּתָּפוּת בַּהֲדֵי כוּתִי. (מגילה כח, סע״א; בדפוס ראשון ובכת״י: גוי)

May I be rewarded, because I have not entered into a partnership with a non-Jew.

** The last plural form is Aramaic.

כְּחִישוּתָא חֻלְשָׁה **weakness; leanness**

כְּחִישוּתָא דְאַתְחִילָה בֵּיהּ (יבמות עט, סע״ב)

weakness that had begun to [affect] him

כְּחַשׁ (כחש: כְּחִישׁ .pass. prt, לִיכְחוּשׁ .fut, לְמִיכְחַשׁ .inf)

כָּחַשׁ; חָלַשׁ **it was/became weak; it was lean**

מֵעִיקָּרָא נְהוֹרָא בְּרִיא, וְהַשְׁתָּא נְהוֹרָא כְּחִישָׁא (קידושין כד, סע״ב)

originally the light (= his eyesight) was normal, and now the light is weak

כִּי

Besides the meanings of this word that are common in Biblical Hebrew (such as *because* and *that*),* the following meanings are more common in the Aramaic of the Talmud:

(1) כְּמוֹ; כְּ־ **like; similar to**

כִּי הַאי תַּנָּא (ברכות ל,א) *like (the opinion of) this tanna*

(2) כַּאֲשֶׁר **when; in these circumstances**

In this sense, it usually precedes a verb.

כִּי קָא מְעַיֵּיל — לְבֵיתָא דְנַפְשֵׁיהּ קָא מְעַיֵּיל (פסחים ו,א)

when he brings in [ḥametz] — he is bringing [it] into his own house

כִּי תַּקִּינוּ רַבָּנַן: בְּסִמְטָא דְלָא דָּחֲקִי רַבִּים (בבא מציעא י,ב)

in what circumstances did the ḥakhamim institute [this method of acquiring an object]: in an alley where multitudes [of people] do not crowd together

(3) אִם **if**

See example below under (וְ)כִי תֵימָא.

(4) כֵּן; כָּךְ **so**

This usage occurs only in the expression לא כִּי ***(Not so!)*. See example under that entry.**

* The Biblical meanings are discussed in גיטין צ,א and in the commentaries thereon and on parallel passages in the Talmud.

וְכִי*

This word is used to introduce a *rhetorical question*. In English its force is expressed by a change in word order and by the speaker's interrogative intonation — rather than by a specific translation of the word.

וְכִי בְּתִשְׁעָה מִתְעַנִּין?! וַהֲלֹא בַּעֲשִׂירִי מִתְעַנִּין! (ברכות ח,ב)

Do we fast on the ninth [of the month of Tishri]?! Indeed we fast on the tenth!

* This usage also occurs in Biblical Hebrew: either with ו־, as in וכי הצילו שומרון מִיָּדִי?! (ישעיהו לו:יט) or כי without ו־ in the parallel pasuk in מלכים ב יח:לד. See also כִּי אִישׁ הָרַגְתִּי לְפִצְעִי (בראשית ד:כג), according to Onkelos and Rashi.

SEE: כלום, אִטוּ, מידי

כִּי אִיתְּמַר כְּשֶׁנֶּאֱמַר ...

In these circumstances was it stated ...; With reference to these cases was it stated ...

This formula defines the scope of an amora's halakha in order to resolve a difficulty that was raised against it.

כִּי אִיתְּמַר דְּאַבָּיֵי — בְּעָלְמָא אִיתְּמַר. (שבועות יח, רע״ב ורש״י שם)

With reference to these cases was the halakha of Abbayé stated: with reference to [cases] elsewhere (not as an interpretation of our mishna).

כִּי אֲתָא רַב ... כַּאֲשֶׁר בָּא רַב ...

When Rav ... came (to Babylonia)

This expression refers to the journeys of certain Babylonian amoraim, such as Rav Dimi and Rabin, from Erets Yisrael to Babylonia. After this reference to his arrival, the Talmud presents a teaching he received from one of the leading Torah authorities in Erets Yisrael, chiefly R. Yoḥanan, and then transmitted to the Babylonian yeshivoth.

כִּי אֲתָא רַב דִּימִי, אֲמַר ר׳ יוֹחָנָן ... (שבת ז,א)

When Rav Dimi came (to Babylonia), [he reported that] R. Yoḥanan had said ...

SEE: כִּי סָלֵיק ר׳ ...

כִּי הַאי גַּוְונָא* כְּגוֹן זֶה

In this manner; in such a case; like this

"לְכוּלֵּי עָלְמָא אַפְקְרִינְהוּ, וְלָךְ לָא אַפְקְרִינְהוּ". וּמִי הָוֵי הֶפְקֵר כִּי הַאי גַּוְונָא?! (בבא מציעא ל,ב)

"I have renounced ownership of them with respect to everyone, but not with respect to you." But is a renunciation like this valid?!

* Sometimes, כִּי הַאי is written as one word, כְּהַאי.

כִּי הֲדָדֵי נִינְהוּ* כְּאֶחָד הֵם; שָׁוִים הֵם

"they are like each other"; they are similar; they are equal

כָּל הֵיכָא דִּכִי הֲדָדֵי נִינְהוּ, מִשְׁתַּעֵי בְּלָשׁוֹן נְקִיָּה. (פסחים ג, רע״ב ורש״י שם)

Wherever [two formulations] are equal [in length], the

Torah speaks with the [more] refined expression.

* Sometimes, כִּי הֲדָדֵי is written as one word, כַּהֲדָדֵי.

SEE: הֲדָדֵי

כִּי הֵיכִי דְּ-

just as — (1) כְּשֵׁם שֶׁ-

כִּי הֵיכִי דְאִיתְרְמִי לְדִידָךְ, אִיתְרְמִי נָמֵי לְחַבְרָךְ. (ב"מ כג,ב)

Just as it happened to you, it may have also happened to your fellow man.

in order that; so that — (2) כְּדֵי שֶׁ-

רְמֵי שְׁבוּעָה עֲלֵיהּ כִּי הֵיכִי דְּלוֹדֵי לֵיהּ בְּכוּלֵּיהּ. (ב"מ ג, רע"ב)

Impose an oath upon him so that he will admit to him about all of it.

וְכִי מָה עִנְיַן ... אֵצֶל ...*

But what connection [does (this) have] with (that)?!

"וַיָּבֹא שְׁלֹמֹה לַבָּמָה אֲשֶׁר בְּגִבְעוֹן יְרוּשָׁלַיִם". וְכִי מָה עִנְיַן גִּבְעוֹן אֵצֶל יְרוּשָׁלַיִם?! (יומא נג, סע"א ע"פ דברי הימים ב א:יג)

"And Sh^e^lomo came to the high place that [was] at Giv'on, Y^e^rushalayim." But what connection [does] Giv'on [have] with Y^e^rushalayim?!

* A similar construction — but without וְכִי — is found in the well-known passage in the Midrash *Torath Kohanim* that is quoted by Rashi and other commentaries to the Torah: מָה עִנְיַן שְׁמִיטָה אֵצֶל הַר סִינַי? (ויקרא כה:א) *What is the connection between the Sabbatical year and Mount Sinai?*

כִּי סָלֵיק ר' ... כַּאֲשֶׁר עָלָה ר' ...

When R. ... went up (to Erets Yisrael)

This expression refers to the journeys of certain amoraim, notably R. Zera, from Babylonia to Erets Yisrael. These amoraim received teachings of the Torah authorities in Erets Yisrael and/or transmitted to them teachings of the Babylonian authorities.

כִּי סָלֵיק ר' זֵירָא, אַשְׁכְּחֵיהּ לְרַ' אַמֵּי דְּיָתֵיב וְקָאָמַר ... (חולין כא, רע"א)

When R. Zera went up (to Eretz Yisrael), he found R. Ammi who was seated and saying ...

SEE: כִּי אֲתָא רַב ...

כִּי פְּלִיגֵי כְּשֶׁנֶּחְלְקוּ ...

In these circumstances [did] they differ ...

This formula defines the scope of a controversy that was previously quoted in the Talmud.

רַב אָמַר: אֵין מַדְלִיקִין מִנֵּר לְנֵר, וּשְׁמוּאֵל אָמַר: מַדְלִיקִין ... כִּי פְּלִיגֵי רַב וּשְׁמוּאֵל מִנֵּר לְנֵר, אֲבָל בִּקְינְסָא אָסַר שְׁמוּאֵל. (שבת כב,א-רע"ב)

Rav said: We must not kindle from one [Hanukka] light to another [Hanukka] light, and Sh^e^muel said: We may kindle [from one to another] ... In these circumstances [did] Rav and Sh^e^muel differ: [about kindling] from one light directly to another light, but by means of a wooden chip [even] Sh^e^muel prohibited.

וְכִי תֵּימָא

And if you should say ... — וְאִם תֹּאמַר ...

This expression is used to introduce a *response* (usually to an objection) that the Talmud tentatively considers but then rejects.

וּמַאי שְׁנָא לְעִנְיַן יֵין נֶסֶךְ ...?! וְכִי תֵּימָא: יֵין נֶסֶךְ דְּרַבָּנַן, חָמֵץ דְּאוֹרַיְיתָא; כָּל דְּתַקּוּן רַבָּנַן כְּעֵין דְּאוֹרַיְיתָא תַּקּוּן. (פסחים ל,ב)

But why are [glazed vessels that have contained hametz and are consequently forbidden for use on Pesah] different from [those that have contained] wine [that has been used] as a libation for idolatry [that are permitted for use]?! And if you should say: [The case of] idolatrous wine is a Rabbinic prohibition, [while] hametz is a Torah prohibition — [I would say] whatever the hakhamim have enacted, they have enacted [with the same force] as Torah law.

כִּי תַּנְיָא הַהִיא כְּשֶׁשְּׁנוּיָה הַהִיא ...

With reference to the following has that [baraitha] been stated ...

The *resolution* of a difficulty or *rejection* of a proof is achieved by limiting the scope of the baraitha that has been cited.

ברייתא: לֹא יֵצֵא הַחַיָּט בְּמַחֲטוֹ הַתְּחוּבָה לוֹ בְּבִגְדוֹ.
תלמוד: מַאי לָאו בְּעֶרֶב שַׁבָּת?! לָא! כִּי תַּנְיָא הַהִיא בְּשַׁבָּת. (שבת יא,ב)

BARAITHA: A tailor is forbidden to go out [into a public domain] with his needle stuck into his coat.
TALMUD: Doesn't this refer to Friday (and provide support for the previous view, which advocated such a prohibition)?! No (= not necessarily)! With reference to the following has that [baraitha] been stated: with reference to the Sabbath.

כִּיוֵּן (כון פִּעֵל: מְכַוֵּין .prt, יְכַוֵּין .fut, לְכַוֵּין .inf)

he directed; he intended

אִם כִּיוֵּן לִבּוֹ (ברכות יג,א: משנה פ"ב מ"א)

if he directed his heart (to the reading of the Sh^e^ma)

SEE: כַּוֵּין, the Aramaic parallel

כֵּיוָן

directly; immediately

וְאֶחָד פּוֹתֵחַ כֵּיוָן (תמיד ל,ב: משנה פ"ג מ"ו)

and one [key] opens directly

כֵּיוָן שֶׁ-; כֵּיוָן דְּ-*

as soon as; once; now that; since

כֵּיוָן דְּמִיטְמַר מֵאִינָשֵׁי, גַּנָּב הוּא. (בבא קמא נז, סע"א)

Since he hides himself from people, he is [categorized as] a thief.

For another example — see כָּל כְּמִינֵיהּ.

* The first form is Hebrew, and the second is Aramaic.

כְּיוֹצֵא בַדָּבָר אַתָּה אוֹמֵר

you may say a similar thing ...; you may apply a similar interpretation (to a second pasuk)

"צַדִּיק כִּי טוֹב" — וְכִי יֵשׁ צַדִּיק טוֹב, וְיֵשׁ צַדִּיק שֶׁאֵינוֹ טוֹב?! אֶלָּא טוֹב לַשָּׁמַיִם וְלַבְּרִיּוֹת — זֶהוּ צַדִּיק טוֹב; טוֹב לַשָּׁמַיִם וְרַע לַבְּרִיּוֹת — זֶהוּ צַדִּיק שֶׁאֵינוֹ טוֹב.
כְּיוֹצֵא בַדָּבָר אַתָּה אוֹמֵר: "אוֹי לְרָשָׁע רָע". וְכִי יֵשׁ רָשָׁע רָע, וְיֵשׁ שֶׁאֵינוֹ רָע?! אֶלָּא רַע לַשָּׁמַיִם וְרַע לַבְּרִיּוֹת — הוּא רָשָׁע רָע; רַע לַשָּׁמַיִם וְאֵינוֹ רַע לַבְּרִיּוֹת — זֶהוּ רָשָׁע שֶׁאֵינוֹ רָע. (קידושין מ,א ע"פ ישעיהו ג:י־יא)

"A righteous man if he is good" — Is there then a righteous man [who is] good and a righteous man who is not good?! Rather [if he is] good towards Heaven and good towards people, this is a righteous man who is good; [if he is] good towards Heaven but evil towards people — this is a righteous man who is not good.
You may apply a similar interpretation (to a second pasuk): "Woe unto a wicked man [who is] evil" — Is there then a wicked man [who is] evil and a wicked man who is not evil?! Rather [if he is] evil towards Heaven and evil towards people, he is a wicked man who is evil; [if he is] evil towards Heaven but not evil towards people, this is a wicked man who is not evil.

כְּיוֹצֵא בוֹ (בָּהּ .f, בָּהֶן .m. pl)

similar to it; similarly

לֹא יַשְׂכִּיר אָדָם כֵּלָיו לְנָכְרִי בְּעֶרֶב שַׁבָּת .... כְּיוֹצֵא בוֹ: אֵין מְשַׁלְּחִין אִיגְּרוֹת בְּיַד נָכְרִי בְּעֶרֶב שַׁבָּת. (שבת יט,א)
A person may not hire out his utensils to a non-Jew on Friday .... Similarly, we are not to send letters through a non-Jew on Friday.

תּוֹלְדוֹתֵיהֶן כְּיוֹצֵא בָהֶן אוֹ לָאו כְּיוֹצֵא בָהֶן? (בבא קמא ב,א)
Are their subcategories [halakhically] similar to them or not similar to them?

כִּיסוּפָא בּוּשָׁה

shame; embarrassment

וְאִתְיְלִיד בֵּיהּ מוּמָא, וּמֵחֲמַת כִּיסוּפָא אֲזַל וַעֲרַק לְעָלְמָא (יבמות קטו,א)
and he was afflicted with a blemish, and on account of shame he went and ran far away
SEE: כְּסַף, אִיכְּסִיף

כֵּיצַד (כְּאֵיזֶה+צַד)*

how? in what manner? in what respect?

מִצְוַת לוּלָב — כֵּיצַד? (סוכה מב,ב: משנה פ"ד מ"ד)
How [was] the commandment of lulav [carried out]?

* See Rambam's Commentary on Mishna: ברכות פ"ו מ"א.
SEE: הָא כֵּיצַד

כִּיתָּנָא פִּשְׁתָּן

flax; linen

הֲוָה קָא שָׁדֵי כִּיתָּנָא בְּפוּרַיָּא (מגילה ה,ב)
he was sowing flax on Purim

כָּל אֵימַת דְּ-

כָּל שָׁעָה שֶׁ- **whenever; as long as**

כָּל אֵימַת דְּבָעֵי, מִימְלִיךְ?! (תמורה כה, סע"א)
Whenever he desires, may he retract?!

כָּל הֵיכָא דְּ- בְּכָל מָקוֹם שֶׁ-; בְּכָל זְמַן שֶׁ-

in all cases where; wherever; whenever

כָּל הֵיכָא דְאִיכָּא לְמִידְרַשׁ דָּרְשִׁינַן. (פסחים כד, רע"ב)
Wherever it is [possible] to make an interpretation, we interpret.

כָּל דְּכֵן

SEE: כָּל שֶׁכֵּן

כָּל כְּמָה דְּ-

(1) כָּל זְמַן שֶׁ- **as long as**

כָּל כְּמָה דְלָא נִתְיָאֲשׁוּ הַבְּעָלִים, בִּרְשׁוּתֵיהּ דְּמָרֵיהּ קָאֵי. (בבא קמא קיא, רע"א)
As long as the owner has not given up hope, [the stolen article] remains in the (legal) possession of its owner.

(2) כָּל כַּמָּה שֶׁ- **as much as; the more** (that)

עַיּוֹלֵי יוֹמָא — כָּל כְּמָה דִּמְקַדְּמִינַן לֵיהּ, עָדִיף (פסחים קה,ב)
[as for] bringing in the [Sabbath] day — the earlier we do it (lit. "the more we do it earlier"), the better
SEE: כַּמָּה דְ-

כָּל כְּמִינֵּיהּ* הַכֹּל מִמֶּנּוּ?!

"Is everything from him?!" Does he have such power?! Is his claim accepted?!

"עֵדוּת שֶׁקֶר הֵעַדְתִּי". כָּל כְּמִינֵּיהּ?! כֵּיוָן שֶׁהִגִּיד, שׁוּב אֵינוֹ חוֹזֵר וּמַגִּיד! (מכות ג,א)
[A witness said:] "I gave false testimony." Is his claim accepted?! Once a witness has testified, he cannot retract and testify again [about the same event].

* The prefix -כְּ, which is used apparently for emphasis, is not translated into English.
SEE: לָאו כָּל כְּמִינֵּיהּ

כָּל עִיקָּר

whatsoever; at all

טוֹב מִזֶּה וּמִזֶּה שֶׁאֵינוֹ נוֹדֵר כָּל עִיקָּר. (נדרים ט, סע"א וש"נ)
Better than [both] this (= a person who vows and violates his vow) and that (= one who vows and fulfills his vow) is one who does not vow at all.

כָּל שֶׁהוּא; כָּל דְּהוּ*

whatever it is; the slightest quantity

ר' שִׁמְעוֹן אוֹמֵר: כָּל שֶׁהוּא — לְמַכּוֹת. (מכות יז,א וש"נ)
R. Shim'on says: [If one eats] the slightest quantity [of a forbidden food], [he is subject] to lashes.

"וְכִחֵשׁ בַּעֲמִיתוֹ" — כָּל דְּהוּ. (שבועות לב,א ע"פ ויקרא ה:כא)
"and he deals falsely with his fellow-man" — [even if he denies a deposit of] the slightest quantity (he is subject to a penalty).

* The first form is Hebrew, and the second is Aramaic.

כָּל שֶׁכֵּן; כָּל דְּכֵן*

all the more so; certainly!

כִּלְאֵי זְרָעִים אֲסוּרִים מִלִּזְרוֹעַ וּמִלְּקַיֵּים, וּמוּתָּרִין בַּאֲכִילָה — וְכָל שֶׁכֵּן בַּהֲנָאָה. (משנה כלאים פ"ח מ"א)

It is forbidden to sow diverse kinds of seeds together or to allow [them] to grow, but it is permitted to eat [the product] — and certainly to derive benefit [therefrom].

* The first form is Hebrew, and the second is Aramaic.

SEE: לֹא כָּל שֶׁכֵּן

כַּלָּה; כַּלְּתָא*

(1) אִשָּׁה הַנִּשֵּׂאת **bride**

כַּלָּה נָאָה וַחֲסוּדָה (כתובות יז,א)

a beautiful and pious bride

(2) אֵשֶׁת בְּנוֹ/בְּנָהּ **daughter-in-law**

מַעֲשֶׂה וְיָלְדָה כַּלָּתוֹ שֶׁל שַׁמַּאי הַזָּקֵן ... (סוכה כח,א: משנה ב:ח)

Once it happened that the daughter-in-law of Shammai the Elder gave birth ...

(3) כִּנּוּס שֶׁל תַּלְמִידֵי חֲכָמִים וַאֲחֵרִים בִּישִׁיבוֹת בָּבֶל

the *kalla*

This term refers to the assembly of scholars, students, and others that was convened in Babylonian yeshivoth during the months of Adar and Elul to study a particular tractate and/or the laws of the impending festivals.

רַב נַחְמָן בַּר יִצְחָק רֵישׁ כַּלָּה הֲוָה. (בבא בתרא כב,א)

Rav Naḥman b. Yitzḥak was head of the kalla.

* The first form is Hebrew, and the second is Aramaic.

כְּלוּם

(1) anything

In this sense, the word is used after negative expressions.

לֹא עָשָׂה וְלֹא כְלוּם (עירובין ס, סע"א: משנה פ"ח מ"ז)

he has not done anything

פּוֹסֵק, וְאֵין בְּכָךְ כְּלוּם (ברכות יד,א)

he may interrupt [his recital of Hallel or his reading of the scroll of Esther], and there is not anything in this (i.e., there is no objection whatsoever)

(2) Is there ...?!

In this sense, the word introduces a *rhetorical question* whose effect is expressed in English by a change in word order and by the intonation of the speaker's voice.

כְּלוּם יֵשׁ אָדָם שֶׁחוֹלֵק בְּדָבָר זֶה?! (ברכות כ, סע"ב)

Is there any person who disputes this matter?!

SEE: אַטּוּ, מִידִי, (וְ)כִי

כְּלוֹמַר (= כְּאִלּוּ לוֹמַר)

as if to say; this means; in other words

For an example — see לָא שְׁמִיעַ לִי כְּלוֹמַר לָא סְבִירָא לִי

כַּלֵּךְ* (= כַּלֵּה + לֵךְ .imp)

Turn away [from ... and] go [to ...]

כַּלֵּךְ מִדִּבְרוֹתֶיךָ אֵצֶל נְגָעִים וְאֹהָלוֹת! (חגיגה יד,א ושי"נ; ע' רש"י שם ובסנהדרין סז, סע"ב)

Turn away from your [aggadic] discourses [and] go to [the laws of] skin diseases and tent coverings (= the profound and complex halakhoth of ritual purity).

* This vocalization and the explanation are based upon Rashi's commentary on the above example and elsewhere. However, some read the word כְּלַךְ, a contraction of לְכָה+לָךְ, *go you*, in keeping with Rashi's comment on שבת קמה,ב.

כַּלֵּךְ לְדֶרֶךְ זוֹ

turn to this [different] approach ...

This expression occurs in Midrash Halakha in the following context: After a tanna has reached a halakhic conclusion on the basis of an analogy between two cases, this expression introduces an alternative conclusion derived from a different analogy.

"בַּסּוּכּוֹת תֵּשְׁבוּ שִׁבְעַת יָמִים" ... נֶאֱמַר כָּאן "יָמִים", וְנֶאֱמַר בְּלוּלָב "יָמִים". מָה לְהַלָּן "יָמִים" — וְלֹא לֵילוֹת, אַף כָּאן "יָמִים" — וְלֹא לֵילוֹת. אוֹ כַּלֵּךְ לְדֶרֶךְ זוֹ: נֶאֱמַר כָּאן "יָמִים" וְנֶאֱמַר בְּמִילּוּאִים "יָמִים". מָה לְהַלָּן "יָמִים" — וַאֲפִילּוּ לֵילוֹת, אַף כָּאן "יָמִים" — וַאֲפִילּוּ לֵילוֹת. (סוכה מג, סע"א ע"פ ויקרא כג:מב)

"You shall dwell in sukkoth seven days." ... Here it is written "days," and with regard to lulav it is written "days." Just as there (it means) "days" — without nights, here too [it means] "days" — without nights. Or turn to this [different] approach: Here it is written "days," and with regard to the installation [of the kohanim] it is written "days." Just as there [it means] "days" — including nights, here too [it means] "days" — including nights.

כְּלָל¹ (כְּלָלוֹת .pl); כְּלָלָא* (כְּלָלֵי .pl)

(1) a general principle; a general rule

זֶה הַכְּלָל: כָּל הָעוֹשֶׂה מְלָאכָה וּמְלַאכְתּוֹ מִתְקַיֶּימֶת, בְּשַׁבָּת — חַיָּיב. (שבת קב, רע"ב: משנה פי"ב מ"א)

This is the general principle: Anyone who performs a [forbidden] labor on the Sabbath and [the product of] his labor endures is guilty [of Sabbath desecration].

וּכְלָלָא הוּא דְּכָל מִצְוַת עֲשֵׂה שֶׁהַזְּמַן גְּרָמָהּ נָשִׁים פְּטוּרוֹת?! (עירובין כז, רע"א)

Is it a general rule that women are exempt from every mitzva that is affected by time?!

(2) a general class; a general category; the general (as opposed to the specific, פְּרָט**)**

This term is used frequently in the Midrashic and Talmudic interpretation of halakhic portions of the Torah — especially in several of the rules of interpretation of R. Yishmael. A כְּלָל**, according to this system, is indicated in the Torah by:**

(a) כָּל**, as in** לְכָל אֲבֵדַת אָחִיךָ**,** ***to every lost object of your***

brother (בבא מציעא כז,א ע״פ דברים כב:ג);
(b) a noun that denotes a general class, such as: הַבְּהֵמָה, *the animal* (ברייתא דר׳ ישמעאל: ע״פ ויקרא א:ב);
(c) a verb that has a general meaning, such as *making,* e.g., לֹא תֵעָשֶׂה, *let it not be made* (מנחות נה, רע״ב ע״פ ויקרא ב:יא).

On the other hand, a פְּרָט is indicated by:
(a) a specific object, such as: שִׂמְלָה, *a garment* (בבא מציעא כז, רע״א: משנה פ״ב מ״ה ע״פ דברים כב,ג);
(b) a verb denoting a specific action, such as: לֹא תֵאָפֶה, *let it not be baked* (מנחות שם ע״פ ויקרא ו:י).

(3) sum; total

שְׁתֵּי כִיתֵּי עֵדִים שֶׁאַחַת אוֹמֶרֶת: מָאתַיִים, וְאַחַת אוֹמֶרֶת: מָנֶה, שֶׁיֵּשׁ בִּכְלַל מָאתַיִים — מָנֶה (סנהדרין לא, רע״א)

two sets of witnesses one of which says: [the debt is] two hundred (zuz), while the other says: a "maneh" (= one hundred zuz), so that within the sum of two hundred there is one hundred (In other words, the testimony of both sets of witnesses indicates that at least one hundred zuz is owed.)

(4) community

אָמַר שְׁמוּאֵל: לְעוֹלָם אַל יוֹצִיא אָדָם אֶת עַצְמוֹ מִן הַכְּלָל. (ברכות מט, סע״ב)

*Sh*e*muel said: A person should never exclude himself from the community.*

* The first form is Hebrew, and the second is Aramaic.

SEE: כְּלָל וּפְרָט ..., פְּרָט וּכְלָל ..., כְּלָל וּפְרָט וּכְלָל ..., פְּרָט, מִדּוֹת, הוּתַּר מִכְּלָלוֹ

כְּלָל[2] adv. **absolutely; at all**

This word is often used at the conclusion of a negative clause.

לֹא הָיוּ מִתְעַנִּין כְּלָל (תענית טו,ב: משנה פ״ב מ״ו)

they would not fast at all

Sometimes, it is written twice before the negative לֹא **for emphasis, thus forming the expression:** כְּלָל כְּלָל לָא, ***not at all***

וְאֵימָא ... מוּקָפִין כְּלָל כְּלָל לָא! (מגילה ב,ב)

But say [that the dwellers in] walled cities [do] not [read] at all!

מִכְּלַל SEE: מִכְּלָל

מִכְּלָלָא SEE: מִכְּלָלָא

כְּלָל וּפְרָט אֵין בַּכְּלָל אֶלָּא מַה שֶּׁבַּפְּרָט

[If] a general class [is written] and [then] a specific item (or items) — the general class includes only the specific item(s).

This statement is one of the *rules of Biblical interpretation* of R. Yishmael, used to explain halakhic passages. When the Torah expresses itself in general terms, the halakha is applied to everything included within those terms. When only specific terms are used, the halakha applies to

the specific items alone — unless it is expanded by means of an analogy to another passage according to one of the rules of interpretation through analogy: קַל וָחוֹמֶר, בִּנְיַן אָב, **or** גְּזֵרָה שָׁוָה. **When the Torah employs a combination of general and specific terms, the application of the halakha is determined exclusively by the sequence of the terms according to the rules of interpretation that apply to such a series. Interpretation through analogy is excluded. For example, in this entry** כְּלָל וּפְרָט, **a general term is followed by a specific term (or terms). In such a series, the halakha applies to the specific item(s) alone, since the specific terms are regarded as explaining the general term.**

״(אָדָם כִּי יַקְרִיב מִכֶּם קָרְבָּן לַה׳) מִן הַבְּהֵמָה״ — כָּלַל; ״מִן הַבָּקָר וּמִן הַצֹּאן״ — פָּרַט; אֵין בַּכְּלָל אֶלָּא מַה שֶּׁבַּפְּרָט. (ברייתא דר׳ ישמעאל: בשלש עשרה המדות ע״פ ויקרא א:ב)

"(When one of you will bring an offering to the Lord) from the beast" — the Torah has generalized; "from the oxen or from the sheep" — it has specified; the general class includes only the specific items.

SEE: כְּלָל, פְּרָט וּכְלָל..., מִדּוֹת, גְּזֵרָה שָׁוָה, קַל וָחוֹמֶר, בִּנְיַן אָב

כְּלָל וּפְרָט וּכְלָל אִי אַתָּה דָן אֶלָּא כְּעֵין הַפְּרָט

[If] a general class [is written] and [then] a specific item (or items) and [then] a general class — you may infer only [items that are] similar to the specific item(s).*

This statement is one of the *rules of Biblical interpretation* of R. Yishmael, used to explain halakhic passages. When a general term is followed by a specific term (or terms) that is in turn followed by a second general term, the halakha neither includes the whole general class (since a specific term has been stated) nor is it restricted to the specific item(s) (since general terms have been stated), but it applies to all items that are similar to the specific term(s) stated in the Biblical text.

״עַל כָּל דְּבַר פֶּשַׁע״ — כָּלַל; ״עַל שׁוֹר, עַל חֲמוֹר, עַל שֶׂה וְעַל שַׂלְמָה״ — פָּרַט; ״עַל כָּל אֲבֵידָה״ — חָזַר וְכָלַל. כְּלָל וּפְרָט וּכְלָל — אִי אַתָּה דָן אֶלָּא כְּעֵין הַפְּרָט: מָה הַפְּרָט מְפוֹרָשׁ דָּבָר הַמִּטַּלְטֵל וְגוּפוֹ מָמוֹן, אַף כָּל דָּבָר הַמִּטַּלְטֵל וְגוּפוֹ מָמוֹן. יָצְאוּ קַרְקָעוֹת שֶׁאֵינָן מִטַּלְטְלִין ..., יָצְאוּ שְׁטָרוֹת שֶׁאַף עַל פִּי שֶׁמִּטַּלְטְלִין אֵין גּוּפָן מָמוֹן. (ב״ק סב, סע״ב ע״פ שמות כב:ח)

[The penalty of double payment, imposed for stealing and embezzling, applies] "with regard to every matter of trespass" — the Torah has generalized; "with regard to an ox, a donkey, a sheep, [or] a garment" — it has specified; "with regard to all missing objects" — it has generalized again. [If] a general class [is written] and [then] specific items and [then] a general class — you

may infer only [items that are] similar to the specific items. Just as the specific items, explicity stated, are things that are movable and of intrinsic value, so too everything that is movable and of intrinsic value [is included]. Real estate has [thus] been excluded, since it is not movable ..., documents have been excluded, since they have no (significant) intrinsic value.

* פְּרָט וּכְלָל וּפְרָט also applies to items כְּעֵין הַפְּרָט, *similar to the specific item*, but these must resemble the specific item(s) stated more closely than in the כלל ופרט וכלל sequence. See נזיר לה,ב.

כְּלָלוֹ שֶׁל דָּבָר; כְּלָלָא דְמִילְּתָא*

The rule of the matter [is] ...

This expression formulates the general principle that was operating in the specific cases previously presented.

שַׁחֲרִית, פָּתַח בְּ"יוֹצֵר אוֹר" וְסִיֵּים בְּ"מַעֲרִיב עֲרָבִים" — לֹא יָצָא; פָּתַח בְּ"מַעֲרִיב עֲרָבִים" וְסִיֵּים בְּ"יוֹצֵר אוֹר" — יָצָא .... כְּלָלוֹ שֶׁל דָּבָר: הַכֹּל הוֹלֵךְ אַחַר הַחִתּוּם. (ברכות יב,א)

*In the morning,** [if] one commenced [the b^e rakha] with [the intention to say] "Who creates light" and concluded with "Who brings forth the evening," he has not fulfilled his obligation; [if] he commenced with [the intention to say] "Who brings forth the evening" and concluded with "Who creates light," he has fulfilled his obligation .... The rule of the matter [is]: everything depends upon the conclusion.*

* The first expression is Hebrew, and the second is Aramaic.

** The text of the b^e rakha before קְרִיאַת שְׁמַע in the morning service commences with יוֹצֵר אוֹר, *Who creates light*, and concludes with יוֹצֵר הַמְּאוֹרוֹת, *Who creates the lights*; in the evening service it commences with מַעֲרִיב עֲרָבִים, *Who brings forth the evening*, and concludes with הַמַּעֲרִיב עֲרָבִים.

כְּלָלֵי וּפְרָטֵי   כְּלָלִים וּפְרָטִים

[the rules of Biblical interpretation involving] general categories and specifics [as formulated in R. Yishmael's system]

For an example — see סוטה טז,א.

SEE: כְּלָל וּפְרָט ..., כְּלָל וּפְרָט וּכְלָל ..., פְּרָט וּכְלָל ..., ריבויי ומיעוטי

כְּלַפֵּי (= כ+ל+אפי)   "כְּלְפְנֵי"; מוּל; לְעֻמַּת

facing; towards; opposite; against

כֹּהֲנִים—פְּנֵיהֶם כְּלַפֵּי הָעָם וַאֲחוֹרֵיהֶם כְּלַפֵּי שְׁכִינָה. (סוטה מ,א)

Kohanim [have] their faces towards the people and their backs towards the Sh^e khina (= the Divine Presence).

כְּלַפֵּי לַיְיא   לְהֶפֶךְ!*

Just the reverse!

This expression is used to point out the *difficulty* that elements stated in a text are formulated in the reverse order of that required by reason or by evidence from other sources. In response to this difficulty, a solution is proposed changing the text so that the elements are transposed.

ברייתא: אֵין לִי אֶלָּא בְּנָכְרִי שֶׁלֹּא כִּיבַּשְׁתּוֹ וְאֵין שָׁרוּי עִמְּךָ בֶּחָצֵר, נָכְרִי שֶׁכִּיבַּשְׁתּוֹ וְשָׁרוּי עִמְּךָ בֶּחָצֵר — מְנַיִין? תַּלְמוּד לוֹמַר: "לֹא יִמָּצֵא".

תלמוד: כְּלַפֵּי לַיְיא?! (פסחים ה,ב ורש"י ור"ח שם)

BARAITHA: I only [know that your ḥametz may not be kept] with a non-Jew whom you have not subjugated and who does not live with you in the [same] courtyard, [but] from where do I [know that your ḥametz may not be kept] with a non-Jew whom you have subjugated and who does live with you in the [same] courtyard? ...

TALMUD: Just the reverse! (It is more logical to be responsible for ḥametz kept with a non-Jew who has been subjugated and lives with you than the reverse!)

* According to R. Ḥananel and R. Nathan of Rome in his *Arukh*, the expression is a variation of כְּלַפֵּי אַלְיָא, *"towards the rump, (= the hindquarters of an animal)," i.e., just the reverse.* Others have suggested that the second word of the expression means *where* and is pronounced לַיְיא. Accordingly, the expression would mean: *Towards where (does that distinction lead)?!*

SEE: אִיפְּכָא מִסְתַּבְּרָא

כְּמַאן אָזְלָא הָא

SEE: (כְּ)מַאן אָזְלָא הָא

כַּמָּה ד-*

(1) כָּל מָה שֶׁ-   **as/so much as; the more that**

כַּמָּה דְּאֶפְשַׁר לְשַׁנּוּיֵי — מְשַׁנִּינַן. (שבת קכח, סע"ב וש"נ)

As much as it is possible to alter [the way the forbidden labor is usually done] we alter [it].

(2) כָּל זְמַן שֶׁ-   **as/so long as**

כַּמָּה דְּלָא שַׁחְטָהּ, לָא עֲבָרֵיהּ לְלָאו. (חולין קמא,א)

So long as he has not slaughtered it (= the mother bird), he has not transgressed a negative commandment.

* This entry is Aramaic, but the next is Hebrew.

SEE: כָּל כַּמָּה ד-

כַּמָּה שֶׁ-

(1) as

כְּמָה שֶׁנֶּאֱמַר (סוטה מב,א: משנה פ"ח מ"א)

as it was stated (in Scripture)

(2) as much as

כְּמָה שֶׁהִזִּיק מְשַׁלֵּם (בבא קמא טו,ב)

he must pay as much as he damaged

כְּמוֹת

like; as

מָצָא פֵּירוֹת בִּכְלִי אוֹ כְּלִי כְּמוֹת שֶׁהוּא (בבא מציעא כד, סע"ב: משנה פ"ב מ"ב)

[if] one found fruit in a vessel or a vessel as it is (= empty)

This word is often used with personal-pronoun suffixes:

like me   כְּמוֹתִי

כְּמוֹתְךָ like you

כְּמוֹתוֹ like him/it (m.)

כְּמוֹתָהּ like her/it (f.)

כְּמוֹתָן like them

שְׁלוּחוֹ שֶׁל אָדָם כְּמוֹתוֹ. (קדושין מב,א)

[The act of] the agent of a person is like [that of the person] himself.

SEE: -כְּוָות, the Aramaic parallel.

כְּמִינְ-*

from מִן .

This Aramaic from is always used with suffixes, as follows:

from you כְּמִינָךְ

from him כְּמִינֵיהּ

from her כְּמִינַהּ

* The -כְּ prefix apparently has an emphatic force, but it is not translated into English.

SEE: כָּל כְּמִינֵיהּ, לָאו כָּל כְּמִינֵיהּ

כְּנִישְׁתָּא*

a gathering; a synagogue כְּנֶסֶת; בֵּית כְּנֶסֶת

* The verbal root כנש appears in the Talmud just a few times in the sense of *gathering* (e.g., סנהדרין ז,א) or *sweeping* (e.g., פסחים מה,ב).

SEE: בֵּי כְנִישְׁתָּא

כְּסִיף pass. prt. (כסף)

ashamed; shameful בּוֹשׁ

כְּסִיפָא לַהּ מִילְּתָא. (קידושין מז, סע"א)

The matter is shameful to her.

SEE: אִיכְּסִיף

כַּסֵּף (כסף פַּעֵל; מְכַסֵּף prt.)

he shamed; he embarrassed בִּיֵּשׁ

SEE: כִּיסוּפָא

כְּעֵין

like (the appearance of or the size of); similar to; in the same manner as

וּמְטַמְּאִין בְּכָל שֶׁהוּא אֲפִילּוּ כְּעֵין הַחַרְדָּל וּבְפָחוֹת מִכֵּן. (נדה מ, רע"א: משנה פ"ה מ"ב)

And they impart ritual uncleanliness whatever [their] quantity, even if [they are] like [the size of] a mustard seed or less than that.

אֲנָא "כְּעֵין חֲדַתָּא" קָאָמֵינָא. (פסחים ל,ב)

I mean "like new" (in appearance).

SEE: עַיִן

כַּף (כוף: כָּיֵיף .prt, לְמֵיכַף .inf.); כְּפָא (כפי: כָּפֵי .prt)

he bent; he forced; he exerted pressure כָּפָה

אָמְרָה: מָאִיס עָלַי — לָא כָּיְיפִינַן לַהּ. (כתובות סג,ב)

[If] she said: He is repulsive to me, we do not exert pressure upon her (to preserve her marriage).

כְּפַת (כפת: כּוֹפֵת .act. prt, כְּפוּת .pass. prt.);
כְּפַת* (כפת: כָּפֵית .act. prt, כְּפִית .pass. prt.)

he tied; he bound; he pressured

כַּפְתֵיהּ וְאוֹדִי. (בבא מציעא כד, רע"א)

He (= an officer of the court) bound him (= the alleged thief), and he confessed.

* The first form is Hebrew, and the second is Aramaic.

כְּרַב (כרב: כָּרֵיב .prt)

he plowed חָרַשׁ

מִכְּדִי מִכְרַב* כָּרְבִי בְּרֵישָׁא, לִיתְנֵי "חוֹרֵשׁ" וַהֲדַר לִיתְנֵי "זוֹרֵעַ"! (שבת עג, רע"ב ורש"י שם)

Since [people] surely plow first (before sowing), let [the tanna] state "plowing" and then let him state "sowing" (in the list of labors forbidden on the Sabbath)!

* The infinitive מִכְרַב, which adds emphasis to the present tense כָּרְבִי, has been expressed by the adverb *surely*.

כְּרוֹךְ וּתְנִי

Combine and teach! כְּרֹךְ וּשְׁנֵה!

A *resolution* of a difficulty within a baraitha or a mishna text: Rearrange the text so that the two statements will be combined into one.

משנה: עַל הַזִּיקִין וְעַל הַזְּוָעוֹת, וְעַל הָרְעָמִים, וְעַל הַבְּרָקִים ... אוֹמֵר: "בָּרוּךְ ... שֶׁכֹּחוֹ וּגְבוּרָתוֹ מָלֵא עוֹלָם". עַל הֶהָרִים, וְעַל הַגְּבָעוֹת, וְעַל הַיַּמִּים ... אוֹמֵר: "בָּרוּךְ ... עוֹשֵׂה מַעֲשֵׂה בְרֵאשִׁית". (ברכות נד, רע"א: משנה פ"ט מ"א)

תלמוד: "עַל הֶהָרִים ...." אַטּוּ כָּל הָנֵי דַּאֲמַרַן עַד הַשְׁתָּא לָאו "מַעֲשֵׂה בְרֵאשִׁית" נִינְהוּ?! אָמַר אַבַּיֵי: כְּרוֹךְ וּתְנִי! (שם נט, סע"א ורש"י שם)

MISHNA: On [witnessing] shooting stars, earthquakes, thunder, and lightning ... one should say: "Blessed Be He ... Whose strength and might fill the world." On [seeing] mountains, hills, and seas ... one should say: "Blessed Be He ... Who fashions the work of creation."
*TALMUD: "On mountains ...." Are not all of these [phenomena] that we have stated up to now [part of] "the work of creation"?! (Why don't we recite: "Who fashions the work of creation" on those as well?) Abbayé said: Combine [the two clauses] and teach [them as one clause, indicating that one must recite both b^erakhoth on each of the phenomena listed]!**

* But this interpretation of Abbayé and its halakhic ramifications have been rejected by Rava and, ultimately, by the codifiers.

כָּרַח- (with suffixes)*

SEE: -בְּעַל כָּרַח

* In post-Talmudic Hebrew, כֹּרַח, *necessity*, is sometimes used without a suffix.

כְּרַךְ (כרך: כָּרֵיךְ .prt)

(1) כָּרַךְ; חִבֵּק; כָּפַל

he wrapped; he embraced; he combined

רַבָּה בַּר רַב הוּנָא הֲוָה כָּרֵיךְ סוּדָרָא אַכַּרְעֵיהּ וְנָפֵיק. (יומא עח,ב)

Rabba b. Rav Huna would wrap a scarf around his foot and go out (on Yom Kippur).

(2) אָכַל **he ate**

כְּרַךְ רִיפְתָּא (תענית כ, סע"ב ועוד)

*he ate bread (which was usually combined with salt and herbs)**

* Compare כּוֹרֵךְ at the Seder (פסחים קטו,א) and כָּרִיךְ, a *sandwich*, in Modern Hebrew.

כְּרַךְ; כְּרַכָּא* **a (fortified) city**

כְּרַכִּין הַמּוּקָּפִין חוֹמָה מִימוֹת יְהוֹשֻׁעַ בִּן נוּן (מגילה ב,א: משנה פ"א מ"א)

cities which have been surrounded by a wall from the days of Y^{e}hoshua b. Nun

seaports — כְּרַכֵּי הַיָּם (שבת כא,א)

* The first form is Hebrew, and the second is Aramaic.

כֶּרֶךְ*

(1) a bundle

הִפְקִידוּ לוֹ בְּכֶרֶךְ אֶחָד (בבא מציעא לז,א)

they entrusted to him [coins to watch] in one bundle

(2) a rolling (of a Torah scroll)

וְלֹא יִקְרְאוּ בוֹ שְׁלֹשָׁה בְּנֵי אָדָם בְּכֶרֶךְ אֶחָד (בבא מציעא כט,ב)

and [if a Torah scroll has been found and is being kept for its owner] three people should not read from it at one rolling

* In Modern Hebrew, this noun also means a *volume (of a book)*.

כַּרְעָא כֶּרַע; רֶגֶל **leg; foot**

standing on one foot — קָאֵי אַחַד כַּרְעָא (ברכות ז,א)

כָּרֵת*/הִכָּרֵת (pl. כְּרֵתוֹת/כְּרִיתוֹת)

extermination (as a Divine punishment)

מֵחֲמִישִּׁים עַד שִׁשִּׁים שָׁנָה — זוֹ הִיא מִיתַת כָּרֵת. (מו"ק כח,א)

[Dying] from [the age of] fifty until [the age of] sixty years — this is death by [Divine] extermination.

* כָּרֵת is probably an abbreviated form of the less frequent הִכָּרֵת (as in משנה חולה פ"א מ"ב), which is a נִפְעַל infinitive meaning *being cut off*. A list of the thirty-six transgressions that are subject to this punishment appears in the Mishna (כריתות ב,א: משנה פ"א מ"א). Its definition is discussed by Biblical and Talmudic commentators in the following sources:

תוספות ד"ה "אשת אח" ליבמות ב,א; רמב"ם הל' תשובה פ"ח ה"א; ורמב"ן לויקרא יח:יט.

כְּשׁוּרָא קוֹרָה **a (wooden) beam**

גַּבְרָא הוּא דְּלָא טָבַע; כְּשׁוּרָא טָבַע. (שבת קח,ב)

It is man who does not sink (in the Dead Sea); a beam does sink.

כְּשֵׁם שֶׁ- **just as**

חַיָּיב אָדָם לְבָרֵךְ עַל הָרָעָה, כְּשֵׁם שֶׁהוּא מְבָרֵךְ עַל הַטּוֹבָה. (ברכות נד,א: משנה פ"ט מ"ה)

A person is bound to recite a b^{e}rakha upon evil, just as he must recite a b^{e}rakha upon good.

כָּשֵׁר* **fit; valid; proper**

נִיקַּב וּסְתָמוֹ — אִם מְעַכֵּב אֶת הַתְּקִיעָה, פָּסוּל; וְאִם לָאו, כָּשֵׁר. (ראש השנה כז, רע"ב: משנה פ"ג מ"ו)

[If] there was a hole [in the shofar] and he sealed it — if it interferes with the blowing, [the shofar] is unfit; but if not, it is fit.

* *Kosher* (or *kasher*) has entered the English language — primarily with regard to food.

SEE: אִיתְכְּשַׁר, אַכְשַׁר, פָּסוּל

כְּשֶׁתִּמְצָא/כְּשֶׁתִּימְצֵי לוֹמַר SEE: (כְּשֶׁ)תִּמְצָא לוֹמַר

כַּת (constr. pl. כִּיתֵּי ,abs. pl. כִּיתּוֹת)

group; set (of two or more witnesses)

שְׁתֵּי כִּיתֵּי עֵדִים (סנהדרין כג,ב ועוד)

two sets of witnesses

כָּתוּב* (pl. כְּתוּבִין) **a *pasuk*; Scripture**

See example in the next entry.

* This Hebrew noun is derived from the passive participle of כתב, meaning *written*.

SEE: שְׁנֵי כְתוּבִין הַבָּאִין כְּאֶחָד אֵין מְלַמְּדִין

כָּתוּב אֶחָד אוֹמֵר ... וְכָתוּב אֶחָד אוֹמֵר ....

One pasuk states ..., while another pasuk states ....

This formula presents an apparent *contradiction* between two p^{e}sukim.

כָּתוּב אֶחָד אוֹמֵר: "שַׁבָּתוֹן זִכְרוֹן תְּרוּעָה", וְכָתוּב אֶחָד אוֹמֵר: "יוֹם תְּרוּעָה יִהְיֶה לָכֶם". (ראש השנה כט,ב ע"פ ויקרא כג:כד ובמדבר כט:א)

One pasuk states (regarding Rosh HaShana): "a solemn rest, a mention of blowing," (implying that the blowing of the shofar is merely mentioned — but not performed), whereas another pasuk states: "a day of blowing for you."

SEE: כְּתִיב ... וּכְתִיב ...

כָּתוֹתֵי* inf. (כתת פָּעֵל) כָּתַת **crush; pulverize**

כָּתוֹתֵי מִכַּתַּת שִׁיעוּרֵיהּ* (סוכה לה,א ועוד)

its (minimum) required quantity is indeed being pulverized

* The infinitive כָּתוֹתֵי, which adds emphasis to the present tense מִכַּתַּת, has been expressed by *indeed* in the English translation.

כְּתִיב* pass. prt. (כתב) כָּתוּב **[it is] written**

This Aramaic word is generally used to introduce a Biblical quotation in the Talmud, just as the Hebrew נֶאֱמַר is used within a mishna or baraitha.

* In post-Talmudic writings, כְּתִיב is often used as a technical term for the *spelling* of a Biblical word — as opposed to the קְרִי, *the masoretic pronunciation*. For an illustration of this distinction, see כְּתִיב ... וְקָרֵינַן ... below.

דִּכְתִיב

for it is written; as it written שֶׁכָּתוּב

טָעָה וְלֹא הִתְפַּלֵּל עַרְבִית, מִתְפַּלֵּל שַׁחֲרִית שְׁתַּיִם — מִשּׁוּם דְּחַד יוֹמָא הוּא, דִּכְתִיב: "וַיְהִי עֶרֶב וַיְהִי בֹקֶר יוֹם אֶחָד" ... (ברכות כו, סע"א ע"פ בראשית א:ה)

[if] one erred and did not recite the night Amida, he may recite the morning Amida twice — since it is one day, as it is written: "And it was evening and it was morning [of] one day" ...

וּכְתִיב בָּתְרֵיהּ

and it is written after it **וְכָתוּב אַחֲרָיו**

After one pasuk has been quoted (usually introduced by either שֶׁנֶּאֱמַר or דִּכְתִיב), this expression introduces another pasuk that appears later on in the same Biblical text. The juxtaposition of the two p^esukim teaches an aggadic lesson.

אָמַר ר׳ יוֹחָנָן: כָּל מָקוֹם שֶׁאַתָּה מוֹצֵא גְבוּרָתוֹ שֶׁל הַקָּדוֹשׁ בָּרוּךְ הוּא אַתָּה מוֹצֵא עַנְוְותָנוּתוֹ .... כָּתוּב בַּתּוֹרָה: "כִּי ה׳ אֱלֹקֵיכֶם הוּא אֱלֹקֵי הָאֱלֹקִים וַאֲדֹנֵי הָאֲדֹנִים ...", וּכְתִיב בָּתְרֵיהּ: "עוֹשֶׂה מִשְׁפַּט יָתוֹם וְאַלְמָנָה". (מגילה לא,א ע״פ דברים י:יז-יח)

R. Yohanan said: Wherever you find [in Scripture] the power of the Holy One Blessed Be He, you [also] find His humility .... It is written in the Torah: "For the Lord your God is the God of gods and the Lord of lords," and it is written after it: "He carries out justice for the orphan and the widow."

SEE: וְאוֹמֵר

כְּתִיב ... וּכְתִיב כָּתוּב ... וְכָתוּב ...

It is written ..., while it is [also] written ...

This formula presents a *contradiction* between two p^esukim or between two elements in the same pasuk.

כְּתִיב: "לַה׳ הָאָרֶץ וּמְלוֹאָהּ", וּכְתִיב: "הַשָּׁמַיִם שָׁמַיִם לַה׳ וְהָאָרֶץ נָתַן לִבְנֵי אָדָם". (ברכות לה, סע״א ע״פ תהלים כד:א וקטו:טז)

It is written: "The earth and its fullness are God's," while it is [also] written: "The heavens are the heavens of God, but the earth He has given to man."

ר׳ יְהוֹשֻׁעַ בֶּן לֵוִי רָמֵי: כְּתִיב: "בְּעִתָּהּ" וּכְתִיב "אֲחִישֶׁנָּה". (סנהדרין צח,א ע״פ ישעיהו ס:כב ורש״י שם)

R. Y^ehoshua raises a problem: It is written [that the Redemption will take place] "in its own time," and it is written: "I (= God) will hasten it."

SEE: כָּתוּב אֶחָד אוֹמֵר ... וְכָתוּב אֶחָד אוֹמֵר ...

כְּתִיב ... וְקָרֵינַן ... כָּתוּב ... וְאָנוּ קוֹרִין ...

It is written ..., and we read ....

This formula presents a word — first, as spelled in the Biblical text, and secondly, as pronounced according to the traditional (Masoretic) reading.

כְּתִיב: כִּי יִתֵּן, וְקָרֵינַן: "כִּי יוּתַּן"! (בבא מציעא כב, רע״ב ע״פ ויקרא יא:לח)

כי יתן *is written (which would ordinarily be pronounced* כִּי יִתֵּן *meaning "if he puts"), and we read* כִּי יוּתַּן *(as if it had a* ו*, meaning "if it be put," a passive form).*

כְּתַנָּאֵי

SEE: (כְּ)תַנָּאֵי

ל

ל-

(1) אֶל; בִּשְׁבִיל **to; for**

As in Biblical Hebrew and Biblical Aramaic, this prefix is used in the Talmud to indicate the indirect object of a verb.

זִיל, שְׁקוֹל לְנַפְשָׁךְ! (ב"מ כד, סע"ב)
Go, take for yourself!

(2) אֶת

In Aramaic — but rarely in Hebrew — this prefix is frequently used as an indicator of a direct object, which is not translated into English.*

אוֹקִירוּ לִנְשַׁיְיכוּ! (ב"מ נט, סע"א)
Honor your wives!

כַּפֶּר נָא לַעֲוֹנוֹת (יומא לה, סע"ב: משנה פ"ג מ"ח)
forgive, please, the sins

Personal-pronoun suffixes are attached to -ל when used in either of the above senses. Here are the most common combinations:**

לֵיהּ	לוֹ; אוֹתוֹ	to/for him; him/it
לַהּ	לָהּ; אוֹתָהּ	to/for her; her/it
לְהוּ	לָהֶם; אוֹתָם	to/for them (m.); them

אֲמַר לֵיהּ רַב אַחָא בְּרֵיהּ דְּרָבָא לְרַב אַשִׁי ... הָנֵי תַּמְרֵי דְזִיקָא — הֵיכִי אָכְלִינַן לְהוּ? (בבא מציעא כב,ב)
*Rav Aha the son of Rava said (to him) to Rav Ashi ... [as for] these wind-blown dates — how are we allowed to eat them (without their owners' permission)?****

* This usage is occasionally found in Biblical Hebrew, e.g.: וְיוֹאָב וַאֲבִישַׁי אָחִיו הָרְגוּ לְאַבְנֵר (שמואל ב ג:ל). For further discussion of the direct-object indicator, see *Grammar for Gemara*: Chapter 9.1.

** For a complete list of the forms, see *Grammar for Gemara:* Chapter 7.321.

*** In this Talmudic quotation, the word לֵיהּ, *to him*, is an indirect object that anticipates *Rav Ashi*. It need not be translated into English, therefore we have presented its translation within parentheses. For a discussion of the anticipatory pronoun, see *Grammar for Gemara*: Chapter 9.2.

לָא ... אֶלָּא ...

not ... but ...; not ... except ...; only

This formula may be rendered into English affirmatively as *only* (like the French *ne ... que ...*).

לא הִתִּירוּ לִרְחוֹץ אֶלָּא פָּנָיו, יָדָיו, וְרַגְלָיו. (שבת מ,א)
They have permitted washing only his face, his hands, and his feet [on the Sabbath].

SEE: אֶלָּא

לֹא אָמַר כְּלוּם

he has not said anything; his statement has no legal validity

This expression is often contrasted to דְּבָרָיו קַיָּימִין, *his words are valid*.

אָמַר לָהֶן אֶחָד: אֲנִי רָאִיתִי אֲבִיכֶם שֶׁהִטְמִין מָעוֹת בְּשִׁידָּה ... וְאָמַר שֶׁל פְּלוֹנִי הֵן ... — בַּבַּיִת, לֹא אָמַר כְּלוּם; בַּשָּׂדֶה, דְּבָרָיו קַיָּימִין. (סנהדרין ל,א ורש"י שם)
[If] a man said to them (= the heirs): I saw your father hiding money in a strongbox ..., and he said: It belongs to So-and-So ... — [if the hiding place is] in the house, his statement has no legal validity (without a second witness); in a field, his words are valid (since he could have taken them secretly, were he dishonest).

לָא אֲמַרַן אֶלָּא ... אֲבָל ...

לֹא אָמַרְנוּ אֶלָּא ..., אֲבָל ...

we have not said ... except for ..., but ...; we have applied [the statement of the amora] only to ..., but ...

This formula is used to limit the scope of an amora's statement.

אָמַר ר' חֶלְבּוֹ אָמַר רַב הוּנָא: הַיּוֹצֵא מִבֵּית הַכְּנֶסֶת אַל יַפְסִיעַ פְּסִיעָה גַּסָּה. אָמַר אַבַּיֵי: לָא אֲמַרַן אֶלָּא לְמִיפַּק — אֲבָל לְמֵיעַל, מִצְוָה לְמִרְהַט .... (ברכות ו,ב)
R. Helbo said, quoting Rav Huna: One who leaves the synagogue must not stride with hasty steps. Abbayé said: We have applied [Rav Huna's statement] only to going away [from the synagogue] — but [as for] going to [the synagogue], it is a mitzva to run ....

SEE: לֵית לַן בַּהּ, which is often used at the conclusion of this formula.

לָא הֲוָה בִּידֵיהּ לֹא הָיָה בְּיָדוֹ.

"It was not in his hand." He did not possess [a tradition].

The hakham was not prepared to answer the question that was posed to him, since he had not received sufficient instruction about such an issue

NOTE: Third-person masculine forms of Aramaic verbs in the imperfect (= "the future") often have a ל prefix. Sometimes, however, the ל prefix represents the first person plural. For example, לִיגְמַר may mean either *let him derive* or *let us derive*. Since these common forms are apt to confuse the learner, many of them have been presented as separate entries at ל — even when the main verbal entry (third person, masculine singular of the past tense, e.g., גְּמַר) appears at its appropriate place. In some of these ל entries, explanations and examples are omitted, and the learner is referred to the main verbal entries for such data. For more information about the conjugation of the Aramic verb, see *Grammar for Gemara*: Chapter 3.

from his teachers to enable him to reach a decision.*

בְּעוּ מִינֵּיהּ: ... "בָּרוּךְ שֶׁהֶחֱיָינוּ וְקִיְּמָנוּ וְהִגִּיעָנוּ לַזְּמַן הַזֶּה — כֹּהֵן מְבָרֵךְ אוֹ אֲבִי הַבֵּן מְבָרֵךְ?! ... לָא הֲוָה בִּידֵיהּ. (פסחים קכא,ב)

*They asked him: ... [As for the b*ᵉ*rakha at the redemption of the first-born:] "Blessed be ... Who has kept us alive and sustained us and brought us to this occasion" — should the kohen recite the b*ᵉ*rakha, or should the father of the son recite the b*ᵉ*rakha? ... He did not possess [a tradition].*

* According to R. Ovadia of Bertinoro in his commentary on אבות פ"ד מט"ו, the Hebrew expression אֵין בְּיָדֵינוּ has a similar meaning (Rabbi Joseph J. Gold ז"ל).

לָא הִיא

SEE: וְדִילְמָא לָא הִיא, וְלָא הִיא

לֹא הָיוּ דְבָרִים מֵעוֹלָם

"Things never were!" It never happened!

This declaration is made by a defendant in denial of a claim put forward by the plaintiff.

אֲמַר לֵיהּ: שְׁלֹשׁ פָּרוֹת מָסַרְתִּי לָךְ וּמֵתוּ כּוּלְּהוּ בִּפְשִׁיעָה, וְאָמַר לֵיהּ אִיהוּ: חֲדָא — לֹא הָיוּ דְבָרִים מֵעוֹלָם! (בבא מציעא ה,א)

He (= the plaintiff) said to him: I delivered three cows to you and they all died out of neglect, and he (= the defendant) said to him: [As for] one [of them], it never happened (= the cow was never given to me in the first place) ...!

לֹא הֲרֵי ... כַּהֲרֵי ...*

[The law] applicable to ... is not applicable to

For an example — see בבא קמא ב, רע"א: משנה פ"א מ"א.

* The literal meaning of הֲרֵי in this context is uncertain. In בבא קמא ד,א the Talmud has equated this expression with לֹא רְאִי ... כִּרְאִי ... See that entry.

לֹא זוֹ אַף זוֹ

Not [only] this, [but] even that

Some texts list cases in a climactic sequence — starting from the most obvious case and progressing until the climax, which is the least obvious and hence the most novel case.

משנה: הוֹרוּ בֵּית דִּין לַעֲבוֹר עַל אַחַת מִכָּל הַמִּצְוֹת הָאֲמוּרוֹת בַּתּוֹרָה, וְהָלַךְ הַיָּחִיד וְעָשָׂה שׁוֹגֵג עַל פִּיהֶם — בֵּין (1) שֶׁעָשׂוּ וְעָשָׂה עִמָּהֶן, בֵּין (2) שֶׁעָשׂוּ וְעָשָׂה אַחֲרֵיהֶן, בֵּין (3) שֶׁלֹּא עָשׂוּ וְעָשָׂה — פָּטוּר, מִפְּנֵי שֶׁתָּלָה בְּבֵית דִּין. (הוריות ב,א: משנה פ"א מ"א)

תלמוד: לֹא זוֹ, אַף זוֹ קָתָנֵי. (שם ב, סע"א וש"נ)

MISHNA: [If] the court ruled [erroneously that one may] violate one of the [negative] commandments that are stated in the Torah, and [an individual] acted [in error, in violation of the commandment] in accordance with their [erroneous] ruling — whether (1) [the judges themselves] acted [in violation of the commandment], and he acted with them, or (2) they acted, and he acted after them, or (3) they did not act, and he [alone] acted [in violation of the commandment] — he is exempt [from a sin offering], because [in his action] he relied upon [the ruling of] the court.

TALMUD: [The tanna] has formulated [this mishna in the sequence]: Not [only] this, [but] even that. (In case 1, his reliance upon the judges is most obvious, since he and they violated the commandment at the same time, whereas in case 3 the judges themselves did not violate the commandment at all, hence his linkage to the judges is least obvious.)

SEE: זוֹ וְאֵין צָרִיךְ לוֹמַר זוֹ

לֹא יְהֵא אֶלָּא

Let him be [regarded] merely [as] ...!

(= Grant him at least the status of ...!)

לֹא יְהֵא אֶלָּא פּוֹעֵל! (בבא מציעא יב, רע"ב)

Let him be [regarded] merely [as] a worker!

לֹא כִּי*

Not so!

זֶה אוֹמֵר: שׁוֹרְךָ הִזִּיק, וְזֶה אוֹמֵר: לֹא כִּי! אֶלָּא בְּסֶלַע לָקָה! (בבא קמא לה, סע"ב: משנה פ"ג מי"א)

One party says: Your ox damaged [mine], and the other says: Not so! Rather it was wounded [by falling] on a rock!

* This usage is sometimes found in Biblical Hebrew, e.g.:

לֹא כִּי! בְּנִי הַחַי וּבְנֵךְ הַמֵּת! (מלכים א ג:כב ותרגום יונתן שם)

Not so! My son is the live one, whereas your son is the dead one!

The fact that there is no *dagesh* in the כ indicates that לא כי should be read as one expression.

לֹא כָּל הֵימֶנּוּ

"not everything is from him"; he does not have the legal power; his claim is not believed (in court)

הַמַּכִּיר כֵּלָיו וּסְפָרָיו בְּיַד אַחֵר ... לֹא כָּל הֵימֶנּוּ. (בבא קמא קיד,ב: משנה פ"י מ"ג)

[If] one [claims that he] recognizes his own tools or books in the possession of another ... his claim is not believed.

SEE: לָאו כָּל כְּמִינֵּיהּ, the Aramaic equivalent.

לֹא כָּל שֶׁכֵּן

is it not all the more so?! shouldn't ... certainly ...?!

This expression is often used as a conclusion to a קַל־וָחוֹמֶר argument.

מִפְּנֵי לוֹמְדֶיהָ עוֹמְדִים — מִפָּנֶיהָ לֹא כָּל שֶׁכֵּן?! (קידושין לג,ב)

[Since we must] stand up before those who study it (= the Torah) — shouldn't [we] certainly [stand up] before it (= the Torah)?!

SEE: כָּל שֶׁכֵּן, קַל וָחוֹמֶר

לָא מִיבָּעֵי (לָא מִיבַּעְיָא .f)

(1) לָא צְרִיךְ **it is not necessary [to state]**

For an example — see לָא מִיבַּעְיָא קָאָמַר.

(2) צְרִיךְ שֶׁלֹּא **it is necessary that ... not; one must not**

הַאי לִישָּׁנָא בִּישָׁא ... לְקַבּוֹלֵי לָא מִיבָּעֵי (נדה סא,א)
[as for] slander ... one must not accept (= believe it)
SEE: מִיבָּעֵי

לָא מִיבַּעְיָא ... אֶלָּא/אֲבָל ...
לֹא צְרִיכָה ... אֶלָּא/אֲבָל ...

It is not necessary (to mention the obvious case) ..., but (even in the more problematic case, the same principle applies). Not only ..., but ...

For an example — see the next entry.
SEE: לֹא זוֹ אַף זוֹ

לָא מִיבַּעְיָא קָאָמַר "אֵינוֹ צָרִיךְ" הוּא אוֹמֵר.

He states [a case of] "not only" ... [but ...].

The Talmud contends that the author of this halakha has formulated the text according to the לָא־מִיבַּעְיָא construction, stating only the climax for emphasis. Then it proceeds to spell out the particulars.

משנה: אֵין מַפְטִירִין אַחַר הַפֶּסַח אֲפִיקוֹמָן.
תלמוד: "לָא מִיבַּעְיָא" קָאָמַר: לָא מִיבַּעְיָא אַחַר מַצָּה — דְּלָא נְפִישׁ טַעְמַיְיהוּ, אֲבָל לְאַחַר הַפֶּסַח דִּנְפִישׁ טַעְמֵיהּ וְלָא מָצֵי עֲבוּרֵיהּ ... (פסחים קיט, סע"ב)

MISHNA: One may not conclude by eating dessert after [eating] the Pesaḥ offering.
TALMUD: [The tanna] states [a case of] "not only [... but ...]": Not only after [eating] matza, the taste of which is not considerable, but [even] after [eating] the Pesaḥ offering, the taste of which is considerable and cannot [easily] be removed ... [is it forbidden to eat].

לֹא מְסָרָךְ* הַכָּתוּב אֶלָּא לַחֲכָמִים

The Torah (by not specifying the particulars of this halakha) has sent you only to the ḥakhamim (for the proper application of the halakha).

לֹא מְסָרָךְ הַכָּתוּב אֶלָּא לַחֲכָמִים לוֹמַר לָךְ אֵיזֶה יוֹם אָסוּר וְאֵיזֶה יוֹם מוּתָּר, אֵי זוֹ מְלָאכָה אֲסוּרָה וְאֵי זוֹ מְלָאכָה מוּתֶּרֶת. (חגיגה יח, סע"א)

The Torah has sent you only to the ḥakhamim [for them] to tell you [on] which day [labor] is forbidden and [on] which day it is permitted (since it is the ḥakhamim who fix the Jewish calendar), [and] which [manner of] labor is forbidden and which is permitted [on the intermediate days of Pesaḥ and Sukkoth].

* This is the reading in בכורות כו,ב, in some manuscripts of חגיגה יח, סע"א, and in R. Ḥananel's commentary there. Our printed editions of חגיגה, however, read לֹא מְסָרָן (instead of לֹא מְסָרָךְ), *Scripture sent them (= the data) only to the ḥakhamim.*

לָא מַשְׁמַע לֵיהּ (pl. לְהוּ)
לֹא מוּבָן לוֹ. אֵינוֹ דוֹרֵשׁ.

For him [the Biblical passage] does not indicate (the conclusion that others have derived). He does not accept the interpretation.

ר' שְׁמוּאֵל בַּר נַחְמָנִי — מַאי טַעְמָא לָא אָמַר מִ"בִּזְמַנֵּיהֶם"? "זְמַן", "זְמַנָּם", "זְמַנֵּיהֶם" לָא מַשְׁמַע לֵיהּ. (מגילה ב,א ע"פ אסתר ט:לא)

[As for] R. Shmuel b. Naḥmanni — for what reason did he not say [that reading the scroll of Esther on several dates is derived] from [the word] "in their times"? For him [the distinction between the words] "time," "their time," and "their times" does not indicate [such a conclusion].
SEE: מַשְׁמַע, דָּרַשׁ

לָא נִצְרְכָה/נִצְרְכָא אֶלָּא*

it is not necessary except; it is needed only

This expression introduces a *resolution* of a difficulty: In response to the contention that the text is superfluous or difficult, it is argued that the text is indeed appropriate because it clarifies the halakha in a particular case or according to a specific tanna.

["וְהוֹדַעְתָּ לָהֶם אֶת הַדֶּרֶךְ יֵלְכוּ בָהּ"] "אֶת הַדֶּרֶךְ" — זוֹ גְּמִילוּת חֲסָדִים ... "בָהּ" — זוֹ קְבוּרָה. הַיְינוּ גְּמִילוּת חֲסָדִים! לֹא נִצְרְכָה אֶלָּא לְזָקֵן וְאֵינוֹ לְפִי כְבוֹדוֹ. (בבא מציעא ל,ב ע"פ שמות יח:כ)

["And you shall teach them the path so that they shall walk in it"] "The path" — this refers to lovingkindness ... "In it — this refers to [the mitzva of] burial. [But] this is [included under the category of] lovingkindness! ["In it"] is needed [to teach the mitzva of burial] only in the case of an elder [whose performing a burial might be regarded as] beneath his dignity (and as such it would not be required unless it be a specific duty).

* In a few instances, אֶלָּא does not appear after לֹא נִצְרְכָה (e.g., בבא מציעא עא,א), but such readings are contradicted by manuscripts.
SEE: לָא צְרִיכָא

לָא סַגִּי/סַגְיָא דְּלָא אִי אֶפְשָׁר שֶׁלֹּא ...

it is not possible that ... not (= it must be)

לָא סַגְיָא דְּלָא מִיתַּפְכָא מַתְנִיתָא (ב"ק סט, סע"א ע"פ כת"י)
it is not possible that the baraitha not be transposed (= the baraitha must be transposed)
SEE: סַגִּי

לָא סַיְימוּהּ קַמֵּיהּ לֹא סִיְּמוּ אוֹתוֹ לְפָנָיו

they had not completed [reciting] it in front of him

In order to explain the reaction of a certain ḥakham to a case that was presented to him, it is argued that he was not told a crucial fact (as in בבא מציעא ס, רע"א) or he was not informed of the final part of a baraitha (as in בבא מציעא עו, סע"ב).
SEE: סַיֵּים

לָא סָלְקָא דַעְתָּךְ   לא תַעֲלֶה עַל דַעְתְּךָ

Let it not occur to your mind!

Do not imagine [such a possibility]!

This expression is a sharp *rejection* of an argument that has been raised. Then the Talmud proceeds to to explain why it is rejected.

מְנָלַן דמניסן מָנינַן? דילמָא מתשרי מָנינַן! לָא סָלְקָא דַעְתָּךְ! (ראש השנה ב,ב)

From where do we know that we count [the year] from [the month of] Nisan? Perhaps we [should] count from Tishri! Do not imagine [such a possibility]!

SEE: סליק

וְלֹא עוֹד אֶלָּא שֶׁ-   and not only that but ...

מפני מָה זָכו בית הלל לקבועַ הֲלָכָה כמותָן? מפני שנוחין וַעֲלובין הָיו, ושונין דבריהן ודברי בית שַׁמַּאי; ולא עוד אלָא שמַּקדימין דבְרי בית שַׁמַּאי לדבְריהן. (עירובין יג,ב)

Why did Beth Hillel merit that the halakha be fixed according to them? Because they were pleasant and humble, and they taught their own rulings and the rulings of Beth Shammai; and not only that, but they mentioned the rulings of Beth Shammai before their own rulings.

לָא פְּלוּג רַבָּנַן   לֹא חִלְּקוּ חֲכָמִים

The ḥakhamim did not differentiate.

In Rabbinic legislation, a decree is sometimes enacted "across the board," irrespective of differences in circumstances.

מחיצות לקלוט דרַבָּנַן .... לָא פלוג רַבָּנַן בין איתַנְהו למחיצות בין לֵיתַנְהו למְחיצות. (בבא מציעא נג,ב)

[The law that] the walls [around Jerusalem have the power] "to retain" [the second tithe] (so that once produce having the status of the second tithe has been brought into the city, it can no longer be redeemed) is an enactment of the ḥakhamim .... The ḥakhamim did not differentiate whether the walls (around Jerusalem) are [standing] or not.

וְלָא פְּלִיגִי

and they do not disagree   (1) וְאֵינָם חֲלוּקִים

The two tannaim or amoraim whose statements diverge are not really in conflict – because of a reason that is immediately presented in the Talmud.

וְלָא פְּלִיגִי: הָא דמְקָרֵב שוקָא; הָא דמְרַחֵק שוקָא. (כתובות ק,א)

and they do not disagree: this [statement refers to a case] where the market-day is near; the other where the market-day is distant. (In other words, each ḥakham refers to a different situation.)

וְלָא פְּלִיגִי: מָר כי אַתְרֵיה, וּמָר כי אַתְרֵיה. (פסחים ג,א וש"נ)

and they do not disagree: one [speaks] according to his own locality, and the other according to his own locality.

וְלָא פְּלִיגִי: הָא לַן, וְהָא לְהוּ. (קידושין כט,ב וש"נ)

and they do not disagree: this is for us (= Babylonian Jewry), and that is for them (= the Jews in Eretz Yisrael).

מָר אָמַר חֲדָא, וּמָר אָמַר חֲדָא — וְלָא פליגי. (ב"מ יא, רע"א)

One speaks of one [situation], and the other speaks of another [situation] — and they do not disagree.

(2) וְכִי אֵינָם חֲלוּקִים?!

Do they [really] not disagree?!

This less common usage presents a *difficulty* or *contradiction.*

וְלָא פליגי?! והָא מיפלָג פליגי! (זבחים ל, רע"ב ורש"י שם: בתמיהָה)

Do they [really] not disagree?! Behold they certainly disagree!

SEE: הָא ... (ו)הָא ...

לָא פְּסִיקָא לֵיהּ   לֹא פָסוּק לוֹ; לֹא בָרוּר לוֹ

[it is] not clear-cut to him

For an example — see פסיקָא ליה.

לָא צְרִיכָא*

The syntax of this expression and its precise translation are uncertain, hence two different interpretations will be presented:

It is not necessary ...   (1) אֵינָהּ צְרִיכָה ...

The difficulty that was raised does not merit serious consideration.**

(2) לֹא! צְרִיכָה ...

No (difficulty)! [This text] is necessary ...

Whatever its literal translation, this expression introduces a *resolution* of a difficulty. In response to the contention that the text is superfluous or difficult, it is argued that the text is indeed appropriate, because it clarifies the halakha in a particular case or according to a specific tanna.

משנה: אָכַל מַעֲשֵׂר שֵׁנִי וְהֶקְדֵּשׁ שֶׁלֹּא נִפְדּוּ ... אֵין מְזַמְּנִין עָלָיו (ברכות מה,א: משנה פ"ז מ"א)

תלמוד: פשיטָא! לָא! צריכָא שֶׁנִּפְדּוּ ולא נִפְדּוּ כְּהִלְכָתָן: מַעֲשֵׂר שֵׁנִי כְּגוֹן שֶׁפְּדָאוֹ עַל גַּבֵּי אַסִּימוֹן ... הֶקְדֵּשׁ שֶׁחִלְּלוֹ עַל גַּבֵּי קַרְקַע (ברכות מז,ב)

MISHNA: [If] one ate [produce of] the second tithe or [of] sacred property that was not redeemed, ... he is not [counted as part of a company] for Birkath HaZimmun (because the food he ate was forbidden).

TALMUD: It is obvious! No! [This halakha in the Mishna] is necessary [in a case] where they were redeemed — but not redeemed properly: the second tithe, where he redeemed it with a token (but not with real money as required) ...; sacred property, where he redeemed it with real estate ...

* In a few instances, לָא צְרִיכָא אֶלָּא occurs in our editions (as in סנהדרין ז,ב), but such readings are contradicted by Talmudic manuscripts, e.g., לָא נִצְרְכָא אֶלָּא (כתי"מ שם). Thus לָא צְרִיכָא is used consistently without an אֶלָּא, while

אֶלָּא consistently includes לָא נִצְרְכָה אֶלָּא. Therefore Jastrow's explanation of לָא צְרִיכָא — with אֶלָּא always understood — is very difficult. Both expressions, however, serve to introduce resolutions of difficulties, and there seems to be no substantial difference between them.

** Compare the Hebrew expression: זוֹ אֵינָה צְרִיכָה לִפְנִים (ב"מ טז, סע"א ורש"י שם), *this need not be [considered] inside.*

SEE: פְּלִיג

לָא קָא מִיבַּעְיָא לַן ... כִּי קָא מִיבַּעְיָא לַן

... אֵין לָנוּ שְׁאֵלָה ...; כְּשֶׁיֵּשׁ לָנוּ שְׁאֵלָה ...

[In such a situation] there is no (halakhic) problem for us; (however) where there is a (halakhic) problem for us [is in the following situation] ...

This formula is used to define the scope of a halakhic problem.

בְּעוֹ מִינֵּיהּ מֵרָבָא: בְּהֶמַת אֲרְנוֹנָא חַיֶּיבֶת בִּבְכוֹרָה אוֹ אֵין חַיֶּיבֶת בִּבְכוֹרָה? כָּל הֵיכָא דְּמָצֵי מְסַלֵּק לֵיהּ בְּזוּזֵי לָא קָא מִיבַּעְיָא לַן דְּחַיָּיב; כִּי קָא מִיבַּעְיָא לַן הֵיכָא דְּלָא מָצֵי מְסַלֵּק לֵיהּ בְּזוּזֵי. מַאי? (פסחים ו,א)

They asked Rava: Are cattle that are liable to [be collected by the Roman authorities as] a tax subject to the (Torah) law of [the] first-born or not subject to the law of [the] first-born? In a case where one can put him (= the tax-collector) off with money (instead of paying an animal) there is no (halakhic) problem for us that it is [indeed] subject [to the law of the first-born]; (however) there is a problem for us where one cannot put him off with money. What is [the ruling]?

SEE: לָא תִּיבָּעֵי לָךְ כִּי תִּיבָּעֵי לָךְ ..., מִיבַּעְיָא

וְלָא קַשְׁיָא

[This situation] is not difficult. וְאֵינָהּ קָשָׁה.

This expression introduces a *resolution* of a difficulty: It is argued that the fact that the two texts contradict one another is not difficult — either because each text deals with a different situation or because each one follows a ruling issued by a different halakhic authority.

משנה: מִי שֶׁבָּא בַּדֶּרֶךְ וְלֹא הָיָה בְיָדוֹ לוּלָב לִיטּוֹל, לִכְשֶׁיִּכָּנֵס לְבֵיתוֹ יִטּוֹל עַל שֻׁלְחָנוֹ. (סוכה לח, רע"א: משנה פ"ג מ"ט)

תלמוד: אָמַרְתָּ: נוֹטְלוֹ עַל שֻׁלְחָנוֹ — לְמֵימְרָא דְּמַפְסִיק, וּרְמִינְהִי: אִם הִתְחִילוּ, אֵין מַפְסִיקִין! אָמַר רַב סָפְרָא: לָא קַשְׁיָא — הָא דְּאִיכָּא שְׁהוּת בַּיּוֹם, הָא דְּלֵיכָּא שְׁהוּת בַּיּוֹם. (סוכה לח,א)

MISHNA: [If] someone was travelling on the road and has no lulav to take [for the mitzva] — when he comes home, he must take [it, even if he remembers in the middle of eating] at his table.

TALMUD: You said: He must take it [even] at his table — indicating that he must interrupt [his meal to do the mitzva]. But note the contradiction between them (= that mishna and the following mishna): If they have begun [to eat a meal], they need not stop [to perform the mitzva]! Rav Safra said: [this] is not difficult. The latter [mishna deals with a case] where there will still be time left in the day [to perform the mitzva], while the former [deals with a case] where there will not be time left.

SEE: קַשְׁיָא, מַאי קוּשְׁיָא, הָא ... (וְ)הָא ..., כָּאן ... כָּאן

לֹא רְאִי ... כִּרְאִי ...

[The law] applicable to ... is not applicable to

לֹא רְאִי הַקֶּרֶן, שֶׁכַּוָּונָתוֹ לְהַזִּיק, כִּרְאִי הַשֵּׁן, שֶׁאֵין כַּוָּונָתוֹ לְהַזִּיק. (בבא קמא ד,א וע' רש"י סוף ד"ה "ולא ראי"*)

The law [of damages] applicable to [one's animal's] "horn" (such as goring) where its intention was to cause damage is not applicable to [damage caused by] the "tooth" (such as the animal's eating) where its intention was not to cause damage.

* Rashi explains: "אֵין דִּין הַכָּתוּב בָּזֶה רָאוּי לִנְהוֹג בָּזֶה." *The law that is written regarding this [case] is not properly applicable to that [case].* It appears that Rashi regards רְאִי as the equivalent of רָאוּי, *proper*, in the sense of *proper to be applied.*

SEE: (וְ)חָזַר הַדִּין לֹא רְאִי זֶה כִּרְאִי זֶה, לֹא הֲרֵי ... כַּהֲרֵי

לָא שְׁמִיעַ לִי כְּלוֹמַר לָא סְבִירָא לִי

לֹא שְׁמַעְתִּי, כְּלוֹמַר: אֵינִי סָבוּר.

It has not been heard by me, in other words: I do not hold [that view].

This declaration is made by an amora who is defending his position against a statement made by an amora of an earlier generation.

For an example — see עירובין קב,ב ושי"נ.

לָא שְׁנָא לֹא שָׁנָה; אֵין הֶבְדֵּל

"It did not differ"; there is no difference

"מִמְכָּר" אֲמַר רַחֲמָנָא אֲבָל לָא שְׂכִירוּת, אוֹ דִילְמָא לָא שְׁנָא? (בבא מציעא נו,ב ע"פ ויקרא כה:יד)

The Torah stated "a sale" (as subject to the prohibition of overcharging) but not a rental — or perhaps there is no difference?

SEE: שְׁנָא

לָא שְׁנָא ... וְלָא שְׁנָא ... לֹא שָׁנָה ... וְלֹא שָׁנָה ...

There is no difference between ... and ...;
It makes no difference whether ... or ...

לָא שְׁנָא בִּרְשׁוּת הָרַבִּים וְלָא שְׁנָא בִּרְשׁוּת הַיָּחִיד — נוֹטֵל וּמַכְרִיז. (בבא מציעא כג,א)

It makes no difference whether [the objects are found lying] in a public thoroughfare or on private property — [he] must pick [them] up and announce [them].

לֹא שָׁנוּ אֶלָּא ... אֲבָל ...

They applied [the text] only ..., but ...

With this formula an amora limits the scope of the halakha in a mishna or a baraitha.

משנה: מְקוֹם שֶׁנָּהֲגוּ לְבָרֵךְ — יְבָרֵךְ; וְשֶׁלֹּא לְבָרֵךְ — לֹא יְבָרֵךְ. (מגילה כא,א: משנה פ"ג מ"א)

תלמוד: אָמַר אַבָּיֵי: לֹא שָׁנוּ אֶלָּא לְאַחֲרֶיהָ, אֲבָל לְפָנֶיהָ מִצְוָה לְבָרֵךְ. (שם כא,ב)

MISHNA: [In] a locality where they were accustomed to recite a bᵉrakha, one should recite a bᵉrakha (in connection with reading the scroll of Esther); [where they were accustomed] not to recite a bᵉrakha, one need not recite a bᵉrakha.

TALMUD: Abbayé said: They applied [the mishna] only to the bᵉrakha after it (= the reading of Esther), but before it there is a duty to recite a bᵉrakha (irrespective of prevailing custom).

SEE: שְׁנוּ

לָא תִיבָּעֵי לָךְ כִּי תִיבָּעֵי לָךְ ...

... לֹא תִהְיֶה לְךָ שְׁאֵלָה; כְּשֶׁתִּהְיֶה לְךָ שְׁאֵלָה ...

(According to one opinion or in one case) there will be no (halakhic) problem for you; (however) there will be a (halakhic) problem for you (according to the other opinion or in a different case).

This formula is used to define the scope of a halakhic problem.

For an example — see בבא קמא ז, סע״ב.

SEE: ... תִּיבָּעֵי, לָא קָא מִיבַּעְיָא לִי ... כִּי קָא מִיבַּעְיָא לִי

לֹא תַעֲשֶׂה*

"Do not do!"; a negative commandment; a (Biblical) prohibition

וְאֵלּוּ עוֹבְרִין בְּלֹא תַעֲשֶׂה: הַמַּלְוֶה, וְהַלֹּוֶה, וְהֶעָרֵב, וְהָעֵדִים. (בבא מציעא עה,א: משנה פ״ה מי״א)

And the following transgress a (Biblical) prohibition [of usury]: The lender, and the borrower, and the cosigner, and the witnesses.

* Sometimes the fuller expression, מִצְוַת לֹא תַעֲשֶׂה, is found.

SEE: לָאו

לָאו

no (1) לֹא

"אִין" וְ"לָאו" וְרַפְיָא בִּידֵיהּ. (שבת קיג,א רש״י שם וש״נ)

"Yes" and "no" — it was weak in his hand. (= He sometimes replied positively and sometimes negatively: He was uncertain about it.)

not (2) לֹא

לָאו אוֹרַח אַרְעָא. (בבא מציעא פד,ב)

It is not the way of the land. (= It is not proper.)

Is it not?! Does it not?! (3) הַאִם לֹא ...?!

לָאו הוּא הַדִּין לְמֶרְחָץ?! (שבת י, סע״א)

Doesn't the same rule apply to a bathhouse?!

(4) מִצְוַת לֹא תַעֲשֶׂה*

"a don't"; a negative commandment; a (Biblical) prohibition

דּוּמְיָא דְלָאו דְ"חֲסִימָה" (מכות יג,ב)

*[a prohibition that is] similar to the prohibition of muzzling***

* In this sense, לָאו is used as a noun and sometimes appears in the plural לָאוֵי or לָאוִין.

** (דברים כה:ד) לֹא תַחְסֹם שׁוֹר בְּדִישׁוֹ, *Don't muzzle an ox while it is threshing,* is regarded as a prototype for prohibitions in the Torah that are subject to the punishment of flogging. Prohibitions *excluded* are described in the entries: לָאו שֶׁאֵין בּוֹ מַעֲשֶׂה, לָאו שֶׁנִּיתַּק לַעֲשֵׂה, and לָאו שֶׁנִּיתַּן לְאַזְהָרַת מִיתַת בֵּית דִּין.

SEE: אִיסּוּר לָאו

לָאו אַדַּעְתַּאי — לֹא עַל דַּעְתִּי.

There are (at least) two different interpretations of this expression:

(1) לֹא הָיִיתִי זָכוּר*; לֹא נָתַתִּי לִבִּי**

I did not recall; I was not aware.

(2) לֹא הָיִיתִי סָבוּר.***

It is not in accordance with my opinion. I do not agree.

* Rashi on שבת צה, סע״א

** Rashi on ברכות כו, רע״א

*** Rashi in the same comment on שבת, quoting his teachers.

וְלָאו אוֹתְבִינֵיהּ חֲדָא זִימְנָא

הַאִם לֹא הֱשַׁבְנוּ (= הִקְשִׁינוּ) עָלָיו פַּעַם אַחַת?!

But did we not (already) refute him once?!

This *rhetorical question* is presented by the Talmud when a second difficulty is raised against an amora's halakha before the first difficulty has been resolved. Since the first difficulty is outstanding, it is argued, why raise a second?

For an example — see פסחים קב,א ורשב״ם שם.

וְלָאו אִיתְּמַר עֲלַהּ — הֲלֹא נֶאֱמַר עָלֶיהָ ...?!

But has it not been stated in connection with it (= this text) ...?!

SEE: הָא אִיתְּמַר עֲלַהּ for explanation and example.

לָאו בְּפֵירוּשׁ אִיתְּמַר אֶלָּא מִכְּלָלָא אִיתְּמַר*

לֹא בְּפֵירוּשׁ נֶאֱמַר, אֶלָּא מִכְּלָל (נֶאֱמַר).

It was not stated explicitly, but by implication.

The halakhic ruling that has been attributed to a particular amora was not actually stated by him. In fact, it was deduced by his students from another ruling of his about a case that is not identical to the one under discussion; hence, their deduction is problematic.

For examples — see ברכות ט,א and בבא מציעא לו,א וש״נ.

* In some cases, the verb אִיתְּמַר is not repeated.

לָאו דַוְקָא — לֹא בְּדִיּוּק [כָּךְ]

not exactly; loosely; not necessarily; not exclusively

For an example — see דַּוְקָא.

לָאו הַבָּא מִכְּלַל עֲשֵׂה

a negative injunction that is inferred from a positive command (without an explicit Biblical prohibition)

"וְאָכְלוּ אֶת הַבָּשָׂר בַּלַּיְלָה הַזֶּה": בַּלַּיְלָה — אִין; בַּיּוֹם — לָא. הַאי לָאו הַבָּא מִכְּלַל עֲשֵׂה הוּא, וְכָל לָאו הַבָּא מִכְּלַל עֲשֵׂה — עֲשֵׂה! (פסחים מא, סע"ב ע"פ שמות יב:ח)

"And they shall eat the flesh (of the Pesaḥ offering) during this night": at night — yes; during the day — no. [But] this (not eating it during the day) is a negative injunction inferred from a positive commandment ("and they shall eat ..."), and every negative injunction inferred from a positive commandment is [considered] a positive commandment (and is not punishable by lashes)!

SEE: אִיסּוּר עֲשֵׂה

לָאו כָּל כְּמִינֵּיהּ* לֹא כָל הֵימֶנּוּ; לֹא הַכֹּל מִמֶּנּוּ

"not everything is from him"; he does not have the legal power; he is not believed (in court)

בִּגְנוּבִין, לָאו כָּל כְּמִינֵּיהּ. לְאַחְזוֹקֵי אֱינִישׁ בְּגַנָּבֵי לָא מַחְזְקִינַן. (שבועות מו,ב)

[If the owner of the house claims that the articles the other man has taken have been] stolen, he is not believed. We do not presume a man to be a thief.

* (1) The prefix -כ, which is apparently used for emphasis, is not translated into English.

(2) Besides the suffix ־ֵיהּ , other suffixes may appear — such as ־ָךְ , *you*, in כְּמִינָךְ, and ־ַהּ , *her*, in כְּמִינַהּ.

SEE: כָּל כְּמִינֵּיהּ

לָאו מִילְּתָא הִיא

"it is not anything" לֹא כְלוּם הוּא

(1) it (= the halakha just quoted) is not correct

מוּתָּר לוֹ לְאָדָם לְהַלְווֹת בָּנָיו וּבְנֵי בֵיתוֹ בְּרִבִּית, כְּדֵי לְהַטְעִימָן טַעַם רִבִּית. וְלָאו מִילְּתָא הִיא, מִשּׁוּם דְּאָתֵי לְמִסְרַךְ. (בבא מציעא עה, סע"א)

One is permitted to lend (money) to his sons and to (other) family members with interest, in order to give them the (bitter) taste of interest. But it (= this halakha) is not correct, because they might get used (to interest).

(2) it is not substantial; it is not significant

For examples — see R. Y°huda in the next entry and מִילְּתָא.

לָאו מִילְּתָא הִיא דַּאֲמַרִי

לֹא כְלוּם הוּא [מַה] שֶׁאָמַרְתִּי ...

What I (previously) said is not correct ...

With this declaration, an amora retracts the explanation or statement he himself proposed. Subsequently, he presents the evidence that convinced him to change his mind.

רַב יוֹסֵף אָמַר: ... כִּי פְּלִיגִי בְּדִיבּוּרָא בְּעָלְמָא. ר' מֵאִיר סָבַר: דִּיבּוּרָא מִילְּתָא הִיא, וְר' יְהוּדָה סָבַר: דִּיבּוּרָא לָאו מִילְּתָא הִיא. הֲדַר אָמַר רַב יוֹסֵף: לָאו מִילְּתָא הִיא דַּאֲמַרִי, דַּאֲפִילּוּ לְר' יְהוּדָה בְּדִיבּוּרָא נַמֵי חַיּוֹבֵי מְחַיֵּיב ... (סנהדרין סא,א)

Rav Yosef said: ... In this case [the tannaim] disagree — in a case of a mere declaration (that one will engage in idolatry): R. Méir holds: A declaration is something [punishable], and R. Y°huda holds: A declaration is not something [punishable]. Subsequently Rav Yosef said: What I (previously) said is not correct, for even according to R. Y°huda one certainly is subject to punishment for a declaration ...

לָאו שֶׁאֵין בּוֹ מַעֲשֶׂה

a Biblical prohibition whose transgression does not involve a physical act

"לֹא תוֹתִירוּ מִמֶּנּוּ עַד בֹּקֶר ..." — ר' יַעֲקֹב אוֹמֵר: ... הֲוָה לֵיהּ לָאו שֶׁאֵין בּוֹ מַעֲשֶׂה, וְכָל לָאו שֶׁאֵין בּוֹ מַעֲשֶׂה אֵין לוֹקִין עָלָיו. (סנהדרין סג, סע"א־רע"ב ע"פ שמות יב:י)

"You shall not leave over any of it (= the Pesaḥ offering) until morning ..." — R. Ya'akov says: ... it is a Biblical prohibition whose transgression does not involve a physical act, and one is not flogged because of (transgressing) a Biblical prohibition that does not involve a physical act.

לָאו שֶׁבִּכְלָלוֹת

a Biblical prohibition that [is stated] in general terms (and includes several distinct Torah prohibitions)

מִנַּיִן לָאוֹכֵל מִן הַבְּהֵמָה קוֹדֶם שֶׁתֵּצֵא נַפְשָׁהּ שֶׁהוּא בְּלֹא תַעֲשֶׂה? תַּלְמוּד לוֹמַר: "לֹא תֹאכְלוּ עַל הַדָּם". דָּבָר אַחֵר: "לֹא תֹאכְלוּ עַל הַדָּם" — לֹא תֹאכְלוּ בָשָׂר וַעֲדַיִין דָּם בַּמִּזְרָק ... ר' עֲקִיבָא אוֹמֵר: מִנַּיִן לְסַנְהֶדְרִין שֶׁהָרְגוּ אֶת הַנֶּפֶשׁ שֶׁאֵין טוֹעֲמִין כְּלוּם כָּל אוֹתוֹ יוֹם? תַּלְמוּד לוֹמַר: "לֹא תֹאכְלוּ עַל הַדָּם" ... וַאֲמַר ר' אַבִין ...: עַל כּוּלָּם אֵינוֹ לוֹקֶה, מִשּׁוּם דַּהֲוָה לֵיהּ לָאו שֶׁבִּכְלָלוֹת. (סנהדרין סג,א ע"פ ויקרא יט:כו)

From where [do we derive that] one who eats of [the flesh of] an animal before it expires violates a negative commandment? The Torah teaches: "Don't eat anything with the blood (= life)!" Another explanation: "Don't eat anything with the blood!" — Don't eat the flesh [of an offering] while the blood is still in the sprinkling vessel. R. Akiva says: From where [do we derive that] a court that has executed a person must not eat anything during that whole day [of the execution]? The Torah teaches: "Don't eat anything with the [shedding of] blood." And R. Abin said: For none of these transgressions is the offender flogged, because it is a Biblical prohibition that is stated in general terms (and includes all the above Torah prohibitions).

לָאו שֶׁנִּיתַּן לְאַזְהָרַת מִיתַת בֵּית דִּין

a Biblical prohibition that was designated as a warning for [an offense punishable by]

death at the hands of the court

The Torah has imposed the death penalty upon one who deliberately violates certain Biblical prohibitions. Such a prohibition is regarded as a warning only against the death penalty; according to the authoritative halakhic view, one who violates it is not subject to flogging — the penalty for violating most Biblical prohibitions.

(1) Therefore, if someone violates the prohibition but the death penalty cannot be imposed because of a technical reason, he is exempt not only from the death penalty but even from the penalty of flogging.

(2) When both an offense punishable by the death penalty and a lesser offense are subsumed under the same prohibition, if one commits the lesser crime, he is exempt not only from the death penalty but even from flogging.

הַמְחַמֵּר אַחַר בְּהֶמְתּוֹ בְּשַׁבָּת פָּטוּר מִכְּלוּם ... דַּהֲוָה לֵיהּ לָאו שֶׁנִּיתַּן לְאַזְהָרַת מִיתַת בֵּית דִּין. (שבת קנד, סע"א ורש"י שם)

*One who drives his (laden) animal on the Sabbath is exempt from any punishment (from the court) ... because it is [a case of] a prohibition that was designated as a warning for [an offense punishable by] death at the hands of the court.**

* The prohibition לֹא תַעֲשֶׂה כָל מְלָאכָה (שמות כ:י), *do not perform any labor*, is the warning against performing any one of the thirty-nine labors on the Sabbath that are subject to the death penalty. As such, it cannot also be the warning for the lesser offense of driving a laden animal, which is subsumed under the same prohibition. As a result, that lesser offense is not subject to flogging.

SEE: ניתן

לָאו שֶׁנִּיתַּק לַעֲשֵׂה

a Biblical prohibition [the punishment of] which has been cancelled by [the performance of] a positive commandment*

After a person violates certain negative commandments, the Torah grants him the opportunity to perform a particular positive commandment instead of incurring the punishment of flogging.

משנה: הַנּוֹטֵל אֵם עַל הַבָּנִים ... מְשַׁלֵּחַ וְאֵינוֹ לוֹקֶה. זֶה הַכְּלָל: כָּל מִצְוַת לֹא תַעֲשֶׂה שֶׁיֵּשׁ בָּהּ קוּם עֲשֵׂה — אֵין לוֹקִין עָלֶיהָ. (חולין קמא, סע"א: משנה פי"ב מ"ד ע"פ דברים כב:ו־ז)

תלמוד: ... לָאו שֶׁנִּיתַּק לַעֲשֵׂה אֵין לוֹקִין עָלָיו. (שם)

MISHNA: [If] one takes the mother [bird] together with the young ..., he must let [the mother bird] go, and he is not punished with flogging. This is the general rule: One is not punished with flogging [for the violation of] any negative commandment that is coupled with a [positive commandment] "get up and do."

*TALMUD: ... One is not punished with flogging for violating a Biblical prohibition [whose punishment] is cancelled by [the performance of] a positive commandment.***

* The translation of the verb ניתק is uncertain. See Rashi on מכות טו, סע"א. Another possibility: A prohibition that has been *transformed* into a positive commandment.

** Whether the actual performance of the positive commandment is essential in order to exempt him from the punishment of flogging is the subject of a debate in the Talmud (מכות טו, א־ב)

לָאִי/לָאִי* בֶּאֱמֶת!

indeed!

לָאִיי! אַפְנוּיֵי מַפְנֵי.** (שבת סד,א ע"פ כת"י ורש"י שם)

Indeed! It (= the Biblical passage) is [redundant and hence] completely free [for interpretation.]

* The etymology may be !?לָא+הִיא, *is it not [so]?!*

** The infinitive אַפְנוּיֵי adds emphasis to the present מַפְנֵי, which has been expressed in English by *completely.*

לְאַלְתַּר* (= עַל+אֲתַר) עַל הַמָּקוֹם; מִיָּד

"on the spot"; immediately; forthwith

צַדִּיקִים גְּמוּרִין נִכְתָּבִין וְנֶחְתָּמִין לְאַלְתַּר לְחַיִּים. (ר"ה טז,ב)

The completely righteous are immediately inscribed and sealed for life.

* From this adverb, Modern Hebrew has developed the verb לְאַלְתֵּר, *to improvise.*

לְבַהֲדֵי

SEE: לַהֲדֵי

לְבַר/לְבָרָא/לְבָרַאי חוּצָה

outside

SEE: (לְ)בַר, בַּר

מִלְּבַר מִבַּחוּץ

from the outside

SEE: (מִלְ)בַר, בַּר

לְבַר מִ- חוּץ מִ-

outside of; except for

SEE: בַּר

לְבָתַר דְּ-

SEE: בָּתַר דְּ-

לְגוֹ לְתוֹךְ; בִּפְנִים.

into; inside

SEE: (לְ)גו

לְגָיו/לְגָאו

לְפָנִים; כְּלַפֵּי פְנִים

inside; to the inside

SEE: (לְ)גָיו

מִלְּגָיו

מִבִּפְנִים

from the inside; from within

SEE: (מִלְ)גָיו

לְגַמְרֵי לַחֲלוּטִין

completely; absolutely

נָפְקָא לַהּ מֵרְשׁוּת אָדוֹן לְגַמְרֵי. (קידושין ד,א)

She leaves the authority of [the] master completely.

לְדִידִי לְדַעְתִּי; לִי עַצְמִי

according to my [opinion]; to me [personally]; to me myself

See the next three entries for examples.

SEE: דִּידִי

לְדִידִי ... אֶלָּא לְדִידְכוּ אודו לִי מִיהָא/מִיהַת דְּ-

לְדַעְתִּי ...; אֶלָּא לְדַעְתְּכֶם, הוֹדוּ לִי מִכָּל מָקוֹם שֶׁ-...

According to my [opinion] (the halakha is ...); but according to your opinion, you should at least agree with me that ...

This *resolution* of a difficulty with regard to a tanna's halakhic statement is sometimes achieved through the *reinterpretation* of the statement, as follows: In formulating his halakha, the tanna took into account his opponents' view only for the sake of argument and stated a halakha that he expects his opponents would concede. In reality, however, this tanna rejects his opponents' opinion entirely.

אָמַר ר׳ יְהוּדָה: ... בֵּיצָה שֶׁנּוֹלְדָה בָּרִאשׁוֹן תֵּאָכֵל בַּשֵּׁנִי .... רָבִינָא אָמַר: ר׳ יְהוּדָה לְדִבְרֵיהֶם דְּרַבָּנַן קָאָמַר לְהוּ: לְדִידִי, אֲפִילּוּ בָּרִאשׁוֹן נַמִי שַׁרְיָא ..., אֶלָּא לְדִידְכוּ, אוֹדוּ לִי מִיהַת דְּבַשֵּׁנִי שַׁרְיָא ...! (ביצה ג, סע״א-רע״ב)

*R. Y*e*huda said: ... An egg laid on the first [day of Rosh HaShana] may be eaten on the second [day] .... (This statement is difficult, because it contradicts another statement of R. Y*e*huda that permits the egg on the first day.) Rabina said: R. Y*e*huda was speaking to the Ḥakhamim according to their point of view (which holds that such an egg may not be eaten, as if to say): According to my [opinion], the egg is permitted even on the first day too ..., but, according to your opinion, you should at least agree with me that it is permitted on the second day!*

לְדִידִי חֲזִי לִי

״לִי עַצְמִי נִרְאָה״; אֲנִי בְּעַצְמִי רָאִיתִי (בְּמוֹ עֵינַי)

I myself saw (with my own eyes)

לְדִידִי חֲזִי לִי ״זָבַת חָלָב וּדְבַשׁ״ דְּכָל אַרְעָא דְיִשְׂרָאֵל. (מגילה ו,א ורש״י שם)

I myself saw "the flow of milk and honey" of all of Eretz Yisrael (with my own eyes).

לְדִידִי מִיפָּרְשָׁא לִי מִינֵּיהּ דְּר׳ ...

לִי עַצְמִי מְפֹרֶשֶׁת מֵר׳ ...

to me [personally], it was explicitly stated by R. ...

With this expression, an amora presents a *version* of the halakha under discussion, in the name of a recognized authority. The amora emphasizes that this version is the correct one, because he himself heard that authority state it explicitly.

For an example — see:

ר׳ יצחק בר נחמני בשם ר׳ יהושע בן לוי (ברכות לד, רע״ב)

לַהּ

to/for her; to/for it (f.) — (1) לָהּ

her/it (f.) — (2) אוֹתָהּ

SEE: -ל and its notes

לַהֲדֵי/לְבַהֲדֵי

מוּל; בְּ-

against; at

אוֹקִי תְּרֵי לַהֲדֵי תְרֵי! (כתובות ב,א)

Set two against two!

SEE: בַּהֲדֵי

לְהֶדְיָא

בְּגָלוּי; יְשִׁירוֹת; מִיָּד

openly; directly; immediately

לָאו אוֹרַח אַרְעָא לְמֵיעַל לְהֶדְיָא. (יומא נא, סע״ב - נב, רע״א)

It is not proper to go directly.

SEE: בְּהֶדְיָא

לַהְדַר/לִיהְדַּר/נַהְדַּר/נִיהְדַּר fut. (הדר אַפְעֵל)

יַחֲזִיר; נַחֲזִיר

let him give back; let us give back

לֵיזִיל לַהְדַּר לִי פֵּירֵי דְמִן הַהוּא יוֹמָא עַד הָאִידָּנָא! (כתובות קד,ב)

Let him go and give me back the produce from that day until now!

SEE: הֲדַר

לְהוּ/לְהוֹן

to them; for them — (1) לָהֶם

them — (2) אוֹתָם

SEE: -ל and its notes

לְהוֹדִיעֲךָ כֹּחוֹ דְּ-

SEE: (לְ)הוֹדִיעֲךָ כחו ד-

לְהַלָּן

there; elsewhere (in the Biblical text)

From the perspective of the Talmud or Midrash, this word refers to a pasuk other than the one currently under discussion (either earlier or later in Scripture).

נֶאֱמַר כָּאן: ״יָקוּם עַל שֵׁם אָחִיו״, וְנֶאֱמַר לְהַלָּן: ״עַל שֵׁם אֲחֵיהֶם יִקָּרְאוּ בְּנַחֲלָתָם״. (יבמות כד,א ע״פ דברים כה:ו ובראשית מח:ו)

Here (in דברים*) it is stated: "He shall succeed in the name of his (dead) brother," and there (in* בראשית*) it is stated: "They shall be called after the name of their brothers with respect to inheritance."*

לוֹג* (pl. לוגין)

log

This measure of volume is equal to the contents of six eggs.

* This measure is also used in ויקרא יד:י. See the table of weights and measurements in Appendix II.

לוֹמַר inf. (אמר)

to say

SEE: אֲמַר, תַּלְמוּד לוֹמַר, כְּלוֹמַר

לוֹקֶה* act. prt. (לקי)

afflicted; punished by flogging

וְאֵלּוּ הֵן הַלּוֹקִין (מכות יג,א: משנה פ״ג מ״א)

and these are [the wrongdoers] who are punished by flogging

* This participle has a passive meaning, even though its form is active. An active meaning — *flogging, inflicting lashes* — is expressed by the active participle of the הִפְעִיל, מַלְקֶה.

SEE: לָקֵי, the Aramaic parallel

לוֹקִים/נוֹקִים fut. (קום אַפְעֵל) יְעַמִּיד; נַעֲמִיד

let him establish; let us establish

For an example — see the next entry.

וְלוֹקְמַהּ/וְלוֹקְמָא בְּ- וְיַעֲמִיד אוֹתָהּ בְּ-...!

But let him establish it (= explain the text) with reference to ...!

וְלוֹקְמַהּ בְּגַזְלָן! (בבא בתרא מד, רע"א)

But let him establish it (= the halakha in the baraitha) with reference to [the case of] a robber!

SEE: אוקים

לְחוּד* לְבַד; בִּפְנֵי עַצְמוֹ **alone; separate**

זְמַן תְּפִלָּה לְחוּד, וּזְמַן תּוֹרָה לְחוּד. (שבת י,א)

There is a separate time for prayer and a separate time for Torah study.

This word is also used with personal-pronoun suffixes:

by himself; by itself (m.)	לְבַדּוֹ	לְחוּדֵיהּ
by herself; by itself (f.)	לְבַדָּהּ	לְחוּדָהּ
by themselves	לְבַדָּם	לְחוּדַיְיהוּ

הָאי לְחוּדֵיהּ קָאֵי, וְהָאי לְחוּדֵיהּ קָאֵי. (סנהדרין פח, סע"ב ועוד)

This one stands by itself, and that one stands by itself.

* This word is popularly pronounced לְחוּד.

לְחַיֵּי "לְחַיִּים"; טוֹב וְיָפֶה

[it is] good; [it is] right; very well

בִּשְׁלָמָא כּוּלְּהוּ — לְחַיֵּי, אֶלָּא "שֶׁלֹּא יְהֵא הִילּוּכְךָ שֶׁל שַׁבָּת כְּהִילּוּכְךָ שֶׁל חוֹל" — מַאי הִיא? (שבת קיג, רע"ב)

Granted all the other [regulations] — very well, but what is [meant by] "that your walking on the Sabbath shall not be like your walking on weekdays"?!

SEE: בִּשְׁלָמָא ... שַׁפִּיר

וְלִטְעֲמִיךְ SEE: (וְלִ)טַעֲמִיךְ

לִיבָּא לֵב **heart; opinion***

הַקָּדוֹשׁ בָּרוּךְ הוּא לִיבָּא בָּעֵי. (סנהדרין קו,ב)

The Holy One Blessed Be He requires the heart.

* Since the heart is regarded as the seat of a person's innermost feelings, inclinations, and thoughts — לִיבָּא has a secondary meaning, *opinion*, mostly in the expression אַלִּיבָּא ד-, *according to the opinion of.*

לִיבְעֵי fut. (בעי) יְהֵא צָרִיךְ; יִצְטָרֵךְ

let him/it require; it should require

לִיבְעֵי שִׁבְעִים וְחַד! (סנהדרין יג, סע"ב).

Let [ordination] require seventy-one [judges]!

SEE: בְּעָא

לִיבְעֵי רַחֲמֵי יְבַקֵּשׁ רַחֲמִים!

"let him seek mercy!" let him pray! he should pray (to God for help)

For an example — see ברכות נה,ב.

לִיגְמַר/לִיגְמוֹר/נִיגְמַר fut. (גמר) יִלְמַד; נִלְמַד

let him learn; let him derive; let us derive

SEE: גְּמַר

וְלִיגְמַר מִינַּהּ

And let us derive from it! וְנִלְמַד מִמֶּנָּה!

This expression is used to raise a *difficulty* that can be paraphrased as follows: Why not regard this case as a prototype and apply its halakha to other cases as well by analogy?!

ברייתא: אם הָיָה כהן והיא בבית הַקְּבָרוֹת או שֶׁהָיָה זָקֵן וְאֵינָהּ לְפִי כְבוֹדוֹ ... לְכָךְ נֶאֱמַר: "וְהִתְעַלַּמְתָּ".

תלמוד: וְלִיגְמַר מִינַּהּ?! (ברכות יט, סע"ב ע"פ דברים כב:א)

BARAITHA: If he was a kohen and it (= a lost article) was in a cemetery, or if he was an elder and [handling] it was not in keeping with his dignity ... for such [situations] it is stated (in the Torah): "And you may hide yourself (and evade the duty of returning the lost article to its owner)."

TALMUD: And let us derive from it (= the baraitha, that human dignity takes precedence over any mitzva in the Torah — a conclusion that is unacceptable)?!

לֵיהּ

to him/it (m.); for him/it	(1) לוֹ
him/it (m.)	(2) אוֹתוֹ

SEE: -לְ and its notes

לֶיהְדַּר/נֶיהְדַּר fut. (הדר)

let him/it go back יַחֲזֹר

וְלֶיהְדַּר וְלִיגְבָּה נִיהֲלֵיהּ! (כתובות קי,א)

And let him go back and collect it for him!

SEE: הֲדַר

לֶיהְדַּר SEE: לַהֲדַר

לֶיהֱוֵי*/נֶיהֱוֵי fut. (הוי: לֶיהֱווּ/נֶיהֱווּ pl.)

let him/it be; it should be יְהֵא; יִהְיֶה

אִי לָא אָתֵינָא עַד תְּלָתִין יוֹמִין, לֶיהֱוֵי גִּיטָּא! (גיטין ל, רע"א)

If I do not arrive within thirty days, let [this] be a (valid) bill of divorce!

* This word is sometimes used in Modern Hebrew in the expression לֶהֱוֵי יָדוּעַ, *let it be known.*

SEE: הֲוָה

לֵיזִיל fut. (אזל) יֵלֵךְ **let him go**

For an example — see לַהֲדַר.

SEE: נֵיזִיל, אֲזַל

לֵיחוּשׁ/נֵיחוּשׁ fut. (חשש) יַחֲשֹׁשׁ; נַחֲשֹׁשׁ

let him suspect; let him be concerned; let him take (the possibility) into account; let us suspect / be concerned / take into account

וְלֵיחוּשׁ דִּילְמָא לָאו אָבִיו הוּא! (חולין יא, רע"ב)

But let us suspect that he is not his father!

SEE: חָשׁ

לֵיחֱזֵי/נֵיחֱזֵי fut. (חזי) יִרְאֶה; נִרְאֶה

let him see; let us see; let's investigate

וְלֵיחֱזֵי הֵיכִי נָהֲגִי! (בבא מציעא פג, רע"ב)

But let's see how [people] conduct themselves!

SEE: חֲזָא

לִיחַיֵּיב/נִיחַיֵּיב prt. (= לִתְחַיֵּיב) (חוב אִתְפָּעַל)

יִתְחַיֵּיב; יְהֵא חַיָּיב; נִתְחַיֵּיב

let him be responsible; let him be obligated; let us be responsible; let us be obligated

וּבְדִינֵי שָׁמַיִם נָמֵי לָא לִיחַיֵּיב! (בבא קמא נו,א)

And let him also not be responsible according to the Heavenly judgment!

SEE: אִיחַיֵּיב

לִיחְשׁוֹב/נִיחְשׁוֹב/נַחְשׁוֹב fut. (חשב)

let him consider; יַחֲשֹׁב; יִמְנֶה; יְפָרֵט

let him enumerate; let him specify

אַטּוּ תַּנָּא כִּי רוֹכְלָא לִיחְשׁוֹב וְלֵיזִיל?! (גיטין לג, רע"א וש"נ)

Should a tanna go on and enumerate (every detail) like a peddler (selling his wares)?!

SEE: חָשֵׁיב

לִיטַמֵּא/לִיטַמֵּי fut. (טמא פַּעֵל)

let it impart ritual uncleanliness יְטַמֵּא

let it impart ritual uncleanliness to a person or to clothes! אָדָם וּבְגָדִים לִיטַמֵּא! (נדה לג,א)

לִיטַּמֵּא/לִיטַּמֵּי fut. (= לִתְטַמֵּי) (טמא אִתְפָּעַל)

let it become ritually unclean יִטָּמֵא

לָא לִיטַּמְּאוּ מִגַּבָּן! (שבת טז, רע"א)

let [the vessels] not become ritually unclean through [an unclean object touching them on] their backs!

SEE: אִיטַּמֵּי

וְלִיטְעֲמֵיךְ SEE: (וְלִ)טְעָמֵיךְ

לִיטְרָא* (pl. לִיטְרִין) **a pound (approximately)**

לִיטְרָא זָהָב יֵשׁ לִי בְּיָדְךָ. (שבועות לח,ב: משנה פ"ו מ"ג)

I have a pound of gold in your possession.

* The Latin equivalent is *libra*, whose abbreviation *lb.* represents *pound* in English.

לָיֵיט prt. (לוט)

"cursing"; condemning; denouncing מְקַלֵּל

אֵין תַּלְמִיד חָכָם רַשַּׁאי לַעֲמוֹד מִפְּנֵי רַבּוֹ בְּשָׁעָה שֶׁעוֹסֵק בַּתּוֹרָה. לָיֵיט עֲלָהּ אַבָּיֵי. (קידושין לג, סע"ב וש"נ)

"A Torah scholar is not permitted to rise before his teacher while he (himself) is engaged in Torah study." Abbayé denounces it (= that teaching).

לַיְיתֵי/לֵיתֵי/נַיְיתֵי/נֵיתֵי fut. (אתא אַפְעֵל)

let him bring יָבִיא

לִטְרַח לֹוֶה וְלַיְיתֵי! (בבא מציעא לה, רע"א)

Let the borrower take the trouble and bring [it]!

SEE: אַיְתִי, לֵיתִי

לֵיכָּא (= לָא+אִיכָּא) אֵין כָּאן; אֵין

it is not; there is not; there is none

וְלֵיכָּא

but it is not; but there is not וְאֵין

This expression is often used to indicate that a halakhic requirement has not been fulfilled.

יָבֵשׁ — "הָדָר" בָּעֵינַן, וְלֵיכָּא (סוכה כט, סע"ב ע"פ ויקרא כג:מ)

a withered (palm branch is not suitable to be used as one of the four species on Sukkoth) — [because] we require a "goodly" one, but it is not

לֵיכָּא ל- אֵין ל- ; אִי אֶפְשָׁר ל-

"there is no [basis] to"; it is impossible to; one cannot

אֶלָּא מֵהָא לֵיכָּא לְמִשְׁמַע מִינַּהּ. (מגילה כב,א ועוד)

But from this [text] one cannot derive [a definitive conclusion].

SEE: אֶלָּא מֵהָא לֵיכָּא לְמִשְׁמַע מִינַּהּ, לֵית

לֵיכוֹל/נֵיכוֹל prt. (אכל) יֹאכַל **let him eat**

כָּל מַאן דִּצְרִיךְ לֵיתֵי וְלֵיכוֹל! (תענית כ, סע"ב)

Let whoever is in need come and eat!

SEE: (לְ)מֵיכַל

לִיכְתּוֹב SEE: לִכְתּוֹב

לֵילַף/נֵילַף fut. (ילף)

let him derive; let us derive יִלְמַד; נִלְמַד

אִי יָלֵיף, לֵילַף כּוּלָּהּ מֵהָתָם! (סנהדרין יד, סע"א)

If he is deriving (the quality of the judges from that pasuk), let him derive everything (including the number of judges) from there!

SEE: יְלַף

לֵימָא/נֵימָא* fut. (אמר)

let him/us say; shall we say יֹאמַר; נֹאמַר

Both לֵימָא and נֵימָא, which are used interchangeably here and in the next six entries as well, introduce a proposal that is ultimately rejected in the course of the Talmudic discussion.*

לֵימָא קְרָא "זְמַן"! (מגילה ב,א ע"פ אסתר ט:לא)

let the pasuk state "time"!

לֵימָא מַתְנִיתִין דְּלָא כְּר' יוֹסֵי? (בבא מציעא ג, רע"א ועוד)

Shall we say [that] our mishna is not in agreement with [the opinion of the tanna] R. Yosé?

לֵימָא תֶּהֱוֵי תְּיוּבְתֵּיהּ דְּר' אַמִי? (תענית יד, רע"ב ועוד)
Shall we say [that] it (= the baraitha or mishna that was just quoted in the Talmud) will constitute a refutation of [the opinion of the amora] R. Ammi?

לֵימָא תְּנַן סְתָמָא כְּר' יוֹסֵי? (שבת מז,ב ועוד)
Shall we say [that] we have taught an anonymous mishna in accordance with [the opinion of the tanna] R. Yosé (and, by implication, against the opinion of his opponent)?

* See: פסחים כא,א תוס' ד"ה "לֵימָא"

SEE: אַמַר and the next six entries.

לֵימָא בְּהָא קָמִיפַּלְגִי
נֹאמַר בְּזֹאת הֵם נֶחֱלָקִים ...?

Shall we say they disagree about this ...?

This formula proposes that the two amoraim or tannaim, whose controversy has just been quoted, really differ about an issue that is more fundamental or more general than we might have thought. Subsequently, this interpretation of the controversy is rejected.

משנה: הַנּוֹדֵר מִן הַמְבוּשָּׁל מוּתָּר בִּצְלִי ... (נדרים מט, רע"א: משנה פ"ו מ"א)
ברייתא: ר' יֹאשִׁיָּה אוֹסֵר. (בבלי שם)
תלמוד: לֵימָא בְּהָא קָמִיפַּלְגִי — דְּר' יֹאשִׁיָּה סָבַר: הַלֵּךְ אַחַר לְשׁוֹן תּוֹרָה, וְתַנָּא דִּילַן סָבַר: בִּנְדָרִים הַלֵּךְ אַחַר לְשׁוֹן בְּנֵי אָדָם?
MISHNA: One who vows [not to eat] what is cooked is permitted [to ... eat what is] roasted ...
BARAITHA: R. Yoshiyya prohibits.
TALMUD: Shall we say they disagree about this — that R. Yoshiyya holds: Follow Biblical language, while our tanna holds: In vows, follow the language of people (= the vernacular)?

SEE: קָמִיפַּלְגִי (which is popularly pronounced קָמִיפְלְגִי)

לֵימָא בִּפְלוּגְתָּא דְּר' ... וְר' ... קָמִיפַּלְגִי
נֹאמַר בְּמַחֲלוֹקֶת בֵּין ר' ... לְבֵין ר' ... חֲלוּקִין?

Shall we say [that] they disagree about [the same issue that is the subject of] the controversy between R. ... and R. ...?

This formula equates a *controversy* between tannaim or between amoraim with another tannaitic *controversy*. Subsequently, this equation is rejected.

לֵימָא רַב וְרַבָּה בַּר בַּר חַנָּה בִּפְלוּגְתָּא דְבֵית שַׁמַּאי וּבֵית הִלֵּל קָמִיפַּלְגִי? (סוכה נו,א)
Shall we say [that] Rav and Rabba, the grandson of Ḥanna, disagree about [the same issue that is the subject of] the controversy between Beth Shammai and Beth Ḥillel?

SEE: קָמִיפַּלְגִי, לֵימָא כְּתַנָּאֵי (popularly pronounced קָמִיפְלְגִי)

לֵימָא כְּתַנָּאֵי* נֹאמַר כְּתַנָּאִים?

Shall we say [that the controversy between the amoraim] is equivalent to [the controversy between these] tannaim?

This expression introduces a baraitha that presents a controversy between two tannaim. It is then argued that this early controversy in the baraitha seems to anticipate a later controversy between two amoraim, which was quoted previously in the Talmud. Such a state of affairs is somewhat disturbing, because if the two controversies are indeed the same, why did the two amoraim present their respective halakhoth as their own independent opinions and fail to acknowledge their respective dependence upon the rulings of the earlier tannaitic authorities? Subsequently, this proposal is rejected, and it is shown that there may be a substantive distinction between the two controversies.

אַמַר שְׁמוּאֵל: שְׁנַיִם שֶׁדָּנוּ — דִּינֵיהֶם דִּין. (סנהדרין ה, סע"ב) אַמַר ר' אַבָּהוּ: שְׁנַיִם שֶׁדָּנוּ דִּינֵי מָמוֹנוֹת — לְדִבְרֵי הַכֹּל, אֵין דִּינֵיהֶן דִּין. לֵימָא כְּתַנָּאֵי? בִּיצוּעַ בִּשְׁלֹשָׁה — דִּבְרֵי ר' מֵאִיר, וַחֲכָמִים אוֹמְרִים: פְּשָׁרָה בְּיָחִיד. (שם ו,א)
*Sh*ᵉ*muel said: [If] two [judges] judged [a case], their judgment is valid ... R. Abbahu said: [If] two judged monetary cases — according to everybody (= all tannaim), their judgment is not valid ... Shall we say [that the controversy between these amoraim] is equivalent to [the following controversy between these] tannaim? Arbitration (which is assumed to be like any other monetary judgment) is by three — [according to] the opinion of R. Méir (like R. Abbahu who said two are not sufficient), but the Ḥakhamim say: Arbitration is by one (and thus two are surely sufficient, like Sh*ᵉ*muel).*

* A proposal of this nature that is eventually accepted in the Talmud is introduced by the word כְּתַנָּאֵי without לֵימָא.

SEE: (כְּ)תַנָּאֵי, לֵימָא בִּפְלוּגְתָּא דְּר' ... וְר' ... קָמִיפַּלְגִי

לֵימָא מְסַיְּעָא* לֵיהּ נֹאמַר מְסַיַּעַת לוֹ?

Shall we say [that the following baraitha or mishna] supports him?

This expression introduces a *proof* from a baraitha or a mishna in support of an amora's halakha. The proof is subsequently rejected.**

אַמַר ר' אַמִי: בִּדְלֵיקָה הִתִּירוּ לוֹמַר: "כָּל הַמְכַבֶּה אֵינוֹ מַפְסִיד". נֵימָא מְסַיַּיע לֵיהּ: נָכְרִי שֶׁבָּא לְכַבּוֹת — אֵין אוֹמְרִים לוֹ: "כַּבֵּה" וְ"אַל תְּכַבֶּה" ...? "כַּבֵּה" הוּא דְלָא אָמְרִינַן לֵיהּ — הָא "כָּל הַמְכַבֶּה אֵינוֹ מַפְסִיד" אָמְרִינַן לֵיהּ! (שבת קכא,א ע"פ המשנה)
R. Ammi said: In [the case of] a blaze [on the Sabbath], [the halakhic authorities] have permitted one to announce: "Whoever extinguishes [it] will not lose." Shall we say [that the following mishna] supports him: [If] a non-Jew comes to extinguish [a fire] — we say to him neither "extinguish!" nor "don't extinguish!" ...? "Extinguish" is what we may not say to him — but "whoever extinguishes will not lose" we may say to him!

* The feminine מְסַיְּיעָא is probably the correct form, since a mishna or a baraitha is taken as feminine. Nevertheless, מסייע — without the final א — occurs frequently.
** A proof from a baraitha that is accepted is introduced by מְסַיְּיעָא לֵיהּ לר׳ ... or ,תַּנְיָא דִּמְסַיְּיעָא לָךְ ,תַּנְיָא נַמִּי הָכִי.

לֵימָא קְרָא

let the pasuk state ...! יֹאמַר הַכָּתוּב ...!

This expression presents an *argument* that is based upon the wording of a pasuk.

אָמַר קְרָא: ״לְקַיֵּים אֶת יְמֵי הַפּוּרִים הָאֵלֶּה בִּזְמַנֵּיהֶם״ — זְמַנִּים הַרְבֵּה תִּיקְּנוּ לָהֶם. הַאי מִיבְּעֵי לֵיהּ לְגוּפֵיהּ! אִם כֵּן, לֵימָא קְרָא ״זְמַן״! מַאי ״זְמַנֵּיהֶם״? זְמַנִּים טוּבָא. (מגילה ב,א ע״פ אסתר ט:לא)

The pasuk has stated: "To confirm the days of Purim in their times" [indicating that] they instituted many times for them (to read the scroll of Esther). (But) isn't [this] text needed for its literal meaning! If [that were] so, let the pasuk state "[at the] time"! What [is the implication of] "their times"? Several times (= Esther may be read on one of several dates).

לֵימָא תֶּיהֱוֵי תְּיוּבְתֵּיהּ דר׳ ...

נֹאמַר תִּהְיֶה תְּשׁוּבָה עַל שֶׁל ר׳ ...?

Shall we say [that] there will be a refutation of [the halakhic opinion of] R. ...?

This expression introduces a *refutation* of the opinion of an amora. The refutation is subsequently rejected.

לֵימָא תֶּיהֱוֵי תְּיוּבְתֵּיהּ דְּרַב הוּנָא בְּתַרְתֵּי? (סוכה ד,ב וש״נ בגליון הש״ס)

Shall we say [that] there will be a refutation of [the halakhic opinion of] Rav Huna with respect to two [points]?

SEE: תְּיוּבְתָּא

לֵיסְטִים

See the next entry.

לֵיסְטִיס* (לִיסְטִים/לִיסְטִין .pl)

robber שׁוֹדֵד

לִיסְטִיס מְזוּיָין — כֵּיוָן דְּמִיטַּמַּר מֵאֱינָשֵׁי — גַּנָּב הוּא. (בבא קמא נז, סע״א ע״פ כת״י)

An armed robber — since he hides himself from the public — is [considered] a thief, (and he must pay double for the stolen object).

הוֹצִיאוּהָ לִיסְטִים — לִיסְטִים חַיָּיבִין. (ב״ק נה, רע״ב: פ״ו מ״א)

[If] the robbers let it (= the animal) out, the robbers are liable.

* In manuscripts and early printed editions, the singular is spelled לִיסְטִיס — corresponding to the Greek form *lestes* — and the plural is לִיסְטִים. In current editions, לִיסְטִים is used in both the singular and the plural.

לֶיעֱבִיד/לֵיעֱבֵד/לֶעֱבִיד/נֶעֱבִיד fut. (עבד)

let him do; let him act יַעֲשֶׂה

אִי כְּר׳ יְהוּדָה סְבִירָא לֵיהּ, לֶיעֱבֵד כְּר׳ יְהוּדָה! (שבת מו,א)

If he holds like [the opinion of] R. Yehuda, let him act in accordance with R. Yehuda!

SEE: עֲבַד

לֵיעוּל/נֵיעוּל fut. (עלל)

let him come; let him enter יָבֹא; יִכָּנֵס

דִּינָא הוּא דְּרַבָּה בַּר הוּנָא לֵיעוּל בְּרֵישָׁא. (מועד קטן כה, רע״ב)

It is proper that Rabba b. Huna should come first.

SEE: עַל

לִיעָרְבִינְהוּ וְלִיתְנִינְהוּ יְעָרְבֵם וְיִשְׁנֵם!

let him combine them and teach them!

A *difficulty*: Why did the tanna list the two cases or items separately, if there is no distinction between them? He should have presented one unified formulation.

ברייתא: שְׁנַיִם שֶׁהָיוּ מוֹשְׁכִין בְּגָמָל וּמַנְהִיגִין בַּחֲמוֹר ... קָנוּ ... (בבא מציעא ח, סע״ב)

תלמוד: ... אִי הָכִי, לִיעָרְבִינְהוּ וְלִתְנִינְהוּ: שְׁנַיִם שֶׁהָיוּ מוֹשְׁכִין וּמַנְהִיגִין בֵּין בְּגָמָל בֵּין בַּחֲמוֹר ... (שם ט, רע״א)

BARAITHA: [If] two [people] were pulling a camel or leading a donkey ... they acquired the animal through these actions] ...

TALMUD: ... If so [= if there is really no distinction between the methods of acquiring a camel and a donkey], let [the tanna] combine [the two clauses] and teach them [thus]: [If] two were pulling or leading a camel or a donkey ...

לִיפְטַר/נִיפְטַר fut. (פטר) יִפְטֹר; נִפְטֹר

let him/us free; let him/us absolve

יַיִן נַמִּי — נִפְטְרֵיהּ פַּת! (ברכות מא, סע״ב)

*[As for] wine too — let [the b^e^rakha over] bread absolve it (from its own b^e^rakha when it is drunk during a meal)!**

* The accepted halakha is that wine always requires its separate b^e^rakha.

SEE: פְּטַר; פָּטוּר

לִיפְטַר/נִיפְטַר (= לִתְפְּטַר) fut. (פטר אִתְפְּעַל)

let him be exempt יִפָּטֵר; יְהֵא פָּטוּר

הַאי דְּקָאָמַר: ״חֶצְיָהּ שֶׁלִּי״ — לֶהֱוֵי כְּמֵשִׁיב אֲבֵידָה וְלִיפָּטַר! (בבא מציעא ח, סע״א)

[As for] the one who says: "Half of it is mine" — let him be [regarded] as one returning a lost article, and let him be exempt (from taking an oath)!

SEE: אִיפְּטַר

לִיפְלוֹג/נִיפְלוֹג fut. (פלג: לִיפְלְגוּ/לִיפְלְגֵי .pl)

let him disagree; let him argue (1) יַחֲלֹק

וְלִיפְלוֹג נַמִּי ר׳ יוֹסֵי בְּהָא! (שבת לט,א)

But let R. Yosé disagree about this, too!

let him distinguish; let him formulate a distinction (2) יַחֲלֹק; יַבְחִין

For an example — see אַדְּתָנֵי ... לִפְלוֹג וְלִיתְנֵי בְּדִידָהּ.

(3) **יַחֲלֹק; יְחַלֵּק; נַחֲלֹק**
let him/us divide; let him/us share
לִיפְלוֹג לִי נַמִּי מִפַּרְדֵּיסֵי וּבוּסְתָּנֵי דִּשְׁתַל! (ב"מ לט, סע"ב)
Let him also share with me the vineyards and gardens that he planted!
SEE: פְּלִיג, אַדְּתָנֵי ... לִפְלוֹג וְלִיתְנֵי בְּדִידֵהּ, פְּלַג

לִיקוּם/לִיקוּ/נֵיקוּם fut. (קום)

let him/it stand; let him get up; let us stand; let us get up **יַעֲמֹד; נַעֲמֹד**
וְאַשִּׁינוּיֵי לִיקוּ וְלִיסְמוֹךְ?! (יבמות צא, סע"ב)
וְאַשִּׁנוּיֵי נֵיקוּם וְלִסְמוֹךְ?! (בבא בתרא קלה,א)
Should we get up and rely upon [forced] explanations?!
SEE: תֵּיקוּ, קָם

לִיקְנֵי/נִיקְנֵי fut. (קני)

let him acquire; let us acquire **יִקְנֶה; נִקְנֶה**
אִי בְּכַסְפָּא, לִיקְנֵי בְּכַסְפָּא! (בבא קמא נא, סע"ב)
If money [was paid], let him acquire [the property] through the money!
SEE: קָנֵי

לִישַׁיְּילֵיהּ fut. (לִישַׁיֵּיל+ֵיהּ) (שאל פָּעֵל)

let him ask him **יִשְׁאַל אוֹתוֹ**
לִישַׁיְּילֵיהּ לְסַפְרָא כַּמָּה כְּתִיב ...! (עבודה זרה ט,א)
let him ask him — the scribe — what number (of years) is written (in official documents) ...!
SEE: שְׁאֵיל

לִישְׁמְעִינַן

SEE: לַשְׁמְעִינַן

לִישָּׁנָא (pl. לִישָּׁנֵי) לָשׁוֹן

(1) tongue; language; expression
מַאי מַשְׁמַע דְּהַאי "עוֹבֵר" לִישָּׁנָא דְּאַקְדּוֹמֵי הוּא? (פסחים ז,ב)
What teaches that this [word] עוֹבֵר *is an expression indicating priority?*

(2) version; reported tradition
For examples, see the next entry and לִישָּׁנָא קַמָּא.

לִישָּׁנָא אַחֲרִינָא לָשׁוֹן אַחֵר

another version
This term introduces a different version of an amora's statement or a different report of a discussion among ḥakhamim.
סְבָרוּהָ: מַאי "מְחִיצָה"? גּוּדָּא ... לִישָּׁנָא אַחֲרִינָא אָמְרֵי לַהּ: סְבָרוּהָ: מַאי "מְחִיצָה"? פְּלוּגְתָּא. (ב"ב ב, סע"ב - ג, רע"א)
[Some scholars] understood it: What does מְחִיצָה *mean? "A wall" ... Some report it [in] another version: [Some scholars] understood it: What does* מְחִיצָה *mean? "A division."*

לִישָּׁנָא בִּישָׁא לָשׁוֹן הָרָע

slander; defamation
מַפִּיק לֵיהּ בְּלִישָּׁנָא בִּישָׁא, דְּאָמַר: הֵיכָא מִשְׁתְּכַח נוּרָא? אֶלָּא בֵּי פְלָנְיָא דְּאִיכָּא בִּשְׂרָא וְכַוְורֵי! (ערכין טו, סע"ב ע"פ שטמ"ק)
he expresses it with slander, for he says: Where is fire to be found? Only in the house of So-and-so where there is meat and fish (roasting all the time)!

לִישָּׁנָא בָּתְרָא הַלָּשׁוֹן הָאַחֲרוֹן

the last version
For an example, see לִישָּׁנָא קַמָּא.

לִישָּׁנָא מְעַלְּיָא לָשׁוֹן מְעֻלָּה; לָשׁוֹן נְקִיָּה

proper language; euphemism
"עוֹשֶׂה שָׁלוֹם וּבוֹרֵא רָע" — מִי קָא אָמְרִינַן כְּדִכְתִיב? אֶלָּא כְּתִיב "רָע", וְקָרֵינַן "הַכֹּל" לִישָּׁנָא מְעַלְּיָא. (ברכות יא, רע"ב ע"פ ישעיהו מה:ז)
"He makes peace and creates evil" — do we read [it in our morning prayers] as it is written? Rather "evil" is written, but we read "[and creates] everything" [as] a euphemism.
For further examples — see יבמות יא,ב וש"נ.

לִישָּׁנָא קַמָּא הַלָּשׁוֹן הָרִאשׁוֹן

the first version
לְלִישָּׁנָא קַמָּא דְּרַב פָּפָּא וַדַּאי לָא תֶּיהֱוֵי תְּיוּבְתָּא; לְלִישָּׁנָא בָּתְרָא לֵימָא תֶּיהֱוֵי תְּיוּבְתָּא? (בבא מציעא לד,א)
With regard to the first version of [the halakha of] Rav Pappa, there would certainly be no refutation; with regard to the last version, shall we say that there will be a refutation?

לִישַׁנֵּי* fut. (שני פָּעֵל) יְתָרֵץ

let him answer
וְלִיטַעְמֵיךְ, לִישַׁנֵּי לֵיהּ הָדֵין! (יבמות מח,ב)
But according to your position, let him (= R. Akiva) answer him [with] that [reply]!
* Do not confuse with לִישָּׁנֵי, the plural of the noun לִישָּׁנָא, *language* or *version*.
SEE: שַׁנֵּי

לִישְׁקוֹל/לִשְׁקוֹל*/נִישְׁקוֹל/נִשְׁקַל fut. (שקל)

let him take **יִטֹּל; יִקַּח**
לִישְׁקוֹל דְּמֵי וְלִיהְדַר! (כתובות פד,א)
Let him take the money and return [it]!
* Do not confuse with לִשְׁקוֹל, *to weigh*, the infinitive of the Hebrew verb שָׁקַל.

לִישְׁתּוֹק/לִשְׁתּוֹק* fut. (שתק)

let him/it be silent **יִשְׁתֹּק**
* Do not confuse with לִשְׁתּוֹק, *to be silent*, the infinitive of the Hebrew verb שָׁתַק.
SEE: אִישְׁתִּיק and the next entry.

לִישְׁתּוֹק קְרָא מִינֵּיהּ יִשְׁתֹּק הַפָּסוּק מִמֶּנּוּ!

Let Scripture be silent about it!
Let the pasuk omit it!
This expression presents an *argument* based upon an apparent redundancy in Scripture.
לִישְׁתּוֹק קְרָא מִינֵּיהּ, וַאֲנָא יָדַעְנָא דִּלְדוֹרוֹת הוּא! (בבא בתרא קכ, רע"ב ע"פ במדבר לו:ו)
Let the pasuk omit it (= this word), and I would have known that it (= the prohibition) is for [all] generations!
SEE: לִיכְתּוֹב ... וְלִישְׁתּוֹק

לית (= לָא+אִית) אֵין **is not; are not**

וְלֵית הִילְכְתָא כְּוָתֵיהּ. (ברכות כב,ב ועוד)

But the halakhic ruling is not like him.

Personal-pronoun suffixes are sometimes appended — just as they are appended to אית — producing the following forms:

לֵיתֵיהּ/לֵיתוֹהִי	אֵינוֹ	he/it (m.) is not
לֵיתָא/לֵיתָהּ	אֵינָהּ	she/it (f.) is not
לֵיתְנְהוּ	אֵינָם	they are not

לֵיתָא לְבָרַיְיתָא מִקַּמֵּי מַתְנִיתִין. (יבמות פג, רע"א)

The baraitha is not [authoritative] in the face of our mishna.

SEE: אית

לית בֵּיהּ (בָּהּ .f.s, בְּהוּ .m. pl) אֵין בּוֹ

"there is not in it"; it does not have; it does not contain

לֵית בֵּיהּ שָׁוֶה פְּרוּטָה (בבא מציעא כו,ב)

it does not have the value of a p'ruta (coin)

SEE: אית ביה

לית לֵיהּ (לַהּ .f.s, לְהוּ .m. pl) אֵין לוֹ

he does not have; he is not entitled to; he does not agree with

SEE: אית ליה

וְלֵית לֵיהּ ל-

But does he not agree with ...?! וְאֵין לוֹ ל-?!

This expression introduces a rhetorical question that points to a *contradiction* between the statement of a tanna or an amora — on the one hand — and a pasuk, a mishna, or an authoritative baraitha — on the other hand.

וְלֵית לֵיהּ לְרַבִּי מַתְנִיתִין "שְׁנַיִם אוֹחֲזִין ..."?! (בבא מציעא ז, סע"א ע"פ כת"י)

But does Rebbi not agree with our mishna: "[If] two are holding a garment ..."?!

לית לַן בַּהּ אֵין לָנוּ בָּהּ (אִיסוּר)

we have no [halakhic objection] to it

וּשְׁתִיָּה ... לָא אֲמַרַן אֶלָּא בְּחַמְרָא וְשִׁיכְרָא, אֲבָל מַיָּא — לֵית לַן בַּהּ. (פסחים קה,א ורש"י שם)

and [as for] drinking (before the recitation of Havdala) ... we have applied [the restriction] only to wine and beer — but [as for the drinking of] water, we have no [halakhic objection] to it.

SEE: לָא אֲמַרַן אֶלָּא ... אֲבָל ...

לֵיתָא/לֵיתָהּ אֵינָהּ

it (f.) is not; it has no substance/validity

SEE: לית, איתא

לֵיתִיב/נֵיתִיב[1] (יתב) .fut יֵשֵׁב **let him sit**

לֵיתִיב מָר אַכָּרִים וּכְסָתוֹת! (מועד קטן טז, סע"ב)

Let the master sit on cushions and bolsters!

לֵיתִיב/נֵיתִיב[2] .fut (נתב)

let him give; let us give יִתֵּן; נִתֵּן

כָּל דְּיָהִיב לֵיהּ — מ"מֵיטַב" לֵיתִיב לֵיהּ! (בבא קמא ז,ב ע"פ שמות כב:ד)

[Of] whatever [commodity] he gives him [as payment] — he must give him the best [quality]!

SEE: יְהַב and its note.

לֵיתֵיהּ/לֵיתוֹהִי אֵינוֹ

it (m.) is not; it has no substance/validity

SEE: לית, איתיה

לֵיתְנְהוּ אֵינָם **they are not; they have no substance/validity**

SEE: לית, איתנהו

לִיתְנֵי/נִיתְנֵי .fut (תני) יִשְׁנֶה; יְלַמֵּד

let him teach; let him state (in a mishna or baraitha)

מַאי שְׁנָא דְּתָנֵי דְעַרְבִית בְּרֵישָׁא?! לִתְנֵי דְשַׁחֲרִית בְּרֵישָׁא! (ברכות ב,א ע"פ הגהות הב"ח)

Why does [the tanna] state [the law] of the evening first?! Let him state [the law] of the morning first!

SEE: תְּנָא

לִכְאוֹרָה* בְּמַבָּט רִאשׁוֹן **at first glance; on the face of it; superficially**

לכאורה, כשמואל רָהֲטָא; כִּי מְעַיְּינַת בָּהּ, הִלְכְתָא כְּוָותֵיהּ דְּרַב. (כתובות נד, סע"א וע' רש"י שם)**

At first glance, [the mishna] goes according to Sh'muel; when you examine it carefully, [you will discover that] the halakha is in accordance with Rav.

* This word occurs only once in the Talmud, but it is often used in the commentaries and in Modern Hebrew. Its etymology is unclear. See the next note.

** In our editions of Rashi's commentary on this passage, he paraphrases לִכְאוֹרָה with פתאם, in the sense of *without thought*, as in פתאם כשור אל טבח יבא (משלי ז:כב). In a different version of Rashi, however, the word is explained as לְאָדָם כָּעוּר = לכעורה, *to a sloppy (or careless) person*. (שיטה מקובצת שם בשם רש"י שבמהדורא קמא)

לִכְתּוֹב/לִיכְתּוֹב/נִכְתּוֹב .fut (כתב)

let him/it write יִכְתֹּב

לִכְתּוֹב קְרָא; לִכְתּוֹב רַחֲמָנָא

יִכְתֹּב הַפָּסוּק/הָרַחְמָן ...! תִּכְתֹּב הַתּוֹרָה ...!

Let the pasuk write ...! Let the Merciful God write ...! Let the Torah write ...!

Both of these expressions present a *difficulty* or a *proof* based upon the wording of a pasuk.

משנה: בֵּית שַׁמַּאי אוֹמְרִים: שְׂאוֹר בִּכְזַיִת, וְחָמֵץ בְּכַכּוֹתֶבֶת. (ביצה ב, רע"א: משנה פ"א מ"א)

תלמוד: מַאי טַעְמַיְיהוּ דְבֵית שַׁמַּאי? אִם כֵּן, לִכְתּוֹב רַחֲמָנָא "חָמֵץ" וְלָא בָּעֵי "שְׂאוֹר"! ... שְׂאוֹר דִּכְתַב רַחֲמָנָא לָמָּה לִי? לוֹמַר לָךְ: שִׁיעוּרוֹ שֶׁל זֶה לֹא שִׁיעוּרוֹ שֶׁל זֶה (שם ז,ב ע"פ שמות יג:ז)

MISHNA: Beth Shammai says: [The minimum amount

of] leavening [that must be removed] is the size of an olive, but [the minimum amount of] ḥametz is the size of a date.

TALMUD: What is the reason of Beth Shammai? [Because] if so (= that the amounts be the same for both ḥametz and leavening), let the Torah write "ḥametz" and it would not need to write "leavening"! ... Why do I need [the word] "leavening" that the Torah wrote? To tell you: The minimum amount of one is not the minimum amount of the other.

לִכְתּוֹב/לִיכְתּוֹב ... וְלִישְׁתּוֹק יִכְתֹּב ... וְיִשְׁתֹּק!

Let [Scripture] write ... and be silent!

This formula presents an *argument* based upon an apparent redundancy in Scripture.

ר׳ שִׁמְעוֹן אָמַר לָךְ: מִכְּדִי בְּעָלְמָא דָּרְשִׁינַן טַעְמָא דִקְרָא, אִם כֵּן לִכְתּוֹב קְרָא: "לֹא יַרְבֶּה לּוֹ נָשִׁים" וְלִישְׁתּוֹק, וַאֲנָא אֲמִינָא: מָה טַעַם לֹא יַרְבֶּה? מִשּׁוּם דְּלֹא יָסוּר! "לֹא יָסוּר" לָמָּה לִי? אֲפִילּוּ אַחַת וּמְסִירָה אֶת לִבּוֹ — הֲרֵי זוֹ לֹא יִשָּׂאֶנָּה. (סנהדרין כא,א ע״פ דברים יז:יז)

R. Shim´on would say to you: Now that we interpret [halakha according to] the reason implied by the pasuk, then let the pasuk write: "He shall not take many wives" and be silent (and not state a reason), and I would say: For what reason should he not take many [wives]? Because [of the danger] that [his heart] might turn away! Why do I need the pasuk to state "[so that his heart] not turn away"? [To teach us that] he should not marry even one woman who would turn his heart away.

SEE: לִישְׁתּוֹק קְרָא מִינֵּיהּ

לְכַתְּחִילָּה/לְכַתְּחִלָּה

(1) at first; in the first place

יוֹצְאָה אִשָּׁה ... בְּכָל דָּבָר שֶׁתִּתֵּן לְתוֹךְ פִּיהָ, וּבִלְבַד שֶׁלֹּא תִתֵּן לְכַתְּחִלָּה בְּשַׁבָּת (שבת סד, רע״א: משנה פ״ו מ:ה)

a woman may go out (into a public domain on the Sabbath) with something in her mouth, provided that she not put [it into her mouth] in the first place on the Sabbath

(2) ideally; with full approval of Jewish law

This term *often* indicates a before-the-fact perspective towards an act, from which Jewish law either approves or disapproves of the act whose performance is being considered.

יֵשׁ קְשָׁרִין שֶׁאֵין חַיָּיבִין עֲלֵיהֶן.... וְיֵשׁ שֶׁמּוּתָּרִין לְכַתְּחִילָּה.... (שבת קיא, סע״ב—קיב, רע״א)

There are some knots for which one is not subject to punishment (for Sabbath desecration)..., and there are some [knots] that are permissible with full approval of Jewish law...

אִם נִתְגָּרְשָׁה, תִּינָּשֵׂא* - לְכַתְּחִלָּה. (גיטין עט,ב)

If [a woman] received a divorce [but she had been alone with her former husband after the bill of divorce had been written for her, but before she received it], she may (still) marry [someone else] – with full approval of Jewish law.

משנה: אַנְדְּרוֹגִינוֹס נוֹשֵׂא ... (יבמות פא,א: משנה פ״ח מ״ו)
תלמוד: "נוֹשֵׂא"** לְכַתְּחִלָּה מַשְׁמַע. (שם פב,ב)

MISHNA: A hermaphrodite may marry ...

TALMUD: [The participle] נוֹשֵׂא *indicates with full approval of Jewish law.*

* According to the Babylonian Talmud, the use of *future tense* (the imperfect תִּנָּשֵׂא) means לְכַתְּחִילָּה.

** Similarly, the use of *present tense* (the participle נוֹשֵׂא) *without* the definite article means לְכַתְּחִילָּה; however, a participle with a definite article prefixed does not mean לְכַתְּחִילָּה but דִּיעֲבַד, *after the fact* (for example הָרוֹחֵץ in שבת קמז, סע״א).

SEE: דִּיעֲבַד

לָמָּה לִי* לְמִיתְנֵי/לְמִיתְנָא לָמָּה לִי לִשְׁנוֹת ...?

Why does [the tanna] state ...?

This expression points out a *difficulty* with the language of a mishna or a baraitha.

לָמָּה לִי לְמִתְנֵי "בְּהֵמָה", וְלָמָּה לִי לְמִתְנֵי "כֵּלִים"? (בבא מציעא לג,ב ע״פ כת״י)

Why does [the tanna] state "an animal," and why does [he] state "utensils"? (= Why is it necessary to mention both words in the mishna?)

* לִי, *for me*, need not be translated into English.

לְמֵימְרָא

SEE: (לְ)מֵימְרָא

לַן

(1) לָנוּ	to us; for us
(2) אוֹתָנוּ	us

SEE: -לְ and its notes

לְעֱבֵיד

SEE: לֶיעֱבֵיד

לְעוֹלָם*

Besides the Biblical meaning *forever*, two common usages of this word occur in the Talmud:

(1) ever; always; under all conditions

In this sense it often introduces a didactic statement.

לְעוֹלָם יְהֵא אָדָם זָהִיר בִּכְבוֹד אִשְׁתּוֹ. (בבא מציעא נט, סע״א)

A person should always be careful about the honor due his wife.

(2) in reality; still; notwithstanding (the difficulty which was raised above)

This usage frequently introduces the *reinstatement* of an interpretation, an opinion, or a resolution of a difficulty that had been presented earlier. The fuller expression לְעוֹלָם אֵימָא לָךְ, *in reality I will say to you*, is often found.

לְעוֹלָם דְּלֵית בְּהוּ סִימָן ... (בבא מציעא כב,ב)**

In reality, [the mishna speaks of a case where] they (= the lost sheaves) have no marks of identification ...

* לָעוֹלָם, with the definite article represented by לָ, means *to*

(or *for*) ***the world,*** as in סנהדרין צ,א: משנה פ"י מ"א
** A fuller presentation of this Talmudic passage appears as an example under (וּדְ)קָאָמְרַתְּ.

לְעוֹלָם לָא תֵּיפוּךְ לְעוֹלָם לא תְּהֲפֹךְ!

In reality, do not reverse (the order of the text)!

For an example — see בבא מציעא ז,ב.
SEE: אֵיפוּךְ, מוּחְלֶפֶת הַשִּׁיטָה

לַעַז*

(1) disrepute; suspicion; discredit

אַתָּה מוֹצִיא לַעַז עַל גִּיטִין הָרִאשׁוֹנִים (גיטין ה, סע"ב)
you would cast discredit upon [the validity of] the letters of divorce [of] former [generations]

(2) a foreign language; any language other than Hebrew

קוֹרִין אוֹתָהּ לַלְּעוֹזוֹת בְּלַעַז (מגילה יז,א: משנה ב:א ע"פ כת"י)
we may read it (= the scroll of Esther) to those speaking a foreign language in (their) foreign language

* According to popular etymology, לע"ז is an acronym for לְשׁוֹן עַם זָר, ***the language of a foreign people,*** but the root לעז really occurs in Biblical Hebrew, as in בֵּית יַעֲקֹב מֵעַם לֹעֵז (תהלים קיד,יא).

לְעֵיל*/לְעֵילָּא לְמַעְלָה

up; above

דְּסָלְקִין לְעֵילָּא וּדְנָחְתִין לְתַתָּא (בבא קמא כג,ב)
those who go up (to Eretz Yisrael) and those who go down (from Eretz Yisrael to Babylonia)

* In the Talmudic commentaries, לְעֵיל is regularly used in the sense of ***earlier in our (Talmudic) text*** as opposed to לְקַמָּן, ***later on in our text.***
SEE: לְהַלָּן, לְקַמָּן

לְעֵילָּא מִ- לִפְנֵי

before; in the presence of

שָׁאוּל שְׁאֵילְתָא לְעֵילָּא מֵרִ' תַּנְחוּם (שבת ל,א ע' רש"י שם)
they asked a question in the presence of R. Tanḥum

לְפוּם לְפִי

according to; as

לְפוּם צַעֲרָא — אַגְרָא. (משנה אבות סוף פרק ה)
According to the suffering is the reward.

לְפוּם חוּרְפָא — שַׁבְּשְׁתָּא. (בבא מציעא צו,ב)
As [great as] the sharpness [so] is the blunder. (= The more clever one is, the greater his error.)

SEE: פּוּם

לְפִי

according to

For an example — see next entry.

לְפִי דַּרְכְּךָ/דַּרְכֵּנוּ

"by your/our way"; incidentally

רְאִיתֶם אֶת טָבִי עַבְדִּי שֶׁהוּא תַּלְמִיד חָכָם וְיוֹדֵעַ שֶׁעֲבָדִים פְּטוּרִין מִן הַסֻּכָּה; לְפִיכָךְ יָשֵׁן הוּא תַּחַת הַמִּטָּה. וּלְפִי דַּרְכֵּנוּ לָמַדְנוּ, שֶׁהַיָּשֵׁן תַּחַת הַמִּטָּה לֹא יָצָא יְדֵי חוֹבָתוֹ. (סוכה כ, סע"ב: משנה פ"ב מ"א)

You have seen Tavi, my slave, who is a Torah scholar and knows that (Canaanite) slaves are exempt from [the duty of] the sukka; therefore he sleeps under the bed. Incidentally, we have learned that one who sleeps under a bed [in a sukka] has not fulfilled his obligation.

For an example of לְפִי דַּרְכְּךָ — see משנה עדויות פ"ב מ"ג.

לְפִי שֶׁ-

because

אֵין אוֹכְלִין אֵזוֹבְיוֹן בְּשַׁבָּת לְפִי שֶׁאֵינוֹ מַאֲכַל בְּרִיאִים. (שבת קט, רע"ב: משנה פי"ד מ"ג)
We may not eat Greek hyssop on the Sabbath, because it is not the food of healthy people (but it is obviously a medicine).

לְפִי תוּמוֹ/תוּמָּהּ

in his/her innocence; innocently

For an example — see מֵסִיחַ.

לְפִיכָךְ

therefore

This word expresses a causal relationship between two clauses. When the causality is not clear, the Talmud questions the appropriateness of the word (as in the example below).

משנה: מָה יְהֵא בְּדָמִים? ... ר' עֲקִיבָא אוֹמֵר: לֹא יִשְׁתַּמֵּשׁ בָּהֶן; לְפִיכָךְ אִם אָבְדוּ, אֵינוֹ חַיָּב בְּאַחֲרָיוּתָן. (בבא מציעא כח,ב: משנה פ"ב מ"ז)
תלמוד: "לְפִיכָךְ" דְּר' עֲקִיבָא לָמָּה לִי? (שם כט, סע"א)
MISHNA: What will be with the money (which the finder has received from the sale of the animal he found)? ... R. Akiva says: He must not use it; therefore if it is lost, he bears no responsibility for it.
TALMUD: Why do I need R. Akiva's "therefore"?

לִפְנֵי וְלִפְנִים

the innermost precincts

אֵין כֹּהֵן גָּדוֹל נִכְנָס בְּבִגְדֵי זָהָב לִפְנַי וְלִפְנִים לַעֲבוֹד עֲבוֹדָה (ראש השנה כו,א)
the kohen gadol does not enter the innermost precincts (= the Holy of Holies) in golden garments to perform the service (on Yom Kippur)

זוֹ צְרִיכָה לִפְנִים — וְלִפְנַי וְלִפְנִים! (בבא מציעא טז,א)
This [contradiction] must be brought inside [the beth midrash for it to be resolved] — and into the innermost precincts [of the beth midrash]!

לִפְנִים

inside; within

זוֹ אֵינָהּ צְרִיכָה לִפְנִים! (בבא מציעא טז,א וע' רש"י שם)
This [contradiction] does not have to [be brought] inside [the beth midrash for it to be resolved]!
SEE: פְּנִים

לִפְנִים מְשׁוּרַת הַדִּין

"inside the line of the law"; in the spirit of generosity (rather than strict legality); **beyond the call of duty; beyond the letter of the law**

אֲבוּהּ דִּשְׁמוּאֵל אַשְׁכַּח הָנָךְ חֲמָרֵי בְּמַדְבְּרָא, וְאַהְדְּרִינְהוּ לְמָרַיְיהוּ לְבָתַר תְּרֵיסַר יַרְחֵי שַׁתָּא — לִפְנִים מְשׁוּרַת הַדִּין. (ב"מ כד,ב)
*Sh*ᵉ*muel's father found some donkeys in the desert, and*

he returned them to their owners twelve months later — beyond the call of duty.

לְצַדְדִין

SEE: (לְ)צַדְדִין

לְקַבֵּל כְּנֶגֶד; מוּל

against; opposite; in the presence of

אַבָּא לְקֳבֵל אַלְפָּא חַמְרָא שָׁתֵי. (מגילה יב,ב ע״פ דניאל ה:א)

My father drank wine in the presence of a thousand [people].

לָקַח (לקח: לוֹקֵחַ .prt, יִקַּח .fut)

(1) he bought; he purchased

This is the meaning in Mishnaic Hebrew.

זֶה אוֹמֵר: עַד שֶׁלֹּא מָכַרְתִּי, וְזֶה אוֹמֵר: מִשֶּׁלָּקַחְתִּי. (בבא מציעא ק, רע״א: משנה פ״ח מ״ד)

One says: [The animal was born] before I sold [its mother], and the other says: [It was born] after I bought [its mother].

(2) he took

This meaning is common in Biblical Hebrew and in Modern Hebrew, but rare in Mishnaic Hebrew.*

נְטִילַת לוּלָב דִּכְתִיב: ״וּלְקַחְתֶּם לָכֶם בַּיּוֹם הָרִאשׁוֹן ...״ (מגילה כ,ב ע״פ ויקרא כג:מ)

taking the lulav, as it is written: "And you shall take for yourselves on the first day ..."

* In Mishnaic and Talmudic Hebrew, *taking* is expressed by the verb נטל (as in נְטִילַת לוּלָב in the example).

לָקֵי (לקי; לִילְקֵי .fut, לְמִילְקָא/לְמִילְקֵי .inf) .prt

afflicted; punished by flogging לוֹקֶה

כֵּיוָן דַּעֲבַר אַמֵּימְרָא דְרַחֲמָנָא, לָקֵי. (תמורה ה, רע״א)

Since he has transgressed the word of God, he is punished by flogging.

SEE: לוֹקֶה and its note

לְקַמֵּיהּ

before him; into his presence לְפָנָיו

לְקַמַּן

before us; into our presence (1) לְפָנֵינוּ

כִּי אָתוּ לְקַמַּן לְדִינָא ... (כתובות יט,א)

when they come before us in court ...

(2) הָלְאָה; לְמַטָּה

further on (in our text); below

כִּדְבָעֵינַן לְמֵימַר לְקַמַּן (בבא מציעא כא,ב)

as we are going to say further on

SEE: כִּדְבָעֵינַן לְמֵימַר לְקַמַּן, לְעֵיל

לְשׁוּם

for the sake of; for the purpose of

For an example, see שׁוּם[1].

לְשׁוֹן הֲבַאי/הֲוָואי

rhetorical exaggeration

דִּבְּרָה תוֹרָה לשון הֲוָואי: ״עָרִים גדולות ובצורות בַּשָּׁמָיִם״. (חולין צ,ב ע״פ דברים א:כח ורש״י לדברים שם)

The Torah (sometimes) spoke with rhetorical exaggeration: "The cities are large and fortified up to heaven."

לְשֵׁם

for the sake of; for the purpose of

לְשֵׁם is often used with personal-pronoun suffixes:

for his/its (m.) own sake לִשְׁמוֹ

for her/its (f.) own sake לִשְׁמָהּ

For examples, see (לְ)שֵׁם.

לַשְׁמְעִינַן/לִישְׁמְעִינַן/נַשְׁמְעִינַן (לַשְׁמַע+ ־ִינַן) .fut

(שמע אַפְעֵל) יַשְׁמִיעַ אוֹתָנוּ; יְלַמֵּד אוֹתָנוּ

let him inform us; let him teach us

This term is used in pointing out a *difficulty* regarding the tanna's or amora's halakhic formulation. It is argued that a somewhat different formulation would have been more logical.

משנה: מְטַבֵּל בַּחֲזֶרֶת עַד שֶׁמַּגִּיעַ לְפַרְפֶּרֶת הַפַּת. (פסחים קיד, סע״א: משנה פ״י מ״ג)

תלמוד: ... לִישְׁמְעִינַן שְׁאָר יְרָקוֹת! (פסחים קיד, רע״ב)

MISHNA: He dips the lettuce (= the bitter herb for "karpas") before he has reached the bitter herb [that is eaten] after the matza.

TALMUD: [Why does the tanna state that the dipping is with a bitter herb?] ... let him teach us [dipping with] other vegetables (not necessarily bitter ones)!

SEE: אַשְׁמְעִינַן

לְשָׁנָה כַּעֲבוֹר שָׁנָה

a year later

זִימְנָא חֲדָא אִיקְלַע אַמֵּימָר לְאַתְרִין .... לְשָׁנָה תוּ אִיקְלַע לְאַתְרִין ... (פסחים קז,א)

Ammemar once happened to come to our town .... A year later he happened to come to our town again ...

לִשְׁקוֹל

SEE: לִישְׁקוֹל

לִשְׁתּוֹק

SEE: לִישְׁתּוֹק

מ

מְאָה   מֵאָה   one hundred

מֵאַחַר שֶׁ-; מֵאַחַר דְּ-*

in view of the fact that; since

וּמֵאַחַר דְּהִלְכְתָא, קְרָא לְמָה לִי? (נדה לב, סע"א)

But since [this law is] a halakhic tradition, why do I need a Biblical source [for it]?

*** The first expression is Hebrew, and the second is Aramaic. The word אַחַר by itself means *after* in the temporal sense. With the מ- prefix, however, it has that meaning only rarely, as in משנה ביכורים פ"ג מ"א.**

מַאי interrog.*

what? what is it?   (1) מַה? מַהוּ?

מַאי "בְּעִיר שֶׁל זָהָב"? (שבת נט, סע"א ע"פ משנה פ"ו מ"א)

What is [the meaning of] "with a golden city"?

what is the halakhic ruling?   (2) מַהוּ הַדִּין?

In this sense, this interrogative pronoun usually appears at the end of the question.

בְּיוֹם הַכִּיפּוּרִים — מַאי? (יומא עח,ב)

What is the halakhic ruling [regarding the wearing of bamboo sandals] on Yom Kippur?

*** Sometimes, מַאי is followed by ד- and serves as a relative pronoun – rather than an interrogative. See מַאי ד- and מַאי דַּהֲוָה הֲוָה.**

וּבְמַאי   וּבְמָה?

And with what [circumstances are we dealing]?

This question — like the full formulation (בְּ)מַאי עָסְקִינַן — introduces a *difficulty*, usually in the form of a dilemma.

For an example — see כתובות לא, רע"ב.

SEE: (בְּ)מַאי עָסְקִינַן

מִמַּאי   מִמָּה? מִנַּיִן לְךָ רְאָיָה?

"From what?" Where is your proof?

(1) This question usually introduces a challenge to a statement that has just been quoted in the Talmud, on the grounds that the statement lacks evidence. It is often followed by דִּילְמָא, *perhaps*.

זֹאת אוֹמֶרֶת: מִצְוֹת צְרִיכוֹת כַּוָּנָה .... מִמַּאי? דִּילְמָא לְעוֹלָם מִצְוֹת אֵין צְרִיכוֹת כַּוָּנָה ... (פסחים קיד, רע"ב)

This [mishna] indicates: Mitzvoth require intention .... Where is the proof? Perhaps in reality mitzvoth do not require intention (and the mishna can be explained differently, so that there will be no proof).

(2) In some instances, this question is immediately answered with a presentation of evidence supporting the previous statement.

תָּנָא הַכְנָסָה נַמֵי "הוֹצָאָה" קָרֵי לַהּ. מִמַּאי? מִדִּתְנַן: הַמּוֹצִיא מֵרְשׁוּת לִרְשׁוּת חַיָּיב — מִי לָא עָסְקִינַן דְּקָא מְעַיֵּיל מֵרְשׁוּת הָרַבִּים לִרְשׁוּת הַיָּחִיד, וְקָא קָרֵי לַהּ "הוֹצָאָה"?! (שבת ב,ב)

The tanna also refers to bringing in as הוֹצָאָה*. Where is the proof? From [the fact] that we stated [in the mishna]: One who is* מוֹצִיא *from one domain to another domain [on the Sabbath] is liable. Are we not (also) dealing with carrying from the public domain into the private domain, and he calls it* הוֹצָאָה *(even though the transfer is from outside to inside)?!*

וּמַאי אוּלְמֵיהּ דְּ... מִ...   וּמָה כֹּחוֹ שֶׁל ... מִ...?

What is the strength (or superiority) of ... over ...?

This formula presents a *difficulty*: Why should this text (or halakha or factor) be regarded as superior to the other one?

מַאי אוּלְמֵיהּ דְּהַאי סְתָמָא מֵהַאי סְתָמָא? (סנהדרין לד,ב)

What is the superiority of this anonymous [mishna] over the other anonymous [mishna]?! (= Why is one more authoritative than the other?)

בְּמַאי אוֹקִימְתָּא   בַּמֶּה הֶעֱמַדְתָּ אוֹתָהּ?

In what [manner] have you set it up?

How have you interpreted it (= the text)?

This question introduces a *difficulty* with regard to an interpretation, which was proposed in the Talmud. According to that proposal, a mishna or baraitha must be set up in accordance with the opinion of only one of the two tannaim involved in a controversy (e.g., ר' ישמעאל בב"ק לו,ב), or it must be explained as dealing with specific circumstances (e.g., כְּשֶׁאֵין סְמוּכִין עַל שׁוּלְחָנוֹ, שם פז,ב, *when they are not dependent on his table*). Now,

---

NOTE: There are many common verbal forms in Aramaic that begin with the consonant מ. Except for the קַל, the present tense of all *binyanim* (e.g., מַגְבֵּי, *causing to be collected* in the (אַפְעֵל) has a מ- prefix, and so does the infinitive of the קַל (e.g., מֵימַר, *to say*). For the convenience of the learner, many of these forms are presented as separate entries at מ — even when the main verbal entry (third person, masculine singular of the past tense, e.g., אַגְבֵּי, *he caused to be collected*, and אֲמַר, *he said*) appears at its appropriate place. Most of these מ entries omit explanations and examples, and the learner is referred to the main verbal entries for such data. For more information about the conjugation of the Aramaic verb, see *Grammar for Gemara*: Chapter 3.

evidence is presented that contradicts the proposed interpretation.

SEE: אוֹקֵי

מַאי אִיכָּא לְמֵימַר

... what is there to say?! ... מַה יֵּשׁ לוֹמַר?!

This rhetorical question is used at the end of a sentence to point out a *difficulty.*

הָנִיחָא לְר׳ יוֹחָנָן, אֶלָּא לְרֵישׁ לָקִישׁ, מַאי אִיכָּא לְמֵימַר?! (יומא עג,ב)

This is reasonable according to R. Yoḥanan, but according to Resh Lakish, what is there to say?!

SEE: אִיכָּא לְמֵימַר

מַאי אִירְיָא מַה תְּפִיסָה [זוֹ]?

"What is [this] seizing (upon this particular case)?" Why did the tanna single out ...?

This expression introduces a *difficulty:* In formulating the mishna or baraitha under discussion, why did the tanna speak of one case in particular — implying that his halakha applies exclusively to it? In reality, there are grounds for applying that halakha to other cases as well!

משנה: עַרְבֵי פְסָחִים סָמוּךְ לְמִנְחָה לֹא יֹאכַל אָדָם עַד שֶׁתֶּחְשַׁךְ. (פסחים צט, רע״א: משנה פ״י מ״א)

תלמוד: מַאי אִירְיָא "עַרְבֵי פְסָחִים"? אֲפִילּוּ עַרְבֵי שַׁבָּתוֹת וְיָמִים טוֹבִים נָמֵי! (שם צט,ב)

MISHNA: On the eves of Pesaḥ festivals one may not dine from before minḥa until it becomes dark.

TALMUD: Why [did the tanna] single out "the eves of Pesaḥ festivals"? [The same rule should] also [apply to] the eves of Sabbaths and [other] festivals as well!

SEE: אִירְיָא

מַאי אִית לָךְ לְמֵימַר

SEE: אֶלָּא מַאי אִית לָךְ לְמֵימַר

מַאי בֵּינַיְיהוּ מַה בֵּינֵיהֶם?

What is [the halakhic difference] between them?

After a controversy has been presented between two ḥakhamim who gave different reasons or different formulations, the Talmud often asks: In what case is there a distinction between the two opinions in the application of the halakha?*

אָמַר רַב חִסְדָּא: לָא לִיסְתּוֹר אֱינִישׁ בֵּי כְנִישְׁתָּא עַד דְּבָנֵי בֵּי כְנִישְׁתָּא אַחֲרִיתִי. אִיכָּא דְּאָמְרִי: מִשּׁוּם פְּשִׁיעוּתָא, וְאִיכָּא דְּאָמְרִי: מִשּׁוּם צְלוֹיֵי. מַאי בֵּינַיְיהוּ? (בבא בתרא ג,ב)

Rav Ḥisda said: One should not demolish one synagogue before he builds another. Some say: on account of neglecting [to build another], and others say: on account of [the interruption of] prayer. What is [the halakhic difference] between them?

The answer to such a query is generally a case that is introduced by the formula אִיכָּא בֵּינַיְיהוּ, *there is [the following halakhic difference] between them,* as in this instance:

אִיכָּא בֵּינַיְיהוּ: דְּאִיכָּא בֵּי כְנִישְׁתָּא אַחֲרִיתִי. (בבא בתרא שם)

There is [the following halakhic difference] between them: [a case] where another synagogue is available. (On the one hand, prayer would not be interrupted; but on the other hand, they might still neglect to build a replacement for the synagogue that has been demolished.)

* In a few instances, the מַאי בֵּינַיְיהוּ question is raised after the halakhic difference has already been stated. In such cases, it seeks the reasoning behind the controversy, like the question (בְּ)מַאי קָמִיפַּלְגִי. See שבת עח, סע״ב and Rashi's comment there.

מַאי דְּ- מַה שֶּׁ-

what; that which; whatever

מַאי דַהֲוָה הֲוָה מַה שֶּׁהָיָה הָיָה.

Whatever occurred has occurred (and it is only of academic interest, with no relevance for normative behavior in the present or in the future).

כֵּיצַד הִלְבִּישָׁן? כֵּיצַד הִלְבִּישָׁן?! מַאי דַהֲוָה הֲוָה. (יומא ה,ב)

How did he dress them? (= In what order were Aharon and his sons dressed in priestly garments?) How did he dress them?! Whatever occurred occurred.

מַאי דּוֹחְקֵיהּ דְּר׳... לְאוֹקוּמֵי מַתְנִיתִין

מַה דָּחְקוֹ שֶׁל ר׳... לְהַעֲמִיד אֶת מִשְׁנָתֵנוּ ...?

What is the [factor that exerted] pressure upon (the amora) R. ... to interpret our mishna (in a less than satisfactory manner — for example, in accordance with a minority tannaitic opinion, rather than with the majority)?

For an example — see שבת קמו,א.

SEE: דְּחַק ,אוֹקֵי

מַאי דִּכְתִיב מַהוּ שֶׁכָּתוּב ...?

What is [the aggadic teaching that can be derived from] what is written (in Scripture)...?

מַאי דִּכְתִיב "וְהַבּוֹר רֵק, אֵין בּוֹ מָיִם"? מִמַּשְׁמָע שֶׁנֶּאֱמַר "וְהַבּוֹר רֵק" — אֵינִי יוֹדֵעַ שֶׁ"אֵין בּוֹ מָיִם"?! אֶלָּא מָה תַּלְמוּד לוֹמַר "אֵין בּוֹ מָיִם"? מַיִם אֵין בּוֹ, אֲבָל נְחָשִׁים וְעַקְרַבִּים יֵשׁ בּוֹ. (שבת כב, רע״א ע״פ בראשית לז:כד וע׳ רש״י שם)

What is [the aggadic teaching that can be derived from] what is written "and the pit was empty, there was no water in it"? From the implication of what was said "and the pit was empty" do I not understand that "there was no water in it"?! What teaching, then, [does] "there is no water in it" [mean] to convey? There is no water in it, but there are snakes and scorpions in it. (Thus the pasuk means that the pit was empty only with regard to water.)

מַאי דַּעְתָּיךְ/דַּעְתָּךְ מַה דַּעְתְּךָ?

"What is your opinion?" What is your reasoning (upon which you base your opinion)?
This question together with the subsequent answer serves to lay the foundation for a *difficulty.*

רַבִינָא אַשְׁכְּחֵיהּ לְרַב אַחָא בְּרֵיהּ דְּרָבָא דַהֲוָה מְהַדַּר אַמְּרִירְתָא. אֲמַר לֵיהּ: מַאי דַּעְתָּיךְ? דִּמְרִירָן טְפֵי! וְהָא "חֲזֶרֶת" תְּנַן ...,
וַאֲמַר ר׳ אוֹשַׁעְיָא: מִצְוָה בַּחֲזֶרֶת! (פסחים לט,א)

Rabina found R. Aḥa, son of Rava, who was seeking "m^erirta" (for the mitzva of bitter herbs at the Seder). He (= Rabina) said to him: What is your reasoning? That they are most bitter! But have we not learnt (in the mishna) "lettuce" ..., and R. Oshaya said: It is [preferable to fulfill the] mitzva with lettuce!

מַאי דָּרַשׁ (pl. דָּרוּשׁ)

What did he interpret? מַה דָּרַשׁ?

מַאי דָּרֵישׁ (pl. דָּרְשִׁי)

What does he interpret? מַה דּוֹרֵשׁ?
This *question* — in either the past or the present tense — is used in two different senses:
(1) For what point did he find support in this Biblical passage? What did he derive from it?*

וְרַבָּנָן, הַאי "לְךָ" מַאי דָּרְשִׁי בֵּיהּ?(סוכה כז,ב ע״פ דברים טז:יג)

And [as for] the Ḥakhamim, for what point do they find support in this [word] לְךָ *(= to you)?*

(2) What pasuk did he interpret in support of this point?

ברייתא: ... וְלֹא פָּחֲתוּ וְלֹא הוֹתִירוּ עַל מַה שֶּׁכָּתוּב בַּתּוֹרָה — חוּץ מִמִּקְרָא מְגִילָּה.
תלמוד: מַאי דְּרוּשׁ? (מגילה יד,א)

BARAITHA: [The prophets] did not subtract [from], nor did they add to what is written in the Torah — except for [the mitzva of] reading the scroll of Esther.
TALMUD: What [pasuk] did they interpret (in support of this new mitzva)?

* In this usage, the verb דרש is followed by בֵּיהּ, *in it*, or בְּהוּ, *in them.*

SEE: דְּרַשׁ

מַאי הַאי מַה זֶה?

What is [the meaning or reason for] this?
This *question* usually appears in the course of an aggadic discussion.

אֲמַר לֵיהּ קֵיסָר לְרַבָּן גַּמְלִיאֵל: יָדַעְנָא אֱלָקַיְיכוּ מַאי קָא עָבִיד .... אִתְנְגִיד וְאִיתְנַח. אֲמַר לֵיהּ: מַאי הַאי? (סנהדרין לט,א ע״פ כת״י)

The (Roman) Emperor said to Rabban Gamliel: I know what your God is doing.... [Rabban Gamliel] became faint and sighed. [The Emperor] said to him: What is this? (= Why are you upset?)

SEE: חַאי מַאי

מַאי הָוֵי מַה יִּהְיֶה?

"What will be?"
Why is it significant? What does it matter?

וְאִי תַקּוּן רַבָּנַן, כִּי לָא אֲמַר — מַאי הָוֵי? (ב״מ י, סע״א)

But if the ḥakhamim have enacted (a law that one automatically acquires objects located within four cubits of himself), what does it matter if he did not declare (that he intends to acquire the object)?

SEE: הָוֵה

מַאי הָוֵי עֲלַהּ מַה יִּהְיֶה עָלֶיהָ?

What will [the halakhic ruling] be about it?
This *question* is asked by the Talmud about a problem or a controversy presented earlier in the discussion that still remains undecided.

הַהִיא מַסּוּתָא דַּהֲווּ מִנְּצוּ עֲלֵיהּ בֵּי תְּרֵי .... מַאי הָוֵי עֲלַהּ דְּמַסּוּתָא? (בבא מציעא ו, רע״ב - ז,א)

[There was] a bathhouse whose [ownership] two people were disputing .... What will [the halakhic ruling] be about it, [i.e.,] the bathhouse?

מַאי הִיא מַה הִיא?

"What is it?"
What does it mean? To what is it referring?
This *question* seeks a clarification of the statement, the expression, or the word that immediately precedes it.

("וְכִבַּדְתּוֹ מֵעֲשׂוֹת דְּרָכֶיךָ") — שֶׁלֹּא יְהֵא הִילּוּכָךְ שֶׁל שַׁבָּת כְּהִילּוּכָךְ שֶׁל חוֹל. מַאי הִיא? (שבת קיג, רע״ב ע״פ ישעיהו נח:יג)

("And you shall honor it by not doing your usual actions") — that your walking on the Sabbath shall not be like your walking on weekdays. What does it mean?

For another example, see אָמְרוּ דָּבָר אֶחָד.

מַאי "וְאוֹמֵר" מַהוּ "וְאוֹמֵר ..."?

What is [the need for] "and it says ..."?
A baraitha or a mishna has cited two different proofs from Scripture, with the second one introduced by the term וְאוֹמֵר, ***and it says.*** **Now the Talmud raises the *difficulty:* Why did the tanna need to quote a second text as proof? The first one should have been sufficient to prove the point! In response, the Talmud shows that the second proof is necessary after all.**

ר׳ מֵאִיר אוֹמֵר: בֵּין כָּךְ וּבֵין כָּךְ אַתֶּם קְרוּיִים בָּנִים, שֶׁנֶּאֱמַר: "בָּנִים סְכָלִים הֵמָּה". וְאוֹמֵר: "בָּנִים לֹא אֵמוּן בָּם"... מַאי "וְאוֹמֵר ..."? (קידושין לו,א ע״פ ירמיהו ד:כב ודברים לב:כ)

R. Méir says: In any event (whether you act like sons or not) you are called sons, as it has been stated: "They are foolish sons," and it says: "[They are] sons in whom there is no faithfulness" ... What is [the need for] "and it says ..." (i.e., the second proof)?

SEE: וְאוֹמֵר

מַאי "וְאִם נַפְשָׁךְ לוֹמַר"

מַהוּ "וְאִם נַפְשָׁךְ לוֹמַר ..."?

What is [the meaning of] "and if it is your desire to say (otherwise)"?

A baraitha has cited two proofs based on Scripture, with the second one introduced by the expression וְאִם נַפְשְׁךָ לוֹמַר, *and if it is your desire to say (otherwise)*. Now the Talmud raises the *difficulty*: Why would you want to say otherwise? What fault do you find with the first proof, presented by the tanna earlier in the baraitha, that compels you to bring a second proof?

For an example — see בבא קמא פג,ב.
SEE: (וְ)אִם נַפְשְׁךָ לוֹמַר

וּמַאי חָזִית   מָה רָאִיתָ?

"What did you see?" On what grounds have you determined to ...? Why?

This question introduces a *difficulty* that is due to apparent arbitrariness.

וּמַאי חָזִית דִסְמַכְתְּ אַהָנֵי? סְמוֹךְ אַהָנֵי! (סנהדרין כז, רע"א)
But on what grounds have you determined to rely upon these [witnesses]? Rely upon those!

SEE: מָה רָאִיתָ

מַאי טַעְמָא   What is the reason? מַהוּ הַטַּעַם?

A *question:* What is the Scriptural basis, the rationale, or the halakhic foundation of the statement that was just quoted in the Talmud?

מְגִילָּה בְּשַׁבָּת לָא קָרֵינַן. מַאי טַעְמָא? (מגילה ד, סע"ב)
We do not read the scroll (of Esther) on the Sabbath. What is the reason?

מַאי לָאו   מַהוּ? הַאִם לֹא (מְדֻבָּר בְּ...)?

What [are the circumstances]? Is it (= the text) not [referring to] ...?*

An introduction to a *proof* or a *refutation* that adopts a particular interpretation of the text that is quoted. The Talmud usually proceeds to reject the argument by offering a different interpretation of that text.

"וְכָתַב לָהּ" — לִשְׁמָהּ. מַאי? לָאו כְּתִיבַת הַגֵּט? לָא! חֲתִימַת עֵדִים. (גיטין כג,א ע"פ דברים כד:א)
"And he shall write for her" — [expressly] for her sake. What [are the circumstances]? Is it (= the pasuk) not [referring to] the writing of the bill of divorce (which must be written expressly for the sake of the woman being divorced)? No! [The pasuk refers to] the signing by the witnesses (hence it is merely their signatures that must be written expressly for her sake — not necessarily the text of the bill of divorce).

* Many prefer to read מַאי לָאו? as a unified idiomatic expression meaning *isn't it (talking about)?* — without translating מַאי literally.

מַאי לְמֵימְרָא

What [does it come] to say?   מַה לּוֹמַר?

This *difficulty* is raised against a proposed interpretation of a mishna, baraitha, or amoraic statement on the grounds that the halakha that emerges is self-evident. The Talmud then proceeds to explain that, in reality, the halakha that emerges from the proposed interpretation is not self-evident.*

ברייתא: טוֹמְנִין בְּגִיזֵי צֶמֶר ... וּבְמוֹכִין וְאֵין מְטַלְטְלִין אוֹתָן ...
תלמוד: הָכִי קָאָמַר: אִם לֹא טָמַן בָּהֶן, אֵין מְטַלְטְלִין אוֹתָן. אִי הָכִי, מַאי לְמֵימְרָא? (שבת מח,א)

BARAITHA: We may store [food] in wool shearings ... and in cloth material (on the Sabbath), but we may not handle them (because they are "muktze") ...
TALMUD: This is what [the baraitha] means: If no one has stored in them, we may not handle them. If so (= according to this explanation), what [is the baraitha coming] to say (since cloth material not meant for Sabbath use is certainly "muktze")?

* If that explanation does not satisfy the Talmud, the *difficulty* is reiterated: וְאַכַּתִּי מַאי לְמֵימְרָא, *but still what [does it come] to say?!* For an example — see ב"מ קג, סע"א.
SEE: (לְ)מֵימְרָא

מַאי מַשְׁמַע   מָה מַשְׁמִיעַ? מָה מְלַמֵּד?

(1) What does it teach? What [support] does [the Biblical passage just now cited] convey (for the halakha or aggada under discussion)?

בַּהֲנָאָה מִנַּיִן? תַּלְמוּד לוֹמַר: "וּבַעַל הַשּׁוֹר נָקִי". מַאי מַשְׁמַע? שִׁמְעוֹן בֶּן זוֹמָא אוֹמֵר: כְּאָדָם שֶׁאוֹמֵר לַחֲבֵירוֹ: "יָצָא פְּלוֹנִי נָקִי מִנְּכָסָיו". (בבא קמא מא,א ע"פ שמות כא:כח)
From where [do I derive the prohibition of deriving] benefit (from the carcass of the ox that was put to death by stoning)? Scripture states: "And the owner of the ox is 'clean.'" What does [this pasuk] teach (in support of this halakha)? Shim'on b. Zoma says: [It is] like a person who says to his friend: "So-and-so has been 'cleaned out' of his property."

(2) What [pasuk] indicates (support for the definition proposed in the Talmud)?

אָמַר רַב יְהוּדָה אָמַר שְׁמוּאֵל: כָּל הַמִּצְוֹת מְבָרֵךְ עֲלֵיהֶן עוֹבֵר לַעֲשִׂיָּיתָן. מַאי מַשְׁמַע דְּהַאי "עוֹבֵר" לִישָּׁנָא דְאַקְדּוֹמֵי הוּא? (פסחים ז,ב)
Rav Y'huda said quoting Sh'muel: For all mitzvot one recites a b'rakha prior (עוֹבֵר) *to performing them. What [pasuk] indicates that this [word]* עוֹבֵר *is an expression denoting "priority"?*

SEE: מַשְׁמַע, מַאי קְרָאָה, מַאי תַּלְמוּדָא

מַאי נִיהוּ (pl. נִינְהוּ)   מַה הוּא?

What is it?

This question is asked by the Talmud in order to identify or clarify the term or expression that has just been used.

תַּרְגּוּם שֶׁבַּתּוֹרָה — מַאי נִיהוּ? "יְגַר שָׂהֲדוּתָא". (שבת קטו, סע"ב ע"פ בראשית לא:מז)

"The Aramaic in the Torah" — what is it? [The expression] יְגַר שָׂהֲדוּתָא (the pile of testimony).

SEE: נִיהוּ

מַאי נָפְקָא לָךְ* מִינַּהּ מַה יּוֹצֵאת לְךָ מִמֶּנָּה?!

"What comes out of it for you?!" What difference does it make to you?!

This rhetorical question indicates a *difficulty*: Why be concerned about something that really makes no difference?!**

אֲמַר לֵיהּ אַבָּיֵי לְרַב יוֹסֵף: הָא דְּרִ' יִצְחָק — גְּמָרָא אוֹ סְבָרָא? אֲמַר לֵיהּ: מַאי נָפְקָא לַן מִינַּהּ?! (עירובין ס, סע"א ותוס' שם)

Abbayé said to Rav Yosef: Is this [ruling] of R. Yitzḥak a received tradition or [is it based upon] reason? He (= Rav Yosef) said to him: What difference does it make to us?!

* Sometimes, the pronoun is לֵיהּ, *to him*, or לַן, *to us*.

** Do not confuse this entry with the next one.

SEE: נְפַק ,נָפְקָא לֵיהּ and its note

לְמַאי נָפְקָא מִינַּהּ לְעִנְיַן מַה, יוֹצֵאת מִמֶּנָּה?

"With regard to what, does something come out of it?" In what case is there a halakhic difference?

This real *question* is followed by an answer that explains the halakhic significance of the point under discussion.*

הֶסְפֵּידָא — יְקָרָא דְחַיֵּי הָוֵי אוֹ יְקָרָא דִשְׁכִיבֵי הָוֵי? לְמַאי נָפְקָא מִינַּהּ? דַּאֲמַר: "לָא תִסְפְּדוּהּ לְהַהוּא גַּבְרָא". (סנהדרין מו, סע"ב)

Is [the purpose of] a eulogy the honor of the living [relatives] or the honor of the dead? In what case is there a halakhic difference? Where [the deceased] had said: "Don't eulogize me!"

* Do not confuse this entry with the previous one.

SEE: נְפַק ,נָפְקָא לֵיהּ and its note; נָפְקָא מִינַּהּ and its note

מַאי עָבֵיד/עָבְדֵי לֵיהּ מַה יַּעֲשֶׂה/יַעֲשׂוּ בּוֹ?

What will he/they do with it?

This question poses a *difficulty* for a specific tanna or amora. According to his opinion, there is a superfluous Biblical word, expression, or pasuk.

וְרִ' אֱלִיעֶזֶר — הַאי "כָּל הָאֶזְרָח (בְּיִשְׂרָאֵל יֵשְׁבוּ בַּסֻּכֹּת)" — מַאי עָבֵיד לֵיהּ? (סוכה כז,ב ע"פ ויקרא כג:מב)

And [as for] R. Eliezer — what will he do with this (superfluous passage): "All the citizens (among the Jewish people shall dwell in sukkoth)," (since according to R. Eliezer, the beginning of the same pasuk already states the obligation of dwelling in sukkoth)?

SEE: עֲבַד

מַאי עֲבִידְתֵּיהּ

מַה מַּעֲשֵׂהוּ (כָּאן)?! מַה מְּקוֹמוֹ (כָּאן)?!

What is its business (here)?! Why is it mentioned (here)?!

This rhetorical question points out a *difficulty*: The text the Talmud has just quoted contains a word, a term, or an element that does not belong in it.

הַדָּר בַּחֲצַר חֲבֵירוֹ שֶׁלֹּא מִדַּעְתּוֹ ... אֵינוֹ צָרִיךְ לְהַעֲלוֹת לוֹ שָׂכָר, וְהַשּׂוֹכֵר בַּיִת מֵרְאוּבֵן מַעֲלֶה שָׂכָר לְשִׁמְעוֹן. שִׁמְעוֹן מַאי עֲבִידְתֵּיהּ? (בבא קמא כא, רע"א)

One who lives in another's courtyard without his (= the owner's) knowledge ... does not have to pay him rent, but one who rents a house from Re'uven must pay rent to Shim'on. Why is Shim'on mentioned here?

* In some instances, a feminine-singular suffix (in עֲבִידְתָּהּ) or a plural suffix (in עֲבִידְתַּיְיהוּ) is used.

SEE: עֲבִידְתָּא ,מַאן דְּכַר שְׁמֵיהּ

בְּמַאי עָסְקִינַן בַּמֶּה אָנוּ עֲסוּקִין?

With what [circumstances] are we dealing?

This question introduces a *difficulty* — usually in the form of a dilemma.

אֲמַר רַב יְהוּדָה: פּוֹתֵחַ אָדָם דֶּלֶת כְּנֶגֶד הַמְּדוּרָה בְּשַׁבָּת. לָיֵיט עֲלַהּ אַבָּיֵי. בְּמַאי עָסְקִינַן? אִילֵימָא בְּרוּחַ מְצוּיָה, מַאי טַעְמָא דְּמַאן דְּאָסַר?! וְאִי בְּרוּחַ שֶׁאֵינָהּ מְצוּיָה, מַאי טַעְמָא דְּמַאן דְּשָׁרֵי?! (שבת קכ,ב ע"פ כת"י)

Rav Yehuda said: One may open a door opposite a fire on the Sabbath. Abbayé condemns this (ruling). (Now the Talmud asks:) With what circumstances are we dealing? If we should say where there is a normal wind [blowing, then] what is the reason of the one who prohibits (since the wind will not fan the flame, even with the door open)?! But if there is an unusual[ly strong] wind [blowing, then] what is the reason of the one who permits (since the wind will fan the flame)?!

SEE: עֲסַק ,הָכָא בְּמַאי עָסְקִינַן

בְּמַאי פְּלִיגֵי

About what do they differ?! בַּמֶּה חֲלוּקִים?!

Usually, this expression introduces a *difficulty* regarding the explanation of a controversy, as if to say: In light of our previous discussion, what case is left for the two disputants to disagree about?

מוֹדֶה הָיָה רִ' יְהוּדָה לַחֲכָמִים בְּזֵיתִים וַעֲנָבִים, וּמוֹדִים חֲכָמִים לְרִ' יְהוּדָה בִּשְׁאָר פֵּירוֹת. אֲמַר לֵיהּ רִ' יִרְמְיָה לְרִ' אַבָּא: אֶלָּא בְּמַאי פְּלִיגֵי?! (שבת קמג,ב)

R. Yehuda agrees with the Ḥakhamim with respect to olives and grapes [that they may not be squeezed on the Sabbath], while the Ḥakhamim agree with R. Yehuda with respect to other fruits [that it is permitted to squeeze them]. R. Yirmeya said to R. Abba: About what [fruits], then, do they differ?!

SEE: פְּלִיג

וּמַאי פָּסְקָא* וּמִפְּנֵי מַה פּוֹסֵק אוֹתָהּ?!

But why would [the tanna] establish it (= such a situation)?!

This question points out a *difficulty* with a proposal that has been put forward to explain the scenario of a mishna or baraitha, on the grounds

that the set of circumstances that has thus been established seems arbitrary.

משנה: [הַמֻּדָּר הֲנָאָה מֵחֲבֵרוֹ] מְלַמְּדוֹ מִדְרָשׁ, הֲלָכוֹת, וְאַגָּדוֹת, אֲבָל לֹא יְלַמְּדֶנּוּ מִקְרָא. (נדרים לה, רע״ב: משנה פ״ד מ״ג)
תלמוד: אָמַר שְׁמוּאֵל: בְּמָקוֹם שֶׁנּוֹטְלִין שָׂכָר עַל הַמִּקְרָא, וְאֵין נוֹטְלִין שָׂכָר עַל הַמִּדְרָשׁ. מַאי פַּסְקָא?! (שם לו, סע״ב)

MISHNA: [If one is under a vow not to benefit from his friend] he may teach him midrash, halakhoth, and aggadoth, but he may not teach him Scripture.
TALMUD: Sh^e^muel said: [The mishna is speaking] of a place where [teachers] receive remuneration for [teaching] Scripture, but they do not receive remuneration for midrash. (But) why would [the tanna] establish it (= such a situation)?! (It is arbitrary to assume that the teachers get paid for teaching Scripture, but not for teaching midrash.)

* According to Rashi פַּסְקָא seems to be a verb from the root פסק, *decide* or *establish. The final* ־ָא is apparently a pronoun suffix, the equivalent of ־ָהּ, which expresses the direct object, *it.* In בבא מציעא לב,ב — our editions of both the Talmudic text and of Rashi read פְּסַקְתְּ, *you established,* a verbal form without a direct-object pronoun suffix. See Rashi's commentary there and on לד,א and טו,א in the same tractate. On the other hand, it has been suggested that פִּסְקָא in this expression is a noun, meaning *decision* or *distinction,* and should be vocalised accordingly. Thus מַאי פִּסְקָא would mean: *What is [the basis for] this decision/distinction?* See Rav E. Z. Melamed, *Eshnav HaTalmud,* p. 48.

SEE: פסק

מַאי קָא מַשְׁמַע לַן   מָה מַשְׁמִיעַ לָנוּ?

What [new point] is he teaching us?

This question points out a *difficulty:* Since the amora's halakha was already known to us from a mishna, a baraitha, or the amora's own statement on another occasion — why did the amora present it again?

אֲמַר רַבָּה בַּר נָתָן: טְעָנוֹ חִטִּין וְהוֹדָה לוֹ בִּשְׂעוֹרִין — פָּטוּר. מַאי קָא מַשְׁמַע לַן? תְּנֵינָא: טְעָנוֹ חִטִּין וְהוֹדָה לוֹ בִּשְׂעוֹרִין — פָּטוּר! (בבא קמא לה, סע״ב)

Rabba b. Nathan said: [If the plaintiff] claimed wheat from him (= the defendant), and he admitted [he owed] him barley — he is exempt. What [new point] is he teaching us? We have [already] learnt (in a mishna): [If the plaintiff] claimed wheat from him and he admitted [he owed] him barley — he is exempt!

SEE: מַשְׁמַע, קָא מַשְׁמַע לַן, פְּשִׁיטָא

מַאי קָאָמַר

What does he mean?   מָה הוּא אוֹמֵר?

This *question* seeks a clarification of the meaning of a mishna, a baraitha, an amoraic statement, or a pasuk — when one or more of its words are obscure, when its syntax is difficult, or when its content seems self-contradictory or superfluous.

The clarification that follows is usually introduced by the term הָכִי קָאָמַר, *this is what he means.*

ברייתא: הָיוּ לְפָנָיו מִינֵי אוֹכָלִים — בּוֹרֵר וְאוֹכֵל, בּוֹרֵר וּמַנִּיחַ; וְלֹא יִבְרוֹר, וְאִם בֵּירֵר חַיָּיב חַטָּאת.
תלמוד: מַאי קָאָמַר? אֲמַר עוּלָּא: הָכִי קָאָמַר ... (שבת עד, רע״א ורש״י שם)

BARAITHA: [If] various foods are before him, he may select and eat, he may select and put aside; but he must not select, and if he does select, he is bound to bring a sin-offering.
TALMUD: What does he (= the tanna) mean (since there are elements in the baraitha that seem to contradict each other)? Ulla said: This is what he means ...

SEE: אָמַר

וּמַאי קוּשְׁיָא

What is the difficulty?!   מַהוּ הַקּשִׁי?!

This rhetorical question introduces the *resolution* of a difficulty.

משנה: מִי שֶׁבָּא בַּדֶּרֶךְ וְלֹא הָיָה בְּיָדוֹ לוּלָב לִיטּוֹל — לִכְשֶׁיִּכָּנֵס לְבֵיתוֹ יִטּוֹל עַל שֻׁלְחָנוֹ. (סוכה לח, רע״א: משנה פ״ג מ״ט)
תלמוד: אַמְרַתְּ: נוֹטְלוֹ עַל שֻׁלְחָנוֹ, לְמֵימְרָא דְמַפְסִיק, וּרְמִינְהִי:
משנה: אִם הִתְחִילוּ, אֵין מַפְסִיקִין! ... (משנה שבת פ״א מ״ב)
תלמוד: אֲמַר רָבָא: מַאי קוּשְׁיָא?! דִּילְמָא הָא דְאוֹרָיְיתָא, הָא דְרַבָּנַן! (שם)

MISHNA: [If] a man was travelling on the road and had no lulav to take (to perform the mitzva), when he comes home he should take [it, even if he remembers while eating] at his table.
TALMUD: You said: He should take it (even) at his table, indicating that he must interrupt [his meal to do so], but note the contradiction between them (= two mishnayoth):
MISHNA: If they have begun (e.g., to eat a meal), they need not stop [in order to pray]! ...
TALMUD: Rava said: What is the difficulty?! Perhaps [this distinction is due to the fact that] the former (= the mitzva of lulav) is of Torah status, (while) the latter (= the mitzva of daily prayer) is of Rabbinic status!

SEE: קוּשְׁיָא, לָא קַשְׁיָא

בְּמַאי קָמִיפַּלְגִי   בַּמֶּה הֵם חֲלוּקִים?

About what [issue] do they disagree?

After a controversy between two ḥakhamim has been presented, the Talmud often seeks to determine the underlying principle in dispute or the reasons of the two disputants.

... בָּעֶרֶב ... קוֹרֵא קְרִיאַת שְׁמַע וּמִתְפַּלֵּל ... ר׳ יְהוֹשֻׁעַ בֶּן לֵוִי אוֹמֵר: תְּפִילּוֹת בְּאֶמְצַע תִּקְנוּם. בְּמַאי קָא מִיפַּלְגִי? אִי בָּעֵית אֵימָא: קְרָא, אִי בָּעֵית אֵימָא: סְבָרָא ... (ברכות ד,ב)

In the evening he should read the Sh^e^ma and recite the Amida ... R. Y^e^hoshua b. Levi says: The Amidoth were arranged [to be said] in the middle (= between the two recitations of Sh^e^ma, so that the Amida *follows Sh*ᵉ*ma in the morning and precedes Sh*ᵉ*ma in the evening). About what [issue] do they disagree? If you want, you may say it is [the interpretation of] a pasuk, or, if you want, it is [a difference in] reasoning...*

SEE: מִיפַּלְגִי and the note about its pronunciation.

מַאי קָסָבַר

What [opinion] does he hold?! מָה הוּא סוֹבֵר?!

This question introduces a *dilemma*, as if to say: Whichever opinion this ḥakham holds on the issue, there is a difficulty.

משנה: מֵאֵימָתַי קוֹרִין אֶת שְׁמַע בְּעַרְבִית? מִשָּׁעָה שֶׁהַכֹּהֲנִים נִכְנָסִים לֶאֱכוֹל בִּתְרוּמָתָן עַד סוֹף הָאַשְׁמוּרָה הָרִאשׁוֹנָה — דִּבְרֵי ר' אֱלִיעֶזֶר. (ברכות ב, רע"א: משנה פ"א מ"א)

תלמוד: מַאי קָסָבַר ר' אֱלִיעֶזֶר?! אִי קָסָבַר שָׁלֹשׁ מִשְׁמָרוֹת הָוֵי הַלַּיְלָה, לֵימָא עַד אַרְבַּע שָׁעוֹת! וְאִי קָסָבַר אַרְבַּע מִשְׁמָרוֹת הָוֵי הַלַּיְלָה, לֵימָא עַד שָׁלֹשׁ שָׁעוֹת! (שם ג, רע"א)

*MISHNA: From when may one recite the Sh*ᵉ*ma in the evening? From the moment the kohanim enter to eat their t*ᵉ*ruma until the end of the first watch — the words of R. Eliezer.*

TALMUD: What [opinion] does R. Eliezer hold?! If he holds that the night has three watches, let him say: "until four hours [have passed]"! But if he holds that night has four watches, let him say: "until three hours [have passed]"!

SEE: סְבַר, מָה נַפְשָׁךְ

מַאי קְרָאָה*/קְרָא

What is the pasuk? מַהוּ הַכָּתוּב?

This *question* asks: What is the Scriptural source for the halakha or aggada that has just been quoted in the Talmud?**

וְתִיקִין הָיוּ גוֹמְרִין אוֹתָהּ עִם הָנֵץ הַחַמָּה כְּדֵי שֶׁיִּסְמוֹךְ גְּאוּלָּה לִתְפִלָּה, וְנִמְצָא מִתְפַּלֵּל בַּיּוֹם. אָמַר ר' זֵירָא: מַאי קְרָאָה? "יִירָאוּךָ עִם שָׁמֶשׁ ..." (ברכות ט,ב ע"פ תהלים עב:ה)

*The pious used to finish it (= the Sh*ᵉ*ma) with sunrise, in order to join [the b*ᵉ*rakha] גָּאַל יִשְׂרָאֵל with [the beginning of] the Amida and consequently recite the Amida by day. R. Zera said: What is the pasuk? "They shall revere you at sunrise ..."*

* Some vocalize this expression מֵאי קְרָאֵהּ? and translate it: *From which pasuk?*

** According to the Ramban in his discussion of the Rambam's "first principle" in the *Sefer HaMitsvoth*, this question seeks a mere support or intimation (אַסְמַכְתָּא) — rather than a real source.

SEE: קְרָא, אֵי, מַאי מַשְׁמַע, מַאי תַּלְמוּדָא

מַאי רְבוּתָא/רְבוּתֵיהּ

"מַהוּ הַגְּדֻלָּה (שֶׁלּוֹ)?" מַהוּ הַחִידּוּשׁ (שֶׁלּוֹ)?

"What is the/his advantage?" What is the/his uniqueness? What is the/his noteworthy point?

ברייתא: אֲפִילּוּ אַגְרִיפַּס הַמֶּלֶךְ ... אוֹתוֹ הַיּוֹם לֹא יֹאכַל עַד שֶׁתֶּחְשַׁךְ.

תלמוד: ... מַאי רְבוּתֵיהּ דְּאַגְרִיפַּס? (פסחים קז, רע"ב)

BARAITHA: Even King Agrippas may not eat on that day (before Pesaḥ) until it becomes dark.

TALMUD: ... what is the uniqueness of Agrippas?

SEE: רְבוּתָא

מַאי שַׁיַּיר דְּהַאי שַׁיַּיר

What [else] did [the tanna] omit that he omitted this? מַה שִּׁיֵּר שֶׁשִּׁיֵּר זֶה?

This *question*, a challenge to the explanation that was just proposed, תָּנָא וְשַׁיַּיר, is based upon the practice of some tannaim to formulate partial lists that omit several items — but never only one item.

SEE: תָּנָא וְשַׁיַּיר

מַאי שְׁנָא*

"[For] what [reason] did it differ?!" How is it unique?! מָה שָּׁנָה?! מַה נִּשְׁתַּנָּה?!

This expression is used to present a *difficulty*.

וְרַב, מַאי שְׁנָא הָנֵי?! (שבת סד,ב)

But [according to] Rav, how are these (ornaments) unique?!

* A parallel expression is found in Mishnaic Hebrew:

מַה שָּׁנָה זֶה מִן הַיּוֹשֵׁב בְּבֵיתוֹ?! (הוריות ג,ב: משנה פ"א מ"ב)

SEE שְׁנָא

מַאי שְׁנָא ד-*

"מַה נִּשְׁתַּנָּה שֶׁ-...?! מַהוּ הַטַּעַם שֶׁ-...?! מַדּוּעַ?!

"[For] what [reason] does it differ that ...?!" What is the reason that ...?! Why ...?!

מַאי שְׁנָא דְּתָנֵי דְּעַרְבִית בְּרֵישָׁא?! לִתְנֵי דְּשַׁחֲרִית בְּרֵישָׁא! (ברכות ב,א ע"פ הגהות הב"ח)

Why does [the tanna] state [the law] of the evening first?! Let him state [the law] of the morning first!

* See previous entry.

מַאי שְׁנָא ... (וּ)מַאי שְׁנָא ...

מַה נִּשְׁתַּנָּה ... מִ- ...?!

What is the difference between ... and ...?!

מַאי שְׁנָא רֵישָׁא וּמַאי שְׁנָא סֵיפָא?! (שבת ע, רע"א ועוד)

What is the difference between the first clause and the latter clause?!

SEE: מַאי שְׁנָא

מַאי תַּלְמוּדָא

What is [the basis for] the deduction [from Scripture]?! מַהוּ הַלִּמּוּד?!

This *question* seeks an explanation of the concise midrashic derivation that has just been quoted in the Talmud.

"בֵּיתֶךָ" — בִּיאָתְךָ, מִן הַיָּמִין. אַתָּה אוֹמֵר: מִן הַיָּמִין, אוֹ אֵינוֹ אֶלָּא מִשְּׂמֹאל?! תַּלְמוּד לוֹמַר: "בֵּיתֶךָ". מַאי תַּלְמוּדָא?! אָמַר

רַבָּה: דֶּרֶךְ בִּיאָתְךָ מִן הַיָּמִין — דְּכִי עָקַר אֱינִישׁ כַּרְעֵיהּ, דְּיָמִינָא עָקַר בְּרֵישָׁא. (מנחות לד,א ע״פ דברים ו:ט)
"(Upon the door-posts of) your house" — as you enter, on the right side. Do you say: On the right side — or perhaps it should really be on the left side? Scripture teaches: "Your house." What is [the basis for] the deduction (from Scripture that "your house" implies the right side)? Rabba said: The way you enter [means] on the right, for when a man lifts his foot [to enter], he lifts his right foot first.
SEE: מַאי מַשְׁמַע, מַאי קְרָאָה, תַּלְמוּד

מַאי תַּקַּנְתֵּיהּ

What is the remedy for him? מַהִי תַּקָּנָתוֹ?
הַאי מַאן דְּמִיבְּעִית ..., מַאי תַּקַּנְתֵּיהּ? לִיקְרֵי קְרִיאַת שְׁמַע! (מגילה ג,א)
[As for] a person who is frightened ..., what is the remedy for him? Let him read the Sh^e^ma!
SEE: תַּקָּנָה

מְאִיס (מאס) pass. prt.

loathsome; repulsive; rejected מָאוּס
שָׁאנֵי בֵּית הַכִּסֵּא דִּמְאִיס (שבת י, רע״ב)
a toilet is different because it is repulsive

מַאן* interrog.

who? whom? מִי?
Who told you so? מַאן אָמַר לָךְ הָכִי? (פסחים ג, סע״ב)
* Sometimes, מַאן is followed by ־ד and serves as a relative pronoun — rather than an interrogative. See ־מַאן ד.

כְּמַאן

like whom? according to whom? כְּמִי?
This *question* often seeks tannaitic support for the opinion or the action of an amora.
אֲבוּהּ דִּשְׁמוּאֵל וְלֵוִי — כִּי הֲווּ בָּעוּ לְמִיפַּק לְאוֹרְחָא, הֲווּ מַקְדְּמִי וּמְצַלּוּ; וְכִי הֲוָה מָטֵי זְמַן קְרִיאַת שְׁמַע, קָרוּ. כְּמַאן? כִּי הַאי תַּנָּא, דְּתַנְיָא: ... הַשְׁכִּים לֵישֵׁב בְּקָרוֹן אוֹ בִסְפִינָה, מִתְפַּלֵּל; וּכְשֶׁיַּגִּיעַ זְמַן קְרִיאַת שְׁמַע, קוֹרֵא. (ברכות ל,א)
When Sh^e^muel's father and Levi would want to go out on the road, they would rise early and recite the Amida; and when the time for reciting the Sh^e^ma would arrive, they would recite [it]. According to whom? According to the following tanna, as it is stated [in a baraitha]: ... [if] one rises early to travel in a carriage or in a boat, he must recite the Amida; and when the time for reciting the Sh^e^ma arrives, he must recite [it].

כְּמַאן אָזְלָא הָא כְּמִי הוֹלֶכֶת זוֹ ...?

"According to whom does this go?"
With whose opinion is this text compatible?
This *question* seeks to determine which of the conflicting opinions quoted previously matches the baraitha or the amoraic statement that follows.
כְּמַאן אָזְלָא הָא דְּאָמַר רַב הוּנָא אָמַר רַב ...? (סוכה ב,ב ועוד)
With whose opinion is this [halakha], which Rav Huna quoted from Rav, compatible?

In response, the Talmud usually names the authority whose opinion is compatible:
כְּמַאן? כְּר׳ זֵירָא. (סוכה שם)
According to whom? According to R. Zera.
Sometimes, however, the Talmud replies that the text quoted is not compatible with any of the opinions that were quoted earlier in the discussion:
According to whom? כְּמַאן? דְּלָא כְּחַד. (שם)
According to none (of the above opinions).
SEE: אֲזַל

מַאן דְּ-

one who; whoever; the one who מִי שֶׁ-
מַאן דִּמְתַרְגֵּם לִי "בַּבָּקָר" אַלִּיבָּא דְּבֶן בַּג בַּג — מוֹבִילְנָא מָאנֵיהּ אֲבַתְרֵיהּ לְבֵי מַסּוּתָא! (עירובין כז, רע״א וש״נ)
[As for] anyone who explains to me [the necessity for the expression] "for oxen" according to b. Bag Bag — I will carry his clothes after him into the bathhouse!

כְּמַאן דְּ-

like one who (1) כְּמִי שֶׁ-
מִיחֲזֵי כְּמַאן דְּאָזֵיל לְחִינְגָּא. (שבת נד, סע״א)
He looks like one who is going to a fair.

as if (2) כְּמוֹ שֶׁ-*
זוּזֵי כְּמַאן דִּפְלִיגֵי דָּמוּ. (בבא מציעא סט, רע״ב)
The money is considered as if [it were] divided.
* In this usage, a form of the verb דָּמֵי, *seems* or *is considered*, is always used — usually at the end of the clause.

מַאן דְּאָמַר מִי שֶׁאוֹמֵר

[the one] who says; [the authority] that holds
מַאן דְּאָמַר חָדָשׁ מַמָּשׁ (עירובין נג,א)
[the one] who says [that he was] actually a new [king]
SEE: אָמַר, (ו)מִי אִיכָּא לְמַאן דְּאָמַר

מַאן דְּכַר שְׁמֵיהּ ... מִי הִזְכִּיר שְׁמוֹ?!

... "who has mentioned its name?!"
Was [this item] stated (earlier in the text)?!
This rhetorical question points out the *difficulty* that one item in this mishna or baraitha is stated out of context.
משנה: וְאֵין הַטַּבָּחִין נֶאֱמָנִין עַל גִּיד הַנָּשֶׁה — דִּבְרֵי ר׳ מֵאִיר. וַחֲכָמִים אוֹמְרִים: נֶאֱמָנִין עָלָיו וְעַל הַחֵלֶב.
תלמוד: "חֵלֶב"! מַאן דְּכַר שְׁמֵיהּ?! (חולין פט,ב: משנה ז:א)
MISHNA: Butchers are not to be trusted with regard to the removal of the sciatic nerve — [this is] the opinion of R. Méir, but the Ḥakhamim say: They are to be trusted with regard to it and with regard to the [removal of forbidden] fat.
TALMUD: [Forbidden] fat! Was it stated (earlier in R. Méir's halakha)?!
Usually, the Talmud immediately presents a *resolution* of this difficulty, introduced by הָכִי קָאָמַר or הָכִי קָתָנֵי, *this is what it says/means*.
הָכִי קָאָמַר: אֵין נֶאֱמָנִין עָלָיו וְעַל הַחֵלֶב — דִּבְרֵי ר׳ מֵאִיר,

וַחֲכָמִים אוֹמְרִים: נֶאֱמָנִין עָלָיו וְעַל הַחֵלֶב. (שם צג, סע"ב ע"פ כת"י וע' רש"י שם)

This is how the mishna should read: They are not to be trusted with regard to it (= the sciatic nerve) nor with regard to the [removal of forbidden] fat — (this is) the opinion of R. Méir, but the Ḥakhamim say: They are to be trusted with regard to it and with regard to the [forbidden] fat.

SEE: דְּכָר, מָאי עֲבִידְתֵּיהּ

מַאן חֲכָמִים ר' ... הִיא

[שֶׁל] מִי [דַּעַת] הַחֲכָמִים? [שֶׁל] ר' ... הִיא.

Whose [opinion has been stated by] the Ḥakhamim? It is [the opinion of] R. ....

This *question* is sometimes raised in the Talmud in order to identify the author of the opinion that was presented in a mishna or baraitha in the name of the Ḥakhamim.

משנה: ... כֹּהֲנִים נוֹשְׂאִין אֶת כַּפֵּיהֶן אַרְבַּע פְּעָמִים בַּיּוֹם: בְּשַׁחֲרִית, בְּמוּסָף, בְּמִנְחָה, וּבִנְעִילַת שְׁעָרִים. (תענית כו, רע"א: משנה פ"ד מ"א. וע' עירובין פג,א וש"נ)

תלמוד: אָמַר רַב נַחְמָן אָמַר רַבָּה בַּר אֲבוּהּ: זוֹ דִּבְרֵי ר' מֵאִיר, אֲבָל חֲכָמִים אוֹמְרִים: שַׁחֲרִית וּמוּסָף יֵשׁ בָּהֶן נְשִׂיאַת כַּפַּיִם; מִנְחָה, וּנְעִילָה אֵין בָּהֶן נְשִׂיאַת כַּפַּיִם. מַאן חֲכָמִים? ר' יְהוּדָה הִיא. (תענית כו,ב)

*MISHNA: The kohanim raise their hands (and pronounce Birkath Kohanim) four times in one day (on Yom Kippur): At the morning service, at the additional service, at the afternoon service, and at the concluding service (= n*ᵉ*ila).*

TALMUD: Rav Naḥman said, quoting Rabba b. Avuh: This is the opinion of R. Méir, but the Ḥakhamim say: In the morning and additional services there is Birkath Kohanim; [while] in the afternoon and concluding services there is no Birkath Kohanim. Whose [opinion has been stated by] the Ḥakhamim? It is [the opinion of] R. Yᵉhuda.

SEE: חֲכָמִים

מַאן שָׁמְעַתְּ לֵיהּ דְּאָמַר אֶת מִי אַתָּה שׁוֹמֵעַ

Whom do you hear that says ...? ?... הָאוֹמֵר

This *question* seeks to identify the tanna who holds the opinion that was anonymously mentioned in the mishna or baraitha that has just been quoted in the Talmud. On the basis of that identification, the Talmud usually proceeds to refute the tanna's opinion, or to bring a proof, or to raise a difficulty.

For an example — see בבא מציעא כד, סע"א.

מַאן תַּנָּא

Who is the tanna ...? ?... מִי הוּא הַתַּנָּא

מַאן תַּנָּא דִּפְלִיג עֲלֵיהּ דְּרַבִּי? רַבָּן שִׁמְעוֹן בֶּן גַּמְלִיאֵל הוּא. (שבת קטז,א)

Who is the tanna who disagrees with [the opinion] of Rebbi? It is Rabban Shim'on b. Gamliel.

*** It is usually possible to determine from the context whether this question should be vocalized** ?מַאן תַּנָּא ***(who is the tanna?)*** **like this entry or** ?מַאן תְּנָא ***(who taught ...?)*** **like the next entry. However, this distinction usually does not alter the meaning of the question significantly.**

SEE: תַּנָּא

Who taught (this text)? ?... מִי שָׁנָה מַאן תְּנָא

For an example — see the next entry.

SEE: תְּנָא

מַאן תְּנָא לְהָא דְּתָנוּ רַבָּנַן

מִי שָׁנָה אֶת זוֹ שֶׁשָּׁנוּ חֲכָמִים?

Who taught this [baraitha] that the ḥakhamim taught?

This *question* seeks to identify which of the tannaim, whose opposing opinions were previously quoted in the Talmud, advocates the opinion contained in the baraitha about to be quoted.

מַאן תְּנָא לְהָא דְּתָנוּ רַבָּנַן: לֹא תְמַלֵּא אִשָּׁה קְדֵרָה ...? לֵימָא בֵּית שַׁמַּאי הִיא וְלֹא בֵּית הִלֵּל?!(שבת יח, רע"ב)

Who taught this [baraitha] that the ḥakhamim taught: A woman must not fill a pot ...? Shall we say it is [the opinion of] Beth Shammai and not [that of] Beth Hillel?!

מָאנָא (מָאנֵי/מָנֵי .pl)

utensil; vessel; garment כְּלִי; בֶּגֶד

SEE: מָנָא**, the more common spelling of the singular**

מָאתַן

two hundred מָאתַיִם

מִבְּעוֹד יוֹם

SEE: (מִבְּ)עוֹד יוֹם

מַבָּרָא/מַעְבָּרָא (עבר)

ferryboat (1) מַעְבֹּרֶת

שְׁמוּאֵל הֲוָה קָא עָבַר בְּמַבָּרָא* (חולין צד,א ורש"י שם)

Shᵉmuel was crossing in a ferryboat

a crossing; a bridge (2) מַעְבָּרָה; גֶּשֶׁר

וְאִי אִיכָּא נַהֲרָא, לָא עָבְרָא; וְאִי אִיכָּא מַבָּרָא, עָבְרָא. (ביצה ז, רע"ב ורש"י שם)

But if there is a river (between the hen and the rooster), [the hen] does not cross over; but if there is a bridge, she does cross over.

*** In the commentary attributed to Rabbenu Gershom, the spelling is** מעברא.

מַגְבֵּי .prt (גבי אַפְעֵל)

causing to be collected; confiscating מַגְבֶּה

SEE: אַגְבֵּי

מְגַדֵּף[1]* .prt (גדף פַּעֵל)

blaspheming; a blasphemer

הַמְגַדֵּף אֵינוֹ חַיָּב עַד שֶׁיְּפָרֵשׁ הַשֵּׁם. (סנהדרין נו, סע"ב: משנה פ"ז מ"ה ע"פ במדבר טו:ל)

A blasphemer is not liable [to punishment] unless he explicitly pronounces the (Divine) Name.

* This entry is Hebrew, and the next is Aramaic.

attacking מִתְקִיף (גדף פָּעֵל) prt. **מְגַדֵּף***[2]

מְגַדֵּף בָּהּ ר׳ אַבָּהוּ** (סנהדרין ג, סע״ב ועוד)

R Abbahu attacks it (= the opinion just now presented)

* This entry is Aramaic, and the previous one is Hebrew.

** See Tosafoth on כתובות ב,ב ד״ה "פשיט".

out of; from מִתּוֹךְ **מִגּוֹ***

For an example — see (מִ)גּוֹ

* Certain arguments and principles that are introduced by the conjunction מִגּוֹ ד- (see next entry) are sometimes referred to by the word מִגּוֹ alone.

SEE: גו

מִגּוֹ ד-/מִיגּוֹ ד-

since; because מִתּוֹךְ שֶׁ-; מִפְּנֵי שֶׁ-

(1) This conjunction is sometimes used in the application of the following rule of evidence, which is called a מִגּוֹ in the Talmud and its commentaries (כתובות טז,א ועוד): In certain cases, the court accepts the plea of a defendant as credible on the ground that, if he intended to lie, he could have invented a better plea than the one he actually presented.

מִיגּוֹ דְּאִי בָּעֵי אָמַר לֵיהּ: "אֲנָא זְבִינְתַּהּ מִינָּךְ", כִּי אָמַר לֵיהּ נַמֵּי: "אַתְּ זַבִּינְתַּהּ לֵיהּ וְזַבְּנָהּ נִיהֲלִי" — מְהֵימַן. (בבא בתרא ג, סע״ב)

Since if [the defendant] wanted [to lie], he could say to him (= the plaintiff): "I bought it (= the property I occupy) from you"; even if he says to him: "You sold it to him (= a third party) who (subsequently) sold it to me" — [the defendant] is believed.

(2) This conjunction is also used to introduce some other principles of Jewish law.

מִגּוֹ דְּהָוְיָא דּוֹפֶן לְעִנְיַן סוּכָּה, הָוְיָא דּוֹפֶן לְעִנְיַן שַׁבָּת. (סוכה ז,א)

Since it is [regarded] as a (legal) wall for a sukka, it is a wall with respect to [defining a private domain for the laws of the] Sabbath.

SEE: מָה לִי לְשַׁקֵּר

מִדְּ- (מִן+ד-)

from [the fact] that; since מִכֵּיוָן שֶׁ-

For an example, see מִדְּקָתָנֵי.

מִדְּאוֹרַיְיתָא

SEE: אוֹרַיְיתָא

מִדָּה

(1) a measure; a measurement

כָּל מִדַּת חֲכָמִים כָּךְ הִיא: בְּאַרְבָּעִים סְאָה הוּא טוֹבֵל; בְּאַרְבָּעִים סְאָה חָסֵר קוֹרְטוֹב אֵינוֹ יָכוֹל לִטְבּוֹל בָּהֶן. (ראש השנה יג,א)

Every [designated] measurement of the ḥakhamim is of this nature: One may take a ritual bath in forty se´a [measures of water], [but] he may not take a ritual bath in forty se´a minus a "kortov" (= a very slight quantity).

(2) characteristic; attribute; manner

מִדַּת חֲסִידוּת שָׁנוּ כָּאן. (בבא מציעא נב,ב)

[The ḥakhamim] are teaching the attribute of piety here. (= They are recommending an action that is not required by Jewish law.)

בְּרִית כְּרוּתָה לִשְׁלֹשׁ עֶשְׂרֵה מִדּוֹת שֶׁאֵינָן חוֹזְרוֹת רֵיקָם. (ראש השנה יז,ב)

A covenant has been made with the thirteen (Divine) attributes that [those who entreat God through them] will not be turned away empty-handed.

(3) principle; rule of interpretation

צֵא וּלְמַד מִשְּׁלֹשׁ עֶשְׂרֵה מִדּוֹת שֶׁהַתּוֹרָה נִדְרֶשֶׁת בָּהֶן! (סנהדרין פו,א)

Go out and learn from the thirteen principles through which the Torah is interpreted!

pushing aside; putting off (פָּעֵל דחי) prt. **מְדַחֵי**

סְפוּקֵי מְסַפְּקָא לֵיהּ וּמְדַחֵי לֵיהּ. (מועד קטן טו, סע״ב)

He (= the amora) is quite uncertain about it (= the relative severity of that case) and pushes it aside (= rebuts arguments from either direction).

SEE: דְּחוּיֵי

מְדִינָה (דון)

(1) "a jurisdiction"; district; country

הַכֹּל כְּמִנְהַג הַמְּדִינָה. (בבא מציעא פג,א: משנה פ״ז מ״א)

Everything depends upon the custom in the country.

(2) the provinces (as opposed to the Beth HaMikdash or Y[e]rushalayim)*

יוֹם טוֹב שֶׁל רֹאשׁ הַשָּׁנָה שֶׁחָל לִהְיוֹת בְּשַׁבָּת — בַּמִּקְדָּשׁ הָיוּ תּוֹקְעִין, אֲבָל לֹא בַּמְּדִינָה. (ר״ה כט,ב ורש״י משנה פ״ד מ״א)

[When] the festival of Rosh HaShana falls on the Sabbath — in the Beth HaMikdash they would blow [the shofar], but not in the provinces.

* Rashi, in his commentary on this mishna, explains the term as including the rest of Y[e]rushalayim and excluding only the Beth HaMikdash; whereas the Rambam, on the same mishna, writes that the term includes all of Erets Yisrael outside of Y[e]rushalayim, since for him מִקְדָּשׁ means all of Y[e]rushalayim.

overseas; the Diaspora **מְדִינַת הַיָּם**

הַמֵּבִיא גֵט מִמְּדִינַת הַיָּם (גיטין ב, רע״א ורש״י שם: משנה פ״א מ״א)

one who delivers a bill of divorce from overseas

מַדְכַּר prt. (דכר אַפְעֵל)

reminding (1) מַזְכִּיר; גּוֹרֵם שֶׁמִּשֶּׁהוּ יִזָּכֵר

מַדְכַּר חַד לְחַבְרֵיהּ (כתובות כ, סע״א)

one (witness) may remind his fellow (witness)

mentioning; reciting (2) מַזְכִּיר; אוֹמֵר

מֵאֵימָתַי מַדְכְּרִינַן: "וְתֵן טַל וּמָטָר"? (תענית י,א)

From when do we [begin to] recite: "And give dew and rain"?
SEE: אַדְכַּר

מַדְלֵי prt. (דלי אַפְעֵל)
raising; elevating מֵרִים; מַגְבִּיהַּ
SEE: מִידְלֵי

מְדַמֵּי prt. (דמי פַּעֵל) מְדַמֶּה **comparing**
ר׳ יְהוֹשֻׁעַ בֶּן לֵוִי מְדַמֵּי מִילְּתָא לְמִילְּתָא. (ברכות יט,א ע"פ כת"י ע׳ רש"י שם)
*R. Y*ehoshua b. Levi compares one case to another (ascribing the same halakhic status to both of them).*

מִדְּקָתָנֵי (= מִ+דְּ+קָא+תָנֵי) כֵּיוָן שֶׁשּׁוֹנֶה
since he teaches (in a mishna or a baraitha)
For an example — see the next entry.

מִדְּקָתָנֵי סֵיפָא ... מִכְּלָל דְּרֵישָׁא ...

כֵּיוָן שֶׁשּׁוֹנֶה ... [בְּ]סֵיפָא, מִזֶּה יוֹצֵא שֶׁ[בְּ]רֵישָׁא [מְדֻבָּר בּ־....]
since he states [in] a latter/later clause ..., by implication it follows that the earlier clause (is dealing with) ....
This formula is used to clarify an earlier clause of a mishna or baraitha by means of an inference from a later clause.
משנה: יוֹצְאִין בָּהֶן ... וְיוֹצְאִין בְּקֶלַח שֶׁלָּהֶן (פסחים לט, רע"א: משנה פ"ב מ"ו)
תלמוד: מִדְּקָתָנֵי סֵיפָא "בְּקֶלַח שֶׁלָּהֶן", מִכְּלָל דְּרֵישָׁא "עָלִין"! (שם לט,ב)
MISHNA: One fulfills the obligation (of eating bitter herbs at the Seder) with them (= the species previously listed) ... and with their stalks.
TALMUD: Since he states [in] a later clause: "(One fulfills the obligation) with their stalks," by implication it follows that [in] the earlier clause ("with them" means "with their) leaves."
SEE: מִדְּ־

מִדְּרַבָּנַן SEE: (מִדְּאוֹרַיְתָא)

מִדְרָשׁ

(1) an interpretation (of a text, based upon a system of interpretive rules)
זֶה מִדְרָשׁ דָּרַשׁ ר׳ אֶלְעָזָר בֶּן עֲזַרְיָה לִפְנֵי חֲכָמִים בַּכֶּרֶם בְּיַבְנֶה: "הַבָּנִים יִירָשׁוּ, וְהַבָּנוֹת יִזּוֹנוּ". מָה הַבָּנִים אֵינָן יוֹרְשִׁין אֶלָּא לְאַחַר מִיתַת הָאָב, אַף הַבָּנוֹת אֵינָן נִזּוֹנוֹת אֶלָּא לְאַחַר מִיתַת אֲבִיהֶן. (כתובות מט,א: משנה פ"ד מ"ו)
*This is an interpretation [of a k*thuba regulation that] R. El'azar b. Azaria expounded before [the] hakhamim at the yeshiva in Yavne: "The sons will inherit (the k*thuba of their mother), and the (unmarried) daughters will be supported (from their father's property)." Just as the sons inherit only after the death of the father, so the daughters must be supported only after their father's death. (This interpretation is derived by analogy from the juxtaposition of these two regulations in the text of the k*thuba.)*
(2) Midrash; a compilation of Biblical interpretation that establishes a Scriptural basis for halakhoth and aggadoth*
בָּקִי ... בְּמִדְרָשׁ, בַּהֲלָכוֹת, וּבָאַגָּדוֹת (תענית טז, סע"א)
well-versed ... in Midrash, halakhoth, and aggadoth
* See Rashi on קידושין מט, סע"א.
SEE: דְּרָשָׁא

מִדְרְשָׁא SEE: בֵּי מִדְרְשָׁא

מָה **what; how; whereas; just as; since**
The following entries illustrate special usages of this word where the common Biblical meaning, the interrogative *what*, is not the best translation.

וּמָה ... אֵינוֹ דִין שֶׁ־

Since ..., (then) is it not logical that ...?!
This formula presents a קַל־וָחֹמֶר argument.
וְדִין הוּא: וּמָה כֶּסֶף, שֶׁאֵין מוֹצִיא, מַכְנִיס — שְׁטָר, שֶׁמּוֹצִיא, אֵינוֹ דִין שֶׁמַּכְנִיס?! (קידושין ה, רע"א)
And it is a logical inference: Since money, which does not set free (= effect a divorce), brings in [to matrimony] — (then) is it not logical that a document, which does set free, should bring in [to matrimony]?!
SEE: דִּין ,קַל וָחוֹמֶר ,(וּ)מָה ... עַל אַחַת כַּמָּה וְכַמָּה

מָה אֲנִי מְקַיֵּים

"How do I establish ...?"
What interpretation do I assign to [this Biblical passage]? What do I learn from ...?
"זָכוֹר" — יָכוֹל בַּלֵּב? כְּשֶׁהוּא אוֹמֵר לֹא תִשְׁכָּח — הֲרֵי שִׁכְחַת הַלֵּב אָמוּר. הָא מָה אֲנִי מְקַיֵּים "זָכוֹר"? בַּפֶּה. (מגילה יח,א ע"פ דברים כה:יז,יט)
זָכוֹר — Could it be [that it means to remember] in the heart [what Amalek did to the Jewish people]? When He says: "Don't forget" — behold [not] forgetting in the heart has been stated! What, then, do I learn from זָכוֹר? Orally (= to read aloud what Amalek did).
SEE: מְקַיֵּים

מָה ... אַף ...

"What is [the nature of] ..., [so] too ..."; Just as ..., [so] also ....
This formula presents an *analogy:* A halakha known to apply to one or more cases is applied to another, similar case as well.
מָה שְׁנַיִם — נִמְצָא אֶחָד מֵהֶן קָרוֹב אוֹ פָּסוּל, עֵדוּתָן בְּטֵילָה; אַף שְׁלֹשָׁה — נִמְצָא אֶחָד מֵהֶן קָרוֹב אוֹ פָּסוּל, עֵדוּתָן בְּטֵילָה. (מכות ה, סע"ב: משנה פ"א מ"א)
Just as [with regard to] two [witnesses] — [if] one of them is discovered to be a relative or [otherwise] disqualified, their testimony is void; [so,] too, [with regard to] three [witnesses] — [if] one of them is

discovered to be a relative or [otherwise] disqualified, their testimony is void.

SEE: הֶיקֵּשׁ, בִּנְיַן אָב, מָה מָּצִינוּ ... אַף ...

בַּמֶּה דְּבָרִים אֲמוּרִים

To what circumstances does [this halakhic statement] apply?

This expression is used in a mishna or baraitha to limit the scope of a halakha.

הַבְּהֵמָה מוּעֶדֶת לֶאֱכוֹל פֵּירוֹת וִירָקוֹת .... בַּמֶּה דְּבָרִים אֲמוּרִים? בִּרְשׁוּת הַנִּיזָּק, אֲבָל בִּרְשׁוּת הָרַבִּים — פָּטוּר. (בבא קמא יט,ב: משנה פ"ב מ"ב)

[The owner of] an animal is considered forewarned with regard to [its] eating fruits and vegetables .... To what circumstances does [this halakha] apply? [To damage the animal caused] on the plaintiff's premises, but [for damage it caused] in the public domain — [its owner] is exempt.

SEE: הָנֵי מִילֵּי

מָה הַצַּד (= מָה הַצַּד הַשָּׁוֶה)

"Just as [the cases that share] a [common] property ..."; a מָה־הַצַּד analogy

This term denotes an analogy based upon a common property shared by two subjects.

תֵּיתֵי בְּ"מָה הַצַּד"! (קידושין כא, רע"א)

Let it be derived through a מָה־הַצַּד analogy!

SEE: בִּנְיַן אָב, (הַ)צַּד הַשָּׁוֶה שֶׁבָּהֶן

מַה טַּעַם קָאָמַר "מָה טַּעַם" הוּא אוֹמֵר.

"What is [the] reason" [the tanna] is stating.

This formula introduces a *resolution* of a redundancy in the text of a mishna or baraitha: A later statement in the text is not redundant as previously argued, but it serves to give the reason for a previous statement.

ברייתא: מָקוֹם שֶׁנָּהֲגוּ לִקְצוֹר — אֵינוֹ רַשַּׁאי לַעֲקוֹר. לַעֲקוֹר — אֵינוֹ רַשַּׁאי לִקְצוֹר. וּשְׁנֵיהֶם מְעַכְּבִין זֶה אֶת זֶה ...
תלמוד: "וּשְׁנֵיהֶן מְעַכְּבִין זֶה אֶת זֶה" — לָמָּה לִי? "מָה טַּעַם" קָאָמַר. מָה טַּעַם לִקְצוֹר אֵינוֹ רַשַּׁאי לַעֲקוֹר, לַעֲקוֹר אֵינוֹ רַשַּׁאי לִקְצוֹר? מִשּׁוּם דִּשְׁנֵיהֶן מְעַכְּבִין זֶה אֶת זֶה. (ב"מ קג, רע"ב)

BARAITHA: [In] a locality where it is customary [in harvesting] to cut [crops], one [who leased a field] must not uproot [them manually]; [where it is customary] to uproot — he must not cut. And either party (= either the owner or the leaseholder) may prevent the other [from altering the usual procedure].
TALMUD: Why do I need [the statement] "and either party can prevent the other"? "What is the reason" [the tanna] is stating. For what reason [where it is customary] to cut must one not uproot; [where it is customary] to uproot must one not cut? Because either party can prevent the other [from altering the usual procedure].

SEE: פְּרוּשֵׁי קָא מְפָרֵשׁ

מַה לְ-... שֶׁ-... תֹּאמַר בְּ-... שֶׁ-...

Whereas (A is potent), [as evidenced by the fact] that ...; can you ascribe [the same power] to (B), which ...?!

This formula presents a *refutation* of a קַל־וָחֹמֶר argument. It shows that A, which was regarded as weaker than B in the course of the קַל וָחֹמֶר, is stronger than B in at least one respect; hence, a strict halakha of A cannot necessarily be attributed to B.

אִיכָּא לְמִיפְרַךְ: מָה לִמְלָאכָה, שֶׁכֵּן נוֹהֶגֶת בְּשַׁבָּתוֹת וְיָמִים טוֹבִים — תֹּאמַר בְּעִינּוּי, שֶׁאֵינוֹ נוֹהֵג בְּשַׁבָּתוֹת וְיָמִים טוֹבִים?! (יומא פא, סע"א)

There are grounds to refute (the קַל וָחֹמֶר that was seeking to prove that a Jew who eats on Yom Kippur has violated a negative commandment, based on the prohibition of labor on Yom Kippur): Whereas a prohibition of labor [is potent] as evidenced by the fact that it also applies to Sabbaths and festivals; can you ascribe [the same power] to fasting, which does not apply to Sabbaths and festivals?!

SEE: אִיכָּא לְמִיפְרַךְ

מַה לִּי*

"What [is it] to me?!"
What [advantage] is there for me ...?!

This expression presents a *rhetorical question.*

For examples — see the next two entries.

* Sometimes, other personal pronouns are used, as in מַה לוֹ.

SEE: לָמָּה לִי

מַה לִּי לְשַׁקֵּר

What [advantage] is there for me to lie?!

This *rhetorical question* is sometimes the basis for the credibility of a plea in court. It is argued: If this party had intended to lie, he would have issued a stronger plea than the one he actually stated.

For an example — see קידושין סד רע"ב וש"נ.

SEE: מִגּוֹ ד-

מַה לִּי ... מַה לִּי ...*

What is [the difference] to me [whether] ... [or] ...?!

מַלְאַךְ הַמָּוֶת — מַה לִּי הָכָא, מַה לִּי הָתָם?! (בבא מציעא לו,ב)

[As for] the angel of death — what [is the difference] to me [whether the animal is] here (= in the thief's house) or there (= elsewhere)?! (= There is no difference, for it would have died in any event.)

* Sometimes, לִי need not be translated into English.

מַה מָּצִינוּ ... אַף ...

Just as we have found ..., also ....

This formula presents an *analogy* teaching that a halakha known to apply to one or more cases should be applied to a similar case as well.*

מָה מָצִינוּ בְּכָל מָקוֹם בָּרְבִיעִית, אַף כָּאן בָּרְבִיעִית. (ר״ה לב,א)

*Just as we have found on every [other] occasion [the sanctity of the holyday is expressed] in the fourth [b*rakha of the Amida], here (= in Musaf of Rosh HaShana) also in the fourth [b*rakha].*

* According to Rashi on שבת כו, רע״ב — this analogy is also called a בִּנְיַן אָב. The expression מָה מָצִינוּ is also used like a noun to denote an analogy of this type:

בְּמַאי גָּמַר מִינֵּיהּ? אִי בְּקַל וָחוֹמֶר אִי בְּמָה מָצִינוּ. (מכות טו,א)

Through what [method] does he derive from it? Either through a קַל־וָחוֹמֶר *analogy or through a* מָה־מָצִינוּ *analogy.*

SEE: מָצִינוּ, מָה ... אַף ... בִּנְיַן אָב

מָה נַפְשָׁךְ מָה רְצוֹנְךָ לוֹמַר?!

(1) What is it your desire [to say]?!
Which position would you adopt?!

This rhetorical question introduces a *dilemma* that confronts the opinion that has just been expressed or implied in the Talmud.*

רַב הוּנָא יְהִיב לֵיהּ לְשַׁמָּעֵיהּ. מָה נַפְשָׁךְ?! אִי שָׁרֵי, לְכוּלֵּי עָלְמָא שָׁרֵי! וְאִי אָסִיר, לְכוּלֵּי עָלְמָא אָסִיר! (חולין קיב,א ע״פ כת״י)

Rav Huna gave it (= bread that had been in contact with bloody meat) to his [Jewish] attendant (exclusively). Which position would you adopt?! If it is permissible, (then) it should be permitted for everyone (to eat it, including Rav Huna himself)! If it is forbidden, (then) it should be forbidden for everybody (including his attendant)!

(2) a מַה־נַפְשָׁךְ argument

זָכָר שָׁקִיל מָנֶה מִמַּה־נַפְשָׁךְ. (בבא בתרא דף קמא, סע״א)

The male receives [the sum of] one hundred zuz by virtue of a מַה־נַפְשָׁךְ *argument.*

* Occasionally, this expression presents two possible alternatives for consideration in *defense* of an opinion, as in בבא מציעא ו,ב.

SEE: מַאי קָסָבַר, נְפַשׁ

וּמָה ... עַל אַחַת כַּמָּה וְכַמָּה

Since ..., (then) ... how much more so!

This formula presents a קַל־וָחוֹמֶר argument.

וּמָה בִּמְקוֹם חִיּוּתֵנוּ אָנוּ מִתְיָרְאִין, בִּמְקוֹם מִיתָתֵנוּ עַל אַחַת כַּמָּה וְכַמָּה! (ברכות סא,ב)

Since we (fish) are afraid [when we are] in the place where we live (= water), (then) in the place where we die (= dry land) how much more so!

SEE: עַל אַחַת כַּמָּה וְכַמָּה, (וּ)מָה ... אֵינוֹ דִּין שֶׁ־

מָה עִנְיַן ... אֵצֶל ...

SEE: (וְ)כִי מָה עִנְיַן ... אֵצֶל ...

וּמָה רָאִיתָ*

"But what did you see?"
On what grounds have you determined to ...?

This question introduces a *difficulty* that is due to apparent arbitrariness.

וּמָה רָאִיתָ לְרַבּוֹת כְּסוּת סוּמָא וּלְהוֹצִיא כְּסוּת לַיְלָה? (שבת כז,ב)

But on what grounds have you determined to include the garment of a blind man (within the mitzva of tzitzith) and to exclude a night-time garment?

* See the Biblical question מָה רָאִיתָ כִּי עָשִׂיתָ אֶת הַדָּבָר הַזֶּה? (בראשית כ:י).

SEE: מַאי חָזֵית, the Aramaic parallel.

מָה שֶׁאֵין כֵּן

which is not so;
which is not the case (with regard to ...)

משנה: הַקּוֹרֵא אֶת הַמְּגִילָּה עוֹמֵד וְיוֹשֵׁב .... (מגילה כא,א: משנה פ״ד מ״א)

ברייתא: תָּנָא: מָה שֶׁאֵין כֵּן בַּתּוֹרָה. (שם)

MISHNA: One may read the scroll (of Esther to fulfill his duty on Purim) either standing or sitting ....

BARAITHA: [A tanna] taught: Which is not the case with regard to the Torah [reading, which must be performed by the reader while he is standing].

מָה תַּלְמוּד לוֹמַר

What teaching [does the Biblical passage mean] to convey?

This question is followed immediately by the tanna's interpretation of a word, a phrase, or a clause — showing that it is not superfluous.

מָה תַּלְמוּד לוֹמַר "לֶחֶם עוֹנִי"? פְּרָט לְעִיסָּה שֶׁנִּילוֹשָׁה בְּיַיִן וְשֶׁמֶן וּדְבַשׁ. (פסחים לו,א ע״פ דברים טז,ג)

What teaching does "the bread of affliction" [mean] to convey? It has excluded (from matza) dough that was kneaded with wine, oil, or honey.

SEE: תַּלְמוּד לוֹמַר

מְהַדֵּר prt. (הדר פָּעֵל)

pursuing zealously; seeking מְחַזֵּר

הַמְהַדְּרִין — נֵר לְכָל אֶחָד וְאֶחָד. (שבת כא,ב ורש״י שם)

*Those who zealously pursue [the mitzvoth] — [they kindle] a candle for each and every person.**

* In our translation of this Hebrew text, we have followed Rashi who explains הַמְהַדְּרִין in accordance with the Aramaic meaning of הדר. However, R. Nathan of Rome in his *Arukh* and the Rambam in his *Mishné Torah* both understood it as a Hebrew term meaning *those who honor [the mitzvoth]*. See רמב״ם הל׳ חנוכה פ״ד ה״א.

SEE: הֲדַר, הֲדַר

מַהֲדַר prt. (הדר אַפְעֵל)

מַחֲזִיר

returning (something); restoring; repeating; replying

For an example, see אַהְדַּר.

לְמֶהְדַּר

SEE: (לְ)מֵיהְדַּר

מָהוּ (= מָה+הוּא)

What is it? What is the halakhic ruling?

This term is often used in the formulation of a halakhic problem.

עִיר שֶׁיֵּשׁ בָּהּ עֲבוֹדָה זָרָה ..., מַהוּ לֵילֵךְ לְשָׁם? (עבודה זרה יא, סע״ב: משנה פ״א מ״ד)

[If there is] an idolatrous [festival] in the town ..., what is the halakhic ruling [as] to going there?

For additional examples, see בָּעֵי מִינֵּיהּ and בְּעָא מִינֵּיהּ.

SEE: מַאי, בַּעְיָא

מַהוּ דְתֵימָא ... קָא מַשְׁמַע לַן

מַהוּ שֶׁתֹּאמַר ...? הוּא מַשְׁמִיעַ לָנוּ.

What is it that you would have supposed ...? He [comes to] teach us.

After a difficulty was raised that a point in a mishna* or baraitha is obvious (פְּשִׁיטָא) and need not be stated, this formula presents a *resolution* of that difficulty. It is argued: If that point had not been stated by the tanna, we might have ruled differently; therefore it was necessary for the tanna to state it.

משנה: נָשִׁים ... פְּטוּרִין מִקְּרִיאַת שְׁמַע. (ברכות כ, סע״א: משנה פ״ג מ״ג)

תלמוד: פְּשִׁיטָא! מִצְוַת עֲשֵׂה שֶׁהַזְּמַן גְּרָמָא הִיא, וְכָל מִצְוַת עֲשֵׂה שֶׁהַזְּמַן גְּרָמָא נָשִׁים פְּטוּרוֹת! מַהוּ דְתֵימָא: הוֹאִיל וְאִית בַּהּ מַלְכוּת שָׁמַיִם? קָא מַשְׁמַע לַן. (שם כ, רע״ב)

*MISHNA: Women ... are exempt from the recitation of Sh*e*ma.*

*TALMUD: It is obvious! It (= the recitation of Sh*e*ma) is a positive commandment bound by time, and women are exempt from all positive commandments bound by time! What is it that you would have supposed: Since it contains [the acceptance of] the kingdom of Heaven [women should be obligated to recite it]? He (= the tanna of the mishna) [comes to] teach us (that they are exempt nevertheless).*

* Rashi (on חולין מב, רע״א) states that this formula usually refers to a mishna.

מְהֵימַן pass. prt. (הימן*)

believed; trustworthy נֶאֱמָן

אַתְּ מְהֵימַנְתְּ לִי בִּשְׁבוּעָה; הָאִיךְ לָא מְהֵימַן לִי בִּשְׁבוּעָה. (בבא מציעא לו,ב)

You are trustworthy to me under oath; the other party is not trustworthy to me under oath (= I do not trust his oath).

* Note the four-letter root, which may have developed from the הִפְעִיל *binyan of* אמן.

מְהֵימַן act. prt. (הימן)

believing; trusting מַאֲמִין

I do not trust you. לָא מְהֵימְנָא* לָךְ. (ב״מ סו, סע״ב)

* מְהֵימְנָא = מְהֵימַן+אֲנָא, *I trust.* See also the previous note.

SEE: הֵימְנֵיהּ

מַהֲבָא

SEE: (מַ)הָכָא

מְהַל (מהל: מָהֵיל .prt, לִימְהַל .fut, לְמִימְהַל .inf)

he circumcised מָלִי

וְהֵיכָא דְלָא מַהֲלֵיהּ אֲבוּהּ, מִחַיְּיבִי בֵּי דִינָא לְמִימְהֲלֵיהּ. (קידושין כט,א)

And in a case where his father did not circumcise him, the court is obligated to circumcise him.

* In Hebrew the root מול means *circumcise* — but the active participle מוֹהֵל, *circumcising* or *circumcisor*, and the passive participle מָהוּל, *circumcised*, indicate the existence of מהל as a Hebrew root as in Aramaic.

מַהֲנֵי prt. (הני אַפְעֵל)

benefiting (1) מְהַנֶּה

דְּאִי טָעֵים בְּצַפְרָא מִידִי, לְאוּרְתָּא לָא הָוָה מַהֲנֵי לֵיהּ מֵיכְלָא (פסחים קח,א)

for if he ate something in the morning, the food would not benefit him in the evening

effective (legally); taking effect (2) מוֹעִיל

וְכִי מַהֲנֵי בַּהּ תְּנַאי? (ביצה ל,ב)

But is a stipulation with regard to it effective?

SEE: אַהֲנֵי

מוּבְהָק* pass. prt. (= מֻבְהָק) (בהק הָפְעַל)

clear; distinct; par excellence

a distinct identifying mark סִימָן מוּבְהָק (ב״מ כז,ב)

his teacher par excellence רַבּוֹ מוּבְהָק (ב״מ לג,א)

* Compare the Biblical בֹּהַק (ויקרא יג:לט).

מוֹדֵי prt. (ידי אַפְעֵל) מוֹדֶה

(1) admitting (responsibility, guilt)

בְּאִינָךְ חַמְשִׁים הָא לָא מוֹדֵי. (בבא מציעא ד, סע״א)

He is not admitting [that he owes] the other fifty.

(2) accepting (his opponent's view); **agreeing**

מוֹדוּ לֵיהּ רַבָּנַן לר׳ שִׁמְעוֹן בֶּן אֶלְעָזָר בְּרוֹב נָכְרִים. (ב״מ כד,א)

The Ḥakhamim agree with R. Shim'on b. El'azar in [a case where] the majority [of the local people] are non-Jews.

(3) thanking; expressing gratitude

אוֹדוּיֵי הוּא דְקָא מוֹדְיָת. (יבמות סב,א)

It was really gratitude that she was expressing (for the birth of her son).*

* The infinitive אוֹדוּיֵי, which strengthens the verb מוֹדְיָת, has been expressed by the adverb *really* in English.

SEE: אוֹדִי

מוֹדַע prt. (ידע אַפְעֵל) מוֹדִיעַ

informing

SEE: אוֹדַע

מוֹדָעָא גִּלּוּי דַּעַת

a notification

In order to cancel the force of a document, one party can issue a declaration in advance in the presence of witnesses claiming that he is about to sign the document under duress.

כָּל מוֹדָעָא דְּלָא כְּתִיב בַּהּ: ״אֲנַן יָדְעִינַן בֵּיהּ בְּאוֹנְסָא דִפְלָנְיָא״ לָאו מוֹדָעָא הִיא. (בבא בתרא מ, סע״א־רע״ב)

Any notification that does not have written in it: "We (the undersigned witnesses) are aware of the coercion imposed upon So-and-so" is not a [valid] notification.

מוּזְהָר (= מֻזְהָר) pass. prt. (זהר הָפְעַל)

warned; prohibited

וְהֵיכָן מוּזְהָר עַל אֲכִילָה? (מכות יט,ב)

And where (in the Torah) is [one] warned against eating (the second tithe in a state of ritual impurity)?

SEE: מַזְהִיר

מוּחְלֶפֶת (= מֻחְלֶפֶת) pass. prt. (חלף הָפְעַל)

reversed; interchanged

See the example referred to in the next entry.

מוּחְלֶפֶת הַשִּׁיטָה

The system should be reversed.

This statement presents a *resolution* of a contradiction. When the opinion of at least one of the two tannaim involved in a controversy contradicts his opinion in another similar controversy, an amora (usually R. Yoḥanan) sometimes proposes that in one of the controversies the two opinions should be reversed. For example (in ביצה ג, סע"א וש"נ), R. Yoḥanan proposes that R. Y^{e}huda holds the opinion that was initially attributed to the Ḥakhamim, and the Ḥakhamim hold the opinion initially attributed to R. Y^{e}huda.

Subsequently, the Talmud proceeds to quote a different amora (usually from Babylonia) who rejects that resolution of the difficulty with the directive לְעוֹלָם לָא תֵּיפוּךְ! *("In reality, do not reverse!")*. Instead, the latter amora resolves the contradiction in a different manner without interchanging opinions.

For an example — see Rabina in ביצה שם ג, רע"ב.

SEE: מַחְלִיף, וְהָא אִיפְּכָא שְׁמַעִינַן לְהוּ, אֵיפוּךְ

מוּטָב pass. prt. (טוב הָפְעַל)

(1) it is better; it is preferable

מוּטָב תֵּיעָקֵר אוֹת אַחַת מֵהַתּוֹרָה, וְאַל תִּשְׁתַּכַּח תּוֹרָה מִיִּשְׂרָאֵל. (תמורה יד,ב ע"פ שיטה מקובצת שם)

It is better [that] one letter be uprooted from the Torah than [that] the Torah be forgotten by the Jewish people.*

(2) the good; the right path

מַחֲזִירָן לְמוּטָב (סנהדרין צז, סע"ב)

he will return them to the right path

* The rule that the Oral Torah not be written down is based on a letter (or two) in the Torah. The rule was uprooted for the preservation of the Torah.

מוֹכַח* prt. (יכח אַפְעֵל) מוֹכִיחַ

(1) "proving"; clear; well-grounded**

אוּמְדָּנָא דְּמוֹכַח שָׁאנֵי. (בבא בתרא קמו, סע"ב)

A well-grounded assumption is exceptional.

(2) reproving; admonishing**

הֲוָה קָא מוֹכַח לַן בְּמִילֵּי דִּשְׁמַיָּא (גיטין נז,ב)

he would admonish us about Heavenly matters

* This form is popularly pronounced מוּכַח.

** The parallel Hebrew noun to the first meaning is הוֹכָחָה, *proof*; whereas the parallel to the second meaning is תּוֹכָחָה, *reproof*.

מוֹכְחָא מִילְּתָא הַדָּבָר מוֹכִיחַ

the matter clarifies; the context is clear

"לְמִי שֶׁעָשָׂה לַאֲבוֹתֵינוּ וְלָנוּ אֶת כָּל הַנִּסִּים הָאֵלּוּ"... הָתָם מוֹכְחָא מִילְּתָא: מַאן עָבֵיד נִיסֵּי? קוּדְשָׁא בְּרִיךְ הוּא. (ברכות נ,א)

"To the One Who has performed all these miracles for our ancestors and for us" ... There the context is clear (that the reference is to the Almighty): Who (is it that) performs miracles? The Holy One Blessed Be He.

מוּם SEE: בַּעַל מוּם

מוּפְלָג (= מֻפְלָג) pass. prt. (פלג הָפְעַל)

(1) removed; distant

מוּפְלָג מִן הַיּוֹבֵל (ערכין כט,ב)

[a time] distant from the Jubilee year

(2) extraordinary; outstanding (in scholarship and/or in advanced years)*

שָׁאנֵי רַב אַחָא בַּר יַעֲקֹב דְּמוּפְלָג. (עירובין סג,א ע' ר"ח שם)

[The case of] Rav Aḥa b. Ya'akov is different, for he is extraordinary.

* A זָקֵן מוּפְלָג is a *remarkably old man* in later Hebrew.

מוּפְנֶה (= מֻפְנֶה) pass. prt. f. (פני הָפְעַל)

free (for interpretation); **available** (for deduction, because it is not needed for the plain sense of the passage)

כָּל גְּזֵירָה שָׁוָה שֶׁאֵינָהּ מוּפְנָה כָּל עִיקָּר — אֵין לְמֵדִין הֵימֶנָּה. (נדה כב, סע"ב)

[As for] any גְּזֵירָה־שָׁוָה *analogy that is not at all free (because its terms are not superfluous) — we cannot deduce from it.*

SEE: מֻפְנֵי

מוֹצִיא prt. (יצא הִפְעִיל)

taking out; removing; bringing forth; extracting; releasing

In addition to its basic meaning, this word is also found in two special senses in Mishnaic Hebrew:

(1) excluding (from a halakha or a category)

וּמוֹצִיא אֲנִי אֶת הַנָּכְרִים שֶׁאֵין מְזוֹנוֹתֵיהֶן עָלֶיךָ (ביצה כא,ב)

but I exclude [preparing food on a festival for the use of] non-Jews, because feeding them is not your responsibility

(2) causing (another) **to fulfill his obligation; performing a duty on behalf of** (others)

כָּל שֶׁאֵינוֹ מְחוּיָּב בְּדָבָר אֵינוֹ מוֹצִיא אֶת הָרַבִּים יְדֵי חוֹבָתָן. (ברכות כ,ב)

Anyone who is not obligated in the matter (= the mitzva) cannot perform the duty on behalf of others.
SEE: מְרַבֶּה אֲנִי, הוֹצִיא, מַפִּיק

הַמּוֹצִיא מֵחֲבֵרוֹ עָלָיו הָרְאָיָה

[If a person] would take [something] away from [the possession of] his fellow man [into his own possession], the [burden of] proof [rests] upon him (= the claimant).

This fundamental rule of evidence means that unless a claimant produces solid evidence for his cause (two witnesses or the equivalent) — he cannot legally collect any part of his claim, and the status quo remains in force.*

שׁוֹר שֶׁהָיָה רוֹדֵף אַחַר שׁוֹר אַחֵר וְהוּזַּק — זֶה אוֹמֵר: שׁוֹרְךָ הִזִּיק, וְזֶה אוֹמֵר: לֹא כִי, אֶלָּא בְסֶלַע לָקָה — הַמּוֹצִיא מֵחֲבֵירוֹ עָלָיו הָרְאָיָה. (בבא קמא לה, סע״א: משנה פ״ג מי״א)

[If] an ox was pursuing the ox of another man and [the latter ox] was [found] injured — one [owner] saying: "Your ox injured [mine]," with the other saying: "Not so, rather it was injured by a rock" — the [burden of] proof [rests] upon him (= the claimant).

* In בבא קמא מו,ב – the Talmud bases this rule on the argument: דְּכָאֵיב לֵיהּ כֵּיבָא הוּא אָזֵיל לְבֵי אָסְיָא.
The one who is suffering pain should go to the doctor. (= The person who is not satisfied with the status quo is the one who should try to remedy the situation.)

מוֹקֵים/מוֹקֵי prt. (קום אַפְעֵל) מַעֲמִיד

setting up (a text as referring to); explaining

This verb often refers to the explanation of a specific text or statement in accordance with a particular opinion or as dealing with particular circumstances. It is usually followed by the direct-object pronoun לַהּ, *it*, which is often omitted in English.

שְׁמוּאֵל מוֹקֵים לַהּ לְמַתְנִיתִין כְּר׳ יְהוּדָה (נדרים ה, רע״ב)
*Sh*ᵉ*muel explains (it) our mishna in accordance with [the opinion of] R. Y*ᵉ*huda*

SEE: (וּ)מִי מָצֵית מוֹקְמַתְּ, אוֹקֵי

מוֹרֵי prt. (ירי אַפְעֵל) מוֹרֶה; פּוֹסֵק

teaching; issuing a halakhic decision

SEE: אוֹרֵי

מוֹתָב מוֹשָׁב

a sitting; a session

at a session of three (judges) בְּמוֹתַב תְּלָתָא (ב״ב קסה,ב)

SEE: מוֹתִיב², יָתֵיב

מוֹתִיב*¹ prt. (תוב אַפְעֵל) מֵשִׁיב; מַקְשֶׁה

replying; refuting; pointing out a difficulty

For an example — see (וּ)מוֹתְבִינַן אַשְׁמַעְתִּין.

* The form מְתִיב is also used in the same sense, and its plural מֵיתִיבֵי is very common.

SEE: אוֹתִיב¹, מְתִיב, מֵיתִיבֵי, הוּא מוֹתִיב לַהּ וְהוּא מְפָרֵק לַהּ

מוֹתִיב² prt. (יתב אַפְעֵל)

seating; installing מוֹשִׁיב

מוֹתְבִינַן לֵיהּ לְצוּרְבָא מֵרַבָּנַן, וּלְעַם הָאָרֶץ נַמֵּי אָמְרִינַן לֵיהּ: ״תֵּיב!״ (שבועות ל,ב)

We (= the judges) seat the Torah scholar, and we also tell the uncultured person: "Be seated!" (when the two oppose each other in a courtroom).

SEE: אוֹתִיב², יָתֵיב

וּמוֹתְבִינַן אַשְׁמַעְתִּין

וּמְשִׁיבִין (= וּמַקְשִׁים) אָנוּ עַל שְׁמוּעָתֵנוּ.

But we may point out a difficulty with our own halakhic teaching.

The amora Rabba uses this expression to introduce a mishna or a baraitha that (apparently) contradicts the halakha that he himself has presented — either in his own name or in the name of his teacher.

רַבָּה וְרַב יוֹסֵף דְּאָמְרֵי תַּרְוַיְיהוּ: הַמַּבְדִּיל בַּתְּפִלָּה צָרִיךְ שֶׁיַּבְדִּיל עַל הַכּוֹס. אָמַר רַבָּה: וּמוֹתְבִינַן אַשְׁמַעְתִּין: טָעָה וְלֹא הִזְכִּיר ... הַבְדָּלָה בְ״חוֹנֵן הַדָּעַת״ אֵין מַחֲזִירִין אוֹתוֹ, מִפְּנֵי שֶׁיָּכוֹל לְאוֹמְרָהּ עַל הַכּוֹס. (ברכות לג,א)

*Rabba and Rav Yosef both say: One who recites Havdala in the Amida must (also) recite Havdala over the cup [of wine]. Rabba said: But we may point out a difficulty with our own halakhic teaching (from the following baraitha): [If] one erred and did not mention Havdala in [the b*ᵉ*rakha of]* חוֹנֵן הַדָּעַת*, we do not make him repeat [the Amida], because he can say it (= Havdala) on the cup (implying that if he did say it in the Amida, he would not have to say it over the cup).*

SEE: שְׁמַעְתָּא, מוֹתִיב¹

מְזַבֵּין prt. (זבן פַּעֵל) מוֹכֵר

selling

SEE: זְבַן, זַבֵּין and its note

מָזַג (מזג: מוֹזֵג .act. prt, מָזוּג .pass. prt);
מְזַג* (מזג: מָזֵיג .act. prt, מְזִיג .pass. prt)

he diluted (wine with water, since pure wine was too strong to drink)**

מָזְגוּ לוֹ כּוֹס רִאשׁוֹן. (פסחים קיד,א: משנה פ״י מ״ב)
They diluted the first cup for him (at the Seder).

diluted wine חַמְרָא מְזִיגָא (עבודה זרה ל,א)

* The first form is Hebrew, and the second is Aramaic.
** In Modern Hebrew, this verb usually means *he poured.*

מִזְדַּבַּן/מִיזְדַּבַּן prt. (זבן אִתְפַּעַל)

being sold נִמְכָּר

חֲדָא חֲדָא מִזְדַּבְּנָן בְּחַמְשִׁין (בבא מציעא צט, רע״ב)
*[if the fifty dates are sold] one by one, they are sold for [a total of] fifty [p*ᵉ*rutoth]*

SEE: זְבַן, זַבֵּין, מְזַבֵּין and its note

מַזְהִיר prt. (זהר הִפְעִיל)**;** **מַזְהַר*** prt. (זהר אַפְעֵל)

warning; prohibiting

אֵין מַזְהִירִין מִן הַדִּין. (מכות ה,ב ורש"י)

We do not [base a] warning on a קַל־וָחֹמֶר *argument (instead of a pasuk).*

* The first form is Hebrew, and the second is Aramaic.

SEE: הִזְהִיר, מוּזְהָר, אַזְהָרָה

מֵזִיד prt. (זוד הִפְעִיל) **acting deliberately (with awareness of wrongdoing)**

בְּשׁוֹגֵג לָא קַנְסוּהּ רַבָּנָן; בְּמֵזִיד קַנְסוּהּ רַבָּנָן. (שבת ג, סע"ב)

For acting unintentionally the ḥakhamim did not punish him; for acting deliberately the ḥakhamim did punish him.

SEE: שָׁגַג

מְחָא (מחי: מָחֵי .prt, לְמִחֵי .fut)

(1) הִכָּה **he hit; he struck**

שְׁקַל פִּנְדָּא דְמָרָא, מַחְיֵיהּ (בבא קמא כז,ב)

he took the handle of a hoe [and] struck him

(2) אָרַג **he wove***

For an example — see אִטּוּ כּוּלְהוּ בְּחַדָא מְחִיתָא מְחִיתִינְהוּ.

* See Rashi's comment on חולין נח,ב explaining this usage.

מְחָאָה **a protest**

מְחָאָה בִּפְנֵי שְׁלֹשָׁה. (בבא בתרא לט, סע"א)

A protest [must be made] in the presence of three [people, in order to be valid].

מָחָה* (מחי: מוֹחֶה .prt)

he protested; he objected

כָּל מִי שֶׁיֵּשׁ בְּיָדוֹ לִמְחוֹת וְאֵינוֹ מוֹחֶה — נֶעֱנָשׁ. (עבודה זרה ח,א)

Whoever has the opportunity to protest [and thereby prevent a transgression] but does not protest — is punished.

* In Biblical Hebrew (e.g., במדבר ה:כג), this verb means *he erased, he wiped out, he destroyed.*

SEE: מִיחָה, מְחֵי

מַחְוֵי prt. (חוי אַפְעֵל)

מַרְאֶה **showing; indicating (by gesture)**

This word is generally used to introduce a brief remark or reply of an amora.

מַחְוֵי לֵיהּ ר' אֲבָהוּ: וּבִשְׁבוּעָה! (בבא מציעא ז,א ורש"י שם)

R. Abbahu indicates to him [with a gesture]: And with an oath! (In order to receive a portion of the garment in dispute, each party must affirm his claim with an oath.)

מְחַוַּורְתָּא pass. prt. (חור פַּעֵל)

מְחֻוֶּרֶת; מְלֻבֶּנֶת; בְּרוּרָה **"bleached"; clear**

SEE: אֶלָּא מְחַוַּורְתָּא כִּדְשַׁנִּינַן מֵעִיקָּרָא

מְחֵי (מחי פַּעֵל: לְמִחוּיֵי .inf)

מִחָה **he protested; he objected**

אִיבָּעֵי לֵיהּ לְמִחוּיֵי (בבא בתרא לה, סע"ב)

he should have protested (that he was still the owner of the property)

SEE: מָחָה, מִיחָה

מְחַיֵּיב prt. (חוב פַּעֵל) מְחַיֵּב

obligating; convicting; declaring guilty

SEE: מִיחַיַּיב

מְחַיֵּיךְ* prt. (חוך פַּעֵל)

צוֹחֵק **laughing; laughing at**

וּמִשּׁוּם דִּסְבִירָא לֵיהּ לְקוּלָּא, מָאן דְּתָנֵי לְחוּמְרָא מְחַיֵּיךְ עֲלֵיהּ?! (עירובין מח, רע"א ע"פ רש"י שם מז, סע"ב)

But because he holds a lenient [opinion], would he laugh at one who teaches a [strict] opinion?!

* In Modern Hebrew, מְחַיֵּיךְ means *smiling.*

SEE: חוּכָא, מַחְכוּ, אַחֵיךְ

מַחֵיל* prt. (חלל אַפְעֵל)

(1) מְחַלֵּל **desecrating; profaning; transferring sanctity from**

(2) מוֹחֵל **forgiving; forgoing; yielding**

* In the second sense, *forgiving,* this verb may be vocalized מָחֵיל — the קַל *binyan* from the root מחל.

SEE: אַחֵיל

מַחֵית* prt. (נחת אַפְעֵל) מוֹרִיד; מַנִּיחַ

lowering; bringing down; placing (down)

* Do not confuse with מָחֵית (= מָחֵי+אַתְּ), *you are flogging.*

SEE: אַחֵית

מַחְכוּ/מְחַיְיכוּ* עֲלַהּ בְּמַעֲרְבָא**

צוֹחֲקִים עָלֶיהָ בַּמַּעֲרָב (= אֶרֶץ יִשְׂרָאֵל).

They laugh at it in the West (= Erets Yisrael). This expression introduces a *difficulty* that was raised in Erets Yisrael with regard to a statement (usually halakhic) that was made by an amora in Babylonia.

כֵּיצַד מְנַפֵּחַ? אָמַר רַב אַדָּא בַּר אַהֲבָה אָמַר רַב: מְנַפֵּחַ מִקִּשְׁרֵי אֶצְבְּעוֹתָיו וּלְמַעְלָה. מַחְכוּ עֲלַהּ בְּמַעֲרְבָא: כֵּיוָן דְּמְשַׁנֵּי, אֲפִילּוּ בְּכוּלַּהּ יְדָא נָמֵי! (ביצה יג, סע"ב - יד,א)

How may one blow away (the chaff from ears of wheat on the Sabbath)? Rav Adda b. Ahava said, quoting Rav: One may blow [only if they are held] from the joints of his fingers upwards. They laugh at it in the West: As long as he does it in an unusual manner, he may even [use] his whole palm!

* In most instances, our printed editions read מַחְכוּ (prt. אַפְעֵל of חוך). However, the *Arukh* and R. Ḥananel have the reading מְחַיְיכוּ (prt. פַּעֵל), as in כריתות ד, סע"א in our editions.

** According to the Talmud (סנהדרין יז,ב), this expression refers to R. Yosé b. Ḥanina. See Tosafoth there.

SEE: מַעַרְבָא, אַחֵיךְ, מְחַיֵּיךְ

בְּמַחְלוֹקֶת שְׁנוּיָה*

[The halakha] taught is controversial.

משנה: הָאוֹכֵל וְהַשּׁוֹתֶה אֵין מִצְטָרְפִין. (יומא עג,ב: משנה ח:ב)
תלמוד: מַאן תַּנָּא? אָמַר רַב חִסְדָּא: בְּמַחְלוֹקֶת שְׁנוּיָה, וְר' יְהוֹשֻׁעַ הִיא, דִּתְנַן ... (שם פא, רע"א ורש"י שם)

MISHNA: Food and drink are not added cumulatively [to make up the minimum quantity of consumption that violates the Yom Kippur fast].

*TALMUD: Who is the tanna [of this halakha in the mishna]? Rav Ḥisda said: [The halakha] taught is controversial, and it [follows the opinion of] R. Y*ᵉ*hoshua, for we have learned (in a different mishna)...*

* In ברכות לח,ב, בְּמַחְלוֹקֶת שְׁנוּיָה is used like כְּתַנָּאֵי to indicate that the very issue two amoraim dispute is the subject of an earlier controversy between two tannaim. In Modern Hebrew, a similar expression, שָׁנוּי בְּמַחְלוֹקֶת, is used to describe a person or an issue as *controversial* — even though the meaning of שָׁנוּי there is not so clear.

SEE: שְׁנָה

מַחְלִיף prt. (חלף אַפְעֵל) מַחֲלִיף **interchanging**

מַחְלֵיף רַבָּה בַּר אֲבוּה וְתָנֵי ... (בבא מציעא צה,ב)

Rabba b. Avuh interchanges [the two opposing opinions] and teaches [the text as follows] ...

SEE: (וְ)הָא אִיפְּכָא שְׁמַעִינַן לְהוּ, מוּחְלֶפֶת הַשִּׁיטָה, אִיפּוּךְ

מְחַלֵּל prt. (חלל פַּעֵל) מְחַלֵּל

(1) desecrating; profaning

קָמְחַלְּלִין* שַׁבְּתָא (שבת קמז, רע"א)

they are desecrating the Sabbath

(2) transferring sanctity from (fruits of the second tithe or of the fourth year to money)

טִבְעָא אַפֵּירָא לָא מְחַלְּלִינַן. (בבא מציעא מד,ב)

We may not transfer sanctity from coins to goods.

* The prefix -קָ is used for emphasis.

SEE: אַחִיל

מְחַמֵּר prt. (חמר פַּעֵל)

driving (a beast of burden from behind)

הַמְחַמֵּר אַחַר בְּהֶמְתּוֹ בְּשַׁבָּת (שבת קנד, סע"א)

one who is driving his animal on the Sabbath

SEE: חֲמָרָא, חַמָּרָא

מֵחֲמַת* **on account of; because of; through**

מֵתָה מֵחֲמַת מְלָאכָה. (בבא מציעא לד,א)

[The animal] died on account of [its] work.

* This word is popularly pronounced מֵחֲמַת. It literally means *through the heat of* or *through the fury of* from the noun חֵמָה or *through the sun (its light or heat) of* from the noun חַמָּה. According to the latter etymology, the word is vocalized מֵחַמַּת.

מַחַת pass. prt. (נחת אַפְעֵל)

lowered; resting; lying מוּרָד; מֻנָּח

מַחֲתָא אוֹרַיְיתָא אַאַרְעָא (נדרים יד, רע"ב)

the Torah [scroll] is lying on the ground

SEE: אַחֵית

מְטָא (מטי: מָטֵי .prt, לֵימְטֵי .fut) "מָצָא"; הִגִּיעַ

"he found"; he reached; he arrived

ר' יוֹחָנָן — כִּי מָטֵי לְהַאי קְרָא, בָּכֵי. (חגיגה ה,א)

[As for] R. Yoḥanan — whenever he reaches this pasuk, he weeps.

SEE: (וּ)מָטוּ בָהּ מִשְּׁמֵיהּ ד-, אַמְטֵי

מַטְבִּיל prt. (טבל הִפְעִיל); **מַטְבֵּיל*** prt. (טבל אַפְעֵל)

dipping; immersing (something, usually for ritual purification)

מִקְוֶה שֶׁיֵּשׁ בּוֹ אַרְבָּעִים סְאָה שֶׁבּוֹ טוֹבְלִין וּמַטְבִּילִין (משנה מקואות פ"א מ"ז)

a ritual bath that contains forty se´a in which [people] immerse [themselves] and immerse [utensils]

* The first form is Hebrew, and the second is Aramaic.

SEE: טְבַל

וּמָטוּ* בָהּ מִשְּׁמֵיהּ דְּ-**
וּמַטִּים בָּהּ [לוֹמַר] בְּשֵׁם ר' ...

and [others] are inclined [to quote it] in the name of R. ...

This expression indicates that another tradition ascribes the same halakha that some quote in the name of an amora to an earlier authority in the chain of halakhic transmission.

אָמַר ר' חִיָּיא בַּר אַבָּא אָמַר ר' יוֹחָנָן, וּמָטוּ בָהּ מִשְּׁמֵיהּ דְּר' יַנַּאי (ראש השנה י, רע"א ורש"י שם)

R. Ḥiyya b. Abba said, quoting R. Yoḥanan, and [others] are inclined [to quote it] in the name of R. Yannai

* We have explained the verb as מַטּוּ, *they tend, they are inclined*, as an אַפְעֵל participle from the root נטי, as Rashi does. Nevertheless, it is also possible to vocalize the verb מָטוּ, *they reach, they arrive* (= מַגִּיעִים), a קַל participle from the root מטי — in the sense of *tracing* the halakha back until we reach an earlier authority.

** Sometimes מִשּׁוּם is used instead of -מִשְּׁמֵיהּ ד.

SEE: מַטִּין, מְטָא

מָטוּתָא/מָטוּ בַּקָּשָׁה **asking a favor**

בְּמָטוּתָא מִינָּךְ*/מִינַּייכוּ

I pray you (s./pl.); please בְּבַקָּשָׁה מִמְּךָ/מִכֶּם

For an example — see ברכות לה,ב.

* בְּמָטוּתָא מִנָּךְ is occasionally used in Modern Hebrew.

מַטִּין prt. pl. (נטי הִפְעִיל) **inclining; favoring**

לָאו "הֲלָכָה" אִיתְּמַר, אֶלָּא "מַטִּין" אִיתְּמַר. (ברכות לג,ב ורש"י)

It was not stated: "[Such is the] halakha" (to be taught publicly), but it was stated: "We are inclined [to that opinion]" (and thus we rule, but only for individuals who ask us).

For another example — see עירובין מו,ב and Rashi's commentary there.

SEE: (וּ)מָטוּ בָהּ מִשְּׁמֵיהּ ד-

מְטַלְטֵל prt. (טול פִּלְפֵּל)* — moving

לָא מְטַלְטְלִינַן לְהוּ (שבת מט, סע"א)

we must not move them (on the Sabbath)

* The first and third letters of the root are duplicated.

SEE: טַלְטֵל

מְטַלְטֵל prt. (= מִתְטַלְטֵל) (טול הִתְפַּלְפֵּל); מְטַלְטֵל* (טול אִתְפַּלְפַּל) — movable; portable

* The first form is Hebrew, and the second is Aramaic.

מְטַלְטְלִין; מְטַלְטְלֵי* — movable properties

נִרְאִין דִּבְרֵי ר' יְהוּדָה בְּקַרְקָעוֹת וְדִבְרֵי ר' שִׁמְעוֹן בְּמְטַלְטְלִין. (עֲרָכִין כח, סע"א: משנה פ"ח מ"ה)

The opinion of R. Y'huda is acceptable regarding real estate, but the opinion of R. Shim'on [is acceptable] with regard to movable properties.

* The first form is Hebrew, and the second is Aramaic. Movable properties are also termed in the Mishna נְכָסִים שֶׁאֵין לָהֶם אַחֲרָיוּת (see that entry) and in post-Talmudic literature נִכְסֵי דְנָיְידֵי.

מְטַמֵּא prt. (טמא פִּעֵל); מְטַמֵּי* prt. (טמי פַּעֵל)

(1) rendering (ritually) unclean; imparting uncleanliness

הַמֵּת ... מְטַמֵּא בְּאֹהֶל (משנה כלים פ"א מ"ד)

a corpse imparts uncleanliness [to everything] within [the same] tent

(2) declaring unclean

ר' מֵאִיר מְטַמֵּא, וַחֲכָמִים מְטַהֲרִים. (משנה נגעים פ"ו מ"ג)

R. Méir declares [it] unclean, while the Ḥakhamim declare [it] clean.

* The first form is Hebrew, and the second is Aramaic.

SEE: מִיטַּמֵּא

מִי

(1) מִי? who?

This common meaning in Hebrew is also used in the Aramaic of the Talmud in the rhetorical question מִי יֵימַר דְּ- *(who can say that ...?)*.

For an example — see that entry.

(2) וְכִי ...? הַאִם ...?

In English, this interrogative usage is expressed by a change in word order and by the intonation of the speaker's voice. It is frequently found in Aramaic and occasionally in Hebrew.*

מִי כָּאן הִלֵּל? (שבת לא,א ורש"י שם) *Is Hillel here?*

מִי אִיכָּא סְפֵיקָא קַמֵּי שְׁמַיָּא? (ברכות ג, סע"ב)

Is there any doubt before Heaven (= from God's perspective)?

(3) הַלְוַאי ...! Oh that ...! Would that ...!

In this sense, מִי is used with the Hebrew imperfect (= the future) to express a wish.**

מִי יְגַלֶּה עָפָר מֵעֵינֶיךָ, רַבָּן יוֹחָנָן בֶּן זַכַּאי! (סוטה כז,ב: משנה פ"ה מ"ב)

Oh that [someone] would remove the dust from your eyes, Rabban Yoḥanan b. Zakkai! (= Would that he were alive today!)

* This usage may have a precedent in Biblical Hebrew:
מִי יָקוּם יַעֲקֹב? (עמוס ז:ב) *shall Ya'akov rise up?*

** This usage is found in Biblical Hebrew:
וּמִי יִתֵּן כָּל עַם ה' נְבִיאִים! (במדבר יא:כט)
and would that all the Lord's people were prophets!

SEE: מִי שֶׁ-, a relative pronoun

וּמִי אִיכָּא לְמַאן דְּאָמַר

הַאִם יֵשׁ מִי שֶׁאוֹמֵר ...?!

Is there any [authority] who maintains ...?!

This expression introduces a *rhetorical question*.

מִי אִיכָּא לְמַאן דְּאָמַר רַקַּת לָאו טְבֶרְיָא הִיא?! (מגילה ו, רע"א)

Is there anyone who maintains [that] Rakath is not [identical with] Tiberias?!

SEE: מַאן דְּאָמַר

מִי אִיכָּא מִידֵּי דְּ-

Is there anything that ...?! הַאִם יֵשׁ דָּבָר שֶׁ- ?!

Can there be such a situation as ...?!

This expression introduces a *rhetorical question*.

מִי אִיכָּא מִידֵּי דְּאֲנַן לָא מָצֵינַן לְמֶעְבַּד, וּשְׁלוּחֵי דִידַן מָצוּ עָבְדִי?! (יומא יט, רע"ב)

Is there anything that we ourselves are unable to perform, yet our agents are able to perform?!

וּמִי אַלִּימָא* מִמַּתְנִיתִין

וְכִי חֲזָקָה הִיא מִמִּשְׁנָתֵנוּ?!

Is [the baraitha] stronger than our mishna?!

This rhetorical question presents a *refutation* of an argument from a baraitha. It contends that just as we have already explained our mishna as not containing conclusive proof with regard to the issue under discussion, we may also explain that the baraitha that has been cited does not contain conclusive proof.

For examples — see שבת יב,א ותוס' שם and ב"מ לד,א.

* In a few passages, the adjective עֲדִיפָא, *better*, is used in this expression rather than אַלִּימָא — without altering the meaning significantly.

SEE: אַלִּים

וּמִי אָמַר ר' ... הָכִי וְהָא אָמַר ר' ...

וְכִי אָמַר ר' ... כָּךְ?! וַהֲלֹא אָמַר ר' ...!

But did R. ... (really) say so?! Did not R. ... say ... !

This formula presents a *contradiction* between two different halakhic positions that were expressed by the same ḥakham.

For an example — see בבא קמא כט,ב.

מִי אָמְרִינַן ... אוֹ דִילְמָא ...

הַאִם אָנוּ אוֹמְרִים ..., אוֹ שֶׁמָּא ...?

Do we say ..., or perhaps ...?

This standard formulation of a *problem* (בָּעְיָא) presents two plausible alternatives.

עַכְבָּר נִכְנָס וְכִכָּר בְּפִיו, וְעַכְבָּר יוֹצֵא וְכִכָּר בְּפִיו — מַהוּ?! מִי אָמְרִינַן הַיְינוּ הַאי דְּעָל וְהַיְינוּ הַאי דִּנְפַק אוֹ דִילְמָא אַחֲרִינָא הוּא? (פסחים י,ב)

What is the law [if] a mouse enters (the house) with a loaf (of bread) in his mouth, and a mouse comes out with a loaf in his mouth? (Does the resident have to search for ḥametz?) Do we say (= assume) that the same [mouse] that entered has come out, or perhaps it is a different one?

SEE: בָּעְיָא[2]

מִי דָמֵי

Is it similar?! וְכִי דּוֹמֶה?!

This rhetorical question introduces a *refutation* of an analogy that was drawn by an amora between two subjects or between two texts.

מִי דָמֵי?! הָתָם טִלְטוּל, הָכָא מְלָאכָה! (שבת קטז, סע״ב)

Is it similar?! There (in the case of rescuing a Torah scroll on the Sabbath with its cover even if the cover contains money) it is [merely a question of] handling (money), (whereas) here (in the case of skinning the hide of the sacrifice) it is [a question of a forbidden] labor (which is much more difficult to permit)!

SEE: דָּמֵי

מִי יֵימַר דְּ-

Who can say that ...?! מִי יֹאמַר שֶׁ-...?!

Who can be certain that ...?!

This expression presents a *rhetorical question.*

מִי יֵימַר דְּמִגַּנְבָא?! (בבא מציעא לד, רע״א)

Who can say that it will be stolen?!

SEE: יֵימַר

מִי כְּתִיב ... כְּתִיב

הַאִם כָּתוּב ...?! ... כָּתוּב!

Is it written ...?! (No!) It is written ...!

This formula presents an *inference* drawn from the precise wording or spelling of a Biblical text.

מִי כְּתִיב: ״חוֹטְאִים״?! ״חַטָּאִים״ כְּתִיב! (ברכות י, רע״א ע״פ תהלים קד:לה)

Is it written ״חוֹטְאִים״ *(which can only be read* חוֹטְאִים, *meaning sinners)?! (No!) It is (actually) written* חטאים *(which can be read* חֲטָאִים, *meaning sins — rather than* חַטָּאִים, *sinners).*

מִי לָא עֲסִיקִינַן/עָסְקִינַן

וְכִי אֵין אָנוּ עֲסוּקִים ...?!

Are we not dealing (also with this case) ...?!

This rhetorical question presents the following argument: The text, currently under discussion in the Talmud, is formulated in such a manner that it also includes a particular case that provides the basis for a *proof* or a *refutation.*

(״מִפְּנֵי שֵׂיבָה תָּקוּם, וְהָדַרְתָּ פְּנֵי זָקֵן״) מָה קִימָה שֶׁאֵין בּוֹ חֶסְרוֹן כִּיס, אַף הִידּוּר שֶׁאֵין בּוֹ חֶסְרוֹן כִּיס. וְקִימָה לֵית בָּהּ חֶסְרוֹן כִּיס?! מִי לָא עָסְקִינַן דְּקָא נָקֵיב מַרְגָּנִיתָא, אַדְּהָכִי וְהָכִי קָאֵים מִקַּמֵּיהּ וּבָטֵיל מִמְּלַאכְתּוֹ?! (קידושין לג, רע״א ורש״י שם ע״פ ויקרא יט:לב)

("Before the aged you shall rise, and you shall honor the presence of an elder.") Just as [the Torah demands] rising that involves no monetary loss, [it] also [demands] honor that does not involve monetary loss. But does rising [never] involve any monetary loss?! Are we not dealing [also] with [a craftsman] who was piercing pearls [so that] while he is standing up before him (= the elder), he is interrupted from his (high-paying) work?!

SEE: עֵסֶק

מִי לֵימָא/נֵימָא

shall we say?! הַאִם נֹאמַר...?!

This expression almost always appears in the context of a controversy between two amoraim. After it has been established that one amora's opinion is disputed by an earlier halakhic authority, it is now argued that such may be the case with respect to the other amora's opinion too.

לִשְׁמוּאֵל וַדַּאי תַּנָּאֵי הִיא; לְרַב מִי לֵימָא תַּנָּאֵי הִיא?! (בבא קמא עה,א)

*According to Sh*e*muel [this issue] is certainly a controversy between tannaim; according to Rav shall we say it is a controversy between tannaim?!*

וּמִי מָצֵית אָמְרַתְּ/מוֹקְמַתְּ ... וְהָא ...

הַאִם אַתָּה יָכוֹל לוֹמַר/לְהַעֲמִיד ...?! וַהֲלֹא ...?!

But [how] can you say/interpret ...?! Is there not (a text that states ...)?!

This formula presents a *refutation* of a statement/interpretation that was quoted earlier in a Talmudic discussion.

For examples — see בבא מציעא ב,א; לג,א.

SEE: אוּקֵי

מִי סָבְרַתְּ

Do you (really) think ...?! הַאִם אַתָּה סָבוּר ...?!

This rhetorical question introduces a *refutation* of an argument that undermines the assumption upon which the argument was based.

ברייתא: ״שׂוֹנֵא״ שֶׁאָמְרוּ שׂוֹנֵא יִשְׂרָאֵל — וְלֹא שׂוֹנֵא אוּמּוֹת הָעוֹלָם.

תלמוד: אִי אָמְרַתְּ צַעַר בַּעֲלֵי חַיִּים דְּאוֹרַיְיתָא, מָה־לִּי שׂוֹנֵא יִשְׂרָאֵל, וּמָה־לִּי שׂוֹנֵא אוּמּוֹת הָעוֹלָם? מִי סָבְרַתְּ אַשּׂוֹנֵא דְּקְרָא קָאֵי?! אַשּׂוֹנֵא דְּמַתְנִיתָא קָאֵי! (ב״מ לב, סע״ב ורש״י שם)

BARAITHA: [The] "enemy" they spoke of is a Jew who is his enemy — not a non-Jewish enemy.

TALMUD: If you say [that relieving] the suffering of an animal is of Torah [origin], what is the difference whether [its owner is] a Jew who is an enemy or a non-Jewish enemy? Do you (really) think [this baraitha] defines [the] "enemy" [mentioned] in the pasuk (שמות כג:ה, *whose laden donkey requires*

assistance)?! (No!) It defines [the] "enemy" [mentioned] in a (previous) baraitha (who needs help to load his animal).
SEE: סְבַר

מִי עֲדִיפָא מִמַּתְנִיתִין SEE: מִי אַלִּימָא מִמַּתְנִיתִין

מִי שֶׁ- **one who; the one who**
מִי שֶׁאָמַר וְהָיָה הָעוֹלָם (קידושין ל,ב ועוד)
"The One Who said and the world came into existence" (= the Creator)

כְּמִי שֶׁ-*

(1) like [the] one who
"הֲרֵינִי נָזִיר ... כְּמִי שֶׁעָקַר דַּלְתוֹת עַזָּה" (נזיר ד,א: משנה א:ב)
"I am hereby a nazarite ... like the one (= Shimshon) who uprooted the gates of Gaza"

(2) as if; as though
קְלוּטָה כְּמִי שֶׁהוּנְחָה דָּמְיָא. (שבת ד, סע"א)
[An object] that is "intercepted" (by the air) is considered as if it had come to rest (according to the law forbidding the transfer of objects from one domain to another on the Sabbath).

* See both usages in the Aramaic expression (כְּ)מַאן דְּ-.

מַיָּא* (מֵי .constr) מַיִם **water**
לָא נְפִישֵׁי מַיָּא (בבא קמא נא,ב) *there is not much water*

* Like its Hebrew counterpart, this noun is usually regarded as plural and takes a plural verb or adjective.

מִיבָּעֵי (= מִתְבָּעֵי: מִיבָּעְיָא .f) prt. (בעי אִתְפְּעֵל)

(1) עוֹמֶדֶת בִּשְׁאֵלָה **it is questionable**
לְרָבָא מִיבָּעְיָא לֵיהּ; לְרַב פָּפָּא פְּשִׁיטָא לֵיהּ. (בבא קמא ג,ב)
For Rava it is questionable; for Rav Papa it is clear.

(2) צָרִיךְ **it is necessary; it is needed**
הַאי מִיבָּעְיָא לֵיהּ לְגוּפֵיהּ! (מגילה ב,א ועוד)
This [Biblical passage] is needed by him for itself (for the meaning indicated by its context)!
SEE: לָא קָא מִיבָּעְיָא לַן, כִּי קָא מִיבָּעְיָא לַן, לָא מִיבָּעֵי/מִיבָּעְיָא, אִיבָּעֵי, הַשְׁתָּא ... מִיבָּעְיָא

... מִיבָּעֵי לֵיהּ

... הָיָה לוֹ [לוֹמַר]! **he should have [said] ...!**
These words are the concluding words of an *objection* that is being raised against a proposed interpretation of a mishna or baraitha. It is contended that if that interpretation were indeed correct, the text under discussion would not have been worded as it stands, but differently. The objection consists of two parts. First, the current wording of the text — which does not fit the proposed interpretation — is recalled. Then, a different wording of the text — which would have been appropriate for that interpretation — is presented as what the tanna *should have said.*

ברייתא: טָעָה וְלֹא הִזְכִּיר ... שְׁאֵלָה בְּבִרְכַּת הַשָּׁנִים אֵין מַחֲזִירִין אוֹתוֹ, מִפְּנֵי שֶׁיָּכוֹל לְאוֹמְרָהּ בְּ"שׁוֹמֵעַ תְּפִלָּה" ....
תלמוד: ... בְּצִבּוּר מַאי טַעְמָא לָא? מִשּׁוּם דְּשָׁמְעָהּ מִשְּׁלִיחַ צִבּוּר. אִי הָכִי, הַאי "מִפְּנֵי שֶׁיָּכוֹל לְאוֹמְרָהּ בְּשׁוֹמֵעַ תְּפִלָּה"? "מִפְּנֵי שֶׁשּׁוֹמֵעַ מִשְּׁלִיחַ צִבּוּר" מִיבָּעֵי לֵיהּ! (ברכות כט, סע"א)

BARAITHA: [If] one made a mistake and did not mention ... the prayer (for rain) in the b'rakha "of the years" (= בָּרֵךְ עָלֵינוּ ...) we do not require him to go back, because he can say it in שׁוֹמֵעַ תְּפִלָּה ....
TALMUD: ... [If he is praying] with the congregation, for what reason does he not [have to go back and say it]? Because he will hear it from the reader (in the repetition of the Amida). If so, [why does the tanna state] this: "Because he can say it in "שׁוֹמֵעַ תְּפִלָּה*? He should have [said]: "Because he will hear it from the reader"!*

לְמִיגְבָּא/מִיגְבֵּי .inf (גבי) לִגְבּוֹת **to collect**
SEE: גְּבֵי

מִיגּוֹ דְ- SEE: מִגּוֹ דְ-

מִידְּחֵי .pass. prt (דחי אִתְפְּעֵל)
נִדְחָה **postponed; disqualified**
SEE: אִידְּחֵי

מִידֵּי (= מִן יְדֵי) **"out of the hands of"; from the status of; from the power of**
לְטַהֲרָהּ מִידֵּי נְבֵילָה (חולין יח,א)
to purify it (= the animal) from the status (= the ritual uncleanliness) of "n'vela"

מִידֵּי

(1) מַשֶּׁהוּ; דָּבָר **something**
טְעֵים מִידֵּי בְּצַפְרָא (שבת י,א)
he ate something in the morning

(2) כְּלוּם **anything (when used with a negative)**
לָא תֵּימָא לִי מִידֵּי! (ב"ק צו,ב) *Don't say anything to me!*
For emphasis, this word is sometimes used with a double negative (which is translated into English as a single negative) as in this example:
וְלָא אֲמַר לֵיהּ וְלָא מִידֵּי (ברכות כז,א ועוד)
and he did not say anything at all to him

(3) כְּלוּם ...?! וְכִי ...?!
When this word introduces *a rhetorical question,* its force is expressed in English by a change in word order and by the speaker's interrogative intonation — rather than by a specific translation. *It is,* for instance, becomes *Is it?*
For examples — see מִידֵּי אִירְיָא, מִידֵּי גַּבֵּי הֲדָדֵי תַּנְיָא, מִידֵּי הוּא טַעְמָא אֶלָּא
SEE: מִי אִיכָּא מִידֵּי דְ-, מִידְּעָם, מִידֵּי אַחֲרִינָא, אַטּוּ, כְּלוּם, (וְ)כִי

מִידֵי אַחֲרִינָא דָּבָר אַחֵר **anything else**

When the Talmud declares that a certain element is a halakhic necessity — to the exclusion of other alternatives, this expression denotes the other *alternatives*.

צֶמֶר וּפִשְׁתִּים, אִין; מִידֵי אַחֲרִינָא, לָא (שבת כז, סע״א)
[a combination of] wool and linen, yes (= it constitutes "sha'atnez"); anything else, no (= it does not constitute "sha'atnez")

מִידֵי אִירְיָא הָא כִּדְאִיתָא וְהָא כִּדְאִיתָא*

וְכִי רְאָיָה הִיא [זוֹ]?!** זוֹ כְּמוֹ שֶׁהִיא, וְזוֹ כְּמוֹ שֶׁהִיא.

Is [this] a proof?! This [case] is unique unto itself, and the other is unique unto itself.

In most instances, this statement is used as a *refutation* of a proof that was based upon the juxtaposition of two cases in a text. The Talmud now argues that no analogy should be drawn from one case to the other because of a significant difference between them.

משנה: לוּלָב וַעֲרָבָה◇ שִׁשָּׁה וְשִׁבְעָה. (סוכה מב,ב: משנה ד:א)
תלמוד: מַאי? לָאו כְּלוּלָב? מַה לוּלָב בִּנְטִילָה, אַף עֲרָבָה בִּנְטִילָה!
מִידֵי אִירְיָא?! הָא כִּדְאִיתָ׳ וְהָא כִּדְאִיתָ׳. (שם מג,ב ע״פ כת״י)◇◇

MISHNA: [The mitzvoth of the] palm branch and willow branch [must be performed on] six and seven [days of the Sukkoth festival, respectively].
TALMUD: What [does it mean]? Is it not [implying that the willow branch is] like [the] palm branch?! Just as [the] palm branch must be taken [into one's hand, rather than be set up at the side of the altar], so too [the] willow branch must be taken! Is [this] a proof?! This (= the mitzva of the palm branch) is unique unto itself, and the other (= the mitzva of the willow branch) is unique unto itself.

* Sometimes, מִידֵי אִירְיָא occurs without הָא כִּדְאִיתָא, but with the same meaning.

** This is Rashi's paraphrase of the statement in his commentary to פסחים ס, סע״א.

◇ Here, the term לוּלָב, *palm branch*, refers to the mitsva of taking all four species, including the citron (אֶתְרוֹג), the myrtle branch (הֲדַס), and the willow branch (עֲרָבָה), on the Sukkoth festival.
Here, the term עֲרָבָה, *willow branch*, refers to a separate mitsva that was performed in the Beth HaMikdash. Nowadays, the separate branch has an additional name, the הוֹשַׁעְנָא, and it is taken in the synagogue only on the seventh day of the Sukkoth festival, *Hosha'na Rabba*.

◇◇ The reading in our printed editions הָא כִּדְאִיתֵיהּ is difficult because the masculine suffix ־ֵיהּ does not match the feminine pronoun הָא. On the other hand, the abbreviation כדאית׳ that is found in manuscripts may represent the feminine כִּדְאִיתָא.

מִידֵי גַּבֵּי הֲדָדֵי תַּנְיָא/תַּנְיָן

כְּלוּם זוֹ אֵצֶל זוֹ שְׁנוּיוֹת?!

Are they (= the two baraithoth) taught together?!

This rhetorical question is a *refutation* of a proof that was based upon the wording of two parallel baraithoth. The Talmud rejects the proof on the grounds that the two baraithoth may have originated from two different authors who employed different literary styles (for example, R. Ḥiyya and R. Osha'ya).

For examples — see שבת יח,א; ב״מ לד, סע״א וש״נ.

מִידֵי דַּהֲוָה אַ-

״דָּבָר שֶׁהָיָה עַל״; בְּדוֹמֶה לְ-

something that is similar to; just like in

לִיבְעֵי תְּרֵי — מִידֵי דַּהֲוָה אַכָּל עֵדִיּוֹת שֶׁבַּתּוֹרָה! (גיטין ב,ב)
Let [the amora] require two [witnesses] — just like in all cases of testimony in the Torah!

מִידֵי הוּא טַעְמָא אֶלָּא

כְּלוּם הַטַּעַם אֵינָהּ אֶלָּא (ל-) ...?!

(1) Is not [this] argument specifically (according to this particular amora) ...?!

Sometimes, this formula presents a *refutation* of a point that has been stated in the Talmud according to the opinion of an amora, on account of a statement made by the same amora that seems to contradict it.

מִידֵי הוּא טַעְמָא אֶלָּא לִשְׁמוּאֵל?! הָאָמַר רַב נַחְמָן אָמַר שְׁמוּאֵל ...! (שבועות לט, סע״ב ורש״י שם)
Is not [this] argument specifically according to Shmuel?! [But] did not Rav Naḥman quote Shmuel as saying ...

(2) Is not the reason (for that halakha) specifically ...?!

This formula is also used to reject a halakhic argument because of the underlying reason for that very halakha.

(1) מְתִיב רַב יוֹסֵף: ״וַיִּתְחַתֵּן שְׁלֹמֹה אֶת (פַּרְעֹה מֶלֶךְ מִצְרַיִם וַיִּקַּח אֶת) בַּת פַּרְעֹה״! גַּיְּירַהּ גַּיְּירַהּ. (2) וְהָא לֹא קִבְּלוּ גֵּרִים לֹא בִּימֵי דָּוִד וְלֹא בִּימֵי שְׁלֹמֹה! (3) מִידֵי הוּא טַעְמָא אֶלָּא לְשׁוּלְחַן מְלָכִים?! הָא לָא צְרִיכָא לֵיהּ! (יבמות עו, סע״א-רע״ב ע״פ מלכים א ג:א)
(1) Rav Yosef raised an objection: "And (King) Shlomo intermarried with (Par'o the king of Egypt, and he took) the daughter of Par'o (as a wife)"! He had her convert (to Judaism). (2) But [did we not learn that] converts were not accepted — neither in the days of David nor in the days of Shlomo?! (3) Is not the reason [for that halakha] specifically [that insincere converts might be motivated by the luxury] of the royal table?! But she (= Par'o's daughter) had no need of it!

מִידְכַּר/מִדְכַּר* inf. (דכר) זָכוֹר **"remember"**

מִידְכַּר* דְּכִירִי אֱינָשֵׁי (בבא מציעא קיב, סע״ב ועוד)
people certainly remember

* The absolute infinitive מִידְכַּר (Heb. זָכוֹר) is used to emphasise another form of the same verb that immediately follows it — in our example, the participle דְּכִירִי. It is best expressed in English by an adverb, such as *certainly, very, indeed*. See *Grammar for Gemara:* Chapter 3.25.
SEE: מִיזְהַר

מִידְּכַר/מִדְּכַר (= מִתְדְּכַר) pass. prt. (דכר אִתְפְּעֵל)
reminded; remembering נִזְכָּר
הַשְׁתָּא דִּמְטָא זְמַן חִיּוּבֵיהּ, רָמֵי אַנַּפְשֵׁיהּ וּמִידְּכַר (בבא מציעא קיג, רע״א ע״פ תוספות וכת״י שם)
now that the time of his obligation has arrived, he casts [the obligation] upon himself and remembers
SEE: אִידְּכַר

מִידַּלֵּי/מִדַּלֵּי* (= מִתְדַּלֵּי) pass. prt. (דלי אִתְפְּעֵל)
raised; elevated מֻגְבָּה
* This word is popularly pronounced מִידְלֵי.
SEE: מַדְלֵי

לְמֵידַן inf. (דון) לָדוּן **to judge; to derive**
SEE: דָּן

מֵידַע; לְמֵידַע* inf. (ידע) יָדוֹעַ; לָדַעַת **to know**
תְּאֵנָה נַמִי מֵידַע יְדִיעַ דְּנָתְרָא (בבא מציעא כא, סע״ב)
a fig also — it is well known that it drops (off the tree)
* These forms are popularly pronounced מֵידַע and לְמֵידַע, respectively. The form without ל- is an absolute infinitive. See the note under מִידְכַּר.
SEE: יְדַע

מִידְּעַם/מִדְּעַם מַשֶּׁהוּ; כְּלוּם
something; anything (with a negative)
לֵיכָּא מִידְּעַם דְּלְיִשְׂרָאֵל שְׁרֵי וּלְגוֹי אָסוּר. (סנהדרין נט, סע״א ע״פ כת״י)
There is not anything that is permitted to a Jew and forbidden to a non-Jew.
SEE: מִידֵּי

מִיהָא/מִיהַת מִכָּל מָקוֹם; עַל כָּל פָּנִים
in any event; however; nevertheless
This word is placed after the first word or the opening expression in a clause.
נְהִי דְּקַטְלָא לֵיכָּא, מַלְקוּת מִיהָא אִיכָּא. (בבא קמא עא, רע״א)
Granted that there is no capital punishment, there should in any event be a punishment of lashes.
SEE: מִיהַת

מֵיהָא/מֵהָא (= מִן+הָא) מִזֹּאת **from this**
שְׁמַע מִינַּהּ, מֵיהָא מַתְנִיתָא, תַּמְנֵי. (פסחים קה, סע״ב)
Deduce from it, from this baraitha, eight [halakhoth].
SEE: פְּשׁוֹט מֵיהָא חֲדָא

מִיהַדַּק (= מִתְהַדַּק) prt. (הדק אִתְפְּעֵל)
fastened; tight מְהֻדָּק
אֲנָא לָא הֲוַאי חָלֵיצְנָא אֶלָּא בְּסַנְדָּלָא דְּטַיְיעָא, דְּמִיהַדַּק טְפֵי. (יבמות קב,א)
I would perform "halitza" only with a Beduin sandal, which [can be] fastened more firmly.

לְמֵיהְדַּר; מֵהְדָּר* inf. (הדר) לַחֲזֹר; חָזוֹר
to go back; to return; to repeat; to retract
* This form (without ל-) is the absolute infinitive. See the note under מִידְכַּר.
SEE: הֲדַר

מִיהוּ אֲבָל **but; however**
אִין, שְׁטָרָא זִיפָא הוּא, מִיהוּ שְׁטָרָא מְעַלְיָא הֲוָה לִי וְאִירְכַס. (בבא בתרא לב, רע״ב)
Yes, it is a forged document, but I did have a proper document and it got lost.

לְמֶיהֱוֵי; מֶיהֱוָה* inf. (הוי) לִהְיוֹת; הָיֹה **to be**
* This form (without ל-) is the absolute infinitive. See the note under מִידְכַּר.
SEE: הֲוָה

מִיהַת*/מִיהָא מִכָּל מָקוֹם; עַל כָּל פָּנִים
in any event; however; nevertheless
This word is placed after the first word or the opening expression in a clause.
וְהָאִיכָּא עֵדִים בִּמְדִינַת הַיָּם?! הַשְׁתָּא מִיהַת לֵיתַנְהוּ קַמָּן. (כתובות כג, סע״א)
But are there not witnesses overseas?! At present, however, they are not before us.
* In some manuscripts, it is sometimes spelled מִיחַת.
SEE: אוֹדוּ לִי מִיהַת, קָתָנֵי מִיהַת

לְמִיזְבַּן inf. (זבן) לִקְנוֹת **to buy**
SEE: זְבַן

מִיזְדַּבַּן
SEE: מִזְדַּבַּן

מִיזְהַר/מִזְהַר* inf. (זהר) הִזָּהֵר **"be careful"**
פֶּסַח בִּזְמַנּוֹ מִיזְהַר זְהִירֵי בֵּיהּ (קידושין נה,ב)
[people] are very careful about the Pesah offering during its [designated] time
* This form (without ל-) is the absolute infinitive. See the note under מִידְכַּר.
SEE: אִיזְדְּהַר

לְמֵיזַל; מֵיזָל* inf. (אזל) לָלֶכֶת; הָלוֹךְ **to go**
* This form (without ל-) is the absolute infinitive. See the note under מִידְכַּר.
SEE: אֲזַל

מִיחָה (מחי פָּעֵל: מְמַחֶה prt.)
he protested; he objected
אֵין מְמַחִין בְּיַד עֲנִיֵּי גוֹיִים בְּלֶקֶט, שִׁכְחָה וּפֵאָה (גיטין נט, רע״ב: משנה פ״ה מ״ח)
we do not object to non-Jewish poor people [gathering] gleanings, forgotten [sheaves], or [produce from] the corner [of the field]
SEE: מָחָה, מְחֵי

לְמֵיחֱזֵי/לְמֶחֱזֵי; מֵיחֱזָא* inf. (חזי)

to see — לִרְאוֹת; רָאֹה

* This form (without -ל) is the absolute infinitive. See the note under מֵידְכַר.

SEE: חֲזָא

מֵיחֲזֵי/מִחֲזֵי/מִתְחֲזֵי/מִיתְחֲזֵי prt. (חזי אִתְפְּעֵל)

it seems; it appears; it looks — נִרְאֶה

מִיחֲזֵי כְּיוֹהֲרָא (ברכות יז,ב) — *it seems like arrogance*

SEE: חֲזָא, חֲזֵי

מִיחַיַּיב (מִתְחַיַּיב) pass. prt. (חוב אִתְפְּעֵל) מְחֻיָּב; חַיָּב

obligated; bound; obliged; responsible

SEE: מְחַיֵּיב

מִיחַלַּף (= מִתְחַלַּף) pass. prt. (חלף אִתְפְּעֵל: לְאִיחַלּוֹפֵי inf.)

interchanged — מִתְחַלֵּף

חֶבֶל בְּחֶבֶל מִיחַלַּף; עֲנִיבָה בְּקְשִׁירָה לָא מִיחַלְּפָא (פסחים יא, סע"א; שבת קיג,א)

one rope might be interchanged (by mistake) with another rope; looping will not be interchanged with tying (a knot)

לְמֵיחַשׁ inf. (חשש) לַחֲשׁוֹשׁ

to be concerned; to take into consideration

SEE: חָשׁ, חֲשָׁשָׁא

מִיטַּמֵּא (= מִתְטַמֵּא) pass. prt. (טמי הִתְפְּעֵל)

becoming (ritually) unclean

אֵלּוּ מִיטַּמְּאִין וּמְטַמְּאִין .... (משנה עוקצין פ"א מ"ג)

The following may become unclean and impart uncleanliness ....

SEE: מְטַמֵּא, אִיטַּמֵּי

לְמִיטְעֵי; מִיטְעָא* inf. (טעי)

to err — לִטְעוֹת; טָעֹה

* This form (without -ל) is the absolute infinitive. See the note under מֵידְכַר.

SEE: טְעָא

מִיַּיאַשׁ/מִיָּאַשׁ (= מִתְיָאֵשׁ) prt. (יאש אִתְפְּעֵל)

despairing; resigning oneself (to a loss); giving up (on a lost article) — מִתְיָאֵשׁ

כְּלָלָא דַאֲבֵידְתָא: כֵּיוָן דַּאֲמַר: "וַוי לֵיהּ לְחֶסְרוֹן כִּיס", מִיָּאַשׁ לֵיהּ מִינַּהּ. (בבא מציעא כג, סע"א)

[This is] the rule of a lost article: Once he says: "Woe is me over the loss of money," he is giving up on it.

מְיַירֵי prt. (ארי אַפְעֵל) מְעֹרֶה (ב-); עוֹסֵק (ב-)

connected (with); dealing (with); speaking (of)

בִּפְלוּגְתָּא לָא קָא מְיַירֵי. (סנהדרין מט,ב)

He is not dealing with controversy.

SEE: (בִּ)פְלוּגְתָּא לָא קָא מְיַירֵי ,אַיְירֵי

מָיֵית prt. (מות: מָיְתָא .f, מָיְתִי .m. pl) מֵת — dying

SEE: מִית

מַיְיתֵי prt. (אתי אַפְעֵל: מַיְיתָא .f, מַיְיתוּ .m. pl)

bringing — מֵבִיא

SEE: אַיְיתֵי

מְיַיתַּר pass. prt. (יתר פַּעֵל)

extra; superfluous — מְיֻתָּר

הֵי מְיַיתַּר? (בבא קמא סז,ב) — *Which [passage] is superfluous (and available for interpretation)?*

SEE: אַיְיתַּר

מִיכַּוֵּין (= מִתְכַּוֵּין) prt. (כון אִתְפְּעֵל)

intending; having intention for — מִתְכַּוֵּן

SEE: אִיכַּוַּון

לְמֵיכַל; מֵיכַל* inf. (אכל) לֶאֱכֹל; אָכוֹל — to eat

גְּזֵירָה דִילְמָא אָתֵי לְמֵיכַל מִינֵּיהּ (פסחים י, סע"ב)

a Rabbinic safeguard so that he not come to eat from it (= ḥametz)

* This form (without -ל) is the absolute infinitive. See the note under מֵידְכַר.

SEE: לֵיכוֹל

מִיכְּסִיף (= מִתְכְּסִיף) pass. prt. (כסף אִתְפְּעֵל)

embarrassed; nonplussed — מִתְבַּיֵּשׁ

SEE: אִיכְּסִיף

מִיל; מִילָא* (pl. מִילִין) אַלְפַּיִם אַמָּה — *mil;*

a measure of distance equal to 2000 cubits

* The first form is Hebrew, and the second is Aramaic. See the table of distances in Appendix II.

מִילֵּי (s. מִילְּתָא) מִלִּים; דְּבָרִים; עִנְיָנִים

words; statements; matters

לֵימָא לַן מָר מֵהָנֵי מִילֵּי מְעַלְּיָיתָא דַּאֲמַרְתְּ מִשְּׁמֵיהּ דְּרַב חִסְדָּא בְּמִילֵּי דְּבֵי כְנִישְׁתָּא! (ברכות ח,א)

Would you tell us some of the outstanding statements that you have said in Rav Ḥisda's name on matters relating to the synagogue?

SEE: הָנֵי מִילֵּי, מְנָא הָנֵי מִילֵּי

לְמֵילַף inf. (ילף) לִלְמֹד — to learn; to derive

SEE: יְלַף

מִילְקָא/מִילְקֵי* inf. (לקי) לָקֹה

"be punished by flogging"; "receive lashes"

* These forms are almost always used as absolute infinitives. See the note under מֵידְכַר.

SEE: לוֹקֶה, לְקֵי

מִילְּתָא/מִלְּתָא* (pl. מִילֵּי)

(1) מִלָּה; דִּבּוּר — word; statement; (halakhic) pronouncement

נֵימָא בֵּיהּ מִילְּתָא. (בבא מציעא טז, סע"ב)

Let us make a statement about it.

(2) דָּבָר; עִנְיָן — thing; matter; point; issue

מִילְּתָא דְּאִיבַּעְיָא לֵיהּ לְרָבָא — פְּשִׁיטָא לֵיהּ לְרַבָּה. (בבא קמא קה, רע"ב)

The matter that was questionable for Rava was clear-cut to Rabba.

(3) דָּבָר שֶׁל מַמָּשׁ; דָּבָר חָשׁוּב

something substantial; a matter of significance; a significant act

רָבָא אָמַר: ... רֵיחָא לָאו מִילְּתָא הִיא. (עבודה זרה סו,ב)

Rava said: ... The smell [of wine whose use is forbidden] is not [considered] something substantial (and thus one is permitted to smell it).

רָבָא אָמַר: ... הַזְמָנָה לָאו מִילְּתָא הִיא. (סנהדרין מז, סע"ב)

Rava said: ... The designation [of a garment for use as a shroud] is not [considered] a significant act [hence the garment is not forbidden for another purpose].

(4) דָּבָר נָכוֹן; כַּהֲלָכָה

a (halakhically) correct point

See (וְ)לָאו מִילְּתָא הִיא and (וְ)לָאו מִילְּתָא הִיא דַּאֲמַרִי for examples.

* מִילְּתָא is sometimes employed as a euphemism for *bereavement* and *mourning*, as in the passage:

אִיתְרַע בֵּיהּ מִילְּתָא (שבת קלו, סע"א ורש"י שם)

or for *bloodletting*, as in: עֲבַד מִילְּתָא (תענית כה,א).

SEE: אִיגַּלַּאי מִילְּתָא, גַּלּוּיֵי מִילְּתָא בְּעָלְמָא הוּא, הוֹאִיל וַאֲתָא לִידָן נֵימָא בָּהּ מִילְּתָא, מוֹכְחָא מִילְּתָא, מְסַתַּיְיעָא מִילְּתָא, תַּלְיָא מִילְּתָא, מִילְּתָא אַגַּב ..., מִילְּתָא דְּאָתְיָא ...

מִילְּתָא אַגַּב אוֹרְחֵיהּ קָא מַשְׁמַע לַן

דָּבָר לְפִי דַּרְכּוֹ הוּא מַשְׁמִיעַ לָנוּ.

He teaches us something in passing.

This statement presents a *resolution* of a difficulty regarding the wording of a halakha. It is proposed that the tanna has formulated the text in this fashion in order to teach a specific halakhic point incidentally.

משנה: מֵאֵימָתַי קוֹרִין אֶת שְׁמַע בְּעַרְבִית? מִשָּׁעָה שֶׁהַכֹּהֲנִים נִכְנָסִים לֶאֱכוֹל בִּתְרוּמָתָן ... (ברכות ב, רע"א: משנה פ"א מ"א)
תלמוד: ... לִיתְנֵי: "מִשְּׁעַת צֵאת הַכּוֹכָבִים"! מִילְּתָא אַגַּב אוֹרְחֵיהּ קָמַשְׁמַע לַן: כֹּהֲנִים אֵימַת קָא אָכְלֵי בִּתְרוּמָה? מִשְּׁעַת צֵאת הַכּוֹכָבִים. (שם ב,א)

MISHNA: From when may we recite the Shema in the evening? From the time that the kohanim enter to eat their teruma ...

TALMUD: Let [the tanna] say "from the time of the appearance of the stars"? He is teaching something in passing: When may the kohanim eat teruma? From the time of the appearance of the stars.

SEE: אַגַּב אוֹרְחֵיהּ

מִילְּתָא דְּאָתְיָא בְּקַל וָחוֹמֶר טָרַח וּכְתַב לַהּ קְרָא

דָּבָר הַנִּלְמָד בְּקַל וָחוֹמֶר — טָרַח וְכָתַב אוֹתוֹ הַכָּתוּב.

(In some instances) a point that is derived through a kal-vaḥomer analogy – Scripture has (nevertheless) taken the trouble to write.

For an example — see פסחים יח,ב ושי"נ.

מִילְּתָא דְּלָא שְׁכִיחָא לָא גְּזַרוּ בַּהּ רַבָּנַן

דָּבָר שֶׁאֵינוֹ מָצוּי לֹא גָּזְרוּ בּוֹ חֲכָמִים.

[With respect to] a case that is not common the ḥakhamim did not issue a decree.

In order to strengthen Torah observance, the ḥakhamim have enacted legislation that prohibits certain activities whose performance might lead a person to violate a Torah prohibition, either through habit or through misunderstanding. Nevertheless, the ḥakhamim have excluded from their own prohibitions rare situations, because there the danger to the observance of Torah prohibitions is only minimal.

For examples, see ביצה ב, סע"ב and עירובין סג, סע"ב ושי"נ.

SEE: מִילְּתָא, גְּזַר, שְׁכִיחַ

מִימְלִיךְ/מִמְּלִיךְ/מִימְּלַךְ (= מִתְמְלִיךְ) prt. (מלך אִתְפְּעֵל) נִמְלָךְ; חוֹזֵר בּוֹ

reconsidering; changing his mind

SEE: אִימְּלִיךְ, נִמְלַךְ

מִימְנַע/מִמְּנַע (= מִתְמְנַע) prt. (מנע אִתְפְּעֵל: לְאִימְּנוֹעֵי inf.) נִמְנָע

restraining oneself; refraining

מִמַּנְעִי וְלָא נָסְבֵי לַהּ (יבמות קיג,א)

[men] would refrain from marrying her

לְמֵימַר/לְמֵימְרָא; מֵימַר* inf. (אמר)

to say לוֹמַר; אָמוֹר

מֵימַר אָמַר: סִימָנָא אִית לִי בְּגַוֵּיהּ; יָהֵיבְנָא סִימָנָא וְשָׁקֵילְנָא לֵיהּ (בבא מציעא כא, רע"ב)

he will probably say (to himself): I have an identifying mark on it; I shall give (= identify) the mark and take it

* This form (without -ל) is the absolute infinitive. See the note under מֵידְכַּר.

SEE: אָמַר, אִיכָּא לְמֵימַר, מַאי אִיכָּא לְמֵימַר, צְרִיכָא לְמֵימַר, לְמֵימְרָא

מֵימְרָא (אמר) מַאֲמָר

a *memra*; a (halakhic or aggadic) statement made by an amora (as opposed to a tanna's statement in a mishna or a baraitha)

מֵימְרָא הִיא, וּמֵימְרָא לְרָבָא לָא סְבִירָא לֵיהּ.* (גיטין מב,ב ורש"י שם וע' בבא בתרא מח, סע"א ורשב"ם שם)

It is a memra, and Rava does not agree with [this] memra.

* According to the Talmud, an amora has the authority to differ with his colleague; hence a contradiction between two *memroth* of two different amoraim presents no difficulty.

SEE: גַּבְרָא אַגַּבְרָא קָא רָמֵית and the note there

לְמֵימְרָא inf. (אמר)

(1) לוֹמַר ...?!

[Is this] to say ...?!

Usually, this term introduces a *difficulty* — a contradiction between the implication of the text just quoted in the Talmud and another text that is about to be quoted.

משנה: עַד כַּמָּה מְזַמְּנִין? עַד כְּזַיִת. ר׳ יְהוּדָה אוֹמֵר: עַד כְּבֵיצָה. (ברכות מה,א: משנה פ״ז מ״ב)
תלמוד: לְמֵימְרָא דְּר׳ מֵאִיר חָשֵׁיב לֵיהּ כְּזַיִת וְר׳ יְהוּדָה כְּבֵיצָה?! וְהָא אִיפְּכָא שָׁמְעִינַן לְהוּ, דִּתְנַן ...?! (שם מט,ב)

*MISHNA: How much [must one have eaten] to be counted as part of a "zimmun"? [A quantity] equivalent to the size of an olive. R. Y*ᵉ*huda says: [A quantity] equivalent to the size of an egg.*
*TALMUD: Is this to say that R. Mé'ir [to whom the first, anonymous opinion in the mishna is attributed] considers it (= the standard quantity) to be the size of an olive, and R. Y*ᵉ*huda the size of an egg?! But have we not heard them [state] the opposite, as we have learned (in another mishna) ...?!*

(2) לוֹמַר ... That is to say ....
Sometimes, the term introduces a *conclusion* derived from the text that was just quoted in the Talmud.

אֲמַר קְרָא: "וַיִּקֹּב ... וַיְקַלֵּל" — לְמֵימְרָא דְּ"נוֹקֵב" קְלָלָה הוּא. (סנהדרין נו,א ע״פ ויקרא כד:יא)
The pasuk stated: "And he blasphemed (from the root נקב*) ... and he cursed." That is to say that* נקב *refers to cursing.*

SEE: אֲמַר, מַאי לְמֵימְרָא

מִינ- (= מִן) from; than

This fuller form of מִן, which never appears by itself, is the form to which personal-pronoun suffixes are attached in Aramaic. Here are some common combinations that result:

מִינֵּיהּ	מִמֶּנּוּ	**from him/it (m.); than he/it**
מִינַּהּ	מִמֶּנָּה	**from her/it (f.); than she/it**
מִינַּיְיהוּ	מֵהֶם	**from them; than they**

For the complete list of forms, see *Grammar for Gemara:* Chapter 7.325

SEE: בַּר מִינַּהּ דְּהָהִיא, בַּר מִינֵּיהּ

וּמִינַּהּ וּמִמֶּנָּה and from it (= that statement)

(1) This term sometimes introduces a *corollary* to the statement that has just been quoted, as if to say: *From this statement we may infer ...*

... אֲבָל לְאַחֲרָיו, אֲפִילּוּ מִיל אֵינוֹ חוֹזֵר. אָמַר רַב אַחָא: וּמִינַּהּ מִיל הוּא דְּאֵינוֹ חוֹזֵר — הָא פָּחוֹת מִמִּיל חוֹזֵר. (פסחים מו,א)
... but as for his [travelling] back (in order to procure water for washing his hands before a meal), even if [the distance] is a "mil" (= two thousand cubits), he need not go back. Rav Aha said: And from it (= that statement, we may infer that) only if the distance is a "mil," he need not go back — but [if] less than a "mil," he must go back.

(2) In some instances, this word introduces a *refutation* of the argument that was just put forward. Here, too, it may be paraphrased: *From this statement we may infer ...*

וְחֶבְרוֹן טְרָשִׁים הֲוַאי?! וְהָא ... תַּנְיָא: אֵילִים מִמּוֹאָב, כְּבָשִׂים מֵחֶבְרוֹן! מִינַּהּ! אַיְּידֵי דְּקַלִּישָׁא אַרְעָא, עָבְדָא רִעְיָא וְשָׁמֵן קִנְיָינָא. (סוטה לד, סע״ב ע״פ כת״י ורש״י שם)
But was Ḥevron a stony area?! ... Is it not stated (in a baraitha): Rams [come] from Moav and lambs from Ḥevron?! From it (= the very statement that was intended to show that Ḥevron was not stony, we may infer that the land was probably stony)! Since the soil is thin, it serves as pasture land, and the flocks grow fat.

(3) This same word also introduces the second stage of a דּוּן־מִינַּהּ־וּמִינַּהּ argument. See that entry for an example.

מִינֵּיהּ וּבֵיהּ* מִמֶּנּוּ וּבוֹ "from it and itself"; from ... itself

מִינֵּיהּ וּבֵיהּ אָבָא לֵיזִיל בֵּיהּ נַרְגָא. (סנהדרין לט,ב ורש״י שם)
The axe (whose handle was made) from the forest itself will go against it (= the forest, by chopping down its trees).

* In post-Talmudic sources and even in modern Hebrew, this expression is used in the sense of *in and of itself, intrinsically,* so that a סְתִירָה מִינֵּיהּ וּבֵיהּ means *an intrinsic contradiction.*

מִינְכַּר/מִנְכַּר (= מִתְנְכַר) pass. prt. (נכר אִתְפְּעֵל) נִכָּר recognizable; distinguishable

הֶיזֵּיקָא דְּמִינְכְּרָא* (בבא קמא ה,א)
a damage that is recognizable

* This form is popularly pronounced מִינְכְּרָא.

מִינַּטַר (= מִתְנְטַר) pass. prt. (נטר אִתְפְּעֵל) נִשְׁמָר; מִשְׁתַּמֵּר guarded; protected; preserved

מִנַּטְרָא* מֵחֲמַת גַּנָּבֵי וּמֵחֲמַת כַּלְבֵי (ביצה טו, סע״א)
it is guarded against thieves and against dogs

* This form is popularly pronounced מִנְטְרָא.

מִינַּסְבָא (= מִתְנַסְבָא) prt. f. (נסב אִתְפְּעֵל) נִשֵּׂאת getting married

אִיתְּתָא דָּיְיקָא וּמִינַּסְבָא* (קידושין עט,א)
a woman carefully investigates, and (only then) she gets married

* This form is popularly pronounced מִינְסְבָא.

SEE: אִינְּסִיבָא

מִינְּצֵי (= מִתְנְצֵי) prt. (נצי* אִתְפְּעֵל) רָב quarreling

הַהִיא מְסוּתָא דַּהֲווּ מִינְּצוּ עֲלַהּ בֵּי תְרֵי ... (ב״מ ו, רע״ב)
There was a bathhouse over which two people were quarreling ...

* The same root is used in אֲנָשִׁים עִבְרִים נִצִּים (שמות ב:יג).

לְמִיסַּק (סלק) inf. לַעֲלוֹת to go up (usually from Babylonia to Erets Yisrael)

בָּעֵי לְמִיסַּק לְאַרְעָא דְיִשְׂרָאֵל (שבת מא,א וש״נ)
he wants to go up to Eretz Yisrael

לְמֵיסַר; מֵיסַר* inf. (אסר)

to forbid; to bind לֶאֱסֹר; לִקְשׁוֹר

* This form (without ל-) is the absolute infinitive. See the note under מֵידְכַר.

SEE: אֲסַר

לְמִיסְרַךְ/לְמִסְרַךְ inf. (סרך)

לְהֵאָחֵז; לְהִגָּרֵר; לְהִתְרַגֵּל

to cling; to adhere; to get used (to)

For an example — see (וְ)לָאו מִילְּתָא הִיא.

מִיסְתְּיָיא/מִסְתְּיָיא*

it is enough דַּי; מַסְפִּיק

This word with pronoun suffixes means *it is enough for me, for you* and so on.

it is enough for me	דַּיִּי	מִיסְתָּאִי
it is enough for you	דַּיְּךָ	מִיסְתְּיָיךְ
it is enough for him	דַּיּוֹ	מִיסְתְּיֵיהּ
it is enough for her	דַּיָּהּ	מִיסְתְּיָיא
it is enough for them	דַּיָּם	מִיסְתְּיֵיהוּ

לָא מִסְתַּיְיהוּ דְּלָא גְּמְרוּ, אֶלָּא מֵיגְמַר נַמֵּי מַגְמְרִי! (שבת קכד, סע"ב ע"פ רש"י שם)

It is not enough for them that they have not learned, but they would even teach (errors to others)!

* The etymology of this word is uncertain, but it may well be related to the Biblical Hebrew מִסַּת in דברים טז:י, which is also found in the Targumim there and elsewhere as a translation of דַּי, e.g., תרגום אונקלוס לויקרא ה:ז.

לְמִיעֲבַד/לְמֶעֱבַד inf. (עבד)

to do; to make לַעֲשׂוֹת

For an example — see הֲוָה לֵיהּ ל-.

SEE: עֲבַד

מִיעוּט; מִיעוּטָא*

(1) a limitation; an exclusion

This term denotes an element in a Biblical text that is interpreted as excluding a certain case from a halakhic category. Such a limitation is indicated by certain special words such as אַךְ or רַק, *only*; מִן (or the prefix מ-), *part of*; or by a superfluous word or phrase.

וְהָא אָמְרַתְּ "בָּהּ" מִיעוּטָא הוּא?! (שבועות ז,ב ע"פ ויקרא ה:ג)

But did you not say [that the word] בָּהּ *(through it, in* לְכֹל טֻמְאָתוֹ אֲשֶׁר יִטְמָא בָּהּ, *whatever his impurity be that he becomes impure through it) is a limitation (indicating that only through this type of impurity does he become impure — not through other types)?!*

(2) a minority

ר' מֵאִיר לְטַעְמֵיהּ דְּחָיֵישׁ לְמִיעוּטָא, וְגָזַר רוּבָּא אַטּוּ מִיעוּטָא. (חולין ו,א)

R. Méir is consistent with his own position [in] that he is concerned about the minority, and he enacts Rabbinic safeguard legislation against [the wine of] all (Cutheans) because of the minority (who worship idols).

(3) the minimum number

מִיעוּט "כְּבָשִׂים" — שְׁנַיִם. (יומא סב,ב ע"פ ויקרא יד:י)

The minimum number [indicated by the plural] "lambs" is two.

* The first form is Hebrew, and the second is Aramaic.

SEE: מִיעֵט, מָעֵט, רִיבּוּי, אֵין מִיעוּט אַחַר מִיעוּט אֶלָּא לְרַבּוֹת

מִיעֵט* (מעט פִּעֵל: מְמַעֵט .prt, לְמַעֵט .inf)

he reduced; he limited (the scope of a halakha); **it excluded** (from a halakhic category)

מִיעֵט רַחֲמָנָא גַּבֵּי מְכָרוּהוּ בֵּית דִּין. "הַעֲנֵק תַּעֲנִיק לוֹ" — "לוֹ", וְלֹא לְמוֹכֵר עַצְמוֹ. (קידושין טו,א ע"פ דברים טו:יד)

The Torah limited [the scope of the mitzva] to [a slave] whom the court sold. "You shall liberally provide him (gifts)" — "him," but not [a slave who] sells himself (into slavery).

* This Hebrew form is used even in Aramaic contexts rather than the Aramaic מַעֵט.

SEE: מִיעוּט, מָעֵט, הוֹצִיא, (לְ)אַפּוּקֵי, רִיבָּה

לְמֵיעַל inf. (עלל)

to come; to enter לָבֹא; לְהִכָּנֵס

SEE: עַל

מִיעָרֵם (מִתְעָרֵם) .prt (ערם אִתְפְּעֵל) מְעָרֵים

employing a stratagem; acting deceptively

SEE: מַעֲרִים, (לְ)אִיעָרוּמֵי

מִיפְּטַר (= מִתְפְּטַר) .prt (פטר אִתְפְּעֵל)

becoming exempt (1) נִפְטָר

דִּילְמָא מוֹדֵי וּמִיפְּטַר* (בבא מציעא לד, רע"א ע"פ כת"י)

perhaps he will confess and become exempt

departing; taking leave (2) נִפְרָד

כִּי הֲווּ מִיפַּטְרֵי* מֵהֲדָדֵי (תענית ה, סע"ב ועוד)

when they were taking leave of each other

* The singular and plural forms are popularly pronounced מִיפְּטַר and מִיפַּטְרֵי, respectively.

SEE: אִיפְּטַר

לְמִיפְטַר imp. (פטר) לִפְטוֹר **to free; to exempt**

For an example — see שבועות כג, סע"א.

SEE: פְּטַר

מִיפְלַג/מִפְלַג* inf. (פלג)

disagree (1) חָלוֹק

הָא מִיפְלַג פְּלִיגִי! (פסחים ק, סע"ב ועוד)

Behold they certainly disagree!

divide; share (2) הִתְחַלֵּק

... אֲבָל מָמוֹנָא — אֵימָא הָנֵי מִיפְלַג פָּלְגִי! (קידושין מג, רע"ב)

... but [as for] money — say [that] these are indeed sharing [it]!

* These forms are absolute infinitives. See the note under מֵידְכַר.

SEE: פְּלִיג, פְּלַג

מִיפַּלְגִי* (= מִתְפַּלְגִי) prt. pl. (פלג אִתְפְּעֵל)

disagreeing; differing; disputing חֲלוּקִים

מִדְּלָא מִיפַּלְגִי בַּאֲבָנִים (ביצה יב,א)

since they are not disagreeing about (carrying) stones

* This common form, which is popularly pronounced מִיפְלְגִי, is plural. A singular form rarely occurs.

SEE: אַדְמִיפַלְגִי ב-... לִיפְלְגוּ ב-, אִיפְלִיג

קָמִיפַּלְגִי/קָא מִיפַּלְגִי*

they disagree; they differ הֵם חֲלוּקִים

* מִיפַּלְגִי is popularly pronounced מִיפְלְגִי.

SEE: (בְּ)מַאי קָמִיפַּלְגִי and the next two entries here.

בְּ... קָמִיפַּלְגִי

they disagree about ... בְּ... הֵם חֲלוּקִים

This formula often presents a response to the question בְּמַאי קָמִיפַּלְגִי? *(about what [issue] do they disagree?)*. It offers an explanation of the *controversy* in terms of different interpretations of a Scriptural passage, different halakhic principles, and so on.

בְּהַאי קְרָא קָמִיפַּלְגִי ... (קידושין טו,ב)

They disagree about [the interpretation of] this pasuk...

בְּהֶכְשֵׁר סוּכָּה קָמִיפַּלְגִי. (סוכה ב,ב)

They disagree about [the minimal area required for] making a sukka valid.

וְהָכָא בִּדְר' אֱלִיעֶזֶר קָא מִיפַּלְגִי. (מנחות קו, רע"ב)

But here they disagree about [the halakha] of R Eliezer (which one amora supports, and the other rejects).

וְקָמִפַּלְגִי בִּפְלוּגְתָּא דְּר' ... וְר' ....*

וַחֲלוּקִים בְּמַחֲלוֹקֶת שֶׁבֵּין ר' ... לְבֵין ר' ....

They disagree about [the same issue that is the subject of] a controversy between R. ... and R. ....

For an example — see שבת יט,ב.

* The verb קָמִיפַּלְגִי sometimes comes at the end of this sentence: בִּפְלוּגְתָּא דְּר' ... וְר' ... קָמִיפַּלְגִי.

מִיפְּסִיל (= מִתְפְּסִיל) pass. prt. (פסל אִתְפְּעֵל)

disqualified; unfit נִפְסַל

SEE: אִיפְּסִיל

לְמִיפְרַךְ/לְמִפְרַךְ inf. (פרך) "לִשְׁבֹּר"; לְהַקְשׁוֹת

"to break"; to refute (an argument)

SEE: אִיכָּא לְמִיפְרַךְ

מִיפְשַׁט/מִפְשַׁט* inf. (פשט)

"be obvious" פָּשׁוּט

מִיפְשַׁט פְּשִׁיטָא לֵיהּ (קידושין י,ב ועוד)

it is indeed obvious to him

* These forms are absolute infinitives. See the note under מִידְכָּר.

מִיקְטַל/מִקְטַל*; לְמִיקְטַל/לְמִקְטַל inf. (קטל)

to kill; to cut הָרוֹג; קָצוֹץ; לַהֲרֹג; לִקְצֹץ

* These forms (without -ל) are absolute infinitives. See the note under מִידְכָּר.

SEE: קְטַל

מִיקְלַע/מִקְלַע (= מִתְקְלַע) prt. (קלע אִתְפְּעֵל)

coming by chance נִקְלָע; מִזְדַּמֵּן

SEE: אִיקְלַע

לְמֵיקַם inf. (קום)

to stand; to be subject to לַעֲמֹד

לְמֵיקַם עֲלַהּ בְּלָאו (יבמות יא,ב)

for her to be subject to a (Biblical) prohibition

SEE: קָם

לְמִיקְנָא/לְמִקְנָא/לְמִיקְנֵי/ לְמִקְנֵי/ לְמִקְנְיָא

to acquire לִקְנוֹת (קני) inf.

SEE: קְנֵי

מִיקְרֵי/מִקְרֵי[1] (= מִתְקְרֵי) prt. (קרא אִתְפְּעֵל)

being called נִקְרָא

SEE: אִיקְרֵי[1]

מִיקְרֵי/מִיקְרֵי[2] (= מִתְקְרֵי) prt. (קרי אִתְפְּעֵל)

happening קוֹרֶה; מִזְדַּמֵּן

SEE: אִיקְרֵי[2]

לְמִיקְרֵי/לְמִקְרֵי/לְמִיקְרָא inf. (קרא)

to read; to call לִקְרֹא

SEE: קְרָא

לְמִירְמָא/לְמִירְמֵי; מִירְמָא* inf. (רמי)

to throw; to cast לְהָטִיל; הָטֵל

* This form (without -ל) is the absolute infinitive. See the note under מִידְכָּר.

SEE: (וְ)אִיכָּא דְּרָמֵי לְהוּ מִירְמָא, רְמָא

מִירְתַת/מִרְתַת (= מִתְרְתַת) prt. (רתת אִתְפְּעֵל)

trembling; afraid רוֹתֵת; רוֹעֵד; פּוֹחֵד

SEE: אִירְתַת

לְמִישְׁקַל/לְמִשְׁקַל; מִישְׁקַל/מִשְׁקַל* inf. (שקל)

to take; to take away לָקַחַת; לָקוֹחַ

* These forms (without -ל) are absolute infinitives. See note under מִידְכָּר. Do not confuse with the Hebrew מִשְׁקָל, *weight*.

SEE: שְׁקַל

לְמִישְׁרֵי/לְמִישְׁרָא; מִישְׁרָא/מִשְׁרָא* inf. (שרי)

לְהַתִּיר; הַתֵּר

to permit; to untie; to begin (breaking bread)

* These forms (without -ל) are absolute infinitives. See the note under מִידְכָּר.

SEE: שְׁרָא

מִישְׁתְּרֵי prt. (שרי אִתְפְּעֵל) מֻתָּר **permitted**

SEE: שְׁרָא, אִישְׁתְּרֵי

מִית (מות*: מָיֵית/מָאֵית .prt, לֵימוּת .fut, לְמֵימַת .inf)

he died מֵת

סְלִיק לְאִיגָּרָא נְפִיל, וּמִית (תענית כט,א)

he went up to the roof and fell, and he died

* For the complete conjugation of this verb, see *Grammar for Gemara*: Chapter 4, Verb 18.

SEE: מָיֵית

מְיַתַּב .pass. prt (יתב פָּעֵל)

quieted; settled; composed מְיֻשָּׁב

מְיַתְּבָא דַּעְתֵּיה

his (physical) senses are restored דַּעְתּוֹ מְיֻשֶּׁבֶת

For examples — see יומא עט,א; פ,ב.

לְמִיתַּב[1]; מִיתָּב* .inf (יתב)

to sit; to live; to dwell לָשֶׁבֶת; יָשׁוֹב

מִיתָּב* יָתְבִינַן, בָּרוֹכֵי לָא מְבָרְכִינַן. (סוכה מז,א)

We must indeed sit (in the sukka on Sh^e^mini Atzereth in the Diaspora, but) we must not recite the b^e^rakha.

* These forms are popularly pronounced מֵיתֵב and לְמֵיתֵב respectively. The form without -ל is an absolute infinitive, rendered by an adverb, e.g., *indeed*. See note under מִידְכַּר.

לְמִיתַּב[2]* .inf (נתב) לָתֵת **to give**

אִילּוּ בָּעֵי לְמִיתְּבָא לֵיהּ בְּמַתָּנָה, מִי לָא יָהֵיב לֵיהּ ?! (ב"ב קכז,ב)

If he would want to give it to him as a gift, could he not give it to him?!

* This form is popularly pronounced לְמֵיתֵב.

SEE: יְהַב and its note.

מִיתְחֲזֵי

SEE: מִיחֲזֵי

לְמֵיתֵי .inf (אתי) לָבוֹא **to come**

SEE: אֲתָא

מֵיתִיבִי* .prt. pl (תוב אַפְעֵל)

replying; refuting; objecting מְשִׁיבִים; מַקְשִׁים

This term introduces a *difficulty* based on a mishna, a baraitha, or a pasuk that contradicts a statement of a specific amora or an anonymous statement.

אֲמַר רַב יוֹסֵף: ... בִּשְׁאָר מִצְוֹת דִּבְרֵי הַכֹּל לֹא יָצָא .... מֵיתִיבִי: לֹא יְבָרֵךְ אָדָם בִּרְכַּת הַמָּזוֹן בְּלִבּוֹ; וְאִם בֵּירֵךְ, יָצָא. (ברכות טו,ב)

Rav Yosef said: ... as for all other mitzvoth (b^e^rakhoth), everyone agrees [that a Jew who recites a b^e^rakha in his heart] has not fulfilled his obligation .... They object to [that halakha on the basis of the following baraitha]: One should not recite Birkath HaMazon in his heart [without saying the words]; but if he did [so], he did fulfill his obligation.

* The Yemenite pronunciation is מְתִיבֵי, ignoring the first י. Among Ashkenasim, it is popularly pronounced מֵיתְבֵי, ignoring the second י.

SEE: מוֹתִיב, מְתִיב, אֵיתִיבֵיהּ

מִיתָנָא[1] הַמֵּת **the dead; the deceased**

אֲנָא בַּר מִיתָנָא אֲנָא, וְנִכְסֵי דִידִי נִינְהוּ. (יבמות לז,ב ע"פ הרי"ף)

I am the son of the deceased, and the property is mine.

מִיתָנָא[2]/מִתָּנָא חֶבֶל **rope**

בְּמַנְעוּל וּקְטִיר בְּמִיתְנָא עָסְקִינַן (עירובין לה,א)

we are dealing with a lock and it is tied with a rope

לְמִיתְנֵי/לְמִתְנֵי/לְמִיתְנָא .inf (תני) לִשְׁנוֹת

to state (in a mishna or a baraitha)

SEE: תְּנָא, אַיְּדֵי דְּבָעֵי לְמִיתְנֵי סֵיפָא, לָמָּה לִי לְמִיתְנֵי, מִשּׁוּם דְּקָא בָּעֵי לְמִיתְנֵי סֵיפָא

מִיתְּסַר .prt (אסר אִתְפְּעִל) נֶאֱסָר **forbidden**

SEE: אִיתְּסַר

מִיתְרְמֵי/מִתְרְמֵי .prt (רמי אִתְפְּעִל)

occurring by chance; happening מִזְדַּמֵּן; קוֹרֶה

SEE: רְמָא, אִיתְרְמִי

מִכְּדִי (מִן+כְּ+דִי) מֵאַחַר שֶׁ- **now that; since**

A clause introduced by this word usually prepares the way for an *objection* or a *difficulty*.

מִכְּדִי אוֹתְבִינְהוּ כָּל הָנֵי קְרָאֵי וְשַׁנִּינְהוּ — חִזְקִיָּה וְרִ' אַבָּהוּ בְּמַאי פְּלִיגִי?! (פסחים כג,ב)

Now that we have raised objections from all these p^e^sukim and answered them — wherein do Ḥizkiyya and R. Abbahu disagree?!

מִכָּל מָקוֹם

(1) in any event; in any case; nevertheless

מִכָּל מָקוֹם קַשְׁיָא! (שבת כא,א ועוד)

Nevertheless (= even though some other difficulty has been resolved), it (= the difficulty originally posed in the Talmud) remains difficult!

(2) in any manner; in all circumstances

In this sense the term is used after the quotation of a Biblical expression that is interpreted as expanding the scope of a halakhic category.

"עָזֹב תַּעֲזוֹב עִמּוֹ" — אֵין לִי אֶלָּא בְּעָלָיו עִמּוֹ; שֶׁאֵין בְּעָלָיו עִמּוֹ מִנַּיִן? תַּלְמוּד לוֹמַר: "עָזֹב תַּעֲזוֹב" — מִכָּל מָקוֹם. (בבא מציעא לא, סע"א ע"פ שמות כג:ה)

"You shall surely help with him [when your neighbor's pack animal is lying under its burden on the road]." I only know [to do so] when the owner is with it; when the owner is not with it, from where [do I learn that I must help]? Scripture teaches: "You shall surely help" — in all circumstances.

* The emphasis provided by the infinitive עָזֹב, *help*, teaches that assistance must *surely* be provided — whatever the circumstances.

מִכְּלַל* **"from the rule of"; from; by implication from**

מִכְּלַל "לָאו" אַתָּה שׁוֹמֵעַ "הֵן". (נדרים יא, רע"א)

From a "no" (= a negative statement) you may infer a "yes" (= a positive statement).

* This preposition is a compound of the prefix -מִ and the noun כְּלָל in the construct state.
SEE: חֲדָא מִכְּלָל חֲבֶרְתָּהּ אִיתְּמַר, לָאו הַבָּא מִכְּלָל עֲשֵׂה

מִכְּלָל שֶׁ-; מִכְּלָל דְּ-* **"from the rule that"; by implication [it follows] that; consequently**

משנה: אֲבוֹת נְזִיקִין ...
תלמוד: מִדְּקָתָנֵי "אֲבוֹת", מִכְּלָל דְּאִיכָּא "תּוֹלָדוֹת"! (ב"ק ב,א)
MISHNA: The principal categories of damage ...
TALMUD: From the fact that [the tanna] specifies "principal categories," by implication it follows that there must (also) be "subordinate categories"!
* The first form is Hebrew, and the second is Aramaic.
SEE: הֲלָכָה מִכְּלָל דִּפְלִיגִי

מִכְּלָלָא מִכְּלָל **by implication**
For an example, see לָאו בְּפֵירוּשׁ אִיתְּמַר אֶלָּא מִכְּלָלָא אִיתְּמַר.

מַכְרִיעַ prt. (כרע הִפְעִיל)
deciding; harmonising; compromising
This term is sometimes applied to the tanna who holds the intermediate position in a three-way controversy.

ברייתא: לֹא יִשְׁתַּטֵּף אָדָם כָּל גּוּפוֹ בֵּין בְּחַמִּין וּבֵין בְּצוֹנִין — דִּבְרֵי ר' מֵאִיר. ר' שִׁמְעוֹן מַתִּיר. ר' יְהוּדָה אוֹמֵר: בְּחַמִּין אָסוּר, בְּצוֹנִין מוּתָּר ...
תלמוד: אָמַר ר' תַּנְחוּם אָמַר ר' יוֹחָנָן ...: כָּל מָקוֹם שֶׁאַתָּה מוֹצֵא שְׁנַיִם חֲלוּקִין וְאֶחָד מַכְרִיעַ — הֲלָכָה כְּדִבְרֵי הַמַּכְרִיעַ. (שבת לט,ב)
BARAITHA: One is forbidden to shower his entire body (on the Sabbath) with either hot or cold water — the opinion of R. Méir. R. Shim'on permits. R. Y'huda says: With hot water it is forbidden, (but) with cold water it is permitted.
TALMUD: R. Tanḥum said in the name of R. Yoḥanan ...: Whenever you find two [authorities] in dispute and a third compromising, the halakha is in accordance with the compromiser (= R. Y'huda in this baraitha).

מַכְשַׁר prt. (כשר אַפְעֵל)
rendering fit; declaring to be fit מַכְשִׁיר
SEE: אַכְשַׁר

מִכַּתַּת pass. prt. (כתת פַּעֵל)
crushed; destroyed כָּתוּת; כָּתוּשׁ
For an example, see כְּתוּתֵי.

מְלוֹג SEE: נִכְסֵי מְלוֹג

מְלַוֶּה prt. (לוי פַּעֵל) **accompanying**
For an example — see סוטה מו, סע"ב.

מַלְוֶה* prt. (לוי הִפְעִיל) **lending; lender; creditor (as opposed to לֹוֶה, borrower)**
הַכּוֹתֵב ... שִׁטְרֵי מִלְוֶה צָרִיךְ שֶׁיַּנִּיחַ מְקוֹם הַמַּלְוֶה, מְקוֹם הַלֹּוֶה, מְקוֹם הַמָּעוֹת, מְקוֹם הַזְּמַן. (גיטין כו,א: משנה פ"ג מ"ב)
[If] one writes ... notes of indebtedness, he must leave space for [the name of] the lender, space for [the name of] the borrower, space for [the amount of] money, [and] space for the date.
* This verbal form is frequently used as a noun.
SEE: בַּעַל חוֹב

מִלְוֶה/מִלְוָה **a loan**
מִלְוֶה לְהוֹצָאָה נִיתְּנָה (קידושין מז,א)
a loan is given for spending

מִלְוֶה בִּשְׁטָר
a loan supported by a promissory note (signed by two witnesses)
For an example — see the next entry.

מִלְוֶה עַל פֶּה **"a verbal loan"; a loan not supported by a promissory note**
דְּבַר תּוֹרָה, אֶחָד מִלְוֶה בִּשְׁטָר וְאֶחָד מִלְוֶה עַל פֶּה גּוֹבֶה מִנְּכָסִים מְשׁוּעְבָּדִים. (בבא בתרא קעה,ב)
[According to] Torah law, one may collect both a loan [supported] by a promissory note and a verbal loan (even) from subjugated properties.
SEE: נְכָסִים

מַלְקוּת (pl. מַלְקִיּוֹת) **the punishment of flogging** (executed by order of the court)

מַלְקִין prt. (לקי הִפְעִיל); **מַלְקֵי*** prt. (לקי אַפְעֵל)
flogging; inflicting the punishment of lashes
מַלְקִינַן לֵיהּ (מכות טז,ב) *we flog him*
* The first form is Hebrew, and the second is Aramaic.
SEE: לוֹקֶה and its note

מִלְּתָא SEE: מִילְּתָא

מְמַאי SEE: (מְ)מַאי

מַמְטֵי prt. (מטי אַפְעֵל)
presenting; bringing מַמְצִיא; מֵבִיא
SEE: אַמְטֵי

מִמֵּילָא* מֵאֵלָיו/מֵאֵלֶיהָ; מֵעַצְמוֹ/מֵעַצְמָהּ
of itself; by itself; automatically
לָא שְׁנָא שַׁלְחָהּ שָׁלוֹחֵי, לָא שְׁנָא אָזְלָה מִמֵּילָא. (בבא קמא ג,א)
It makes no difference whether he actually sent it (= his animal), or whether it went by itself.
* This Aramaic word is often used in Modern Hebrew in the above senses and with the meaning *in any case.*

מַמָּשׁ*
(1) substance; reality; significance
This noun is used in either a physical or an abstract sense.
טַעְמוֹ וְלֹא מַמָּשׁוֹ (חולין קח, רע"א)
its flavor, but not its substance
אִם יֵשׁ מַמָּשׁ בִּדְבָרָיו, שׁוֹמְעִין לוֹ. (סנהדרין מ,א: משנה ה:ד)

If there is substance to his words, they (= the judges) listen to him.

(2) really; literally

This adverbial usage is common (even today).

"עַיִן תַּחַת עַיִן" — מַמָּשׁ. (בבא קמא פד,א ע"פ שמות כא:כד)

"An eye for an eye" — literally.

לא "קָטָן" קָטָן מַמָּשׁ, אֶלָּא גָּדוֹל וְסָמוּךְ עַל שֻׁלְחַן אָבִיו זֶהוּ "קָטָן". (בבא מציעא יב, רע"ב)

"A minor" does not mean a minor really (in terms of age), but an adult who is maintained at his father's table is considered "a minor".

* This word is derived from the root משש as in the pasuk כַּאֲשֶׁר יְמַשֵּׁשׁ הָעִוֵּר בָּאֲפֵלָה (דברים כח:כט), *as a blind man feels [his way] in the darkness.* From מַמָּשׁ a new verb מִמֵּשׁ has been created in Modern Hebrew, meaning *he realized* or *he carried out.*

מִמַּשְׁמָע

SEE: (מִ)מַּשְׁמָע

מִן

from; than

As in Hebrew, this word is often used in Aramaic with personal-pronoun suffixes. In the Talmud, these suffixes are almost always attached to the fuller spelling מִינ-.

SEE: מִינ- and its suffixes.

מָנָא/מָאנָא (pl. מָאנֵי/מָנֵי)

(1) כְּלִי **utensil; vessel**

הָא קָמְתַקֵּן מָנָא! (שבת קמו,ב)

Behold he is making a utensil (on the Sabbath)!

(2) בֶּגֶד **garment; clothes***

ר' יוֹחָנָן קָרֵי לְמָאנֵיהּ "מְכַבְּדוֹתַי". (שבת קיג, סע"ב)

R. Yoḥanan calls his clothes "my honorers" (because clothing lends dignity to a person).

* In Mishnaic Hebrew the noun כֵּלִים is also used in the sense of clothes, as in בְּנוֹת יְרוּשָׁלַיִם יוֹצְאוֹת בִּכְלֵי לָבָן שְׁאוּלִין (תענית כו,ב: משנה פ"ד מ"ח).

מְנָא (= מִן+אָן)

מְנַיִן? **From where? What is the source?**

מְנָא יָדְעִינַן? (בבא קמא נט, רע"ב ועוד)

From where do we know?

מְנָא אָמֵינָא לַהּ

מְנַיִן אֲנִי אוֹמֵר אוֹתָהּ? **From where do I say it?**

With this question an amora introduces *evidence* from a mishna or a baraitha (or occasionally from a pasuk or from the statement of an earlier amora) to bolster the opinion he has presented.

For an example — see קידושין יב, סע"ב.

מְנָא הָא מִילְּתָא דַּאֲמוּר רַבָּנַן

מְנַיִן דָּבָר זֶה שֶׁאָמְרוּ חֲכָמִים ...?

What is the source of the statement that the ḥakhamim have made ...?

With this question an amora seeks a *Biblical source* for a halakhic or aggadic teaching taught by earlier authorities.

אֲמַר לֵיהּ רַבָּה לְרָבָא בַּר מָארִי: מְנָא הָא מִילְּתָא דַּאֲמוּר רַבָּנַן: בְּנֵי בָנִים הֲרֵי הֵן כְּבָנִים? (יבמות סב,ב)

Rabba said to Rava b. Mori: What is the source of the statement that the ḥakhamim have made: Grandchildren are [considered] like children?

מְנָא הָא מִילְּתָא דְּאָמְרִי אֱנָשֵׁי

מְנַיִן דָּבָר זֶה שֶׁאוֹמְרִים אֲנָשִׁים ...?

From where is [the Biblical source of] the maxim that people say ...?

This question introduces a *popular maxim,* for which a basis can be found in Scripture.

מְנָא הָא מִילְּתָא דְּאָמְרִי אֱנָשֵׁי: בֵּירָא דְּשָׁתִית מִינֵּיהּ לָא תִשְׁדֵּי בֵיהּ קָלָא? ... דִּכְתִיב: ... "לֹא תְתַעֵב מִצְרִי כִּי גֵר הָיִיתָ בְאַרְצוֹ". (בבא קמא צב,ב ע"פ דברים כג:ח)

From where is [the Biblical source of] the maxim that people say: Into the well from which you have drunk — do not throw a clod of earth!? (= Don't pay back evil for good!) ... as it is written: "Do not despise an Egyptian, because you have been a stranger in his land."

SEE: אָמְרִי אֱנָשֵׁי

מְנָא הָנֵי* מִילֵּי מְנַיִן הַדְּבָרִים הָאֵלּוּ?

From where [do we derive] these things?

This question seeks a *source* for a statement in a mishna, in a baraitha, or by an amora. The answer is a Scriptural interpretation.**

משנה: וְהַנָּשִׁים בִּכְלַל הַנֶּזֶק. (בבא קמא יד, רע"ב: משנה א:ג)

תלמוד: מְנָהָנֵי מִילֵּי? אָמַר רַב יְהוּדָה אָמַר רַב ...: אָמַר קְרָא: "אִישׁ אוֹ אִשָּׁה כִּי יַעֲשׂוּ מִכָּל חַטֹּאת הָאָדָם" — הִשְׁוָה הַכָּתוּב אִשָּׁה לְאִישׁ לְכָל עוֹנָשִׁין שֶׁבַּתּוֹרָה. (שם טו,א ע"פ במדבר ה:ו)

MISHNA: Women are subject to [the laws of] damages...

TALMUD: From where [do we derive] these things? Rav Y^ehuda said quoting Rav ...: The pasuk states: "When a man or a woman commit any of the transgressions against a fellow human being" — Scripture has equated woman with man regarding all the penalties in the Torah.

* מְנָא הָנֵי is sometimes written as one word, מְנָהָנֵי.

** In some instances, the Scriptural interpretation is a mere allusion or support (see אַסְמַכְתָּא), as Rashi notes in his commentary on ביצה טו, רע"ב.

SEE: הָנֵי מִילֵּי

מְנָא ל- מְנַיִן ל-?

"From where is it to ...?" Where is the source?

The interrogative מְנָא is often followed by the preposition ל- with a personal-pronoun suffix in order to form a *question.*

מְנָא לָךְ? מְנַיִן לְךָ? **"From where is it to you?" What is your source? How do you derive?**

What is his source?	מִנַּיִן לוֹ?	מְנָא לֵיהּ?
What is our source?	מִנַּיִן לָנוּ?	מְנָא לַן?
What is their source?	מִנַּיִן לָהֶם?	מְנָא לְהוּ?

For an example — see מְנָלַן, which is often used as a contraction of מְנָא+לַן.

וּמְנָא תֵימְרָא* וּמִנַּיִן אַתָּה אוֹמְרָהּ?

And from where would you say it?

This *question* seeks a source for a halakha stated in a mishna, a baraitha, or by an amora's statement.

וּמְנָא תֵימְרָא דִלְהֶפְסֵד מְרוּבֶּה חָשְׁשׁוּ, וּלְהֶפְסֵד מוּעָט לֹא חָשְׁשׁוּ? (פסחים כ,ב)

And from where would you say that [the Rabbinical authorities] were concerned about a substantial loss, but they were not concerned about a slight loss?

* תֵּימְרָא = תֵּימְרָה with the final א- equal to a final ה-.

a maneh **מָנֶה***

This silver coin or weight equals one hundred *zuz.*

מָנֶה לִי בְּיָדְךָ! (שבועות לח,ב: משנה פ"ו מ"א)

A maneh of mine is in your hand (= You owe me one hundred zuz)!

* See the table of coins and weights in Appendix II.

ע' יחזקאל מה:יב ורש"י שם.

מָנָה¹ (מני: מוֹנֶה .prt)

he counted; he enumerated

Scripture has enumerated מָנָה הַכָּתוּב (ברכות כד,א ועוד)

מָנוּ חֲכָמִים (פסחים מג,א ועוד)

[the] hakhamim have enumerated (in a mishna)

SEE: מָנֵי

portion; share (usually of food) **מָנָה²; מְנָתָא***

מָנָה יָפָה לְשַׁבָּת (ביצה טו, רע"ב)

a fine portion for the Sabbath

* The first form is Hebrew, and the second is Aramaic.

מִנְהָג; מִנְהָגָא*

(1) custom (in some cases, a practice that originated as a voluntary restriction beyond the normative requirements of Jewish law)

אֲמִינָא לָךְ אֲנָא אִיסוּרָא, וְאַתְּ אָמְרַתְּ לִי מִנְהָגָא! (יבמות יג, סע"ב; נדה סו, סע"א)

I speak to you of a legal prohibition, but you quote me a custom!

(2) the established halakhic practice (though not announced to the public)

מַאן דְּאָמַר "מִנְהָג" — מִידְרַשׁ לָא דָּרְשִׁינַן, אוֹרוֹיֵי מוֹרֵינַן. (תענית כו,ב וע' רש"י לעירובין מו,ב)

[According to] the one who says "(the) established halakhic practice (is like R. Me'ir)" — we do not expound [the decision in a public discourse], (yet) we do teach it (to any individual who asks us).

* The first form is Hebrew, and the second is Aramaic.

SEE: נְהַג

מְנָהָנֵי מִילֵּי SEE: מְנָא הָנֵי מִילֵּי

מַנּוּ (= מַאן הוּא)

who is he? who is it (m.)? מִי הוּא?

דָּרֵשׁ רַב נַחְמָן מִשּׁוּם רַבֵּינוּ — וּמַנּוּ? שְׁמוּאֵל. (ברכות לח,ב)

Rav Nahman expounded in the name of our master — and who is it? Sh'muel.

SEE: מַנִּי

placing מֵנִיחַ (נוח אַפְעֵל) act. prt. **מַנַּח¹**

כִּי מַנַּח תְּפִילִּין אַדְּרָעֵיהּ (ברכות ס,ב)

when he places t'fillin on his arm

SEE: אַנַּח

placed מֻנָּח (נוח אַפְעֵל) pass. prt. **מַנַּח²**

הָא מַנַּח כָּסָא קַמַּן (פסחים קג, סע"א)

behold the cup is placed before us

SEE: אַנַּח

מָנֵי (מני: לִימְנֵי .fut, לְמִימְנֵי .inf) prt.

he counts; he enumerates מוֹנֶה

אַמֵּימָר מָנֵי יוֹמֵי, וְלָא מָנֵי שָׁבוּעֵי. (מנחות סו,א)

*Ammemar counts days (of the Omer), but he does not count weeks.**

* According to the accepted halakhic norm, we do count weeks as well.

SEE: מָנָה¹

מַנִּי (= מַאן הִיא)

who is she? who is it (f.)? (1) מִי הִיא?

אֲמַר לְהוּ רַב חִסְדָּא לִבְנָתֵיהּ: ... וְכִי קָרֵי אֱינִישׁ אַבָּבָא, לָא תֵּימְרוּן: "מַנּוּ?" אֶלָּא "מַנִּי?" (שבת קמ,ב ע"פ כת"י)

Rav Hisda said to his daughters: ... and when someone calls at the door, do not say: "Who is it (m.)?" but [say]: "Who is it (f.)?"

whose is it? (2) שֶׁל מִי הִיא?

This term is used to raise a question: Whose [opinion] is [being presented in the text under discussion]?

For an example, see the next entry.

SEE: מַנּוּ

מַנִּי מַתְנִיתִין [שֶׁל] מִי הִיא מִשְׁנָתֵנוּ?

Whose [opinion] is [presented by] our mishna?

מַנִּי מַתְנִיתִין? לָא ר' יְהוּדָה וְלָא ר' שִׁמְעוֹן וְלָא ר' יוֹסֵי הַגְּלִילִי! (פסחים כח, סע"א)

Whose [opinion] is [presented by] our mishna? It is neither R. Y'huda['s] nor R. Shim'on['s] nor [that of] R. Yosé, the Galilean!

SEE: מַתְנִיתִין מַנִּי

מִנַּיִין/מִנַּיִן (= מִן+אַיִן)

From where [is it derived]?

מִנַּיִן לְסִיכָה שֶׁהִיא כִשְׁתִיָּה בְּיוֹם הַכִּיפּוּרִים? (שבת פו,א: משנה פ"ט מ"ד)

From where [is it derived] that on Yom Kippur annointing is [forbidden] like drinking?

מִנְיָן; מִנְיָינָא/מִנְיָנָא*

(1) a count; a counting

כָּל דָּבָר שֶׁבְּמִנְיָן — צָרִיךְ מִנְיָן אַחֵר לְהַתִּירוֹ (ביצה ה,א)

[as for] any restriction that (was voted) by a count (of judges) — another count is required in order to cancel it (even if the reason no longer applies)

(2) a number; a quorum

מִנְיָינָא ... לְמַעוּטֵי מַאי? (קידושין ג,א ועוד)

What [does] the number [stated in the text come] to exclude?

* The first form is Hebrew, and the others are Aramaic.

מְנַכֵּי prt. (נכי פָּעֵל) מְנַכֶּה — deducting

מַאי דְּאַפְסֵיד מְנַכֵּינַן לֵיהּ, וְאִידָךְ יָהֲבִינַן לֵיהּ. (ב"מ קט, סע"א)

We deduct the amount of the loss he has caused, but we give him the rest.

מְנָלַן (= מְנָא+לַן) מִנַּיִן לָנוּ?

"From where [is it] to us?" How do we derive [it]? What is our source (usually in Scripture)?

משנה: מְגִילָּה נִקְרֵאת בְּאַחַד עָשָׂר.... (מגילה ב,א: משנה א:א)

תלמוד: מְנָלַן? (שם ב,א)

MISHNA: The scroll of Esther may be read on the eleventh (of Adar) .... TALMUD: What is our source?

* In some instances, the source is merely an allusion or a support (see אַסְמַכְתָּא), as in our example where the Talmud subsequently paraphrases מְנָלַן with הֵיכָא רְמִיזָא (*where is it hinted?*).

SEE: מְנָא ל-

מְנַמְנֵם* prt. (נום פַּלְפֵּל)** מִתְנַמְנֵם — dozing

הֲוָה יָתֵיבְנָא בְּפִירְקָא וַהֲוָה קָא מְנַמְנֵם, וַחֲזַאי בְּחֵילְמָא ... (שבת נו, סע"ב)

I was sitting at the lecture and dozing, and I saw in a dream ...

* Sometimes, מְנַמְנֵם is a euphemism for *dying*. See "Rashi's" comment on מועד קטן כח,א.

** The first and third letters of the root נום) are duplicated to form נמנם).

מְנַקֵּיט prt. (נקט פָּעֵל)

gathering; compiling — מְלַקֵּט

מְנַקֵּיט אַבָּיֵי תּוֹמְרֵי מַתְנְיָיתָא וְתָנֵי. (שבת קלח,א ורש"י שם)

Abbayé [was] compiling rules from baraithoth and reciting them.

מְנָת

SEE: עַל מְנָת

מְנָתָא

SEE: מָנָה

מְסָאַב pass. prt. (סאב פָּעֵל) — unclean

וְנֶאֱכָלִין בְּיָדַיִם מְסָאָבוֹת (חולין לג,א: משנה פ"ב מ"ח)

and they may be eaten with "unclean" hands

SEE: יִסְתָּאַב

מְסָאנָא נַעַל — shoe

For an example, see סַיֵּים.

מְסַגֵּי prt. (סגי פָּעֵל)

הוֹלֵךְ; עוֹבֵר — **walking; passing**

SEE: סַגֵּי

מַסְהִיד prt. (סהד אַפְעֵל) מֵעִיד — testifying

For an example, see בַּר קְטָלָא.

SEE: אַסְהִיד

מָסוֹר* (pl. מָסוֹרוֹת) — informer; traitor

שָׁאנֵי מָסוֹר דְּדִיבּוּרָא הוּא. (בבא קמא ה,א ע"פ כת"י)

[The case of] an informer is different, because it is [through] speech [that he causes damage].

* In current editions of the Talmud and in Modern Hebrew, the form is מוֹסֵר.

SEE: מְסַר

מָסוֹרֶת

(1) a tradition (aggadic or halakhic)

מָסוֹרֶת בְּיָדָם מֵאֲבוֹתֵיהֶם שֶׁשָּׁם הָאָרוֹן נִגְנַז. (משנה שקלים ו:א)

They had a tradition from their forefathers that the holy ark was hidden there.

עוֹף טָהוֹר נֶאֱכָל בְּמָסוֹרֶת. נֶאֱמָן הַצַּיָּיד לוֹמַר: עוֹף זֶה טָהוֹר מָסַר לִי רַבִּי. (חולין סג, סע"ב)

Kosher birds may be eaten according to tradition. A hunter is trusted if he says: My master has transmitted [a tradition] to me: "This [species of] bird is kosher."

(2) the accepted spelling (of the consonantal Biblical text)*

For an example, see יֵשׁ אֵם לַמָּסוֹרֶת.

* In later Hebrew, the term מָסוֹרָה (Masora) refers to the traditions — dealing with the spelling, the vocalisation, and the accentuation of the Biblical text — that are contained in the annotations published in some editions of the מִקְרָאוֹת גְּדוֹלוֹת.

SEE: מְסַר

מַסוּתָא/מַסְחוּתָא

SEE: בֵּי מַסוּתָא

מַסֵּי prt. (אסי אַפְעֵל) מְרַפֵּא — curing

אִיכָּא מַכָּה, מַסֵּי; לֵיכָּא מַכָּה, מַרְפֵּי. (שבת קיא,א)

[If] there is a wound, [vinegar] cures; [if] there is no wound, it causes weakness.

SEE: אַסְיָא

מֵסִיחַ prt. (סוח הִפְעִיל) — talking

מֵסִיחַ לְפִי תוּמּוֹ (בבא קמא קיד,ב ועוד)

he is talking in his innocence (= informally, in ignorance of the legal ramifications)

SEE: סָח

מְסַיֵּים prt. (סום פָּעֵל)

(1) מְסַיֵּים — **completing**

(2) מְצַיֵּין — **specifying**

SEE: סַיֵּים

מְסַיֵּיעַ prt. (סיע פָּעֵל); **מְסַיֵּיעַ*** (סיע פַּעֵל)

assisting; supporting (a ḥakham in his halakha)

וּמִקְרָא מְסַיְּיעוֹ (סנהדרין צא,ב)

and a pasuk supports him

* The first form is Hebrew, and the second is Aramaic.

SEE: לֵימָא מְסַיֵּיעַ לֵיהּ, תַּנְיָא דִּמְסַיֵּיעַ לָךְ and the next entry.

מְסַיֵּיעַ/מְסַיְּיעָא לֵיהּ לְר׳ ...

מְסַיֵּיעַ/מְסַיֶּיעֶת לְר׳ ... **It supports R. ...**

This formula is used to indicate that the text (usually a baraitha) quoted previously in the Talmud comprises a *proof* for the opinion of the amora that is about to be quoted.

ברייתא: אֵין בֵּין תִּשְׁעָה בְּאָב לְיוֹם הַכִּיפּוּרִים, אֶלָּא שֶׁזֶּה סְפֵקוֹ אָסוּר, וְזֶה סְפֵקוֹ מוּתָּר ...

תלמוד: הָא לְכָל דִּבְרֵיהֶם זֶה וָזֶה שָׁוִין. מְסַיֵּיעַ לֵיהּ לְר׳ אֶלְעָזָר, דְּאָמַר ר׳ אֶלְעָזָר: אָסוּר לוֹ לְאָדָם שֶׁיּוֹשִׁיט אֶצְבָּעוֹ בְּמַיִם בְּתִשְׁעָה בְּאָב, כְּדֶרֶךְ שֶׁאָסוּר לְהוֹשִׁיט אֶצְבָּעוֹ בְּיוֹם הַכִּיפּוּרִים. (פסחים נד,ב ע״פ כת״י)

BARAITHA: There is no difference between the Ninth of Av and Yom Kippur except that [regarding] the latter its doubtful case is forbidden, but [regarding] the former its doubtful case is permitted.

TALMUD: But regarding all [other] regulations, the two are alike. [This baraitha] supports R. El'azar, for R. El'azar said: It is forbidden for a person to dip his finger into water on the Ninth of Av, just as he is forbidden to dip his finger into water on Yom Kippur.

מַסִּיק¹ prt. (סלק הִפְעִיל)*

heating; kindling; firing (an oven)

הוּא מַסִּיק וְאִשְׁתּוֹ אוֹפָה. (פסחים קטז, רע״א)

He fires (the oven), and his wife bakes.

* This entry is Hebrew, but the next is Aramaic.

מַסִּיק² prt. (סלק אַפְעֵל)*

מַעֲלֶה; קוֹרֵא; מַעֲלֶה עַל הַדַּעַת; מַסִּיק (מַסְקָנָה); נוֹשֶׁה

bringing up; naming; considering (with דַּעְתָּא); concluding; having a (monetary) claim

הַהוּא גַּבְרָא דַּהֲוָה מַסִּיק בְּחַבְרֵיהּ זוּזֵי ... (נדרים כה,א)

There was a man who had a claim regarding money against his fellow man ...

For examples of the other meanings of this verb, see אַסִּיק.

* This entry is Aramaic, but the previous one is Hebrew.

מַסֶּכְתָּא* מַסֶּכֶת

"a web"; a tractate (from the Mishna, Tosefta, or the Talmud)

כִּי קָאֵי רַבִּי בְּהָא מַסֶּכְתָּא, לָא תְּשַׁיְּילֵיהּ בְּמַסֶּכְתָּא אַחֲרִיתִי! (שבת ג, רע״ב)

When Rebbi is engaged in [the study of] this tractate, don't ask him [questions] in another tractate!

* This noun is derived from the verb נָסַךְ, *he wove*. Similarly, *text* in English is derived from the Latin *textus*, *a web*.

מְסַלֵּיק prt. (סלק פַּעֵל)

removing; dismissing מְסַלֵּק

מָצֵי מְסַלֵּק לֵיהּ בְּזוּזֵי (פסחים ו, רע״א)

he can dismiss him with [a payment of] money

מְסֻפָּק (מְסֻפֶּקֶת .f) pass. prt. (ספק פֻּעַל)

doubtful מְסֻפָּק

For an example — see the next entry.

מְסַפְּקָא לֵיהּ מְסֻפֶּקֶת לוֹ; הוּא מְסֻפָּק

it is doubtful to him; he is in doubt

מְסַפְּקָא לֵיהּ אִי גְּנוּחֵי גָנַח אִי יְלוּלֵי יָלֵיל. (ר״ה לד, סע״א)

He (= R. Abbahu) is in doubt whether [it is like a person] sighing or [a person] wailing.

מַסְקָנָא מַסְקָנָה; סִיּוּם; סוֹף

the upshot; the conclusion; the end

וּמַסְקָנָא בְּכוֹסוֹת פְּלִיגֵי. (זבחים פא, סע״ב)

And the conclusion is [that] they disagree regarding the vessels.

SEE: אַסִּיק

מָסַר (מוֹסֵר act. prt., מָסוּר pass. prt.);

מְסַר* (מָסַר act. prt., מְסִיר pass. prt.)

he handed over; he transmitted

* The first form is Hebrew, and the second is Aramaic.

SEE: לֹא מְסָרָךְ הַכָּתוּב אֶלָּא לַחֲכָמִים, מָסוּר

מָסַר עַצְמוֹ; מְסַר נַפְשֵׁיהּ*

"he gave himself over"; he devoted himself; he submitted himself (to martyrdom); he risked his life

כָּל מִצְוָה שֶׁמָּסְרוּ יִשְׂרָאֵל עַצְמָן עָלֶיהָ בִּשְׁעַת הַשְּׁמָד ... עֲדַיִין מוּחְזֶקֶת הִיא בְּיָדָם. (שבת קל,א ע״פ כת״י)

Every commandment for which the Jewish people risked their lives at a time of religious persecution ... is still observed resolutely by them.

* The first expression is Hebrew, and the second is Aramaic.

מִסְתַּבַּר (מִסְתַּבְּרָא .f) prt. (סבר אִתְפַּעַל) מִסְתַּבֵּר

it is logical; it is convincing; it makes sense

מִסְתַּבַּר טַעֲמֵיהּ דְּר׳ מֵאִיר דְּקָמְסַיֵּיעַ לֵיהּ קְרָא. (יומא לו,ב)

The opinion of R. Méir is [more] convincing because the pasuk supports him.

For an additional example — see אִיפְּכָא מִסְתַּבְּרָא.

SEE: הָכִי נָמֵי מִסְתַּבְּרָא

מִסְתְּיָיא SEE: מִיסְתְּיָיא

מִסְתַּיַּיע prt. (סיע אִתְפַּעַל)

aided; assisted מִסְתַּיֵּיעַ; נֶעֱזָר

מִסְתַּיְּיעָא מִילְּתָא הָעִנְיָן מִסְתַּיֵּיעַ

"The matter is aided (from Heaven)."

The goal is realized.

ר׳ חֲנִינָא וְר׳ הוֹשַׁעְיָא — הֲוָה קָא מִשְׁתַּקֵּיד ר׳ יוֹחָנָן לְמִיסְמְכִינְהוּ; לָא הֲוָה מִסְתַּיְּיעָא מִילְּתָא. (סנהדרין יד,א)

[As for] R. Hanina and R. Hoshaya — R. Yohanan was intent upon ordaining them, (but that) goal was not realized.

מִסְתְּפֵי prt. (ספי אִתְפְּעֵל) **יָרֵא** **afraid**

מִסְתְּפֵינָא מִמַּלְכוּתָא. (בבא בתרא ד,א)

I am afraid of the (Roman) government.

לְמֶעֱבַד SEE: (לְ)מֶיעְבַד

מָעָה (מָעִין .pl)**; מַעֲתָא*** (מָעֵי .pl) **ma'a**

This silver coin or weight is equal to one sixth of a *dinar*.**

"עֶשְׂרִים גֵּרָה — הַשֶּׁקֶל", וּמְתַרְגְּמִינַן "עֶשְׂרִין מָעִין", וְתַנְיָא: שֵׁשׁ מָעָה כֶּסֶף — דִּינָר. (בכורות נ,א ע"פ שמות ל:יג ות"א ורש"י)

"Twenty gêras [equal] a shekel," and we translate "twenty ma'as," and it is stated (in a baraitha): Six ma'as of silver [equal] a dinar.

* The first form is Hebrew, and the second is Aramaic.

** See the table of coins and weights in Appendix II.

SEE: מָעוֹת

מֵעוֹלָם **ever; from time immemorial**

This adverb is commonly used with a negative, usually לֹא, in the sense of *never*.

מִי שֶׁלֹּא רָאָה יְרוּשָׁלַיִם בְּתִפְאַרְתָּהּ לֹא רָאָה כְּרַךְ נֶחְמָד מֵעוֹלָם. (סוכה נא,א)

One who has not seen Jerusalem in its glory has never seen a beautiful city.

SEE: לֹא הָיוּ דְבָרִים מֵעוֹלָם

מְעוּשֶּׂה (= מְעֻשֶּׂה) pass. prt. (עשי פֻּעַל)

forced; given under coercion

גֵּט הַמְעוּשֶּׂה (גיטין פח, רע"ב: משנה פ"ט מ"ח)

a bill of divorce given under coercion

SEE: מְעַשֶּׂה

מָעוֹת pl. (מָעָה .s) **money; coins***

אָסוּר לְהַרְצוֹת מָעוֹת כְּנֶגֶד נֵר חֲנוּכָּה. (שבת כב,א)

It is forbidden to count money by the Hanukka light.

* The coins may be made of copper, silver, or gold.

SEE: מָעָה

מַעֵט (מעט פַּעֵל: לְמַעוֹטֵי .inf)* **מִעֵט**

he reduced; he limited; he excluded (from a halakhic category)

This verb is often used in explaining why a particular word or expression in a Biblical passage or in a mishna or baraitha is not superfluous.

"זוֹ הִיא רְשׁוּת הַיָּחִיד" — לְמַעוֹטֵי מַאי? לְמַעוֹטֵי הָא דְּרַבִּי יְהוּדָה דִּתְנַן ... (שבת ו, סע"א)

"This [alone] is [the definition of] a private domain." What [does this wording "this is" come] to exclude? [It comes] to exclude the [additional case] of R. Y'huda that we learned [in a mishna] ...

* In our printed editions, the past tense of this Aramaic verb occurs only with personal-pronoun suffixes, as in מַעֲטֵיהּ קְרָא, *Scripture has excluded it* (קידושין יד, סע"א). Otherwise, the Hebrew form מִיעֵט is used.

SEE: הוֹצִיא, (לְ)אַפּוֹקֵי, רַבִּי, מִיעֵט

מְעַיֵּיל prt. (עלל פַּעֵל)

bringing in; inserting מֵבִיא; מַכְנִיס

כָּל כִּי הַאי זוּגָא — חַלּוֹפֵי ר' יוֹחָנָן וּמְעַיְּילֵי ר' יוֹנָתָן. (סוכה ד, סע"ב וש"נ)

Whenever this pair [of hakhamim is mentioned we] change [the name of] R. Yohanan and insert [the name of] R. Yonathan.

SEE: עָל

מֵעֵין **"from the color of"; similar to; a reflection of; an abstract of**

מֵעֵין עוֹלָם הַבָּא (ברכות נז,ב)

a reflection of the world-to-come

מֵעֵין שְׁמוֹנֶה עֶשְׂרֵה (ברכות כח,ב: משנה פ"ד מ"ג)

an abstract of the Eighteen (B'rakhoth of the Amida)

מֵעִיקָּרָא "מֵעִיקָּרוֹ שֶׁל דָּבָר"; מִתְּחִילָּה; בָּרִאשׁוֹנָה

"from the root (of the matter)"; originally; at the outset; at first

אֶלָּא מְחַוַּורְתָּא כִּדְשַׁנִּינַן מֵעִיקָּרָא. (מכות ב, רע"ב ועוד)

But the clear explanation is [the one] which we had proposed originally.

SEE: עִיקָּרָא

מֵעִיקָּרָא ... וְהַשְׁתָּא ... מִתְּחִלָּה ... וְעַכְשָׁיו ...

originally ... and now ...

מֵעִיקָּרָא ... וּלְבַסּוֹף ... מִתְּחִלָּה ... וּלְבַסּוֹף ...

originally ... and ultimately ...

מֵעִיקָּרָא מַאי סָבַר, וּלְבַסּוֹף מַאי סָבַר? (מו"ק טז, רע"ב ועוד)

What did he think originally, and what did he think ultimately? (= Why did he change his mind?)

מְעַכֵּב prt. (עכב פִּעֵל/פַּעֵל)*

detaining; preventing; invalidating (by its omission); is indispensable

הַתְּכֵלֶת אֵינָהּ מְעַכֶּבֶת אֶת הַלָּבָן, וְהַלָּבָן אֵינוֹ מְעַכֵּב אֶת הַתְּכֵלֶת. (מנחות לח,א: משנה פ"ד מ"א)

[Absence of] the blue thread does not invalidate the white (in the commandment of tzitzith), and [absence of] the white does not invalidate the blue.

כַּפָּרָה לָא מְעַכְּבָא. (ברכות ב, סע"א)

[The bringing of] a sin offering [by a kohen who was ritually unclean] is not indispensable (in order for the kohen to resume eating t'ruma).

* The פִּעֵל *binyan* is Hebrew, and the פַּעֵל is Aramaic.

מַעֲלֶה prt. (עלי הִפְעִיל)

(1) raising; bringing up (upon the altar); enhancing; elevating (to a higher level of sanctity)

מַעֲלִין בַּקֹּדֶשׁ, וְלֹא מוֹרִידִין. (משנה שקלים פ"ו מ"ד)

We elevate [to a higher level] of sanctity, but we do not downgrade.

(2) accounting; crediting; considering

In this usage, the subject is the Almighty or the Torah, and the context is aggadic.

For an example — see the next entry.

מַעֲלֶה עָלָיו הַכָּתוּב כְּאִילּוּ

the Torah regards him as if ...

כָּל הַמְקַיֵּים נֶפֶשׁ אַחַת מִיִּשְׂרָאֵל — מַעֲלֶה עָלָיו הַכָּתוּב כְּאִילּוּ קִיֵּים עוֹלָם מָלֵא. (סנהדרין לז, סע"א: משנה פ"ד מ"ה)

[As for] anyone who rescues the life of a single Jew — the Torah regards him as if he had saved an entire world.

מַעֲלֵי

מַעֲלֵי adj. (m.s. emph. or f.s. מַעַלְיָא)

excellent; beneficial; proper מְעֻלֶּה; טוֹב; כָּשֵׁר

לְמֵימְרָא דְחוֹמֶץ מַעֲלֵי לְשִׁינַּיִים?! (שבת קיא,א)

Is this to say that vinegar is beneficial for the teeth?!

שְׁטָרָא מַעַלְיָא (בבא בתרא לב, רע"ב ועוד)

a proper document (as opposed to a forged one)

SEE: לִישָּׁנָא מַעַלְיָא, מַעַלְיוּתָא

מַעֲלֵי

מַעֲלֵי constr. "כְּנִיסַת"; עֶרֶב

"the coming of"; the day before

SEE: עַל and the next entry

מַעֲלֵי שַׁבְּתָא

the day before the Sabbath; Friday עֶרֶב שַׁבָּת

For an example — see .שבת קיט, רע"א

מַעַלְיוּתָא

excellence; benefit; advantage מַעֲלָה; יִתְרוֹן

אֲמַר רַב יוֹסֵף: כַּמָּה מַעַלְיָא הָא שְׁמַעְתָּא ...! אֲמַר לֵיהּ אַבַּיֵי: מַאי מַעַלְיוּתָא? (ברכות יד,ב)

Rav Yosef said: How excellent is this halakhic teaching ...! Abbayé said to him: What is [its] excellence?

SEE: מַעֲלֵי, גְּרִיעוּתָא

מַעַרְבָא

the West; Erets Yisrael הַמַּעֲרָב **(since it is located west of Babylonia)**

אֲתָא אִיגַּרְתָּא מִמַּעַרְבָא ... (שבת קטו, רע"א ועוד)

a letter (containing a halakhic ruling) arrived from Eretz Yisrael ...

SEE: מְחַכּוּ עֲלָהּ בְּמַעַרְבָא

מַעֲרִים

מַעֲרִים prt. (ערם הִפְעִיל); **מְעָרֵים*** prt. (ערם אִפְעֵל)

employing a stratagem (in order to get around a prohibition); acting deceptively

כּוֹתֵב אָדָם תְּפִילִּין וּמְזוּזוֹת לְעַצְמוֹ ... וּלְאֲחֵרִים בְּטוֹבָה — דִּבְרֵי ר' מֵאִיר. ר' יְהוּדָה אוֹמֵר: מַעֲרִים וּמוֹכֵר אֶת שֶׁלּוֹ וְחוֹזֵר וְכוֹתֵב לְעַצְמוֹ. (מועד קטן יט, רע"א)

*A person may write [parchments for] t*ᵉ*fillin or m*ᵉ*zuzoth (on Ḥol HaMoed despite the prohibition of other writing) for himself ... and for others as a favor — [this is] the opinion of R. Méir. R. Y*ᵉ*huda says: He may employ a stratagem and sell his own and write again for himself.*

* The first form is Hebrew, and the second is Aramaic.

SEE: (לְ)אִיעֲרוּמֵי

מַעֲשֶׂה

מַעֲשֶׂה* prt. (עשי פַּעֵל)

causing; forcing

גָּדוֹל הַמְעַשֶּׂה מִן הָעוֹשֶׂה. (בבא בתרא ט, סע"א)

One who causes [others to do good] is greater than the doer.

SEE: מְעוּשֶּׂה

* Do not confuse this verbal form with the noun מַעֲשֶׂה, the next entry.

מַעֲשֶׂה

(1) an act

For an example — see .לָאו שֶׁאֵין בּוֹ מַעֲשֶׂה

(2) conduct; practice (as opposed to theory)

לֹא הַמִּדְרָשׁ הוּא הָעִיקָּר אֶלָּא הַמַּעֲשֶׂה. (משנה אבות פ"א מי"ז)

It is not study that is the most important but practice.

(3) incident; case

בָּא מַעֲשֶׂה לִפְנֵי חֲכָמִים (סנהדרין לג,א ועוד)

a case came before the ḥakhamim

SEE: הֲלָכָה לְמַעֲשֶׂה

מַעֲשֶׂה בְּ-

[There was] an incident with regard to ...; It once happened that ...

מַעֲשֶׂה בְּחָסִיד אֶחָד שֶׁהָיָה מִתְפַּלֵּל בַּדֶּרֶךְ ... (ברכות לב, סע"ב)

It once happened that a certain pious man was praying by the roadside ...

מַעֲשֶׂה וְ-

[There was] a case and ...; It once happened that ...

מַעֲשֶׂה וְגָזְרוּ תַּעֲנִית בַּחֲנוּכָּה בְּלוֹד ... (ראש השנה יח,ב)

It once happened that [the ḥakhamim] decreed a fast day on Ḥanukka in Lod ...

מַעֲשֶׂה לִסְתּוֹר

Is [the] incident [quoted] to contradict?!

This rhetorical question points out the following *difficulty*: After a halakha was presented in a mishna, an incident is quoted in the mishna that appears to contradict that halakha — instead of serving as an illustration of that halakha, as we would have expected. In response, the Talmud presents a resolution of the difficulty that is introduced by the formula .חַסּוּרֵי מִחַסְּרָא וְהָכִי קָתָנֵי

For an example, see .חַסּוּרֵי מִחַסְּרָא וְהָכִי קָתָנֵי

מַעֲשֶׂה רַב*

The practice (of the ḥakhamim) is most significant (rather than a teaching that was stated but not necessarily carried out).

תלמוד: בְּעָא מִינֵּיהּ אַבַּיֵי מֵרַבָּה: שְׁמָנִים שֶׁאָמְרוּ חֲכָמִים אֵין מַדְלִיקִין בָּהֶן בַּשַּׁבָּת — מַהוּ שֶׁיִּתֵּן לְתוֹכָן שֶׁמֶן כָּל שֶׁהוּא

וְיַדְלִיק? ... אֲמַר לֵיהּ: אֵין מַדְלִיקִין .... אֵיתִיבֵיהּ:
ברייתא: כָּרַךְ דָּבָר שֶׁמַּדְלִיקִין בּוֹ עַל גַּבֵּי דָּבָר שֶׁאֵין מַדְלִיקִין בּוֹ. רַבָּן שִׁמְעוֹן בֶּן גַּמְלִיאֵל אוֹמֵר: שֶׁל בֵּית אַבָּא הָיוּ כּוֹרְכִין פְּתִילָה עַל גַּבֵּי אֱגוֹז וּמַדְלִיקִין.
תלמוד: קָתָנֵי מִיהַת: מַדְלִיקִין. אַדְמוֹתְבַתְּ לֵיהּ מִדְּרַבָּן שִׁמְעוֹן בֶּן גַּמְלִיאֵל, סַיְיעֵיהּ מִדְּתַנָּא קַמָּא! הָא לָא קַשְׁיָא: מַעֲשֶׂה רַב. (שבת כא,א ע"פ כת"י וש"נ)

TALMUD: Abbayé asked Rabba: [As for] oils that the ḥakhamim said we may not kindle with them for the Sabbath — what is the law as far as putting a bit of [permitted] oil into them and kindling? ... [Rabba] said to him: We may not kindle .... He objected to him:
BARAITHA: [If] one wrapped something (= a wick) with which we may not kindle [for the Sabbath] on top of something with which we may kindle, we may not kindle with it. Rabban Shim'on b. Gamliel says: In my father's home we used to wrap a wick around a nut and kindle.
TALMUD: [The tanna] states at any rate: We may kindle (a permitted substance that was combined with a forbidden substance in contradiction to Rabba's ruling above). Instead of your objecting to him (= Rabba) from Rabban Shim'on b. Gamliel, support him from the first (anonymous) tanna in the baraitha (who forbids kindling with a permitted substance combined with a forbidden substance). The practice (in Rabban Gamliel's home) is most significant.

* The adjective רַב is used here to mean *great* or *significant* as in Aramaic.

SEE: רַב

מַעֲשֶׂה שֶׁהָיָה

an incident (bearing halakhic implications) that has occurred

For an example — see סנהדרין יט, סע"א.

מֵעֵת לְעֵת*

from [a specific] time [on one day] to [exactly the same] time [on the next day]; full astronomical day(s)

אִילּוּ יוֹם הֻלַּדְתּוֹ — לָא בָּעֵינַן מֵעֵת לְעֵת (שבת קלז, סע"א)

as for (the eight days for circumcision from) the day of his birth — we do not require full astronomical days

* Compare the Biblical phrase מֵעֵת אֶל עֵת, which occurs in דברי הימים א ט:כה.

מֵעַתָּה

SEE: אֱמוֹר מֵעַתָּה, אֶלָּא מֵעַתָּה

מַפִּיק* prt. (נפק אַפְעֵל)

taking out; bringing forth; excluding מוֹצִיא

See additional definitions and examples under אַפֵּיק.

* In Hebrew grammar, מַפִּיק is the term used for the dot inserted in a final ה in order to indicate that it is to be pronounced as a consonantal *h* as in נְתָנָהּ (= נָתַן אוֹתָהּ), *he gave it* — as opposed to a final ה that merely indicates a vowel as in נָתְנָה, *she gave*. Thus, מַפִּיק means one should *bring forth* or *produce* the *h* sound.

SEE: מַפָּק

מַפִּישׁ prt. (נפש אַפְעֵל)

increasing; extending מַרְבֶּה

SEE: אַפֵּישׁ

מַפְנֵי pass. prt. (פני אַפְעֵל) מֻפְנֶה

free (for interpretation); available (for deduction)

SEE: מוּפְנֶה

מַפַּק pass. prt. (נפק אַפְעֵל)

taken out; excluded מוּצָא

הָא דְּרַבִּי מַפְּקָא מִדְּר' מֵאִיר וּמַפְּקָא מִדְּרַבָּנַן. (יומא לב,ב ורש"י שם)

This [statement] of Rebbi is excluded (= differs) from that of R. Méir and from that of the Ḥakhamim.

SEE: מַפֵּיק

מַפְקַר pass. prt. (פקר אַפְעֵל)

renouncing ownership מַפְקִיר

SEE: אַפְקַר

מְפָרֵק[1] prt. (פרק פִּעֵל: מְפוֹרָק .pass. prt)*

taking apart; unloading

חוֹלֵב חַיָּיב מִשּׁוּם מְפָרֵק. (שבת צה,א ורש"י שם)

One who milks (on the Sabbath) is bound [to bring a guilt-offering] because of "unloading" (the udder of its contents).

* This entry is Hebrew, but the next is Aramaic.

SEE: פָּרַק

מְפָרֵק[2] prt. (פרק פָּעֵל)*

resolving (a difficulty) מְתָרֵץ

הוּא חָכָם — דְּאִי מַקְשׁוּ לֵיהּ, מְפָרֵק לְהוּ. (ברכות כז, סע"ב)

He is a ḥakham — so that if [people] point out a difficulty to him, he will resolve it.

* This entry is Aramaic, but the previous one is Hebrew.

SEE: הוּא מוֹתִיב לַהּ וְהוּא מְפָרֵק לַהּ, פֵּירוּקָא

מִצְוָה

commandment

SEE: בַּר מִצְוָה

מִצְוַת לֹא תַעֲשֶׂה

a commandment of "do not do!"; a (Biblical) prohibition

SEE: לֹא תַעֲשֶׂה; לָאו

מִצְוַת עֲשֵׂה

a commandment of "do!"; a positive (Biblical) commandment

SEE: עֲשֵׂה

מָצֵי prt. (מצי) יָכוֹל

he is able; he can

Like its Hebrew counterpart יָכוֹל, this Aramaic verb is often used as a helping verb — but with one difference: מָצֵי is usually followed by a participle (for example, מָצֵי אָמַר); whereas יָכוֹל is followed by an infinitive (for example, יָכוֹל לוֹמַר), as in the English usage, *he is able to say*.

מִי אִיכָּא מִידֵי דַּאֲנַן לָא מָצֵינַן עָבְדִינַן, וְאִינְהוּ מָצוּ עָבְדִי?! (קידושין כג,ב)
Is there anything that we ourselves cannot do, but they (= our agents) can do (on our behalf)?!

* The masculine plural form is either מָצֵי or מָצוּ.
SEE: (ו)מִי מָצֵית אָמְרַתְּ, (ו)מִי מָצֵית מוֹקְמַתְּ, אַמְצֵי

מַצִּיל prt. (נצל אַפְעֵל) מַצִּיל **saving; rescuing**
SEE: (לְ)אַצּוֹלֵי

מָצִינוּ 1st pers. pl. (מצא) **we found**
This Mishnaic Hebrew form is the equivalent of the Biblical Hebrew מָצָאנוּ.
וְכִי הֵיכָן מָצִינוּ יוֹם שֶׁמִּקְצָתוֹ אָסוּר בַּעֲשִׂיַּת מְלָאכָה וּמִקְצָתוֹ מוּתָּר בַּעֲשִׂיַּת מְלָאכָה?! (פסחים ב,ב)
Where, then, have we found a day during part of which work is forbidden, while during the other part work is permitted?!
SEE: מָה מָצִינוּ

מְצִיעָא (מְצִיעֲתָא .f, מְצִיעָאֵי .m. pl) אֶמְצָעִי **middle; central**
SEE: בָּבָא

מְצִיעֲתָא הָאֶמְצָעִית
the middle clause; the intermediary part
This term denotes the middle clause of a mishna or a baraitha — as opposed to the רֵישָׁא, *the first clause*, and the סֵיפָא, *the last clause*.
רֵישָׁא וְסֵיפָא דְּאִיכָּא עֵדִים; מְצִיעֲתָא דְּלֵיכָּא עֵדִים. (כתובות כג,ב)
The first clause and the last clause [of the baraitha refer to cases] where there are witnesses; the middle clause where there are no witnesses.
SEE: רֵישָׁא, סֵיפָא

מְצַלֵּי prt. (צלי פַּעֵל) מִתְפַּלֵּל **praying; reciting the Amida**
רַב מְצַלֵּי שֶׁל שַׁבָּת בְּעֶרֶב שַׁבָּת מִבְּעוֹד יוֹם (ברכות כז,א)
Rav recites the Amida of the Sabbath on Friday while it is still day
SEE: צַלִּי

מַצְלֵי prt. (צלי אַפְעֵל) מַטֶּה **turning; bending; perverting**
מַצְלֵי דִינָא (סנהדרין קט,ב)
"the perverter of justice" (an epithet applied to one of the judges in S^edom)

מֶצְרָא מֵצַר; גְּבוּל **boundary**
SEE: בַּר מֶצְרָא

מָקוֹם **place; case; situation**
בְּמָקוֹם שֶׁיֵּשׁ עֵדִים (בבא מציעא מג,ב)
in a case where there are witnesses
SEE: מִכָּל מָקוֹם

הַמָּקוֹם **the Omnipresent; God**
בִּזְמַן שֶׁיִּשְׂרָאֵל עוֹשִׂים רְצוֹנוֹ שֶׁלַּמָּקוֹם* (ברכות לה, ב ועוד)
at a time when the Jewish people is acting in accordance with the will of God

* This form is currently written as two separate words (שֶׁל מָקוֹם) without the definite article -הַ. Nevertheless, the original spelling is שֶׁלַּמָּקוֹם with the definite article expressed by -לַ- (= לְהַ). See שֶׁל and its note.

מְקַיֵּים prt. (קום פַּעֵל) **establishing; maintaining**
For an example — see (ו)מָה אֲנִי מְקַיֵּים.

מַקִּישׁ prt. (נקש הִפְעִיל); **מַקִּישׁ** prt. (נקש אַפְעֵל)*
comparing; drawing an analogy (between two subjects, usually because of their juxtaposition in Scripture)
מַקִּישׁ הֲוָיָה לִיצִיאָה — מָה יְצִיאָה בִּשְׁטָר, אַף הֲוָיָה נַמֵּי בִּשְׁטָר. (קידושין ה, רע״א וש״נ ע״פ דברים כד:ב)
[A pasuk] compares "becoming [a wife]" to "departing" (= divorce) — just as divorce is effected through a document, so marriage may also be effected through a [marriage] document.

* The הִפְעִיל binyan is Hebrew, and the אַפְעֵל is Aramaic.
SEE: מַקְשִׁינַן, הִקִּישׁ, אַקִּישׁ, הֶיקֵּשׁ, מַקְשֵׁי

מִקַּמֵּי
(1) לִפְנֵי **before; prior to**
הָא מִקַּמֵּי דַּאֲתָא רַב לְבָבֶל, וְהָא לְבָתַר דַּאֲתָא רַב לְבָבֶל. (עירובין כח, סע״א)
One [ruling was issued] before Rav came to Babylonia, while the other [was issued] after Rav came to Babylonia.

(2) מִפְּנֵי **in the face of; on account of**
לָא דָּחִינַן אִיסּוּרָא מִקַּמֵּי מָמוֹנָא (בבא מציעא ל, סע״א)
we do not put aside a prohibition in the face of a monetary matter
This word, in both its senses, is also used with personal-pronoun suffixes (most commonly -יהּ *him* or *its*) as in the next entry.

מִקַּמֵּיהּ
(1) מִלְּפָנָיו **from before him; from his presence**
מַדְלֵי תַּכָּא מִקַּמֵּיהּ (פסחים קטו, סע״ב)
they were removing the tray from before him

(2) מִפָּנָיו **"on account of his presence"; in his honor**
נֵיקוּ מִקַּמֵּיהּ, דְּגַבְרָא דָּחִיל חֶטְאִין הוּא! (שבת לא, רע״ב)
Let us rise in his honor, since he is a man [who] fears sins!
SEE: לְקַמָּן

מַקְנֵי prt. (קני אַפְעֵל) מַקְנֶה **transferring possession; selling**
SEE: אַקְנֵי

מִקְרָא*

(1) a reading

הִגִּיעַ זְמַן הַמִּקְרָא (ברכות יג,א: משנה פ"ב מ"א)

*the time for the reading (of Sh*ma) arrived*

(2) the written Torah; Scripture

בֶּן חָמֵשׁ שָׁנִים לַמִּקְרָא. (משנה אבות פ"ה מכ"א)

Five-years old [is the appropriate age] to [begin the study of] Scripture.

(3) *pasuk*; Biblical verse

וּשְׁנֵיהֶם מִקְרָא אֶחָד דָּרְשׁוּ (ברכות ד,ב ועוד)

and each of them (= the two ḥakhamim who disagree) found support [for his opinion] in one (and the same) pasuk

* This Hebrew word should not be confused with the Aramaic מִקְּרָא, *from a pasuk.*

SEE: יֵשׁ אֵם לַמִּקְרָא, קְרָא

מְקָרַב pass. prt. (קרב פָּעַל)

nearby; close מְקֹרָב; קָרוֹב

ר' מֵאִיר לָא קָאָמַר אֶלָּא בְּעַכּוֹ, דִּמְקָרְבָא; אֲבָל בְּבָבֶל, דִּמְרַחֲקָא — לָא. (גיטין ו,א)

R. Méir is only talking about [a place like] Acco, which is nearby; but regarding Babylonia, which is distant — [he is] not [talking].

SEE: מְרַחֵק

מַקְרֵי prt. (קרא אַפְעֵל) מַקְרִיא; מְלַמֵּד

reading to another; teaching (Scripture)

SEE: אַקְרֵי

מַקְרֵי דַרְדְּקֵי מְלַמֵּד תִּינוֹקוֹת

a teacher of schoolchildren (whose curriculum was primarily the written Torah)

וַאֲמַר רָבָא: סַךְ מַקְרֵי דַרְדְּקֵי עֶשְׂרִין וְחַמְשָׁה יָנוּקֵי. (בבא בתרא כא, סע"א ורש"י שם)

And Rava said: The number [of pupils assigned to one] teacher of schoolchildren is twenty-five.

מְקַרְקְעֵי קַרְקָעוֹת

land; real estate

For an example — see אַגַּב מְקַרְקְעֵי.

מַקְשֵׁי prt. (קשי אַפְעֵל)* מַקְשֶׁה

pointing out a difficulty; raising an objection

כִּי הֲוָה מַקְשֵׁי ר' פִּנְחָס בֶּן יָאִיר קוּשְׁיָא, הֲוָה מְפָרֵק לֵיהּ ר' שִׁמְעוֹן בֶּן יוֹחַאי (שבת לג, סע"ב)

when R. Pinḥas b. Ya'ir would raise a difficulty, R. Shim'on b. Yoḥai would answer him

* This verb should not be confused with the next entry.

SEE: אַקְשֵׁי

מַקְּשֵׁי prt. pl. (נקש אַפְעֵל)

comparing מַקִּישִׁים

מַקְּשִׁינַן לוּלָב לְאֶתְרוֹג (סוכה לא,א ע"פ ויקרא כג:מ)

we compare [the law of the] lulav to [the law of the] ethrog

SEE: מַקִּישׁ, the singular form

מָר*

(1) the master; sir

This word, which basically means *master*, is used as a respectful mode of address — mostly by a disciple addressing his master. In this sense, it may be regarded as the equivalent of מָרִי, *my master.*

מִי בָּדֵיל מָר? (ברכות כז, רע"ב)

Has my master ceased (doing work before the Sabbath)?

Abbayé and Rava used to designate their master, Rabba, in this manner — even when Rabba was not present.

אֲמַר אַבַּיֵי: מֵרֵישׁ הֲוָה אָמֵינָא ..., אֲמַר לִי מָר .... (חולין קה,ב)

Abbayé said: At first I used to think ..., [but then] my master told me (differently) ....

(2) Mar

This word also serves as a title that precedes the proper names of several Babylonian amoraim who did not receive ordination, e.g., מָר זוּטְרָא, מָר עוּקְבָא.

In some instances, the title is added at the end of an amora's proper name, forming one word.

אַמֵימָר (= אַמֵי+מָר); מָרֵימָר (= מָרֵי+מָר)

A few Babylonian amoraim are called מָר — without the addition of a proper name.

מָר בַּר רַב אַשִׁי; מָר בְּרֵיהּ דְּרַבִינָא

* While Sephardic Jews pronounce this word *mor*, pronunciation among Ashkenazic Jews is *mar*. In Israeli Hebrew, the word is often used as a title (מַר כֹּהֵן, *Mr. Cohen*), and it is vocalized מַר, in accordance with the Ashkenazi pronunciation.

SEE: אֲמַר מָר, מָרָא

מָר ... וּמָר ... חָכָם אֶחָד ..., וְחָכָם אֶחָד ...

One master (or authority) ..., and/while the other ....

With this formula, the Talmud presents an explanation of a *controversy* (or an apparent controversy) between two authorities.

מָר סָבַר תְּחוּמִין דְּאוֹרַיְיתָא; וּמָר סָבַר תְּחוּמִין דְּרַבָּנָן. (סוטה ל,ב)

One authority (= R. Akiva) holds that the limits (beyond which one may not walk on the Sabbath) are of Torah authority, while the other (= R. Eliezer, son of R. Yosé the Galilean) holds that the limits are of Rabbinic authority.

מָר כִּי אַתְרֵיהּ, וּמָר כִּי אַתְרֵיהּ. (פסחים ג,א ושי"נ)

One authority [is speaking] of his locality, while the other [is speaking] of his locality (but there is no substantial disagreement, since each one is reporting the practice that prevails in a different area).

מָר אָמַר חֲדָא, וּמָר אָמַר חֲדָא — וְלָא פְּלִיגִי. (בבא מציעא יא, רע״א ועוד)

One is speaking of one [situation], and the other is speaking of another [situation] — but they do not disagree.

מָרָא (מָר .abs, מָרֵי .constr)

(1) אֲדוֹן **master***

כְּעַבְדָּא קַמֵּי מָרֵיהּ (שבת י,א ע״פ כת״י)

like a slave in the presence of his master

מָרָא דִשְׁמַעְתָּא (סוכה מז,א ועוד)

"the master of the halakha" (= the authority who has presented the halakha in the beth midrash)

מָרָא דְעוּבְדָא (ביצה כט,ב וש״נ ורש״י שם)

a master of [scrupulous] behavior

מָרָא דְאַרְעָא דְיִשְׂרָאֵל (יומא ט, סע״ב וש״נ)

"the master of the land of Israel" (= its supreme halakhic authority)

(2) בְּעָלִים **owner**

מָרֵי חִטַּיָא (ברכות סד,א וש״נ ורש״י שם)

"the owner of wheat" (= a scholar who has collected many halakhoth)

(3) מַר; דֶּקֶר **hoe; spade**

בָּעֵינָא חוּטְרָא לִידָא וּמָרָא לִקְבוּרָה (כתובות סד,א ע״פ כת״י)

I need a staff for my hand and a spade for burial

* מָרָא דְאַתְרָא, *the master of the place (= the community rabbi)*, is a post-Talmudic usage that has entered Hebrew.

מַרְבֶּה prt. (רבי הִפְעִיל) **increasing; doing much**

אֶחָד הַמַּרְבֶּה וְאֶחָד הַמַּמְעִיט — וּבִלְבַד שֶׁיְּכַוֵּין לִבּוֹ לַשָּׁמַיִם. (מנחות קי, סע״א וש״נ: משנה פי״ג מי״א)

One who does much and one who does little are the same — provided that he directs his heart to Heaven.

מְרַבֶּה* prt. (רבי פִּעֵל) **including; extending**

* Although this word is popularly pronounced מַרְבֶּה, the vocalization מְרַבֶּה is supported by *Codex Assemani 66* (the vocalized manuscript of *Torath Kohanim*) and by the forms רִיבָּה and לְרַבּוֹת, which are definitely *binyan* פִּעֵל.
SEE: מְרַבֵּי, the parallel Aramaic form

מְרַבֶּה אֲנִי **I include**

This expression is used in Midrash Halakha in explaining which *additional case* the extra Scriptural word (or words) comes to incorporate within the halakha.

"וּרְאִיתֶם אוֹתוֹ" — פְּרָט לִכְסוּת לַיְלָה ... מְרַבֶּה אֲנִי כְּסוּת סוּמָא, שֶׁיֶּשְׁנָהּ בִּרְאִיָּה אֵצֶל אֲחֵרִים, וּמוֹצִיא אֲנִי כְּסוּת לַיְלָה, שֶׁאֵינָהּ בִּרְאִיָּה אֵצֶל אֲחֵרִים. (שבת כז,ב ע״פ במדבר טו:לט)

"And you shall see it (= tzitzith)" — to the exclusion of a night garment ... I include a garment of a blind man, which is seen by others, but I exclude a night garment, which is not seen by others.

מְרַבֵּי* prt. (רבי פַּעֵל)

מְרַבֶּה; מְגַדֵּל **including; raising**

* This form is popularly pronounced מַרְבֵּי.
SEE: מְרַבֶּה, רַבִּי and its note

מַרְגְּלָא pass. prt. f. (רגל אַפְעֵל)

מֻרְגֶּלֶת; שְׁגוּרָה **habitual; familiar**

מַרְגְּלָא בְּפוּמֵיהּ ד־* שְׁגוּרָה בְּפִיו שֶׁל ...

The [following was a] familiar [saying] from the mouth of ...

This expression introduces an aggadic or halakhic saying that a particular ḥakham had received from his teacher and repeated often to others.

מַרְגְּלָא בְּפוּמֵיהּ דְּרָבָא: תַּכְלִית חָכְמָה תְּשׁוּבָה וּמַעֲשִׂים טוֹבִים. (ברכות יז,א ורש״י שם)

The [following was a] familiar [saying] from the mouth of Rava: The purpose of wisdom (= the mastery of Torah) is the return [to God] and [the practice of] good deeds.

* See Rashi's commentary on סנהדרין ג, רע״ב. This expression is similar to הוּא הָיָה אוֹמֵר, *he used to say*, in the Mishna, especially in the tractate *Avoth*. According to *Yad Rama* on the same passage, מַרְגְּלָא is an Aramaic noun meaning a *pearl*, like the Hebrew noun מַרְגָּלִית, in the next entry.

מַרְגָּלִית; מַרְגָּנִיתָא* **pearl; jewel**

Besides this literal meaning, this word sometimes denotes a matter of value, especially an apt statement.**

מַרְגָּלִית טוֹבָה הָיְתָה בְּיֶדְכֶם. (חגיגה ג, סע״א)

There was a "fine jewel" in your hand.

אִי לָאו דְּדָלַאי לָךְ חַסְפָּא, לָא מַשְׁכַּחַתְּ מַרְגָּנִיתָא תּוּתָהּ. (בבא מציעא יז, רע״ב וש״נ)

If I had not lifted the clay fragment for you, you would not have found the pearl underneath it.

* The first form is Hebrew, and the second is Aramaic.
** In English there is a similar expression, *a pearl of wisdom*.

מְרַחַק pass. prt. (רחק פֻּעַל)

מְרֻחָק; רָחוֹק **distant; far removed**

For an example, see מְקָרַב.

מֵרֵישׁ מֵרֹאשׁ; מִתְּחִלָּה **at first; initially**

This adverb is regularly followed by the verb הֲוָה (often by הֲוָה אֲמִינָא, *I used to think*), and it introduces the opinion formerly held by the speaker.

וְאָמַר ר׳ אַבָּהוּ: מֵרֵישׁ הֲוָה אֲמִינָא עִינְוְתָנָא אֲנָא. כֵּיוָן דְּחָזֵינָא לֵיהּ לְר׳ אַבָּא דְּמִן עַכּוֹ ..., אֲמִינָא לָאו עִינְוְתָנָא אֲנָא. (סוטה מ,א)

R. Abbahu said: At first, I used to think I was a humble person. Now that I have seen R. Abba of Acco ..., I realize [that] I am not a humble person.

מֵרַע prt. (רעע אַפְעֵל)

מֵרַע; מַחֲלִישׁ **impairing; harming**

מָרַע לֵיהּ לְדִיבּוּרֵיהּ! (בבא מציעא ה,ב)
He would be impairing his own statement (= plea)!

מְרַע pass. prt. (מרע)
dangerously ill חוֹלֶה אָנוּשׁ
* This word is commonly pronounced מֻרַע as if it were connected with the word רַע, *evil.* The pronunciation מְרַע is supported by the vocalization in Targum Onkelos, for example, (לבראשית מח:א) .הָא אֲבוּךְ מְרַע The noun ,מַרְעִין *diseases*, is also found in the Talmud.
SEE: שְׁכִיב מְרַע

מְשָׁא (משי: מְשֵׁי .prt)
he washed (his hands) רָחַץ; נָטַל (יָדָיו)
רַב מְשָׁא יְדֵיהּ, וּקְרָא קְרִיאַת שְׁמַע, וְאַנַּח תְּפִילִּין, וְצַלִּי. (ברכות יד,ב)
*Rav washed his hands, recited the Sh*ᵉ*ma, and put on t*ᵉ*fillin, and recited the Amida.*

מְשַׁבַּשְׁתָּא pass. prt. f. (שבש פַּעֵל)
faulty; corrupt (with respect to a text) מְשֻׁבֶּשֶׁת
כָּל מַתְנִיתָא דְלָא תַנְיָא בֵּי ר׳ חִיָּיא וּבֵי ר׳ אוֹשַׁעְיָא מְשַׁבַּשְׁתָּא הִיא. (חולין קמא, סע״א ורש״י שם)
Any baraitha which has not been taught in the school of R. Ḥiyya or in the school of R. Osha'ya is faulty (and is therefore rejected).
SEE: מִשְׁתַּבֵּשׁ, מִתָּרַצְתָּא

מְשַׁדַּר prt. (שדר פַּעֵל)
sending שׁוֹלֵחַ
SEE: שַׁדַּר

מְשַׁהֵי prt. (שהי פַּעֵל)
delaying; detaining מַשְׁהֶה; מְעַכֵּב
SEE: שַׁהִי

מַשֶּׁהוּ (= מָה שֶּׁהוּא)
"whatever it is"; the slightest quantity; anything
חָמֵץ בִּזְמַנּוֹ ... אָסוּר בְּמַשֶּׁהוּ. (פסחים ל, רע״א)
[The eating of] leaven in its time (= during Pesaḥ itself) is forbidden (even) of the slightest quantity.

מְשַׁוֵּי prt. (שוי פַּעֵל)
making; appointing עוֹשֶׂה
it makes it a utensil מְשַׁוֵּי לֵיהּ מָנָא (שבת נח,ב)
he may appoint an agent מְשַׁוֵּי שְׁלִיחַ (גיטין כט,ב)
SEE: שַׁוִּי

מַשְׁוֵי prt. (שוי אַפְעֵל)
levelling; straightening מְשַׁוֶּה; מְיַשֵּׁר
הָא קָא מַשְׁוֵי גוּמוֹת! (שבת קמ, סע״ב)
Behold he is levelling holes (in the ground)!

מִשּׁוּם
in the name of (1) מִשֵּׁם, בְּשֵׁם
אָמַר ר׳ יוֹחָנָן מִשּׁוּם ר׳ שִׁמְעוֹן בֶּן יוֹחַאי (ברכות ז,ב)
R. Yoḥanan said in the name of R. Shim'on b. Yoḥai

because of; on account of (2) מֵחֲמַת
on account of danger מִשּׁוּם סַכָּנָה (יבמות קיד,א)

under the category of; (3) בִּכְלָל; מֵאִיסּוּר
because of the prohibition of
כָּל הַכּוֹבֵשׁ שְׂכַר שָׂכִיר עוֹבֵר ... מִשּׁוּם בַּל תַּעֲשׁוֹק אֶת רֵעֲךָ. (בבא מציעא קיא,א ע״פ ויקרא יט:יג)
Anyone who withholds the wages of a hired hand transgresses ... because of the prohibition of "do not oppress your fellow man."
SEE: ... מִשּׁוּם ר׳ ... אָמַר ר׳ ... (בְּ)שֵׁם, שׁוּם

מִשּׁוּם ד- מִשּׁוּם שֶׁ-; מִפְּנֵי שֶׁ-
because of [the fact] that; because
טָעָה וְלֹא הִתְפַּלֵּל עַרְבִית — מִתְפַּלֵּל שַׁחֲרִית שְׁתַּיִם, מִשּׁוּם דְּחַד יוֹמָא הוּא. (ברכות כו, סע״א)
[If] one erred and did not recite the Amida in the evening — he should recite the Amida twice in the morning, because it is (all) one day.

מִשּׁוּם דְּקָא* בָּעֵי לְמִיתְנָא סֵיפָא ... תְּנָא נַמֵּי רֵישָׁא ...
מִשּׁוּם שֶׁרוֹצָה לִשְׁנוֹת בְּסוֹפָהּ ..., שָׁנָה אַף בְּרֹאשָׁהּ ...
Since [the tanna] wants to state ... [in] the latter clause, he also stated ... [in] the first clause.
This formula appears in the following context: A difficulty was raised in the Talmud that a specific term or phrase in the first clause of a mishna or baraitha is inappropriate. Now this formula is used to present a *resolution* of the difficulty, insisting that the term — although inappropriate (or even imprecise) if the first clause were to stand by itself — is indeed appropriate for the text as a whole, in order for that term to be consistent with a parallel term in the latter clause.
משנה: הָאִשָּׁה נִקְנֵית בְּשָׁלֹשׁ דְּרָכִים וְקוֹנָה אֶת עַצְמָהּ בִּשְׁתֵּי דְרָכִים. (קידושין ב, רע״א: משנה פ״א מ״א)
תלמוד: ... נִיתְנֵי הָכָא "הָאִישׁ קוֹנֶה"! מִשּׁוּם דְּקָא בָּעֵי לְמִיתְנָא סֵיפָא: "וְקוֹנָה אֶת עַצְמָהּ" — בְּדִידַהּ, תְּנָא נַמֵּי רֵישָׁא בְּדִידַהּ. (שם ב, רע״ב)
MISHNA: A wife is acquired in three ways, and she acquires herself (= her freedom from marriage) in two ways.
TALMUD: ... [Instead of "a wife is acquired"] let [the tanna] state here: "The man acquires"! Since [the tanna] wants to state: "and she acquires herself" [in] the latter clause — with her as the subject, he also stated ["a wife is acquired" in] the first clause — with her as the subject.
* Sometimes: דְּבָעֵי — without קָא.

מִשּׁוּם הָכִי מִשּׁוּם כָּךְ
because of this; accordingly; it follows that
For an example — see ... אִי אָמְרַתְּ בִּשְׁלָמָא.

מִשּׁוּם שֶׁנֶּאֱמַר

since it is stated (in the Torah)

See explanation and example under (מ)מַשְׁמָע שֶׁנֶּאֱמַר.

מְשׁוּעְבָּד pass. prt. (עבד שַׁפְעֵל)

subjugated; obligated

SEE: שִׁעְבֵּד ,נְכָסִים מְשׁוּעְבָּדִים ,מְשַׁעְבָּד ,מִשְׁתַּעְבַּד

מְשַׁח (משח: מוֹשֵׁחַ .prt) **he annointed** (with oil)

מִפְּנֵי מָה מְשָׁחוּ אֶת שְׁלֹמֹה? (הוריות יא,ב)

Why did they annoint Sh^elomo?

SEE: מִשְׁחָא

מְשַׁח* (משח: מָשַׁח .prt) מָדַד **he measured**

מָשְׁחִינַן לְהוּ תְּחוּמָא (עירובין עג,א)

we measure the [Sabbath] limit for them

* The Hebrew noun מָשׁוֹחוֹת, *measurers* or *surveyors*, occurs in the Mishna (עירובין נב, סע"ב ורש"י שם: משנה פ"ד מי"א).

SEE: מִשְׁחָא

מִשְׁחָא

(1) שֶׁמֶן **oil**

שְׁרָגָא דְמִשְׁחָא שְׁרֵי לְטַלְטוּלֵהּ. (שבת מו,א)

*It is permissible to handle a lamp of (olive) oil (on the Sabbath).**

(2) מִדָּה **measure**

בְּמִשְׁחָא נֵיתֵיב לֵיהּ, וּבְמִשְׁחָא נִשְׁקוֹל מִינֵּיהּ. (שבת יט, סע"א)

He should give (his garment) to him (= the laundryman) according to measure (= its size), and he should get [it] back from him according to measure (so that if it shrank, he would be compensated).

* See Rashi and Tosafoth there who discuss under what circumstances it is permitted.

SEE: מְשַׁח

מַשְׁכָּא עוֹר **skin; hide**

דְּמָא וְתַרְבָּא לְדִידַן, מַשְׁכָּא וּבִישְׂרָא לְדִידְכוּ. (חולין לט, סע"ב)

The blood and the fat (of the rams that are to be slaughtered) are to be ours, [while] the hide and the meat will be yours.

מַשְׁכַּח prt. (שכח אַפְעֵל) מוֹצֵא **finding**

SEE: אַשְׁכַּח

מַשְׁכַּחַתְּ (= מַשְׁכַּח+אַתְּ) אַתָּה מוֹצֵא **you find**

מַשְׁכַּחַתְּ לַהּ אַתָּה מוֹצֵא אוֹתָהּ **you find it**

This expression refers to the application of principles or texts to particular circumstances.

SEE: הֵיכִי מַשְׁכַּחַתְּ לַהּ

מִשְּׁמֵיהּ מִשְּׁמוֹ; בִּשְׁמוֹ **in his name**

For an example — see (מ)שְּׁמֵיהּ.

מִשְּׁמֵיהּ דִּגְמָרָא SEE: (מ)שְּׁמֵיהּ דִּגְמָרָא

לְמִשְׁמַע inf. (שמע) לִשְׁמֹעַ; לִלְמֹד; לְהָבִין

to hear; to learn; to understand

SEE: אֶלָּא מֵהָא לֵיכָּא לְמִשְׁמַע מִינָּהּ

מַשְׁמַע¹ act. prt. (שמע אַפְעֵל) מַשְׁמִיעַ

causing to understand; teaching

SEE: אַשְׁמַע ,מַאי מַשְׁמַע ,קָא מַשְׁמַע לַן

מַשְׁמַע² pass. prt. (שמע אַפְעֵל) מוּבָן

understood; indicated

SEE: לָא מַשְׁמַע לֵיהּ

מַשְׁמָע (מַשְׁמָעוֹת .pl)

meaning; the plain sense (of a pasuk)

For examples, see the next four entries.

בְּמַשְׁמָע **within the meaning** (of the pasuk)

See example under the next entry.

מִמַּשְׁמָע שֶׁנֶּאֱמַר*

from the meaning of what is stated (in the Torah)

"אַךְ אֲשֶׁר יֵאָכֵל לְכָל נֶפֶשׁ הוּא לְבַדּוֹ יֵעָשֶׂה לָכֶם". מִמַּשְׁמָע שֶׁנֶּאֱמַר "לְכָל נֶפֶשׁ", שׁוֹמֵעַ אֲנִי אֲפִילוּ נֶפֶשׁ בְּהֵמָה בְּמַשְׁמָע. (ביצה כא, סע"א ע"פ שמות יב:טז)

"Only that which is to be eaten by every living creature — that alone may be produced by you." From the meaning of what is stated: "by every living creature," I understand [that] even an animal [is included] within the meaning [of the pasuk].

* מִשּׁוּם שֶׁנֶּאֱמַר and מִתּוֹךְ שֶׁנֶּאֱמַר are used similarly.

כְּמַשְׁמָעוֹ **like its plain sense; literally**

"הַיָּרֵא וְרַךְ הַלֵּבָב" — כְּמַשְׁמָעוֹ, שֶׁאֵינוֹ יָכוֹל לַעֲמוֹד בְּקִשְׁרֵי הַמִּלְחָמָה וְלִרְאוֹת חֶרֶב שְׁלוּפָה. (סוטה מד, סע"א: משנה פ"ח מ"ה ע"פ דברים כ:ח)

"The fearful and the faint-hearted" — like its plain sense, one who cannot stand in the battle ranks and see a drawn sword.

מַשְׁמָעוֹת דּוֹרְשִׁין אִיכָּא בֵּינַיְיהוּ

מַשְׁמָעוֹת דּוֹרְשִׁין יֵשׁ בֵּינֵיהֶם.

[The only difference] between them is [their ways of] interpreting the meanings [of Biblical texts].

With this statement an amora contends that the two tannaim (or early amoraim) who are in disagreement differ only about which Biblical passage constitutes a basis for the halakha under discussion. There is no substantive difference between them about the halakha itself.

ברייתא: "אֲשֶׁר תֹּאבַד" — פְּרָט לַאֲבֵידָה שֶׁאֵין בָּהּ שָׁוֶה פְרוּטָה. ר' יְהוּדָה אוֹמֵר: "וּמְצָאתָהּ" — פְּרָט לַאֲבֵידָה שֶׁאֵין בָּהּ שָׁוֶה פְּרוּטָה.

תלמוד: מַאי בֵּינַיְיהוּ? אָמַר אַבָּיֵי: מַשְׁמָעוֹת דּוֹרְשִׁין אִיכָּא בֵּינַיְיהוּ. (בבא מציעא כז,א ע"פ דברים כב:ג)

BARAITHA: "That will be lost" (this otherwise superfluous Biblical expression indicates a significant loss) — excluding a lost article worth less than a p^eruta (= a small coin). R. Y^ehuda says: "And you will find it" ("it" indicates a significant find) — excluding a lost article worth less than a p^eruta.
TALMUD: What is [the difference] between them (= the first tanna and R. Y^ehuda)? Abbayé said: [The only difference] between them is [their respective ways of] interpreting the meanings [of Biblical texts in order to find support for the halakha].

מְשַׁמֵּת prt. (שמת פַּעֵל)

excommunicating מְנַדֶּה

מְשַׁמְּתִינַן לֵיהּ עַד דִּמְקַבֵּיל עֲלֵיהּ כָּל אוֹנְסָא דְּאָתֵי מֵחֲמָתֵיהּ. (בבא קמא קיד,א)
We excommunicate him until he accepts upon himself [the responsibility for] any mishap that might occur on account of him.

מִשְׁנָה

learning; instruction (1) לִמּוּד

כֵּיצַד סֵדֶר מִשְׁנָה? מֹשֶׁה לָמַד מִפִּי הַגְּבוּרָה. נִכְנַס אַהֲרֹן וְשָׁנָה לוֹ מֹשֶׁה ... (עירובין נד,ב)
In what manner was the order of instruction? Moshe [Rabbenu] learned from the Almighty. Aharon entered and Moshe taught him ...

mishna; (2) קֹבֶץ שֶׁל הֲלָכוֹת שֶׁל תַּנָּאִים
a collection of halakhoth of tannaim
In this sense, the term usually refers to the *Mishna* of R. Y^ehuda HaNasi (= Rebbi), which is also termed מִשְׁנָתֵינוּ, *our Mishna.*

זוֹ שֶׁשְּׁנוּיָה בְּמִשְׁנַת בַּר קַפָּרָא (בבא בתרא קנד,ב)
this [halakha] which is taught in the mishna of bar Kappara

בְּמִשְׁנָתֵינוּ קָאָמְרִינַן, וְהָא בָּרַיְיתָא הִיא! (ברכות יט,א)
We say [the cases are formulated] in our Mishna, but this is a baraitha!

halakha; teaching; (3) הֲלָכָה; מַאֲמָר
a statement (formulated either in the Mishna or in a baraitha)

בִּימֵי רַבִּי נִשְׁנֵית מִשְׁנָה זוֹ. (בבא מציעא לג, רע"ב ורש"י שם)
This halakha was taught in the days of Rebbi.

כָּךְ הִיא הַצָּעָה שֶׁל מִשְׁנָה ... (סנהדרין נא, סע"א ורש"י שם)
Such is the text of the statement (= baraitha) ...
SEE: אֵינָהּ מִשְׁנָה, סְתָם מִשְׁנָה, מַתְנִיתָא, בָּרַיְיתָא

מִשְׁנָה יְתֵירָה

a superfluous clause (in the Mishna)

מִמִּשְׁנָה יְתֵירָה, אַשְׁמְעִינַן דִּרְאִיָּה לָא קָנֵי. (ב"מ ב, סע"א)
Through the superfluous clause, he (= the tanna) has taught us that sighting [an object] does not establish ownership.

וּמִשְׁנָה לֹא זָזָה מִמְּקוֹמָהּ

and the halakha did not move from its place
In some instances, a halakhic teaching has been retained intact in the Mishna, even though it was subsequently rejected or shown to be superfluous.
For examples, see שבועות ד,א ורש"י שם; יבמות ל,א וש"נ.

מִשְׁנָה רִאשׁוֹנָה

an early halakha
(as opposed to the halakha of a later tanna who disagrees)

זוֹ מִשְׁנַת ר' עֲקִיבָא, אֲבָל מִשְׁנָה רִאשׁוֹנָה ... (סנהדרין כז,ב: משנה פ"ג מ"ד)
This is the halakha of R. Akiva, but an early halakha (teaches otherwise ...)

מְשַׁנֵּי prt. (שני פַּעֵל)

(1) מְשַׁנֶּה
changing; altering; doing differently

כַּמָּה דְּאֶפְשָׁר לְשַׁנּוֹיֵי, מְשַׁנֵּינַן (שבת קכח, סע"ב וש"נ)
as much as it is possible to alter (the manner of performing this activity on the Sabbath), we alter (it, so that it does not fall within the category of a forbidden labor)

answering; resolving; reconciling (2) מְתָרֵץ
(a difficulty or a contradiction)

... רָמֵי מַתְנְיָיאתָא אַהֲדָדֵי וּמְשַׁנֵּי (ב"מ פא,א ע"פ כת"י)
... [he] pits the (two) mishnayoth against each other and resolves (the contradiction between them)
SEE: שְׁנָא, שַׁנֵּי

מְשַׁעְבֵּד prt. (עבד שַׁפְעֵל)

obligating; subjugating מְשַׁעְבֵּד
SEE: שַׁעְבֵּיד

מְשַׁעְבַּד pass. prt. (עבד שַׁפְעֵל)

obligated; subjugated; mortgaged מְשֻׁעְבָּד
SEE: שַׁעְבֵּיד

מְשַׁעְבְּדֵי pl. נְכָסִים מְשֻׁעְבָּדִים

"subjugated" properties (that were sold to a third party)*

בִּשְׁטָרָא דְּאִית בֵּיהּ זְמַן, גָּבֵי מִמְּשַׁעְבְּדֵי. (בבא מציעא ז, סע"א)
With a document that has a date [written] in it, one may collect a debt from "subjugated" properties.

* For a fuller explanation, see נְכָסִים מְשׁוּעְבָּדִים.

מַמָּשָׁא

substance; reality; significance מַמָּשׁ

עֲבוֹדָה זָרָה לֵית בָּהּ מַמָּשָׁא. (עבודה זרה נה,א)
Idolatry has no substance.

מִשְׁתַּבַּח prt. (שבח אִתְפַּעַל)

being full of praise (for) מִשְׁתַּבֵּחַ

מִשְׁתַּבַּח לֵיהּ רַב חִסְדָּא לְרַב הוּנָא בְּדְרַב הַמְנוּנָא דְּאָדָם גָּדוֹל הוּא. (קידושין כט, סע"ב)

Rav Ḥisda is full of praise for Rav Hamnuna in front of Rav Huna [declaring] that he is a great man (in Torah learning).

מִשְׁתַּבֵּשׁ prt. (שבשׁ אִתְפְּעֵל)

erring; mistaken טוֹעֶה

מַאן דְּתָנֵי "לִיבָּה" לָא מִשְׁתַּבֵּשׁ ... וּמַאן דְּתָנֵי "נִיבָּה" לָא מִשְׁתַּבֵּשׁ. (בבא קמא ס, רע"א)

One who teaches (the word) לִיבָּה* *(in the mishna) is not mistaken ..., and one who teaches (the word)* נִיבָּה* *is not mistaken.*

* Both verbs denote *fanning flames.*

SEE: מְשַׁבַּשְׁתָּא

מִשְׁתְּכַח prt. (שכח אִתְפְּעֵל)

discovered נִמְצָא

SEE: אִישְׁתְּכַח

מִשְׁתַּעְבַּד prt. (עבד אִשְׁתַּפְעַל)

obligated; subjugated; mortgaged מְשֻׁעְבָּד

מִטַּלְטְלֵי — מִי מִשְׁתַּעְבְּדֵי לִכְתוּבָּה?! (נדרים סה, סע"ב)

Are movable properties (automatically) mortgaged to a marriage contract (so that a widow or divorcee can collect her settlement from them)?!

SEE: שַׁעְבֵּיד, מְשַׁעְבַּד, מְשׁוּעְבָּד

מִשְׁתַּעֵי prt. (שעי אִתְפַּעַל)

speaking; expressing itself (1) מְדַבֵּר

מִשְׁתַּעֵי קְרָא הָכִי (סנהדרין לח, סע"ב)

Scripture expresses itself in this manner

telling; relating (an incident) (2) מְסַפֵּר

ר' יוֹחָנָן מִשְׁתַּעֵי: זִימְנָא חֲדָא הֲוָה קָא אָזְלִינַן בִּסְפִינְתָּא ... (בבא בתרא עד, סע"א)

R. Yoḥanan relates: Once we were travelling in a ship...

מָתָא עִיר; מָקוֹם

city; town; place

קְבִיעַ בֵּי דוֹאַר בְּמָתָא. (שבת יט,א)

There is a permanent post office in the town.

SEE: בַּר מָתָא

מִתּוֹךְ

out of; (immediately) from

אֵין עוֹמְדִין לְהִתְפַּלֵּל אֶלָּא מִתּוֹךְ כֹּבֶד רֹאשׁ. (ברכות ל,ב: משנה פ"ה מ"א)

One should not stand up to pray except out of a serious attitude.

מִתּוֹךְ שֶׁ-

since; because

מִתּוֹךְ שֶׁיָּכוֹל לוֹמַר לוֹ: הֶחֱזַרְתִּיו לָךְ, כִּי אָמַר לֵיהּ: לְקוּחָה הִיא בְּיָדִי — מְהֵימַן. (בבא בתרא מה, סע"א)

Since he could say to him: I have returned it to you, if he says to him: It was purchased by me — he is believed.

SEE: מִיגּוֹ דְּ-

since it is stated (in the Torah) **מִתּוֹךְ שֶׁנֶּאֱמַר**

This expression is used in a Midrashic context in a manner similar to (מִ)מַּשְׁמַע שֶׁנֶּאֱמַר.

מְתִיב/מוֹתִיב prt. (תוב אַפְעֵל) מֵשִׁיב; מַקְשֶׁה

refuting; raising an objection

This term introduces a *difficulty* that one amora poses against a halakha of another amora. The difficulty is based upon a mishna, a baraitha, or a pasuk.

אָמַר רַב יְהוּדָה: סָפֵק קָרָא קְרִיאַת שְׁמַע, סָפֵק לֹא קָרָא — אֵינוֹ חוֹזֵר וְקוֹרֵא ... מַאי טַעְמָא? קְרִיאַת שְׁמַע דְּרַבָּנַן .... מְתִיב רַב יוֹסֵף: "וּבְשָׁכְבְּךָ וּבְקוּמֶךָ"! (ברכות כא,א ע"פ דברים ו:ז)

*Rav Yhuda said: [If a man is in] doubt [about whether] he has recited the Sh*e*ma or not — he need not go back and recite [it]. What is the reason? The reading of Sh*e*ma is a Rabbinic mitzva.... Rav Yosef raises a difficulty: "[You shall recite these words] at the time when you retire and at the time when you rise" (indicating that the mitzva of reciting the Sh*e*ma is from the Torah)!*

SEE: אוֹתִיב, אֵיתִיבֵיהּ, מֵיתִיבֵי

מְתִיבְתָּא (מְתִיבָתָא .pl)

session; lesson; lecture (1) שִׁיעוּר; פֶּרֶק

יָתִיב וְקָא מְסַיֵּים מְתִיבְתָּא דְיוֹמָא לְרַבָּנַן (בבא קמא קיז,א)

[he was] sitting and going over the day's lecture for the ḥakhamim

***yeshiva;* Rabbinical academy** (2) יְשִׁיבָה

מְתִיבָתָא בְּגִירְסַיְיהוּ טְרִידִי. (גיטין ו,א)

The yeshivoth are engrossed in their studies.

מַתְנֵי prt. (תני אַפְעֵל)

teaching (1) מַשְׁנֶה; מְלַמֵּד

(a mishna, a baraitha, or an amora's statement)

ברייתא: הָיוּ לְפָנָיו שְׁנֵי מִינֵי אוֹכָלִין וּבֵירֵר וְאָכַל ...

תלמוד: רַב אַשִׁי מַתְנֵי: פָּטוּר, וְר' יִרְמְיָה מִדִּפְתִּי מַתְנֵי: חַיָּיב. (שבת עד,א)

BARAITHA: [If] two types of food were before him (on the Sabbath), and he selected [one] and ate [it] ...

*TALMUD: Rav Ashi teaches: He is exempt (from punishment for Sabbath desecration for selecting one species from a mixture of different species), while R. Yirm*e*ya of Difti teaches: He is subject to punishment.**

אַמֵּימָר מַתְנֵי לְהָא דְּרַב חִסְדָּא בְּהָדֵ לִישָּׁנָא. (תענית ו, סע"א)

Ammemar teaches this [statement] of Rav Ḥisda in the following words.

* Thus the two amoraim have reported two different versions of the halakhic ruling in the baraitha.

stipulating; making a stipulation (2) מַתְנֶה

הָכָא מוֹכֵר קָא מַתְנֵי (בבא מציעא סו, רע"א)

here [it is the] seller [who is] making a stipulation

SEE: תְּנָאִי, אַתְנִי, אִיכָּא דְּמַתְנֵי לַהּ לְהָא שְׁמַעְתָּא בְּאַפֵּי נַפְשָׁהּ, and the next entry.

מַתְנֵי אַ-   מַשְׁנָה עַל

he teaches [the amora's comment as] referring to [a particular case or a specific text]; he applies [the statement] to ...

משנה: בַּכֹּל מְעָרְבִין ... חוּץ מִן הַמַּיִם וּמִן הַמֶּלַח, וְהַכֹּל נִיקָּח בְּכֶסֶף מַעֲשֵׂר חוּץ מִן הַמַּיִם וּמִן הַמֶּלַח. (עירובין כו, סע"ב: משנה פ"ג מ"א)

תלמוד: ר' אֶלְעָזָר וְר' יוֹסֵי בַּר חֲנִינָא: חַד מַתְנֵי אַעֵירוּב וְחַד מַתְנֵי אַמַּעֲשֵׂר. חַד מַתְנֵי אַעֵירוּב: לֹא שָׁנוּ אֶלָּא מַיִם בִּפְנֵי עַצְמָן וּמֶלַח בִּפְנֵי עַצְמוֹ דְּאֵין מְעָרְבִין, אֲבָל מַיִם וּמֶלַח מְעָרְבִין; וְחַד מַתְנֵי אַמַּעֲשֵׂר: לֹא שָׁנוּ אֶלָּא מַיִם בִּפְנֵי עַצְמָן וּמֶלַח בִּפְנֵי עַצְמוֹ דְּאֵין נִיקָּחִין, אֲבָל מַיִם וּמֶלַח נִיקָּחִין בְּכֶסֶף מַעֲשֵׂר. (שם כז,א)

MISHNA: An "eruv" may be made with anything except water or salt, and anything may be bought with the money of the [second] tithe (to be eaten in Jerusalem) except water or salt.

TALMUD: R. El'azar and R. Yosé b. Ḥanina [differ]: One teaches (the following exception as) referring to an "eruv," and the other as referring to the [second] tithe. One applies [it] to an "eruv": They meant that only water by itself and salt by itself may not be used as an "eruv," but salt-water may be used as an "eruv"; while the other applies [it] to the [second] tithe: They meant that only water by itself and salt by itself may not be purchased (with money of the second tithe), but salt-water may be purchased.

SEE: אִיכָּא דְּמַתְנֵי לַהּ/לְהָא אַ- and the previous entry

מַתְנֵי לַהּ בְּהֶדְיָא   מַשְׁנֶה אוֹתָהּ בְּפֵרוּשׁ

he teaches it explicitly

With this expression the Talmud quotes an amora who presents a clear-cut position about an issue that was in doubt earlier in the course of the Talmudic discussion.

בָּעֵי רַב בִּיבִי בַּר אַבַּיֵי: הִדְבִּיק פַּת בַּתַּנּוּר — הִתִּירוּ לוֹ לִרְדּוֹתָהּ קוֹדֶם שֶׁיָּבוֹא לִידֵי ... אוֹ לֹא הִתִּירוּ? ... רַב אַחָא בְּרֵיהּ דְּרָבָא מַתְנֵי לַהּ בְּהֶדְיָא: אָמַר רַב בִּיבִי בַּר אַבַּיֵי: הִדְבִּיק פַּת בַּתַּנּוּר — הִתִּירוּ לוֹ לִרְדּוֹתָהּ קוֹדֶם שֶׁיָּבֹא לִידֵי אִיסּוּר .... (שבת ד,א ורש"י)

Rav Bibbi b. Abbayé raises a (halakhic) problem: [If] one pasted bread [dough] to [the inside wall of] the oven (on the Sabbath) — did they permit him to detach it before he violates [a Sabbath prohibition when the bread becomes baked] ... or did they not permit? ... Rav Aḥa b. Rava teaches it explicitly: Rav Bibbi b. Abbayé said: [If] one pasted bread [dough] to [the inside wall of] the oven — they permitted him to detach it before he violates a Sabbath prohibition ...*

*** Ordinarily, it is forbidden to detach the dough from the wall of the oven on the Sabbbath.**

מַתְנִיתָא* (= מַתְנִיתָא בָּרַיְיתָא; מַתְנְיָיתָא .pl)

מִשְׁנָה חִיצוֹנִית; בָּרַיְיתָא

an outside teaching; a baraitha

כִּי אֲתָא רַב חַגַּי מִדָּרוֹמָא, אֲתָא וְאַיְתִי מַתְנִיתָא בִּידֵיהּ. (בבא קמא מב, סע"א)

When Rav Ḥaggai came [back] from the Darom (= the South), he came and brought a baraitha with him.

מַתְנְיָיתָא מִי לָא קַשְׁיָין אַהֲדָדֵי?! (עירובין ג,א)

Don't the (two) baraithoth contradict each other?!

* Occasionally, מַתְנִיתָא refers to a *mishna*, and the plural מַתְנְיָיתָא refers to *mishnayoth*. For examples, see:
ב"מ מח,א ע"פ משנה מעילה פ"ה מ"ד; יבמות צא, סע"ב ע"פ משנה גיטין פ"ח מ"ה-מ"ט.

SEE: בָּרַיְיתָא, מַתְנִיתִין

מַתְנִיתָא לָא שְׁמִיעַ לֵיהּ

הוּא לֹא שָׁמַע אֶת הַבָּרַיְיתָא.

He has not heard of [this specific] baraitha.

For an example — see פסחים קא,ב.
SEE: בָּרַיְיתָא לָא שְׁמִיעַ לֵיהּ and its note.

בְּמַתְנִיתָא תְּנָא   בִּבְרַיְיתָא שָׁנָה ...

[A tanna] taught in a baraitha ...

This expression introduces a baraitha (usually anonymous) that presents aggadic or halakhic material dealing with the same topic as a previously-quoted amoraic statement. The baraitha is not identical with the amoraic statement: it either disagrees with one point, or offers a different interpretation, or presents supplementary data.*

אֲמַר רַב יְהוּדָה אֲמַר שְׁמוּאֵל: "מְקוֹשֵׁשׁ" מַעֲבִיר אַרְבַּע אַמּוֹת בִּרְשׁוּת הָרַבִּים הֲוָה. בְּמַתְנִיתָא תְּנָא: תּוֹלֵשׁ הֲוָה. (שבת צו,ב ע"פ במדבר ט:לב)

Rav Yhuda said quoting Shmuel: [The offense of the] gatherer (of wood) was carrying [it] four cubits in the public domain. [A tanna] taught in a baraitha: He was detaching (branches from a tree).

*** The expression וְאָמְרִי לַהּ בְּמַתְנִיתָא תְּנָא, *and some say [a tanna] taught in a baraitha*, presents the view that the statement that is about to be quoted is a baraitha — not merely the opinion of the *amora* to whom it has been attributed.**

For an example see — ברכות נא,ב.

מַתְנִיתִין*   מִשְׁנָתֵנוּ

our mishna

The Mishna, compiled by R. Yhuda HaNasi (= Rebbi), or any one of its statements is called *our mishna* — in contradistinction to a *baraitha*, a teaching of tannaim that was not included in the Mishna.

מַתְנִיתִין מַאן תַּקְּינַהּ? רַבִּי. (יבמות סד,ב)

Who compiled our Mishna? Rebbi (= R. Yhuda HaNasi).

שָׁבְקַתְּ מַתְנִיתִין וְעָבְדַתְּ כִּבְרַיְיתָא?! (סוכה יט,ב)

Are you ignoring our mishna and acting in accordance with a baraitha?!

* In our printed editions of the Talmud, the abbreviation 'מתני is used to indicate the beginning of each mishna of the tractate.

SEE: מִשְׁנָה, מַתְנִיתָא

מַתְנִיתִין דְּלָא כִּי הַאי תַּנָּא

מִשְׁנָתֵנוּ אֵינֶנָּה כְּמוֹ הַתַּנָּא הַזֶּה ...

Our mishna is not in accordance with [the opinion of] the following tanna ...

This statement points out that the halakha stated by the tanna of our mishna is actually the subject of a controversy with another tanna whose view is now presented in a baraitha.

משנה: כְּרַכִּין הַמּוּקָּפִין חוֹמָה מִימוֹת יְהוֹשֻׁעַ בִּן נוּן קוֹרִין בַּחֲמִשָּׁה עָשָׂר ... (מגילה ב, רע"א: משנה פ"א מ"א)
תלמוד: מַתְנִיתִין דְּלָא כִּי הַאי תַּנָּא, דְּתַנְיָא: ר' יְהוֹשֻׁעַ בֶּן קָרְחָה אוֹמֵר: כְּרַכִּין הַמּוּקָּפִין חוֹמָה מִימוֹת אֲחַשְׁוֵרוֹשׁ קוֹרִין בַּחֲמִשָּׁה עָשָׂר. (שם ב,ב)

MISHNA: Cities surrounded by a wall from the days of Y^ehoshua b. Nun read [the scroll of Esther] on the fifteenth [of Adar] ...

TALMUD: Our mishna is not in accordance with [the opinion of] the following tanna, for it is stated (in a baraitha): R. Y^ehoshua b. Korḥa says: Cities surrounded by a wall from the days of Aḥashverosh read on the fifteenth.

מַתְנִיתִין הִיא

It is our mishna! מִשְׁנָתֵנוּ הִיא!

The issue under discussion has been settled in our mishna; hence there is no room for doubt about it.

For an example — see שבת צט,ב.

מַתְנִיתִין מַנִּי

מִשְׁנָתֵנוּ [שֶׁל] מִי הִיא?

Whose [opinion] is [presented by] our mishna?

For an example — see שבת לז,א.

SEE: מַנִּי מַתְנִיתִין

מַתְנִיתִין נַמֵּי דַּיְקָא דְּקָתָנֵי

אַף מִשְׁנָתֵנוּ מְדֻיֶּקֶת, שֶׁהוּא שׁוֹנֶה ...

[The wording of] our mishna is also precise (and supportive of what was just proposed), for [the tanna] states ...

For an example — see שבת ב, סע"ב.

SEE: דַּיְקָא נַמֵּי, מַתְנִיתִין קַשְׁיָתֵיהּ

מַתְנִיתִין קַשְׁיָתֵיהּ

מִשְׁנָתֵנוּ הָיְתָה קָשָׁה לוֹ.

Our mishna was perplexing to him.

This statement is made by the amora Rava in the following context: It has been charged that the statement made by an earlier amora is without foundation. Rava answers this charge by arguing that the particular wording of our mishna provides a basis for the amora's statements, because otherwise the mishna would be difficult to explain.

For an example — see בבא מציעא כו, סע"ב.

SEE: מַתְנִיתִין נַמֵּי דַּיְקָא דְּקָתָנֵי, קַשְׁיָתֵיהּ

מַתְקִיף

prt. (תקף אַפְעֵל) מַתְקִיף; מַקְשֶׁה

attacking; pointing out a difficulty

מַתְקִיף לַהּ רַב ...

רַב ... מַתְקִיף אוֹתָהּ; רַב ... מַקְשֶׁה עָלֶיהָ

Rav ... attacks it; Rav ... points out a difficulty with it

This expression introduces a *difficulty* that is usually based upon a logical argument. In most instances, an amora attacks another amora's halakha, argument, or interpretation that was just quoted in the Talmud. Occasionally, the object of the attack is a baraitha (e.g., שבועות לד,א) or even a mishna (בבא מציעא לג, סע"ב ורש"י שם).

הָיוּ לְפָנָיו מִינֵי אוֹכָלִין ... אֲמַר עוּלָּא: ... בּוֹרֵר וְאוֹכֵל לְבוֹ בַּיּוֹם ... וּלְמָחָר לֹא יִבְרוֹר, וְאִם בֵּירֵר חַיָּיב חַטָּאת. מַתְקִיף לַהּ רַב חִסְדָּא: וְכִי מוּתָּר לֶאֱפוֹת לְבוֹ בַּיּוֹם?! (שבת ע"ד,א ורש"י שם)

[If] there were [several] kinds of foodstuffs before him [on the Sabbath] ... Ula said: ... he may select [one of them for] eating on the same day (the Sabbath) ... but for the next day he must not select, and if he did select, he is obligated [to bring] a sin-offering [for the Sabbath desecration of selecting one item that was intermingled with others]. Rav Ḥisda attacks it: [If indeed selecting is categorized as a forbidden labor, how is it permitted to select for use on the Sabbath itself?!] Is it permitted to bake for [eating] on the same [Sabbath] day?!

מְתָרֵץ/מְתָרֵיץ

prt. (תרץ פַּעֵל)

resolving; explaining (a text) מְתָרֵץ; מְיַשֵּׁב

SEE: תָּרֵיץ and the next entry.

... מְתָרֵץ לְטַעְמֵיהּ, וְ... מְתָרֵץ לְטַעְמֵיהּ

... מְתָרֵץ לְשִׁטָּתוֹ, וְ... מְתָרֵץ לְשִׁטָּתוֹ.

[One amora] would explain [the baraitha] according to his opinion, and [the opposing amora] would explain [it] according to his opinion.

After a baraitha has been quoted that seems to contradict both sides of an amoraic controversy, the Talmud uses this formula to show how each amora could explain the baraitha so that it would be in harmony with his position after all.

For an example — see רבה ורבא בבבא מציעא כב, סע"ב.

SEE: (לְ)טַעְמֵיהּ

מְתָרַצְתָּא

pass. prt. f. (תרץ פַּעֵל)

genuine; correct מְיֻשֶּׁרֶת; נְכוֹנָה

וּמַאן נֵימָא לַן דִּמְתָרַצְתָּא הִיא? דִּילְמָא מְשַׁבַּשְׁתָּא הִיא! (פסחים צט, סע"ב)

But who can tell us that [the baraitha] is genuine? Perhaps [its text] is faulty!

SEE: מְשַׁבַּשְׁתָּא

נ

נָאִים SEE: נָיִים

נֶאֱמַר (אמר נִפְעַל)

it was stated; it was said (in a pasuk)*

For examples, see the next two entries.

* On one occasion, this word does not refer to a Biblical passage, but it is used in one mishna to introduce a quotation from the previous mishna. See:
בכורות נז,ב: משנה פ"ט מ"ה-מ"ו, אבל ע' שיטה מקובצת שם.

שֶׁנֶּאֱמַר **for it was stated ...; as it was said ...**

This term introduces a Biblical passage that is quoted by a tanna as a *source* for his statement.

חַיָּב אָדָם לְבָרֵךְ עַל הָרָעָה כְּשֵׁם שֶׁהוּא מְבָרֵךְ עַל הַטּוֹבָה, שֶׁנֶּאֱמַר: "וְאָהַבְתָּ אֵת ה' אֱלֹקֶיךָ ... וּבְכָל מְאֹדֶךָ" — בְּכָל מִדָּה וּמִדָּה שֶׁהוּא מוֹדֵד לְךָ, הֱוֵי מוֹדֶה לוֹ בִּמְאֹד מְאֹד. (ברכות נד,א: משנה פ"ט מ"ה ע"פ דברים ו:ה)

A person should recite a b^erakha over evil just as he does over good, as it was said: "And you shall love the Lord your God ... and with every measure of yours" — with every measure that He measures to you, you shall thank Him very much.

נֶאֱמַר ... וְנֶאֱמַר ...

It was stated (in one passage) **..., and it was stated** (in another passage) **...**

This formula presents an *analogy* between two Biblical passages that teaches a halakhic or aggadic point.

אֶת זוֹ דָּרַשׁ שִׁמְעוֹן בֶּן זוֹמָא: נֶאֱמַר בְּמַעֲשֵׂה בְרֵאשִׁית "יוֹם אֶחָד", וְנֶאֱמַר בְּאוֹתוֹ וְאֶת בְּנוֹ "יוֹם אֶחָד"; מָה "יוֹם אֶחָד" הָאָמוּר בְּמַעֲשֵׂה בְרֵאשִׁית, הַיּוֹם הוֹלֵךְ אַחַר הַלַּיְלָה — אַף "יוֹם אֶחָד" הָאָמוּר בְּאוֹתוֹ וְאֶת בְּנוֹ, הַיּוֹם הוֹלֵךְ אַחַר הַלַּיְלָה. (חולין פג, סע"א: משנה פ"ה מ"ה)

Shim'on b. Zoma presented this interpretation: It was stated in the account of creation "one day," and it was stated in [the prohibition of slaughtering] him (= an animal) and his offspring (on the same day) "one day"; just as [regarding] "one day" that is stated in the account of creation, the day follows the night — [regarding] "one day" that is stated in [the prohibition of slaughtering] him and his offspring too, the day follows the night.

נְבֵילָה/נְבֵלָה; נְבִילְתָא* *n^evela;*

the carcass of an animal that died without a halakhic slaughtering

כָּל שֶׁנִּפְסְלָה בִשְׁחִיטָתָהּ — נְבֵלָה. (חולין לב, סע"א: משנה ב:ד)

*Any [animal] that has been disqualified through [a fault in] its slaughtering is [classified as] n^evela (i.e., it must not be eaten,** and it conveys ritual uncleanliness**).*

* The first two forms are Hebrew, and the last is Aramaic.

** See the p^esukim לא תאכלו כָל נְבֵלָה (דברים יד:כא) and הַנֹּגֵעַ בְּנִבְלָתָהּ יִטְמָא עַד הָעָרֶב (ויקרא יא:לט).

SEE: טְרֵיפָה

נְגַד (נגד: נָגֵיד .prt)

he pulled; he stretched out מָשַׁךְ

נְגִידוּ מִינֵּיהּ מֵיכְלֵיהּ! (גיטין סח,ב)

Pull away his food from him!

SEE: אַגָּדָה and its note.

נַגֵּיד (נגד פַּעֵל: מְנַגֵּיד .prt, נַגּוֹדֵי .inf)

he flogged; he administered lashes הִלְקָה

ר' שֵׁילָא נַגְדֵיהּ לְהַהוּא גַּבְרָא. (ברכות נח,א)

R. Sheela administered lashes to a certain man.

נְגַה

(1) הֵאִיר **it became bright**

נְגַהּ לֵיהּ טוּבָא (יומא כח, רע"ב) *it has become too bright*

(2) אֵחַר **he was late**

נְגַה לְצַלּוֹיֵי (שבת י,א ורש"י שם) *he was (too) late to pray*

(3) הִמְתִּין **he waited**

נְגַה לֵיהּ, וְלָא אֲתָא. (יבמות צג, סע"א ורש"י שם)

He waited for him, but he did not come.

נְגַהֵי constr. אוֹר לְ-* **"light"; the night before***

בְּפַלְגָא אוּרְתָּא דִתְלֵיסַר, נְגַהֵי אַרְבְּסַר (ברכות ד,א ורש"י שם)

at midnight of the night after the thirteenth, the night before the fourteenth

* This definition is in keeping with the conclusion of the discussion in פסחים ג,א — but in contrast to what had been assumed in פסחים ב,א. See קָא סָלְקָא דַעְתָּךְ.

NOTE: First person plural forms of Aramaic verbs in the imperfect (= the future) usually have a נ prefix. Sometimes, however, the נ prefix represents the third person, masculine singular. For example, נִיגְמַר may mean either *let us derive* or *let him derive*. Since these common forms are apt to confuse the learner, many of them have been presented as separate entries at נ — even when the main verbal entry (third person, masculine singular of the past tense, e.g., גְּמַר, *he derived*) appears at its appropriate place. In some of these נ entries, the explanations and examples are omitted, and the learner is referred to the main verbal entries for such data. For more information about the conjugation of the Aramaic verb, see *Grammar for Gemara*: Chapter 3.

נְהַג (נהג: act. part. נָהֵיג, pass. part. נְהִיג) נָהַג

(1) he has become accustomed; he followed a practice; he acted

הָאִידָּנָא נְהוּג עָלְמָא לְמִיקְרֵי "כִּי תוֹלִיד בָּנִים..." (מגילה לא, רע"ב ע"פ דברים ד:כה)

*nowadays the world has become accustomed to read [the Torah portion on Tish'a b*ᵉ*Av, beginning with:] "When you will beget children ..."*

וְלֵיחְזֵי הֵיכִי נָהֲגִי! (בבא מציעא פג, רע"ב)

But let us see how [people] act!

(2) it applied

לָא נָהֲגָא מִצְוַת שִׁבְעָה בְּרֶגֶל (מועד קטן יט, סע"ב)

the mitzva of "shiv'a" (= the seven-day mourning period) does not apply during a festival

SEE: מִנְהָג

נַהְדַּר/נֵיהְדַּר fut. (הדר אַפְעֵל)

let him give back יַחֲזִיר

SEE: לַהְדַּר, אַהְדַּר

נֶהְדַּר

SEE: נֵיהְדַּר

נְהוֹרָא (נהור .abs) אוֹר **light; eyesight**

נְהוֹרָא דִשְׁרָגָא (פסחים ז, סע"ב) *the light of a candle*

SEE: סַגִּי נְהוֹר

נְהִי fut. (הוי)

"let it be"; granted; even though "יְהִי"; נָנִּיחַ

נְהִי דַעֲנִיִּים דְּהָכָא מִיָּאֲשִׁי, אִיכָּא עֲנִיִּים בְּדוּכְתָּא אַחֲרִיתִי דְּלָא מִיָּאֲשִׁי! (ב"מ כא,ב)

Granted that the poor people here have given up hope, (yet) there are poor people elsewhere who have not given up hope!

נְהִי נַמֵּי אֲפִילוּ יְהִי; אֲפִילוּ נָנִּיחַ **even granted**

נְהִי נַמֵּי דְמִחַיֵּיב בִּגְנֵבָה וַאֲבֵדָה, בְּאוֹנְסֶיהָ ... מִי מִחַיֵּיב?! (יבמות סו,ב)

Even granted that he is liable for theft and loss, is he liable for accidents to it ...?!

SEE: נַמֵּי

נְהִיר pass. prt. (נהר)

clear; known בָּרוּר; יָדוּעַ

אָמַר שְׁמוּאֵל: נְהִירִין לִי שְׁבִילֵי דִשְׁמַיָּא כִּשְׁבִילֵי דִנְהַרְדְּעָא ... (ברכות נח,ב)

*Sh*ᵉ*muel said: The paths of the sky are as clear to me as the streets of N*ᵉ*hard*ᵉ*a ...*

נְהִירְנָא (בבא בתרא צא,ב ורשב"ם שם)*

It is clear to me (= I remember)

* This form appears six times on that page.

נַהֲמָא* לֶחֶם **bread**

נַהֲמָא הוּא דְסָעִיד; חַמְרָא לָא סָעִיד. (ברכות לה, סע"ב)

It is bread that sustains; wine does not sustain.

* The letters נ and ה in the Aramaic נַהֲמָא are respectively parallel to the ל and ח in the Hebrew לֶחֶם.

נוֹטָרִיקוֹן **shorthand; abbreviation**

This term denotes a *method of interpretation* of Biblical words in which either: (1) each letter of the word is taken as a representation for a whole word, or (2) a single Biblical word is broken down into components.* Both types are illustrated in the example below.

ר' יוֹחָנָן דִּידֵיהּ אָמַר: "אָנֹכִי" נוֹטָרִיקוֹן — אֲנָא נַפְשִׁי כְּתַבִית יְהַבִית ... דְּבֵי ר' יִשְׁמָעֵאל תָּנָא: "כַּרְמֶל" — כַּר מָלֵא. (שבת קה,א ע"פ שמות כ:ב; ויקרא כג:יד)

R. Yoḥanan himself said: אנכי *(= I, in "I am the Lord your God") is an abbreviation [for]* אֲנָא *I,* נַפְשִׁי *Myself,* כְּתַבִית *wrote [the Torah, and]* יְהַבִית *gave [it to the Jewish people] ... the school of R. Yishmael taught:* כַּרְמֶל *[means]* כַּר+מָלֵא, *[like] a full cushion.*

* This method appears in the list of thirty-two rules of aggadic interpretation ascribed to R. Eliezer b. R. Yosé the Galilean.

נוֹקִים fut. (קום אַפְעֵל)

let us/him set up נַעֲמִיד; יַעֲמִיד

SEE: לוֹקִים, אוֹקֵי

נוּרָא (נור .abs) אֵשׁ **fire; a blaze**

דְּכִירְנָא כַּד הֲוָה יָתֵיבְנָא אַחַר י"ז שׁוּרָן אֲחוֹרֵיהּ דְּרַב קַמֵּיהּ דְּרַבִּי וְנָפְקֵי זִיקוּקֵי דְנוּר* מִפּוּמֵיהּ דְּרַב לְפוּמֵיהּ דְּרַבִּי וּמִפּוּמֵיהּ דְּרַבִּי לְפוּמֵיהּ דְּרַב, וְלֵית אֲנָא יָדַע מָה הֵן אָמְרִין ... (חולין קלז, סע"ב)

I (= R. Yoḥanan) recall when I was sitting before Rebbi, seventeen rows behind Rav, and "sparks of fire" were travelling from the mouth of Rav to the mouth of Rebbi and from the mouth of Rebbi to the mouth of Rav, but I did not understand what they were saying ...

* In Modern Hebrew, זִקּוּקִין דִּנוּר means *fireworks.*

נוֹתֵן prt. (נתן) **giving; indicating; pointing**

SEE: (וְה)דִין נוֹתֵן, (וְ)הִיא הַנּוֹתֶנֶת

נִזְקָק prt. (זקק נִפְעַל)

attached (to); engaged (in); attending (to)

בֵּית דִּין נִזְקָקִין אֲפִילוּ לִפְחוֹת מִשָּׁוֶה פְרוּטָה. (ב"מ נה, סע"א)

*The court attends even to [a case involving] less than the value of a p*ᵉ*ruta (= a small coin).*

נֶזֶק (pl. נְזָקִין/נִזְקִין)**; נִיזְקָא/נִזְקָא*** **damage**

גְּרָמָא בִּנְזָקִין (בבא קמא ס,א; ב"ב כב, סע"ב ע"פ כת"י)

the indirect causation of damages

כּוּלָּהּ נְזִיקִין חֲדָא מַסֶּכְתָּא הִיא (בבא קמא קב, סע"א)

*The whole of N*ᵉ*zikin (= Bava Kamma, Bava Metzia and Bava Bathra) comprises one tractate (in the Mishna).*

* The first form is Hebrew, and the others are Aramaic.

נָח (נוח: act. prt. נָיֵיחַ, pass. prt. נִיחָא, fut. לֵינַח, מֵינַח (inf. נָח **he rested**

נָח נַפְשֵׁיה
"his soul rested"; he died — נִפְטַר; מֵת

כִּי נָח נַפְשֵׁיה דְּר' יוֹחָנָן, יָתִיב ר' אַמִי שִׁבְעָה וּשְׁלֹשִׁים. (מועד קטן כה,ב)

When R. Yoḥanan died, R. Ammi (his disciple) observed [the mourning periods of] seven and thirty (days).

נָחוֹתֵי* **"descenders"; travellers** — יוֹרְדִים

This term refers to the scholars who travelled from Erets Yisrael to Babylonia (and back) and reported the teachings of the halakhic authorities in Erets Yisrael to their Babylonian counterparts (and vice versa).

כִּי אֲתָא רַבִין וְכָל נָחוֹתֵי, אָמְרִי ... (סוכה מג,ב ורש"י שם)

When Rabin and all the (other) travellers (from Eretz Yisrael) arrived, they reported ...

* In the Talmud Yerushalmi, the term נְחוֹתָה was added to the names of several amoraim e.g., ר' אַבְדּוּמָא נְחוֹתָה, because of their journeys to the Diaspora.

SEE: נְחַת

נָחוֹתֵי יַמָּא **seafarers** — יוֹרְדֵי הַיָּם

שְׁאִילְתִּינְהוּ לְכָל נָחוֹתֵי יַמָּא וַאֲמָרוּ לִי: עוֹף אֶחָד יֵשׁ בִּכְרַכֵּי הַיָּם וְקִיק שְׁמוֹ. (שבת כא, רע"א)

I inquired of all the seafarers, and they told me: There is a certain bird in the seaports, and its name is "kik."

נֶחֱזֵי SEE: נִיחְזֵי

נְחַת/נְחֵית (נחת*: נָחֵית .prt, לֵיחוּת .fut, לְמֵיחַת .inf)
he went down; he descended — יָרַד

הַהוּא דִּנְחֵית קַמֵּיהּ דְּרַבָּה ... (ברכות יד, רע"ב)

*[There was] a certain man who went down** (to lead the prayer service) in the presence of Rabba ...*

* This verb is common in Aramaic (in the Targumim it is the standard translation of the Hebrew ירד) but rare in Hebrew (איוב יז:טז). It is used in Modern Hebrew, primarily for the *landing* of aircraft.

** In Talmudic times, the שְׁלִיחַ צִיבּוּר was stationed in a place lower than the rest of the synagogue.

ע' ברכות י,ב ע"פ תהלים קל:א — "מִמַּעֲמַקִּים קְרָאתִיךָ".

SEE: נָחוֹתֵי, אַחֵית

נְטִירוּתָא **watching; safeguarding** — שְׁמִירָה

he accepted קַבֵּיל עֲלֵיהּ נְטִירוּתָא (בבא קמא מז, סע"ב)
upon himself [the responsibility of] safeguarding

SEE: נְטַר

נְטַר (נטר: נָטַר .prt, לֵינְטַר .fut, לְמֵינְטַר .inf)
(1) נָטַר; שָׁמַר
he watched; he guarded;* he protected

נְטַר כְּדְנָטְרֵי אֱינָשֵׁי (בבא מציעא צג, רע"ב)

he guarded as people [usually] guard

(2) הִמְתִּין **he waited**

רַבָּנַן אַכּוּלַּהּ מִילְּתָא פְּלִיגֵי, וְנָטְרֵי לֵיהּ לְר' מֵאִיר עַד דְּמַסְּיֵק לַהּ לְמִילְּתָא, וַהֲדַר פְּלִיגֵי עֲלֵיהּ. (חולין פו,א)

The Ḥakhamim disagree with the whole statement (expressed in the earlier and later clauses in the mishna), but they wait until R. Méir has completed the (presentation of his) statement, and then they express their disagreement with him.

* The contemporary group calling itself נָטוֹרֵי קַרְתָּא (popularly pronounced *Neturé Karta*) sees itself as *the guardians of the city (of Yerushalayim).*

SEE: נְטִירוּתָא, אַגַר נְטַר לֵיהּ

נַטַּר (נטר פַּעֵל: מְנַטַּר .prt, לְנַטּוֹרֵי .inf)
he guarded (carefully) — שָׁמַר

אִיבָּעֵי לָךְ לְנַטּוֹרֵי לְכוּלֵּיהּ בַּקְרָךְ (בבא קמא כד,ב)

you must guard your entire herd (carefully)

נִיבְעֵי .fut (בעי) נְבַקֵּשׁ; נִשְׁאַל; יִשְׁאַל; יְהֵא צָרִיךְ
let us request/ask; let him ask; let it need

SEE: לִיבְעֵי, בְּעָא

נִיגְמַר/נִגְמַר/נִגְמוֹר .fut (גמר) נִלְמַד; יִלְמַד
let us learn/derive; let him learn/derive

SEE: לִיגְמַר, גְּמַר

נִידּוֹן pass. prt. (דון נִפְעַל)
judged; discussed; inferred (from)

For an example — see דַּיּוֹ לַבָּא מִן הַדִּין לִהְיוֹת כַּנִּידּוֹן.

נִיהְדַּר/נֶהְדַּר .fut (הדר) יַחֲזֹר **let him go back**

SEE: לֶיהְדַּר, הֲדַר

נִיהְדַּר SEE: נֶהְדַּר

נִיהוּ (נִיהִי .f, נִינְהוּ .m. pl) הוּא **it; it is; is it**

The forms נִיהוּ, נִיהִי, and נִינְהוּ are often used instead of אִיהוּ, אִיהִי, and אִינְהוּ respectively — in questions and at the conclusion of other clauses.

הֵי נִיהוּ "קְנֵה הַלֵּב"? (חולין מה,ב)

Which is "the artery of the heart"?

הִיא נִיהִי דְּלָא מְהֵימְנָא — הָא עֵד אֶחָד מְהֵימָן! (יבמות צד,א)

She (= the woman herself) it is who is not believed — but one (impartial) witness is believed!

SEE: מַאי נִיהוּ

נֶיהֱוֵי .fut (הוי) יִהְיֶה **let it be**

SEE: יְהֵא, לֶיהֱוֵי, הֲוָה

נִיהֲלַהּ לָהּ **to her**
נִיהֲלֵיהּ לוֹ **to him**

These pronouns are used to express an *indirect object* instead of the usual לֵיהּ, לַהּ, and so on — when one of those pronouns is already used in the sentence as the direct object (e.g., לֵיהּ, *it*, in the first example), or when a personal-pronoun suffix appended to the verb serves as the direct object (e.g., ־ַהּ in אֲמַרִיתַהּ, *I told it*, in the second example).*

שָׁקִיל לֵיהּ וְיָהֵיב לֵיהּ נִיהֲלַהּ (גיטין כא, סע"ב)
he may take it and give it to her

אֲנָא אֲמַרִיתַהּ נִיהֲלֵיהּ אַמַּתְנִיתִין, וְהוּא אֲמָרַהּ אַבָּרַיְיתָא. (עירובין כט,א ורש"י שם)
I told it (= a halakha) to him in connection with our mishna, but he stated it in connection with a baraitha.

* For a table of all the נִיהֲל- forms, see *Grammar for Gemara:* Chapter 7.322.

נֵיזִיל fut. (אזל) נֵלֵךְ; יֵלֵךְ
let us/him go
SEE: לֵיזִיל, אֲזַל

נִיזָּק pass. prt. (נזק נִפְעַל)
an injured party; a victim of a damage
שׁוֹר הַמַּזִּיק בִּרְשׁוּת הַנִּיזָּק (בבא קמא טו,ב: משנה פ"א מ"ד)
ox causing damage on the injured party's property

נִיזְקָא/נִזְקָא
SEE: נֶזֶק

נִיחָא* pass. prt. (נוח) נוֹחַ; נוֹחָה
(1) gentle; convenient; easy
מִיטְרָא נִיחָא (תענית ג, סע"ב) *a gentle rain*
לָא נִיחָא תַּשְׁמִישְׁתֵּיהּ (שבת ז,א) *its use is not convenient*

(2) it is pleasing
In this sense, נִיחָא is often followed by a personal pronoun as an indirect object, so that נִיחָא לֵיהּ means *it is pleasing to him, he is pleased, he likes.*
אִיכָּא דְנִיחָא לֵיהּ בְּחַמְרָא וְלָא נִיחָא לֵיהּ בְּחַלָּא. (ב"ב פד,ב)
There is [a person] who likes wine but does not like vinegar.
נִיחָא לֵיהּ לְאִינִישׁ דְּתִיעָבֵיד מִצְוָה בְּמָמוֹנֵיהּ. (ב"מ כט,ב וש"נ)
A person is pleased that a mitzva be done with his property.

(3) it is appropriate; it is satisfactory; it fits (= there is no difficulty)
לְרָבָא נִיחָא; לְרַבָּה קַשְׁיָא. (גיטין ד,ב)
According to Rava, [the baraitha] fits; (whereas) according to Rabba, it is difficult.

* The masculine singular form that one would expect, נִיחַ, is not found in the Talmud. The form נִיחָא serves for both masculine and feminine.
SEE: הֲנִיחָא

נֵיחוּשׁ prt. (חשש)
let us/him be concerned נָחֹשׁ
SEE: לֵיחוּשׁ, חָשׁ

נִיחוּתָא נוֹחוּת; נַחַת
mildness; gentleness; ease (of mind)
צָרִיךְ לְמֵימְרִינְהוּ בְּנִיחוּתָא, כִּי הֵיכִי דְּלִיקַבְּלִינְהוּ מִינֵּיהּ. (שבת לד,א; גיטין ז, רע"א)
He should say them (= these things) with gentleness, so that they will accept them from him.

* In his commentary on the Talmud, Rashi uses the term בְּנִיחוּתָא to denote an indicative statement or a proof — as opposed to his term בִּתְמִיהָה, *in wonderment*, which characterizes objections and rhetorical questions. For example — see Rashi on ברכות טז, סע"א.
SEE: נָח

נִיחֱזֵי/נֶחֱזֵי
SEE: לֶיחֱזֵי, חֲזָא

נֶיחֱזֵי אֲנַן נִרְאֶה אֲנַחְנוּ
let's see (for ourselves);* let's investigate
Since one aspect of the position of an earlier authority is unknown to us, let us endeavor to clarify that aspect ourselves either through logical analysis or by examining an authoritative source.
וּשְׁאֵילְתֵּיהּ לְרַב נַחְמָן, וַאֲמַר לִי: מִינֵּיהּ דְּמַר שְׁמוּאֵל לָא שְׁמִיעַ לִי, אֶלָּא נֶחֱזֵי אֲנַן (ברכות מט,ב)
and he (= Rav Amram) asked Rav Nahman, and he said to me: I have not heard [this point] from Shmuel, but let us investigate (the issue on our own)

* The verb חזי, *see*, is not necessarily meant literally. The amora Rav Yosef uses this expression several times — even though he was blind, e.g., in גיטין לג,ב; מד, סע"ב.

נִיחַיֵּיב
SEE: לִיחַיֵּיב

נִיחְשׁוֹב/נַחְשׁוֹב fut. (חשב) יַחְשֹׁב; יִמְנֶה; יְפָרֵט
let him consider; let him enumerate/specify
SEE: לִיחְשׁוֹב, חָשֵׁיב

נִיטְפַּל/נִטְפַּל (טפל נִפְעַל: נִטְפָּל prt.)
(1) he joined; he attached himself
וְאִם כֵּן עָנַשׁ הַכָּתוּב לַנִּטְפָּל לְעוֹבְרֵי עֲבֵירָה כְּעוֹבְרֵי עֲבֵירָה, עַל אַחַת כַּמָּה וְכַמָּה יְשַׁלֵּם שָׂכָר לַנִּטְפָּל לְעוֹשֵׂי מִצְוָה כְּעוֹשֵׂי מִצְוָה. (מכות ה, סע"ב: משנה פ"א מ"ז)
And if Scripture has thus punished one who attaches himself to criminal offenders like criminal offenders, how much more will [the Almighty] grant a reward to one who attaches himself to performers of a mitzva like performers of a mitzva.

(2) he addressed; he accosted
כְּשֶׁחָרַב הַבַּיִת בַּשְּׁנִיָּה, רַבּוּ פְרוּשִׁין בְּיִשְׂרָאֵל שֶׁלֹּא לֶאֱכוֹל בָּשָׂר וְשֶׁלֹּא לִשְׁתּוֹת יַיִן. נִטְפַּל לָהֶם ר' יְהוֹשֻׁעַ, אָמַר לָהֶן: בָּנַי! מִפְּנֵי מָה אִי אַתֶּם אוֹכְלִין בָּשָׂר, וְאֵין אַתֶּם שׁוֹתִים יַיִן? (ב"ב ס,ב)
When the Beth HaMikdash was destroyed the second time, ascetics who refrained from eating meat and from drinking wine became numerous in Israel. R. Yhoshua accosted them [and] said to them: My sons! Why do you not eat meat and not drink wine?

נַיֵּיד prt. (נוד) נָד; נָע
moving; mobile; animate
שָׁאנֵי מִטַּלְטְלֵי דְּנָיְידֵי מִמִּטַּלְטְלֵי דְּלָא נָיְידֵי.* (ב"ק יב, רע"ב)
Animate movables (= slaves) are different from inanimate movables.

* In post-Talmudic Hebrew, the term נִכְסֵי דְּלָא נָיְידֵי (acronym: נדל"ן) means *immovable property, real estate.* See also the note on the next entry.

נֵייח* .prt (נוח) נָח **resting; at rest; stationary**

גּוּפוֹ נֵייח; יָדוֹ לֹא נֵייח (שבת ג, סע״א)

His body is at rest; his hand is not at rest.

* In Modern Hebrew, the adjective נַיָּח is used in contradistinction to נַיָּד, *mobile.* מַשְׁגְּרֵי טִילִים נַיָּחִים וְנַיָּדִים means *stationary and mobile missile launchers.*

SEE: נָח

נֵיים/נָאֵים .prt (נום)

sleeping; dosing יָשֵׁן; מְנַמְנֵם

For example, see אָמִינָא כִּי נֵיים וְשָׁכֵיב רַב אֲמַר לְהָא שְׁמַעְתָּא

SEE: נִים

נֵייתֵי/נַיְתֵי .fut (אתי אַפְעֵל)

let him bring יָבִיא

SEE: לַיְיתֵי, נֵיתֵי, אַתְּיָא

נֵיכוּל .fut (אכל) נֹאכַל; יֹאכַל **let us/him eat**

SEE: לֵיכוּל

נִיכְתּוֹב

SEE: נִכְתּוֹב

נֵילַף .fut (ילף) נִלְמַד; יִלְמַד **let us/him derive**

SEE: לֵילַף, יְלַף

נִים (נום: נֵיים/נָאֵים .prt)

he slept; he was dosing יָשֵׁן, נִמְנֵם

נִים וְלָא נִים, תִּיר וְלָא תִּיר (פסחים קכ, רע״ב וש״נ)

he was asleep but not asleep, awake but not awake

נֵימָא .fut (אמר)

let us/him say; shall we say נֹאמַר; יֹאמַר

SEE: לֵימָא, אֲמַר

נִימָא (.pl נִימִין) חוּט **thread; string**

אֵין בֵּין טִיפָּה לְטִיפָּה אֶלָּא כִּמְלֹא נִימָא. (תענית ט,ב)

There is only the breadth of a thread between one drop and another.

נִינְהוּ (.f. pl נִינְהִי*) הֵם **they are; are they**

הָנֵי הִלְכְתָא נִינְהוּ?! הָנֵי קְרָאֵי נִינְהוּ! (נדרים עב, ב ע״פ כת״י)

*Are these halakhoth [based on oral tradition]?! (No!) They are [based on] p*e*sukim!*

* In our printed editions, נִינְהוּ is used for the plural — masculine as well as feminine. Sometimes, however, נִינְהִי is found in manuscripts as a distinct feminine plural form. For example, see ברכות לד,א according to the Munich Manuscript.

SEE: נִיהוּ, אָמוֹרָאֵי נִינְהוּ וְאַלִּיבָּא דְּר׳ יוֹחָנָן, אִיהוּ

נֵיעוּל .fut (עלל) יָבוֹא **let him come**

SEE: לֵיעוּל, עַל

נִיפְלוֹג .fut (פלג) יַחֲלֹק; יַבְחִין; נַחֲלֹק

let him disagree; let him distinguish; let him/us divide

SEE: לִיפְלוֹג, פְּלִיג, פְּלַג

נֵיקוּם .fut (קום)

let us/him stand נַעֲמֹד; יַעֲמֹד

SEE: לֵיקוּם, קָם

נִיקְנֵי .fut (קני) נִקְנֶה; יִקְנֶה **let us/him acquire**

SEE: לִיקְנֵי, קְנֵי

נִישְׁקוֹל

SEE: נִשְׁקוֹל

נֵיתֵי/נֵייתֵי* .fut (אתי)

let him/us come יָבֹא; נָבֹא

נֵיתֵי מָר וְנִיתְנֵי! (הוריות יג, סע״ב ועוד)

Let the master come and teach!

* נֵיתֵי, *let him come,* also occurs several times.

SEE: נַיְתֵי, אֲתָא, לֵיתֵי

נַיְתֵי

SEE: נֵייתֵי

נִיתֵּיב

SEE: לִיתֵּיב[1], לִיתֵּיב[2]

נִיתַּן (נתן נִפְעַל: נִיתָּן .pass. prt, יִנָּתֵן .fut)

it was given; it was put

Besides this common meaning, the following usages are found in the Talmud:

(1) it was permitted

לֹא נִיתַּן לְאַחוֹתוֹ (מועד קטן כו,ב)

it is not permitted to sew it (= the garment torn by a mourner for a parent)

(2) it was intended; it was meant; it was designated

רוֹב עֵצִים לְהַסָּקָה נִיתְּנוּ. (נדרים סב,ב)

Most wood was meant for heating.

נִיתְנֵי .fut (תני) יִשְׁנֶה; יְלַמֵּד; נְלַמֵּד

let him/us teach (in a mishna or baraitha)

SEE: לִיתְנֵי, תְּנָא

נְכֵי .pass. prt (נכי) פָּחוֹת; חָסֵר **less; minus**

חַמְשִׁין נְכֵי חֲדָא* (בבא מציעא צט, רע״ב)

fifty minus one (= forty-nine)

* The same construction is also used in Mishnaic Hebrew: אַרְבָּעִים חָסֵר אַחַת (שבת ע״ג סע״א: משנה פ״ז מ״ב)

נְכַס (נכס: נָכֵיס .prt, כּוֹס .imp)

he slaughtered שָׁחַט

וְהָאִידָּנָא נָכֵיס אַבָּא לְפוּם בְּרָא (סנהדרין כה, סע״ב ורש״י שם)

and now he will "slaughter" the father before the son

נִכְסֵי מְלוֹג* **"properties to pluck"**

These are properties — usually houses, real estate, or slaves — that a wife brings with her upon marriage (or that she inherits after marriage) under the following terms: The properties continue to belong to her, with the husband benefiting only from their "fruits" (such as rent, produce of a field, or the work of a slave) as long as the couple is married. He does not have the right to sell them or to give them away without her approval, nor is she permitted to sell them or to give them away during the marriage without his permission. Upon divorce or death of the husband, the property reverts to her absolute control.

בְּאוּשָׁא הִתְקִינוּ: הָאִשָּׁה שֶׁמָּכְרָה בְּנִכְסֵי מְלוֹג בְּחַיֵּי בַּעְלָהּ וּמֵתָה — הַבַּעַל מוֹצִיא מִיַּד הַלָּקוֹחוֹת. (בבא מציעא לה, סע"א)

In Usha [the ḥakhamim] enacted: [As for] a wife who sold some "properties to pluck" during the life of her husband and died — the husband may take them away from the purchasers.

* The term is derived from the root מלג, *to pluck* (as in ביצה לד,א), since the husband may "pluck" (= gain from) its produce.

SEE: נִכְסֵי צֹאן בַּרְזֶל

נִכְסֵי צֹאן בַּרְזֶל **"properties of iron sheep"**

These are properties that a wife transfers to her husband upon marriage under the following terms: He is permitted to do with them as he pleases, but he is held responsible for them to the extent of their worth at the time of the marriage. Their worth is thus as unchangeable as iron.

For an example — see בבא קמא פט,א. See also צֹאן בַּרְזֶל in בבא מציעא סט, סע"ב ורש"י שם.

SEE: נִכְסֵי מְלוֹג

נְכָסִים; נִכְסִין/נִכְסֵי* **property**

For examples — see the two previous entries and the next four entries.

* The first form is Hebrew, and the others are Aramaic. In the Mishna and the Talmud, this noun is always in the plural. Modern Hebrew, however, sometimes uses the singular נֶכֶס in the sense of *an asset* or *a valuable commodity*.

נְכָסִים בְּנֵי חוֹרִין; בְּנֵי חָרֵי*

"free" properties

Properties belonging to a debtor (usually a borrower) at the time the debt was incurred and supported by a promissory note are automatically mortgaged to that debt and may be seized by the creditor up to the amount of the debt as repayment. If the properties still remain in the possession of the debtor, they are termed *"free" properties*, since they are not under obligation to a third party.

אֵין נִפְרָעִין מִנְּכָסִים מְשׁוּעְבָּדִים בִּמְקוֹם שֶׁיֵּשׁ נְכָסִים בְּנֵי חוֹרִין. (גיטין מח,ב: משנה פ"ה מ"ב)

Compensation may not be exacted from "subjugated" properties (that have been sold to a third party) where there are "free" properties available (from which the debt may be collected).

* The first expression is Hebrew, and בְּנֵי חָרֵי is Aramaic.

SEE: בְּנֵי חוֹרִין, נְכָסִים מְשׁוּעְבָּדִים

נְכָסִים מְשׁוּעְבָּדִים; מְשַׁעְבְּדֵי*

"subjugated" properties

Properties belonging to a debtor (usually a borrower) at the time the debt was incurred and supported by a promissory note are automatically mortgaged to that debt. They may be seized by the creditor as repayment — up to the amount of the debt — even from a third party to whom they were sold in the meantime. If the properties have already been transferred to a third party, they are termed *"subjugated" properties*, in that they are subjugated to the third party.

מִנְּכָסִים מְשׁוּעְבָּדִים כֵּיצַד? מָכַר נְכָסָיו לַאֲחֵרִים, וְהִיא נִפְרַעַת מִן הַלָּקוֹחוֹת — לֹא תִפָּרַע אֶלָּא בִשְׁבוּעָה. (כתובות פז, סע"א: משנה פ"ט מ"ח)

How [does a widow or a divorcee collect her marriage contract] from mortgaged properties? [If her husband] had sold his property to others, and she seeks to be paid from the purchaser — she is not to be paid unless [she takes] an oath [that she is really entitled to payment].

* The first expression is Hebrew, and מְשַׁעְבְּדֵי is Aramaic.

SEE: נְכָסִים בְּנֵי חוֹרִין, שִׁעְבֵּד

נְכָסִים שֶׁאֵין לָהֶם אַחֲרָיוּת (= מִטַּלְטְלִין)

property which does not offer security (= movable property)

This term is appropriate because, even though a creditor may collect his debt from movable properties still in the debtor's possession, movables do not provide security to the creditor, since they can be concealed or transferred to another party.

וּ[נְכָסִים] שֶׁאֵין לָהֶם אַחֲרָיוּת אֵינָן נִקְנִין אֶלָּא בִמְשִׁיכָה (קידושין כו, רע"א: משנה פ"א מ"ה)

but [property] which does not offer security may be acquired only by pulling (the object to be acquired into one's possession)

SEE: מִטַּלְטְלִין

נְכָסִים שֶׁיֵּשׁ לָהֶם אַחֲרָיוּת (= קַרְקָעוֹת)

property which offers security (= real estate; land and houses)

This term is appropriate because land provides security to a creditor, since it cannot be concealed by the debtor. If the loan was supported by a promissory note, the land remains liable to seizure even if subsequently sold to someone else.

נְכָסִים שֶׁיֵּשׁ לָהֶם אַחֲרָיוּת נִקְנִין בְּכֶסֶף וּבִשְׁטָר וּבַחֲזָקָה. (קידושין כו, רע"א: משנה פ"א מ"ה)

Property which offers security is acquired by money, by a document, or by taking possession (by a formal act of acquisition, such as building a fence around it).

SEE: מְקַרְקְעֵי

נִכְתּוֹב/נִיכְתּוֹב fut. (כתב)

let him/it write יִכְתֹּב

SEE: לִכְתּוֹב

נַמֵּי

This word is always placed *after* the word with which it is connected.

... also; ... too **(1) ... גַּם כֵּן**

הַשְׁתָּא נַמֵּי (בבא מציעא ה, סע״א ועוד)
now also

even; indeed* **(2) ... אֲפִילוּ**

even granted he is liable נְהִי נַמֵּי דְּמִחַיַּיב (יבמות סו,ב)

yes, it is indeed so אִין, הָכִי נַמֵּי (חגיגה ד,א ועוד)

* **Sometimes, נַמֵּי expresses emphasis that need not be rendered in translation.**

SEE: אִי נַמֵּי, נְהִי נַמֵּי, הָכִי נַמֵּי, אִין הָכִי נַמֵּי

נִמְלַךְ (מלך נִפְעַל: נִמְלָךְ .prt, לִימָּלֵךְ .inf)

(1) he consulted (with)

הָיָה לוֹ לִימָּלֵךְ בְּיִרְמְיָהוּ, וְלֹא נִמְלַךְ (תענית כב,ב)

*he (= the king) should have consulted with Yirm*ᵉ*yahu, but he did not consult*

(2) he reconsidered; he changed his mind

כָּתַב לְגָרֵשׁ אֶת אִשְׁתּוֹ, וְנִמְלַךְ ... פָּסוּל לְגָרֵשׁ בּוֹ. (גיטין כד, סע״א: משנה פ״ג מ״א)

[If] he wrote [a bill of divorce] to divorce his wife, and he changed his mind ... [the document] is invalid for divorcing with it.

SEE: אִימְּלִיךְ, **the Aramaic equivalent**

נִמְנוּ (מני נִפְעַל) .pl

they were counted; they voted

נִמְנוּ וְגָמְרוּ

they voted and reached a decision

For an example — see סנהדרין עד,א.

נִמְצָא (מצא נִפְעַל; יִמָּצֵא .fut)

(1) he/it was found; he found himself

נִמְצָא עוֹמֵד בַּמִּזְרָח, מַחֲזִיר פָּנָיו לַמַּעֲרָב; בַּמַּעֲרָב, מַחֲזִיר פָּנָיו לַמִּזְרָח. (ברכות ל,א)

[If] one found himself standing east [of the Holy of Holies when he was about to recite the Amida], he should face westward; [if] west, he should face eastward.

(2) it was discovered; it turned out; he concluded (after a thorough analysis)

... נִמְצְאוּ כָּל יִשְׂרָאֵל מְכַוְּנִין אֶת לִבָּם לְמָקוֹם אֶחָד. (ברכות שם)

... it turned out [that] all of the Jewish people were directing their hearts to one place.

SEE: אִישְׁתְּכַח

נִמְצֵאתָ אַתָּה אוֹמֵר

you conclude (after examining the matter and) say

נִמְצֵאתָ אַתָּה אוֹמֵר: בִּשְׁלֹשָׁה מְקוֹמוֹת קָדְשׁוּ בְכוֹרוֹת לְיִשְׂרָאֵל — בְּמִצְרַיִם, וּבַמִּדְבָּר, וּבִכְנִיסָתָן לָאָרֶץ. (בכורות ד, סע״ב)

You conclude (and) say: In three places the first-born became sanctified for Israel — in Egypt, and in the wilderness, and at their entrance into Erets Yisrael.

SEE: אִם תִּמְצָא לוֹמַר, (כְּשֶׁתִּמְצָא לוֹמַר

נְסַב/נְסֵיב (נְסֵיב .prt, לִנְסֵיב .fut, מֵינְסַב .inf)

(1) לָקַח; תָּפַס

he took; he mentioned (in a text); he quoted

אַיְידֵי דִּנְסֵיב רֵישָׁא "שָׁמְרוֹ", תְּנָא סֵיפָא "וַאֲנִי אֶשְׁמְרֶנּוּ" (בבא קמא מח, סע״ב)

since the first clause mentioned "watch it," the final clause stated "and I will watch it" (so that the two clauses be parallel)

הָתָם אַגַּב גְּרָרָא נְסָבָהּ (בבא מציעא ד, סע״ב)

there he mentioned it incidentally

וְנָסְבִין חַבְרַיָּיא לְמֵימַר (חולין יד, רע״א, ע׳ רש״י שם)

and the ḥaverim take [upon themselves] to say

he took a wife; he married **(2) נָשָׂא אִשָּׁה**

כִּי נְסֵיב אֱינִישׁ אִתְּתָא (ברכות ח,א)

when a man marries a woman

* **See Targum Onkelos and the commentary of Rashi on** בראשית מג:טו. **Rashi explains the difference between** נְסַב **and** דְּבַר.

SEE: כְּדֵי נַסְבָהּ, אַנְסֵיב, אִינְסִיבָא, דְּבַר

נִסְכָּא*

a piece of **חֲתִיכַת מַתֶּכֶת**
(raw, unminted) metal (usually silver)

הַהוּא גַּבְרָא דַּחֲטַף נִסְכָּא מֵחַבְרֵיהּ ... (בבא בתרא לג, סע״ב)

One man seized a piece of metal from his fellow man...

* **This noun is related to the Hebrew verb** נָסַךְ, ***he cast (metal).***

נַעֲבֵיד/נֵיעֲבֵד (עבד) נַעֲשֶׂה; יַעֲשֶׂה

let us/him do

SEE: לֶיעֱבֵיד, עֲבַד

נַעֲנָה (ענה נִפְעַל)

(1) he was answered; his request was granted

... וּכְשֶׁאָמַר: "זְכוֹר לְאַבְרָהָם לְיִצְחָק וּלְיִשְׂרָאֵל עֲבָדֶיךָ", מִיָּד נַעֲנָה. (שבת ל,א ע״פ שמות לב:יג)

... and when he (= Moshe Rabbenu) said: "Remember Avraham, Yitzḥak, and Yisrael Your servants," he was immediately answered.

(2) he began by saying; he began to speak*

In this sense, this verb is used together with the verb אמר.

כְּשֶׁחָלָה ר׳ אֱלִיעֶזֶר נִכְנְסוּ אַרְבָּעָה זְקֵנִים לְבַקְּרוֹ — ר׳ טַרְפוֹן וְר׳ יְהוֹשֻׁעַ וְר׳ אֶלְעָזָר בֶּן עֲזַרְיָה וְר׳ עֲקִיבָא. נַעֲנָה ר׳ טַרְפוֹן וְאָמַר ... נַעֲנָה ר׳ יְהוֹשֻׁעַ וְאָמַר ... (סנהדרין קא, סע״א)

*When R. Eliezer took sick, four elders came in to visit him — R. Tarfon, R. Y*ᵉ*hoshua, R. El'azar b. Azarya, and R. Akiva. R. Tarfon began by saying ... R. Y*ᵉ*hoshua began by saying ...*

(3) he was humbled; he submitted himself**

נַעֲנֵיתִי לָךְ, מְחוֹל לִי! (ברכות כח,א)

I am humbled before you, forgive me!

* **This meaning is found in Biblical Hebrew, e.g., in the**

pasuk: וְעָנִיתָ וְאָמַרְתָּ (דברים כו:ה ורש"י וראב"ע שם).
** This meaning is found in Biblical Hebrew, e.g., in the pasuk: עַד מָתַי מֵאַנְתָּ לֵעָנֹת מִפָּנָי (שמות י:ג ות"א ורש"י שם).

נַעֲרָה **maiden**

This term refers to a girl between twelve and twelve-and-a-half years old who has reached puberty. She is בַּת מִצְוָה, *obligated by the commandments*, but she is not fully considered an adult according to Jewish law in terms of her personal status.

For an example — see כתובות מ,ב: משנה פ"ג מ"ח.
SEE: בּוֹגֶרֶת

נַעֲשָׂה כְּאוֹמֵר **it becomes as if he says ...**

This formula presents a *legal fiction* that presumes that one of the parties to a conflict made a certain statement.

נַעֲשָׂה כְּאוֹמֵר לוֹ: לִכְשֶׁתִּגָּנֵב וְתִרְצֶה וּתְשַׁלְּמֵנִי — הֲרֵי פָּרָתִי קְנוּיָה לְךָ מֵעַכְשָׁיו. (בבא מציעא לד, רע"א)
It becomes as if he has said to him: If it will be stolen, and you will be willing to pay me, behold my cow is transferred to you from now.

נַפְּחָא נַפָּח **blacksmith**

ר' יִצְחָק נַפְּחָא (בבא מציעא כד, סע"ב ועוד)
R. Yitzhak, the blacksmith

נְפִישׁ pass. prt. (נפש) מְרֻבֶּה

(1) much; considerable

נְפִישׁ טִירְחַיְיהוּ (בבא מציעא כא, סע"א)
Their bother (to pick them up) is considerable.

(2) many; numerous; more numerous

הָנָךְ נְפִישָׁן. (שבת כה, רע"ב) *Those are more numerous.*

נְפַק (נפק:* נָפֵיק .prt, לִיפּוֹק .fut, פּוּק .imp, לְמִיפַּק .inf)

(1) יָצָא he went out; it came out; it resulted

נְפַק מִילְּתָא מִבֵּינַיְיהוּ. (בבא קמא יט, רע"ב ועוד)
A matter (= a halakhic point) came out of [the discussion] between them.

נָפֵיק מִינֵּיהּ חוּרְבָּא (שבת כט,ב ורש"י שם ועוד)
misfortune will result from it

(2) יָצָא; נִלְמַד it was derived

וְהָא מֵהָכָא נָפְקָא?! מֵהָתָם נָפְקָא! (למשל סנהדרין נו,א)
But is it derived from here?! It is derived from there!

(3) יָצָא יְדֵי חוֹבָתוֹ he fulfilled his obligation

דִּבְעִידָּנָא דְּאַגְבְּהֵיהּ נְפַק בֵּיהּ (פסחים ז,ב ע"פ כת"י)
for at the moment he picked it up (= the lulav with the other three species), he fulfilled his obligation

* For the full conjugation of this verb, see *Grammar for Gemara*: Chapter 4, Verb 6.
SEE: אַפֵּיק, יָצָא

נְפַק דָּק וְאַשְׁכַּח יָצָא, עִיֵּן (בְּסֵפֶר), וּמָצָא

he went out, examined [his sources], and found [an answer]

In order to determine the halakha in a particular case, an amora sometimes had to study whatever sources were available to him — usually a mishna or a baraitha.

אֲמַר לֵיהּ רַב חִסְדָּא לְרַבָּה: פּוּק עַיֵּין בָּהּ, דְּלְאוּרְתָּא בָּעֵי מִינָּךְ רַב הוּנָא! נְפַק דָּק וְאַשְׁכַּח, דִּתְנַן ... (בבא מציעא יח, רע"ב)
Rav Ḥisda said to Rabba: Go out [and] look into it, for in the evening Rav Huna will ask you [about the case]! He went out, examined [his sources], and found [an answer], as we learned in a mishna ...

נָפְקָא לֵיהּ "יוֹצֵאת לוֹ"; הוּא לוֹמֵד אוֹתָהּ

it is derived by him; he derives it

כָּל אִיסּוּרִין שֶׁבַּתּוֹרָה — מְנָא לֵיהּ דַּאֲסוּרִין בַּהֲנָאָה? נָפְקָא לֵיהּ מִ"לַּכֶּלֶב תַּשְׁלִיכוּן אוֹתוֹ" — אוֹתוֹ אַתָּה מַשְׁלִיךְ לַכֶּלֶב, וְאִי אַתָּה מַשְׁלִיךְ לַכֶּלֶב כָּל אִיסּוּרִין שֶׁבַּתּוֹרָה. (פסחים כא,סע"ב-כב,רע"א ע"פ שמות כב:ל)
[As far as] all foods forbidden by the Torah — from where [does he derive that] one is forbidden to benefit from them? He derives it from: "You shall cast it (= a carcass) to the dogs" — "it" you may cast to the dogs (as dog food and thus benefit from it), but you may not cast to the dogs any (other) foods forbidden by the Torah.

נָפְקָא מִינַּהּ יוֹצֵאת מִמֶּנָּה

it is derived from it; the halakhic difference (or significance) is*

"סִימָן לִשְׁפֵלָה שִׁקְמָה." נָפְקָא מִינַּהּ לְמִקָּח וּמִמְכָּר. (פסחים נג,א ורש"י שם)
"A characteristic of lowland is the sycamore tree." The halakhic significance is with respect to buying and selling. (If there is a transaction of lowland, it must contain a sycamore tree.)

* In colloquial speech among students of the Talmud and in Modern Hebrew, נָפְקָא מִינָּה is also used as a noun, meaning *difference*, as in the translation of this entry.

נֶפֶשׁ **soul; life; person; desire; wish**

Besides the common Biblical meanings of this Hebrew noun: *soul, life* or *person* — another important meaning in the Talmud and in midrᵉshé halakha is *desire* or *wish*.*

For examples, see מָה נַפְשָׁךְ and (וְ)אִם נַפְשָׁךְ לוֹמַר.
* This usage also occurs in Biblical Hebrew, as in the pasuk: אִם יֵשׁ אֶת נַפְשְׁכֶם לִקְבֹּר אֶת מֵתִי (בראשית כג:ח ורש"י שם).

נַפְשָׁא נֶפֶשׁ **soul; life; person**

עַבְדֵּיהּ דְּיַנַּאי מַלְכָּא קְטַל נַפְשָׁא. (סנהדרין יט,א)
The slave of King Yannai killed a person.

The Aramaic -נַפְשׁ is often used with personal-pronoun suffixes in the sense of *himself, herself,* and so on.*

himself; itself (m.)	עַצְמוֹ	נַפְשֵׁיה
herself; itself (f.)	עַצְמָהּ	נַפְשַׁהּ
themselves	עַצְמָם	נַפְשַׁיְיהוּ

קַמָּאֵי הֲווֹ קָא מָסְרֵי נַפְשַׁיְיהוּ אַקְּדוּשַּׁת הַשֵּׁם. (ברכות כ,א)

The earlier (generations) used to sacrifice their lives for the sanctity of God.

* For a complete listing of the forms thus produced, see *Grammar for Gemara:* Chapter 7.34.

SEE: אַדַּעְתָּא דְנַפְשֵׁיהּ, (בְּ)אַפֵּי נַפְשֵׁיהּ, טַעְמָא דְנַפְשֵׁיהּ קָאָמַר, נָח נַפְשֵׁיהּ, קָרֵי אַנַּפְשֵׁיהּ

נְקוֹט ... בִּידָךְ תְּפֹס ... בְּיָדְךָ!

"Hold ... in your hand!" Adopt (this principle or ruling as a guide for your halakhic decisions)!

נְקוֹט הַאי כְּלָלָא בִּידָךְ! (שבת קמז,א וש"נ)

Adopt this general rule!

Adopt [the ruling] of Rav! נְקוֹט דְּרַב בִּידָךְ! (שבת כד,א)

נְקַט (נקט: נָקֵיט act. prt., נְקִיט pass. prt., לִינְקוֹט fut., נְקוֹט imp., לְמִינְקַט inf.)

(1) אָחַז; תָּפַס he held; he seized

נָקֵיט חֶפְצָא בִּידֵיהּ* (שבועות לח, סע"ב)

he was holding a (sacred) object in his hand

(2) נָקַט he mentioned (in a text); he used (an expression)

וְתַנָּא חֲדָא מִינַּיְיהוּ נָקַט (סוטה ת,א וע' יבמות מח,ב וש"נ)

but the tanna used one of them (by way of example, even though the rule applies to other instances as well)

לִישָּׁנָא מְעַלְּיָא הוּא דְּנָקַט (פסחים ג,א וש"נ)

a euphemism is what he used

* The Hebrew expression נְקִיטַת חֵפֶץ is also used in this context by the Rambam and other post-Talmudic authorities. See רמב"ם הל' שבועות פי"א הי"א.

נָקְטִינַן* (= נָקְטֵי act. prt. + אֲנַן); נְקִיטִינַן* (= נְקִיטֵי pass. prt. + אֲנַן)

תְּפוּסִים אָנוּ; מְקֻבָּל בְּיָדֵינוּ

we hold; we have a tradition

An amora (most commonly Abbayé) uses this term to introduce an important statement, usually a halakha, that he received from his teachers.

אָמַר אַבַּיֵי: נְקִיטִינַן — שְׁנַיִם שֶׁאָכְלוּ כְּאַחַת מִצְוָה לֵיחָלֵק. (ברכות מה,ב)

Abbayé said: We have a tradition — [if] two persons have eaten together, it is [their] duty to separate (to recite Birkath HaMazon individually).

* These two forms both occur in the Talmud without any significant distinction between them in meaning or usage.

SEE: גְּמִיר

נִרְאָה (ראי נִפְעַל: נִרְאָה prt.)

(1) it was seen; it appeared [to be]

נִרְאִין כְּאוֹהֲבִין בִּשְׁעַת הֲנָאָתָן, וְאֵין עוֹמְדִין לוֹ לָאָדָם בִּשְׁעַת דָּחְקוֹ. (משנה אבות פ"ב מ"ג)

They (= the governmental authorities) appear [to be his] friends when it is to their advantage, but they don't stand up for a person in a time of his distress.

(2) it was fit

נִרְאָה וְנִדְחָה (סוכה לג,ב)

it had been fit but was (later) disqualified

(3) it was acceptable

נִרְאִין* דִּבְרֵי ר' אֱלִיעֶזֶר בְּשַׁבָּת וְדִבְרֵי ר' יְהוֹשֻׁעַ בְּחוֹל. (בבא מציעא נד,א)

The opinion of R. Eliezer is acceptable with respect to [eating on] the Sabbath, and the opinion of R. Y^e^hoshua [is acceptable] with respect to [eating on] a weekday.

* Rashi (לעירובין מו,ב) and Tosafoth (שם ד"ה ר' אסי) differ as to the halakhic significance of this term.

נַרְגָּא גַּרְזֶן ax

שְׁדָא בֵּיהּ נַרְגָּא (פסחים לב, סע"ב)

"he swung an ax at it" (= he refuted the statement)

נַשׁ

SEE: בַּר נַשׁ

נָשָׁא

SEE: בֵּי נָשָׁא

נָשָׂא וְנָתַן "he took and he gave";

he dealt; he conducted business; he debated

Did you deal faithfully? נָשָׂאתָ וְנָתַתָּ בֶּאֱמוּנָה? (שבת לא,א)

SEE: שַׁקְלָא וְטַרְיָא

נָשִׂיא; נְשִׂיאָה* *Nasi;* Patriarch

This title was accorded to the president of the Sanhedrin who was also recognized as the leader of the Jewish people during the Second Temple period. The second in rank was the *av beth din.*

ר' יְהוּדָה הַנָּשִׂיא הַיְינוּ רַבִּי. (שבת לב,ב וש"נ)

R. Y^e^huda HaNasi is identical with Rebbi.

* The first form is Hebrew, and the second is Aramaic.

SEE: בֵּי נְשִׂיאָה, אַב בֵּית דִּין

נִשְׁקוֹל/נִישְׁקוֹל fut. (שקל) יִטֹּל let him take

SEE: לִישְׁקוֹל, שְׁקַל

ס

סְאָה (סְאִין .pl, סָאתַיִים dual) **s^e a**

This measure of volume is equal to the contents of 144 eggs.*

כָּל מָקוֹם שֶׁיֵּשׁ בּוֹ אַרְבָּעִים סְאָה טוֹבְלִין וּמַטְבִּילִין. (משנה מקואות פ"ה מ"ו)

[In] any place containing forty s^e as [of water] one may immerse [oneself] and immerse [vessels].

* See the table of measurements in Appendix II.

סָבָא (סַבְתָּא .f)

(1) זָקֵן adj. **older; elder**

רַב הַמְנוּנָא סָבָא* (פסחים קה, רע"א ועוד)

Rav Hamnuna the elder

(2) זָקֵן n. **an old man; an elder**

תְּנָא לֵיהּ הַהוּא סָבָא מִשּׁוּם ר׳ שִׁמְעוֹן (ברכות ה, רע"ב)

a certain elder taught him in the name of R. Shim'on

(3) אֲבִי הָאָב; אֲבִי הָאֵם **grandfather****

נֵיכְלֵיהּ אַרְיָא לְסָבָא! (כתובות עב,ב)

May a lion devour [your] grandfather!

* This usage of the Aramaic word to describe certain amoraim — probably to distinguish between them and others bearing the same name — parallels the Hebrew usage, like הִלֵּל הַזָּקֵן in משנה שביעית פ"י מ"ג.

** סָבָא is used frequently in Modern Hebrew — usually in this sense. It is popularly pronounced סָבָּא (by analogy with אַבָּא) — even in the name of the Israeli city that is properly vocalised כְּפַר סָבָא.

SEE: סַבְתָּא

סָבוּר; כְּסָבוּר (סְבוּרָה .f, סְבוּרִים .m. pl)

thinking; holding

This Hebrew passive participle has an active meaning. It is sometimes preceded by a -כ prefix, which may add a bit of emphasis.*

כְּסָבוּר רְשׁוּת הַיָּחִיד, וְנִמְצֵאת רְשׁוּת הָרַבִּים (שבת עג,א)

he was thinking [it is] a private domain, but it was discovered [to be] a public domain

* This usage may have a Biblical precedent in the emphatic -כ in כִּי הוּא כְּאִישׁ אֱמֶת (נחמיה ז:ב וראב"ע שם).

SEE: סבר

סְבוּר* מִינַּהּ

סָבְרוּ מִמֶּנָּה **they understood from it**

The students assumed a particular interpretation of an amoraic statement. Subsequently, the interpretation was found to be wanting in light of another amoraic statement.

אֲמַר שְׁמוּאֵל: אֵין קִידּוּשׁ אֶלָּא בִּמְקוֹם סְעוּדָה. סְבוּר מִינַּהּ: הָנֵי מִילֵּי מִבַּיִת לְבַיִת, אֲבָל מִמָּקוֹם לְמָקוֹם בְּחַד בֵּיתָא — לָא. אֲמַר לְהוּ רַב עָנָן בַּר תַּחְלִיפָא: זִימְנִין סַגִּיאִין הֲוָה קָאֵימְנָא קַמֵּיהּ דִּשְׁמוּאֵל וְנָחִית מֵאִיגְּרָא לְאַרְעָא וַהֲדַר מְקַדֵּשׁ. (פסחים קא,א)

Sh^e muel said: Kiddush is valid only in the place where the meal is eaten. They understood from it (= this statement) that [only in] the following circumstances [is the Kiddush invalid: where they moved] from [one] house [after reciting Kiddush] to [eat the meal in another] house, but not [where the meal is eaten after moving merely] from [one] place to [another] place within one house. Rav Anan b. Taḥlifa said to them: Many times I was standing before Sh^e muel, and he went down from the upper story to the ground floor and recited Kiddush again.

* The Aramaic form סְבוּר is a third-person, masculine-plural form of the past tense, the equivalent of סָבְרוּ. See *Grammar for Gemara:* Chapter 3.21.

SEE: סְבַר

סְבִירָא לֵיהּ הוּא סָבוּר **he holds; he thinks**

ר׳ חִיָּיא כְּר׳ מֵאִיר סְבִירָא לֵיהּ. (בבא מציעא ג,ב)

R. Ḥiyya holds [the same opinion] as R. Méir.

שְׁמוּאֵל טַעְמָא דְתַנָּא דִידַן קָאָמַר, וְלֵיהּ לָא סְבִירָא לֵיהּ. (בבא מציעא יב,א)

Sh^e muel [merely] states the reason of our tanna, but he himself does not agree with him.

SEE: סְבַר

סְבַר (סבר: סָבַר .act. prt, סְבִיר .pass. prt, לִיסְבַּר .fut)

(1) סָבַר **he held (an opinion)**

וְסָבַר ר׳ יוֹסֵי קָטָן אִית לֵיהּ זְכִיָּה מִדְּאוֹרַיְיתָא?! (ב"מ יב,א)

But does R. Yosé [really] hold that a minor has a right to acquire things according to the law of the Torah?!

(2) חָשַׁב; הֵבִין **he thought; he considered; he assumed; he understood**

סָבַר לְמֶיעְבַּד עוּבְדָא כְּמַתְנִיתִין (ראש השנה כז,א)

he considered issuing a ruling in accordance with our mishna

SEE: (וְ)אַתְּ לָא תִּסְבְּרָא ,(וְ)תִסְבְּרָא, the next five entries, and the previous three entries.

קָסָבַר (= קָא+סָבַר)

הוּא סוֹבֵר **he thinks; he holds (an opinion)**

קָסָבַר רָבָא: סִימָן הֶעָשׂוּי לִידָּרֵס הָוֵי סִימָן. (בבא מציעא כב,ב)

Rava holds: An (identifying) mark that is liable to be trampled upon is [considered] an (identifying) mark.

SEE: מַאי קָסָבַר

סְבַר וְקַבֵּיל* "חָשַׁב וְקִבֵּל"; הִתְחַיֵּב

"he thought (about it) and accepted (it)"; he has committed himself

חַיְיתָא דִקְטִירֵי סַבְרַתְּ וְקַבִּילַתְּ! (בבא מציעא ט, רע"א וש"נ)

You have committed yourself to [the purchase of] "a bag of knots" (= something of no value)!

* According to the סֵפֶר זִכָּרוֹן (a super-commentary on Rashi's Torah commentary by R. Avraham Bakrat, a refugee from the Spanish expulsion of 1492) on שמות טו:יג, this expression means סָבַל וְקִבֵּל, *he bore [it] and accepted [it]* — with ר replacing ל.

סָבַר לַהּ* כְּוָותֵיהּ בַּחֲדָא וּפְלִיג עֲלֵיהּ בַּחֲדָא

סוֹבֵר כְּמוֹתוֹ בְּאַחַת, וְחוֹלֵק עָלָיו בְּאַחַת.

He holds like him (= a specific tanna) with regard to one [point], but disagrees with him about another.

This proposal is presented as a *resolution* of a difficulty. After it was first assumed that this ḥakham (usually an amora) fully agreed with the opinion of a specific tanna, a contradiction arose between the two opinions. Now it is proposed that the ḥakham does not totally accept the opinion of the tanna after all, but he agrees with him about one issue and not about another.

For an example — see בבא מציעא כד, רע"ב.

* The pronoun לַהּ, *it*, is difficult to translate. Perhaps the literal translation is *he understands it (= the matter) like him.*

סְבָרָא

(1) סְבָרָה; דָּבָר הַנִּלְמָד בְּדֶרֶךְ הֶגְיוֹנִית

reason; an argument based on reason (as opposed to גְּמָרָא, *a received tradition*, or to קְרָא, *a Biblical source*)

הָא לָמָּה לִי קְרָא? סְבָרָא הוּא: דְּכָאֵיב לֵיהּ כֵּיבָא הוּא אָזֵיל לְבֵי אָסְיָא. (בבא קמא מו,ב)

But why do I need a pasuk (as a source for the halakha that the burden of proof is on the claimant, הַמּוֹצִיא מֵחֲבֵירוֹ עָלָיו הָרְאָיָה*)? There is an argument based on reason: The one who is suffering pain (who seeks to alter the status quo) should go to the doctor.*

(2) הֲבָנָה; טַעַם

understanding; rationale (behind a halakha)

גְּמָרָא גְמִירְנָא; סְבָרָא לָא יָדַעְנָא. (יומא לג, סע"א)

I have learned the halakha from tradition; (but) I do not know [its] rationale.

SEE: אִיבָּעֵית אֵימָא קְרָא אִיבָּעֵית אֵימָא סְבָרָא

סְבָרוּהָ

סָבְרוּ אוֹתָהּ

they understood it; they assumed

Some scholars in the beth midrash proposed an interpretation of a mishna or a baraitha that would prove a certain point. Subsequently, their interpretation is usually rejected.*

סְבָרוּהָ דְּכוּלֵּי עָלְמָא: סִימָן הַבָּא מֵאֵילָיו הָוֵי סִימָן (ב"מ כג,א)

they assumed that all [the tannaim would agree]: an identification mark that may have come by itself is a [valid] identification mark

* Exceptions are discussed by Tosafoth on בבא בתרא ב,א.

SEE: קָא סָלְקָא דַעְתָּךְ

סַבְתָּא

(1) זְקֵנָה **old woman**

הַהִיא סַבְתָּא דַּהֲוְיָא לַהּ תְּלָת בְּנָתָא ... (בבא מציעא לט, רע"ב)

There was an old woman who had three daughters ...

(2) אֵם הָאָב; אֵם הָאֵם **grandmother***

נִכְסַי לְסַבְתָּא. (בבא בתרא קכה, רע"ב ורשב"ם שם)

[I hereby bequeath] my possessions to [my] grandmother.

* This Aramaic noun is used in Modern Hebrew — usually in this second sense.

SEE: סָבָא

סְגָא

(סגי: סָגֵי .prt);

סְגֵי[1]

(סגי פָּעַל: מְסַגֵּי .prt, לְסַגּוֹיֵי .inf)

הָלַךְ **he walked; he passed; it circulated**

פְּסָלַתּוּ מַלְכוּת ... לָא סָגֵי כְּלָל (ב"מ מו, סע"ב ורש"י שם)

[a coin that] the government has invalidated ... does not circulate at all

SEE: סוּגְיָא

סַגִּי[2]*

(1) דַּי **enough**

בִּתְרֵי סַגִּי (בבא מציעא לב, רע"א)

it is enough with two (witnesses)

(2) רַב **much; abundant**

For an example — see סַגִּי נְהוֹר, the next entry.

(3) אֶפְשָׁר **possible**

For an example, see לָא סַגִּי דְלָא.

* This adjective is spelled שַׂגִּיא in Biblical Hebrew and Biblical Aramaic. See איוב לו:כו and דניאל ב:ו.

סַגִּי נְהוֹר*

"רַב אוֹר"; עִוֵּר

"abundant of light" (euphemistically)**; blind**

רַב שֵׁשֶׁת סַגִּי נְהוֹר הֲוָה (ברכות נח,א)

Rav Shesheth was blind

* A Hebrew euphemism for blindness, מְאוֹר עֵינַיִם, *the light of eyes*, is also found in the Talmud in חגיגה ה,ב. In later Hebrew literature, the term לְשׁוֹן סַגִּי נְהוֹר, *an expression of "much light,"* refers to any euphemism in which a meaning opposite to the literal meaning is intended.

SEE: סוּמָא

סַגִּיאִין

(סַגִּיאָן .f. pl) רַבִּים **many**

וְעָקָן סַגִּיאָן עֲתִידָן לְמֵיתֵי עַל עָלְמָא (סנהדרין יא, א)

and many troubles are destined to come upon the world

SEE: זִימְנִין סַגִּיאִין

סְגֵיד*

(סגד: סָגֵיד .prt)

הִשְׁתַּחֲוָה **he bowed**

חֲזָא אַנְדַּרְטָא וּסְגֵיד לֵיהּ (סנהדרין סב, סע"א)

he saw a statue and bowed down to it

* The Modern Hebrew מִסְגָּד, which is derived from the same root, means *a mosque.*

סָגָן* (constr. סְגַן)
high official; superintendent

ר' חֲנִינָא סְגַן הַכֹּהֲנִים (פסחים יד, רע"א: משנה פ"א מ"ו)
R. Hanina, the superintendent of the kohanim

* In Modern Hebrew, this word means *a deputy (official)*. Thus, a סְגַן יוֹשֵׁב רֹאשׁ is *a vice-chairman*. In the Israeli army, a סֶגֶן is *a lieutenant*. In Biblical Hebrew and Biblical Aramaic, it appears only in the plural (e.g., in עזרא ט:ב and דניאל ג:ב).

סַדְיָא
SEE: בֵּי סַדְיָא

סֵדֶר; סִידְרָא*
order; arrangement; section

This term sometimes designates any one of the six *sections* (or *orders*) of the Mishna. They are all mentioned by name in שבת לא, סע"א.

(1) סֵדֶר זְרָעִים *the order of seeds*
(dealing with agricultural halakha, prefaced by a tractate on the Sh^e^ma, the Amida and b^e^rakhoth)

(2) סֵדֶר מוֹעֵד *the order of festivals*

(3) סֵדֶר נָשִׁים *the order of women*
(dealing mainly with family life, marriage, and divorce)

(4) סֵדֶר נְזִיקִין *the order of damages*
(dealing with civil law, criminal law, and government)

(5) סֵדֶר קָדָשִׁים *the order of sacred matters*
(dealing with the Temple service and offerings)

(6) סֵדֶר טְהָרוֹת *the order of purities*

The Mishna as a whole is also referred to as the שִׁשָּׁה סְדָרִים in Hebrew and the שִׁיתָּא סִדְרֵי in Aramaic. The acronym for both expressions, שַׁ"ס, is applied to the Talmud as well.

וּמַתְנֵינָא שִׁיתָּא סִדְרֵי לְשִׁיתָּא יָנוּקֵי (כתובות קג, סע"ב)
and I was teaching the six sections (= the whole mishna) to six schoolboys

* The first form is Hebrew, and the second is Aramaic.
SEE: פְּסִיק סִידְרָא, where the Aramaic סִידְרָא refers to a *section* from נביאים or כְּתוּבִים.

סָהֲדָא* עֵד
a witness

לָא אִיבְּרוּ סָהֲדֵי אֶלָּא לְשַׁקָּרֵי. (קידושין סה, סע"ב)
[The institution of] witnesses was created only against liars [but witnesses are not essential in order to make a business transaction valid].

* This noun also occurs in Biblical Hebrew where it is spelled with a שׁ: הִנֵּה בַשָּׁמַיִם עֵדִי, וְשָׂהֲדִי בַּמְּרוֹמִים (איוב טז:יט).

סָהֲדוּתָא* עֵדוּת
testimony

כְּמַאן מְקַבְּלִינַן הָאִידָּנָא סָהֲדוּתָא מֵעַם הָאָרֶץ? (חגיגה כב,א)
According to whom (= which tanna) do we nowadays accept testimony from an uneducated person?

* This Aramaic noun occurs in the Torah, where it is spelled with a שׁ: יְגַר שָׂהֲדוּתָא (בראשית לא:מז).

סוּגְיָא* (= סֻגְיָא) מַהֲלָךְ
course; trend

וַעֲבַד כְּחַד מִינַּיְיהוּ, וְסוּגְיָא דִשְׁמַעְתָּא כְּאִידָךְ (סנהדרין לג,א; ע' רש"י שם שגרס "סוגיא דעלמא")
and [the hakham] ruled according to one of them (= the two disputing opinions), but the course of the discussion [tends] towards the other

* In Modern Hebrew, the noun סֻגְיָה means *a topic (for discussion), a subject, a problem.*
SEE: סְגָא

סוּדָר; סוּדָרָא*
scarf (which also covered the head)

כִּי פָּרִיס סוּדָרָא עַל רֵישֵׁיהּ (ברכות ס,ב)
when he arranges a scarf on his head

The scarf is also the classical object that is symbolically handed over by one party to the other to affirm an agreement. This procedure is termed קִנְיַן סוּדָר.

וְאִי אָמְרַתְּ מַטְבֵּעַ נִקְנָה בַּחֲלִיפִין, נִיקְנוּ לֵיהּ מָעוֹת לְהָאִיךְ אַגַּב סוּדָר! (בבא מציעא מו, רע"א ע"פ כת"י)
But if you say a coin may be acquired through exchange, let them transfer the money to the other party by means of a scarf!

* The first form is Hebrew, and the second is Aramaic.
SEE: חֲלִיפִין, קִנְיָן

סוּמָא; סַמְיָא*
a blind man

סוּמָא וּמִי שֶׁאֵינוֹ יָכוֹל לְכַוֵּין אֶת הָרוּחוֹת יְכַוֵּין לִבּוֹ כְּנֶגֶד אָבִיו שֶׁבַּשָּׁמַיִם. (ברכות ל,א)
A blind man or anyone who cannot tell directions (so that he cannot pray facing the direction of Jerusalem) should direct his heart towards his Father Who is in Heaven.

* The first form is Hebrew (and is pronounced by the Sephardim as סוֹמָא), and the second is Aramaic.
SEE: סַמֵּי, סַגִּי נְהוֹר

סוּמָק* אָדוֹם
red

דִּילְמָא דְּמָא דְּהַהוּא גַּבְרָא סוּמָק טְפֵי! (פסחים כה,ב)
Perhaps the blood of the other person is redder!

* The noun סֹמֶק, *redness, rouge,* or *blush,* and the verb הִסְמִיק, *it became red, he blushed,* have both entered Modern Hebrew.

סוֹף סוֹף
ultimately; after all; be that as it may

סוֹף סוֹף, מַתְנִיתָא הֵיכִי מְתָרְצָא? (בבא קמא י, רע"ב)
Be that as it may, how can the baraitha be explained?

סוֹפֵג (ספג) prt.
absorbing

סוֹפֵג אֶת הָאַרְבָּעִים
"he absorbs the forty"; he must receive the forty (in practice: thirty-nine) **lashes** (prescribed by the Torah)

For an example — see חולין עח,א: משנה פ"ה מ"א.
SEE: לוֹקֶה

סוֹפֵר; סָפְרָא*
(1) scribe

הַאי סָפְרָא דַּיְקָנָא כַּתְבֵיהּ. (עבודה זרה י, רע"א)
An accurate scribe wrote this (document).

(2) a (school) teacher

קִנְאַת סוֹפְרִים תַּרְבֶּה חָכְמָה. (בבא בתרא כב, רע"א)

Jealousy among teachers will increase wisdom.

(3) a Torah scholar; one of the *Sof^{e}rim*

The *Sof^{e}rim* were the Torah leaders of the Jewish people for several hundred years, from the time of Ezra until the time of the tannaim. In some passages, the term סוֹפְרִים is the equivalent of רַבָּנַן or חֲכָמִים, as in the example below.

בְּשֶׁל תּוֹרָה הַלֵּךְ אַחַר הַמַּחְמִיר; בְּשֶׁל סוֹפְרִים הַלֵּךְ אַחַר הַמֵּיקֵל. (עבודה זרה ז, סע"א)

[In controversies about laws] of Torah origin, follow the stricter view; in those of the Sof^{e}rim, follow the more lenient view.

* The first form is Hebrew, and the second is Aramaic.

SEE: דִּבְרֵי סוֹפְרִים

סָח* (סוח: סָח .prt) **he talked; he told**

סָח לִי זָקֵן אֶחָד מֵאַנְשֵׁי יְרוּשָׁלַיִם (גיטין נז, רע"ב)

one of the elders of Jerusalem told me

* According to Rashi, לָשׂוּחַ in בראשית כד:סג has a similar meaning, even though it is spelled with a שׂ. In Modern Hebrew too, the verb שָׂח means *he conversed*, and a שִׂיחָה is *a conversation* or *an informal talk*.

סְחוֹר סְחוֹר סָבִיב **around**

נְזִירָא סְחוֹר סְחוֹר! לְכַרְמָא לָא תִקְרַב! (שבת יג, סע"א וש"נ)

O Nazarite, [go] around! Do not approach the vineyard!

* The Hebrew verb סָחַר means *he moved around* or *he traded*, and סְחַרְחַר means *he circulated* or *he was dizzy*.

סִידְרָא SEE: פְּסֵיק סִידְרָא, סֵדֶר

סִיהֲרָא/סַהֲרָא*

the moon; moonlight סַהַר; יָרֵחַ

לָא אִיבְּרִי סִיהֲרָא אֶלָּא לְגִירְסָא. (עירובין סה,א)

Moonlight was created just for learning (Torah).

* According to the explanation of R. Avraham ibn Ezra, the noun הַסַּהַר in שיר השירים ז:ג is a Hebrew parallel of this Aramaic noun. In Modern Hebrew, סַהַר is occasionally used as *moon*, with חֲצִי סַהַר meaning *a crescent*.

סַיֵּים (סום פָּעֵל: מְסַיֵּים .prt)

(1) סִיֵּם; הִשְׁלִים **he completed; he concluded**

פָּתַח בַּחֲדָא, וְסַיֵּים בְּתַרְתֵּי (ברכות מט,א)

he began by [mentioning] one [phrase], and he concluded by [mentioning] both [phrases]

(2) כִּוֵּן; צִיֵּן בְּדִיּוּק

he specified; he indicated clearly

לָא מְסַיְּימִי קְרָאֵי. (בבא מציעא לא, סע"א ורש"י שם)

The p^{e}sukim do not specify (which one refers to loading the animal and which to unloading).

SEE: לָא סַיְּימוּהָ קַמֵּיהּ, תִּסְתַּיֵּים

סָיֵים (סום) .prt נוֹעֵל **putting on [shoes]**

הֲוָה סָיֵים מְסָאנֵי אוּכָּמֵי (תענית כב,א)

he was putting on black shoes

סַיֵּיעַ (סיע פָּעֵל: מְסַיֵּיעַ .prt, לְסַיּוּעַ .inf);

סַיֵּיעַ* (סיע פָּעֵל: מְסַיֵּיעַ .prt, לְסַיּוֹעֵי .inf)

he supported

תָּנֵי ר' חִיָּיא לְסַיּוֹעֵיהּ לְרַב. (שבועות מ,א)

R. Ḥiyya teaches (a baraitha) to support Rav.

* The first verb is Hebrew, and the second is Aramaic.

SEE: סַיַּיעְתָּא

סַיִיף; סַיְיפָא* **sword**

מִנַּיִן לַמּוּמָתִים בְּסַיִיף שֶׁהוּא מִן הַצַּוָּאר?** (כתובות לז,ב)

From where [do we deduce] regarding those executed by the sword that it (= the execution) is [done] at the neck?

* The first form is Hebrew, and the second is Aramaic. The Aramaic noun סַיָּיפָא, *a swordsman*, also occurs in the Talmud (עבודה זרה יז:ב). The Modern Hebrew equivalent, סַיָּף, is a participant in the sport of סִיּוּף, *fencing*.

** This mode of execution is also referred to as הֶרֶג. See סנהדרין מט, רע"ב: משנה פ"ז מ"א.

סָיֵיר (סור) .prt בּוֹדֵק; מְבַקֵּר

inspecting; visiting; superintending

אַבַּיֵי הֲוָה סָיֵיר נִכְסֵיהּ כָּל יוֹמָא וְיוֹמָא. (חולין קה,א)

Abbayé used to inspect his property every day.

* In modern Hebrew, the verb סִיֵּר (in the פִּעֵל conjugation) means *he toured* or *he scouted*, and a סִיּוּר means *a tour, an expedition*, or *a patrol*.

סִיכְּתָא (סִיכֵּי .pl) יָתֵד **peg**

הַאי מַאן דִּשְׁדָא סִיכְּתָא לְאַתּוּנָא חַיָּיב מִשּׁוּם מְבַשֵּׁל. (שבת עד,ב ורש"י שם)

One who threw a [moist wooden] peg into the oven is liable on account of cooking (on the Sabbath).

סִילְקָא סֶלֶק **beet; beets**

מַאי שְׁנֵי תַבְשִׁילִין? אָמַר רַב הוּנָא: סִילְקָא וְאָרוּזָא. (פסחים קיד, סע"ב)

What should the two cooked dishes (at the Seder) be? Rav Huna said: Beets and rice.

סַיַּיעְתָּא/סִיַּעְתָּא*

(1) עֶזְרָה **help; assistance**

סִיַּעְתָּא דִשְׁמַיָּא** (ב"ב נה, סע"א) *the help of Heaven*

(2) רְאָיָה **support; proof**

לָא תְיוּבְתָּא וְלָא סַיַּיעְתָּא (בבא מציעא מח,א)

[there would be] neither a refutation nor a support

* Do not confuse this Aramaic noun with the Hebrew סִיעָתוֹ, *his group, his followers, his colleagues* (from סִיעָה), usually in the phrase חִזְקִיָּה וְסִיעָתוֹ, *[King] Hizkiya and his colleagues*, as in בבא בתרא טו, רע"א.

** The Aramaic בְּסַיַּיעְתָּא דִשְׁמַיָּא, abbreviated בס"ד, is in common use today among religious Jews — especially on

the top of a letterhead — as an alternative to בְּעֶזְרַת הַשֵּׁם, which is abbreviated בע"ה or ב"ה.
SEE: סַיֵּיע

סִימֵּא (סמא פִּעֵל: מְסַמֵּא .prt) **he blinded**

סִימֵּא אֶת עֵינוֹ, נוֹתֵן לוֹ דְּמֵי עֵינוֹ. (בבא קמא פה,ב)
[If] he blinded someone's eye, he must pay him (= the victim) the value of his eye.
SEE: סוּמָא, סַמִּי

סִימָן; סִימָנָא*

(1) sign; indication

מֵאֵימָתַי מַתְחִילִין לִקְרוֹת קְרִיאַת שְׁמַע בְּעַרְבִית? ... מִשָּׁעָה שֶׁהַכֹּהֲנִים זַכָּאִין לֶאֱכוֹל בִּתְרוּמָתָן. סִימָן לַדָּבָר: צֵאת הַכּוֹכָבִים. (ברכות ב,ב)
From what time may we begin to recite the Shᵉma in the evening? ... From the time the kohanim are entitled to eat their tᵉruma. A sign for [this] matter [is] the appearance of the stars.

(2) a mark of identification (to prove ownership)

יָהִיבְנָא סִימָנָא, וְשָׁקִילְנָא לֵיהּ. (בבא מציעא כא, רע"ב)
I shall declare [my] identification mark [on the lost article], and I will receive it.

(3) a mnemonic aid; a device employed to assist the memory

אֵין תּוֹרָה נִקְנֵית אֶלָּא בְּסִימָנִין. (עירובין נד סע"ב ורש"י שם)
Torah may be mastered only with [the help of] mnemonic aids.

(a) Mnemonic devices are employed by certain tannaim (for example, R. Yᵉhuda in the Pesaḥ Haggada who formulated דצ"ך עד"ש באח"ב for *the ten plagues*) and amoraim (notably, Rav Naḥman b. Yitsḥak), and by the Talmud itself — in order to facilitate the recall of important data. The mnemonic usually consists of a word or a series of words that form a phrase, a clause, or a sentence. Occasionally (e.g., in שבת צ,ב), a Biblical or a Talmudic passage is used — but in a different sense from its original meaning. These mnemonics are generally introduced by the term וְסִימָנָךְ, *and your mnemonic aid [is]*, and they follow the material to which they refer.

בְּבֵי רַב אָמְרִי: רַב שָׁרֵי, וּשְׁמוּאֵל אָסַר. בִּנְהַרְדְּעָא אָמְרִי: רַב אָסַר, וּשְׁמוּאֵל שָׁרֵי. אָמַר רַב נַחְמָן בַּר יִצְחָק: וְסִימָנָךְ — אֵלּוּ מְקִילִין לְעַצְמָן, וְאֵלּוּ מְקִילִין לְעַצְמָן. (כתובות ו, רע"א)
In the school of Rav they say: Rav permits, while Shᵉmuel forbids. In Nᵉhardᵉa (Shᵉmuel's city) they say: Rav forbids, while Shᵉmuel permits. Rav Naḥman b. Yitsḥak said: And your mnemonic (to remember who says what) is: These make it easier for themselves, and those make it easier for themselves. (According to the school of Rav, it is Rav who holds the lenient view, and according to the authorities in Shᵉmuel's area, it is Shᵉmuel who is lenient).

(b) A more common type of mnemonic, which may actually be of post-Talmudic origin, refers to a series of statements that are about to be presented in sequence in the Talmud. These mnemonics consist of either a group of words or a group of letters — with one word or letter taken from each one of the statements that follow. The group of words or the acronym (רָאשֵׁי תֵּבוֹת) thus formed by the letters sometimes has a meaning. In our printed editions of the Talmud, these mnemonics are enclosed within parentheses together with the word סִימָן, which appears either before or after the mnemonic itself.

(עֲמָלֵק סימן) תָּנוּ רַבָּנַן: עָרֵב מֵעִיד לַלֹּוֶה ... מַלְוֶה מֵעִיד לַלֹּוֶה ... לוֹקֵחַ רִאשׁוֹן מֵעִיד לַלּוֹקֵחַ שֵׁנִי ... קַבְּלָן ... מֵעִיד ... (בבא בתרא מו,סע"ב-מז,רע"א)
(עמלק is a mnemonic aid) The ḥakhamim taught: A cosigner (עָרֵב) may testify in behalf of the borrower ... A lender (מַלְוֶה) may testify in behalf of the borrower ... The first purchaser (לוֹקֵחַ) may testify in behalf of the second purchaser ... A contractor (קַבְּלָן) may testify ...

For a mnemonic composed of words — see ברכות נז,ב.

* The first form is Hebrew, and the second is Aramaic.

סִיַּיעְתָּא SEE: סִיַּיעְתָּא

סֵיפָא* הַסּוֹף; סוֹפָהּ **the end; its end**

This term denotes a later clause (or portion) of a mishna, a baraitha, or a pasuk. Sometimes it refers to the *latter* of two clauses, and sometimes to the *last* of several clauses.

See the next two entries for examples.

* In some manuscripts of the Talmud, the word is spelled סופא (or סופה). That may have been the original form, which became סֵיפָא by analogy with רֵישָׁא.

SEE: אַיְּידֵי דִתְנָא רֵישָׁא ... תְּנָא נַמֵּי סֵיפָא ...‚ אֵימָא סֵיפָא‚ מַאי שְׁנָא רֵישָׁא וּמַאי שְׁנָא סֵיפָא‚ מִדְּקָתָנֵי סֵיפָא ... מִכְּלַל דְּרֵישָׁא ...‚ מִשּׁוּם דְּקָא בָעֵי לְמִיתְנָא סֵיפָא ... תְּנָא נַמֵּי רֵישָׁא ...‚ שַׁפֵּיל לְסֵיפֵיהּ דִּקְרָא‚ תָּנָא סֵיפָא לְגַלּוּיֵי אַרֵישָׁא

סֵיפָא אִיצְטְרִיכָא לֵיהּ

סוֹפָהּ (שֶׁל הַהֲלָכָה) הוּצְרְכָה לוֹ.

He needed [to state] its latter clause.

In response to the difficulty that the mishna or baraitha under discussion is redundant, the following *resolution* is sometimes proposed: The latter clause of the same text contains a novel point, and the previous clause has been formulated as its foundation or as a contrast to it.

ברייתא: הַשּׁוֹאֵל סֵפֶר תּוֹרָה מֵחֲבֵירוֹ, הֲרֵי זֶה לֹא יַשְׁאִילֶנּוּ לְאַחֵר; פּוֹתְחוֹ וְקוֹרֵא בוֹ, וּבִלְבַד שֶׁלֹּא יִלְמוֹד בּוֹ בִּתְחִילָּה ...
תלמוד: פּוֹתְחוֹ וְקוֹרֵא בוֹ. פְּשִׁיטָא! לְמַאי כּוּ* שַׁיְילֵיהּ מִינֵּיהּ? סֵיפָא אִיצְטְרִיכָא לֵיהּ: וּבִלְבַד שֶׁלֹּא יִלְמוֹד בּוֹ בִּתְחִילָּה. (בבא מציעא כט,ב ע"פ כת"י)
BARAITHA: [If] one borrows a Torah scroll from his fellow man, he may not lend it to another; he may

open it and read it, provided that he does not study [a passage] in it for the first [time] ...
TALMUD: He may open it and read it. [This is] obvious! For what, then, did he borrow it from him? He (= the tanna) needed [to state] its latter clause: Provided that he does not study [a passage] in it for the first [time].

* See כּוּ and its notes.

סֵיפָא אֲתַאן ל–   סוֹפָהּ בָּאנוּ ל–...

[With] its latter clause, we have come to (a different halakhic situation or to a different halakhic position).
In response to the difficulty that the latter clause in the mishna or baraitha is superfluous or inconsistent with the previous clause(s), it is sometimes proposed — as a *resolution* of that difficulty — that the latter clause refers to a different case or that it presents the opinion of a different tanna.

משנה: לֹא יֵשֵׁב אָדָם לִפְנֵי הַסַּפָּר סָמוּךְ לְמִנְחָה עַד שֶׁיִּתְפַּלֵּל ... וְאִם הִתְחִילוּ, אֵין מַפְסִיקִין. מַפְסִיקִין לִקְרִיאַת שְׁמַע, וְאֵין מַפְסִיקִין לִתְפִלָּה. (שבת ט, רע"ב: משנה פ"א מ"ב)
תלמוד: הָא תָּנָא לֵיהּ רֵישָׁא "אֵין מַפְסִיקִין"! סֵיפָא אֲתַאן לְדִבְרֵי תוֹרָה, דְּתַנְיָא: חֲבֵרִים שֶׁהָיוּ עוֹסְקִים בַּתּוֹרָה מַפְסִיקִין לִקְרִיאַת שְׁמַע, וְאֵין מַפְסִיקִין לִתְפִלָּה. (שבת יא,א)

MISHNA: A person must not sit down before the barber close to minḥa [time], until he has recited the [minḥa] Amida ... But if they (already) began [the haircut], they need not stop [for minḥa, provided there will be enough time left to pray]. They must stop for the reading of the Shᵉma, but not for the Amida.
TALMUD: But [the tanna has already] stated [in] the first clause: "They need not stop" (and so it is redundant for him to state: "They must stop ... but not for the Amida")! [With] its latter clause, we have come to [the case of] Torah study (rather than haircuts), as it is taught (in a baraitha): Scholars who are engaged in Torah [study] must stop for the recitation of the Shᵉma, but not for the Amida.
SEE: אֲתַאן

סִיפֵּק   SEE סִפֵּק

סִיפְרָא/סִפְרָא (pl. סִיפְרֵי/סִפְרֵי)

(1) סֵפֶר   **book**
וּנְחֶמְיָה בֶּן חֲכַלְיָה - מַאי טַעְמָא לָא אִיקְרֵי סִיפְרָא עַל שְׁמֵיהּ?* (סנהדרין צג, סע"ב)
As for Nᵉḥemia b. Ḥakhalia — for what reason was the book not called by his name?

(2) סֵפֶר תּוֹרַת כֹּהֲנִים   ***Sifra; Torath Kohanim***
The Midrash halakha of tannaim to וַיִּקְרָא is known by either name.
סְתָם סִפְרָא — ר' יְהוּדָה. (סנהדרין פו, רע"א ורש"י שם)
[The author of] an anonymous statement in the Sifra [is] R. Yᵉhuda (b. Ilai).

* In the Talmud (בבא בתרא יד,ב), the Biblical book that we nowadays call Nᵉḥemia is considered part of Ezra and does not have a separate name. Rashi also followed that system, since he gave the Book of Ezra as the source of pᵉsukim that we now have in the Book of Nᵉḥemia. For example, see Rashi on מגילה ג,א.

סִיפְרֵי/סִפְרֵי   ***Sifré*** **(= "books")**
This name is applied to the Midrash halakha of the tannaim to בְּמִדְבַּר and the Midrash halakha to דְּבָרִים. They are two separate works.
סְתָם סִפְרֵי — ר' שִׁמְעוֹן. (סנהדרין פו, רע"א ורש"י שם)
[The author of] an anonymous statement in the Sifré [is] R. Shim'on (b. Yoḥai).

סֵירוּגִין   **piecemeal; at intervals**
קְרָאָהּ סֵירוּגִין ... יָצָא. (מגילה יז,א: משנה פ"ב מ"ב)
[If] he read it (= the Scroll of Esther) piecemeal, he has fulfilled his obligation.

סִיתְוָא/סִיתְוָוא/סִתְוָא
חוֹרֶף*   **winter; the rainy season**
אִיכָּא חַד גַּבְרָא בִּיהוּדָאֵי דְּקָא מְבַטֵּל תְּרֵיסַר אַלְפֵי גַּבְרֵי מִיִּשְׂרָאֵל, יַרְחָא בְּקַיְיטָא וְיַרְחָא בְּסִתְוָא, מִכְּרָגָא דְּמַלְכָּא. (בבא מציעא פו, רע"א)
*There is one man (= Rabba) among the Jews who holds back twelve thousand men of Israel from [the payment of] the royal poll-tax, one month in the summer and one month in the winter (by having them attend the kalla** sessions).*

* In the semi-tropical climate of Eretz Yisrael, there are two distinct seasons — a rainy winter and a dry summer; hence, סְתָיו in Biblical Hebrew and סִיתְוָא in the Aramaic of the Talmud and the Targumim mean *the rainy season*:
כִּי הִנֵּה הַסְּתָו עָבָר, הַגֶּשֶׁם חָלַף הָלַךְ לוֹ. (שיר השירים ב:יא)
וְקִיטָא וְסִתְוָא (= וְקַיִץ וָחֹרֶף) (ת"א לבראשית ח:כב)
In Modern Hebrew, however, סְתָו means *autumn*.
** See כַּלָּה.

סְכַר; סְכַר* (סכר)   **he blocked up; he dammed**
יִשְׂרָאֵל סָכְרוּ לֵיהּ, וְיִשְׂרָאֵל כְּרוּ לֵיהּ. (בבא מציעא כד,ב)
Jews dammed it (= the river), and Jews dredged it.

* The first form is Hebrew, and the second is Aramaic. In Modern Hebrew, a סֶכֶר is *a dam*.

סְלֵיק (סלק:* סָלֵיק .prt, לִיסַּק .fut, סַק .imp, לְמִיסַּק .inf)

(1) עָלָה   **he went up; he ascended**
כִּי סְלֵיק ר' זֵירָא (חולין כא, רע"א)
when R. Zera went up (to Eretz Yisrael)

(2) נִגְמַר   **it finished; it was completed****
סְלֵיק עִנְיָנָא (מגילה כג, רע"ב)   *the subject was completed*

(3) עָלָה; הוֹעִיל   **it was effective**
סָלְקָא טְבִילָה לְכוּלֵּיהּ גּוּפֵיהּ דְּמָנָא (חגיגה כב,א)
the immersion is effective for the entire body of the vessel

it happened; it befell — **(4) קָרָה**

כָּל דַּהֲוָה סָלְקָא לֵיהּ, אָמַר: גַּם זוֹ לְטוֹבָה. (סנהדרין קח, סע"ב ורש"י שם)

Whatever would befall him, he would say: This too is for the best.

* For the full conjugation of this verb, see *Grammar for Gemara:* Chapter 4, Verb 7.

** It is customary to print at the conclusion of each tractate of the Talmud: .... וּסְלִיקָא לַהּ מַסֶּכֶת ..., ... *and tractate ... has been completed.*

SEE: סָלְקָא דַּעְתָּךְ, סָלְקָא דַּעְתָּךְ אֲמִינָא, לָא סָלְקָא דַּעְתָּךְ, כִּי סָלֵיק ר', סָלֵיק, אַסִּיק

סֶלַע*

(1) *sela*

This silver coin or weight was equal to two *shekels* in Talmudic times and to one Biblical *shekel.*

כָּל "כֶּסֶף" הָאָמוּר בַּתּוֹרָה סְתָם — סֶלַע (בכורות נ,א)

*every [time the term] "silver" is stated in the Torah [with reference to money] without qualification [it means] "sela"***

(2) rock; boulder; a clod of earth

as hard as a rock — קָשֵׁי כְּסֶלַע (קידושין כו,ב)

* See the table of coins and weights in Appendix II.

** For example: וְעָנְשׁוּ אוֹתוֹ מֵאָה כֶסֶף (דברים כב:יט). See Targum Onkelos there.

SEE: שֶׁקֶל

סַלֵּק (סלק פָּעֵל: מְסַלֵּק .prt, לְסַלּוֹקֵי .inf)

he removed; he dismissed — סַלֵּק

בָּתַר דְּסַלִּיקוּ תְּפִילַּיְיהוּ (נדה נא, סע"ב)

*after they removed their t*e*fillin*

SEE: סָלֵיק and its note.

סָלְקָא דַּעְתָּךְ (= סָלְקָא אַדַּעְתָּךְ?!) הַאִם עוֹלֶה עַל דַּעְתְּךָ?!

"Would it arise on your mind?!"

Would you think?! Do you [really] think?!

This expression, which often appears at the end of a rhetorical question, points out a *difficulty.*

בְּשַׁבָּת סָלְקָא דַּעְתָּךְ?! (גיטין ח,ב)

Would you think [it may be done] on the Sabbath?!

SEE: סָלֵיק

סָלְקָא דַּעְתָּךְ אֲמִינָא ... עוֹלֶה עַל דַּעְתְּךָ לוֹמַר

it would have occurred to you [that] I might say ...

This expression is used to present a *resolution* of the difficulty that a pasuk or a halakha is superfluous.

(הֲלָכָה כְּר' יְהוֹשֻׁעַ בֶּן קָרְחָה אִיצְטְרִיךְ. סָלְקָא דַּעְתָּךְ אֲמִינָא: יָחִיד וְרַבִּים הֲלָכָה כְּרַבִּים. קָא מַשְׁמַע לָן: הֲלָכָה כְּיָחִיד. (בבא קמא קב,א)

*It was necessary to state [that the halakha is according to the view of] R. Y*e*hoshua b. Korha (and the ruling is not redundant). It would have occurred to you [that] I might say: [If there is a controversy between] an individual and a majority, the halakha is in accordance with the majority. [Rav Huna] teaches us: The halakha (in this particular case) is according to [the view of] the individual (= R. Y*e*hoshua b. Korha).*

SEE: סָלֵיק

סְמוּכִים/סְמוּכִין

juxtaposition

This term usually denotes an analogy between two matters based upon their location in two adjacent *p*e*sukim* or two adjacent *parashoth.* The analogy teaches a halakhic or aggadic point.*

ר' יְהוּדָה לָא דָּרֵישׁ סְמוּכִין בְּכָל הַתּוֹרָה כּוּלָּהּ, וּבְמִשְׁנֵה תוֹרָה דָּרֵישׁ (ברכות כא,ב; יבמות ד,א)

*R. Y*e*huda does not interpret [on the basis of] juxtaposition througout the whole Torah, but in the Book of D*e*varim he does [so] interpret*

For an example of סְמוּכִים, see (וּ)סְמִיךְ לֵיהּ — an expression that often presents such an analogy.

* In תוספות לסוכה לא,א — it is stated that the difference between a הֶיקֵּשׁ (see that entry) and סְמוּכִים is the following: A הֶיקֵּשׁ compares two items that appear within the same pasuk, whereas סְמוּכִים compares items located in two different p*e*sukim. This distinction, however, has been challenged by other authorities. See *Encyclopedia Talmudith,* vol. 10, p. 561 (הֶיקֵּשׁ).

סְמִי imp. (סמי פָּעֵל)

erase! omit! — **(1) מְחוֹק!**

As a *resolution* of a difficulty with regard to the text of a mishna or baraitha or of a contradiction between it and another text — it is sometimes proposed that a word, a phrase, or even a whole text be eliminated.

סְמִי מִכָּאן "קְצִירָה"! (פסחים נו, רע"ב)

Omit [the mention of] "reaping" from here (= the mishna).

blind! — **(2) סַמֵּא!**

Blind the eye of this [idol]! — סְמִי עֵינֵיהּ דְּדֵין! (ר"ה כד,ב)

SEE: אֵיסַמְיֵיהּ, סוּמָא

סַמְיָא

SEE: סוּמָא

סְמִיךְ pass. prt. (סמך)

near; adjacent — **(1) סָמוּךְ**

For an example, see the next entry: (וּ)סְמִיךְ לֵיהּ.

thick; solid — **(2) סָמִיךְ; עָבֶה; מוּצָק**

מַיָּא כִּי אַרְעָא סְמִיכְתָּא דָּמֵי. (גיטין ח, רע"א)

The water [in a river] is [regarded] as solid ground.

וּסְמִיךְ לֵיהּ וְסָמוּךְ לוֹ

and adjacent to it

This expression introduces a second Biblical passage immediately after the quotation of a passage that precedes it in the Biblical source. The juxtaposition of the two passages teaches a halakhic or aggadic point by analogy.

"וּמַכֵּה נֶפֶשׁ בְּהֵמָה יְשַׁלְּמֶנָּה — נֶפֶשׁ תַּחַת נָפֶשׁ", וּסְמִיךְ לֵיהּ: "וְאִישׁ כִּי יִתֵּן מוּם בַּעֲמִיתוֹ, כַּאֲשֶׁר עָשָׂה כֵּן יֵעָשֶׂה לּוֹ". (בבא קמא פג,ב ע"פ ויקרא כד:יח-יט)
"And a person who kills a beast must pay for it — a beast for a beast," and adjacent to it: "And if a person maims his fellow man, as he has done so it must be done to him." (The analogy teaches that just as the penalty for killing an animal is monetary compensation, so too is the penalty for wounding a human being.)

SEE: סְמוּכִין, הֶיקֵּשׁ

סְמַךְ (סמך: סָמֵיךְ .act. prt, סְמִיךְ .pass. prt, לִסְמוֹךְ .fut, לְמִיסְמַךְ .inf) סָמַךְ

(1) he depended upon; he relied upon
וּמַאי חֲזֵית דְּסָמְכַתְּ אַהֲנֵי? סְמוֹךְ אַהֲנֵי! (סנהדרין כז, רע"א)
But on what basis have you determined to rely on these (witnesses)? Rely upon those!

(2) it was committed
In this sense, the verb is used with דַּעַת, *mind.*
הָכָא סָמְכָא דַּעְתֵּיהּ (בבא מציעא טז, סע"א)
his mind is committed (to the deal)

(3) he conferred rabbinical ordination upon
סַמְכֵיהּ ר' יְהוּדָה בֶּן בָּבָא (סנהדרין יד:א)
R. Y'huda b. Bava conferred rabbinical ordination upon him

(4) he connected
שַׁחֲרִית, הֵיכִי מָצֵי סָמֵיךְ? (ברכות ד,ב)
[In the] morning prayer, how can he connect (the b'rakha גָּאַל יִשְׂרָאֵל *with the Amida)?*

סִמְכָא SEE: בַּר סִמְכָא

סַנְהֶדְרִין/סַנְהֶדְרֵי* (סַנְהֶדְרָיוֹת .pl) **Sanhedrin**
This term, which is of Greek origin, refers to courts that functioned during the time of the Mishna and the Talmud.
סַנְהֶדְרֵי גְדוֹלָה הָיְתָה שֶׁל שִׁבְעִים וְאֶחָד, וּקְטַנָּה — שֶׁל עֶשְׂרִים וּשְׁלֹשָׁה. (סנהדרין ב,א: משנה פ"א מ"ו ע"פ כת"י)
The great Sanhedrin was [composed] of seventy-one [judges], and the lesser Sanhedrin [was composed] of twenty-three.
סַנְהֶדְרִין הַהוֹרֶגֶת אֶחָד בְּשָׁבוּעַ נִקְרֵאת חוֹבְלָנִית. (מכות ז,א: משנה פ"א מ"י)
A Sanhedrin that executes one [person] within seven years is called destructive.

* The form סַנְהֶדְרֵי is consistently found in manuscripts in the combinations סַנְהֶדְרֵי גְדוֹלָה and סַנְהֶדְרֵי קְטַנָּה.

סָנֵי (סני) act. prt. שׂוֹנֵא **hating**
הַהִיא חֲמָתָא דַּהֲוָת סָנְיָא לְכַלָּתָהּ ... (שבת כו, רע"א ע"פ כת"י)
There was a mother-in-law who hated her daughter-in-law ...

סְנֵי (סני) pass. prt. שָׂנוּי **hated; hateful**
דַּעֲלָךְ סְנֵי לְחַבְרָךְ לָא תַּעֲבֵיד! (שבת לא,א)
What is hateful to you do not do to your fellow man!

סְפַד (ספד: סָפֵד .prt, לְמִיסְפַּד .inf)
סָפַד; הִסְפִּיד **he mourned; he eulogized**
ר' זֵירָא סַפְדֵיהּ לְהָהוּא מֵרַבָּנַן בְּבֵי כְנִישְׁתָּא (מגילה כח,ב)
R. Zera eulogized one of the hakhamim in the synagogue.

סַפּוֹקֵי .inf (ספק פָּעֵל: מְסַפַּק .pass. prt)
סָפֵק; הָיָה בְּסָפֵק **"be in doubt"**

סַפּוֹקֵי מְסַפְּקָא לֵיהּ
סָפֵק מְסֻפָּק לוֹ **he is certainly in doubt**
רַב אַסִּי סַפּוֹקֵי מְסַפְּקָא לֵיהּ, וְעָבֵיד הָכָא לְחוּמְרָא וְהָכָא לְחוּמְרָא. (ביצה ד,ב ורש"י שם)
Rav Assi is certainly in doubt, and [hence] he rules here strictly, and he rules there strictly.

* This infinitive is used to strengthen the passive participle, מְסַפְּקָא, and it is best translated by an adverb in English, such as *certainly* or *surely.*

סָפֵי (ספי) prt. מַאֲכִיל **giving to eat; feeding**
מִי קָא סָפוּ לָךְ מֵאַלְיָה? (פסחים ג,ב)
Do they give you to eat from the tail?

סִפֵּק (ספק פִּעֵל: מְסַפֵּק .prt, יְסַפֵּק .fut);
סַפֵּק* (ספק פַּעֵל: מְסַפֵּק .prt) **he supplied**
מְסַפְּקִים מַיִם וּמָזוֹן לַאֲחֵיהֶם שֶׁבִּכְרַכִּים. (מגילה ד,ב)
They supply water and food to their brethren in the cities.

* The first form is Hebrew, and the second is Aramaic.

סֶפֶק/סִיפֶק **ability; opportunity; enough**
הָיָה סִיפֵק בְּיָדָם לִמְחוֹת, וְלֹא מִיחוּ. (סוכה כט,ב)
They had the opportunity to protest, but they did not protest.
לֹא סֶפֶק לִשְׂכַר עֲמָלוֹ וּמְזוֹנוֹ (בבא מציעא סח,ב)
there is not enough for payment for his work and his food

סָפֵק; סְפֵיקָא*
a doubt; a doubtful case; an uncertainty
וְכָל סְפֵק נְפָשׁוֹת דּוֹחֶה אֶת הַשַּׁבָּת (יומא פג,א: משנה פ"ח מ"ז)
and any doubtful case of [danger to] life supersedes the observance of the Sabbath

* The first form is Hebrew, and the second is Aramaic.

סְפֵק ... סְפֵק ...
[There is] a doubt whether ... or ...
סְפֵק חֲשֵׁיכָה סְפֵק אֵינָהּ חֲשֵׁיכָה. (שבת לד,א: משנה פ"ב מ"ז)
[There is] a doubt whether it is night or whether it is not night.

סָפֵק סְפֵיקָא

"a doubt of a doubt"; a double doubt

When there are two independent reasons to doubt whether a prohibition is present, Jewish law treats the case leniently.

כֵּיוָן דְּאִיכָּא דְּפָתְחִי לְשׁוּם מָמוֹנָא, הֲוָה לֵיהּ סְפֵק סְפֵיקָא. (עבודה זרה ע, סע"א ורש"י שם)

Since there are some [thieves] who open [the wine casks in their search] for money (without handling the wine), it is [a case of] a double doubt. (Wine that has been indeed handled by a non-Jew may not be drunk by a Jew. In this case, there is a double doubt whether the wine was indeed handled by a non-Jew. First, it is doubtful whether it was a Jew or a non-Jew who opened a the cask, and second, even if it was a non-Jew, it is doubtful whether he actually handled the wine. Therefore, it is permitted for a Jew to drink the wine.)

סָפְרָא

SEE: סוֹפֵר

סִפְרָא

SEE: סִיפְרָא

סִפְרֵי

SEE: סִיפְרֵי

סַק

imp. (סלק) עֲלֵה! **go up!**

קוּם, סַק לְאַרְעָא דְיִשְׂרָאֵל! (בבא קמא קיז,א)

Arise [and] go up to Eretz Yisrael!

SEE: סְלֵיק

סָרֵי

prt. (סרי)

stinking; decayed; rotten מַסְרִיחַ

אַשְׁכְּחֵיה רוֹעֶה וַאֲמַר לֵיהּ: גַּנְבָא סָרְיָא! (ב"מ צג, סע"ב ורש"י)

A shepherd found him (= the thief) and said to him: (You) rotten thief!

סְרִיק

pass. prt. (סרק) רֵק **empty**

מְעוּבֶּרֶת ... מֵעִיקָּרָא גוּפָא סְרִיקָא וְהַשְׁתָּא גוּפָא מַלְיָא (יבמות פז, סע"א-רע"ב)

a pregnant woman ... at first an empty body and now a full body

SEE: בּוּקֵי סְרִיקֵי, סְרָק

סָרֵס

(סרס פִּעֵל: מְסָרֵס **act. prt.**, מְסוֹרָס **pass. prt.**, סָרֵס **imp.**)

he castrated; he mutilated;

he transposed; he reversed

סָרֵס הַמִּקְרָא וְדָרְשֵׁהוּ! (ב"ב קיט, ב ורשב"ם ע"פ במדבר כז:ב)

Reverse [the order of the words in] the pasuk and expound it! (= Interpret the pasuk as if the order of some of its words has been changed!)

"בְּכָל הַמָּקוֹם אֲשֶׁר אַזְכִּיר אֶת שְׁמִי אָבוֹא אֵלֶיךָ [וּבֵרַכְתִּיךָ] ..." "בְּכָל מָקוֹם" סָלְקָא דַעְתָּךְ?! אֶלָּא מִקְרָא זֶה מְסוֹרָס הוּא: "בְּכָל מָקוֹם אֲשֶׁר אָבוֹא אֵלֶיךָ וּבֵרַכְתִּיךָ — שָׁם אַזְכִּיר אֶת שְׁמִי". (סוטה לח,א ע"פ שמות סוף פרק כ)

"In every place where I cause My Name to be mentioned I will come to you and bless you ..." Would it arise on your mind that it means "every place"?! But [some words in] this pasuk [must be] transposed: "In every place where I will come to you and bless you, I will cause My Name to be mentioned."

סְרָק

emptiness; barrenness

אֵיזֶהוּ אִילַן סְרָק? כָּל שֶׁאֵינוֹ עוֹשֶׂה פֵּירוֹת. (משנה כלאים ו:ה)

What is [considered] a tree of barrenness (= a barren tree)? Any tree that does not produce fruit.

SEE: סְרִיק

סְתִימְתָּאָה

הַתַּנָּא שֶׁדְּבָרָיו מוּבָאִים סְתָם בַּמִּשְׁנָה

the tanna whose opinion is quoted anonymously in the mishna

זוֹ דִּבְרֵי ר' עֲקִיבָא סְתִימְתָּאָה. (מגילה ב,א ורש"י שם)

This is the opinion of R. Akiva, the tanna whose opinion is quoted anonymously in the mishna.

SEE: סְתָם

סָתַם

(סתם: סוֹתֵם **act. prt.**, סָתוּם **pass. prt.**);

סְתַם*

(סתם: סָתֵים **act. prt.**, סְתִים **pass. prt.**)

(1) he enclosed; he closed up; he concealed

שׁוֹפָר שֶׁ-... נִיקַּב וּסְתָמוֹ ... (ר"ה כז, סע"א-רע"ב: משנה ג:ו)

a ram's horn that ... was punctured, and [someone] closed it (= the hole) up

יִלְמַד סָתוּם מִן הַמְּפוֹרָשׁ! (יומא נט, רע"א ורש"י שם)

Let him learn the case that is "concealed" (= unspecified) from [the case] that is described explicitly!

(2) he formulated (a text) anonymously (in keeping with one tannaitic opinion, thereby implying that it is the normative opinion)

מַאן סְתַם לַן לְמַתְנִיתִין? רַבִּי .... יוֹם טוֹב דְּקִיל וְאָתֵי לְזַלְזוּלֵי בֵּיהּ — סְתַם לַן כְּר' יְהוּדָה דְּמַחְמִיר. (ביצה ב, רע"ב ע"פ רש"י)

Who formulated our mishna for us anonymously? Rebbi .... [With respect to] a festival that is less stringent (than the Sabbath), and [a person] might come to treat it lightly — he formulated [the mishna] for us anonymously in keeping with [the opinion of] R. Y'huda who is strict.

* The first form is Hebrew, and the second is Aramaic.

SEE: מַאן חֲכָמִים

סְתָם*; סְתָמָא**

(1) the unspecified, the unknown; the ordinary

סְתָם יֵינָן (עבודה זרה עד, סע"א ע"פ רש"י שם)

"their ordinary wine"; wine of heathens about which it is not known whether it has been poured as a libation to an idol or not

(2) without specifying

This noun is sometimes used as an adverb.

הַמַּלְוֶה אֶת חֲבֵירוֹ סְתָם אֵינוֹ רַשַּׁאי לְתוֹבְעוֹ פָּחוֹת מִשְּׁלֹשִׁים יוֹם. (מכות ג,ב)

[If] one lends [money] to his fellow man without specifying [the date the loan is due], he may not claim [it] from him within thirty days.

(3) an anonymous statement

סְתָם מַתְנִיתִין — ר' מֵאִיר; סְתָם תּוֹסֶפְתָּא — ר' נְחֶמְיָה; סְתָם סִפְרָא — ר' יְהוּדָה; סְתָם סִפְרֵי — ר' שִׁמְעוֹן; וְכוּלְּהוּ אַלִּיבָּא דְר' עֲקִיבָא. (סנהדרין פו, רע"א וש"נ ורש"י שם)

[The author of] an anonymous statement in our Mishna [is] R. Méir; [the author of] an anonymous statement in the Toseftha [is] R. N^eḥemia; [the author of] an anonymous statement in the Sifra [is] R. Y^ehuda; [the author of] an anonymous statement in the Sifré [is] R. Shim'on; and all of them are in accordance with [the teachings of] R. Akiva.

סְתָמָא דְמִילְתָא

סְתָמָא דְמַתְנִיתִין וּמַחֲלוֹקֶת בְּבָרַיְיתָא ... הֲלָכָה כִּסְתָם. (יבמות מב, סע"ב)

[If there is] an anonymous statement in our Mishna and a controversy [about the same issue] in a baraitha, the halakhic ruling is in accordance with the anonymous statement.

* This word is popularly pronounced סְתַם by Ashkenasic Jews (like the Sephardic pronunciation).

** The first form is Hebrew, and the second is Aramaic.

סְתָמָא דְמִילְתָא סְתָמוֹ שֶׁל דָּבָר ordinarily

סְתָמָא דְמִילְתָא: כִּי מִתְרַע בְּאֱנִישׁ מִילְתָא, בְּרֵישָׁא גָּנַח וַהֲדַר יַלֵּיל. (ראש השנה לד, סע"א)

Ordinarily, when a tragedy befalls a person, at first he sighs, and subsequently he wails.

ע

עֲבַד (עבד:* עָבֵיד act. prt., עֲבִיד pass. prt., לֶיעֱבֵיד fut., עֲבֵיד imp., לְמֶיעְבַּד inf.)

he did; he acted; he made — עָשָׂה

כָּל דְּעָבֵיד רַחֲמָנָא — לְטַב עָבֵיד. (ברכות ס, סע"ב)
Everything that the Merciful One does — He does for the best.

דַּעֲבַד כְּמָר עֲבַד, וְדַעֲבַד כְּמָר עֲבַד. (ברכות כז, סע"א)
He who has acted according to one authority has acted [properly], and he who has acted according to the other has acted [properly].

רַב אַשִׁי עֲבַד הִלּוּלָא לִבְרֵיהּ. (ברכות לא, רע"א)
Rav Ashi made a wedding feast for his son.

* For the full conjugation of this verb, see *Grammar for Gemara*: Chapter 4, Verb 4.

SEE: דְּיַעֲבַד, מַאי עָבֵיד לֵיהּ, and the next three entries

עֲבַד עוּבְדָא "עָשָׂה מַעֲשֶׂה"; פָּסַק הֲלָכָה

"he did an act"; he issued a halakhic ruling (about an actual case that came before him)

עֲבַד רַבָּה עוּבְדָא בְּהַהוּא גִיטָּא דְּאִישְׁתְּכַח בֵּי כִיתָּנָא בְּפוּמְבְּדִיתָא — כִּשְׁמַעְתֵּיהּ. (גיטין כז,א)
Rabba issued a ruling concerning a bill of divorce that was found among the flax in Pumb'ditha — according to his halakha (that such a document is valid and should be delivered to the wife).

עֲבִיד pass. prt. — עָשׂוּי — **made; done**

Besides this basic meaning, this form is also used in the following two senses, like its Hebrew equivalent:

(1) destined (to); is about (to)

כָּל מִילְּתָא דַּעֲבִידָא לְאִיגַּלּוּיֵי — לָא מְשַׁקְּרֵי בַּהּ אֱינָשֵׁי. (ראש השנה כב,ב וש"נ)
[Regarding] any matter that is destined to come to light — people do not lie.

(2) likely (to)

לָא עֲבִיד אֱינִישׁ דִּמְשַׁוֵּי נַפְשֵׁיהּ רַשִׁיעָא. (קידושין נ,א)
A man is not likely to make himself a criminal (= to incriminate himself).

עֲבִידְתָּא

(1) עֲבוֹדָה; מְלָאכָה; מַעֲשֶׂה — **work; labor**

אֲנָא עֲבַדִי עֲבִידְתָּא גַּבָּךְ. (ב"מ ג,א) *I did the work for you.*

(2) מַעֲשֶׂה — **doings; business**

For an example — see מַאי עֲבִידְתֵּיהּ.

עֲבַר (עבר: עָבַר prt., לֶיעֱבַר fut., לְמֶיעְבַּר inf.)

(1) עָבַר — **he passed; he crossed**

הֲוָה עָבַר בְּמַבָּרָא (כתובות קה,ב)
he was crossing in a ferryboat

(2) עָבַר (עַל) — **he trespassed; he violated**

וְקָעָבַר אַ"לִפְנֵי עִוֵּר לֹא תִתֵּן מִכְשֹׁל"! (קידושין לב,א ע"פ ויקרא יט:יד)
and he is violating (the Biblical prohibition): "You shall not place an obstacle before a blind man!"

עַבַּר (עבר פִּעֵל: מְעַבַּר prt., לִיעַבַּר fut., לְעַבּוֹרֵי inf.)

(1) הֶעֱבִיר — **he caused to pass; he displaced; he deposed**

הַהוּא טַבָּחָא דְּאִישְׁתְּכַח דִּנְפָקָא טְרֵיפְתָּא מִתּוּתֵי יְדֵיהּ — פַּסְלֵיהּ רַב נַחְמָן וְעַבְּרֵיהּ. (סנהדרין כה,א)
[As for] a certain ritual slaughterer who was found to have a t'refa animal pass through his hands — Rav Naḥman disqualified him (as a slaughterer) and deposed him.

(2) עִבֵּר — **he declared a leap (= thirteen-month) year or a full (= thirty-day) month**

עַבְּרוּהּ לֶאֱלוּל* (ראש השנה כ,א)
they have declared Elul a full (= thirty-day) month

* Literally: *they declared it full, Elul.*

עַד — **up to; until**

עַד דְּ- — SEE: עַד שֶׁ-

עַד הֵיכָן

until where? how far? to what extent?

עַד הֵיכָן כִּיבּוּד אָב וָאֵם? (קידושין לא,א)
How far [must] honor for father and mother [extend]?

עַד וְלֹא עַד בִּכְלָל — **until and not including**
עַד וְעַד בִּכְלָל — **until and including**

משנה: ר' יְהוּדָה אוֹמֵר: (תְּפִלַּת הַשַּׁחַר) עַד אַרְבַּע שָׁעוֹת. (ברכות כו,א: משנה פ"ד מ"א)
תלמוד: אִיבַּעְיָא לְהוּ: עַד וְעַד בִּכְלָל — אוֹ דִּלְמָא עַד וְלֹא עַד בִּכְלָל? (שם כו, סע"ב)
MISHNA: R. Y'huda says: [The morning Amida must be recited] until four hours (in the day).
TALMUD: They asked: [Does "until" mean] until and including [the fourth hour] — or perhaps [it means] until and not including [the fourth hour]?

עַד כָּאן לָא פְּלִיגִי ... אֶלָּא ...

עַד כָּאן אֵינָם חֲלוּקִים ... אֶלָּא ...

Until here do (the tannaim) disagree — only (about the following circumstances) ...

This formula is used in the Talmud to limit the scope of a controversy that has just been quoted.

ברייתא: אָמַר לִשְׁלֹשָׁה: "צְאוּ וְקַדְּשׁוּ לִי הָאִשָּׁה", אֶחָד שָׁלִיחַ וּשְׁנַיִם עֵדִים — דִּבְרֵי בֵית שַׁמַּאי, וּבֵית הִלֵּל אוֹמְרִים: כּוּלָּם שְׁלוּחִין הֵן, וְאֵין שָׁלִיחַ נַעֲשֶׂה עֵד.
תלמוד: עַד כָּאן לָא פְלִיגִי אֶלָּא בִשְׁלֹשָׁה, אֲבָל בִּשְׁנַיִם דִּבְרֵי הַכֹּל לָא. (קידושין מג, סע"א)

BARAITHA: [If] one said to three: "Go forth and betroth the woman for me," one is [his] agent and [the other] two witnesses — [this is] the opinion of Beth Shammai, but Beth Hillel says: They are all [his] agents, and an agent cannot be a witness.
TALMUD: Until here do [Beth Shammai and Beth Hillel] disagree — only with three [people], but with two — according to both opinions [the betrothal can] not [be effected].

עַד כָּאן לָא קָאָמַר ... אֶלָּא ...
עַד כָּאן אֵינוֹ אוֹמֵר ... אֶלָּא ...

Until here does [the tanna] state [his halakha] only (with regard to the following circumstances)

This formula is used in the Talmud to limit the scope of a halakha or of a controversy that has just been quoted.

משנה: הַקּוֹרֵא אֶת שְׁמַע וְלֹא הִשְׁמִיעַ לְאָזְנוֹ — יָצָא. ר' יוֹסֵי אוֹמֵר: לֹא יָצָא. (ברכות טו,א: משנה פ"ב מ"ג)
תלמוד: עַד כָּאן לָא קָאָמַר ר' יוֹסֵי "לֹא יָצָא" — אֶלָּא גַּבֵּי קְרִיאַת שְׁמַע דְּאוֹרָיְיתָא, אֲבָל תְּרוּמָה מִשּׁוּם בְּרָכָה הוּא, וּבְרָכָה דְּרַבָּנָן. (שם)

MISHNA: One who recites the Shma but did not make it audible to his ear has (nevertheless) fulfilled his obligation. R. Yosé says: He has not fulfilled his obligation.
*TALMUD: Until here does R. Yosé state "he has not fulfilled his obligation" — only with regard to the recitation of the Sh*ᵉ*ma, [a mitzva] from the Torah, but [with regard to] t*ᵉ*ruma [where the issue is] because of the b*ᵉ*rakha, and a b*ᵉ*rakha is of Rabbinic status (it is quite conceivable that R. Yosé would accept a b*ᵉ*rakha that is not made audible to the ear).*

SEE: לָא ... אֶלָּא ...

עַד שֶׁ-; עַד דְּ-*

(1) until

הַמְתֵּן לוֹ עַד דִּמְסַיֵּים! (ברכות לג,ב)

Wait for him until he finishes!

(2) while

עַד דְּקָאֵי בְּשַׁחֲרִית, פָּרֵישׁ מִילֵּי דְּשַׁחֲרִית. (ברכות ב,א)

While he is dealing with [the topic of] the morning, he expounds [other] matters relating to the morning.

(3) unless

הַקּוֹרֵא אֶת הַמְּגִילָּה ... לֹא יָצָא עַד שֶׁתְּהֵא כְתוּבָה אַשּׁוּרִית** (מגילה יז,א: משנה פ"ב מ"א-מ"ב)

*One who reads the scroll (of Esther) ... has not fulfilled his obligation unless it is written [in the] "Assyrian" [script]***

(4) before; instead of

שָׁאַל ר' חֲנִינָא בֶּן עָגוּל אֶת ר' חִיָּיא בַּר אַבָּא: מִפְּנֵי מָה בְּדִבְּרוֹת הָרִאשׁוֹנִים לֹא נֶאֱמַר בָּהֶן "טוֹב" וּבְדִבְּרוֹת הָאַחֲרוֹנִים נֶאֱמַר בָּהֶן "טוֹב"? אָמַר לוֹ: עַד שֶׁאַתָּה שׁוֹאֲלֵנִי לָמָּה נֶאֱמַר בָּהֶן "טוֹב", שְׁאָלֵנִי אִם נֶאֱמַר בָּהֶן "טוֹב"! (בבא קמא נד,סע"ב-נה,רע"א)

R. Hanina b. Agul asked R. Hiyya b. Abba: Why is "well-being" not mentioned in the first [version of the] Decalogue (שמות כ), *but "well-being" is mentioned in the second [version of the] Decalogue* (דברים ה)*? He answered him: Before you ask me WHY "well-being" is mentioned in it, ask me WHETHER "well-being" is mentioned in it!*

* שֶׁ- is Hebrew, and דְּ- is Aramaic.

** This is the Hebrew script in use today in the five scrolls and in the Torah.

עַד שֶׁלֹּא
not yet; before

הִשְׁכִּים לִשְׁנוֹת עַד שֶׁלֹּא קָרָא קְרִיאַת שְׁמַע — צָרִיךְ לְבָרֵךְ. (ברכות יא,ב)

*[If] one arose to learn Torah before having recited the Sh*ᵉ*ma — he must recite Birkath [HaTorah prior to this learning].*

עֲדָא f. זֹאת
this

עֲדָא אָמְרָה ... (ב"מ ס,א ורש"י שם ועוד)

This [is to] say ...

SEE: הָא, דָּא

עֲדֵי אֵלּוּ
these

עֲדֵי גוּבְרִין ... (גיטין מה, סע"א ורש"י שם)

These are men ...

SEE: אִילֵּין

עֲדַיִין
still; yet

אָמַר ר' מֵאִיר: נִמְנוּ וְרַבּוּ בֵית שַׁמַּאי עַל בֵּית הִלֵּל ... אָמַר ר' יוֹסֵי: עֲדַיִין מַחְלוֹקֶת בִּמְקוֹמָהּ עוֹמֶדֶת. (משנה מקוואות ד:א)

R. Méir said: They voted and Beth Shammai outnumbered Beth Hillel ... [whereas] R. Yosé said: The controversy still stands in its place (as it was).

עָדִיף; עֲדִיף*
better; superior; preferable

תַּלְמוּד תּוֹרָה וּמִקְרָא מְגִילָּה - מִקְרָא מְגִילָּה עָדִיף. (מגילה ג,ב)

[If one must choose between two mitzvoth] the study of Torah versus the reading of the scroll of Esther — the reading of the scroll of Esther is preferable.

וּמִי עֲדִיפָא מִמַּתְנִיתִין?! (בבא קמא מז,ב)

Is [this baraitha that is now being cited as a proof] any better than our mishna?!

עֲדִיף also appears with a personal-pronoun subject suffix:

I am better	עֲדִיפְנָא (= עֲדִיף אֲנָא)
you are better	עֲדִיפַתְּ (= עֲדִיף אַתְּ)
we are better	עֲדִיפִינַן (= עֲדִיפֵי אֲנַן)

* The first form is Hebrew, and the second is Aramaic.

עוֹבָדָא* (pl. עוֹבָדִין) מַעֲשֶׂה

(1) an act; conduct; an activity

מָרֵי דְעוֹבָדָא (שבת לז, סע"ב וש"נ ורש"י שם)

a master of conduct (= a scrupulous person)

מִיחֲזֵי כְּעוּבְדִין דְּחוֹל (ביצה כח,א)
it seems like weekday activities (and hence it should be prohibited on a festival)

(2) case; occurrence; incident

For examples, see (בְּ)דִידִי הֲוָה עוּבְדָא and עֲבַד עוּבְדָא.

* Most Ashkenazic Jews pronounce this word עוֹבְדָא, and it has thus entered Modern Hebrew, meaning *a fact*.

SEE: גּוּפָא דְעוּבְדָא הֵיכִי הֲוָה

עוּבָּר (= עֻבָּר) embryo

רוֹב הַיּוֹלְדוֹת לְתִשְׁעָה - עוּבָּרָהּ נִיכָּר לִשְׁלִישׁ יָמֶיהָ. (יבמות לז,א)
[As for] most women who give birth at [the end of] nine [months] — her embryo (= pregnancy) is discernible at [the end of] a third of her days (= after three months).

עוּבָּרָה* (= עֻבָּרָה) a pregnant woman

עוּבָּרוֹת וּמֵינִיקוֹת מִתְעַנּוֹת וּמַשְׁלִימוֹת בּוֹ, כְּדֶרֶךְ שֶׁמִּתְעַנּוֹת וּמַשְׁלִימוֹת בְּיוֹם הַכִּפּוּרִים. (פסחים נד,ב)
Pregnant women and nursing mothers must fast a complete fast on it (= Tish'a b^eAv), just as they fast a complete fast on Yom Kippur.

* The Kaufman manuscript of the Mishna vocalises עוֹבָרָה, and some Sephardic Jews pronounce it that way.

עוֹד more; additional; again; still

וְעוֹד

(1) and furthermore; and moreover

This word introduces an *additional statement* of a tanna, an amora, or an *additional difficulty* that is pointed out by the Talmud.

הֲלָכָה אֲנִי אוֹמֵר; וְעוֹד מִקְרָא מְסַיְּיעֵנִי. (יבמות עז, סע"ב)
I am stating a halakhic tradition; and moreover a pasuk supports me.

וְעוֹד, כָּל מִצְוֹת עֲשֵׂה נְחַיְּיבִינְהוּ מִדְּרַבָּנַן! (ברכות כ,ב)
And furthermore (if women are indeed obligated in Kiddush through Rabbinic enactment) let us obligate them in all positive commandments through Rabbinic enactment!

(2) and a little bit more

שְׁמוֹנֶה אַמּוֹת וְעוֹד (משנה כלאים פ"ו מ"ו)
eight cubits and a little bit more

SEE: (וְ)לֹא עוֹד אֶלָּא שֶׁ-, חֲדָא וְעוֹד קָאָמַר

מִבְּעוֹד יוֹם while it is still day

לֹא כְסָּהוּ מִבְּעוֹד יוֹם, לֹא יְכַסֶּנּוּ מִשֶּׁתֶּחְשַׁךְ. (שבת נא, רע"א: משנה פ"ד מ"ב)
[If] he had not insulated it (= the cooked food) while it was still day (= before the onset of the Sabbath), he must not insulate it after it becomes dark (= on the Sabbath).

לְעַוּוֹתֵי inf. (עות פָּעֵל)

לְעַוֵּת; לְקַלְקֵל **to pervert; to impair**

לְתַקּוֹנֵי שַׁדַּרְתִּיךְ — וְלָא לְעַוּוֹתֵי. (קידושין מב, רע"ב וש"נ)
I sent you to benefit [me] — but not to impair [my cause].

עוֹלָם*

In Biblical Hebrew, this word denotes *long duration, everlastingness, antiquity,* and *futurity.* In Mishnaic Hebrew and in Modern Hebrew, there is an additional meaning: *world.*

בִּשְׁבִילִי נִבְרָא הָעוֹלָם. (סנהדרין לז, סע"א: משנה פ"ד מ"ה)
The world was created for me.

* There are two Biblical passages where this word has been explained as meaning *world*, but that explanation is debatable: גַּם אֶת הָעֹלָם נָתַן בְּלִבָּם (קהלת ג:יא וראב"ע שם) and עוֹלָם חֶסֶד יִבָּנֶה (תהלים פט:ג וראב"ע ורש"י שם).

SEE: לְעוֹלָם, מֵעוֹלָם לֹא, עָלְמָא

עוֹרְבָא פָּרַח* עוֹרֵב פּוֹרֵחַ. A raven is flying.

This expression is an evasive response on the part of a hakham to a difficulty or a problem that he was not ready to answer on the spot.

For examples, see ביצה כא, רע"א and חולין קכד,ב.

On both passages, Rashi equates it with the expression הִשִּׂיאוֹ לְדָבָר אַחֵר (עבודה זרה כט,ב: משנה פ"ב מ"ה), *he diverted him to something else*.

* This expression is occasionally used in Modern Hebrew.

עִידִית the best (land); the highest grade (of real estate)

"מֵיטַב שָׂדֵהוּ וּמֵיטַב כַּרְמוֹ יְשַׁלֵּם" ... ר' עֲקִיבָא אוֹמֵר: לֹא בָא הַכָּתוּב אֶלָּא לִגְבּוֹת לַנִּיזָּקִין מִן הָעִידִית. (בבא קמא ו,ב ע"פ שמות כב:ד)
"He must pay the best of his field or the best of his vineyard" ... R. Akiva says: Scripture only intended to teach that [payment of damages] be collected from the best land for the injured party.

עִידָּנָא* (constr. עִידַּן)

(1) זְמַן time; period

בְּעִידָּנָא דְּקָא מַסְהֲדִי, גַּבְרָא בַּר קְטָלָא הוּא (מכות ה,א)
by the time that they gave their (false) testimony, the man had (already) been sentenced to death

(2) זְמַן קָבוּעַ; שִׁיעוּר קָבוּעַ בְּתוֹרָה a fixed time; a regular [Torah] learning session

הַאי צוּרְבָא מֵרַבָּנַן לָא לִפְתַּח בְּעִידָּנֵיהּ בְּאוּרְתָּא דִּתְלֵיסַר ... (פסחים ד,א ורש"י שם)
a Torah scholar may not begin his regular learning session on the night following the thirteenth (of Nisan, so that he not neglect the search for hametz)

* In Modern Hebrew, עִדָּן means *era* or *epoch*.

עַיֵּיל (עלל פָּעֵל: prt. מְעַיֵּיל, fut. לְעַיֵּיל, imp. עַיֵּיל, inf. לְעַיּוֹלֵי)

הֵבִיא; הִכְנִיס **he brought in**

עַיְּילָהּ וְאַפְּקָהּ — אַפָּקָה מִשְּׂכִירוּת וְעַיְּילָהּ לִשְׁאֵילָה. (ב"מ לה,ב)
He brought it (= the animal) in, and he took it out —

he took it out of [the status of] hiring and brought it into [the status of] borrowing.
SEE: עַל

עַיֵּין (עין פַּעֵל: מְעַיֵּין .prt, לְעַיֵּין .fut, עַיֵּין .imp, לְעַיּוֹנֵי .inf)

he analyzed (1) עַיֵּן

הָא לְמִיגְרַס; הָא לְעַיּוֹנֵי. (תענית י,ב)
This [halakha refers] to reviewing [texts] by heart; the other to analyzing [them].

he examined; he investigated (2) בָּדַק

יְתִיב רַב שִׁימִי בַּר חִיָּיא קַמֵּיהּ דְּרַב וְקָא מְעַיֵּין בָּהּ: אִי אִית בָּהּ שָׁוֶה פְּרוּטָה, אִין; אִי לָא, לָא. (קידושין יב, סע"א)
Rav Shimi b. Ḥiyya was sitting before Rav and he was examining it (= an object used to contract a marriage): if it is worth a p^eruta, yes (= the marriage is valid); if not, [it is] not.

לְעֵיל; לְעֵילָּא

SEE: לְעֵיל, לְעֵילָּא

עִילָּאָה עֶלְיוֹן

upper

חַם לְתוֹךְ צוֹנֵן ... רַב אָמַר: עִילָּאָה גָּבַר. (פסחים עו,א)
[If] hot [meat falls] into cold [milk] ... Rav said: The upper [substance] prevails (in other words, it is assumed that the hot meat heats up the cold milk).

עִילָּוֵי עַל

on; upon; on top of

This preposition is often used with personal-pronoun suffixes:*

on him; on it (m.)	עָלָיו	עִילָּוֵיהּ
on her; on it (f.)	עָלֶיהָ	עִילָּוַהּ

רְוִיחָא תַּתָּאָה, וּמְצִיעָא עִילָּוֵיהּ, וְזוּטָא עִילָּוֵי מְצִיעָא. (בבא מציעא כה, רע"א)
The widest [coin] is the bottom one, the medium-sized one is on top of it, and the smallest is on top of the medium-sized one.

* For a full list of the forms thus created, see *Grammar for Gemara:* Chapter 7.323.
SEE: עַל, אַ-

עַיִן; עֵינָא*

(1) eye
For examples, see עַיִן הָרַע and עַיִן רָעָה.

(2) appearance; form; color**
כְּדֵי שֶׁיִּקְלוֹט הָעַיִן (שבת יז, סע"ב: משנה פ"א מ"ו)
enough [time] for [the wool] to absorb the color (of the dye)

* The first form is Hebrew, and the second is Aramaic.
** This meaning also occurs in Biblical Hebrew in the pasuk וְעֵינוֹ כְּעֵין הַבְּדֹלַח (במדבר יא:ז).
SEE: בְּעֵינָא, בְּעֵינֵיהּ, בְּעֵינַיְיהוּ, כְּעֵין, מֵעֵין

עַיִן הָרַע; עֵינָא בִּישָׁא*

the evil eye

לָא קָא מִסְתְּפֵי מָר מֵעֵינָא בִּישָׁא? (בבא מציעא פד,א)
Isn't the master afraid of the evil eye?
* The first expression is Hebrew, and the second is Aramaic.

עַיִן יָפָה

a benevolent eye; good will; a generous person
For an example — see the next entry.

עַיִן רָעָה

an evil eye; ill will; stinginess; a stingy person

שִׁיעוּר תְּרוּמָה: עַיִן יָפָה — אֶחָד מֵאַרְבָּעִים ... וְהַבֵּינוֹנִית — מֵחֲמִישִּׁים, וְהָרָעָה — מִשִּׁשִּׁים. (משנה תרומה פ"ד מ"ג)
The proper quantity of t^eruma: a generous person [gives] one-fortieth (of his crop), and an average person one-fiftieth, and a stingy person one-sixtieth.

עִיקָּרָא עִיקָּר

(1) root
the root of the date-palm עִיקָּרָא דְּדִיקְלָא (סוכה לו,ב)

(2) the essence; the basis; the beginning
מֵעִיקָּרָא דְּדִינָא פִּירְכָא (קידושין ד,ב)
[there is] a refutation [of the argument] from the basis of the analogy (= from the initial premise)
SEE: מֵעִיקָּרָא

עַל (עלל:* עָלֵיל .prt, לֵיעוֹל .fut, עוֹל .imp, לְמֵיעַל .inf)

he came; he entered בָּא; נִכְנַס

ר' חִיָּיא בַּר אַבָּא חֲלַשׁ; עַל לְגַבֵּיהּ ר' יוֹחָנָן. (ברכות ה,ב)
R. Ḥiyya b. Abba became ill; R. Yoḥanan came to [visit] him.

* For the full conjugation of this verb, see *Grammar for Gemara:* Chapter 4, Verb 16. Do not confuse this Aramaic verb with the Hebrew verb, עָלָה, *he went up*. The Aramaic עַל does not mean *he went up*, but rather *he went in*. On the other hand, עָלָה may occasionally be explained in the same sense as the Aramaic עַל, *he entered*. (See יואל ד:יב and ירמיה ד:כט.)

עַל

on; upon; on top of; against; with reference to; on account of
In Aramaic as in Hebrew, this preposition is often used with personal-pronoun suffixes:*

on him; on it (m.)	עָלָיו	עֲלֵיהּ
on her; on it (f.)	עָלֶיהָ	עֲלַהּ

שִׁיעְבּוּדָא עֲלֵיהּ** דִּידֵיהּ רַמְיָא (בבא קמא ח, רע"ב)
the liability remains upon him

* For a full list of the forms thus created, see *Grammar for Gemara:* Chapter 7.323.
** The construction עֲלֵיהּ דִּידֵיהּ means literally "*on it, that of him.*" See *Grammar for Gemara:* Chapter 9.2.
SEE: עִילָּוֵי, אַ-

עַל אַחַת כַּמָּה וְכַמָּה*

how much more so; all the more so

וּמָה דְּבָרִים שֶׁדַּרְכָּן לַעֲשׂוֹתָן בְּפַרְהֶסְיָא — אָמְרָה תּוֹרָה: "הַצְנֵעַ לֶכֶת", דְּבָרִים שֶׁדַּרְכָּן לַעֲשׂוֹתָן בְּצִנְעָא — עַל אַחַת כַּמָּה וְכַמָּה! (סוכה מט,ב; מכות כד,א ע"פ מיכה ו:ח)
If [regarding] matters that people generally do in public

because — **עַל שׁוּם שֶׁ-**

For an example — see שׁוּם[1].

עָלָה (עלי: עוֹלֶה .prt, יַעֲלֶה .fut, עֲלֵה .imp, לַעֲלוֹת .inf)

he went up; he rose

Besides the common meaning in Biblical Hebrew, several other usages appear in the Mishna and Talmud:

(1) it counted; it was counted

שַׁבָּת עוֹלָה וְאֵינָהּ מַפְסֶקֶת. (מועד קטן יט,א: משנה פ״ג מ״ה)

The Sabbath counts (as one of the seven days of mourning), but it does not discontinue (the mourning after the Sabbath).

(2) it was neutralized

תְּרוּמָה עוֹלָה בְּאֶחָד וּמֵאָה. (משנה תרומות פ״ד מ״ז)

*T*ruma is neutralized in one hundred and one parts. (A ratio of 100:1 is required.)*

(3) he achieved; he was successful

This is the meaning of the expression עָלָה בְּיָדוֹ, literally *"it came up into his hand."*

הַרְבֵּה עָשׂוּ כְּרִ׳ יִשְׁמָעֵאל, וְעָלְתָה בְּיָדָן. (ברכות לה,ב)

Many acted like R. Yishmael, and they were successful.

SEE: סְלֵיק, the Aramaic equivalent

עֲלָיךְ אֲמַר קְרָא — עָלֶיךָ אָמַר הַכָּתוּב ...

With regard to you (in anticipation of your argument), the pasuk has stated ...

אֲמַר לֵיהּ רַב פָּפִּי לְרַב פָּפָּא: ... מוּתָּר לַעֲשׂוֹת מוּגְמָר בְּיוֹם טוֹב? ... אֲמַר לֵיהּ: עֲלָיךְ אֲמַר קְרָא: "אַךְ אֲשֶׁר יֵאָכֵל לְכָל נֶפֶשׁ" — דָּבָר הַשָּׁוֶה לְכָל נֶפֶשׁ. (כתובות ז,א ע״פ שמות יב: טז)

Rav Pappi said to Rav Pappa: ... Is it permitted to make a perfume (by placing spices upon coals) on a festival? ... [Rav Pappa] said to him: With regard to you the pasuk says: "Only that which is eaten by every person" — something which is useful for everybody.

עָלְמָא הָעוֹלָם — **the world**

בְּהַאי עָלְמָא (קידושין לט,ב ועוד) — *in this world*

SEE: כּוּלֵּי עָלְמָא, עוֹלָם

דְּעָלְמָא

(1) שֶׁל הָעוֹלָם — **of the world**

רוּבָּא דְעָלְמָא (קידושין ו,א ועוד) *the majority of the world*

(2) לֹא שֶׁל עַצְמוֹ; שֶׁל אֲחֵרִים

not his own; of others

הָא בְּמֵת דִּידֵיהּ, הָא בְּמֵת דְּעָלְמָא. (שבת קה, רע״ב)

This [text refers] to his own deceased [relative]; the other [refers] to the deceased of others.

(3) רָגִיל — **in general; ordinary**

אֱינִישׁ דְּעָלְמָא (ראש השנה כב,ב)

an ordinary person; a layman (as opposed to a great scholar)

the Torah states: "Walk humbly," how much more so [regarding] matters they generally do in private!

* A more complete form of this expression appears in the Tosefta: עַל אַחַת כַּמָּה וְכַמָּה קוּלִּין וַחֲמוּרִין יֵשׁ לַדָּבָר (תוספתא ברכות פ״ז הי״ט)

SEE: לֹא כָּל שֶׁכֵּן

עַל גַּב/גַּבֵּי

(1) on (top of); by the side of; over

עַל גַּבֵּי מִטָּה (שבת יב,ב) — *on a bed*

(2) on the basis of; by means of; through

מַעֲשֵׂר שֵׁנִי ... שֶׁפְּדָאוֹ עַל גַּבֵּי אֲסִימוֹן* (ברכות מז,ב)

*[produce of] the second tithe ... which he had redeemed** by means of a metal slug*

This Hebrew expression is also used with personal-pronoun suffixes:

on him/it (m.); by him/it (m.) — עַל גַּבָּיו

on her/it (f.); by her/it (f.) — עַל גַּבָּהּ

on them; by them — עַל גַּבֵּיהֶם/גַּבָּן

כְּשֶׁיִּשְׂרָאֵל עוֹמֵד עַל גַּבָּיו (חולין ג,א ועוד)

when a Jew is standing over him

* In modern Israel, an אֲסִימוֹן is a *telephone token.*

** Literally: *that he had redeemed it*

SEE: גַּבֵּי, אַף עַל גַּב

עַל יַד עַל יַד — **little by little; gradually**

רוֹעֶה שֶׁעָשָׂה תְּשׁוּבָה — אֵין מְחַיְּיבִין אוֹתוֹ לִמְכּוֹר מִיָּד, אֶלָּא מוֹכֵר עַל יַד עַל יַד. (בבא קמא פ,א)

A shepherd who has repented (raising sheep and goats in the cultivated fields of Eretz Yisrael) is not required to sell [them all] immediately, but he may sell [them off] little by little.

עַל כָּרְח- — **against the will of ...; of necessity**

In the Talmud, this expression is always used with personal-pronoun suffixes — usually with the prefix -בְּ.

SEE: -בְּעַל כָּרְח and the next entry

עַל כָּרְחָךְ — **against your will; of necessity**

This term is used to introduce a Talmudic conclusion, as if to say: Of necessity you must conclude that ...

עַל כָּרְחָךְ כְּרַב שֵׁשֶׁת סְבִירָא לֵיהּ. (קידושין כח,ב)

Of necessity [you must conclude that] he (= Resh Lakish) agrees with Rav Shesheth.

עַל מְנַת

(1) on condition that

מַתָּנָה עַל מְנַת לְהַחֲזִיר (סוכה מא,ב)

a gift [given] on condition that it be returned

(2) in order (to); with the intention (of); with a view (towards)

הַקּוֹרֵעַ עַל מְנַת לִתְפּוֹר שְׁתֵּי תְפִירוֹת (שבת עג, סע״ב: משנה ז:ב)

one who tears in order to sew two stitches

worldly **(4) שֶׁל הָעוֹלָם**

מִילֵּי דְעָלְמָא (ברכות ג,ב)

worldly matters (as opposed to spiritual, Torah matters)

עַם הָאָרֶץ (pl. עַמֵּי הָאָרֶץ)

(1) ignoramus; an illiterate, uncultured person (as opposed to a תַּלְמִיד חָכָם)

וְלֹא עַם הָאָרֶץ חָסִיד (משנה אבות פ״ב מ״ה)

and an ignoramus is not a pious person

(2) a person who is not scrupulous (regarding the laws of t^e^rumoth and tithes and laws of ritual purity — as opposed to a חָבֵר)

אַל תְּהִי רָגִיל אֵצֶל עַם הָאָרֶץ, שֶׁסּוֹפוֹ לְהַאֲכִילְךָ טְבָלִים. (נדרים כ,א ע״פ כת״י)

Do not associate with an "am ha'aretz" frequently, for he will eventually give you untithed produce to eat.

עַמְמִין גּוֹיִים gentiles; non-Jews

אֲמַר רָבָא: מֵת — בְּיוֹם טוֹב רִאשׁוֹן יִתְעַסְּקוּ בּוֹ עַמְמִין; בְּיוֹם טוֹב שֵׁנִי יִתְעַסְּקוּ בּוֹ יִשְׂרָאֵל ... (ביצה ו, רע״א ע״פ כת״י)

Rava said: [As for] a corpse — on the first day of a festival, (only) non-Jews should attend to it; on the second day of a festival Jews should attend to it ...*

* The terms "first day of a festival" and "second day of a festival" that are used by the Babylonian amora Rava apply only outside Erets Yisrael, where second days of festivals are observed — i.e., on the second and eighth days of Pesaḥ, on the second day of Sukkoth and on the ninth (= Simḥath Torah), and on the second day of Shavu'oth.

עַמְרָא (abs. and constr. עֲמַר) צֶמֶר wool

״תְּכֵלֶת״ עַמְרָא הוּא. (יבמות ד,ב ע״פ במדבר טו:לח)

[The term] תְּכֵלֶת [refers to blue] wool.

עֲמַר גּוּפְנָא (שבת קי,ב)

"wool of the vine" (= the Hebrew צֶמֶר גֶּפֶן, cotton)

עִנְיָן; עִנְיָינָא*

(1) subject (of study); topic; passage; context

אֵין לוֹ אֶלָּא מַה שֶּׁאָמוּר בָּעִנְיָן. (חולין קל,א: משנה פ״י מ״א)

He receives only what is stated in the passage.

הָכָא מֵעִנְיָינֵיהּ דִּקְרָא, וְהָתָם מֵעִנְיָינֵיהּ דִּקְרָא. (סכות ח,א)

Here [it must be interpreted] in keeping with the context of the pasuk, and there in keeping with the context of the pasuk.

(2) connection; relation; bearing

For examples, see:

(וְ)כִי מָה עִנְיָן ... אֵצֶל ..., אִם אֵינוֹ עִנְיָן ל ... תְּנֵהוּ עִנְיָן ל־

* The first form is Hebrew, and the second is Aramaic.

SEE: דָּבָר הַלָּמֵד מֵעִנְיָנוֹ, וַיִּ״ו מוֹסִיף עַל עִנְיָן רִאשׁוֹן

עֲסַק (עסק: עָסֵיק, act. prt. עָסֵיק, pass. prt.)

he was occupied (with); he dealt (with) עָסַק

The m. pl. participle combined with the suffix ־נַן, we, is very common:

עָסְקִינַן* (= עָסְקִי+אֲנַן) **we are dealing (with)**

עֲסִיקִינַן (= עֲסִיקִי+אֲנַן) **we are dealing (with)**

אַטּוּ בְּשׁוּפְטָנֵי עֲסִיקִינַן דְּיָהֲבֵי בְּכַלְיָא רַבָּא וְשָׁקְלֵי בְּכַלְיָא זוּטָא?! (בבא מציעא מ,א ע״פ כת״י)

Are we dealing with fools who give out [merchandise] with a large measure and take [it] back with a small measure?!

* In our printed editions, the active עָסְקִינַן is the common form; in manuscripts, the passive עֲסִיקִינַן predominates.

SEE: (בְּ)מַאי עָסְקִינַן, הָכָא בְּמַאי עֲסִיקִינַן, אִיעֲסַק

עֵצָה טוֹבָה קָא מַשְׁמַע לַן

He is (merely) telling us some good advice.

The text that has been quoted in the Talmud does not necessarily teach us a normative requirement, but it recommends a certain procedure as advisable.

For examples, see עירובין לט,א and גיטין כב,ב ושי״נ.

עֲצֶרֶת* (= חַג הַשָּׁבוּעוֹת)

***Shavu'oth*; the Feast of Weeks**

In the Midrash and Talmud, this is the standard name for the festival of Shavu'oth.

אֵין מְבִיאִין בִּיכּוּרִים קוֹדֶם לָעֲצֶרֶת. (משנה ביכורים פ״א מ״ג)

One may not bring the first fruits before Shavu'oth.

* The literal meaning of this Biblical word is a matter of dispute among the commentators to ויקרא כג:לו where it is used in connection with the eighth day of Sukkoth, now called שְׁמִינִי עֲצֶרֶת. See the commentary of the Ramban who draws an analogy between that day and Shavu'oth.

עֲקַר (עקר: עָקַר .prt, לְמִיעְקַר .inf) עָקַר

he uprooted; he eradicated; he detached; he lifted; he moved

וְכִי עָקַר אֱינִישׁ, כַּרְעֵיהּ דְּיַמִּינָא עָקַר בְּרֵישָׁא (יומא יא,ב)

and when a man moves, he lifts his right foot first

עֲרַאי temporariness; casualness; chance

This Hebrew noun is often used in an adjectival or adverbial sense.

בִּנְיַן עֲרַאי לֹא אָסְרָה תוֹרָה. (ביצה לב, סע״ב)

The Torah did not forbid temporary building.

אוֹכְלִין וְשׁוֹתִין עֲרַאי חוּץ לַסּוּכָּה. (סוכה כה,א: פ״ב מ״ד)

Casual eating and casual drinking are permitted outside the sukka.

עָרֵיב (ערב פַּעֵל: מְעָרֵב .prt, לִיעָרֵב .fut, לְעָרוּבֵי .inf)

(1) עֵרַב; עִרְבֵּב he mixed

אִי בְּעֵית לְעָרוּבֵי, מִי הֲוָה שְׁרֵי לָךְ?! (בבא מציעא מ,ב)

If you had wanted to mix [them], would it have been permitted to you?!

(2) עֵרַב; עָשָׂה עֵרוּב he arranged an eruv

אֲבוּהּ דִּשְׁמוּאֵל מְעָרֵב אַכּוּלַּהּ נְהַרְדְּעָא (ביצה טז,ב)

Sh^e^muel's father arranged an eruv for the whole [city of] N^e^hard^e^a

עַרְסָא* עֶרֶשׂ; מִטָּה **bed**

כַּד הֲוָה קְצִיר וּרְמֵי בְּעַרְסֵיהּ (בבא בתרא קנג, סע"א)
when he was sick and lying in his bed

* The Hebrew noun עֲרִיסָה, *a crib*, occurs in ב"ב קלא,ב and is used in Modern Hebrew. The expression found in the Bible, עַל עֶרֶשׂ דְּוָי (תהלים מא,ד), *on (one's) sick bed*, is also used in Modern Hebrew, and so is שִׁיר עֶרֶשׂ, *lullaby*.

עַרְעֵר (עור פַּלְפֵּל: מְעַרְעֵר .prt)

עִרְעֵר **he contested; he challenged**

הַשְׁתָּא בַּעַל לָא קָא מְעַרְעֵר, אֲנַן נֵיקוּם וּנְעַרְעֵר עֲלַהּ?! (גיטין ה, רע"ב)
Now that the husband is not challenging (the legitimacy of the bill of divorce), shall we stand up and challenge it?!

עַרְעָר **a challenge**

אֵין עַרְעָר פָּחוֹת מִשְּׁנַיִם. (בבא בתרא לב,א ושי"נ)
There is no [valid] challenge (to someone's ownership) by less than two [witnesses].

עֲרַק* (ערק: עָרִיק .prt)

בָּרַח; נָס **he ran away; he fled**

עֲרַק טְשָׁא בְּהַהוּא בֵּי בָנֵי (קידושין לט, סע"ב)
he ran away and hid in a bathhouse

* In Modern Hebrew, the verb עָרַק is used in a special sense, *he deserted (from the army)*, and an עָרִיק is *a deserter*.

עֲשֵׂה

"Do!"; a positive (Biblical) commandment

יָבֹא עֲשֵׂה וְיִדְחֶה לֹא תַעֲשֶׂה (שבת קלג,א ושי"נ)
let the positive commandment come and supersede the negative commandment (when the two commandments are in conflict with each other)

SEE: אִיסוּר עֲשֵׂה, חַיָּיבֵי עֲשֵׂה, קוּם וַעֲשֵׂה, לָאו הַבָּא בִּכְלַל עֲשֵׂה

עַשַּׂר (עשר פַּעֵל: מְעַשַּׂר .prt, לְעַשַּׂר .fut, לְעַשּׂוֹרֵי .inf)

עִשֵּׂר **he tithed**

דִּלְמָא אָתֵי לְעַשּׂוֹרֵי בְּיוֹם טוֹב (חגיגה ח,א)
perhaps he will come to tithe on a festival

עַשְׂרָה SEE: בֵּי עַשְׂרָה

מֵעַתָּה

from now; consequently; according to this

For examples, see אֶלָּא מֵעַתָּה and אֱמוֹר מֵעַתָּה.

עַתִּיק* יָשָׁן **old; ancient**

חַמְרָא עַתִּיקָא (עבודה זרה סו, רע"א) *old wine*

* This adjective also appears in Biblical Hebrew (e.g., דבה"י א ד:כב) and in Biblical Aramaic (e.g., דניאל ז:ט).

עַתִּיר* עָשִׁיר **rich; wealthy**

וּמַקְרֵינָא לִבְנֵי עֲנִיֵּי כִּבְנֵי עַתִּירֵי (תענית כד, סע"א)
and I teach the children of the poor as [I teach] the children of the wealthy

* This adjective is also used in Modern Hebrew, especially in the expression עָתִיר נְכָסִים, *rich in property*.

פ

פּוּמָא (פּוּם* abs. and constr.)

mouth; opening פֶּה

לָא הֲוָה פָּסֵיק פּוּמֵיהּ מִגִּירְסָא (שבת ל, רע"ב ועוד)

his mouth did not cease [reciting Torah] learning

יָתֵיב אַפּוּמָא דִמְטַלַּלְתָּא (סוכה ג,א)

sitting at the opening of the sukka

* This form is vocalized פֹּום in Yemenite editions of Targum Onkelos.

SEE: אַפּוּמָא ד־, לְפוּם

פּוּק imp. (נפק) צֵא! **go out!**

פּוּק חֲזִי מַאי עַמָּא דָּבַר

צֵא וּרְאֵה מַה נּוֹהֵג הָעָם!

Go out [and] see what people do!

When the halakha is unsettled about a specific issue, it is sometimes determined by the actual practice of the common people.

משנה: הַשּׁוֹתֶה מַיִם לִצְמָאוֹ מְבָרֵךְ שֶׁהַכֹּל נִהְיֶה בִּדְבָרוֹ. ר׳ טַרְפוֹן אוֹמֵר: בּוֹרֵא נְפָשׁוֹת רַבּוֹת וְחֶסְרוֹנָן. (ברכות מד, סע"א ורש"י שם וש"נ: משנה פ"ו מ"ח)

תלמוד: אֲמַר לֵיהּ רָבָא בַּר רַב חָנָן לְאַבָּיֵי ... הִלְכְתָא מַאי? אֲמַר לֵיהּ: פּוּק חֲזִי מַאי עַמָּא דָּבַר! (שם מה, רע"א)

MISHNA: [If] one drinks water to [quench] his thirst, he recites (before drinking) ... שֶׁהַכֹּל. *R. Tarfon says: (He recites before drinking)* ... בּוֹרֵא נְפָשׁוֹת.

TALMUD: Rava b. Rav Ḥanan said to Abbayé ...: What is the halakha? [Abbayé] said to him: Go out [and] see what people do!

SEE: נְפַק

פּוּק תְּנִי לְבָרָא צֵא וּשְׁנֵה בַחוּץ!

Go out [and] recite [the baraitha] outside (the beth midrash)!

The baraitha that has been presented is not genuine, and so the halakha it contains is not acceptable.

תָּנֵי ר׳ אַבָּהוּ קַמֵּיהּ דְּר׳ יוֹחָנָן: כָּל הַמְקַלְקְלִין פְּטוּרִין חוּץ מֵחוֹבֵל וּמַבְעִיר. אֲמַר לֵיהּ: פּוּק, תְּנִי לְבָרָא! חוֹבֵל וּמַבְעִיר אֵינָהּ מִשְׁנָה. (שבת קו, רע"א וש"נ)

R. Abbahu teaches before R. Yoḥanan: All who effect damage (by their actions) are exempt (from desecrating the Sabbath) except for he who wounds and he who sets fire (to a stack of grain). [R. Yoḥanan] said to him: Go out [and] recite it outside (the beth midrash)! "Wounding" and "setting fire" is not an [authentic] teaching.

SEE: אֵינָהּ מִשְׁנָה

פּוּרְתָּא מְעַט **a little**

טוּבָא גָרֵיר; פּוּרְתָּא סָעֵיד. (ברכות לה, סע"ב)

[Drinking] a lot (of wine) stimulates (the appetite); a little is filling.

פָּטוּר; פְּטִיר* pass. prt. (פטר)

exempt (from punishment or responsibility)

כָּל פְּטוּרֵי דְשַׁבָּת פָּטוּר אֲבָל אָסוּר — בַּר מֵהָנֵי תְּלָת דְּפָטוּר וּמוּתָּר ... (שבת ג, רע"א ורש"י ותוס׳ שם)

All the exemptions [stated] with regard to the Sabbath are [cases where a person is] exempt (from punishment) but forbidden (to perform the act) — except for these three [cases] where he is exempt and [the act is] permitted ...

אַתְּ הוּא דִמְחַיַּיבְתְּ, אֲבָל כּוּלֵּי עָלְמָא פְּטִירֵי. (סוכה כה,ב)

*You are obligated (to wear t*ᵉ*fillin), but all [other mourners] are exempt.*

* The first form is Hebrew, and the second is Aramaic.

an exemption **פְּטוּר; פְּטוּרָא***

מֵהֶן לְחִיּוּב, וּמֵהֶן לִפְטוּר (שבת ב,ב)

some of them [refer] to obligation and some of them [refer] to exemption

For another example, see the previous entry.

* The first form is Hebrew, and the second is Aramaic.

SEE: פְּטַר

פָּטַר (פטר: פּוֹטֵר a. prt., פָּטוּר p. prt., לִפְטוֹר inf.);

פְּטַר* (פטר: פָּטַר a. prt., פְּטִיר p. prt., לְמִיפְטַר inf.)

(1) he released; he dismissed; he divorced

בֵּית שַׁמַּאי אוֹמְרִים: פּוֹטֵר אָדָם אֶת אִשְׁתּוֹ בְּגֵט יָשָׁן, וּבֵית הִלֵּל אוֹסְרִין. וְאֵיזֶהוּ גֵט יָשָׁן? כָּל שֶׁנִּתְיַחֵד עִמָּהּ אַחַר שֶׁכְּתָבוֹ לָהּ. (גיטין עט,ב: משנה פ"ח מ"ד)

Beth Shammai says: A man may divorce his wife with an old bill of divorce, but Beth Hillel prohibits [the practice]. And what is [considered] "an old bill of divorce"? Any case in which [the husband] has been alone with her (= his wife) after he (or his scribe) wrote it for [divorcing] her.

(2) he freed (from punishment, responsibility, or obligation)**; he acquitted; he exempted**

אָנוּס רַחֲמָנָא פַּטְרֵיהּ. (נדרים כז,א וש"נ)

The Torah exempted one who was prevented by unavoidable circumstances.

מְבָרֵךְ עַל הָעִיקָּר וּפוֹטֵר אֶת הַטְּפֵלָה (ברכות מד, רע"א: משנה פ"ו מ"ז)

*he recites a b*ᵉ*rakha over the main [food] and (thereby) exempts the secondary one (from a b*ᵉ*rakha)*

* The first verb is Hebrew, and the second is Aramaic.

פַּיֵּיס (פוס פָּעַל: מְפַיֵּיס .prt, לְפַיּוֹסֵי .inf) **פַּיֵּס**

he appeased; he made peace; he quieted

אֲזַל פַּיְּיסֵיה לְבַעַל דִּינֵיה (מועד קטן טז,א)

he went [and] appeased his opponent

פֵּירוּקָא פֵּרוּק; תֵּרוּץ

a resolution (of a difficulty); a reply

בְּקוּשְׁיָא דר' זֵירָא וּבְפֵירוּקָא דְאַבָּיֵי פְּלִיגֵי. (בבא קמא יד,א)

They disagree with regard to the difficulty of R. Zera and the resolution of Abbayé.

SEE: מְפָרֵק

בְּפֵירוּשׁ

clearly; explicitly

For an example, see לָאו בְּפֵירוּשׁ אִיתְּמַר אֶלָּא מִכְּלָלָא.

פִּירְכָא "שְׁבִירָה"; קֻשְׁיָא; סְתִירָה

a refutation; a contradiction

לְר' אֱלִיעֶזֶר, פֵּירוּקָא דְרָבָא פִּירְכָא הִיא! (יבמות עט, סע"ב)

The reply of Rava is a contradiction to [the opinion of] R. Eliezer!

SEE: פְּרַךְ

פִּירְקָא

chapter (1) פֶּרֶק

בְּכוּלֵּיהּ פִּרְקִין הֲלָכָה כְּבֵית הִלֵּל — בַּר מֵהָא דַהֲלָכָה כְּבֵית שַׁמַּאי. (ברכות נב,ב)

Throughout our whole chapter, the halakhic ruling is in accordance with Beth Hillel — except for this [instance] where the halakhic ruling is in accordance with the Beth Shammai.

(2) דְּרָשָׁה בְּצִבּוּר

a public lecture (delivered on the Sabbath before a general audience)

כִּי הֲוָה דָּרֵישׁ ר' מֵאִיר בְּפִירְקֵיהּ, הֲוָה דָּרֵישׁ תִּילְתָּא שְׁמַעְתָּא, תִּילְתָּא אַגַּדְתָּא, תִּילְתָּא מַתְלֵי. (סנהדרין לח, סע"ב)

When R. Méir would deliver his public lecture, he would devote one-third [to] halakha, one-third [to] aggada, [and] one-third [to] parables.

פְּלַג (פלג:* פָּלֵיג .act. prt, פְּלִיג .pass. prt, לִיפְלוֹג .fut, לְמִיפְלַג .inf)

(1) חָלַק **he divided** (into shares);

he distributed; he received (a portion)

אֲזַל רַב סַפְרָא, פְּלַג לֵיהּ בְּלָא דַעְתֵּיהּ דְּאִיסּוּר בְּאַפֵּי בֵּי תְרֵי. (בבא מציעא לא, סע"ב)

Rav Safra went, and he divided it without Issur's knowledge in the presence of two people.

פְּלַג רִיפְתָּא לִינוּקֵי (תענית כג, רע"ב)

he distributed the bread to the children

(2) חִלֵּק; הִבְדִּיל **he separated;**

he differentiated; he drew a distinction

נִכְתּוֹב רַחֲמָנָא: "מִפְּנֵי שֵׂיבָה זָקֵן תָּקוּם וְהָדַרְתָּ"! מַאי שְׁנָא דִּפְלַגִינְהוּ רַחֲמָנָא? (קידושין לב, סע"ב ע"פ ויקרא יט:לב)

Let the Torah write (in one clause): "You shall rise before and honor שֵׂיבָה *[and]* "זָקֵן *— why did the Torah differentiate between them (=* שֵׂיבָה *and* זָקֵן*, by writing: You shall rise before* שֵׂיבָה*, and honor the presence of a* זָקֵן*)?*

* For the full conjugation of this verb, see *Grammar for Grammar*: Chapter 4, Verb 1.

SEE: פְּלִיג, לָא פְלוּג רַבָּנַן, אִיפְּלִיג

פַּלְגָא/פַּלְגוּ (.pl פַּלְגֵי) חֲצִי **half**

פַּלְגָא עֲלַי וּפַלְגָא עֲלָךְ (שבת פט,ב)

half [the responsibility] is upon me and half upon you

פַּלְגְאָה

an argumentative person בַּעַל מַחֲלֹקֶת

This epithet refers to an amora who frequently disagrees with his colleagues.

וּמְקַמֵּי פַּלְגְאָה נֵיקוּם?! (גיטין סב, סע"א ורש"י שם)

Shall we stand up for [such] an argumentative person?!

פְּלוּגְתָּא*

controversy; a difference of opinion מַחֲלֹקֶת

See examples under the next four entries.

* In one Talmudic discussion (בבא בתרא ב,רע"ב-ג,א), this Aramaic noun is used as a translation of the Hebrew noun מְחִיצָה, *a dividing wall.*

SEE: בַּר פְּלוּגְתָּא

וּבִפְלוּגְתָּא דְהָנֵי תַנָּאֵי

וּבְמַחֲלֹקֶת שֶׁל הַתַּנָּאִים הָאֵלֶּה ...

And [it is the subject] of a controversy between these tannaim ...

This expression usually indicates that the halakhic *controversy* between two tannaim that has been presented in the Talmud is equivalent to another *controversy* between two other tannaim that is about to be quoted.

מָר סָבַר: צָרִיךְ אֶגֶד, וּמָר סָבַר: אֵין צָרִיךְ אֶגֶד. וּבִפְלוּגְתָּא דְהָנֵי תַנָּאֵי, דְּתַנְיָא: לוּלָב, בֵּין אָגוּד בֵּין שֶׁאֵינוֹ אָגוּד, כָּשֵׁר; ר' יְהוּדָה אוֹמֵר: אָגוּד כָּשֵׁר, שֶׁאֵינוֹ אָגוּד פָּסוּל. (סוכה יא,ב)

One (= R. Shim'on b. Y'hotzadak) holds: [The four species] must be tied together, and the others (= the Hakhamim) hold: They need not be tied together. And [their controversy is the subject] of a controversy between these tannaim, as it is stated (in a baraitha): A lulav is valid — whether it is tied together [with the other three species] or not tied together; R. Y'huda says: [If] tied together, it is valid, [but if] not tied together, it is invalid.

פְּלוּגְתָּא דְר' ... וְר' ...

מַחֲלֹקֶת בֵּין ר' ... לְבֵין ר' ...

[the halakha depends upon the outcome of] the controversy between R. ... and R. ...

הִנִּיחַ בְּזָוִית זוֹ וּמָצָא בְּזָוִית אַחֶרֶת — פְּלוּגְתָּא דְרַבָּן שִׁמְעוֹן בֶּן גַּמְלִיאֵל וְרַבָּנַן (פסחים י, רע"ב)

[if] one placed [hametz] in one corner and (then) found [hametz] in another corner — [the halakha of whether he must search for more hametz depends upon the outcome of] the controversy between Rabban Shim'on b. Gamliel and the Hakhamim

בִּפְלוּגְתָּא דר׳ ... וְר׳ ... קָמִיפַּלְגִי*

בְּמַחֲלֹקֶת בֵּין ר׳ ... לְבֵין ר׳ ... חֲלוּקִים.

They disagree about [the same issue that is the subject of] a controversy between R. ... and R. ....

For an example — see פסחים כט,ב.

* The verb קָמִיפַּלְגִי sometimes comes at the beginning of this sentence — rather than at the end. See the entry (וְקָ)מִיפַּלְגִי בִּפְלוּגְתָּא דְר׳ ... וְר׳ .... When the equation between the two controversies is tentative and ultimately rejected by the Talmud, this formula is preceded by לֵימָא *(shall we say?)*.

SEE: מִיפַּלְגִי, לֵימָא בִּפְלוּגְתָּא דְר׳ ... וְר׳ ... קָמִיפַּלְגִי

בִּפְלוּגְתָּא לָא קָא מַיְירִי

הוּא אֵינוֹ עוֹסֵק בְּמַחֲלֹקֶת.

He is not dealing with controversy.

The author of this text included only halakhoth that are unanimously accepted, and he omitted those that are subject to controversy.

For an example — see סנהדרין מט,ב.

פְּלוֹנִי (פְלוֹנִית .f)**; פְּלַן/פְּלָנְיָא*** (פְּלָנִיתָא .f)

So-and-so; John Doe; such and such

This term is used as a fictitious name for a person or a designation of an unspecified place or time-unit and so on.

פְּלוֹנִי שֶׁלָּמַד תּוֹרָה: רְאוּ כַּמָּה נָאִים דְּרָכָיו! כַּמָּה מְתוּקָּנִים מַעֲשָׂיו! (יומא פו,א)

So-and-so who has learned Torah: See how pleasant are his ways! How fine is his behavior!

מָקוֹם פְּלוֹנִי (מכות ב,א ועוד)
such and such a place

חַמְרֵיה דִּפְלָנְיָא בַּר פְּלָנִיתָא (שבת סו,ב)
the wine of So-and-so, son of (Mrs.) So-and-so

* The first form is Hebrew, and the others are Aramaic.

פְּלַח (פלח:* פָּלַח .prt)

he served; he worshipped עָבַד

מִדִּפְלַחוּ יִשְׂרָאֵל לָעֵגֶל (עבודה זרה נג,ב)
since the Israelites served the [golden] calf

* The Hebrew noun פֻּלְחָן, *worship*, comes from the same root. In the Targumim, the verb is also used to translate the Hebrew verb עָבַד in the sense of *he worked*, as in Targum Onkelos to בראשית כט:טו.

פְּלִיג (פלג) **pass. prt.**

divided (1) מְחֻלָּק

זוּזֵי כְּמַאן דִּפְלִיגֵי דָּמוּ. (בבא מציעא סט, סע״א-רע״ב)
The money is considered as if already divided.

disagreeing; differing (in opinion); conflicting (2) חָלוּק

For examples, see the next two entries.

SEE: ״הֲלָכָה״ מִכְּלָל דִּפְלִיגִי, (וְ)לָא פְלִיגִי, כּוּלֵּי עָלְמָא לָא פְלִיגִי, כִּי פְלִיגִי, פְּלַג

וּפְלִיגָא דִידֵיהּ אַדִּידֵיהּ וַחֲלוּקָה שֶׁלּוֹ עַל שֶׁלּוֹ

"and his (statement) conflicts with his"

The statement, which has just been quoted in the Talmud in the name of an amora, contradicts another statement of the same amora, which the Talmud now proceeds to quote.

For an example — see שבת יג, סע״א.

וּפְלִיגָא דְר׳ ... (= וּפְלִיגָא אַדְּר׳ ...)

וַחֲלוּקָה עַל [דִּבְרֵי] ר׳ ...

And [this statement] disagrees with [the statement] of R. ...

The statement which was quoted in the Talmud above in the name of one hakham (usually an amora) is in conflict with the statement of another hakham, which the Talmud now proceeds to quote.

הֵבִיאוּ לִפְנֵיהֶם תְּאֵנִים וַעֲנָבִים בְּתוֹךְ הַסְּעוּדָה — אָמַר רַב הוּנָא: טְעוּנִים בְּרָכָה לִפְנֵיהֶם ... וּפְלִיגָא דְר׳ חִיָּיא, דְּאָמַר ר׳ חִיָּיא: פַּת פּוֹטֶרֶת כָּל מִינֵי מַאֲכָל, וְיַיִן פּוֹטֵר כָּל מִינֵי מַשְׁקִים. (ברכות מא,ב ורש״י שם)

[If] figs or dates were brought before him during the meal — Rav Huna said: A b^e^rakha must be recited before [eating] them ... And [that statement] disagrees with [the statement] of R. Hiyya, for R. Hiyya said: [A b^e^rakha recited over] bread exempts all types of food [subsequently eaten in the meal from a b^e^rakha of their own], and [a b^e^rakha over] wine exempts all types of drinks [from a separate b^e^rakha].

פְּלַן/פְּלָנְיָא SEE: פְּלוֹנִי

argumentation; dialectics **פִּלְפּוּל; פִּלְפּוּלָא***

אִי חַס וְשָׁלוֹם מִשְׁתַּכְּחָא תּוֹרָה מִיִּשְׂרָאֵל, מְהַדְרְנָא לַהּ מִפִּילְפּוּלִי (ב״מ פה,ב)

If, God forbid, the Torah were to be forgotten by the Jewish people, I would restore it through my argumentation.

* The first form is Hebrew, and the second is Aramaic.

towards evening לִפְנוֹת עֶרֶב **פַּנְיָא***

הַהוּא יוֹמָא אַפַּנְיָא** דְּמַעֲלֵי שַׁבְּתָא הֲוָה. (ב״מ מט, סע״א)

That day it was towards the evening before the Sabbath (= late Friday afternoon).

* The root פני expresses the idea of *turning.*

** The prefix -אַ on is best left untranslated in this case.

the inside; the interior **פְּנִים**

זְבִיחָה מְיוּחֶדֶת שֶׁהִיא עֲבוֹדַת פְּנִים וְחַיָּיבִין עָלֶיהָ מִיתָה (סנהדרין ס,ב ע״פ שמות כב:יט)

slaughtering [an animal] is unique, since it is a service [performed] in the interior [of the Beth HaMikdash], and [people who slaughter as an idolatrous practice] incur [the] death [penalty] on account of it

This Hebrew noun is often used with a prefix in an adverbial sense.

inside; within בִּפְנִים
towards the inside; inside; within לִפְנִים
from the inside; from within מִבִּפְנִים

SEE: לִפְנִים, לִפְנֵי וְלִפְנִים, לִפְנִים מִשּׁוּרַת הַדִּין

פָּסוּל; פְּסִיל* (פסל) pass. prt.

invalid; unfit; disqualified

לוּלָב הַגָּזוּל וְהַיָּבֵשׁ פָּסוּל. (סוכה כט,ב: משנה פ"ג מ"א)

A stolen or a dry palm branch is unfit (for use as a lulav on Sukkoth).

* The first form is Hebrew, and the second is Aramaic.

פְּסוּל; פְּסוּלָא* a disqualification; a flaw

כֹּהֵן שֶׁנִּמְצָא בוֹ פְּסוּל ... יוֹצֵא וְהוֹלֵךְ לוֹ. (משנה מדות פ"ה מ"ד)

A kohen in whom there was discovered a disqualification ... would leave and go away (from the Temple service).

* The first form is Hebrew, and the second is Aramaic.

פְּסוּקָא פָּסוּק; כָּתוּב *pasuk*; Biblical verse

For an example, see פְּסַק.

SEE: קְרָא, כָּתוּב

פְּסֵיד (פסד: פָּסֵיד act. prt., פְּסִיד pass. prt.)

he incurred a loss; it spoiled נִפְסַד; נִתְקַלְקֵל

בִּיְדַיִם קָא פָּסֵיד (בבא קמא קטז,א)

he incurs a loss through [an act done by his own] hands

SEE: אַפְסֵיד

פְּסֵידָא הֶפְסֵד loss; disadvantage

אִי אִיכָּא פְּסֵידָא דְיַתְמֵי (בבא מציעא מב,ב)

if there is a loss for the orphans

פָּסֵיק סִידְרָא

קוֹרֵא פָּרָשָׁה שֶׁל נְבִיאִים אוֹ שֶׁל כְּתוּבִים

he was reciting (and studying) a Biblical section (from נְבִיאִים or כְּתוּבִים)*

רַב הֲוָה פָּסֵיק סִידְרָא קַמֵּיהּ דְּרַבִּי. (יומא פז, סע"א ורש"י שם)

Rav was reciting a Biblical section before Rebbi.

* See also Tosafoth שבת כד, סע"א ד"ה "שאלמלא".

פְּסִיק* רֵישֵׁיהּ וְלָא יָמוּת

הוּא חוֹתֵךְ אֶת רֹאשׁוֹ, וְלֹא יָמוּת?!

"He cuts off its (= an animal's) head, and it will not die?!"

This rhetorical question serves as a metaphor for a *case where the negative consequence of a person's act is inevitable.* It is quoted in the Talmud to limit the application of R. Shim'on's principle that a person is not responsible for an unintentional result of his action. If the result has the character of פְּסִיק רֵישֵׁיהּ (i.e., it is inevitable), then R. Shim'on agrees that the person is held responsible for that result — as if it really were his intention.**

For examples, see שבת קלג,א ור"ח שם ושי"נ.

* This form is popularly pronounced פָּסִיק, as a passive participle, *having been cut off,* but Rashi (in his comment on סוכה לג,ב) seems to regard it as an active form.

** In his *Arukh* (s.v. פסק and סבר), R. Nathan of Rome stipulates that by definition a פְּסִיק רֵישֵׁיהּ must be נִיחָא לֵיהּ, *[the result must be] pleasing to him.* Many authorities, however, disagree with that stipulation. See, for example, שבת קג,א תוספות ד"ה "לא".

פְּסִיקָא לֵיהּ פְּסוּקָה לוֹ; בְּרוּרָה לוֹ

clear-cut to him (without any exceptions or distinctions); definite for him

מִילְּתָא דִּפְסִיקָא לֵיהּ קָתָנֵי; מִילְּתָא דְּלָא פְּסִיקָא לֵיהּ לָא קָתָנֵי. (תמורה כג, רע"ב ורש"י שם)

[The tanna] is stating the case that is clear-cut to him; he is not stating the case that is not clear-cut to him.

SEE: פְּסַק

פְּסַל (פסל: פּוֹסֵל a. prt., פָּסוּל p. prt., לִפְסוֹל inf.);
פְּסַל* (פסל: פָּסֵל a. prt., פְּסִיל p. prt., לְמִיפְסַל inf.)

he disqualified; he invalidated; he declared invalid

אָתֵי בַּעַל וּמְעַרְעֵר וּפָסֵיל לֵיהּ (גיטין ג, רע"א)

the husband may come and challenge [the bill of divorce] and invalidate it

הָעוֹשֶׂה סֻכָּתוֹ כְּמִין צְרִיף ... ר' אֱלִיעֶזֶר פּוֹסֵל, מִפְּנֵי שֶׁאֵין לָהּ גַּג, וַחֲכָמִים מַכְשִׁירִין. (סוכה יט, רע"ב: משנה פ"א מי"א)

[If] one makes his sukka like a (cone-shaped) hut ... R. Eliezer declares [it] invalid, since it has no roof; while the Ḥakhamim declare [it] valid.

* The first verb is Hebrew, and the second is Aramaic.

פְּסַק (פסק: פָּסֵיק act. prt., פְּסִיק pass. prt.)

he cut (off); he severed (1) פָּסַק; חָתַךְ

For an example, see פְּסִיק רֵישֵׁיהּ וְלָא יָמוּת.

he separated; he divided (2) פָּסַק

כָּל פְּסוּקָא דְּלָא פַּסְקֵיהּ מֹשֶׁה — אֲנַן לָא פָּסְקִינַן לֵיהּ. (מגילה כב, רע"א וש"נ)

[As for] any pasuk that Moshe has not separated [as an independent verse] — we do not separate it.

he stopped; he ceased (3) נִפְסַק

קָלָא דְּפָסֵיק (מועד קטן יח, רע"ב; יבמות כה, רע"א)

a rumor that ceases (as opposed to a persistent rumor)

he set; he established; he stated categorically; he decided (4) קָבַע; פָּסַק הֲלָכָה

כְּבָר פַּסְקָהּ תַּנָּא דְּבֵי ר' יִשְׁמָעֵאל. (יבמות פז,א ועוד)

The tanna of the school of R. Yishmael has already decided it (= the halakha).

he recited a pasuk (5) **קָרָא פְּסוּק**

פְּסַק לִי יְנוּקָא פְּסוּקָא (גיטין סח,א)
the boy has recited the pasuk to me

SEE: קָא פָּסֵיק וְתָנֵי, (וּ)מַאי פִּסְקָא, פָּסֵיק סִידְרָא, פְּסוּקָא, פְּסִיקָא לֵיהּ

children pl. ***פְּעוֹטוֹת**

(from the age of six who understand business transactions)

הַפְּעוֹטוֹת — מִקְחָן מִקָּח, וּמִמְכָּרָן מִמְכָּר בְּמִטַּלְטְלִין. (גיטין נט,א: משנה פ"ה מ"ז)
[As for] children — their purchase is a [valid] purchase, and their sale is a [valid] sale with respect to movables.

* In modern Israel, a פָּעוֹטוֹן is a *nursery* that cares for babies less than three years old.

פָּקַע (פקע: פּוֹקֵעַ .prt); ***פְּקַע** (פקע: פָּקַע .prt)

(1) it burst; it was split

the roof burst פְּקַע אִיגָּרָא (פסחים פה, סע"ב)

(2) it was removed; it ceased

כֵּיוָן דְּמִית לֵיהּ, פְּקַע קְדוּשָּׁתֵיהּ מִינַּהּ. (יבמות נו, סע"א)
Once [her husband who was a kohen] died, his sanctity was removed from her.

* The first form is Hebrew, and the second is Aramaic.

openly; publicly בְּגָלוּי ***בְּפַרְהֶסְיָא**

זָעַקְנוּ בִּצְנְעָא וְלֹא נַעֲנֵינוּ; נְבַזֶּה עַצְמֵנוּ בְּפַרְהֶסְיָא. (תענית טז, רע"א)
We have cried out in private, but we were not answered; let us humiliate ourselves publicly.

* This adverb is also used in Modern Hebrew — sometimes with a Hebraized spelling פַּרְהֶסְיָה.

פְּרוּטָה (פְּרוּטוֹת, פְּרִיטֵי* .pl)

p[e]***ruta*; the smallest copper coin**

A p[e]ruta is worth one-eighth of an *issar.*** For many halakhoth, it is regarded as the minimal legal quantity.

הָאִשָּׁה מִתְקַדֶּשֶׁת בְּשָׁוֶה פְּרוּטָה (ב"מ נה,א: משנה פ"ד מ"ז)
a woman may be married by [accepting something] worth a p[e]*ruta*

* The first plural form is Hebrew and the second Aramaic.
** See the table of coins in Appendix II.

פָּרוֹשֵׁי* קָא מְפָרֵשׁ

he is really explaining פָּרֵשׁ הוּא מְפָרֵשׁ

This expression is used to present a *new interpretation* of a mishna or a baraitha in order to refute an argument based on that text. According to this proposal, the latter clause of the text comprises an explanation of an earlier clause — rather than a different halakhic statement.

ברייתא: זִימּוּן בִּשְׁלֹשָׁה.
תלמוד: מַאי זִימּוּן? אִילֵימָא בִּרְכַּת זִימּוּן, וְהָתַנְיָא:
ברייתא: זִימּוּן בִּשְׁלֹשָׁה; בִּרְכַּת זִימּוּן בִּשְׁלֹשָׁה!
תלמוד: וְכִי תֵּימָא פָּרוֹשֵׁי קָא מְפָרֵשׁ: מַאי זִימּוּן? בִּרְכַּת זִימּוּן ... (סנהדרין ח,א)

BARAITHA: "Zimmun" [must be done] with three [people].

TALMUD: What is "zimmun"? If we say [it means] "the b[e]*rakha of zimmun" (that invites people to recite Birkath HaMazon), but it is stated (in another baraitha):*

BARAITHA: Zimmun [must be done] with three [people]; the b[e]*rakha of zimmun [must be done] with three [people]! (This implies that "zimmun" is not the same as "the b*[e]*rakha of zimmun" because there are two separate statements.)*

TALMUD: But if you reply: [The tanna] is really explaining: What is "zimmun"? (He is explaining that) it is "the b[e]*rakha of zimmun" ...*

* The absolute infinitive פָּרוֹשֵׁי adds emphasis to the verb מְפָרֵשׁ, which is best expressed in English by an adverb, such as *really.*

SEE: מַה טַעַם קָאָמַר, פָּרֵישׁ[1]

iron בַּרְזֶל **פַּרְזְלָא**

מְסָרֵיקְנָא לִבְשָׂרַיְיכוּ בְּמַסְרְקֵי דְפַרְזְלָא (גיטין נז,ב)
I will comb your flesh with combs of iron

פָּרַט (פרט: יִפְרוֹט .fut)

he specified; he stated explicitly

כָּל מָקוֹם שֶׁנֶּאֱמַר "עֵד" הֲרֵי כָּאן שְׁנַיִם עַד שֶׁיִּפְרוֹט לְךָ הַכָּתוּב "אֶחָד". (סוטה ב, רע"ב; סנהדרין ל, סע"א)
Wherever [in Scripture the word] עֵד *is stated, it means two [witnesses]* unless Scripture specifies* "[עֵד] אֶחָד" *(= one witness).*

* עֵד is thus understood to mean *testimony*, as in גַּלְעֵד (בראשית לא:מז), whose Aramaic parallel is יְגַר שָׂהֲדוּתָא, *the mound for testimony*, in the same pasuk.

פְּרָט; פְּרָטָא*

a specific item; a detail; a particular

This term is used frequently in Midrashic and Talmudic interpretation in contradistinction to כְּלָל, *a general category.*

For examples, see: כְּלָל וּפְרָט אֵין בַּכְּלָל אֶלָּא מַה שֶׁבַּפְּרָט, כְּלָל וּפְרָט וּכְלָל אִי אַתָּה דָן אֶלָּא כְּעֵין הַפְּרָט

* The first form is Hebrew, and the second is Aramaic.

פָּרַט וְכָלַל נַעֲשָׂה כְּלָל מוּסָף עַל הַפְּרָט

[The Torah] has specified and it has generalised — the general class becomes an addition to the specific item (so as to include everything contained within the class).

This *rule of Biblical interpretation* is used to explain halakhic passages. When a specific term is

followed by a general term, the halakha applies to everything included within the general category, and the specific or specifics are regarded as illustrative examples of the general class.

"כִּי יִתֵּן אִישׁ אֶל רֵעֵהוּ חֲמוֹר אוֹ שׁוֹר אוֹ שֶׂה" — פְּרָט; "וְכָל בְּהֵמָה" — כְּלָל; נַעֲשָׂה כְּלָל מוֹסִיף עַל הַפְּרָט, וְרַבִּי כָּל מִילֵּי. (ברייתא דרי ישמעאל: בשלש עשרה מדות, ע״פ שמות כב:ט)

"If a man delivers to his neighbor a donkey or an ox or a sheep" — [the Torah] has specified; "or any beast" — it has generalized; the general class becomes an addition to the specific item, so that it (= the general class) has included everything (= all animals).

SEE: כְּלָל

פְּרָט לְ- **"a specification as against"; to the exclusion of**

"לֶחֶם עֹנִי" — פְּרָט לְעִיסָה הַנִּילוֹשָׁה בְּיַיִן וְשֶׁמֶן וּדְבַשׁ. (פסחים לו,א ע״פ דברים טז:ג)

"The bread of affliction" — to the exclusion of dough that was kneaded with wine or oil or honey (which may not be used to fulfill the obligation of eating matza at the Pesaḥ Seder).

פְּרֵיךְ¹ (פרך: act. prt. פָּרֵיךְ, pass. prt. פְּרִיךְ, fut. לִיפְרוֹךְ, inf. לְמִיפְרַךְ) שׁוֹבֵר; מַקְשֶׁה; סוֹתֵר

breaking; refuting; contradicting

פְּרֵיךְ רַב אַחַאי.* (קידושין יג,א ושי״נ) *Rav Aḥai refutes (the argument that was just presented).*

* See the discussion of Tosafoth כתובות ב,ב ד״ה "פשיט".

SEE: אִיכָּא לְמִיפְרַךְ, פִּירְכָא

פָּרֵיךְ² (פרך פָּעֵל: prt. מְפָרֵיךְ, imp.) **refute!** הַקְשֵׁה!

אֶלָּא פָּרֵיךְ הָכִי ... ! (בבא מציעא ד,א ועוד)

But refute [it] thus ... !

פָּרֵישׁ¹ (פרש פָּעֵל: act. prt. מְפָרֵשׁ, pass. prt. מְפָרַשׁ, imp. פָּרֵישׁ, inf. לְפָרוֹשֵׁי)

(1) פֵּרַשׁ; הִסְבִּיר **he explained; he interpreted**

תָּנָה גְּמִיר לַהּ לְהָא מַתְנִיתָא, וְלָא יָדַע לֵיהּ לְפָרוֹשַׁהּ (בבא בתרא קכא, רע״א)

he has learned this baraitha, but he did not know [how] to explain it

(2) פֵּרַשׁ; בֵּיאֵר בְּפֵרוּשׁ **he specified; he stated explicitly**

טַעְמָא, דְּפָרֵישׁ — הָא לָא פָּרֵישׁ, דַּעְתֵּיהּ אַכְּזַיִת. (שבועות כב,ב)

The reason [we know he means even the slightest quantity is] that he specified [so] — but if he did not specify, [it is assumed that] his intention is for the size of an olive.

פָּרֵישׁ² (פרש) prt. פּוֹרֵשׁ **going away; refraining**

For an example — see פְּרַשׁ.

פְּרַס

(1) a piece; half a loaf; a quantity equal to the volume of four eggs (according to Rashi*) or three eggs (according to the Rambam)**

כְּדֵי אֲכִילַת פְּרַס (כריתות יב,ב: משנה פ״ג מ״ג)

within [the time it takes for] eating half a loaf

(2) (in the term בֵּית הַפְּרָס) an extended area* (of ritual impurity on account of scattered bones of the dead)**

הַחוֹרֵשׁ אֶת הַקֶּבֶר הֲרֵי זֶה עוֹשֶׂה בֵּית הַפְּרָס. (משנה אהלות פי״ז מ״א ע׳ רמב״ם ורע״ב שם)

[If] one plows over a grave, he thereby creates an extended area (of ritual impurity).

* See Rashi's commentary on עירובין ד, סע״א.

** See the Rambam's commentary on the Mishna, on עירובין פ״ח מ״ב. See also שלחן ערוך, אורח חיים תריב:ד and the table of measurements in Appendix II.

*** This translation follows the explanation of the Rambam ibid. According to Rashi on נדה נז,א), the word פְּרָס here means *broken* — referring to *crushed bones.*

פַּרְסָה (pl. פַּרְסָאוֹת); **פַּרְסָא*** (pl. פַּרְסֵי) *parasang*

This measure of distance is equal to 8,000 cubits or four *mil*.

* The first form is Hebrew, and the second is Aramaic. See the table of distances in Appendix II.

פְּרַק* (פרק: prt. פּוֹרֵק, inf. לִפְרוֹק)

he unloaded; he cast off; he released

כָּל שֶׁבְּשֶׁלּוֹ פּוֹרֵק וְטוֹעֵן, בְּשֶׁל חֲבֵירוֹ נַמִּי פּוֹרֵק וְטוֹעֵן. (ב״מ ל,ב)

Whoever would unload and load [the burden of] his own [pack-animal], [in similar circumstances] he must also unload and load that of his fellow man.

פָּרְקוּ עוֹל שָׁמַיִם מִצַּוְּארֵיהֶם (סנהדרין קיא, סע״ב)

they have cast off the yoke of Heaven from their necks

* This verb is also found in Biblical Hebrew as in: וּפָרַקְתָּ עֻלּוֹ מֵעַל צַוָּארֶךָ (בראשית כז:מ)

פְּרַק* (פרק: prt. פָּרֵיק, fut. לִיפְרוֹק, inf. לְמִיפְרַק)

he redeemed פָּדָה

וּפָרֵיק לַהּ אַרְבַּע וְחָמֵשׁ שְׁנִין מִקַּמֵּי יוֹבֵל (ב״מ עט, סע״א)

and he may redeem it (= his former property) four or five years before the Jubilee year

* This verb occurs in Biblical Hebrew in this sense in וַיִּפְרְקֵנוּ מִצָּרֵינוּ (תהלים קלו:כד). The noun פֻּרְקָן, *redemption*, in the prayers יְקוּם פֻּרְקָן מִן שְׁמַיָּא and עַל הַנִּסִּים וְעַל הַפֻּרְקָן, is derived from the same root.

פְּרַשׁ (פרש: prt. פָּרֵישׁ, fut. לִיפְרוֹשׁ, inf. לְמִיפְרַשׁ)

(1) פָּרַשׁ; נִבְדַּל; נִתְרַחֵק **he separated himself; he went away; he withdrew; he refrained**

מִשּׁוּם שַׁבָּת קָא פָּרֵישׁ (שבת ע,ב ורש״י שם)

he would refrain [from these labors] on account of [being informed that it is] the Sabbath

(2) פָּרַשׁ; בֵּאֵר **he explained; he specified**

דָּמֵי הַאי מֵרַבָּנַן כְּמַאן דְּלָא פָּרְשֵׁי אֱינָשֵׁי שְׁמַעְתָּא. (עירובין סו, סע״א ורש״י)

This scholar is like people who cannot explain a halakha.

SEE: פָּרֵישׁ

פַּשׁ (פוש: פָּיֵישׁ .prt) **נִשְׁאַר** **it remained**

דַּל חַד קְרָא לְגוּפֵיהּ — פָּשׁוּ לְהוּ תְּלָתָא. (סוכה ו,ב)

Deduct one Scriptural source for [the law] itself — (and) there remain three [extra words to indicate the walls of the sukka].

SEE: אַפֵּישׁ

פְּשׁוֹט מֵיהָא*/מֵהָא חֲדָא פְּשֹׁט מִזֹּאת אַחַת!

Solve, from the following, one [of the problems that have been raised]!

This exclamation introduces evidence from a baraitha or from an amoraic statement that solves one of several problems that had been previously raised in the Talmud.

אִיבַּעְיָא לְהוּ: "הוֹצִיאוּהָ" — מַהוּ? "עִזְבוּהָ" — מַהוּ? "הַתִּירוּהָ" — מַהוּ? "הַנִּיחוּהָ" — מַהוּ? "הוֹעִילוּ לָהּ" — מַהוּ? "עֲשׂוּ לָהּ כַּדָּת" — מַהוּ? פְּשׁוֹט מֵיהָא חֲדָא, דְּתַנְיָא: "עֲשׂוּ לָהּ כַּדָּת" ... לֹא אָמַר כְּלוּם. (גיטין סה,ב ורש"י שם)

They had a halakhic problem: [If a man says to his agent for delivering a bill of divorce]: "Put her out" — what is the law? (= would the divorce be valid?) "Let her go" — what is the law? "Release her" — what is the law? "Let her be" — what is the law? "Confer a benefit upon her" — what is the law? "Do to her according to the law" — what is the law? Solve from the following [baraitha] one [of the problems], as it is stated: "Do to her according to the law" — his statement has no legal validity (and the divorce is invalid).

* Rashi interprets this word as a contraction of מִן+הָא, *from this* or *from the following* — even if spelled מיהא with a י vowel letter — where it could be vocalized מִיהָא and translated as *at least*.

SEE: פְּשַׁט, מִיהָא

פְּשׁוּטוֹ; פְּשָׁטֵיהּ* **its simple meaning***

אֵין מִקְרָא יוֹצֵא מִידֵי פְּשׁוּטוֹ. (שבת סג,א; יבמות יא,ב; כד,א)

*A pasuk does not depart from its simple meaning. (Even when the passage is interpreted in a midrashic manner, its simple meaning is still valid, too.)***

פְּשָׁטֵיהּ דִּקְרָא בְּמַאי כְּתִיב? (עירובין כג,ב וש"נ)

What is the simple meaning of the pasuk (as opposed to the midrashic interpretation that has just been presented)?

* The first form is Hebrew, and the second is Aramaic. Both forms are usually translated *its simple meaning* or *its literal meaning* (i.e., of the pasuk). Nevertheless, when the Talmud uses the expression פְּשָׁטֵיהּ דִּקְרָא (in עירובין כג,ב and in the other five passages listed in the margin there), the Biblical interpretation presented does not necessarily appear to be *simple* or *literal*. In order to evade this difficulty, it has been proposed that the term refers not to the *nature* of the interpretation but to its *authority* or its *acceptance*, since פָּשׁוּט sometimes means *widespread*, as in the expression מִנְהָג פָּשׁוּט, *a widespread custom* (e.g., as used by the Rambam in (הל' חנוכה פ"ד ה"ג). Thus פְּשָׁטֵיהּ דִּקְרָא would be translated *the standard meaning* or *the accepted meaning of the pasuk*.

** This interpretation was advocated by the Ramban in his critique of the Rambam's *Second Root* (or *Principle*) of his *Sefer HaMitsvoth* and by Rashi's grandson, the Rashbam, in his commentary to בראשית לז:ב. The Rambam, however, adopted a different position.

פְּשַׁט (פשט: פָּשֵׁיט .act. prt, פְּשִׁיט .pass. prt, לִפְשׁוֹט .fut, פְּשׁוֹט .imp, לְמִיפְשַׁט .inf)

(1) **פְּשַׁט** **he solved (a halakhic problem)**

וַהֲדַר פְּשַׁטוּ לָהּ מִבָּרַיְיתָא (ברכות ב, רע"ב)

and then they solved it (= the halakhic problem) from a baraitha

(2) **פְּשַׁט; הִתְפַּשֵּׁט** **he extended; it spread**

פָּשֵׁיט אִיסוּרֵיהּ בְּכוּלֵּיהּ יָרֵךְ (חולין צא,א)

its forbidden substance spreads throughout the entire thigh

SEE: בָּתַר דְּבַעְיָא הֲדַר פַּשְׁטַהּ, פְּשׁוֹט מֵיהָא חֲדָא, תִּפְשַׁט

פְּשִׁיטָא פְּשׁוּטָה; מוּבֶנֶת מֵאֵלֶיהָ

simple; clear-cut; obvious; self-evident

לְרַבָּה, פְּשִׁיטָא לֵיהּ; לְרָבָא, מִיבַּעְיָא לֵיהּ. (בבא קמא יז,ב)

For Rabba [the halakha] is clear-cut; for Rava it is questionable.

(1) This term often comprises an exclamation that points out the *difficulty* that the statement just presented is obvious and hence redundant.*

משנה: נָשִׁים ... פְּטוּרִין מִקְּרִיאַת שְׁמַע. (ברכות כ, סע"א־רע"ב: משנה פ"ג מ"ג)

תלמוד: קְרִיאַת שְׁמַע? פְּשִׁיטָא! מִצְוַת עֲשֵׂה שֶׁהַזְּמַן גְּרָמָא הִיא, וְכָל מִצְוֹת עֲשֵׂה שֶׁהַזְּמַן גְּרָמָא נָשִׁים פְּטוּרוֹת! (ברכות כ, רע"ב)

MISHNA: Women ... are exempt from the reading of Sh^e^ma.

TALMUD: [From] the reading of Sh^e^ma? [It is] obvious! It is a positive commandment that is time-bound, and [we already know that] women are exempt [from] all positive commandments that are time-bound!

(2) This term is also used in a different context — in an introduction to a halakhic problem. It indicates that the halakha is quite clear in the following case (or cases) — in contrast to another case mentioned subsequently where the halakha needs to be investigated.

פְּשִׁיטָא: אָמַר לָהּ לְאִשְׁתּוֹ: "הֲרֵי אַתְּ בַּת חוֹרִין" — לֹא אָמַר וְלֹא כְלוּם ... אָמַר לָהּ לְאִשָּׁה: "הֲרֵי אַתְּ לְעַצְמֵךְ" — מַהוּ? (גיטין פה, רע"ב)

It is obvious [that if a man] said to his wife (in a bill of divorce): "You are a free woman" — he has said nothing (and the divorce is invalid, because a wife is not enslaved). [If] he said to a woman: "you are on your own" — what is the halakhic ruling?

* See חידושי הר"ן לפסחים כא,ב.

SEE: מִיפְשַׁט, צְרִיכָא לְמֵימַר

פְּשִׁיעוּתָא פְּשִׁיעָה **criminal negligence**

כָּל "לָא יָדַעְנָא" פְּשִׁיעוּתָא הִיא. (בבא מציעא לה,א)

Any [case where the custodian of an article says:] "I don't know [where I put it]" is [a case of] criminal negligence.

פְּשַׁע (פשע: פָּשַׁע .prt, לְמִיפְשַׁע .inf)

פָּשַׁע **he was negligent; he acted negligently**

דִּילְמָא פָּשַׁע וְלָא מְבַטֵּל לֵיהּ (פסחים ו, סע"ב)

perhaps he will act negligently and not declare it (= his ḥametz) null and void

פְּתַח (פתח: פָּתַח .act. prt, פְּתִיחַ .pass. prt, לִפְתַּח .fut, לְמִיפְתַּח .inf)

פָּתַח; הִתְחִיל **he opened; he began**

פָּתַח בְּ"בוֹר" וּמְסַיֵּים בְּ"כוֹתֶל"! (בבא בתרא יז, רע"ב)

[The tanna] opens [the mishna] with [a case] of "a pit," and he concludes with [a case of] "a wall"! (Why does he switch cases?)

צ - ק

צָאִית SEE: צָיֵית

צֹאן בַּרְזֶל SEE: נִכְסֵי צֹאן בַּרְזֶל

הַצַּד הַשָּׁוֶה שֶׁבָּהֶן the element common to (both of) them; their common denominator

This term is used in the derivation of halakhoth through the method of (מִשְּׁנֵי כְתוּבִים) בִּנְיַן אָב. A halakha already in force in two Biblical cases sharing a common property is now applied to a third case that also has the same property.

For an example — see the second example under בִּנְיַן אָב.
SEE: מָה הַצַּד

לִצְדָדִין קָתָנֵי לִצְדָדִים הוּא שׁוֹנֶה.

[The tanna] is teaching [his halakha] about separate cases.

As a *resolution* of a difficulty, a halakhic statement is sometimes reinterpreted so that it refers partially to one case and partially to another.

תלמוד: אֲמַר רַב: שְׂכִיר שָׁעוֹת דְּיוֹם גּוֹבֶה כָּל הַיּוֹם, שְׂכִיר שָׁעוֹת דְּלַיְלָה גּוֹבֶה כָּל הַלַּיְלָה .... תְּנַן:
משנה: שְׂכִיר שָׁעוֹת גּוֹבֶה כָּל הַלַּיְלָה וְכָל הַיּוֹם.
תלמוד: תְּיוּבְתָּא דְרַב! אָמַר לָךְ רַב: לִצְדָדִין קָתָנֵי: שְׂכִיר שָׁעוֹת דְּיוֹם גּוֹבֶה כָּל הַיּוֹם, שְׂכִיר שָׁעוֹת דְּלַיְלָה גּוֹבֶה כָּל הַלַּיְלָה. (בבא מציעא קיא,א)

TALMUD: Rav said: A man hired to work [a number of] daylight hours collects (his wages) during that day; a man hired to work [a number of] night hours collects during that night .... We have learned (in our mishna):
MISHNA: A man hired to work [a number of] hours collects during that night and during that day.
TALMUD: [This constitutes] a refutation of [the statement of] Rav! Rav would say to you: [The tanna of our mishna] is teaching [his halakha] about separate cases: A man hired to work [a number of] daylight hours collects during that day; a man hired to work [a number of] night hours collects during that night.

צְוַוח (צוח: צָוַח .prt) צָוַח; צָעַק

he shouted; he cried out; he protested

שָׁתִיק מֵעִיקָּרָא וַהֲדַר צָוַוח (בבא מציעא ו,א)
he is silent in the beginning, and subsequently he protests

וּצְוַוח רֵישׁ לָקִישׁ כִּי כְרוּכְיָא* (קידושין מד, סע"א ורש"י שם)
and Resh Lakish "cried out like a crane" (= he protested loudly)

* This expression has entered post-Talmudic Hebrew.

צַוְותָא*

company; companionship חֶבְרָה; הִתְחַבְּרוּת

אֲפִילּוּ בַּר שֵׁשׁ נַמִי בְּצַוְותָא דְאִמֵּיהּ נִיחָא לֵיהּ (עירובין פב,ב)
even a six-year-old likes the company of his mother

* In Modern Hebrew, the expression בְּצַוְותָא means *together* or *in friendship*.

צוּרְבָא מֵרַבָּנַן* תַּלְמִיד חָכָם (צָעִיר)

a (young) Torah scholar

וַאֲמַר רָבָא: הַאי צוּרְבָא מֵרַבָּנַן דְּרָתַח — אוֹרָיְיתָא הוּא דְּקָא מַרְתְּחָא לֵיהּ. (תענית ד, רע"א ו"רש"י" שם)
And Rava said: [As for] a (young) Torah scholar who becomes excited — it is the Torah that is exciting him.

* The etymology is probably as follows: The verb צרב means *burn* or *ignite*, and so צוּרְבָא מֵרַבָּנַן is literally: *one who has been ignited (= inspired) by the ḥakhamim.*

צָיֵית/צָאִית .prt (צות)

listening to; obeying נִשְׁמָע לְ־; מְצַיֵּת

וְאִי לָא צָיֵית דִּינָא, מְשַׁמְּתִינַן לֵיהּ (מועד קטן יד,ב)
and if one does not obey the halakhic decision, we excommunicate him

צְלוֹתָא* תְּפִלָּה

prayer; the Amida

בְּשַׁבְּתָא בֵּין בִּצְלוֹתָא בֵּין בְּקִידּוּשָׁא "מְקַדֵּשׁ הַשַּׁבָּת" ... (פסחים קיז,ב)
On the Sabbath, both in the Amida and in Kiddush [one says:] "He who sanctifies the Sabbath" ...

* Do not confuse with צִילוּתָא, *clarity (of mind)*, which is found in מגילה כח,ב. See the next entry.

צַלִּי (צלי פָּעֵל: מְצַלֵּי .prt, לְצַלּוֹיֵי .inf)

he prayed; he recited the Amida הִתְפַּלֵּל

רַב צַלִּי שֶׁל שַׁבָּת בְּעֶרֶב שַׁבָּת. (ברכות כז,ב)
Rav recited the Amida for the Sabbath on Friday.

בְּצִנְעָא* בַּסֵּתֶר; בַּחֲשַׁאי

secretly; privately

עָשָׂה עִמּוֹ בְּפוּמְבֵּי, וּבִקֵּשׁ לַעֲשׂוֹת עִמּוֹ בְּצִנְעָא (ב"ב קמה,ב)
[if] he rendered service to him in public, and [the latter] wanted to render service to him privately

* This Aramaic word is used in Modern Hebrew with the Hebraized spelling, צְנְעָה.

צַעַר (צער פָּעֵל: מְצַעֵר .prt, לְצַעוֹרֵי .inf)

he inflicted pain; he annoyed צִעֵר

לְצַעוֹרַהּ קָא מִיכַּוֵּין (גיטין לב,א)
he intends to annoy her (= his wife)

צַפְרָא בֹּקֶר

morning

עַד חֲצוֹת נַמִי צַפְרָא הוּא (ברכות כז,א)
until noon is also morning

צָר (צרר: צָיֵיר .prt, לְמֵיצַר .inf)

he wrapped; he tied (around) צָרַר; קָשַׁר

הַאי סוּדָרָא דִּתְפִלִּין דְּאַזְמְנֵיהּ לְמֵיצַר בֵּיהּ תְּפִלִּין — צָר בֵּיהּ

תְּפִלִּין, אָסוּר לְמֵיצַר בֵּיהּ זוּזֵי. (ברכות כג,ב)
[As for] a t^efillin bag that he has designated for wrapping t^efillin in it — [once] he has wrapped t^efillin in it, it is forbidden to wrap money in it.

צָרִיךְ וְאֵין לוֹ תַּקָּנָה

he must, and there is no remedy for him (if he does not)

The procedure that is required is halakhically indispensable.

ברייתא: נָזִיר מְמוֹרָט — בֵּית שַׁמַּאי אוֹמְרִים: צָרִיךְ הַעֲבָרַת תַּעַר.
תלמוד: וְאָמַר רַב אֲבִינָא: כְּשֶׁאוֹמְרִים בֵּית שַׁמַּאי "צָרִיךְ" — צָרִיךְ וְאֵין לוֹ תַּקָּנָה. (יומא סא,ב; ע' ברכות טו,ב וש"נ)
BARAITHA: [As for] a bald nazirite — Beth Shammai says: He must undergo shaving (his head) with a razor. TALMUD: And Rav Abina said: When Beth Shammai says "he must," [it means] he must (have his head shaved), and there is no remedy for him (= since it is impossible to shave a bald head, he must remain a nazirite indefinitely).

צְרִיכָא

pass. prt. f. (צרד*: צְרִיכִי m. pl.)
צְרִיכָה

it is necessary

This term introduces an argument that explains why two or more allegedly redundant points or cases — which appear in a mishna, a baraitha, an amora's statement, or in the Torah — are really necessary, since one point cannot be inferred from the other. This type of an argument is called a צְרִיכוּתָא by some commentators.

אָמַר רָבָא: לָמָּה לִי דִּכְתַב רַחֲמָנָא לָאו בְּרִבִּית, לָאו בְּגָזֵל, וְלָאו בְּאוֹנָאָה? צְרִיכִי, דְּאִי כְּתַב רַחֲמָנָא לָאו בְּרִבִּית, מִשּׁוּם דְּחִידּוּשׁ הוּא דַּאֲפִילּוּ בְּלֹוֶה אַסְרַהּ רַחֲמָנָא; וְאִי כְּתַב רַחֲמָנָא לָאו בְּגָזֵל, מִשּׁוּם דִּבְעַל כָּרְחֵיהּ; אֲבָל אוֹנָאָה — אֵימָא לָא! (ב"מ סא,א)
Rava said: Why did the Torah write a (separate) prohibition against usury, a (separate) prohibition against robbery, and a (separate) prohibition against overcharging (or underpaying)? (Are not all three actions basically alike — the illegal taking of another's property?!) They are necessary, for if the Torah had written the prohibition against usury, [one could have argued, that is] because [usury] is [a] unique [prohibition], since the Torah has forbidden it even for the borrower (the victim); and if the Torah had written the prohibition against robbery, [one could have argued, that is] because [it is carried out] against his (= the victim's) will; but [as for] overcharging [where the prohibition is only against the offender — not against his victim, and the victim participates with his consent], I might say [that it is] not [forbidden]!

* For the full conjugation of this verb, see *Grammar for Gemara*: Chapter 4, Verb 3

SEE: לֹא נִצְרְכָה אֶלָּא, לָא צְרִיכָא, and the next entry

צְרִיכָא לְמֵימַר

... הַאִם צְרִיכָה לוֹמַר?!

... is it necessary to state?!

This *rhetorical question* argues that a specific halakha need not be stated, because it is too obvious.

אֲמַר אִיהוּ: "גְּלִימָא", וַאֲמַר אִיהוּ: "גְּלִימָא" — צְרִיכָא לְמֵימַר דִּכְמָה דְּלָא אֲמַר סִימָנִין לָא יָהֲבִינַן לֵיהּ?! (ב"מ כח,ב ע"פ כת"י)
[if] he (= the finder) said: "[I found] a cloak," and he (= the person who claims ownership) said: "[I lost] a cloak" — is it necessary to state that as long as he does not state marks of identification, we do not give [the lost article] to him?!

SEE: פְּשִׁיטָא

קָא/קָ-

A contraction of the participle קָאֵים (from the root קום) is often placed before another participle — either as a separate word, קָא, or as an attached prefix, -קָ. It has an emphatic effect that is difficult to translate into English.

SEE: קָא מַשְׁמַע לַן, קָא סָלְקָא דַעְתָּךְ, קָא פָּסֵיק וְתָנֵי, (וּדְ)קָא קַשְׁיָא לָךְ, (קָ)אֲמִינָא, (קָ)אָמַר, (קָ)אָמְרָה, (קָ)אָמְרִי, (קָ)אָמְרִינַן, (קָ)אָמְרִיתוּ, (קָ)אָמְרַתְּ, (קָ)אָרֵי, (קָ)אָתוּ, (קָ)אָתֵי, (קָ)אָתְיָא, (קָ)מִיפַּלְגִי, (קָ)סָבַר, (קָ)תָנֵי, קָם

קָא אֲמִינָא

SEE: (קָ)אֲמִינָא

קָא אָמְרִי

SEE: (קָ)אָמְרִי

קָא אָמְרִינַן

SEE: (קָ)אָמְרִינַן

קָא אָמְרַתְּ

SEE: (קָ)אָמְרַתְּ

קָא מִיפַּלְגִי

SEE: (קָ)מִיפַּלְגִי

קָא מַשְׁמַע לַן

הוּא מַשְׁמִיעַ לָנוּ

he lets us hear; he teaches us

In response to the contention (or implication) that a statement is superfluous, it is sometimes argued that the statement does indeed clarify a point that is not obvious or that is subject to misinterpretation. This argument often begins with the expressions מַהוּ דְּתֵימָא, or הֲוָה אֲמִינָא, or סָלְקָא דַעְתָּךְ אֲמִינָא, and closes with קָא מַשְׁמַע לַן.

For examples, see מַהוּ דְּתֵימָא and סָלְקָא דַעְתָּךְ אֲמִינָא.

SEE: מַאי קָא מַשְׁמַע לַן, מִילְּתָא אַגַּב אוֹרְחָא קָא מַשְׁמַע לַן

קָא סָבַר

SEE: (קָ)סָבַר

קָא סָלְקָא דַעְתָּךְ

עוֹלָה עַל דַּעְתְּךָ

it occurs to your mind; you would assume

An introduction to an assumption that the Talmud initially adopts but subsequently rejects.

משנה: אוֹר לְאַרְבָּעָה עָשָׂר בּוֹדְקִין אֶת הֶחָמֵץ לְאוֹר הַנֵּר.
תלמוד: מַאי "אוֹר"? רַב הוּנָא אָמַר: נַגְהֵי, וְרַב יְהוּדָה אָמַר:

לֵילֵי. קָא סָלְקָא דַעְתָּךְ: מַאן דַּאֲמַר נַגְהֵי, נַגְהֵי מַמָּשׁ, וּמַאן דַּאֲמַר לֵילֵי, לֵילֵי מַמָּשׁ. (פסחים ב, רע"א)

... אֶלָּא בֵּין רַב הוּנָא וּבֵין רַב יְהוּדָה, דְּכוּלֵּי עָלְמָא "אוֹר" אוּרְתָּא הוּא, וְלָא פְּלִיגִי: מָר כִּי אַתְרֵיהּ, וּמָר כִּי אַתְרֵיהּ — בְּאַתְרֵיהּ דְּרַב הוּנָא קָרוּ נַגְהֵי, וּבְאַתְרֵיהּ דְּרַב יְהוּדָה קָרוּ לֵילֵי. (שם ג,א)

MISHNA: On the "light" of the fourteenth (of Nisan) we search for ḥametz by the light of a candle.

TALMUD: What is [the meaning of] "light"? Rav Huna said: Day, and Rav Yehuda said: Night. You would assume: the one who said "day" really [means] "day," and the one who said "night" really [means] "night."

*... Rather, both Rav Huna and Rav Y*e*huda [agree that] "light" (in the mishna) means "evening," and they do not disagree: One authority [is speaking] according to (the dialect of) his locality, while the other [is speaking] according to (the dialect of) his locality — in Rav Huna's locality they call [evening] "day,"* and in Rav Y*e*huda's locality they call [it] "night."*

* According to R. Nathan of Rome in his *Arukh*, they take נַגְהֵי, *"light,"* as a euphemism for *evening*. Compare entry סַגֵּי נְהוֹר and its note.

SEE: מַהוּ דְּתֵימָא, הֲוָה אָמִינָא, סְבוּר מִינָּהּ, סְבָרוּהָ

קָא פָּסֵיק וְתָנֵי הוּא פּוֹסֵק וְשׁוֹנֶה ...

[The tanna] states categorically ...

This expression is used to draw the following *inference*: Since the halakha has been formulated in general categories — without distinguishing between different cases — it applies "across the board." The Talmud proceeds to raise an objection against the application of the halakha to a certain case.

משנה: לוּלָב הַגָּזוּל וְהַיָּבֵשׁ פָּסוּל. (סוכה כט,ב: משנה פ"ג מ"א)
תלמוד: קָא פָּסֵיק וְתָנֵי — לָא שְׁנָא בְּיוֹם טוֹב רִאשׁוֹן וְלָא שְׁנָא בְּיוֹם טוֹב שֵׁנִי .... גָּזוּל — בִּשְׁלָמָא יוֹם טוֹב רִאשׁוֹן, דִּכְתִיב "לָכֶם", מִשֶּׁלָּכֶם — אֶלָּא בְּיוֹם טוֹב שֵׁנִי, אַמַּאי לָא?! (שם כט, סע"ב ע"פ ויקרא כג:מ)

MISHNA: A stolen lulav (= a palm branch) or a dry one is invalid [for use as one of the four species on Sukkoth].

TALMUD: [The tanna] states [that it is invalid] categorically — there is no distinction between the first day of the festival and the second day of the festival .... [As for] a stolen lulav — it is reasonable [that it is invalid for the mitzva] on the first day of the festival, for it is written (in the Torah) "for you," [i.e, it must be] yours — but on the second day of the festival (when the mitzva is only a Rabbinic enactment), why [is a stolen lulav] not [valid]?!

וְדָקָא קַשְׁיָא לָךְ ... וְ(זֶה) שֶׁקָּשָׁה לְךָ ...

And [as for] what [was] difficult for you ...

This expression recalls a *difficulty* that had been raised earlier in the Talmudic discussion. The Talmud proceeds to resolve the difficulty and to reinstate the explanation that had been rejected because of that difficulty.

וְדָקָא קַשְׁיָא לָךְ דְּרַבָּה! דְּרַבָּה תַּנָּאֵי הִיא. (שבת קמט,א)

And [as for] what [was] difficult for you [based upon the statement] of Rabba! [The statement] of Rabba [need not be accepted, because] it is [a subject of controversy between two] tannaim.

קָא תָנֵי SEE: (קָאתָנֵי)

קָאֵי/קָאֵים prt. (קום: קָיְימָא .f, קָיְימִי/קָיְימִין .m. pl, קָיְימָן .f. pl)

rising; standing; referring (to) קָם; עוֹמֵד

This participle is often used with a word that has a prepositional prefix -אַ to mean *basing oneself upon* or *referring to.*

מִי סָבְרַתְּ ר' חֶלְבּוֹ אַרֵישָׁא קָאֵי?! אַסֵּיפָא קָאֵי! (שבת לז,א)

Do you really hold [that] R. Ḥelbo is referring to the beginning [of the mishna]?! He is referring to the latter clause [in the mishna]!

תַּנָּא אַקְּרָא קָאֵי. (ברכות ב,א)

The tanna (who formulated our mishna) bases himself upon a pasuk.

SEE: קָא, קָם, -אַ

קָאֵימְנָא* (= קָאֵים .prt+אֲנָא) עוֹמֵד אֲנִי **I stand**

זִימְנִין סַגִּיאִין הֲוָה קָאֵימְנָא קַמֵּיהּ דְּרַב (פסחים קו, רע"ב)

on many occasions I used to stand before Rav

* Do not confuse with קָאֲמִינָא.

SEE: קָם

קָאֲמִינָא (= קָא+אֲמִינָא) SEE: אֲמִינָא

קָאָמַר (= קָא+אָמַר) SEE: אָמַר

קָאָמְרָה (= קָא+אָמְרָה) SEE: אָמְרָה

קָאָמְרִי (= קָא+אָמְרִי) SEE: אָמְרִי

קָאָמְרִינַן (= קָא+אָמְרִינַן) SEE: אָמְרִינַן

קָאָמְרִיתוּ (= קָא+אָמְרִיתוּ) SEE: אָמְרִיתוּ

קָאָמְרַתְּ (= קָא+אָמְרַתְּ) SEE: אָמְרַתְּ

קָאָרֵי (= קָא+אָרֵי) SEE: אָרֵי

קָאָתוּ (= קָא+אָתוּ) SEE: אָתוּ

קָאָתֵי (= קָא+אָתֵי) SEE: אָתֵי

קָאָתְיָא (= קָא+אָתְיָא) SEE: אָתְיָא

קַב* *kav*

This measure of volume is equal to 24 eggs.

* See the table of weights in Appendix II.

קַבֵּיל (קבל פָּעֵל: מְקַבֵּל .prt, לְקַבֵּל .fut, קַבֵּיל .imp, לְקַבּוּלֵי .inf)

he received; he accepted; he undertook קִבֵּל

אֲכִילָה וּשְׁתִיָּה קַבֵּיל עֲלֵיהּ. (ברכות יד,א)
he accepted upon himself [to refrain from] eating and drinking

קְבִיעַ (קבע) pass. prt.

set; established; permanent קָבוּעַ

קְבִיעַ בֵּי דוֹאַר בְּמָתָא. (שבת יט,א)
There is a permanent post office in town.
SEE: קְבַע

קַבָּלָה*

(1) receiving; acceptance

שְׁלִיחַ לְקַבָּלָה (גיטין כא,א)
an agent for receiving (a bill of divorce)

(2) received tradition (formulated in נְבִיאִים or כְּתוּבִים)

קָפַץ נַחְשׁוֹן בֶּן עַמִּינָדָב וְיָרַד לַיָּם תְּחִילָּה ... וְעָלָיו מְפֹרָשׁ בְּקַבָּלָה: "הוֹשִׁיעֵנִי אֱלֹקִים, כִּי בָאוּ מַיִם עַד נָפֶשׁ ..." (סוטה לז, רע"א ע"פ תהלים סט:ב)
Naḥshon son of Amminadav leaped forward and descended into the sea first ... and about him it is clearly taught in a received tradition [that he cried out]: "Save me, O God, for the water has come up to [my] neck ..."

* Since the Middle Ages two additional meanings of the term קַבָּלָה have gained currency:
(1) a tradition received and transmitted through the oral Torah (רמב"ם הל' קדוש החודש פי"א ה"ג; הל' מלכים יב:ב)
(2) *Kabbala*; esoteric lore; Jewish mysticism, as presented in various works, especially *the Zohar*
SEE: דִּבְרֵי קַבָּלָה

קַבְּלַהּ מִינֵּיהּ אוֹ לָא קַבְּלַהּ מִינֵּיהּ

קִבְּלָהּ מִמֶּנּוּ אוֹ לֹא קִבְּלָהּ מִמֶּנּוּ?

Did he accept it (= the opinion) from him (= his colleague), or did he not accept it from him?

This *question* is sometimes raised by the Talmud to determine the reaction of a tanna or an amora to the argument of a colleague against the halakha he has presented.

For an example — see חגיגה יד,א.

קְבַע (קבע: קָבַע act. prt., קְבִיעַ pass. prt., לְמִיקְבַּע inf.)

he set; he established; he fixed קָבַע

קְבַעִיתוּ לַהּ נַמֵּי בִּגְמָרָא? (עירובין לב,ב)
Have you also established it (= this explanation) as a part of the (standard) learning?

קְדַם* (קדם: קָדֵים prt.) קָדַם

he acted early; he preceded; he anticipated

כְּבָר קְדַמוּךְ רַבָּנַן. (שבת יט,א ושי"נ)
The ḥakhamim have already anticipated you (by recommending measures to counter your trickery).

* Sometimes, קַדֵּים (in the פַּעֵל binyan) is used with the same meaning as קְדַם.
SEE: אַקְדֵּים

קֳדָם לִפְנֵי

before; in the presence of

אֲמַרִית קֳדָם רַבִּי (שבת קנו,א)
I spoke in the presence of my master

This word is also used with personal-pronoun suffixes:

before me	לְפָנַי	קֳדָמַי
before you (m.s.)	לְפָנֶיךָ	קֳדָמָךְ
before him	לְפָנָיו	קֳדָמוֹהִי
before us	לְפָנֵינוּ	קֳדָמַנָא
before you (m. pl.)	לִפְנֵיכֶם	קֳדָמֵיכוֹן

SEE: קַמֵּי

קַדְמָאָה* (קַדְמָיְתָא f.s., קַדְמָאֵי m.pl., קַדְמָיָיתָא f.pl.)

first רִאשׁוֹן

רָבָא יוֹמָא קַדְמָאָה דְחָלֵישׁ ... (נדרים מ,א)
[As for] Rava, on the first day that he becomes ill ...

* In the more common forms like קַמָּא and קַמַּיְיתָא, the ד has been omitted and replaced by a *dagesh* in the מ.

קוּלָּא קַל; קֻלָּה

leniency; the easier practice

סְפֵק דְרַבָּנַן — לְקוּלָּא. (שבת לד,א)
A doubtful case in a law of Rabbinic origin [is treated] with leniency.
SEE: קַל וְחוֹמֶר

קוּם וַעֲשֵׂה*

"get up and do!"

a mitsva act that one must perform (e.g., eating matza on Pesaḥ)

For an example — see שֵׁב וְאַל תַּעֲשֶׂה.
* This term is not identical with a מִצְוַת עֲשֵׂה.
For example, שַׁבַּת שַׁבָּתוֹן (ויקרא טז:לא) is a מִצְוַת עֲשֵׂה, to refrain from working and eating on Yom Kippur, yet it cannot be described as קוּם וַעֲשֵׂה but as שֵׁב וְאַל תַּעֲשֶׂה.

קוּשְׁטָא אֱמֶת

truth

מֵרֵישׁ הֲוָה אָמִינָא: לֵיכָּא קוּשְׁטָא בְּעָלְמָא! (סנהדרין צז,א)
Initially I used to think: There is no truth in the world!

קוּשְׁיָא

difficulty; objection; contradiction קֹשִׁי

For examples, see הֲדַר קוּשְׁיַין לְדוּכְתֵּיהּ and (וּ)מַאי קוּשְׁיָא.
SEE: קַשְׁיָא

קַטִין דַּק; צַר; קָטָן

fine; thin; small

הַאי יְנוּקָא דְקַטִין (שבת קלד,א)
a baby that is thin

הָנֵי חַמְשִׁין זוּזֵי דְמֵי דְאַרְעָא קְטִינָא. (כתובות צא,ב)
These fifty zuz are the price of the small [plot of] land.

קְטַל (קטל: קָטֵיל prt., לִיקְטוֹל fut., קְטוֹל imp., לְמִיקְטַל inf.)

he killed (1) הָרַג

See the example below, which contains both usages.

(2) חָתַךְ; קָצַר **he cut; he reaped**

קְטוֹל אַסְפַּסְתָּא בְּשַׁבְּתָא וּשְׁדִי לְחֵיוָתָא - וְאִי לָא, קָטֵילְנָא לָךְ! (סנהדרין עד,ב ורש״י שם)

[A tyrant threatens a Jew:] Cut some grass on the Sabbath and throw [it] to the wild animals — but if [you do] not, I shall kill you!

קְטָלָא הֶרֶג; מִיתָה; מִיתַת בֵּית דִּין

killing; death; the death penalty

מָסְרָה נַפְשָׁהּ לִקְטָלָא (סנהדרין עג,ב)

"she gave herself over to death" (= she risked her life)

אַתְרוּ בֵיהּ מַלְקוֹת וְלָא אַתְרוּ בֵיהּ קְטָלָא (סנהדרין ט, רע״א)

they warned him [that the crime he was about to commit is subject to] flogging, but they did not warn him [that it is subject to] the death penalty

SEE: בַּר קְטָלָא

קְטַר (קטר: קָטַר prt., לְמִיקְטַר inf.)

he tied קָשַׁר

סָיֵים דִּיַמִּינֵיהּ וְלָא קָטַר, וְסָיֵים דִּשְׂמָאלֵיהּ וְקָטַר, וַהֲדַר קָטַר דִּיַמִּינֵיהּ. (שבת סא,א)

He puts on his right [shoe] but does not tie [it], and he puts on his left [shoe] and ties [it], and then he ties his right [shoe].

קַיְיטָא/קַיְטָא* קַיִץ*

summer

שִׁילְהֵי דְקַיְיטָא קָשְׁיָא מִקַּיְיטָא. (יומא כט, רע״א)

The end of the summer is harsher than the (rest of the) summer.

* The Aramaic ט is parallel to the Hebrew צ (as in the Aramaic עֵיטָא = עֵצָה). The Modern Hebrew קַיְטָנָה, a *summer (day) camp*, is derived from the Aramaic form.

קַיְימָא

SEE: בֶּן קַיְימָא

קָיְימָא* (קום) prt. עוֹמֶדֶת

standing

* This form is popularly pronounced קַיְימָא.

קַיְימָא לַן עוֹמֶדֶת לָנוּ; מְקֻבָּל בְּיָדֵינוּ

it has been established for us; it is accepted by us

This term introduces a *received tradition*, usually of halakhic significance.

קַיְימָא לַן דְּעַד צֵאת הַכּוֹכָבִים לָאו לֵילְיָא הוּא. (מגילה כ,ב)

It is accepted by us that until the appearance of the stars it is not (considered) night.

SEE: קָם, קִים לְהוּ רַבָּנַן

קִים (קום) pass. prt. עוֹמֵד; מְקֻבָּל; בָּרוּר

standing; accepted; certain

שְׁבָעָתוֹ הָעַיִן, קִים לֵיהּ בְּגַוַּויְיהוּ וּמְהַדְרִינַן לֵיהּ. (ב״מ כג, סע״ב)

[If his] eye is familiar with them (= the lost vessels),

he is certain about them, and we must return [them] to him.

SEE: קָם

קִים לְהוּ לְרַבָּנַן מְקֻבָּל בִּידֵי הַחֲכָמִים

it has been accepted by the ḥakhamim

קִים לְהוּ לְרַבָּנַן דִּבְהָכִי מִיתַּבָא דַּעְתֵּיהּ. (יומא עט,א)

It has been accepted by the ḥakhamim that with such [a quantity of food] his senses are restored.

SEE: קַיְימָא לַן

קִים לֵיהּ בִּדְרַבָּה מִינֵּיהּ

SEE: קָם לֵיהּ בְּ-

קִימְעָא* מְעַט

a little

אֵלֵךְ לְבֵיתִי, וְאוֹכַל קִימְעָא, וְאֶשְׁתֶּה קִימְעָא, וְאִישַׁן קִימְעָא. (ברכות ד, רע״ב)

I shall go to my house, and I shall eat a little, and I shall drink a little, and I shall sleep a little.

* This (apparently) Aramaic word occurs only in Hebrew passages in the Talmud!

קַל* וָחוֹמֶר

"leniency and strictness"; an inference from the minor to the major; an argument a fortiori

This term usually refers to *a halakhic inference* from a halakha of lesser consequence to one of greater consequence or vice versa. Thus, if a restriction applies to a festival whose status is relatively lower, it must certainly be applied to the Sabbath whose status is relatively higher. Or, if some activity is permitted on the Sabbath, it must certainly be permitted on a festival. Since the קַל־וָחוֹמֶר inference is based upon logic, it need not be received as a tradition from one's teacher.**

אָדָם דָּן קַל וָחוֹמֶר מֵעַצְמוֹ (נדה יט,ב ושי״ן)

A person may draw an inference from the minor to the major by himself.

In some instances, this term is best translated informally as *all the more so*, like כָּל שֶׁכֵּן.

לֹא עוֹלִין בָּאִילָן, וְלֹא רוֹכְבִין עַל גַּבֵּי בְהֵמָה, וְלֹא שָׁטִין עַל פְּנֵי הַמַּיִם .... כָּל אֵלּוּ בְּיוֹם טוֹב אָמְרוּ — קַל וָחוֹמֶר בַּשַּׁבָּת. (ביצה לו,ב: משנה כ״ה מ״ב)

One may not climb a tree, ride an animal, or float on the surface of the water .... All these [restrictions] they stated with regard to a festival — all the more so with regard to the Sabbath.

* The vocalization קַל is difficult since it seems to indicate that the word is an adjective. In order that the word be taken as a noun (like its parallel חוֹמֶר), the vocalization קֹל may be more appropriate.

** For examples of קַל־וָחוֹמֶר inferences, see the entries (וּ)מָה ... עַל אַחַת כַּמָּה וְכַמָּה and (וּ)מָה ... אֵינוֹ דִין שֶׁ ....

SEE: קוּלָּא, דִּין

קָם (קום: קָאֵי/קָאֵים* act. prt., קִים pass. prt., לֵיקוּם/לֵיקוּ fut., קוּם imp., לְמֵיקַם inf.)

(1) **עָמַד** — **he stood**

אֲזַל רַב שֵׁשֶׁת, קָם אַבָּבָא. (עירובין יא,ב)

Rav Shesheth went, (and) he stood at the gate.

(2) **קָם** — **he stood up; he rose**

ר' אִלְעַי וְר' יַעֲקֹב בַּר זַבְדִּי הֲווֹ יָתְבִי. חֲלֵיף וְאָזֵיל ר' שִׁמְעוֹן בַּר אַבָּא וְקָמוּ מִקַּמֵּיהּ. (קידושין לג,ב)

R. Illai and R. Ya'akov b. Zavdi were seated. R. Shim'on b. Abba passed by, and they rose out of respect for him.

* For the full conjugation of this verb, see *Grammar for Gemara*: Chapter 4, Verb 17.

SEE: קָא, קָאֵי, קָאֵימְנָא, קָיְימָא, קִים

קם בְּ-

(1) עָמַד בְּ-; הִסְכִּים

he adopted (a position); he agreed with

קָם אַבַּיֵּי בְּשִׁיטָתֵיהּ דְּרָבָא (שבת צב,א)

Abbayé adopted the (halakhic) position of Rava

(2) עָמַד עַל

he made certain about; he ascertained

קָמוּ רַבָּנַן בְּמִילְּתָא (בבא מציעא יט,א)

the ḥakhamim made certain about the matter

קם לֵיהּ בְּ- "עָמַד לוֹ בְּ-"; חָל עָלָיו (דִּין ...)

he was subject to (the law of)

קָם לֵיהּ בְּ"אֲשֶׁר לֹא יִבְנֶה" (יבמות לב, רע"א ע"פ דברים כה:ט)

he would be subject to [the law of] "one who would not build up (his deceased brother's family)"

קָם לֵיהּ בִּדְרַבָּה מִינֵּיהּ (כתובות לג, סע"ב ועוד*)

*he was subject to the greater (punishment)***

* In a few passages the text reads קִים לֵיהּ, *he is subject to.*

** One who commits a crime that entails two punishments (e.g., the death penalty and monetary payment) receives only the sterner punishment, not the lesser one.

קַמָּא* (קַמַּיְיתָא f.s., קַמָּאֵי m. pl., קַמַּיְיתָא f. pl.)

first — רִאשׁוֹן

תְּרֵי כָּסֵי קַמָּאֵי בָּעוּ הֲסִיבָּה ... (פסחים קח,א)

*The first two cups [of wine at the Seder] require reclining ...***

* The fuller forms — with a ד, such as קַדְמָאָה — are also used occasionally.

** According to the halakhic conclusion, all four cups require reclining.

SEE: קַדְמָאָה, בָּבָא, לִישָּׁנָא קַמָּא, תַּנָּא קַמָּא

קַמֵּי/לְקַמֵּי לִפְנֵי

before; in front of; in the presence of

This preposition is often used with personal-pronoun suffixes.

before me	לְפָנַי	(לְ)קַמַּאי
before you	לְפָנֶיךָ	(לְ)קַמָּךְ
before him/it (m.)	לְפָנָיו	(לְ)קַמֵּיהּ
before her/it (f.)	לְפָנֶיהָ	(לְ)קַמַּהּ
before us	לְפָנֵינוּ	(לְ)קַמָּן
before them	לִפְנֵיהֶם	(לְ)קַמַּיְיהוּ

SEE: לְקַמָּן, מִקַּמֵּי, מִקַּמֵּיהּ, קֳדָם

קַמֵּיהּ* דְּ-

"before him, that [is]"; before — לִפְנֵי

אַבַּיֵּי הֲוָה יָתֵיב קַמֵּיהּ דְּרַבָּה (בבא מציעא ל, רע"ב)

Abbayé was sitting before Rabba

* The suffix ־ֵיהּ, *him*, anticipates the object (i.e., רַבָּה in the example).

קָמִיפַּלְגִי (= קָא+מִיפַּלְגִי)

SEE: מִיפַּלְגִי

קָמַשְׁמַע לַן

SEE: קָא מַשְׁמַע לַן

קָנֵי (קני: קָנֵי act. prt., קְנֵי pass. prt., לִיקְנֵי fut., קְנֵי imp., לְמִיקְנָא inf.) קוֹנֶה

acquiring; purchasing; entering into a legal transaction (or commitment)

אִיהוּ לָא קָנֵי, לְאַחֲרִינֵי מַקְנֵי?! (בבא מציעא ח,א)

[Since] he does not acquire [for himself], can he transfer to others?!

SEE: קִנְיָן

קִנְיָן

(1) ownership; acquisition; transfer of ownership; transaction

כָּל קִנְיָן בְּטָעוּת חוֹזֵר. (גיטין יד,א)

Any transaction [to which one of the parties agreed] through an error must be retracted.

(2) a mode of acquisition; an act that formalizes an agreement; affirmation

One symbolic act that formalizes a transaction or other agreements is the קִנְיָן סוּדָר*, which is accomplished by handing over a scarf, a shoe** or another object from one party to the other. Sometimes, this procedure is simply called קִנְיָן.

קִנְיָן — בִּפְנֵי שְׁנַיִם. (בבא בתרא מ, רע"א ורשב"ם ותוס' שם)

Affirmation [by means of a scarf is carried out] in the presence of two [witnesses].

* See בבא מציעא מז,א.

** See רות ד:ז.

SEE: קָנֵי, סוּדָר, חֲלִיפִין

קְנַס (קנס: קָנֵיס prt., לִקְנוֹס/נִקְנוֹס fut.)

he fined; he punished — קָנַס; עָנַשׁ

עָבַר וְשִׁהָה — מַאי? מִי קְנָסוּהוּ רַבָּנַן אוֹ לָא? (שבת לח,א ורש"י שם)

[If] one transgressed (the Sabbath law) and let [food] stay [on the oven] — what is the halakhic ruling (about eating it)? Did the hakhamim punish him (and forbid it) or not?

קְנָס*

a fine; a punishment

This payment, which was imposed only by the

ordained authorities in Erets Yisrael, is either a fixed sum of money or an amount more than or less than the damage caused. It is not normal compensation.

אֵינוֹ מְשַׁלֵּם קְנָס עַל פִּי עַצְמוֹ (שבועות לו,ב: משנה פ"ה מ"ד)
one does not [have to] pay a fine on the basis of himself (=his own admission)

* It has been suggested that this word has been derived from the Latin *census*.

קַסָבַר (= קָא+סָבַר) SEE: סָבַר

קָסָלְקָא דַעְתָּךְ SEE: קָא סָלְקָא דַעְתָּךְ

קָפֵיד prt. (קפד) מַקְפִּיד (עַל); מְדַקְדֵּק (בְּ-)
caring (about); particular (with regard to)
This Aramaic verb is followed either by -אַ or by עַל with a personal-pronoun suffix.

קָפְדִיתוּ אַמָּנָא? (חולין קז,א)
Are you particular about the vessel?

כֵּיוָן דְּקָפֵיד עֲלַיְיהוּ, לָא מְטַלְטְלִינַן לְהוּ (שבת מט, סע"א)
since one cares about them, we may not handle them (on the Sabbath)

SEE: אַ-, אִיקְפַּד

קָפָסֵיק וְתָנֵי SEE: קָא פָסֵיק וְתָנֵי

קְרָא (pl. קְרָאֵי) מִקְרָא; פָּסוּק
***pasuk*; a Biblical passage** (or any part thereof)
an (apparently) redundant pasuk קְרָא יְתֵירָא

קְרָא וּמַתְנִיתָא מְסַיְּיעֵי לֵיהּ. (גיטין מח, סע"א; ב"ק כב, סע"ב)
A pasuk and a baraitha support him (= the amora).

Two p^{e}sukim are written (פסחים ד,ב) תְּרֵי קְרָאֵי כְּתִיבֵי.
(that appear to contradict each other).

SEE: כְּתוּב, פְּסוּקָא, מִקְרָא, אָמַר קְרָא, עָלֶיךָ אָמַר קְרָא

קָרָא (קרא: prt. קוֹרֵא, fut. יִקְרָא, inf. לִקְרוֹת);
קְרָא* (קרא: act. prt. קָרֵי, pass. act. קְרֵי, fut. לִקְרֵי, imp. קְרִי, inf. לְמִיקְרֵי)

he read; he called; he termed; he cited
This verb often refers to reciting p^{e}sukim and mastering them.

אִם רָגִיל לִקְרוֹת — קוֹרֵא; וְאִם לָאו — קוֹרִין לְפָנָיו. וּבַמֶּה קוֹרִין לְפָנָיו? בְּאִיּוֹב, וּבְעֶזְרָא ... (יומא יח, סע"ב: משנה א:ו)
[On Yom Kippur night] if [the kohen gadol] is familiar with reading [Scripture], he would read; but if not, they would read to him. And from what would they read to him? From [the book of] Job, or Ezra, ...

מַאן דְּקָרֵי וְתָנֵי (מגילה כט,א וכתובות יז, סע"א ורש"י שם)
one who reads (= is well-versed in Scripture) and recites (= is well-versed in the oral law)

See further examples under the entries that follow.

* The first verb is Hebrew, and the second is Aramaic.

SEE: אַל תִּקְרֵי ... אֶלָּא ...

קָרָא עָלָיו הַמִּקְרָא הַזֶּה
He cited regarding him this pasuk ...; He applied the following pasuk to him ...
The speaker applies a Biblical passage to a person whose situation has just been described in the Talmud.

כְּשֶׁנֶּאֶמְרוּ דְּבָרִים לִפְנֵי ר' יוֹסֵי, קָרָא עָלָיו הַמִּקְרָא הַזֶּה: "שְׂפָתַיִם יִשָּׁק מֵשִׁיב דְּבָרִים נְכוֹחִים". (גיטין ט, רע"א ע"פ משלי כד: כו)
When the words (of R. Shim'on) were said before R. Yosé he applied to him (= R. Shim'on) the following pasuk: "The lips should kiss one who gives straight-forward answers."

SEE: קָרֵי אַנַּפְשֵׁיהּ ..., קָרֵי עֲלֵיהּ ...

קְרָאָה הַפָּסוּק **the pasuk**
SEE: מַאי קְרָאָה

קָרֵי אַנַּפְשֵׁיהּ
He cites regarding himself ... קוֹרֵא עַל עַצְמוֹ ...
The speaker applies either a Biblical passage or a popular saying to his own situation.

For an example — see פסחים קו,א ע"פ קהלת ב:יד.
SEE: קָרָא עָלָיו הַמִּקְרָא הַזֶּה

קְרִי בֵּיהּ קְרָא בּוֹ ...!
"Read into it!"; Read it (as if it said) **...!**
This expression presents a Biblical interpretation that *explains* the text *as if* it were vocalized or written differently from the Masoretic tradition.

אָמַר קְרָא: "אֲשֶׁר תִּקְרְאוּ אֹתָם" — קְרִי בֵּיהּ "אַתֶּם"! (ראש השנה כד,א ע"פ ויקרא כג:ד)
The pasuk stated: "(These are the festivals of the Lord) that you shall proclaim them" — read it אַתֶּם, *"you" (instead of* אֹתָם, *"them" — to emphasize that the people should actually proclaim the sanctification of the month).*

SEE: אַל תִּקְרֵי ... אֶלָּא ..., יֵשׁ אֵם לַמִּקְרָא

קְרִי כָּאן קְרָא כָּאן ...! **Read here ...!**
This expression cites a Biblical passage to support the halakha under consideration.

קְרִי כָּאן: "כִּי יִקָּרֵא" — פְּרָט לִמְזוּמָּן. (בבא מציעא קב, סע"א ע"פ דברים כב:ו)
Read here: "If [a bird's nest] chance (before you)" — excluding [one that is] at hand (on your property).

קָרֵי לֵיהּ קוֹרֵא אוֹתוֹ ... **he calls it ...;**
he designates it (by a certain term)

זֶה נִיסָן וְקָרֵי לֵיהּ "רִאשׁוֹן" (ראש השנה ז,א ע"פ שמות יב:ב)
this is [the month of] Nisan, and [the Torah] calls it "the first [month]"

קְרֵי עֲלֵיהּ

he cites regarding him ... קוֹרֵא עָלָיו ...

קָרֵינָא בֵּיהּ אֲנִי קוֹרֵא בּוֹ ...

I cite with regard to him/it (m.); I apply to him/it (m.) ...

The speaker applies either a Biblical passage or a popular saying to a person whose situation has just been described in the Talmud.

אִמּוֹ מִיִּשְׂרָאֵל "מִקֶּרֶב אַחֶיךָ" קָרֵינָא בֵּיהּ. (קידושין עו,ב ע"פ דברים יז:טו)

[If] his mother is Jewish, I apply to him [the passage] "from among your brethren (you may set a king upon yourselves)," (hence he is eligible for public office).

For another example — see ב"מ פג,ב ע"פ משלי כא:כג.

SEE: קָרֵינַן בֵּיהּ, קָרָא עָלָיו הַמִּקְרָא הַזֶּה

קָרֵינַן אָנוּ קוֹרְאִים **we read; we call**

This word is often used with reference to the (Masoretic) reading of the Biblical text.

מִי קָרֵינַן "עָנִי"?! "עוֹנִי" קָרֵינַן! (פסחים לו,א ע"פ דברים טז:ג)

Do we read [the word עני *as if it were vocalized]* עָנִי*, "poor (bread)"?! (No!) We read* עני *"(the bread of) affliction"!*

SEE: כְּתִיב ... וְקָרֵינַן ...

קָרֵינַן בֵּיהּ אָנוּ קוֹרְאִים בּוֹ

we cite [the Biblical passage] with regard to him/it (m.)

SEE: קְרֵי לֵיהּ, קָרֵינָא בֵּיהּ

קַשׁוּ קְרָאֵי אַהֲדָדֵי קָשִׁים הַפְּסוּקִים זֶה עַל זֶה!

"The p°sukim are difficult one against the other!" The p°sukim contradict each other!

וְ"דֶּרֶךְ" לְשׁוֹן נְקֵבָה הוּא, דִּכְתִיב: "וְהוֹדַעְתָּ לָהֶם אֶת הַדֶּרֶךְ יֵלְכוּ בָהּ" ... וְאַשְׁכְּחַן "דֶּרֶךְ" דְּאִיקְּרִי לְשׁוֹן זָכָר, דִּכְתִיב: "בְּדֶרֶךְ אֶחָד יֵצְאוּ אֵלֶיךָ, וּבְשִׁבְעָה דְרָכִים יָנוּסוּ לְפָנֶיךָ" אִי הָכִי, קַשׁוּ קְרָאֵי אַהֲדָדֵי! (קידושין ב,ב ע"פ שמות יח:כ ודברים כח:ז)

and [the noun] דֶּרֶךְ *("a path") is feminine, as it is written: "And you shall let them know the path in which (*בָּהּ*, f.) they should walk" ... But we have found* דֶּרֶךְ *that is treated as a masculine [noun], as it is written: "In one (*אֶחָד*, m.) path they will come forth to [attack] you, and in seven (*שִׁבְעָה*, m.) paths they will flee [from] before you." If so, the [two] p°sukim contradict each other!*

קְשֵׁי (קשי: תִּיקְשֵׁי/תִּקְשֵׁי .fut) נִתְקַשָּׁה

it was difficult; he found... difficult; he was perplexed (by)

הָא מִילְּתָא קְשׁוּ בָהּ רַבָּה וְרַב יוֹסֵף עֶשְׂרִין וְתַרְתֵּין שְׁנִין וְלָא אִיפְּרְקָה ... (בבא קמא סו, סע"ב ע"פ כת"י)

Rabba and Rav Yosef found this matter difficult for twenty-two years, and it was not resolved ...

SEE: תִּיקְשֵׁי לָךְ

קָשֵׁי (קַשְׁיָא .f.s, קַשְׁיָין .f. pl)

difficult; contradictory קָשֶׁה

קַשְׁיָא .f קָשֶׁה! **It is difficult!**

This term often appears at the conclusion of a Talmudic discussion, indicating that the *difficulty* previously raised against a halakha remains unresolved.*

For an example — see שבת כב,ב and the next entry.

* For the distinction between the terms קַשְׁיָא (or the noun קוּשְׁיָא) and תְּיוּבְתָּא, see the note on the latter.

For the distinction between a קוּשְׁיָא and a בַּעְיָא, see ²בַּעְיָא.

SEE: אִי קַשְׁיָא, הָא קַשְׁיָא, הָא גוּפָא קַשְׁיָא, הָא לָא קַשְׁיָא, (וּדְ)קָא קַשְׁיָא לָךְ ..., לָא קַשְׁיָא

קַשְׁיָא דְר' ... אַדְּר' ... (הַהֲלָכָה הַזֹּאת) שֶׁל ר' ... קָשָׁה עַל (הֲלָכָה אַחֶרֶת) שֶׁל ר' ...!

[This halakhic statement] of R. ... is contradictory to [another halakhic statement] of R. ... (i.e., the same tanna).

With this formula, the Talmud argues that one of the tannaim involved in the controversy just quoted contradicts his own statement, which is contained in a different mishna or baraitha.

קַשְׁיָא דְר' יְהוּדָה אַדְּר' יְהוּדָה; קַשְׁיָא דְרַבָּנַן אַדְּרַבָּנַן. (פסחים יא,א)

[The halakhic statement] of R. Y°huda is contradictory to [another halakhic statement] of R. Y°huda; [the halakhic statement] of the Ḥakhamim is contradictory to [another halakhic statement] of the [same] Ḥakhamim.

For another example, see ... תְּרֵי תַנָּאֵי וְאַלִּיבָּא דְר'.

קַשְׁיָין אַהֲדָדֵי קָשׁוֹת זוֹ עַל זוֹ!

"They are difficult one against the other!" They contradict each other!

There is a *contradiction* between the two halakhoth (of tannaim) that have been quoted in the Talmud.

תַּנְיָא: מַחְזֶקֶת רֹאשׁוֹ וְרוּבּוֹ וְשׁוּלְחָנוֹ כְּשֵׁרָה ... וְתַנְיָא אִידָךְ: אֲפִילּוּ אֵינָהּ מַחְזֶקֶת אֶלָּא רֹאשׁוֹ וְרוּבּוֹ כְּשֵׁרָה — וְאִילּוּ שׁוּלְחָנוֹ לָא קָתָנֵי. קַשְׁיָין אַהֲדָדֵי! (סוכה ג,א)

It is stated (in one baraitha): [Only a sukka large enough to] hold a man's head, most of his body, and his table is fit [for the mitzva] ... But it is stated [in] another [baraitha]: Even if it holds only his head and most of his body, it is fit — whereas "his table" is not stated. They (= the two baraithoth) contradict each other!

קַשְׁיָתֵיהּ (= קָשֶׁת .f + ־ֵיהּ)

it was difficult for him הָיְתָה קָשָׁה לוֹ

SEE: מַתְנִיתִין קַשְׁיָתֵיהּ, קְשֵׁי

קָתָנֵי (= קָא+תָנֵי)

SEE: תָּנֵי

ר

רְאִי

SEE: לא רְאִי ... כִּרְאִי ...

רְאָיָה*

proof; evidence

"לא רָאִינוּ" אֵינוֹ רְאָיָה. (משנה עדיות פ"ב מ"ב)

[The fact that people claim:] "We did not witness [a particular event]" does not constitute [sufficient] evidence [that the event did not occur].

* Many Ashkenazic Jews pronounce this noun רַאְיָה.

SEE: אַף עַל פִּי שֶׁאֵין רְאָיָה לַדָּבָר זֵכֶר לַדָּבָר, (וּ)מָה רָאִיתָ, (הַ)מּוֹצִיא מֵחֲבֵירוֹ עָלָיו הָרְאָיָה, (מִ)שָּׁם רְאָיָה

רְאִיָּה/רְאִיָּיה

(1) seeing; sighting; sight

אַשְׁמְעִינַן דִּרְאִיָּה לָא קָנֵי (בבא מציעא ב, סע"א)

[the tanna] has taught us that sighting [an article] does not acquire [it]

(2) an appearance (at the Beth HaMikdash)*

הַכֹּל חַיָּיבִין בִּרְאִיָּה (חגיגה ב, רע"א: משנה פ"א מ"א)

all (males) are obligated in the appearance (at the Beth HaMikdash on the three pilgrim festivals)

(3) an appearance (of discharge)

תָּלָה הַכָּתוּב אֶת הַזָּכָר בִּרְאִיּוֹת וְאֶת הַנְּקֵבָה בְּיָמִים. (כריתות ח,ב ע"פ ויקרא טו:ב,ג,כה)

Scripture has made [the defilement of] the male dependent upon [the number of] appearances [of discharge] and [that of] the female dependent upon [the number of] days [of discharge].

* This obligation is based on the Biblical verse:
שָׁלוֹשׁ פְּעָמִים בַּשָּׁנָה יֵרָאֶה כָל זְכוּרְךָ אֶת פְּנֵי ה' אֱלֹקֶיךָ בַּמָּקוֹם אֲשֶׁר יִבְחָר ... (דברים טז:טז)
It is sometimes called רֵאָיוֹן (משנה פאה א:א).

רַב

(1) teacher (of Torah)

עֲשֵׂה לְךָ רַב (משנה אבות פ"א מ"ו)

acquire a teacher for yourself

(2) master

עֲבָדִים הַמְשַׁמְּשִׁים אֶת הָרַב (משנה אבות פ"א מ"ג)

slaves who are serving a master

(3) *Rav* ...*

This word is also used as a title of amoraim who were ordained in Babylonia. Their halakhic authority was inferior to that of amoraim ordained in Erets Yisrael, and they were not given the title רַבִּי like the latter. The Babylonian amoraim were not authorised to impose fines (קְנָסוֹת), nor to rule that a first-born animal had a defect permitting its private use and consumption.

(4) *Rav*

The proper noun *Rav* is often used without a name after it to refer to ר' אַבָּא אֲרִיכָא, the famous amora who was active in Babylonia after the compilation of the Mishna. In several baraithoth** he is called *R. Abba*, and his colleague Sh^e^muel called him *Abba.**** When Rav's halakhic statement is contradicted by a mishna or a baraitha (and no other means of reconciliation is available), the Talmud sometimes replies that Rav has the authority to disagree with the opinion of a tanna.

רַב תַּנָּא הוּא וּפָלֵיג. (עירובין נ,ב ושי"נ)

Rav is [as authoritative as] a tanna, and he disagrees.

(5) big; large; great; significant גָּדוֹל

This word is also the absolute form of the Aramaic adjective that comprises the next entry.

* When the title רַב comes before a name that begins with the letter א followed by a consonant articulated by the lips (= ב, מ, פ), the title sometimes combines with the proper name to form a single word (with the א omitted).
רַב אַבָּא > רַבָּה, רָבָא; רַב אַבִין > רַבִין;
רַב אַמִי > רַמִי; רַב אֶפְרַיִם > רַפְרָם.
See *Arukh*, s.v. אביי.
** See ברכות מט, רע"א; כתובות פא, סע"א.
*** See חולין מה,ב ורש"י שם; שבת נג,א ורש"י שם.
SEE: מַעֲשֵׂה רַב, רַבָּנוּ, בֵּי רַב/רַבָּנַן

רַבָּא/רַבָּה

(abs. רַב, f.s. רַבְּתָא/רַבָּתִי, m. pl. רַבְרְבֵי)

big; large; great גָּדוֹל

יְהֵא שְׁמֵיהּ רַבָּא מְבָרַךְ ... (ברכות נז, רע"א)

May His great Name be a source of blessing ...

ר' חִיָּיא רַבָּה (שבת לח, רע"ב) *R. Ḥiyya, the great*

רַבָּה*

teacher רַב; מוֹרֶה

הָא בְּרַבָּה; הָא בְּתַלְמִידָא. (פסחים קיז,א)

This [statement speaks] of a teacher; (whereas) that [speaks] of a student.

* רַבָּה (= רַב אַבָּא) is also the name of an important Babylonian amora. See the first note on רַב.

רִבּוּי

SEE: רִיבּוּי

לְרַבּוּיֵי

SEE: רַבִּי

לְרַבּוֹת

SEE: רִיבָּה

רְבוּתָא

greatness; advantage; a noteworthy point; uniqueness גְּדֻלָּה; יִתְרוֹן; חִדּוּשׁ

רֵישָׁא רְבוּתָא קָא מַשְׁמַע לָן (שבת קמז, רע"ב)

the first clause (of our mishna) does teach us a noteworthy point (and hence it is not superfluous) ...

SEE: מַאי רְבוּתָא

רַבִּי/רְבִּי*

(1) ***Räbbi*** **(= my teacher)**
This title is applied to tannaim,** to amoraim of Erets Yisrael, and to Babylonian amoraim who were ordained in Erets Yisrael.

(2) ***Rebbi; R. Y***^{e}***huda HaNasi***
The word *Rebbi* by itself — without a proper name after it — refers to ר׳ יְהוּדָה הַנָּשִׂיא, who compiled the Mishna. In aggadic passages, he is sometimes called רַבֵּנוּ הַקָּדוֹשׁ, *our holy teacher* (as in שבת קיח,ב), and רְבִּי רַבָּה, *Rebbi the Great* (חולין נא,א ורש״י שם).

* The pronunciation varies among different Jewish communities — רַבִּי or רְבִּי (especially for *R. Y*^{e}*huda HaNasi*) among Ashkenasic Jews and רִבִּי among Sephardic Jews. Because of this uncertainty, this dictionary regularly uses an abbreviation, *R.* or ר׳.

** Tannaim who were active prior to the destruction of the second Beth HaMikdash are generally mentioned by name alone, without titles. See examples in Pirké Avoth:
יוֹסֵי בֶּן יוֹעֶזֶר; שִׁמְעוֹן בֶּן שֶׁטַח; הִלֵּל; שַׁמַּאי; עֲקַבְיָה בֶּן מַהֲלַלְאֵל
On the other hand, the absence of a title before the name of a later tanna or an amora indicates that the ḥakham was not officially ordained, e.g., שִׁמְעוֹן בֶּן עַזַּאי; סוּמְכוֹס; שְׁמוּאֵל.

בְּרַבִּי

SEE: בְּרִיבִּי

רָבֵי prt. (רבי)

growing　　　גָּדֵל

חַאי מֵאַרְעָא קָא רָבֵי. (עירובין כח,ב)
This grows from the ground.

רַבִּי (רבי פָּעֵל: מְרַבֵּי .prt, לְרַבּוּיֵי .inf)

he included; he widened (the scope)　　　רִבָּה

SEE: אַיְיתִי, חֲבִיא, מָעֵט, רִיבָּה and the next entry.

רַבִּי רַחֲמָנָא　　רִבָּה הָרַחֲמָן; הַתּוֹרָה רִבְּתָה

The Torah has included ... (into a halakha by using an additional word)
For an example — see פסחים עח,א.

רְבִיעִית; רְבִיעֲתָא* (= רְבִיעִית הַלֹּג)

a quarter of a *log* (in liquid measure)
* The first form is Hebrew, and the second is Aramaic. See the table of measurements at the end of this volume.
SEE: רוֹבַע

רַבָּן (= רַבֵּנוּ)

Rabban **(= our teacher)**
This Hebrew title is applied to the heads of the Sanhedrin until the death of Rabban Gamliel, the son of R. Y^{e}huda HaNasi, including:
רַבָּן יוֹחָנָן בֶּן זַכַּאי; רַבָּן גַּמְלִיאֵל; רַבָּן שִׁמְעוֹן בֶּן גַּמְלִיאֵל.
SEE: נָשִׂיא

רַבָּנָא　　רַבֵּנוּ

Rabbana **(= our teacher)**
This Aramaic title precedes the names of certain amoraim, e.g., רַבָּנָא נְחֶמְיָה, אֲחוּהּ דְּרֵישׁ גָּלוּתָא (שבת כ,ב)
Rabbana N^{e}*ḥemia, the brother of the exilarch*

רַבָּנַן

(1) חֲכָמֵינוּ; הַחֲכָמִים
our *ḥakhamim*; the *ḥakhamim*
This Aramaic noun is sometimes used with reference to Torah sages in general, like the Hebrew term חֲכָמִים when used in its general sense. This usage is very common when this noun appears with the prefix -דְּ, forming דְּרַבָּנַן. See the next entry and its first example.

(2) הַחֲכָמִים　　**the *Ḥakhamim***
This term often refers to a group of anonymous tannaim, who present an opinion that differs with the view of a tanna who is mentioned by name. Sometimes, the anonymous opinion referred to by the term רַבָּנַן is that of the תַּנָּא קַמָּא. Occasionally, it refers to an opinion ascribed to a tanna whose identity is known, e.g., בֶּן עַזַּאי in סוטה כא,ב.

(3) תַּלְמִידֵי בֵּית הַמִּדְרָשׁ; בְּנֵי יְשִׁיבָה　　**students (in the beth midrash); yeshiva students**

רַבָּנַן דְּבֵי רַב אַשִׁי (מנחות סו,א ועוד)
the students in the beth midrash of Rav Ashi

SEE: הָאי מֵרַבָּנַן, הַהוּא מֵרַבָּנַן, צוּרְבָא מֵרַבָּנַן, תָּנוּ רַבָּנַן, חֲכָמִים

דְּרַבָּנַן　　שֶׁל הַחֲכָמִים

of the *ḥakhamim*

(1) of Rabbinic status (as opposed to a mitsva of Torah status)

מַצָּה בִּזְמַן הַזֶּה דְאוֹרַיְיתָא, וּמָרוֹר דְּרַבָּנַן. (פסחים קכ,א)
[The eating of] matza nowadays is [a mitzva] of Torah status, whereas [the eating of] bitter herbs is of Rabbinic status.

(2) advocated by the Ḥakhamim (as opposed to the opinion of a different tanna)

לְדִבְרֵיהֶם דְּרַבָּנַן קָאָמַר לְהוּ (שבת מה,ב)
[the tanna] was talking to them according to the opinion advocated by the Ḥakhamim

SEE: קַשְׁיָא דְּר׳ ... אַדְּר׳ ...، חֲכָמִים, אַסְמַכְתָּא¹, אוֹרַיְיתָא

מִדְּרַבָּנַן　　מִדִּין חֲכָמִים

from Rabbinic law; according to Rabbinic enactment

מוּתָּר מִן הַתּוֹרָה וְאָסוּר מִדְּרַבָּנַן. (חולין צב,ב)
It is permissible according to the law of the Torah but forbidden according to Rabbinic enactment.

רַבָּנַן בָּתְרָאֵי

הַחֲכָמִים הָאַחֲרוֹנִים　　**the later Ḥakhamim**

In a three-way controversy between (1) an anonymous tanna (תַּנָּא קַמָּא), (2) another tanna identified by name, and (3) the Ḥakhamim — the Talmud refers to the last disputants as רַבָּנַן בָּתְרָאֵי.
For an example — see עבודה זרה ז,ב.
SEE: תַּנָּא קַמָּא

רַבְרְבֵי pl. (רַבְרְבָתָא .f. pl) גְּדוֹלִים **big; great**

תְּרֵי גַּבְרֵי רַבְרְבֵי (שבת כג,ב ועוד)

two great men (= ḥakhamim)

SEE: גַּבְרָא רַבָּה, רַבָּא

רְהַט* (רהט: רָהֵיט .prt) רָץ **he ran**

שִׁיתִּין רָהוֹטֵי רְהוּט וְלָא מְטוֹ לְגַבְרָא דְמִצַּפְרָא כְּרַךְ. (ב"ק צב,ב)

Sixty runners ran [after him], but they did not overtake the man who had eaten (breakfast) in the morning.

* In post-Talmudic Hebrew, the adjective רָהוּט is used. The phrase עִבְרִית רְהוּטָה means *fluent Hebrew.*

רוּבָּא רֹב **the majority**

זִיל בָּתַר רוּבָּא! (חולין יא, רע"א) *Follow the majority!*

רוֹבַע* **a quarter of a *kav***

* See the table of measurements in Appendix II.

SEE: רְבִיעִית

רְוַוח (רוח: רָוַוח .act. prt, רְוִיחַ .pass. prt)

it became relieved; it was at ease; it widened הִתְרַוַּח; הִתְרַחֵב

הוֹאִיל וַאֲתָא מִיטְרָא, הַשְׁתָּא רְוַוח עָלְמָא. (תענית כג,ב ורש"י שם)

Since rain has come, now the world is at ease.

SEE: אַרְוַוח

רְוָוחָא

ampleness; profit; comfort; ease רֶוַח

מֵעִיקָּרָא הֲווֹ עָיְילִי בָהּ בְּדוֹחְקָא, וְהַשְׁתָּא עָיְילִי בָהּ בִּרְוָוחָא. (בבא בתרא נג,א)

Initially they would go through it (= the hole in the fence) with difficulty, but now they go through it with ease.

SEE: אַרְוַוח

רוּמְיָא "הֲטָלָה"; קוּשְׁיָא

"the hurling" (of one source against another); a contradiction

מַאי רוּמְיָא?! (כתובות לו,א) *What is the contradiction?!*

SEE: קוּשְׁיָא, רְמָא

רָחֵים prt. (רחם) אוֹהֵב **loving***

לָא לִידוּן אֱינִישׁ דִּינָא לְמַאן דְּרָחֵים לֵיהּ וְלָא לְמַאן דְּסָנֵי לֵיהּ. (כתובות קה,ב)

One should not judge the case of [a person] whom he loves nor of [a person] whom he hates.

* This is the meaning of the verb in the קַל *binyan* as in Targum Onkelos (ויקרא יט:יח ועוד). In the פַּעֵל *binyan*, it means *he pitied, he showed mercy*, like the פִּעֵל in Hebrew.

קָא מְרַחֵם מָר אַעֲנְיָא (מועד קטן כח, סע"א)

you show mercy to a poor man

רַחֲמֵי רַחֲמִים **mercy; compassion**

צְלוֹתָא רַחֲמֵי הִיא (ברכות כו, סע"א)

prayer is [a request for Divine] mercy

SEE: בְּעָא

רַחֲמָנָא הָרַחֲמָן; הַתּוֹרָה

the Merciful (God); the Torah

רַחֲמָנָא לִיצְּלַן! (תענית ט,ב) *May the Merciful save us!*

SEE: גַּלֵּי רַחֲמָנָא and the next entry.

רַחֲמָנָא אֲמַר הַתּוֹרָה אָמְרָה

The Merciful (God) said; the Torah said

For an example, see the more common אֲמַר רַחֲמָנָא.

רִיבָּה (רבי פִּעֵל: מְרַבֶּה .prt, לְרַבּוֹת .inf)

he included; he widened (the scope of a halakha)

This verb indicates that a Biblical text has an extra word or letter that teaches a certain point.

"אֶת ה' אֱלֹקֶיךָ תִּירָא" — לְרַבּוֹת תַּלְמִידֵי חֲכָמִים. (פסחים כב,ב ע"פ דברים ו:יג)

"You shall revere the Lord your God" — [the word את *is written] to include [reverence towards] Torah scholars.*

SEE: רַבִּי, הֵבִיא, אַיְיתִי

רִיבָּה וּמִיעֵט וְרִיבָּה רִיבָּה הַכֹּל

[Scripture] extended and limited and extended — it has (thereby) included everything.

This statement is one of the *rules of Biblical interpretation* (מִדּוֹת) of R. Akiva that are used to interpret halakhic passages. According to R. Akiva, this sequence of terms in the Torah that are regarded as extensions and limitations, respectively, leaves the general category intact with the exclusion of only that which is clearly exceptional.

ברייתא: הַגּוֹזֵל שָׂדֶה מֵחֲבֵירוֹ וּשְׁטָפָהּ נָהָר, חַיָּיב לְהַעֲמִיד לוֹ שָׂדֶה — דִּבְרֵי ר' אֱלִיעֶזֶר ...

תלמוד: ר' אֱלִיעֶזֶר דָּרֵישׁ רִיבּוּיֵי וּמִיעוּטֵי. "וְכִחֵשׁ בַּעֲמִיתוֹ" — רִיבָּה, "בְּפִקָּדוֹן אוֹ בִתְשׂוּמֶת יָד" — מִיעֵט, "אוֹ מִכֹּל אֲשֶׁר יִשָּׁבַע ... (וְשִׁלַּם אֹתוֹ)" — חָזַר וְרִיבָּה: רִיבָּה וּמִיעֵט וְרִיבָּה — רִיבָּה הַכֹּל. מַאי רִיבָּה? רִיבָּה כָּל מִילֵּי. וּמַאי מִיעֵט? מִיעֵט שְׁטָרוֹת. (שבועות לז,ב ע"פ ויקרא ה:כא,כד)

BARAITHA: [If] one steals a field from his fellow man and (then) a river flooded it, he is obligated to restore a field to him — [these are] the words of R. Eliezer ...

TALMUD: R. Eliezer expounds extensions and limitations. "And he falsely denied [something of] his fellow man" — [this expression] extended [the law]; "regarding a charge or a loan" — [this] limited [its scope]; "or anything about which he may swear ... (he must pay for it)" — [this] extended once again: [Scripture] extended and limited and extended — it has (thereby) included everything. What has it included? It has included everything. But what has it excluded? It has excluded documents (which are unlike the particulars stated in the pasuk since their value is not intrinsic).

רִיבּוּי; רִיבּוּיָא/רִבּוּיָא*

(1) much; majority

בִּדְרַבָּנָן נָמֵי רִבּוּיָא הוּא דְּבָעֵינָן (יבמות פב, סע"א)
even with regard to [a prohibition] of Rabbinic status, it is a majority that we require

(2) an inclusion; an extension

This term denotes an amplification of the scope of a halakhic category through an apparently extra expression, word or letter in a Biblical text.

"וְכָל בְּהֶמְתֶּךָ" רִיבּוּיָא הוּא. (בבא קמא נד,ב ע"פ דברים ה:יד)
[The Biblical expression] "and all your animals" is an inclusion (of work done by all animals into the prohibition of labor on the Sabbath).

* The first form is Hebrew, and the second is Aramaic.
SEE: מִיעוּט

רִיבּוּיֵי וּמִיעוּטֵי רִבּוּיִים וּמִעוּטִים

[the rules of Biblical interpretation through] extensions and limitations (according to the system of R. Akiva, e.g., (רִיבָּה וּמִיעֵט וְרִיבָּה)
SEE: כְּלָלֵי וּפְרָטֵי

רִיבְעָא רֶבַע **one-fourth; a quarter**

רִיפְתָּא לֶחֶם; כִּכָּר **bread; loaf**

כְּרַךְ רִיפְתָּא (תענית כ, סע"ב ועוד)
he ate bread
SEE: כְּרַךְ

רֵישׁ גָּלוּתָא רֹאשׁ הַגּוֹלָה

"the chief of the exile"; the exilarch

The authority of this leader of the Babylonian Jewish community was recognized by the government. In some cases, he participated in halakhic discussions in the beth midrash.

בְּעָא מִינֵּיה רֵישׁ גָּלוּתָא מֵרַבָּה בַּר הוּנָא (שבת קטו,ב)
the exilarch asked Rabba b. Huna

רֵישָׁא (abs. and constr. רֵישׁ)

the head; the beginning הָרֹאשׁ

This word often serves as a technical term denoting *the first* (or *earlier*) *clause* of the text under discussion — usually a mishna or a baraitha, but occasionally a Biblical passage or an amora's statement. This term is used in contradistinction to סֵיפָא, *the latter* (or *last*) *clause*. Occasionally, both רֵישָׁא and סֵיפָא are contrasted to מְצִיעֲתָא, *the middle clause*.
SEE: מְצִיעֲתָא, סֵיפָא

רֵישָׁא ר' ... וְסֵיפָא ר' ...*

הָרֹאשׁ הוּא (לְפִי) ר' ..., וְהַסּוֹף הוּא (לְפִי) ר' ...?!

Does the first clause (in the mishna or baraitha follow the opinion of) R. ..., while the latter clause (follows the opinion of) R. ...?!

This formula usually constitutes a *rhetorical question* that points out that two clauses in the same text are inconsistent with each other — unless they are viewed as the opinions of two different tannaim. In response, either the divided authorship is reluctantly accepted, or the contradiction between the two clauses is reconciled according to the opinion of one of the tannaim.

For an example — see ר' ישמעאל ור' עקיבא בב"מ מא,א.
* Occasionally, this formula is not a rhetorical question, but it presents an interpretation of the text under discussion.
For an example — see רבי והחכמים בעירובין לד,ב.
SEE: אֲתָאן ל-, תַּבְרָא

רְמָא (רמי: רָמֵי .prt, לִירְמֵי .fut, רְמֵי .imp, לְמִירְמֵי .inf)

(1) הִשְׁלִיךְ; זָרַק; הֵטִיל **he threw; he thrust**

רְמָא לֵיה תּוֹרָא (נדה לג,ב)
he thrust before him an ox (= served him some beef)

(2) הֵטִיל; הִקְשָׁה

he pitted (one source against another); he pointed out a contradiction (between two sources)

This verb is frequently used in presenting a *contradiction* between two mishnayoth, between two baraithoth, between a mishna and a baraitha, between two psukim, between two halakhic statements of the same amora, or between the Masoretic reading (= the קְרִי) and spelling (= the כְּתִיב) of the same Biblical word.

רְמָא לֵיה תּוֹרָא, רְמָא לֵיה מַתְנְיָיתָא אַהֲדָדֵי. (נדה לג,ב)
he thrust before him an ox (= served him some beef), (and) he pointed out a contradiction between two mishnayoth before him

ר' זֵירָא רָמֵי מַתְנִיתִין אַבָּרַיְיתָא, וּמְשַׁנֵּי. (גיטין כז, סע"ב)
R. Zera points out a contradiction between our mishna and a baraitha, and he resolves [it].

ר' אַבָּהוּ רָמֵי: כְּתִיב: "זָכָר וּנְקֵבָה בְּרָאָם", וּכְתִיב: "כִּי בְּצֶלֶם אֱלֹקִים עָשָׂה אֶת הָאָדָם". (ברכות סא,א ע"פ בראשית ה:ב; ט:ו)
R. Abbahu points out a contradiction: It is written (in the Torah): "Male and female He created them (plural)," and it is written: "For he made man (singular) in the image of God."

וּרְמֵי דְּר' יוֹחָנָן אַדְּר' יוֹחָנָן, וּרְמֵי דְּרֵישׁ לָקִישׁ אַדְּרֵישׁ לָקִישׁ! (עירובין יא, סע"א)
Pit [this halakhic statement] of R. Yoḥanan against [another halakhic statement] of R. Yoḥanan, and pit [this halakhic statement] of Resh Lakish against [another halakhic statement] of Resh Lakish!

רַב פָּפָּא רָמֵי: כְּתִיב: "כִּי יתן", וְקָרֵינַן: "כִּי יוּתַּן". (בבא מציעא כב, רע"ב ע"פ ויקרא יא:לח)
Rav Pappa points out a contradiction: It is written (in the Torah): כִּי יתן *(usually read* יִתֵּן *— "if he will place"), but we read:* כִּי יוּתַּן*, "if it will be placed."*

* This verb does occur in Biblical Hebrew, for example:

סוּס וְרֹכְבוֹ רָמָה בַיָּם (שמות טו:א, כא), *the horse and its rider He threw into the sea.*

SEE: אִיכָּא דְּרָמֵי לְהוּ מִירְמָא, גַּבְרָא אַגַּבְרָא קָא רָמֵית, קַשְׁיָא, שְׁדָא, רוּמְיָא, וּרְמִינְהוּ

וּרְמִינְהוּ* (= וּרְמִי+אִינְהוּ) **וְהָטֵל אוֹתָם!**

"And pit them (against each other)!" But note the contradiction between them!

This term is used by the Talmud to introduce a *contradiction* between two sources — usually, of equal authority, e.g., two tannaitic statements or two p^esukim.**

For an example — see לָא קַשְׁיָא.

* In our printed editions of the Talmud, וּרְמִינְהוּ, with a masculine-plural suffix, is the common form, but older editions and manuscripts read וּרְמִינְהִי, with a feminine-plural suffix, e.g., in שבת כא,ב. Since the suffix *them*, usually refers to mishnayoth and baraithoth whose gender is feminine, the spelling וּרְמִינְהִי appears to be more correct.

** See: ריטב"א לבבא בתרא מב,א ד"ה "למימרא". There are, however, some exceptions, e.g., שבת כא,א where this term introduces a baraitha that contradicts an amora's halakha. (יד מלאכי ס' רן)

SEE: רְמָא

רַעֲוָא רָצוֹן **will; desire**

For an example — see יְהֵא רַעֲוָא.

רַשַּׁאי (f. רְשָׁאָה, m. pl. רַשָּׁאִין)

entitled; permitted*

הַחוֹבֵל בְּעַצְמוֹ, אַף עַל פִּי שֶׁאֵינוֹ רַשַּׁאי, פָּטוּר. (בבא קמא צ,ב: משנה פ"ח מ"ו)

One who wounds himself, even though he is not permitted √[to do so], is exempt [from punishment].

* In one mishna (according to our texts) this word is used to mean *obligated*. One of the Tosafists explained this word in the same way in some other cases as well.
ערכין כח, סע"ב רש"י ותוס' ושטמ"ק שם: משנה פ"ח מ"ז.

רְתַח* (רתח: prt. רָתַח, inf. לְמִירְתַּח)

רְתַח; כָּעַס he boiled; he became angry

אֶיחֱזֵי אִי רְתַח אִי לָא רָתַח. (קידושין לב,א)

I will see whether he becomes angry or not.

* The phrase בְּעִידַּן רִיתְחָא is used in Modern Hebrew in the sense of *in a moment of rage*, whereas we find in the Talmud (כתובות קו,א; ובבא קמא סו,ב ורש"י שם) that it means *at the time of (Divine) wrath = during an epidemic.*

ש

שְׁאֵיל (שאל: שָׁאֵיל .prt, לִישְׁאוֹל .fut, לְמִישְׁאַל .inf)

(1) שָׁאַל; הֶעֱלָה שְׁאֵלָה

he asked; he posed a halakhic problem

אֲתָא שַׁיְילֵיהּ לְרַב יוֹסֵף. (שבת צט, רע"ב)

He came (and) posed it (= the halakhic problem) to Rav Yosef.

(2) שָׁאַל; בִּקֵּשׁ וְקִבֵּל חֵפֶץ מֵחֲבֵירוֹ לְהִשְׁתַּמֵּשׁ בּוֹ חִנָּם וּלְהַחֲזִירוֹ בְּאוֹתוֹ מַצָּב

he borrowed (articles to be used and returned intact)

הַהוּא גַּבְרָא דִשְׁאֵיל נַרְגָּא מֵחַבְרֵיהּ ... (בבא מציעא צו, סע"ב)

There was a man who borrowed an ax from his fellow man ...

SEE: אוֹשִׁיל, יְזַף

שֶׁאֵין תַּלְמוּד לוֹמַר SEE: (שֶׁ)אֵין תַּלְמוּד לוֹמַר

שָׁאנֵי/שָׁנֵי prt. (שני)

it is different; it is exceptional שׁוֹנֶה

This word is used to present *a distinction* that resolves a difficulty or a contradiction between two sources. The expression שָׁאנֵי הָתָם, *it is different in that case*, is very common.

מָר סָבַר ["עַל ..."] לְמַפְרֵעַ מַשְׁמַע .... מֵיתִיבֵי: ... נְטָלוֹ לָצֵאת בּוֹ, אוֹמֵר: "אֲשֶׁר קִדְּשָׁנוּ בְּמִצְוֹתָיו וְצִוָּנוּ עַל נְטִילַת לוּלָב"! שָׁאנֵי הָתָם דִּבְעִידָּנָא דְאַגְבְּהַהּ, נְפַק בַּהּ. (פסחים ז,א)

One (amora) holds that [the use of the preposition עַל *before a verbal noun] implies that an event took place in the past. They refute [from this baraitha]: Once he has taken it (= the lulav) in order to fulfill his obligation with it, he should recite: ... "Who has sanctified us with His commandments and commanded us about the taking of the lulav" (hence it would appear that* עַל *anticipates the act that he is about to perform)! In that case (= lulav) it is different, for at the very moment he lifted it up, he had already fulfilled his obligation.*

שֶׁאֲנִי אוֹמֵר SEE: (שֶׁ)אֲנִי אוֹמֵר

שֶׁב/שְׁבַע f. שֶׁבַע **seven**

שֵׁב וְאַל תַּעֲשֶׂה* **"stay put and don't do!" an act that one must refrain from performing; a prohibited act**

כִּי קָא חָשֵׁיב שֵׁב וְאַל תַּעֲשֶׂה; קוּם וַעֲשֵׂה לָא קָא חָשֵׁיב. (סנהדרין נח, סע"ב)

When [the tanna lists the seven mitzvoth that apply to the sons of Noaḥ], he lists prohibited acts; [but] he does not list mitzva acts that one must perform.

* This term is not identical with a לֹא תַעֲשֶׂה (מִצְוַת), which must be formulated negatively in the Torah. For example, an אִיסּוּר עֲשֵׂה or a לָאו הַבָּא מִכְּלַל עֲשֵׂה is not a לֹא תַעֲשֶׂה; nevertheless it is a prohibited act, which can be described as שֵׁב וְאַל תַּעֲשֶׂה.

SEE: לֹא תַעֲשֶׂה, קוּם וַעֲשֵׂה

בְּשִׁבְּבוּתֵיהּ SEE: בְּשִׁיבְבוּתֵיהּ

שָׁבוּעַ

(1) (a period of) seven years*

הָיָה שְׂכִיר שַׁבָּת, שְׂכִיר חֹדֶשׁ, שְׂכִיר שָׁנָה, שְׂכִיר שָׁבוּעַ — נוֹתֵן לוֹ שְׂכַר שַׁבָּת. (בבא מציעא נח,א)

If [a worker] was hired by the week, by the month, by the year, or by seven years — [his employer] must pay him wages for the Sabbath.

(2) week

This is the common Biblical meaning.* It is also found in the Mishna and Talmud — mostly in passages dealing with the laws of ritual purity. Otherwise a week is usually שַׁבָּת (as in the previous example).

מִיטַּמְּאִין בְּשָׁבוּעַ אֶחָד, שֶׁהוּא שִׁבְעַת יָמִים (משנה נגעים ג:ד)

they may become ritually unclean for one week, which is seven days

* In the Book of Daniel, there are some instances where שָׁבוּעַ means *a seven-year period*.

שְׁבוּת **an activity prohibited on the Sabbath or on a festival by decree of the ḥakhamim; a Rabbinic Sabbath prohibition**

אֲמִירָה לְנָכְרִי שְׁבוּת. (שבת קנ,א)

Telling a non-Jew [to perform a forbidden labor on the Sabbath] is a Rabbinic Sabbath prohibition.

SEE: גְּזֵירָה

שַׁבֵּישׁ (שבש פַּעֵל: מְשַׁבֵּשׁ .prt, שַׁבֵּישׁ .inf) שִׁבֵּשׁ; הִטְעָה

he declared erroneous; he found fault with

וּמַאי חֲזֵית דִּמְשַׁבְּשַׁתְּ קְרָאֵי? שַׁבֵּישׁ מַתְנִי'!* (יומא עא,א)

But on what basis do you find fault with [the order of] the p^esukim? Find fault with [the order in] the mishna!

* Our printed versions read מַתְנִיתָא, which usually means *baraitha*, but the Munich Manuscript has מַתְנִי', which could be read מַתְנִיתִין, *our mishna*. The latter reading seems better, because it is a mishna that is under discussion in the Talmudic passage.

SEE: מְשַׁבַּשְׁתָּא, שַׁבֶּשְׁתָּא

שַׁבְסַר/שִׁיבְסַר שִׁבְעָה עָשָׂר **seventeen**

שַׁבְסְרֵי/שִׁיבְסְרֵי f. שְׁבַע עֶשְׂרֵה **seventeen**

שְׁבַע/שַׁב f. שֶׁבַע **seven**

שִׁבְעָא/שִׁבְעָה שִׁבְעָה **seven**

שִׁבְעִין שִׁבְעִים **seventy**

שְׁבַק (שבק: שָׁבֵיק .prt, לִישְׁבּוֹק .fut, שְׁבוֹק .imp, לְמִישְׁבַּק .inf)

(1) עָזַב; הִנִּיחַ **he left aside; he abandoned**

וְרַב שָׁבֵיק מַתְנִיתִין וְעָבֵיד כְּבָרַיְיתָא?! (בבא קמא צו,ב)

But does Rav abandon our mishna and rule in accordance with a baraitha?!

(2) הִרְשָׁה; הִנִּיחַ **he permitted; he allowed**

לָא שְׁבַקְתֵּיהּ גַּלּוֹיֵי רֵישֵׁיהּ (שבת קנו,ב)

she did not allow him to uncover his head

שַׁבֶּשְׁתָּא שִׁיבּוּשׁ; טָעוּת **confusion; an error**

וַאֲמַר רָבָא: ... שַׁבֶּשְׁתָּא מְמֵילָא נָפְקָא. רַב דִּימִי מִנְּהַרְדְּעָא אֲמַר: ... שַׁבֶּשְׁתָּא — כֵּיוָן דְּעָל, עָל. (בבא בתרא כא, סע"א)

And Rava said: ... an error goes away by itself. Rav Dimi from N^e^hard^e^a said: ... once an error has entered, it has entered (and cannot easily be eradicated).

SEE: מְשַׁבַּשְׁתָּא, שַׁבֵּישׁ

שַׁבָּת **the Sabbath; a week***

שַׁבָּת שֶׁחָל תִּשְׁעָה בְּאָב לִהְיוֹת בְּתוֹכָהּ (תענית כו, רע"ב: משנה פ"ד מ"ז)

the week during which Tish'a b^e^Av falls

* This meaning is also found in the Torah: שֶׁבַע שַׁבָּתוֹת תְּמִימֹת תִּהְיֶינָה (ויקרא כג:טו), *they must be seven complete weeks.*

SEE: שָׁבוּעַ

שְׁגַג (שגג: שׁוֹגֵג .prt) **he erred; he transgressed out of ignorance** (of the halakha)

בְּשׁוֹגֵג לָא קַנְסוּהָ רַבָּנַן (שבת ג, סע"ב)

for transgressing out of ignorance the ḥakhamim did not punish him

SEE: מֵזִיד

שְׁגָגָה **an unintended wrongdoing**

דָּבָר שֶׁחַיָּיבִין עַל ... שִׁגְגָתוֹ חַטָּאת (סנהדרין סו, רע"א: משנה פ"ז מ"ח)

an offense [whose perpetrators] are liable to [bring] ... a sin offering (when it is) an unintended wrongdoing

SEE: זָדוֹן

שְׁדָא (שדי: שָׁדֵי .act. prt, שְׁדֵי .pass. prt, לִישְׁדֵי .fut, שְׁדִי .imp, לְמִישְׁדָא .inf)

הִשְׁלִיךְ; זָרַק; הֵטִיל **he threw; he cast**

הָא מִילְּתָא הֲוַאי בִּידַן, וַאֲתָא ר' חֲנִינָא שְׁדָא בֵּיהּ נַרְגָּא. (ראש השנה יג, סע"א וסוכה יב, רע"א ורש"י שם)

This matter was "in our hand" (as a halakhic ruling), but R. Ḥanina came along (and) "cast an ax into it" (= he refuted the halakhic ruling).

SEE: רְמָא

שַׁדַּר* (שדר פָּעֵל: מְשַׁדַּר .prt, לִישַׁדַּר .fut, שַׁדַּר .imp, לְשַׁדּוֹרֵי .inf)

שָׁלַח **he sent**

לְתַקּוֹנֵי שַׁדַּרְתִּיךְ — וְלָא לְעַוּוֹתֵי! (קידושין מב, רע"ב ורש"י)

I sent you to benefit [me] — not to cause [me] injury!

* The verb שִׁדֵּר is used in Modern Hebrew to mean *he broadcasted*. Thus רְשׁוּת הַשִּׁידּוּר is *the Broadcasting Authority*.

SEE: שָׁלַח

שְׁהָא (שהי: שָׁהֵי .prt)

שָׁהָה **he waited; he delayed**

שְׁהָא לְמוֹצָאֵי שַׁבָּת שִׁיעוּר לְמִקְבְּרִינְהוּ (בבא מציעא מב,א)

he waited after the conclusion of the Sabbath long enough to bury them (= the coins)

שַׁהִי (שהי פָּעֵל: מְשַׁהֵי .prt, לְשַׁהֵי .fut, לְשַׁהוֹיֵי .inf)

הִשְׁהָה **he delayed (something); he permitted delay**

כָּל שֶׁהוֹיֵי מִצְוָה לָא מְשַׁהֵינַן. (יבמות לט, סע"א)

We surely do not permit any delay of [the performance of] a mitzva.

שׁוֹגֵג SEE: שָׁגַג

שָׁוֶה adj. **equal; equivalent; worth**

שָׁוֶה פְּרוּטָה (קידושין ב, רע"א: משנה פ"א מ"א)

worth a p^e^ruta (= a small coin)

פִּיו וְלִבּוֹ שָׁוִין. (משנה תרומות פ"ג מ"ח)

"His mouth and his heart are equal" (= He says what he has on his mind)

שְׁוַור (שור)

קָפַץ; דִּלֵּג **he jumped; he leaped**

חַזְיֵיהּ רֵישׁ לָקִישׁ וּשְׁוַור לְיַרְדְּנָא אַבָּתְרֵיהּ. (בבא מציעא פד,א)

Resh Lakish saw him (= R. Yoḥanan) and jumped into the Jordan [River] after him.

שָׁוֵי adj. (שָׁוְיָא .f.s, שָׁווּ .m. pl)

(1) שָׁוֶה **worth; valued**

מֵעִיקָּרָא שָׁוְיָא זוּזָא, וּלְבַסּוֹף שָׁוְיָא אַרְבְּעָה. (בבא מציעא מג,א)

It was originally worth one zuz, but eventually it was worth four.

(2) זוֹל **worth its price; inexpensive; cheap**

אַיְּידֵי דְּצוֹר אֲתוּ דְּשָׁוֵי חַמְרָא (עבודה זרה לד,ב ורש"י שם)

they came through Tzor (= Tyre) where wine is inexpensive

שַׁוִּי (שוי פָּעֵל: מְשַׁוֵּי .prt, לְשַׁוֵּי .fut, לְשַׁוּוֹיֵי .inf)

עָשָׂה **he made**

שַׁוְּיֵיהּ שְׁלִיחַ. (ב"מ כב,א)

He made him [his] agent.

SEE: מְשַׁוֵּי

וְשָׁוִין

and they are equal; and they (both) agree

This word is used to introduce a halakha that is agreed to by two tannaim who have just expressed their disagreement about a related halakha in the (same) mishna or baraitha.

וְעוֹשֶׂה תַּבְשִׁיל מֵעֶרֶב יוֹם טוֹב וְסוֹמֵךְ עָלָיו לַשַּׁבָּת. בֵּית שַׁמַּאי אוֹמְרִים: שְׁנֵי תַבְשִׁילִין, וּבֵית הִלֵּל אוֹמְרִים: תַּבְשִׁיל אֶחָד. וְשָׁוִין בְּדָג וּבֵיצָה שֶׁעָלָיו שֶׁהֵן שְׁנֵי תַבְשִׁילִין. (ביצה טו,ב: משנה ב:א)

And one may prepare a cooked dish from before the festival (that occurs on Friday) and rely on it for the Sabbath (that is, as part of his preparations for the Sabbath meals). Beth Shammai says: Two cooked dishes [are required], while Beth Hillel says: One cooked dish. And they [both] agree with regard to fish [cooked] with egg on it that they are [considered] two cooked dishes.*

* This procedure is known as עֵירוּב תַּבְשִׁילִין.

שׁוּם¹

(1) name; category; a [Biblical] prohibition

In the Targumim,* שׁוּם is the standard Aramaic translation of the Hebrew noun שֵׁם. It has entered Mishnaic Hebrew with the above meanings, like שֵׁם. For examples, see שֵׁם.

The noun שׁוּם is also used with prepositional prefixes and after the preposition עַל:

for the sake of; for the purpose of — לְשׁוּם

for the sake of marriage — לְשׁוּם אִישׁוּת (קידושין ד, סע"ב)

in the name of; because of; under the category/prohibition of — מִשּׁוּם

For examples, see מִשּׁוּם.

because — מִשּׁוּם שֶׁ–; מִשּׁוּם דְּ–

For an example — see מִשּׁוּם דְּ–, the Aramaic form.

in commemoration of [the fact] that; because — עַל שׁוּם שֶׁ–

מָרוֹר — עַל שׁוּם שֶׁמֵּרְרוּ הַמִּצְרִיִּים אֶת חַיֵּי אֲבוֹתֵינוּ בְּמִצְרַיִם. (פסחים קטז, רע"ב: משנה פ"י מ"ה)

A bitter herb [is eaten at the Seder] — in commemoration of [the fact] that the Egyptians embittered the lives of our ancestors in Egypt.

(2) any; any trace of

Unlike שֵׁם, שׁוּם is sometimes used in this sense in a negative context.**

שׁוּם קוֹרְבָה אָסוּר (שבת יג, סע"א)

any intimacy is forbidden

* In Yemenite editions of Onkelos, it is vocalized שׂוּם.

** This usage has become common in post-Talmudic Hebrew and in Modern Hebrew, in such expressions as שׁוּם דָּבָר and בְּשׁוּם אֹפֶן.

שׁוּם²; שׁוּמָא* — **an estimate; an appraisal**

שׁוּם כֶּסֶף (בבא קמא יד, רע"ב: משנה פ"א מ"ג)

appraisal [of damages by the court must be made in terms of] money

* The first form is Hebrew, and the second is Aramaic and is also presented as a separate entry below.

שׁוּם³; תּוּמָא* — **garlic**

כִּקְלִיפַּת הַשּׁוּם** (משנה מקואות פ"ו מ"ט)

like [the thinness of] the skin of garlic

* The first form is Hebrew, and the second is Aramaic.

** In the Talmud (e.g., בכורות נח,א) and in later Hebrew, this phrase is sometimes used metaphorically to indicate worthlessness.

שׁוּמָא¹ שׁוּם — **an estimate; an appraisal; evaluated property**

שׁוּמָא הָדַר. (בבא מציעא לה, סע"א)

Evaluated property [that was confiscated in payment of a debt] returns [to its owner].

SEE: שׁוּם²

שׁוּמָא² בְּלִיטָה בְעוֹר הַגּוּף

mark; mole (on a person's skin)

שׁוּמָא סִימָן מוּבְהָק הוּא. (בבא מציעא כז,ב)

A mole is [regarded as] a clear sign of identification.

שׂוֹנְאֵיהֶן שֶׁל יִשְׂרָאֵל

"the enemies of Israel" (= Israel)

This is a *euphemism* for *the Jewish people*. It is used in passages that condemn them to severe punishment.

בְּאוֹתָהּ שָׁעָה נִתְחַיְּיבוּ שׂוֹנְאֵיהֶן שֶׁל יִשְׂרָאֵל כְּלָיָה שֶׁהֶחֱנִיפוּ אֶת אַגְרִיפַּס. (סוטה מא,ב ע"פ כת"י בתוספתא ז:טז: "נתחייבו ישראל")

At that moment "the enemies of Israel" became liable to extermination because they flattered Agrippa.

שׂוֹנְאֵיהֶן שֶׁל תַּלְמִידֵי חֲכָמִים

"the enemies of Torah scholars" (= Torah scholars)

Like the previous entry, this is a *euphemism*.

For an example — see ברכות סג,ב ושי"נ.

שׁוּפְרָא יֹפִי — **beauty; the beautiful**

May women have your beauty! — שׁוּפְרָךְ לִנְשֵׁי! (ב"מ פד,א)

שׁוּפְרֵי שׁוּפְרֵי (פסחים ג,ב)

"the beautiful of the beautiful" (= the best quality)

שׁוּקָא שׁוּק; חוּץ — **the market; outside**

אִי לָאו תּוֹרָה, כַּמָּה נַחְמָן בַּר אַבָּא אִיכָּא בְּשׁוּקָא. (קידושין לג, סע"א)

Were it not for Torah [learning], there are a number of [people named] Nahman b. Abba (like me) outside.

שְׁחַט (שחט: שָׁחֵיט .prt, לִשְׁחוֹט .fut, לְמִישְׁחַט .inf)

he slaughtered — שָׁחַט

דִּלְמָא בְּסַכִּין פְּגוּמָה שָׁחֵיט? (חולין ג,ב)

Perhaps he is slaughtering with a defective knife?

בְּשִׁיבְבוּתֵיהּ/שִׁבְבוּתֵיהּ בִּשְׁכֵנוּתוֹ; בִּשְׁכוּנָתוֹ
in his vicinity; in his neighborhood
הָנְהוּ בִּרְיוֹנֵי דַּהֲווּ בְּשִׁבָבוּתֵיהּ דְּרִ' מֵאִיר ... (ברכות י, רע"א)
There were some outlaws in the vicinity of R. Méir ...*
* Literally: *"in his vicinity, that of R. Méir"*

שִׁיבְסַר/שַׁבְסַר שִׁבְעָה עָשָׂר **seventeen**

שִׁיבְסְרֵי/שַׁבְסְרֵי f. שְׁבַע עֶשְׂרֵה **seventeen**

שִׁיטָה[1] (pl. שִׁיטִין) **line; row**
הִרְחִיק אֶת הָעֵדִים שְׁנֵי שִׁיטִין מִן הַכְּתָב — פָּסוּל. (ב"ב קסב,א)
[If the signatures of] the witnesses were placed two lines away from the text [of the document], [the document] is invalid.

שִׁיטָה[2]**; שִׁיטְתָא*** **a line of reasoning; system; opinion; a (halakhic) position**
קָם אַבַּיֵי בְּשִׁיטְתֵיהּ דְּרָבָא. (שבת צב,א)
Abbayé adopted the (halakhic) position of Rava.
* The first form is Hebrew, and the second is Aramaic.
SEE: מוּחְלֶפֶת הַשִּׁיטָה

שָׁיֵיךְ (שָׁיְיכָא .f, שָׁיְיכֵי .m. pl) שַׁיָּךְ; קָשׁוּר
belonging; subject (to); connected (with)
שָׁיֵיךְ בְּמִצְוֹת (בבא קמא טו, רע"א)
subject to the commandments

שַׁיֵּיל* (שׁאל פַּעֵל: מְשָׁאֵיל/מְשַׁיֵּיל .prt, לִישַׁיֵּיל .fut, לְשַׁיּוֹלֵי .inf) שָׁאַל **he asked; he borrowed**
* This verb in the פַּעֵל *binyan* has the same meaning as the קַל form, שְׁאֵיל. For an example, see that entry.

שָׁיֵיף (שׁוף) .prt מוֹרֵחַ **rubbing**
שָׁיֵיף לַהּ לִבְרַתֵּיהּ בְּגוֹהַרְקֵי דְּעָרְלָה (פסחים כה,ב ורש"י שם)
[Rabina] was rubbing his daughter (for medicinal purposes) with the undeveloped fruit of "orla" (= fruit of a tree less than three years old)*
* Literally: *"her, his daughter"*

שַׁיֵּיר (שׁאר פַּעֵל: מְשַׁיֵּיר .prt, שַׁיּוֹרֵי .inf) שִׁיֵּר; הִשְׁאִיר
he left out; he omitted; he left over
בְּשָׂדֶה לָא שַׁיֵּיר וְלָא מִידֵי (בבא בתרא סב,ב)
in the field [itself], he has not left over anything at all
SEE: תְּנָא וְשַׁיַּיר

שְׁיָירָא/שְׁיָירָה; שְׁיָירְתָא* **caravan**
אִיכָּא שְׁיָירְתָא דְּאָזְלֵי וְאָתוּ הָתָם (בבא קמא קיב, סע"ב)
there are caravans that come and go there
* The first two forms are Hebrew, and the third is Aramaic.

שִׁיכְרָא/שִׁכְרָא
an intoxicating beverage; beer שֵׁכָר
מַהוּ לְקַדּוּשֵׁי אַשִּׁיכְרָא? (פסחים קז,א)
What is the halakhic ruling [with regard] to reciting kiddush over beer?

שִׁילְהֵי* constr. סוֹף **the end of; the conclusion of**
אָמַר רַב כָּהֲנָא: הֲוָה יָתֵיבְנָא בְּשִׁילְהֵי פִּירְקֵיהּ דְּרָבָא ... (בבא מציעא סד,א ורש"י שם)
Rav Kahana said: I was sitting (in the audience) at the conclusion of Rava's lecture ...
* This Aramaic noun is also used in Modern Hebrew, where it is often spelled שִׁלְהֵי.

שִׁינּוּיָא
תֵּירוּץ **resolution (of a difficulty); answer**
For an example — see the next entry.

שִׁינּוּיָא דְּחִיקָא תֵּירוּץ דָּחוּק
a forced reply; a strained solution
שִׁינּוּיָא דְּחִיקָא לָא מְשַׁנֵּינַן לָךְ. (בבא קמא קו,א ושׁ"נ)
We do not respond to you (with) a forced reply.
SEE: שַׁנִּי

שִׁינָּנָא
Two different explanations have been offered for this term (of affection) that Sh^emuel uses when addressing his distinguished student, Rav Y^ehuda b. Y^eheskel.*
(1) שִׁנָּן; גְּדוֹל הַשִּׁנַּיִם **having large teeth**
(2) שָׁנוּן **sharp; keen (in Torah learning)**
For an example — see ברכות לו,א ושׁ"נ.
* Both explanations and etymologies are given by R. Nathan of Rome in his *Arukh*.

שִׁיעְבּוּד; שִׁיעְבּוּדָא SEE: שִׁעְבּוּד

שִׁיפּוּלֵי* constr. שׁוּלֵי
the edge of; the hem of; the bottom of
וְנָקְטֵי לֵיהּ בְּשִׁיפּוּלֵי גְּלִימֵיהּ (תענית כג,ב)
and they would take hold of him by the hem of his garment
* This Aramaic noun is also used in Modern Hebrew, where it is often spelled שִׁפּוּלֵי.

שִׁיפּוּרָא שׁוֹפָר ***shofar*; a ram's horn**
Besides the blowing on Rosh HaShana, the sound of the *shofar* was sometimes used to herald an important announcement.
נְפַק שִׁיפּוּרָא מִבֵּית רַבָּן גַּמְלִיאֵל דִּשְׁכֵיב. (ב"מ נט, סע"ב)
The [sound of the] shofar issued forth from Rabban Gamliel's house [indicating] that he had died.

שִׁירָא מֶשִׁי **silk**

שִׁירָאֵי/שִׁירָאִין בִּגְדֵי מֶשִׁי **silk garments**
רַב הוּנָא קְרַע שִׁירָאֵי בְּאַנְפֵּי רַבָּה בְּרֵיהּ (קידושין לב,א)
Rav Huna tore silk garments in front of his son Rabba

שֵׁית f. שֵׁשׁ **six**

שִׁיתָּא שִׁשָּׁה **six**

שִׁיתִּין/שִׁתִּין sixty שִׁשִּׁים

שֵׁיתְסַר sixteen שִׁשָּׁה עָשָׂר

שֵׁיתְסְרֵי/שֵׁית סְרֵי f. sixteen שֵׁשׁ עֶשְׂרֵה

שְׁכִיב (שכב: שָׁכֵיב act. prt., שְׁכִיב pass. prt.)

he lay; he slept; he died שָׁכַב; יָשַׁן; מֵת

For examples, see יְקָרָא and שִׁיפּוּרָא.

שְׁכִיב מְרַע "שׁוֹכֵב חוֹלֶה"; חוֹלֶה אָנוּשׁ

someone gravely ill; a dying man

דִּבְרֵי שְׁכִיב מְרַע כִּכְתוּבִין וְכִמְסוּרִין דָּמוּ. (גיטין טו,א וש"נ)

The instructions of a dying man [have the same force] as if they were written and delivered.

SEE: מְרַע

שְׁכִיחַ* (שכח) pass. prt.

found; common; frequent מָצוּי

שִׁיקְרָא שְׁכִיחַ; קוּשְׁטָא לָא שְׁכִיחַ. (שבת קד,א)

Falsehood is common; the truth is not common.

* This word is often used as an adjective in Modern Hebrew.

SEE: מִילְּתָא דְּלָא שְׁכִיחָא לָא גְּזַרוּ בַּהּ רַבָּנַן, אַשְׁכַּח

שֶׁל of

In Biblical Hebrew, שֶׁל never appears as an independent word. Instead, we find אֲשֶׁר לְ-, as in הַצֹּאן אֲשֶׁר לְאָבִיהָ (בראשית כט:ט) *the flock of her father,* and (rarely) the form -שֶׁל prefixed to a noun, as in מִטָּתוֹ שֶׁלִּשְׁלֹמֹה (שיר השירים ג:ז), *the bed of (King) Sh'lomo.* In manuscripts of the Mishna and the Talmud, -שֶׁל still occurs as a prefix — whereas in almost all printed editions it has become a separate word. In some instances, a definite article, which was indicated by the vowel under the לּ, has become lost in this process.

יָדוֹ שֶׁלֶּעָנִי* (משנה שבת פ"א מ"א ע"פ כת"י קאופמן. בדפוס: יָדוֹ שֶׁל עָנִי)

the hand of the poor man

* The לֶ indicates that it means יָדוֹ שֶׁל הֶעָנִי.

שְׁלוּחָא SEE: שָׁלִיחַ

שְׁלַח (שלח: שָׁלַח a. prt., שְׁלִיחַ p. prt., לִישְׁלַח fut.);

שַׁלַּח (שלח פָּעֵל: מְשַׁלַּח prt., לְשַׁלּוֹחֵי inf.)

(1) שְׁלַח he sent; he sent a message*

שְׁלַח לְהוּ ר' יְהוֹשֻׁעַ לְבֵי מִדְרְשָׁא (ברכות כח,א)

R. Y'hoshua sent (the following) message to (the scholars in) the beth midrash

(2) פָּשַׁט; הִפְשִׁיט he took off (clothes or hide); he undressed; he stripped**

שְׁלִיחַ עַרְטִלָּאֵי וּרְמֵי מְסָאנֵי (כתובות סה, רע"ב ורש"י שם)

stripped naked but wearing shoes

* In מגילה ז, סע"א this verb is used in the sense of *sending a message*, in contrast to שְׁדַר, which appears just before it in the sense of *sending an object*.

** Also appearing in the Talmud is the Hebrew noun שֶׁלַח, *hide*, and the Aramaic nouns שַׁלְחָא, *hide*, and שַׁלָּחָא, *a remover of hides*.

שְׁלַחוּ מִתָּם

they sent (a message) from there שָׁלְחוּ מִשָּׁם

This expression introduces a communication from the halakhic authorities in Erets Yisrael to those in Babylonia.

שְׁלַחוּ מִתָּם: הִזָּהֲרוּ בְּמִנְהַג אֲבוֹתֵיכֶם בִּידֵיכֶם! (ביצה ד, סע"ב)

They sent (a message) from there: Give heed to the custom of your ancestors [which you have received] "in your hands"!

שָׁלִיחַ (שְׁלִיחַ constr., שְׁלוּחַ- with suffixes, שְׁלוּחִין pl.);

שְׁלִיחָא/שְׁלוּחָא* agent; deputy; representative

שְׁלוּחוֹ שֶׁל אָדָם כְּמוֹתוֹ (קידושין מא,ב וש"נ)

[an act performed by] the agent of a person is like [an act performed by] himself

* The first form is Hebrew, and the last forms are Aramaic.

שְׁלִיחַ (שלח pass. prt.) stripped

For an example — see שְׁלַח.

שְׁלִיחַ לְהוֹלָכָה an agent for delivery (usually of a bill of divorce)

In a divorce, the "hand" of the husband's agent is legally regarded as the "hand" of the husband. Accordingly, the wife is not legally divorced until the bill of divorce comes into her possession (or that of her agent*). Until that moment, the husband can still retract, even though he has already handed the document to his agent.

For an example — see גיטין סב,ב.

* Her agent is called a שְׁלִיחַ לְקַבָּלָה. See that entry below.

שְׁלִיחַ לְקַבָּלָה an agent for receiving (usually a bill of divorce)

In a divorce, the "hand" of the wife's agent is legally regarded as the "hand" of the wife. Accordingly, the wife is legally divorced as soon as her agent receives the bill of divorce from the husband (or from his agent*) — irrespective of where the wife happens to be at that moment. Thereafter, the husband cannot retract, even though the document has not actually reached her.

For an example — see גיטין סב,ב.

* His agent is called a שְׁלִיחַ לְהוֹלָכָה. See that entry above.

שְׁלִיחַ צִיבּוּר*; שְׁלִיחָא דְצִיבּוּרָא**

"the representative of the congregation"; the leader of public prayer; the cantor; the reader

שְׁלִיחַ צִיבּוּר מוֹצִיא אֶת הָרַבִּים יְדֵי חוֹבָתָן. (ראש השנה לג,ב: משנה פ״ד מ״ט)
The leader of public prayer performs the duty in behalf of the congregation (who listen to his recitation of the Amida).

* See note under חַזָּן.

** The first form is Hebrew, and the second is Aramaic.

שְׁלִים* (שלם: שְׁלִים .pass. prt) נִגְמַר; הֻשְׁלַם

it was finished; it was completed

וּשְׁלִים עִיבִידְתָּא בְּפַלְגָא דְיוֹמָא (בבא מציעא עז,א)
and the work was completed in half a day

* A plural form of the active participle, שָׁלְמִין/שָׁלְמֵי, also occurs a few times with the same meaning.

שַׁלֵּים (שלם פַּעֵל: מְשַׁלֵּם .prt, לְשַׁלֵּם .fut, שַׁלֵּים .imp, לְשַׁלּוֹמֵי .inf) שִׁלֵּם

he paid

מָמוֹן מְעַלְיָא בָּעֵי שַׁלּוֹמֵי לֵיהּ (גיטין נג, רע״ב)
he must pay him the full value

בִּשְׁלָמָא ״בְּשָׁלוֹם״; נוֹחַ הַדָּבָר

"at peace"; it is appropriate; it is reasonable

This term is generally used to introduce a *difficulty,* as in the next entry.*

* In נזיר מז, סע״א — it introduces a *halakhic problem,* as פְּשִׁיטָא sometimes does.

SEE: אִי אָמְרַתְּ בִּשְׁלָמָא

בִּשְׁלָמָא ... אֶלָּא .... נוֹחַ הַדָּבָר ..., אֶלָּא ....

[This] is reasonable (with regard to one case or according to one opinion), but (regarding the other case* or according to the other opinion) ....**

בִּשְׁלָמָא שׁוֹמֵר חִנָּם מִשְׁתְּבַע דְּלָא פְּשַׁע בָּהּ, אֶלָּא שׁוֹמֵר שָׂכָר — אַמַּאי מִשְׁתְּבַע? כִּי לָא פְּשַׁע נַמֵּי, שַׁלּוֹמֵי בָּעֵי! (ב״מ פב, סע״ב)
[The case of] the unpaid watchman is reasonable [for] he swears that he was negligent with regard to it (= that for which he accepted responsibility), but about what would the paid watchman swear? Even if he was not negligent, he must pay!

בִּשְׁלָמָא לְאַבָּיֵי נִיחָא,*** אֶלָּא לְרָבָא קַשְׁיָא! (בבא בתרא יז, ב)
It is appropriate according to [the opinion of] Abbayé, but according to Rava it is difficult!

* In this usage, this formula functions like the entry תִּינַח.

** In this usage, this formula functions like the entry הָנִיחָא.

*** The words בִּשְׁלָמָא and נִיחָא reinforce each other.

שְׁלַף (שלף: שָׁלֵיף .prt, לְמִישְׁלַף .inf);

שַׁלֵּף (שלף פַּעֵל: מְשַׁלֵּף .prt, שַׁלּוֹפֵי .inf)

שָׁלַף; חָלַץ; הוֹצִיא; עָקַר

he took off; he removed; he uprooted

אֲמַר לֵיהּ רַב כָּהֲנָא לִשְׁמוּאֵל: מִמַּאי דְּהַאי ״וְחָלְצָה נַעֲלוֹ מֵעַל רַגְלוֹ״ מִישְׁלַף הוּא ...? (יבמות קב,ב)
Rav Kahana said to Sh'muel: Where is the proof that this [expression] "and she shall perform 'halitza' on his shoe from his foot" means "removing"...?

שָׁם (שׁוּם: שָׁיֵים prt) שָׂם; הֶעֱרִיךְ; אָמַד

he estimated; he appraised; he evaluated

בְּדִנְיָזִק שָׁיְימִינַן. (בבא קמא ו,ב־ז,א)
We appraise (the damage) from [the best property of] the victim.

שֵׁם; שׁוּם; שְׁמָא*

(1) name**

שְׁמָא בִשְׁמָא מִיחַלַף. (גיטין יא,א ע״פ כת״י)
[One] name is interchanged with [another] name.

(2) a halakhic category; a halakhic principle

לֹא מִן הַשֵּׁם הוּא זֶה, אֶלָּא מִשּׁוּם ... (פסחים פד,א)
This is not because of the halakhic principle (just cited), but because of (this halakhic principle) ...

(3) a Biblical prohibition; a *pasuk*

כָּל הַכּוֹבֵשׁ שְׂכַר שָׂכִיר עוֹבֵר בַּחֲמִשָּׁה שֵׁמוֹת הַלָּלוּ וַעֲשֵׂה. (בבא מציעא קיא,א)
Anyone withholding the wages of a hired man transgresses these five Biblical prohibitions and [one] positive commandment.

... לוֹקִין וּמְשַׁלְּמִין, שֶׁלֹּא הַשֵּׁם הַמְּבִיאָן לִידֵי מַכּוֹת מְבִיאָן לִידֵי תַשְׁלוּמִין. (מכות ד, סע״א ורש״י שם: משנה פ״א מ״ב)
[These witnesses who have been convicted of false testimony] are flogged and must (also) pay compensation, because the pasuk that subjects them to lashes is not [the same pasuk] that subjects them to monetary compensation.

* The first form is Hebrew, the second is used in both Hebrew and Aramaic, and the third is Aramaic.

** הַשֵּׁם (with the definite article) often denotes *the name of God,* as in יומא לט,ב.

SEE: שׁוּם[1], כְּשֵׁם שֶׁ־, (לְ)שֵׁם

in the name of; on behalf of **בְּשֵׁם**

כָּל הָאוֹמֵר דָּבָר בְּשֵׁם אוֹמְרוֹ מֵבִיא גְאוּלָּה לָעוֹלָם. (אבות פ״ו* מ״ו; מגילה טו,א)
Anyone who quotes a statement in the name of its author is bringing redemption to the world.

* The sixth chapter of Pirké Avoth, which is also known as פֶּרֶק קִנְיַן תּוֹרָה, is not an integral part of the Mishnaic tractate but a collection of baraithoth.

SEE: מִשּׁוּם, מִשְּׁמֵיהּ דְּ־

just as **כְּשֵׁם שֶׁ־**

SEE: כשם שֶׁ־

"for the name of"; for the sake of; for the purpose of **לְשֵׁם/לְשׁוּם**

כָּל מַעֲשָׂיו לְשֵׁם שָׁמַיִם (ביצה טז,א)
All his actions [were done] for the sake of Heaven.

לְשֵׁם is often used with personal-pronoun suffixes:

for his/its own sake לִשְׁמוֹ

for her/its (f.) own sake לִשְׁמָהּ

הָיָה ר׳ בְּנָאָה אוֹמֵר: כָּל הָעוֹסֵק בַּתּוֹרָה לִשְׁמָהּ, תּוֹרָתוֹ נַעֲשֵׂית לוֹ סַם חַיִּים. (תענית ז,א)

R. Banna'a used to say: [As for] anyone who engages in the study of Torah for its own sake, his Torah will become an elixir of life for him.

SEE: ¹שׁוּם

מִשָּׁם רְאָיָה

[Can you really bring] a proof from there?!

This rhetorical question is used in the following situation: A halakhic issue is the subject of controversy between two tannaitic opinions expressed in a baraitha. One tanna attempted to support his halakhic opinion by citing evidence from a specific incident that took place in tannaitic times (or, in some cases, from a pasuk). With the rhetorical question מִשָּׁם רְאָיָה, another tanna introduces a *refutation* of that proof. In his refutation, the latter tanna argues that the incident (or pasuk) cited is not analogous to the case under halakhic debate.

משנה: סוּכָּה גְבוֹהָה לְמַעְלָה מֵעֶשְׂרִים אַמָּה פְּסוּלָה, ור׳ יְהוּדָה מַכְשִׁיר. (סוכה ב, רע״ב: משנה פ״א מ״א)

תלמוד: אָמַר ר׳ יְהוּדָה: מַעֲשֶׂה בְּהֵילֵנִי הַמַּלְכָּה שֶׁהָיְתָה סוּכָּתָהּ גְּבוֹהָה מֵעֶשְׂרִים אַמָּה, וְהָיוּ זְקֵנִים נִכְנָסִין וְיוֹצְאִין לְשָׁם וְלֹא אָמְרוּ לָהּ דָּבָר. אָמְרוּ לוֹ: מִשָּׁם רְאָיָה?! אִשָּׁה הָיְתָה וּפְטוּרָה מִן הַסּוּכָּה. (שם ב,ב ע׳ שבת כט,ב וש״נ)

MISHNA: A sukka more than twenty cubits tall is invalid, but R. Y^e^huda declares [it] valid.

TALMUD: R. Y^e^huda said: There was an incident involving Queen Heleni whose sukka was taller than twenty cubits, and the elders were entering it and departing from it and said nothing (against its validity). [The Hakhamim who invalidated such a sukka in the mishna] said to him: [Can you really bring] a proof from there? She was a woman and [thus] exempt from [the mitzva] of sukka.*

* This queen was a convert to Judaism.

the destruction (of Judaism) הַשְׁמָד; שְׁמָדָא*

* The first form is Hebrew, and the second is Aramaic.

SEE: גְּזֵירַת מַלְכוּת

שְׁמוּעָה

(1) report

שְׁמוּעָה רְחוֹקָה (מועד קטן כ,א)

a report [of a death received thirty days] late

(2) tradition

הוּא אוֹמֵר מִפִּי הַשְּׁמוּעָה, וְהֵן אוֹמְרִין: כָּךְ הוּא בְּעֵינֵינוּ. (סנהדרין פח, סע״א)

He states: [My halakhic opinion is based] upon tradition, and they state: This is [how the halakha seems to be] in our eyes (= based upon our own reasoning).

(3) halakha

וְאֵין אוֹמְרִים שְׁמוּעָה וְהַגָּדָה בְּבֵית הָאֵבֶל. (מו״ק כג, רע״א)

and one may state neither a halakha nor an aggada in a house of mourning.

SEE: שְׁמַעְתָּא

שַׁמּוּתִי מִתַּלְמִידֵי שַׁמַּאי*

a disciple of the school of Shammai

הֵיאַךְ מַנִּיחִין דִּבְרֵי חֲכָמִים וְעוֹשִׂין כְּר׳ אֱלִיעֶזֶר — חֲדָא: דְּר׳ אֱלִיעֶזֶר שַׁמּוּתִי הוּא, וְעוֹד: יָחִיד וְרַבִּים, הֲלָכָה כְּרַבִּים ...?! (שבת קל,ב ור״ח, ורש״י, ותוס׳ שם: ע׳ נדה ז,ב ורש״י, ותוס׳, ותוס׳ הרא״ש שם)

how can they disregard the opinion of the Hakhamim and follow [the opinion] of R. Eliezer — (in view of the following facts) firstly: that R. Eliezer is a disciple of the school of Shammai, and furthermore: [when] an individual [authority disagrees] with many [authorities], the halakha follows the many ...?!

* This explanation is preferred by R. Hananel, the *Arukh*, and the Tosafoth. Another explanation, *excommunicated*, is given by Rashi and mentioned in the *Arukh*. According to the latter explanation, see שַׁמְתָּא and שַׁמֵּת.

שְׁמַט (prt. שָׁמֵיט :שמט)

he removed; he detached שְׁמַט

אַדְּהָכִי וְהָכִי שָׁמֵיט וְאָכֵיל פֵּירֵי. (בבא בתרא קסט, רע״ב)

In the meantime he would be removing the fruit and eating [it].

... שְׁמֵיהּ ... (f. ... שְׁמַהּ ...)

[As for] ... its name is ...; ... is considered valid ... שְׁמוֹ ...; ... נֶחְשָׁב

כִּיבּוּשׁ יָחִיד שְׁמֵיהּ כִּיבּוּשׁ. (גיטין ח, רע״ב)

The conquest (of additional territory) by an individual is considered a valid conquest (and thus this territory becomes an integral part of Eretz Yisrael).

SEE: שֵׁם

מִשְּׁמֵיהּ דְּ- "מִשְּׁמוֹ שֶׁל"; בְּשֵׁם

"from his name, [that] of ..."; in the name of

וִיתֵיב רַב חִסְדָּא וְקָאָמַר מִשְּׁמֵיהּ דְּרַב הוּנָא ... וְתוּ יְתֵיב רַב חִסְדָּא וְקָאָמַר מִשְּׁמֵיהּ דְּנַפְשֵׁיהּ ... (פסחים קא,ב)

Rav Hisda was sitting and expounding in the name of Rav Huna ... and subsequently Rav Hisda was sitting and expounding in the name of himself (= in his own name) ...

SEE: ... אָמַר ר׳ ... מִשּׁוּם ר׳

מִשְּׁמֵיהּ דִּגְמָרָא בְּשֵׁם מָסֹרֶת

quoting an accepted tradition (current in the beth midrash)

ר׳ מֵאִיר ...: מַעֲשֵׂר רִאשׁוֹן אָסוּר לְזָרִים ... מַאי טַעְמֵיהּ דְּר׳ מֵאִיר? אָמַר רַב אַחָא בְּרֵיהּ דְּרַבָּה מִשְּׁמֵיהּ דִּגְמָרָא (יבמות פה,סע״ב־פו,רע״א ורש״י שם)

R. Méir ...: The first tithe is forbidden to non-Kohanim ... What is R. Méir's reason? ... Rav Aha the son of Rabba stated, quoting an accepted tradition

SEE: גְּמָרָא

שְׁמַע (שמע: שָׁמַע act. prt., שְׁמִיעַ pass. prt., לִישְׁמַע fut., שְׁמַע imp., לְמִשְׁמַע inf.)

he heard; שָׁמַע

he listened; he accepted; he derived

For examples, see the next three entries.

SEE: מַאן שָׁמְעַתְּ לֵיהּ דְּאָמַר, בָּרַיְיתָא/מַתְנִיתָא לָא שְׁמִיעַ לֵיהּ, לָא שְׁמִיעַ לִי כְּלוֹמַר לָא סְבִירָא לִי

שְׁמַע מִינַּהּ שְׁמַע מִמֶּנָּה! לְמַד מִמֶּנָּה!

Deduce from it! (= There is proof from here!)

This expression introduces an *inference* that the Talmud has drawn from the text of a mishna, a baraitha, or an amora's halakha. Sometimes the expression is repeated after the inference for emphasis.

שְׁמַע מִינַּהּ: [שַׁמָּשׁ] בָּעֵי הֲסִיבָּה. שְׁמַע מִינַּהּ! (פסחים קח, סע"א)

Deduce from it: [A waiter] is required to recline [at the Seder table]. Deduce from it!

SEE: אֶלָּא לָאו

שְׁמַע מִינַּהּ תְּלָת

Deduce from it three! שְׁמַע מִמֶּנָּה שָׁלֹשׁ!

Three separate halakhoth may be derived from the statement or from the incident that has just been quoted in the Talmud.

For examples — see פסחים ד, רע"א ושם ה, סע"א.

שְׁמַע מִינַּהּ תַּרְתֵּי שְׁמַע מִמֶּנָּה שְׁתַּיִם!

שָׁמְעַתְּ מִינַּהּ תַּרְתֵּי שׁוֹמֵעַ אַתָּה מִמֶּנָּה שְׁתַּיִם!

Deduce (or "you may deduce") **from it two (halakhoth)!**

In most instances, this assertion marks the conclusion of a *proof* that both of the halakhic points under discussion should be derived from the same pasuk.

(1) "וְטָמֵא טָמֵא יִקְרָא": טוּמְאָה קוֹרְאָה לוֹ וְאוֹמֶרֶת לוֹ: פְּרוֹשׁ! (2) הַהוּא מִיבָּעֵי לֵיהּ לְכִדְתַנְיָא: "וְטָמֵא טָמֵא יִקְרָא": צָרִיךְ לְהוֹדִיעַ צַעֲרוֹ לָרַבִּים, וְרַבִּים מְבַקְּשִׁים עָלָיו רַחֲמִים. (3) אִם כֵּן, לִיכְתּוֹב: "וְטָמֵא יִקְרָא"! מַאי "וְטָמֵא טָמֵא"? שָׁמְעַתְּ מִינַּהּ תַּרְתֵּי! (מועד קטן ה,א ע"פ ויקרא יג:מה)

(1) "And he (= the person suffering from tzara'ath) shall cry out: 'Unclean! Unclean!'" [Thus] impurity cries out [to the passerby] and tells him: "Keep off!" (2) That [Biblical passage] is needed by him for [the halakha] stated (in a baraitha): "And he shall cry out: 'Unclean! Unclean!'" [Thus] he should make his distress known to the public, so that the public will pray in his behalf. (3) If so (= that only the latter halakha is indicated by this passage), let [the Torah] write: "And he shall cry out: 'Unclean!'" Why [does it write:] "Unclean! Unclean!"? You may deduce from it two (halakhoth)!

שַׁמָּעָא* שַׁמָּשׁ **an attendant; a servant**

(often a disciple serving his master)

מִסְתְּמִיךְ וְאָזִיל ר' יַנַּאי אַכַּתְפָּא דְּר' שִׂמְלַאי, שַׁמָּעֵיהּ. (בבא בתרא קיא,א)

R. Yannai [was] walking along leaning against the shoulder of R. Simlai, his attendant.

* The verb שַׁמַּע, *he ministered to* or *he served*, is also found in the Talmud.

שְׁמַעְתָּא (שְׁמַעְתָּתָא pl.)

(1) שְׁמוּעָה; הֲלָכָה **a tradition; a halakha**

(or an explanation of a halakha) of an amora

מָר אָמַר לֵיהּ: לֵימָא מָר שְׁמַעְתָּא! וּמָר אָמַר לֵיהּ: לֵימָא מָר אַגַּדְתָּא! (בבא קמא ס,ב ע"פ כת"י)

One said to him: Would the master say a halakha? But the other said: Would the master say an aggada?

תְּלָת מַתְנְיָיתָא וְתַרְתֵּי שְׁמַעְתָּתָא (נדה כו, סע"א וע' רש"י)

three baraithoth and two (amoraic) halakhoth

עֲבַד רַב נַחְמָן עוּבְדָא בֵּי רֵישׁ גָּלוּתָא כִּשְׁמַעְתֵּיהּ. (ב"מ סו,א)

Rav Naḥman issued a halakhic ruling with regard to [the case of] the exilarch in accordance with his own halakha.

(2) לִמּוּד הֲלָכָה **the study of halakha**

יוֹמָא חַד מְשַׁכְתֵּיהּ שְׁמַעְתָּא. (כתובות סב,ב)

On one occasion the study of halakha kept him (late).

SEE: שְׁמוּעָה

שְׁמַעְתִּי (שמע) **"I heard";**

I received (a halakha from my teachers)

זוֹ לֹא שָׁמַעְתִּי; כַּיּוֹצֵא בָהּ שָׁמַעְתִּי. (מגילה כב, רע"א ועוד)

I have not received [a halakha about] this [case]; I have received [a halakha about a case] similar to it.

שִׁמְשֵׁי SEE: בֵּי שִׁמְשֵׁי

שַׁמֵּת (שמת פִּעֵל: מְשַׁמֵּת prt., לְשַׁמֵּת fut., לְשַׁמּוֹתֵי inf.)

he excommunicated; he banned נִדָּה; הֶחֱרִים

שַׁמְּתֵיהּ וְעַבְרֵיהּ וְאַכְרֵיז אַבִּישְׂרֵיהּ דִּטְרֵפָה הוּא. (חולין יח,א)

[The rabbi] excommunicated him (= the ritual slaughterer), removed him (from his job) and announced that his meat (that he had slaughtered) was "t^erefa" (and hence forbidden to be eaten).

SEE: שַׁמּוֹתֵי and its note

שַׁמְתָּא/שְׁמָתָא נִדּוּי **excommunication**

לִיהֱוֵי הַהוּא גַּבְרָא בְּשַׁמְתָּא! (מועד קטן יז,א)*

May "that fellow" (= you) be under excommunication!

* On the same page, Rav and Sh^emuel dispute the etymology of this word.

שְׁנָא (שני: שָׁאנֵי/שָׁנֵי prt.)

it differed; שָׁנָה; הָיָה שׁוֹנֶה

it was different; it made a difference

For examples — see לָא שְׁנָא and מַאי שְׁנָא.

שֶׁנֶּאֱמַר SEE: (שֶׁאֱמַר)

שָׁנָה (שני: שונה .act. prt, שָׁנוּי .pass. prt, ישנה .fut, לִשְׁנוֹת .inf)

(1) he did [it] again; he repeated

חַיָּיב אָדָם לִקְרוֹת אֶת הַמְּגִילָּה בַּלַּיְלָה וּלְשׁוֹנוֹתָהּ בַּיּוֹם (מגילה ד,א)

a person is obligated to read the scroll (of Esther) at night and to read it again during the day

(2) he taught; he stated

שָׁנוּ חֲכָמִים בִּלְשׁוֹן הַמִּשְׁנָה. (אבות: ריש פ"ו, "קנין תורה")*

The hakhamim taught in the language of the Mishna.

(3) he learned; he studied (the oral Torah)

אָמַר לוֹ: בְּנִי, קָרִיתָ? ... שָׁנִיתָ? (בבא בתרא ח,א)

He said to him: My son, have you read (Scripture)? Have you studied (the oral Torah)?

(4) it was different**

הורו בית דין, וְיָדְעוּ שֶׁטָּעוּ, וְחָזְרוּ בָּהֶן ... וְהָלַךְ וְעָשָׂה עַל פִּיהֶן ... ר' אֱלִיעֶזֶר אוֹמֵר: סָפֵק. אֵיזֶהוּ סָפֵק? יָשַׁב לוֹ בְּתוֹךְ בֵּיתוֹ — חַיָּיב; הָלַךְ לוֹ לִמְדִינַת הַיָּם — פָּטוּר .... מַה שָּׁנָה זֶה מִן הַיּוֹשֵׁב בְּבֵיתוֹ? (הוריות ג,ב: משנה פ"א מ"ב)

[If] the court ruled, and [then the judges] realized that they had erred and reversed themselves ... and he went and acted in accordance with their (original) ruling ... R. Eliezer says: There is a doubt (about his guilt). Which case is treated as a doubt (requiring him to bring a suspensive guilt offering, אָשָׁם תָּלוּי*)? [If] he stayed in his house — he is obligated (to bring a suspensive guilt offering); [if] he went overseas — he is exempt .... How is this [person who went overseas] different from one who stays in his house?*

* See the note on the entry (ב)שֵׁם.

** This meaning is occasionally found in Biblical Hebrew, as in .אֲנִי ה' לֹא שָׁנִיתִי (מלאכי ג:ו)

SEE: כָּאן שָׁנָה רַבִּי, תַּבְרָא מִי שֶׁשָּׁנָה זוֹ לֹא שָׁנָה זוֹ, מִשְׁנָה, תְּנָא, (ב)מַחְלוֹקֶת שְׁנוּיָה

... שָׁנוּ (שני) **they taught ...**

This verb is used at the end of a sentence limiting the scope of a mishna or a baraitha to particular circumstances. The *limitation* often resolves a difficulty.

משנה: הָעוֹבֵר לִפְנֵי הַתֵּיבָה בְּיוֹם טוֹב שֶׁל רֹאשׁ הַשָּׁנָה — הַשֵּׁנִי מַתְקִיעַ. (ראש השנה לב,ב: משנה פ"ד מ"ז)

תלמוד: ... תְּקִיעָה נַמִי נַעֲבֵיד בְּרִאשׁוֹן, מִשּׁוּם דִּזְרִיזִין מַקְדִּימִין לְמִצְוֹות! אֲמַר ר' יוֹחָנָן: בִּשְׁעַת הַשְּׁמָד שָׁנוּ. (שם)

MISHNA: [Regarding those] who pass before the ark (to lead the prayers) on the holyday of Rosh HaShana, the second one (who leads the Musaf prayer) directs the blowing (of the shofar).

TALMUD: ... let us have the blowing performed by the first one (who leads the Shaharith prayer), since the zealous perform mitzvoth early! R. Yohanan said: They taught [this mishna] with regard to a time of religious persecution (when the government forbade blowing the shofar in the morning).

SEE: לֹא שָׁנוּ אֶלָּא ... אֲבָל ...

שָׁנֵי SEE: שְׁאנֵי

שַׁנִּי (שני פִּעֵל: מְשַׁנֵּי .prt, לִישַׁנֵּי .fut, לְשַׁנּוּיֵי .inf)

(1) תָּרֵץ **he resolved** (a difficulty); **he answered**

אֵיתִיבֵיהּ כָּל הָנֵי תְּיוּבָתָא, וְשַׁנֵּי לֵיהּ כִּדְשַׁנִּינַן. (ביצה יח, סע"א)

He refuted him [with] all these refutations, and he answered him as we had answered.

(2) שִׁנָּה **he changed; he made a distinction**

מִדְּשַׁנֵּי קְרָא בְּדִיבּוּרֵיהּ (קידושין לה,ב ע"פ ויקרא יט:כז)

since Scripture made a distinction in its [mode of] expression (by using a plural suffix in the first clause and a singular suffix in the second clause)

SEE: שִׁינּוּיָא, מְחַוַּורְתָּא

שְׁנֵי כְתוּבִים הַבָּאִין כְּאֶחָד אֵין מְלַמְּדִין*

Two Biblical passages that present the same point do not teach (about other cases).

A בִּנְיַן־אָב analogy may not apply a halakha that has already been stated in two Biblical passages to other cases. Since the halakha had to be stated in both passages, neither passage was capable of extending the halakha to other cases.

נִיהֲווּ שֵׁן וָעַיִן כִּשְׁנֵי כְתוּבִים הַבָּאִים כְּאֶחָד, וְכָל שְׁנֵי כְתוּבִים הַבָּאִים כְּאֶחָד אֵין מְלַמְּדִין! (קידושין כד, סע"א ורש"י שם וש"נ ע"פ שמות כא:כו־כז)

Let [the cases of] "a tooth" and "an eye" (where their deprivation causes a heathen slave to go free) be two Biblical passages that present the same point, and whenever two Biblical passages present the same point, [they] do not teach [about other cases, e.g., regarding the deprivation of other limbs]!

If it can be shown that the cases in the two passages are significantly different from each other so that it was indeed necessary for the halakha to be stated in both passages, then the בִּנְיַן־אָב analogy may indeed be applied to other cases.

צְרִיכָא: דְּאִי כְּתַב רַחֲמָנָא שֵׁן, הֲוָה אָמִינָא אֲפִילּוּ שֵׁן דְּחָלָב, כְּתַב רַחֲמָנָא עַיִן; וְאִי כְּתַב רַחֲמָנָא עַיִן, הֲוָה אָמִינָא מָה עַיִן שֶׁנִּבְרָא עִמּוֹ אַף כָּל שֶׁנִּבְרָא עִמּוֹ, אֲבָל שֵׁן לָא; צְרִיכָא. (קידושין כד, סע"א־רע"ב)

It is necessary: for if the Torah had written [only the case of] "a tooth," I would have said even [the deprivation] of a baby tooth [would cause the slave to go free, hence] the Torah wrote "an eye" (an organ that ordinarily lasts a lifetime); and if the Torah had written [only the case of] "an eye," I would have said just as an eye is created with him (= together with the rest of his body) so too every limb that is created with him [would cause the slave to go free], but [the deprivation of] a tooth [that develops later] would not.

It is necessary [to state both, and so their halakha can be applied to other limbs as well].

* This rule is the majority view, held by the Ḥakhamim, but it is disputed by R. Y^{e}huda in קידושין לה,א.
SEE: בִּנְיַן אָב

שַׁעְבֵּד (עבד שפעל: מְשַׁעְבֵּד a. prt., מְשׁוּעְבָּד p. prt.);
שַׁעְבֵּיד* (עבד שַׁפְעֵל: מְשַׁעְבֵּד a. prt., מְשַׁעְבַּד p. prt.)
he enslaved; he subjugated
he subjugated himself שַׁעְבֵּיד נַפְשֵׁיהּ (ב"מ יג, רע"א)
* The first verb is Hebrew, and the second is Aramaic.

שִׁעְבּוּד/שִׁיעְבּוּד; שִׁעְבּוּדָא/שִׁיעְבּוּדָא*
subjugation; a mortgage; a lien
דְּבַר תּוֹרָה, אֶחָד מַלְוֶה בִּשְׁטָר וְאֶחָד מַלְוֶה עַל פֶּה, גּוֹבֶה מִנְּכָסִים מְשׁוּעְבָּדִים. מַאי טַעְמָא? שִׁעְבּוּדָא דְּאוֹרָיְיתָא. (ב"ב קעה,ב)
According to Torah law, both a loan supported by a promissory note and an oral loan may be collected from subjugated properties. What is the reason? The [automatic] mortgaging [of properties to a debt] is [a halakha] of Biblical status.
* The first forms are Hebrew, and the latter are Aramaic.
SEE: נְכָסִים מְשׁוּעְבָּדִים

שַׁפִּיר
good; (it is) well; (it is) satisfactory יָפֶה; טוֹב
This adjective is often used at the end of a clause introduced by either אִי אָמְרַתְּ בִּשְׁלָמָא, (בִּ)שְׁלָמָא, or הָנִיחָא.
אִי אָמְרַתְּ בִּשְׁלָמָא מִשּׁוּם כְּבוֹד אָבִיו — שַׁפִּיר. (סנהדרין מח,א)
If you agree that [this regulation was enacted] on account of respect for his father — [it is] well.

שַׁפִּיר דָּמֵי "דּוֹמֶה יָפֶה"; מֻתָּר
[it is] considered proper; [it is] permissible
כָּל מִידֵי דְּאָתֵי מִמֵּילָא שַׁפִּיר דָּמֵי. (שבת יט, סע"א)
Everything (= every Sabbath labor) that occurs automatically is permissible.
SEE: דָּמֵי

שַׁפִּיר קָאָמַר לֵיהּ/לְהוּ יָפֶה הוּא אוֹמֵר לוֹ/לָהֶם!
"He is telling him/them well!" He is refuting him (= his colleague) very convincingly!
Sometimes a mishna or a baraitha presents a controversy between two tannaim in which one tanna poses an argument against his colleague that is not refuted. Thereupon the Talmud remarks that the tanna has indeed formulated an impressive argument against his colleague's position. By implication, the Talmud is asking what reply could have been presented by that colleague in his own defense. Then the Talmud proposes a possible defense that the latter tanna might have presented.

ברייתא: מֵאֵימָתַי מַתְחִילִין לִקְרוֹת שְׁמַע בְּעַרְבִין? ... ר' מֵאִיר אוֹמֵר: מִשָּׁעָה שֶׁהַכֹּהֲנִים טוֹבְלִין לֶאֱכוֹל בִּתְרוּמָתָן. אָמַר לוֹ ר' יְהוּדָה: וַהֲלֹא כֹּהֲנִים מִבְּעוֹד יוֹם הֵם טוֹבְלִים?!
תלמוד: שַׁפִּיר קָאָמַר לֵיהּ ר' יְהוּדָה לְר' מֵאִיר! וְר' מֵאִיר הָכִי קָאָמַר לֵיהּ: ... אֲנָא אַבֵּין הַשְּׁמָשׁוֹת דְּר' יוֹסֵי קָא אָמִינָא, דְּאָמַר ר' יוֹסֵי: בֵּין הַשְּׁמָשׁוֹת כְּהֶרֶף עַיִן — זֶה נִכְנָס, וְזֶה יוֹצֵא, וְאִי אֶפְשָׁר לַעֲמוֹד עָלָיו. (ברכות ב, סע"ב)

BARAITHA: From when may we begin to recite the Sh^{e}ma at night? ... R. Méir says: From the time the kohanim immerse themselves (just before twilight) in order to eat their t^{e}ruma. R. Y^{e}huda said to him: But don't the kohanim immerse themselves while it is still day?!
TALMUD: R. Y^{e}huda is refuting R. Méir convincingly! But this [is what] R. Méir could say to him: ... I am speaking of "twilight" [according to the definition] of R. Yosé, for R. Yosé says: "Twilight" is as [long as] the twinkling of an eye — one (= night) enters, and the other (= day) leaves, and it is impossible to discern it. (Thus, the immersion of the kohanim takes place late enough to be termed "the time when people go to sleep," in accordance with בְּשָׁכְבְּךָ *in the Torah.)*

שַׁפִּיר קָאָמְרַתְּ
You are saying well! יָפֶה אַתָּה אוֹמֵר!
This expression is used by one amora to express his agreement with the statement of his fellow amora.
For an example — see כתובות קט,ב.

שָׁקַל (שקל: שׁוֹקֵל act.prt., שָׁקוּל pass.prt., יִשְׁקוֹל fut.)
he weighed; he balanced; he weighed out (in payment)**; he contributed** (half a shekel)**; he considered**
אֵין בֵּית דִּין שָׁקוּל. (סנהדרין ב, רע"ב: משנה פ"א מ"ו)
A court should not be weighted evenly. (= It should not have an even number of judges.)
SEE: תְּקַל, the parallel Aramaic verb.

שְׁקַל* (שקל: שָׁקֵיל act. prt., שְׁקִיל pass. prt., לִישְׁקוֹל fut., שְׁקוֹל imp., לְמִישְׁקַל inf.)
he took לָקַח; נָטַל
שְׁקִילָא טִיבוּתָיךְ וְשַׁדְיָא אַחִיזְרֵי! (בבא מציעא סג, רע"ב וש"נ)
May your favor be taken and cast among the thorns! (= You are not doing me any favor!)
חַד שָׁקֵיל וְטָרֵי** בַּהֲדֵי רַבֵּיהּ (חגיגה יא,ב)
one [student] "takes and gives" (= discusses the halakhic topic) with his teacher

* Do not confuse this Aramaic verb with the Hebrew verb of the previous entry.
** The Aramaic expression שַׁקְלָא וְטַרְיָא, literally *taking and giving*, is used in Modern Hebrew in the sense of *discussion*, *debate*, or *negotiations* — just like the Hebrew מַשָּׂא וּמַתָּן. Compare the English expression, *give and take*.

שֶׁקֶל *shekel*

This silver coin or weight was equal to two silver *dinars*, i.e., half a *sela**, in Talmudic times.

* The Biblical shekel, שֶׁקֶל הַקֹּדֶשׁ, was double the value of the Talmudic *shekel* and equal to the Talmudic *sela*. Targum Onkelos consistently translates the Biblical word שֶׁקֶל as סַלְעָא, e.g., on שמות ל:יג. See the table of coins and weights in Appendix II.

שְׁרָא (שרי: שָׁרֵי .act. prt, שְׁרֵי .pass. prt, לִישְׁרֵי .fut, לְמִישְׁרָא .inf)

(1) הִתִּיר (קֶשֶׁר) **he untied; he unraveled**

שָׁרֵי חַד, וְקָטַר חַד. (שבת עד,ב)

He unties one [knot], and he ties another.

(2) פָּתַר **he solved; he settled**

שְׁרִי לֵיהּ תִּגְרֵיהּ ...! (קידושין ע, רע"ב וע' רש"י שם)

Settle his case ...!

(3) הִתִּיר (אִיסּוּר); נָתַן רְשׁוּת **he permitted**

כָּל דַּאֲסַר לַן רַחֲמָנָא, שְׁרָא לַן כְּוָותֵיהּ. (חולין קט,ב)

[For] everything that the Merciful (God) has forbidden to us [in the Torah], He has permitted us [something similar to it].

(4) מָחַל **he forgave**

שְׁרָא לֵיהּ מָרֵיהּ! (יומא פו,א)

May his Master forgive him (for his misdeeds)!

(5) הִתְחִיל **he began**

מִיּוֹם שֶׁחָרַב בֵּית הַמִּקְדָּשׁ, שְׁרוֹ חַכִּימַיָּא לְמִיהְוֵי כְּסָפְרַיָּא (סוטה מט, סע"א: "משנה פ"ט מט"ו")

from the day the Beth HaMikdash was destroyed, the ḥakhamim began to be [only] like school teachers

(6) בָּצַע **he broke bread***

לִישְׁרֵי לַן מָר! (ברכות מו, רע"א וע' רש"י שם)

Let the master break bread for us!

* The noun שֵׁירוּתָא, *a meal*, is also found occasionally.

שְׁתוּת; שְׁתוּתָא* שִׁשִּׁית **one-sixth**

* The first form is Hebrew, and the second is Aramaic. See the table of fractions in Appendix II.

שָׁתֵי prt. (שתי) שׁוֹתֶה **drinking**

SEE: אִישְׁתִּי

שִׁתִּין

SEE: שִׁיתִּין

שְׁתֵיק (שתק: שָׁתֵיק .prt, לִישְׁתּוֹק .fut, מִישְׁתַּק .inf)

שָׁתַק **he was silent**

SEE: אִישְׁתִּיק

ת

תָּא imp. (אתי) בּוֹא! come!

This imperative is often followed immediately by another imperative.

תָּא חֲזִי ...! (גיטין נז,א ועוד) *Come (and) see ...!*

SEE: אֲתָא

תָּא שְׁמַע בּוֹא וּשְׁמַע! Come [and] hear!

This expression introduces a mishna, a baraitha, a pasuk, or an early amora's statement or practice that is quoted either as *proof* for the opinion of an amora, or as a *resolution* of a problem, or as a *difficulty.*

רַב צַלִּי שֶׁל שַׁבָּת בְּעֶרֶב שַׁבָּת — אוֹמֵר קְדוּשָּׁה עַל הַכּוֹס אוֹ אֵינוֹ אוֹמֵר קְדוּשָּׁה עַל הַכּוֹס? תָּא שְׁמַע, דְּאָמַר רַב נַחְמָן אָמַר שְׁמוּאֵל: מִתְפַּלֵּל אָדָם שֶׁל שַׁבָּת בְּעֶרֶב שַׁבָּת וְאוֹמֵר קְדוּשָּׁה עַל הַכּוֹס. (ברכות כז,ב)

Rav recited the Amida for the Sabbath on Friday — does one say Kiddush over a cup (of wine) or not (afterwards)? Come [and] hear, that Rav Naḥman quoted Sh[e]*muel saying: A person may recite the Amida for the Sabbath on Friday and say Kiddush over a cup (of wine).*

תָּאגָא SEE: תָּגָא

תְּבַר (תבר: תָּבַר, act. prt. תָּבֵיר, pass. prt. תְּבִיר, fut. לִיתְבַּר)

he broke שָׁבַר

מָנָא תְבִירָא תְּבַר! (בבא קמא יז, סע"ב) *He broke a broken utensil (therefore he is not liable for the damage)!*

SEE: תַּבְרָא

תַּבְרָא/תַּבְרָה

(1) סְתִירָה **refutation; contradiction***

מִצַּדָּהּ תַּבְרָא. (קידושין עד,ב; זבחים יג,ב)

The refutation (of the analogy) "is at its side" (= is clear).

(2) שֶׁבֶר; צָרָה; אָסוֹן **trouble; calamity**

מַאי קָא גָרֵים לְהוּ תַּבְרָא? (עבודה זרה ב,א)

What causes them the calamity?

(3) שׁוֹבֵר **a document that "breaks" (= cancels) another document; receipt; voucher**

שְׁטָרָךְ אִירְכַס לִי. אֶכְתּוֹב לָךְ תַּבְרָא. (בבא בתרא קעא, ב)

I lost your document (of indebtedness). I will write you a receipt.

* See the next entry.

תַּבְרָא/תַּבְרָה* מִי שֶׁשָּׁנָה זוֹ לֹא שָׁנָה זוֹ

There is a contradiction! The one who taught this (statement) did not teach that (statement)!

This exclamation asserts that the apparent contradiction between two clauses of an anonymous mishna** can be resolved only if one presumes that the clauses are really statements of different tannaim who are in disagreement.

משנה: הַמִּתְכַּוֵּין לְהוֹצִיא לְפָנָיו וּבָא לוֹ לְאַחֲרָיו — פָּטוּר; לְאַחֲרָיו וּבָא לוֹ לְפָנָיו — חַיָּיב. (שבת צב, רע"ב: משנה פ"י מ"ד)
תלמוד: אָמַר ר' אֶלְעָזָר: תַּבְרָא! מִי שֶׁשָּׁנָה זוֹ לֹא שָׁנָה זוֹ! (שם)

MISHNA: [If] one intends to carry out [an object] in front of him, and it shifts [to be] behind him — he is exempt [from punishment]; [if he intends to carry it] in back of him, and it shifts in front of him — he is subject [to punishment].

TALMUD: R. El'azar said: There is a contradiction! The one who taught this (= that he is subject to punishment) did not teach that (= that he is exempt)!

* We have translated תַּבְרָא, *contradiction*, which is consistent with Rashi's comment on כתובות עה,ב. According to Rabbenu Ḥananel, however, the word is an oath. His opinion is quoted by the Tosafoth there and by R. Nathan of Rome in his *Arukh*. It is also possible to understand this form as an imperative of the verb תְּבַר with a 3rd person f.s. suffix — either תַּבְרָה or תַּבְרָא — meaning *split it (into two)!*

** In one extraordinary instance, the contradiction is between R. Méir's halakha as recorded in a mishna as opposed to a halakha of his in a baraitha. See:
בבא מציעא פב,ב ושיטה מקובצת שם בשם ר' חננאל

תָּגָא/תָּאגָא

(1) כֶּתֶר **crown**

וּדְאִשְׁתַּמֵּשׁ בְּתָגָא חֲלַף (מגילה כח,ב ורש"י שם: משנה אבות א:יג)

and one who exploited the crown (of Torah learning) has passed (from the world)

(2) תָּג **crown = the crown-like portions of certain letters in a Torah scroll***

מַאי טַעְמָא אִית לֵיהּ תָּאגָא? (מנחות כט,ב ע' רש"י ותוס' שם)

Why does [this letter] have a crown?

* In the post-Talmudic work, מַסֶּכֶת סוֹפְרִים, a תָּג is one of the crown-like decorations written on top of the letters שעטנז גץ.

תָּדִיר; תְּדִירָא* **constant; regular; frequent**

תָּדִיר וְשֶׁאֵינוֹ תָּדִיר — תָּדִיר קוֹדֵם. (ברכות נא. סע"ב וע' זבחים פט, רע"א: משנה פ"י מ"א)

[As for a] constant [duty] and [one] not [so] constant — [the] constant [duty] takes precedence.

* The first form is Hebrew, and the second is Aramaic.

תֵּדַע* fut. 2nd pers. m.s. (ידע)

You should know (that such is the case) ...

This term is used to introduce a *proof* that corroborates the halakhic statement or the explanation just now quoted in the Talmud.

אֵינוֹ נֶהֱרָג עַד שֶׁיֹּאמַר: "כָּךְ הוּא בְּעֵינַי", וְהֵן אוֹמְרִים: "מִפִּי הַשְּׁמוּעָה". תֵּדַע, שֶׁהֲרֵי לֹא הָרְגוּ אֶת עֲקַבְיָא בֶּן מַהֲלַלְאֵל. (סנהדרין פח, סע"א)

[A rebellious elder] is not executed unless he says: "Thus it [appears] in my eyes," and they (= his colleagues) say: "[Our ruling has been received] from tradition." You should know (that such is the case), for [the Sanhedrin] did not execute Akavia b. Mahalalel.

* The Talmud Yerushalmi uses the fuller form:
תֵּדַע לָךְ שֶׁהוּא כֵן (ירושלמי סנהדרין פ"ח ה"א)

תְּהֵא fut. 3rd pers. f.s. (היי)

Let it be ...; Let it refer to ...

This term introduces a *resolution* of a difficulty that restricts the text under discussion to a particular situation.

הֵיכִי מָצֵי סָמִיךְ?! וְהָא אָמַר ר' יוֹחָנָן: בִּתְחִלָּה הוּא אוֹמֵר: "ה' שְׂפָתַי תִּפְתָּח ..."?! אָמַר ר' אֶלְעָזָר: תְּהֵא בִּתְפִלַּת הַמִּנְחָה. (ברכות ט, סע"ב ע"פ תהלים נא:יז)

How can one connect [the brakha גָּאַל יִשְׂרָאֵל *with the beginning of the Amida]? Did not R. Yohanan say: At the beginning [of the Amida] one must recite:* ה' שְׂפָתַי תִּפְתָּח ... *?! R. El'azar said: Let it (= the duty to say:* ה' שְׂפָתַי תִּפְתָּח ... *) refer to the afternoon service.**

* Nowadays, however, ה' שְׂפָתַי תִּפְתָּח is recited before every Amida.

תָּהֵי prt. (תהי: תְּהֵי .imp)

(1) **מֵרִיחַ** — **smelling**

תָּהֵי לֵיהּ בְּקַנְקַנֵּיהּ (ב"ב כב,א ורש"י; שבת קח,א ורש"י שם)

smell his vessel (to determine the quality of the wine) (= examine his Torah learning to determine whether he is really a Torah scholar!)

(2) **תּוֹהֶה; תָּמֵהַּ** — **wondering**

תָּהֵי בָּהּ ר' אֶלְעָזָר. אָמַר ר' זֵירָא: מַאי תְּהִיָּא דר' אֶלְעָזָר? (עירובין סו,א ורש"י שם)

R. El'azar [was] wondering about it (= the halakha). R. Zera said: What is [the reason for] the wonderment of R. El'azar?

תּוּ (= תוב)

שׁוּב; עוֹד — **again; furthermore; in addition**

לְשָׁנָה תּוּ אִיקְלַע לְאַתְרִין ... (פסחים קז,א)

A year later he chanced upon our town again ...

וְתוּ לָא* — **וְשׁוּב לֹא; וְלֹא יוֹתֵר**

and no more; and no further

וְלֵימָא הַאי פְּסוּקָא וְתוּ לָא?! (ברכות יב,ב)

But let him say this pasuk and no more?!

* This expression is also used in Modern Hebrew.

וְתוּ לָא מִידֵי — **וְעוֹד לֹא כְלוּם.**

There is nothing more [to be said about this issue].

This expression is used to signify the end of some Talmudic discussions.

For an example — see .סוכה לו, רע"ב וש"נ ורש"י שם

וְתוּ לֵיכָּא וְהָא אִיכָּא — **וְאֵין עוֹד? וַהֲלֹא יֵשׁ ...!**

But are there no more? Behold there is ...!

This formula introduces a *difficulty:* How could the tanna or amora declare that there is a specific number of instances of a certain phenomenon, when we have discovered (at least) one more instance?!

אָמַר רַב הוּנָא: בִּשְׁלֹשָׁה מְקוֹמוֹת נֶחְלְקוּ שַׁמַּאי וְהִלֵּל ... וְתוּ לֵיכָּא? וְהָא אִיכָּא: הִלֵּל אוֹמֵר: לִסְמוֹךְ, וְשַׁמַּאי אוֹמֵר: שֶׁלֹּא לִסְמוֹךְ! (שבת טו,א)

Rav Huna said: In three places Shammai and Hillel disagreed ... But are there no more? Behold there is [the following instance]: Hillel says: One must lean [his hands upon the head of an animal sacrifice during a festival], and Shammai says: One must not lean [his hands during a festival]!

תּוֹךְ

SEE: מִתּוֹךְ, גּוֹ

תּוֹךְ כְּדֵי דִיבּוּר

within as much [time] as [needed for] an utterance

משנה: מִי שֶׁאָמַר: "הֲרֵינִי נָזִיר", וְשָׁמַע חֲבֵירוֹ וְאָמַר: "וַאֲנִי", "וַאֲנִי" — כּוּלָּם נְזִירִים. (נזיר כ, ב: משנה פ"ד מ"א)

תלמוד: רֵישׁ לָקִישׁ ... אָמַר: וְהוּא שֶׁהִתְפִּיסוּ כּוּלָּן בְּתוֹךְ כְּדֵי דִיבּוּר. וְכַמָּה תּוֹךְ כְּדֵי דִיבּוּר? כְּדֵי שְׁאֵלַת שָׁלוֹם. וְכַמָּה כְּדֵי שְׁאֵלַת שָׁלוֹם? כְּדֵי שֶׁאוֹמֵר שָׁלוֹם תַּלְמִיד לְרַב ("שָׁלוֹם עָלֶיךָ, רַבִּי"). (שם וש"נ)

MISHNA: [If] one said: "I hereby become a nazirite," and his friend heard [him] and said: "Me, too" [and another one said:] "Me, too" — they are all nazirites.

TALMUD: Resh Lakish said: Provided that all of them attached [their vow] within as much [time] as [needed for] an utterance. And how long is "within as much [time] as [needed for] an utterance"? As much as a greeting. And how long is "as much as a greeting"? As long as [it takes] for a disciple to greet his master (with the three Hebrew words: "Shalom to-you, my-master").

SEE: כְּדֵי, מִתּוֹךְ

תּוֹכִיחַ fut. 3rd pers. f.s. (יכח הִפְעִיל) **Let it prove!**

SEE: יוֹכִיחַ

תּוּמָא

SEE: שׁוּם[1]

תּוֹר; תּוֹרָא*

(1) **turtle-dove**

תּוֹרִין — גְּדוֹלִים כְּשֵׁרִים; קְטַנִּים פְּסוּלִים. (חולין כב, סע"א)

[As for] turtle-doves — large ones are fit [to be offered on the altar]; small ones are disqualified.

(2) line; row; turn

תּוֹרָא בָּרָא דְשִׂיפְּתֵיהּ (ברכות לט,א)

the outer line (= the edge) of his lip

* The first form is Hebrew, and the second is Aramaic.

תּוֹרָא (abs. תּוֹר) שׁוֹר **ox**

סוֹף סוֹף דְּמֵי תוֹרָא מְעַלְיָא בָּעֵי לְשַׁלּוֹמֵי! (בבא קמא לו,א)

Ultimately he must pay the value of a good ox!

תּוּרְגְּמָן (= תְּרְגְּמָן)

(1) translator; interpreter

"עַל פִּי שְׁנַיִם עֵדִים" — שֶׁלֹּא תְּהֵא סַנְהֶדְרִין שׁוֹמַעַת מִפִּי הַתּוּרְגְּמָן. (מכות ו,ב: משנה פ"א מ"ט ע"פ דברים יז:ו)

"Through the mouth of two witnesses" — so that the Sanhedrin not hear [evidence] from the mouth of the interpreter.

(2) speaker; the man who stood near the ḥakham who was lecturing and repeated the lecture to the audience in a loud voice

וְר' חֲנַנְיָה בֶּן עֲקַבְיָא לְתוּרְגְּמָן וְתוּרְגְּמָן הִשְׁמִיעַ לָרַבִּים (מועד קטן כא,א)

and R. Ḥanania b. Akavia [spoke] to a speaker, and the speaker spoke aloud to the public

SEE: אָמוֹרָא, תַּרְגֵּם

תּוֹרֶף **the substantive part** (of a document)

This portion of a document spells out the particulars of the transaction: the names of the parties, the date, and — in a financial deal — the amount of money and a description of the merchandise involved.

שַׁתְּקוּ שָׁתוּקֵי לְבַעַל עַד דְּכָתְבִיתוּ לֵיהּ לְתוֹרֶף דְּגִיטָּא (גיטין פד, סע"ב)

keep the husband silent (from stipulating any conditions) until you write the substantive part of the bill of divorce

SEE: טוֹפֶס

תּוּתֵי* תַּחַת **under; beneath**

יוֹמָא חַד יָתִיב קָא גָרֵיס תּוּתֵי דִּיקְלָא (שבת קנו,ב)

one day he was sitting, studying under a palm tree

This preposition is also used with personal-pronoun suffixes, chiefly:

תּוּתֵיהּ תַּחְתָּיו **under it** (m.)

* This word, which is popularly pronounced תּוּתֵי, is a shortened form of תְּחוֹתֵי (which seldom occurs).

SEE: תַּתָּאָה, תַּתָּא

לְכַתְּחִילָּה/לְכַתְּחִלָּה SEE: לְכַתְּחִילָּה

תֵּיבָה; תֵּיבוּתָא*

Besides the Biblical meanings of this noun — *a box* or *(Noah's) ark* — there are two additional

usages in the Hebrew of the Talmud.

(1) the holy ark (containing Torah scrolls)**

לָמָּה שְׁלִיחַ צִיבּוּר יוֹרֵד לִפְנֵי הַתֵּיבָה? (ראש השנה לד,ב)

Why does the leader of public prayer go down before the holy ark (and repeat the Amida)?

(2) word

הֲפוֹךְ אֶת הַתֵּיבָה וְדוֹרְשֶׁהּ! (שבת נה,ב ע"פ בראשית מט:ד)

Reverse [the order of the letters in] the word (פַּחַז) *and interpret it (as the initials of several other words)!*

* The first form is Hebrew, and the second is Aramaic.

** In this sense, הַתֵּיבָה is used with the definite article. In Talmudic times, *the ark*, which was also called the אָרוֹן, was portable. In the contemporary synagogue, the table or desk from which the reader leads the congregation in prayer is sometimes called the תֵּיבָה.

תִּיבָּעֵי* (= תִּתְבָּעֵי) fut. 3rd pers. f.s. (בעי אִתְפְּעֵל)

(1) תִּשָּׁאֵל

it will be a question; let it be a question

In this sense, this verb usually refers to a halakhic problem and its application.

For an example, see לָא תִּיבָּעֵי לָךְ כִּי תִּיבָּעֵי לָךְ.

she/it should require (2) תְּהֵא צְרִיכָה

אִי אִשְׁתּוֹ הִיא, תִּיבָּעֵי גֵּט! (יבמות קח,א)

If she is (indeed) his wife, she should require a bill of divorce (in order to marry someone else)!

* In certain tractates (תמורה, נזיר, נדרים), תִּיבָּעֵי indicates that a halakhic problem remains unresolved — just like תֵּיקוּ in most tractates.

For examples — see נדרים י,ב; תמורה יג, סע"ב ורש"י שם.

SEE: אִיבָּעֵי, תֵּיקוּ

תֶּיהֱוֵי fut. 3rd pers. f.s. (הוי)

let it be; it will be תְּהֵא; תִּהְיֶה

For an example, see ... לֵימָא תֶּיהֱוֵי תְּיוּבְתֵּיהּ דר'.

SEE: הֲוָה

תְּיוּבְתָּא

refutation; contradiction תְּשׁוּבָה; סְתִירָה

Both תְּיוּבְתָּא and תְּשׁוּבָה — from the Aramaic תוב and the Hebrew שוב respectively — mean *a response* in the sense of a *refutation*, not *a resolution*.

For examples, see the next entry, and see the entry ... לֵימָא תֶּיהֱוֵי תְּיוּבְתֵּיהּ דר'.

* Occasionally, תְּיוּבְתָּא is the equivalent of תְּשׁוּבָה in the sense of *return (to God), repentance*, as in תענית כג,ב.

תְּיוּבְתָּא דר' ...

תְּשׁוּבָה לר' ...; קוּשְׁיָא [לְדַעְתּוֹ] שֶׁל ר' ...

[This constitutes] a refutation of [the opinion of] R. ...

This expression rejects the opinion of an amora because of a contradiction from a mishna or a baraitha. When the word תְּיוּבְתָּא is repeated after the amora's name, it denotes that the refutation is final.*

תְּיוּבְתָּא דְּרַב פָּפָּא תְּיוּבְתָּא, וְהִילְכְתָא כְּוָותֵיהּ דְּרַב פָּפָּא. תְּיוּבְתָּא וְהִילְכְתָא?! (עירובין טז,ב)

The refutation of Rav Pappa['s opinion] is a refutation, and the halakhic ruling is in accordance with Rav Pappa. [Is there both] a refutation and a halakhic ruling [in favor]?!

* According to Rabbenu Ḥananel (quoted in the *Arukh*), R. Yitsḥak Alfasi (גיטין פרק ז'), and Rashi (on סנהדרין עב,א), תְּיוּבְתָּא usually indicates that a halakhic opinion has been clearly and definitely rejected; whereas קַשְׁיָא, *[it is] difficult*, does not mean that the difficult opinion must be rejected. For a different distinction — see the Rashbam in his commentary on בבא בתרא נב, רע"ב.

תִּילְתָּא* שְׁלִישׁ **one-third**

תִּילְתָּא יָהֲבִינַן לַהּ לְאַחְתָּא (בבא מציעא לט,ב)

we give one-third [of the estate] to the sister

* See the table of fractions in Appendix II.

תֵּימָא/תֵּימַר (אמר) fut. 2nd pers. m.s.

you will say תֹּאמַר

For examples, see מַהוּ דְתֵימָא, אֲפִילוּ תֵּימָא, and (וְ)כִי תֵּימָא.

תְּמִיהָ* **astonishment; wonder**

כָּל דְּבָרֶיךָ אֵינָן אֶלָּא דִבְרֵי תְמִיהָ! (פסחים עב, סע"ב)

All your words are nothing but words [that arouse] astonishment!

* In Talmudic commentaries, this word is often used to introduce a difficulty, as in Tosafoth בבא מציעא כא, סע"א.

תִּימְצֵי

SEE: תִּמְצָא

תִּינוֹק (pl. תִּינוֹקוֹת) **"a suckling"; child; boy**

תִּינוֹקוֹת שֶׁל בֵּית רַבָּן **schoolchildren**

אֵין מְבַטְּלִין תִּינוֹקוֹת שֶׁל בֵּית רַבָּן — אֲפִילוּ לְבִנְיַן בֵּית הַמִּקְדָּשׁ. (שבת קיט, סע"ב)

We do not cause schoolchildren to neglect [their Torah studies] — even for the building of the Beth HaMikdash.

תֵּינַח (נוח) fut. 3rd pers. f.s.

it would be appropriate תּוּנַח; תְּהֵא נוֹחָה

This term introduces the following *difficulty:* Whereas the statement or the explanation that has just been proposed fits one of the cases under discussion, it does not fit another case.*

אָמַר לְפָנָיו: רִבּוֹנוֹ שֶׁלָּעוֹלָם! בַּמָּה אֵדַע? אָמַר לוֹ: קְחָה לִי עֶגְלָה מְשׁוּלֶּשֶׁת וְגוֹ'. אָמַר לְפָנָיו: רִבּוֹנוֹ שֶׁלָּעוֹלָם! תֵּינַח בִּזְמַן שֶׁבֵּית הַמִּקְדָּשׁ קַיָּים, בִּזְמַן שֶׁאֵין בֵּית הַמִּקְדָּשׁ קַיָּים מָה תְּהֵא עֲלֵיהֶם? (מגילה לא,ב ע"פ בראשית טו: ח־ט)

*He (= Avraham) said before Him: Lord of the universe! By what (means) will I know (that my descendants can obtain forgiveness)? He said to him: Take me a heifer three-years old ....** He said before Him: Lord of the universe! [That answer] is appropriate for the time when the Beth HaMikdash is standing, [but] in the time when the Beth HaMikdash will not be standing, what will become of them (since they will have no means to obtain forgiveness)?*

* Compare הָנִיחָא which introduces an objection on the grounds that a proposal is consistent with only one opinion.

** The Divine response indicates that the Jewish people will obtain forgiveness through the *korbanoth*.

SEE: (וְ)הָתִינַח, (בִּ)שְׁלָמָא

וְתִיסְבְּרָא

SEE: (וְ)תִסְבְּרָא

תִּיסְגֵי/תִּסְגֵי (סגי) fut. 3rd pers. f.s.

let it be enough תַּסְפִּיק; תִּהְיֶה דַי

וְתִיסְגֵי לָךְ בְּחַד! (שבת לג,ב)

But it should be enough for you with one!

תֵּיפוּךְ (אפך) fut. 2nd pers. m.s.

you will reverse תַּהֲפֹךְ

SEE: לְעוֹלָם לָא תֵּיפוּךְ, אֵיפוּךְ, מוּחְלֶפֶת הַשִּׁיטָה

תֵּיפוֹק (נפק) fut. 3rd pers. f.s.

it will go out; let it go out תֵּצֵא

תֵּיפּוֹק לֵיהּ* "תֵּצֵא לוֹ!" יִלְמַד אוֹתָהּ!

let it be derived by him! let him derive it!

This expression introduces the following *difficulty:* Why not derive the same point through a simpler or more fundamental reason, source, or interpretation — than the one that has been previously cited?**

רֶמֶז לְעֵדִים זוֹמְמִין שֶׁלּוֹקִין מִנַּיִין? ... וְתֵיפּוֹק לֵיהּ מִ"לֹּא תַעֲנֶה"! (סנהדרין י,א ומכות ב,ב ע"פ שמות כ:יג)

Where [in the Torah] is there an allusion to [the law that] false witnesses are (sometimes) subject to flogging? ... (In response, a complicated derivation is presented whereupon the Talmud asks:) But let him derive it (instead) from (the pasuk): "You shall not testify (falsely)" (since the standard punishment for violating a negative command is flogging)!

* תֵּיפּוֹק לִי, *let me derive it*, and תֵּיפּוֹק לְהוּ, *let them derive it*, also occur in the Talmud in the same sense.

** Occasionally, תֵּיפּוֹק לֵיהּ introduces an argument *against* the halakha that has been presented, as in גיטין פד, רע"ב.

תֵּיקוּ (= תֵּיקוּם) (קום) fut. 3rd pers. f.s.

Let it stand! תַּעֲמֹד!

This term appears at the conclusion of some Talmudic discussions to indicate that the problem that was under consideration remains unresolved.*

בָּעֵי רַב פָּפָּא: בֵּין פְּסוּקָא לִפְסוּקָא, מַהוּ? תֵּיקוּ! (ברכות ח, סע"א)

Rav Pappa poses a problem: What is the halakhic ruling [about leaving the synagogue] between [the reading of one] pasuk and [another] pasuk? Let it stand.

* Popular etymology explains תֵּיקוּ as initials of the words תִּשְׁבִּי יְתָרֵץ קוּשְׁיוֹת וּבְעָיוֹת, *the Tishbi (= Eliyahu the prophet) will solve difficulties and problems.*

** Occasionally, in our printed editions and, more frequently, in manuscripts — a fuller expression is used:

לָא יָדְעִינַן; תֵּיקוּ. (בבא קמא מג,ב ועוד)

We don't know [the answer]; let it stand.

SEE: תִּיבָּעֵי and its note

תֵּיקְשֵׁי לָךְ

it will be difficult for you תִּקְשֶׁה לְךָ

This term is used in the course of Talmudic debates to present a *difficulty.*

וּלְטַעֲמֵיךְ תֵּיקְשֵׁי לָךְ הִיא גוּפָא! (בבא קמא כח,ב ועוד)

But according to your position, this [point] itself will be difficult!

SEE: קְשֵׁי

תֵּיר

SEE: אִיתְּעַר

תֵּירוּצָא

a resolution (of a difficulty) תֵּרוּץ

This Aramaic noun occurs only once in our editions of the Talmud.* Nevertheless, its Hebrew form is used in commentaries on the Talmud and in discussions about Talmudic topics — even in our own day. In Modern Hebrew, it often means *an excuse* or *a rationalization.*

* It does appear once in current editions of the Talmud (i.e., in יומא יז,ב), but that reading is contradicted by the versions found in manuscripts and in Rashi's commentary on that passage.

SEE: תָּרֵיץ

תֵּיתֵי (אתי) fut. 3rd pers. f.s.

it will come; it will be derived תָּבוֹא

מֵהֵיכָא תֵּיתֵי? (חולין סו,א ועוד)

From where will it be derived?

תֵּיתֵי לִי תָּבוֹא לִי (בְּרָכָה); יְשֻׁלַּם שְׂכָרִי

"may it come to me"; may I be rewarded

תֵּיתֵי לִי דְקַיֵּימִית שָׁלֹשׁ סְעוּדוֹת בְּשַׁבָּת. (שבת קיח, סע"ב ורש"י שם קיט, רע"א)

May I be rewarded, for I have fulfilled [the duty of eating] three meals on the Sabbath.

תֵּיתִיב (יתב) fut. 2nd pers. m.s.

you will sit (1) תֵּשֵׁב

For an example — see קידושין לו,ב ורש"י.

you will give (2) תִּתֵּן

For an example — see קידושין נב,ב.

SEE: לֵיתִיב, נֵיתִיב, (לְ)מֵיתַב

תְּלָא (תלי: תָּלֵי, act. prt. תְּלֵי, pass. prt. לִיתְלֵי, fut. לְמִיתְלָא (inf.

he hung; he made dependent (1) תָּלָה

בְּ"פֶטֶר רֶחֶם" תְּלָא רַחֲמָנָא. (קידושין כט,ב ע"פ שמות לד:יט)

The Torah has made [the definition of a first-born] dependent upon the [first] opening of the womb.

הָא בְּהָא תַּלְיָא. (שבת קלה,ב ורש"י)

This is dependent upon that (= The two issues are interdependent).

he attributed; he assumed (2) תָּלָה; הִנִּיחַ

אִינְקְבָה רֵיאָה הֵיכָא דִמְמַשְׁמְשָׁא יְדֵיהּ דְטַבָּחָא — תָּלִינַן אוֹ לָא תָּלִינַן? (חולין מט,א)

[If] a lung was perforated where the hand of the butcher handles [it] — do we attribute [the perforation to the butcher's hand] or do we not (since the lung may have been perforated prior to the slaughtering)?

SEE: אַתְלֵי

תְּלֵיסַר

thirteen שְׁלֹשָׁה עָשָׂר

תְּלֵיסְרֵי/תְּלָת־סְרֵי/תְּלָת־עַשְׂרֵי f.

thirteen שְׁלֹשׁ עֶשְׂרֵה

תַּלְמוּד; תַּלְמוּדָא*

(1) study; learning

הַתַּלְמוּד מֵבִיא לִידֵי מַעֲשֶׂה. (קידושין מ,ב)

Study leads to practice.

(2) a teaching (usually based upon, or at least supported by, a Biblical passage)

לְתַלְמוּדוֹ הוּא בָא (ראש השנה לד,א)

It (= the Biblical passage) comes for its own teaching.

a clearly-formulated teaching תַּלְמוּד עָרוּךְ (שבועות מ,ב)

(3) discussion; analysis; the Talmud (which is primarily a discussion of the Mishna)

בֶּן חָמֵשׁ עֶשְׂרֵה לְתַלְמוּד. (משנה אבות פ"א מכ"א)

A fifteen-year old is ready for (Talmudic) analysis.

הֲוָה גְמִירְנָא לְכוּלֵּיהּ תַּלְמוּדָא (שבת סג,א)

I had studied the entire Talmud

* The first form is Hebrew, and the second is Aramaic.

SEE: גְּמָרָא, מַאי תַּלְמוּדָא

תַּלְמוּד לוֹמַר

A (Biblical) teaching says; Scripture teaches

This term introduces a *Biblical passage* that is quoted to clarify a halakhic or aggadic point.

יָכוֹל יִתְפַּלֵּל אָדָם לְכָל רוּחַ שֶׁיִּרְצֶה? תַּלְמוּד לוֹמַר: "נֶגֶד יְרוּשָׁלַיִם". (ברכות לא,א ע"פ דניאל ו:יא)

Could it be that a person may pray (the Amida) in any direction that he wishes? Scripture teaches: "Towards Jerusalem."

SEE: (שֶׁ)אֵין תַּלְמוּד לוֹמַר, מַה תַּלְמוּד לוֹמַר

תַּלְמִיד חָבֵר

disciple-colleague תַּלְמִיד חָבֵר

This expression indicates a dual relationship between two ḥakhamim, but the classical commentators differ as to its definition. In his commentary on עירובין סג, רע"א, Rashi indicates that the two individuals are ḥakhamim of equal caliber so that they are essentially colleagues. If one of them has acquired some Torah knowledge from the other, he is *a disciple of a colleague*. On the other hand, according to the Rashbam's commentary on the Talmudic example in this entry, this expression refers to two successive stages in a relationship between two ḥakhamim: One ḥakham was originally a disciple of the other, his master. Subsequently, the disciple developed in Torah learning to such an extent that he became a colleague of his master, so that now he is both *disciple and colleague*.

בֶּן עַזַּאי תַּלְמִיד חָבֵר דְּר׳ עֲקִיבָא הֲוָה. (בבא בתרא קנח, סע״ב)

Ben Azzai was a disciple-colleague of R. Akiva.

תַּלְמִיד חָכָם (pl. תַּלְמִידֵי חֲכָמִים)

"the student of a ḥakham"; a Torah scholar

מַמְזֵר תַּלְמִיד חָכָם קוֹדֵם לְכֹהֵן גָּדוֹל עַם הָאָרֶץ. (הוריות יג,א: משנה פ״ג מ״ח)

An illegitimate son [who is] a Torah scholar takes precedence over a high priest [who is] an ignoramus.

תְּלָת f. שָׁלֹשׁ three

SEE: שְׁמַע מִינָּהּ תְּלָת

תְּלָתָא שְׁלֹשָׁה three

תְּלָתִין שְׁלֹשִׁים thirty

מִתָּם מִשָּׁם (= מֵאֶרֶץ יִשְׂרָאֵל) from there

This word occurs only in the expression שְׁלַחוּ מִתָּם.

SEE: תַּמָּן, הָתָם, שְׁלַחוּ מִתָּם

תְּמַהּ* (תמה: תְּמֵיהַּ/תְּמֵהַּ .prt, תִּתְמַה .fut, תְּמַה .imp)

he wondered; he was amazed

For an example — see the next entry.

* The term בִּתְמִיהָה, *in astonishment*, is frequently used by Rashi in his commentary to indicate that a clause should be read as a *rhetorical question*, while בְּנִיחוּתָא, *gently*, indicates that a clause be read as an indicative statement. See, for example, Rashi's comment on this Talmudic passage:

ברייתא: בִּיְּישׁוֹ עָרוֹם — חַיָּב.

תלמוד: עָרוֹם בַּר בּוֹשֶׁת הוּא?! (בבא קמא פו, רע״ב ורש״י שם: בִּתְמִיהָה)

BARAITHA: [If] one embarrassed a naked man, he is liable to pay (for the embarrassment he caused — even though the victim was naked and apparently not sensitive to embarrassment).

TALMUD: Is a naked man subject to shame?!

(Rashi comments that the last sentence must be read *in astonishment*.)

SEE: אַל תִּתְמַהּ, אַתְמוֹהֵי מַתְמְהָהּ

תְּמֵיהַנִי/תְּמֵיהַּ־אֲנִי אִם I wonder whether ...

אָמַר ר׳ אֶלְעָזָר בֶּן עֲזַרְיָה: תְּמֵיהַנִי אִם יֵשׁ בַּדּוֹר הַזֶּה שֶׁיּוֹדֵעַ לְהוֹכִיחַ. (ערכין טז,ב)

R. El'azar b. Azarya said: I wonder whether there is anyone in this generation who knows how to give reproof.

תַּמָּן* שָׁם there

בְּאַתְרָא דְּלֵית גְּבַר, תַּמָּן הֲוֵי גְּבַר! (ברכות סג,א)

In a place where there is no man, there [you should] be a man!

* This word is used regularly in the Targumim and in the Talmud Yerushalmi. It occurs infrequently in the Babylonian Talmud — mostly in aphorisms, in narrative passages based in Erets Yisrael, and in the tractate נְדָרִים.

SEE: הָתָם, the common word for *there* in the Babylonian Talmud.

תַּמְנֵי f. שְׁמוֹנֶה eight

תַּמְנֵי סְרֵי f. שְׁמוֹנֶה עֶשְׂרֵה eighteen

תְּמָנְיָא שְׁמוֹנָה eight

תְּמָנֵיסַר שְׁמוֹנָה עָשָׂר eighteen

תְּמָנַן שְׁמוֹנִים eighty

תִּמָּצֵא/תִּימָּצֵי* fut. 2nd pers. m.s. (מצא נפעל)

"you will be found"; you will conclude (after examining the matter)

For an example, see next entry.

* This word is used only in the next entry and in אִם תִּמָּצֵא/תִּימָּצֵי לוֹמַר. It is popularly pronounced תִּמְצָא or תִּימְצֵי as if it were from the קַל *binyan*, but we have vocalized it as a נִפְעַל form in keeping with the parallel expression נִמְצֵאתָ אַתָּה אוֹמֵר in the past tense, where the verb נִמְצֵאתָ is clearly נִפְעַל.

SEE: אִם תִּמָּצֵא לוֹמַר, נִמְצֵאתָ אַתָּה אוֹמֵר

כְּשֶׁתִּמָּצֵא/כְּשֶׁתִּימָּצֵי לוֹמַר לְדִבְרֵי ר׳ ... לְדִבְרֵי ר׳ ...

When [you analyse this controversy between the tannaim] you will conclude: According to the opinion of R. ...; according to the opinion of R. ....

With this formula, an amora or the Talmud itself presents an *analysis of the controversy* between two tannaim previously quoted in a mishna or a baraitha.

משנה: אֶחָד אוֹמֵר בִּשְׁתֵּי שָׁעוֹת, וְאֶחָד אוֹמֵר בְּשָׁלֹשׁ שָׁעוֹת — עֵדוּתָן קַיֶּימֶת. אֶחָד אוֹמֵר בְּשָׁלֹשׁ, וְאֶחָד אוֹמֵר בְּחָמֵשׁ — עֵדוּתָן בְּטֵלָה. דִּבְרֵי ר׳ מֵאִיר. ר׳ יְהוּדָה אוֹמֵר: עֵדוּתָן קַיֶּימֶת. (פסחים יא,ב ע״פ משנה סנהדרין פ״ה מ״ג)

תלמוד: אָמַר אַבַּיֵּי: כְּשֶׁתִּמָּצֵא לוֹמַר: לְדִבְרֵי ר׳ מֵאִיר אֵין אָדָם טוֹעֶה וְלֹא כְּלוּם, לְדִבְרֵי ר׳ יְהוּדָה אָדָם טוֹעֶה חֲצִי שָׁעָה. (פסחים שם ורש״י שם)

MISHNA: [If] one [witness] says [the murder took place] at the second hour [in the day], and the other says at the third hour — their testimony is valid. [If] one says at the third hour, and the other says at the fifth hour — their testimony is void. [This is] the opinion of R. Méir. R. Yᵉhuda says: Their testimony is valid.

TALMUD: Abbayé said: When [you analyze this controversy between the tannaim] you will conclude: According to the opinion of R. Méir, a person does not err at all [with regard to the hour, but the two witnesses are referring to the same time, which one calls the end of the second hour and the other calls the beginning of the third]; according to the opinion of R. Yᵉhuda, a person may err by one-half hour [and the murder took place in the middle of the fourth hour, so that the one who says at the third hour means the end of the third, and his error is being a half-hour too early; whereas the one who says at the fifth hour means the beginning of the fifth, and his error is being a half-hour too late].

dates תְּמָרִים pl. **תַּמְרֵי**

... הָנֵי תַּמְרֵי דְזִיקָא הֵיכִי אָכְלִינַן לְהוּ? (ב"מ כב,ב ורש"י שם)

... how can we eat dates [that were blown down] by the wind (perhaps they are still the property of their owners)?

תְּנָא/תָּנָא (תני: act. prt. תָּנֵי, pass. prt. f. תַּנְיָא, fut. לִיתְנֵי, imp. תְּנִי, inf. לְמִיתְנֵי/לְמִיתְנָא)

(1) שָׁנָה; לָמַד; לִמֵּד

he learned; he taught; he stated; he listed

The term תְּנָא* often introduces a brief baraitha containing a remark or a note on a mishna that either explains the mishna, supplies a missing detail, or limits its scope.

משנה: הַקּוֹרֵא אֶת הַמְּגִילָּה עוֹמֵד וְיוֹשֵׁב. (מגילה כא,א: משנה פ"ד מ"א)

ברייתא: תָּנָא: מַה שֶּׁאֵין כֵּן בַּתּוֹרָה. (שם)

MISHNA: One may read the scroll (of Esther to fulfill his duty on Purim) — either standing or sitting.

BARAITHA: [A tanna] taught: Which is not the case with regard to [the reading of] the Torah.

he repeated (2) שָׁנָה; עָשָׂה שֵׁנִית

Scripture repeated it. תְּנָא בֵּיהּ קְרָא (ב"ק פה,א ועוד)

* In this sense, the word is traditionally pronounced תָּנָא — perhaps because of the influence of the Hebrew parallel שָׁנָה. This pronunciation is corroborated by the spelling תאנא, which is found occasionally, e.g., in קידושין ס, רע"ב. For the complete conjugation of this verb, see *Grammar for Gemara*: Chapter 4, Verb 13.

SEE: מַאן תְּנָא, שָׁנָה

tanna תַּנָּא; שׁוֹנֶה (pl. תַּנָּאֵי) **תַּנָּא**

(1) a ḥakham whose statements are recorded in the Mishna or in baraithoth; one who formulates mishnayoth or baraithoth

The tannaim lived during a period of almost three hundred years — from the time of Hillel and Shammai (the generation before the common era) until the generation after R. Yᵉhuda HaNasi, the compiler of the Mishna (in the middle of the third century). This term is used in contrast to the term אָמוֹרָא, *amora*, which designates ḥakhamim of the subsequent period.

תְּרֵי תַנָּאֵי וּתְרֵי אָמוֹרָאֵי דִּפְלִיגֵי אַהֲדָדֵי (עירובין ז, רע"א)

two tannaim and two amoraim who disagree with each other (each pair in their own historical period)

(2) an expert at committing halakhoth to memory who recited mishnayoth and baraithoth by heart before the Rosh HaYeshiva during the amoraic period and into gaonic times

Questions that arose in the beth midrash about the proper wording of the text were referred to the tanna because of his expertise. This tanna was not necessarily a profound scholar.

תָּנֵי תַנָּא, וְלָא יָדַע מַאי אָמַר. (סוטה כב, רע"א)

A tanna is reciting (a baraitha), but he does not know what he is saying.

SEE: אָמוֹרָא, תַּנָּאֵי, תַּנָּא בָּרָא, תַּנָּא דִידָן

תַּנָּא בָּרָא הַתַּנָּא הַחִיצוֹן

"the tanna outside" (of the mishna); the tanna of the baraitha

The tanna who has taught the halakha that appears in the baraitha that has just been quoted — is contrasted to תַּנָּא דִידָן, *our tanna*, who has taught the halakha that appears in our mishna.

תַּנָּא דִידָן סָבַר: אֵין צָרִיךְ לְהָבִיא רְאָיָה, וְתַנָּא בָּרָא סָבַר: צָרִיךְ לְהָבִיא רְאָיָה. (בבא בתרא קעג, רע"א)

Our tanna holds: It is not necessary [for the holder of a bond] to bring proof [that it is his], while the tanna of the baraitha holds: It is necessary to bring proof.

SEE: בָּרַיְיתָא, תַּנָּא דִידָן

תְּנָא דְבֵי ר' ... שָׁנָה שֶׁל בֵּית ר' ...

[one] of [the ḥakhamim from] the beth midrash of R. ... taught

תְּנָא דְבֵי ר' יִשְׁמָעֵאל (סוטה ג,א ועוד)

[one] of [the ḥakhamim from] the beth midrash of R. Yishmael taught

our tanna; הַתַּנָּא שֶׁלָּנוּ **תַּנָּא דִידָן**

the tanna whose opinion is stated in our mishna (anonymously)

תַּנְיָא: ר' יְהוֹשֻׁעַ בֶּן קָרְחָה אוֹמֵר: כְּרַכִּין הַמּוּקָּפִין חוֹמָה מִימוֹת אֲחַשְׁוֵרוֹשׁ קוֹרִין בַּחֲמִשָּׁה עָשָׂר ... וְתַנָּא דִידָן ... מוּקֶּפֶת חוֹמָה מִימוֹת יְהוֹשֻׁעַ בִּן נוּן. (מגילה ב,ב ע"פ משנה שם פ"א מ"א)

It is taught [in a baraitha]: R. Yᵉhoshua b. Korḥa says: Cities that are surrounded by a wall from the days of Aḥashverosh read [the scroll of Esther] on the fifteenth [of Adar] ..., but [according to] our tanna ... [only if] it is surrounded by a wall from the days of Y^ehoshua b. Nun.

SEE: תְּנָא בָּרָא

תָּנָא וְשַׁיֵּיר   שָׁנָה וְשִׁיֵּר.

He stated (some), but he omitted (others).

In formulating a mishna or a baraitha, a tanna sometimes presents a *partial listing* of items or cases that are included within a halakha. In light of this practice, the Talmud argues that an omission of some items does not prove that they are to be excluded from the halakha.

יְלַמְּדֵנוּ רַבֵּנוּ: אֵשֶׁת אֲחִי אֲבִי הָאָב וַאֲחוֹת אֲבִי הָאָב, מָהוּ? תָּא שְׁמַע: מָה הֵן שְׁנִיּוֹת? ... וְלָא קָחָשֵׁיב לְהוּ בַּהֲדַיְיהוּ! תָּנָא וְשַׁיֵּיר. (יבמות כא, סע"ב)

Will our teacher instruct us: What is the halakha (with regard to marrying) the wife of the brother of one's father's father or the sister of one's father's father? Come [and] hear: What are the prohibitions of the second degree? [The list that is presented] does not [count them (= these two relatives) among them! [The tanna] stated (some), but he omitted (others).

Sometimes, the Talmud asks מַאי שַׁיֵּיר דְּהַאי שַׁיֵּיר? *What [else] did [the tanna] omit that he omitted this?* This challenge to תָּנָא וְשַׁיֵּיר is based upon the tannaitic practice of formulating either comprehensive lists or lists missing several items, but never lists from which only one item is missing.

וְתַנָּא מַייתֵי לַהּ מֵהָכָא
וְתַנָּא מֵבִיא אוֹתָהּ מִכָּאן.

And a tanna deduces it from here.

The Talmud has quoted an amora as having deduced the halakha or aggada under consideration (or support for it) from one Biblical passage. With this introduction, the Talmud now presents a *tanna's derivation* of the same halakha from a different Biblical passage.

For an example — see ביצה טו,ב.

SEE: וְהַאי תַּנָּא מַייתֵי לַהּ מֵהָכָא

תְּנָא סֵיפָא לְגַלּוֹיֵי רֵישָׁא
שָׁנָה סוֹפָהּ לְגַלּוֹת רֹאשָׁהּ.

[The tanna] stated the latter clause in order to clarify the first clause.

After an amora's interpretation of a mishna or a baraitha is attacked because of the alleged redundancy of its latter clause — it is sometimes argued that the latter clause is not really redundant because it serves to clarify the meaning of the first clause by contrast.

משנה: (רישא) הַמַּחֲלִיף פָּרָה בַּחֲמוֹר וְיָלְדָה ... — זֶה אוֹמֵר: עַד שֶׁלֹּא מָכַרְתִּי, וְזֶה אוֹמֵר: מִשֶּׁלָּקַחְתִּי — יַחֲלוֹקוּ ... (סיפא) זֶה אוֹמֵר: אֵינִי יוֹדֵעַ, וְזֶה אוֹמֵר: אֵינִי יוֹדֵעַ — יַחֲלוֹקוּ. (בבא מציעא ק, רע"א: משנה פ"ח מ"ד)

תלמוד: ... הַשְׁתָּא בָּרִי וּבָרִי אָמַר: יַחֲלוֹקוּ, שֶׁמָּא וְשֶׁמָּא מִיבַּעְיָא! אִי מִשּׁוּם הָא, לָא אִירְיָא. תְּנָא סֵיפָא לְגַלּוֹיֵי רֵישָׁא: שֶׁלֹּא תֹּאמַר רֵישָׁא שֶׁמָּא וְשֶׁמָּא, אֲבָל בָּרִי וּבָרִי לָא; תְּנָא סֵיפָא שֶׁמָּא וְשֶׁמָּא, מִכְּלָל דְּרֵישָׁא בָּרִי וּבָרִי, וַאֲפִילּוּ הָכִי יַחֲלוֹקוּ. (בבא מציעא ק,א)

MISHNA: (1) [If] one barters a donkey for a cow and [the latter] gives birth — one (= the seller of the cow) says: [It gave birth] before I sold [it], and the other (= the purchaser of the cow) says: [It gave birth] after I bought [it] — they must split [the value of the new-born calf]. (2) [If] one says: I don't know [when it gave birth], and the other one says: I don't know — they must split.

TALMUD: Now [that in the first clause where both parties issue] definite [pleas], [the tanna] says: They split [the value of the new-born calf] — is there any question [that in the second clause where both parties plead] "perhaps" [that the parties should split, and so the second clause is superfluous]?! If [your argument is] because of this [mishna], there is no proof. [The tanna] stated the latter clause in order to clarify the first clause, so that you not say the first clause [refers to a case where] both [parties plead] "perhaps," implying that if both [issue a] definite [plea], [they do] not [split]; [therefore the tanna] formulated the latter clause [where both plead] "perhaps," [and] it follows that the first clause [by contrast, refers to] definite [pleas], and even so they split.

SEE: גַּלֵּי, אִי מִשּׁוּם הָא לָא אִירְיָא

תַּנָּא קַמָּא   הַתַּנָּא הָרִאשׁוֹן   the first tanna

This term denotes the tanna whose statement is presented first in a mishna or first in a baraitha. Usually, it designates an anonymous tanna as in בבא מציעא כט,ב. In some instances, however, it refers to a specific tanna who was mentioned by name in the text — as in פסחים כח, רע"ב.

SEE: אֲתָאן לְתַנָּא קַמָּא

וְתַנָּא/וְתַנָּא תוּנָא

This expression, which introduces a mishna or a baraitha that an amora has quoted to corroborate his own halakha, has been translated by the classical commentators in two different ways:

and the tanna taught*   (1) וְהַתַּנָּא שָׁנָה

and our tanna taught**   (2) וְשָׁנָה הַתַּנָּא שֶׁלָּנוּ

וַאֲמַר רַב חִסְדָּא: מָכַר לוֹ שָׁוֶה שֵׁשׁ בְּחָמֵשׁ, וְהוּזְלוּ וְעָמְדוּ עַל שָׁלֹשׁ — ... מוֹכֵר יָכוֹל לַחֲזוֹר בּוֹ, וְלֹא לוֹקֵחַ .... וְתַנָּא תוּנָא: רָעוֹת וְנִמְצְאוּ יָפוֹת — מוֹכֵר יָכוֹל לַחֲזוֹר בּוֹ, וְלֹא לוֹקֵחַ. (בבא בתרא פד,א ורשב"ם שם)

And Rav Ḥisda said: [If] one sold him [an article] worth six [sh^ekalim] for five, and it became cheaper and stood at three — ... the seller may retract, but not the purchaser .... And the tanna taught: [If articles were sold as] inferior, and they turned out to be superior — the seller can retract, but not the purchaser.

* According to Rabbenu Ḥananel (on בבא מציעא ג,א) and R. Nathan of Rome in his *Arukh*, the first word is the noun תַּנָּא, *the tanna*, and תּוּנָא is a verb in the past tense, a variant of תְּנָא, *he taught*.

** According to Rashi (on בבא מציעא ג,א) and the Rashbam (on the passage quoted above as an example), the first word is the verb תְּנָא, *(he) taught*, and it should be vocalised accordingly. They explain תּוּנָא as a noun meaning *our tanna*, with the suffix נָא- used as the first-person-plural possessive pronoun, *our*.

SEE: תַּנָּא, תְּנָא/תָּנָא

a stipulation; a condition תְּנַאי; תְּנָאָה*

מִכְּדִי כָּל תְּנַאי מֵהֵיכָא גָּמְרִינַן? מִתְּנַאי בְּנֵי גָד וּבְנֵי רְאוּבֵן. תְּנָאָה דְאֶפְשַׁר לְקַיּוֹמֵיהּ עַל יְדֵי שְׁלִיחַ כִּי הָתָם הָוֵי תְּנָאָה; תְּנָאָה דְלָא אֶפְשַׁר לְקַיּוֹמֵיהּ עַל יְדֵי שְׁלִיחַ כִּי הָתָם לָא הָוֵי תְּנָאָה. (כתובות עד,א ע"פ במדבר לב:כט־ל)

*Now from where do we derive [the validity] of any stipulation? From the stipulation [made by Moshe Rabbenu with the tribes of Gad and Rᵉuven ("if the children of Gad and the children of Rᵉuven will cross the Jordan with you, every man armed for battle before the Lord, and land shall be conquered before you — you shall give them the land of Gil'ad for a possession").** A stipulation where it is possible to perform it (= the transaction) through an agent as in that case (where Moshe was to give them the land through his agent Yᵉhoshua) is a [valid] stipulation; a stipulation where it is not possible to perform it (= the transaction) through an agent as in that case is not a [valid] stipulation.*

* The first form is Hebrew, and the second is Aramaic.

** That stipulation is regarded as the prototype. Some of the other features that are also derived from this prototype are the following:

(1) The stipulation must be doubled (תְּנַאי כָּפוּל), so that it contains both a positive and a negative formulation, e.g., *"If .. will cross the Jordan ..; but if they will not .."*

(2) The positive clause must precede the negative clause (הֵן קוֹדֵם לְלָאו), e.g., *"If .. will cross .."* must precede *"if they will not cross .."*

(3) The *if-clause* must precede the principal clause (תְּנַאי קוֹדֵם לְמַעֲשֶׂה), e.g., *"If .. will cross .."* must precede *"you shall give them .."*

כְּתַנָּאֵי [כְּ[מַחֲלֹקֶת] תַּנָּאִים

[It is] like [a controversy between] tannaim.

תַּנָּאֵי הִיא [מַחֲלֹקֶת] תַּנָּאִים הִיא

It is [a controversy between] tannaim.

(1) These two expressions usually indicate that the halakha, quoted in the name of an amora — or the controversy between two amoraim — was already the subject of an earlier controversy between two tannaim that is about to be quoted.

אֲמַר רַב הוּנָא לְרַבָּה בְּרֵיהּ: חֲטוֹף וּבְרֵיךְ! לְמֵימְרָא דִמְבָרֵךְ עָדִיף מִמַּאן דְּעָנֵי "אָמֵן"? וְהָתַנְיָא: ר' יוֹסֵי אוֹמֵר: גָּדוֹל הָעוֹנֶה "אָמֵן" יוֹתֵר מִן הַמְבָרֵךְ! ... תַּנָּאֵי הִיא, דְּתַנְיָא: ... מְמַהֲרִין לַמְבָרֵךְ יוֹתֵר מִן הָעוֹנֶה "אָמֵן". (ברכות נג,ב)

Rav Huna said to his son Rabba: Seize [the cup of wine], and recite the bᵉrakha! Is it to say that the one who recites a bᵉrakha is superior to one who answers "Amen"? But is it not stated [in a baraitha]: R. Yosé says: The one who answers "Amen" is greater than the one who recites the bᵉrakha! ... It is [a controversy between] tannaim, since it is stated [in another baraitha]: ... the one who recites a bᵉrakha is rewarded more quickly than the one who says "Amen."

(2) In some instances, these expressions indicate that two anonymous mishnayoth or baraithoth that contradict each other represent the opinions of two different tannaim; hence there is no need to resolve that contradiction.

תְּנַן: הָעוֹבֵד עֲבוֹדַת כּוֹכָבִים — עוֹבֵד, אִין; אוֹמֵר, לָא. וְהָאֲנַן תְּנַן: הָאוֹמֵר אֶעֱבוֹד, אֵלֵךְ וְאֶעֱבוֹד?! ... רַב יוֹסֵף אֲמַר: תַּנָּאֵי שַׁקַּלְתְּ מֵעָלְמָא? תַּנָּאֵי הִיא, דְּתַנְיָא: הָאוֹמֵר: בּוֹאוּ וְעִבְדוּנִי — ר' מֵאִיר מְחַיֵּיב, וְר' יְהוּדָה פּוֹטֵר. (סנהדרין סא,א)

We have learned (in a mishna): One who engages in idolatry [is executed] — serving [the idol], yes; saying [that he would do so], no. But have we not learned [in another mishna that if one says]: I will serve [idols] or I will go and serve ... [he is executed]?! ... Rav Yosef said: Have you eliminated tannaim from the world?! [This issue] is [a controversy between] tannaim, as it is stated [in a baraitha]: If one says: Come and worship me — R. Méir declares [him] liable [to the death penalty], while R. Yᵉhuda exempts [him].

SEE: לֵימָא כְּתַנָּאֵי, (וְ)הָנֵי תַּנָּאֵי כְּהָנֵי תַּנָּאֵי

they taught; they stated (תני) תָּנוּ/תְּנוֹ/תָּנוּ*

For examples, see the next two entries.

* The vocalisation and the explanation of this verbal form are somewhat controversial. It is popularly pronounced תָּנוּ and understood as a past tense — parallel to the Hebrew שָׁנוּ, which probably influenced its pronunciation. According to the usual pattern in Aramaic, the past tense should be vocalised תְּנוֹ — as the Yemenites pronounce it — or perhaps תְּנוּ. It is also possible to regard the תָּנוּ pronunciation as an Aramaic participle, the equivalent of the Hebrew שׁוֹנִים, *teaching*.

SEE: תְּנֵינָא לְהָא דְתָנוּ רַבָּנַן, תְּנָא/תָּנָא

the ḥakhamim taught תָּנוּ רַבָּנַן שָׁנוּ חֲכָמִים

This expression usually* introduces a baraitha that begins with an anonymous statement.

תָּנוּ רַבָּנַן: הַמִּתְפַּלֵּל צָרִיךְ שֶׁיְּכַוֵּין לִבּוֹ לַשָּׁמַיִם ...** (ברכות לא,א)

The ḥakhamim taught: One who is praying must direct his heart to Heaven ...

* Occasionally, it introduces a mishna as in פסחים לז,א.

** In the very next line in this Talmudic passage, another baraitha that begins אָמַר ר' יְהוּדָה is introduced by the term תַּנְיָא, *it is taught* — apparently since the name of a tanna is mentioned at the outset. Compare תַּנְיָא and its note.

SEE: תָּנוּ and its note.

תָּנוּ רַבָּנַן ... תַּנְיָא אִידָךְ ...
שָׁנוּ חֲכָמִים ..., שְׁנוּיָה אַחֶרֶת ....

The hakhamim taught ..., [and] another [baraitha] is taught ....

This formula presents two baraithoth that deal with halakhoth that are related to each other. The halakhoth are complementary — not contradictory.

תָּנוּ רַבָּנַן: "לֹא תִּגְנוֹב" — בְּגוֹנֵב נְפָשׁוֹת הַכָּתוּב מְדַבֵּר ...; תַּנְיָא אִידָךְ: "לֹא תִּגְנוֹבוּ" — בְּגוֹנֵב מָמוֹן הַכָּתוּב מְדַבֵּר .... (סנהדרין פו,א ע"פ שמות כ:טו וויקרא יט:יא)

The hakhamim teach: "Thou shalt not steal" — Scripture is speaking of stealing human beings (= kidnapping) ...; another [baraitha] is taught: "Thou shalt not steal" — Scripture is speaking of stealing money ....

SEE: תָּנֵי חֲדָא ... וְתַנְיָא אִידָךְ ....

תְּנֵי imp. (תני) שְׁנֵה ...! Read ...! State ...!

This imperative proposes a textual correction or an interpretation of a mishna or baraitha.

משנה: וְאֵלּוּ חַיָּיב לְהַכְרִיז: ... צִבּוּרֵי פֵירוֹת .... (בבא מציעא כד, סע"ב: משנה פ"ב מ"ב)

תלמוד: תְּנֵי: צִבּוּר פֵּירוֹת! (שם כה,א)

MISHNA: And these are [the found articles that] one must announce: ... heaps of fruit ....

TALMUD: Read: "A heap of fruit!"

SEE: פּוּק תְּנֵי לְבָרָא

תָּנֵי prt. (תני: תָּנוּ .pl)

he teaches; he states שׁוֹנֶה

ר' חִיָּיא תָּנֵי כְּוָותֵיהּ דְּרַב, וְכוּלְּהוּ תַּנָּאֵי תָּנוּ כְּוָותֵיהּ דִּשְׁמוּאֵל. (פסחים ח, סע"ב)

R. Hiyya teaches [a baraitha] in accordance with [the opinion of] Rav, while all the tannaim (= the experts at committing halakhoth to memory) teach [a baraitha] in accordance with [the opinion of] Sh^emuel.

SEE: אַדְּתָנֵי...לִיפְלוֹג וְלִיתְנֵי בְּדִידָהּ, הוּא תָּנֵי לָהּ וְהוּא אָמַר לָהּ

קָתָנֵי (= קָא+תָּנֵי)

he teaches; [the tanna] states הוּא שׁוֹנֶה

SEE: הָכִי קָתָנֵי

תָּנֵי וַהֲדַר מְפָרֵשׁ שׁוֹנֶה וְאַחַר כָּךְ מְפָרֵשׁ.

[The tanna first] states [the general rule], and then he explains [the specifics].

In response to the argument that two clauses of a mishna or a baraitha are redundant, the Talmud sometimes resolves that difficulty by contending that one clause constitutes a general principle, while the other clause spells out the particulars.

משנה: ... נְכָסִים שֶׁהֵן שֶׁל בְּנֵי בְרִית ... (ב"ק ט,ב: משנה א:ב)

תלמוד: לְמַעוּטֵי דְנָכְרִי. הָא קָתָנֵי לַהּ לְקַמָּן: שׁוֹר שֶׁל יִשְׂרָאֵל שֶׁנָּגַח שׁוֹר שֶׁל נָכְרִי — פָּטוּר!?* תָּנֵי וַהֲדַר מְפָרֵשׁ. (בבא קמא יג, רע"ב ע"פ כת"י)

MISHNA: ... property that belongs to children of the covenant ... [if damaged, compensation must be paid]

TALMUD: Excluding [the property] of a non-Jew [from the law of compensation]. But did not [the tanna] state it later: [As for] an ox of a Jew that gored an ox of a non-Jew [the owner] is exempt [from paying compensation]?! [The tanna first] states [the general rule that only the damaging of property belonging to Jews requires compensation], and then he explains [the specifics].*

* "Since non-Jews do not hold a person responsible for his animal that caused damage, hence we rule according to their laws" (רמב"ם הלכות נזקי ממון פ"ח ה"ה). See also R. Menahem HaMeiri in *Beth HaB^ehira* on this passage.

SEE: פָּרוֹשֵׁי קָא מְפָרֵשׁ

תָּנֵי חֲדָא ... וְתַנְיָא אִידָךְ ....
[תַּנָּא] שׁוֹנֶה אַחַת ..., וּשְׁנוּיָה אַחֶרֶת ....

[A tanna] teaches one [baraitha] ..., whereas another [baraitha] is taught ....

This formula presents two baraithoth that are apparently in direct conflict with each other. Subsequently, the Talmud resolves the contradiction.

תָּנֵי חֲדָא: הָעוֹנֶה "אָמֵן" אַחַר בִּרְכוֹתָיו הֲרֵי זֶה מְשׁוּבָּח, וְתַנְיָא אִידָךְ: הֲרֵי זֶה מְגוּנֶּה. (ברכות מה, סע"ב)

[A tanna] teaches one [baraitha]: One who answers "Amen" after his own b^erakhoth is worthy of praise, whereas another [baraitha] is taught: He is worthy of condemnation.

SEE: תָּנוּ רַבָּנַן ... תַּנְיָא אִידָךְ ...

קָתָנֵי מִיהַת/מִיהָא ... הוּא שׁוֹנֶה מִכָּל מָקוֹם ...

[The tanna] states at any rate ...

Immediately after a fairly lengthy baraitha has been quoted in full, this formula is used to introduce an *excerpt* from the same baraitha, which constitutes a basis for the argument that is about to be presented.

משנה: הַמַּפְקִיד פֵּירוֹת אֵצֶל חֲבֵירוֹ — אֲפִילּוּ הֵן אוֹבְדִין — לֹא יִגַּע בָּהֶן. רַבָּן שִׁמְעוֹן בֶּן גַּמְלִיאֵל אוֹמֵר: מוֹכְרָן בִּפְנֵי בֵית דִּין מִפְּנֵי שֶׁהוּא כְּמֵשִׁיב אֲבֵידָה לַבְּעָלִים. (ב"מ לח, א: משנה ג:ו)

תלמוד: ... אָמַר ר' יוֹחָנָן: ... יוֹתֵר מִכְּדֵי חֶסְרוֹנָן — דִּבְרֵי הַכֹּל: מוֹכְרָן בְּבֵית דִּין .... מֵיתִיבִי:

ברייתא: הַמַּפְקִיד פֵּירוֹת אֵצֶל חֲבֵירוֹ וְהִרְקִיבוּ; יַיִן וְהֶחְמִיץ; שֶׁמֶן וְהִבְאִישׁ; דְּבַשׁ וְהִדְבִּישׁ — הֲרֵי זֶה לֹא יִגַּע בָּהֶן, דִּבְרֵי ר' מֵאִיר; וַחֲכָמִים אוֹמְרִים: עוֹשֶׂה לָהֶן תַּקָּנָה וּמוֹכְרָן בְּבֵית דִּין ....

תלמוד: קָתָנֵי מִיהַת: "פֵּירוֹת ... וְהִרְקִיבוּ". מַאי? לָאו אֲפִילּוּ יוֹתֵר מִכְּדֵי חֶסְרוֹנָן?! (שם)

disagreement with the Hakhamim — not an explanation of their opinion)!

* An exceptional usage of this term introducing a *mishna* occurs in ברכות לז,ב. See Rashi's commentary there.

R. ... teaches שׁוֹנֶה ר' ... **תָּנֵי ר' ...***

This expression introduces an amora's presentation of a baraitha. Especially common are תָּנֵי ר' חִיָּיא as in ברכות לז, סע"ב and תָּנֵי רַב יוֹסֵף as in ברכות ח,ב.

* Baraithoth introduced in this manner are apparently not accorded the same authority as other baraithoth, for in some instances amoraim reject them.

תָּנֵי תַּנָּא קַמֵּיהּ דר' ... שׁוֹנֶה תַּנָּא לִפְנֵי ר' ...

A tanna recites [a baraitha] before R. ...

This formula introduces a baraitha that a tanna (= an expert at committing statements to memory) recited before the Rosh HaYeshiva. The latter proceeds to explain the baraitha, to object to it, to alter its wording, to supplement its teaching, to express agreement or disagreement with it, or to have his students comment upon it.

תָּנֵי תַּנָּא קַמֵּיהּ דר' יוֹחָנָן: כָּל הָעוֹסֵק בַּתּוֹרָה, וּבִגְמִילוּת חֲסָדִים, וְקוֹבֵר אֶת בָּנָיו — מוֹחֲלִין לוֹ עַל כָּל עֲוֹנוֹתָיו. אֲמַר לֵיהּ ר' יוֹחָנָן: בִּשְׁלָמָא תּוֹרָה וּגְמִילוּת חֲסָדִים, דִּכְתִיב ..., אֶלָּא קוֹבֵר אֶת בָּנָיו — מְנַיִן? (ברכות ה, סע"א-רע"ב)

A tanna recites [a baraitha] before R. Yohanan: Everyone who is involved in Torah [study], or in [acts of] loving-kindness, or who buries his children — their sins are forgiven. R. Yohanan said to him: [Regarding] Torah [study] and [acts of] loving-kindness it is correct, for it is written ..., but [regarding one] who buries his children — from where [is it derived]?

SEE: תַּנָּא

it is taught שְׁנוּיָה (תני) pass. prt. f. **תַּנְיָא**

This term usually introduces a baraitha* with the name of a tanna mentioned before the first statement.

תַּנְיָא:** אָמַר ר' יְהוּדָה: כָּךְ הָיָה מִנְהָגוֹ שֶׁל ר' עֲקִיבָא ... (ברכות לא,א)

[A baraitha] is taught: R. Y^ehuda said: Such was the custom of R. Akiva ...

* Occasionally, it introduces a mishna, as in פסחים יט,א.

** On the other hand, the baraitha quoted in the previous line of the Talmud is introduced by תָּנוּ רַבָּנַן, since it does not begin with the name of a tanna.

SEE: וְהָתַנְיָא

וְתַנְיָא אִידָךְ*

and another [baraitha] is taught שְׁנוּיָה אַחֶרֶת

* See תָּנוּ רַבָּנַן ... תַּנְיָא אִידָךְ and תָּנֵי חֲדָא ... וְתַנְיָא אִידָךְ. Note the difference between the two entries.

תַּנְיָא דִּמְסַיְּיעָא* לָךְ שְׁנוּיָה שֶׁמְּסַיַּיעַת לְךָ ...

[A baraitha] is taught that supports you ...

This expression introduces a baraitha that one

MISHNA: [If] one deposits fruit for safekeeping with his friend — even if it is spoiling — [the latter] must not touch it. Rabban Shim'on b. Gamliel says: He should sell it under the supervision of the court because he is like someone returning a lost article to the owner.

TALMUD: ... R. Yohanan said: ... [if it is spoiling at] more than the normal rate of spoilage, [according to] the opinion of everybody: He should sell it under the supervision of the court .... They raise an objection:

BARAITHA: [If] one deposits fruit for safekeeping with his friend, and it has become rotten; wine, and it soured; oil, and it became rancid; honey, and it turned rancid — [the latter] must not touch it, [according to] the opinion of R. Méir; but the Hakhamim say: He should remedy their [situation] and sell them under the supervision of the court ....

TALMUD: [The tanna] states at any rate: "Fruit ..., and it has become rotten." What [is the case]? Is it not referring to spoiling at] more than the normal rate of spoilage (thereby contradicting R. Yohanan's statement that there is no controversy in such a case)?!

SEE: מִיהָא, מִיהַת

וְתָנֵי עֲלַהּ ... וְשׁוֹנֶה עָלֶיהָ ...

and [the tanna of the following baraitha] states on it ...

This expression introduces a baraitha* that supplements the mishna or the baraitha that has just been quoted. The combination of the two texts is usually presented in order to point out a *difficulty*, a *contradiction*, or a *proof*.

אָמַר ר' יְהוֹשֻׁעַ בֶּן לֵוִי: כָּל מָקוֹם שֶׁאָמַר ר' יְהוּדָה "אֵימָתַי" בְּמִשְׁנָתֵנוּ, אֵינוֹ אֶלָּא לְפָרֵשׁ דִּבְרֵי חֲכָמִים ... וְ"אֵימָתַי" לְפָרֵשׁ הוּא?! וְהָא תְּנַן: וְאֵלּוּ הֵן הַפְּסוּלִים: הַמְשַׂחֵק בְּקוּבְיָא ... אָמַר ר' יְהוּדָה: אֵימָתַי? בִּזְמַן שֶׁאֵין לוֹ אוּמָנוּת אֶלָּא הִיא, אֲבָל יֵשׁ לוֹ אוּמָנוּת שֶׁלֹּא הִיא — הֲרֵי זֶה כָּשֵׁר. וְתָנֵי עֲלַהּ בְּבָרַיְיתָא: וַחֲכָמִים אוֹמְרִים: בֵּין שֶׁאֵין לוֹ אוּמָנוּת אֶלָּא הִיא וּבֵין שֶׁיֵּשׁ לוֹ אוּמָנוּת שֶׁלֹּא הִיא — הֲרֵי זֶה פָּסוּל! (עירובין פב, רע"א ע"פ משנה סנהדרין פ"ג מ"ג)

R. Y^ehoshua b. Levi said: Wherever R. Y^ehuda said "when [does this apply]" in our Mishna — it is only [meant] to explain the words of the Hakhamim [which were quoted previously — not to disagree with them]. But does [the expression] "when" [mean] to explain?! Behold we have learned [in a mishna]: And the following are disqualified [as witnesses]: The dice player ... R. Y^ehuda said: When? In a case where he has no other occupation except this (= dice-playing), but [if] he has another occupation besides this — he is fit. And [the tanna] in the [following] baraitha states on it (= the mishna): But the Hakhamim say: Whether he has no other occupation except for this or he has an occupation other than this he is disqualified (hence the Hakhamim and R. Y^ehuda differ and R. Y^ehuda's statement in the mishna expresses a

amora quotes in order to corroborate a statement of another amora. In some instances, the second amora rejects the proof.

For an example — see בבא מציעא לא, רע"א.

* The feminine participle מְסַיְּיעָא is the proper form, agreeing with the feminine תַּנְיָא, but the spelling מסייע occurs frequently — perhaps as an abbreviation.

SEE: מְסַיֵּיעַ

תַּנְיָא כְּוָותֵיהּ דְּר' ... שְׁנוּיָה כְּמוֹ ר' ...

[A baraitha] is taught like R. ...

This expression introduces a baraitha that corroborates a statement of an amora.

תַּנְיָא כְּוָותֵיהּ דְּר' יוֹחָנָן ... (בבא מציעא לד,א)

[A baraitha] is taught like R. Yoḥanan ...

SEE: כְּוָותֵיהּ דְּ-

תַּנְיָא נַמֵּי הָכִי אַף שְׁנוּיָה כָּךְ ...

[A baraitha] is also taught thus ...

This expression introduces a baraitha that corroborates a statement of an amora or a statement of the Talmud.

אָמַר אַבַּיֵי: ... לִקְרִיאַת שְׁמַע כְּוָתִיקִין, דְּאָמַר ר' יוֹחָנָן: וְתִיקִין הָיוּ גּוֹמְרִין אוֹתָהּ עִם הָנֵץ הַחַמָּה. תַּנְיָא נַמֵּי הָכִי: וְתִיקִין הָיוּ גּוֹמְרִין אוֹתָהּ עִם הָנֵץ הַחַמָּה ... (ברכות ט,ב)

Abbayé said: ... regarding the reading of the Sh'ma, [we follow the practice] of the pious, as R. Yoḥanan stated: The pious would complete it (= the Sh'ma) at sunrise. [A baraitha] is also taught thus: The pious would complete it at sunrise.

תְּנֵינָא (= תְּנֵי אֲנָא) שׁוֹנֶה אֲנִי I teach

This word is used to introduce a baraitha.

For an example — see שבת כג,ב ורש"י שם.

תְּנֵינָא (תני) 1st pers. pl. שָׁנִינוּ we have stated; we have learned; we have taught

SEE: תְּנַן

תְּנֵינָא חֲדָא זִימְנָא שָׁנִינוּ פַּעַם אַחַת ...!

We have (already) learned (this) once ...!

The verb תְּנֵינָא — with or without חֲדָא זִימְנָא — presents the *difficulty* that the halakha previously quoted is superfluous, since it has already been taught in the mishna or baraitha about to be quoted. In most instances, the Talmud responds that there is a new element in the halakha quoted that was not mentioned in the mishna or baraitha, and so it is not superfluous.

משנה: שְׁלשָׁה שֶׁאָכְלוּ כְּאַחַת אֵינָן רַשָּׁאִין לֵיחָלֵק ... (ברכות נ, סע"א: משנה פ"ז מ"ד)

תלמוד: מַאי קָא מַשְׁמַע לַן? תְּנֵינָא חֲדָא זִימְנָא: שְׁלשָׁה שֶׁאָכְלוּ כְּאַחַת חַיָּיבִין לְזַמֵּן! (שם ע"פ פ"ז מ"א)

MISHNA: Three [men] who ate together are not permitted to split up [to recite Birkath HaMazon individually] ...

TALMUD: What does it [come to] teach us? We have [already] learned [this] once [in a previous mishna]: Three [men] who ate together are obligated to recite Birkath HaZimmun (and to say Birkath HaMazon together)!

SEE: אַף אֲנַן נַמֵּי תְּנֵינָא

תְּנֵינָא לְהָא דְּתָנוּ רַבָּנַן

שָׁנִינוּ אֶת זוֹ שֶׁשָּׁנוּ חֲכָמִים.

We have [thus] stated [in the mishna] what the ḥakhamim have stated (in the baraitha that is about to be quoted).

This expression introduces a baraitha whose halakhic content is corroborated by the text of the mishna under discussion.*

משנה: כָּל מִצְוֹת הַבֵּן עַל הָאָב — אֲנָשִׁים חַיָּיבִין וְנָשִׁים פְּטוּרוֹת. (קידושין כט,א: משנה פ"א מ"ז)

תלמוד: תְּנֵינָא לְהָא דְּתָנוּ רַבָּנַן: הָאָב חַיָּיב בִּבְנוֹ לְמוּלוֹ, וְלִפְדּוֹתוֹ, וּלְלַמְּדוֹ תּוֹרָה, וּלְהַשִּׂיאוֹ אִשָּׁה, וּלְלַמְּדוֹ אוּמָנוּת; וְיֵשׁ אוֹמְרִים: אַף לְהַשִּׁיטוֹ בְּמַיִם. (שם)

MISHNA: All obligations toward a son [that are incumbent] upon a parent — men (= fathers) are obligated [to perform], and women (= mothers) are exempt [from them].

TALMUD: We have (thus) stated (in the mishna) what the ḥakhamim have stated (in the following baraitha): A father is obligated to circumcise his son, and to redeem him (if he is the first-born child), and to teach him Torah, and to marry him off, and to teach him a trade; and some say: to teach him how to swim, too.

* See Rashi's commentary on בבא קמא יד, רע"ב.

תְּנֵיתוּהָ שְׁנִיתֶם אוֹתָהּ you have learnt it

With this word, an amora (chiefly Rav Shesheth) introduces a mishna or a baraitha as comprising the *solution* to the problem that was posed to him.

בְּעוֹ מִינֵּיהּ מֵרַב שֵׁשֶׁת: מִנְיָן הָוֵי סִימָן אוֹ לָא הָוֵי סִימָן? אֲמַר לְהוּ רַב שֵׁשֶׁת: תְּנֵיתוּהָ: מָצָא כְּלִי כֶּסֶף ... הֲרֵי זֶה לֹא יַחֲזִיר עַד שֶׁיִּתֵּן אוֹת אוֹ עַד שֶׁיְּכַוֵּין מִשְׁקְלוֹתָיו ... וּמִדְּמִשְׁקָל הָוֵי סִימָן, מִדָּה וּמִנְיָן נַמֵּי הָוֵי סִימָן. (בבא מציעא כג, רע"ב)

They asked Rav Shesheth: Is number [considered] a mark of identification or not (for a person to return items that he found)? Rav Shesheth said to them: You have learnt it: [If] one found a vessel of silver ..., one should not return it unless [someone] identifies [it with] an identifying mark or states its weight accurately. And since weight is [considered] an identifying mark, size and number are also [considered] identifying marks.

תְּנַן (תני) 1st pers. pl. שָׁנִינוּ we have stated; we have learned; we have taught

(1) This term introduces a mishna* from the same chapter — usually the very mishna that the

Talmud is due to take up, the one reprinted in our editions at the head of the Talmudic discussion. A mishna is often quoted by the Talmud in order to raise a *difficulty* or to provide *proof* with regard to a point that was presented earlier in the discussion.

אִתְּמַר: שְׁנַיִם שֶׁאָכְלוּ כְּאַחַת — פְּלִיגִי רַב וְרִ׳ יוֹחָנָן. חַד אָמַר: אִם רָצוּ לְזַמֵּן, מְזַמְּנִין; וְחַד אָמַר: אִם רָצוּ לְזַמֵּן, אֵין מְזַמְּנִין. תְּנַן: שְׁלֹשָׁה שֶׁאָכְלוּ כְּאַחַת — חַיָּיבִין לְזַמֵּן. שְׁלֹשָׁה — אִין; שְׁנַיִם — לָא! (ברכות מה,א)

It was stated: [As for] two who ate together — Rav and R. Yoḥanan disagree. One says: If they wish to recite Birkath HaZimmun, they may recite Birkath HaZimmun; while the other says: If they wish to recite Birkath HaZimmun, they may not recite Birkath HaZimmun. We learned (in the mishna): Three who have eaten together are obligated to recite Birkath HaZimmun — three, yes; [but] two, no!

(2) תְּנַן is also used at the end of a clause — usually when the correct reading of the mishna or its interpretation is being clarified.

"אֵלּוּ" תְּנַן אוֹ "וְאֵלּוּ" תְּנַן? (שבת יג,ב)

Have we stated "these are" [in the mishna text], or have we stated "and these are"?

* Occasionally, תְּנַן introduces a baraitha – as in ברכות לו,א.

SEE: תְּנֵינָא, וְהָתְנַן, וְהָא אֲנַן תְּנַן, תְּנַן הָתָם

תְּנַן הָתָם שָׁנִינוּ שָׁם **we learned there**

This expression usually introduces a mishna from a different tractate (e.g., משנה פאה פ"ח מ"ז quoted in בבא בתרא ט,א)* or from a different chapter in the same tractate (e.g., משנה בבא מציעא פ"ח מ"ג quoted in בבא מציעא פ, סע"ב). Occasionally, it introduces a mishna from the same chapter (e.g., משנה פסחים א:ד quoted in פסחים ד,ב; see Rashi's comment there) or even a baraitha (e.g., קידושין מ, סע"א; see Tosefoth there). The text thus presented inaugurates a Talmudic discussion. In some instances, a contradiction is pointed out between that text and our mishna (e.g., בבא מציעא שם). In other instances, there is a discussion and explanation of that text, since it deals with an aspect of the topic the Talmud has been discussing (e.g., פסחים שם).

* תְּנַן הָתָם often introduces a mishna from a tractate that has no Babylonian Talmud.

וְתִסְבְּרָא/וְתִיסְבְּרָא* (= וְתִסְבְּרָה) fut. (סבר)
כְּלוּם אַתָּה סָבוּר כָּךְ?!

Do you (really) maintain it (= that opinion)?!

This word introduces a *difficulty* — usually with regard to the opinion of an amora.

אָמַר ר׳ יִרְמְיָה וְאִיתֵּימָא ר׳ חִיָּיא בַּר אַבָּא: מנצפ"ך צופים אֲמָרוּם. וְתִיסְבְּרָא?! וְהָכְתִיב: "אֵלֶּה הַמִּצְוֹת" — שֶׁאֵין הַנָּבִיא רַשַּׁאי לְחַדֵּשׁ דָּבָר מֵעַתָּה! (שבת קד, רע"א ע"פ ויקרא כז:לד)

R. Yirm^e^ya — and someone says R. Ḥiyya b. Abba — said: The prophets proclaimed מנצפ"ך *(= the distinct forms of those letters at the end of a word,* ם נ צ ף ך*). Do you (really) maintain it (= that it was the prophets who originated them)?! But is it not written: "These are the mitzvoth" — [teaching] that a prophet is not permitted to originate anything from now on!***

* This final א־ָ is a personal-pronoun suffix that is equivalent to final ה־ָ.

** The proper form of the letters is of halakhic significance in such mitzvoth as t^e^fillin and m^e^zusa.

SEE: סְבַר, (וְ)אַתְּ לָא תִּסְבְּרָא

תִּסְתַּיֵּים fut. (סים אִתְפָּעַל)

תִּתְבָּרֵר* **let it be settled; let it be clarified**

Sometimes a controversy is presented between two amoraim without any indication as to which of the two amoraim held which opinion. In order to fill this gap in the tradition, the Talmud examines other statements about the issue in dispute that may indicate which amora said what.**

פְּלִיגִי בַּהּ אֲבוּהּ דְּרַב אוֹשַׁעְיָא וּבַר קַפָּרָא — חַד אָמַר: אֵין מִתְאַחִין, וְחַד אָמַר: מִתְאַחִין. תִּסְתַּיֵּים דַּאֲבוּהּ דְּרַב אוֹשַׁעְיָא דְּאָמַר: אֵין מִתְאַחִין, דְּאָמַר רַב אוֹשַׁעְיָא: אֵין מִתְאַחִין. מִמַּאן שְׁמִיעַ לֵיהּ? לָאו מֵאֲבוּהּ?! (מועד קטן כד, סע"א)

The father of Rav Oshaya and Bar Kappara disagreed about it — one said: [One's garments that were torn because of mourning] may not be sewed up, while the other said: They may be sewed up. Let it be settled that Rav Oshaya's father is [the one] who said: They may not be sewed up, for Rav Oshaya said: They may not be sewed up. From whom did he hear it? Was it not from his father?!

* See Rashi on מגילה כז, רע"א.

** In some instances where the identification thus determined is conclusive, the term תִּסְתַּיֵּים is repeated after the evidence is cited, as in ברכות מה,ב.

SEE: חַד אָמַר ... וְחַד אָמַר ..., סַיֵּים

תָּפֵל* **without salt; tasteless**

בָּשָׂר — בֵּין תָּפֵל בֵּין מָלִיחַ מוּתָּר לְטַלְטְלוֹ. (שבת קכח, סע"א)

[As for] meat — it is permitted to handle it (on the Sabbath) whether it be without salt or salted.

* This adjective is occasionally used in Biblical Hebrew, e.g., in הֲיֵאָכֵל תָּפֵל מִבְּלִי מֶלַח? (איוב ו:ו).

SEE: טָפֵל

תִּפְשׁוֹט (פשט) fut. 2nd pers. s. תִּפְשֹׁט

you may solve; you may settle (a halakhic problem)

For an example — see בבא קמא יז, סע"ב.

SEE: פְּשַׁט

תַּקֵּין (תקן: מְתַקֵּין act. prt., מְתַקַּן pass. prt., לִיתַקֵּין fut.)

he established; תִּקֵּן; הִתְקִין
he instituted (a Rabbinic enactment)

כָּל דְּתַקּוּן רַבָּנַן, כְּעֵין דְּאוֹרָיְיתָא תַּקּוּן. (פסחים ל,ב ושי"נ)

Whatever the ḥakhamim have instituted, they have

instituted [with strictness] similar to Torah law.
SEE: אַתְקֵין

תְּקֵיף (תקף: תְּקֵיף prt.)

(1) נִתְחַזֵּק it was strong; it was heavy; it became severe
כִּי תְּקֵיף גְּזֵירְתָא (שבת לג,ב)
when the decree became severe

(2) תָּקַף it overpowered; he seized
תְּקֵיף לְהוּ יִצְרָא דַעֲבֵירָה (עבודה זרה סט, סע״ב)
the passion for (sexual) immorality would overpower them

(3) הֶחֱמִיץ it turned into vinegar; it became sour
תְּקֵיף הַהוּא חַמְרָא. (ב״מ קו,ב) *That wine became sour.*
SEE: מַתְקֵיף

תַּקִּיף חָזָק; קָשֶׁה strong; tough
וְאִי אֱינִישׁ תַּקִּיפָא הוּא דְּלָא יָהֵיב מַתָּנָה ... (ב״מ סד, רע״א)
But if he is a tough guy who does not give presents ...

תְּקַל* (תקל: תָּקֵיל act. prt., תְּקִיל pass. prt.)

he weighed שָׁקַל
זִיל, שְׁלִים לַהּ טָבִין וּתְקִילִין! (בבא מציעא מד,ב)
Go (and) pay her current and [full-]weight (coins)!

* This verb can be found in דניאל ה:כז, which is quoted in סנהדרין כב,א: תְּקֵל תְּקַלְתָּא בְמֹאזַנְיָא. The Aramaic nouns מַתְקָל, *weight*, and תִּיקְלָא, *shekel*, also occur in the Talmud.

SEE: שָׁקַל

תַּקָּנָה; תַּקַּנְתָּא*

(1) a remedy; welfare
מִפְּנֵי תַקָּנַת הַשְּׁבוּיִין (גיטין מה,א: משנה פ״ד מ״ו)
because of the welfare of the captives
לֵית לֵיהּ תַּקַּנְתָּא (יומא כז, סע״ב) *it has no remedy*

(2) an enactment; Rabbinic legislation
וְתַקַּנְתָּא לְתַקַּנְתָּא לָא עָבְדִינַן (בבא מציעא ה, רע״ב)
and we do not make [one] enactment to [protect another] enactment

* The first form is Hebrew, and the second is Aramaic.

SEE: מַאי תַּקַּנְתֵּיהּ

תַּרְגֵּם (רגם תַּפְעֵל: מְתַרְגֵּם prt.)

(1) תִּרְגֵּם (מֵעִבְרִית לַאֲרָמִית)
he translated (from Hebrew into Aramaic)
״יוֹם תְּרוּעָה יִהְיֶה לָכֶם״ — וּמְתַרְגְּמִינַן: ״יוֹם יַבָּבָא יְהֵא לְכוֹן״ (ראש השנה לג,ב ע״פ במדבר כט:א ות״א שם)
"a day of תְּרוּעָה it must be for you" — and we translate (into Aramaic): "a day of יַבָּבָא (= blowing) it must be for you"

(2) פֵּרֵשׁ he explained; he interpreted
In this sense, this verb usually refers to an amora's *resolution* of a difficulty, achieved by reinterpreting a mishna or a baraitha.

תַּרְגְּמָהּ רַב פָּפָּא בִּלְסְטִיס מְזוּיָין. (ב״מ כב, רע״א ע״פ כת״י)
Rav Pappa interpreted it (= the word גַּנָּב in the baraitha) as "an armed robber."
SEE: הָכָא תַרְגִּימוּ, תּוּרְגְּמָן

תַּרְגְּמַהּ ר׳ ... אַלִּיבָּא דְּר׳ ...
ר׳ ... פֵּרֵשׁ אוֹתָהּ לְפִי דַעְתּוֹ שֶׁל ר׳ ...

R. ... interpreted it in accordance with the opinion of R. ...

This formula presents one amora's *resolution* of a difficulty with regard to the opinion of that amora's opponent or his teacher's opponent. Even though intellectual honesty moves him to defend his opponent's point of view, nevertheless he really disagrees with him and maintains that his own opinion is the halakha.*
תַּרְגְּמַהּ רָבָא אַלִּיבָּא דְאַבַּיֵי. (סוכה יט, רע״א ורש״י שם)
Rava interpreted it in accordance with the opinion of Abbayé.

* See שבת נב, סע״ב for a list of Talmudic passages with this expression.

תַּרְוַיְיהוּ

the two of them; both of them שְׁנֵיהֶם
תַּרְוַיְיהוּ מִן הַמִּקְרָא הַזֶּה (סנהדרין צ,ב)
both [points are deduced] from the following passage
SEE: (ד)אָמְרִי תַּרְוַיְיהוּ, תְּרֵי

תְּרֵי/תְּרֵין שְׁנַיִם two

This number is sometimes used with personal-pronoun suffixes:

the two of us; both of us — תַּרְוַיְינַן שְׁנֵינוּ
the two of you; both of you — תַּרְוַיְיכוּ שְׁנֵיכֶם
the two of them; both of them — תַּרְוַיְיהוּ שְׁנֵיהֶם

SEE: בֵּי תְּרֵי, תַּרְוַיְיהוּ

תְּרֵי גַוְונֵי

There are two types of ... שְׁנֵי מִינֵי ...

In order to explain away a contradiction or a redundancy, the Talmud sometimes proposes that the same term refers to two different cases.
וּתְרֵי גַוְונֵי קָטָן: ... קָטָן שֶׁלֹּא הִגִּיעַ לְחִינּוּךְ ... קָטָן שֶׁהִגִּיעַ לְחִינּוּךְ ... (ברכות טו, רע״ב; מגילה יט,ב)
*and there are two types of minors: ... a minor who has not reached the age of education (who is not fit to perform the mitzva of reading the scroll of Esther, and) ... a minor who has reached the age of education (who is fit to read it according to R. Y*huda).*

תְּרֵי תַנָּאֵי אַלִּיבָּא* דְּר׳ ...
שְׁנֵי תַנָּאִים [חֲלוּקִים] לְדַעַת ר׳ ...

[The statements] are [made by] two [different] tannaim, [who disagree] about the opinion of R. ... (an earlier tanna).

A *resolution* of a difficulty: After the statement of a tanna in one mishna or baraitha is quoted as contradicting another statement of the same tanna in another mishna or baraitha, the Talmud sometimes replies that the contradiction presents no real difficulty, because two different tannaim who are disciples of that tanna have issued two different reports of their master's statement.**

משנה: מֵאֵימָתַי קוֹרִין אֶת שְׁמַע בְּעַרְבִית? מִשָּׁעָה שֶׁהַכֹּהֲנִים נִכְנָסִים לֶאֱכוֹל בִּתְרוּמָתָן ... דִּבְרֵי ר' אֱלִיעֶזֶר. (ברכות ב, רע"א: משנה פ"א מ"א)

ברייתא: ... מִשָּׁעָה שֶׁקִּדֵּשׁ הַיּוֹם בְּעַרְבֵי שַׁבָּתוֹת — דִּבְרֵי ר' אֱלִיעֶזֶר. (שם ב,ב)

תלמוד: קַשְׁיָא דר' אֱלִיעֶזֶר אַדר' אֱלִיעֶזֶר! תְּרֵי תַנָּאֵי אַלִּיבָּא דר' אֱלִיעֶזֶר. (שם ג, רע"א)

MISHNA: From when do we read the Sh^ema in the evening? From the time the kohanim [who have purified themselves] enter to eat the t^eruma ... [this is] the opinion of R. Eliezer.

BARAITHA: ... From the time the day is sanctified on Sabbath eve — [this is] the opinion of R. Eliezer.

TALMUD: [This statement of] R. Eliezer is contradictory to [the other statement] of R. Eliezer! [The statements] are [made by] two [different] tannaim [who disagree] about the opinion of R. Eliezer.

* In some instances: וְאַלִּיבָּא, *and [they disagree] about the opinion of.*

** The different reports may have developed because their teacher had actually changed his mind and presented a new statement that one of the two disciples did not hear. See, for example, the controversy between Rav and Levi with regard to Rebbi's opinion in ביצה כד,ב.

SEE: אָמוֹרָאֵי נִינְהוּ וְאַלִּיבָּא דר' יוֹחָנָן

תְּרֵיסַר שְׁנֵים עָשָׂר* **twelve**

* This word is used in Modern Hebrew to mean *a dozen.*

תָּרֵיץ (תרץ פַּעֵל: prt. מְתָרֵץ, imp. תָּרֵיץ, inf. לְתָרוֹצֵי)

(1) תֵּרֵץ; יִשֵּׁב; תִּקֵּן **he resolved (a difficulty); he explained (a difficult text); he corrected (a difficult text)**

תָּרֵצְתְּ קוֹשֵׁר, מַתִּיר — מַאי אִיכָּא לְמֵימַר? (שבת עד, סע"ב)

You have explained [the source in the construction of the Tabernacle for] tying [a knot], (but) what can be said [about a source for] untying [a knot]?

וְלָאו תָּרוֹצֵי קָא מְתָרְצַתְּ לַהּ?! תָּרֵיץ הָכִי! (ב"מ קטו, רע"א)

But aren't you (already) correcting it (= the text of the baraitha)?! (Then) correct [it] this way!

(2) יִשֵּׁר; זָקַף **he staightened; he stood erect**

מְתָרֵץ תָּרוֹצֵי וְיָתֵיב וּמִשְׁתַּעֵי בַּהֲדֵיהּ!

he would certainly [have to] straighten [himself] and sit up in order to talk with him!

SEE: תֵּירוּצָא

תָּרֵיץ וְאֵימָא* הָכִי תָּרֵץ וֶאֱמוֹר כָּךְ!

Resolve (the difficulty) and say thus!

This expression introduces the *resolution* of a textual difficulty that is achieved either by correcting the text (as in the example below) or by limiting the scope of the case.

ר' שִׁמְעוֹן (אוֹמֵר: אֵינוֹ חַיָּיב) עַד שֶׁיִּכְתּוֹב אֶת הַשֵּׁם כּוּלּוֹ. וּמִי מָצֵית אָמְרַתְּ הָכִי?! וְהָתַנְיָא: ר' שִׁמְעוֹן אוֹמֵר: "וְעָשָׂה אַחַת" — יָכוֹל עַד שֶׁיִּכְתּוֹב אֶת הַשֵּׁם כּוּלּוֹ? תַּלְמוּד לוֹמַר: "מֵאַחַת". תָּרֵיץ וְאֵימָא הָכִי: יָכוֹל עַד שֶׁיִּכְתּוֹב אֶת הַפָּסוּק כּוּלּוֹ? תַּלְמוּד לוֹמַר "מֵאַחַת". (שבת קג,ב ע"פ ויקרא ד:ב)

R. Shim'on [says: One is not guilty of desecrating the Sabbath by writing] unless he writes the whole word. But can you (really) say so?! Has it not been taught (in a baraitha): R. Shim'on says: "And he shall do one" — you might [think that he is not guilty] unless he writes the whole word? Scripture teaches: "[Part] of one" (even if it does not comprise a complete word). Resolve (the difficulty) and say thus: You might [think that he is not guilty] unless he writes the whole pasuk? Scripture teaches: "[Part] of one" (not a whole pasuk, but a word).

* In some instances, תָּרֵיץ הָכִי occurs without the word וְאֵימָא.

תַּרְעָא (constr. תְּרַע)

(1) שַׁעַר **gate**

וְתַרְעָא לְדָרְתָּא עָבֵיד (שבת לא, רע"ב)

and he makes a gate for a courtyard

(2) שַׁעַר; מְחִיר **price; the market value**

אַפְקוּעֵי תַּרְעָא (בבא בתרא צ,א) *raising the price*

תַּרְעוֹמֶת **complaint; resentment; argument**

נְתָנוֹ לְבֶן לֵוִי אַחֵר — אֵין לוֹ עָלָיו אֶלָּא תַּרְעוֹמֶת. (ב"מ סט,א)

[If] he gave it (= a tithe that had been promised to one levite) to another levite — he (= the first levite) only has [cause] for a complaint against him (but he has no legal recourse for this breach of promise).

תַּרְתֵּי/תַּרְתֵּין f. שְׁתַּיִם **two**

תַּרְתֵּי שְׁתַּיִם?! **Two?! Both?!**

This *rhetorical question* indicates that two elements in the halakhic statements just quoted are paradoxical (as in the example below) or redundant (as in תַּרְתֵּי לָמָּה לִי, the next entry).

כּוֹפִין וּמְבַקְשִׁין — תַּרְתֵּי?! (קידושין סה,א)

They (= the judges) compel [him to grant his wife a divorce] and they request him [to do so]. Both?! (How can granting a divorce be both mandatory and voluntary?!)

תַּרְתֵּי לָמָּה לִי

Why do I [need] two? **לָמָּה לִי שְׁתַּיִם?**

This question poses the following *difficulty*: Why are there two separate halakhoth — when one may be logically inferred from the other?

משנה: וְכָל הַמִּתְחַיֵּיב בְּנַפְשׁוֹ אֵין מְשַׁלֵּם מָמוֹן, שֶׁנֶּאֱמַר: "וְאִם לֹא יִהְיֶה אָסוֹן, עָנוֹשׁ יֵעָנֵשׁ". (כתובות לו,ב: משנה פ"ג מ"ב ע"פ שמות כא:כב)

תלמוד: "כְּדֵי רִשְׁעָתוֹ" — מִשּׁוּם רִשְׁעָה אַחַת אַתָּה מְחַיְּיבוֹ, וְאִי אַתָּה מְחַיְּיבוֹ מִשּׁוּם שְׁתֵּי רִשְׁעִיּוֹת ... תַּרְתֵּי לָמָּה לִי? (שם לז, סע"א ע"פ דברים כה:ב)

MISHNA: But anyone who is convicted of the death penalty does not have to pay money (for his crime), as it was stated: "And if there be no death, he must certainly be punished" (to pay damages — implying that if a death did occur because of his action, he is exempt from paying damages).

TALMUD: "According to his evil" — on account of one evil you require him to be punished (for one act), but you do not require him to be punished on account of two evils (involved in the same act) ... Why do I need two (derivations of the same principle)?

SEE: הָא תּוּ לָמָּה לִי

תַּרְתֵּי מַשְׁמַע

(1) לְ... שְׁתֵּי מַשְׁמָעֻיּוֹת שׁוֹנוֹת.

[The word] ... has two different meanings.

"דָּמִים" תַּרְתֵּי מַשְׁמַע.* (מגילה יד, רע"ב ורש"י שם)

[The word] "blood" has two different meanings (menstrual blood, and the spilling of blood = murder).

(2) ... פֵּירוּשׁוֹ שְׁתַּיִם.

[The use of a noun in the plural] indicates [a minimum of] two.

"בַּסּוּכּוֹת" תַּרְתֵּי מַשְׁמַע. (סוכות ט,ב)

[The word] "in-the-sukkoth" indicates [a minimum of] two [walls for a sukka].

* See the note on the entry דָּמִים.

תַּרְתֵּי סְרֵי f.

twelve שְׁתֵּים עֶשְׂרֵה

תְּשׁוּבָה

return; repentance; reply

For an example — see בַּעַל תְּשׁוּבָה.

תַּתָּא/תַּתָּאֵי

below; down לְמַטָּה

דְּסָלְקִין לְעֵילָּא וּדְנָחְתִין לְתַתָּא (בבא קמא קיג, סע"ב)

those that go up (to Eretz Yisrael) and those who go down (to Babylonia)

SEE: תּוֹתֵי

תַּתָּאָה (pl. תַּתָּאֵי)

lower; lowest; the bottom תַּחְתּוֹן

רְוִיחָא תַּתָּאָה וּמְצִיעָא עִילָּוֵיהּ ... (בבא מציעא כה, סע"א)

The broadest [coin] is the lowest, and the medium-sized one is on top of it ...

SEE: תּוֹתֵי

APPENDIX I

Abbreviations and Acronyms

ACRONYMS (ראשי תיבות) IN THE TALMUD

The following section contains a comprehensive list of the Hebrew and Aramaic *acronyms* (= רָאשֵׁי תֵיבוֹת) that appear in the standard editions of the Babylonian Talmud. Each acronym represents two or more words and has a double apostrophe *before* its last letter (e.g., א״א = אִי אֶפְשָׁר). Some common *abbreviations* of individual words are also presented with a single apostrophe *after* the last letter (e.g., א׳ = אֶחָד). In addition, the names of Hebrew/Aramaic letters that are spelled out in the Talmud with a double apostrophe like acronyms (e.g., אל״ף = the letter *alef*) are included, since they might be mistaken for acronyms. Each item is resolved into its Hebrew or Aramaic component parts in the middle column, and an English translation is presented in the left-hand column.

א

NOTE: **Sometimes the letter א at the beginning of an item is *not* an initial representing a separate word (as in א״א = אִי אֶפְשָׁר) but the Aramaic *prefix* -אַ (= Hebrew עַל) meaning *on, with reference to,* etc., (as in the acronym אדר״א = אַדְּרַבִּי אֱלִיעֶזֶר).**

English	Hebrew/Aramaic	Acronym
one	אֶחָד/אַחַת	**א׳**
[1] [it is] impossible	אִי אֶפְשָׁר	**א״א[1]**
[2] if you say	אִי אָמְרַתְּ	**א״א[2]**
if you say ... it is well	אִי אָמְרַתְּ בִּשְׁלָמָא ...	**אא״ב**
unless	אֶלָּא אִם כֵּן	**אא״כ**
[1] (the letters) *alef* [and] *beth*	(האותיות) "א", "ב"	**א״ב[1]**
[2] there is [the following difference] between them	אִיכָּא בֵּינַיְיהוּ	**א״ב[2]**
if you want, say!	אִיבָּעֵית, אֵימָא!	**אב״א**
(the letters) *alef, beth,* [and] *gimmel*	(האותיות) "א", "ב", "ג"	**אב״ג**
if you want, say!	אִי בָּעֵית, אֵימָא!	**אבע״א**
[1] there are [some] who say	אִיכָּא דְּאָמְרִי	**א״ד[1]**
[2] or perhaps	אוֹ דִּילְמָא	**א״ד[2]**
on that [statement] of R. ...[a]	אַדְּרַבִּי ...	**אדר׳**
on that [statement] of R. Eliezer	אַדְּרַבִּי אֱלִיעֶזֶר	**אדר״א**
on that [statement] of Rabban Gamliel	אַדְּרַבָּן גַּמְלִיאֵל	**אדר״ג**
on that [statement] about Rosh Ḥodesh (= the first of the month)	אַדְּרֹאשׁ חוֹדֶשׁ	**אדר״ח**
on that [statement] of Resh Lakish	אַדְּרֵישׁ לָקִישׁ	**אדר״ל**
on that [statement] of R. Méir	אַדְּרַבִּי מֵאִיר	**אדר״מ**
on that [statement] of R./Rabban Shim′on	אַדְּרַבִּי/אַדְּרַבָּן שִׁמְעוֹן	**אדר״ש**
on that [statement] of Rabban Shim′on son of Gamliel	אַדְּרַבָּן שִׁמְעוֹן בֶּן גַּמְלִיאֵל	**אדרשב״ג**
if so	אִי הָכִי	**א״ה**
Yes, [it is] indeed so!	אִין, הָכִי נַמֵי!	**אה״נ**
the nations of the world	אוּמּוֹת הָעוֹלָם	**או״ה**
the nations of the world	אוּמּוֹת הָעוֹלָם	**אוה״ע**
says	אוֹמֵר	**אומ׳**
afterwards	אַחַר כָּךְ	**אח״כ**
(the letters) *alef, ḥeth,* [and] *samekh*	(האותיות) "א", "ח", "ס"	**אח״ס**
Erets Yisrael	אֶרֶץ יִשְׂרָאֵל	**א״י**
if you want, say!	אִי בָּעֵית, אֵימָא!	**איבע״א**

---

[a] **Among Ashkenazic Jews, רבי is usually pronounced רַבִּי when it appears as a title followed by a proper name, e.g., רַבִּי מֵאִיר, רַבִּי יְהוּדָה. We have rendered this usage as "R." in English. When רבי refers to R. Y^e^huda HaNasi, the compiler of the Mishna, it is usually pronounced רֶבִּי, which we have transliterated as "Rebbi." On the other hand, Sephardic Jews usually pronounce this word רַבִּי in both cases. We have vocalized according to the Ashkenazic tradition.**

there is/are	אִיכָּא	איכ'
if so	אִם כֵּן/כָּךְ	א"כ
on everybody	אַכּוּלֵּי עָלְמָא	אכ"ע
[1] he said to him	אֲמַר לוֹ; אֲמַר לֵיהּ	א"ל[1]
[2] (the letters) *alef* [and] *lamed*	(האותיות) "א", "ל"	א"ל[2]
(the letter) *alef*	(האות) "א"	אל"ף
"our God, King of the universe"[b]	"אֱלוֹקֵינוּ, מֶלֶךְ הָעוֹלָם"	אמ"ה
we say	אָמְרִינַן	אמרי'
on/against our mishna	אַמַּתְנִיתִין	אמתני'
or else	אִי נַמִּי	א"נ
even though	אַף עַל גַּב	אע"ג
on idolatry	אַעֲבוֹדָה זָרָה	אע"ז
even though	אַף עַל פִּי	אע"פ
even though	אַף עַל פִּי	אעפ"י
in spite of that; nevertheless	אַף עַל פִּי כֵן	אעפ"כ
even so	אֲפִילּוּ הָכִי	אפ"ה
even	אֲפִילּוּ	אפי'
he/she does not need; there is no need	אֵינוֹ צָרִיךְ; אֵינָהּ צְרִיכָה; אֵין צוֹרֶךְ	א"צ
there is no need to say	אֵין צוֹרֶךְ לוֹמַר	אצ"ל
the pasuk states	אָמַר קְרָא	א"ק
"Who has sanctified us with His mitzvoth and commanded us"[b]	"אֲשֶׁר קִדְּשָׁנוּ בְּמִצְוֹתָיו וְצִוָּנוּ"	אקב"ו
R. .../Rebbi/Rav ... said*	אָמַר רַבִּי .../רַבִּי/רַב ...	א"ר
R. Eliezer/El'azar said	אָמַר רַבִּי אֱלִיעֶזֶר/אֶלְעָזָר	אר"א
Rabba grandson of Ḥanna said	אָמַר רַבָּה בַּר בַּר חָנָה	ארבב"ח
Rabban Gamliel said	אָמַר רַבָּן גַּמְלִיאֵל	אר"ג
R. Y^{e}huda/Yosé/Yoḥanan/Y^{e}hoshua said	אָמַר רַבִּי יְהוּדָה/יוֹסֵי/יוֹחָנָן/יְהוֹשֻׁעַ	אר"י
R. Y^{e}hoshua son of Levi said	אָמַר רַבִּי יְהוֹשֻׁעַ בֶּן לֵוִי	אריב"ל
Resh Lakish said	אָמַר רֵישׁ לָקִישׁ	אר"ל
Rav Naḥman said	אָמַר רַב נַחְמָן	אר"נ
R. Akiva said	אָמַר רַבִּי עֲקִיבָא	אר"ע
Rav Pappa said	אָמַר רַב פָּפָּא	אר"פ
R. Shim'on said	אָמַר רַבִּי שִׁמְעוֹן	אר"ש
Rabban Shim'on son of Gamliel said	אָמַר רַבָּן שִׁמְעוֹן בֶּן גַּמְלִיאֵל	ארשב"ג
R. Shim'on son of Lakish said	אָמַר רַבִּי שִׁמְעוֹן בֶּן לָקִישׁ	ארשב"ל
[1] if you would say	אִם תֹּאמַר	א"ת[1]
[2] (the letters) *alef* [and] *tav*	(האותיות) "א", "ת"	א"ת[2]
if (upon examining the issue) you conclude and say	אִם תִּמְצָא לוֹמַר	את"ל

ב

NOTE: Sometimes the letter ב at the beginning of an item is *not* an initial representing a separate word (as in ב"ד = בֵּית דִּין) but the *prefix* -ב meaning *in, by,* or *with* (as in בא"י = בְּאֶרֶץ יִשְׂרָאֵל).

two	שְׁנַיִם/שְׁתַּיִם	ב'
people; the son of El'azar	בְּנֵי אָדָם; בֶּן אֶלְעָזָר	ב"א
in (combinations of pairs of letters whose numerical value add up to ten, like) *alef* [and] *teth; beth* [and] *ḥeth*	בְּ(אותיות) "א", "ט"; "ב", "ח"	באטב"ח

---

[b] These words comprise part of the text of a *b^{e}rakha.*

* See note a

[1] in Erets Yisrael	בְּאֶרֶץ יִשְׂרָאֵל	בא"י[1]
[2] "Blessed are You, O God"*	"בָּרוּךְ אַתָּה, הַשֵּׁם"	בא"י[2]
with (the letter) *alef*	בְּ(אות) "א"	באל"ף
with (the letters) *alef, beth;* alphabetically	בְּ(אותיות) "א", "ב"	באל"ף בי"ת
with (the letter) beth	בְּ(אות) "ב"	בב'
in court	בְּבֵית דִּין	בב"ד
in the synagogue	בְּבֵית הַכְּנֶסֶת	בבהכ"נ
in the beth midrash	בְּבֵית הַמִּדְרָשׁ	בבהמ"ד
in the cemetery	בְּבֵית הַקְּבָרוֹת	בבה"ק
[1] grandson of Ḥanna	בַּר בַּר חַנָּה	בב"ח[1]
[2] with [regard to] a creditor	בְּבַעַל חוֹב	בב"ח[2]
in the synagogue	בְּבֵית הַכְּנֶסֶת	בביהכ"נ
on/with three	בְּ(מספר) 3	בג'
son of Gamliel	בֶּן גַּמְלִיאֵל	ב"ג
with regard to (the letter) *gimmel*	בְּ(אות) "ג"	בגימ"ל
with a *g^ezera-shava* [analogy]	בִּגְזֵרָה שָׁוָה	בגז"ש
with a *g^ezera-shava* [analogy]	בִּגְזֵרָה שָׁוָה	בג"ש
court	בֵּית דִּין	ב"ד
on/with four	בְּ(מספר) 4	בד'
To what [circumstances] do the words [apply]?	בַּמֶּה דְּבָרִים אֲמוּרִים?	בד"א
with regard to [the halakha] of Rebbi**	בִּדְרֶבִּי	בדר'
regarding [the statement] of R. Ḥiyya/Ḥanina	בִּדְרַבִּי חִיָּיא/חֲנִינָא	בדר"ח
with regard to [the statement] of R. Yosé	בִּדְרַבִּי יוֹסִי	בדר"י
in/with (regard to) words of Torah (learning)	בְּדִבְרֵי תוֹרָה	בד"ת
[1] synagogue	בֵּית הַכְּנֶסֶת	ב"ה[1]
[2] Beth (= the school of) Hillel	בֵּית הִלֵּל	ב"ה[2]
[3] Blessed Be He	בָּרוּךְ הוּא	ב"ה[3]
[1] with (regard to) God	בַּשֵּׁם	בה'[1]
[2] on/with five	בְּ(מספר) 5	בה'[2]
Beth (= the school of) Hillel says	בֵּית הִלֵּל אוֹמְרִים	בה"א
Monday, Thursday, and Monday	(ימי) שֵׁנִי, חֲמִישִׁי, וְשֵׁנִי	בה"ב
in/with (the letter) *hé*	בְּ(אות) "ה"	בה"י
synagogue	בֵּית הַכְּנֶסֶת	בהכ"נ
lavatory	בֵּית הַכִּסֵּא	בהכ"ס
beth midrash	בֵּית הַמִּדְרָשׁ	בהמ"ד
Birkath HaMazon (= Grace after Meals)	בִּרְכַּת הַמָּזוֹן	בהמ"ז
the Holy Temple	בֵּית הַמִּקְדָּשׁ	בהמ"ק
with (regard to) the Holy One Blessed Be He	בְּהַקָּדוֹשׁ בָּרוּךְ הוּא	בהקב"ה
flesh and blood	בָּשָׂר וָדָם	ב"ו
on/with six	בְּ(מספר) 6	בו'
son of Zakkai	בֶּן זַכַּאי	ב"ז
on/with seven	בְּ(מספר) 7	בז'
nowadays	בִּזְמַן הַזֶּה	בזה"ז
[1] creditor	בַּעַל חוֹב	ב"ח[1]
[2] animals	בַּעֲלֵי חַיִּים	ב"ח[2]
on/with eight	בְּ(מספר) 8	בח'
in [a place] outside of Erets Yisrael	בְּחוּצָה לָאָרֶץ	בחו"ל

* See note b

** See note a

בחוש״מ	בְּחוּלּוֹ שֶׁל מוֹעֵד	on the intermediate days of a festival
בחי״ת	בְּ(אות) ״ח״	in (the letter) *heth*
בח״ל	בְּחוּצָה לָאָרֶץ	in [a place] outside of Erets Yisrael
בט׳	בְּ(מספר) 9	on/with nine
בט״ו	בְּ(מספר) 15	on/with fifteen
בט״ז	בְּ(מספר) 16	on/with sixteen
בט״ע	בְּ(אותיות) ״ט״, ״ע״	in (the letters) *teth* [and] *ayin*
ב״י[1]	בֶּן יוֹסֵי	[1] the son of Yosé
ב״י[2]	בְּ(מספר) 10	[2] on/with ten
בי׳	בֵּיהּ	with/in him; with/in it (m.)
בי״א	בְּ(מספר) 11	on/with eleven
בי״ב	בְּ(מספר) 12	on/with twelve
בי״ג	בְּ(מספר) 13	on/with thirteen
בי״ד	בְּ(מספר) 14	on/with fourteen
ביה״כ	בְּיוֹם הַכִּפּוּרִים	on Yom Kippur
ביה״ש	בֵּין הַשְּׁמָשׁוֹת	during twilight
ביו״ד	בְּ(אות) ״י״	in/with (the letter) *yod*
ביוה״כ	בְּיוֹם הַכִּפּוּרִים	on Yom Kippur
ביו״ט	בְּיוֹם טוֹב	on a festival
בי״ז	בְּ(מספר) 17	on/with seventeen
בי״ח	בְּ(מספר) 18	on/with eighteen
בי״ט[1]	בְּיוֹם טוֹב	[1] on a festival
בי״ט[2]	בְּ(מספר) 19	[2] on/with nineteen
ביי׳/בי״י	בַּשֵּׁם	with (regard to) God
ביע״ל קג״ם	בְּ(הלכות) ״יֵאוּשׁ שֶׁלֹּא מִדַּעַת״, ״עֵד זוֹמֵם״, ״לְחִי הָעוֹמֵד מֵאֵלָיו״, ״קִדּוּשִׁין שֶׁלֹּא נִמְסְרוּ לְבִיאָה״, גִּלּוּי דַּעְתָּא בְּגִיטָּא״, ״מוּמָר אוֹכֵל נְבֵילוֹת לְהַכְעִיס״	(the names of six halakhoth in which Abbayé's opinion is accepted against Rava's)
בי״ת	(האות) ״ב״	(the letter) *beth*
בכ״א	בְּ(מספר) 21	on/with twenty-one
בכ״ג[1]	בְּכֹהֵן גָּדוֹל	[1] with regard to the high priest
בכ״ג[2]	בְּ(מספר) 23	[2] on/with twenty-three
בכ״ד	בְּ(מספר) 24	on/with twenty-four
בכ״ה	בְּ(מספר) 25	on/with twenty-five
בכ״ט	בְּ(מספר) 29	on/with twenty-nine
בכ״מ	בְּכָל מָקוֹם	in every place; wherever
ב״ל	בֶּן לֵוִי/לָקִישׁ	son of Levi/Lakish
בל׳	בְּ(מספר) 30	on/with thirty
בלה״ק	בִּלְשׁוֹן הַקֹּדֶשׁ	in the holy tongue (= Hebrew)
בל״ו	בְּ(מספר) 36	on/with thirty-six
בלמ״ד	בְּ(אות) ״ל״	in/with (the letter) *lamed*
בל״ת	בְּלֹא תַעֲשֶׂה	with (regard to) a negative commandment
ב״ם	(האותיות) ״ב״, ״מ״	(the letters) *beth* [and] *mem*
במ״ג	בְּ(מספר) 43	on/with forty-three
במד״א	בַּמֶּה דְּבָרִים אֲמוּרִים?	To what [circumstances] do the words [apply]?
במ״ה	בְּ(מספר) 45	on/with forty-five
במ״ו	בְּ(מספר) 46	on/with forty-six
במוצ״ש	בְּמוֹצָאֵי שַׁבָּת	on the conclusion of the Sabbath (= Saturday night)

on the conclusion of the Sabbath (= Saturday night)	בְּמוֹצָאֵי שַׁבָּת	במו"ש
"Creator of varieties of foods"[b]	"בּוֹרֵא מִינֵי מְזוֹנוֹת"	במ"מ
on the conclusion of the Sabbath (= Saturday night)	בְּמוֹצָאֵי שַׁבָּת	במ"ש
in our mishna	בְּמַתְנִיתִין	במתני'
on/with fifty	בְּ(מספר) 50	בנ'
people	בְּנֵי אָדָם	בנ"א
in [such a quantity that] it imparts taste	בְּנוֹתֵן טַעַם	בנ"ט
on/with sixty	בְּ(מספר) 60	בס'
with a Torah scroll	בְּסֵפֶר תּוֹרָה	בס"ת
son of Asaria	בֶּן עֲזַרְיָה	ב"ע
on/with seventy	בְּ(מספר) 70	בע'
with (regard to) an ignorant man	בְּעַם הָאָרֶץ	בע"ה
the owner; the landlord; the host	בַּעַל הַבַּיִת	בעה"ב
in the world to come	בָּעוֹלָם הַבָּא	בעוה"ב
in this world	בָּעוֹלָם הַזֶּה	בעוה"ז
with (regard to) idolatry	בַּעֲבוֹדָה זָרָה	בע"ז
creditor; creditors	בַּעַל/בַּעֲלֵי חוֹב	בע"ח
against his/her will	בְּעַל כָּרְחֵיהּ/כָּרְחַהּ	בע"כ
with regard to a worshiper(s) of stars and planets	בְּעוֹבֵד/בְעוֹבְדֵי כּוֹכָבִים וּמַזָּלוֹת	בעכו"ם
on the day before Pesaḥ	בְּעֶרֶב פֶּסַח; בְּעַרְבֵי פְּסָחִים	בע"פ
on the day before the Sabbath (= on Friday)	בְּעֶרֶב שַׁבָּת	בע"ש
[1] "Creator of the fruit ..."[b]	"בּוֹרֵא פְּרִי"	ב"פ[1]
[2] twice	שְׁתֵּי פְעָמִים	ב"פ[2]
with eighty	בְּ(מספר) 80	בפ'
"Creator of the fruit of the ground"[b]	"בּוֹרֵא פְּרִי הָאֲדָמָה"	בפה"א
"Creator of the fruit of the vine"[b]	"בּוֹרֵא פְּרִי הַגָּפֶן"	בפה"ג
"Creator of the fruit of the tree"[b]	"בּוֹרֵא פְּרִי הָעֵץ"	בפה"ע
with (regard to) being fruitful and multiplying	בִּפְרִיָּה וּרְבִיָּה	בפו"ר
"in my presence it was written and signed"	"בְּפָנַי נִכְתַּב וּבְפָנַי נֶחְתַּם"	בפ"נ ובפ"נ
a (Heavenly) echo	בַּת קוֹל	ב"ק
with a *kal-vaḥomer* [argument]	בְּקַל וָחוֹמֶר	בק"ו
in/with (regard to) the recitation of Sh^{e}ma	בִּקְרִיאַת שְׁמַע	בק"ש
the son of Rebbi/R. .../Rav ...*	בֶּן רַבִּי/רַבִּי .../רַב ...	ב"ר
with (regard to) R. ...*	בְּרַבִּי ...	בר'
son of R. El´asar	בֶּן רַבִּי אֶלְעָזָר	בר"א
[1] son of Rabban Gamliel	בֶּן רַבָּן גַּמְלִיאֵל	בר"ג[1]
[2] with (regard to) Rabban Gamliel	בְּרַבָּן גַּמְלִיאֵל	בר"ג[2]
[1] on Rosh HaShana	בְּרֹאשׁ הַשָּׁנָה	בר"ה[1]
[2] in a public domain	בִּרְשׁוּת הָרַבִּים	בר"ה[2]
in a private domain	בִּרְשׁוּת הַיָּחִיד	ברה"י
in a public domain	בִּרְשׁוּת הָרַבִּים	ברה"ר
on Rosh Ḥodesh (= the first of the month)	בְּרֹאשׁ חֹדֶשׁ	בר"ח
[1] son of R. Y^{e}huda	בֶּן רַבִּי יְהוּדָה	בר"י[1]
[2] with (regard to) R. Yosé	בְּרַבִּי יוֹסֵי	בר"י[2]
his son	בְּרֵיהּ	ברי'
with two hundred forty-eight	בְּ(מספר) 248	ברמ"ח
with (regard to) R. Akiva	בְּרַבִּי עֲקִיבָא	בר"ע

---

[b] These words comprise part of the text of a *b^{e}rakha*.

* See note a

[1] son of R. Shim'on	בן רבי שמעון	בר״ש[1]
[2] with (regard to) R. Shim'on	בְּרַבִּי שִׁמְעוֹן	בר״ש[2]
with (regard to) Rabban Shim'on son of Gamliel	בְּרַבָּן שִׁמְעוֹן בֶּן גַּמְלִיאֵל	ברשב״ג
Beth (= the school of) Shammai	בֵּית שַׁמַּאי	ב״ש
Beth (= the school of) Shammai says	בֵּית שַׁמַּאי אוֹמְרִים	בש״א
in *Shir HaShirim* (= the Song of Songs)	בְּשִׁיר הַשִּׁירִים	בשה״ש
with (the declaration): "Today is the Sabbath!"	בְּ"שַׁבָּת הַיּוֹם"	בשה״י
with (regard to) a promissory note	בִּשְׁטָר חוֹב	בשט״ח
with (regard to) semen	בְּשִׁכְבַת זֶרַע	בש״ז
with (regard to) someone gravely ill	בִּשְׁכִיב מְרַע	בשכ״מ
with (regard to) Torah scholars	בְּתַלְמִידֵי חֲכָמִים	בת״ח
after him/it (m.)	בָּתְרֵיהּ	בתרי׳

ג

three	(המספר) 3	ג׳
(the letters) *gimmel* [and] *daleth*	(האותיות) "ג", "ד"	ג״ד
(the letters) *gimmel* [and] *resh*	(האותיות) "ג", "ר"	ג״ר
a *g*[e]*zera-shava* [analogy]	גְּזֵירָה שָׁוָה	גז״ש
three handbreadths	שְׁלֹשָׁה טְפָחִים	ג״ט
(the letter) *gimmel*	(האות) "ג"	גימ״ל
(the letters) *gimmel, yod,* [and] *pé*	(האותיות) "ג", "י", "פ"	גי״ף
G[e]mara; Talmud	גְּמָרָא	גמ׳
(the letters) *gimmel* [and] *nun*	(האותיות) "ג", "נ"	ג״ן
non-Jews, women, animals, [or] Samaritans	גוֹיִם, נָשִׁים, בְּהֵמָה, כּוּתִים	גנב״ך
the garden of Eden	גַּן עֵדֶן	ג״ע
three times	שָׁלֹשׁ פְּעָמִים	ג״פ
(the letters) *gimmel* [and] *tzadé*	(האותיות) "ג", "צ"	ג״ץ
a *g*[e]*zera-shava* [analogy]	גְּזֵרָה שָׁוָה	ג״ש

ד

NOTE: Sometimes the letter ד at the beginning of an item is *not* an initial representing a separate word (as in ד״א = דָּבָר אַחֵר) but an Aramaic *prefix* -דְּ. It is equivalent either to the Hebrew -שֶׁ, *because* or *that* (as in דא״א = דְּאִי אֶפְשָׁר) or to the Hebrew שֶׁל, *of* (as in דא״י = דְּאֶרֶץ יִשְׂרָאֵל).

[1] four	(המספר) 4	ד׳[1]
[2] (the letter) *daleth*	(האות) "ד"	ד׳[2]
[1] something else	דָּבָר אַחֵר	ד״א[1]
[2] four cubits	אַרְבַּע אַמּוֹת	ד״א[2]
because [it is] impossible	דְּאִי אֶפְשָׁר	דא״א
of Erets Yisrael	דְּאֶרֶץ יִשְׂרָאֵל	דא״י
because if so	דְּאִם כֵּן/כָּךְ	דא״כ
because he said to him	דַּאֲמַר לֵיהּ	דא״ל
because we say	דְּאָמְרִינַן	דאמרי׳
because even if	דְּאִי נָמֵי	דא״נ
because even though	דְּאַף עַל גַּב	דאע״ג
because even though	דְּאַף עַל פִּי	דאע״פ
because/that even	דַּאֲפִילּוּ	דאפי׳

because there is no need	דְּאֵין צוֹרֶךְ	דא"צ
because a pasuk says	דְּאָמַר קְרָא	דא"ק
because R. .../Rav ... said*	דְּאָמַר רַבִּי .../רב	דא"ר
because R. Eliezer said	דְּאָמַר רַבִּי אֱלִיעֶזֶר	דאר"א
because R. Ḥanina said	דְּאָמַר רַבִּי חֲנִינָא	דאר"ח
because R. Yehoshua son of Levi said	דְּאָמַר רַבִּי יְהוֹשֻׁעַ בֶּן לֵוִי	דאריב"ל
because Resh Lakish said	דְּאָמַר רֵישׁ לָקִישׁ	דאר"ל
because R. Akiva said	דְּאָמַר רַבִּי עֲקִיבָא	דאר"ע
because R. Shim'on said	דְּאָמַר רַבִּי שִׁמְעוֹן	דאר"ש
because R. Shim'on son of Lakish said	דְּאָמַר רַבִּי שִׁמְעוֹן בֶּן לָקִישׁ	דארשב"ל
because in court	דִּבְבֵית דִּין	דבב"ד
of/because a court	דְּבֵית דִּין	דב"ד
of/because Beth (= the school of) Hillel	דְּבֵית הִלֵּל	דב"ה
because on a festival	דִּבְיוֹם טוֹב	דביו"ט
of (the letter) *beth*	דְּ(האות) "ב"	דבי"ת
of "Creator of varieties of foods"**	דְּ"בּוֹרֵא מִינֵי מְזוֹנוֹת"	דבמ"מ
of the owner; of the landlord; of the host	דְּבַעַל הַבַּיִת	דבע"ה
of the owner; of the landlord; of the host	דְּבַעַל הַבַּיִת	דבעה"ב
of/because a creditor	דְּבַעַל חוֹב	דבע"ח
because against his will	דִּבְעַל כָּרְחוֹ	דבע"כ
because on Rosh HaShana	דִּבְרֹאשׁ הַשָּׁנָה	דבר"ה
of/because Beth (= the school) of Shammai	דְּבֵית שַׁמַּאי	דב"ש
of non-Jews, women, animals, [or] Samaritans	דְּגוֹיִם, נָשִׁים, בְּהֵמָה, כּוּתִים	דגנב"ך
of (the letter) *daleth*	דְּ(האות) "ד"	דדל"ת
the words (= opinion) of everyone	דִּבְרֵי הַכֹּל	ד"ה
because he had; because he should have	דַּהֲוָה לֵיהּ	דהו"ל
of (the letter) *hé*	דְּ(האות) "ה"	דה"י
because he had; because he should have	דַּהֲוָה לֵיהּ	דה"ל
of/because the Holy One Blessed Be He	דְּהַקָּדוֹשׁ בָּרוּךְ הוּא	דהקב"ה
of (the letter) *vav*	דְּ(האות) "ו"	דוי"ו
of (the letter) *ḥeth*	דְּ(האות) "ח"	דחי"ת
of/because Yom Kippur	דְּיוֹם הַכִּפּוּרִים	דיה"כ
of/because Yom Kippur	דְּיוֹם הַכִּפּוּרִים	דיוה"כ
of/because a festival	דְּיוֹם טוֹב	די"ט
of/because a high priest	דְּכֹהֵן גָּדוֹל	דכ"ג
for in this manner; of such a case	דְּכִי הַאי גַּוְונָא	דכה"ג
of/because everyone	דְּכוּלֵּי עָלְמָא	דכ"ע
(the letters) *daleth, kaf,* [and] *pé*	(האותיות) "ד", "כ", "פ"	דכ"ף
(the letters) *daleth, kaf,* [and] *tzadé*	(האותיות) "ד", "כ", "צ"	דכ"ץ
which is according to R. Méir	דִּכְרַבִּי מֵאִיר	דכר"מ
for/as it is written	דִּכְתִיב	דכתי'
of [the halakha of] Beth (= the school of) Shammai	דִּלְבֵית שַׁמַּאי	דלב"ש
for according to everyone	דִּלְכוּלֵּי עָלְמָא	דלכ"ע
of/because (the letter) *lamed*	דְּ(האות) "ל"	דלמ"ד
because according to R. Méir	דִּלְרַבִּי מֵאִיר	דלר"מ
because according to R. Shim'on	דִּלְרַבִּי שִׁמְעוֹן	דלר"ש
(the letter) *daleth*	(האות) "ד"	דל"ת
of/because the one who says	דְּמַאן דְּאָמַר	דמ"ד

* See note a
** See note b

דמ״ס	דְמַר סָבַר	for one hakham holds (the opinion)
דמ״ע	דְמִצְוַת עֲשֵׂה	of/because a positive commandment
דמתני׳	דְמַתְנִיתִין	of our mishna
ד״ס	(האותיות) "ד", "ס"	(the letters) *daleth* [and] *samekh*
דס״ד	דְסָלְקָא דַעְתָּךְ	for it would arise [upon] your mind
דסד״א	דְסָלְקָא דַעְתָּךְ אֲמִינָא	for it would arise [upon] your mind [that] I'd say
דע״ז	דַעֲבוֹדָה זָרָה	of/because idolatry
דע״י	דְעַל יְדֵי	for by means of
דעכו״ם	דְעוֹבֵד/דְעוֹבְדֵי כוֹכָבִים וּמַזָּלוֹת	of/because the worshiper(s) of stars and planets
דפ׳	דְ(מספר) 80	of eighty
ד״ק[1]	(האותיות) "ד", "ק"	[1] (the letters) *daleth* [and] *kof*
ד״ק[2]	דִינִים, קִלְלַת הַשֵּׁם	[2] civil law [and] blaspheming the Divine Name
דקא״ל	דְקָאָמַר לֵיהּ	because he is saying to him
דקב״ה	דְקוּדְשָׁא בְּרִיךְ הוּא	of the Holy One Blessed Be He
דק״ו	דְקַל וָחוֹמֶר	of/because a *kal-vahomer* [argument]
דקוב״ה	דְקוּדְשָׁא בְּרִיךְ הוּא	of [His] Holiness Blessed Be He
דקו״ף	דְ(האות) "ק"	of (the letter) *kof*
דקי״ל	דְקַיְימָא לַן	for it has been established for us
ד״ר	דִבְרֵי רַבִּי	the words (= opinion) of Rebbi*
דר׳	דְרַבִּי ...	of R. ...*
דר״א	דְרַבִּי אֱלִיעֶזֶר/אֶלְעָזָר	of R. Eliezer/El'azar
דראב״י	דְרַבִּי אֱלִיעֶזֶר בֶּן יַעֲקֹב	of R. Eliezer son of Ya'akov
דר״ג	דְרַבָּן גַמְלִיאֵל	of Rabban Gamliel
דר״ה	דְרֹאשׁ הַשָּׁנָה	of Rosh HaShana
דר״ח[1]	דְרֹאשׁ חֹדֶשׁ	[1] of Rosh Hodesh (= the first of the month)
דר״ח[2]	דְרַבִּי חֲנִינָא	[2] of R. Hanina
דר״ט	דְרַבִּי טַרְפוֹן	of R. Tarfon
דר״י	דְרַבִּי יְהוּדָה/יוֹסֵי/יוֹחָנָן/ יִשְׁמָעֵאל/יְהוֹשֻׁעַ	because R. Y^e^huda/Yosé/Yohanan/ Yishmael/Y^e^hoshua
דריב״ל	דְרַבִּי יְהוֹשֻׁעַ בֶּן לֵוִי	of R. Y^e^hoshua son of Levi
דר״ל	דְרֵישׁ לָקִישׁ	of Resh Lakish
דר״מ	דְרַבִּי מֵאִיר	of/because R. Méir
דר״נ	דְרַב נַחְמָן	of Rav Nahman
דר״ע	דְרַבִּי עֲקִיבָא	of R. Akiva
דרע״א	דְרַבִּי עֲקִיבָא אוֹמֵר	because R. Akiva says
דרקב״ש	דְרוֹעִים, קַיָּיצִים, בּוֹרְגָנִים, שׁוֹמְרֵי פֵּירוֹת	of shepherds, watchmen of drying fruit, city-guards, [or] orchard-keepers
דר״ש	דְרַבִּי שִׁמְעוֹן	of R. Shim'on
דרשב״ג	דְרַבָּן שִׁמְעוֹן בֶּן גַמְלִיאֵל	of/because Rabban Shim'on son of Gamliel
דרשב״ל	דְרַבִּי שִׁמְעוֹן בֶּן לָקִישׁ	of/because R. Shim'on son of Lakish
דשלב״ל	דָבָר שֶׁלֹּא בָא לְעוֹלָם	something that has not [yet] come into the world
ד״ת	דִבְרֵי תוֹרָה	words of Torah
דת״ק	דְתַנָּא קַמָּא	of/because the first tanna
דת״ר	דְתָנוּ רַבָּנַן	because the Hakhamim taught

ה

ה׳[1]	הַשֵּׁם	[1] God
ה׳[2]	(המספר) 5	[2] five

* See note a

ה״א¹	(האות) ״ה״	[1] (the letter) *hé*
ה״א²	הֲוָה אֲמִינָא	[2] I would have said
הב״ע	הָכָא בְּמַאי עָסְקִינַן?	With what [circumstances] are we involved here?
ה״ג	הַאי גַּוְונָא	this manner
ה״ד	הֵיכִי דָמֵי?	How? What is the case?
הד״ס	הֲבָאָה, וִידּוּי, אָסוּר	bringing, declaration, forbidden
ה״ה	הוּא הַדִּין	this is [also] the rule
ה״ו	(האותיות) ״ה״, ״ו״	(the letters) *hé* [and] *vav*
הו״א	הֲוָה אֲמִינָא	I would have said
הו״ל	הֲוָה לֵיהּ	he had; he should have
ה״ז	הֲרֵי זֶה	behold it is
הזי״ו ל״ך	״הַאֲזִינוּ״, ״זְכוֹר״, ״יַרְכִּבֵהוּ״, ״וַיַּרְא״ ״לוּ״ (וי״א: ״לוּלֵי״), ״כִּי״	(the first words in six p^e^sukim that divide up *Parashath Ha'azinu*)
ה״ט	הַיְינוּ טַעְמָא	this is the reason
ה״י	(האות) ״ה״	(the letter) *hé*
הי״ט	הַיּוֹם טוֹב	the festival
ה״ל	הֲוָה לֵיהּ	he had; he should have
הל״מ	הֲלָכָה לְמֹשֶׁה מִסִּינַי	halakha [transmitted] to Moshe from Sinai
הל״ק	(האותיות) ״ה״, ״ל״, ״ק״	(the letters) *hé, lamed,* [and] *kof*
ה״מ	הָנֵי מִילֵּי	"these words"; it applies only [in a case]
ה״ם	(הסיומת) ״הֶם״	(the Hebrew suffix) *-hem (= their)*
המע״ה	הַמּוֹצִיא מֵחֲבֵירוֹ עָלָיו הָרְאָיָה.	One who seeks to take [something] away from his fellow man [has] the [burden of] proof upon him.
ה״נ¹	הָכָא נַמִּי	[1] here too
ה״נ²	הָכִי נַמִּי	[2] so too
הנ״מ	הָנֵי מִילֵּי	"these words"; it applies only [in a case]
ה״ע	(האותיות) ״ה״, ״ע״	(the letters) *hé* [and] *ayin*
העוה״ב	הָעוֹלָם הַבָּא	the world to come
העוה״ז	הָעוֹלָם הַזֶּה	this world
העכו״ם	הָעוֹבֵד/הָעוֹבְדֵי כּוֹכָבִים וּמַזָּלוֹת	the worshiper/s of stars and planets
ה״ץ	(האותיות) ״ה״, ״צ״	(the letters) *hé* [and] *tzadé*
ה״ק	הָכִי קָאָמַר/קָתָנֵי	thus he is saying/teaching; this [is what] he means
הקב״ה	הַקָּדוֹשׁ בָּרוּךְ הוּא	the Holy One Blessed Be He
הש״ס	הַ״שִּׁשָּׁה סְדָרִים״	the six orders (of the Mishna); the Talmud

ו

NOTE: The letter ו is almost always the *prefix* -ו, usually meaning *and*. It is *not* an initial representing a separate word.

ו׳	(המספר) 6	six
וא׳	וְאֶחָד/וְאַחַת	and one
וא״א¹	וְאִי אָמְרַתְּ	[1] but if you say
וא״א²	וְאִי אֶפְשָׁר	[2] and [it is] impossible
ואב״א	וְאִי בָּעֵית, אֵימָא!	and if you want, say!
ואבע״א	וְאִי בָּעֵית, אֵימָא!	and if you want, say!
וא״ד	וְאִיכָּא דְאָמְרִי	and there are [some] who say; and others say
וא״ו	(האות) ״ו״	(the letter) *vav*
ואח״כ	וְאַחַר כָּךְ	and afterwards

and Erets Yisrael	וְאֶרֶץ יִשְׂרָאֵל	וא״י
and if you want, say!	וְאִי בָּעֵית, אֵימָא!	ואיב״א
and if you want, say!	וְאִי בָּעֵית, אֵימָא!	ואיבע״א
[1] and he said to him	וְאָמַר לוֹ; וַאֲמַר לֵיהּ	וא״ל[1]
[2] and some say it; but some quote it	וְאָמְרִי לַהּ	וא״ל[2]
and alternatively	וְאִי נַמִּי	וא״נ
and even though	וְאַף עַל גַּב	ואע״ג
and even though	וְאַף עַל פִּי	ואע״פ
and in spite of that; and nevertheless	וְאַף עַל פִּי כֵן	ואעפ״כ
and even so	וַאֲפִילּוּ הָכִי	ואפ״ה
and even	וַאֲפִילּוּ	ואפי׳
and he does not need; and there is no need	וְאֵינוֹ צָרִיךְ; וְאֵין צוֹרֶךְ	וא״צ
and there is no need to say	וְאֵין צוֹרֶךְ לוֹמַר	ואצ״ל
and R. .../Rebbi/Rav ... said*	וַאֲמַר רַבִּי .../רַבִּי/רַב ...	וא״ר
and R. Y^ehoshua son of Levi said	וַאֲמַר רַבִּי יְהוֹשֻׁעַ בֶּן לֵוִי	ואריב״ל
and Resh Lakish said	וַאֲמַר רֵישׁ לָקִישׁ	ואר״ל
but if you say (= argue)	וְאִם תֹּאמַר; וְאִי תֵּימָא	וא״ת
and if (upon examining the issue) you conclude [and] say	וְאִם תִּמְצָא לוֹמַר	ואת״ל
and two; and the second	וּשְׁנַיִם; וְהַשֵּׁנִי	וב׳
and in court	וּבְבֵית דִּין	ובב״ד
and with (regard to) a g^e*zera-shava* [argument]	וּבִגְזֵרָה שָׁוָה	ובג״ש
and the court	וּבֵית דִּין	וב״ד
and with (the letter) *daleth*	וּבְ(אות) ״ד״	ובדל״ת
and with respect to that [statement] of Resh Lakish	וּבִדְרֵישׁ לָקִישׁ	ובדר״ל
and on five; and on the fifth	וּבַחֲמִשָּׁה; וּבַחֲמִישִׁי	ובה׳
and Beth (= the school of) Hillel	וּבֵית הִלֵּל	וב״ה
and Beth Hillel says	וּבֵית הִלֵּל אוֹמְרִים	ובה״א
and in the six orders (of the Mishna); and in the Talmud	וּבְהַ״שִּׁשָּׁה סְדָרִים״	ובהש״ס
and on seven; and on the seventh	וּבְשִׁבְעָה; וּבַשְּׁבִיעִי	ובז׳
and a creditor	וּבַעַל חוֹב	וב״ח
and in [a place] outside of Erets Yisrael	וּבְחוּצָה לָאָרֶץ	ובחו״ל
and in [a place] outside of Erets Yisrael	וּבְחוּצָה לָאָרֶץ	ובח״ל
and on fourteen; and on the fourteenth	וּבְ(מספר) 14	ובי״ד
and on Yom Kippur	וּבְיוֹם הַכִּפּוּרִים	ובי״ה
and a lavatory	וּבֵית הַכִּסֵּא	וביהכ״ס
and on Yom Kippur	וּבְיוֹם הַכִּפּוּרִים	וביוה״כ
and on eighteen; and on the eighteenth	וּבְ(מספר) 18	ובי״ח
and on a festival	וּבְיוֹם טוֹב	ובי״ט
and on twenty-five	וּבְ(מספר) 25	ובכ״ה
and in our mishna	וּבְמַתְנִיתִין	ובמתני׳
and a creditor	וּבַעַל חוֹב	ובע״ח
and we require	וּבָעֵינַן	ובעי׳
and with (regard to) worshiper(s) of stars and planets	וּבְעוֹבֵד/וּבְעוֹבְדֵי כוֹכָבִים וּמַזָּלוֹת	ובעכו״ם
and with (the formula) "provided that"	וּבְ״עַל מְנָת״	ובע״מ
and with a *kal-vaḥomer* [argument]	וּבְקַל וָחוֹמֶר	ובק״ו
and on Rosh HaShana	וּבְרֹאשׁ הַשָּׁנָה	ובר״ה

* See note a

and in a public domain	וּבִרְשׁוּת הָרַבִּים	וברה"ר
and Beth (= the school of) Shammai	וּבֵית שַׁמַּאי	וב"ש
and in the six orders (of the Mishna); and in the Talmud	וּבְשִׁשָּׁה סְדָרִים"	ובש"ס
and three	וְ(המספר) 3	וג'
and so on (in the pasuk quoted)	וְגוֹמֵר	וגו'
and four	וְ(המספר) 4	וד'
and another matter	וְדָבָר אַחֵר	וד"א
and that [statement] of everyone	וּדְכוּלֵּי עָלְמָא	ודכ"ע
and [as for] what he said to him	וְדְקָאָמַר לֵיהּ	ודקא"ל
and that [statement] of R. ...*	וּדְרַבִּי ...	ודר'
and that [statement] of Resh Lakish	וּדְרֵישׁ לָקִישׁ	ודר"ל
[1] and God	וְהַשֵּׁם	וה'[1]
[2] and five	וְ(המספר) 5	וה'[2]
and with what [circumstances] are we dealing here?	וְהָכָא בְּמַאי עָסְקִינַן?	והב"ע
but has not R. .../Rav ... said!*	וְהָא אָמַר רַבִּי .../רב ...!	והא"ר
and how? and what is the case?	וְהֵיכִי דָמֵי?	וה"ד
and this is [also] the rule	וְהוּא הַדִּין	וה"ה
and (the letter) *hé*	וְ(האות) "ה"	וה"י
and behold it is written!	וְהָכְתִיב!	והכתי'
and he had; and he should have	וַהֲוָה לֵיהּ	וה"ל
"and these words"; and it applies only [in a case]	וְהָנֵי מִילֵּי	וה"מ
and here too	וְהָכָא נַמִּי	וה"נ
"and these words"; and it applies only [in a case]	וְהָנֵי מִילֵּי	והנ"מ
and thus he is saying/teaching; and this [is what] he means	וְהָכִי קָאָמַר/קָתָנֵי	וה"ק
and the Holy One Blessed Be He	וְהַקָּדוֹשׁ בָּרוּךְ הוּא	והקב"ה
(the letter) *vav*	(האות) "ו"	ו"ו
(the letters) *vav*	(האותיות) "ו"	ווי"ן
and seven; and the seventh	וְשִׁבְעָה; וְהַשְּׁבִיעִי	וז'
and the [other] one says	וְחַד אָמַר	וח"א
and the intermediary days of the festival	וְחוּלּוֹ שֶׁלַּמּוֹעֵד	וחוש"מ
and the Ḥakhamim say	וַחֲכָמִים אוֹמְרִים	וחכ"א
and fifteen; and the fifteenth	וְ(המספר) 15	וט"ו
and there are [some who] say; and others say	וְיֵשׁ אוֹמְרִים	וי"א
and twelve; and the twelfth	וְ(המספר) 12	וי"ב
and thirteen; and the thirteenth	וְ(המספר) 13	וי"ג
and fourteen; and the fourteenth	וְ(המספר) 14	וי"ד
and (the letter) *vav*	וְ(האות) "ו"	וי"ו
and Yom Kippur	וְיוֹם הַכִּפּוּרִים	ויוה"כ
and a festival	וְיוֹם טוֹב	ויו"ט
and eighteen; and the eighteenth	וְ(המספר) 18	וי"ח
and the evil inclination	וְיֵצֶר הָרַע	ויצה"ר
and twenty; and the twentieth	וְ(המספר) 20	וכ'
and a high priest	וְכֹהֵן גָּדוֹל	וכ"ג
and like that [statement] of R. ...*	וְכִדְרַבִּי ...	וכדר'
and like that [statement] of R. Elieser	וְכִדְרַבִּי אֱלִיעֶזֶר	וכדר"א
and like that [statement] of R. Yehuda	וְכִדְרַבִּי יְהוּדָה	וכדר"י
and so he says	וְכֵן הוּא אוֹמֵר	וכה"א

* See note a

and in this manner	[illegible]	[illegible]
and so on (in the mishna, baraitha, or memra quoted)	וְכוּלֵּיהּ	וכו'
and twenty-eight	וְ(המספר) 28	וכ"ח
and everywhere/wherever	וְכָל מָקוֹם	וכ"מ
and like [the opinion of the] one who says	וּכְמַאן דְּאָמַר	וכמ"ד
and everybody (= all the disputants)	וְכוּלֵּי עָלְמָא	וכ"ע
and (the letter) *kaf*	וְ(האות) "כ"	וכ"ף
and like R. ...*	וּכְרַבִּי ...	וכר'
and like R. Shim'on	וּכְרַבִּי שִׁמְעוֹן	וכר"ש
and like Rabban Shim'on son of Gamliel	וּכְרַבָּן שִׁמְעוֹן בֶּן גַּמְלִיאֵל	וכרשב"ג
and how much more so! and certainly!	וְכָל שֶׁכֵּן!	וכ"ש
and if you should say	וְכִי תֵימָא	וכ"ת
and it is written (in Scripture)	וּכְתִיב	וכתי'
and thirty	וְ(המספר) 30	ול'
and according to Beth (= the school of) Hillel	וּלְבֵית הִלֵּל	ולב"ה
and according to Beth (= the school of) Shammai	וּלְבֵית שַׁמַּאי	ולב"ש
and to/for God	וְלַשֵּׁם	ולה'
and to (the letter) *vav*	וּלְ(אות) "ו"	ולוי"ו
and to/for twelve	וּלְ(מספר) 12	ולי"ב
and for Yom Kippur	וּלְיוֹם הַכִּפּוּרִים	וליוה"כ
and according to the one who says	וּלְמַאן דְּאָמַר	ולמ"ד
and to/for good deeds	וּלְמַעֲשִׂים טוֹבִים	ולמע"ט
and to/for the world to come	וּלְעוֹלָם הַבָּא	ולעוה"ב
and to/for a worshiper of stars and planets	וּלְעוֹבֵד כּוֹכָבִים וּמַזָּלוֹת	ולעכו"ם
and it is not difficult	וְלָא קַשְׁיָא	ול"ק
and to/for recitation of *Sh*e*ma*	וְלִקְרִיאַת שְׁמַע	ולק"ש
and according to R. ...*	וּלְרַבִּי ...	ולר'
and according to R. Elieser/El'asar	וּלְרַבִּי אֱלִיעֶזֶר/אֶלְעָזָר	ולר"א
and according to Rabban Gamliel	וּלְרַבָּן גַּמְלִיאֵל	ולר"ג
and according to R. Y*e*huda	וּלְרַבִּי יְהוּדָה	ולר"י
and according to Resh Lakish	וּלְרֵישׁ לָקִישׁ	ולר"ל
and according to R. Méir	וּלְרַבִּי מֵאִיר	ולר"מ
and according to R. Akiva	וּלְרַבִּי עֲקִיבָא	ולר"ע
and according to Rabban Shim'on	וּלְרַבִּי שִׁמְעוֹן	ולר"ש
and according to Rabban Shim'on son of Gamliel	וּלְרַבָּן שִׁמְעוֹן בֶּן גַּמְלִיאֵל	ולרשב"ג
and there is no difference	וְלָא שְׁנָא	ול"ש
and a negative commandment; and a prohibition	וְלֹא תַעֲשֶׂה	ול"ת
and according to the first tanna	וּלְתַנָּא קַמָּא	ולת"ק
and the one who says	וּמַאן דְּאָמַר	ומ"ד
and from [the fact] that he said to him	וּמִדְּאָמַר לֵיהּ	ומדא"ל
and from that [statement] of Rabban Gamliel	וּמִדְּרַבָּן גַּמְלִיאֵל	ומדר"ג
and from that [statement] of Rav Nahman	וּמִדְּרַב נַחְמָן	ומדר"נ
and from that [statement] of R. Akiva	וּמִדְּרַבִּי עֲקִיבָא	ומדר"ע
and from that [statement] of Rabban Shim'on son of Gamliel	וּמִדְּרַבָּן שִׁמְעוֹן בֶּן גַּמְלִיאֵל	ומדרשב"ג
and from God	וּמֵהַשֵּׁם	ומה'
and what is the reason?	וּמַאי טַעְמָא?	ומ"ט
and in any event	וּמִכָּל מָקוֹם	ומ"מ

* See note a

ומנ״ל	וּמְנָא לַן?	and from where do we know?
ומ״ס	וּמָר סָבַר	and [the other] ḥakham holds (the opinion)
ומרז״ן	(האותיות) "ו", "מ", "ר", "ז", "נ"	(the letters) *vav, mem, resh, zayin,* [and] *nun*
ומ״ש	וּמַאי שְׁנָא?	and what is the difference?
ומש״ה	וּמִשּׁוּם הָכִי	and because of this
ומתני׳	וּמַתְנִיתִין	and our mishna
ונאמ׳	וְנֶאֱמַר	and it was said
וס״ד	וְסָלְקָא דַעְתָּךְ	and it would arise [upon] your mind
וס״ל	וּסְבִירָא לֵיהּ	and he holds (the opinion)
וסמ״ך	וְ(האות) "ס"	and (the letter) *samekh*
וס״ת	וְסֵפֶר תּוֹרָה	and a Torah scroll
וע״ג	וְ(המספר) 73	and seventy-three
וע״ז	וַעֲבוֹדָה זָרָה	and idolatry
וע״י	וְעַל יְדֵי	and by means of
וע״כ	וְעַד כָּאן	and thus far
וע״פ	וְעַל פִּי	and according to
ו״ף	(האותיות) "ו", "פ"	(the letters) *vav* [and] *fé*
וצד״י	וְ(האות) "צ"	and (the letter) *tzadé*
וק׳	וְ(המספר) 100	and (the number) one hundred
וקיי״ל	וְקַיְימָא לַן	and it has been established for us
וקי״ל	וְקַיְימָא לַן	and it has been established for us
וקמ״ל	וְקָא מַשְׁמַע לַן	and it/he informs us
וק״ש	וּקְרִיאַת שְׁמַע	and the recitation of *Sh[e]ma*
ור׳	וְרַבִּי ...	and R. ...*
ור״א	וְרַבִּי אֱלִיעֶזֶר/אֶלְעָזָר	and R. Eliezer/El'azar
וראב״ע	וְרַבִּי אֶלְעָזָר בֶּן עֲזַרְיָה	and R. El'azar the son of Azarya
ור״ג	וְרַבָּן גַּמְלִיאֵל	and Rabban Gamliel
ורה״י	וּרְשׁוּת הַיָּחִיד	and the private domain
ורה״ר	וּרְשׁוּת הָרַבִּים	and the public domain
ור״ח	וְרֹאשׁ חֹדֶשׁ	and Rosh Ḥodesh (= and the first of the month)
ור״י	וְרַבִּי יְהוּדָה/יְהוֹשֻׁעַ	and R. Y[e]huda/Y[e]hoshua
וריב״ל	וְרַבִּי יְהוֹשֻׁעַ בֶּן לֵוִי	and R. Y[e]hoshua son of Levi
ור״כ	וְרַב כָּהֲנָא	and Rav Kahana
ור״ל	וְרֵישׁ לָקִישׁ	and Resh Lakish
ור״מ	וְרַבִּי מֵאִיר	and R. Méir
ור״ע	וְרַבִּי עֲקִיבָא	and R. Akiva
ור״ש	וְרַבִּי שִׁמְעוֹן	and R. Shim'on
ורשב״ג	וְרַבָּן שִׁמְעוֹן בֶּן גַּמְלִיאֵל	and Rabban Shim'on son of Gamliel
ושי״ן	וְ(האות) "ש"	and (the letter) *shin*
וש״מ	וּשְׁמַע מִינַּהּ!	and derive from it!
וש״ס	וְ"שִׁשָּׁה סְדָרִים"	and six orders (of the Mishna); and the Talmud
ות״ח	וְתַלְמִידֵי חֲכָמִים	and Torah scholars
ותני׳	וְתַנְיָא	and it is stated (in a baraitha)
ות״ק	וְתַנָּא קַמָּא	and the first tanna
ות״ת	וְתַלְמוּד תּוֹרָה	and the study of Torah

* See note a

ז

ז׳	7 (המספר)	seven
ז״ח	(האותיות) ״ז״, ״ח״	(the letters) *zayin* [and] *ḥeth*
ז״ע	(האותיות) ״ז״, ״ע״	(the letters) *zayin* [and] *ayin*
ז״ץ	(האותיות) ״ז״, ״צ״	(the letters) *zayin* [and] *tzadé*

ח

ח׳	8 (המספר)	eight
ח״ו	חַס וְשָׁלוֹם!	far be it! Heaven forbid!
חי״ת	(האות) ״ח״	(the letter) *ḥeth*
חכ״א	חֲכָמִים אוֹמְרִים	the Ḥakhamim say
ח״נ	חֲצִי נֶזֶק	half [the value of] the damage
ח״ס	(האותיות) ״ח״, ״ס״	(the letters) *ḥeth* [and] *samekh*
ח״ק	(האותיות) ״ח״, ״ק״	(the letters) *ḥeth* [and] *kof*
ח״ר	(האותיות) ״ח״, ״ר״	(the letters) *ḥeth* [and] *resh*
חש״ו	חֵרֵשׁ, שׁוֹטֶה, וְקָטָן	a deaf-mute, an idiot, and/or a minor

ט

ט׳	9 (המספר)	nine; the ninth
ט״ב[1]	9 בְּאָב	[1] the ninth of Av
ט״ב[2]	טוּמְאָה, בִּיעוּר	[2] ritual defilement [and] removal
ט״ו	15 (המספר)	fifteen; the fifteenth
ט״ז	16 (המספר)	sixteen; the sixteenth
ט״י	(האותיות) ״ט״, ״י״	(the letters) *teth* [and] *yod*
טי״ת	(האות) ״ט״	(the letter) *teth*
ט״ן	(האותיות) ״ט״, ״נ״	(the letters) *teth* [and] *nun*
ט״ר	(האותיות) ״ט״, ״ר״	(the letters) *teth* [and] *resh*

י

י׳	10 (המספר)	ten
י״א[1]	11 (המספר)	[1] eleven; the eleventh
י״א[2]	יֵשׁ אוֹמְרִים	[2] there are some [who] say; others say
י״ב	12 (המספר)	twelve; the twelfth
יב״ח	12 חֳדָשִׁים	twelve months
י״ג	13 (המספר)	thirteen; the thirteenth
י״ד	14 (המספר)	fourteen; the fourteenth
י״ה	יוֹם הַכִּפּוּרִים	Yom Kippur
יה״כ	יוֹם הַכִּפּוּרִים	Yom Kippur
יהנ״ק	יַיִן, הַבְדָּלָה, נֵר, קִדּוּשׁ	wine, Havdala, candle, Kiddush[c]
יה״ר	יְהִי רָצוֹן	may it be (Your) will
יו״ד	(האות) ״י״	(the letter) *yod*
יוה״כ	יוֹם הַכִּפּוּרִים	Yom Kippur
יו״ט	יוֹם טוֹב	festival
י״ז	17 (המספר)	seventeen; the seventeenth
י״ח	18 (המספר)	eighteen; the eighteenth
י״ט[1]	יוֹם טוֹב	[1] festival
י״ט[2]	19 (המספר)	[2] nineteen; the nineteenth

---

[c] Each of these words refers to the text of a separate *b^e^rakha*.

God	הַשֵּׁם	י"י
God	הַשֵּׁם	יי'
wine that was poured (as an offering for idolatry)	יַיִן נֶסֶךְ	יי"נ
it is [possible] to say; one may say	יֵשׁ לוֹמַר	י"ל
(the letters) *yod* [and] *mem*	(האותיות) "י", "מ"	י"ם
wine, candle, Havdala, Kiddush[c]	יַיִן, נֵר, הַבְדָּלָה, קִדּוּשׁ	ינה"ק
the evil inclination	יֵצֶר הָרַע	יצה"ר
wine, Kiddush, "time", candle, Havdala[c]	יַיִן, קִדּוּשׁ, זְמַן (= שֶׁהֶחֱיָינוּ), נֵר, הַבְדָּלָה	יקזנ"ה
wine, Kiddush, candle, Havdala[c]	יַיִן, קִדּוּשׁ, נֵר, הַבְדָּלָה	יקנ"ה
wine, Kiddush, candle, Havdala, "time"[c]	יַיִן, קִדּוּשׁ, נֵר, הַבְדָּלָה, זְמַן (= שֶׁהֶחֱיָינוּ)	יקנה"ז
(the letters) *yod* [and] *shin*	(האותיות) "י", "ש"	י"ש

כ

NOTE: The letter כ at the beginning of an item is often a *prefix* -כְּ, *as* or *like* (as in כדר"פ = כִּדְרַב פָּפָּא), rather than an initial representing a separate word (as in כ"מ = כָּל מָקוֹם).

[1] twenty; the twentieth	(המספר) 20	כ"[1]
[2] (the letter) *kaf*	(האות) "כ"	כ"[2]
but; except	כִּי אִם	כ"א
twenty-two	(המספר) 22	כ"ב
like two	כְּ(מספר) 2	כב'
like Beth (= the school of) Hillel	כְּבֵית הִלֵּל	כב"ה
like Beth (= the school of) Shammai	כְּבֵית שַׁמַּאי	כב"ש
high priest	כֹּהֵן גָּדוֹל	כ"ג
like three; like the third	כִּשְׁלֹשָׁה; כִּשְׁלִישִׁי	כג'
twenty-four	(המספר) 24	כ"ד
like that [statement] of R. ...*	כִּדְרַבִּי ...	כדר'
like that [statement] of R. Elieser	כִּדְרַבִּי אֱלִיעֶזֶר	כדר"א
like that [statement] of R. Tarfon	כִּדְרַבִּי טַרְפוֹן	כדר"ט
like that [statement] of Resh Lakish	כִּדְרֵישׁ לָקִישׁ	כדר"ל
like that [statement] of Rav Pappa	כִּדְרַב פָּפָּא	כדר"פ
twenty-five	(המספר) 25	כ"ה
like God	כְּהַשֵּׁם	כה'
[1] the high priest	כֹּהֵן הַגָּדוֹל	כה"ג[1]
[2] in this manner	כִּי הַאי גַּוְונָא	כה"ג[2]
the rest of it (= the mishna, baraitha, or memra quoted)	כּוּלֵּיהּ	כו'
twenty-six	(המספר) 26	כ"ו
[1] twenty-seven	(המספר) 27	כ"ז[1]
[2] all the time (that); whenever	כָּל זְמַן	כ"ז[2]
twenty-eight	(המספר) 28	כ"ח
(the letters) *kaf* [and] *lamed*	(האותיות) "כ", "ל"	כ"ל
everywhere; wherever	כָּל מָקוֹם	כ"מ
(the letters) *kaf* [and] *mem*	(האותיות) "כ", "מ"	כ"ם
like the one who says	כְּמַאן דְּאָמַר	כמ"ד
the great assembly	כְּנֶסֶת הַגְּדוֹלָה	כנה"ג
everybody (= all the disputants)	כּוּלֵּי עָלְמָא	כ"ע
like a worshiper of stars and planets	כְּעוֹבֵד כּוֹכָבִים וּמַזָּלוֹת	כעכו"ם
like R. ...**	כְּרַבִּי ...	כר'

[c] Each of these words refers to the text of a separate b'rakha.

* See note a

like R. Elieser/El'asar	כְּרַבִּי אֱלִיעֶזֶר/אֶלְעָזָר	כר"א
like Rabban Gamliel	כְּרַבָּן גַּמְלִיאֵל	כר"ג
like Rav Huna	כְּרַב הוּנָא	כר"ה
like the private domain	כִּרְשׁוּת הַיָּחִיד	כרה"י
like the public domain	כִּרְשׁוּת הָרַבִּים	כרה"ר
like R. Yᵉhuda/Yosé/Yoḥanan	כְּרַבִּי יְהוּדָה/יוֹסֵי/יוֹחָנָן	כר"י
like R. Yᵉhoshua son of Levi	כְּרַבִּי יְהוֹשֻׁעַ בֶּן לֵוִי	כריב"ל
like Resh Lakish	כְּרֵישׁ לָקִישׁ	כר"ל
like R. Méir	כְּרַבִּי מֵאִיר	כר"מ
like R. Akiva	כְּרַבִּי עֲקִיבָא	כר"ע
like R. Shim'on	כְּרַבִּי שִׁמְעוֹן	כר"ש
like R. Shim'on son of El'asar	כְּרַבִּי שִׁמְעוֹן בֶּן אֶלְעָזָר	כרשב"א
like Rabban Shim'on son of Gamliel	כְּרַבָּן שִׁמְעוֹן בֶּן גַּמְלִיאֵל	כרשב"ג
like R. Shim'on son of Lakish	כְּרַבִּי שִׁמְעוֹן בֶּן לָקִישׁ	כרשב"ל
[1] how much more so!	כָּל שֶׁכֵּן!	כ"ש[1]
[2] the slightest amount	כָּל שֶׁהוּא	כ"ש[2]
when the Holy One Blessed Be He	כְּשֶׁהַקָּדוֹשׁ בָּרוּךְ הוּא	כשהקב"ה
like an unpaid guardian	כְּשׁוֹמֵר חִנָּם	כש"ח
like a paid guardian	כְּשׁוֹמֵר שָׂכָר	כש"ש
it is written (in Scripture)	כְּתִיב	כתי'
[1] if you would say	כִּי תֵימָא	כ"ת[1]
[2] (the letters) *kaf* [and] *tav*	(האותיות) "כ", "ת"	כ"ת[2]
like Torah scholars	כְּתַלְמִידֵי חֲכָמִים	כת"ח
like the first tanna	כְּתַנָּא קַמָּא	כת"ק

ל

NOTE: The letter ל at the beginning of an item is often the *prefix* ל-, which is either translated *to, for, according to* (as in לְבֵית הַכְּנֶסֶת = לבהכ"נ) or not translated into English at all when it is a direct-object indicator (like the Hebrew אֶת). Sometimes, however, it is an initial representing a separate word (as in לִישָּׁנָא אַחֲרִינָא = ל"א).

thirty	(המספר) 30	ל'
another version	לִישָּׁנָא אַחֲרִינָא	ל"א
to/for one	לְאֶחָד/לְאַחַת	לא'
to Erets Yisrael	לְאֶרֶץ יִשְׂרָאֵל	לא"י
thirty-two	(המספר) 32	ל"ב
to/for two	לְ(מספר) 2	לב'
to court	לְבֵית דִּין	לב"ד
[1] to/for a synagogue	לְבֵית הַכְּנֶסֶת	לב"ה[1]
[2] to/according to/for Beth (= the school of) Hillel	לְבֵית הִלֵּל	לב"ה[2]
[3] for maintenance of the Beth HaMikdash	לְבֶדֶק הַבַּיִת	לב"ה[3]
to/for the synagogue	לְבֵית הַכְּנֶסֶת	לבהכ"נ
to/for the synagogue	לְבֵית הַכְּנֶסֶת	לביהכ"נ
to/for the beth midrash	לְבֵית הַמִּדְרָשׁ	לביהמ"ד
to/for the landlord/owner/host	לְבַעַל הַבַּיִת	לבעה"ב
to/for a creditor	לְבַעַל חוֹב	לבע"ח
to/according to/for Beth (= the school of) Shammai	לְבֵית שַׁמַּאי	לב"ש
thirty-three	(המספר) 33	ל"ג

לג'	לְ(מספר) 3	to/for three
ל"ד	(המספר) 34	thirty-four
לד'	לְ(מספר) 4	to/for four
לד"ה	לְדִבְרֵי הַכֹּל	according to the words (= opinion) of everyone
לדר'	לְדְרַבִּי ...	according to R. ...*
לד"ת	לְדִבְרֵי תּוֹרָה	to/for words of Torah
לה'	לְהַשֵּׁם	to God
להד"מ	לֹא הָיוּ דְבָרִים מֵעוֹלָם!	The events never took place!
להקב"ה	לְהַקָּדוֹשׁ בָּרוּךְ הוּא	to the Holy One Blessed Be He
לה"ר	לָשׁוֹן הָרָע	"the evil tongue"; slander
ל"ו	(המספר) 36	thirty-six
לוי"ו	לְ(אות) "ו"	to/for (the letter) *vav*
לז'	לְ(מספר) 7	to/for seven
ל"ט	(המספר) 39	thirty-nine
לט'	לְ(מספר) 9	to/for nine
לט"ו	לְ(מספר) 15	to/for fifteen
לט"ז	לְ(מספר) 16	to/for sixteen
לי"[1]	לֵיהּ	[1] to for/it (m.); him/it (m.)
לי"[2]	לְ(מספר) 10	[2] to/for ten
לי"ד	לְ(מספר) 14	to/for tourteen
לי"ו	לְ(מספר) 16	to/for sixteen
ליוה"כ	לְיוֹם הַכִּפּוּרִים	to/for Yom Kippur
ליו"ט	לְיוֹם טוֹב	to/for a festival
לי"ט	לְיוֹם טוֹב	to/for a festival
ליצה"ר	לְיֵצֶר הָרָע	to/for the evil inclination
לי"ך		SEE: הזי"ן ל"ך
לכ"ג	לְכֹהֵן גָּדוֹל	to/for a high priest
לכ"ד	לְ(מספר) 24	regarding twenty-four
לכדר"ש	לְכִדְרַבִּי שִׁמְעוֹן	for [the halakha that is] like that [statement] of R. Shim'on
לכ"ע	לְכוּלֵּי עָלְמָא	according to everybody (= the disputants)
ליצה"ר	לְיֵצֶר הָרָע	to/for the evil inclination
לכדר'	לְכִדְרַבִּי ...	for [the halakha that is] like that [statement] of R. ...*
לכ"ש	לֹא כָּל שֶׁכֵּן!	is it not all the more so!
ל"ל[1]	לָמָּה לִי?	[1] why do I need?
ל"ל[2]	לֵית לָן	[2] we do not have
ללה"ר	לְלָשׁוֹן הָרָע	to/for the "evil tongue"; to/for slander
ללע"ט	לְלֵב, עַיִן, טְחוֹל	for the heart, the eye, [and] the spleen
למ"ד[1]	לְמַאן דְּאָמַר	[1] according to the one who says
למ"ד[2]	(האות) "ל"	[2] (the letter) *lamed*
למ"ה	לִמְדִינַת הַיָּם	to a country overseas
למה"ד	(מָשָׁל) לְמָה הַדָּבָר דּוֹמֶה?	To what (parable) is this matter similar?
למוצ"ש	לְמוֹצָאֵי שַׁבָּת	on the night after the Sabbath (= Saturday night)
למ"ש	לְמוֹצָאֵי שַׁבָּת	on the night after the Sabbath (= Saturday night)
למתני'	לְמַתְנִיתִין	to/for our mishna
לנט"י	לִנְטִילַת יָדַיִם	for the washing of the hands
לס"ת	לְסֵפֶר תּוֹרָה	to/for a Torah scroll
לעוה"ב	לָעוֹלָם הַבָּא	to the world to come
לע"ז	לַעֲבוֹדָה זָרָה	for/to idolatry
לעי"ן	לְ(אות) "ע"	to (the letter) *ayin*

* See note a

לעכו"ם	לְעוֹבֵד כּוֹכָבִים וּמַזָּלוֹת	to a worshiper of stars and planets
לע"ל	לֶעָתִיד לָבֹא	for the future [that is] to come
לע"ש	לְעֶרֶב שַׁבָּת	to/for the day before the Sabbath; to/for Friday
ל"פ	לָא פְּלִיגֵי	they do not disagree
ל"ק	לָא קַשְׁיָא	it is not difficult
לק"ש	לִקְרִיאַת שְׁמַע	for the recitation of *Sh^{e}ma*
לר'	לְרַבִּי .../לְרֶבִּי	to/according to/for R. .../Rebbi*
לר"א	לְרַבִּי אֱלִיעֶזֶר/אֶלְעָזָר	to/for R. Eliezer/El'azar
לרבב"ח	לְרַבָּה בַּר בַּר חָנָה	to Rabba the grandson of Ḥanna
לר"ג	לְרַבָּן גַּמְלִיאֵל	to/according to/for Rabban Gamliel
לר"ה[1]	לִרְשׁוּת הָרַבִּים	[1] to a public domain
לר"ה[2]	לְרַב הוּנָא	[2] according to Rav Huna
לר"ה[3]	לְרֹאשׁ הַשָּׁנָה	[3] to/for Rosh HaShana
לרה"י	לִרְשׁוּת הַיָּחִיד	to a private domain
לרה"ר	לִרְשׁוּת הָרַבִּים	to a public domain
לר"ח	לְרֹאשׁ חֹדֶשׁ	to/for Rosh Hodesh (= the first of the month)
לר"י	לְרַבִּי יוֹחָנָן	to/according to/for R. Yoḥanan
לריב"ל	לְרַבִּי יְהוֹשֻׁעַ בֶּן לֵוִי	to/according to/for R. Y^{e}hoshua son of Levi
לר"ל	לְרֵישׁ לָקִישׁ	to/according to/for Resh Lakish
לר"מ	לְרַבִּי מֵאִיר	to/according to/for R. Méir
לרמ"ת	לְרֹאשׁ, מֵעַיִם, תַּחְתּוֹנִיּוֹת	for the head, the intestines, [and] abdominal illnesses
לר"נ	לְרַב נַחְמָן	to/according to/for Rav Naḥman
לר"ע	לְרַבִּי עֲקִיבָא	to/according to/for R. Akiva
לר"פ	לְרַב פָּפָּא	to/according to/for Rav Pappa
לר"ש	לְרַבִּי שִׁמְעוֹן	to/according to/for R. Shim'on
לרשב"א	לְרַבִּי שִׁמְעוֹן בֶּן אֶלְעָזָר	to/according to/for R. Shim'on son of El'azar
לרשב"ג	לְרַבָּן שִׁמְעוֹן בֶּן גַּמְלִיאֵל	to/according to/for Rabban Shim'on son of Gamliel
לרשב"ל	לְרַבִּי שִׁמְעוֹן בֶּן לָקִישׁ	to/according to/for R. Shim'on son of Lakish
ל"ש[1]	לֹא שָׁנוּ	[1] they did not teach (this text)
ל"ש[2]	לָא שְׁנָא	[2] "it did not differ"; there is no difference
לש"ס	לַ"שִּׁשָּׁה סְדָרִים"	to/for the six orders [of the Mishna]; to/for the Talmud
ל"ת	לֹא תַעֲשֶׂה	"don't do"; a negative commandment
לת"ח	לְתַלְמִיד חָכָם	to/for a Torah scholar
לת"ק	לְתַנָּא קַמָּא	according to the first tanna
לת"ת	לְתַלְמוּד תּוֹרָה	to/for the study of Torah

מ

NOTE: The letter מ at the beginning of an item often represents the *prefix* -מִ, *from* (as in מדקא"ל = מִדְקָאָמַר לֵיהּ), rather than an initial representing a separate word (as in מא"ל = מַאי אִיכָּא לְמֵימַר).

מ'	40 (המספר)	forty
מא'	מֵאֶחָד	from/than one
מא"י	מֵאֶרֶץ יִשְׂרָאֵל	from Erets Yisrael
מא"ל	מַאי אִיכָּא לְמֵימַר?	what is [it possible] to say?
מאפ"ו	"מָשְׁכוּ", "אִם", "פְּסָל", "וַיְדַבֵּר"	(words that begin Torah readings on the intermediate days of Pesaḥ)
מב'	מִ(המספר) 2	from two
מב"ד	מִבֵּית דִּין	from court

---

* See note a

מב"ח	מִבַּעַל חוֹב	from a creditor
מבע"ה	מִבַּעַל הַבַּיִת	from the owner/landlord/host
מבעה"ב	מִבַּעַל הַבַּיִת	from the owner/landlord/host
מבעו"י	מִבְּעוֹד יוֹם	from while [it is] still day
מג'	מֵ(המספר) 3	from three
מגימ"ל	מֵ(האות) "ג"	from (the letter) *gimmel*
מ"ד[1]	מַאן דְּאָמַר	[1] the one who says
מ"ד[2]	מַאי דִּכְתִיב?	[2] What [is the meaning of] that which is written?
מ"ד[3]	מַהוּ דְתֵימָא?	[3] What [is it] that you would say?
מד'	מֵ(המספר) 4	from four
מדקא"ל	מִדְּקָאָמַר לֵיהּ	from that [statement] that he says to him
מדר'	מִדְּרַבִּי ...	from that [statement] of R. ...*
מדר"ל	מִדְּרֵישׁ לָקִישׁ	from that [statement] of Resh Lakish
מד"ס	מִדִּבְרֵי סוֹפְרִים	from the words of the Sof[e]rim (= the early ḥakhamim)
מדר"א	מִדְּרַבִּי אֱלִיעֶזֶר	from that [statement] of R. Eliezer
מדר"נ	מִדְּרַבִּי נַחְמָן	from that [statement] of R. Naḥman
מדר"ש	מִדְּרַבִּי שִׁמְעוֹן	from that [statement] of R. Shim'on
מדרשב"א	מִדְּרַבִּי שִׁמְעוֹן בֶּן אֶלְעָזָר	from that [statement] of R. Shim'on son of El'azar
מדרשב"ג	מִדְּרַבָּן שִׁמְעוֹן בֶּן גַּמְלִיאֵל	from that [statement] of Rabban Shim'on son of Gamliel
מד"ת	מִדִּבְרֵי תוֹרָה	from the words of the Torah
מ"ה	(המספר) 45	forty-five
מה"[1]	מֵהַשֵּׁם	[1] from God
מה"[2]	מֵ(המספר) 5	[2] from five
מה"מ	מְנָא הָנֵי מִילֵּי?	From where [do we derive] these things?
מה"ש	מַלְאֲכֵי הַשָּׁרֵת	the angels in the service (of God)
מה"ת	מִן הַתּוֹרָה	from the Torah
מז'	מֵ(המספר) 7	from seven
מ"ח	(המספר) 48	forty-eight
מח'	מֵ(המספר) 8	from eight
מח"ל	מֵחוּצָה לָאָרֶץ	from outside of Erets Yisrael
מחפ"ז	מִיתָה, חוֹמֶשׁ, פִּדְיוֹן, זָרִים	death, a fifth, redemption, non-*kohanim*
מחש"ו	מֵחֵרֵשׁ, שׁוֹטֶה, וְקָטָן	from a deaf-mute, an idiot, and/or a minor
מ"ט	מַאי טַעְמָא?	What is the reason?
מט'	מֵ(המספר) 9	from nine
מי'	מֵ(המספר) 10	from ten
מיוה"כ	מִיּוֹם הַכִּפּוּרִים	from Yom Kippur
מיו"ט	מִיּוֹם טוֹב	from a festival
מי"ח	מֵ(המספר) 18	from eighteen
מי"ט	מִיּוֹם טוֹב	from a festival
מ"כ	מֵ(המספר) 20	from twenty
מ"ל	מַה לִּי ...?	What [difference is there] to me [whether ... or ...]?
מל'	מֵ(המספר) 30	from thirty
מ"מ[1]	מִכָּל מָקוֹם	[1] in any event
מ"מ[2]	מִינֵי מְזוֹנוֹת	[2] "(Who creates) varieties of foods"**
מ"ם	(האות) "מ"	(the letter) *mem*
ממ"ד	מִמַּאן דְּאָמַר	from the one who says
ממ"ה[1]	מִמְּדִינַת הַיָּם	[1] from a country overseas
ממ"ה[2]	מֶלֶךְ מַלְכֵי הַמְּלָכִים	[2] the King of the kings of the kings

* See note a

** See note b

from a "what-is-your-desire–[to-say" dilemma]	מִמַּה נַפְשָׁךְ	ממ"נ
from our mishna	מִמַּתְנִיתִין	ממתני'
From where [do we derive] these things?	מְנָא הָנֵי מִילֵּי?	מנה"מ
the scroll [of Esther], [the] miracle, [and] "Who gave us life"**	מְגִילָּה, נֵס, "שֶׁהֶחֱיָנוּ"	מנ"ח
[1] From where do we [know]?	מְנָא לָן?	מנ"ל[1]
[2] From where does he [know]?	מְנָא לֵיהּ?	מנ"ל[2]
(the letters) *mem, nun, tzadé, pé* [and] *kaf*	(האותיות) "מ", "נ", "צ", "פ", "כ"	מנצפ"ך
one [ḥakham] holds (the opinion)	מָר סָבַר	מ"ס
from sixty	מִ(המספר) 60	מס'
a positive commandment	מִצְוַת עֲשֵׂה	מ"ע
from idolatry	מֵעֲבוֹדַת גִּלּוּלִים	מע"ג
from an ignorant person	מֵעַם הָאָרֶץ	מע"ה
from idolatry	מֵעֲבוֹדָה זָרָה	מע"ז
from the day before a festival	מֵעֶרֶב יוֹם טוֹב	מעיו"ט
from the day before a festival	מֵעֶרֶב יוֹם טוֹב	מעי"ט
from a worshiper of stars and planets	מֵעוֹבֵד כּוֹכָבִים וּמַזָּלוֹת	מעכו"ם
from [one] time to [another] time [24 hours later]	מֵעֵת לָעֵת	מעל"ע
from the day before the Sabbath; from Friday	מֵעֶרֶב שַׁבָּת	מע"ש
from a *kal-vaḥomer* [argument]	מִקַּל וָחוֹמֶר	מק"ו
from the recitation of *Sh^ema*	מִקְּרִיאַת שְׁמַע	מק"ש
from R. ...**	מֵרַבִּי ...	מר'
from R. Eliezer	מֵרַבִּי אֱלִיעֶזֶר	מר"א
from Rosh HaShana	מֵרֹאשׁ הַשָּׁנָה	מר"ה
from the private domain	מֵרְשׁוּת הַיָּחִיד	מרה"י
from the public domain	מֵרְשׁוּת הָרַבִּים	מרה"ר
from Rosh Ḥodesh (= the first of the month)	מֵרֹאשׁ חוֹדֶשׁ	מר"ח
from (the letter) *resh*	מֵ(האות) "ר"	מרי"ש
from Rav Naḥman	מֵרַב נַחְמָן	מר"נ
[In] what [way] did it differ? What is the difference?	מַאי שְׁנָא?	מ"ש
that which is not so	מַה שֶּׁאֵין כֵּן	משא"כ
because of this	מִשּׁוּם הָכִי	מש"ה
because of this	מִשּׁוּם הָכִי	משו"ה
in his name	מִשְּׁמֵיהּ	משמי'
from the six "orders" [of the Mishna]; from the Talmud	מִ"שִּׁשָּׁה סְדָרִים"	מש"ס
our mishna	מַתְנִיתִין	מתני'
from the first tanna	מִתַּנָּא קַמָּא	מת"ק
from six hundred thirteen	מִ(המספר) 613	מתרי"ג

נ

[1] fifty	(המספר) 50	נ"[1]
[2] (the letter) *nun*	(האות) "נ"	נ"[2]
[1] fifty-one	(המספר) 51	נ"א[1]
[2] a different version (of the text)	נֹסַח אַחֵר; נוּסְחָא אַחֲרִינָא	נ"א[2]
fifty-two	(המספר) 52	נ"ב
candle, Havdala, wine, Kiddush*	נֵר, הַבְדָּלָה, יַיִן, קִדּוּשׁ	נהי"ק
(the Hebrew suffix) *–nu* (= us)	(הסיומת) "נוּ"	נ"ו
(the letter) *nun*	(האות) "נ"	נו"ן
it imparts taste	נוֹתֵן טַעַם	נ"ט

* See note c.

** See note a.

נט״י	נְטִילַת יָדַיִם	the washing of the hands
ניה״ק	נֵר, יַיִן, הַבְדָּלָה, קִדּוּשׁ	candle, wine, Havdala, Kiddush*
נ״מ	נָפְקָא מִינַּהּ	[a halakhic distinction] is derived from it
נקי״ה	נֵר, קִדּוּשׁ, יַיִן, הַבְדָּלָה	candle, Kiddush, wine, Havdala*
נ״ש	נֶזֶק שָׁלֵם	the full [value of] the damage
נשג״א	נִדָּה, שִׁפְחָה, גּוֹיָה, אֵשֶׁת אִישׁ	a menstruous woman, a maid-servant, a non-Jewess, a married woman**
נשג״ז	נִדָּה, שִׁפְחָה, גּוֹיָה, זוֹנָה	a menstruous woman, a maid-servant, a non-Jewess, a promiscuous woman**
נת״ר	נְעִילַת הַסַּנְדָּל, תַּשְׁמִישׁ הַמִּטָּה, רְחִיצַת יָדַיִם	wearing shoes, marital relations, washing hands**

ס

ס׳	(המספר) 60	sixty
ס״א	(המספר) 61	sixty-one
ס״ד	סָלְקָא דַעְתָּךְ	it would arise [upon] your mind
סד״א	סָלְקָא דַעְתָּךְ אֲמִינָא	it would arise [upon] your mind [that] I might say
סי׳	סִימָן	sign; mnemonic
ס״ך	סֵרוּס, כִּלְאַיִים	castration [and] intermingling (of different species)
ס״ל	סְבִירָא לֵיהּ	he holds (an opinion)
סמ״ך	(האות) ״ס״	(the letter) *samekh*
ס״ע	(האותיות) ״ס״, ״ע״	(the letters) *samekh* [and] *ayin*
ס״ת	סֵפֶר תּוֹרָה	a Torah scroll

ע

ע״א	(המספר) 71	seventy-one
עאכ״ו	עַל אַחַת כַּמָּה וְכַמָּה!	even more so!
עאכו״כ	עַל אַחַת כַּמָּה וְכַמָּה!	even more so!
ע״ג[1]	עַל גַּב/גַּבֵּי	[1] "on the back of"; upon
ע״ג[2]	עֲבוֹדַת גִּלּוּלִים	[2] idolatry
ע״ה	עַם הָאָרֶץ	an ignorant person
עוה״ב	עוֹלָם הַבָּא	the world to come
ע״ז[1]	עֲבוֹדָה זָרָה	[1] idolatry
ע״ז[2]	עַל זֶה	[2] on this
ע״י[1]	עַל יְדֵי	[1] by means of; through
ע״י[2]	עַל יָדוֹ	[2] through him
עיו״ט	עֶרֶב יוֹם טוֹב	the day before a festival
עי״ן	(האות) ״ע״	(the letter) *ayin*
ע״כ[1]	עַד כָּאן	[1] until here; thus far
ע״כ[2]	עַל כָּרְחָךְ	[2] against your will
עכו״ם[1]	עוֹבֵד/עוֹבְדֵי כּוֹכָבִים וּמַזָּלוֹת	[1] worshiper(s) of stars and planets
עכו״ם[2]	עֲבוֹדַת כּוֹכָבִים וּמַזָּלוֹת	[2] the worship of stars and planets
ע״מ	עַל מְנָת	on condition that; with a view towards
ע״ע	עֶבֶד עִבְרִי	a Hebrew slave
ע״פ	עַל פִּי	according to; by means of
ער״ה	עֶרֶב רֹאשׁ הַשָּׁנָה	the day before the New Year
ע״ש[1]	עַל שֵׁם	[1] "in the name of"; because of

* See note c.

** Each of these terms refers to a *prohibition*.

ע"ש[2]	עֶרֶב שַׁבָּת	[2] the day before the Sabbath; Friday

פ

פ"[1]	(האות) "פ"	[1] (the letter) *pé*
פ"[2]	(המספר) 80	[2] eighty
פ"א[1]	(האות) "פ"	[1] (the letter) *pé*
פ"א[2]	(המספר) 81	[2] eighty-one
פה"א	"פְּרִי הָאֲדָמָה"	"the fruit of the earth"*
פה"י	"פֶּסַח הַיּוֹם!"	"Today is the Pesaḥ [festival]!"
פז"ר	פַּיִיס, זְמַן (= "שהחינו"), רגל	lottery, "time,"* a pilgrim festival
פח"ז	פְּרִיעַת הָרֹאשׁ, חֲזָרַת קֶרַע לַאֲחוֹרָיו, זְקִיפַת הַמִּטָּה	uncovering the head, turning the torn side of the garment backwards, tilting up the bed**

צ

צד"י	(האות) "צ"	(the letter) *tzadé*
צ"ל	צָרִיךְ לוֹמַר	one needs to say

ק

ק'	(המספר) 100	one hundred
קא"ר	קָאָמַר רַבִּי ...	R. ... is saying***
ק"ג	(המספר) 103	one hundred three
ק"ד	(המספר) 104	one hundred four
קא"ל	קָאָמַר לֵיהּ	he is saying to him
קב"ה	קוּדְשָׁא בְּרִיךְ הוּא	the Holiness Blessed Be He
ק"ו	קַל וָחוֹמֶר	a *kal-vaḥomer* [argument]
קוב"ה	קוּדְשָׁא בְּרִיךְ הוּא	the Holiness Blessed Be He
קו"ף	(האות) "ק"	(the letter) *kof*
קיי"ל	קַיְימָא לַן	it has been established for us
קי"ל	קַיְימָא לַן	it has been established for us
קינ"ה	קִדּוּשׁ, יַיִן, נֵר, הַבְדָּלָה	Kiddush, wine, candle, Havdala****
קמ"ל	קָא מַשְׁמַע לַן	he teaches us; he informs us
קני"ה	קִדּוּשׁ, נֵר, יַיִן, הַבְדָּלָה	Kiddush, candle, wine, Havdala****
קס"ד	קָא סָלְקָא דַּעְתָּךְ	it would arise [on] your mind; you might think
ק"פ	(המספר) 180	one hundred eighty
ק"ש	קְרִיאַת שְׁמַע	the recitation of *Shema*
קש"ב	קָרְבָּן, שִׁיר, בְּרָכָה	the offering, the psalm, the berakha

ר

ר'	רַבִּי .../רֶבִּי	R. .../Rebbi***
ר"א	רַבִּי אֱלִיעֶזֶר/אֶלְעָזָר	R. Eliezer/El'azar
רא"א	רַבִּי אֱלִיעֶזֶר אוֹמֵר	R. Eliezer says
ראב"י	רַבִּי אֶלְעָזָר בֶּן יַעֲקֹב	R. El'azar son of Ya'akov
ראב"ע	רַבִּי אֶלְעָזָר בֶּן עֲזַרְיָה	R. El'azar son of Azarya
רבב"ח	רַבָּה בַּר בַּר חָנָה	Rabba grandson of Ḥanna
רבש"ע	רִבּוֹנוֹ שֶׁלָּעוֹלָם	Lord of the world
ר"ג	רַבָּן גַּמְלִיאֵל	Rabban Gamliel

* See note b

** Each of these terms refers to a *mourning practice*.

*** See note a

**** See note c

[1] Rav Huna	רַב הוּנָא	ר"ה[1]
[2] Rosh HaShana	רֹאשׁ הַשָּׁנָה	ר"ה[2]
a private domain	רְשׁוּת הַיָּחִיד	רה"י
a public domain	רְשׁוּת הָרַבִּים	רה"ר
[1] Rav Ḥisda; R. Ḥanina	רַב חִסְדָּא; רַבִּי חֲנִינָא	ר"ח[1]
[2] Rosh Ḥodesh (= the first of the month); days of Rosh Ḥodesh	רֹאשׁ חֹדֶשׁ; רָאשֵׁי חֳדָשִׁים	ר"ח[2]
R. Tarfon	רַבִּי טַרְפוֹן	ר"ט
R. Yoḥanan/Y^ehuda/Yosé/ Yishmael/Y^ehoshua	רַבִּי יוֹחָנָן/יְהוּדָה/יוֹסֵי/ יִשְׁמָעֵאל/יְהוֹשֻׁעַ	ר"י
Rabban Yoḥanan son of Zakkai	רַבָּן יוֹחָנָן בֶּן זַכַּאי	ריב"ז
R. Y^ehoshua son of Levi	רַבִּי יְהוֹשֻׁעַ בֶּן לֵוִי	ריב"ל
R. Yosé the Galilean	רַבִּי יוֹסֵי הַגְּלִילִי	ריה"ג
(the letter) *resh*	(האות) "ר"	רי"ש
Resh Lakish (= R. Shim'on son of Lakish)	רֵישׁ לָקִישׁ	ר"ל
R. Méir	רַבִּי מֵאִיר	ר"מ
two hundred forty-eight	248 (המספר)	רמ"ח
Rav Naḥman; R. N^ehemia	רַב נַחְמָן; רַבִּי נְחֶמְיָה	ר"נ
Rav Naḥman son of Yitsḥak	רַב נַחְמָן בַּר יִצְחָק	רנב"י
R. Akiva	רַבִּי עֲקִיבָא	ר"ע
R. Akiva says	רַבִּי עֲקִיבָא אוֹמֵר	רע"א
R. Akiva	רַבִּי עֲקִיבָא	רע"ק
Rav Pappa; R. Pinḥas	רַב פָּפָּא; רַבִּי פִּנְחָס	ר"פ
shepherds, watchmen of drying fruit, city-guards, [or] orchard-keepers	רוֹעִים, קַיְּיצִים, בּוּרְגָּנִים, שׁוֹמְרֵי פֵּירוֹת	רקב"ש
R. Shim'on	רַבִּי שִׁמְעוֹן	ר"ש
R. Shim'on says	רַבִּי שִׁמְעוֹן אוֹמֵר	רש"א
R. Shim'on son of El'azar	רַבִּי שִׁמְעוֹן בֶּן אֶלְעָזָר	רשב"א
Rabban Shim'on son of Gamliel	רַבָּן שִׁמְעוֹן בֶּן גַּמְלִיאֵל	רשב"ג
R. Shim'on son of Lakish	רַבִּי שִׁמְעוֹן בֶּן לָקִישׁ	רשב"ל
R. Shim'on son of Yoḥai	רַבִּי שִׁמְעוֹן בַּר יוֹחָאי	רשב"י

ש

NOTE: Sometimes the letter ש at the beginning of an item is *not* an initial representing a separate word (as in ש"ד = שְׁפִיר דָּמֵי) but the Hebrew *prefix* -שֶׁ, meaning *for* or *that* (as in שא"א = שֶׁאִי אֶפְשָׁר).

because [it is] impossible	שֶׁאִי אֶפְשָׁר	שא"א
because even though	שֶׁאַף עַל פִּי	שאע"פ
because/that even	שֶׁאֲפִילוּ	שאפי'
which does not need; which has no need	שֶׁאֵינוֹ צָרִיךְ; שֶׁאֵין צוֹרֶךְ	שא"צ
for there is no need to say	שֶׁאֵין צוֹרֶךְ לוֹמַר	שאצ"ל
for R. ... /Rav ... said*	שֶׁאָמַר רַבִּי/רַב	שא"ר
that/for people	שֶׁבְּנֵי אָדָם	שב"א
that is in Erets Yisrael	שֶׁבְּאֶרֶץ יִשְׂרָאֵל	שבא"י
because in court	שֶׁבְּבֵית דִּין	שבב"ד
because a court	שֶׁבֵּית דִּין	שב"ד
because at/with five	שֶׁבְּ(מספר) 5	שבה'
because the Holy Temple	שֶׁבֵּית הַמִּקְדָּשׁ	שבהמ"ק

* See note a

שבר"ה	שֶׁבִּרְשׁוּת הָרַבִּים	that [is] in a public domain
שברה"ר	שֶׁבִּרְשׁוּת הָרַבִּים	that [is] in a public domain
שב"ש	שֶׁבֵּית שַׁמַּאי	because Beth (= the school of) Shammai
שבש"א	שֶׁבֵּית שַׁמַּאי אוֹמְרִים	because Beth Shammai says
ש"ד	שַׁפִּיר דָּמֵי	it is good
שה"י	"שַׁבָּת הַיּוֹם!"	"Today is the Sabbath!"
שהי'	שֶׁהָיָה	because/that it was
שהקב"ה	שֶׁהַקָּדוֹשׁ בָּרוּךְ הוּא	because/that the Holy One Blessed Be He
ש"ז	שִׁכְבַת זֶרַע	semen
ש"ח	שׁוֹמֵר חִנָּם	an unpaid watchman
שט"ח	שְׁטַר חוֹב	a promissory note
שי"ן	(האות) "ש"	(the letter) *shin*
שכ"ג	שֶׁכֹּהֵן גָּדוֹל	because a high priest
שכ"מ	שְׁכִיב מְרַע	someone gravely ill; a dying man
ש"מ	שְׁמַע מִינַּהּ!	Derive from it!
שמר"ה	שֶׁמֵּרֹאשׁ הַשָּׁנָה	because from Rosh HaShana
שנא'	שֶׁנֶּאֱמַר	because it has been stated
ש"ס	"שִׁשָּׁה סְדָרִים"	six orders (of the Mishna); the Talmud
שס"ה	(המספר) 365	three hundred sixty-five
שעכו"ם	שֶׁעוֹבְדֵי כּוֹכָבִים וּמַזָּלוֹת	because the worshipers of stars and planets
שע"ג	שֶׁעַל גַּבֵּי	which is upon
ש"פ	שָׁוֶה פְּרוּטָה	worth a *p[e]ruta* (coin)
שצ"ל	שֶׁצָּרִיךְ לוֹמַר	because he must say
שקה"ח	שְׁקִיעַת הַחַמָּה	sunset
שר'	שֶׁרַבִּי ...	because/that R. ...*
שר"א	שֶׁרַבִּי אֱלִיעֶזֶר	because/that R. Elieser
שר"ג	שֶׁרַבָּן גַּמְלִיאֵל	because Rabban Gamliel
שרה"י	שֶׁרְשׁוּת הַיָּחִיד	because/that a private domain
שרה"ר	שֶׁרְשׁוּת הָרַבִּים	because/that a public domain
שר"י	שֶׁרַבִּי יְהוּדָה/יוֹסֵי	because/that R. Y[e]huda/Yosé
שר"ע	שֶׁרַבִּי עֲקִיבָא	because R. Akiva
ש"ש	שֵׁם שָׁמַיִם	the name of Heaven
ש"ת	(האותיות) "ש", "ת"	(the letters) *shin* [and] *tav*

ת

ת"ח	תַּלְמִיד חָכָם; תַּלְמִידֵי חֲכָמִים	a Torah scholar; Torah scholars
תי"ו	(האות) "ת"	(the letter) *tav*
ת"ל	תַּלְמוּד לוֹמַר	a (Biblical) teaching says; Scripture teaches
תני'	תַּנְיָא	it is taught
תנ"ה	תַּנְיָא נַמֵּי הָכִי	[A baraitha] is also taught thus.
ת"ק	תַּנָּא קַמָּא	the first tanna
ת"ר	תָּנוּ רַבָּנָן	the ḥakhamim taught
ת"ש	תָּא שְׁמַע!	Come [and] hear!
תש"ת	תְּקִיעָה, שְׁבָרִים, תְּקִיעָה	*teki'a* (= straight sound from the shofar), broken sounds, *teki'a*
ת"ת	תַּלְמוּד תּוֹרָה	the study of Torah

* See note a

APPENDIX II

Measures, Weights, Coins and Numbers

INTRODUCTION

The following tables present most of the units of measurement and all of the Aramaic numbers that appear in the Talmud. Before using the tables, please take note of the following:

(1) In the left-hand column, the Hebrew terms are listed in order, beginning with the smallest measure (at the top) to the largest (at the bottom). The terms are also listed in the same order from left to right in the top row.

(2) If you select one of the terms in the left column, e.g. אֶצְבַּע, and read *across* – from left to right – you learn that an אֶצְבַּע *equals* 1/4 of a טֶפַח, 1/12 of a זֶרֶת, 1/24 of an אַמָּה, etc.

(3) If, on the other hand, you begin with an אֶצְבַּע from the top row and read *down*, you learn that 4 אֶצְבָּעוֹת *constitute* a טֶפַח, 12 *constitute* a זֶרֶת, 24 *constitute* an אַמָּה, etc.

(4) The precise width of the אֶצְבַּע (the thumb), a basic unit of measurement that affects many other measurements in Jewish law, is subject to controversy among the halakhic authorities. The most well-known opinions today are those expressed respectively by Rav Avraham Ḥayyim Na'eh and Rav Avraham Yesha'ya Karelitz (the *Ḥazon Ish*). The two columns at the right of the table translate the measurements into contemporary terms according to each opinion. The metric measurements were taken from מידות ושיעורי תורה, by Rav Ḥayyim P. Beinish, who has graciously granted his permission for the use of these tables in this appendix.

(1) LENGTH

	אֶצְבַּע	טֶפַח	זֶרֶת	אַמָּה	רִיס	מִיל	פַּרְסָה	רא"ח נאה	חזו"א
אצבע fingerbreadth	1	1/4	1/12	1/24	1/6,400	1/48,000	1/192,000	2 cm. .79 in.	2.4 cm. .94 in.
טפח handbreadth	4	1	1/3	1/6	1/1,600	1/12,000	1/48,000	8 cm. 3.15 in.	9.6 cm. 3.78 in.
זרת span	12	3	1	1/2	3/1,600	1/4,000	1/16,000	24 cm. 9.45 in.	28.8 cm. 11.34 in.
אמה cubit	24	6	2	1	3/800	1/2,000	1/8,000	48 cm. 18.9 in.	57.6 cm. 22.7 in.
ריס *ris*	6,400	1,600	$533^{1/3}$	$266^{2/3}$	1	2/15	1/30	128 m. 139 yd.	153.6 m 167 yd.
מיל *mil*	48,000	12,000	4,000	2,000	7.5	1	1/4	960 m. 1,049 yd.	1,152 m. 1,258 yd.
פרסה *parasang*	192,000	48,000	16,000	8,000	30	4	1	3.84 km. 2.4 mi.	4.608 km. 2.88 mi.

The distance covered by an average man in a day's walk is 10 פרסאות.
The time it takes him to walk a מיל is 18 minutes.
The time it takes him to walk a פרסה is 72 minutes.

(2) AREA

Please take note of the instructions that appear in the introduction to the appendix, and apply them to this table as well.

	אַמָּה עַל אַמָּה	בֵּית רוֹבַע	בֵּית סְאָה	בֵּית כּוֹר	רא"ח נאה	חזו"א
אמה על אמה square cubit	1	6/625	1/2,500	1/75,000	2,304 cm.^{2} 357.1 in.^{2}	3,318 cm.^{2} 514.3 in.^{2}
בית רובע * space for sowing 1/4 of a *kav*	$104^{1/6}$	1	1/24	1/720	24 m.^{2} 28.7 yd.^{2}	34.56 m.^{2} 41.33 yd.^{2}
בית סאה* space for sowing a *s^ea*	2,500	24	1	1/30	576 m.^{2} 688.9 yd.^{2}	829.4 m.^{2} 992 yd.^{2}
בית כור* space for sowing a *kor*	75,000	720	30	1	17,280 m.^{2} 20,666.6 yd.^{2}	24,883 m.^{2} 29,759.7 yd.^{2}

A גְּרִיס, *split bean*, is an area equal to 9 square עֲדָשׁוֹת, *lentils*, or 36 square שְׂעָרוֹת, *hairs*.**
Most authorities have equated the area of a גְּרִיס with the area of a circle whose diameter is approximately 20 mm.

(c. 21 mm. כמעט :מעיל צדקה; 20.3 mm. :חזון איש; 19 mm. :דרכי תשובה)

* These terms indicate *the minimum amount of space required to sow specific quantities of grain.*

** משנה נגעים פ"ו מ"א.

(3) VOLUME

Please take note of the instructions that appear in the introduction to the appendix, and apply them to this table as well.

	בֵּיצָה	רְבִיעִית	לוֹג	קַב	עִשָּׂרוֹן	סְאָה	אֵיפָה	כּוֹר	רא״ח נאה	חזו״א
ביצה	1	2/3	1/6	1/24	5/216	1/144	1/432	1/4,320	.0576 lit.**	.1 lit.
רביעית	1.5	1	1/4	1/16	5/144	1/96	1/288	1/2,880	.086 lit.	.15 lit.
לוג (רובע)*	6	4	1	1/4	5/36	1/24	1/72	1/720	.345 lit.	.6 lit.
קב	24	16	4	1	5/9	1/6	1/18	1/180	1.38 lit.	2.4 lit.
עשרון (עומר)*	43.2	28.8	7.2	1.8	1	3/10	1/10	1/100	2.49 lit.	4.32 lit.
סאה	144	96	24	6	3 1/3	1	1/3	1/30	8.29 lit.	14.4 lit.
בת (איפה)*	432	288	72	18	10	3	1	1/10	24.88 lit.	43.2 lit.
כור (חומר)*	4,320	2,880	720	180	100	30	10	1	248.83 lit.	432 lit.

The following measures appear in the Talmud occasionally:

קוֹרְטוֹב = 1/16 of a רְבִיעִית   תַּרְקַב = 1/2 of a סְאָה   לֶתֶךְ = 1/2 of a כּוֹר

The following important measures are subject to dispute in the sources.

We present the rulings stated in R. Yosef Karo's *Shulḥan Arukh.*

זַיִת (olive) = 1/2 of a בֵּיצָה (ש״ע או״ח תפ״ו)***   גְּרוֹגֶרֶת (fig) = 1/3 of a בֵּיצָה (ש״ע או״ח שס״ח:ג)

כּוֹתֶבֶת (date) = a bit less than a בֵּיצָה (ש״ע או״ח תרי״ב:א)****

פְּרַס = four ביצים according to Rashi but three ביצים according to the Rambam.

Both opinions are recorded in the *Shulḥan Arukh* (ש״ע או״ח תרי״ב:ג).

---

* When a second term is added in parentheses in the left-hand column, the first term is used for a *liquid* measure, and the one in parentheses is used for *dry* measure.

** A *liter* (1,000 cubic centimeters) is approximately equal to a U.S. quart.

*** According to another opinion, it is a bit less than 1/3 of a ביצה.See ביאור הגר״א ומשנה ברורה שם.

**** This quantity, which is the maximum a sick person can eat at once on Yom Kippur, has been set by some authorities at 30 cubic centimeters.

(4) COINS AND WEIGHTS

(1) Please take note of the first three instructions that appear in the introduction to the appendix, and apply them to this table as well.
(2) The value of all the coins - even those made of copper or gold - is based upon the weight of *silver* coins in Talmudic times. Rashi (in his commentary on שמות כא:לב) and the Rambam (in his commentary on משנה בכורות פ"ח מ"ו) disagree about the weight equivalencies in pure silver. The weights that are presented in the right-hand column, both in *grams* and in *Troy ounces* (for Americans), follow the opinion of the Rambam, which has been accepted as *halakha* in the ***Shulḥan Arukh*** (חושן משפט פ"ח:א).*
(3) The coins designated below as silver were also common measures of *weight* in Talmudic times, as was the ככר (= 60 מנה).

	פְּרוּטָה	אִיסָר	פּוּנְדְּיוֹן	מָעָה	דִּינַר־כֶּסֶף	שֶׁקֶל	סֶלַע	דִּינַר־זָהָב	מָנֶה	weight of pure-silver equivalent
copper פרוטה	1	1/8	1/16	1/32	1/192	1/384	1/768	1/4,800	**1/19,200**	.022 gm. .00071 oz.
(**) איסר	8	1	1/2	1/4	1/24	1/48	1/96	1/600 •	1/2,400	.177 gm. .00569 oz.
(**) פונדיון	16	2	1	1/2	1/12	1/24	1/48	1/300	1/1,200	.35 gm. .01125 oz.
(silver) מעה	32	4	2	1	1/6	1/12	1/24	1/150	1/600	.7 gm. .02251 oz.
(silver) דינר	192	24	12	6	1	1/2	1/4	1/25	1/100	4.25 gm. .13664 oz.
(silver) שקל	384	48	24	12	2	1	1/2	2/25	1/50	8.5 gm. .27328 oz.
(silver) סלע	768	96	48	24	4	2	1	4/25	1/25	17 gm. .54657 oz.
(gold) דינר	4,800	600	300	150	25	$12^{1/2}$	$6^{1/4}$	1	1/4	106.25 gm. 3.41604 oz.
(silver) מנה	19,200	2,400	1,200	600	100	50	25	4	1	425 gm. 13.66417 gm.

* According to Rashi, the weights are 16.7% less, and a סלע, for example, is 14.16 grams instead of 17 grams. On the other hand, some authorities follow a system that sets the weight at about 13% more than the Rambam, so that a סלע weighs 19.2 grams. See also the note of the Ramban on this issue, which is printed at the very end of his commentary of the Torah. For a full discussion of the subject, see Rav Ḥayyim P. Beinish's מדות ושיעורי תורה.

(5) NUMBERS

In Aramaic as in Hebrew, the distinction between masculine and feminine in numerals *three* to *ten* is the reverse of what would be expected. The numbers that are treated as masculine (e.g., the Aramaic תְּלָתָא and the Hebrew שְׁלשָׁה) have feminine suffixes — not the ones that are treated as feminine (e.g., the Aramaic תְּלָת and the Hebrew שָׁלשׁ).

CARDINAL NUMBERS

Masculine			Feminine	
Aramaic	Hebrew		Aramaic	Hebrew
חַד	אֶחָד	1	חֲדָא	אַחַת
תְּרֵי, תְּרֵין	שְׁנֵי, שְׁנַיִם	2	תַּרְתֵּי, תַּרְתֵּין	שְׁתֵּי, שְׁתַּיִם
תְּלָתָא	שְׁלשָׁה	3	תְּלָת	שָׁלשׁ
אַרְבְּעָה	אַרְבָּעָה	4	אַרְבַּע, אַרְבְּעִי	אַרְבַּע
חַמְשָׁא, חַמְשָׁה	חֲמִשָּׁה	5	חֲמֵשׁ	חָמֵשׁ
שִׁיתָּא	שִׁשָּׁה	6	שֵׁת	שֵׁשׁ
שִׁבְעָא, שִׁבְעָה	שִׁבְעָה	7	שַׁב, שְׁבַע	שֶׁבַע
תְּמָנְיָא	שְׁמוֹנָה	8	תַּמְנֵי	שְׁמוֹנֶה
תִּשְׁעָה	תִּשְׁעָה	9	תְּשַׁע	תֵּשַׁע
עַשְׂרָה	עֲשָׂרָה	10	עֲשַׂר	עֶשֶׂר
חַד סַר, חַדְסַר	אַחַד עָשָׂר	11	חַד סְרֵי	אַחַת עֶשְׂרֵה
תְּרֵיסַר	שְׁנֵים עָשָׂר	12	תַּרְתֵּי סְרֵי	שְׁתֵּים עֶשְׂרֵה
תְּלֵיסַר	שְׁלשָׁה עָשָׂר	13	תְּלֵיסְרֵי, תְּלָת סְרֵי, תְּלָת עַשְׂרֵי	שְׁלשׁ עֶשְׂרֵה
אַרְבֵּיסַר, אַרְבְּסַר	אַרְבָּעָה עָשָׂר	14	אַרְבַּסְרֵי, אַרְבַּע סְרֵי	אַרְבַּע עֶשְׂרֵה
חֲמֵיסַר	חֲמִישָּׁה עָשָׂר	15	חֲמֵסְרֵי	חֲמֵשׁ עֶשְׂרֵה
שֵׁיתְסַר	שִׁשָּׁה עָשָׂר	16	שֵׁיתְסְרֵי, שֵׁית סְרֵי	שֵׁשׁ עֶשְׂרֵה
שִׁיבְסַר, שַׁבְסַר	שִׁבְעָה עָשָׂר	17	שַׁבְסְרֵי, שִׁיבְסְרֵי	שְׁבַע עֶשְׂרֵה
תְּמָנֵיסַר	שְׁמוֹנָה עָשָׂר	18	תַּמְנֵי סְרֵי	שְׁמוֹנֶה עֶשְׂרֵה
תְּשַׁסַר	תִּשְׁעָה עָשָׂר	19	תְּשַׁסְרֵי	תְּשַׁע עֶשְׂרֵה

Common Gender

Aramaic		Hebrew
עַשְׂרִין	20	עֶשְׂרִים
תְּלָתִין	30	שְׁלשִׁים
אַרְבְּעִין	40	אַרְבָּעִים
חַמְשִׁין, חַמְשִׁי	50	חֲמִשִּׁים
שִׁיתִּין, שִׁיתִּי, שִׁתִּין	60	שִׁשִּׁים
שִׁבְעִין	70	שִׁבְעִים
תְּמָנַן	80	שְׁמוֹנִים
תִּשְׁעִין	90	תִּשְׁעִים
מְאָה	100	מֵאָה
מָאתַן	200	מָאתַיִם
תְּלָת מְאָה	300	שְׁלשׁ מֵאוֹת
אַלְפָּא	1000	אֶלֶף
תְּרֵי אַלְפֵי	2000	אַלְפַּיִם
רִבּוֹא	10000	רִבּוֹא
שִׁיתִּין רִיבְוָותָא	600000	שִׁשִּׁים רִבּוֹא

ORDINAL NUMBERS

Masculine			Feminine	
Aramaic	Hebrew		Aramaic	Hebrew
קַמָּא, קַדְמָאָה	רִאשׁוֹן	1st	קַמַּיְיתָא, קַדְמַיְיתָא	רִאשׁוֹנָה
תִּנְיָינָא	שֵׁנִי	2nd		
תְּלִיתָאִי	שְׁלִישִׁי	3rd	תְּלִיתָאָה	שְׁלִישִׁית
רְבִיעָאָה	רְבִיעִי	4th		
שְׁבִיעָאָה	שְׁבִיעִי	7th	שְׁבִיעָתָא	שְׁבִיעִית
עֲשִׂירָאָה	עֲשִׂירִי	10th		
בָּתְרָא	אַחֲרוֹן	last	בָּתְרַיְיתָא	אַחֲרוֹנָה

FRACTIONS

Aramaic		Hebrew
פַּלְגָא	1/2	חֲצִי
תִּילְתָּא	1/3	שְׁלִישׁ
רִיבְעָא, רְבִיעָתָא	1/4	רֶבַע, רְבִיעִית
חוּמְשָׁא	1/5	חֹמֶשׁ
שְׁתוּתָא	1/6	שְׁתוּת, שִׁשִּׁית
עִישּׂוּרָא	1/10	עֲשִׂירִית